THE HARRODIAN SCHOOL

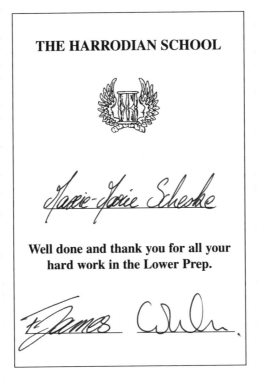

Marie-Josie Scheske

**Well done and thank you for all your
hard work in the Lower Prep.**

F. James Aulu.

CHAMBERS

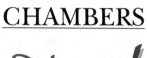

CHAMBERS

THESAURUS

CHAMBERS

CHAMBERS
An imprint of Chambers Harrap Publishers Ltd
7 Hopetoun Crescent
Edinburgh, EH7 4AY

Previous edition published 2000
This edition published by Chambers Harrap Publishers Ltd 2004

© Chambers Harrap Publishers Ltd 2004

We have made every effort to mark as such all words
which we believe to be trademarks. We should also like to
make it clear that the presence of a word in the dictionary, whether
marked or unmarked, in no way affects its legal
status as a trademark.

All rights reserved. No part of this publication may be reproduced,
stored in a retrieval system, or transmitted by
any means, electronic, mechanical, photocopying or
otherwise, without the prior permission of the publisher.

A CIP catalogue record for this book is available from the
British Library.

ISBN 0550 10074 1

Designed and typeset by Chambers Harrap Publishers Ltd, Edinburgh
Printed in Norway

Contents

Preface

The *Chambers School Thesaurus* is specially designed for use by students aged 10-14 and is an ideal companion to the *Chambers School Dictionary*.

Colour is used in the thesaurus to highlight particular parts of entries and thus make them easier to use. For example, where a word has more than one meaning, illustrative examples are given to guide users to the relevant group of synonyms. These illustrative examples are presented in colour, making them instantly recognizable.

While the main purpose of a thesaurus is to provide the user with synonyms (alternatives) for words and phrases, this thesaurus also contains antonyms (opposites) and these are clearly indicated by the symbol ➤. Hyponyms answer the question, 'What kinds of ... are there?', and there are over 80 hyponym boxes in the *School Thesaurus*. A useful list of these boxes is to be found on page xv.

This new edition contains an increased number of **Word Study** and **Word Workshop** panels, while existing panels have been updated and expanded. **Word Study** panels focus on idiomatic ways of expressing certain concepts, eg anger, fear or surprise. **Word Workshop** panels suggest alternatives to words that students may be tempted to overuse when speaking or writing, eg **nice**, **really** or **great**. You will find a list of these panels on page xiv.

At the back there is a selection of word games to help students use synonyms in a fun way. There are also helpful sections on **Using Words Well** and **Using Words Creatively**, which provide invaluable information on choosing the right words for the context, and on avoiding potential difficulties.

Whether seeking out alternative or opposite words, or simply browsing for pleasure, students will, we hope, enjoy using this handy yet comprehensive wordfinder.

To help make best use of Chambers School titles, teachers can download photocopiable versions of the panels, along with games and exercises, from our website at www.chambers.co.uk

Contributors

Project Editor
Elaine O'Donoghue

Editor
Kay Cullen

Editorial Assistance
Hilary Bates   Helen Birkbeck

Publishing Manager
Patrick White

Prepress
Clair Cameron

How to use the Thesaurus

accommodate

Headwords appear in bold at the beginning of each entry.

accommodate *verb*
1 accommodate someone in a hotel: lodge, board, put up, house, shelter.
2 we try to accommodate all our customers: oblige, help, assist, aid, serve, provide, supply, comply, conform.

accommodating *adjective*
obliging, indulgent, helpful, co-operative, willing, kind, considerate, unselfish, sympathetic, friendly, hospitable.
🔁 disobliging, selfish.

accommodation

Many examples are given of word families (hyponyms).

Types of accommodation include:

apartment, bedsit, bedsitter, digs (*infml*), dwelling, flat, halls of residence, hostel, lodgings, pad (*infml*), residence, rooms, shelter, squat (*infml*); bed and breakfast, boarding-house, guest-house, hotel, inn, motel, pension, timeshare, villa, youth hostel; barracks, billet, married quarters.
⇨ *See also* **building**; **house**; **room**.

Example sentences show the meaning of each synonym block.

accompany *verb*
1 accompany someone on holiday: escort, attend, convoy, chaperon(e), usher, conduct, follow.
2 a book accompanied by a study guide: coexist, coincide, belong to, go with, complement, supplement.

Where the entry is not split down into separate meanings, synonyms are simply listed after the headword.

accomplice *noun* assistant, helper, abettor, mate, henchman, conspirator, collaborator, ally, confederate, partner, associate, colleague, participator, accessory.

accomplish *verb* achieve, attain, do, perform, carry out, execute, fulfil, discharge, finish, complete, conclude, consummate, realize, effect, bring about, engineer, produce, obtain.

x

death

Running heads show the first and last headword on each page.

deal *noun*
1 cause a great deal of trouble: quantity, amount, extent, degree, portion, share.
2 a better deal: agreement, contract, understanding, pact, transaction, bargain, buy.
3 it's your deal: round, hand, distribution.
► *verb*
1 deal the cards/deal out punishment: apportion, distribute, share, dole out, divide, allot, dispense, assign, mete out, give, bestow.
2 dealing in antiques: trade, negotiate, traffic, bargain, treat.
◆**deal with** attend to, concern, see to, manage, handle, cope with, treat, consider, oversee.

The sign ◆ indicates a phrasal verb.

dealer *noun*
trader, merchant, wholesaler, marketer, merchandiser.

dear *adjective*
1 my dear friend: loved, beloved, treasured, valued, cherished, precious, favourite, esteemed, intimate, close, darling, familiar.
2 a car was too dear so I bought a bike: expensive, high-priced, costly, overpriced, pricey (*infml*).
⊞**1** disliked, hated. **2** cheap.
► *noun*
beloved, loved one, precious, darling, treasure.

Parts of speech or word class, eg *noun*, *verb* and *adjective* are spelled out in full. A new part of speech within an entry appears on a new line.

death *noun*
1 cause many deaths/death by hanging: decease, end, finish, loss, demise, departure, fatality, cessation, passing, expiration, dissolution.
2 the death of communism: destruction, ruin, undoing, annihilation, downfall, extermination, extinction, obliteration, eradication.
⊞**1** life, birth.
⇨ *See also* **Word Study panel.**

The sign ⊞ indicates antonyms – words that mean the opposite of the headword.

Word Study or Word Workshop panels are indicated at the relevant entry.

xi

Pronunciation

This thesaurus provides help in cases where a word can be pronounced in more than one way depending on its meaning. Pronunciations are designed to be immediately understandable. The syllables are separated by hyphens, and the stressed syllable (the syllable pronounced with most emphasis) is shown in thick black type. Any vowel or group of vowels which is pronounced with an unemphasized 'uh' sound is shown in italic type. Pronunciations are given directly after the part of speech, for example:

> **abuse** *verb* /*a*-**byooz**/
> ....
> ▸ *noun* /*a*-**byoos**/

A few sounds are difficult to show in normal English letters. Here is a guide to the letter combinations that are used to show these sounds.

Consonants
'ng'	shows the sound as in ri**ng**
'ngg'	shows the sound as in fi**ng**er
'th'	shows the sound as in **th**in
'dh'	shows the sound as in **th**is
'sz'	shows the sound as in deci**s**ion, mea**s**ure
'kh'	shows the sound as in lo**ch**

Vowels
'uw'	shows the sound as in b**oo**k, p**u**t
'oo'	shows the sound as in m**oo**n, l**o**se
'ah'	shows the sound as in **ar**m, d**a**nce
'aw'	shows the sound as in s**aw**, ign**o**re
'er'	shows the sound as in f**er**n, b**ir**d, h**ear**d
'ei'	shows the sound as in d**ay**, s**a**me
'ai'	shows the sound as in m**y**, p**i**ne
'oi'	shows the sound as in b**oy**, s**oi**l
'oh'	shows the sound as in b**o**ne, n**o**, th**ough**
'ow'	shows the sound as in n**ow**, b**ough**

Sound combinations

'eer'	shows the sound as in n**ear**, b**eer**, t**ier**
'eir'	shows the sound as in h**air**, c**are**, th**ere**
'oor'	shows the sound as in p**oor**, s**ure**
'air'	shows the sound as in f**ire**, h**igher**

Abbreviations

fml	formal
infml	informal
US	United States

List of Panels

List of Hyponym Boxes

accommodation
amphibians
anatomical terms
animals
area
arts and crafts
artists and artisans
biology terms
birds
bones
books
buildings
cats
celebrations
chemistry terms
church services
clothes
clouds
collective nouns
collectors and
  enthusiasts
colours
communication
computer terms
dogs
educational
  establishments
entertainment
family members
fish, shellfish and
  crustaceans
flowers
fruit
geography terms
houses
insects and arachnids
invertebrates
language terms
literary terms
literature, types of
mammals
manias

marsupials
mathematics
meals
molluscs
music, types of
musical terms
musical instruments
painting terms
party
phobias
physics terms
plants
poems
political terms
punctuation marks
regions, geographical
regions, administrative
religions
reptiles
rodents
rooms
sciences
shapes
shops
smells
songs
sports
storms
story, types of
study, subjects of
taste
theatrical forms
time
travel, methods of
travel, forms of
trees
vegetables
vehicles
weather
wood
writers
zodiac signs

abandon *verb*
1 abandon one's loved ones: desert, leave, forsake, ditch (*infml*), leave in the lurch (*infml*), maroon, strand, leave behind.
2 abandon ship: vacate, evacuate, quit.
3 abandon an activity: renounce, resign, give up, forgo, relinquish, surrender, yield, waive, drop.
F3 1 support, maintain, keep.
3 continue.

abashed *adjective*
ashamed, shamefaced, embarrassed, mortified, humiliated, humbled, confused, bewildered, nonplussed, confounded, perturbed, discomposed, disconcerted, taken aback, dumbfounded, floored (*infml*), dismayed.
F3 unabashed, composed, at ease.

abate *verb*
1 the storm abated: decrease, reduce, lessen, diminish, decline, sink, dwindle, taper off, fall off.
2 anger/pain abated: moderate, ease, relieve, alleviate, mitigate, remit, pacify, quell, subside, let up (*infml*), weaken, wane, slacken, slow, fade.
F3 1 increase. **2** strengthen.

abbreviate *verb*
shorten, cut, trim, clip, truncate, curtail, abridge, summarize, précis, abstract, digest, condense, compress, reduce, lessen, shrink, contract.
F3 extend, lengthen, expand, amplify.

abbreviation *noun*
shortening, clipping, curtailment, abridgement, summarization, summary, synopsis, résumé, précis, abstract, digest, compression, reduction, contraction.
F3 extension, expansion, amplification.

abdicate *verb*
renounce, give up, relinquish, cede, surrender, yield, forgo, abandon, quit, vacate, retire, resign, step down (*infml*).

abdomen *noun*
belly, guts, stomach, tummy (*infml*), paunch, midriff.

abdominal *adjective*
ventral, intestinal, visceral, gastric.

abduct *verb*
carry off, run away with, run off with (*infml*), make off with, spirit away, seduce, kidnap, snatch, seize, appropriate.

aberration *noun*
deviation, straying, wandering, divergence, irregularity, nonconformity, anomaly, oddity, peculiarity, eccentricity, quirk, freak, lapse, defect.
F3 conformity.

abhor *verb*
hate, detest, loathe, abominate, shudder at, recoil from, shrink from, spurn, despise.
F3 love, adore.

abhorrent *adjective*
detestable, loathsome, abominable, execrable (*fml*), heinous (*fml*), obnoxious, odious, hated, hateful, horrible, horrid, offensive, repugnant, repellent, repulsive, revolting, nauseating, disgusting, distasteful.
F3 delightful, attractive.

abide *verb*
1 I can't abide that smell: bear, stand,

endure, tolerate, put up with, stomach (*infml*), accept.
2 (*fml*) **truths that abide**: remain, last, endure, continue, persist.
◆ **abide by** obey, observe, follow, comply with, adhere to, conform to, submit to, go along with, agree to, fulfil, discharge, carry out, stand by, hold to, keep to.

ability *noun*
1 the ability to teach: capability, capacity, faculty, facility, potentiality, power.
2 someone of great ability: skill, dexterity, deftness, adeptness, competence, proficiency, qualification, aptitude, talent, gift, endowment, knack, flair, touch, expertise, know-how (*infml*), genius, forte, strength.
E3 1 inability. **2** incompetence, weakness.

able *adjective*
1 are you able to tell us what he said?: allowed, permitted, free, willing.
2 a very able candidate: capable, fit, dexterous, adroit, deft, adept, competent, proficient, qualified, practised, experienced, skilled, accomplished, clever, expert, masterly, skilful, ingenious, talented, gifted, strong, powerful, effective, efficient.
E3 1 unable. **2** incapable, incompetent, ineffective.

abnormal *adjective*
odd, strange, singular, peculiar, curious, queer, weird, eccentric, paranormal, unnatural, uncanny, extraordinary, exceptional, unusual, uncommon, unexpected, irregular, anomalous, aberrant (*fml*), erratic, wayward, deviant, divergent, different.
E3 normal, regular, typical.

abnormality *noun*
oddity, peculiarity, singularity, eccentricity, strangeness, bizarreness, unnaturalness, unusualness, irregularity, exception, anomaly, deformity, flaw, aberration, deviation, divergence, difference.
E3 normality, regularity.

abolish *verb*
do away with, annul, nullify, invalidate,

quash, repeal, rescind, revoke, cancel, obliterate, blot out, suppress, destroy, eliminate, eradicate, get rid of (*infml*), stamp out, end, put an end to, terminate, subvert, overthrow, overturn.
E3 create, retain, authorize, continue.

abominable *adjective*
loathsome, detestable, hateful, horrid, horrible, abhorrent (*fml*), odious, repugnant, repulsive, repellent, disgusting, revolting, obnoxious, nauseating, foul, vile, heinous (*fml*), atrocious, appalling, terrible, reprehensible, contemptible, despicable, wretched.
E3 delightful, pleasant, desirable.

abort *verb*
miscarry, terminate, end, stop, arrest, halt, check, frustrate, thwart, nullify, call off, fail.
E3 continue.

abortion *noun*
miscarriage, termination, frustration, failure, misadventure.
E3 continuation, success.

abortive *adjective*
failed, unsuccessful, fruitless, unproductive, barren, sterile, vain, idle, futile, useless, ineffective, unavailing.
E3 successful, fruitful.

about *preposition*
1 write about a subject: regarding, concerning, relating to, referring to, connected with, concerned with, as regards, with regard to, with respect to, with reference to.
2 somewhere about the house: close to, near, nearby, beside, adjacent to.
3 walk about the town: round, around, surrounding, encircling, encompassing, throughout, all over.
▶ *adverb*
1 about twenty: around, approximately, roughly, in the region of, more or less, almost, nearly, approaching, nearing.
2 run about: to and fro, here and there, from place to place.
◆ **about to** on the point of, on the verge of, all but, ready to, intending to, preparing to.

above *preposition*
over, higher than, on top of, superior to, in excess of, exceeding, surpassing, beyond, before, prior to.
E∃ below, under.
► *adverb*
overhead, aloft, on high, earlier.
E∃ below, underneath.
► *adjective*
above-mentioned, above-stated, foregoing, preceding, previous, earlier, prior.

abrasive *adjective*
1 abrasive material: scratching, scraping, grating, rough, harsh, chafing, frictional (*fml*).
2 an abrasive person: galling, irritating, annoying, sharp, biting, caustic, hurtful, nasty, unpleasant.
E∃ **1** smooth. **2** pleasant.

abreast *adjective*
1 walk abreast: side by side, level, next to each other.
2 keep abreast of the news: in touch, up to date, informed, acquainted, knowledgeable, in the picture (*infml*), au fait, conversant (*fml*), familiar.
E∃ **2** unaware, out of touch.

abridge *verb*
shorten, cut (down), prune, curtail, abbreviate, contract, reduce, decrease, lessen, summarize, précis, abstract, digest, condense, compress, concentrate.
E∃ expand, amplify, pad out (*infml*).

abroad *adverb*
overseas, in foreign parts, out of the country, far and wide, widely, extensively.
E∃ at home.

abrupt *adjective*
1 abrupt departure: sudden, unexpected, unforeseen, surprising, quick, rapid, swift, hasty, hurried, precipitate (*fml*).
2 an abrupt drop: sheer, precipitous, steep, sharp.
3 an abrupt reply/manner: brusque, curt, terse, short, brisk, snappy, gruff, rude, uncivil, impolite, blunt, direct.
E∃ **1** gradual, slow, leisurely. **3** expansive, ceremonious, polite.

abscond *verb*
run away, run off, make off, decamp, flee, fly, escape, bolt, quit, clear out (*infml*), disappear.

absence *noun*
1 absence from school: truancy, non-attendance, non-appearance, absenteeism, non-existence.
2 absence of colour: lack, need, want, deficiency, dearth, scarcity, unavailability, default, omission, vacancy.
E∃ **1** presence, attendance, appearance. **2** existence.

absent *adjective*
1 absent from school/the meeting: missing, not present, away, out, unavailable, gone, lacking, truant.
2 an absent smile: inattentive, daydreaming, dreamy, faraway, elsewhere, absent-minded, vacant, vague, distracted, preoccupied, unaware, oblivious, unheeding.
E∃ **1** present. **2** alert, aware.

absent-minded *adjective*
forgetful, scatterbrained, absent, abstracted, withdrawn, faraway, distracted, preoccupied, absorbed, engrossed, pensive, musing, dreaming, dreamy, inattentive, unaware, oblivious, unconscious, heedless, unheeding, unthinking, impractical.
E∃ attentive, practical, matter-of-fact.

absolute *adjective*
1 in absolute confidence/silence: utter, total, complete, entire, full, thorough, exhaustive, supreme, definitive, conclusive, final, categorical, definite, unequivocal, unquestionable, decided, decisive, positive, sure, certain, genuine, pure, perfect, sheer, unmixed, unqualified, downright, out-and-out, outright.
2 absolute power/ruler: omnipotent, totalitarian, autocratic, tyrannical, despotic, dictatorial, sovereign, unlimited, unrestricted.

absolutely *adverb*
utterly, totally, dead, completely, entirely, fully, wholly, thoroughly, exhaustively, perfectly, supremely, unconditionally, conclusively, finally,

categorically, definitely, positively,
unequivocally, unambiguously,
unquestionably, decidedly, decisively,
surely, certainly, infallibly, genuinely,
truly, purely, exactly, precisely.

absolve verb
excuse, forgive, exonerate, clear,
pardon, acquit, let off (infml).

absorb verb
1 absorb liquid/facts: take in, ingest,
drink in, imbibe, suck up, soak up,
consume, devour, engulf, digest,
assimilate, understand, receive, hold,
retain.
2 absorb your attention: engross,
involve, fascinate, enthral, monopolize,
preoccupy, occupy, fill (up).
E3 1 exude.

absorbing adjective
interesting, amusing, entertaining,
diverting, engrossing, preoccupying,
intriguing, fascinating, captivating,
enthralling, spellbinding, gripping,
riveting, compulsive, unputdownable
(infml).
E3 boring, off-putting.

abstain verb
refrain, decline, refuse, reject, resist,
forbear (fml), shun, avoid, keep from,
stop, cease, desist, give up, renounce,
forgo, go without, deny oneself.
E3 indulge.

abstemious adjective
abstinent, self-denying, self-
disciplined, disciplined, sober,
temperate, moderate, sparing, frugal,
austere, ascetic, restrained.
E3 intemperate, gluttonous, luxurious.

abstract adjective
non-concrete, conceptual, intellectual,
hypothetical, theoretical, unpractical,
unrealistic, general, generalized,
indefinite, metaphysical,
philosophical, academic, complex,
abstruse (fml), deep, profound, subtle.
E3 concrete, real, actual.

absurd adjective
ridiculous, ludicrous, preposterous,
fantastic, incongruous, illogical,
paradoxical, implausible, untenable,
unreasonable, irrational, nonsensical,
meaningless, senseless, foolish, silly,

stupid, idiotic, crazy, daft (infml),
farcical, comical, funny, humorous,
laughable, risible, derisory.
E3 logical, rational, sensible.

abundant adjective
plentiful, in plenty, full, filled, well-
supplied, ample, generous, bountiful,
rich, copious, profuse, lavish,
exuberant, teeming, overflowing.
E3 scarce, sparse.

abuse verb /a-**byooz**/
1 abuse authority: misuse, misapply,
exploit, take advantage of.
2 abuse children: oppress, wrong, ill-
treat, maltreat, hurt, injure, molest,
damage, spoil, harm.
3 abuse immigrants: insult, swear at,
defame (fml), libel, slander, smear,
disparage (fml), malign, revile, scold,
upbraid (fml).
E3 2 cherish, care for. **3** compliment,
praise.
▶ noun /a-**byoos**/
1 the abuse of privilege/drugs: misuse,
misapplication, exploitation,
imposition, oppression, wrong,
maltreatment.
2 child/physical abuse: mistreatment,
maltreatment, ill-treatment, cruelty,
hurt, injury, molestation, assault,
damage.
3 shout abuse: insults, obscenities,
invective, defamation (fml), libel,
slander, disparagement (fml),
reproach, scolding, upbraiding (fml),
tirade.
E3 2 care, attention. **3** compliment,
praise.

abusive adjective
insulting, offensive, rude, scathing,
hurtful, injurious, cruel, destructive,
defamatory, libellous, slanderous,
derogatory, disparaging, pejorative,
vilifying, maligning, reviling,
censorious, reproachful, scolding,
upbraiding.
E3 complimentary, polite.

abyss noun
gulf, chasm, crevasse, fissure, gorge,
canyon, crater, pit, depth, void.

academic adjective
1 she's very academic: scholarly,

erudite, learned, well-read, studious, bookish, scholastic, pedagogical, educational, instructional, literary, highbrow.
2 an academic, not practical, approach: theoretical, hypothetical, conjectural, speculative, notional, abstract, impractical.
▸ *noun*
professor, don, master, fellow, lecturer, tutor, student, scholar, man of letters.

accelerate *verb*
1 the car/driver accelerated: quicken, speed, speed up, go faster, pick up/ gather speed, step on it (*infml*).
2 accelerate a process: speed up, hasten, hurry, step up, expedite, precipitate (*fml*), stimulate, facilitate, advance, further, promote.
F₃ 1, 2 decelerate, slow down.

accent *noun*
pronunciation, enunciation, articulation, brogue, twang (*infml*), tone, pitch, intonation, inflection, accentuation, stress, emphasis, intensity, force, cadence, rhythm, beat, pulse, pulsation.

accentuate *verb*
accent, stress, emphasize, underline, highlight, intensify, strengthen, deepen.
F₃ play down, weaken.

accept *verb*
1 accept a gift: take, receive, obtain, acquire, gain, secure.
2 accept a decision: acknowledge, recognize, admit, allow, approve, agree to, consent to, take on, adopt.
3 accept ill-treatment: tolerate, put up with, stand, bear, abide, face up to, yield to.
F₃ 1 refuse, turn down. **2** reject.

acceptable *adjective*
satisfactory, tolerable, moderate, passable, adequate, all right, OK (*infml*), so-so (*infml*), unexceptionable, admissible, suitable, conventional, correct, desirable, pleasant, gratifying, welcome.
F₃ unacceptable, unsatisfactory, unwelcome.

accepted *adjective*
authorized, approved, ratified,

sanctioned, agreed, acknowledged, recognized, admitted, confirmed, acceptable, correct, conventional, orthodox, traditional, customary, time-honoured, established, received, universal, regular, standard, normal, usual, common.
F₃ unconventional, unorthodox, controversial.

access *noun*
admission, admittance, entry, entering, entrance, gateway, door, key, approach, passage, road, path, course.
F₃ exit, outlet.

accessible *adjective*
1 accessible from the motorway: reachable, get-at-able (*infml*), attainable, handy.
2 facilities made accessible to everyone: possible, obtainable, available, on hand, ready, achievable, convenient, near, nearby.
3 an accessible book: user-friendly, understandable, intelligible, easy to understand.
F₃ 1 inaccessible, remote. **3** incomprehensible, unintelligible.

accessory *noun*
1 computer accessories: extra, supplement, addition, appendage, attachment, extension, component, fitting, accompaniment.
2 accessories to match an outfit: decoration, adornment, frill, trimming.
3 an accessory to a crime: accomplice, partner, associate, colleague, confederate, assistant, helper, help, aid.

accident *noun*
1 happen by accident: chance, hazard, fortuity (*fml*), luck, fortune, fate, serendipity, contingency, fluke.
2 an accident with boiling water: misfortune, mischance, misadventure, mishap, casualty, blow, calamity, disaster.
3 a road accident: collision, crash, shunt (*infml*), prang (*slang*), pile-up (*infml*), smash.

accidental *adjective*
unintentional, unintended,

inadvertent, unplanned, uncalculated, unexpected, unforeseen, unlooked-for, chance, fortuitous (*fml*), flukey (*infml*), uncertain, haphazard, random, casual, incidental.
F3 intentional, deliberate, calculated, premeditated.

acclaim *verb*
praise, commend, extol (*fml*), exalt, honour, hail, salute, welcome, applaud, clap, cheer, celebrate.
▶ *noun*
acclamation, praise, commendation, homage, tribute, eulogy, exaltation, honour, welcome, approbation (*fml*), approval, applause, ovation, clapping, cheers, cheering, shouting, celebration.
F3 criticism, disapproval.

accommodate *verb*
1 **accommodate someone in a hotel**: lodge, board, put up, house, shelter.
2 **we try to accommodate all our customers**: oblige, help, assist, aid, serve, provide, supply, comply, conform.

accommodating *adjective*
obliging, indulgent, helpful, co-operative, willing, kind, considerate, unselfish, sympathetic, friendly, hospitable.
F3 disobliging, selfish.

accommodation

Types of accommodation include:

apartment, bedsit, bedsitter, digs (*infml*), dwelling, flat, halls of residence, hostel, lodgings, pad (*infml*), residence, rooms, shelter, squat (*infml*); bed and breakfast, boarding-house, guest-house, hotel, inn, motel, pension, timeshare, villa, youth hostel; barracks, billet, married quarters. ⇨ *See also* **building**;**house**; **room**.

accompany *verb*
1 **accompany someone on holiday**: escort, attend, convoy, chaperon(e), usher, conduct, follow.
2 **a book accompanied by a study guide**: coexist, coincide, belong to, go with, complement, supplement.

accomplice *noun*
assistant, helper, abettor, mate, henchman, conspirator, collaborator, ally, confederate, partner, associate, colleague, participator, accessory.

accomplish *verb*
achieve, attain, do, perform, carry out, execute, fulfil, discharge, finish, complete, conclude, consummate, realize, effect, bring about, engineer, produce, obtain.

accomplished *adjective*
skilled, professional, practised, proficient, gifted, talented, skilful, adroit, adept, expert, masterly, consummate, polished, cultivated.
F3 unskilled, inexpert, incapable.

accomplishment *noun*
1 **the accomplishment of a task**: achievement, attainment, doing, performance, carrying out, execution, fulfilment, discharge, finishing, completion, conclusion, consummation, perfection, realization, fruition, production.
2 **a writer of considerable accomplishment**: skill, art, aptitude, faculty, ability, capability, proficiency, gift, talent, forte.
3 **no mean accomplishment**: exploit, feat, deed, stroke, triumph.

according to *preposition*
in accordance with, in keeping with, obedient to, in conformity with, in line with, consistent with, commensurate with, in proportion to, in relation to, after, in the light of, in the manner of, after the manner of.

account *noun*
1 **an account of what happened**: narrative, story, tale, chronicle, history, memoir, record, statement, report, communiqué, write-up, version, portrayal, sketch, description, presentation, explanation.
2 **the accounts of a business**: ledger, book, books, register, inventory.
3 **pay an account**: statement, invoice, bill, tab, charge, reckoning, computation, tally, score, balance.
◆ **account for** explain, elucidate, illuminate, clear up, rationalize, justify,

vindicate, answer for, put paid to, destroy, kill.

accountable *adjective*
answerable, responsible, liable, amenable, obliged, bound.

accumulate *verb*
gather, assemble, collect, amass, aggregate, cumulate, accrue, grow, increase, multiply, build up, pile up, hoard, stockpile, stash (*infml*), store.
Fa disseminate.

accurate *adjective*
correct, right, unerring, precise, exact, well-directed, spot-on (*infml*), faultless, perfect, word-perfect, sound, authentic, factual, true, truthful, just, proper, close, faithful, well-judged, careful, rigorous, scrupulous, meticulous, strict, minute.
Fa inaccurate, wrong, imprecise, inexact.

accusation *noun*
charge, allegation, imputation, indictment, denunciation, impeachment, recrimination, complaint, incrimination.

accuse *verb*
charge, indict, impugn (*fml*), denounce, arraign, impeach, cite, allege, attribute, impute (*fml*), blame, censure, recriminate, incriminate, criminate, inform against.
Fa defend.

accustomed *adjective*
used, in the habit of, given to, confirmed, seasoned, hardened, inured, disciplined, trained, adapted, acclimatized, acquainted, familiar, wonted, habitual, routine, regular, normal, usual, ordinary, everyday, conventional, customary, traditional, established, fixed, prevailing, general.
Fa unaccustomed, unusual.

ache *verb*
1 *my neck aches*: hurt, be sore, suffer, agonize, throb, pound, twinge, smart, sting.
2 *aching to tell her*: yearn, long, pine, hanker, desire, crave, hunger, thirst, itch.
▶ *noun*
an ache in my neck: pain, hurt,
soreness, suffering, anguish, agony, throb, throbbing, pounding, pang, twinge, smarting, stinging.

achieve *verb*
accomplish, attain, reach, get, obtain, acquire, procure, gain, earn, win, succeed, manage, do, perform, carry out, execute, fulfil, finish, complete, consummate, effect, bring about, realize, produce.
Fa miss, fail.

achievement *noun*
1 *the achievement of our aims*: accomplishment, attainment, acquirement, performance, execution, fulfilment, completion, success, realization, fruition.
2 *great achievements*: act, deed, exploit, feat, effort.

acid *adjective*
1 *tastes acid*: sour, bitter, tart, vinegary, sharp, pungent, acidic, acerbic, caustic, corrosive.
2 *an acid remark*: stinging, biting, mordant (*fml*), cutting, incisive, trenchant (*fml*), harsh, hurtful.

acknowledge *verb*
1 *acknowledge an error*: admit, confess, own up to, declare, recognize, accept, grant, allow, concede.
2 *acknowledged us with a nod*: greet, address, notice, salute, recognize.
3 *acknowledge a letter*: answer, reply to, respond to, confirm.
Fa 1 deny. **2** ignore.

acquaint *verb*
accustom, familiarize, tell, notify, advise, inform, brief, enlighten, divulge, disclose, reveal, announce.

acquaintance *noun*
1 *my acquaintance with them*: familiarity, intimacy, relationship, association, fellowship, companionship.
2 *some acquaintance with art*: familiarity, awareness, knowledge, understanding, experience.
3 *friends and acquaintances*: friend, companion, colleague, associate, contact.

acquire *verb*
buy, purchase, procure, appropriate,

obtain, get, cop (*slang*), receive, collect, pick up, gather, net, gain, secure, earn, win, achieve, attain, realize.
F3 relinquish, forfeit.

acquit *verb*
absolve, clear, reprieve, let off, exonerate, exculpate (*fml*), excuse, vindicate, free, liberate, deliver, relieve, release, dismiss, discharge, settle, satisfy, repay.
F3 convict.

acrid *adjective*
pungent, sharp, stinging, acid, sour, tart, burning, caustic, acerbic.

acrimonious *adjective*
bitter, biting, cutting, trenchant (*fml*), sharp, virulent, severe, spiteful, censorious, abusive, ill-tempered.
F3 peaceable, kindly.

act *noun*
1 acts of bravery: deed, action, undertaking, enterprise, operation, manoeuvre, move, step, doing, execution, accomplishment, achievement, exploit, feat, stroke.
2 put on an act: pretence, make-believe, sham, fake, feigning, dissimulation, affectation, show, front.
3 an act of parliament: law, statute, ordinance, edict, decree, resolution, measure, bill.
4 a juggler's act: turn, item, routine, sketch, performance, gig (*slang*).
▶ *verb*
1 act in a certain way: behave, be, move, do, conduct, exert, work.
2 the drug will act soon: take effect, have an effect, work, operate, function.
3 the gear acts as a brake: work, function, serve, operate, do, do the job of.
4 act upset: pretend, feign, put on, assume, simulate.
5 act in a play: mimic, imitate, impersonate, portray, represent, mime, play, perform, enact.
◆ **act on 1** act on orders: carry out, fulfil, comply with, conform to, obey, follow, heed, take.
2 natural enzymes acting on the skin: affect, influence, alter, modify, change, transform.

acting *adjective*
temporary, provisional, interim, stopgap, supply, stand-by, substitute, reserve.

action *noun*
1 his prompt action: act, move, deed, exploit, feat, accomplishment, achievement, performance, effort, endeavour, enterprise, undertaking, proceeding, process, activity.
2 people of action: liveliness, spirit, energy, vigour, power, force.
3 put an idea into action: exercise, exertion, work, functioning, operation, mechanism, movement, motion.
4 killed in action: warfare, battle, conflict, combat, fight, fray, engagement, skirmish, clash.
5 a legal action: litigation, lawsuit, suit, case, prosecution.

activate *verb*
start, initiate, trigger, set off, fire, switch on, set in motion, mobilize, propel, move, stir, rouse, arouse, stimulate, motivate, prompt, animate, energize, impel, excite, galvanize.
F3 deactivate, stop, arrest.

active *adjective*
1 an active person: busy, occupied, on the go (*infml*), industrious, diligent, hardworking, forceful, spirited, vital, forward, dynamic.
2 active members: enterprising, enthusiastic, devoted, engaged, involved, committed, militant, activist.
3 active for his age: agile, nimble, sprightly, light-footed, quick, alert, animated, lively, energetic, vigorous.
4 the system is active: in operation, functioning, working, running.
F3 1 passive. 3 inert, dormant. 4 inactive.

activity *noun*
1 there is always a lot of activity around the town centre: liveliness, life, activeness, action, motion, movement, commotion, bustle, hustle, industry, labour, exertion, exercise.
2 holiday activities: occupation, job, work, act, deed, project, scheme, task, venture, enterprise, endeavour,

undertaking, pursuit, hobby, pastime, interest.
F3 1 inactivity.

actor *noun*
actress, play-actor, comedian, tragedian, ham, player, performer, artist, impersonator, mime.

actual *adjective*
real, existent, substantial, tangible, material, physical, concrete, positive, definite, absolute, certain, unquestionable, indisputable, confirmed, verified, factual, truthful, true, genuine, legitimate, bona fide, authentic, realistic.
F3 theoretical, apparent, imaginary.

actually *adverb*
in fact, as a matter of fact, as it happens, in truth, in reality, really, truly, indeed, absolutely.

acumen *noun*
astuteness, shrewdness, sharpness, keenness, quickness, penetration, insight, intuition, discrimination, discernment, judgement, perception, sense, wit, wisdom, intelligence, cleverness, ingenuity.

acute *adjective*
1 an acute shortage: severe, intense, extreme, violent, dangerous, serious, grave, urgent, crucial, vital, decisive, sharp, cutting, poignant, distressing.
2 an acute mind: sharp, keen, incisive, penetrating, astute, shrewd, judicious (*fml*), discerning, observant, perceptive.
F3 1 mild, slight.

adapt *verb*
alter, change, qualify, modify, adjust, convert, remodel, customize, fit, tailor, fashion, shape, harmonize, match, suit, conform, comply, prepare, familiarize, acclimatize.

adaptable *adjective*
alterable, changeable, variable, modifiable, adjustable, convertible, conformable, versatile, plastic, malleable, flexible, compliant, amenable, easy-going.
F3 inflexible, refractory.

adaptation *noun*
alteration, change, shift,

transformation, modification, adjustment, accommodation, conversion, remodelling, reworking, reshaping, refitting, revision, variation, version.

add *verb*
append, annex, affix, attach, tack on, join, combine, supplement, augment.
F3 take away, remove.
◆ **add up 1 add up numbers**: add, sum up, tot up, total, tally, count (up), reckon, compute.
2 the total adds up to 200: amount, come to, constitute, include.
3 it doesn't add up: be consistent, hang together, fit, be plausible, be reasonable, make sense, mean, signify, indicate.
F3 1 subtract.

addict *noun*
1 a chess addict: enthusiast, fan, buff (*infml*), fiend, freak (*infml*), devotee, follower, adherent.
2 a drug addict: drug taker, drug user, user (*infml*), dope-fiend, junkie (*infml*).

addiction *noun*
dependence, craving, compulsion, habit, obsession.

addition *noun*
1 the addition of a conservatory: adding, annexation, accession, extension, enlargement, increasing, increase, gain.
2 an addition to the report: adjunct, supplement, additive, addendum, appendix, appendage, accessory, attachment, extra, increment.
3 addition of numbers: summing-up, totting-up, totalling, counting, reckoning, inclusion.
F3 1 removal. **3** subtraction.
◆ **in addition** additionally, too, also, as well, besides, moreover, further, furthermore, over and above.

additional *adjective*
added, extra, supplementary, spare, more, further, increased, other, new, fresh.

address *noun*
1 one's home/business address: residence, dwelling, abode (*fml*), house, home, lodging, direction,

whereabouts, location, situation, place.
2 the president's address to the nation: speech, talk, lecture, sermon, oration (*fml*), discourse, dissertation.
▶ *verb*
1 addressing me in his normal tone of voice: speak to, talk to, greet, salute, hail.
2 addressed his remarks to me: direct, convey, communicate.
♦ **address (yourself) to** deal with, attend to, apply (yourself) to, focus on, tackle.

adept *adjective*
skilled, accomplished, expert, masterly, experienced, versed, practised, polished, proficient, able, adroit, deft, nimble.

adequate *adjective*
enough, sufficient, commensurate, requisite, suitable, fit, able, competent, capable, serviceable, acceptable, satisfactory, passable, tolerable, fair, respectable, presentable.
E∃ inadequate, insufficient.

adhere *verb*
1 barnacles adhering to the hull: stick, glue, paste, cement, fix, fasten, attach, join, link, combine, coalesce, cohere, hold, cling, cleave to.
2 adhere to the agreement: observe, follow, abide by, comply with, fulfil, obey, keep, heed, respect, stand by.

adherent *noun*
supporter, upholder, advocate, partisan, follower, disciple, satellite, henchman, hanger-on, votary, devotee, admirer, fan, enthusiast, freak (*infml*), nut (*infml*).

adhesive *adjective*
sticky, tacky, self-adhesive, gummed, gummy, gluey, adherent, adhering, sticking, clinging, holding, attaching, cohesive.
▶ *noun*
glue, gum, paste, cement.

adjacent *adjective*
adjoining, abutting, touching, contiguous, bordering, alongside, beside, juxtaposed, next-door, neighbouring, next, closest, nearest, close, near.
E∃ remote, distant.

adjoining *adjective*
adjacent to, abutting, touching, meeting, bordering, neighbouring, alongside, next to.

adjourn *verb*
interrupt, suspend, discontinue, break off, delay, stay, defer, postpone, put off, recess, retire.
E∃ assemble, convene.

adjust *verb*
1 adjust one's plans/the volume: modify, change, adapt, alter, convert, dispose, shape, remodel, fit, suit, accommodate, measure, rectify, regulate, balance, temper, tune, fine-tune, fix, set, arrange, compose, settle, square.
2 adjust to new conditions: accustom, habituate, acclimatize, reconcile, harmonize, conform.
E∃ 1 disarrange, upset.

ad-lib *verb*
improvise, make up, invent, extemporize (*fml*).
▶ *adverb*
impromptu, spontaneously, extemporaneously (*fml*), off the cuff (*infml*), off the top of one's head (*infml*).

administer *verb*
1 administer an organization: govern, rule, lead, head, preside over, officiate, manage, run, organize, direct, conduct, control, regulate, superintend, supervise, oversee.
2 administer the medicine: give, provide, supply, distribute, dole out, dispense, measure out, mete out, execute, impose, apply.

administrative *adjective*
governmental, legislative, authoritative, directorial, managerial, management, executive, organizational, regulatory, supervisory.

admirable *adjective*
praiseworthy, commendable, laudable, creditable, deserving, worthy, respected, fine, excellent, superior, wonderful, exquisite, choice, rare, valuable.
E∃ contemptible, despicable, deplorable.

admiration *noun*
esteem, regard, respect, reverence, veneration, worship, idolism, adoration, affection, approval, praise, appreciation, pleasure, delight, wonder, astonishment, amazement, surprise.
🔁 contempt.

admire *verb*
esteem, respect, revere, venerate, worship, idolize, adore, approve, praise, laud (*fml*), applaud, appreciate, value.
🔁 despise, censure.

admirer *noun*
follower, disciple, adherent, supporter, fan, enthusiast, devotee, worshipper, idolizer, suitor, boyfriend, girlfriend, sweetheart, lover.
🔁 critic, opponent.

admission *noun*
confession, acknowledgement, granting, recognition, acceptance, allowance, concession, affirmation, declaration, profession, disclosure, divulgence, revelation, exposé.
🔁 denial.

admit *verb*
1 admit I was wrong: confess, own (up), grant, acknowledge, recognize, accept, allow, concede, agree, affirm, declare, profess, disclose, divulge, reveal.
2 be admitted to the palace: let in, allow to enter, give access, accept, receive, take in, introduce, initiate.
🔁 **1** deny. **2** shut out, exclude.

adolescence *noun*
teens, puberty, youth, minority, boyhood, girlhood, development, immaturity, youthfulness, boyishness, girlishness.

adolescent *adjective*
teenage, young, youthful, juvenile, boyish, girlish, growing, developing, pubescent.
▸ *noun*
teenager, young person, young adult, youth, juvenile, minor.

adopt *verb*
take on, accept, assume, take up, appropriate, embrace, follow, choose, select, take in, foster, support,
maintain, back, endorse, ratify, approve.
🔁 repudiate, disown.

adorable *adjective*
lovable, dear, darling, precious, appealing, sweet, winsome, charming, enchanting, captivating, winning, delightful, pleasing, attractive, fetching.
🔁 hateful, abominable.

adore *verb*
love, cherish, dote on, admire, esteem, honour, revere, venerate, worship, idolize, exalt, glorify.
🔁 hate, abhor.

adorn *verb*
decorate, deck, bedeck, ornament, crown, trim, garnish, gild, enhance, embellish, doll up (*infml*), enrich, grace.

adult *adjective*
grown-up, of age, full-grown, fully grown, developed, mature, ripe, ripened.
🔁 immature.

adulterate *verb*
contaminate, pollute, taint, corrupt, defile (*fml*), debase, dilute, water down, weaken, doctor (*infml*).
🔁 purify.

advance *verb*
1 advance to the next stage: proceed, go forward, move on, move forward, go ahead, progress, push on (*infml*).
2 advance his career considerably: accelerate, speed, further, promote, improve, boost, upgrade, foster, support, assist, benefit, facilitate.
3 technology advanced very rapidly: improve, develop, prosper, thrive.
4 advance an idea: present, submit, suggest, allege, cite, put/bring forward, offer, provide, supply.
5 advance a sum of money: lend, loan, pay beforehand, pay, give.
🔁 **1** retreat. **2** retard, impede.
▸ *noun*
1 an important technological advance: progress, forward movement, onward movement, headway, step, advancement, breakthrough, development, growth, increase, improvement.

2 *an advance on his salary*: deposit, down payment, prepayment, credit, loan.
Ⓕ **1** retreat, recession.
◆ **in advance** beforehand, previously, early, earlier, sooner, ahead, in front, in the lead, in the forefront.
Ⓕ later, behind.

advanced *adjective*
leading, foremost, ahead, forward, precocious, progressive, forward-looking, avant-garde, ultra-modern, sophisticated, complex, higher.
Ⓕ backward, retarded, elementary.

advantage *noun*
1 *the advantages of electric light*: asset, blessing, benefit, good, welfare, interest, service, help, aid, assistance, use, avail, convenience, usefulness, utility, profit, gain, start.
2 *an advantage over other candidates*: lead, edge (*infml*), upper hand, superiority, precedence, pre-eminence, sway.
Ⓕ **1** disadvantage, drawback, hindrance.

advantageous *adjective*
beneficial, favourable, opportune, convenient, helpful, useful, worthwhile, valuable, profitable, gainful, remunerative, rewarding.
Ⓕ disadvantageous, adverse, damaging.

adventure *noun*
exploit, venture, undertaking, enterprise, risk, hazard, escapade, chance, speculation, experience, incident, occurrence.

adventurous *adjective*
daring, intrepid, bold, audacious, headstrong, impetuous, reckless, rash, risky, venturesome, enterprising.
Ⓕ cautious, wary, prudent.

adverse *adjective*
hostile, antagonistic, opposing, opposite, counter, contrary, conflicting, counter-productive, negative, disadvantageous, unfavourable, inauspicious, unfortunate, unlucky, inopportune, detrimental, harmful, noxious,
injurious, hurtful, unfriendly, uncongenial.
Ⓕ advantageous, favourable.

adversity *noun*
misfortune, ill fortune, bad luck, ill luck, reverse, hardship, hard times, misery, wretchedness, affliction, suffering, distress, sorrow, woe, trouble, trial, tribulation, calamity, disaster, catastrophe.
Ⓕ prosperity.

advertise *verb*
publicize, promote, push, plug (*infml*), praise, hype (*infml*), trumpet, blazon, herald, announce, declare, proclaim, broadcast, publish, display, make known, inform, notify.

advertisement *noun*
advert (*infml*), ad (*infml*), commercial, publicity, promotion, plug (*infml*), hype (*infml*), display, blurb, announcement, notice, poster, bill, placard, leaflet, circular, handout, propaganda.

advice *noun*
1 *gave her some good advice*: warning, caution, do's and don'ts, injunction, instruction, counsel, help, guidance, direction, suggestion, recommendation, opinion, view.
2 *a remittance advice*: notification, notice, memorandum, communication, information, intelligence.

advisable *adjective*
recommended, sensible, wise, prudent, judicious (*fml*), sound, profitable, beneficial, desirable, suitable, fitting, appropriate, apt, fit, proper, correct.
Ⓕ inadvisable, foolish.

advise *verb*
1 *advised him to say nothing*: counsel, guide, warn, forewarn, caution, instruct, teach, tutor, suggest, recommend, commend, urge.
2 *advised us of his arrival*: notify, inform, tell, acquaint, make known, report.

adviser *noun*
counsellor, consultant, authority, guide, teacher, tutor, instructor, coach, helper, aide, right-hand man, mentor, confidant(e), counsel, lawyer.

advocate *verb*
defend, champion, campaign for, press for, argue for, plead for, justify, urge, encourage, advise, recommend, propose, promote, endorse, support, uphold, patronize, adopt, subscribe to, favour, countenance.
Fa impugn (*fml*), disparage (*fml*), deprecate (*fml*).

affable *adjective*
friendly, amiable, approachable, open, expansive, genial, good-humoured, good-natured, mild, benevolent, kindly, gracious, obliging, courteous, amicable, congenial, cordial, warm, sociable, pleasant, agreeable.
Fa unfriendly, reserved, reticent, cool.

affair *noun*
1 a curious affair: business, transaction, operation, proceeding, undertaking, activity, project, responsibility, interest, concern, matter, question, issue, subject, topic, circumstance, happening, occurrence, incident, episode, event.
2 have an affair: relationship, liaison, intrigue, love affair, romance, amour.

affect *verb*
1 affecting the climate/doesn't affect us: concern, regard, involve, relate to, apply to, bear upon, impinge upon, act on, change, transform, alter, modify, influence, sway, prevail over, attack, strike, impress, interest, stir, move, touch, upset, disturb, perturb, trouble, overcome.
2 affect an air of indifference: adopt, assume, put on, feign, simulate, imitate, fake, counterfeit, sham, pretend, profess, aspire to.

affectation *noun*
airs, pretentiousness, mannerism, pose, act, show, appearance, façade, pretence, sham, simulation, imitation, artificiality, insincerity.
Fa artlessness, ingenuousness.

affected *adjective*
assumed, put-on, feigned, simulated, artificial, fake, counterfeit, sham, phoney (*infml*), contrived, studied, precious, mannered, pretentious,
pompous, stiff, unnatural, insincere.
Fa genuine, natural.

affection *noun*
fondness, attachment, devotion, love, tenderness, care, warmth, feeling, kindness, friendliness, goodwill, favour, liking, partiality, inclination, penchant, passion, desire.
Fa dislike, antipathy.

affectionate *adjective*
fond, attached, devoted, doting, loving, tender, caring, warm, warm-hearted, kind, friendly, amiable, cordial.
Fa cold, undemonstrative.

affirm *verb*
confirm, corroborate, endorse, ratify, certify, witness, testify, swear, maintain, state, assert, declare, pronounce.
Fa refute, deny.

affirmative *adjective*
agreeing, concurring, approving, assenting, positive, confirming, corroborative, emphatic.
Fa negative, dissenting.

afflict *verb*
strike, visit, trouble, burden, oppress, distress, grieve, pain, hurt, wound, harm, try, harass, beset, plague, torment, torture.
Fa comfort, solace.

affliction *noun*
distress, grief, sorrow, misery, depression, suffering, pain, torment, disease, illness, sickness, plague, curse, cross, ordeal, trial, tribulation, trouble, hardship, adversity, misfortune, calamity, disaster.
Fa comfort, consolation, solace, blessing.

affluent *adjective*
wealthy, rich, moneyed, loaded (*infml*), flush (*infml*), well-off, prosperous, well-to-do, opulent, comfortable.
Fa poor, impoverished.

afford *verb*
1 can't afford a holiday: have enough for, be able to pay, spare, allow, manage.
2 afford some relief: provide, supply, furnish, give, grant, offer, impart, produce, yield, generate.

affront *noun*
offence, insult, slur, rudeness, discourtesy, disrespect, indignity, snub, slight, wrong, injury, abuse, provocation, vexation, outrage.
F3 compliment.

afraid *adjective*
frightened, scared, alarmed, terrified, fearful, timorous, daunted, intimidated, faint-hearted, cowardly, reluctant, apprehensive, anxious, nervous, timid, distrustful, suspicious.
F3 unafraid, brave, bold, confident.

after *preposition*
following, subsequent to, as a result of, in consequence of, behind, below.
F3 before.

again *adverb*
once more, once again, another time, over again, afresh, anew, encore.

against *preposition*
1 against the wall: abutting, adjacent to, close up to, touching, in contact with, on.
2 against the proposal/against our wishes: opposite to, facing, fronting, in the face of, confronting, opposing, versus, opposed to, in opposition to, hostile to, resisting, in defiance of, in contrast to.
F3 2 for, pro.

age *noun*
1 the age of steam: era, epoch, day, days, generation, date, time, period, duration, span, years, aeon.
2 age was creeping up on him: old age, maturity, elderliness, seniority, dotage, senility, decline.
F3 2 youth.
► *verb*
grow old, decline, deteriorate, degenerate.

agent *noun*
1 a travel/estate/government agent: representative, rep (*infml*), broker, middleman, go-between, intermediary, negotiator, mover, doer, performer, operator, operative, functionary, worker.
2 the agent of change: instrument, vehicle, channel, means, agency, cause, force.

aggravate *verb*
1 aggravate the problem: exacerbate, worsen, inflame, increase, intensify, heighten, magnify, exaggerate.
2 (*infml*) don't aggravate him!: annoy, irritate, vex, needle (*infml*), get on someone's nerves (*infml*), exasperate, incense, provoke, tease, pester, harass.
F3 1 improve, alleviate. **2** appease, mollify.

aggressive *adjective*
argumentative, quarrelsome, contentious, belligerent, warlike, pugnacious (*fml*), hostile, offensive, provocative, intrusive, invasive, bold, assertive, pushy (*infml*), go-ahead, forceful, vigorous, zealous, ruthless, destructive.
F3 peaceable, friendly, submissive, timid.

aggrieved *adjective*
wronged, offended, hurt, injured, insulted, maltreated, ill-used, resentful, pained, distressed, saddened, unhappy, upset, annoyed.
F3 pleased.

aghast *adjective*
shocked, appalled, horrified, horror-struck, thunderstruck, stunned, stupefied, amazed, astonished, astounded, startled, confounded, dismayed.

agile *adjective*
active, lively, nimble, spry, sprightly, mobile, flexible, limber, lithe, fleet, quick, swift, brisk, prompt, sharp, acute, alert, quick-witted, clever, adroit, deft.
F3 clumsy, stiff.

agitate *verb*
1 the noise and bustle agitated them: rouse, arouse, stir up, excite, stimulate, incite, inflame, ferment, work up, worry, trouble, upset, alarm, disturb, unsettle, disquiet, discompose, fluster, ruffle, flurry, unnerve, confuse, distract, disconcert.
2 agitating the leaves/the water: shake, rattle, rock, stir, beat, churn, toss, convulse.
F3 1 calm, tranquillize.

agitator *noun*
troublemaker, rabble-rouser, revolutionary, stirrer (*infml*), inciter, instigator.

agony *noun*
anguish, torment, torture, pain, spasm, throes, suffering, affliction, tribulation, distress, woe, misery, wretchedness.

agree *verb*
1 agree with each other: concur, see eye to eye, get on, settle, accord, match, suit, fit, tally, correspond, conform.
2 agree to his offer: consent, allow, permit, assent, accede, grant, admit, concede, yield, comply.
E3 1 disagree, differ, conflict. **2** refuse.

agreement *noun*
1 the final agreement: settlement, compact, covenant, treaty, pact, contract, deal, bargain, arrangement, understanding.
2 be in agreement: concurrence, accord, concord, unanimity, union, harmony, sympathy, affinity, compatibility, similarity, correspondence, consistency, conformity, compliance, adherence, acceptance.
E3 2 disagreement.

agricultural *adjective*
farming, farmed, cultivated, rural, pastoral, bucolic (*fml*), agrarian, agronomic.

ahead *adverb*
forward, onward, leading, at the head, in front, in the lead, winning, at an advantage, advanced, superior, to the fore, in the forefront, in advance, before, earlier on.

aid *noun*
help, assistance, prop, support, relief, benefit, subsidy, donation, contribution, funding, grant, sponsorship, patronage, favour, encouragement, service.
E3 hindrance, impediment, obstruction.
▸ *verb*
help, assist, support, subsidize, sustain, promote, boost, encourage, expedite, facilitate, ease.
E3 hinder, impede, obstruct.

ailment *noun*
illness, sickness, complaint, malady, disease, infection, disorder, affliction, infirmity, disability, weakness.

aim *verb*
1 aim their guns at: point, direct, take aim, level, train, sight, zero in on (*infml*), target.
2 aiming to get into Oxford or Cambridge: aspire, want, wish, seek, resolve, purpose, intend, propose, mean, plan, design, strive, try, attempt, endeavour.
▸ *noun*
aspiration, ambition, hope, dream, desire, wish, plan, design, scheme, purpose, motive, end, intention, object, objective, target, mark, goal, direction, course.

aimless *adjective*
pointless, purposeless, unmotivated, irresolute, directionless, rambling, undirected, unguided, stray, chance, random, haphazard, erratic, unpredictable, wayward.
E3 purposeful, positive, determined.

air *noun*
1 open the window to get a little air: oxygen, breath, puff, waft, draught, breeze, wind.
2 birds flying in the air: sky, heavens, atmosphere.
3 an air of indifference: appearance, look, aspect, aura, bearing, demeanour, manner, character, effect, impression, feeling, quality.
▸ *verb*
1 air a room: ventilate, aerate, freshen.
2 air an opinion: utter, voice, express, give vent to, make known, declare, communicate, tell, reveal, disclose, divulge, expose, make public, broadcast, publish, circulate, disseminate, exhibit, display, parade, publicize.

airless *adjective*
unventilated, stuffy, musty, stale, suffocating, stifling, sultry, muggy, close, heavy, oppressive.
E3 airy, fresh.

airy *adjective*
1 a bright and airy office: roomy,

spacious, open, well-ventilated.
2 his manner was airy: cheerful, happy,
light-hearted, high-spirited, lively,
nonchalant, offhand.
E3 1 airless, stuffy, close, heavy,
oppressive.

alarm *noun*
1 jumped back in alarm: fright, scare,
fear, terror, panic, horror, shock,
consternation, dismay, distress,
anxiety, nervousness, apprehension,
trepidation, uneasiness.
2 sound the alarm: danger signal, alert,
warning, distress signal, siren, bell,
alarm-bell, fire alarm, tocsin (*fml*).
E3 1 calmness, composure.
▶ *verb*
frighten, scare, startle, put the wind up
(*infml*), terrify, panic, unnerve, daunt,
dismay, distress, agitate.
E3 reassure, calm, soothe.

alarming *adjective*
frightening, scary, startling, terrifying,
unnerving, daunting, ominous,
threatening, dismaying, disturbing,
distressing, shocking, dreadful.
E3 reassuring.

alert *adjective*
attentive, wide-awake, watchful,
vigilant, on the lookout, sharp-eyed,
observant, perceptive, sharp-witted,
on the ball (*infml*), on your toes (*infml*),
quick, nimble, ready, prepared, careful,
heedful, circumspect (*fml*), wary.
E3 slow, listless, unprepared.
▶ *verb*
warn, forewarn, notify, inform, tip off,
signal, make aware.

alias *noun*
pseudonym, false name, assumed
name, nom de guerre, nom de plume,
pen name, stage name, nickname,
sobriquet (*fml*).
▶ *preposition*
also known as, a.k.a. (*infml*), also
called, otherwise.

alibi *noun*
defence, justification, story,
explanation, excuse, pretext, reason.

alien *adjective*
strange, unfamiliar, outlandish,
incongruous, foreign, exotic,

extraterrestrial, extraneous, remote,
estranged, separated, opposed,
contrary, conflicting, antagonistic,
incompatible.
E3 akin.
▶ *noun*
foreigner, immigrant, newcomer,
stranger, outsider.
E3 native.

alight¹ *verb*
passengers alighting from buses:
descend, get down, dismount, get off,
disembark, land, touch down, come
down, come to rest, settle, light, perch.
E3 ascend, board.

alight² *adjective*
eyes alight with excitement: lighted,
lit, ignited, on fire, burning, blazing,
ablaze, flaming, fiery, lit up,
illuminated, bright, radiant, shining,
brilliant.
E3 dark.

align *verb*
1 aligned the two edges of the fabric:
straighten, range, line up, make
parallel, even (up), adjust.
2 aligned themselves with Labour:
ally, side, sympathize, associate,
affiliate, join, co-operate, agree.

alike *adjective*
similar, resembling, comparable, akin,
analogous, corresponding, equivalent,
equal, the same, identical, duplicate,
parallel, even, uniform.
E3 dissimilar, unlike, different.
▶ *adverb*
similarly, analogously,
correspondingly, equally, in common.

alive *adjective*
1 didn't know if he was alive or dead:
living, having life, live, animate,
breathing, existent, in existence, real.
2 alive with insects: full of, overflowing
with, crawling with (*infml*), teeming
with, abounding in.
E3 1 dead, extinct.

all *adjective*
1 all people are equal/all Europe was
at war: each, every, each and every,
every single, every one of, the whole of,
every bit of.
2 go with all speed: complete, entire,

full, total, utter, outright, perfect, greatest.
E3 1 no, none.
▶ *noun*
everything, sum, total, aggregate, total amount, whole amount, whole, entirety, the lot (*infml*), comprehensiveness, utmost, universality.
E3 nothing, none.
▶ *adverb*
completely, entirely, wholly, fully, totally, utterly, altogether.

allay *verb*
alleviate, relieve, soothe, ease, smooth, calm, quiet, quell, pacify, mollify, soften, blunt, lessen, reduce, diminish, check, moderate.
E3 exacerbate, intensify.

allegation *noun*
accusation, charge, claim, profession, assertion, affirmation, declaration, statement, testimony, plea.

allege *verb*
assert, affirm, declare, state, attest (*fml*), maintain, insist, hold, contend, claim, profess, plead.

alleged *adjective*
supposed, reputed, inferred, so-called, professed, declared, stated, claimed, described, designated, doubtful, dubious, suspect, suspicious.

allegiance *noun*
loyalty, fidelity, faithfulness, constancy, duty, obligation, obedience, devotion, support, adherence, friendship.
E3 disloyalty, enmity.

allergic *adjective*
sensitive, hypersensitive, susceptible, affected, incompatible, averse, disinclined, opposed, hostile, antagonistic.
E3 tolerant.

alleviate *verb*
relieve, soothe, ease, palliate (*fml*), mitigate, soften, cushion, dull, deaden, allay, abate, lessen, reduce, diminish, check, moderate, temper, subdue.
E3 aggravate.

alliance *noun*
confederation, federation, association, affiliation, coalition, league, bloc,

cartel, conglomerate, consortium, syndicate, guild, union, partnership, marriage, agreement, compact, bond, pact, treaty, combination, connection.
E3 separation, divorce, estrangement, enmity, hostility.

allocate *verb*
assign, designate, budget, allow, earmark, set aside, allot, apportion, share out, distribute, dispense, mete.

allot *verb*
divide, ration, apportion, share out, distribute, dispense, mete, dole out (*infml*), allocate, assign, designate, budget, allow, grant, earmark, set aside.

all-out *adjective*
complete, full, total, undivided, comprehensive, exhaustive, thorough, intensive, thoroughgoing, wholesale, vigorous, powerful, full-scale, no-holds-barred (*infml*), maximum, utmost, unlimited, unrestrained, resolute, determined.
E3 perfunctory (*fml*), half-hearted.

allow *verb*
1 allow the children to stay up late: permit, let, enable, authorize, sanction, approve, tolerate, put up with (*infml*), endure, suffer.
2 allow two hours for the journey: allot, allocate, assign, apportion, afford, give, provide.
3 allow that he had a point: admit, confess, own, acknowledge, concede, grant.
E3 1 forbid, prevent. **3** deny.
◆ **allow for** take into account, make provision for, make allowances for, provide for, foresee, plan for, arrange for, bear in mind, keep in mind, consider, include.
E3 discount.

allowance *noun*
1 their weekly allowance of milk and eggs: allotment, lot, amount, allocation, portion, share, ration, quota.
2 give him an allowance of £200 a month: payment, remittance, pocket money, grant, maintenance, stipend, pension, annuity.

3 an allowance against tax: rebate, reduction, deduction, discount, concession, subsidy, weighting.

alloy *noun*
blend, compound, composite, amalgam, combination, mixture, fusion, coalescence.

all right *adjective*
1 it was all right, I suppose: satisfactory, passable, unobjectionable, acceptable, allowable, adequate, fair, average, OK (*infml*).
2 are you all right?: well, healthy, unhurt, uninjured, unharmed, unimpaired, whole, sound, safe, secure.
Ea 1 unacceptable, inadequate.

allude *verb*
mention, refer to, speak of, hint at, imply, insinuate, touch on/upon, suggest.

ally *noun*
confederate, associate, consort, partner, sidekick, colleague, co-worker, collaborator, helper, helpmate, accomplice, accessory, friend.
Ea antagonist, enemy.
▶ *verb*
confederate, affiliate, league, associate, collaborate, join forces, band together, team up, fraternize, side, join, connect, link, marry, unite, unify, amalgamate, combine.
Ea estrange, separate.

almighty *adjective*
1 the almighty Caesar: omnipotent, all-powerful, supreme, absolute, great, invincible.
2 an almighty bang: enormous, severe, intense, overwhelming, overpowering, terrible, awful, desperate.
Ea 1 impotent, weak.

almost *adverb*
nearly, well-nigh, practically, virtually, just about, as good as, all but, close to, not far from, approaching, nearing, not quite, about, approximately.

alone *adjective*
only, sole, single, unique, solitary, separate, detached, unconnected, isolated, apart, by oneself, by itself, on one's own, lonely, lonesome, deserted,

abandoned, forsaken, forlorn, desolate, unaccompanied, unescorted, unattended, solo, single-handed, unaided, unassisted, mere.
Ea together, accompanied, escorted.

aloof *adjective*
distant, remote, offish, standoffish, haughty, supercilious, unapproachable, inaccessible, detached, forbidding, cool, chilly, cold, unsympathetic, unresponsive, indifferent, uninterested, reserved, unforthcoming, unfriendly, unsociable, formal.
Ea sociable, friendly, concerned.

aloud *adverb*
out loud, audibly, intelligibly, clearly, plainly, distinctly, loudly, resoundingly, sonorously, noisily, vociferously.
Ea silently.

also *adverb*
too, as well, and, plus, along with, including, as well as, additionally, in addition, besides, further, furthermore, moreover.

alter *verb*
change, vary, diversify, modify, qualify, shift, transpose, adjust, adapt, convert, turn, transmute, transform, reform, reshape, remodel, recast, revise, amend, emend, tweak (*infml*).
Ea fix.

alteration *noun*
change, variation, variance, difference, diversification, shift, transposition, modification, adjustment, adaptation, conversion, transformation, transfiguration, metamorphosis, reformation, reshaping, remodelling, revision, amendment.
Ea fixity.

alternate *verb* /ol-te-neit/
interchange, reciprocate, rotate, take turns, follow one another, replace each other, substitute, change, alter, vary, oscillate, fluctuate, intersperse.
▶ *adjective* /ol-tern-at/
alternating, every other, every second, interchanging, reciprocal, rotating, alternative.

alternative *noun*
option, choice, selection, preference,

other, recourse, substitute, back-up.
▶ *adjective*
substitute, second, another, other, different, unorthodox, unconventional, fringe, alternate.

altogether *adverb*
totally, completely, entirely, wholly, fully, utterly, absolutely, quite, perfectly, thoroughly, in all, all told, in toto, all in all, as a whole, on the whole, generally, in general.

altruistic *adjective*
unselfish, self-sacrificing, disinterested, public-spirited, philanthropic, charitable, humanitarian, benevolent, generous, considerate, humane.
Fᴀ selfish.

always *adverb*
every time, consistently, invariably, without exception, unfailingly, regularly, repeatedly, continually, constantly, perpetually, unceasingly, eternally, endlessly, evermore, forever, ever, twenty-four-seven (*infml*).
Fᴀ never.

amalgamate *verb*
merge, blend, mingle, commingle, intermix, homogenize, incorporate, alloy, integrate, compound, fuse, coalesce, synthesize, combine, unite, unify, ally.
Fᴀ separate.

amateur *noun*
non-professional, layman, ham (*infml*), dilettante, dabbler, enthusiast, fancier, buff (*infml*).
Fᴀ professional.
▶ *adjective*
non-professional, lay, unpaid, unqualified, untrained, amateurish, inexpert, unprofessional.
Fᴀ professional.

amaze *verb*
surprise, startle, astonish, astound, stun, stupefy, daze, floor (*infml*), stagger, dumbfound, flabbergast (*infml*), shock, dismay, disconcert, confound, bewilder.

amazement *noun*
surprise, astonishment, shock, dismay, confusion, perplexity, bewilderment, admiration, wonderment, wonder, marvel.

ambassador *noun*
emissary, envoy, legate, diplomat, consul, plenipotentiary, deputy, representative, agent, minister, apostle.

ambiguity *noun*
double meaning, double entendre, equivocality, equivocation, enigma, puzzle, confusion, obscurity, unclearness, vagueness, woolliness, dubiousness, doubt, doubtfulness, uncertainty.
Fᴀ clarity.

ambiguous *adjective*
double-meaning, equivocal, multivocal, double-edged, back-handed, cryptic, enigmatic, puzzling, confusing, obscure, unclear, vague, indefinite, woolly, confused, dubious, doubtful, uncertain, inconclusive, indeterminate.
Fᴀ clear, definite.

ambition *noun*
1 his ambition to be a jockey: aspiration, aim, goal, target, objective, intent, purpose, design, object, ideal, dream, hope, wish, desire, yearning, longing, hankering, craving, hunger.
2 a woman of ambition: enterprise, drive, push, thrust, striving, eagerness, commitment, zeal.
Fᴀ **2** apathy, diffidence.

ambitious *adjective*
1 an ambitious politician who wants to get to the top: aspiring, hopeful, desirous, intent, purposeful, pushy (*infml*), bold, assertive, go-ahead, enterprising, driving, energetic, enthusiastic, eager, keen, striving, industrious, zealous.
2 Isn't this plan a trifle ambitious?: formidable, hard, difficult, arduous, strenuous, demanding, challenging, exacting, impressive, grandiose, elaborate.
Fᴀ **1** lazy, unassuming. **2** modest, uninspiring.

ambivalent *adjective*
contradictory, conflicting, clashing, warring, opposed, inconsistent, mixed, confused, fluctuating,

vacillating, wavering, hesitant, irresolute, undecided, unresolved, unsettled, uncertain, unsure, doubtful, debatable, inconclusive.
F3 unequivocal.

amble *verb*
walk, saunter, toddle (*infml*), stroll, promenade, wander, drift, meander, ramble.
F3 stride, march.

ambush *verb*
lie in wait, waylay, surprise, trap, ensnare.

amenable *adjective*
accommodating, flexible, open, agreeable, persuadable, compliant, willing, tractable, submissive, responsive, susceptible, liable, responsible.
F3 intractable.

amend *verb*
revise, correct, rectify, emend, fix, repair, mend, remedy, redress, reform, change, alter, adjust, modify, qualify, enhance, improve, ameliorate (*fml*), better.
F3 impair, worsen.

amends *noun*
atonement, expiation, requital, satisfaction, recompense, compensation, indemnification, indemnity, reparation, redress, restoration, restitution.

amid *preposition*
amidst, midst, in the midst of, in the thick of, among, amongst, in the middle of, surrounded by.

among *preposition*
amongst, between, in the middle of, surrounded by, amid, amidst, midst, in the midst of, in the thick of, with, together with.

amount *noun*
quantity, number, sum, total, sum total, whole, entirety, aggregate, lot, quota, supply, volume, mass, bulk, measure, magnitude, extent, expanse.
◆ **amount to** add up to, total, aggregate, come to, make, equal, mean, be tantamount to, be equivalent to, approximate to, become, grow.

amphibian

Amphibians include:
axolotl, bullfrog, congo eel, eft, frog, horned toad, midwife toad, natterjack, newt, salamander, toad, tree frog.

ample *adjective*
1 a room of ample proportions: large, big, extensive, expansive, broad, wide, full, voluminous, roomy, spacious, commodious, great.
2 there were ample supplies/opportunities: considerable, substantial, handsome, generous, bountiful, munificent, liberal, lavish, copious, abundant, plentiful, plenty, unrestricted, profuse, rich.
F3 2 insufficient, inadequate, meagre.

amplify *verb*
enlarge, magnify, expand, dilate, fill out, bulk out, add to, supplement, augment, increase, extend, lengthen, widen, broaden, develop, elaborate, enhance, boost, intensify, strengthen, deepen, heighten, raise.
F3 reduce, decrease, abridge.

amputate *verb*
cut off, remove, sever, dissever, separate, dock, lop, curtail, truncate.

amuse *verb*
entertain, divert, regale, make laugh, tickle (*infml*), crease (*infml*), slay (*infml*), cheer (up), gladden, enliven, please, charm, delight, enthral, engross, absorb, interest, occupy, recreate, relax.
F3 bore, displease.

amusement *noun*
entertainment, diversion, distraction, fun, enjoyment, pleasure, delight, merriment, mirth, hilarity, laughter, joke, prank, game, sport, recreation, hobby, pastime, interest.
F3 boredom, monotony.

amusing *adjective*
funny, humorous, hilarious, comical, laughable, ludicrous, droll, witty, facetious, jocular, jolly, enjoyable, pleasant, charming, delightful, entertaining, interesting.
F3 dull, boring.

anaemic *adjective*
bloodless, ashen, chalky, livid, pasty, pallid, sallow, pale, wan, colourless, insipid, weak, feeble, ineffectual, enervated, frail, infirm, sickly.
Ea ruddy, sanguine, full-blooded.

anaesthetize *verb*
desensitize, numb, deaden, dull, drug, dope, stupefy.

analogy *noun*
comparison, simile, metaphor, likeness, resemblance, similarity, parallel, correspondence, equivalence, relation, correlation, agreement.

analyse *verb*
break down, separate, divide, take apart, dissect, anatomize, reduce, resolve, sift, investigate, study, examine, scrutinize, review, interpret, test, judge, evaluate, estimate, consider.

analysis *noun*
breakdown, separation, division, dissection, reduction, resolution, sifting, investigation, enquiry, study, examination, scrutiny, review, exposition, explication, explanation, interpretation, test, judgement, opinion, evaluation, estimation, reasoning.
Ea synthesis.

analytic *adjective*
analytical, dissecting, detailed, in-depth, searching, critical, questioning, enquiring, inquisitive, investigative, diagnostic, systematic, methodical, logical, rational, interpretative, explanatory, expository (*fml*), studious.

anarchic *adjective*
lawless, ungoverned, anarchistic, libertarian, nihilist, revolutionary, rebellious, mutinous, riotous, chaotic, disordered, confused, disorganized.
Ea submissive, orderly.

anarchy *noun*
lawlessness, unrule, misrule, anarchism, revolution, rebellion, insurrection, mutiny, riot, pandemonium, chaos, disorder, confusion.
Ea rule, control, order.

anatomical terms

Anatomical terms include:
aural, biceps, bone, cardiac, cartilage, cerebral, dental, diaphragm, dorsal, duodenal, elbow, epidermis, epiglottis, Fallopian tubes, funny bone (*infml*), gastric, gingival, gristle, groin, gullet, hamstring, helix, hepatic, hock, intercostal, jugular, lachrymal, ligament, lumbar, mammary, membral, muscle, nasal, neural, ocular, oesophagus, optical, pectoral, pedal, pulmonary, renal, spine, tendon, triceps, umbilicus, uterus, uvula, voice box, windpipe, wisdom tooth, womb. →*See also* **bone**.

ancestor *noun*
forebear, forefather, progenitor (*fml*), predecessor, forerunner, precursor, antecedent.
Ea descendant.

ancestry *noun*
ancestors, forebears, forefathers, progenitors (*fml*), parentage, family, lineage, line, descent, blood, race, stock, roots, pedigree, genealogy, extraction, derivation, origin, heritage, heredity.

anchor *verb*
moor, berth, tie up, make fast, fasten, attach, affix, fix.

ancient *adjective*
1 ancient manuscripts: old, aged, time-worn, age-old, antique, antediluvian, prehistoric, fossilized, primeval, immemorial.
2 an ancient record-player: old-fashioned, out-of-date, antiquated, archaic, obsolete, bygone, early, original.
Ea **1** recent, contemporary. **2** modern, up-to-date.

anecdote *noun*
story, tale, yarn, sketch, reminiscence.

angelic *adjective*
cherubic, seraphic, celestial, heavenly, divine, holy, pious, saintly, pure, innocent, unworldly, virtuous, lovely, beautiful, adorable.
Ea devilish, fiendish.

anger noun

annoyance, irritation, antagonism, displeasure, irritability, temper, pique, vexation, ire, rage, fury, wrath, exasperation, outrage, indignation, gall, bitterness, rancour, resentment.
E3 forgiveness, forbearance.
▶ verb

annoy, irritate, aggravate (*infml*), wind up (*infml*), vex, irk, rile, miff (*infml*), needle (*infml*), nettle, bother, ruffle, provoke, antagonize, offend, affront, gall, madden, enrage, incense, infuriate, exasperate, outrage.
E3 please, appease, calm.
⇨ *See also* **Word Study** *panel.*

angle noun

1 form an angle : corner, nook, bend, flexure, hook, crook, elbow, knee, edge, point.
2 look at something from a different angle : aspect, outlook, facet, side, approach, direction, position, standpoint, viewpoint, point of view, slant, perspective.

angry adjective

annoyed, cross, irritated, aggravated (*infml*), displeased, uptight (*infml*), irate, mad (*infml*), enraged, incensed, infuriated, furious, raging, passionate, heated, hot, exasperated, outraged, indignant, bitter, resentful.
E3 content, happy, calm.
⇨ *See also* **Word Study** *panel.*

animal noun

creature, mammal, beast, brute, barbarian, savage, monster, cur, pig, swine.

Animals include:

aardvark, antelope, ape, armadillo, baboon, badger, bear, beaver, bison, buffalo, bull, camel, caribou, cat, cheetah, chimpanzee, cougar, cow, deer, dog, dolphin, eland, elephant, elk, ermine, ferret, fox, gazelle, gerbil, giant panda, gibbon, giraffe, gnu, goat, gorilla, grizzly bear, hamster, hare, hedgehog, hippopotamus, horse, hyena, impala, jaguar, kangaroo, koala, lemur, leopard, lion, llama, mink, mole, mongoose, monkey, moose, mouse, ocelot, orang-utan, otter, panda, panther, pig, platypus, polar bear, polecat, puma, rabbit, racoon, rat, reindeer, rhinoceros, seal, sealion, sheep, skunk, squirrel, tiger, wallaby, walrus, weasel, whale, wolf, wolverine, wombat, zebra. ⇨*See also* **amphibian**; **bird**; **cat**; **dog**; **fish**; **insect**; **mammal**; **marsupial**; **reptile**; **rodent**.

animated adjective

lively, spirited, buoyant, vibrant, ebullient, vivacious, alive, vital, quick, brisk, vigorous, energetic, active, passionate, impassioned, vehement, ardent, fervent, glowing, radiant, excited, enthusiastic, eager.
E3 lethargic, sluggish, inert.

animosity noun

ill feeling, ill-will, acrimony, bitterness, rancour, resentment, spite, malice, malignity, malevolence, hate, hatred, loathing, antagonism, hostility, enmity, feud.
E3 goodwill.

annex verb

1 annexing part of northern France : acquire, appropriate, seize, usurp, occupy, conquer, take over.
2 annexed to the main report : add, append, affix, attach, fasten, adjoin, join, connect, unite, incorporate.

annexe noun

wing, extension, attachment, addition, supplement, expansion.

annihilate verb

eliminate, eradicate, obliterate, erase, wipe out, liquidate (*infml*), murder, assassinate, exterminate, extinguish, raze, destroy, abolish.

announce verb

declare, proclaim, report, state, reveal, disclose, divulge, make known, notify, intimate, promulgate, propound, publish, broadcast, advertise, publicize, blazon.
E3 suppress.

announcement noun

declaration, proclamation, report, statement, communiqué, dispatch, bulletin, notification, intimation,

There are a great number of expressions and phrases used to talk or write about **anger**, and you might choose some of those listed below to add variety and interest to your speech or writing. Be careful, however, because many of these phrases are fairly informal and would not normally be used in formal written work.

being angry

be up in arms
be beside yourself with anger
have/get the hump
be hopping mad
foam at the mouth
have kittens

gnash your teeth
be in a temper
look like thunder
be on the warpath
be fit to be tied
be ticked off (*US*)

suddenly becoming angry

go up in the air
go ballistic (*slang*)
raise Cain
cut up rough
go off the deep end
fly into a rage
blow a fuse/gasket

go mental (*slang*)
fly off the handle
lose your head
blow/flip your lid
lose your rag
throw a wobbly (*slang*)
see red

go spare (*slang*)
blow your stack
throw a tantrum
lose your temper
blow your top
hit the roof

making someone angry

make someone's blood boil
drive someone mad
get a rise out of someone
get someone's dander up

set someone's teeth on edge
stir up a hornet's nest
drive someone up the wall

speaking angrily to someone

send someone away with a flea
  in their ear
give someone hell
let fly
do your nut
give someone a piece of your
  mind
tear into someone

rant and rave
read the riot act
give someone the rough side
  of your tongue
cause/raise a stink
tear someone off a strip
jump down someone's throat

being in a bad mood

be like a bear with a sore head   get out of bed on the wrong side

revelation, disclosure, divulgence, publication, broadcast, advertisement.

announcer *noun*
broadcaster, newscaster, newsreader, commentator, compère, master of ceremonies, MC, town crier, herald, messenger.

annoy *verb*
irritate, rile, needle (*infml*), aggravate (*infml*), displease, anger, vex, irk, madden, exasperate, tease, provoke, ruffle, trouble, disturb, bother, pester, plague, harass, molest.
F3 please, gratify, comfort.

annoyance *noun*
1 just a minor annoyance: nuisance, pest, disturbance, bother, trouble, bore, irritant, bind (*infml*), pain (*infml*), headache (*infml*), tease, provocation.
2 express one's annoyance: irritation, aggravation (*infml*), displeasure, anger, vexation, exasperation, harassment.
F3 2 pleasure.
⇨ See also **Word Study** panel.

annoyed *adjective*
irritated, cross, displeased, angry, vexed, piqued, exasperated, provoked, harassed.
F3 pleased.

annoying *adjective*
irritating, aggravating (*infml*), vexatious, irksome, troublesome, bothersome, tiresome, trying, maddening, exasperating, galling, offensive, teasing, provoking, harassing.
F3 pleasing, welcome.

annul *verb*
nullify, invalidate, undo, void, rescind, suspend, cancel, abolish, quash, repeal, revoke, negate, retract, recall, reverse.
F3 enact, restore.

anomalous *adjective*
abnormal, atypical, exceptional, irregular, inconsistent, incongruous, deviant, freakish, eccentric, peculiar, odd, unusual, singular, rare.
F3 normal, regular, ordinary.

anonymous *adjective*
unnamed, nameless, unsigned, unacknowledged, unspecified, unidentified, unknown, incognito, faceless, impersonal, nondescript, unexceptional.
F3 named, signed, identifiable, distinctive.

answer *noun*
1 gave them his answer: reply, acknowledgement, response, reaction, rejoinder, retort, riposte, comeback, retaliation, rebuttal, vindication, defence, plea.
2 the answer to the riddle: solution, explanation.
▶ *verb*
1 answer a letter/query: reply, acknowledge, respond, react, retort, retaliate, refute, solve.
2 answer a need: fulfil, fill, meet, satisfy, match up to, correspond, correlate, conform, agree, fit, suit, serve, pass.
◆ **answer back** talk back, retort, riposte, retaliate, contradict, disagree, argue, dispute, rebut.

answerable *adjective*
liable, responsible, accountable, chargeable, blameworthy, to blame.

antagonism *noun*
hostility, opposition, rivalry, antipathy, ill feeling, ill-will, animosity, friction, discord, dissension, contention, conflict.
F3 rapport, sympathy, agreement.

antagonize *verb*
alienate, estrange, disaffect, repel, embitter, offend, insult, provoke, annoy, irritate, anger, incense.
F3 disarm.

anthology *noun*
selection, collection, compilation, compendium, digest, treasury, miscellany.

anticipate *verb*
1 trying to anticipate any problems: forestall, pre-empt, intercept, prevent, obviate, preclude.
2 eagerly anticipate his arrival: expect, foresee, predict, forecast, look for, await, look forward to, hope for, bank on, count upon.

anticlimax *noun*
comedown, let-down, disappointment, fiasco, bathos (*fml*).

WORD *study*   annoyance

There are many lively phrases used to express feelings of **annoyance**. Be careful, as some of these phrases are fairly informal.

annoying someone

drive someone round the bend/ twist
drive someone mad
get someone's goat
get on someone's nerves
try the patience of a saint
get under someone's skin
drive someone up the wall
get on someone's wick (*slang*)
bug someone (*slang*)

rattle someone's cage
ruffle someone's feathers
make someone's hackles rise
get up someone's nose
rub it in
tread/step on someone's toes
rub someone up the wrong way
get someone's back up
wind someone up

being annoyed

be browned off
have had it up to here

be hot under the collar

things people say when they are annoyed

give me a break!
what's the big idea?
for heaven's sake!
I don't know
for crying out loud!

do you mind?
for goodness sake!
knock it off!
for Pete's sake!
that's the last straw!

antics *noun*
foolery, tomfoolery, silliness, buffoonery, clowning, frolics, capers, skylarking, playfulness, mischief, tricks, monkey-tricks, pranks, stunts, doings.

antidote *noun*
remedy, cure, counter-agent, antitoxin, neutralizer, countermeasure, corrective.

antipathy *noun*
aversion, dislike, hate, hatred, loathing, abhorrence (*fml*), distaste, disgust, repulsion, antagonism, animosity, ill-will, bad blood, enmity, hostility,
opposition, incompatibility.
🗲 sympathy, affection, rapport.

antique *adjective*
antiquarian, ancient, old, veteran, vintage, quaint, antiquated, old-fashioned, outdated, archaic, obsolete.
▶ *noun*
antiquity, relic, bygone, period piece, heirloom, curio, museum piece, curiosity, rarity.

antiseptic *adjective*
disinfectant, medicated, aseptic, germ-free, clean, pure, unpolluted,

uncontaminated, sterile, sterilized, sanitized, sanitary, hygienic.

▶ *noun*

disinfectant, germicide, bactericide, purifier, cleanser.

antisocial *adjective*
asocial, unacceptable, disruptive, disorderly, rebellious, belligerent, antagonistic, hostile, unfriendly, unsociable, uncommunicative, reserved, retiring, withdrawn, alienated, unapproachable.
F3 sociable, gregarious.

anxiety *noun*
worry, concern, care, distress, nervousness, apprehension, dread, foreboding, misgiving, uneasiness, restlessness, fretfulness, impatience, suspense, tension, stress.
F3 calm, composure, serenity.

anxious *adjective*
worried, concerned, nervous, apprehensive, afraid, fearful, uneasy, restless, fretful, impatient, in suspense, on tenterhooks, tense, taut, distressed, disturbed, troubled, tormented, tortured.
F3 calm, composed.

apart *adverb*
1 live apart/stand apart: separately, independently, individually, singly, alone, on one's own, by oneself, privately, aside, to one side, away, afar, distant, aloof, excluded, isolated, cut off, separated, divorced, separate, distinct.
2 fall/tear apart: to pieces, to bits, into parts, in pieces, in bits.

apathetic *adjective*
uninterested, uninvolved, indifferent, cool, unemotional, emotionless, impassive, unmoved, unconcerned, cold, unfeeling, numb, unresponsive, passive, listless, unambitious.
F3 enthusiastic, involved, concerned, feeling, responsive.

ape *verb*
copy, imitate, echo, mirror, parrot, mimic, take off, caricature, parody, mock, counterfeit, affect.

apocryphal *adjective*
unauthenticated, unverified, unsubstantiated, unsupported, questionable, spurious, equivocal, doubtful, dubious, fabricated, concocted, fictitious, imaginary, legendary, mythical.
F3 authentic, true.

apologetic *adjective*
sorry, repentant, penitent, contrite, remorseful, conscience-stricken, regretful, rueful.
F3 unrepentant, impenitent, defiant.

apology *noun*
acknowledgement, confession, excuse, explanation, justification, vindication, defence, plea.
F3 defiance.

appal *verb*
horrify, shock, outrage, disgust, dismay, disconcert, daunt, intimidate, unnerve, alarm, scare, frighten, terrify.
F3 reassure, encourage.

appalling *adjective*
horrifying, horrific, harrowing, shocking, outrageous, atrocious, disgusting, awful, dreadful, frightful, terrible, dire, grim, hideous, ghastly, horrible, horrid, loathsome, daunting, intimidating, unnerving, alarming, frightening, terrifying.
F3 reassuring, encouraging.

apparatus *noun*
machine, appliance, gadget, device, contraption, equipment, gear, tackle, outfit, tools, implements, utensils, materials, machinery, system, mechanism, means.

apparent *adjective*
seeming, outward, visible, evident, noticeable, perceptible, plain, clear, distinct, marked, unmistakable, obvious, manifest, patent, open, declared.
F3 hidden, obscure.

apparently *adverb*
seemingly, ostensibly, outwardly, superficially, plainly, clearly, obviously, manifestly, patently.

appeal *noun*
1 an appeal for calm/mercy: request, application, petition, suit, solicitation, plea, entreaty, supplication, prayer, invocation.

2 have great appeal: attraction, allure, interest, fascination, enchantment, charm, attractiveness, winsomeness, beauty, charisma, magnetism.

▸ *verb*

1 appeal for help: ask, request, call, apply, address, petition, sue, solicit, plead, beg, beseech, implore, entreat, supplicate, pray, invoke, call upon.

2 appeals to the young: attract, draw, allure, lure, tempt, entice, invite, interest, engage, fascinate, charm, please.

appear *verb*

1 appear out of nowhere: arrive, enter, turn up, attend, materialize, develop, show (up), come into sight, come into view, loom, rise, surface, arise, occur, crop up, come to light, come out, emerge, issue, be published.

2 appeared to be dead: seem, look, turn out.

3 appear in a show: act, perform, play, take part.

F3 1 disappear, vanish.

appearance *noun*

1 the appearance of a new political party: appearing, arrival, advent, coming, rise, emergence, début, introduction.

2 have a strange appearance: look, expression, face, aspect, air, bearing, demeanour, manner, looks, figure, form, semblance, show, front, guise, illusion, impression, image.

F3 1 disappearance.

⇨ *See also* **Word Study** *panel.*

appendix *noun*

addition, appendage, adjunct, addendum, supplement, epilogue, codicil, postscript, rider.

appetite *noun*

hunger, stomach, relish, zest, taste, propensity, inclination, liking, desire, longing, yearning, craving, eagerness, passion, zeal.

F3 distaste.

appetizing *adjective*

mouthwatering, tempting, inviting, appealing, palatable, tasty, delicious, scrumptious (*infml*), succulent, piquant, savoury.

F3 disgusting, distasteful.

applaud *verb*

clap, cheer, acclaim, compliment, congratulate, approve, commend, praise, laud (*fml*), eulogize (*fml*), extol (*fml*).

F3 criticize, censure.

applause *noun*

ovation, clapping, cheering, cheers, acclaim, acclamation, accolade, congratulation, approval, commendation, praise.

F3 criticism, censure.

applicable *adjective*

relevant, pertinent, apposite, apt, appropriate, fitting, suited, useful, suitable, fit, proper, valid, legitimate.

F3 inapplicable, inappropriate.

applicant *noun*

candidate, interviewee, contestant, competitor, aspirant, suitor, petitioner, inquirer.

application *noun*

1 an application for a driving licence: request, appeal, petition, suit, claim, inquiry.

2 has many applications: relevance, pertinence (*fml*), function, purpose, use, value.

3 he shows great application: diligence, industry, effort, commitment, dedication, perseverance, keenness, attentiveness.

apply *verb*

1 apply for a job: request, ask for, requisition, put in for, appeal, petition, solicit, sue, claim, inquire.

2 apply oneself to a task: address, buckle down, settle down, commit, devote, dedicate, give, direct, concentrate, study, persevere.

3 apply new methods: use, exercise, utilize, employ, bring into play, engage, harness, ply, wield, administer, execute, implement, assign, direct, bring to bear, practise, resort to.

4 applies to us all: refer, relate, be relevant, pertain, fit, suit.

5 apply ointment: put on, spread on, lay on, cover with, paint, anoint, smear, rub.

appoint *verb*

1 appoint a new minister: name, nominate, elect, install, choose, select,

WORD *study*

appearance

Here are some of the many expressions used when referring to the **appearance** of someone or something. Note that some of these expressions are rude or offensive, and it would be very bad manners to use them to refer to someone directly.

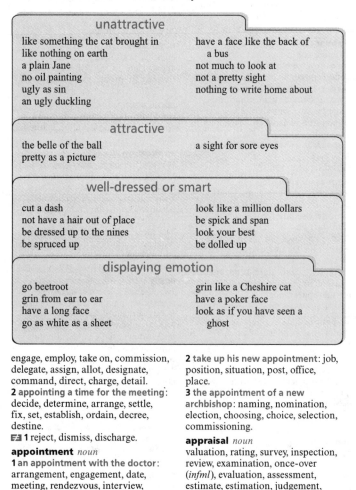

unattractive

like something the cat brought in
like nothing on earth
a plain Jane
no oil painting
ugly as sin
an ugly duckling

have a face like the back of
   a bus
not much to look at
not a pretty sight
nothing to write home about

attractive

the belle of the ball
pretty as a picture

a sight for sore eyes

well-dressed or smart

cut a dash
not have a hair out of place
be dressed up to the nines
be spruced up

look like a million dollars
be spick and span
look your best
be dolled up

displaying emotion

go beetroot
grin from ear to ear
have a long face
go as white as a sheet

grin like a Cheshire cat
have a poker face
look as if you have seen a
   ghost

engage, employ, take on, commission, delegate, assign, allot, designate, command, direct, charge, detail.
2 appointing a time for the meeting: decide, determine, arrange, settle, fix, set, establish, ordain, decree, destine.

F∃ 1 reject, dismiss, discharge.

appointment *noun*
1 an appointment with the doctor: arrangement, engagement, date, meeting, rendezvous, interview, consultation.

2 take up his new appointment: job, position, situation, post, office, place.
3 the appointment of a new archbishop: naming, nomination, election, choosing, choice, selection, commissioning.

appraisal *noun*
valuation, rating, survey, inspection, review, examination, once-over (*infml*), evaluation, assessment, estimate, estimation, judgement, reckoning, opinion, appreciation.

appreciate *verb*
1 appreciate art: enjoy, relish, savour, prize, treasure, value, cherish, admire, respect, regard, esteem, like, welcome, take kindly to.
2 appreciate in value: grow, increase, rise, mount, inflate, gain, strengthen, improve, enhance.
3 appreciate that you have had difficulties: understand, comprehend, perceive, realize, recognize, acknowledge, sympathize with, know.
F3 1 despise. **2** depreciate.

appreciative *adjective*
1 appreciative of his generosity: grateful, thankful, obliged, indebted, pleased.
2 appreciative of beauty: admiring, encouraging, enthusiastic, respectful, sensitive, responsive, perceptive, knowledgeable, conscious, mindful.
F3 1 ungrateful.

apprehensive *adjective*
nervous, anxious, worried, concerned, uneasy, doubtful, suspicious, mistrustful, distrustful, alarmed, afraid.
F3 assured, confident.

apprentice *noun*
trainee, probationer, student, pupil, learner, novice, beginner, starter, recruit, newcomer, tiro.
F3 expert.

approach *verb*
1 approaching the border: advance, move towards, draw near, near, gain on, catch up, reach, meet.
2 approached me for help: apply to, appeal to, sound out.
3 approached the job with a positive attitude: begin, commence, set about, undertake, introduce, mention.
4 approaching perfection: resemble, be like, compare with, approximate, come close.
▶ *noun*
1 the approach of winter: advance, coming, advent, arrival.
2 the approach to his estate: access, road, avenue, way, passage, entrance, doorway, threshold.
3 an approach from a rival company:

application, appeal, overture, proposition, proposal.
4 take another approach: attitude, manner, style, technique, procedure, method, means.

appropriate *adjective* /a-**proh**-pri-at/
applicable, relevant, pertinent, to the point, well-chosen, apt, fitting, right, suitable, fit, befitting, becoming, proper, correct, spot-on (*infml*), well-timed, timely, seasonable, opportune.
F3 inappropriate, irrelevant, unsuitable.
▶ *verb* /a-**proh**-pri-eit/
seize, take, expropriate (*fml*), commandeer, requisition, confiscate, impound, assume, usurp, steal, filch, pilfer, purloin (*fml*).

approval *noun*
1 win their approval: admiration, esteem, regard, respect, good opinion, liking, appreciation, approbation (*fml*), favour, recommendation, praise, commendation, acclaim, acclamation, honour, applause.
2 gain approval for the scheme: agreement, concurrence, assent, consent, permission, leave, sanction, authorization, licence, mandate, go-ahead, green light (*infml*), blessing, OK (*infml*), certification, ratification, validation, confirmation, support.
F3 1 disapproval, condemnation.

approve *verb*
1 approve of their methods: admire, esteem, regard, like, appreciate, favour, recommend, praise, commend, acclaim, applaud.
2 approve a proposal: agree to, assent to, consent to, accede to, allow, permit, pass, sanction, authorize, mandate, bless, countenance, OK (*infml*), ratify, rubber-stamp (*infml*), validate, endorse, support, uphold, second, back, accept, adopt, confirm.
F3 1 disapprove, condemn.

approximate *adjective* /ap-**rok**-sim-at/
estimated, guessed, rough, inexact, loose, close, near, like, similar, relative.
F3 exact.
▶ *verb* /ap-**rok**-sim-eit/
approach, border on, verge on, be tantamount to, resemble.

approximately *adverb*
roughly, around, about, circa, more or less, loosely, approaching, close to, nearly, just about.

apt *adjective*
1 an apt comment : relevant, applicable, apposite, appropriate, fitting, suitable, fit, seemly, proper, correct, accurate, spot-on (*infml*), timely, seasonable.
2 an apt pupil : clever, gifted, talented, skilful, expert, intelligent, quick, sharp.
3 apt to be noisy : liable, prone, given, disposed, likely, ready.
F₃ 1 inapt. **2** stupid.

aptitude *noun*
ability, capability, capacity, faculty, gift, talent, flair, facility, proficiency, cleverness, intelligence, quickness, bent, inclination, leaning, disposition, tendency.
F₃ inaptitude.

arbitrary *adjective*
1 an arbitrary decision : random, chance, capricious, inconsistent, discretionary, subjective, instinctive, unreasoned, illogical, irrational, unreasonable.
2 govern in an arbitrary manner : despotic, tyrannical, dictatorial, autocratic, absolute, imperious, magisterial, domineering, overbearing, high-handed, dogmatic.
F₃ 1 reasoned, rational, circumspect (*fml*).

arbitrate *verb*
judge, adjudicate, referee, umpire, mediate, settle, decide, determine.

arbitration *noun*
judgement, adjudication, intervention, mediation, negotiation, settlement, decision, determination.

arbitrator *noun*
judge, adjudicator, arbiter, referee, umpire, moderator, mediator, negotiator, intermediary, go-between.

arch *noun*
archway, bridge, span, dome, vault, concave, bend, curve, curvature, bow, arc, semicircle.
▶ *verb*
bend, curve, bow, arc, vault, camber.

archaic *adjective*
antiquated, old-fashioned, outmoded, old hat (*infml*), passé, outdated, out-of-date, obsolete, old, ancient, antique, quaint, primitive.
F₃ modern, recent.

archetype *noun*
pattern, model, standard, form, type, prototype, original, precursor, classic, paradigm, ideal.

architect *noun*
designer, planner, master builder, prime mover, originator, founder, instigator, creator, author, inventor, engineer, maker, constructor, shaper.

archives *noun*
records, annals, chronicles, memorials, papers, documents, deeds, ledgers, registers, roll.

ardent *adjective*
fervent, fiery, warm, passionate, impassioned, fierce, vehement, intense, spirited, enthusiastic, eager, keen, dedicated, devoted, zealous.
F₃ apathetic, unenthusiastic.

arduous *adjective*
hard, difficult, tough, rigorous, severe, harsh, formidable, strenuous, tiring, taxing, fatiguing, exhausting, backbreaking, punishing, gruelling, uphill, laborious, onerous.
F₃ easy.

area *noun*
1 a run-down area of the city : neighbourhood, environment, environs, locality, quarter, sector, department, precinct, enclave, terrain, district, region, zone.

Types of urban area include:
built-up area, catchment area, city, development area, dockland, estate, ghetto, ghost town, hamlet, home-town, industrial park, inner city, manor, market town, metropolis, new town, outskirts, port, quarter, red-light district, rural district, satellite town, shanty town, suburb, village.

2 an area of desert/ocean : expanse, stretch, section, sector, tract, patch, breadth, width, portion.

3 an area of study/knowledge : field, sphere, branch, subject.

argue *verb*
1 arguing over every little detail : quarrel, squabble, bicker, row, wrangle, haggle, remonstrate, join, take issue, fight, feud, fall out, disagree, dispute.
2 argue the point : question, debate, discuss.
3 argued that it couldn't be so : reason, assert, contend, hold (*fml*), maintain, claim, plead, exhibit, display, show, manifest, demonstrate, indicate, denote, prove, evidence, suggest, imply.

argument *noun*
1 a heated argument : quarrel, squabble, row, wrangle, controversy, debate, discussion, dispute, disagreement, clash, conflict, fight, feud.
2 putting forward his argument : reasoning, reason, logic, assertion, contention, claim, demonstration, defence, case, synopsis, summary, theme.

argumentative *adjective*
quarrelsome, contentious, polemical, opinionated, belligerent, perverse, contrary.
E3 complaisant.

arid *adjective*
1 arid landscape : dry, parched, waterless, desiccated, torrid, barren, infertile, unproductive, desert, waste.
2 found the subject arid : dull, uninteresting, boring, monotonous, tedious, dry, sterile, dreary, colourless, lifeless, spiritless, uninspired.
E3 **1** fertile. **2** lively.

arise *verb*
1 main point arising from the discussion : originate, begin, start, commence, derive, stem, spring, proceed, flow, emerge, issue, appear, come to light, crop up, occur, happen, result, ensue, follow.
2 (*fml*) arose from his bed/chair : rise, get up, stand up.

aristocracy *noun*
upper class, gentry, nobility, peerage, ruling class, gentility, élite.
E3 common people.

aristocrat *noun*
noble, patrician, nobleman, noblewoman, peer, peeress, lord, lady.
E3 commoner.

aristocratic *adjective*
upper-class, highborn, well-born, noble, patrician, blue-blooded (*infml*), titled, lordly, courtly, gentle, thoroughbred, élite.
E3 plebeian, vulgar.

arm[1] *noun*
1 with folded arms : limb, upper limb, appendage.
2 the air arm of the fighting forces : branch, projection, extension, offshoot, section, division, detachment, department.

arm[2] *verb*
arm someone with weapons/information : provide, supply, furnish, issue, equip, rig, outfit, ammunition, prime, prepare, forearm, gird, steel, brace, reinforce, strengthen, fortify, protect.

arms *noun*
1 arms race : weapons, weaponry, firearms, guns, artillery, instruments of war, armaments, ordnance, munitions, ammunition.
2 the family arms : coat-of-arms, armorial bearings, insignia, heraldic device, escutcheon, shield, crest, heraldry, blazonry.

army *noun*
armed force, military, militia, land forces, soldiers, troops, legions, cohorts, multitude, throng, host, horde.

aroma *noun*
smell, odour, scent, perfume, fragrance, bouquet, savour.

aromatic *adjective*
perfumed, fragrant, sweet-smelling, balmy, redolent, savoury, spicy, pungent.

around *preposition*
1 all around : surrounding, round, encircling, encompassing, enclosing, on all sides of, on every side of.
2 around a dozen : approximately, roughly, about, circa, more or less.

▶ *adverb*

1 jump around: everywhere, all over, in all directions, on all sides, about, here and there, to and fro.

2 stay around: close, close by, near, nearby, at hand.

arouse *verb*
rouse, startle, wake up, waken, awaken, instigate, summon up, call forth, spark, kindle, inflame, whet, sharpen, quicken, animate, excite, prompt, provoke, stimulate, galvanize, goad, spur, incite, agitate, stir up, whip up.
🔁 calm, lull, quieten.

arrange *verb*
1 arranging the cards in his hand: order, tidy, range, array, marshal, set out, dispose, distribute, position, lay out, align, group, class, classify, sift, categorize, sort (out), file, systematize, methodize, regulate, adjust.
2 arrange a meeting: organize, co-ordinate, prepare, fix, plan, project, design, devise, contrive, determine, settle.
3 arrange music: adapt, set, score, orchestrate, instrument, harmonize.
🔁 **1** untidy, disorganize, muddle.

arrangement *noun*
1 change the arrangement of the furniture: order, array, display, disposition, layout, line-up, grouping, classification, structure, system, method, set-up, organization, preparation, planning, plan, scheme, design, schedule.
2 come to an arrangement with someone: agreement, settlement, contract, terms, compromise.
3 a musical arrangement: adaptation, version, interpretation, setting, score, orchestration, instrumentation, harmonization.

array *noun*
arrangement, display, show, exhibition, exposition, assortment, collection, assemblage, muster, order, formation, line-up, parade.

arrest *verb*
1 arrest a criminal: capture, catch, seize, nick (*infml*), run in, apprehend, detain.

2 arrest its development: stop, stem, check, restrain, inhibit, halt, interrupt, stall, delay, slow, retard, block, obstruct, impede, hinder.

arrival *noun*
appearance, entrance, advent, coming, approach, occurrence.
🔁 departure.

arrive *verb*
reach, get to, appear, materialize, turn up, show up (*infml*), roll up (*infml*), enter, come, occur, happen.
🔁 depart, leave.

arrogant *adjective*
haughty, supercilious, disdainful, scornful, contemptuous, superior, condescending, patronizing, high and mighty, lordly, overbearing, high-handed, imperious, self-important, presumptuous, assuming, insolent, proud, conceited, boastful.
🔁 humble, unassuming, bashful.

art *noun*
1 study art: fine art, painting, sculpture, drawing, artwork, craft, artistry, draughtsmanship, craftsmanship.

Arts and crafts include:

fresco, oil painting, painting, portraiture, watercolour; architecture, caricature, drawing, illustration, sketching; calligraphy, engraving, etching, lithography; film, graphics, photography, video; marquetry, modelling, origami, sculpture, woodcarving, woodcraft; ceramics, cloisonné, collage, enamelling, jewellery, metalwork, mosaic, pottery, stained glass; batik, crochet, embroidery, knitting, needlework, patchwork, silk-screen printing, spinning, tapestry, weaving.

2 the art of public speaking: skill, knack, technique, method, aptitude, facility, dexterity, finesse, ingenuity, mastery, expertise, profession, trade.
3 with the art of a conjurer: artfulness, cunning, craftiness, slyness, guile, deceit, trickery, astuteness, shrewdness.

artful *adjective*
cunning, crafty, sly, foxy, wily, tricky, scheming, designing, deceitful, devious, subtle, sharp, shrewd, smart, clever, masterly, ingenious, resourceful, skilful, dexterous.
F3 artless, naïve, ingenuous.

article *noun*
1 article in a magazine: feature, report, story, account, piece, review, essay, commentary, composition, paper.
2 a few articles of jewellery: item, thing, object, commodity, unit, part, constituent, piece, portion, division.

articulate *adjective*
distinct, well-spoken, clear, lucid, intelligible, comprehensible, vocal, understandable, coherent, fluent, expressive, meaningful.
F3 inarticulate, incoherent.

artificial *adjective*
1 an artificial smile: false, fake, bogus, counterfeit, spurious, phoney (*infml*), pseudo, specious, sham, insincere, assumed, affected, mannered, forced, contrived, made-up, feigned, pretended, simulated, imitation, mock.
2 artificial flowers: synthetic, plastic, man-made, manufactured, non-natural, unnatural.
F3 1 genuine, true. **2** real, natural.

artisan *noun*
craftsman, craftswoman, artificer, journeyman, expert, skilled worker, mechanic, technician.

artist

Types of artist and artisan include:

architect, blacksmith, carpenter, cartoonist, designer, draughtsman, draughtswoman, engraver, goldsmith, graphic designer, illustrator, installation artist, painter, photographer, potter, printer, sculptor, silversmith, weaver, video artist; craftsman, craftswoman, master.

artistic *adjective*
aesthetic, ornamental, decorative, beautiful, exquisite, elegant, stylish, graceful, harmonious, sensitive, tasteful, refined, cultured, cultivated, skilled, talented, creative, imaginative.
F3 inelegant, tasteless.

artistry *noun*
craftsmanship, workmanship, skill, craft, talent, flair, brilliance, genius, finesse, style, mastery, expertise, proficiency, accomplishment, deftness, touch, sensitivity, creativity.
F3 ineptitude.

as *conjunction, preposition*
1 he waved as the train drew out: while, when.
2 as her mother was before her: such as, for example, for instance, like, in the manner of.
3 as he was working late, I asked him to lock up: because, since, seeing that, considering that, inasmuch as, being.
◆ **as for** with reference to, as regards, with regard to, on the subject of, in connection with, in relation to, with relation to, with respect to.

ascend *verb*
rise, take off, lift off, go up, move up, slope upwards, climb, scale, mount, tower, float up, fly up, soar.
F3 descend, go down.

ascent *noun*
1 their ascent of Everest: ascending, ascension, climb, climbing, scaling, escalation, rise, rising, mounting.
2 a steep ascent: slope, gradient, incline, ramp, hill, elevation.
F3 1 descent.

ascertain *verb*
find out, learn, discover, determine, fix, establish, settle, locate, detect, identify, verify, confirm, make certain.

ascribe *verb*
attribute, credit, accredit (*fml*), put down, assign, impute (*fml*), charge, chalk up to (*infml*).

ashamed *adjective*
sorry, apologetic, remorseful, contrite, guilty, conscience-stricken, sheepish, embarrassed, blushing, red-faced, mortified, humiliated, abashed, humbled, crestfallen, distressed, confused, reluctant, hesitant, shy, self-

conscious, bashful, modest, prudish.
F3 shameless, unashamed, proud,
defiant.

aside *adverb*
apart, on one side, in reserve, away, out
of the way, separately, in isolation,
alone, privately, secretly.
▶ *noun*
digression, parenthesis, departure,
soliloquy, stage whisper, whisper.

ask *verb*
1 ask for help/advice: request, appeal,
petition, sue, plead, beg, entreat,
implore, clamour, beseech, pray,
supplicate, crave, demand, order, bid,
require, seek, solicit, invite, summon.
2 ask awkward questions: inquire,
query, question, interrogate, quiz, press.
3 ask him out/round: invite, have round,
entertain.

asleep *adjective*
sleeping, napping, snoozing, fast
asleep, sound asleep, dozing,
slumbering, dormant (*fml*), resting,
inactive, inert, unconscious, numb.

aspect *noun*
**1 view the problem from a different
aspect/an aspect of his life**: angle,
direction, detail, side, facet, feature,
dimension, standpoint, point of view,
view.
2 take on a more promising aspect:
appearance, look, air, manner,
bearing, demeanour, mien (*fml*), face,
expression, countenance.
3 a house with a northern aspect:
direction, outlook, view, situation,
position, prospect.

aspire *verb*
aim, intend, purpose, seek, pursue,
hope, dream, wish, desire, yearn, long,
crave, hanker.

aspiring *adjective*
would-be, aspirant, striving,
endeavouring, ambitious, enterprising,
keen, eager, hopeful, optimistic,
wishful, longing.

assault *noun*
1 an assault on the nerves: attack,
offensive, onslaught, blitz, strike, raid,
invasion, incursion, storm, storming,
charge.

2 charged with assault: battery,
grievous bodily harm, GBH (*infml*),
mugging (*infml*), rape, abuse.
▶ *verb*
attack, charge, invade, strike, hit,
assail, set upon, fall on, beat up (*infml*),
mug (*infml*), rape, molest, abuse.

assemble *verb*
1 assemble in the playground: gather,
congregate, muster, rally, convene,
meet, join up, flock, group, collect,
accumulate, amass, bring together,
round up, marshal, mobilize.
2 assemble a model aeroplane:
construct, build, put together, piece
together, compose, make, fabricate,
manufacture.
F3 1 scatter, disperse. 2 dismantle.

assembly *noun*
1 an assembly of bishops: gathering,
rally, meeting, convention, conference,
convocation (*fml*), congress, council,
group, body, company, congregation,
flock, crowd, multitude, throng,
collection, assemblage.
2 assembly of the components:
construction, building, fabrication,
manufacture.

assert *verb*
affirm, attest (*fml*), swear, testify to,
allege, claim, contend, maintain,
insist, stress, protest, defend, vindicate,
uphold, promote, declare, profess,
state, pronounce, lay down, advance.
F3 deny, refute.

assertive *adjective*
bold, confident, self-assured, forward,
pushy (*infml*), insistent, emphatic,
forceful, firm, decided, strong-willed,
dogmatic, opinionated, presumptuous,
assuming, overbearing, domineering,
aggressive.
F3 timid, diffident.

assess *verb*
gauge, estimate, evaluate, appraise,
review, judge, consider, weigh, size up,
compute, determine, fix, value, rate,
tax, levy, impose, demand.

assessment *noun*
gauging, estimation, estimate,
evaluation, appraisal, review,
judgement, opinion, consideration,

calculation, determination, valuation, rating, taxation.

asset *noun*
strength, resource, virtue, plus (*infml*), benefit, advantage, blessing, boon, help, aid.
F3 liability.

assets *noun*
estate, property, possessions, goods, holdings, securities, money, wealth, capital, funds, reserves, resources, means.

assign *verb*
1 assigned them various tasks : allocate, apportion, grant, give, dispense, distribute, allot, consign, delegate, name, nominate, designate, appoint, choose, select, determine, set, fix, specify, stipulate.
2 to what do you assign your popularity? : attribute, accredit (*fml*), ascribe, put down.

assignment *noun*
commission, errand, task, project, job, position, post, duty, responsibility, charge, appointment, delegation, designation, nomination, selection, allocation, consignment, grant, distribution.

assist *verb*
help, aid, abet, rally round, co-operate, collaborate, back, second, support, reinforce, sustain, relieve, benefit, serve, enable, facilitate, expedite, boost, further, advance.
F3 hinder, thwart.

assistance *noun*
help, aid, succour, co-operation, collaboration, backing, support, reinforcement, relief, benefit, service, boost, furtherance.
F3 hindrance, resistance.

assistant *noun*
helper, helpmate, aide, right-hand man, auxiliary, ancillary, subordinate, backer, second, supporter, accomplice, accessory, abettor, collaborator, colleague, partner, ally, confederate, associate.

associate *verb*
1 don't associate the one with the other : connect, link, couple, correlate, identify, put together.
2 associate with bad company : socialize, mingle, mix, fraternize, consort, hang around (*infml*).

association *noun*
1 an association of women's groups : organization, corporation, company, partnership, league, alliance, coalition, confederation, confederacy, federation, affiliation, consortium, cartel, union, syndicate, society, club, fraternity, fellowship, clique, group, band.
2 a close association : bond, tie, connection, correlation, relation, relationship, involvement, intimacy, friendship, companionship, familiarity.

assorted *adjective*
miscellaneous, mixed, varied, different, differing, heterogeneous (*fml*), diverse, sundry, various, several, manifold (*fml*).

assortment *noun*
miscellany, medley, pot-pourri, jumble, mixture, variety, diversity, collection, selection, choice, arrangement, grouping.

assume *verb*
1 assumed that it was correct : presume, surmise, accept, take for granted, expect, understand, deduce, infer, guess, postulate, suppose, think, believe, imagine, fancy.
2 assume a disguise : affect, take on, feign, counterfeit, simulate, put on, pretend.
3 assume command : undertake, adopt, embrace, seize, commandeer, appropriate, usurp, take over.

assumed *adjective*
false, bogus, counterfeit, fake, phoney (*infml*), sham, affected, feigned, simulated, pretended, made-up, fictitious, hypothetical.
F3 true, real, actual.

assumption *noun*
presumption, surmise, inference, supposition, guess, conjecture, theory, hypothesis, premise, postulate, idea, notion, belief, fancy.

assure *verb*
affirm, guarantee, warrant, pledge,

promise, vow, swear, tell, convince, persuade, encourage, hearten, reassure, soothe, comfort, boost, strengthen, secure, ensure, confirm.

assured adjective
1 his future was assured: sure, certain, indisputable, irrefutable, confirmed, positive, definite, settled, fixed, guaranteed, secure.
2 an assured young woman: self-assured, confident, self-confident, self-possessed, bold, audacious, assertive.
F3 1 uncertain. 2 shy.

astonish verb
surprise, startle, amaze, astound, stun, stupefy, daze, stagger, floor (infml), dumbfound, flabbergast (infml), shock, confound, bewilder.

astounding adjective
surprising, startling, amazing, astonishing, stunning, breathtaking, stupefying, overwhelming, staggering, shocking, bewildering.

astray adverb
adrift, off course, lost, amiss, wrong, off the rails (infml), awry, off the mark.

astute adjective
shrewd, prudent, sagacious (fml), wise, canny, knowing, intelligent, sharp, penetrating, keen, perceptive, perspicacious (fml), discerning, subtle, clever, crafty, cunning, sly, wily.
F3 stupid, slow.

asylum noun
haven, sanctuary, refuge, shelter, retreat, safety.

asymmetrical adjective
unsymmetrical, unbalanced, uneven, crooked, awry, unequal, disproportionate, irregular.
F3 symmetrical.

atheist noun
unbeliever, non-believer, disbeliever, sceptic, infidel, pagan, heathen, free-thinker.

athletic adjective
fit, energetic, vigorous, active, sporty, muscular, sinewy, brawny, strapping, robust, sturdy, strong, powerful, well-knit, well-proportioned, wiry.
F3 puny.

atmosphere noun
1 pollution in the atmosphere: air, sky, aerospace, heavens, ether.
2 a hotel with a pleasant atmosphere: ambience, environment, surroundings, aura, feel, feeling, mood, spirit, tone, tenor, character, quality, flavour.

atom noun
molecule, particle, bit (infml), morsel, crumb, grain, spot, speck, mite, shred, scrap, hint, trace, scintilla, jot, iota, whit.

atrocious adjective
shocking, appalling, abominable, dreadful, terrible, horrible, hideous, ghastly, heinous (fml), grievous, savage, vicious, monstrous, fiendish, ruthless.
F3 admirable, fine.

attach verb
1 attach a label: affix, stick, adhere, fasten, fix, secure, tie, bind, weld, join, unite, connect, link, couple, add, annex.
2 attach too much significance to: ascribe, attribute, impute (fml), assign, put, place, associate, relate to, belong.
F3 1 detach, unfasten.

attachment noun
1 an attachment for the drill/to the will: accessory, fitting, fixture, extension, appendage, extra, supplement, addition, adjunct, codicil.
2 form an attachment: fondness, affection, tenderness, love, liking, partiality, loyalty, devotion, friendship, affinity, attraction, bond, tie, link.

attack noun
1 a military/verbal attack: offensive, blitz, bombardment, invasion, incursion, foray, raid, strike, charge, rush, onslaught, assault, battery, aggression, criticism, censure, abuse.
2 have an attack: seizure, fit, convulsion, paroxysm, spasm, stroke.
▶ verb
1 attacked by Vikings/a gang: invade, raid, strike, storm, charge, assail, assault, set about, set upon, fall on, lay into, do over (slang).
2 attacked in the press: criticize,

censure, blame, denounce, revile, malign, abuse.
F3 1 defend, protect.

attacker *noun*
assailant, mugger (*infml*), aggressor, invader, raider, critic, detractor, reviler, abuser, persecutor.
F3 defender, supporter.

attain *verb*
accomplish, achieve, fulfil, complete, effect, realize, earn, reach, touch, arrive at, grasp, get, acquire, obtain, procure, secure, gain, win, net.

attainment *noun*
accomplishment, achievement, feat, fulfilment, completion, consummation, realization, success, ability, capability, competence, proficiency, skill, art, talent, gift, aptitude, facility, mastery.

attempt *noun*
try, endeavour, shot (*infml*), go (*infml*), effort, struggle, bid, undertaking, venture, trial, experiment.
▶ *verb*
try, endeavour, aspire, seek, strive, undertake, tackle, venture, experiment.

attend *verb*
1 attend school/a meeting: be present, go to, frequent, visit.
2 wasn't attending to what was being said: pay attention, listen, hear, heed, mind, mark, note, notice, observe.
3 attended by her lady-in-waiting: escort, chaperon(e), accompany, usher, follow, guard, look after, take care of, care for, nurse, tend, minister to, help, serve, wait on.
◆ **attend to** deal with, see to, take care of, look after, manage, direct, control, oversee, supervise.

attendant *noun*
aide, helper, assistant, auxiliary, steward, waiter, servant, page, retainer, guide, marshal, usher, escort, companion, follower, guard, custodian.

attention *noun*
alertness, vigilance, concentration, heed, notice, observation, regard, mindfulness, awareness, recognition, thought, contemplation, consideration, concern, care, treatment, service.
F3 inattention, disregard, carelessness.

attentive *adjective*
1 an attentive audience: alert, awake, vigilant, watchful, observant, concentrating, heedful, mindful, careful, conscientious.
2 an attentive husband: considerate, thoughtful, kind, obliging, accommodating, polite, courteous, devoted.
F3 1 inattentive, heedless. 2 inconsiderate.

attitude *noun*
feeling, disposition, mood, aspect, manner, bearing, pose, posture, stance, position, point of view, opinion, view, outlook, perspective, approach.

attract *verb*
pull, draw, lure, allure, entice, seduce, tempt, invite, induce, incline, appeal to, interest, engage, fascinate, enchant, charm, bewitch, captivate, excite.
F3 repel, disgust.

attraction *noun*
pull, draw, magnetism, lure, allure, bait, enticement, inducement, seduction, temptation, invitation, appeal, interest, fascination, enchantment, charm, captivation.
F3 repulsion.

attractive *adjective*
pretty, fair, fetching, good-looking, handsome, beautiful, gorgeous, stunning (*infml*), glamorous, lovely, pleasant, pleasing, agreeable, appealing, winning, enticing, seductive, tempting, inviting, interesting, engaging, fascinating, charming, captivating, magnetic.
F3 unattractive, repellent.

attribute *verb* /a-**trib**-yoot/
ascribe, accredit (*fml*), credit, impute (*fml*), assign, put down, blame, charge, refer, apply.
▶ *noun* /**a**-trib-yoot/
property, quality, virtue, point, aspect, facet, feature, trait, characteristic, idiosyncrasy, peculiarity, quirk, note, mark, sign, symbol.

audible *adjective*
clear, distinct, recognizable, perceptible, discernible, detectable, appreciable.
🔁 inaudible, silent, unclear.

audience *noun*
spectators, onlookers, house, auditorium, listeners, viewers, crowd, turnout, gathering, assembly, congregation, fans, devotees, regulars, following, public.

auspicious *adjective*
favourable, propitious, encouraging, cheerful, bright, rosy, promising, hopeful, optimistic, fortunate, lucky, opportune, happy, prosperous.
🔁 inauspicious, ominous.

austere *adjective*
1 an austere building: stark, bleak, plain, simple, unadorned, grim, forbidding.
2 life at the monastery was austere: severe, stern, strict, cold, formal, rigid, rigorous, exacting, hard, harsh, spartan, grave, serious, solemn, sober, abstemious, self-denying, restrained, economical, frugal, ascetic, self-disciplined, puritanical, chaste.
🔁 1 ornate, elaborate.

authentic *adjective*
genuine, true, real, actual, certain, bona fide, legitimate, honest, valid, original, pure, factual, accurate, true-to-life, faithful, reliable, trustworthy.
🔁 false, fake, counterfeit, spurious.

authenticate *verb*
guarantee, warrant, vouch for, attest (*fml*), authorize, accredit (*fml*), validate, certify, endorse, confirm, verify, corroborate.

author *noun*
1 a famous author: writer, novelist, dramatist, playwright, composer, pen, penman, penwoman.
2 the principal author of the reforms: creator, founder, originator, initiator, parent, prime mover, mover, inventor, designer, architect, planner, maker, producer.

authoritarian *adjective*
strict, disciplinarian, severe, harsh, rigid, inflexible, unyielding, dogmatic, absolute, autocratic, dictatorial, despotic, tyrannical, oppressive, domineering, imperious.
🔁 liberal.

authoritative *adjective*
scholarly, learned, official, authorized, legitimate, valid, approved, sanctioned, accepted, definitive, decisive, authentic, factual, true, truthful, accurate, faithful, convincing, sound, reliable, dependable, trustworthy.
🔁 unofficial, unreliable.

authority *noun*
1 assert one's authority over others: sovereignty, supremacy, rule, sway, control, dominion, influence, power, force, government, administration, officialdom.
2 have no legal authority to enter the premises: authorization, permission, sanction, permit, warrant, licence, credentials, right, prerogative, mandate.
3 an authority on antiques: expert, pundit, connoisseur, specialist, professional, master, scholar.

authorize *verb*
legalize, validate, ratify, confirm, license, entitle, accredit (*fml*), empower, enable, commission, warrant, permit, allow, consent to, sanction, approve, give the go-ahead.

automatic *adjective*
1 an automatic washing machine: automated, self-activating, mechanical, mechanized, programmed, self-regulating, computerized, push-button, robotic, self-propelling, unmanned.
2 an automatic response: spontaneous, reflex, involuntary, unwilled, unconscious, unthinking, natural, instinctive, routine, necessary, certain, inevitable, unavoidable, inescapable.

autonomous *adjective*
self-governing, sovereign, independent, self-determining, free.

auxiliary *adjective*
ancillary, assistant, subsidiary, accessory, secondary, supporting,

supportive, helping, assisting, aiding, extra, supplementary, spare, reserve, back-up, emergency, substitute.

available *adjective*
free, vacant, to hand, within reach, at hand, accessible, handy, convenient, on hand, ready, on tap, obtainable.
🖃 unavailable.

avenge *verb*
take revenge for, take vengeance for, punish, requite, repay, retaliate.

average *adjective*
mean, medial, median, middle, intermediate, medium, moderate, satisfactory, fair, mediocre, middling, indifferent, so-so (*infml*), passable, tolerable, undistinguished, run-of-the-mill, ordinary, everyday, common, usual, normal, regular, standard, typical, unexceptional.
🖃 extreme, exceptional, remarkable.
▶ *noun*
mean, mid-point, norm, standard, rule, par, medium.
🖃 extreme, exception.
▶ *verb*
find the mean, equalize, standardize, normalize.

averse *adjective*
reluctant, unwilling, loth, disinclined, ill-disposed, hostile, opposed, antagonistic, unfavourable.
🖃 willing, keen, sympathetic.

aversion *noun*
dislike, hate, hatred, loathing, abhorrence (*fml*), abomination, horror, phobia, reluctance, unwillingness, distaste, disgust, revulsion, hostility, opposition, antagonism.
🖃 liking, sympathy, desire.

avert *verb*
turn away, deflect, turn aside, parry, fend off, ward off, stave off, forestall, frustrate, prevent, obviate, avoid, evade.

avid *adjective*
eager, earnest, keen, enthusiastic, fanatical, devoted, dedicated, zealous, ardent, fervent, intense, passionate, insatiable, ravenous, hungry, thirsty, greedy, grasping, covetous.
🖃 indifferent.

avoid *verb*
evade, elude, sidestep, dodge, shirk, duck (*infml*), escape, get out of, bypass, circumvent, balk, prevent, avert, shun, abstain from, refrain from, steer clear of.

awake *adjective*
wakeful, wide-awake, aroused, alert, vigilant, watchful, observant, attentive, conscious, aware, sensitive, alive.

award *verb*
give, present, distribute, dispense, bestow, confer, accord, endow, gift, grant, allot, apportion, assign, allow, determine.
▶ *noun*
prize, trophy, decoration, medal, presentation, dispensation, bestowal, conferral, endowment, gift, grant, allotment, allowance, adjudication, judgement, decision, order.

aware *adjective*
conscious, alive to, sensitive, appreciative, sentient, familiar, conversant (*fml*), acquainted, informed, enlightened, au courant, knowing, knowledgeable, cognizant, mindful, heedful, attentive, observant, sharp, alert, on the ball (*infml*), shrewd, sensible.
🖃 unaware, oblivious, insensitive.

awe *noun*
wonder, veneration, reverence, respect, admiration, amazement, astonishment, fear, terror, dread, apprehension.
🖃 contempt.

awe-inspiring *adjective*
wonderful, sublime, magnificent, stupendous, overwhelming, breathtaking, stupefying, stunning, astonishing, amazing, impressive, imposing, majestic, solemn, moving, awesome, formidable, daunting, intimidating, fearsome.
🖃 contemptible, tame.

awful *adjective*
terrible, dreadful, fearful, frightful, ghastly, unpleasant, nasty, horrible, hideous, ugly, gruesome, dire, abysmal, atrocious, horrific, shocking, appalling, alarming, spine-chilling.

▣ wonderful, excellent.

awkward *adjective*
1 too awkward to be a good dancer:
clumsy, unco-ordinated, ungainly,
gauche, inept, inexpert, unskilful,
bungling, ham-fisted, graceless,
ungraceful, inelegant.
2 feeling awkward in their presence:
uncomfortable, ill at ease,
embarrassed.
3 he's just being awkward: obstinate,
stubborn, unco-operative, irritable,
touchy, prickly, rude, unpleasant.
4 an awkward problem/size:
cumbersome, unwieldy, inconvenient,
difficult, fiddly, delicate, troublesome,
perplexing.
▣ 1 graceful, elegant. 2 comfortable,
relaxed. 3 amenable, pleasant. 4
convenient, handy.

axe *noun*
hatchet, chopper, cleaver, tomahawk,
battle-axe.
▸ *verb*
cancel, terminate, discontinue,
remove, withdraw, eliminate, get rid of,
throw out, dismiss, discharge, sack
(*infml*), fire (*infml*).

babble *verb*
1 babbling incoherently: chatter, gabble, jabber, cackle, mutter, mumble, murmur.
2 stream babbling over the rocks: burble, gurgle.

baby *noun*
infant, babe (*fml*), new-born, child, toddler.

babyish *adjective*
childish, juvenile, puerile (*fml*), infantile, silly, foolish, soft (*infml*), baby, young, immature, naïve.
F∃ mature, precocious.

back *noun*
rear, stern, end, tail, tail end, hind part, hindquarters, posterior, reverse.
F∃ front, face.
▶ *adjective*
rear, end, tail, posterior, hind, hindmost, reverse.
F∃ front.
▶ *verb*
1 back into the garage/out of the room: go backwards, reverse, recede, regress, backtrack, retreat, retire, withdraw, back away, recoil.
2 back the Labour candidate/a new business venture: support, sustain, assist, side with, champion, advocate, encourage, promote, boost, favour, sanction, countenance, endorse, second, sponsor, finance, subsidize, underwrite.
F∃ 1 advance, approach. **2** oppose.
◆ **back down** concede, yield, give in, surrender, submit, retreat, withdraw, back-pedal (*infml*).
◆ **back out** abandon, give up, chicken out (*infml*), withdraw, pull out (*infml*), resign, recant, go back on, cancel.

◆ **back up** confirm, corroborate, substantiate, endorse, second, champion, support, reinforce, bolster, assist, aid.
F∃ contradict, let down.

backbone *noun*
1 a chair that supports the backbone: spine, spinal column, vertebrae, vertebral column.
2 the backbone of the company: mainstay, support, core, foundation.
3 a coward with no backbone: courage, mettle, pluck, nerve, grit, determination, resolve, tenacity, steadfastness, toughness, stamina, strength, character, power.
F∃ 3 spinelessness, weakness.

backfire *verb*
recoil, rebound, ricochet, boomerang, miscarry, fail, flop.

background *noun*
1 the background of the story: setting, surroundings, environment, context, circumstances.
2 with a science background/from a different background: record, history, credentials, experience, grounding, preparation, education, upbringing, breeding, culture, tradition.

backing *noun*
support, accompaniment, aid, assistance, helpers, championing, advocacy, encouragement, moral support, favour, sanction, promotion, endorsement, seconding, patronage, sponsorship, finance, funds, grant, subsidy.

backlash *noun*
reaction, response, repercussion, reprisal, retaliation, recoil, backfire.

backward *adjective*
1 a backward step : retrograde, retrogressive, regressive.
2 a backward child/region : slow, dull, immature, retarded, subnormal, stupid, behind, behindhand, underdeveloped.
3 backward in making suggestions : shy, bashful, reluctant, unwilling, hesitant, hesitating, wavering.
E3 1 forward. 2 precocious.

bacteria *noun*
germs, bugs (*infml*), microbes, micro-organisms, bacilli.

bad *adjective*
1 a bad smell/habit/experience/accident : unpleasant, disagreeable, nasty, undesirable, unfortunate, distressing, adverse, detrimental, harmful, damaging, injurious, serious, grave, severe, harsh.
2 a bad person : evil, wicked, sinful, criminal, corrupt, immoral, vile.
3 bad workmanship/service/eyesight : poor, inferior, substandard, imperfect, faulty, defective, deficient, unsatisfactory, useless.
4 this meat/milk/butter is bad : rotten, mouldy, decayed, spoilt, putrid, rancid, sour, off, tainted, contaminated.
5 a bad child : naughty, mischievous, ill-behaved, disobedient.
6 a bad time to call : inconvenient, unfortunate, unsuitable, inappropriate.
E3 1 good, pleasant, mild, slight. 2 good, virtuous. 3 excellent, skilled. 4 fresh. 5 well-behaved. 6 good.
⇨ *See also* **Word Workshop** *panel.*

badge *noun*
identification, emblem, device, insignia, sign, mark, token, stamp, brand, trademark, logo.

badly *adverb*
1 badly injured/damaged : greatly, extremely, exceedingly, intensely, deeply, acutely, bitterly, painfully, seriously, desperately, severely, critically, crucially.
2 behave badly : wickedly, criminally, immorally, shamefully, unfairly.
3 go/spell/drive badly : wrong,

wrongly, incorrectly, improperly, defectively, faultily, imperfectly, inadequately, unsatisfactorily, poorly, incompetently, negligently, carelessly.
4 turn out badly : unfavourably, adversely, unfortunately, unsuccessfully.
E3 1 slightly. 2 well, virtuously. 3 well, correctly, competently. 4 successfully.

bad-tempered *adjective*
irritable, cross, crotchety, crabbed, crabby, snappy, grumpy, querulous (*fml*), petulant, cantankerous, fractious, stroppy (*infml*).
E3 good-tempered, genial, agreeable.

baffle *verb*
puzzle, perplex, mystify, bemuse, bewilder, confuse, confound, bamboozle (*infml*), flummox (*infml*), daze, upset, disconcert, foil, thwart, frustrate, hinder, check, defeat, stump (*infml*).
E3 enlighten, help.

bag *noun*
container, sack, case, suitcase, grip, carrier, hold-all, handbag, shoulder-bag, satchel, rucksack, haversack, backpack.
▶ *verb*
1 (*infml*) bag the front seat : obtain, acquire, get, gain, corner, take, grab, appropriate, commandeer, reserve.
2 bag a couple of rabbits : catch, capture, trap, land, kill, shoot.

baggage *noun*
luggage, suitcases, bags, belongings, things, equipment, gear (*infml*), paraphernalia, impedimenta (*fml*).

baggy *adjective*
loose, slack, roomy, ill-fitting, billowing, bulging, floppy, sagging, droopy.
E3 tight, firm.

bail *noun*
security, surety, pledge, bond, guarantee, warranty.

bail out[1] *verb*
bail out a troubled company : help, aid, assist, relieve, rescue, finance.

bail out[2]**, bale out** *verb*
bailed out just before the plane/company crashed : get out, get clear, withdraw, retreat, quit, back out, escape.

bait *noun*
lure, incentive, inducement, bribe, temptation, enticement, allurement, attraction.
F3 disincentive.

balance *verb*
1 balance a ball on its nose: steady, poise, stabilize.
2 balance the two sides of the scales/ ledger: level, square, equalize, equate, match, counterbalance, adjust.
3 balanced the lower mark with the higher one: offset, counteract, neutralize.
4 balancing the risks and benefits: compare, consider, weigh (up), estimate.
F3 1 unbalance, overbalance.
▶ *noun*
1 lose one's balance/strike a good balance between two things: equilibrium, steadiness, stability, evenness, symmetry, equality, parity, equity, equivalence, correspondence.
2 the balance of one's mind: composure, self-possession, poise, equanimity.
3 demand the balance of their bill: remainder, rest, residue, surplus, difference.
F3 1 imbalance, instability.

balcony *noun*
terrace, veranda, gallery, upper circle, gods.

bald *adjective*
1 a completely bald head/a bald patch: bald-headed, hairless, smooth, uncovered.
2 bald of all vegetation: bare, naked, bleak, stark, barren, treeless.
3 a bald statement: forthright, direct, straight, plain, simple, unadorned, outright, downright, straightforward.
F3 1 hairy, hirsute. **3** adorned.

bale out ⇨ *see* **bail out²**.

balk, baulk *verb*
flinch, recoil, shrink, jib, boggle, hesitate, refuse, resist, evade, disconcert, check, stall.

ball *noun*
sphere, globe, orb, globule, drop,
conglomeration, pellet, pill, shot, bullet, slug (*infml*).

ballot *noun*
poll, polling, vote, voting, election, referendum, plebiscite.

ban *verb*
forbid, prohibit, disallow, proscribe, bar, exclude, ostracize, outlaw, banish, suppress, restrict.
F3 allow, permit, authorize.

banal *adjective*
trite, commonplace, ordinary, everyday, humdrum, boring, unimaginative, hackneyed, clichéd, stock, stereotyped, corny (*infml*), stale, threadbare, tired, empty.
F3 original, fresh, imaginative.

band¹ *noun*
a metal band: strip, belt, ribbon, tape, bandage, binding, tie, ligature, bond, strap, cord, chain.

band² *noun*
1 a band of disciples: troop, gang, crew, group, herd, flock, party, body, association, company, society, club, clique.
2 a rock/jazz/dance band: group, orchestra, ensemble.

bandit *noun*
robber, thief, brigand, marauder, outlaw, highwayman, pirate, buccaneer, hijacker, cowboy, gunman, desperado, gangster.

bandy¹ *verb*
bandy words about: exchange, swap, trade, barter, interchange, reciprocate, pass, toss, throw.

bandy² *adjective*
he has bandy legs: bow-legged, curved, bowed, bent, crooked.

bang *noun*
1 a bang on the head: blow, hit, knock, bump, crash, collision, smack, punch, thump, wallop (*infml*), stroke, whack (*infml*).
2 a loud bang: explosion, detonation, pop, boom, clap, peal, clang, clash, thud, thump, slam, noise, report, shot.
▶ *verb*
1 bang one's head/a nail in: strike, hit,

Your writing will have added interest if you try to avoid repeating **bad** too often. The following lists offer some suggestions for synonyms that you might use instead.

a person's character

disagreeable	unpleasant
evil	wicked

bad behaviour

disobedient	mischievous	rude
ill-behaved	naughty	

something, eg fruit or milk, that has gone bad

decayed	putrid	sour
mouldy	rancid	
off	rotten	

feeling bad

annoyed	upset	unwell

something that has a harmful effect

adverse	dangerous	unhealthy
damaging	harmful	

something that has been done or made badly

defective	inferior	unsatisfactory
faulty	poor	useless
imperfect	substandard	

bad   WORD *workshop*

The following passage shows ways in which you can use other words to avoid repeating **bad**. Try describing things instead of simply saying they were bad.

> 'I have had such a ~~bad~~ *terrible* day,.' moaned Asif. 'What happened?' asked Innes. 'First of all,' replied Asif, 'the weather was ~~bad~~ *awful* and I got soaked on my way to school. Then I got a ~~bad~~ *poor* mark in French.' 'Don't feel too ~~bad~~ *upset* about that,' said Innes, 'at least you're not in trouble for being ~~bad~~ *disobedient* in class.'
>
> 'At lunch-time the milk was ~~bad~~ *off*,' continued Asif, 'and I couldn't drink it because I'm sure it would have been ~~bad~~ *harmful* to drink. Then I went to the cinema with Hilary but the film was ~~bad~~ *useless* and we left before it had ended. Now I feel ~~bad~~ *unwell* and I'm sure I have a cold because of the ~~bad~~ *dreadful* weather this morning. I hope tomorrow isn't as ~~bad~~ *unpleasant*!'

Have you ever had such a terrible day? Describe it, but remember to use as many different substitutes for **bad** as you can.

bash, knock, bump, rap, drum, hammer, pound, thump.
2 fireworks banging: explode, burst, detonate, boom, echo, resound, crash, slam, clatter, clang, peal, thunder.

▶ *adverb*
straight, directly, headlong, right, precisely, slap, smack, hard, noisily, suddenly, abruptly.

banish *verb*
expel, eject, evict, deport, transport,

exile, outlaw, ban, bar, debar, exclude, shut out, ostracize, excommunicate, dismiss, oust, dislodge, remove, get rid of, discard, dispel, eliminate, eradicate.

E3 recall, welcome.

bank¹ *noun*

investment bank: accumulation, fund, pool, reservoir, depository, repository, treasury, savings, reserve, store, stock, stockpile, hoard, cache.

▶ *verb*

banked the cheque: deposit, save, keep, store, accumulate, stockpile.

E3 spend.

bank² *noun*

a grassy bank: heap, pile, mass, edge, mound, earthwork, ridge, rampart, slope, embankment, side, tilt, shore.

▶ *verb*

1 banked up the earth: heap, pile, stack, mass, amass, accumulate, mound, drift.

2 aeroplane banked sharply: slope, incline, pitch, slant, tilt, tip.

bank³ *noun*

a bank of computers: array, panel, bench, group, tier, rank, line, row, series, succession, sequence, train.

bankrupt *adjective*

1 a bankrupt business: insolvent, in liquidation, ruined, failed, beggared, destitute, impoverished, broke (*infml*), gone bust (*infml*).

2 bankrupt of ideas: spent, exhausted, depleted, lacking.

E3 1 solvent, wealthy.

banter *noun*

joking, jesting, pleasantry, badinage, repartee, word play, chaff, chaffing, kidding (*infml*), ribbing, derision, mockery, ridicule.

baptize *verb*

christen, name, call, term, style, title, introduce, initiate, enrol, recruit, immerse, sprinkle, purify, cleanse.

bar *noun*

1 a resort with good bars and restaurants: public house, pub (*infml*), inn, tavern, saloon, lounge, counter.

2 a gold/chocolate bar: slab, block, lump, chunk, wedge, ingot, nugget.

3 an iron bar/a five-bar gate: rod, stick, shaft, pole, stake, stanchion, batten, cross-piece, rail, railing, paling, barricade.

4 a bar to progress: obstacle, impediment, hindrance, obstruction, barrier, stop, check, deterrent.

▶ *verb*

1 barred from entering: exclude, debar, ban, forbid, prohibit, prevent, preclude, hinder, obstruct, restrain.

2 bar the door: barricade, lock, bolt, latch, fasten, secure.

barbaric *adjective*

barbarous, primitive, wild, savage, fierce, ferocious, cruel, inhuman, brutal, brutish, uncivilized, uncouth, vulgar, coarse, crude, rude.

E3 humane, civilized, gracious.

bare *adjective*

1 bare legs/a bare hillside: naked, nude, unclothed, undressed, stripped, denuded, uncovered, exposed.

2 the bare truth/essentials: plain, simple, unadorned, unfurnished, bald, stark, basic, essential.

E3 1 clothed. 2 decorated, detailed.

barely *adverb*

hardly, scarcely, only just, just, almost.

bargain *noun*

1 make a bargain: deal, transaction, contract, treaty, pact, pledge, promise, agreement, understanding, arrangement, negotiation.

2 the best place to find bargains: discount, reduction, snip, giveaway, special offer.

▶ *verb*

negotiate, haggle, deal, trade, traffic, barter, buy, sell, transact, contract, covenant, promise, agree.

barge *verb*

bump, hit, collide, impinge, shove, elbow, push (in), muscle in, butt in, interrupt, gatecrash, intrude, interfere.

bark *noun, verb*

yap, woof, yelp, snap, snarl, growl, bay, howl.

barrage *noun*

bombardment, shelling, gunfire, cannonade, broadside, volley, salvo, burst, assault, attack, onset, onslaught, deluge, torrent, stream, storm, hail, rain, shower, mass, profusion.

barren *adjective*
arid, dry, desert, desolate, empty, flat, treeless, waste, unproductive, useless.
🔁 fertile, productive, useful.

barricade *noun*
blockade, obstruction, barrier, fence, stockade, bulwark, rampart, protection.
▸ *verb*
block, obstruct, bar, fortify, defend, protect.

barrier *noun*
1 build a barrier across the road: wall, fence, railing, barricade, blockade, boom, rampart, fortification, ditch, frontier, boundary, bar, check.
2 a barrier to success: obstacle, hurdle, stumbling block, impediment, obstruction, hindrance, handicap, limitation, restriction, drawback, difficulty.

barter *verb*
exchange, swap, trade, traffic, deal, negotiate, bargain, haggle.

base *noun*
1 the base of the statue: bottom, foot, pedestal, plinth, stand, rest, support, foundation, bed, groundwork.
2 the element that forms the base: basis, fundamental, essential, principal, key, heart, core, essence, root, origin, source.
3 a naval base/the base for operations: headquarters, centre, post, station, camp, settlement, home, starting point.
▸ *verb*
1 base oneself somewhere: establish, locate, station.
2 a theory based on observation: found, ground, build, construct, derive, depend, hinge.

baseless *adjective*
groundless, unfounded, unsupported, unsubstantiated, unauthenticated, unconfirmed, unjustified, uncalled-for, gratuitous.
🔁 justifiable.

basic *adjective*
fundamental, elementary, primary,

root, underlying, key, central, inherent, intrinsic, essential, indispensable, vital, necessary, important.
🔁 inessential, minor, peripheral.

basically *adverb*
fundamentally, at bottom, at heart, inherently, intrinsically, essentially, principally, primarily.

basics *noun*
fundamentals, rudiments, principles, essentials, necessaries, practicalities, brass tacks (*infml*), grass roots, bedrock, rock bottom, core, facts.

basin *noun*
bowl, dish, sink, crater, cavity, hollow, depression, dip.

basis *noun*
base, bottom, footing, support, foundation, ground, groundwork, fundamental, premise, principle, essential, heart, core, thrust.

bask *verb*
sunbathe, lie, lounge, relax, laze, wallow, revel, delight in, enjoy, relish, savour.

basket *noun*
hamper, creel, pannier, punnet, trug, bassinet.

bass *adjective* /beis/
deep, low, low-toned, resonant.

batch *noun*
lot, consignment, parcel, pack, bunch, set, assortment, collection, assemblage, group, contingent, amount, quantity.

bath *noun*
wash, scrub, soak (*infml*), shower, douche, tub, sauna, Jacuzzi®.
▸ *verb*
bathe, wash, clean, soak, shower.

bathe *verb*
1 bathe the wound: wash, clean, cleanse, rinse, immerse, soak.
2 bathe in the Mediterranean: swim, go swimming, paddle.
3 bathed in sunshine: steep, flood, cover, suffuse.

batter *verb*
beat, pound, pummel, buffet, smash, dash, pelt, lash, thrash, wallop (*infml*), abuse, maltreat, ill-treat, manhandle,

maul, assault, hurt, injure, bruise, disfigure, mangle, distress, crush, demolish, destroy, ruin, shatter.

battered *adjective*
beaten, abused, ill-treated, injured, bruised, weather-beaten, dilapidated, tumbledown, ramshackle, crumbling, damaged, crushed.

battle *noun*
war, warfare, hostilities, action, conflict, strife, combat, fight, engagement, encounter, attack, fray, skirmish, clash, struggle, contest, campaign, crusade, row, disagreement, dispute, debate, controversy.
▶ *verb*
fight, combat, war, feud, contend, struggle, strive, campaign, crusade, agitate, clamour, contest, argue, dispute.

baulk ⇨*see* **balk**.

bay *noun*
gulf, bight, inlet, sound, cove, estuary.

be *verb*
1 to be or not to be?: exist, breathe, live, be alive.
2 will be for centuries to come: stay, remain, abide (*fml*), last, endure, persist, continue, survive, stand, prevail.
3 how can that be?: happen, occur, arise, come about, take place, come to pass, befall, develop.

beach *noun*
sand, sands, shingle, shore, strand, seashore, seaside, water's edge, coast, seaboard.

bead *noun*
drop, droplet, drip, globule, glob (*infml*), blob, dot, bubble, pearl, jewel, pellet.

beam *noun*
1 a beam of light: ray, shaft, gleam, glint, glimmer, glow.
2 oak/steel beam: plank, board, timber, rafter, joist, girder, spar, boom, bar, support.
▶ *verb*
1 sunlight beaming down/sun beaming all day: emit, radiate, shine, glare, glitter, glow, glimmer.

2 pictures beamed around the world: broadcast, transmit.
3 beam with pleasure: smile, grin.

bear *verb*
1 bear pain/inconvenience: tolerate, stand, put up with, cope with, endure, abide, suffer, take (*infml*).
2 bear something's weight: hold, carry, support, take.
3 bear a grudge: sustain, maintain, harbour, cherish.
4 bear a child/fruit: give birth to, breed, propagate, beget (*fml*), engender, produce, generate, develop, yield, bring forth.
5 bearing the names of the fallen: display, exhibit, show, have.
6 bearing the coffin: carry, convey, transport, transfer, move, take, bring.
◆ **bear out** confirm, endorse, support, uphold, prove, demonstrate, justify corroborate, substantiate, vindicate.
◆ **bear up** persevere, soldier on, carry on, suffer, endure, survive, withstand.
◆ **bear with** tolerate, put up with, endure, suffer, forbear (*fml*), be patient with, make allowances for.

bearable *adjective*
tolerable, endurable, sufferable, supportable, sustainable, acceptable, manageable.
Eঘ unbearable, intolerable.

bearer *noun*
carrier, conveyor, porter, courier, messenger, runner, holder, possessor.

bearing *noun*
1 have no bearing on the matter: relevance, significance, connection, relation, reference.
2 of military bearing: demeanour, manner, mien (*fml*), air, aspect, attitude, behaviour, comportment (*fml*), poise, deportment, carriage, posture.

bearings *noun*
orientation, position, situation, location, whereabouts, course, track, way, direction, aim.

beast *noun*
animal, creature, brute, monster, savage, barbarian, pig, swine, devil, fiend.

beat *noun*
1 feel the rapid beat of its heart :
pulsation, pulse, stroke, throb, thump,
palpitation, flutter.
2 two beats to the bar : rhythm, time,
tempo, metre, measure, rhyme, stress,
accent.
3 a policeman on his beat : round,
rounds, territory, circuit, course,
journey, way, path, route.
▶ *verb*
1 beat the child/beaten by his father :
whip, flog, lash, tan (*infml*), cane, strap,
thrash, lay into, hit, punch, strike,
swipe, knock, bang, wham, bash,
pound, hammer (*infml*), batter, buffet,
pelt, bruise.
2 beating faintly : pulsate, pulse, throb,
thump, race, palpitate, flutter, vibrate,
quiver, tremble, shake, quake.
3 beat the enemy/all comers : defeat,
trounce, hammer (*infml*), slaughter
(*infml*), conquer, overcome,
overwhelm, vanquish (*fml*), subdue,
surpass, excel, outdo, outstrip, outrun.
◆ **beat up** (*infml*) attack, assault,
knock about, knock around, batter, do
over (*infml*).

beautiful *adjective*
attractive, fair, pretty, lovely, good-
looking, handsome, gorgeous, radiant,
ravishing, stunning (*infml*), pleasing,
appealing, alluring, charming,
delightful, fine, exquisite.
F3 ugly, plain, hideous.

beautify *verb*
embellish, enhance, improve, grace,
gild, garnish, decorate, ornament,
deck, bedeck, adorn, array, glamorize.
F3 disfigure, spoil.

beauty *noun*
attractiveness, fairness, prettiness,
loveliness, (good) looks, glamour,
handsomeness, appeal, allure, charm,
grace, elegance, symmetry, excellence.
F3 ugliness, repulsiveness.

because *conjunction*
as, for, since, owing to, in that, on
account of, by reason of, thanks to.

beckon *verb*
summon, motion, gesture, signal, nod,
wave, gesticulate, call, invite, attract,

pull, draw, lure, allure, entice, tempt,
coax.

become *verb*
1 become a handsome young man :
turn, grow, get, change into, develop
into.
2 green becomes you : suit, befit,
flatter, enhance, grace, embellish,
ornament, set off, harmonize.

bed *noun*
1 sleeping on a bed : divan, couch,
bunk, berth, cot, mattress, pallet, sack
(*infml*).
2 riverbed/seabed : watercourse,
channel, bottom.
3 on a bed of gravel : layer, stratum,
substratum, matrix, base, bottom,
foundation, groundwork.
4 bed of flowers : garden, border,
patch, plot.

bedraggled *adjective*
untidy, unkempt, dishevelled,
disordered, scruffy, slovenly, messy,
dirty, muddy, muddied, soiled, wet,
sodden, drenched.
F3 neat, tidy, clean.

before *adverb*
ahead, in front, in advance, sooner,
earlier, formerly, previously.
F3 after, later.

beforehand *adverb*
in advance, preliminarily, already,
before, previously, earlier, sooner.

beg *verb*
request, require, desire, crave, beseech,
plead, entreat, implore, pray,
supplicate, petition, solicit, cadge,
scrounge, sponge.

begin *verb*
1 begin a new life/business/term :
start, commence, set about, embark on,
set in motion, activate, originate,
initiate, introduce, found, institute,
instigate.
2 began in the 18th century : arise,
emerge, appear.
F3 **1** end, finish, cease.

beginner *noun*
novice, tiro, starter, learner, trainee,
apprentice, student, freshman, fresher,
recruit, cub, tenderfoot (*US*), fledgling.
F3 veteran, old hand, expert.

beginning *noun*
1 the beginning of the story/race/process: start, commencement, onset, outset, opening, preface, prelude, introduction, initiation, establishment, inauguration, inception, starting point.
2 the beginning of time/life/democracy: birth, dawn, origin, source, fountainhead, root, seed, emergence, rise.
F₃1 end, finish.

behalf *noun*
sake, account, good, interest, benefit, advantage, profit, name, authority, side, support.

behave *verb*
act, react, respond, work, function, run, operate, perform, conduct oneself, acquit oneself, comport oneself (*fml*).

behaviour *noun*
conduct, manner, manners, actions, doings, dealings, ways, habits, action, reaction, response, functioning, operation, performance, comportment (*fml*).

behead *verb*
decapitate, execute, guillotine.

behind *adverb*
after, following, next, subsequently, behindhand, late, overdue, in arrears, in debt.
▶ *preposition*
1 who's behind all this?: causing, responsible for, instigating, initiating.
2 behind you all the way: supporting, backing, for.

beige *adjective*
buff, fawn, mushroom, camel, sandy, khaki, coffee, ecru, neutral.

being *noun*
1 put her whole being into the performance: existence, actuality, reality, life, animation, essence, substance, nature, soul, spirit.
2 a living being/a being from another planet: creature, animal, beast, human being, mortal, person, individual, thing, entity.

belief *noun*
1 demonstrate their belief in the project: conviction, persuasion, credit, trust, reliance, confidence, assurance, certainty, sureness.
2 it's my belief that it will end soon: presumption, expectation, feeling, intuition, impression, notion, theory, view, opinion, judgement.
3 religious beliefs: ideology, faith, creed, doctrine, dogma, tenet, principle.
F₃1 disbelief.

believable *adjective*
credible, imaginable, conceivable, acceptable, plausible, possible, likely, probable, authoritative, reliable, trustworthy.
F₃ unbelievable, incredible, unconvincing.

believe *verb*
1 can't believe anything they say: accept, wear (*infml*), swallow (*infml*), credit, trust, count on, depend on, rely on.
2 believed that it cured baldness: swear by, hold (*fml*), maintain.
3 he believes that it may work: assume, postulate, presume, gather, speculate, conjecture, guess, imagine, think, consider, reckon, suppose, deem, judge.
F₃1 disbelieve, doubt.

believer *noun*
convert, proselyte, disciple, follower, adherent, devotee, zealot, supporter, upholder.
F₃ unbeliever, sceptic.

belittle *verb*
demean, minimize, play down, trivialize, dismiss, underrate, undervalue, underestimate, lessen, diminish, detract from, deprecate (*fml*), decry, disparage (*fml*), run down, deride, scorn, ridicule.
F₃ exaggerate, praise.

belong *verb*
fit, go with, be part of, attach to, link up with, tie up with, be connected with, relate to.

belongings *noun*
possessions, property, chattels (*fml*), goods, effects, things, stuff (*infml*), gear (*infml*), paraphernalia.

below *adverb*
beneath, under, underneath, down, lower, lower down.
≠above.
▶ *preposition*
1 the valley below: under, underneath, beneath.
2 below him in rank: inferior to, lesser than, subordinate to, subject to.
≠above.

belt *noun*
1 a leather belt: sash, girdle, waistband, girth, strap.
2 a belt of rain/cultivated land: strip, band, swathe, stretch, tract, area, region, district, zone, layer.

bench *noun*
1 a wooden bench: seat, form, settle, pew, ledge, counter, table, stall, workbench, worktable.
2 come before the bench: court, courtroom, tribunal, judiciary, judicature, judge, magistrate.

bend *verb*
curve, turn, deflect, swerve, veer, diverge, twist, contort, flex, shape, mould, buckle, bow, incline, lean, stoop, crouch.
≠straighten.
▶ *noun*
curvature, curve, arc, bow, loop, hook, crook, elbow, angle, corner, turn, twist, zigzag.

beneath *adverb*
below, under, underneath, lower, lower down.
▶ *preposition*
1 waves crashing on the rocks beneath: under, underneath, below, lower than.
2 beneath contempt: unworthy of, unbefitting.

beneficial *adjective*
advantageous, favourable, useful, helpful, profitable, rewarding, valuable, improving, edifying, wholesome.
≠harmful, detrimental, useless.

benefit *noun*
advantage, good, welfare, interest, favour, help, aid, assistance, service, use, avail, gain, profit, asset,

blessing, plus (*infml*).
≠disadvantage, harm, damage.
▶ *verb*
help, aid, assist, serve, avail, advantage, profit, improve, enhance, better, further, advance, promote.
≠hinder, harm, undermine.

benevolent *adjective*
philanthropic, humanitarian, charitable, generous, liberal, munificent, altruistic, benign, humane, kind, kindly, well-disposed, compassionate, caring, considerate.
≠mean, selfish, malevolent.

benign *adjective*
1 a benign expression on his face: benevolent, good, gracious, gentle, kind, obliging, friendly, amiable, genial, sympathetic.
2 a benign tumour: curable, harmless.
3 the climate was benign: favourable, propitious, beneficial, temperate, mild, warm, refreshing, restorative, wholesome.
≠1 hostile. **2** malignant. **3** harmful, unpleasant.

bent *noun*
tendency, inclination, leaning, preference, ability, capacity, faculty, aptitude, facility, gift, talent, knack, flair, forte.
▶ *adjective*
1 bent wire/wheel/back: angled, curved, bowed, arched, folded, doubled, twisted, hunched, stooped.
2 (*infml*) a bent lawyer: dishonest, crooked (*infml*), illegal, criminal, corrupt, untrustworthy.
≠1 straight, upright. **2** honest, straight.
◆ **bent on** determined, resolved, set, fixed, inclined, disposed.

bequeath *verb*
will, leave, bestow, gift, endow, grant, settle, hand down, pass on, impart, transmit, assign, entrust, commit.

berserk *adjective*
mad, crazy, demented, insane, amok, maniacal, deranged, frantic, frenzied, wild, raging, furious, violent, rabid, raving.
≠sane, calm.

beside *preposition*
alongside, abreast of, next to, adjacent,

abutting, bordering, neighbouring, next door to, close to, near, overlooking.

besides *preposition*
apart from, other than, in addition to, over and above.
▸ *adverb*
also, as well, too, in addition, further, additionally, furthermore, moreover.

besiege *verb*
1 besieging the city : lay siege to, blockade, surround, encircle, confine.
2 besieged by biting flies : trouble, bother, importune, assail, beset, beleaguer, harass, pester, badger, nag, hound, plague.

besotted *adjective*
infatuated, doting, obsessed, smitten, bewitched, hypnotized, spellbound, intoxicated.
E3 indifferent, disenchanted.

best *adjective*
optimum, optimal, first, foremost, leading, unequalled, unsurpassed, matchless, incomparable, supreme, crème de la crème, greatest, highest, largest, finest, excellent, outstanding, superlative, first-rate, first-class, perfect.
E3 worst.
▸ *adverb*
greatly, extremely, exceptionally, excellently, superlatively.
E3 worst.
▸ *noun*
finest, cream, prime, élite, top, first, pick, choice, favourite.
E3 worst.

bestow *verb*
award, present, grant, confer, endow, bequeath, commit, entrust, impart, transmit, allot, apportion, accord, give, donate, lavish.
E3 withhold, deprive.

bet *noun*
wager, flutter (*infml*), gamble, speculation, risk, venture, stake, ante, bid, pledge.
▸ *verb*
wager, gamble, punt, speculate, risk,

hazard, chance, venture, lay, stake, bid, pledge.

betray *verb*
1 betray a friend : inform on, dupe, shop (*slang*), sell (out), double-cross, desert, abandon, grass (*slang*), forsake.
2 betray one's emotions : disclose, give away, tell, divulge, expose, reveal, show, manifest.
E3 1 defend, protect. 2 conceal, hide.

betrayal *noun*
treachery, treason, sell-out, disloyalty, unfaithfulness, double-dealing, duplicity, deception, trickery, falseness.
E3 loyalty, protection.

better *adjective*
1 a better deal/example : superior, bigger, larger, longer, greater, worthier, finer, surpassing, preferable.
2 getting better : improving, progressing, on the mend (*infml*), recovering, fitter, healthier, stronger, recovered, restored.
E3 1 inferior. 2 worse.

between *preposition*
mid, amid, amidst, among, amongst.

beware *verb*
watch out, look out, mind, take heed, steer clear of, avoid, shun, guard against.

bewildered *adjective*
confused, muddled, uncertain, disoriented, nonplussed, bamboozled (*infml*), baffled, puzzled, perplexed, flummoxed (*infml*), mystified, bemused, surprised, stunned.
E3 unperturbed, collected.

beyond *preposition*
past, further than, apart from, away from, remote from, out of range of, out of reach of, above, over, superior to.

biased *adjective*
slanted, angled, distorted, warped, twisted, loaded, weighted, influenced, swayed, partial, predisposed, prejudiced, one-sided, unfair, bigoted, blinkered, jaundiced.
E3 impartial, fair.

bicker *verb*
squabble, row, quarrel, wrangle, argue,

scrap, spar, fight, clash, disagree, dispute.
F3 agree.

bid *verb*
1 he bid more than the painting was worth : offer, proffer, tender, submit, propose.
2 (*fml*) bid me go/enter : ask, request, desire, instruct, direct, command, enjoin, require, charge, call, summon, invite, solicit.
▸ *noun*
1 a higher bid : offer, tender, sum, amount, price, advance, submission, proposal.
2 his latest bid to climb the mountain : attempt, effort, try, go (*infml*), endeavour, venture.

big *adjective*
1 big ears/big muscles/a big house : large, great, sizable, considerable, substantial, huge, enormous, immense, massive, colossal, gigantic, mammoth, burly, bulky, extensive, spacious, vast.
2 a big occasion/a big step : important, significant, momentous, serious, main, principal, eminent, prominent, influential.
3 that's big of you : generous, magnanimous, gracious, unselfish.
F3 1 small, little. 2 insignificant, unknown.
⇨ *See also* **Word Workshop** *panel.*

bigoted *adjective*
prejudiced, biased, intolerant, illiberal, narrow-minded, narrow, blinkered, closed, dogmatic, opinionated, obstinate.
F3 tolerant, liberal, broad-minded, enlightened.

bigotry *noun*
prejudice, discrimination, bias, injustice, unfairness, intolerance, narrow-mindedness, chauvinism, jingoism, sectarianism, racism, racialism, sexism, dogmatism, fanaticism.
F3 tolerance.

bill *noun*
1 pay the telephone bill : invoice, statement, account, charges, reckoning, tally, score.

2 a parliamentary bill : proposal, measure, legislation.
▸ *verb*
invoice, charge, debit.

bind *verb*
1 bind the two pieces together with tape/bind their wounds : attach, fasten, secure, clamp, tie, lash, truss, strap, bandage, cover, wrap.
2 bound the members of the group together : unite, unify, weld, fuse.
3 bound by a solemn oath : oblige, force, compel, constrain, necessitate, restrict, require, confine, restrain.

binding *adjective*
obligatory, compulsory, mandatory, necessary, requisite, permanent, conclusive, irrevocable, unalterable, indissoluble, unbreakable, strict.

biography *noun*
life story, life, history, autobiography, memoirs, recollections, curriculum vitae, account, record.

biology

Terms used in biology include:
amino acid, anatomy, bacillus, bacteria, bacteriology, biochemistry, bionics, botanist, botany, cell, chromosome, class, corpuscle, cybernetics, cytology, cytoplasm, Darwinism, deoxyribonucleic acid (DNA), diffusion, ecology, ecosystem, ectoplasm, embryo, embryology, endocrinology, endoplasmic reticulum (ER), enzyme, evolution, excretion, extinction, flora and fauna, food chain, fossil, gene, genetic engineering, genetic fingerprinting, genetics, germ, homeostasis, meiosis, membrane, metabolism, microbe, micro-organism, mitosis, molecule, mutation, natural selection, nuclear membrane, nucleus, nutrition, organism, osmosis, palaeontology, pathology, photosynthesis, physiology, pollution, protein, protoplasm, reproduction, respiration, reticulum, ribonucleic acid (RNA), ribosome, secretion, symbiosis, taxonomy, virus, zoology.

bird

Birds include:

blackbird, bluetit, bullfinch, chaffinch, crow, cuckoo, dove, dunnock, goldfinch, greenfinch, jackdaw, jay, linnet, magpie, martin, nightingale, pigeon, raven, robin, rook, shrike, skylark, sparrow, starling, swallow, swift, thrush, tit, twite, wagtail, warbler, woodpecker, wren, yellowhammer; albatross, auk, avocet, bittern, coot, cormorant, crane, curlew, dipper, duck, eider, flamingo, gannet, goose, guillemot, heron, kingfisher, lapwing, mallard, moorhen, peewit, petrel, pelican, plover, puffin, seagull, snipe, stork, swan, teal, tern; buzzard, condor, eagle, falcon, hawk, kestrel, kite, osprey, owl, sparrowhawk, vulture; emu, kiwi, ostrich, peacock, penguin; chicken, grouse, partridge, pheasant, quail, turkey; bird of paradise, budgerigar, budgie (*infml*), canary, cockatiel, cockatoo, kookaburra, lovebird, macaw, mockingbird, myna bird, parakeet, parrot, toucan.

birth *noun*
1 the birth of their son/a difficult birth: childbirth, parturition (*fml*), confinement, delivery, nativity.
2 of noble birth: ancestry, family, parentage, descent, line, lineage, genealogy, pedigree, blood, stock, race, extraction, background, breeding.
3 the birth of the nation: beginning, rise, emergence, origin, source, derivation.

birthplace *noun*
place of origin, native town, native country, homeland, fatherland, mother country, roots, provenance, source, fount.

bisect *verb*
halve, divide, separate, split, intersect, cross, fork, bifurcate.

bit *noun*
fragment, part, segment, piece, slice, crumb, morsel, scrap, atom, mite, whit, jot, iota, grain, speck.

◆ **bit by bit** gradually, little by little, step by step, piecemeal.
F∃ wholesale.

bite *verb*
1 bite the apple/one's lip: chew, masticate (*fml*), munch, gnaw, nibble, champ, crunch, crush.
2 the dog bit her hand: nip, pierce, wound, tear, rend.
3 cold wind biting their cheeks: smart, sting, tingle.
4 when the measures start to bite: take effect, grip, hold, seize, pinch.
▶ *noun*
1 a dog bite/the bite of the whip: nip, wound, sting, smarting, pinch.
2 a bite to eat: snack, refreshment, mouthful, morsel, taste.
3 sauce with a bit of bite: pungency, piquancy, kick (*infml*), punch.

biting *adjective*
1 biting wind: cold, freezing, bitter, harsh, severe.
2 biting criticism: cutting, incisive, piercing, penetrating, raw, stinging, sharp, tart, caustic, scathing, cynical, hurtful.
F∃ 1 mild. **2** bland.

bitter *adjective*
1 bitter taste/fruit: sour, tart, sharp, acid, vinegary, unsweetened.
2 became old and bitter: resentful, embittered, jaundiced, cynical, rancorous, acrimonious, acerbic, hostile.
3 a bitter wind/dispute: intense, severe, harsh, fierce, cruel, savage, merciless, painful, stinging, biting, freezing, raw.
F∃ 1 sweet. **2** contented. **3** mild.

bizarre *adjective*
strange, odd, queer, curious, weird, peculiar, eccentric, way-out (*infml*), outlandish, ludicrous, ridiculous, fantastic, extravagant, grotesque, freakish, abnormal, deviant, unusual, extraordinary.
F∃ normal, ordinary.

black *adjective*
1 black hair: jet-black, coal-black, jet, ebony, sable, inky, sooty.
2 the sky became black: dark, unlit,

moonless, starless, overcast, dingy, gloomy, sombre, funereal.
3 black with soot: filthy, dirty, soiled, grimy, grubby.
E3 2 bright. **3** clean.

blacken *verb*
1 faces blackened by coal-dust: darken, dirty, soil, smudge, cloud.
2 blackening someone's character: defame (*fml*), malign, slander, libel, vilify (*fml*), revile, denigrate, detract, smear, sully (*fml*), stain, tarnish, taint, defile (*fml*), discredit, dishonour.
E3 2 praise, enhance.

blackmail *noun*
extortion, chantage, hush money (*infml*), intimidation, protection, pay-off, ransom.
▸ *verb*
extort, bleed, milk, squeeze, hold to ransom, threaten, lean on (*infml*), force, compel, coerce, demand.

black out *verb*
1 black out for a few seconds: faint, pass out, collapse, flake out (*infml*).
2 blacking out the sun/the radio: darken, eclipse, cover up, conceal, suppress, withhold, censor, gag.

blackout *noun*
1 a news blackout: suppression, censorship, cover-up (*infml*), concealment, secrecy.
2 suffer from headaches and blackouts: faint, coma, unconsciousness, oblivion.
3 used candles and torches during the blackout: power failure, power cut.

blade *noun*
edge, knife, dagger, sword, scalpel, razor, vane.

blame *noun*
censure, criticism, stick (*infml*), reprimand, reproof, reproach, recrimination, condemnation, accusation, charge, rap (*infml*), incrimination, guilt, culpability, fault, responsibility, accountability, liability, onus.
▸ *verb*
accuse, charge, tax, reprimand, chide, reprove, upbraid (*fml*), reprehend (*fml*), admonish, rebuke, reproach, censure, criticize, find fault with,

disapprove, condemn.
E3 exonerate, vindicate.

blameless *adjective*
innocent, guiltless, clear, faultless, perfect, unblemished, stainless, virtuous, sinless, upright, above reproach, irreproachable, unblamable, unimpeachable.
E3 guilty, blameworthy.

bland *adverb*
1 a bland design/appearance: boring, monotonous, humdrum, tedious, dull, uninspiring, uninteresting, unexciting, nondescript.
2 a bland tasting mixture/a bland smile: characterless, flat, insipid, tasteless, weak, mild, smooth, soft, gentle, non-irritant.
E3 1 lively, stimulating.

blank *adjective*
1 a blank page: empty, unfilled, void, clear, bare, unmarked, plain, clean, white.
2 a blank stare: expressionless, deadpan, poker-faced, impassive, apathetic, glazed, vacant, uncomprehending.
▸ *noun*
space, gap, break, void, emptiness, vacancy, vacuity, nothingness, vacuum.

blanket *noun*
covering, coating, coat, layer, film, carpet, rug, cloak, mantle, cover, sheet, envelope, wrapper, wrapping.
▸ *verb*
cover, coat, eclipse, hide, conceal, mask, cloak, surround, muffle, deaden, obscure, cloud.

blare *verb*
trumpet, clamour, roar, blast, boom, resound, ring, peal, clang, hoot, toot, honk.

blasé *adjective*
nonchalant, offhand, unimpressed, unmoved, unexcited, jaded, weary, bored, uninterested, uninspired, apathetic, indifferent, cool, unconcerned.
E3 excited, enthusiastic.

blasphemous *adjective*
profane, impious, sacrilegious, godless, ungodly, irreligious, irreverent.

WORD *workshop*   big

Try not to use the word **big** too often in your writing. Some possible synonyms are listed below under broad categories of meaning.

big in size, amount etc.

colossal	great	massive
considerable	huge	sizeable
enormous	humungous *(infml)*	spacious
extensive	immense	vast
gigantic	mammoth	

a big person or creature

bulky	hefty	stocky
burly	large	tall
giant	muscular	well-built

someone or something important

eminent	main	serious
famous	momentous	significant
important	principal	well-known
influential	prominent	

kind, considerate, etc. behaviour or acts

generous	gracious	magnanimous unselfish

blasphemy *noun*
profanity, curse, expletive, cursing, swearing, execration (*fml*), impiety, irreverence, sacrilege, desecration, violation, outrage.

blast *noun*
1 destroyed in the blast: explosion, detonation, bang, crash, clap, crack, volley, burst, outburst, discharge.
2 a blast of cold air: draught, gust, gale, squall, storm, tempest.
3 the blast of trumpets: sound, blow, blare, roar, boom, peal, hoot, wail, scream, shriek.
▶ *verb*
1 blasting the rocks in the quarry:

big   WORD *workshop*

In the following article, there are suggestions for how synonyms might be used to avoid repeating **big**.

The Daily News

momentous
Yesterday was a ~~big~~ day for
Enormous
the town of Hillgrove. ~~Big~~

crowds turned out for the

return of the local boy Darren
famous
Songster who is ~~big~~ in pop
burly
music. The ~~big~~ man, who
sprawling
grew up in the ~~big~~ suburb of

Sunnymeadow was delighted

massive
by the ~~big~~ reception. 'It is
generous
very ~~big~~ of people to come

out to welcome me,' he

announced. 'I have
huge
travelled to many ~~big~~ cities
important
and attended ~~big~~ events but
huge
it is always a ~~big~~ pleasure

to come home.'

Try writing a newspaper article about some important event. Use as many different words as you can instead of **big**.

---

explode, blow up, burst, shatter, destroy, demolish, ruin, assail, attack.
2 music blasting from the loudspeakers: sound, blare, roar, boom, peal, hoot, wail, scream, shriek.

blatant *adjective*
flagrant, brazen, barefaced, arrant, open, overt, undisguised, ostentatious, glaring, conspicuous, obtrusive, prominent, pronounced, obvious, sheer, outright, unmitigated.

blaze *noun*
fire, flames, conflagration, bonfire, flare-up, explosion, blast, burst, outburst, radiance, brilliance, glare,

flash, gleam, glitter, glow, light, flame.
▶ *verb*
burn, flame, flare (up), erupt, explode, burst, fire, flash, gleam, glare, beam, shine, glow.

bleach *verb*
whiten, decolorize, fade, pale, lighten.

bleak *adjective*
1 a bleak prospect: gloomy, sombre, leaden, grim, dreary, dismal, wintry, depressing, joyless, cheerless, comfortless, hopeless, discouraging, disheartening.
2 a bleak hillside/landscape: cold,

chilly, raw, weather-beaten,
unsheltered, windy, windswept,
exposed, open, barren, bare, empty,
desolate, gaunt.
F3 1 bright, cheerful.

bleed *verb*
1 bleed heavily/bleeding from a gash:
haemorrhage, gush, spurt, flow, run,
exude, weep, ooze, seep, trickle.
2 bleeding him dry: drain, suck dry,
exhaust, squeeze, milk, sap, reduce,
deplete.

blemish *noun*
1 a facial blemish: flaw, imperfection,
defect, fault, deformity, disfigurement,
birthmark, naevus, spot, mark, speck,
smudge, blotch.
2 a long service record without
blemish: blot, stain, taint, disgrace,
dishonour.
▶ *verb*
flaw, deface, disfigure, spoil, mar,
damage, impair, spot, mark, blot,
blotch, stain, sully (*fml*), taint, tarnish.

blend *verb*
1 blend the ingredients: merge,
amalgamate, coalesce, compound,
synthesize, fuse, unite, combine, mix,
mingle.
2 flavours/colours that blend well:
harmonize, complement, fit, match.
F3 1 separate.

bless *verb*
1 bless the wine/the little children:
anoint, sanctify, consecrate, hallow,
dedicate, ordain.
2 bless his name: praise, extol (*fml*),
magnify, glorify, exalt, thank.
3 blessed the undertaking/blessed
with children: approve, countenance,
favour, grace, bestow, endow, provide.
F3 1 curse. **2** condemn.

blessed *adjective*
1 Christ's blessed name: holy, sacred,
hallowed, sanctified, revered, adored,
divine.
2 a blessed relief: happy, contented,
glad, joyful, joyous.
3 live a blessed existence: lucky,
fortunate, prosperous, favoured,
endowed.
F3 1 cursed.

blessing *noun*
1 the blessing of the bread:
consecration, dedication, benediction,
grace, thanksgiving, invocation.
2 a real blessing in disguise: benefit,
advantage, favour, godsend, windfall,
gift, gain, profit, help, service.
3 give a proposal one's blessing:
approval, concurrence, backing,
support, authority, sanction, consent,
permission, leave.
F3 2 curse, blight. **3** condemnation.

blight *verb*
spoil, mar, injure, undermine, ruin,
wreck, crush, shatter, destroy,
annihilate, blast, wither, shrivel,
frustrate, disappoint.
F3 bless.

blind *adjective*
1 a blind person: sightless, unsighted,
unseeing, eyeless, purblind, partially
sighted.
2 blind faith/panic: impetuous,
impulsive, hasty, rash, reckless, wild,
mad, indiscriminate, careless,
heedless, mindless, unthinking,
unreasoning, irrational.
3 blind to their distress: ignorant,
oblivious, unaware, unconscious,
unobservant, inattentive, neglectful,
indifferent, insensitive, thoughtless,
inconsiderate.
4 a blind alley: closed, obstructed,
hidden, concealed, obscured.
F3 1 sighted. **2** careful, cautious. **3**
aware, sensitive.

bliss *noun*
blissfulness, ecstasy, euphoria, rapture,
joy, happiness, gladness, blessedness,
paradise, heaven.
F3 misery, hell, damnation.

blissful *adjective*
ecstatic, euphoric, elated, enraptured,
rapturous, delighted, enchanted,
joyful, joyous, happy.
F3 miserable, wretched.

blister *noun*
sore, swelling, cyst, boil, abscess, ulcer,
pustule, pimple, carbuncle.

bloated *adjective*
swollen, puffy, blown up, inflated,
distended, dilated, expanded,

enlarged, turgid, bombastic.
F3 thin, shrunken, shrivelled.

blob *noun*
drop, droplet, globule, glob (*infml*),
bead, pearl, bubble, dab, spot, lump,
mass, ball, pellet, pill.

block *noun*
1 a block of stone: piece, lump, ingot,
mass, chunk, hunk, square, cube,
brick, bar.
2 a mental block/writer's block:
obstacle, barrier, bar, jam, blockage,
stoppage, resistance, obstruction,
impediment, hindrance, let, delay.
▸ *verb*
choke, clog, plug, stop up, dam up,
close, bar, obstruct, impede, hinder,
stonewall, stop, check, arrest, halt,
thwart, scotch, deter, veto.

blockage *noun*
blocking, obstruction, stoppage,
occlusion, block, clot, jam, log-jam,
congestion, hindrance, impediment.

blood *noun*
extraction, birth, descent, lineage,
family, kindred, relations, ancestry,
descendants, kinship, relationship.

bloodcurdling *adjective*
horrifying, chilling, spine-chilling,
hair-raising, terrifying, frightening,
scary, dreadful, fearful, horrible,
horrid, horrendous.

bloodshed *noun*
killing, murder, slaughter, massacre,
blood-bath, butchery, carnage, gore,
bloodletting.

bloodthirsty *adjective*
murderous, homicidal, warlike, savage,
barbaric, barbarous, brutal, ferocious,
vicious, cruel, inhuman, ruthless.

bloom *noun*
1 heavy with blooms: blossom, flower,
bud.
2 in the bloom of youth: prime,
heyday, perfection, blush, flush, glow,
rosiness, beauty, radiance, lustre,
health, vigour, freshness.
▸ *verb*
bud, sprout, grow, wax, develop,
mature, blossom, flower, blow, open.
F3 fade, wither.

blossom *noun*
bloom, flower, bud.
▸ *verb*
develop, mature, bloom, flower, blow,
flourish, thrive, prosper, succeed.
F3 fade, wither.

blot *noun*
spot, stain, smudge, blotch, smear,
mark, speck, blemish, flaw, fault,
defect, taint, disgrace.
▸ *verb*
spot, mark, stain, smudge, blur, sully
(*fml*), taint, tarnish, spoil, mar,
disfigure, disgrace.
◆ **blot out** obliterate, cancel, delete,
erase, expunge (*fml*), darken, obscure,
shadow, eclipse.

blotch *noun*
patch, splodge, splotch, splash,
smudge, blot, spot, mark, stain,
blemish.

blotchy *adjective*
spotty, spotted, patchy, uneven, smeary,
blemished, reddened, inflamed.

blow[1] *verb*
1 blow on the hot soup/wind blowing
the dry leaves around: breathe, exhale,
pant, puff, waft, fan, flutter, float, flow,
stream, rush, whirl, whisk, sweep,
fling, buffet, drive, blast.
2 blow a horn: play, sound, pipe,
trumpet, toot, blare.
◆ **blow over** die down, subside, end,
finish, cease, pass, vanish, disappear,
dissipate, fizzle out, peter out.
◆ **blow up 1** blew up the dam/the oven
blew up: explode, go off, detonate,
burst, blast, bomb.
2 blew up when he heard the news:
lose one's temper, blow one's top
(*infml*), erupt, hit the roof (*infml*), rage,
go mad (*infml*), go ballistic (*infml*).
3 blow up a balloon/the image: inflate,
pump up, swell, fill (out), puff up,
bloat, distend, dilate, expand, enlarge,
magnify, exaggerate, overstate.

blow[2] *noun*
1 blow to the head: concussion, box,
cuff, clip, clout, swipe, biff (*infml*),
bash, slap, smack, whack (*infml*),
wallop (*infml*), belt (*infml*), buffet, bang,
clap, knock, rap, stroke, thump, punch.

2 a blow to hopes of lasting peace: misfortune, affliction, reverse, setback, comedown, disappointment, upset, jolt, shock, bombshell, calamity, catastrophe, disaster.

blue *adjective*

1 blue sky/shades of blue: azure, sapphire, cobalt, ultramarine, navy, indigo, aquamarine, turquoise, Cyan.
2 feeling blue: depressed, low, down in the dumps (*infml*), dejected, downcast, dispirited, down-hearted, despondent, gloomy, glum, dismal, sad, unhappy, miserable, melancholy, morose, fed up (*infml*).
E3 2 cheerful, happy.

blueprint *noun*

archetype, prototype, model, pattern, design, outline, draft, sketch, pilot, guide, plan, scheme, project.

bluff *verb*

lie, pretend, feign, sham, fake, deceive, delude, mislead, hoodwink, blind, bamboozle (*infml*), fool.
▶ *noun*
lie, idle boast, bravado, humbug, pretence, show, sham, fake, fraud, trick, subterfuge, deceit, deception.

blunder *noun*

mistake, error, solecism (*fml*), howler (*infml*), bloomer (*infml*), clanger (*infml*), inaccuracy, slip, boob (*infml*), indiscretion, gaffe, faux pas, slip-up (*infml*), oversight, fault.
▶ *verb*
stumble, flounder, bumble, err, slip up (*infml*), miscalculate, misjudge, bungle, botch, fluff (*infml*), mismanage.

blunt *adjective*

1 a blunt knife/pencil: unsharpened, dull, worn, pointless, rounded, stubbed.
2 a blunt approach: frank, candid, direct, forthright, unceremonious, explicit, plain-spoken, honest, downright, outspoken, tactless, insensitive, rude, impolite, uncivil, brusque, curt, abrupt.
E3 1 sharp, pointed. **2** subtle, tactful.
▶ *verb*
dull, take the edge off, dampen, soften, deaden, numb, anaesthetize, alleviate,

allay, abate, weaken.
E3 sharpen, intensify.

blur *noun*

smear, smudge, blotch, haze, mist, fog, cloudiness, fuzziness, indistinctness, muddle, confusion, dimness, obscurity.

blurred *adjective*

out of focus, fuzzy, unclear, indistinct, vague, ill-defined, faint, hazy, misty, foggy, cloudy, bleary, dim, obscure, confused.
E3 clear, distinct.

blurt out *verb*

exclaim, cry, gush, spout, utter, tell, reveal, disclose, divulge, blab (*infml*), let out, leak, let slip, spill the beans (*infml*).
E3 bottle up, hush up.

blush *verb*

flush, redden, colour, glow.

blushing *adjective*

flushed, red, rosy, glowing, confused, embarrassed, ashamed, modest.
E3 pale, white, composed.

bluster *noun*

boasting, crowing, bravado, bluff, swagger.

blustery *adjective*

windy, gusty, squally, stormy, tempestuous, violent, wild, boisterous.
E3 calm.

board *noun*

1 a wooden board: sheet, panel, slab, plank, beam, timber, slat.
2 the board of directors: committee, council, panel, jury, commission, directorate, directors, trustees, advisers.
3 bed and board: meals, food, provisions, rations.
▶ *verb*
get on, embark, mount, enter, catch.

boast *verb*

brag, crow, claim, exaggerate, talk big (*infml*), bluster, trumpet, vaunt, strut, swagger, show off, exhibit.
E3 belittle, deprecate (*fml*).

boastful *adjective*

proud, conceited, vain, swollen-headed, big-headed (*infml*), puffed up, bragging, crowing, swanky (*infml*),

cocky, swaggering.
F3 modest, self-effacing, humble.

bob *verb*
bounce, hop, skip, spring, jump, leap,
twitch, jerk, jolt, shake, quiver, wobble,
oscillate, nod, bow, curtsy.
◆ **bob up** appear, emerge, arrive, show
up (*infml*), materialize, rise, surface,
pop up, spring up, crop up, arise.

bodily *adjective*
physical, corporeal, carnal, fleshly,
real, actual, tangible, substantial,
concrete, material.
F3 spiritual.
▸ *adverb*
altogether, en masse, collectively, as a
whole, completely, fully, wholly,
entirely, totally, in toto.

body *noun*
1 the human body/scars on his head
and body: anatomy, physique, build,
figure, trunk, torso.
2 a dead body: corpse, cadaver,
carcase, stiff (*slang*).
3 a large body of men: company,
association, society, corporation,
confederation, bloc, cartel, syndicate,
congress, collection, group, band,
crowd, throng, multitude, mob,
mass.
4 shampoo infusing hair with body
and shine: consistency, density, solidity,
firmness, bulk, mass, substance,
essence, fullness, richness.

bog *noun*
marsh, swamp, fen, mire, quagmire,
quag, slough, morass, quicksands,
marshland, swampland, wetlands.
◆ **bog down** encumber, hinder,
impede, overwhelm, deluge, sink,
stick, slow down, slow up, delay, retard,
halt, stall.

bogus *adjective*
false, fake, counterfeit, forged, dummy,
fraudulent, phoney (*infml*), spurious,
sham, pseudo, artificial, imitation.
F3 genuine, true, real, valid.

bohemian *adjective*
artistic, arty (*infml*), unconventional,
unorthodox, nonconformist, offbeat,
alternative, eccentric, way-out
(*infml*), bizarre, exotic.

F3 bourgeois, conventional, orthodox.

boil[1] *verb*
1 boil water/potatoes: simmer, stew,
brew, gurgle, bubble, steam.
2 boil with rage: erupt, explode, fizz,
rage, seethe, rave, storm, effervesce,
froth, foam, fulminate (*fml*), fume.
◆ **boil down** reduce, concentrate,
distil, condense, digest, abstract,
summarize, abridge.

boil[2] *noun*
a boil on the skin: pustule, abscess,
gumboil, ulcer, tumour, pimple,
carbuncle, blister, inflammation.

boiling *adjective*
1 a boiling cauldron: turbulent,
gurgling, bubbling, steaming.
2 it's boiling outside: hot, baking,
roasting, scorching, blistering.
3 boiling with rage: angry, indignant,
incensed, infuriated, enraged, furious,
fuming, flaming.

boisterous *adjective*
exuberant, rumbustious (*infml*),
rollicking, bouncy, turbulent,
tumultuous, loud, noisy, clamorous,
rowdy, rough, disorderly, riotous,
wild, unrestrained, unruly,
obstreperous.
F3 quiet, calm, restrained.

bold *adjective*
1 a bold fighter: fearless, dauntless,
daring, audacious, brave, courageous,
valiant, heroic, gallant, intrepid,
adventurous, venturesome,
enterprising, plucky, spirited,
confident, outgoing.
2 a bold pattern: eye-catching,
striking, conspicuous, prominent,
strong, pronounced, bright, vivid,
colourful, loud, flashy, showy,
flamboyant.
3 bold behaviour: brazen, brash,
forward, shameless, unabashed,
cheeky (*infml*), impudent, insolent.
F3 1 cautious, timid, shy. 2 faint,
restrained.

bolt *noun*
bar, rod, shaft, pin, peg, rivet, fastener,
latch, catch, lock.
▸ *verb*
1 bolt the door: fasten, secure,

bar, latch, lock.

2 bolt at the first sign of trouble: abscond, escape, flee, fly, run, sprint, rush, dash, hurtle.

3 bolt one's food: gulp, wolf, gobble, gorge, devour, cram, stuff (*infml*).

bomb verb
bombard, shell, torpedo, attack, blow up, destroy.

bombard verb
attack, assault, assail, pelt, pound, strafe, blast, bomb, shell, blitz, besiege, hound, harass, pester.

bond noun
1 form a lasting bond between them: connection, relation, link, tie, union, affiliation, attachment, affinity.
2 gave them his bond: contract, covenant, agreement, pledge, promise, word, obligation.
3 throw off their bonds: fetter, shackle, manacle, chain, cord, band, binding.
► verb
connect, fasten, bind, unite, fuse, glue, gum, paste, stick, seal.

bone

Human bones include:

carpal, clavicle, coccyx, collarbone, femur, fibula, hip-bone, humerus, ilium, ischium, mandible, maxilla, metacarpal, metatarsal, patella, pelvic girdle, pelvis, pubis, radius, rib, sacrum, scapula, shoulderblade, skull, sternum, stirrup bone, temporal, thigh-bone, tibia, ulna, vertebra.

bonus noun
advantage, benefit, plus (*infml*), extra, perk (*infml*), commission, dividend, premium, prize, reward, honorarium, tip, gratuity, gift, handout.
F∃ disadvantage, disincentive.

bony adjective
thin, lean, angular, lanky, gawky, gangling, skinny, scrawny, emaciated, rawboned, gaunt, drawn.
F∃ fat, plump.

book noun
volume, tome, publication, work, booklet, tract.

Types of book include:

audio book, bestseller, e-book, hardback, paperback; fiction, novel, romantic novel, story, thriller; annual, children's book, picture-book, primer; almanac, anthology, atlas, A to Z, catalogue, compendium, concordance, cookbook, dictionary, directory, encyclopedia, gazetteer, guidebook, handbook, lexicon, manual, omnibus, pocket companion, reference book, thesaurus, yearbook; album, diary, exercise book, Filofax®, jotter, journal, ledger, notebook, pad, scrapbook, sketchbook, textbook; hymnal, hymn-book, lectionary, libretto, manuscript, missal, prayer book, psalter. ⇨*See also* **literature**; **story**.

book verb
reserve, bag (*infml*), engage, charter, procure, order, arrange, organize, schedule, programme.
F∃ cancel.

boom noun
1 an economic boom: increase, growth, expansion, gain, upsurge, jump, spurt, boost, upturn, improvement, advance, escalation, explosion.
2 the boom of the big guns: bang, clap, crash, roar, thunder, rumble, reverberation, blast, explosion, burst.
F∃ **1** failure, collapse, slump, recession, depression.

boon noun
blessing, advantage, benefit, godsend, windfall, favour, kindness, gift, present, grant, gratuity.
F∃ disadvantage, blight.

boorish adjective
uncouth, oafish, loutish, ill-mannered, rude, coarse, crude, vulgar, unrefined, uncivilized, uneducated, ignorant.
F∃ polite, refined, cultured.

boost noun
improvement, enhancement, expansion, increase, rise, jump, increment, addition, supplement, booster, lift, hoist, heave, push, thrust,

help, advancement, promotion, praise, encouragement, fillip.

E3 setback, blow.

▸ *verb*

raise, elevate, improve, enhance, develop, enlarge, expand, amplify, increase, augment, heighten, lift, hoist, jack up, heave, push, thrust, help, aid, assist, advance, further, promote, advertise, plug (*infml*), praise, inspire, encourage, foster, support, sustain, bolster, supplement.

E3 hinder, undermine.

booth *noun*
kiosk, stall, stand, hut, box, compartment, cubicle, carrel.

booty *noun*
loot, plunder, pillage, spoils, swag (*slang*), haul, gains, takings, pickings, winnings.

border *noun*
1 the border between two countries/ across national borders: boundary, frontier, bound, bounds, confine, confines, limit, demarcation, borderline, margin, fringe, periphery, surround, perimeter, circumference, edge, rim, brim, verge, brink.
2 a lace border: trimming, frill, valance, skirt, hem, frieze.

border on *verb*
1 bordering on our land: adjoin, abut, touch, impinge, join, connect, communicate with.
2 bordering on lunacy: resemble, approximate, approach, verge on.

bore[1] *verb*
boring a hole: drill, mine, pierce, perforate, penetrate, sink, burrow, tunnel, undermine.

bore[2] *verb*
travelling bores him: tire, weary, fatigue, jade, trouble, bother, worry, irritate, annoy, vex, irk.

E3 interest, excite.

▸ *noun* (*infml*)

a bit of a bore: nuisance, bother, bind (*infml*), drag (*infml*), pain (*infml*), headache (*infml*).

E3 pleasure, delight.

boring *adjective*
tedious, monotonous, routine, repetitious, uninteresting, unexciting, uneventful, dull, dreary, humdrum, commonplace, trite, unimaginative, uninspired, dry, stale, flat, insipid, tiresome.

E3 interesting, exciting, stimulating, original.

borrow *verb*
steal, pilfer, filch, lift, plagiarize, crib, copy, imitate, mimic, echo, take, draw, derive, obtain, adopt, use, scrounge, cadge, sponge, appropriate, usurp.

E3 lend.

boss *noun*
employer, governor, master, owner, captain, head, chief, leader, supremo, administrator, executive, director, manager, foreman, gaffer, superintendent, overseer, supervisor.

◆ **boss around** order around, order about, domineer, tyrannize, bully, bulldoze, browbeat, push around, dominate.

bossy *adjective*
authoritarian, autocratic, tyrannical, despotic, dictatorial, domineering, overbearing, oppressive, lordly, high-handed, imperious, insistent, assertive, demanding, exacting.

E3 unassertive.

bother *verb*
disturb, inconvenience, harass, hassle (*infml*), pester, plague, nag, annoy, irritate, irk, molest, trouble, worry, concern, alarm, dismay, distress, upset, vex.

▸ *noun*

inconvenience, trouble, problem, difficulty, hassle (*infml*), fuss, bustle, flurry, nuisance, pest, annoyance, irritation, aggravation (*infml*), vexation, worry, strain.

bottle *noun*
phial, flask, carafe, decanter, flagon, demijohn.

◆ **bottle up** hide, conceal, restrain, curb, hold back, suppress, inhibit, restrict, enclose, contain.

E3 unbosom, unburden.

bottom *noun*
underside, underneath, sole, base, foot, plinth, pedestal, support,

foundation, substructure, ground, floor, bed, depths, nadir.
F3 top.

bottomless *adjective*
deep, profound, fathomless, unfathomed, unplumbed, immeasurable, measureless, infinite, boundless, limitless, unlimited, inexhaustible.
F3 shallow, limited.

bounce *verb*
spring, jump, leap, bound, bob, ricochet, rebound, recoil.
▶ *noun*
1 give one's hair bounce: spring, bound, springiness, elasticity, give, resilience, rebound, give.
2 he's full of bounce: ebullience, exuberance, vitality, vivacity, energy, vigour, go (*infml*), zip (*infml*), dynamism, animation, liveliness.

bound¹ *adjective*
1 bound hand and foot: fastened, secured, fixed, tied (up), chained, held, restricted, bandaged.
2 bound by the agreement: liable, committed, duty-bound, obliged, required, forced, compelled, constrained, destined, fated, doomed, sure, certain.

bound² *verb*
a big dog came bounding towards us: jump, leap, vault, hurdle, spring, bounce, bob, hop, skip, frisk, gambol, frolic, caper, prance.
▶ *noun*
jumped the wall in one bound: jump, leap, vault, spring, bounce, bob, hop, skip, gambol, frolic, caper, dance, prance.

boundary *noun*
border, frontier, barrier, line, borderline, demarcation, bounds, confines, limits, margin, fringe, verge, brink, edge, perimeter, extremity, termination.

boundless *adjective*
unbounded, limitless, unlimited, unconfined, countless, untold, incalculable, vast, immense, measureless, immeasurable, infinite, endless, unending, interminable,

inexhaustible, unflagging, indefatigable.
F3 limited, restricted.

bounds *noun*
confines, limits, borders, marches, margins, fringes, periphery, circumference, edges, extremities.

bounty *noun*
1 benefit from the king's bounty: generosity, liberality, munificence, largesse, almsgiving, charity, philanthropy, beneficence (*fml*), kindness.
2 earn a bounty: reward, recompense, premium, bonus, gratuity, gift, present, donation, grant, allowance.

bouquet *noun*
1 bouquet of flowers: bunch, posy, nosegay, spray, corsage, buttonhole, wreath, garland.
2 savour the wine's bouquet: aroma, smell, pong (*infml*), odour, scent, perfume, fragrance.

bourgeois *adjective*
middle-class, materialistic, conservative, traditional, conformist, conventional, unadventurous, dull, humdrum, banal, commonplace, trite, unoriginal, unimaginative.
F3 bohemian, unconventional, original.

bout *noun*
1 a boxing bout: fight, battle, engagement, encounter, struggle, set-to, match, contest, competition, round, heat.
2 a bout of illness: period, spell, time, stint, turn, go (*infml*), term, stretch, run, course, session, spree, attack, fit.

bow *noun* /bow/
bob, curtsy, genuflection, inclination, bending, nod, kowtow, salaam, salutation, acknowledgement.
▶ *verb*
1 bow one's head: incline, bend, nod, bob, curtsy, genuflect, kowtow, salaam, stoop.
2 bow to pressure: yield, give in, consent, surrender, capitulate, submit, acquiesce, concede, accept, comply, defer.
◆ **bow out** withdraw, pull out (*infml*),

desert, abandon, defect, back out, chicken out (*infml*), retire, resign, quit, stand down, step down, give up.

bowl[1] *noun*
a washing-up bowl: receptacle, container, vessel, dish, basin, sink.

bowl[2] *verb*
bowl a ball: throw, hurl, fling, pitch, roll, spin, whirl, rotate, revolve.
◆ **bowl over** surprise, amaze, astound, astonish, stagger, stun, dumbfound, flabbergast (*infml*), floor (*infml*).

box[1] *noun*
a wooden box: container, receptacle, case, crate, carton, packet, pack, package, present, chest, coffer, trunk, coffin.
◆ **box in** enclose, surround, circumscribe, cordon off, hem in, corner, trap, confine, restrict, imprison, cage, coop up, contain.

box[2] *verb*
learn to box/box someone's ears: fight, spar, punch, hit, strike, slap, buffet, cuff, clout, sock (*infml*), wallop (*infml*), whack (*infml*).

boxer *noun*
pugilist, fighter, prizefighter, sparring partner, flyweight, featherweight, lightweight, welterweight, middleweight, heavyweight.

boy *noun*
son, lad, youngster, kid (*infml*), nipper (*infml*), stripling, youth, fellow.

boycott *verb*
refuse, reject, embargo, ban, prohibit, disallow, bar, exclude, blacklist, outlaw, ostracize, cold-shoulder, ignore, spurn.
F3 encourage, support.

bracing *adjective*
fresh, crisp, refreshing, reviving, strengthening, fortifying, tonic, rousing, stimulating, exhilarating, invigorating, enlivening, energizing, brisk, energetic, vigorous.
F3 weakening, debilitating.

brag *verb*
boast, show off, crow, bluster.
F3 be modest, deprecate (*fml*).

braid *verb*
plait, interweave, interlace, intertwine,

weave, lace, twine, entwine, ravel, twist, wind.
F3 undo, unravel.

brain *noun*
1 use your brain: cerebrum, grey matter, head, mind, intellect, nous, brains (*infml*), intelligence, wit, reason, sense, common sense, shrewdness, understanding.
2 one of the brains of the operation: mastermind, intellectual, highbrow, egghead (*infml*), scholar, expert, boffin, genius, prodigy.

brainy *adjective* (*infml*)
intellectual, intelligent, clever, smart, bright, brilliant.
F3 dull, stupid.

brake *noun*
check, curb, rein, restraint, control, restriction, constraint, drag.
▶ *verb*
slow, decelerate, retard, drag, slacken, moderate, check, halt, stop, pull up.
F3 accelerate.

branch *noun*
1 the branch of a tree: bough, limb, sprig, shoot, offshoot.
2 a different branch of the company: department, office, part, section, arm, wing, division, subsection, subdivision.
◆ **branch out** diversify, vary, develop, expand, enlarge, extend, broaden out, increase, multiply, proliferate, ramify.

brand *noun*
make, brand-name, tradename, trademark, logo, mark, symbol, sign, emblem, label, stamp, hallmark, grade, quality, class, kind, type, sort, line, variety, species.
▶ *verb*
mark, stamp, label, type, stigmatize, burn, scar, stain, taint, disgrace, discredit, denounce, censure.

brandish *verb*
wave, flourish, shake, raise, swing, wield, flash, flaunt, exhibit, display, parade.

brave *adjective*
courageous, plucky, unafraid, fearless, dauntless, undaunted, bold, audacious, daring, intrepid, stalwart, hardy, stoical, resolute, stout-hearted,

valiant, gallant, heroic, indomitable.
E3 cowardly, afraid, timid.
▸ *verb*
face, confront, defy, challenge, dare,
stand up to, face up to, suffer, endure,
bear, withstand.
E3 capitulate.

bravery *noun*
courage, pluck, guts (*infml*),
fearlessness, dauntlessness, boldness,
audacity, daring, intrepidity,
stalwartness, hardiness, fortitude,
resolution, stout-heartedness,
valiance, valour, gallantry, heroism,
indomitability, grit, mettle, spirit.
E3 cowardice, faint-heartedness,
timidity.

brawl *noun*
fight, punch-up (*infml*), scrap, scuffle,
dust-up (*infml*), mêlée, free-for-all, fray,
affray, broil, fracas, rumpus, disorder,
row, argument, quarrel, squabble,
altercation (*fml*), dispute, clash.

brazen *adjective*
blatant, flagrant, brash, brassy, bold,
forward, saucy, pert, barefaced,
impudent, insolent, defiant, shameless,
unashamed, unabashed, immodest.
E3 shy, shamefaced, modest.

breach *noun*
1 a breach of the rules: violation,
contravention, infringement, trespass
(*fml*), disobedience, offence,
transgression, lapse, disruption.
2 heal the breach between them:
quarrel, disagreement, dissension,
difference, variance, schism, rift,
rupture, split, division, separation,
parting, estrangement, alienation,
disaffection, dissociation.
3 a breach in the hull: break, crack,
rift, rupture, fissure, cleft, crevice,
opening, aperture, gap, space, hole,
chasm.

bread *noun*
loaf, roll, food, provisions, diet, fare,
nourishment, nutriment, sustenance,
subsistence, necessities.

breadth *noun*
width, broadness, wideness, latitude,
thickness, size, magnitude, measure,
scale, range, reach, scope, compass,
span, sweep, extent, expanse, spread,
comprehensiveness, extensiveness,
vastness.

break *verb*
1 broke a bone/window: fracture,
crack, snap, split, sever, separate,
divide, rend, smash, disintegrate,
splinter, shiver, shatter, ruin, destroy,
demolish.
2 break the law: violate, contravene,
infringe, breach, disobey, flout.
3 break for lunch: pause, halt, stop,
discontinue, interrupt, suspend, rest.
**4 break a wild horse/break someone's
spirit**: subdue, tame, weaken, enfeeble,
impair, undermine, demoralize.
5 break the news: tell, inform, impart,
divulge, disclose, reveal, announce.
6 break a record: exceed, beat, better,
excel, surpass, outdo, outstrip.
E3 1 mend. **2** keep, observe, abide by.
◆ **break away** separate, split, part
company, detach, secede, leave, depart,
quit, run away, escape, flee, fly.
◆ **break down 1 the bus broke down**:
fail, stop, pack up (*infml*), conk out
(*infml*), seize up.
2 break down in tears: collapse, crack
up (*infml*).
3 break down the total price: analyse,
dissect, separate, itemize, detail.
◆ **break in 1 thieves broke in during
the night**: burgle, rob, raid, invade.
2 broke into our conversation:
interrupt, butt in, interpose, interject,
intervene, intrude, encroach,
impinge.
◆ **break off 1 broke off in my hand**:
detach, snap off, sever, separate, part,
divide, disconnect.
2 he broke off to answer the phone:
pause, interrupt, suspend, discontinue,
halt, stop, cease, end, finish, terminate.
◆ **break out 1 fighting broke out**: start,
begin, commence, arise, emerge,
happen, occur, erupt, flare up, burst
out.
2 break out of prison: escape, abscond,
bolt, flee.
◆ **break up 1 break up old machinery/
pack-ice breaking up**: dismantle, take
apart, demolish, destroy, disintegrate,
divide.

2 break up with one's partner: split up, part, separate, divorce.
3 the party broke up at midnight: disband, disperse, dissolve, adjourn, suspend, stop, finish, terminate.
▶ *noun*
1 a break in the pipe: fracture, crack, split, rift, rupture, schism, separation, tear, gash, fissure, cleft, crevice, rent, opening, gap, hole, breach.
2 have a break for coffee: interval, intermission, interlude, interruption, pause, halt, lull, let-up (*infml*), respite, rest, breather (*infml*), time out, holiday.
3 give/get a break: opportunity, chance, advantage, fortune, luck.

breakable *adjective*
brittle, fragile, delicate, flimsy, insubstantial, frail.
Fᴈ unbreakable, durable, sturdy.

breakdown *noun*
1 a mechanical/mental breakdown: failure, collapse, disintegration, malfunction, interruption, stoppage.
2 a breakdown of the figures: analysis, dissection, itemization, classification, categorization.

break-in *noun*
burglary, house-breaking, robbery, raid, invasion, intrusion, trespass.

breakthrough *noun*
discovery, find, finding, invention, innovation, advance, progress, headway, step, leap, development, improvement.

breath *noun*
1 lose one's breath/take a deep breath: air, breathing, respiration, inhalation, exhalation, sigh, gasp, pant, gulp.
2 not a breath of wind: breeze, puff, waft, gust.
3 not a breath of scandal: hint, suggestion, suspicion, whiff, undertone, whisper, murmur.

breathe *verb*
1 breathe deeply: respire, inhale, exhale, expire, sigh, gasp, pant, puff.
2 not breathe a word: say, utter, express, voice, articulate, murmur, whisper, impart, tell.
3 breathe life into: instil, imbue, infuse, inject, inspire.

breathless *adjective*
1 feel breathless: short-winded, out of breath, panting, puffing, puffed (out), exhausted, winded, gasping, wheezing, choking.
2 breathless anticipation: expectant, impatient, eager, agog, excited, feverish, anxious.

breathtaking *adjective*
awe-inspiring, impressive, magnificent, overwhelming, amazing, astonishing, stunning, exciting, thrilling, stirring, moving.

breed *verb*
1 breed rapidly/successfully: reproduce, procreate, multiply, propagate, hatch, bear, bring forth, rear, raise, bring up, educate, train, instruct.
2 breed discontent: produce, create, originate, arouse, cause, occasion, engender, generate, make, foster, nurture, nourish, cultivate, develop.
▶ *noun*
species, strain, variety, family, ilk, sort, kind, type, stamp, stock, race, progeny (*fml*), line, lineage, pedigree.

breeding *noun*
1 the breeding of domestic animals: reproduction, procreation, nurture, development, rearing, raising, upbringing, education, training, background, ancestry, lineage, stock.
2 have good breeding: manners, politeness, civility, gentility, urbanity, refinement, culture, polish.
Fᴈ 2 vulgarity.

breeze *noun*
wind, gust, flurry, waft, puff, breath, draught, air.

breezy *adjective*
1 a breezy day: windy, blowing, fresh, airy, gusty, blustery, squally.
2 a breezy manner: animated, lively, vivacious, jaunty, buoyant, blithe, debonair, carefree, cheerful, easy-going (*infml*), casual, informal, light, bright, exhilarating.
Fᴈ 1 still. **2** staid, serious.

brevity *noun*
briefness, shortness, terseness, conciseness, succinctness, pithiness,

crispness, incisiveness, abruptness, curtness, impermanence, ephemerality, transience, transitoriness.

▣ verbosity, permanence, longevity.

brew verb

1 let the tea brew/brew beer: infuse, stew, boil, seethe, ferment, prepare, soak, steep, mix, cook.
2 some devilment brewing: plot, scheme, plan, project, devise, contrive, concoct, hatch, excite, foment, build up, gather, develop.

bribe noun

incentive, inducement, allurement, enticement, back-hander (infml), kickback, payola, refresher (infml), sweetener (infml), hush money (infml), protection money.
▶ verb
corrupt, suborn, buy off, reward.

bridal adjective

wedding, nuptial (fml), marriage, matrimonial, marital, conjugal.

bridge noun

arch, span, causeway, link, connection, bond, tie.
▶ verb
span, cross, traverse, fill, link, connect, couple, join, unite, bind.

brief adjective

1 a brief description: short, terse, succinct, concise, pithy, crisp, compressed, thumbnail, laconic, abrupt, sharp, brusque, blunt, curt, surly.
2 a brief interruption/stay: short-lived, momentary, ephemeral, transient, fleeting, passing, transitory, temporary, limited, cursory, hasty, quick, swift, fast.
▣ 1 long. 2 lengthy.
▶ noun
1 a brief for the task in hand: orders, instructions, directions, remit, mandate, directive, advice, briefing, data, information.
2 a lawyer's brief: outline, summary, précis, dossier, case, defence, argument.
▶ verb
instruct, direct, explain, guide, advise,

prepare, prime, inform, fill in (infml), gen up (infml).

briefing noun

meeting, conference, preparation, priming, filling-in (infml), gen (infml), low-down (infml), information, advice, guidance, directions, instructions, orders.

bright adjective

1 bright lights/sunshine: luminous, illuminated, radiant, shining, beaming, flashing, gleaming, glistening, glittering, sparkling, twinkling, shimmering, glowing, brilliant, resplendent, glorious, splendid, dazzling, glaring, blazing, intense, vivid.
2 merry and bright/a bright smile: happy, cheerful, glad, joyful, merry, jolly, lively, vivacious.
3 the future looks bright: promising, propitious, auspicious, favourable, rosy, optimistic, hopeful, encouraging.
4 a very bright child: clever, brainy (infml), smart, intelligent, quick-witted, quick, sharp, acute, keen, astute, perceptive.
5 a bright colour: clear, transparent, translucent, lucid.
6 a bright day: fine, sunny, cloudless, unclouded.
▣ 1 dull. 2 sad. 3 depressing. 4 stupid. 5 muddy. 6 dark.

brighten verb

1 brighten a dark corner/the weather brightened up: light up, illuminate, lighten, clear up.
2 brightening the tarnished metal: polish, burnish, rub up, shine, gleam, glow.
3 she brightened a little when she got the news: cheer up, gladden, hearten, encourage, enliven, perk up.
▣ 1 darken. 2 dull, tarnish.

brilliance noun

1 his brilliance with figures: talent, virtuosity, genius, greatness, distinction, excellence, aptitude, cleverness.
2 a gem's brilliance/the brilliance of the emperor's court: radiance, brightness, sparkle, dazzle, intensity,

vividness, gloss, lustre, sheen, glamour, glory, magnificence, splendour.

brilliant *adjective*
1 a brilliant pianist: gifted, talented, accomplished, expert, skilful, masterly, exceptional, outstanding, superb, illustrious, famous, celebrated.
2 a brilliant star: sparkling, glittering, scintillating, dazzling, glaring, blazing, intense, vivid, bright, shining, glossy, showy, glorious, magnificent, splendid.
3 a brilliant idea/analysis: clever, brainy (*infml*), intelligent, quick, astute.
F3 1 undistinguished. **2** dull. **3** stupid.

brim *noun*
rim, perimeter, circumference, lip, edge, margin, border, brink, verge, top, limit.

bring *verb*
1 bring the children/an umbrella: carry, bear, convey, transport, fetch, take, deliver, escort, accompany, usher, guide, conduct, lead.
2 bring disease/despair/hope: cause, produce, engender, create, prompt, provoke, force, attract, draw.
◆ **bring about** cause, occasion, create, produce, generate, effect, accomplish, achieve, fulfil, realize, manage, engineer, manoeuvre, manipulate.
◆ **bring in** earn, net, gross, produce, yield, fetch, return, accrue, realize.
◆ **bring off** achieve, accomplish, fulfil, execute, discharge, perform, succeed, win.
◆ **bring on** cause, occasion, induce, lead to, give rise to, generate, inspire, prompt, provoke, precipitate (*fml*), expedite, accelerate, advance.
F3 inhibit.
◆ **bring out 1** bring out her best features: emphasize, stress, highlight, enhance, draw out.
2 bring out a new magazine: publish, print, issue, launch, introduce.
◆ **bring up 1** bring up children: rear, raise, foster, nurture, educate, teach, train, form.
2 bring up a subject: introduce, broach, mention, submit, propose.
3 bring up one's food: vomit, puke (*slang*), regurgitate, throw up (*infml*).

brink *noun*
verge, threshold, edge, margin, fringe, border, boundary, limit, extremity, lip, rim, brim, bank.

brisk *adjective*
1 her manner was brisk and efficient: energetic, vigorous, quick, snappy, lively, spirited, active, busy, bustling, agile, nimble, alert.
2 a brisk walk: invigorating, exhilarating, stimulating, bracing, refreshing, fresh.
F3 1 lazy, sluggish.

bristle *noun*
hair, whisker, stubble, spine, prickle, barb, thorn.

bristly *adjective*
hairy, whiskered, bearded, unshaven, stubbly, rough, spiny, prickly, spiky, thorny.
F3 clean-shaven, smooth.

brittle *adjective*
breakable, fragile, delicate, frail, crisp, crumbly, crumbling, friable, shattery, shivery.
F3 durable, resilient.

broad *adjective*
1 a broad avenue/river: wide, large, vast, roomy, spacious, capacious, ample, extensive, widespread.
2 a broad category: wide-ranging, far-reaching, encyclopedic, catholic, eclectic, all-embracing, inclusive, comprehensive, general, sweeping, universal, unlimited.
F3 1 narrow. **2** restricted.

broadcast *verb*
air, show, transmit, beam, relay, televise, report, announce, publicize, advertise, publish, circulate, promulgate, disseminate, spread.
▸ *noun*
transmission, programme, show.

broaden *verb*
widen, thicken, swell, spread, enlarge, expand, extend, stretch, increase, augment, develop, open up, branch out, diversify.

broad-minded *adjective*
liberal, tolerant, permissive, enlightened, free-thinking, open-

minded, receptive, unbiased, unprejudiced.

F3 narrow-minded, intolerant, biased.

brochure *noun*
leaflet, booklet, pamphlet, prospectus, broadsheet, handbill, circular, handout, folder.

broke *adjective* (*infml*)
insolvent, penniless, bankrupt, bust, ruined, skint (*infml*), impoverished, destitute.

F3 solvent, rich, affluent.

broken *adjective*
1 a broken leg/toy/pipe: fractured, burst, ruptured, severed, separated, dud (*slang*), faulty, defective, out of order, shattered, destroyed, demolished, kaput (*slang*).
2 a broken line/voice: disjointed, disconnected, fragmentary, discontinuous, interrupted, intermittent, spasmodic, erratic, hesitating, stammering, halting, imperfect.
3 a broken man: beaten, defeated, crushed, demoralized, down, weak, feeble, exhausted, tamed, subdued, oppressed.

F3 1 mended. 2 continuous, fluent.

broken-down *adjective*
dilapidated, worn-out, ruined, kaput (*slang*), collapsed, decayed, inoperative, out of order.

brood *verb*
ponder, ruminate, meditate, muse, mull over, go over, rehearse, dwell on, agonize, fret, mope.
▶ *noun*
clutch, chicks, hatch, litter, young, offspring, issue, progeny (*fml*), children, family.

brother *noun*
sibling, relation, relative, comrade, friend, mate, partner, colleague, associate, fellow, companion, monk, friar.

brotherhood *noun*
fraternity, association, society, league, confederation, confederacy, alliance, union, guild, fellowship, community, clique.

browbeat *verb*
bully, coerce, dragoon, bulldoze, awe, cow, intimidate, threaten, tyrannize, domineer, overbear, oppress, hound.

F3 coax.

brown *adjective*
mahogany, chocolate, coffee, hazel, bay, chestnut, umber, sepia, tan, tawny, russet, rust, rusty, brunette, dark, dusky, sunburnt, tanned, bronzed, browned, toasted.

browse *verb*
1 browsing through the dictionary: leaf through, flick through, dip into, skim, survey, scan, peruse.
2 animals browsing on the vegetation: graze, pasture, feed, eat, nibble.

bruise *noun*
contusion, discoloration, black eye, shiner (*infml*), mark, blemish, injury.
▶ *verb*
discolour, blacken, mark, blemish, pound, pulverize, crush, hurt, injure, insult, offend, grieve.

brush[1] *verb*
1 brush the floor: clean, sweep, flick, burnish, polish, shine.
2 brushing against her cheek: touch, contact, graze, kiss, stroke, rub, scrape.
◆ **brush aside** dismiss, pooh-pooh, belittle, disregard, ignore, flout, override.
◆ **brush off** disregard, ignore, slight, snub, cold-shoulder, rebuff, dismiss, spurn, reject, repulse, disown, repudiate.
◆ **brush up 1** brush up my French: revise, relearn, improve, polish up, study, read up, swot (*infml*).
2 wash and brush up: refresh, freshen up, clean, tidy.

brush[2] *noun*
hiding in the brush: scrub, thicket, bushes, shrubs, brushwood, undergrowth, ground cover.

brush[3] *noun*
a brush with the law: confrontation, encounter, clash, conflict, fight, scrap, skirmish, set-to, tussle, dust-up (*infml*), fracas.

brusque *adjective*
abrupt, sharp, short, terse, curt, gruff, surly, discourteous, impolite, uncivil,

blunt, tactless, undiplomatic.
F3 courteous, polite, tactful.

brutal *adjective*
animal, bestial, beastly, brutish,
inhuman, savage, bloodthirsty, vicious,
ferocious, cruel, inhumane,
remorseless, pitiless, merciless,
ruthless, callous, insensitive, unfeeling,
heartless, harsh, gruff, rough, coarse,
crude, rude, uncivilized, barbarous.
F3 kindly, humane, civilized.

brutality *noun*
savagery, bloodthirstiness, viciousness,
ferocity, cruelty, inhumanity, violence,
atrocity, ruthlessness, callousness,
roughness, coarseness, barbarism,
barbarity.
F3 gentleness, kindness.

brute *noun*
animal, beast, swine, creature,
monster, ogre, devil, fiend, savage,
sadist, bully, lout.

bubble *noun*
blister, vesicle, globule, ball, drop,
droplet, bead.
▶ *verb*
effervesce, fizz, sparkle, froth, foam,
seethe, boil, burble, gurgle.

bubbly *adjective*
1 **bubbly champagne**: effervescent,
fizzy, sparkling, carbonated, frothy,
foaming, sudsy.
2 **a bubbly personality**: lively, bouncy,
happy, merry, elated, excited,
irrepressible.
F3 **1** flat, still. **2** dull, lethargic.

bucket *noun*
pail, can, bail, scuttle, vessel.

buckle *noun*
clasp, clip, catch, fastener.
▶ *verb*
1 **buckle my shoe**: fasten, clasp, catch,
hook, hitch, connect, close, secure.
2 **metal buckled/legs buckled under
him**: bend, warp, twist, distort, bulge,
cave in, fold, wrinkle, crumple,
collapse.

bud *noun*
shoot, sprout, germ, embryo.

budding *adjective*
potential, promising, embryonic,

burgeoning, developing, growing,
flowering.

budge *verb*
move, stir, shift, remove, dislodge,
push, roll, slide, propel, sway,
influence, persuade, convince, change,
bend, yield, give (way).

budget *noun*
finances, funds, resources, means,
allowance, allotment, allocation,
estimate.
▶ *verb*
plan, estimate, allow, allot, allocate,
apportion, ration.

buff[1] *verb*
buffing the leather with a soft cloth:
polish, burnish, shine, smooth, rub,
brush.

buff[2] (*infml*) *noun*
a film buff: expert, connoisseur,
enthusiast, fan, admirer, devotee,
addict, fiend, freak.

buffet[1] *noun* /buwf-ei/
a railway buffet: snack-bar, counter,
café, cafeteria.

buffet[2] *verb* /buf-it/
buffeted by the storm: batter, hit,
strike, knock, bang, bump, push,
shove, pound, pummel, beat, thump,
box, cuff, clout, slap.
▶ *noun*
blow, knock, bang, bump, jar, jolt,
push, shove, thump, box, cuff, clout,
slap, smack.

bug *noun*
1 **a tummy bug**: virus, bacterium,
germ, microbe, micro-organism,
infection, disease.
2 **bugs in the computer program**:
fault, defect, blemish, imperfection,
flaw, failing, error, gremlin
(*infml*).
▶ *verb*
1 **bug their offices**: tap, spy on, listen
in.
2 (*infml*) **don't bug me with
questions!**: annoy, irritate, vex, irk,
needle (*infml*), bother, disturb, harass,
badger.

build *noun*
physique, figure, body, form, shape,
size, frame, structure.

▸ *verb*

1 build a house/a wall/a lasting peace : erect, raise, construct, fabricate, make, form, constitute, assemble, knock together, develop, enlarge, extend, increase, augment, escalate, intensify.
2 build an organization : base, found, establish, institute, inaugurate, initiate, begin.

F⋑ **1** destroy, demolish, knock down, lessen.

◆ **build up** strengthen, reinforce, fortify, extend, expand, develop, amplify, increase, escalate, intensify, heighten, boost, improve, enhance, publicize, advertise, promote, plug (*infml*), hype (*infml*).

F⋑ weaken, lessen.

building *noun*
edifice, dwelling, construction, fabrication, structure, architecture.

Types of building include:

block of flats, bungalow, cabin, castle, chateau, cottage, farmhouse, house, mansion, palace, villa; abbey, cathedral, chapel, church, monastery, mosque, pagoda, synagogue, temple; café, cinema, college, factory, garage, gymnasium, hospital, hotel, inn, library, multiplex, museum, observatory, office block, power station, prison, pub (*infml*), public house, restaurant, school, shop, silo, skyscraper, sports hall, store, theatre, tower block, warehouse; barracks, fort, fortress, mausoleum, monument; barn, beach hut, boathouse, dovecote, gazebo, lighthouse, mill, outhouse, pavilion, pier, shed, stable, summerhouse, windmill. ⇨*See also* **house**; **shop**.

build-up *noun*
1 a build-up of tension :enlargement, expansion, development, increase, gain, growth, escalation.
2 gave him a good build-up : publicity, promotion, plug (*infml*), hype (*infml*).
3 a build-up of arms: accumulation, mass, load, heap, stack, store, stockpile.

F⋑ **1** reduction, decrease.

bulge *verb*
swell, puff out, bulb, hump, dilate, expand, enlarge, distend, protrude, project, sag.

▸ *noun*
swelling, bump, lump, hump, distension (*fml*), protuberance (*fml*), projection.

bulk *noun*
size, magnitude, dimensions, extent, amplitude, bigness, largeness, immensity, volume, mass, weight, substance, body, preponderance, majority, most.

bulky *adjective*
substantial, big, large, huge, enormous, immense, mammoth, massive, colossal, hulking, hefty, heavy, weighty, unmanageable, unwieldy, awkward, cumbersome.

F⋑ insubstantial, small, handy.

bullet *noun*
shot, pellet, ball, slug (*infml*), missile, projectile.

bulletin *noun*
report, newsflash, dispatch, communiqué, statement, announcement, notification, communication, message.

bully *noun*
persecutor, tormentor, browbeater, intimidator, bully-boy, heavy (*infml*), ruffian, tough, thug.

▸ *verb*
persecute, torment, terrorize, bulldoze, coerce, browbeat, bullyrag, intimidate, cow, tyrannize, domineer, overbear, oppress, push around.

bump *verb*
1 bump one's head against the door : hit, strike, knock, bang, crash, collide (with).
2 bumping along on the uneven surface : jolt, jerk, jar, jostle, rattle, shake, bounce.

◆ **bump into** meet, encounter, run into, chance upon, come across.

◆ **bump off** (*infml*) kill, murder, assassinate, eliminate, liquidate (*infml*), do in (*infml*), top (*slang*).

▸ *noun*
1 hit the other car with a bump : blow,

hit, knock, bang, thump, thud, smash, crash, collision, impact, jolt, jar, shock.
2 a bump on the head : lump, swelling, bulge, hump, protuberance (*fml*).

bumper *adjective*
plentiful, abundant, large, great, enormous, massive, excellent, exceptional.
F∃ small.

bumpy *adjective*
jerky, jolting, bouncy, choppy, rough, lumpy, knobbly, uneven, irregular.
F∃ smooth, even.

bunch *noun*
1 a bunch of keys : bundle, sheaf, tuft, clump, cluster, batch, lot, heap, pile, stack, mass, number, quantity, collection, assortment.
2 a bunch of flowers : bouquet, posy, spray.
3 a bunch of thugs : gang, band, troop, crew, team, party, gathering, flock, swarm, crowd, mob, multitude.

bundle *noun*
bunch, sheaf, roll, bale, truss, parcel, package, packet, carton, box, bag, pack, batch, consignment, group, set, collection, assortment, quantity, mass, accumulation, pile, stack, heap.

bungle *verb*
mismanage, foul up (*infml*), mess up (*infml*), ruin, spoil, mar, botch, fudge, blunder.

buoy *noun*
float, marker, signal, beacon.
◆ **buoy up** support, sustain, raise, lift, boost, encourage, cheer, hearten.
F∃ depress, discourage.

buoyant *adjective*
1 in buoyant mood : light-hearted, carefree, bright, cheerful, happy, joyful, lively, animated, bouncy.
2 a buoyant container : floatable, floating, afloat, light, weightless.
F∃ 1 depressed, despairing. **2** heavy.

burden *noun*
cargo, load, weight, dead-weight, encumbrance, millstone, onus, responsibility, obligation, duty, inconvenience, imposition, strain, stress, worry, anxiety, care, trouble,
trial, affliction, sorrow.
▶ *verb*
load, weigh down, encumber, saddle, handicap, bother, worry, tax, strain, overload, lie heavy on, oppress, overwhelm.
F∃ unburden, relieve.

bureau *noun*
service, agency, office, branch, department, division, counter, desk.

bureaucracy *noun*
administration, government, ministry, civil service, the authorities, the system, officialdom, red tape, regulations.

burglar *noun*
housebreaker, robber, thief, pilferer, trespasser.

burglary *noun*
housebreaking, break-in, robbery, theft, stealing, trespass.

burly *adjective*
big, well-built, hulking, hefty, heavy, stocky, sturdy, brawny, beefy, muscular, athletic, strapping, strong, powerful.
F∃ small, puny, thin, slim.

burn *verb*
1 fire burning/burn the rubbish : flame, blaze, flare, flash, glow, flicker, smoulder, smoke, ignite, light, kindle, incinerate, cremate.
2 burn one's finger/burn the food : scald, scorch, singe, char, toast, sear.
3 burn with indignation : smart, sting, hurt, tingle, fume, simmer, seethe.

burning *adjective*
1 a burning lamp : ablaze, aflame, afire, fiery, flaming, blazing, flashing, gleaming, glowing, smouldering, alight, lit, illuminated.
2 a burning sensation : hot, scalding, scorching, searing, piercing, acute, smarting, stinging, prickling, tingling, biting, caustic, pungent.
3 burning desire : ardent, fervent, eager, earnest, intense, vehement, passionate, impassioned, frantic, frenzied, consuming.
4 burning issue : urgent, pressing, important, significant, crucial, essential, vital.
F∃ 2 cold. **3** apathetic. **4** unimportant.

burrow *noun*
warren, hole, earth, set, den, lair, retreat, shelter, tunnel.
► *verb*
tunnel, dig, delve, excavate, mine, undermine.

burst *verb*
puncture, rupture, tear, split, crack, break, fragment, shatter, shiver, disintegrate, explode, blow up, erupt, gush, spout, rush, run.

bury *verb*
1 bury the dead: inter, entomb, lay to rest, shroud.
2 buried under snow: sink, submerge, immerse, plant, implant, embed, conceal, hide, cover, enshroud, engulf, enclose.
3 buried in his books: engross, occupy, engage, absorb.
⊟1 disinter, exhume. **2** uncover.

bushy *adjective*
hairy, thick, dense, luxuriant, shaggy.

business *noun*
1 the business sector: trade, commerce, industry, manufacturing, dealings, transactions, bargaining, trading, buying, selling.
2 a successful business: company, firm, corporation, establishment, venture, organization, concern, enterprise.
3 went about his business quietly: job, occupation, work, employment, trade, profession, line, calling, career, vocation, duty, task, responsibility.
4 that's not our business: affair, matter, issue, subject, topic, question, problem, point.

businesslike *adjective*
professional, efficient, thorough, systematic, methodical, organized, orderly, well-ordered, well-organized, practical, matter-of-fact, precise, correct, formal, impersonal.
⊟ inefficient, disorganized.

bustle *verb*
dash, rush, scamper, scurry, hurry, hasten, scramble, fuss.
► *noun*
activity, stir, commotion, tumult, agitation, excitement, fuss, ado, flurry, hurry, haste.

busy *adjective*
1 busy at the office: occupied, engaged, tied up (*infml*), employed, working, slaving.
2 keep oneself busy: active, lively, energetic.
3 a busy street: crowded, swarming, teeming, bustling.
4 had a busy day: hectic, eventful, strenuous, tiring.
5 her busy fingers: restless, tireless, diligent, industrious.
⊟1 idle. **2** idle, lazy. **3** quiet. **4** quiet, restful. **5** idle.

busybody *noun*
meddler, nosey parker (*infml*), intruder, pry, gossip, eavesdropper, snoop, snooper, troublemaker.

butt[1] *noun*
the butt of his rifle: stub, end, tip, tail, base, foot, shaft, stock, handle, haft.

butt[2] *noun*
the butt of their jokes: target, mark, object, subject, victim, laughing-stock, dupe.

butt[3] *verb*
butt the gate open: hit, bump, knock, buffet, push, shove, ram, thrust, punch, jab, prod, poke.
◆ butt in interrupt, cut in, interpose, intrude, meddle, interfere.

buy *verb*
purchase, invest in (*infml*), pay for, procure, acquire, obtain, get.
⊟ sell.
► *noun*
purchase, acquisition, bargain, deal.

buyer *noun*
purchaser, shopper, consumer, customer, vendee, emptor.
⊟ seller, vendor.

buzz *verb*
1 bees buzzing: hum, drone, murmur, whirr, sussurate (*fml*).
2 buzz with excitement: hum, throb, pulse, bustle.

by *preposition*
near, next to, beside, along, over, through, via, past.
► *adverb*
near, close, handy, at hand, past, beyond, away, aside.

bypass *verb*
avoid, dodge, sidestep, skirt,
circumvent, ignore, neglect, omit.

by-product *noun*
consequence, result, side-effect, fallout

(*infml*), repercussion, after-effect.

bystander *noun*
spectator, onlooker, looker-on,
watcher, observer, witness, eye-
witness, passer-by.

cabin *noun*
1 the captain's cabin : berth, quarters, compartment, room.
2 log cabin : hut, shack, lodge, chalet, cottage, shed, shelter.

cable *noun*
1 an electric cable : line, rope, cord, chain, hawser, wire, flex, lead.
2 sent a cable : telegram, telegraph, message, wire.

cache *noun*
store, hoard, stock, stockpile, dump, supply, repository (*fml*), hiding-place, stash (*infml*).

cadge *verb*
scrounge, sponge, beg, hitch.

café *noun*
coffee shop, tea shop, tea room, coffee bar, cafeteria, snack bar, bistro, brasserie, restaurant.

caged *adjective*
shut up, locked up, cooped up, confined, fenced in, imprisoned, incarcerated.
Ea free.

cajole *verb*
coax, persuade, wheedle, flatter, sweet-talk (*infml*), butter up (*infml*), tempt, lure, seduce, entice, beguile, inveigle (*fml*), mislead, dupe.
Ea bully, force, compel.

cake *noun*
1 tea and cakes : gâteau, fancy, madeleine, bun, pie, flan, pastry, sponge, tart.
2 cake of soap : lump, mass, bar, slab, block.
▶ *verb*
coat, cover, encrust, dry, harden, solidify, consolidate, coagulate, congeal, thicken.

calamity *noun*
disaster, catastrophe, mishap, trial, misadventure, mischance, misfortune, adversity, reverse, tribulation, ruin, affliction, distress, tragedy, downfall.
Ea blessing, godsend.

calculate *verb*
compute, work out, count, enumerate, reckon, figure, determine, weigh, rate, value, estimate, gauge, judge, consider, plan, intend, aim.

calculating *adjective*
crafty, cunning, sly, devious, scheming, designing, contriving, sharp, shrewd.
Ea artless, naïve.

calculated *adjective*
considered, deliberate, purposeful, intended, intentional, planned, premeditated.

calibre *noun*
1 guns of different calibres : diameter, bore, gauge, size, measure.
2 candidates of the right calibre : talent, gifts, strength, worth, merit, quality, character, ability, capacity, faculty, stature, distinction.

call *noun*
1 a call for assistance : cry, exclamation, shout, yell, scream.
2 a telephone call/doctor has several calls to make : ring, visit, summons, invitation.
3 calls for his resignation : appeal, request, plea, order, command, claim, announcement, signal.
4 there's no call for it : demand, need, occasion, cause, excuse, justification, reason, grounds, right.
▶ *verb*
1 they call him Bob : name, christen,

baptize, title, entitle, dub, style, term, label, designate.
2 he called her name : shout, yell, exclaim, cry.
3 she called us all in for a meeting : summon, invite, bid, send for, order, convene, assemble.
4 I'll call you later : telephone, phone, ring (up), contact.
◆ **call for 1** calls for drastic action : demand, require, need, necessitate, involve, entail, occasion, suggest.
2 called for me at six o'clock : fetch, collect, pick up.
◆ **call off** cancel, drop, abandon, discontinue, break off, withdraw.

calling *noun*
mission, vocation, career, profession, occupation, job, trade, business, line, work, employment, field, province, pursuit.

callous *adjective*
heartless, hard-hearted, cold, indifferent, uncaring, unsympathetic, unfeeling, insensitive, hardened, thick-skinned.
F3 kind, caring, sympathetic, sensitive.

calm *adjective*
1 told us to remain calm : composed, self-possessed, collected, cool, dispassionate, unemotional, impassive, unmoved, placid, sedate, unflappable, imperturbable, unexcitable, laid-back (*infml*), relaxed, unexcited, unruffled, unflustered, unperturbed, undisturbed, untroubled, unapprehensive.
2 calm waters : smooth, still, windless, unclouded, mild, tranquil, serene, peaceful, quiet, uneventful, restful.
F3 1 excitable, worried, anxious.
2 rough, wild, stormy.
▶ *verb*
compose, soothe, relax, sedate, tranquillize, hush, quieten, placate, pacify.
F3 excite, worry.
▶ *noun*
calmness, stillness, tranquillity, serenity, peacefulness, peace, quiet, hush, repose.
F3 storminess, restlessness.

camouflage *noun*
disguise, guise, masquerade, mask, cloak, screen, blind, front, cover, concealment, deception.
▶ *verb*
disguise, mask, cloak, veil, screen, cover, conceal, hide, obscure.
F3 uncover, reveal.

campaign *noun*
crusade, movement, promotion, drive, push, offensive, attack, battle, expedition, operation.
▶ *verb*
crusade, promote, push, advocate, fight, battle.

cancel *verb*
call off, abort, abandon, drop, abolish, annul, quash, rescind, revoke, repeal, countermand, delete, erase, obliterate, eliminate.
◆ **cancel out** offset, compensate, make up for, counterbalance, neutralize, nullify, wipe out.

candid *adjective*
frank, open, truthful, honest, sincere, forthright, straightforward, ingenuous, guileless, simple, plain, clear, unequivocal, blunt, outspoken.
F3 guarded, evasive, devious.

candidate *noun*
applicant, aspirant, contender, contestant, competitor, entrant, runner, possibility, nominee, claimant, pretender, suitor.

canopy *noun*
awning, covering, shade, shelter, sunshade, umbrella.

canvass *verb*
electioneer, agitate, campaign, solicit, ask for, seek, poll.

canyon *noun*
gorge, ravine, gully, valley, chasm, abyss, defile (*fml*).

capability *noun*
ability, capacity, faculty, power, potential, means, facility, competence, qualification, skill, proficiency, talent.
F3 inability, incompetence.

capable *adjective*
able, competent, efficient, qualified, experienced, accomplished, skilful,

capacity *noun*
1 the capacity of the jug: volume, space, room, size, dimensions, magnitude, extent, compass, range, scope.
2 have the capacity to make people laugh: capability, ability, faculty, power, potential, competence, efficiency, skill, gift, talent, genius, cleverness, intelligence, aptitude, readiness.
3 in her capacity as president: role, function, position, office, post, job, appointment.

cape[1] *noun*
the Cape of Good Hope: headland, head, promontory, point, ness, peninsula.

cape[2] *noun*
a long black cape: cloak, shawl, wrap, robe, poncho, mantle, cope, coat.

capital *noun*
1 the capital of Brazil: most important city, administrative centre, centre of government.
2 write in capitals: block letter, block capital, capital letter, upper-case letter.
3 the capital to start a business: funds, finance, principal, money, cash, savings, investment(s), wealth, means, wherewithal, resources, assets, property, stock.
▶ *adjective*
1 capital cities: principal, important, leading, prime, main, major, chief, foremost.
2 a capital crime: serious, punishable by death.

capitalize on *verb*
profit from, take advantage of, exploit, cash in on (*infml*).

capitulate *verb*
surrender, throw in the towel (*infml*), yield, give in, relent, submit, succumb, fall.
E3 fight on.

capsize *verb*
overturn, turn over, turn turtle, invert, keel over, upset.

capsule *noun*
1 take the medicine in capsule form: pill, tablet, lozenge.
2 a seed capsule/space capsule: receptacle, shell, sheath, pod, module.

captivate *verb*
charm, enchant, bewitch, beguile, fascinate, enthral, hypnotize, mesmerize, lure, allure, seduce, win, attract, enamour, infatuate, enrapture, dazzle.
E3 repel, disgust, appal.

captive *noun*
prisoner, hostage, slave, detainee, internee, convict.
▶ *adjective*
imprisoned, caged, confined, restricted, secure, locked up, enchained, enslaved, ensnared.
E3 free.

captivity *noun*
custody, detention, imprisonment, incarceration, internment, confinement, restraint, bondage, duress, slavery, servitude.
E3 freedom.

capture *verb*
catch, trap, snare, take, seize, nab (*infml*), arrest, apprehend, imprison, secure.

car *noun*
automobile, motor car, motor, vehicle.

care *noun*
1 full of care: worry, anxiety, stress, strain, pressure, concern, trouble, distress, affliction, tribulation, vexation.
2 drive without due care: carefulness, caution, prudence, forethought, vigilance, watchfulness, pains, meticulousness, attention, heed, regard, consideration, interest.
3 in their care: keeping, custody, guardianship, protection, ward, charge, responsibility, control, supervision.
E3 2 carelessness, thoughtlessness, inattention, neglect.
▶ *verb*
worry, mind, bother.
◆ **care for 1** caring for the elderly: look after, nurse, tend, mind, watch over,

protect, minister to, attend.
2 don't care for it much: like, be fond of, love, be keen on, enjoy, delight in, want, desire.

career *noun*
vocation, calling, life-work, occupation, pursuit, profession, trade, job, employment, livelihood.

carefree *adjective*
unworried, untroubled, unconcerned, blithe, breezy, happy-go-lucky, cheery, light-hearted, cheerful, happy, easy-going (*infml*), laid-back (*infml*).
F3 worried, anxious, despondent.

careful *adjective*
1 be careful: cautious, prudent, circumspect (*fml*), judicious (*fml*), wary, chary, vigilant, watchful, alert, attentive, mindful.
2 a careful study: meticulous, painstaking, conscientious, scrupulous, thorough, detailed, punctilious, particular, accurate, precise, thoughtful.
F3 1 careless, inattentive, thoughtless, reckless. **2** careless.

careless *adjective*
1 a careless remark: unthinking, thoughtless, inconsiderate, uncaring, unconcerned, heedless, unmindful, forgetful, remiss, negligent, irresponsible, unguarded.
2 careless work: inaccurate, messy, untidy, disorderly, sloppy, neglectful, slipshod, slapdash, hasty, cursory, offhand, casual.
F3 1 thoughtful, prudent. **2** careful, accurate, meticulous.

caress *verb*
stroke, pet, fondle, cuddle, hug, embrace, kiss, touch, rub.

cargo *noun*
freight, load, pay-load, lading, tonnage, shipment, consignment, contents, goods, merchandise, baggage.

caricature *noun*
cartoon, parody, lampoon, burlesque, satire, send-up, take-off, imitation, representation, distortion, travesty.

carnage *noun*
bloodshed, blood-bath, butchery,
slaughter, killing, murder, massacre, holocaust.

carnival *noun*
festival, fiesta, gala, jamboree, fête, fair, holiday, jubilee, celebration, merrymaking, revelry.

carriage *noun*
1 a railway carriage: coach, wagon, car, vehicle.
2 the charge for carriage: carrying, conveyance, transport, transportation, delivery, postage.

carry *verb*
1 carrying goods/electricity: bring, convey, transport, haul, move, transfer, relay, release, conduct, take, fetch.
2 carried the entire weight: bear, shoulder, support, underpin, maintain, uphold, sustain, suffer, stand.
3 the amendment was carried: pass, vote for, accept, adopt, sanction, ratify.
4 carry a risk: bear, involve, mean, entail.
5 carry the story: cover, contain, display, show, present, communicate, print, broadcast.
6 we don't carry that brand: stock, sell, have, have for sale.
◆ **carry on 1 try to carry on regardless**: continue, proceed, last, endure, maintain, keep on, persist, persevere.
2 carry on a business: operate, run, manage, administer.
3 children carrying on: misbehave, mess about (*infml*), play up (*infml*).
F3 1 stop, finish.
◆ **carry out** do, perform, undertake, discharge, conduct, execute, implement, fulfil, accomplish, achieve, realize, bring off.

cartoon *noun*
comic strip, animation, sketch, drawing, caricature, parody.

cartridge *noun*
cassette, canister, cylinder, tube, container, case, capsule, shell, magazine, round, charge.

carve *verb*
cut, slice, hack, hew, chisel, chip, sculpt, sculpture, shape, form, fashion, mould, etch, engrave, incise, indent.

case¹ *noun*
1 let me carry your case : receptacle, holder, suitcase, trunk.
2 a case of champagne : container, crate, box, carton, casket, chest.
3 a display case : cabinet, showcase.
4 a waterproof/metal case : casing, cartridge, shell, capsule, sheath, cover, jacket, wrapper.

case² *noun*
1 in this case : circumstances, context, state, condition, position, situation, contingency, occurrence, occasion, event.
2 a medical case/a clear case of too much too soon : specimen, example, instance, illustration, point.
3 a legal case : lawsuit, suit, trial, proceedings, action, process, cause, argument, dispute.

cash *noun*
money, hard money, ready money, bank-notes, notes, coins, change, legal tender, currency, hard currency, dough (*infml*), bullion, funds, resources, wherewithal.
▸ *verb*
encash, exchange, realize, liquidate.

cast *verb*
1 casting the seed on the earth : throw, hurl, lob, pitch, fling, toss, sling, shy, launch, impel, drive, direct, project, shed, emit, diffuse, spread, scatter.
2 cast in bronze : mould, shape, form, model, found.
▸ *noun*
1 a cast of thousands : company, troupe, actors, players, performers, entertainers, characters, dramatis personae.
2 make a cast of the footprint : casting, mould, shape, form.

castle *noun*
stronghold, fortress, citadel, keep, tower, château, palace.

casual *adjective*
1 a casual meeting/remark : chance, fortuitous (*fml*), accidental, unintentional, unpremeditated, unexpected, unforeseen, irregular, random, occasional, incidental, superficial, cursory.

2 a casual attitude : nonchalant, blasé, lackadaisical, negligent, couldn't-care-less (*infml*), apathetic, indifferent, unconcerned, informal, offhand, relaxed, laid-back (*infml*).
3 casual work : temporary, irregular, occasional, part-time, short-term.
4 casual clothes : informal, comfortable, relaxed, leisure.
F3 1 deliberate, planned. **2** formal. **3** permanent. **4** formal.

casualty *noun*
injury, loss, death, fatality, victim, sufferer, injured person, wounded, dead person.

cat

Breeds of cat include:
Abyssinian, American shorthair, Balinese, Birman, Bombay, British longhair, British shorthair, Burmese, Carthusian, chinchilla, Cornish rex, Cymric, Devon rex, domestic tabby, Egyptian Mau, Exotic shorthair, Foreign Blue, Foreign spotted shorthair, Foreign White, Havana, Himalayan, Japanese Bobtail, Korat, Maine Coon, Manx, Norwegian Forest, Persian, rag-doll, rex, Russian Blue, Scottish Fold, Siamese, silver tabby, Singapura, Somali, Tiffany, Tonkinese, Tortoiseshell, Turkish Angora, Turkish Van.

catalogue *noun*
list, inventory, roll, register, roster, schedule, record, table, index, directory, gazetteer, brochure, prospectus.

catastrophe *noun*
disaster, calamity, cataclysm, debacle, fiasco, failure, ruin, devastation, tragedy, blow, reverse, mischance, misfortune, adversity, affliction, trouble, upheaval.

catch *noun*
1 the catch on the bracelet : fastener, clip, hook, clasp, hasp, latch, bolt.
2 what's the catch? : disadvantage, drawback, snag, hitch, obstacle, problem.

▶ *verb*

1 catch a ball : seize, grab, take, hold, grasp, grip, clutch.
2 catch a thief : capture, trap, entrap, snare, ensnare, hook, net, arrest, apprehend.
3 Did you catch what he said? : hear, understand, perceive, recognize.
4 try to catch them red-handed : surprise, expose, unmask, find (out), discover, detect, discern.
5 catch a cold : contract, get, develop, go down with.
F3 1 drop. **2** release, free. **3** miss.
◆ **catch up** gain on, draw level with, overtake.

catching *adjective*
infectious, contagious, communicable, transmittable.

catchy *adjective*
memorable, haunting, popular, melodic, tuneful, attractive, captivating.
F3 dull, boring.

categorical *adjective*
absolute, total, utter, unqualified, unreserved, unconditional, downright, positive, definite, emphatic, direct, unequivocal, clear, explicit, express.
F3 tentative, qualified, vague.

category *noun*
class, classification, group, grouping, sort, type, section, division, department, chapter, head, heading, grade, rank, order, list.

cater *verb*
cook, provide, supply, furnish, serve.

catholic *adjective*
broad, wide, wide-ranging, universal, global, general, comprehensive, inclusive, all-inclusive, all-embracing, liberal, tolerant, broad-minded.
F3 narrow, limited, narrow-minded.

cattle *noun*
cows, bulls, oxen, livestock, stock, beasts.

cause *noun*
1 what was the cause of the argument? : source, origin, beginning, root, basis, spring, originator, creator, producer, maker, agent, agency.
2 the causes of war : reason, motive,

grounds, motivation, stimulus, incentive, inducement, impulse.
3 a worthy cause : object, purpose, end, ideal, belief, conviction, movement, undertaking, enterprise.
F3 1 effect, result, consequence.
▶ *verb*
begin, give rise to, lead to, result in, occasion, bring about, effect, produce, generate, create, precipitate (*fml*), motivate, stimulate, provoke, incite, induce, force, compel.
F3 stop, prevent.

caustic *adjective*
corrosive, acid, burning, stinging, biting, cutting, mordant (*fml*), trenchant (*fml*), keen, pungent, bitter, acrimonious, sarcastic, scathing, severe.
F3 soothing, mild.

caution *noun*
1 show a little more caution : care, carefulness, prudence, vigilance, watchfulness, alertness, heed, discretion, forethought, deliberation, wariness.
2 a police caution : warning, caveat, injunction, admonition, advice, counsel.
F3 1 carelessness, recklessness.
▶ *verb*
warn, alert, advise, counsel, forewarn.

cautious *adjective*
careful, prudent, circumspect (*fml*), judicious (*fml*), vigilant, watchful, alert, heedful, discreet, tactful, chary, wary, cagey (*infml*), guarded, tentative, softly-softly, unadventurous.
F3 incautious, imprudent, heedless, reckless.

cave *noun*
cavern, grotto, hole, pothole, hollow, cavity.
◆ **cave in** collapse, subside, give way, yield, fall, slip.

cavity *noun*
hole, gap, dent, hollow, crater, pit, well, sinus, ventricle.

cease *verb*
stop, desist, refrain, pack in (*infml*), halt, call a halt, break off, discontinue,

finish, end, conclude, terminate, fail, die.
ᴇᴤbegin, start, commence.

ceaseless *adjective*
endless, unending, never-ending, eternal, everlasting, continuous, non-stop, incessant, interminable, constant, perpetual, continual, persistent, untiring, unremitting.
ᴇᴤoccasional, irregular.

celebrate *verb*
commemorate, remember, observe, keep, rejoice, toast, drink to, honour, exalt, glorify, praise, extol (*fml*), eulogize (*fml*), commend, bless, solemnize.

celebrated *adjective*
famous, well-known, famed, renowned, illustrious, glorious, eminent, distinguished, notable, prominent, outstanding, popular, acclaimed, exalted, revered.
ᴇᴤunknown, obscure, forgotten.

celebration *noun*
commemoration, remembrance, observance, anniversary, jubilee, festival, gala, merrymaking, jollification, revelry, festivity, party, rave-up (*infml*).

Celebrations include:

anniversary, banquet, baptism, bar mitzvah, birthday, centenary, christening, coming-of-age, commemoration, feast, festival, fête, gala, graduation, harvest festival, homecoming, Independence Day, jubilee, marriage, May Day, name-day, party, reception, remembrance, retirement, reunion, saint's day, thanksgiving, tribute, wedding. ⇨*See also* **party**.

celebrity *noun*
personage, dignitary, VIP (*infml*), luminary, worthy, personality, name, big name, star, superstar.
ᴇᴤnobody, nonentity.

cemetery *noun*
burial-ground, graveyard, churchyard.

censor *verb*
cut, edit, blue-pencil, bowdlerize, expurgate.

censure *noun*
condemnation, blame, disapproval, criticism, admonishment, admonition, reprehension, reproof, reproach, rebuke, reprimand, telling-off (*infml*).
ᴇᴤpraise, compliments, approval.
▶ *verb*
condemn, denounce, blame, criticize, castigate (*fml*), admonish, reprehend (*fml*), reprove, upbraid (*fml*), reproach, rebuke, reprimand, scold, tell off (*infml*).
ᴇᴤpraise, compliment, approve.

central *adjective*
middle, mid, inner, interior, focal, main, chief, key, principal, primary, fundamental, vital, essential, important.
ᴇᴤperipheral, minor, secondary.

centre *noun*
middle, mid-point, bull's-eye, heart, core, nucleus, pivot, hub, focus, crux.
ᴇᴤedge, periphery, outskirts.

ceremonial *adjective*
formal, official, stately, solemn, ritual, ritualistic.
ᴇᴤinformal, casual.

ceremony *noun*
1 *wedding ceremony*: service, rite, commemoration, observance, celebration, function, parade.
2 *without ceremony*: etiquette, protocol, decorum, propriety, formality, form, niceties, ceremonial, ritual, pomp, show.

certain *adjective*
1 *I'm sure he's telling the truth/it's now certain that they will win*: sure, positive, assured, confident, convinced, undoubted, indubitable, convincing, unquestionable, incontrovertible, undeniable, irrefutable, plain, conclusive, absolute, true.
2 *it was certain to happen sometime*: inevitable, unavoidable, bound, fated, destined.
3 *a certain person we both know/below a certain point*: specific, special, particular, individual, precise, express, fixed, established, settled, decided, definite.

4 one of the few certain things in life: dependable, reliable, trustworthy, constant, steady, stable.
F₃ 1 uncertain, unsure, hesitant, doubtful. **2** unlikely. **4** unreliable.

certainly *adverb*
of course, naturally, definitely, for sure, undoubtedly, doubtlessly.

certainty *noun*
sureness, positiveness, assurance, confidence, conviction, faith, trust, truth, validity, fact, reality, inevitability.
F₃ uncertainty, doubt, hesitation.

certificate *noun*
document, award, diploma, qualification, credentials, testimonial, guarantee, endorsement, warrant, licence, authorization, pass, voucher.

certify *verb*
declare, attest (*fml*), aver (*fml*), assure, guarantee, endorse, corroborate, confirm, vouch, testify, witness, verify, authenticate, validate, authorize, license.

chain *noun*
1 prisoners in chains: fetter, manacle, restraint, bond, link, coupling, union.
2 chain of events: sequence, succession, progression, string, train, series, set.
▶ *verb*
tether, fasten, secure, bind, restrain, confine, fetter, shackle, manacle, handcuff, enslave.
F₃ release, free.

challenge *noun*
dare, defiance, confrontation, provocation, test, trial, hurdle, obstacle, question, ultimatum.
▶ *verb*
1 challenge him to fight: dare, defy, throw down the gauntlet, confront, brave, accost, provoke, test, tax, try.
2 challenge the decision: dispute, question, query, protest, object to.

champion *noun*
winner, victor, conqueror, hero, guardian, protector, defender, vindicator, patron, backer, supporter, upholder, advocate.

chance *noun*
1 come across it by chance/take a

chance: accident, fortuity (*fml*), coincidence, fluke (*infml*), luck, fortune, providence, fate, destiny, risk, gamble, speculation.
2 a chance of winning millions: possibility, prospect, probability, likelihood, odds.
3 a second chance: opportunity, opening, occasion, time.
F₃ 1 certainty.
▶ *adjective*
fortuitous (*fml*), casual, accidental, inadvertent, unintentional, unintended, unforeseen, unlooked-for, random, haphazard, incidental.
F₃ deliberate, intentional, foreseen, certain.

change *verb*
1 changing into a butterfly/prices keep changing: alter, modify, convert, reorganize, reform, remodel, restyle, transform, transfigure, metamorphose, mutate, vary, fluctuate, vacillate, shift.
2 change one thing for another: swap, exchange, trade, switch, transpose, substitute, replace, alternate, interchange.
▶ *noun*
alteration, modification, conversion, transformation, metamorphosis, mutation, variation, fluctuation, shift, exchange, transposition, substitution, interchange, difference, diversion, novelty, innovation, variety, transition, revolution, upheaval.

changeable *adjective*
variable, mutable, fluid, kaleidoscopic, shifting, mobile, unsettled, uncertain, unpredictable, unreliable, erratic, irregular, inconstant, fickle, capricious, volatile, unstable, unsteady, wavering, vacillating.
F₃ constant, reliable.

channel *noun*
1 an irrigation channel: duct, conduit, main, groove, furrow, trough, gutter, canal, flume, watercourse, waterway, strait, sound.
2 channel of communication: route, course, path, avenue, way, means, medium, approach, passage.

▶ *verb*
direct, guide, conduct, convey, send, transmit, force.

chaos *noun*
disorder, confusion, disorganization, anarchy, lawlessness, tumult, pandemonium, bedlam.
F3 order.

chaotic *adjective*
disordered, confused, disorganized, topsy-turvy, deranged, anarchic, lawless, riotous, tumultuous, unruly, uncontrolled.
F3 ordered, organized.

chapter *noun*
part, section, division, clause, topic, episode, period, phase, stage.

character *noun*
1 the place has a character all its own : personality, nature, disposition, temperament, temper, constitution, make-up, individuality, peculiarity, feature, attributes, quality, type, stamp, calibre, reputation, status, position, trait.
2 Chinese characters : letter, figure, symbol, sign, mark, type, cipher, rune, hieroglyph, ideograph.
3 a bit of a character : eccentric, oddball (*infml*), case (*infml*).
4 characters in a play : individual, person, sort, type, role, part.

characteristic *noun*
peculiarity, idiosyncrasy, mannerism, feature, trait, attribute, property, quality, hallmark, mark, symptom.
▶ *adjective*
distinctive, distinguishing, individual, idiosyncratic, peculiar, specific, special, typical, representative, symbolic, symptomatic.
F3 uncharacteristic, untypical.

charge *verb*
1 charge a high price : ask, demand, levy, exact, debit.
2 charge him with theft : accuse, indict, impeach, incriminate, blame.
3 charged forward : attack, assail, storm, rush.
▶ *noun*
1 high charges : price, cost, fee, rate, amount, expense, expenditure, outlay, payment.

2 a charge of murder : accusation, indictment, allegation, imputation.
3 the charge of the Light Brigade : attack, assault, onslaught, sortie, rush.
4 in your charge : custody, keeping, care, safekeeping, guardianship, ward, trust, responsibility, duty.

charitable *adjective*
philanthropic, humanitarian, kind, benevolent, benign, compassionate, sympathetic, understanding, considerate, generous, magnanimous, liberal, tolerant, broad-minded, lenient, forgiving, indulgent, gracious.
F3 uncharitable, inconsiderate, unforgiving.

charity *noun*
1 show a bit of charity : generosity, bountifulness, alms-giving, beneficence (*fml*), philanthropy, unselfishness, altruism, benevolence, kindness, goodness, humanity, compassion, tender-heartedness, love, affection, clemency, indulgence.
2 dispense/live on charity : alms, gift, handout, aid, relief, assistance.
F3 **1** selfishness, malice.

charm *noun*
1 have a lot of charm : attraction, allure, magnetism, appeal, desirability, fascination, enchantment, spell, sorcery, magic.
2 lucky charm : trinket, talisman, amulet, fetish, idol.
▶ *verb*
please, delight, enrapture, captivate, fascinate, beguile, enchant, bewitch, mesmerize, attract, allure, cajole, win, enamour.
F3 repel.

charming *adjective*
pleasing, delightful, pleasant, lovely, captivating, enchanting, attractive, fetching, appealing, sweet, winsome, seductive, winning, irresistible.
F3 ugly, unattractive, repulsive.

chart *noun*
diagram, table, graph, map, plan, blueprint.
▶ *verb*
map, map out, sketch, draw, draft, outline, delineate, mark, plot, place.

charter *noun*
right, privilege, prerogative, authorization, permit, licence, franchise, concession, contract, indenture (*fml*), deed, bond, document.
▶ *verb*
hire, rent, lease, commission, engage, employ, authorize, sanction, license.

chase *verb*
pursue, follow, hunt, track, drive, expel, rush, hurry.

chasm *noun*
gap, opening, gulf, abyss, void, hollow, cavity, crater, breach, rift, split, cleft, fissure, crevasse, canyon, gorge, ravine.

chat *noun*
talk, conversation, natter (*infml*), gossip, chinwag (*infml*), tête-à-tête, heart-to-heart, rap (*infml*).
▶ *verb*
talk, crack, natter (*infml*), gossip (*infml*), chatter, rabbit (on) (*infml*).

chatty *adjective*
talkative, gossipy, newsy, friendly, informal, colloquial, familiar.
E3 quiet.

cheap *adjective*
1 a cheap hotel: inexpensive, reasonable, dirt-cheap, bargain, reduced, cut-price, knock-down, budget, economy, economical.
2 a cheap trick/made of cheap materials: tawdry, tatty, cheapo (*infml*), shoddy, inferior, second-rate, worthless, vulgar, common, poor, paltry, mean, contemptible, despicable, low.
E3 1 expensive, costly. **2** superior, noble, admirable.

cheat *verb*
defraud, swindle, diddle, short-change, do (*infml*), rip off (*slang*), fleece, con (*infml*), double-cross, mislead, deceive, dupe, fool, trick, hoodwink, bamboozle (*infml*), beguile.
▶ *noun*
cheater, dodger, fraud, swindler, shark (*infml*), con man (*infml*), extortioner,

double-crosser, impostor, charlatan, deceiver, trickster, rogue.

check *verb*
1 check the brakes/his work/the figures: examine, inspect, scrutinize, give the once-over (*infml*), investigate, probe, test, monitor, study, research, compare, cross-check, confirm, verify.
2 checked its progress: curb, bridle, restrain, control, limit, repress, inhibit, damp, thwart, hinder, impede, obstruct, bar, retard, delay, stop, arrest, halt.
▶ *noun*
1 a health check: examination, inspection, scrutiny, once-over (*infml*), check-up, investigation, audit, test, research.
2 a check on growth: curb, restraint, control, limitation, constraint, inhibition, damper, blow, disappointment, reverse, setback, frustration, hindrance, impediment, obstruction, stoppage.

cheeky *adjective* (*infml*)
impertinent, impudent, insolent, disrespectful, forward, brazen, pert, saucy (*infml*), audacious.
E3 respectful, polite.

cheer *verb*
1 cheering their team: acclaim, hail, clap, applaud.
2 cheered by the news: comfort, console, brighten, gladden, warm, uplift, elate, exhilarate, encourage, hearten.
E3 1 boo, jeer. **2** dishearten.
▶ *noun*
acclamation, hurrah, bravo, applause, ovation.
◆ **cheer up** encourage, hearten, take heart, rally, buck up (*infml*), perk up (*infml*).

cheerful *adjective*
happy, glad, contented, joyful, joyous, blithe, carefree, light-hearted, cheery, good-humoured, sunny, optimistic, enthusiastic, hearty, genial, jovial, jolly, merry, lively, animated, bright, chirpy, breezy, jaunty, buoyant, sparkling, upbeat (*infml*).
E3 sad, dejected, depressed.

chemistry

Terms used in chemistry include:

acid, alkali, analytical chemistry, atom, atomic number, atomic structure, base, biochemistry, bond, buffer, catalysis, catalyst, chain reaction, chemical bond, chemical compound, chemical element, chemical equation, chemical reaction, chemist, chlorination, combustion, compound, corrosion, covalent bond, crystal, cycle, decomposition, diffusion, dissociation, distillation, electrochemical cell, electrode, electron, electrolysis, emulsion, fermentation, fixation, formula, free radical, gas, halogen, hydrolysis, immiscible, inert gas, inorganic chemistry, ion, ionic bond, isomer, isotope, lipid, liquid, litmus paper, litmus test, mass, matter, metallic bond, mixture, mole, molecule, neutron, noble gas, nucleus, organic chemistry, oxidation, periodic table, pH, physical chemistry, polymer, proton, radioactivity, reaction, reduction, respiration, salt, solids, solution, solvent, subatomic particles, substance, suspension, symbol, synthesis, valency.

chew verb
masticate (*fml*), gnaw, munch, champ, crunch, grind.

chief adjective
leading, foremost, uppermost, highest, supreme, grand, arch, premier, principal, main, key, central, prime, prevailing, predominant, pre-eminent, outstanding, vital, essential, primary, major.
minor, unimportant.
▶ noun
ruler, chieftain, lord, master, supremo, head, principal, leader, commander, captain, governor, boss, director, manager, superintendent, superior, ringleader.

chiefly adverb
mainly, mostly, for the most part, predominantly, principally, primarily, essentially, especially, generally, usually.

child noun
youngster, kid (*infml*), nipper (*infml*), brat (*infml*), baby, infant, toddler, tot (*infml*), minor, juvenile, offspring, issue, progeny (*fml*), descendant.

childhood noun
babyhood, infancy, boyhood, girlhood, schooldays, youth, adolescence, minority, immaturity.

childish adjective
babyish, boyish, girlish, infantile, puerile (*fml*), juvenile, immature, silly, foolish, frivolous.
mature, sensible.

childlike adjective
innocent, naïve, ingenuous, artless, guileless, credulous, trusting, trustful, simple, natural.

chill verb
1 chill the fruit salad: cool, refrigerate, freeze, ice.
2 chilled by his threatening tone: frighten, terrify, dismay, dishearten, discourage, depress, dampen.
1 warm, heat.

chilly adjective
1 chilly weather: cold, fresh, brisk, crisp, nippy (*infml*), wintry.
2 a chilly response: cool, frigid, unsympathetic, unwelcoming, aloof, stony, unfriendly, hostile.
1 warm. 2 friendly.

chink noun
crack, rift, cleft, fissure, crevice, slot, opening, aperture, gap, space.

chip noun
1 chips on the paintwork: notch, nick, scratch, dent, flaw.
2 wood chips: fragment, scrap, wafer, sliver, flake, shaving, paring.

choice noun
option, alternative, selection, variety, pick, preference, say, decision, dilemma, election, discrimination, choosing, opting.
▶ adjective
best, superior, prime, plum, excellent, fine, exquisite, exclusive, select, hand-

picked, special, prize, valuable,
precious.
F3 inferior, poor.

choke *verb*
1 tried to choke her: throttle, strangle,
asphyxiate, suffocate, stifle, smother,
suppress.
2 leaves choking the gutters: obstruct,
constrict, congest, clog, block, dam,
bar, close, stop.
3 smoke made him choke: cough, gag,
retch.

choose *verb*
pick, select, single out, designate,
predestine, opt for, plump for, vote for,
settle on, fix on, adopt, elect, prefer,
wish, desire, see fit.

choosy *adjective* (*infml*)
selective, discriminating, picky (*infml*),
fussy, particular, finicky, fastidious,
exacting.
F3 undemanding.

chop *verb*
cut, hack, hew, lop, sever, truncate,
cleave, divide, split, slash.
◆ **chop up** cut (up), slice (up), divide,
cube, dice, mince.

christen *verb*
baptize, name, call, dub, title, style,
term, designate, inaugurate, use.

chronic *adjective*
1 a chronic illness/shortage/liar:
incurable, deep-seated, recurring,
incessant, persistent, inveterate,
confirmed, habitual, ingrained, deep-
rooted.
2 (*infml*) his singing was chronic:
awful, terrible, dreadful, appalling,
atrocious.
F3 **1** acute, temporary.

chubby *adjective*
plump, podgy, fleshy, flabby, stout,
portly, rotund, round, tubby,
paunchy.
F3 slim, skinny.

chuckle *verb*
laugh, giggle, titter, snigger, chortle,
snort, crow.

chunk *noun*
lump, hunk, mass, wodge (*infml*),
wedge, block, slab, piece, portion.

church *noun*
chapel, house of God, cathedral,
minster, abbey, temple.

*Names of church services
include:*

baptism, christening, Christingle,
communion, confirmation,
dedication, Eucharist, evening
service, evensong, funeral, High
Mass, Holy Communion, Holy
Matrimony, Lord's Supper, marriage,
Mass, memorial service, Midnight
Mass, morning prayers, morning
service, nuptial Mass, Requiem Mass,
Vigil Mass.

cinema *noun*
1 interested in cinema: films, pictures,
movies (*infml*), big screen.
2 go to the local cinema: picture-house,
multiplex, fleapit (*infml*), flicks (*slang*).

circle *noun*
1 draw a circle/move in circles: ring,
hoop, loop, round, disc, sphere, globe,
orb, cycle, turn, revolution, circuit, orbit,
circumference, perimeter, coil, spiral.
2 circle of friends: group, band,
company, crowd, set, clique, coterie,
club, society, fellowship, fraternity.
▸ *verb*
1 belt circling her waist/circle the
globe: ring, loop, encircle, surround,
gird, encompass, enclose, hem in,
circumscribe, circumnavigate.
2 circling faster and faster: rotate,
revolve, pivot, gyrate, whirl, turn, coil,
wind.

circuit *noun*
lap, orbit, revolution, tour, journey,
course, route, track, round, beat,
district, area, region, circumference,
boundary, bounds, limit, range,
compass, ambit.

circuitous *adjective*
roundabout, indirect, oblique, devious,
tortuous, winding, meandering,
rambling, labyrinthine.
F3 direct, straight.

circular *adjective*
round, annular, ring-shaped, hoop-
shaped, disc-shaped.

▶ *noun*
handbill, leaflet, pamphlet, notice, announcement, advertisement, letter.

circulate *verb*
spread, diffuse, broadcast, publicize, publish, issue, propagate, pass round, distribute.

circumference *noun*
circuit, perimeter, rim, edge, outline, boundary, border, bounds, limits, extremity, margin, verge, fringe, periphery.

circumstances *noun*
details, particulars, facts, items, elements, factors, conditions, state, state of affairs, situation, position, status, lifestyle, means, resources.

cite *verb*
quote, name, specify, enumerate, mention, refer to, advance, bring up.

citizen *noun*
city-dweller, townsman, townswoman, inhabitant, denizen, resident, householder, taxpayer, subject.

city *noun*
metropolis, town, municipality, conurbation.

civic *adjective*
city, urban, municipal, borough, community, local, public, communal.

civil *adjective*
1 he was very civil to me: polite, courteous, well-mannered, well-bred, courtly, refined, civilized, polished, urbane, affable, complaisant, obliging, accommodating.
2 civil affairs: domestic, home, national, internal, interior, state, municipal, civic.
F₃ 1 uncivil, discourteous, rude. 2 international, military.

civilization *noun*
progress, advancement, development, education, enlightenment, cultivation, culture, refinement, sophistication, urbanity.
F₃ barbarity, primitiveness.

civilize *verb*
tame, humanize, educate, enlighten, cultivate, refine, polish, sophisticate, improve, perfect.

civilized *adjective*
advanced, developed, educated, enlightened, cultured, refined, sophisticated, urbane, polite, sociable.
F₃ uncivilized, barbarous, primitive.

claim *verb*
1 claimed he had been cheating: allege, pretend, profess, state, affirm, assert, maintain, contend, hold (*fml*), insist.
2 claim a refund: ask, request, require, need, demand, exact, take, collect.

clammy *adjective*
damp, moist, sweaty, sweating, sticky, slimy, dank, muggy, heavy, close.

clamp *noun*
vice, grip, press, brace, bracket, fastener.
▶ *verb*
fasten, secure, fix, clinch, grip, brace.

clan *noun*
tribe, family, house, race, society, brotherhood, fraternity, sect, faction, group, band, set, clique.

clap *verb*
1 clapped as he took a bow: applaud, acclaim, cheer.
2 clapping him on the back: slap, smack, pat, wallop (*infml*), whack (*infml*), bang.

clarify *verb*
explain, throw light on, illuminate, elucidate, gloss, define, simplify, resolve, clear up.
F₃ obscure, confuse.

clarity *noun*
clearness, transparency, lucidity, simplicity, intelligibility, comprehensibility, explicitness, unambiguousness, obviousness, definition, precision.
F₃ obscurity, vagueness, imprecision.

clash *noun*
1 the clash of the cymbals: crash, bang, jangle, clatter, noise.
2 a clash with the police: conflict, confrontation, showdown, fight, disagreement, brush.

clasp *noun*
fastener, buckle, clip, pin, hasp, hook, catch.

▶ *verb*

hold, grip, grasp, clutch, embrace, enfold, hug, squeeze, press.

class *noun*

1 a class of people/animals/plants: category, classification, group, set, section, division, department, sphere, grouping, order, league, rank, status, caste, quality, grade, type, genre, sort, kind, species, genus, style.
2 a geography class: lesson, lecture, seminar, tutorial, course.

▶ *verb*

categorize, classify, group, sort, rank, grade, rate, designate, brand.

classic *adjective*

typical, characteristic, standard, regular, usual, traditional, time-honoured, established, archetypal, model, exemplary, ideal, best, finest, first-rate, definitive, masterly, excellent, ageless, immortal, undying, lasting, enduring, abiding.
F3 unrepresentative, second-rate.

classical *adjective*

elegant, refined, pure, traditional, excellent, well-proportioned, symmetrical, harmonious, restrained.
F3 modern, inferior.

classify *verb*

categorize, class, group, pigeonhole, sort, grade, rank, arrange, dispose, distribute, systematize, codify, tabulate, file, catalogue.

clean *adjective*

1 clean laundry/a clean record: washed, laundered, sterile, aseptic, antiseptic, hygienic, sanitary, sterilized, decontaminated, purified, pure, unadulterated, fresh, unpolluted, uncontaminated, immaculate, spotless, unstained, unsoiled, unsullied, perfect, faultless, flawless, unblemished.
2 a clean life: innocent, guiltless, virtuous, upright, moral, honest, honourable, respectable, decent, chaste.
3 clean lines: smooth, regular, straight, neat, tidy.
F3 1 dirty, polluted. **2** dishonourable, indecent. **3** rough.

▶ *verb*

wash, bath, launder, rinse, wipe, sponge, scrub, scour, mop, swab, sweep, vacuum, dust, freshen, deodorize, cleanse, purge, purify, decontaminate, disinfect, sanitize, sterilize, clear, filter.
F3 dirty, defile (*fml*).

clear *adjective*

1 is that clear?: plain, distinct, patent, comprehensible, intelligible, coherent, lucid, explicit, precise, unambiguous, well-defined, apparent, evident, obvious, manifest, conspicuous, unmistakable, unquestionable.
2 clear about his instructions: sure, certain, positive, definite, convinced.
3 clear water/clear glass: transparent, limpid, crystalline, glassy, see-through, clean, unclouded, colourless.
4 a clear day: cloudless, unclouded, fine, bright, sunny, light.
5 the road was clear: unobstructed, unblocked, open, free, empty, unhindered, unimpeded.
6 his voice was clear: audible, perceptible, pronounced, distinct, recognizable.
F3 1 unclear, vague, ambiguous, confusing. **2** unsure, muddled. **3** opaque, cloudy. **4** dull. **5** blocked. **6** inaudible, indistinct.

▶ *verb*

1 clear the drain/a path: unblock, unclog, decongest, free, rid, extricate, disentangle, loosen.
2 clear the windscreen/decks: clean, wipe, erase, cleanse, refine, tidy, empty.
3 cleared of all charges: acquit, exculpate (*fml*), exonerate, absolve, vindicate, excuse, justify, free, liberate, release, let go.
F3 1 block. **2** dirty, defile (*fml*). **3** condemn.

◆ **clear up 1** clear up the misunderstanding: explain, clarify, elucidate, unravel, solve, resolve, answer.
2 clear up the mess: tidy, order, sort, rearrange, remove.

clergyman *noun*

churchman, cleric, ecclesiastic (*fml*), divine, man of God, minister, priest, reverend, father, vicar, pastor, padre, parson, rector, canon, dean, deacon, chaplain, curate, presbyter, rabbi.

clerical *adjective*
office, secretarial, white-collar, administrative.

clever *adjective*
intelligent, brainy (*infml*), bright, smart, witty, gifted, expert, knowledgeable, adroit, apt, able, capable, quick, quick-witted, sharp, keen, shrewd, knowing, discerning, cunning, ingenious, inventive, resourceful, sensible, rational.
F3 foolish, stupid, senseless, ignorant.

cliché *noun*
platitude, commonplace, banality, truism, chestnut, stereotype.

client *noun*
customer, patron, regular, buyer, shopper, consumer, user, patient, applicant.

cliff *noun*
bluff, face, rock-face, scar, scarp, escarpment, crag, overhang, precipice.

climate *noun*
weather, temperature, setting, milieu, environment, ambience, atmosphere, feeling, mood, temper, disposition, tendency, trend.

climax *noun*
culmination, height, high point, highlight, acme, zenith, peak, summit, top, head.
F3 nadir, low point.

climb *verb*
ascend, scale, shin up, clamber, mount, rise, soar, top.
♦ **climb down** retract, eat one's words, back down, retreat.

cling *verb*
clasp, clutch, grasp, grip, stick, adhere, cleave, fasten, embrace, hug.

clip *verb*
trim, snip, cut, prune, pare, shear, crop, dock, poll, truncate, curtail, shorten, abbreviate.

clique *noun*
circle, set, coterie, group, bunch, pack, gang, crowd, faction, clan.

cloak *noun*
cape, mantle, robe, wrap, coat, cover, shield, mask, front, pretext.

clog *verb*
block, choke, stop up, bung up, dam, congest, jam, obstruct, impede, hinder, hamper, burden.
F3 unblock.

close[1] *verb* /klohz/
1 close the gate: shut, fasten, secure, lock, bar, obstruct, block, clog, plug, cork, stop up.
2 closing the meeting: end, finish, complete, conclude, terminate, wind up, stop, cease.
F3 1 open, separate. **2** start.
▶ *noun*
the close of play: end, finish, completion, conclusion, culmination, ending, finale, dénouement, termination, cessation, stop, pause.

close[2] *adjective* /klohs/
1 a close neighbour: near, nearby, at hand, neighbouring, adjacent, adjoining.
2 Christmas is very close: impending, imminent.
3 a close friend/we're very close: intimate, dear, familiar, attached, devoted, loving.
4 it's close in here: oppressive, heavy, muggy, humid, sultry, sweltering, airless, stifling, suffocating, stuffy, unventilated.
5 close with money: miserly, mean, parsimonious, tight (*infml*), stingy, niggardly.
6 they're very close about their activities: secretive, uncommunicative, taciturn, private, secret, confidential.
7 a close match/translation: exact, precise, accurate, strict, literal, faithful.
8 pay close attention: fixed, intense, concentrated, keen.
9 a close weave: dense, solid, packed, cramped.
F3 1, 2 far, distant. **3** cool, unfriendly. **4** fresh, airy. **5** generous. **6** open. **7** rough.

clot *verb*
coalesce, curdle, coagulate, congeal, thicken, solidify, set, gel.

clothes *noun*
clothing, garments, wear, attire, garb,

gear (*infml*), togs (*infml*), outfit, get-up (*infml*), dress, costume, wardrobe, vestments.

Clothes include:

caftan, dinner-gown, evening dress, frock, kimono, sari, shirtwaister; culottes, dirndl, divided skirt, kilt, mini skirt, pencil skirt, pinafore skirt, sarong; blouse, boiled shirt, cardigan, dress shirt, fleece, guernsey, jersey, jumper, polo neck, polo shirt, pullover, shirt, smock, sweater, sweat-shirt, tabard, tank top, tee-shirt, T-shirt, tunic, turtleneck, twinset, waistcoat; bell-bottoms, Bermuda shorts, breeches, Capri pants, cargo pants, combat trousers, cords, denims, drainpipes, dungarees, flannels, hipsters, hot pants, jeans, jodhpurs, Levis®, 501s®, leggings, palazzo pants, pedal-pushers, plus-fours, shorts, slacks; boiler suit, catsuit (*US*), coveralls, double-breasted jacket, dress suit, jumpsuit, leisure suit, lounge suit, morning suit, overall, shell suit, single-breasted jacket, three-piece suit, trouser suit, tracksuit, wet suit; basque, body stocking, bra, brassière, briefs, camiknickers, camisole, corset, French knickers, girdle, garter, g-string, hosiery, liberty bodice, lingerie, panties, pantihose, pants, petticoat, shift, slip, stockings, suspender belt, suspenders, teddy, thong, tights; boxer-shorts or boxers, singlet, string vest, underpants, vest, Y-fronts; bathing costume, bikini, leotard, salopette, swimming costume, swimming trunks, swimsuit; bed-jacket, bedsocks, dressing-gown, housecoat, negligee, nightdress, nightie (*infml*), nightshirt, pyjamas; anorak, biker jacket, blazer, bomber jacket, cagoule, duffel coat, jacket, overcoat, mac (*infml*), parka, raincoat; belt, bow tie, braces, cravat, cummerbund, earmuffs, glove, leg warmers, mitten, muffler, necktie, pashmina, scarf, shahtoosh, shrug, shawl, sock, stole, tie; burka, veil, yashmak.

cloud *noun*
vapour, haze, mist, fog, gloom, darkness, obscurity.

Types of cloud include:

altocumulus, altostratus, cirrocumulus, cirrostratus, cirrus, cumulonimbus, cumulus, fractocumulus, fractostratus, nimbostratus, stratocumulus, stratus.

▶ *verb*
mist, fog, blur, dull, dim, darken, shade, shadow, overshadow, eclipse, veil, shroud, obscure, muddle, confuse, obfuscate (*fml*).
🖅 clear.

cloudy *adjective*
nebulous, hazy, misty, foggy, blurred, blurry, opaque, milky, muddy, dim, indistinct, obscure, dark, murky, sombre, leaden, lowering, overcast, dull, sunless.
🖅 clear, bright, sunny, cloudless.

club *noun*
1 be a member of a club: association, society, company, league, guild, order, union, fraternity, group, set, circle, clique.
2 carrying a heavy club: bat, stick, mace, bludgeon, truncheon, cosh (*infml*), cudgel.

clue *noun*
hint, tip, suggestion, idea, notion, lead, tip-off, pointer, sign, indication, evidence, trace, suspicion, inkling, intimation.

clump *noun*
cluster, bundle, bunch, mass, tuft, thicket.

clumsy *adjective*
bungling, ham-fisted, unhandy, unskilful, inept, bumbling, blundering, lumbering, gauche, ungainly, gawky (*infml*), unco-ordinated, awkward, ungraceful, uncouth, rough, crude, ill-made, shapeless, unwieldy, heavy, bulky, cumbersome.
🖅 careful, graceful, elegant.

cluster *noun*
bunch, clump, batch, group, knot, mass, crowd, gathering, collection, assembly.

▸ *verb*
bunch, group, gather, collect,
assemble, flock.

clutch *verb*
hold, clasp, grip, hang on to, grasp,
seize, snatch, grab, catch, grapple,
embrace.

clutter *noun*
litter, mess, jumble, untidiness,
disorder, disarray, muddle, confusion.
▸ *verb*
litter, encumber, fill, cover, strew,
scatter.

coach *noun*
trainer, instructor, tutor, teacher.
▸ *verb*
train, drill, instruct, teach, tutor, cram,
prepare.

coalition *noun*
merger, amalgamation, combination,
integration, fusion, alliance, league,
bloc, compact, federation,
confederation, confederacy,
association, affiliation, union.

coarse *adjective*
1 coarse cloth: rough, unpolished,
unfinished, uneven, lumpy,
unpurified, unrefined, unprocessed.
2 coarse humour: bawdy, ribald,
earthy, smutty, vulgar, crude, offensive,
foul-mouthed, boorish, loutish, rude,
impolite, indelicate, improper,
indecent, immodest.
🔁 1 smooth, fine. 2 refined,
sophisticated, polite.

coast *noun*
coastline, seaboard, shore, beach,
seaside.
▸ *verb*
free-wheel, glide, slide, sail, cruise,
drift.

coat *noun*
1 the fox's coat turns white: fur, hair,
fleece, pelt, hide, skin.
2 a coat of paint: layer, coating,
covering.
▸ *verb*
cover, paint, spread, smear, plaster.

coax *verb*
persuade, cajole, wheedle, sweet-talk
(*infml*), soft-soap, flatter, beguile,
allure, entice, tempt.

code *noun*
1 a code of conduct: ethics, rules,
regulations, principles, system,
custom, convention, etiquette,
manners.
2 written in code: cipher, secret
language.

coherent *adjective*
articulate, intelligible, comprehensible,
meaningful, lucid, consistent, logical,
reasoned, rational, sensible, orderly,
systematic, organized.
🔁 incoherent, unintelligible,
meaningless.

coil *verb*
wind, spiral, convolute, curl, loop,
twist, writhe, snake, wreathe, twine,
entwine.
▸ *noun*
roll, curl, loop, ring, convolution,
spiral, corkscrew, helix, twist.

coin *verb*
invent, make up, think up, conceive,
devise, formulate, originate, create,
fabricate, produce.
▸ *noun*
piece, bit, money, cash, change, small
change, loose change, silver, copper.

coincide *verb*
coexist, synchronize, agree, concur,
correspond, square, tally, accord,
harmonize, match.

coincidence *noun*
chance, accident, eventuality, fluke
(*infml*), luck, fortuity (*fml*).

coincidental *adjective*
chance, accidental, casual,
unintentional, unplanned, flukey
(*infml*), lucky, fortuitous (*fml*).
🔁 deliberate, planned.

cold *adjective*
1 a cold bedroom/cold outside:
unheated, cool, chilled, chilly, chill,
shivery, nippy, parky (*infml*), raw,
biting, bitter, wintry, frosty, icy, glacial,
freezing, frozen, arctic, polar.
2 cold and distant: unsympathetic,
unmoved, unfeeling, stony, frigid,
unfriendly, distant, aloof, standoffish,
reserved, undemonstrative,
unresponsive, indifferent, lukewarm.
🔁 1 hot, warm. 2 friendly, responsive.

▶ *noun*

coldness, chill, chilliness, coolness, frigidity, iciness.

F3 warmth.

collaborate *verb*

conspire, collude, work together, co-operate, join forces, team up, participate.

collapse *verb*

1 collapse with exhaustion: faint, pass out, crumple.

2 collapse in ruins: fall, sink, founder, fail, fold (*infml*), fall apart, disintegrate, crumble, subside, cave in.

▶ *noun*

failure, breakdown, flop, debacle, downfall, ruin, disintegration, subsidence, cave-in, faint, exhaustion.

colleague *noun*

workmate, co-worker, team-mate, partner, collaborator, ally, associate, confederate, confrère, comrade, companion, aide, helper, assistant, auxiliary.

collect *verb*

gather, assemble, congregate, convene, muster, rally, converge, cluster, aggregate, accumulate, amass, heap, hoard, stockpile, save, acquire, obtain, secure.

F3 disperse, scatter.

collected *adjective*

composed, self-possessed, placid, serene, calm, unruffled, unperturbed, imperturbable, cool.

F3 anxious, worried, agitated.

collection *noun*

1 a strange collection of people: gathering, assembly, convocation (*fml*), congregation, crowd, group, cluster.

2 a museum collection/a collection of small objects: accumulation, hoard, conglomeration, mass, heap, pile, stockpile, store.

3 a collection of poems: set, assemblage, assortment, anthology, compilation.

collective *adjective*

united, combined, concerted, co-operative, joint, common, shared, corporate, democratic, composite, aggregate, cumulative.

F3 individual.

collective nouns

Collective nouns (by animal) include:

shrewdness of apes, cete of badgers, sloth of bears, swarm of bees, obstinacy of buffaloes, clowder of cats, drove of cattle, brood of chickens, bask of crocodiles, murder of crows, herd of deer, pack of dogs, school of dolphins, dole of doves, team of ducks, parade of elephants, busyness of ferrets, charm of finches, shoal of fish, skulk of foxes, army of frogs, gaggle/skein of geese, tribe of goats, husk of hares, cast of hawks, brood of hens, bloat of hippopotamuses, string of horses, pack of hounds, troop of kangaroos, kindle of kittens, exaltation of larks, leap of leopards, pride of lions, swarm of locusts, tittering of magpies, troop of monkeys, watch of nightingales, family of otters, parliament of owls, pandemonium of parrots, covey of partridges, muster of peacocks, rookery of penguins, nye of pheasants, litter of pigs, school of porpoises, bury of rabbits, colony of rats, unkindness of ravens, crash of rhinoceroses, building of rooks, pod of seals, flock of sheep, murmuration of starlings, ambush of tigers, rafter of turkeys, turn of turtles, gam of whales, rout of wolves, descent of woodpeckers, zeal of zebras.

collectors and enthusiasts

Names of collectors and enthusiasts include:

zoophile (animals), antiquary (antiques), tegestollogist (beer mats), campanologist (bell-ringing), ornithologist (birds), bibliophile (books), audiophile (broadcast and recorded sound), lepidopterist (butterflies), cartophilist (cigarette cards), numismatist (coins/medals), conservationist (countryside), environmentalist (the environment), xenophile (foreigners), gourmet (good food), gastronome (good-living), discophile (gramophone records), chirographist (hand-writing), hippophile (horses), entomologist (insects), phillumenist (matches/matchboxes), monarchist (the monarchy), deltiologist (postcards), arachnologist (spiders/arachnids), philatelist (stamps), arctophile (teddy bears), etymologist (words).

collide *verb*
crash, bump, smash, clash, conflict, confront, meet.

collision *noun*
impact, crash, bump, smash, accident, pile-up, clash, conflict, confrontation, opposition.

colloquial *adjective*
conversational, informal, familiar, everyday, vernacular, idiomatic.
🖃 formal.

colony *noun*
settlement, outpost, dependency, dominion, possession, territory, province.

colossal *adjective*
huge, enormous, immense, vast, massive, gigantic, mammoth, monstrous, monumental.
🖃 tiny, minute.

colour *noun*
1 all the colours of the rainbow/lose its colour: hue, shade, tinge, tone, tincture, tint, dye, paint, wash, pigment, pigmentation, coloration, complexion.
2 put colour in her cheeks: rosiness, ruddiness, glow.

The range of colours includes:
red, crimson, scarlet, vermilion, cherry, cerise, magenta, maroon, burgundy, ruby, orange, tangerine, apricot, coral, salmon, peach, amber, brown, chestnut, mahogany, bronze, auburn, rust, copper, cinnamon, chocolate, tan, sepia, taupe, beige, fawn, yellow, lemon, canary, ochre, saffron, topaz, gold, chartreuse, green, eau de nil, emerald, jade, bottle, avocado, sage, khaki, turquoise, aquamarine, cobalt, blue, sapphire, gentian, indigo, navy, violet, purple, mauve, plum, lavender, lilac, pink, rose, magnolia, cream, ecru, milky, white, grey, silver, charcoal, ebony, jet, black.

▶ *verb*
1 colouring her drawing: paint, crayon, dye, tint, stain, tinge.
2 she coloured when he complimented her: blush, flush, redden.
3 colour one's judgement: affect, bias, prejudice, distort, pervert, exaggerate, falsify.

colourful *adjective*
1 colourful robes: multicoloured, kaleidoscopic, variegated, vivid, bright, brilliant, rich, intense.
2 a colourful description: vivid, graphic, picturesque, lively, stimulating, exciting, interesting.
🖃 **1** colourless, drab.

colourless *adjective*
1 colourless liquid/complexion: transparent, clear, neutral, bleached, washed out, faded, pale, pallid, ashen, sickly, anaemic.
2 a colourless performance: insipid, lacklustre, dull, dreary, drab, plain, characterless, unmemorable, uninteresting, tame.
🖃 **1** colourful. **2** bright, exciting.

column *noun*
1 a column of marble: pillar, post, shaft, upright, support, obelisk.
2 a column of figures/tanks: list, line, row, rank, file, procession, queue, string.

comb *verb*
1 comb one's hair: groom, neaten, tidy, untangle.
2 combing the countryside: search, hunt, scour, sweep, sift, screen, rake, rummage, ransack.

combat *noun*
war, warfare, hostilities, action, battle, fight, skirmish, struggle, conflict, clash, encounter, engagement, contest, bout, duel.
▶ *verb*
fight, battle, strive, struggle, contend,

contest, oppose, resist, withstand, defy.

combine *verb*
merge, amalgamate, unify, blend, mix, integrate, incorporate, synthesize, compound, fuse, bond, bind, join, connect, link, marry, unite, pool, associate, co-operate.
F∃ divide, separate, detach.

come *verb*
advance, move towards, approach, near, draw near, reach, attain, arrive, enter, appear, materialize, happen, occur.
F∃ go, depart, leave.
◆ **come about** happen, occur, come to pass, transpire, result, arise.
◆ **come across** find, discover, chance upon, happen upon, bump into, meet, encounter, notice.
◆ **come along** arrive, happen, develop, improve, progress, rally, mend, recover, recuperate.
◆ **come apart** disintegrate, fall to bits, break, separate, split, tear.
◆ **come between** separate, part, divide, split up, disunite, estrange, alienate.
◆ **come down** descend, fall, reduce, decline, deteriorate, worsen, degenerate.
◆ **come in** enter, appear, show up (*infml*), arrive, finish.
◆ **come off** happen, occur, take place, succeed.
◆ **come on** begin, appear, advance, proceed, progress, develop, improve, thrive, succeed.
◆ **come out** result, end, conclude, terminate.
◆ **come out with** say, state, affirm, declare, exclaim, disclose, divulge.
◆ **come round 1** come round from the anaesthetic: recover, wake, awake.
2 with a little gentle persuasion, he'll probably come round: yield, relent, concede, allow, grant, accede.
◆ **come through** endure, withstand, survive, prevail, triumph, succeed, accomplish, achieve.
◆ **come up** rise, arise, happen, occur, crop up.

comedy *noun*
farce, slapstick, clowning, hilarity, drollery, humour, wit, joking, jesting, facetiousness.

comfort *verb*
ease, soothe, relieve, alleviate, assuage (*fml*), console, cheer, gladden, reassure, hearten, encourage, invigorate, strengthen, enliven, refresh.
▶ *noun*
1 no comfort to him/you've been a great comfort: consolation, compensation, cheer, reassurance, encouragement, alleviation, relief, help, aid, support.
2 live in comfort/all the comforts of home: ease, relaxation, luxury, snugness, cosiness, well-being, satisfaction, contentment, enjoyment.
F∃ 1 distress. **2** discomfort.

comfortable *adjective*
1 a comfortable bed/pair of shoes: snug, cosy, comfy (*infml*), relaxing, restful, easy, convenient, pleasant, agreeable, enjoyable, delightful.
2 comfortable with the decision: at ease, relaxed, contented, happy.
3 a comfortable living: affluent, well-off, well-to-do, prosperous.
F∃ 1 uncomfortable, unpleasant. **2** uneasy, nervous. **3** poor.

comic *adjective*
funny, hilarious, side-splitting, comical, droll, humorous, witty, amusing, entertaining, diverting, joking, facetious, light, farcical, ridiculous, ludicrous, absurd, laughable, priceless (*infml*), rich (*infml*).
F∃ tragic, serious.

command *noun*
1 give the command: commandment, decree, edict, precept (*fml*), mandate, order, bidding, charge, injunction, directive, direction, instruction, requirement.
2 be in command: power, authority, leadership, control, domination, dominion, rule, sway, government, management.
▶ *verb*
1 commanded that they stop: order, bid, charge, enjoin, direct, instruct,

require, demand, compel.
2 commanding the army: lead, head, rule, reign, govern, control, dominate, manage, supervise.

commemorate *verb*
celebrate, solemnize, remember, memorialize, mark, honour, salute, immortalize, observe, keep.

commend *verb*
1 commend his bravery: praise, compliment, acclaim, extol (*fml*), applaud, approve, recommend.
2 commend them to God: commit, entrust, confide, consign, deliver, yield.
F∃ 1 criticize, censure.

comment *noun*
statement, remark, observation, note, annotation, footnote, explanation, elucidation, illustration, exposition, commentary, criticism.
▶ *verb*
say, mention, interpose, interject, remark, observe, note.

commentary *noun*
narration, voice-over, analysis, description, review, critique, explanation, notes, treatise.

commentator *noun*
sportscaster, broadcaster, reporter, narrator, critic, annotator, interpreter.

commerce *noun*
trade, traffic, business, dealings, relations, dealing, trafficking, exchange, marketing, merchandising.

commercial *adjective*
trade, trading, business, sales, profit-making, profitable, sellable, saleable, popular, monetary, financial, mercenary, venal.

commission *noun*
1 undertake a commission: assignment, mission, errand, task, job, duty, function, appointment, employment, mandate, warrant, authority, charge, trust.
2 the commission investigating war crimes: committee, board, delegation, deputation, representative.
3 commission on a sale: percentage, cut (*infml*), rake-off (*infml*), allowance, fee.
▶ *verb*
nominate, select, appoint, engage,

employ, authorize, empower, delegate, depute, send, order, request, ask for.

commit *verb*
1 commit a crime: do, perform, execute, enact, perpetrate.
2 commit his soul to God: entrust, confide, commend, consign, deliver, hand over, give, deposit.
◆ **commit oneself** decide, undertake, promise, pledge, bind oneself.

commitment *noun*
undertaking, guarantee, assurance, promise, word, pledge, vow, engagement, involvement, dedication, devotion, adherence, loyalty, tie, obligation, duty, responsibility, liability.
F∃ vacillation, wavering.

committee *noun*
council, board, panel, jury, commission, advisory group, think-tank, working party, task force.

common *adjective*
1 a common problem: familiar, customary, habitual, usual, daily, everyday, routine, regular, frequent, widespread, prevalent, general, universal, standard, average, ordinary, plain, simple, workaday, run-of-the-mill, undistinguished, unexceptional, conventional, accepted, popular, commonplace.
2 don't be so common!: vulgar, coarse, unrefined, crude, inferior, low, ill-bred, loutish, plebeian.
3 a common stairway/purpose: communal, public, shared, mutual, joint, collective.
F∃ 1 uncommon, unusual, rare, noteworthy. **2** tasteful, refined.

commonplace *adjective*
ordinary, everyday, common, humdrum, pedestrian, banal, trite, widespread, frequent, hackneyed, stock, stale, obvious, worn out, boring, uninteresting, threadbare.
F∃ memorable, exceptional.

commotion *noun*
agitation, hurly-burly, turmoil, tumult, excitement, ferment, fuss, bustle, ado, to-do (*infml*), uproar, furore, ballyhoo (*infml*), hullabaloo (*infml*), racket, hubbub, rumpus, fracas, disturbance, bust-up (*infml*), disorder, riot.

communal *adjective*
public, community, shared, joint, collective, general, common.
F3 private, personal.

communicate *verb*
1 communicate information: announce, declare, proclaim, report, reveal, disclose, divulge, impart, inform, acquaint, intimate, notify, publish, disseminate, spread, diffuse, transmit, convey.
2 communicate with each other: talk, converse, commune, correspond, write, phone, telephone, contact.

communication *noun*
information, intelligence, intimation, disclosure, contact, connection, transmission, dissemination.

Forms of communication include:

media, mass media, broadcasting, radio, wireless, television, TV, cable TV, digital TV, satellite, subscription TV, pay TV, pay-per-view, video, video-on-demand, teletext; telecommunications, data communication, information technology (IT); the Internet, the net, World Wide Web; newspaper, press, news, newsflash, magazine, journal, advertising, publicity, poster, leaflet, pamphlet, brochure, catalogue; post, dispatch, correspondence, letter, postcard, aerogram, email, telegram, Telemessage®, cable, wire (*infml*), chain letter, junk mail, mailshot; conversation, word, message, dialogue, speech, gossip, grapevine (*infml*); notice, bulletin, announcement, communiqué, circular, memo, note, report; telephone, mobile phone, cell phone, MMS (multimedia messaging service), SMS (short message service), text message, intercom, answering machine, walkie-talkie, bleeper, tannoy, teleprinter, facsimile, fax, computer, word processor, typewriter, dictaphone, megaphone, loud-hailer; radar, Morse code, semaphore, Braille, sign language.

communicative *adjective*
talkative, voluble, expansive, open, informative, chatty, sociable, friendly, forthcoming, outgoing, extrovert, unreserved, free, frank, candid.
F3 quiet, reserved, reticent, secretive.

community *noun*
district, locality, population, people, populace, public, residents, nation, state, colony, commune, kibbutz, settlement, society, association, fellowship, brotherhood, fraternity.

commute *verb*
1 commute the death sentence to life imprisonment: reduce, decrease, shorten, curtail, lighten, soften, mitigate, remit, adjust, modify, alter, change, exchange, alternate.
2 commute by train: travel, journey.

compact *adjective*
small, short, brief, terse, succinct, concise, condensed, compressed, close, dense, impenetrable, solid, firm.
F3 large, rambling, diffuse.

companion *noun*
fellow, comrade, friend, buddy (*infml*), crony (*infml*), chum (*infml*), pal (*infml*), intimate, confidant(e), ally, aide, confederate, colleague, associate, partner, mate, consort, escort, chaperon, attendant, assistant, accomplice, follower.

company *noun*
1 a manufacturing company: firm, business, concern, association, corporation, establishment, house, partnership, syndicate, cartel, consortium.
2 a company of soldiers: troupe, group, band, ensemble, set, circle, crowd, throng, body, troop, crew, party, assembly, gathering, community, society.
3 have company: guests, visitors, callers.
4 good company/look forward to your company: society, companionship, fellowship, support, attendance, presence.

comparable *adjective*
similar, alike, related, akin, cognate, corresponding, analogous, equivalent,

tantamount, proportionate, commensurate, parallel, equal.
F3 dissimilar, unlike, unequal.

compare *verb*
liken, equate, contrast, juxtapose, balance, weigh, correlate, resemble, match, equal, parallel.

comparison *noun*
juxtaposition, analogy, parallel, correlation, relationship, likeness, resemblance, similarity, comparability, contrast, distinction.

compartment *noun*
section, division, subdivision, category, pigeonhole, cubbyhole, niche, alcove, bay, area, stall, booth, cubicle, locker, carrel, cell, chamber, berth, carriage.

compassionate *adjective*
kind-hearted, kindly, tender-hearted, tender, caring, warm-hearted, benevolent, humanitarian, humane, merciful, clement, lenient, pitying, sympathetic, understanding, supportive.
F3 cruel, indifferent.

compatible *adjective*
harmonious, consistent, congruous, matching, consonant, accordant, suitable, reconcilable, adaptable, conformable, sympathetic, like-minded, well-matched, similar.
F3 incompatible, antagonistic, contradictory.

compel *verb*
force, make, constrain, oblige, necessitate, drive, urge, impel, coerce, pressurize, hustle, browbeat, bully, strongarm, bulldoze, press-gang, dragoon.

compelling *adjective*
forceful, coercive, imperative, urgent, pressing, irresistible, overriding, powerful, cogent, persuasive, convincing, conclusive, compulsive, incontrovertible, irrefutable, gripping, enthralling, spellbinding, mesmeric.
F3 weak, unconvincing, boring.

compensate *verb*
balance, counterbalance, cancel, neutralize, counteract, offset, redress, satisfy, requite, repay, refund, reimburse, indemnify, recompense,

reward, remunerate, atone, redeem, make good, restore.

compensation *noun*
amends, redress, satisfaction, requital, repayment, refund, reimbursement, indemnification, indemnity, damages, reparation, recompense, reward, payment, remuneration, return, restoration, restitution, consolation, comfort.

compete *verb*
vie, contest, fight, battle, struggle, strive, oppose, challenge, rival, emulate, contend, participate, take part.

competent *adjective*
capable, able, adept, efficient, trained, qualified, well-qualified, skilled, experienced, proficient, expert, masterly, equal, fit, suitable, appropriate, satisfactory, adequate, sufficient.
F3 incompetent, incapable, unable, inefficient.

competition *noun*
1 a swimming competition: contest, championship, tournament, cup, event, race, match, game, quiz.
2 competition between the brothers: rivalry, opposition, challenge, contention, conflict, struggle, strife, competitiveness, combativeness.
3 the competition looks strong: competitors, rivals, opponents, challengers, field.

competitive *adjective*
combative, contentious, antagonistic, aggressive, pushy (*infml*), ambitious, keen, cut-throat.

competitor *noun*
contestant, contender, entrant, candidate, challenger, opponent, adversary, antagonist, rival, emulator, competition, opposition.

complacent *adjective*
smug, self-satisfied, gloating, triumphant, self-righteous, unconcerned.
F3 diffident, concerned, discontented.

complain *verb*
protest, grumble, grouse, gripe, beef, carp, fuss, lament, bemoan, bewail, moan, whine, groan, growl.

complaint *noun*
1 received several complaints about his behaviour: protest, objection, grumble, grouse, gripe, beef, moan, grievance, dissatisfaction, annoyance, fault-finding, criticism, censure, accusation, charge.
2 a chest complaint: ailment, illness, sickness, disease, malady, malaise, indisposition, affliction, disorder, trouble, upset.

complementary *adjective*
reciprocal, interdependent, correlative, interrelated, corresponding, matching, twin, fellow, companion.
E3 contradictory, incompatible.

complete *adjective*
1 feel a complete fool/complete nonsense: utter, total, absolute, downright, out-and-out, thorough, perfect.
2 the job isn't complete yet: finished, ended, concluded, over, done, accomplished, achieved.
3 a complete version of the report/ have our complete attention: unabridged, unabbreviated, unedited, unexpurgated, integral, whole, entire, full, undivided, intact.
E3 1 partial. **2** incomplete. **3** abridged.
▶ *verb*
finish, end, close, conclude, wind up, terminate, finalize, settle, clinch, perform, discharge, execute, fulfil, realize, accomplish, achieve, consummate, crown, perfect.

complex *adjective*
complicated, intricate, elaborate, involved, convoluted, circuitous, tortuous, devious, mixed, varied, diverse, multiple, composite, compound, ramified.
E3 simple, easy.
▶ *noun*
1 a shopping complex: structure, system, scheme, organization, establishment, institute, development.
2 has a bit of a complex about his weight: fixation, obsession, preoccupation, hang-up (*infml*), phobia.

complexion *noun*
1 a pale/dark complexion: skin, colour, colouring, pigmentation.
2 put a different complexion on things: look, appearance, aspect, light, character, nature, type, kind.

complicated *adjective*
complex, intricate, elaborate, involved, convoluted, tortuous, difficult, problematic, puzzling, perplexing.
E3 simple, easy.

complication *noun*
difficulty, drawback, snag, obstacle, problem, ramification, repercussion, complexity, intricacy, elaboration, convolution, tangle, web, confusion, mixture.

compliment *noun*
flattery, admiration, favour, approval, congratulations, tribute, honour, accolade, bouquet, commendation, praise, eulogy.
E3 insult, criticism.

complimentary *adjective*
1 she was very complimentary about my work: flattering, admiring, favourable, approving, appreciative, congratulatory, commendatory, eulogistic.
2 complimentary ticket: free, gratis, honorary, courtesy.
E3 1 insulting, unflattering, critical.

comply *verb*
agree, consent, assent, accede, yield, submit, defer, respect, observe, obey, fall in, conform, follow, perform, discharge, fulfil, satisfy, meet, oblige, accommodate.
E3 defy, disobey.

component *noun*
part, constituent, ingredient, element, factor, item, unit, piece, bit, spare part.

compose *verb*
1 what is this material composed of?: constitute, make up, form.
2 compose a song/letter: create, invent, devise, write, arrange, produce, make, form, fashion, build, construct, frame.
3 compose herself before the performance: calm, soothe, quiet, still, settle, tranquillize, quell, pacify, control, regulate.

composition *noun*
1 composition of a letter: making, production, formation, creation, invention, design, formulation, writing, compilation.
2 the composition of the soil/of the painting: constitution, make-up, combination, mixture, form, structure, configuration, layout, arrangement, organization, harmony, consonance, balance, symmetry.
3 a musical composition: work, opus, piece, study, exercise.

compound *noun*
alloy, blend, mixture, medley, composite, amalgam, synthesis, fusion, composition, amalgamation, combination.

comprehend *verb*
understand, conceive, see, grasp, fathom, penetrate, tumble to (*infml*), realize, appreciate, know, apprehend, perceive, discern, take in, assimilate.
Ⓔ misunderstand.

comprehensive *adjective*
thorough, exhaustive, full, complete, encyclopedic, compendious, broad, wide, extensive, sweeping, general, blanket, inclusive, all-inclusive, all-embracing, across-the-board.
Ⓔ partial, incomplete, selective.

compress *verb*
press, squeeze, crush, squash, flatten, jam, wedge, cram, stuff, compact, concentrate, condense, contract, telescope, shorten, abbreviate, summarize.
Ⓔ expand, diffuse.

comprise *verb*
consist of, include, contain, incorporate, embody, involve, encompass, embrace, cover.

compromise *noun*
bargain, trade-off, settlement, agreement, concession, give and take, co-operation, accommodation, adjustment.
Ⓔ disagreement, intransigence.

compulsive *adjective*
1 makes for compulsive viewing: irresistible, overwhelming, overpowering, uncontrollable, compelling, driving, urgent.

2 a compulsive liar: obsessive, hardened, incorrigible, irredeemable, incurable, hopeless.

compulsory *adjective*
obligatory, mandatory, imperative, forced, required, requisite, set, stipulated, binding, contractual.
Ⓔ optional, voluntary, discretionary.

computer *noun*
personal computer, PC, mainframe, processor, word-processor, data processor.

Computer terms include:

types of computer: mainframe, microcomputer, minicomputer, PC (personal computer), Apple Mac®, Mac (*infml*), iMac®, desktop, laptop, notebook, palmtop, handheld; hardware: chip, silicon chip, circuit board, motherboard, CPU (central processing unit), card, graphics card, sound card, video card, disk drive, floppy drive, hard drive, joystick, joypad, keyboard, light pen, microprocessor, modem, cable modem, monitor, mouse, pointer, printer, bubblejet printer, dot-matrix printer, inkjet printer, laser printer, screen, scanner, terminal, touchpad, trackball, VDU (visual display unit); software: program, application, abandonware, freeware, shareware; memory: backing storage, external memory, immediate access memory, internal memory, magnetic tape, RAM (Random Access Memory), ROM (Read Only Memory), CD-R (Compact Disc Recordable), CD-ROM (Compact Disc Read Only Memory), DVD-ROM (Digital Versatile Disc Read Only Memory); disks: Compact Disc (CD), Digital Versatile Disc (DVD), magnetic disk, floppy disk, hard disk, optical disk, zip disk; programming languages: BASIC, C, C++, COBOL, Delphi, FORTRAN, Java®, Pascal; web: email or e-mail, hit, hyperlink, Internet, international services digital network (ISDN), intranet, uniform resource locator (URL), World Wide Web (WWW); miscellaneous: access, ASCII, autosave, backup, binary, BIOS (Basic Input/Output System), bitmap, boot, cold boot, reboot, warm boot, buffer, bug, bus, byte, gigabyte, kilobyte, megabyte, terabyte, cache, character, character code, client-server, compression, computer game, computer graphics, computer literate, computer simulation, cracking, cursor, data, databank, database, Data Protection Act, debugging, default, desktop publishing (DTP), digitizer, directory, dots per inch (dpi), DOS (disk operating system), editor, file, format, FTP (File Transfer Protocol), function, grammar checker, graphics, GUI (graphical user interface), hacking, icon, installation, interface, Linux, login, log off, log on, Mac OS (Macintosh® operating system), macro, menu, message box, metafile, MS-DOS (Microsoft® disk operating system), mouse mat, multimedia, network, output, P2P (peer-to-peer), package, password, peripheral, pixel, platform, port, parallel port, serial port, protocol, script, scripting language, scroll bar, scrolling, shell, shellscript, spellchecker, spreadsheet, sprite, subdirectory, template, toggle, toolbar, Unicode, Unix®, upgrade, user-friendly, user interface, utilities, video game, virtual reality (VR), virus, virus checker, wide area network (WAN), window, Windows®, word processing, workstation, worm, WYSIWYG (what you see is what you get).

con verb (*infml*)
trick, hoax, dupe, deceive, mislead, inveigle (*fml*), hoodwink, bamboozle (*infml*), cheat, double-cross, swindle, defraud, rip off (*infml*), rook.

conceal verb
hide, obscure, disguise, camouflage, mask, screen, veil, cloak, cover, bury, submerge, smother, suppress, keep dark, keep quiet, hush up (*infml*).
E∃ reveal, disclose, uncover.

concede verb
1 have to concede that she was right: admit, confess, acknowledge, allow, recognize, own, grant, accept.
2 conceding two goals in the first ten minutes: yield, give up, surrender, relinquish, forfeit, sacrifice.
E∃ 1 deny.

conceited adjective
vain, boastful, swollen-headed, bigheaded (*infml*), egotistical, self-important, cocky, self-satisfied, complacent, smug, proud, arrogant, stuck-up (*infml*), toffee-nosed (*infml*).
E∃ modest, self-effacing, diffident, humble.

concentrate verb
1 concentrating around the centre: focus, converge, centre, cluster, crowd, congregate, gather, collect, accumulate.
2 can't concentrate on work: apply oneself, think, pay attention, attend.
3 concentrated the solution: condense, evaporate, reduce, thicken, intensify.
E∃ 1 disperse. 3 dilute.

concept noun
idea, notion, plan, theory, hypothesis, thought, abstraction, conception, conceptualization, visualization, image, picture, impression.

concern verb
1 concerned about their safety: upset, distress, trouble, disturb, bother, worry.
2 concerns your daughter: relate to, refer to, regard, involve, interest, affect, touch.
▶ noun
1 a cause for concern: anxiety, worry, unease, disquiet, care, sorrow, distress.
2 grateful for your concern: regard, consideration, attention, heed, thought.
3 it's not my concern: responsibility, duty, charge, job, task, field, business, affair, matter, problem, interest, involvement.
4 a new concern: company, firm, business, corporation, establishment,

enterprise, organization.
E3 1 joy. 2 indifference.

concerned *adjective*
1 concerned parents: anxious, worried, uneasy, apprehensive, upset, unhappy, distressed, troubled, disturbed, bothered, attentive, caring.
2 the people concerned: connected, related, involved, implicated, interested, affected.
E3 1 unconcerned, indifferent, apathetic.

concerning *preposition*
about, regarding, with regard to, as regards, respecting, with reference to, relating to, in the matter of.

concise *adjective*
short, brief, terse, succinct, pithy, compendious, compact, compressed, condensed, abridged, abbreviated, summary, synoptic.
E3 diffuse, wordy.

conclude *verb*
1 I conclude that they were innocent: infer, deduce, assume, surmise, suppose, reckon, judge.
2 conclude their discussions: end, close, finish, complete, consummate, cease, terminate, culminate.
3 conclude a deal: settle, resolve, decide, establish, determine, clinch.
E3 2 start, commence.

conclusive *adjective*
final, ultimate, definitive, decisive, clear, convincing, definite, undeniable, irrefutable, indisputable, incontrovertible, unarguable, unanswerable, clinching.
E3 inconclusive, questionable.

concoct *verb*
fabricate, invent, devise, contrive, formulate, plan, plot, hatch, brew, prepare, develop.

concrete *adjective*
real, actual, factual, solid, physical, material, substantial, tangible, touchable, perceptible, visible, firm, definite, specific, explicit.
E3 abstract, vague.

condemn *verb*
disapprove, upbraid (*fml*), reproach, castigate (*fml*), blame, disparage (*fml*),
revile, denounce, censure, slam (*infml*), slate (*infml*), convict.
E3 praise, approve.

condense *verb*
1 condensing the novel: shorten, curtail, abbreviate, abridge, précis, summarize, encapsulate, contract, compress, compact.
2 condenses on the cold glass: distil, precipitate (*fml*), concentrate, reduce, thicken, solidify, coagulate.
E3 1 expand. 2 dilute.

condescend *verb*
deign, see fit, stoop, bend, lower oneself, patronize, talk down.

condition *noun*
1 the condition of the country: state, circumstances, case, position, situation, predicament, plight.
2 a condition of the contract: requirement, obligation, prerequisite, terms, stipulation, proviso, qualification, limitation, restriction, rule.
3 a heart condition: disorder, defect, weakness, infirmity, problem, complaint, disease.
4 out of condition: fitness, health, state, shape, form, fettle, nick (*infml*).

conditions *noun*
surroundings, environment, milieu, setting, atmosphere, background, context, circumstances, situation, state.

condone *verb*
forgive, pardon, excuse, overlook, ignore, disregard, tolerate, brook, allow.
E3 condemn, censure.

conducive *adjective*
leading, tending, contributory, productive, advantageous, beneficial, favourable, helpful, encouraging.
E3 detrimental, adverse, unfavourable.

conduct *noun*
1 good conduct: behaviour, comportment (*fml*), actions, ways, manners, bearing, attitude.
2 the conduct of their affairs: administration, management, direction, running, organization,

operation, control, supervision,
leadership, guidance.
▶ *verb*
1 conducting the meeting: administer,
manage, run, organize, orchestrate,
chair, control, handle, regulate.
**2 conduct oneself in a dignified
manner**: behave, acquit, comport
oneself (*fml*), act.
3 conducts heat: convey, carry, bear,
transmit.
4 conducted me to my seat: lead,
accompany, escort, usher, guide,
direct, pilot, steer.

confer *verb*
1 conferring with his colleagues:
discuss, debate, deliberate, consult,
talk, converse.
2 conferring some benefit: bestow,
award, present, give, grant, accord,
impart, lend.

conference *noun*
meeting, convention, congress,
convocation (*fml*), symposium, forum,
discussion, debate, consultation.

confess *verb*
admit, confide, own (up), come clean
(*infml*), grant, concede, acknowledge,
recognize, affirm, assert, profess,
declare, disclose, divulge, expose.
E⊒ deny, conceal.

confide *verb*
confess, admit, reveal, disclose,
divulge, whisper, breathe, tell, impart,
unburden.
E⊒ hide, suppress.

confidence *noun*
certainty, faith, credence, trust,
reliance, dependence, assurance,
composure, calmness, self-possession,
self-confidence, self-reliance, self-
assurance, boldness, courage.
E⊒ distrust, diffidence.

confident *adjective*
sure, certain, positive, convinced,
assured, composed, self-possessed,
cool, self-confident, self-reliant, self-
assured, unselfconscious, bold,
fearless, dauntless, unabashed.
E⊒ doubtful, diffident.

confidential *adjective*
secret, top secret, classified, restricted,

hush-hush (*infml*), off-the-record,
private, personal, intimate, privy.

confine *verb*
enclose, circumscribe, bound, limit,
restrict, cramp, constrain, imprison,
incarcerate, intern, cage, shut up,
immure, bind, shackle, trammel,
restrain, repress, inhibit.
E⊒ free.

confirm *verb*
1 confirm her version of events:
endorse, back, support, reinforce,
strengthen, fortify, validate, prove,
authenticate, corroborate,
substantiate, verify, evidence.
**2 confirmed his position in the
company**: establish, fix, settle, clinch,
ratify, sanction, approve.
3 confirm that he will go: affirm,
assert, assure, pledge, promise,
guarantee.
E⊒ 1 refute, deny.

confirmed *adjective*
inveterate, entrenched, dyed-in-the-
wool, rooted, established, long-
established, long-standing, habitual,
chronic, seasoned, hardened,
incorrigible, incurable.

confiscate *verb*
seize, appropriate, expropriate (*fml*),
remove, take away, impound,
sequester, commandeer.
E⊒ return, restore.

conflict *noun*
1 a conflict of interest: difference,
variance, discord, contention,
disagreement, dissension, dispute,
opposition, antagonism, hostility,
friction, strife, unrest, confrontation.
2 the conflict in the Balkans: battle,
war, warfare, combat, fight, contest,
engagement, skirmish, set-to, fracas,
brawl, quarrel, feud, encounter, clash.
E⊒ 1 agreement, harmony, concord.
▶ *verb*
differ, clash, collide, disagree,
contradict, oppose, contest, fight,
combat, battle, war, strive, struggle,
contend.
E⊒ agree, harmonize.

conform *verb*
agree, accord, harmonize, match,

correspond, tally, square, adapt, adjust, accommodate, comply, obey, follow.

Ea differ, conflict, rebel.

confront *verb*
face, meet, encounter, accost, address, oppose, challenge, defy, brave, beard.

Ea evade.

confrontation *noun*
encounter, clash, collision, showdown, conflict, disagreement, fight, battle, quarrel, set-to, engagement, contest.

confuse *verb*
1 confusing her further : puzzle, baffle, perplex, mystify, confound, bewilder, disorient, disconcert, fluster, upset, embarrass, mortify.
2 don't confuse the blue and the brown wires : muddle, mix up, mistake, jumble, disarrange, disorder, tangle, entangle, involve, mingle.

Ea 1 enlighten, clarify.

confused *adjective*
1 looked confused/a confused old lady : puzzled, baffled, perplexed, flummoxed (*infml*), nonplussed, bewildered, disorientated.
2 a confused mess of dirty plates and cutlery : muddled, jumbled, disarranged, disordered, untidy, disorderly, higgledy-piggledy (*infml*), chaotic, disorganized.

Ea 2 orderly.

congested *adjective*
clogged, blocked, jammed, packed, stuffed, crammed, full, crowded, overcrowded, overflowing, teeming.

Ea clear.

congratulate *verb*
praise, felicitate (*fml*), compliment, wish well.

Ea commiserate.

congregate *verb*
gather, assemble, collect, muster, rally, rendezvous, meet, convene, converge, flock, crowd, throng, mass, accumulate, cluster, clump, conglomerate.

Ea disperse.

conical *adjective*
cone-shaped, pyramidal, tapering, tapered, pointed.

connect *verb*
join, link, unite, couple, combine, fasten, affix, attach, relate, associate, ally.

Ea disconnect, cut off, detach.

connected *adjective*
joined, linked, united, coupled, combined, related, akin, associated, affiliated, allied.

Ea disconnected, unconnected.

connection *noun*
junction, coupling, fastening, attachment, bond, tie, link, association, alliance, relation, relationship, interrelation, contact, communication, correlation, correspondence, relevance.

Ea disconnection.

conquer *verb*
1 conquering the Aztecs : defeat, beat, overthrow, vanquish (*fml*), rout, overrun, best, worst, get the better of, overcome, surmount, win, succeed, triumph, prevail, overpower, master, crush, subdue, quell, subjugate, humble.
2 conquer Everest/the market : seize, take, annex, occupy, possess, acquire, obtain.

Ea 1 surrender, yield, give in.

conscience *noun*
principles, standards, morals, ethics, scruples, qualms.

conscientious *adjective*
diligent, hardworking, scrupulous, painstaking, thorough, meticulous, punctilious, particular, careful, attentive, responsible, upright, honest, faithful, dutiful.

Ea careless, irresponsible, unreliable.

conscious *adjective*
1 remained conscious during the operation : awake, alive, responsive, sentient, sensible, rational, reasoning, alert.
2 conscious of his failings/a conscious decision : aware, self-conscious, heedful, mindful, knowing, deliberate, intentional, calculated, premeditated, studied, wilful, voluntary.

Ea 1 unconscious. 2 unaware, involuntary.

consciousness *noun*
awareness, sentience, sensibility, knowledge, intuition, realization, recognition.
🗗 unconsciousness.

consecutive *adjective*
sequential, successive, continuous, unbroken, uninterrupted, following, succeeding, running.
🗗 discontinuous.

consent *verb*
agree, concur, accede, assent, approve, permit, allow, grant, admit, concede, acquiesce, yield, comply.
🗗 refuse, decline, oppose.
▶ *noun*
agreement, concurrence, assent, approval, permission, go-ahead, green light (*infml*), sanction, concession, acquiescence, compliance.
🗗 disagreement, refusal, opposition.

consequence *noun*
1 have serious consequences: result, outcome, issue, end, upshot, effect, side effect, repercussion.
2 of no consequence: importance, significance, concern, value, weight, note, eminence, distinction.
🗗 **1** cause. **2** unimportance, insignificance.

conservation *noun*
keeping, safe-keeping, custody, saving, economy, husbandry, maintenance, upkeep, preservation, protection, safeguarding, ecology, environmentalism.
🗗 destruction.

conservative *adjective*
Tory, right-wing, hidebound, diehard, reactionary, establishmentarian, unprogressive, conventional, traditional, moderate, middle-of-the-road, cautious, guarded, sober.
🗗 left-wing, radical, innovative.
▶ *noun*
Tory, right-winger, die-hard, stick-in-the-mud, reactionary, traditionalist, moderate.
🗗 left-winger, radical.

conserve *verb*
keep, save, store up, hoard, maintain,

preserve, protect, guard, safeguard.
🗗 use, waste, squander.

consider *verb*
1 consider your options: ponder, deliberate, reflect, contemplate, meditate, muse, mull over, chew over, examine, study, weigh, respect, remember, take into account.
2 consider it an honour: regard, deem, think, believe, judge, rate, count.

considerable *adjective*
great, large, big, sizable, substantial, tidy (*infml*), ample, plentiful, abundant, lavish, marked, noticeable, perceptible, appreciable, reasonable, tolerable, respectable, important, significant, noteworthy, distinguished, influential.
🗗 small, slight, insignificant, unremarkable.

considerate *adjective*
kind, thoughtful, caring, attentive, obliging, helpful, charitable, unselfish, altruistic, gracious, solicitous, sensitive, tactful, discreet.
🗗 inconsiderate, thoughtless, selfish.

consist of *verb*
comprise, be composed of, contain, include, incorporate, embody, embrace, involve, amount to.

consistency *noun*
1 of the consistency of porridge: viscosity, thickness, density, firmness.
2 the consistency of her playing is impressive: steadiness, regularity, evenness, uniformity, sameness, identity, constancy, steadfastness.
3 ensure that there is consistency in our dealings with each other: agreement, accordance, coherence, correspondence, congruity, compatibility, harmony.
🗗 **3** inconsistency.

consistent *adjective*
1 a consistent winner: steady, stable, regular, uniform, unchanging, undeviating, constant, persistent, unfailing, dependable.
2 consistent with the facts: agreeing, accordant, consonant, congruous, coherent, compatible, harmonious, logical.
🗗 **1** irregular, erratic. **2** inconsistent.

console *verb*
comfort, cheer, hearten, encourage, relieve, soothe, calm.
F3 upset, agitate.

consolidate *verb*
reinforce, strengthen, secure, stabilize, unify, unite, join, combine, affiliate, amalgamate, fuse, cement, compact, condense, thicken, harden, solidify.

conspicuous *adjective*
apparent, visible, noticeable, marked, clear, obvious, evident, patent, manifest, prominent, striking, blatant, flagrant, glaring, ostentatious, showy, flashy, garish.
F3 inconspicuous, concealed, hidden.

conspire *verb*
plot, scheme, intrigue, manoeuvre, connive, collude, hatch, devise.

constant *adjective*
1 constant noise/interruptions:
continuous, unbroken, never-ending, non-stop, endless, interminable, ceaseless, incessant, eternal, everlasting, perpetual, continual, unremitting, relentless, persistent.
2 a constant temperature/needs constant attention: resolute, persevering, unflagging, unwavering, stable, steady, unchanging, unvarying, changeless, immutable, invariable, unalterable, fixed, permanent, firm, even, regular, uniform.
3 a constant friend: loyal, faithful, staunch, steadfast, dependable, trustworthy, true, devoted.
F3 1 variable, irregular, fitful, occasional. **3** disloyal, fickle.

constituent *adjective*
component, integral, essential, basic, intrinsic, inherent.
▶ *noun*
ingredient, element, factor, principle, component, part, bit, section, unit.
F3 whole.

constitute *verb*
represent, make up, compose, form, comprise, create, establish, set up, found.

constrain *verb*
1 felt constrained to tell the whole truth: force, compel, oblige, necessitate, drive, impel, urge.
2 constrained by lack of money: limit, confine, constrict, restrain, check, curb, bind.

constraint *noun*
1 the constraint of legislation: force, duress, compulsion, coercion, pressure, necessity, deterrent.
2 the constraint of a large and expensive family: restriction, limitation, hindrance, restraint, check, curb, damper.

constrict *verb*
squeeze, compress, pinch, cramp, narrow, tighten, contract, shrink, choke, strangle, inhibit, limit, restrict.
F3 expand.

construct *verb*
build, erect, raise, elevate, make, manufacture, fabricate, assemble, put together, compose, form, shape, fashion, model, design, engineer, create, found, establish, formulate.
F3 demolish, destroy.

constructive *adjective*
practical, productive, positive, helpful, useful, valuable, beneficial, advantageous.
F3 destructive, negative, unhelpful.

consult *verb*
refer to, ask, question, interrogate, confer, discuss, debate, deliberate.

consultant *noun*
adviser, expert, authority, specialist.

consultation *noun*
discussion, deliberation, dialogue, conference, meeting, hearing, interview, examination, appointment, session.

consume *verb*
1 consuming large quantities of food:
eat, drink, swallow, devour, gobble, polish off (*infml*), ingest.
2 consume energy: use, absorb, spend, expend, deplete, drain, exhaust, use up, dissipate, squander, waste.
3 consumed in the flames: destroy, demolish, annihilate, devastate, ravage.

consumer *noun*
user, end-user, customer, buyer, purchaser, shopper.

contact *noun*
touch, impact, juxtaposition, contiguity, communication, meeting, junction, union, connection, association.
▸ *verb*
approach, apply to, reach, get hold of, get in touch with, telephone, phone, ring, call, notify.

contagious *adjective*
infectious, catching, communicable, transmissible, spreading, epidemic.

contain *verb*
1 contains additives/containing the major organs: include, comprise, incorporate, embody, involve, embrace, enclose, hold, accommodate.
2 contain one's feelings: repress, stifle, restrain, control, check, curb, limit.
E∃ 1 exclude.

container *noun*
receptacle, vessel, holder.

contaminate *verb*
infect, pollute, adulterate, taint, soil, sully (*fml*), defile (*fml*), corrupt, deprave, debase, stain, tarnish.
E∃ purify.

contemplate *verb*
1 contemplating the meaning of life: meditate, reflect on, ponder, mull over, deliberate, consider, regard, view, survey, observe, study, examine, inspect, scrutinize.
2 couldn't contemplate losing: expect, foresee, envisage, plan, design, propose, intend, mean.

contemporary *adjective*
1 contemporary architecture: modern, current, present, present-day, recent, latest, up-to-date, fashionable, up-to-the-minute, ultra-modern.
2 contemporary with the Surrealists: contemporaneous, coexistent, concurrent, synchronous, simultaneous.
E∃ 1 out-of-date, old-fashioned.

contempt *noun*
scorn, disdain, condescension, derision, ridicule, mockery, disrespect, dishonour, disregard, neglect, dislike, loathing, detestation.
E∃ admiration, regard.

contemptible *adjective*
despicable, shameful, ignominious, low, mean, vile, detestable, loathsome, abject, wretched, pitiful, paltry, worthless.
E∃ admirable, honourable.

contemptuous *adjective*
scornful, disdainful, sneering, supercilious, condescending, arrogant, haughty, high and mighty, cynical, derisive, insulting, disrespectful, insolent.
E∃ humble, respectful.

content *noun*
substance, matter, essence, gist, meaning, significance, text, subject matter, ideas, contents, load, burden.
▸ *adjective*
satisfied, fulfilled, contented, untroubled, pleased, happy, willing.
E∃ dissatisfied, troubled.

contented *adjective*
happy, glad, pleased, cheerful, comfortable, relaxed, content, satisfied.
E∃ discontented, unhappy, annoyed.

contentment *noun*
contentedness, happiness, gladness, pleasure, gratification, comfort, ease, complacency, peace, peacefulness, serenity, equanimity, content, satisfaction, fulfilment.
E∃ unhappiness, discontent, dissatisfaction.

contents *noun*
1 the contents of the package: constituents, parts, elements, ingredients, content, load, items.
2 the contents of the book: chapters, divisions, subjects, topics, themes.

contest *noun*
competition, game, match, tournament, encounter, fight, battle, set-to, combat, conflict, struggle, dispute, debate, controversy.
▸ *verb*
1 contest the decision: dispute, debate, question, doubt, challenge, oppose, argue against, litigate, deny, refute.
2 contesting one with the other: compete, vie, contend, strive, fight.
E∃ 1 accept.

contestant *noun*
competitor, contender, player, participant, entrant, candidate, aspirant, rival, opponent.

context *noun*
background, setting, surroundings, framework, frame of reference, situation, position, circumstances, conditions.

continual *adjective*
constant, perpetual, incessant, interminable, eternal, everlasting, regular, frequent, recurrent, repeated.
F3 occasional, intermittent, temporary.

continue *verb*
resume, recommence, carry on, go on, proceed, persevere, stick at, persist, last, endure, survive, remain, abide (*fml*), stay, rest, pursue, sustain, maintain, lengthen, prolong, extend, project.
F3 discontinue, stop.

continuity *noun*
flow, progression, succession, sequence, linkage, interrelationship, connection, cohesion.
F3 discontinuity.

continuous *adjective*
unbroken, uninterrupted, consecutive, non-stop, endless, ceaseless, unending, unceasing, constant, unremitting, prolonged, extended, continued, lasting.
F3 discontinuous, broken, sporadic.

contort *verb*
twist, distort, warp, wrench, disfigure, deform, misshape, convolute, gnarl, knot, writhe, squirm, wriggle.

contour *noun*
outline, silhouette, shape, form, figure, curve, relief, profile, character, aspect.

contract *verb* /kon-**trakt**/
1 wood contracts when it gets cold: shrink, lessen, diminish, reduce, shorten, curtail, abbreviate, abridge, condense, compress, constrict, narrow, tighten, tense, shrivel, wrinkle.
2 contract pneumonia: catch, get, go down with, develop.
3 contracted to build two warships: pledge, promise, undertake, agree, stipulate, arrange, negotiate, bargain.

F3 1 expand, enlarge, lengthen.
▶ *noun* /**kon**-trakt/
bond, commitment, engagement, covenant, treaty, convention, pact, compact, agreement, transaction, deal, bargain, settlement, arrangement, understanding.

contradict *verb*
deny, disaffirm, confute, challenge, oppose, impugn (*fml*), dispute, counter, negate, gainsay.
F3 agree, confirm, corroborate.

contradictory *adjective*
contrary, opposite, paradoxical, conflicting, discrepant, inconsistent, incompatible, antagonistic, irreconcilable, opposed, repugnant.
F3 consistent.

contraption *noun*
contrivance, device, gadget, apparatus, rig, machine, mechanism.

contrary *adjective*
1 /**kon**-tra-ri/ take the contrary view: opposite, counter, reverse, conflicting, antagonistic, opposed, adverse, hostile.
2 /kon-**treir**-ri/ a contrary child: perverse, awkward, disobliging, difficult, wayward, obstinate, intractable, cantankerous, stroppy (*infml*).
F3 1 like, similar. **2** obliging.
▶ *noun*
opposite, converse, reverse.

contrast *noun*
difference, dissimilarity, disparity, divergence, distinction, differentiation, comparison, foil, antithesis, opposition.
F3 similarity.
▶ *verb*
compare, differentiate, distinguish, discriminate, differ, oppose, clash, conflict.

contravene *verb*
infringe, violate, break, breach, disobey, defy, flout, transgress.
F3 uphold, observe, obey.

contribute *verb*
donate, subscribe, chip in (*infml*), add, give, bestow, provide, supply, furnish, help, lead, conduce.
F3 withhold.

contrite *adjective*
sorry, regretful, remorseful, repentant, penitent, conscience-stricken, chastened, humble, ashamed.

contrived *adjective*
unnatural, artificial, false, forced, strained, laboured, mannered, elaborate, overdone.
✍ natural, genuine.

control *verb*
1 the policeman controlled the traffic: lead, govern, rule, command, direct, manage, oversee, supervise, superintend, run, operate.
2 control the temperature: regulate, adjust, monitor, verify.
3 control one's temper: restrain, check, curb, subdue, repress, hold back, contain.
▶ *noun*
1 have full control: power, charge, authority, command, mastery, government, rule, direction, management, oversight, supervision, superintendence, discipline, guidance.
2 controls on spending: restraint, check, curb, repression.
3 fiddle with the controls: instrument, dial, switch, button, knob, lever.

controversial *adjective*
contentious, polemical, disputed, doubtful, questionable, debatable, disputable.

controversy *noun*
debate, discussion, war of words, polemic, dispute, disagreement, argument, quarrel, squabble, wrangle, strife, contention, dissension.
✍ accord, agreement.

convenience *noun*
1 the convenience of everything being in one place/for the convenience of our guests: accessibility, availability, handiness, usefulness, use, utility, serviceability, service, benefit, advantage, help, suitability, fitness.
2 all modern conveniences: facility, amenity, appliance, gadget.
✍ 1 inconvenience.

convenient *adjective*
nearby, at hand, accessible, available, handy, useful, commodious, beneficial, helpful, labour-saving, adapted, fitted, suited, suitable, fit, appropriate, opportune, timely, well-timed.
✍ inconvenient, awkward.

conventional *adjective*
traditional, orthodox, formal, correct, proper, prevalent, prevailing, accepted, received, expected, unoriginal, ritual, routine, usual, customary, regular, standard, normal, ordinary, straight, stereotyped, hidebound, pedestrian, commonplace, common, run-of-the-mill.
✍ unconventional, unusual, exotic.

converge *verb*
focus, concentrate, approach, merge, coincide, meet, join, combine, gather.
✍ diverge, disperse.

conversation *noun*
talk, chat, gossip, discussion, discourse, dialogue, exchange, communication, chinwag (*infml*), tête-à-tête.

convert *verb*
1 convert the loft into a third bedroom: alter, change, turn, transform, adapt, modify, remodel, restyle, revise, reorganize.
2 convert them to Catholicism: win over, convince, persuade, reform, proselytize.

convey *verb*
carry, bear, bring, fetch, move, transport, send, forward, deliver, transfer, conduct, guide, transmit, communicate, impart, tell, relate, reveal.

convict *verb*
condemn, sentence, imprison.
▶ *noun*
criminal, felon, culprit, prisoner.

conviction *noun*
assurance, confidence, fervour, earnestness, certainty, firmness, persuasion, view, opinion, belief, faith, creed, tenet, principle.

convince *verb*
assure, persuade, sway, win over, bring round, reassure, satisfy.

convincing *adjective*
persuasive, cogent, powerful, telling,

impressive, credible, plausible, likely, probable, conclusive, incontrovertible.
F3 unconvincing, improbable.

convoluted *adjective*
twisting, winding, meandering, tortuous, involved, complicated, complex, tangled.
F3 straight, straightforward.

convulsion *noun*
1 have convulsions: fit, seizure, paroxysm, spasm, cramp, contraction, tic, tremor.
2 a convulsion of anger: eruption, outburst, furore, disturbance, commotion, tumult, agitation, turbulence, upheaval.

cook up *verb*
concoct, prepare, brew, invent, fabricate, contrive, devise, plan, plot, scheme.

cool *adjective*
1 a cool breeze/climate: chilly, fresh, breezy, nippy, cold, chilled, iced, refreshing.
2 a cool exterior: calm, unruffled, unexcited, composed, self-possessed, level-headed, unemotional, quiet, relaxed, laid-back (*infml*).
3 a cool reception: unfriendly, unwelcoming, cold, frigid, lukewarm, half-hearted, unenthusiastic, apathetic, uninterested, unresponsive, uncommunicative, reserved, distant, aloof, standoffish.
F3 1 warm, hot. 2 excited, angry. 3 friendly, welcoming.
▸ *verb*
1 cool the lemonade: chill, refrigerate, ice, freeze, fan.
2 cool his ardour: moderate, lessen, temper, dampen, quiet, abate, calm, allay, assuage (*fml*).
F3 1 warm, heat. 2 excite.
▸ *noun*
coolness, calmness, collectedness, composure, poise, self-possession, self-discipline, self-control, control, temper.

co-operate *verb*
collaborate, work together, play ball (*infml*), help, assist, aid, contribute, participate, combine, unite, conspire.

co-operation *noun*
helpfulness, assistance, participation, collaboration, teamwork, unity, co-ordination, give-and-take.
F3 opposition, rivalry, competition.

co-operative *adjective*
1 she was very co-operative: helpful, supportive, obliging, accommodating, willing.
2 a co-operative venture: collective, joint, shared, combined, united, concerted, co-ordinated.
F3 1 unco-operative, rebellious.

co-ordinate *verb*
organize, arrange, systematize, tabulate, integrate, mesh, synchronize, harmonize, match, correlate, regulate.

cope *verb*
manage, carry on, survive, get by, make do.
◆ **cope with** deal with, encounter, contend with, struggle with, grapple with, wrestle with, handle, manage, weather.

copy *noun*
duplicate, carbon copy, photocopy, Photostat®, Xerox®, facsimile, reproduction, print, tracing, transcript, transcription, replica, model, pattern, archetype, representation, image, likeness, counterfeit, forgery, fake, imitation, borrowing, plagiarism, crib.
F3 original.
▸ *verb*
duplicate, photocopy, reproduce, print, trace, transcribe, forge, counterfeit, simulate, imitate, impersonate, mimic, ape, parrot, repeat, echo, mirror, follow, emulate, borrow, plagiarize, crib.

cord *noun*
string, twine, rope, line, cable, flex, connection, link, bond, tie.

core *noun*
kernel, nucleus, heart, centre, middle, nub, crux, essence, gist, nitty-gritty (*infml*).
F3 surface, exterior.

corner *noun*
1 round the corner: angle, joint, crook, bend, turning.

2 a shady corner of the garden: nook, cranny, niche, recess, alcove, cavity, hole, hideout, hide-away, retreat.

corpse *noun*
body, stiff (*slang*), carcase, skeleton, remains, cadaver.

correct *verb*
rectify, put right, right, emend, remedy, cure, debug, redress, adjust, regulate, improve, amend.

▶ *adjective*

1 the correct answer/correct in every detail: right, accurate, precise, exact, strict, true, truthful, word-perfect, faultless, flawless.

2 the correct way to address the queen: proper, acceptable, OK (*infml*), standard, regular, just, appropriate, fitting.

F∃1 incorrect, wrong, inaccurate.

correspond *verb*

1 their version of events doesn't correspond with ours: match, fit, answer, conform, tally, square, agree, concur, coincide, correlate, accord, harmonize, dovetail, complement.

2 corresponded with her over a number of years: communicate, write.

corresponding *adjective*
matching, complementary, reciprocal, interrelated, analogous, equivalent, similar, identical.

corrode *verb*
erode, wear away, eat away, consume, waste, rust, oxidize, tarnish, impair, deteriorate, crumble, disintegrate.

corrosive *adjective*
corroding, acid, caustic, cutting, abrasive, erosive, wearing, consuming, wasting.

corrupt *adjective*
rotten, unscrupulous, unprincipled, unethical, immoral, fraudulent, shady (*infml*), dishonest, bent (*infml*), crooked (*infml*), untrustworthy, depraved, degenerate, dissolute.
F∃ethical, virtuous, upright, honest, trustworthy.

▶ *verb*
contaminate, pollute, adulterate, taint, defile (*fml*), debase, pervert, deprave, lead astray, lure, bribe, suborn.
F∃purify.

corruption *noun*
unscrupulousness, immorality, impurity, depravity, degeneration, degradation, perversion, distortion, dishonesty, crookedness (*infml*), fraud, shadiness (*infml*), bribery, extortion, vice, wickedness, iniquity (*fml*), evil.
F∃honesty, virtue.

cosmetic *adjective*
superficial, surface.
F∃essential.

cosmetics *noun*
make-up, grease paint.

cosmopolitan *adjective*
worldly, worldly-wise, well-travelled, sophisticated, urbane, international, universal.
F∃insular, parochial, rustic.

cost *noun*

1 the cost of bread/high running costs: expense, outlay, payment, disbursement (*fml*), expenditure, charge, price, rate, amount, figure, worth.

2 to my cost: detriment, harm, injury, hurt, loss, deprivation, sacrifice, penalty, price.

costly *adjective*

1 costly jewellery: expensive, dear, pricey (*infml*), exorbitant, excessive, lavish, rich, splendid, valuable, precious, priceless.

2 a costly mistake: harmful, damaging, disastrous, catastrophic, loss-making.
F∃1 cheap, inexpensive.

costume *noun*
outfit, uniform, livery, robes, vestments, dress, clothing, get-up (*infml*), fancy dress.

cosy *adjective*
snug, comfortable, comfy (*infml*), warm, sheltered, secure, homely, intimate.
F∃uncomfortable, cold.

council *noun*
committee, panel, board, cabinet, ministry, parliament, congress, assembly, convention, conference.

counsel *noun*

1 give good counsel: advice, suggestion, recommendation,

guidance, direction, information, consultation, deliberation, consideration, forethought.
2 counsel for the defence : lawyer, advocate, solicitor, attorney, barrister.
▶ *verb*
advise, warn, caution, suggest, recommend, advocate, urge, exhort, guide, direct, instruct.

count *verb*
1 counting sheep/count up to 100 : number, enumerate, list, include, reckon, calculate, compute, tell, check, add, total, tot up, score.
2 that doesn't count : matter, signify, qualify.
3 count yourself lucky : consider, regard, deem, judge, think, reckon, hold.
▶ *noun*
numbering, enumeration, poll, reckoning, calculation, computation, sum, total, tally.
◆ **count on** depend on, rely on, bank on, reckon on, expect, believe, trust.

counter *adverb*
against, in opposition, conversely.
▶ *adjective*
contrary, opposite, opposing, conflicting, contradictory, contrasting, opposed, against, adverse.
▶ *verb*
parry, resist, offset, answer, respond, retaliate, retort, return, meet.

counteract *verb*
neutralize, counterbalance, offset, countervail, act against, oppose, resist, hinder, check, thwart, frustrate, foil, defeat, undo, negate, annul, invalidate.
E3 support, assist.

counterfeit *verb*
fake, forge, fabricate, copy, imitate, impersonate, pretend, feign, simulate, sham.
▶ *adjective*
fake, false, phoney (*infml*), forged, copied, fraudulent, bogus, pseudo, sham, spurious, imitation, artificial, simulated, feigned, pretended.
E3 genuine, authentic, real.
▶ *noun*
fake, forgery, copy, reproduction, imitation, fraud, sham.

counterpart *noun*
equivalent, opposite number, complement, supplement, match, fellow, mate, twin, duplicate, copy.

countless *adjective*
innumerable, myriad, numberless, unnumbered, untold, incalculable, infinite, endless, immeasurable, measureless, limitless.
E3 finite, limited.

country *noun*
1 a foreign country/several European countries : state, nation, people, kingdom, realm, principality.
2 a walk in the country : countryside, green belt, farmland, provinces, sticks (*infml*), backwoods, wilds.
3 difficult country for smaller vehicles : terrain, land, territory.
E3 **2** town, city.
▶ *adjective*
rural, provincial, agrarian, rustic, agricultural, pastoral, bucolic (*fml*), landed.
E3 urban.

countryside *noun*
landscape, scenery, country, green belt, farmland, outdoors.

county *noun*
shire, province, region, area, district.

couple *noun*
pair, brace, twosome, duo.

coupon *noun*
voucher, token, slip, check, ticket, certificate.

courage *noun*
bravery, pluck, guts (*infml*), fearlessness, dauntlessness, heroism, gallantry, valour, boldness, audacity, nerve, daring, resolution, fortitude, spirit, mettle.
E3 cowardice, fear.

courageous *adjective*
brave, plucky, fearless, dauntless, indomitable, heroic, gallant, valiant, lion-hearted, hardy, bold, audacious, daring, intrepid, resolute.
E3 cowardly, afraid.

course *noun*
1 English/computer course : curriculum, syllabus, classes,

lessons, lectures, studies.
2 the course of events: flow, movement, advance, progress, development, furtherance, order, sequence, series, succession, progression.
3 during the course of the trial: duration, time, period, term, passage.
4 along the river's course: direction, way, path, track, road, route, channel, trail, line, circuit, orbit, trajectory, flight path.
5 course of action: plan, schedule, programme, policy, procedure, method, mode.

court *noun*
1 the highest court in the land: law-court, bench, bar, tribunal, trial, session.
2 number six Meadow Court: courtyard, yard, quadrangle, square, cloister, forecourt, enclosure.
3 the king's court: entourage, attendants, retinue, suite, train, cortège.

courteous *adjective*
polite, civil, respectful, well-mannered, well-bred, ladylike, gentlemanly, gracious, obliging, considerate, attentive, gallant, courtly, urbane, debonair, refined, polished.
E3 discourteous, impolite, rude.

courtesy *noun*
politeness, civility, respect, manners, breeding, graciousness, consideration, attention, gallantry, urbanity.
E3 discourtesy, rudeness.

cove *noun*
bay, bight, inlet, estuary, firth, fiord, creek.

cover *verb*
1 covered her face: hide, conceal, obscure, shroud, veil, screen, mask, disguise, camouflage.
2 covered with mud: coat, spread, daub, plaster, encase, wrap, envelop, clothe, dress.
3 covered the young plants: shelter, protect, shield, guard, defend.
4 cover a topic: deal with, treat, consider, examine, investigate, encompass, embrace, incorporate,

embody, involve, include, contain, comprise.
E3 1 uncover. **2** strip. **3** expose. **4** exclude.
▶ *noun*
1 a book/bed/dust cover: coating, covering, top, lid, veil, screen, mask, front, façade, jacket, wrapper, case, envelope, clothing, dress, bedspread, canopy.
2 take cover/give cover: shelter, refuge, protection, shield, guard, defence, concealment, disguise, camouflage.
◆ **cover up** conceal, hide, whitewash, dissemble (*fml*), suppress, hush up, keep dark, repress.
E3 disclose, reveal.

covering *noun*
layer, coat, coating, blanket, film, veneer, skin, crust, shell, casing, housing, wrapping, clothing, top, protection, mask, overlay, cover, shelter, roof.

cover-up *noun*
concealment, whitewash, smokescreen, front, façade, pretence, conspiracy, complicity.

covet *verb*
envy, begrudge, crave, long for, yearn for, hanker for, want, desire, fancy (*infml*), lust after.

coward *noun*
craven, faint-heart, chicken (*infml*), scaredy-cat, wimp (*infml*), renegade, deserter.
E3 hero.

cowardice *noun*
cowardliness, faint-heartedness, timorousness, spinelessness.
E3 courage, valour.

cowardly *adjective*
faint-hearted, craven, fearful, timorous, scared, unheroic, chicken-hearted, chicken-livered, chicken (*infml*), yellow (*infml*), spineless, weak, weak-kneed, soft (*infml*).
E3 brave, courageous, bold.

cower *verb*
crouch, grovel, skulk, shrink, flinch, cringe, quail, tremble, shake, shiver.

coy *adjective*
modest, demure, prudish, diffident,

shy, bashful, timid, shrinking, backward, retiring, self-effacing, reserved, evasive, arch, flirtatious, coquettish, skittish, kittenish.
F3 bold, forward.

crack *verb*
1 ice cracking/cracked a plate: split, burst, fracture, break, snap, shatter, splinter, chip.
2 thunder roared and lightening cracked: explode, burst, pop, crackle, snap, crash, clap, slap, whack (*infml*).
3 crack a code: decipher, work out, solve.
▶ *noun*
1 a crack in the marble: break, fracture, split, rift, gap, crevice, fissure, chink, line, flaw, chip.
2 the crack of the whip: explosion, burst, pop, snap, crash, clap, blow, smack, slap, whack (*infml*).
3 what did you mean by that crack?: joke, quip, witticism, gag (*infml*), wisecrack, gibe, dig.
▶ *adjective* (*infml*)
first-class, first-rate, top-notch (*infml*), excellent, superior, choice, hand-picked.
◆ **crack down on** clamp down on, end, stop, put a stop to, crush, suppress, check, repress, act against.
◆ **crack up** go mad, go to pieces, break down, collapse.

cradle *noun*
1 a baby's cradle: cot, crib, bed.
2 the cradle of civilization: source, origin, spring, wellspring, fount, fountain-head, birthplace, beginning.
▶ *verb*
hold, support, rock, lull, nurse, nurture, tend.

craft *noun*
1 arts and crafts/the craft of boat-building: skill, expertise, mastery, talent, knack, ability, aptitude, dexterity, cleverness, art, handicraft, handiwork.
2 learning his craft: trade, business, calling, vocation, job, occupation, work, employment.
3 a sturdy little craft: vessel, boat, ship, aircraft, spacecraft, spaceship.

craftsmanship *noun*
artistry, workmanship, technique, dexterity, expertise, mastery.

crafty *adjective*
sly, cunning, artful, wily, devious, subtle, scheming, calculating, designing, deceitful, fraudulent, sharp, shrewd, astute, canny.
F3 artless, naïve.

cram *verb*
stuff, jam, ram, force, press, squeeze, crush, compress, pack, crowd, overfill, glut, gorge.

cramped *adjective*
narrow, tight, uncomfortable, restricted, confined, crowded, packed, squashed, squeezed, overcrowded, jam-packed, congested.
F3 spacious.

crash *noun*
1 car crash: accident, collision, bump, smash, pile-up, smash-up (*infml*), wreck.
2 fell to the ground with a crash: bang, clash, clatter, clang, thud, thump, boom, thunder, racket, din.
3 the stock-market crash: collapse, failure, ruin, downfall, bankruptcy, depression.
▶ *verb*
1 crashed into the wall: collide, hit, knock, bump, bang.
2 crashing into a thousand pieces: break, fracture, smash, dash, shatter, splinter, shiver, fragment, disintegrate.
3 the stock market crashed: fall, topple, pitch, plunge, collapse, fail, fold (up), go under, go bust (*infml*).

crave *verb*
hunger for, thirst for, long for, yearn for, pine for, hanker after, fancy (*infml*), desire, want, need, require.
F3 dislike.

craving *noun*
appetite, hunger, thirst, longing, yearning, hankering, lust, desire, urge.
F3 dislike, distaste.

crawl *verb*
1 crawled under the table: creep, inch, edge, slither, wriggle.
2 crawl to the boss: grovel, cringe, toady, fawn, flatter, suck up (*infml*).

craze *noun*
fad, novelty, fashion, vogue, mode, trend, rage (*infml*), thing (*infml*), obsession, preoccupation, mania, frenzy, passion, infatuation, enthusiasm.

crazy *adjective*
1 a crazy person/idea: mad, insane, lunatic, unbalanced, deranged, demented, crazed, zany, potty (*infml*), barmy (*infml*), daft (*infml*), off one's head (*infml*), silly, foolish, idiotic, senseless, unwise, imprudent, nonsensical, absurd, ludicrous, ridiculous, preposterous, outrageous, half-baked, impracticable, irresponsible, wild, berserk.
2 (*infml*) crazy about golf: enthusiastic, fanatical, zealous, ardent, passionate, infatuated, enamoured, smitten, mad, wild.
F∃1 sane, sensible. **2** indifferent.

creak *verb*
squeak, groan, grate, scrape, rasp, scratch, grind, squeal, screech.

crease *noun*
fold, line, pleat, tuck, wrinkle, pucker, ruck, crinkle, corrugation, ridge, groove.
▶ *verb*
fold, pleat, wrinkle, pucker, crumple, rumple, crinkle, crimp, corrugate, ridge.

create *verb*
invent, coin, formulate, compose, design, devise, concoct, hatch, originate, initiate, found, establish, set up, institute, cause, occasion, produce, generate, engender, make, form, appoint, install, invest, ordain.
F∃ destroy.

creative *adjective*
artistic, inventive, original, imaginative, inspired, visionary, talented, gifted, clever, ingenious, resourceful, fertile, productive.
F∃ unimaginative.

creator *noun*
maker, inventor, designer, architect, author, originator, initiator.

creature *noun*
animal, beast, bird, fish, organism, being, mortal, individual, person, man, woman, body, soul.

credentials *noun*
diploma, certificate, reference, testimonial, recommendation, accreditation, authorization, warrant, licence, permit, passport, identity card, papers, documents, deed, title.

credibility *noun*
integrity, reliability, trustworthiness, plausibility, probability.
F∃ implausibility.

credit *noun*
acknowledgement, recognition, thanks, approval, commendation, praise, acclaim, tribute, glory, fame, prestige, distinction, honour, reputation, esteem, estimation.
F∃ discredit, shame.
▶ *verb*
believe, swallow (*infml*), accept, subscribe to, trust, rely on.
F∃ disbelieve.

creditable *adjective*
honourable, reputable, respectable, estimable, admirable, commendable, praiseworthy, good, excellent, exemplary, worthy, deserving.
F∃ shameful, blameworthy.

creed *noun*
belief, faith, persuasion, credo, catechism, doctrine, principles, tenets, articles, canon, dogma.

creep *verb*
inch, edge, tiptoe, steal, sneak, slink, crawl, slither, worm, wriggle, squirm, grovel, writhe.

creepy *adjective*
eerie, spooky, sinister, threatening, frightening, scary, terrifying, hair-raising, nightmarish, macabre, gruesome, horrible, unpleasant, disturbing.

crest *noun*
1 the crest of the hill: ridge, crown, top, peak, summit, pinnacle, apex, head.
2 crest of feathers on a helmet: tuft, tassel, plume, comb, mane.
3 the family crest: insignia, device, symbol, emblem, badge.

crevice *noun*
crack, fissure, split, rift, cleft, slit, chink, cranny, gap, hole, opening, break.

crew *noun*
team, party, squad, troop, corps, company, gang, band, bunch, crowd, mob, set, lot, posse (*infml*).

crime *noun*
law-breaking, lawlessness, delinquency, offence, felony, misdemeanour, misdeed, wrongdoing, misconduct, transgression, violation, sin, iniquity (*fml*), vice, villainy, wickedness, atrocity, outrage.

criminal *noun*
law-breaker, crook, felon, delinquent, offender, outlaw, wrongdoer, miscreant (*fml*), culprit, convict, prisoner.
▶ *adjective*
illegal, unlawful, illicit, lawless, wrong, culpable, indictable, crooked (*infml*), bent (*infml*), dishonest, corrupt, wicked, scandalous, deplorable.
F3 legal, lawful, honest, upright.

cringe *verb*
shrink, recoil, shy, start, flinch, wince, quail, tremble, quiver, cower, crouch, bend, bow, stoop, grovel, crawl, creep.

cripple *verb*
lame, paralyse, disable, handicap, injure, maim, mutilate, damage, impair, spoil, ruin, destroy, sabotage, weaken, incapacitate, debilitate.

crippled *adjective*
lame, paralysed, disabled, handicapped, incapacitated.

crisis *noun*
emergency, extremity, crunch (*infml*), catastrophe, disaster, calamity, dilemma, quandary, predicament, difficulty, trouble, problem.

crisp *adjective*
1 **a crisp biscuit**: crispy, crunchy, brittle, crumbly, firm, hard.
2 **a crisp autumn day**: bracing, invigorating, refreshing, fresh, brisk.
3 **a crisp reply**: terse, pithy, snappy, brief, short, clear, incisive.
F3 1 soggy, limp, flabby. 2 muggy. 3 wordy, vague.

criterion *noun*
standard, norm, touchstone, benchmark, yardstick, measure, gauge, rule, principle, canon, test.

critic *noun*
reviewer, commentator, analyst, pundit, authority, expert, judge, censor, carper, fault-finder, attacker, knocker (*infml*).

critical *adjective*
1 **at the critical moment**: crucial, vital, essential, all-important, momentous, decisive, urgent, pressing, serious, grave, dangerous, perilous.
2 **a critical study**: analytical, diagnostic, penetrating, probing, discerning, perceptive.
3 **make critical remarks**: derogatory, uncomplimentary, disparaging, disapproving, censorious, carping, fault-finding, nit-picking (*infml*).
F3 1 unimportant. 3 complimentary, appreciative.

criticism *noun*
1 **received much criticism**: condemnation, disapproval, disparagement (*fml*), fault-finding, censure, blame, brickbat, flak (*infml*).
2 **literary criticism**: review, critique, assessment, evaluation, appraisal, judgement, analysis, commentary, appreciation.
F3 1 praise, commendation.
⇨ *See also* **Word Study** *panel.*

criticize *verb*
1 **criticize her work**: condemn, slate (*infml*), slam (*infml*), knock (*infml*), disparage (*fml*), carp, find fault (with), censure, blame.
2 **criticize a literary work**: review, assess, evaluate, appraise, judge, analyse.
F3 1 praise, commend.

crockery *noun*
dishes, tableware, china, porcelain, earthenware, stoneware, pottery.

crook *noun*
criminal, thief, robber, swindler, cheat, shark (*infml*), rogue, villain, con man (*infml*).

crooked *adjective*
1 **a crooked nose**: askew, skew-whiff

WORD *study* criticism

Here are some of the informal and more formal phrases used to express **criticism**.

criticizing severely

give someone/something bad press
put the boot in (*slang*)
give someone an ear-bashing
pull something to pieces
pour scorn on someone/something
give someone the rough side of your tongue
take someone to task
cast aspersions on

pull something to bits
haul someone over the coals
pick holes in something
give someone a rap over the knuckles
tear someone/something to shreads
give someone stick (*slang*)
give someone a rough time

criticism

a put-down

a dressing-down

(*infml*), awry, lopsided, asymmetric, irregular, uneven, off-centre, tilted, slanting, bent, angled, hooked, curved, bowed, warped, distorted, misshapen, deformed, twisted, tortuous, winding, zigzag.
2 (*infml*) **something crooked about this business/a crooked lawyer**: illegal, unlawful, illicit, criminal, nefarious, dishonest, deceitful, bent (*infml*), corrupt, fraudulent, shady (*infml*), shifty, underhand, treacherous, unscrupulous, unprincipled, unethical.
F3 1 straight. **2** straight, honest.

crop *noun*
growth, yield, produce, fruits, harvest, vintage, gathering.
▸ *verb*
cut, snip, clip, shear, trim, pare, prune, lop, shorten, curtail.
◆ **crop up** arise, emerge, appear, arrive, occur, happen.

cross *adjective*
1 makes me very cross: irritable, annoyed, angry, vexed, shirty (*infml*),

bad-tempered, ill-tempered, crotchety, grumpy, grouchy, irascible, crabby, short, snappy, snappish, surly, sullen, fractious, fretful, impatient.
2 strong cross winds made the take-off difficult: transverse, crosswise, oblique, diagonal, intersecting, opposite, reciprocal.
F3 1 placid, pleasant.
▸ *verb*
1 cross the river: go across, traverse, ford, bridge, span.
2 our paths cross now and again: intersect, meet, criss-cross, lace, intertwine.
3 crossing French cattle with British ones: crossbreed, interbreed, mongrelize, hybridize, cross-fertilize, cross-pollinate, blend, mix.
4 don't cross him: thwart, frustrate, foil, hinder, impede, obstruct, block, oppose.
▸ *noun*
1 have a cross to bear: burden, load, affliction, misfortune, trouble, worry, trial, tribulation, grief, misery, woe.

2 a collie/golden retriever cross:
crossbreed, hybrid, mongrel, blend,
mixture, amalgam, combination.
3 a cross on a chain: crucifix.

crouch *verb*
squat, kneel, stoop, bend, bow, hunch,
duck, cower, cringe.

crowd *noun*
1 a crowd of demonstrators: throng,
multitude, host, mob, masses,
populace, people, public, riff-raff,
rabble, horde, swarm, flock, herd,
pack, press, crush, squash, assembly,
company, group, bunch, lot,
2 kick the ball into the crowd:
spectators, gate, attendance,
audience.
3 not one of our crowd: set, circle,
clique.
▶ *verb*
gather, congregate, muster, huddle,
mass, throng, swarm, flock, surge,
stream, push, shove, elbow, jostle,
press, squeeze, bundle, pile, pack,
congest, cram, compress.

crowded *adjective*
full, filled, packed, jammed, jam-
packed, congested, cramped,
crammed, overcrowded,
overpopulated, busy, teeming,
swarming, overflowing.
🔁empty, deserted.

crown *noun*
1 a crown of thorns: coronet, diadem,
tiara, circlet, wreath, garland.
2 the Wimbledon crown: prize, trophy,
reward, honour, laurels.
3 the powers of the crown: sovereign,
monarch, king, queen, ruler,
sovereignty, monarchy, royalty.
4 the crown of the hill: top, tip, apex,
crest, summit, pinnacle, peak, acme.
▶ *verb*
**1 crowning him king/Olympic
champion:** enthrone, anoint, adorn,
festoon, honour, dignify, reward.
**2 saw the award as crowning her
career:** top, cap, complete, fulfil,
consummate, perfect.

crucial *adjective*
urgent, pressing, vital, essential, key,
pivotal, central, important,

momentous, decisive, critical,
trying, testing, searching.
🔁unimportant, trivial.

crude *adjective*
1 crude oil: raw, unprocessed,
unrefined, rough, coarse, unfinished,
unpolished.
2 a crude dwelling: rough, natural,
primitive, makeshift.
3 a crude remark: vulgar, coarse, rude,
indecent, obscene, gross, dirty, lewd.
🔁**1** refined, finished. **3** polite, decent.

cruel *adjective*
fierce, ferocious, vicious, savage,
barbarous, bloodthirsty, murderous,
cold-blooded, sadistic, brutal,
inhuman, inhumane, unkind,
malevolent, spiteful, callous, heartless,
unfeeling, merciless, pitiless, flinty,
hard-hearted, stony-hearted,
implacable, ruthless, remorseless,
relentless, unrelenting, inexorable,
grim, hellish, atrocious, bitter,
harsh, severe, cutting, painful,
excruciating.
🔁kind, compassionate, merciful.

cruelty *noun*
ferocity, viciousness, savagery,
barbarity, bloodthirstiness,
murderousness, violence, sadism,
brutality, inhumanity, spite, venom,
callousness, heartlessness, hard-
heartedness, mercilessness,
ruthlessness, tyranny, harshness,
severity.
🔁kindness, compassion, mercy.

crumble *verb*
fragment, break up, decompose,
disintegrate, decay, degenerate,
deteriorate, collapse, crush, pound,
grind, powder, pulverize.

crusade *noun*
campaign, drive, push, movement,
cause, undertaking, expedition, holy
war, jihad.

crush *verb*
1 crush the garlic cloves: squash,
compress, squeeze, press, pulp, break,
smash, pound, pulverize, grind,
crumble.
2 crushing her dress: crumple, wrinkle.
3 the rebels were crushed: conquer,

vanquish (*fml*), demolish, devastate, overpower, overwhelm, overcome, quash, quell, subdue, put down, humiliate, shame, abash.

crust *noun*
surface, exterior, outside, covering, coat, coating, layer, film, skin, rind, shell, scab, incrustation, caking, concretion.

crux *noun*
nub, heart, core, essence.

cry *verb*
1 cry pathetically: weep, sob, blubber, wail, bawl, whimper, snivel.
2 crying for help: shout, call, exclaim, roar, bellow, yell, scream, shriek, screech, yelp.
▶ *noun*
1 have a good cry: weep, sob, blubber, wail, bawl, whimper, snivel.
2 a cry for help: shout, call, plea, exclamation, roar, bellow, yell, scream, shriek, yelp.

cryptic *adjective*
enigmatic, ambiguous, equivocal, puzzling, perplexing, mysterious, strange, bizarre, secret, hidden, veiled, obscure, abstruse, esoteric, dark, occult.
F3 straightforward, clear, obvious.

cuddle *verb*
hug, embrace, clasp, hold, nurse, nestle, snuggle, pet, fondle, caress.

cuddly *adjective*
cuddlesome, lovable, huggable, plump, soft, warm, cosy.

cue *noun*
signal, sign, nod, hint, suggestion, reminder, prompt, incentive, stimulus.

culminate *verb*
climax, end (up), terminate, close, conclude, finish, consummate.
F3 start, begin.

culprit *noun*
guilty party, offender, wrongdoer, miscreant (*fml*), law-breaker, criminal, felon, delinquent.

cult *noun*
1 religious cults: sect, denomination, school, movement, party, faction.

2 become something of a cult: craze, fad, fashion, vogue, trend.

cultivate *verb*
1 cultivating the land/rice: farm, till, work, plough, grow, sow, plant, tend, harvest.
2 cultivating new talent: foster, nurture, cherish, help, aid, support, encourage, promote, further, work on, develop, train, prepare, polish, refine, improve, enrich.
F3 2 neglect.

cultural *adjective*
artistic, aesthetic, liberal, civilizing, humanizing, enlightening, educational, edifying, improving, enriching, elevating.

culture *noun*
1 ancient cultures/Western culture: civilization, society, lifestyle, way of life, customs, mores.
2 a man of culture: cultivation, taste, education, enlightenment, breeding, gentility, refinement, politeness, urbanity.

cultured *adjective*
cultivated, civilized, advanced, enlightened, educated, well-read, well-informed, scholarly, highbrow, well-bred, refined, polished, genteel, urbane.
F3 uncultured, uneducated, ignorant.

cumbersome *adjective*
awkward, inconvenient, bulky, unwieldy, unmanageable, burdensome, onerous, heavy, weighty.
F3 convenient, manageable.

cunning *adjective*
crafty, sly, artful, wily, tricky, devious, subtle, deceitful, guileful, sharp, shrewd, astute, canny, knowing, deep, imaginative, ingenious, skilful, deft, dexterous, sneaky.
F3 naïve, ingenuous, gullible.
▶ *noun*
craftiness, slyness, artfulness, trickery, deviousness, subtlety, deceitfulness, guile, sharpness, shrewdness, astuteness, ingenuity, cleverness, adroitness.

cup *noun*
mug, tankard, beaker, goblet, chalice, trophy.

curb *verb*
restrain, constrain, restrict, contain, control, check, moderate, bridle, muzzle, suppress, subdue, repress, inhibit, hinder, impede, hamper, retard.
🖅 encourage, foster.

curdle *verb*
coagulate, congeal, clot, thicken, turn, sour, ferment.

cure *verb*
1 cure the illness: heal, remedy, correct, restore, repair, mend, relieve, ease, alleviate, help.
2 cure the ham: preserve, dry, smoke, salt, pickle, kipper.
▶ *noun*
remedy, antidote, panacea, medicine, specific, corrective, restorative, healing, treatment, therapy, alleviation, recovery.

curiosity *noun*
1 his curiosity irritated her: inquisitiveness, nosiness, prying, snooping, interest.
2 a bit of a curiosity: oddity, rarity, freak, phenomenon, spectacle.

curious *adjective*
1 the neighbours are too curious about our activities: inquisitive, nosey, prying, meddlesome, questioning, inquiring, interested.
2 a curious sight: odd, queer, funny (*infml*), strange, peculiar, bizarre, mysterious, puzzling, extraordinary, unusual, rare, unique, novel, exotic, unconventional, unorthodox, quaint.
🖅 1 uninterested, indifferent. 2 ordinary, usual, normal.

curl *verb*
crimp, frizz, wave, ripple, bend, curve, meander, loop, turn, twist, wind, wreathe, twine, coil, spiral, corkscrew, scroll.
🖅 uncurl.
▶ *noun*
wave, kink, swirl, twist, ringlet, coil, spiral, whorl.

curly *adjective*
wavy, kinky, curling, spiralled, corkscrew, curled, crimped, permed, frizzy, fuzzy.
🖅 straight.

currency *noun*
1 European currencies: money, legal tender, coinage, coins, notes, bills.
2 give currency to their beliefs: acceptance, publicity, popularity, vogue, circulation, prevalence, exposure.

current *adjective*
present, on-going, existing, contemporary, present-day, modern, fashionable, up-to-date, up-to-the-minute, trendy (*infml*), popular, widespread, prevalent, common, general, prevailing, reigning, accepted.
🖅 obsolete, old-fashioned.
▶ *noun*
draught, stream, jet, flow, drift, tide, course, trend, tendency, undercurrent, mood, feeling.

curse *noun*
1 shouting curses: swear word, oath, expletive, obscenity, profanity, blasphemy.
2 put a curse on someone/congestion is the curse of city life: jinx, anathema, bane, evil, plague, scourge, affliction, trouble, torment, ordeal, calamity, disaster.
🖅 2 blessing, advantage.
▶ *verb*
1 cursed loudly: swear, blaspheme, condemn, denounce, fulminate (*fml*).
2 cursed with backache: blight, plague, scourge, afflict, trouble, torment.
🖅 2 bless.

curtail *verb*
shorten, truncate, cut, trim, abridge, abbreviate, lessen, decrease, reduce, restrict.
🖅 lengthen, extend, prolong.

curtain *noun*
blind, screen, backdrop, hanging, drapery, tapestry.

curve *verb*
bend, arch, arc, bow, bulge, hook, crook, turn, wind, twist, spiral, coil.
▶ *noun*
bend, turn, arc, trajectory, loop, camber, curvature.

curved *adjective*
bent, arched, bowed, rounded, humped, convex, concave, crooked, twisted, sweeping, sinuous, serpentine.
F∃ straight.

cushion *noun*
pad, buffer, shock absorber, bolster, pillow, headrest, hassock.
▶ *verb*
soften, deaden, dampen, absorb, muffle, stifle, suppress, lessen, mitigate, protect, bolster, support.

custody *noun*
1 be granted custody of the children: keeping, possession, charge, care, safe-keeping, protection, preservation, custodianship, trusteeship, guardianship, supervision.
2 in police custody: detention, confinement, imprisonment, incarceration.

custom *noun*
tradition, usage, use, habit, routine, procedure, practice, policy, way, manner, style, form, convention, etiquette, formality, observance, ritual.

customary *adjective*
traditional, conventional, accepted, established, habitual, routine, regular, usual, normal, ordinary, everyday, familiar, common, general, popular, fashionable, prevailing.
F∃ unusual, rare.

customer *noun*
client, patron, regular, punter (*infml*), consumer, shopper, buyer, purchaser, prospect.

cut *verb*
1 cut hair/the cake/my finger/a hole in something: clip, trim, crop, shear, mow, shave, pare, chop, hack, hew, slice, carve, divide, part, split, bisect, dock, lop, sever, prune, excise, incise,
penetrate, pierce, stab, wound, nick, gash, slit, slash, lacerate, score, engrave, chisel, sculpt.
2 cutting tax/the text: reduce, decrease, lower, shorten, curtail, abbreviate, abridge, condense, précis, edit, delete.
3 he cut me dead: ignore, cold-shoulder, spurn, avoid, snub, slight, rebuff, insult.
▶ *noun*
1 a deep cut: incision, wound, nick, gash, slit, slash, rip, laceration.
2 spending cuts: reduction, decrease, lowering, cutback, saving, economy.
◆ **cut down 1** cut down a tree: fell, hew, lop, level, raze.
2 cut down our expenses: reduce, decrease, lower, lessen, diminish.
◆ **cut in** interrupt, butt in, interject, interpose, intervene, intrude.
◆ **cut off 1** cut off his head/the supply: sever, amputate, separate, isolate, disconnect, block, obstruct, intercept.
2 cut off her allowance: stop, end, halt, suspend, discontinue, disown, disinherit.
◆ **cut out** excise, extract, remove, delete, eliminate, exclude, debar, stop, cease.
◆ **cut up** chop, dice, mince, dissect, divide, carve, slice, slash.

cutback *noun*
cut, saving, economy, retrenchment, reduction, decrease, lowering, lessening.

cutting *adjective*
1 a cutting remark: sharp, keen, pointed, trenchant (*fml*), incisive, wounding, stinging, mordant (*fml*), caustic, acid, scathing, sarcastic, malicious.
2 a cutting wind: biting, bitter, raw, chill, penetrating, piercing.
▶ *noun*
clipping, extract, piece.

cycle *noun*
circle, round, rotation, revolution, series, sequence, phase, period, era, age, epoch, aeon.

cylinder *noun*
column, barrel, drum, reel, bobbin, spool, spindle.

cynic *noun*
sceptic, doubter, pessimist, killjoy, spoilsport (*infml*), scoffer, knocker (*infml*).

cynical *adjective*
sceptical, doubtful, doubting, distrustful, disillusioned, disenchanted, pessimistic, negative, scornful, derisive, contemptuous, sneering, scoffing, mocking, sarcastic, sardonic, ironic.

dab *verb*
pat, tap, daub, swab, wipe.

daft *adjective*
1 a daft thing to say: foolish, crazy, silly, stupid, absurd, dotty (*infml*), idiotic, inane.
2 he's gone daft: insane, mad, lunatic, simple, crazy, mental, potty (*infml*).
3 (*infml*) daft about her: infatuated.
Ⓕ1 sensible. **2** sane.

daily *adjective*
a daily occurrence: regular, routine, everyday, customary, common, commonplace, ordinary, diurnal (*fml*).

dainty *adjective*
1 dainty little thing: delicate, elegant, exquisite, refined, fine, graceful, neat, charming, delectable, petite.
2 a dainty eater: fastidious, fussy, particular, scrupulous, nice (*fml*).
Ⓕ1 gross, clumsy.

dam *noun*
barrier, barrage, embankment, blockage, obstruction, hindrance.
▶ *verb*
block, confine, restrict, check, barricade, staunch, stem, obstruct.

damage *noun*
harm, injury, hurt, destruction, devastation, loss, suffering, mischief, mutilation, impairment, detriment.
Ⓕ repair.
▶ *verb*
harm, injure, hurt, spoil, ruin, impair, mar, wreck, deface, mutilate, weaken, tamper with, play havoc with, incapacitate.
Ⓕ mend, repair, fix.

damp *noun*
dampness, moisture, clamminess, dankness, humidity, wet, dew, drizzle, fog, mist, vapour.
Ⓕ dryness.
▶ *adjective*
moist, wet, clammy, dank, humid, dewy, muggy, drizzly, misty, soggy.
Ⓕ dry, arid.

dampen *verb*
1 dampen the cloth: moisten, wet, spray.
2 dampen their enthusiasm: discourage, dishearten, deter, dash, dull, deaden, restrain, check, depress, dismay, reduce, lessen, moderate, decrease, diminish, muffle, stifle, smother.
Ⓕ1 dry. **2** encourage.

dance *noun*
ball, hop (*infml*), knees-up (*infml*), social, shindig (*infml*).

danger *noun*
1 in danger of falling: insecurity, endangerment, jeopardy, precariousness, liability, vulnerability.
2 the dangers of smoking: risk, threat, peril, hazard, menace.
Ⓕ1 safety, security. **2** safety.

dangerous *adjective*
unsafe, insecure, risky, threatening, breakneck, hairy (*infml*), hazardous, perilous, precarious, reckless, treacherous, vulnerable, menacing, exposed, alarming, critical, severe, serious, grave, daring, nasty.
Ⓕ safe, secure, harmless.

dangle *verb*
hang, droop, swing, sway, flap, trail.

dank *adjective*
damp, moist, clammy, dewy, slimy, soggy.
Ⓕ dry.

dappled *adjective*
speckled, mottled, spotted, stippled, dotted, flecked, freckled, variegated, bespeckled, piebald, checkered.

dare *verb*
1 wouldn't dare ask him: risk, venture, brave, hazard, adventure, endanger, stake, gamble.
2 daring her to jump: challenge, defy, goad, provoke, taunt.
▶ *noun*
challenge, provocation, taunt, gauntlet.

daring *adjective*
bold, adventurous, intrepid, fearless, brave, plucky, audacious, dauntless, reckless, rash, impulsive, valiant.
F3 cautious, timid, afraid.
▶ *noun*
boldness, fearlessness, courage, bravery, nerve, audacity, guts (*infml*), intrepidity, defiance, pluck, rashness, spirit, grit, gall, prowess.
F3 caution, timidity, cowardice.

dark *adjective*
1 a dark room: unlit, overcast, black, dim, unilluminated, shadowy, murky, cloudy, dusky, dingy.
2 a dark mood: gloomy, grim, cheerless, dismal, bleak, forbidding, sombre, sinister, mournful, ominous, menacing, drab.
3 dark secrets: hidden, mysterious, obscure, secret, unintelligible, enigmatic, cryptic, abstruse (*fml*).
F3 1 light. 2 bright, cheerful. 3 comprehensible.
▶ *noun*
1 scared of the dark: darkness, dimness, night, night-time, nightfall, gloom, dusk, twilight, murkiness.
2 stay in the dark: concealment, secrecy, obscurity.
F3 1 light. 2 openness.

dart *verb*
1 swallows darting about after insects: dash, bound, sprint, flit, flash, fly, rush, run, race, spring, tear.
2 darting a glance in her direction: throw, hurl, fling, shoot, sling, launch, propel, send.
▶ *noun*
bolt, arrow, barb, shaft.

dash *verb*
1 must dash: rush, dart, hurry, race, sprint, run, bolt, tear.
2 dashing the boat against the rocks: smash, strike, lash, pound, throw, crash, hurl, fling.
3 dash their hopes: crush, smash, shatter, discourage, disappoint, dampen, confound, blight, ruin, destroy, spoil, frustrate.
▶ *noun*
1 a dash of lemon juice: drop, pinch, touch, flavour, soupçon, suggestion, hint, bit, little.
2 make a dash for the bus: sprint, dart, bolt, rush, spurt, race, run.

data *noun*
information, documents, facts, input, statistics, figures, details, materials.

date *noun*
1 an earlier/later date: time, age, period, era, stage, epoch.
2 have a date with destiny: appointment, engagement, assignation, meeting, rendezvous.
3 met her date outside the cinema: escort, steady (*infml*), partner, friend.

daunt *verb*
discourage, dishearten, put off, deter, intimidate, overawe, unnerve, alarm, dismay, frighten, scare.
F3 encourage.

dawdle *verb*
delay, loiter, lag, hang about, dally, trail, potter, dilly-dally (*infml*).
F3 hurry.

dawn *noun*
1 get up at dawn: sunrise, daybreak, morning, daylight.
2 the dawn of a new era of prosperity: beginning, start, emergence, onset, origin, birth, advent.
F3 1 dusk. 2 end.

day *noun*
1 during the day: daytime, daylight.
2 in the days of Henry VIII: age, period, time, date, era, generation, epoch.
F3 1 night.
◆ **day after day** regularly, continually, endlessly, persistently, monotonously, perpetually, relentlessly.

◆ **day by day** gradually, progressively, slowly but surely, steadily.

daydream *noun*
fantasy, imagining, reverie, castles in the air, pipe dream, vision, musing, wish, dream, figment.

daze *verb*
stun, stupefy, shock, bewilder, confuse, baffle, dumbfound, amaze, surprise, startle, perplex, astonish, flabbergast (*infml*), astound, stagger.
▸ *noun*
bewilderment, confusion, stupor, trance, shock, distraction.

dazzle *verb*
1 bright sunlight dazzled him: daze, blind, confuse, blur.
2 dazzled the audience with their skill: fascinate, impress, overwhelm, awe, overawe, amaze, astonish, bewitch, stupefy.

dead *adjective*
1 dead on arrival at hospital: lifeless, deceased, inanimate, defunct, departed, late, gone.
2 fingers went dead: unresponsive, apathetic, dull, indifferent, insensitive, numb, cold, frigid, lukewarm, torpid.
3 dead on his feet: exhausted, tired, worn out, dead-beat (*infml*).
4 dead centre: exact, absolute, perfect, unqualified, utter, outright, complete, entire, total, downright.
E3 1 alive. 2 lively. 3 refreshed.

deaden *verb*
reduce, blunt, muffle, lessen, quieten, suppress, weaken, numb, diminish, stifle, alleviate, anaesthetize, desensitize, smother, check, abate, allay, dampen, hush, mute, paralyse.
E3 heighten.

deadlock *noun*
standstill, stalemate, checkmate, impasse, dead end, halt.

deadly *adjective*
1 deadly poison: lethal, fatal, dangerous, venomous, destructive, pernicious, malignant, murderous, mortal.
2 his lectures are absolutely deadly: dull, boring, uninteresting, tedious, monotonous.

3 a deadly aim: unerring, effective, true.
E3 1 harmless. 2 exciting.

deaf *adjective*
1 go deaf: hard of hearing, stone-deaf.
2 deaf to their pleas: unconcerned, indifferent, unmoved, oblivious, heedless, unmindful.
E3 2 aware, conscious.

deafening *adjective*
piercing, ear-splitting, booming, resounding, thunderous, roaring.
E3 quiet.

deal *noun*
1 cause a great deal of trouble: quantity, amount, extent, degree, portion, share.
2 a better deal: agreement, contract, understanding, pact, transaction, bargain, buy.
3 it's your deal: round, hand, distribution.
▸ *verb*
1 deal the cards/deal out punishment: apportion, distribute, share, dole out, divide, allot, dispense, assign, mete out, give, bestow.
2 dealing in antiques: trade, negotiate, traffic, bargain, treat.
◆ **deal with** attend to, concern, see to, manage, handle, cope with, treat, consider, oversee.

dealer *noun*
trader, merchant, wholesaler, marketer, merchandiser.

dear *adjective*
1 my dear friend: loved, beloved, treasured, valued, cherished, precious, favourite, esteemed, intimate, close, darling, familiar.
2 a car was too dear so I bought a bike: expensive, high-priced, costly, overpriced, pricey (*infml*).
E3 1 disliked, hated. 2 cheap.
▸ *noun*
beloved, loved one, precious, darling, treasure.

death *noun*
1 cause many deaths/death by hanging: decease, end, finish, loss, demise, departure, fatality, cessation, passing, expiration, dissolution.

WORD study

death

People are often reluctant to refer in a direct way to **death**, and there are therefore many phrases that allow you to avoid using the word itself.

to die

breathe your last
cash in your chips (*slang*)
pop your clogs (*slang*)
give up the ghost
lose your life
snuff it (*slang*)
pass away
go belly up (*US slang*)

kick the bucket (*slang*)
shuffle off this mortal coil
bite the dust
depart this life
meet your maker
go the way of all flesh
peg out (*slang*)

dying young

go to an early grave

be cut off in your prime

dead

pushing up the daisies (*slang*)
six feet under (*slang*)
at rest

dead as a doornail/dodo
put to the sword
gone to the happy hunting-
ground

approaching death

someone's days are numbered
not be long for this world
your number is up

be at death's door
your hour has come

to murder someone

bump someone off (*slang*)
do someone in (*slang*)

do away with someone
rub someone out (*slang*)

2 the death of communism:
destruction, ruin, undoing, downfall,
annihilation, extermination,
extinction, obliteration, eradication.
F3 1 life, birth.
⇨ See also **Word Study** panel.

debase *verb*
degrade, demean, devalue, defile (*fml*),
sully (*fml*), pollute, corrupt, adulterate,
taint, lower, reduce.

debatable *adjective*
questionable, uncertain, disputable,
contestable, controversial, arguable,
open to question, doubtful,
contentious, undecided, unsettled,
problematical, dubious, moot.
F3 unquestionable, certain,
incontrovertible.

debate *verb*
1 debating the point: dispute, argue,

discuss, contend, wrangle.
2 debating whether to go: consider, deliberate, ponder, reflect, meditate on, mull over, weigh.
▶ *noun*
discussion, argument, controversy, disputation, deliberation, reflection, consideration, contention, dispute, polemic.

debris *noun*
remains, ruins, rubbish, waste, wreck, wreckage, litter, fragments, rubble, trash, pieces, bits, sweepings, drift.

debt *noun*
indebtedness, obligation, debit, arrears, due, liability, duty, bill, commitment, claim, score.
F3 credit, asset.

debut *noun*
introduction, launching, beginning, entrance, presentation, inauguration, première, appearance, initiation.

decadent *adjective*
corrupt, debased, debauched, depraved, dissolute, immoral, degenerate, degraded, self-indulgent, decaying, declining.
F3 moral.

decay *verb*
1 plant material decays to form compost: rot, go bad, putrefy, decompose, spoil, perish, mortify.
2 this area is slowly decaying: decline, deteriorate, disintegrate, corrode, crumble, waste away, degenerate, wear away, dwindle, shrivel, wither, sink.
F3 2 flourish, grow.

deceased *adjective*
dead, departed, former, late, lost, defunct, expired, gone, finished, extinct.

deceit *noun*
deception, pretence, cheating, misrepresentation, fraud, duplicity, trickery, fraudulence, double-dealing, underhandedness, fake, sham, subterfuge, swindle, treachery, hypocrisy, artifice, ruse, cunning, slyness, craftiness, imposition, shift, abuse.
F3 honesty, openness, frankness.

deceitful *adjective*
dishonest, deceptive, deceiving, false, insincere, untrustworthy, double-dealing, fraudulent, two-faced (*infml*), treacherous, duplicitous, guileful, tricky (*infml*), underhand, sneaky, counterfeit, crafty, hypocritical, designing, illusory.
F3 honest, open.

deceive *verb*
mislead, delude, cheat, betray, fool, take in (*infml*), trick, dissemble (*fml*), hoax, con (*infml*), have on (*infml*), take for a ride (*infml*), double-cross (*infml*), dupe, kid (*infml*), swindle, impose upon, bamboozle (*infml*), two-time (*infml*), lead on, outwit, hoodwink, beguile, ensnare, camouflage, abuse.

decent *adjective*
1 not decent: respectable, proper, fitting, decorous, chaste, seemly, suitable, modest, appropriate, presentable, pure, fit, becoming, befitting, nice.
2 very decent of you: kind, obliging, courteous, helpful, generous, polite, gracious.
3 a decent salary/effort: adequate, acceptable, satisfactory, reasonable, sufficient, tolerable, competent.
F3 1 indecent. 2 disobliging.

deception *noun*
deceit, pretence, trick, cheat, fraud, lie, dissembling (*fml*), deceptiveness, insincerity, con (*infml*), sham, fallacy, subterfuge, artifice, hypocrisy, bluff, treachery, hoax, fraudulence, duplicity, ruse, snare, leg-pull (*infml*), illusion, wile, guile, craftiness, cunning.
F3 openness, honesty.

deceptive *adjective*
dishonest, false, fraudulent, misleading, unreliable, illusive, fake, illusory, spurious, mock, fallacious, ambiguous, specious.
F3 genuine, artless, open.

decide *verb*
choose, determine, resolve, reach a decision, settle, elect, opt, judge, adjudicate, conclude, fix, purpose, decree.

decidedly *adverb*
definitely, certainly, undeniably, indisputably, absolutely, undisputedly, unmistakably, unquestionably, positively, unambiguously, distinctly, emphatically.

decipher *verb*
decode, unscramble, crack, construe, interpret, make out (*infml*), figure out (*infml*), understand.

decision *noun*
1 the final decision: result, conclusion, outcome, verdict, finding, settlement, judgement, arbitration, ruling.
2 act with decision: determination, decisiveness, firmness, resolve, purpose.
E⒮ 2 indecision.

decisive *adjective*
1 have decisive evidence: conclusive, definite, definitive, absolute, final.
2 he's usually very decisive: resolute, determined, decided, positive, firm, forceful, forthright, strong-minded.
3 a decisive moment in history: significant, critical, crucial, influential, momentous, fateful.
E⒮ 1 inconclusive. **2** indecisive, hesitant. **3** insignificant.

declaration *noun*
1 a declaration of guilt: affirmation, acknowledgement, assertion, statement, testimony, attestation, disclosure, profession, revelation.
2 a public declaration: announcement, notification, pronouncement, edict, proclamation, manifesto.

declare *verb*
1 declare that it was so: affirm, assert, claim, profess, maintain, state, attest (*fml*), certify, confess, confirm, disclose, reveal, show, aver, swear, testify, witness, validate.
2 declared his intention: announce, proclaim, pronounce, decree, broadcast.

decline *noun*
deterioration, dwindling, lessening, decay, degeneration, weakening, worsening, failing, downturn, diminution, falling-off, recession, slump, abatement.

E⒮ improvement, rise.
▶ *verb*
1 decline his invitation: refuse, reject, turn down, deny, forgo.
2 decline in value/her health is declining: diminish, decrease, dwindle, lessen, fall, sink, wane, flag.

decode *verb*
decipher, interpret, crack (*infml*), figure out (*infml*), unscramble, translate, transliterate, uncipher.
E⒮ encode.

decorate *verb*
1 decorate the tree: ornament, adorn, beautify, embellish, trim, deck, grace, enrich, prettify, trick out.
2 decorating the bedroom: renovate, do up (*infml*), paint, paper, colour, refurbish.
3 was decorated for bravery: honour, crown, garland.

decoration *noun*
1 Christmas decorations/a style with little decoration: ornament, frill, adornment, ornamentation, trimming, embellishment, beautification, garnish, flourish, enrichment, elaboration, scroll, bauble.
2 a decoration for valour: award, medal, order, badge, garland, crown, colours, ribbon, laurel, star, emblem.

decorative *adjective*
ornamental, fancy, adorning, beautifying, embellishing, non-functional, pretty, ornate, enhancing.
E⒮ plain.

decorum *noun*
propriety, seemliness, etiquette, good manners, respectability, protocol, behaviour, decency, dignity, grace, deportment, restraint, politeness, modesty, breeding.
E⒮ impropriety, indecorum, bad manners.

decoy *noun*
lure, trap, enticement, inducement, ensnarement, pretence, attraction, bait.

decrease *verb*
lessen, lower, diminish, dwindle, decline, fall off, reduce, subside, abate,

cut down, contract, drop, ease, shrink, taper, wane, slim, slacken, peter out, curtail.
F3 increase.

▶ *noun*

lessening, reduction, decline, falling-off, dwindling, loss, diminution, abatement, cutback, contraction, downturn, shrinkage, subsidence.
F3 increase.

decree *noun*
order, command, law, ordinance, regulation, ruling, statute, act, edict, fiat, proclamation, mandate, precept (*fml*).

▶ *verb*

order, command, rule, lay down, dictate, decide, determine, ordain, prescribe, proclaim, pronounce.

decrepit *adjective*
dilapidated, run-down, rickety, broken-down, worn-out, tumbledown, clapped-out (*infml*).

dedicate *verb*
1 dedicating himself to his studies: devote, commit, assign, give over to, pledge, present, offer, sacrifice, surrender.
2 dedicating the church to St Agnes: consecrate, bless, sanctify, set apart, hallow.
3 dedicated the book to her husband: inscribe, address.

dedicated *adjective*
devoted, committed, enthusiastic, single-minded, whole-hearted, single-hearted, zealous, given over to, purposeful.
F3 uncommitted, apathetic.

dedication *noun*
1 shows exceptional dedication: commitment, devotion, single-mindedness, whole-heartedness, allegiance, attachment, adherence, faithfulness, loyalty, self-sacrifice.
2 dedication of the chapel: consecration, hallowing, presentation.
3 a dedication to his parents: inscription, address.
F3 1 apathy.

deduce *verb*
derive, infer, gather, conclude, reason, surmise, understand, draw, glean.

deduct *verb*
subtract, take away, remove, reduce by, decrease by, knock off (*infml*), withdraw.
F3 add.

deduction *noun*
1 powers of deduction/my deduction is that he is guilty: inference, reasoning, finding, conclusion, corollary, assumption, result.
2 the deduction of tax: subtraction, reduction, decrease, diminution, abatement, withdrawal, discount, allowance.
F3 2 addition, increase.

deed *noun*
1 the deeds of the knights of old: action, act, achievement, performance, exploit, feat, fact, truth, reality.
2 a deed of sale: document, contract, record, title, transaction, indenture (*fml*).

deep *adjective*
1 a deep gorge: bottomless, unplumbed, fathomless, cavernous, yawning.
2 his books are too deep for me to understand: obscure, mysterious, difficult, recondite (*fml*), abstruse, esoteric.
3 a deep person: wise, perceptive, discerning, profound, learned, astute.
4 a deep sleep: intense, serious, earnest, extreme.
5 a deep groan/voice: low, bass, resonant, booming.
F3 1 shallow, open. **2** clear, plain, open. **3** superficial. **4** light. **5** high.

deep-seated *adjective*
ingrained, entrenched, deep-rooted, fixed, confirmed, deep, settled.
F3 eradicable, temporary.

deface *verb*
damage, spoil, disfigure, blemish, impair, mutilate, mar, sully (*fml*), tarnish, vandalize, deform, obliterate, injure, destroy.
F3 repair.

defamation *noun* (*fml*)
vilification (*fml*), aspersion (*fml*), slander, libel, disparagement (*fml*), slur, smear, innuendo, scandal.
F3 commendation, praise.

default *verb*
fail, evade, defraud, neglect, dodge, swindle, backslide.

defeat *verb*
1 defeat one's enemies: conquer, beat, overpower, subdue, overthrow, worst, repel, subjugate, overwhelm, rout, ruin, trounce, thrash (*infml*), thump (*infml*), quell, vanquish (*fml*).
2 the problem defeated him: frustrate, confound, get the better of, disappoint, foil, thwart, baffle, checkmate.
▶ *noun*
1 heavy defeat on the battlefield: conquest, beating, rout, repulsion, subjugation, vanquishment (*fml*), thrashing (*infml*).
2 defeat on a specific issue: frustration, failure, setback, downfall, thwarting, disappointment, checkmate.

defect *noun*
imperfection, fault, flaw, deficiency, failing, mistake, inadequacy, blemish, error, bug (*infml*), shortcoming, want, weakness, frailty, lack, spot, absence, taint.

defective *adjective*
faulty, imperfect, out of order, flawed, deficient, broken, abnormal.
E3 in order, operative.

defence *noun*
1 the castle provided defence against attack: protection, resistance, security, fortification, cover, safeguard, shelter, guard, shield, deterrence, barricade, bastion, immunity, bulwark, rampart, buttress.
2 evidence offered in his defence: justification, explanation, excuse, argument, exoneration, plea, vindication, pleading, alibi, case.
E3 1 attack, assault. **2** accusation.

defenceless *adjective*
unprotected, undefended, unarmed, unguarded, vulnerable, exposed, helpless, powerless.
E3 protected, guarded.

defend *verb*
1 defending their borders: protect, guard, safeguard, shelter, fortify, secure, shield, screen, cover, contest.

2 a lawyer defending the accused: support, stand up for, stand by, uphold, endorse, vindicate, champion, argue for, speak up for, justify, plead.
E3 1 attack. **2** accuse.

defer *verb*
delay, postpone, put off, adjourn, hold over, shelve, suspend, procrastinate, prorogue (*fml*), protract, waive.

defiant *adjective*
challenging, resistant, antagonistic, aggressive, rebellious, insubordinate, disobedient, intransigent, bold, contumacious (*fml*), insolent, obstinate, unco-operative, provocative.
E3 compliant, submissive.

deficiency *noun*
1 a deficiency of able candidates: shortage, lack, inadequacy, scarcity, insufficiency, dearth, want, scantiness, absence, deficit.
2 highlight the deficiencies in the system: imperfection, shortcoming, weakness, fault, defect, flaw, failing, frailty.
E3 1 excess, surfeit. **2** perfection.

deficit *noun*
shortage, shortfall, deficiency, loss, arrears, lack, default.
E3 excess.

define *verb*
1 defining the boundaries of the estate: bound, limit, delimit, demarcate, mark out.
2 define the meaning: explain, characterize, describe, interpret, expound, determine, designate, specify, spell out, detail.

definite *adjective*
1 a definite job offer: certain, settled, sure, positive, fixed, decided, assured, determined, guaranteed.
2 his answer was a quite definite 'no': clear, clear-cut, exact, precise, specific, explicit, particular, obvious, marked.
E3 1 indefinite. **2** vague.

definitely *adverb*
positively, surely, unquestionably, absolutely, certainly, categorically, undeniably, clearly, doubtless, unmistakably, plainly, obviously, indeed, easily.

definition *noun*
1 the definition of boundaries: delineation, demarcation, delimitation.
2 a dictionary definition: explanation, description, interpretation, exposition, clarification, elucidation.
3 gives the picture definition: distinctness, clarity, precision, clearness, focus, contrast, sharpness.

definitive *adjective*
decisive, conclusive, final, authoritative, standard, correct, ultimate, reliable, exhaustive, perfect, exact, absolute, complete.
F∃interim.

deflect *verb*
deviate, diverge, turn (aside), swerve, veer, sidetrack, twist, avert, wind, glance off, bend, ricochet.

deformed *adjective*
distorted, misshapen, contorted, disfigured, crippled, crooked, bent, twisted, warped, buckled, defaced, mangled, maimed, marred, ruined, mutilated.

defraud *verb*
cheat, swindle, dupe, fleece, sting (*infml*), rip off (*infml*), do (*infml*), diddle (*infml*), rob, trick, con (*infml*), rook, deceive, delude, mislead, fool, embezzle, beguile.

deft *adjective*
adept, handy, dexterous, nimble, skilful, adroit, agile, expert, nifty (*infml*), proficient, able, neat, clever.
F∃clumsy, awkward.

defy *verb*
1 defy the authorities: challenge, confront, resist, dare, brave, face, repel, spurn, beard, flout, withstand, disregard, scorn, despise, defeat, provoke, thwart.
2 his writings defy categorization: elude, frustrate, baffle, foil.
F∃**1** obey. **2** permit.

degenerate *verb*
decline, deteriorate, sink, decay, rot, slip, worsen, regress, fall off, lapse, decrease.
F∃improve.

degrade *verb*
dishonour, disgrace, debase, abase, shame, humiliate, humble, discredit, demean, lower, weaken, impair, deteriorate, cheapen, adulterate, corrupt.
F∃exalt.

degree *noun*
1 of high degree: grade, class, rank, order, position, standing, status.
2 to a great degree: extent, measure, range, stage, step, level, intensity, standard.

deign *verb*
condescend, stoop, lower oneself, consent, demean oneself.

deity *noun*
god, goddess, divinity, godhead, idol, demigod, demigoddess, power, immortal.

dejected *adjective*
downcast, despondent, depressed, downhearted, disheartened, down, low, melancholy, disconsolate, sad, miserable, cast down, gloomy, glum, crestfallen, dismal, wretched, doleful, morose, spiritless.
F∃cheerful, high-spirited, happy.

delay *noun*
hold-up, check, setback, postponement, interruption, pause, lull, interval, wait.
▶ *verb*
1 delay progress: obstruct, hinder, impede, hold up, check, hold back, set back, stop, halt, detain.
2 delay the wedding: defer, put off, postpone, procrastinate, suspend, shelve, hold over, stall.
3 don't delay, buy today: dawdle, linger, lag, loiter, dilly-dally (*infml*), tarry, hang back (*infml*).
F∃**1** accelerate. **2** bring forward. **3** hurry.

delegate *noun*
representative, agent, envoy, messenger, deputy, ambassador, commissioner.
▶ *verb*
authorize, appoint, depute, charge, commission, assign, empower, entrust, devolve, consign, designate, nominate, name, hand over.

delete *verb*
erase, remove, cross out, cancel, rub out, strike (out), obliterate, edit (out), blot out, efface (*fml*), expunge (*fml*).
Ｅ３ add, insert.

deliberate *adjective*
1 a deliberate mistake: intentional, planned, calculated, prearranged, premeditated, willed, conscious, designed, considered, advised.
2 deliberate way of speaking: careful, unhurried, thoughtful, methodical, cautious, circumspect (*fml*), studied, prudent, slow, ponderous, measured, heedful.
Ｅ３ **1** unintentional, accidental. **2** hasty.
▸ *verb*
consider, ponder, reflect, think, cogitate, meditate, mull over, debate, discuss, weigh, consult.

deliberation *noun*
consideration, reflection, thought, calculation, forethought, meditation, rumination, study, debate, discussion, consultation, speculation.

delicacy *noun*
1 the delicacy of her features: daintiness, fineness, elegance, exquisiteness, lightness, precision.
2 treat the matter with some delicacy: sensitivity, subtlety, finesse, tact, discrimination, niceness.
3 provided guests with local delicacies: titbit, dainty, taste, sweetmeat, savoury, relish.
Ｅ３ **1** coarseness, roughness. **2** tactlessness.

delicate *adjective*
1 delicate lace: fine, fragile, dainty, exquisite, flimsy, elegant, graceful.
2 a delicate child: frail, weak, ailing, faint.
3 delicate workmanship: sensitive, scrupulous, discriminating, careful, accurate, precise.
4 a delicate blue: subtle, muted, pastel, soft.
Ｅ３ **1** coarse, clumsy. **2** healthy.

delicious *adjective*
1 the food was delicious: appetizing, palatable, tasty, delectable,

scrumptious (*infml*), mouth-watering, succulent, savoury.
2 a delicious breeze: enjoyable, pleasant, agreeable, delightful.
Ｅ３ **1** unpalatable. **2** unpleasant.

delight *noun*
bliss, happiness, joy, pleasure, ecstasy, enjoyment, gladness, rapture, transport, gratification, jubilation.
Ｅ３ disgust, displeasure.
▸ *verb*
please, charm, gratify, enchant, tickle, thrill, ravish.
Ｅ３ displease, dismay.
◆ **delight in** enjoy, relish, like, love, appreciate, revel in, take pride in, glory in, savour.
Ｅ３ dislike, hate.

delighted *adjective*
charmed, elated, happy, pleased, enchanted, captivated, ecstatic, thrilled, overjoyed, jubilant, joyous.
Ｅ３ disappointed, dismayed.

delightful *adjective*
charming, enchanting, captivating, enjoyable, pleasant, thrilling, agreeable, pleasurable, engaging, attractive, pleasing, gratifying, entertaining, fascinating.
Ｅ３ nasty, unpleasant.

delinquency *noun*
crime, offence, wrongdoing, misbehaviour, misconduct, law-breaking, misdemeanour, criminality.

delirious *adjective*
demented, raving, incoherent, beside oneself, deranged, frenzied, light-headed, wild, mad, frantic, insane, crazy, ecstatic.
Ｅ３ sane.

deliver *verb*
1 deliver a parcel: convey, bring, send, give, carry, supply.
2 deliver him to the court: surrender, hand over, relinquish, yield, transfer, grant, entrust, commit.
3 deliver a speech: utter, speak, proclaim, pronounce.
4 deliver a blow: administer, inflict, direct.
5 deliver us from evil: set free, liberate, release, emancipate.

delivery *noun*
1 the delivery of letters and parcels: conveyance, consignment, dispatch, transmission, transfer, surrender.
2 a halting delivery: articulation, enunciation, speech, utterance, intonation, elocution.
3 an easy delivery: childbirth, labour, confinement.

delude *verb*
deceive, mislead, beguile, dupe, take in, trick, hoodwink, hoax, cheat, misinform.

delusion *noun*
illusion, hallucination, fancy, misconception, misapprehension, deception, misbelief, fallacy.

demand *verb*
1 demanded that he come/demand payment: ask, request, call for, insist on, solicit, claim, exact.
2 demands your strict attention: necessitate, need, require, involve.
▶ *noun*
1 a demand from the boss: request, question, claim, order, inquiry, desire, interrogation.
2 no demand for their products: need, necessity, call.

demanding *adjective*
hard, difficult, challenging, exacting, taxing, tough, exhausting, wearing, back-breaking, insistent, pressing, urgent, trying.
🗲 easy, undemanding, easy-going.

demean *verb*
lower, humble, degrade, humiliate, debase, abase, descend, stoop, condescend.
🗲 exalt, enhance.

demeanour *noun*
bearing, manner, deportment, conduct, behaviour, air.

demented *adjective*
mad, insane, lunatic, out of one's mind, crazy, loony (*infml*), deranged, unbalanced, frenzied.
🗲 sane.

democratic *adjective*
self-governing, representative, egalitarian, autonomous, popular, populist, republican.

demolish *verb*
1 demolishing the building: destroy, dismantle, knock down, pull down, flatten, bulldoze, raze, tear down, level.
2 demolish the opposition: ruin, defeat, destroy, annihilate, wreck, overturn, overthrow.
🗲 **1** build up.

demonstrable *adjective*
verifiable, provable, arguable, attestable, self-evident, obvious, evident, certain, clear, positive.
🗲 unverifiable.

demonstrate *verb*
1 demonstrates the efficiency of the police: show, display, prove, establish, exhibit, substantiate, manifest, testify to, indicate.
2 demonstrated the technique: show, explain, illustrate, describe, teach.
3 students demonstrating: protest, march, parade, rally, picket, sit in.

demonstration *noun*
1 sufficient demonstration of his stupidity: proof, confirmation, affirmation, substantiation, validation, evidence, testimony, manifestation, expression.
2 demonstration of how a computer works: display, exhibition, explanation, illustration, description, exposition, presentation, test, trial.
3 an anti-war demonstration: protest, march, demo (*infml*), rally, picket, sit-in, parade.

demonstrative *adjective*
affectionate, expressive, expansive, emotional, open, loving.
🗲 reserved, cold, restrained.

demoralize *verb*
discourage, dishearten, dispirit, undermine, depress, deject, crush, lower, disconcert.
🗲 encourage.

demote *verb*
downgrade, degrade, relegate, reduce.
🗲 promote, upgrade.

den *noun*
lair, hideout, hole, retreat, study, hide-away, shelter, sanctuary, haunt.

denial *noun*
1 issue an outright denial:

contradiction, negation, dissent, repudiation, disavowal, disclaimer, dismissal, renunciation.
2 denial of their rights: refusal, rebuff, rejection, prohibition, veto.

denomination *noun*
1 (*fml*) all plants and animals have Latin denominations: classification, category, class, kind, sort, term, title.
2 worshippers of several denominations: religion, persuasion, sect, belief, faith, creed, communion, school.

denote *verb*
indicate, stand for, signify, represent, symbolize, mean, express, designate, typify, mark, show, imply.

denounce *verb*
condemn, censure, accuse, revile, decry, attack, inform against, betray, impugn (*fml*), vilify (*fml*), fulminate (*fml*).
Ⓕ acclaim, praise.

dense *adjective*
1 a dense forest: compact, thick, compressed, condensed, close, close-knit, heavy, solid, opaque, packed, impenetrable, crowded.
2 he can sometimes be a bit dense: stupid, thick (*infml*), crass, dull, slow, slow-witted.
Ⓕ **1** thin, sparse. **2** quick-witted, clever.

dent *noun*
hollow, depression, dip, concavity, indentation, crater, dimple, dint, pit.
▶ *verb*
depress, bend, push in, buckle, crumple, indent.

denunciation *noun*
condemnation, denouncement, censure, accusation, incrimination, invective, criticism.
Ⓕ praise.

deny *verb*
1 deny the accusation: contradict, oppose, refute, disagree with, disaffirm, disprove.
2 denied her faith/her own brother: disown, disclaim, renounce, repudiate, recant.
3 deny them basic human rights:

refuse, turn down, forbid, reject, withhold, rebuff, veto.
Ⓕ **1** admit. **3** allow.

depart *verb*
1 he departed soon afterwards/ departing from Southampton: go, leave, withdraw, exit, make off, quit, decamp, take one's leave, absent oneself, set off, remove, retreat, migrate, escape, disappear, retire, vanish, do a bunk (*infml*).
2 departing from the script: deviate, digress, differ, diverge, swerve, veer.
Ⓕ **1** arrive, return. **2** keep to.

department *noun*
1 a government department: division, branch, subdivision, section, sector, office, station, unit.
2 not my department: sphere, realm, province, domain, field, area, concern, responsibility, speciality, line.

departure *noun*
1 the departure of several colleagues: exit, going, leave-taking, removal, withdrawal, retirement, exodus.
2 a departure from the usual rules: deviation, digression, divergence, variation, innovation, branching (out), difference, change, shift, veering.
Ⓕ **1** arrival, return.

depend on *verb*
1 depend on his income: rely upon, count on, bank on (*infml*), calculate on, reckon on (*infml*), build upon, trust in, lean on, expect.
2 depends on several factors: hinge on, rest on, revolve around, be contingent upon (*fml*), hang on.

dependable *adjective*
reliable, trustworthy, steady, trusty, responsible, faithful, unfailing, sure, honest, conscientious, certain.
Ⓕ unreliable, fickle.

dependent *adjective*
1 a dependent infant/dependent on his parents: reliant, helpless, weak, immature, vulnerable.
2 whether we go or not is dependent on the weather: conditional on, determined by, decided by, dictated by, subject to, contingent on (*fml*).
Ⓕ **1** independent.

depict *verb*
portray, illustrate, delineate, sketch, outline, draw, picture, paint, trace, describe, characterize, detail.

deplete *verb*
empty, drain, exhaust, evacuate, use up, expend, run down, reduce, lessen, decrease.

deplorable *adjective*
1 a deplorable state of affairs: awful, grievous, lamentable, pitiable, regrettable, unfortunate, wretched, distressing, sad, miserable, dire, heartbreaking, melancholy, disastrous, appalling.
2 deplorable behaviour: reprehensible, disgraceful, scandalous, shameful, dishonourable, disreputable.
F31 excellent. 2 commendable.

deplore *verb*
1 deplored the suffering they witnessed: grieve for, lament, mourn, regret, bemoan, rue.
2 deplore violence: censure, disapprove of, condemn, denounce.
F32 extol (*fml*).

deploy *verb*
dispose, arrange, position, station, use, utilize, distribute.

deport *verb*
expel, banish, exile, extradite, transport, expatriate, oust.

depose *verb*
demote, dethrone, downgrade, dismiss, unseat, topple, disestablish, displace, oust.

deposit *verb*
1 deposits its eggs on a leaf: lay, drop, place, put, settle, dump (*infml*), park, precipitate (*fml*), sit, locate.
2 deposit funds in a savings account: save, store, hoard, bank, amass, consign, entrust, lodge, file.
▶ *noun*
1 muddy deposits which formed the rocks: sediment, accumulation, dregs, precipitate (*fml*), lees, silt.
2 put down a deposit: security, stake, down payment, pledge, retainer, instalment, part payment, money.

depot *noun*
1 an arms depot: storehouse, store,

warehouse, depository, repository, arsenal.
2 a bus depot: station, garage, terminus.

depraved *adjective*
corrupt, debauched, degenerate, perverted, debased, dissolute, immoral, base, shameless, licentious, wicked, sinful, vile, evil.
F3moral, upright.

depreciate *verb*
1 depreciate the price by 50%: devalue, deflate, downgrade, decrease, reduce, lower, drop, fall, lessen, decline, slump.
2 depreciate someone's efforts: disparage (*fml*), belittle, undervalue, underestimate, underrate, slight.
F31 appreciate. 2 overrate.

depress *verb*
1 it depressed him: deject, sadden, dishearten, discourage, oppress, upset, daunt.
2 depressing their energy levels: weaken, undermine, sap, tire, drain, exhaust, weary, impair, reduce, lessen, lower.
3 depressing demand: devalue, bring down, lower.
F31 cheer. 2 fortify. 3 increase, raise.

depressed *adjective*
1 feeling depressed: dejected, low-spirited, melancholy, dispirited, sad, unhappy, low, down, downcast, disheartened, fed up (*infml*), miserable, moody, cast down, discouraged, glum, downhearted, distressed, despondent, morose, crestfallen, pessimistic.
2 the depressed peoples of the world: poor, disadvantaged, deprived, destitute.
F31 cheerful. 2 affluent.

depressing *adjective*
dejecting, dismal, bleak, gloomy, saddening, cheerless, dreary, disheartening, sad, melancholy, sombre, grey, black, daunting, discouraging, heartbreaking, distressing, hopeless.
F3cheerful, encouraging.

depression *noun*
1 go into a deep depression: dejection, despair, despondency, melancholy, low

spirits, sadness, gloominess, doldrums, blues (*infml*), glumness, dumps (*infml*), hopelessness.

2 the Great Depression: recession, slump, stagnation, hard times, decline, inactivity.

3 a depression in the rock: indentation, hollow, dip, concavity, dent, dimple, valley, pit, sink, dint, bowl, cavity, basin, impression, dish, excavation.

F3 1 cheerfulness. 2 prosperity, boom. 3 convexity, protuberance (*fml*).

deprive *verb*
1 depriving them of their land: dispossess, strip, divest, denude, bereave, expropriate (*fml*), rob.
2 depriving him of sweets: deny, withhold, refuse.

F3 1 endow. 2 provide.

deprived *adjective*
poor, needy, underprivileged, disadvantaged, impoverished, destitute, lacking, bereft.

F3 prosperous.

depth *noun*
1 the depth of the water: deepness, profoundness, extent, measure, drop.
2 the farthest depths: lowest point, remotest area, bed, floor, bottom, deep, abyss.
3 a mind of great depth: wisdom, insight, discernment, penetration.
4 depth of feeling: intensity, strength, seriousness.

F3 1 shallowness. 2 surface.

deputize *noun*
represent, stand in for, substitute, replace, understudy, double.

deputy *noun*
representative, agent, delegate, proxy, substitute, second-in-command, ambassador, commissioner, lieutenant, surrogate, subordinate, assistant, locum.

deranged *adjective*
disordered, demented, crazy, mad, lunatic, insane, unbalanced, disturbed, confused, frantic, delirious, distraught, berserk.

F3 sane, calm.

derelict *adjective*
abandoned, neglected, deserted,

forsaken, desolate, discarded, dilapidated, ruined.

derisive *adjective*
mocking, scornful, contemptuous, disrespectful, irreverent, jeering, disdainful, taunting.

F3 respectful, flattering.

derivation *noun*
source, origin, root, beginning, etymology, extraction, foundation, genealogy, ancestry, basis, descent, deduction, inference.

derivative *adjective*
unoriginal, acquired, copied, borrowed, derived, imitative, obtained, second-hand, secondary, plagiarized, cribbed (*infml*), hackneyed, trite.

▶ *noun*
derivation, offshoot, by-product, development, branch, outgrowth, spin-off, product, descendant.

derive *verb*
1 derive some benefit: gain, obtain, get, draw, extract, receive, procure, acquire, borrow.
2 deriving from a Latin word: originate, arise, spring, flow, emanate, descend, proceed, stem, issue, follow, develop.
3 what do you derive from these facts?: infer, deduce, trace, gather, glean.

derogatory *adjective*
insulting, pejorative, offensive, disparaging, depreciative, critical, defamatory, injurious.

F3 flattering.

descend *verb*
1 descending from 30,000 feet: drop, go down, fall, plummet, plunge, tumble, swoop, sink, arrive, alight, dismount, dip, slope, subside.
2 descending into farce: degenerate, deteriorate.
3 descend to their level: condescend, deign, stoop.
4 descended from apes: originate, proceed, spring, stem.

F3 1 ascend, rise.

descendants *noun*
offspring, children, issue, progeny

ml), successors, lineage, line, seed
(*ml*).

escent *noun*
a steep descent: fall, drop, plunge,
dip, decline, incline, slope.
their descent into poverty:
comedown, debasement, degradation.
of Norman descent: ancestry,
parentage, heredity, family tree,
genealogy, lineage, extraction,
origin.
F3 1 ascent, rise.

escribe *verb*
describe your feelings/described her
attacker: portray, depict, delineate,
illustrate, characterize, specify, draw,
define, detail, explain, express, tell,
narrate, outline, relate, recount,
present, report, sketch.
describing a circle in the air: mark
out, trace.

escription *noun*
a good description of the thief:
portrayal, representation, account,
characterization, delineation,
depiction, sketch, presentation, report,
outline, explanation, exposition,
narration.
a vehicle of some description: sort,
type, kind, variety, specification, order.

escriptive *adjective*
illustrative, explanatory, expressive,
detailed, graphic, colourful, pictorial,
vivid.

esert[1] *noun* /**dez**-ert/
the Sahara desert: wasteland,
wilderness, wilds, void.
adjective
desert island: bare, barren, waste,
wild, uninhabited, uncultivated, dry,
arid, infertile, desolate, sterile, solitary.

esert[2] *verb* /di-**zert**/
desert his family/the soldier deserted:
abandon, forsake, leave, maroon,
strand, decamp, defect, give up,
renounce, relinquish, jilt, abscond,
quit.
F3 stand by, support.

eserted *adjective*
abandoned, forsaken, empty, derelict,
desolate, godforsaken, neglected,
underpopulated, stranded, isolated,

bereft, vacant, betrayed, lonely,
solitary, unoccupied.
F3 populous.

deserter *noun*
runaway, absconder, escapee, truant,
renegade, defector, traitor, fugitive,
betrayer, apostate, backslider,
delinquent.

deserve *verb*
earn, be worthy of, merit, be entitled to,
warrant, justify, win, rate, incur.

deserved *adjective*
due, earned, merited, justifiable,
warranted, right, rightful, well-earned,
suitable, proper, fitting, fair, just,
appropriate, apt, legitimate, apposite.
F3 gratuitous, undeserved.

deserving *adjective*
worthy, estimable, exemplary,
praiseworthy, admirable,
commendable, laudable, righteous.
F3 undeserving, unworthy.

design *noun*
1 a design for the garden: blueprint,
draft, pattern, plan, prototype, sketch,
drawing, outline, model, guide.
2 of a different design: style, shape,
form, figure, structure, organization,
arrangement, composition,
construction, motif.
3 his design to be a millionaire: aim,
intention, goal, purpose, plan, end,
object, objective, scheme, plot, project,
meaning, target, undertaking.
▶ *verb*
1 was designed to float: plan, plot,
intend, devise, purpose, aim, scheme,
shape.
2 design a dress: sketch, draft, outline,
draw (up).
3 designing a computer program:
invent, originate, conceive, create,
think up, develop, construct, fashion,
form, model, fabricate, make.

designer *noun*
deviser, originator, maker, stylist,
inventor, creator, contriver, fashioner,
architect, author.

designing *adjective*
artful, crafty, scheming, conspiring,
devious, intriguing, plotting, tricky,
wily, sly, deceitful, cunning, guileful,

underhand, sharp, shrewd.
F3 artless, naïve.

desirable *adjective*
1 find it desirable to accept his offer:
advantageous, profitable, worthwhile,
advisable, appropriate, expedient,
beneficial, preferable, sensible, eligible,
good, pleasing.
2 a desirable woman: attractive,
alluring, seductive, fetching, tempting.
F3 1 undesirable. **2** unattractive.

desire *verb*
1 desire his approval: ask, request,
petition, solicit.
**2 does madam desire anything
further?**: want, wish for, covet, long
for, need, crave, hunger for, yearn for,
fancy (*infml*), hanker after.
▶ *noun*
want, longing, wish, need, yearning,
craving, hankering, appetite, aspiration.

desist *verb*
stop, cease, leave off, refrain,
discontinue, end, break off, give up,
halt, abstain, suspend, pause, peter
out, remit, forbear (*fml*).
F3 continue, resume.

desolate *adjective*
1 a desolate landscape: deserted,
uninhabited, abandoned, bare, arid,
unfrequented, barren, bleak, gloomy,
dismal, dreary, lonely, god-forsaken,
forsaken, waste, depressing.
2 left feeling desolate: forlorn, bereft,
depressed, dejected, forsaken, lonely,
despondent, distressed, melancholy,
miserable, gloomy, disheartened,
dismal, downcast, solitary, wretched.
F3 1 populous. **2** cheerful.
▶ *verb*
devastate, lay waste, destroy, despoil,
spoil, wreck, denude, depopulate, ruin,
waste, ravage, plunder, pillage.

despair *noun*
despondency, gloom, hopelessness,
desperation, anguish, wretchedness,
inconsolableness, melancholy, misery.
F3 cheerfulness, resilience.
▶ *verb*
lose heart, lose hope, give up, give
in, collapse, surrender.
F3 hope.

despatch ⇨*see* **dispatch**.

desperate *adjective*
1 a desperate situation: hopeless,
inconsolable, wretched, despondent,
abandoned.
2 a desperate act: reckless, rash,
impetuous, audacious, daring,
dangerous, do-or-die, foolhardy, risky,
hazardous, hasty, precipitate (*fml*),
wild, violent, frantic, frenzied,
determined.
3 a desperate hurry: critical, acute,
serious, severe, extreme,
urgent.
F3 1 hopeful. **2** cautious.

desperately *adverb*
dangerously, critically, gravely,
hopelessly, seriously, severely,
badly, dreadfully, fearfully,
frightfully.

desperation *noun*
1 desperation in his voice: despair,
despondency, anguish, hopelessness,
misery, agony, distress, pain, sorrow,
trouble, worry, anxiety.
2 driven to desperation: recklessness,
rashness, frenzy, madness,
hastiness.

despicable *adjective*
contemptible, vile, worthless,
detestable, disgusting, mean, wretched,
disgraceful, disreputable, shameful,
reprobate.
F3 admirable, noble.

despise *verb*
scorn, deride, look down on, disdain,
condemn, spurn, undervalue, slight,
revile, deplore, dislike, detest,
loathe.
F3 admire.

despite *preposition*
in spite of, notwithstanding, regardless
of, in the face of, undeterred by,
against, defying.

despondent *adjective*
depressed, dejected, disheartened,
downcast, down, low, gloomy, glum,
discouraged, miserable, melancholy,
sad, sorrowful, doleful, despairing,
heart-broken, inconsolable, mournful,
wretched.
F3 cheerful, heartened, hopeful.

despot *noun*
autocrat, tyrant, dictator, oppressor, absolutist, boss.

despotism *noun*
autocracy, totalitarianism, tyranny, dictatorship, absolutism, oppression, repression.
F3 democracy, egalitarianism, liberalism, tolerance.

destination *noun*
1 have a definite destination in mind: goal, aim, objective, object, purpose, target, end, intention, aspiration, design, ambition.
2 reach one's destination safely: journey's end, terminus, station, stop.

destined *adjective*
1 destined to be a success: fated, doomed, inevitable, predetermined, ordained, certain, foreordained, meant, unavoidable, inescapable, intended, designed, appointed.
2 goods destined for the United States: bound, directed, en route, headed, heading, scheduled, assigned, booked.

destiny *noun*
fate, doom, fortune, karma, lot, portion (*fml*), predestiny, kismet.

destitute *adjective*
1 destitute refugees: poor, penniless, poverty-stricken, impoverished, down-and-out (*infml*), distressed, bankrupt.
2 destitute of ideas: lacking, needy, wanting, devoid of, bereft, innocent of, deprived, deficient, depleted.
F3 1 prosperous, rich.

destroy *verb*
1 destroy the city/the environment: demolish, ruin, raze, devastate, ravage, shatter, wreck, smash.
2 destroyed his career/their trust: ruin, wreck, nullify, undo, undermine, waste, smash, crush.
3 the dog had to be destroyed: kill, dispatch, slay (*fml*), annihilate, eliminate.
F3 1 build up. 3 create.

destruction *noun*
1 the destruction of the city: ruin, devastation, shattering, crushing, wreckage, demolition, defeat,

downfall, overthrow, ruination, desolation, undoing, wastage, havoc, ravagement.
2 destruction of thousands of rare species: annihilation, extermination, eradication, elimination, extinction, slaughter, massacre, end, liquidation, nullification.
F3 2 creation.

destructive *adjective*
1 destructive storms: devastating, damaging, catastrophic, disastrous, deadly, harmful, fatal, disruptive, lethal, ruinous, detrimental, hurtful, malignant, nullifying, slaughterous.
2 destructive criticism: adverse, hostile, negative, discouraging, disparaging, contrary, undermining, subversive, vicious.
F3 1 creative. 2 constructive.

desultory *adjective*
random, erratic, aimless, disorderly, haphazard, irregular, spasmodic, inconsistent, undirected, unco-ordinated, unsystematic, loose, unmethodical, fitful, disconnected, capricious.
F3 systematic, methodical.

detach *verb*
separate, disconnect, unfasten, disjoin, cut off, disengage, remove, undo, uncouple, sever, dissociate, isolate, loosen, free, unfix, unhitch, segregate, divide, disentangle, estrange.
F3 attach.

detachment *noun*
1 display a certain detachment: aloofness, remoteness, coolness, unconcern, indifference, impassivity, disinterestedness, neutrality, impartiality, objectivity, fairness.
2 detachment of the wings: separation, disconnection, disunion, disengagement.
3 a detachment of infantry: squad, unit, force, corps, brigade, patrol, task force.

detail *noun*
particular, item, factor, element, aspect, component, feature, point, specific, ingredient, attribute, count, respect, technicality, complication,

intricacy, triviality, fact, thoroughness, elaboration, meticulousness, refinement, nicety.

▶ *verb*

1 detailing his requirements: list, enumerate, itemize, specify, catalogue, recount, relate.

2 was detailed to carry out regular patrols: assign, appoint, charge, delegate, commission.

detailed *adjective*
comprehensive, exhaustive, full, blow-by-blow (*infml*), thorough, minute, exact, specific, particular, itemized, intricate, elaborate, complex, complicated, meticulous, descriptive.
F3 cursory, general.

detain *verb*
delay, hold (up), hinder, impede, check, retard, slow, stay, stop.

detect *verb*

1 detect gas: notice, ascertain, note, observe, perceive, recognize, discern, distinguish, identify, sight, spot, spy.

2 detecting the culprits: uncover, catch, discover, disclose, expose, find, track down, unmask, reveal.

detective *noun*
investigator, private eye (*infml*), sleuth (*infml*), sleuth-hound (*infml*).

detention *noun*
detainment, custody, confinement, imprisonment, restraint, incarceration, constraint, quarantine.
F3 release.

deter *verb*
discourage, put off, inhibit, intimidate, dissuade, daunt, turn off (*infml*), check, caution, warn, restrain, hinder, frighten, disincline, prevent, prohibit, stop.
F3 encourage.

deteriorate *verb*

1 the weather/their relationship deteriorated: worsen, decline, degenerate, depreciate, go downhill (*infml*), fail, fall off, lapse, slide, relapse, slip.

2 the building is deteriorating rapidly: decay, disintegrate, decompose, weaken, fade.
F3 1 improve. 2 progress.

determination *noun*
resoluteness, tenacity, firmness, will-power, perseverance, persistence, purpose, backbone, guts (*infml*), grit (*infml*), steadfastness, will, insistence, conviction, dedication, drive, fortitude.
F3 irresolution.
⇨ *See also* **Word Study** *panel.*

determine *verb*

1 she determined that she wasn't cut out for the job: decide, settle, resolve, make up one's mind, choose, conclude, fix on, elect, clinch, finish.

2 to determine what had happened: discover, establish, find out, ascertain, identify, check, detect, verify.

3 will determine the result: affect, influence, govern, control, dictate, direct, guide, regulate, ordain.

determined *adjective*
resolute, firm, purposeful, strong-willed, single-minded, persevering, persistent, strong-minded, steadfast, tenacious, dogged, insistent, intent, fixed, convinced, decided, unflinching.
F3 irresolute, wavering.

deterrent *noun*
hindrance, impediment, obstacle, repellent, check, bar, discouragement, obstruction, curb, restraint, difficulty.
F3 incentive, encouragement.

detest *verb*
hate, abhor, loathe, abominate, execrate (*fml*), dislike, recoil from, deplore, despise.
F3 adore, love.

detestable *adjective*
hateful, loathsome, abhorrent (*fml*), abominable, repellent, obnoxious, execrable (*fml*), despicable, revolting, repulsive, repugnant, offensive, vile, disgusting, accursed (*fml*), heinous (*fml*), shocking, sordid.
F3 adorable, admirable.

detour *noun*
deviation, diversion, indirect route, circuitous route, roundabout route, digression, byroad, byway, bypath, bypass.

WORD*study*   determination

There are many expressions and phrases used to express various degrees of **determination**, and you might choose to use some of those listed below to add variety to your speech or writing.

things people say to show determination

over my dead body
not for all the tea in China
where there's a will there's a way
at all costs

not for love nor money
never say die
come hell or high water
do or die

doing something with determination

grasp the nettle
move heaven and earth to do
   something

take the bull by the horns
go to great lengths to do
   something

continue doing something with determination

stay the course
hold your ground
dig your heels in
rise to the occasion
stop at nothing
put your foot down
put up a good fight
keep a stiff upper lip

hang on like grim death
stick to your guns
keep at it
stay the pace
pull out all the stops
stand fast
hang tough (*US*)
leave no stone unturned

being determined

hell bent on (doing) something
set one's mind on (doing) something

dead-set on (doing) something
mean business

detract (from) *verb*
diminish, subtract from, take away from, reduce, lessen, lower, devaluate, depreciate, belittle, disparage (*fml*).
Ⅎ add to, enhance, praise.

detriment *noun*
damage, harm, hurt, disadvantage, loss, ill, injury, disservice, evil, mischief, prejudice.
Ⅎ advantage, benefit.

detrimental *adjective*
damaging, harmful, hurtful, adverse,

disadvantageous, injurious, prejudicial, mischievous, destructive.
Ⅎ advantageous, favourable, beneficial.

devastating *adjective*
1 devastating storms: destructive, disastrous.
2 a devastating argument: effective, incisive, overwhelming, stunning.

devastation *noun*
destruction, desolation, havoc, ruin, wreckage, ravages, demolition,

annihilation, pillage, plunder, spoliation.

develop *verb*
1 develop further: advance, evolve, expand, progress, foster, flourish, mature, prosper, branch out.
2 developing his argument: elaborate, amplify, augment, enhance, unfold.
3 developed the steam engine: create, invent, acquire, contract, begin, generate.
4 what developed after that: result, come about, grow, ensue, arise, follow, happen.

development *noun*
1 rapid development: growth, evolution, advance, blossoming, elaboration, furtherance, progress, unfolding, expansion, extension, spread, increase, improvement, maturity, promotion, refinement, issue.
2 a new development: occurrence, happening, event, change, outcome, situation, result, phenomenon.

deviate *verb*
diverge, veer, turn (aside), digress, swerve, vary, differ, depart, stray, yaw, wander, err, go astray, go off the rails (*infml*), drift, part.

deviation *noun*
divergence, aberration, departure, abnormality, irregularity, variance, variation, digression, eccentricity, anomaly, deflection, alteration, disparity, discrepancy, detour, fluctuation, change, quirk, shift, freak.
≠conformity, regularity.

device *noun*
1 a device for peeling apples: tool, implement, appliance, gadget, contrivance, contraption (*infml*), apparatus, utensil, instrument, machine.
2 a crafty device: scheme, ruse, strategy, plan, plot, gambit, manoeuvre, wile, trick, dodge (*infml*), machination.
3 a device on his shield: emblem, symbol, motif, logo (*infml*), design, insignia, crest, badge, shield.

devil *noun*
demon, Satan, fiend, evil spirit, arch-fiend, Lucifer, imp, Evil One, Prince of Darkness, Adversary, Beelzebub, Mephistopheles, Old Nick (*infml*), Old Harry (*infml*).

devious *adjective*
1 a devious plan/person: underhand, deceitful, dishonest, disingenuous, double-dealing, scheming, tricky (*infml*), insidious, insincere, calculating, cunning, evasive, wily, sly, slippery (*infml*), surreptitious, treacherous, misleading.
2 by devious means/a devious route: indirect, circuitous, rambling, roundabout, wandering, winding, tortuous, erratic.
≠2 straightforward.

devise *verb*
invent, contrive, plan, plot, design, conceive, arrange, formulate, imagine, scheme, construct, concoct, forge, frame, project, shape, form.

devoid *adjective*
lacking, wanting, without, free, bereft, destitute, deficient, deprived, barren, empty, vacant, void.
≠endowed.

devote *verb*
dedicate, consecrate, commit, give oneself, set apart, set aside, reserve, apply, allocate, allot, sacrifice, enshrine, assign, appropriate, surrender, pledge.

devoted *adjective*
dedicated, ardent, committed, loyal, faithful, devout, loving, staunch, steadfast, true, constant, fond, unswerving, tireless, concerned, attentive, caring.
≠indifferent, disloyal.

devotee *noun*
enthusiast, fan (*infml*), fanatic, addict, aficionado, follower, supporter, zealot, adherent, admirer, disciple, buff (*infml*), freak (*infml*).

devotion *noun*
1 his devotion to duty: dedication, commitment, consecration, ardour, loyalty, allegiance, adherence, zeal, support, love, passion, fervour, fondness, attachment, adoration, affection, faithfulness, reverence,

steadfastness, regard, earnestness.
2 religious devotion: devoutness, piety,
godliness, faith, holiness, spirituality.
3 made his devotion: prayer,
worship.
F3 1 inconstancy. **2** irreverence.

devour *verb*
1 devoured everything on the table:
eat, consume, guzzle, gulp, gorge,
gobble, bolt, wolf down, swallow, stuff
(*infml*), cram, polish off (*infml*),
gourmandize (*fml*), feast on, relish,
revel in.
2 green spaces devoured by the ever-
expanding city: destroy, consume,
absorb, engulf, ravage, dispatch.

devout *adjective*
1 a devout plea: sincere, earnest,
devoted, fervent, genuine, staunch,
steadfast, ardent, passionate, serious,
whole-hearted, constant, faithful,
intense, heartfelt, zealous, unswerving,
deep, profound.
2 a devout Catholic: pious, godly,
religious, reverent, prayerful, saintly,
holy, orthodox.
F3 1 insincere. **2** irreligious.

dexterous *adjective*
deft, adroit, agile, able, nimble,
proficient, skilful, clever, expert, nifty
(*infml*), nippy, handy, facile, nimble-
fingered, neat-handed, adept.
F3 clumsy, inept, awkward.

diabolical *adjective*
devilish, fiendish, demonic, hellish,
evil, infernal, wicked, vile, dreadful,
outrageous, shocking, disastrous,
excruciating, atrocious.

diagnose *verb*
identify, determine, recognize,
pinpoint, distinguish, analyse, explain,
isolate, interpret, investigate.

diagnosis *noun*
identification, verdict, explanation,
conclusion, answer, interpretation,
analysis, opinion, investigation,
examination, scrutiny.

diagonal *adjective*
oblique, slanting, cross, crosswise,
sloping, crooked, angled, cornerways.

diagram *noun*
plan, sketch, chart, drawing, figure,

representation, schema, illustration,
outline, graph, picture, layout, table.

dial *noun*
circle, disc, face, clock, control.
▶ *verb*
phone, ring, call (up).

dialect *noun*
idiom, language, regionalism, patois,
provincialism, vernacular, argot,
jargon, accent, lingo (*infml*), speech,
diction.

dialogue *noun*
1 enter into a dialogue with them:
conversation, interchange, discourse,
communication, talk, exchange,
discussion, converse, debate,
conference.
2 write the dialogue for the school
play: lines, script.

diary *noun*
journal, day-book, logbook, chronicle,
yearbook, appointment book,
engagement book.

diatribe *noun*
tirade, invective, abuse, harangue,
attack, onslaught, denunciation,
criticism, insult, reviling, upbraiding.
F3 praise, eulogy.

dictate *verb*
1 dictate a letter: say, speak, utter,
announce, pronounce, transmit.
2 dictate the terms: command, order,
direct, decree, instruct, rule.
▶ *noun*
command, decree, precept (*fml*),
principle, rule, direction, injunction,
edict, order, ruling, statute,
requirement, ordinance, law, bidding,
mandate, ultimatum, word.

dictator *noun*
despot, autocrat, tyrant, supremo
(*infml*), Big Brother (*infml*).

dictatorial *adjective*
tyrannical, despotic, totalitarian,
authoritarian, autocratic, oppressive,
imperious, domineering, bossy (*infml*),
absolute, repressive, overbearing,
arbitrary, dogmatic.
F3 democratic, egalitarian, liberal.

diction *noun*
speech, articulation, language,

elocution, enunciation, intonation, pronunciation, inflection, fluency, delivery, expression, phrasing.

dictionary *noun*
lexicon, glossary, thesaurus, vocabulary, wordbook, encyclopaedia, concordance.

die *verb*
1 die young : decease, perish, pass away, expire, depart, breathe one's last, peg out (*infml*), snuff it (*infml*), bite the dust (*infml*), kick the bucket (*infml*).
2 sound of their voices died away : dwindle, fade, ebb, sink, wane, wilt, wither, peter out, decline, decay, finish, lapse, end, disappear, vanish, subside.
3 (*infml*) dying for an ice cream : long for, pine for, yearn, desire.
E3 1 live.

diehard *noun*
reactionary, intransigent, hardliner, blimp (*infml*), ultra-conservative, old fogey (*infml*), stick-in-the-mud (*infml*), rightist, fanatic, zealot.

diet *noun*
1 a healthy diet : food, nutrition, provisions, sustenance, rations, foodstuffs, subsistence.
2 go on a diet : fast, abstinence, regimen.
▶ *verb*
lose weight, slim, fast, reduce, abstain, weight-watch (*infml*).

differ *verb*
1 his views differ from mine : vary, diverge, deviate, depart from, contradict, contrast.
2 we differ on the subject of exercise : disagree, argue, conflict, oppose, dispute, dissent, be at odds with, clash, quarrel, fall out, debate, contend, take issue.
E3 1 conform. 2 agree.

difference *noun*
1 no difference between them : dissimilarity, unlikeness, discrepancy, divergence, diversity, variation, variety, distinctness, distinction, deviation, differentiation, contrast, disparity, singularity, exception.
2 settle their differences : disagreement, clash, dispute, conflict, contention, controversy.

3 split the difference : remainder, rest.
E3 1 conformity. 2 agreement.

different *adjective*
1 different to mine : dissimilar, unlike, contrasting, divergent, inconsistent, deviating, at odds, clashing, opposed.
2 different colours : varied, various, diverse, miscellaneous, assorted, disparate, many, numerous, several, sundry, other.
3 he has always felt different : unusual, unconventional, unique, distinct, distinctive, extraordinary, individual, original, special, strange, separate, peculiar, rare, bizarre, anomalous.
E3 1 similar. 2 same. 3 conventional.

differentiate *verb*
distinguish, tell apart, discriminate, contrast, separate, mark off, individualize, particularize.

difficult *adjective*
1 a difficult journey : hard, laborious, demanding, arduous, strenuous, tough, wearisome, uphill, formidable.
2 a difficult problem : complex, complicated, intricate, involved, abstruse, obscure, dark, knotty, thorny, problematical, perplexing, abstract, baffling, intractable.
3 a difficult child : unmanageable, perverse, troublesome, trying, unco-operative, tiresome, stubborn, obstinate, intractable.
E3 1 easy. 2 straightforward. 3 manageable.
⇨ *See also* **Word Study** *panel.*

difficulty *noun*
1 in great difficulty : hardship, trouble, labour, arduousness, painfulness, trial, tribulation, awkwardness.
2 in financial difficulties : predicament, dilemma, quandary, perplexity, embarrassment, plight, distress, fix (*infml*), mess (*infml*), jam (*infml*), spot (*infml*), hiccup (*infml*), hang-up.
3 encounter many difficulties : problem, obstacle, hindrance, hurdle, impediment, objection, opposition, block, complication, pitfall, protest, stumbling block.
E3 1 ease.
⇨ *See also* **Word Study** *panel.*

Here are some familiar expressions used to talk or write about **difficulties** and **difficult situations**.

in difficulty

with your back to the wall
out of your depth
in the hot seat
in a tight spot
up against it
in hot water
in a pickle/fix/jam
in at the deep end
up a gum tree

up the creek without a paddle (*slang*)
out of the frying pan into the fire
in the soup
in trouble
in deep water
bogged down
(skate) on thin ice
have your work cut out

a difficult situation

a catch-22 situation
a pretty kettle of fish
a sticky situation
a fate worse than death
not a bowl of cherries
no picnic
no mean feat

a vicious circle
a no-win situation
a hard nut to crack
not a bed of roses
a tall order
the devil of a job

to cause difficulties for yourself

bite off more than you can chew
make a rod for your own back
open a can of worms

make a meal of something
tie yourself in knots

to cause difficulties for others

set the cat among the pigeons
lead someone a dance
make waves
throw a spanner in the works

set someone by the ears
box someone into a corner
rock the boat
leave someone in the lurch

to face difficulty

put a brave face on it
(keep going) to the bitter end
keep your chin up

keep your end up
have a cross to bear
weather the storm

to survive difficulty

ride out the storm
squeeze home
be over the hump

be off the hook
be out of the woods
be home and dry

diffident *adjective*
unassertive, modest, shy, timid, self-conscious, self-effacing, insecure, bashful, abashed, meek, reserved, withdrawn, tentative, shrinking, inhibited, hesitant, reluctant, unsure, shamefaced.
F3 assertive, confident.

diffuse *verb*
spread, scatter, disperse, distribute, propagate, dispense, disseminate, circulate, dissipate.
F3 concentrate.

dig *verb*
1 dig a hole: excavate, penetrate, burrow, mine, quarry, scoop, tunnel, till, gouge, delve, pierce.
2 digging me in the ribs: poke, prod.
3 digging for clues: investigate, probe, go into, research, search.
◆ **dig up** discover, unearth, uncover, disinter, expose, extricate, exhume, find, retrieve, track down.
F3 bury, obscure.

digest *verb*
1 digest one's food: absorb, assimilate, incorporate, process, dissolve.
2 have to digest this information: take in, absorb, understand, assimilate, grasp, study, consider, contemplate, meditate, ponder.
▶ *noun*
summary, abridgement, abstract, précis, synopsis, résumé, reduction, abbreviation, compression, compendium.

dignified *adjective*
stately, solemn, imposing, majestic, noble, august, lordly, lofty, exalted, formal, distinguished, grave, impressive, reserved, honourable.
F3 undignified, lowly.

dignitary *noun*
worthy, notable, VIP (*infml*), high-up, personage, bigwig (*infml*).

dignity *noun*
stateliness, propriety, solemnity, decorum, courtliness, grandeur, loftiness, majesty, honour, eminence, importance, nobility, self-respect, self-esteem, standing, poise, respectability, greatness, status, pride.

digress *verb*
diverge, deviate, stray, wander, go off at a tangent, drift, depart, ramble.

dilapidated *adjective*
ramshackle, shabby, broken-down, neglected, tumbledown, uncared-for, rickety, decrepit, crumbling, run-down, worn-out, ruined, decayed, decaying.

dilate *verb*
distend, enlarge, expand, spread, broaden, widen, increase, extend, stretch, swell.
F3 contract.

dilemma *noun*
quandary, conflict, predicament, problem, catch-22 (*infml*), difficulty, puzzle, embarrassment, perplexity, plight.

diligent *adjective*
assiduous (*fml*), industrious, hardworking, conscientious, painstaking, busy, attentive, tireless, careful, meticulous, persevering, persistent, studious.
F3 negligent, lazy.

dilute *verb*
adulterate, water down, thin (out), attenuate (*fml*), weaken, diffuse, diminish, decrease, lessen, reduce, temper, mitigate.
F3 concentrate.

dim *adjective*
1 a dim corner/a dim light: dark, dull, dusky, cloudy, shadowy, gloomy, sombre, dingy, lacklustre, feeble.
2 a dim outline: indistinct, blurred, hazy, ill-defined, obscure, misty, unclear, foggy, fuzzy, vague, faint, weak.
3 he's too dim to understand: stupid, dense, obtuse, thick (*infml*), doltish.
F3 1 bright. 2 distinct. 3 bright, intelligent.
▶ *verb*
darken, dull, obscure, cloud, blur, fade, tarnish, shade.
F3 brighten, illuminate.

dimension(s) *noun*
extent, measurement, measure, size, scope, magnitude, largeness, capacity, mass, scale, range, bulk, importance, greatness.

diminish *verb*
1 the light diminished: decrease, lessen, reduce, lower, contract, decline, shrink, dwindle, recede, taper off, wane, weaken, abate, fade, sink, subside, ebb, slacken, cut.
2 diminishing her efforts: belittle, disparage (*fml*), deprecate (*fml*), devalue.
FI 1 increase. **2** exaggerate.

diminutive *adjective*
undersized, small, tiny, little, miniature, minute, infinitesimal, wee, petite, midget, mini (*infml*), teeny (*infml*), teeny-weeny (*infml*), Lilliputian, dinky (*infml*), pint-size(d) (*infml*), pygmy, pocket(-sized).
FI big, large, oversized.

din *noun*
noise, row, racket, clash, clatter, clamour, pandemonium, uproar, commotion, crash, hullabaloo (*infml*), hubbub, outcry, shout, babble.
FI quiet, calm.

dine *verb*
eat, feast, sup, lunch, banquet, feed.

dingy *adjective*
dark, drab, grimy, murky, faded, dull, dim, shabby, soiled, discoloured, dirty, dreary, gloomy, seedy, sombre, obscure, run-down, colourless, dusky, worn.
FI bright, clean.

dinner *noun*
meal, supper, tea (*infml*), banquet, feast, spread, repast (*fml*).

dip *verb*
1 dipping his biscuit in his tea: plunge, immerse, submerge, duck, dunk, bathe, douse, sink.
2 dip below the horizon: descend, decline, drop, fall, subside, slump, sink, lower.
▶ *noun*
1 a dip in the road: hollow, basin, decline, hole, concavity, incline, depression, fall, slope, slump, lowering.
2 go for a quick dip: bathe, immersion, plunge, soaking, ducking, swim, drenching, infusion, dive.

diplomacy *noun*
1 learn to use a little diplomacy when dealing with sensitive issues: tact, tactfulness, finesse, delicacy, discretion, savoir-faire, subtlety, skill, craft.
2 international diplomacy: statecraft, statesmanship, politics, negotiation, manoeuvring.

diplomat *noun*
go-between, mediator, negotiator, ambassador, consul, envoy, conciliator, peacemaker, moderator, politician.

diplomatic *adjective*
tactful, politic, discreet, judicious (*fml*), subtle, sensitive, prudent, discreet.
FI tactless.

dire *adjective*
1 a dire warning: desperate, urgent, grave, drastic, crucial, extreme, alarming, ominous.
2 (*infml*) the music was dire: disastrous, dreadful, awful, appalling, calamitous, catastrophic.

direct *verb*
1 direct the company: control, manage, run, administer, organize, lead, govern, regulate, superintend, supervise.
2 directing us to stay where we were: instruct, command, order, charge.
3 directed me to the next set of shelves: guide, lead, conduct, point.
4 directed the missiles at the main cities: aim, point, focus, turn.
▶ *adjective*
1 a direct route: straight, undeviating, through, uninterrupted.
2 a direct approach: straightforward, outspoken, blunt, frank, unequivocal, sincere, candid, honest, explicit.
3 a direct meeting: immediate, first-hand, face-to-face, personal.
FI 1 circuitous. **2** equivocal. **3** indirect.

direction *noun*
1 direction of traffic: control, administration, management, government, supervision, guidance, leadership.
2 go in the other direction: route, way, line, road.

directions *noun*
instructions, guidelines, orders, briefing, guidance, recommendations, indication, plan.

directive *noun*
command, instruction, order, regulation, ruling, imperative, dictate, decree, charge, mandate, injunction, ordinance, edict, fiat, notice.

directly *adverb*
1 will be back directly: immediately, instantly, promptly, right away, speedily, forthwith, instantaneously, quickly, soon, presently, straightaway, straight.
2 spoke very directly: frankly, bluntly, candidly, honestly.

director *noun*
manager, head, boss, chief, controller, executive, principal, governor, leader, organizer, supervisor, administrator, producer, conductor.

dirt *noun*
1 dig in the dirt: earth, soil, clay, dust, mud.
2 covered in dirt: filth, grime, muck, mire, excrement, stain, smudge, slime, tarnish.

dirty *adjective*
filthy, grimy, grubby, mucky, soiled, unwashed, foul, messy, muddy, polluted, squalid, dull, miry, scruffy, shabby, sullied, clouded, dark.
E3 clean.

disability *noun*
handicap, impairment, disablement, disorder, inability, incapacity, infirmity.

disable *verb*
cripple, lame, incapacitate, damage, handicap, impair, debilitate, disqualify, weaken, immobilize, invalidate, paralyse, prostrate.

disabled *adjective*
handicapped, incapacitated, impaired, infirm, crippled, lame, immobilized, maimed, weak, weakened, paralysed, wrecked.
E3 able, able-bodied.

disadvantage *noun*
drawback, snag, hindrance, handicap, impediment, inconvenience, flaw,

nuisance, weakness, trouble.
E3 advantage, benefit.

disadvantaged *adjective*
deprived, underprivileged, poor, handicapped, impoverished, struggling.
E3 privileged.

disaffected *adjective*
disloyal, hostile, estranged, alienated, antagonistic, rebellious, dissatisfied, disgruntled, discontented.
E3 loyal.

disagree *verb*
1 disagree about how to go about it: dissent, oppose, quarrel, argue, bicker, fall out (*infml*), wrangle, fight, squabble, contend, dispute, contest, object.
2 the two sets of readings disagree: conflict, clash, diverge, contradict, counter, differ, deviate, depart, run counter to, vary.
E3 1 agree. 2 correspond.

disagreeable *adjective*
1 disagreeable old man: bad-tempered, ill-humoured, difficult, peevish, rude, surly, churlish, irritable, contrary, cross, brusque.
2 a disagreeable taste: disgusting, offensive, repulsive, repellent, obnoxious, unsavoury, objectionable, nasty.
E3 1 amiable, pleasant. 2 agreeable.

disagreement *noun*
1 had a disagreement over who should drive: dispute, argument, conflict, altercation (*fml*), quarrel, clash, dissent, falling-out, contention, strife, misunderstanding, squabble, tiff (*infml*), wrangle.
2 the disagreement in the figures is quite significant: difference, variance, unlikeness, disparity, discrepancy, deviation, discord, dissimilarity, incompatibility, divergence, diversity, incongruity.
E3 1 agreement, harmony. 2 similarity.

disappear *verb*
1 spots will disappear gradually: vanish, wane, recede, fade, evaporate, dissolve, ebb.
2 they disappeared as soon as the

police arrived: go, depart, withdraw, retire, flee, fly, escape, scarper (*infml*), hide.
3 dinosaurs disappeared millions of years ago: end, expire, perish, pass.
F3 1 appear. 3 emerge.

disappearance *noun*
vanishing, fading, evaporation, departure, loss, going, passing, melting, desertion, flight.
F3 appearance, manifestation.

disappointed *adjective*
let down, frustrated, thwarted, disillusioned, dissatisfied, miffed (*infml*), upset, discouraged, disgruntled, disheartened, distressed, down-hearted, saddened, despondent, depressed.
F3 pleased, satisfied.

disappointment *noun*
1 couldn't hide her disappointment: frustration, dissatisfaction, disenchantment, disillusionment, displeasure, discouragement, distress, regret.
2 the match was a bit of a disappointment: failure, let-down, setback, comedown, blow, misfortune, fiasco, disaster, calamity, washout (*infml*), damp squib (*infml*), swiz (*infml*), swizzle (*infml*).
F3 1 pleasure, satisfaction, delight. **2** success.

disapproval *noun*
censure, condemnation, criticism, displeasure, reproach, objection, dissatisfaction, denunciation, dislike.
F3 approval, approbation (*fml*).

disapprove of *verb*
censure, condemn, blame, take exception to, object to, deplore, denounce, disparage (*fml*), dislike, reject, spurn.
F3 approve of.

disarray *noun*
disorder, confusion, chaos, mess, muddle, shambles (*infml*), tangle, disorganization, clutter, untidiness, unruliness, jumble, indiscipline, upset.
F3 order.

disaster *noun*
calamity, catastrophe, misfortune,

reverse, tragedy, blow, accident, act of God, cataclysm, debacle, mishap, failure, flop (*infml*), fiasco, ruin, stroke, trouble, mischance, ruination.
F3 success, triumph.

disastrous *adjective*
calamitous, catastrophic, cataclysmic, devastating, ruinous, tragic, unfortunate, dreadful, dire, terrible, destructive, ill-fated, fatal, miserable.
F3 successful, auspicious.

disband *verb*
disperse, break up, scatter, dismiss, demobilize, part company, separate, dissolve.
F3 assemble, muster.

disbelief *noun*
unbelief, incredulity, doubt, scepticism, suspicion, distrust, mistrust, rejection.
F3 belief.

disc *noun*
1 the bright disc of the sun: circle, face, plate, ring.
2 the DJ will spin a couple of discs: record, album, LP, CD.
3 a storage container for the discs: disk, diskette, hard disk, floppy disk, CD-ROM.

discard *verb*
reject, abandon, dispose of, get rid of, jettison, dispense with, cast aside, ditch (*infml*), dump (*infml*), drop, scrap, shed, remove, relinquish.
F3 retain, adopt.

discern *verb*
perceive, make out, observe, detect, recognize, see, ascertain, notice, determine, discover, descry, discriminate, distinguish, differentiate, judge.

discernible *adjective*
perceptible, noticeable, detectable, appreciable, distinct, observable, recognizable, visible, apparent, clear, obvious, plain, patent, manifest, discoverable.
F3 imperceptible.

discerning *adjective*
discriminating, perceptive, astute, clear-sighted, sensitive, shrewd, wise,

sharp, subtle, sagacious (*fml*), penetrating, acute, piercing, critical, eagle-eyed.

Fa dull, obtuse.

discharge *verb*

1 discharge the prisoner: liberate, free, pardon, release, clear, absolve, exonerate, acquit, relieve, dismiss.

2 discharge one's duty: execute, carry out, perform, fulfil, dispense.

3 discharging a gun: fire, shoot, let off, detonate, explode.

4 discharged him for incompetence: emit, sack (*infml*), remove, fire (*infml*), expel, oust, eject.

Fa 1 detain. **2** neglect. **4** appoint.

▶ *noun*

1 his discharge from prison: liberation, release, acquittal, exoneration.

2 discharge from the chemical plant: emission, secretion, ejection.

3 the discharge of his duty: execution, accomplishment, fulfilment.

Fa 1 confinement, detention. **2** absorption. **3** neglect.

disciple *noun*

follower, convert, proselyte, adherent, believer, devotee, supporter, learner, pupil, student, acolyte.

disciplinarian *noun*

authoritarian, taskmaster, autocrat, stickler, despot, tyrant.

discipline *noun*

1 military discipline: training, exercise, drill, practice.

2 harsh discipline: punishment, chastisement, correction.

3 the discipline of his painting technique: strictness, restraint, regulation, self-control, orderliness.

4 an expert in that discipline: subject, area of study, field of study, branch, speciality.

Fa 3 indiscipline.

▶ *verb*

1 were disciplined in all the necessary skills: train, instruct, drill, educate, exercise, break in.

2 moral rules that discipline their behaviour: check, control, constrain, correct, restrain, govern.

3 he will be severely disciplined:

punish, chastise, chasten, penalize, reprimand, castigate (*fml*).

disclose *verb*

1 disclose details of the case: divulge, make known, reveal, tell, confess, let slip, relate, publish, communicate, impart, leak (*infml*).

2 opens up disclosing the brightly-coloured centre: expose, reveal, uncover, lay bare, unveil.

Fa 1, 2 conceal.

discomfort *noun*

ache, pain, uneasiness, malaise, trouble, distress, disquiet, hardship, vexation, irritation, annoyance.

Fa comfort, ease.

disconcerting *adjective*

disturbing, confusing, upsetting, unnerving, alarming, bewildering, off-putting (*infml*), distracting, embarrassing, awkward, baffling, perplexing, dismaying, bothersome.

disconnect *verb*

cut off, disengage, uncouple, sever, separate, detach, unplug, unhook, part, divide.

Fa attach, connect.

disconsolate *adjective*

desolate, dejected, dispirited, sad, melancholy, unhappy, wretched, miserable, gloomy, forlorn, inconsolable, crushed, heavy-hearted, hopeless.

Fa cheerful, joyful.

discontent *noun*

uneasiness, dissatisfaction, disquiet, restlessness, fretfulness, unrest, impatience, vexation, regret.

Fa content.

discontented *adjective*

dissatisfied, fed up (*infml*), disgruntled, unhappy, browned off (*infml*), cheesed off (*infml*), disaffected, miserable, exasperated, complaining.

Fa contented, satisfied.

discontinue *verb*

stop, end, finish, cease, break off, terminate, halt, drop, suspend, abandon, cancel, interrupt.

Fa continue.

discord *noun*

1 discord amongst the back-benchers:

dissension, disagreement, discordance, clashing, disunity, incompatibility, conflict, difference, dispute, contention, friction, division, opposition, strife, split, wrangling.
2 harmony and discord: dissonance, disharmony, cacophony (*fml*), jangle, jarring, harshness.
⊟1 concord, agreement. **2** harmony.

discordant *adjective*
1 a discordant comment: disagreeing, conflicting, at odds, clashing, contradictory, incongruous, incompatible, inconsistent.
2 a discordant note: dissonant, cacophonous (*fml*), grating, jangling, jarring, harsh.
⊟1 concordant. **2** harmonious.

discount *verb*
1 discount his version of events: disregard, ignore, overlook, disbelieve, gloss over.
2 discounting many items of stock: reduce, deduct, mark down, knock off (*infml*).
▶ *noun*
reduction, rebate, allowance, cut, concession, deduction, mark-down.

discourage *verb*
1 discouraged by the exam results: dishearten, dampen, dispirit, depress, demoralize, dismay, unnerve, deject, disappoint.
2 discourage visitors: deter, dissuade, hinder, put off, restrain, prevent.
⊟1 hearten. **2** encourage.

discover *verb*
1 discover a hidden valley: find, uncover, unearth, dig up, disclose, reveal, light on, locate, trace.
2 discover the truth: ascertain, determine, realize, notice, recognize, perceive, see, find out, spot, discern, learn, detect.
3 discovered penicillin: originate, invent, pioneer.
⊟1 miss. **2** conceal, cover (up).

discovery *noun*
1 a new discovery: breakthrough, find, origination, introduction, innovation, invention, exploration.
2 their discovery of the facts:

disclosure, detection, revelation, location.

discredit *verb*
disparage (*fml*), dishonour, degrade, defame (*fml*), disgrace, slander, slur, smear, reproach, vilify (*fml*).
⊟ honour.

discreditable *adjective*
dishonourable, disreputable, disgraceful, reprehensible, scandalous, blameworthy, shameful, infamous, degrading, improper.
⊟ creditable.

discreet *adjective*
tactful, careful, diplomatic, politic, prudent, cautious, delicate, judicious (*fml*), reserved, wary, sensible.
⊟ tactless, indiscreet.

discrepancy *noun*
difference, disparity, variance, variation, inconsistency, dissimilarity, discordance, divergence, disagreement, conflict, inequality.

discretion *noun*
1 had too much discretion to mention it: tact, diplomacy, judiciousness, caution, prudence, wisdom, circumspection, discernment, judgement, care, carefulness, consideration, wariness.
2 would like more discretion on how to spend the budget: choice, freedom, preference, will, wish.
⊟1 indiscretion, imprudence.

discriminate *verb*
distinguish, differentiate, discern, tell apart, make a distinction, segregate, separate.
⊟ confuse, confound.
◆ **discriminate (against)** be prejudiced, be biased, victimize.

discriminating *adjective*
discerning, fastidious, selective, critical, perceptive, particular, tasteful, astute, sensitive, cultivated.

discrimination *noun*
1 racial discrimination: bias, prejudice, intolerance, unfairness, bigotry, favouritism, inequity (*fml*), racism, sexism.
2 his choice shows discrimination: discernment, judgement, acumen,

perception, acuteness, insight, penetration, subtlety, keenness, refinement, taste.

discuss *verb*
debate, talk about, confer, argue, consider, deliberate, converse, consult, examine.

discussion *noun*
debate, conference, argument, conversation, dialogue, exchange, consultation, discourse, deliberation, consideration, analysis, review, examination, scrutiny, seminar, symposium.

disdainful *adjective*
scornful, contemptuous, derisive, haughty, aloof, arrogant, supercilious, sneering, superior, proud, insolent.
E₃ respectful.

disease *noun*
illness, sickness, ill-health, infirmity, complaint, disorder, ailment, indisposition, malady, condition, affliction, infection, epidemic.
E₃ health.

diseased *adjective*
sick, ill, unhealthy, ailing, unsound, contaminated, infected.
E₃ healthy.

disembark *verb*
land, arrive, alight, debark.
E₃ embark.

disengage *verb*
disconnect, detach, loosen, free, extricate, undo, release, liberate, separate, disentangle, untie, withdraw.
E₃ connect, engage.

disentangle *verb*
1 disentangle the ropes: loose, free, extricate, disconnect, untangle, disengage, detach, unravel, separate, unfold.
2 disentangle the situation: resolve, clarify, simplify.
E₃ 1 entangle.

disfigure *verb*
deface, blemish, mutilate, scar, mar, deform, distort, damage, spoil.
E₃ adorn, embellish.

disgrace *noun*
shame, ignominy, disrepute,
dishonour, disfavour, humiliation, defamation (*fml*), discredit, scandal, reproach, slur, stain.
E₃ honour, esteem.
▶ *verb*
shame, dishonour, abase, defame (*fml*), humiliate, disfavour, stain, discredit, reproach, slur, sully (*fml*), taint, stigmatize.
E₃ honour, respect.

disgraceful *adjective*
shameful, dishonourable, disreputable, ignominious, scandalous, shocking, unworthy, dreadful, appalling.
E₃ honourable, respectable.

disguise *verb*
1 disguised as a beggar: conceal, cover, camouflage, mask, hide, dress up, cloak, screen, veil, shroud.
2 disguised the truth: falsify, deceive, dissemble (*fml*), misrepresent, fake, fudge.
E₃ 1 reveal, expose.
▶ *noun*
concealment, camouflage, cloak, cover, costume, mask, front, façade, masquerade, deception, pretence, travesty, screen, veil.

disgust *verb*
offend, displease, nauseate, revolt, sicken, repel, outrage, put off.
E₃ delight, please.
▶ *noun*
revulsion, repulsion, repugnance, distaste, aversion, abhorrence (*fml*), nausea, loathing, detestation, hatred.

disgusted *adjective*
repelled, repulsed, revolted, offended, appalled, outraged.
E₃ attracted, delighted.

disgusting *adjective*
repugnant, repellent, revolting, offensive, sickening, nauseating, odious, foul, unappetizing, unpleasant, vile, obscene, abominable, detestable, objectionable, nasty.
E₃ delightful, pleasant.

dish *noun*
plate, bowl, platter, food, recipe.
◆ **dish out** distribute, give out, hand out, hand round, dole out, allocate,

mete out, inflict.

◆ **dish up** serve, present, ladle, spoon, dispense, scoop.

dishearten *verb*
discourage, dispirit, dampen, cast down, depress, dismay, dash, disappoint, deject, daunt, crush, deter.
F∃ encourage, hearten.

dishevelled *adjective*
tousled, unkempt, uncombed, untidy, bedraggled, messy, ruffled, slovenly, disordered.
F∃ neat, tidy.

dishonest *adjective*
untruthful, fraudulent, deceitful, false, lying, deceptive, double-dealing, cheating, crooked (*infml*), treacherous, unprincipled, swindling, shady (*infml*), corrupt, disreputable.
F∃ honest, trustworthy, scrupulous.

dishonesty *noun*
deceit, falsehood, fraud, criminality, falsity, cheating, treachery, trickery, duplicity (*fml*), shadiness (*infml*).
F∃ honesty, truthfulness.
⇨ *See also* **Word Study** *panel.*

dishonour *verb*
disgrace, shame, humiliate, debase, defile (*fml*), degrade, defame (*fml*), discredit, demean, debauch.
F∃ honour.
▸ *noun*
disgrace, abasement (*fml*), humiliation, shame, degradation, discredit, disrepute, indignity, ignominy, reproach, slight, slur, scandal, insult, disfavour, outrage, aspersion (*fml*), abuse, discourtesy.
F∃ honour.

disillusioned *adjective*
disenchanted, disabused, undeceived, disappointed.

disinclined *adjective*
averse, reluctant, resistant, indisposed, loath, opposed, hesitant.
F∃ inclined, willing.

disinfect *verb*
sterilize, fumigate, sanitize, decontaminate, cleanse, purify, purge, clean.
F∃ contaminate, infect.

disintegrate *verb*
break up, decompose, fall apart, crumble, rot, moulder, separate, splinter.

disinterested *adjective*
unbiased, neutral, impartial, unprejudiced, dispassionate, detached, uninvolved, open-minded, equitable, even-handed, unselfish.
F∃ biased, concerned.

disjointed *adjective*
1 disjointed communities:
disconnected, dislocated, divided, separated, disunited, displaced, broken, split, disarticulated.
2 disjointed speech: incoherent, aimless, confused, disordered, loose, unconnected, bitty, rambling, fitful, spasmodic.
F∃ 2 coherent.

dislike *verb*
hate, detest, object to, loathe, abhor, abominate, disapprove, shun, despise, scorn.
F∃ like, favour.
⇨ *See also* **Word Study** *panel.*
▸ *noun*
hatred, disapproval, distaste, loathing, abhorrence (*fml*), antipathy.

dislodge *verb*
displace, eject, remove, oust, extricate, shift, move, uproot.

disloyal *adjective*
treacherous, faithless, false, traitorous, two-faced (*infml*), unfaithful, apostate, unpatriotic.
F∃ loyal, trustworthy.

dismal *adjective*
dreary, gloomy, depressing, bleak, cheerless, dull, drab, low-spirited, melancholy, sad, sombre, lugubrious, forlorn, despondent, dark, sorrowful, long-faced (*infml*), hopeless, discouraging.
F∃ cheerful, bright.

dismantle *verb*
demolish, take apart, disassemble, strip.
F∃ assemble, put together.

dismay *noun*
consternation, alarm, distress, apprehension, agitation, dread, fear,

WORD study   dishonesty

There are lots of expressions used to refer to **dishonesty** or **dishonest behaviour** in an indirect way. Remember, while many of these expressions might be used in formal contexts, you would be less likely to use them in formal written work.

deceiving someone

feed/shoot someone a line
sell someone a pup (*slang*)
take someone for a ride
laugh up your sleeve
rip someone off (*slang*)
pull a fast one

put one over on someone
have the shirt off someone's back
pull the wool over someone's eyes

telling lies

tell a white lie
lie through your teeth
be economical with the truth
a pack of lies

tell porkies
speak with a forked tongue
spin a yarn
a tissue of lies

a dishonest person

a snake in the grass

a wolf in sheep's clothing

behave dishonestly

cook the books
have light fingers
be up to no good
be on the take

be on the fiddle
have your fingers in the till
wheel and deal

dishonest activity

funny business
in bad faith
funny money
foul play
sleight of hand
under the table

under the counter
a put-up job
monkey business
sharp practice
on the sly
dirty tricks

---

trepidation, fright, horror, terror, discouragement, disappointment.
F3 boldness, encouragement.

dismember *verb*
disjoint, amputate, dissect, dislocate, divide, mutilate, sever.
F3 assemble, join.

dismiss *verb*
1 the class was dismissed: discharge, free, let go, release, send away.

WORD study   dislike

There are many phrases to express **dislike**. You can also check the panel at **like** to find ways of expressing the opposite.

dislike someone or something strongly

have something against
make someone's flesh crawl *or* creep
not stand the sight of

hold in contempt
have no time for
be sick to the back teeth of

not keen on or impressed by someone or something

take exception to something
turn your nose up at something
not have a good word to say about
not what it's cracked up to be
not to your taste

not take kindly to something
have a thing about
not someone's cup of tea
leave a lot to be desired

something or someone which is disliked

pet hate
bête noir

bugbear
thorn in your flesh/side

---

2 dismiss employees: sack (*infml*), make redundant, lay off, fire (*infml*).
3 dismiss it from your mind: discount, disregard, reject, repudiate, set aside, shelve, spurn, banish.
F∃2 appoint. **3** retain, accept.

disobey   *verb*
contravene, infringe, violate, transgress, flout, disregard, defy, ignore, resist, rebel.
F∃ obey.

disorder   *noun*
1 try to sort out the disorder: confusion, chaos, muddle, disarray, mess, untidiness, shambles (*infml*), clutter, disorganization, jumble.
2 charged with public disorder: disturbance, tumult, riot, confusion, commotion, uproar, fracas, brawl, fight, clamour, quarrel.
3 a disorder of the nervous system: illness, complaint, disease, sickness, disability, ailment, malady, affliction.

F∃1 neatness, order. **2** law and order, peace.

disorderly   *adjective*
1 in disorderly piles: disorganized, confused, chaotic, irregular, messy, untidy.
2 a disorderly crowd of fans: unruly, undisciplined, unmanageable, obstreperous, rowdy, turbulent, rebellious, lawless.
F∃1 neat, tidy. **2** well-behaved.

disorganized   *verb*
1 a disorganized pile of papers: confused, jumbled, chaotic, shambolic (*infml*), disordered, disturbed, disarranged, muddled.
2 his life is so disorganized: unmethodical, careless, unorganized, unsystematic, unstructured.

disown   *verb*
repudiate, renounce, disclaim, deny, cast off, disallow, reject, abandon.
F∃ accept, acknowledge.

disparaging *adjective*
derisive, derogatory, mocking, scornful, critical, insulting, snide (*infml*).
E3 flattering, praising.

dispassionate *adjective*
detached, objective, impartial, neutral, disinterested, impersonal, fair, cool, calm, composed.
E3 biased, emotional.

dispatch, despatch *verb*
1 dispatching the goods: send, transmit, forward, consign.
2 dispatched his opponent/duty: dispose of, finish, perform, discharge, conclude.
3 dispatched him with a single shot to the head: kill, murder, execute.
E3 1 receive.

dispense *verb*
1 dispense medicines: distribute, give out, apportion, allot, allocate, assign.
2 dispense justice: administer, apply, implement, enforce, discharge, execute, operate, mete out.
◆ **dispense with** dispose of, get rid of, abolish, discard, omit, disregard, cancel, forgo, ignore, waive.

disperse *verb*
scatter, dispel, spread, distribute, diffuse, dissolve, break up, dismiss, separate.
E3 gather.

displace *verb*
1 displacing some slates: dislodge, move, shift, misplace, disturb, dislocate.
2 displacing his rivals: depose, oust, remove, replace, dismiss, discharge, supplant, eject, evict, succeed, supersede.

display *verb*
1 display goods for sale: show, present, demonstrate, exhibit.
2 display irritation: betray, disclose, reveal, show, expose.
3 displaying her tan: show off, flourish, parade, flaunt.
E3 1 conceal. 2 disguise.
▶ *noun*
show, exhibition, demonstration, presentation, parade, spectacle, revelation, array.

displeasure *noun*
offence, annoyance, disapproval, irritation, resentment, disfavour, anger, indignation, wrath.
E3 pleasure.

dispose of *verb*
1 dispose of the matter quickly: deal with, decide, settle.
2 dispose of waste: get rid of, discard, scrap, destroy, dump (*infml*), jettison.
E3 2 keep.

disposed *adjective*
liable, inclined, predisposed, prone, likely, apt, minded, subject, ready, willing.
E3 disinclined.

disposition *noun*
character, nature, temperament, inclination, make-up, bent, leaning, predisposition, constitution, habit, spirit, tendency, proneness.

disproportionate *adjective*
unequal, uneven, incommensurate, excessive, unreasonable.
E3 balanced.

disprove *verb*
refute, rebut, confute, discredit, invalidate, contradict, expose.
E3 confirm, prove.

dispute *verb* /dis-**pyoot**/
argue, debate, question, contend, challenge, discuss, doubt, contest, contradict, deny, quarrel, clash, wrangle, squabble.
E3 agree.
▶ *noun* /**dis**-pyoot/
argument, debate, disagreement, controversy, conflict, contention, quarrel, wrangle, feud, strife, squabble.
E3 agreement, settlement.

disqualify *verb*
debar, preclude, rule out, disentitle, eliminate, prohibit.
E3 qualify, accept.

disquiet *noun*
anxiety, worry, concern, nervousness, uneasiness, restlessness, alarm, distress, fretfulness, fear, disturbance, trouble, unrest.
E3 calm, reassurance.

disregard *verb*
1 if you have paid please disregard this letter: ignore, overlook, discount, neglect, pass over, disobey, make light of, turn a blind eye to (*infml*), brush aside.
2 disregarding the fans who had waited all night: slight, snub, despise, disdain, disparage (*fml*).
F3 1 heed, pay attention to. **2** respect.

disrepair *noun*
dilapidation, deterioration, decay, collapse, ruin, shabbiness.
F3 good repair.

disreputable *adjective*
1 a disreputable affair: disgraceful, discreditable, dishonourable, unrespectable, notorious, scandalous, infamous, shameful, shady, base, contemptible, low, mean, shocking.
2 a disreputable old jacket: scruffy, shabby, seedy, unkempt.
F3 1 respectable. **2** smart.

disrespectful *adjective*
rude, discourteous, impertinent, impolite, impudent, insolent, uncivil, unmannerly, cheeky, insulting, irreverent, contemptuous.
F3 polite, respectful.

disrupt *verb*
disturb, disorganize, confuse, interrupt, break up, unsettle, intrude, upset.

dissatisfaction *noun*
discontent, displeasure, dislike, discomfort, disappointment, frustration, annoyance, irritation, exasperation, regret, resentment.
F3 satisfaction.

dissect *verb*
1 dissect the frog: dismember, anatomize.
2 dissecting the evidence: analyse, investigate, scrutinize, examine, inspect, pore over.

dissent *verb*
disagree, differ, protest, object, refuse, quibble.
F3 assent.
▶ *noun*
disagreement, difference, dissension,

discord, resistance, opposition, objection.
F3 agreement, conformity.

disservice *noun*
disfavour, injury, wrong, bad turn, harm, unkindness, injustice.
F3 favour.

dissident *noun*
dissenter, protestor, noncomformist, rebel, agitator, revolutionary.
F3 assenter.

dissimilar *adjective*
unlike, different, divergent, disparate, unrelated, incompatible, mismatched, diverse, various, heterogeneous (*fml*).
F3 similar, like.

dissipate *verb*
1 dissipating his inheritance: spend, waste, squander, expend, consume, deplete, fritter away, burn up.
2 the clouds dissipated: disperse, vanish, disappear, dispel, diffuse, evaporate, dissolve.
F3 1 accumulate. **2** appear.

dissociate *verb*
separate, detach, break off, disunite, disengage, disconnect, cut off, disband, divorce, disrupt, isolate, segregate.
F3 associate, join.

dissolute *adjective*
dissipated, debauched, degenerate, depraved, wanton, abandoned, corrupt, immoral, licentious, lewd, wild.
F3 restrained, virtuous.

dissolve *verb*
1 when all the sugar has dissolved: evaporate, disintegrate, liquefy, melt.
2 dissolved into dust: decompose, disintegrate, disperse, break up, disappear, crumble.
3 dissolve the marriage: end, terminate, separate, sever, divorce.

dissuade *verb*
deter, discourage, put off, disincline.
F3 persuade.

distance *noun*
space, interval, gap, extent, range, reach, length, width.
F3 closeness.

distant *adjective*
1 distant stars: far, faraway, far-flung, out-of-the-way, remote, outlying, abroad, dispersed.
2 he is always a little distant with strangers: aloof, cool, reserved, stand-offish (*infml*), formal, cold, restrained, stiff.
E3 1 close. 2 approachable.

distaste *noun*
dislike, aversion, repugnance, disgust, revulsion, loathing, abhorrence (*fml*).
E3 liking.

distasteful *adjective*
disagreeable, offensive, unpleasant, objectionable, repulsive, obnoxious, repugnant, unsavoury, loathsome, abhorrent (*fml*).
E3 pleasing.

distinct *adjective*
1 two distinct languages: separate, different, detached, individual, dissimilar.
2 a distinct lack of enthusiasm: clear, plain, evident, obvious, apparent, marked, definite, noticeable, recognizable.
E3 2 indistinct, vague.

distinction *noun*
1 made no distinction between rich and poor: differentiation, discrimination, discernment, separation, difference, dissimilarity, contrast.
2 an obvious distinction: characteristic, peculiarity, individuality, feature, quality, mark.
3 a man of distinction: renown, fame, celebrity, prominence, eminence, importance, reputation, greatness, honour, prestige, repute, superiority, worth, merit, excellence, quality.
E3 3 unimportance, obscurity.

distinctive *adjective*
characteristic, distinguishing, individual, peculiar, different, unique, singular, special, original, extraordinary, idiosyncratic.
E3 ordinary, common.

distinguish *verb*
1 distinguish one from the other: differentiate, tell apart, discriminate,

determine, categorize, characterize, classify.
2 distinguish his features: discern, perceive, identify, ascertain, make out, recognize, see, discriminate.

distinguished *adjective*
famous, eminent, celebrated, well-known, acclaimed, illustrious, notable, noted, renowned, famed, honoured, outstanding, striking, marked, extraordinary, conspicuous.
E3 insignificant, obscure, unimpressive.

distort *verb*
1 distorting the image: deform, contort, bend, misshape, disfigure, twist, warp.
2 distorting the facts: falsify, misrepresent, pervert, slant, colour, garble.

distract *verb*
divert, sidetrack, deflect, occupy.

distracted *adjective*
confused, disconcerted, bewildered, confounded, disturbed, perplexed, puzzled.

distraught *adjective*
agitated, anxious, overwrought, upset, distressed, distracted, beside oneself, worked up, frantic, hysterical, raving, mad, wild, crazy.
E3 calm, untroubled.

distress *noun*
1 his distress was obvious: anguish, grief, misery, sorrow, heartache, affliction, suffering, torment, wretchedness, sadness, worry, anxiety, desolation, pain, agony.
2 financial distress: adversity, hardship, poverty, need, privation (*fml*), destitution, misfortune, trouble, difficulties, trial.
E3 1 content. 2 comfort, ease.
▶ *verb*
upset, afflict, grieve, disturb, trouble, sadden, worry, torment, harass, harrow, pain, agonize, bother.
E3 comfort.

distribute *verb*
1 distribute the money to children's charities: dispense, allocate, dole out, dish out, share, deal, divide, apportion.
2 distribute the leaflets: deliver, hand

out, spread, issue, circulate, diffuse,
disperse, scatter.
F3 2 collect.

distribution noun
1 distribution of aid: allocation,
division, sharing.
2 the distribution of goods:
circulation, spreading, scattering,
delivery, dissemination, supply,
dealing, handling.
F3 2 collection.

district noun
region, area, quarter, neighbourhood,
locality, sector, precinct, parish, locale,
community, vicinity, ward.

distrust verb
mistrust, doubt, disbelieve, suspect,
question.
F3 trust.
▶ noun
mistrust, doubt, disbelief, suspicion,
misgiving, wariness, scepticism,
question, qualm.
F3 trust.

disturb verb
1 disturbing his rest: disrupt,
interrupt, distract.
2 disturbed by the news: agitate,
unsettle, upset, distress, worry, fluster,
annoy, bother.
3 disturbing the neat piles of papers:
disarrange, disorder, confuse, upset.
F3 2 reassure. **3** order.

disturbance noun
1 causing disturbance: disruption,
agitation, interruption, intrusion,
upheaval, upset, confusion,
annoyance, bother, trouble, hindrance.
2 a disturbance in the town centre:
disorder, uproar, commotion, tumult,
turmoil, fracas, fray, brawl, riot.
F3 1 peace. **2** order.

disuse noun
neglect, decay, abandonment,
discontinuance.
F3 use.

ditch noun
trench, dyke, channel, gully, furrow,
moat, drain, level, watercourse.

dither verb
hesitate, shilly-shally (infml), waver,
vacillate.

dive verb
plunge, plummet, dip, submerge, jump,
leap, nose-dive, fall, drop, swoop,
descend, pitch.
▶ noun
plunge, lunge, header, jump, leap,
nose-dive, swoop, dash, spring.

diverge verb
1 the veins diverge to form capillaries:
divide, branch, fork, separate, spread,
split.
2 diverging from the matter at hand:
deviate, digress, stray, wander.
3 this is where opinions diverge: differ,
vary, disagree, dissent, conflict.
F3 1 converge. **3** agree.

diverse adjective
various, varied, varying, sundry,
different, differing, assorted,
dissimilar, miscellaneous, discrete,
separate, several, distinct.
F3 similar, identical.

diversify verb
vary, change, expand, branch out,
spread out, alter, mix, assort.

diversion noun
1 a diversion off the motorway:
deviation, detour.
2 a puppet theatre and other
diversions: amusement,
entertainment, distraction, pastime,
recreation, relaxation, play, game.

diversity noun
variety, dissimilarity, difference,
variance, assortment, range, medley.
F3 similarity, likeness.

divert verb
1 diverting the stream: deflect,
redirect, reroute, side-track, avert,
distract, switch.
2 tried to divert them by singing
songs: amuse, entertain, occupy,
distract, interest.

divide verb
1 divide the orange into segments:
split, separate, part, cut, break up,
detach, bisect, disconnect.
2 dividing the money equally:
distribute, share, allocate, deal out,
allot, apportion.
3 dividing families: disunite, separate,
estrange, alienate.

4 divide the men from the boys:
classify, group, sort, grade, segregate.
E3 1 join. **2** collect. **3** unite.

divine *adjective*
1 he is almost divine: godlike,
superhuman, supernatural, celestial,
heavenly, angelic, spiritual.
2 divine worship: holy, sacred,
sanctified, consecrated, transcendent,
exalted, glorious, religious, supreme.
E3 1 human. **2** mundane.

division *noun*
1 the division of cells: separation,
detaching, parting, cutting, disunion.
2 a division in the Cabinet: breach,
rupture, split, schism, disunion,
estrangement, disagreement, feud.
3 division of his estate amongst his
children: distribution, sharing,
allotment.
4 head of the sales division: section,
sector, segment, part, department,
branch.
E3 1 union. **2** unity. **3** collection. **4**
whole.

divorce *noun*
dissolution, annulment, break-up,
split-up, rupture, separation, breach,
disunion.
▶ *verb*
separate, part, annul, split up, sever,
dissolve, divide, dissociate.
E3 marry, unite.

divulge *verb*
disclose, reveal, communicate, tell,
leak (*infml*), impart, confess, betray,
uncover, let slip, expose, publish,
proclaim.

dizzy *adjective*
1 feeling dizzy: giddy, faint, light-
headed, woozy (*infml*), shaky, reeling.
2 dizzy with excitement: confused,
bewildered, dazed, muddled.

do *verb*
1 do a play: perform, carry out,
execute, accomplish, achieve, fulfil,
implement, complete, undertake,
work, put on, present, conclude, end,
finish.
2 don't know what to do: behave, act,
conduct oneself.
3 do the repairs: fix, prepare, organize,

arrange, deal with, look after, manage,
produce, make, create, cause, proceed.
4 that'll do nicely: suffice, satisfy, serve.
▶ *noun* (*infml*)
function, affair, event, gathering, party,
occasion.
◆ **do away with** get rid of, dispose of,
exterminate, eliminate, abolish,
discontinue, remove, destroy, discard,
kill, murder.
◆ **do up 1** do up your laces: fasten, tie,
lace.
2 doing up their house: renovate,
restore, decorate, redecorate,
modernize, repair.
◆ **do without** dispense with, abstain
from, forgo, give up, relinquish.

docile *adjective*
tractable, co-operative, manageable,
submissive, obedient, amenable,
controlled, obliging.
E3 truculent, unco-operative.

dock *noun*
harbour, wharf, quay, boat-yard, pier,
waterfront, marina.
▶ *verb*
anchor, moor, drop anchor, land,
berth, put in, tie up.

doctor *noun*
physician, general practitioner, GP,
medic (*infml*), medical officer,
consultant, clinician.
▶ *verb*
alter, tamper with, falsify,
misrepresent, pervert, adulterate,
change, disguise, dilute.

doctrine *noun*
dogma, creed, belief, tenet, principle,
teaching, precept (*fml*), conviction,
opinion, canon.

document *noun*
paper, certificate, deed, record, report,
form, instrument (*fml*).

dodge *verb*
avoid, elude, evade, swerve, side-step,
shirk, shift.
▶ *noun*
trick, ruse, ploy, wile, scheme,
stratagem, machination, manoeuvre.

dog *noun*
hound, cur, mongrel, canine, puppy,
pup, bitch, mutt (*infml*), pooch (*infml*).

Breeds of dog include:

Afghan hound, alsatian, basset-hound, beagle, Border collie, borzoi, bulldog, bull-mastiff, bull-terrier, cairn terrier, chihuahua, chow, cocker spaniel, collie, corgi, dachshund, Dalmatian, Doberman pinscher, foxhound, fox-terrier, German Shepherd, golden retriever, Great Dane, greyhound, husky, Irish wolfhound, Jack Russell, King Charles spaniel, Labrador, lhasa apso, lurcher, Maltese, Old English sheepdog, Pekingese, pit bull terrier, pointer, poodle, pug, Rottweiler, saluki, sausage-dog (*infml*), schnauzer, Scottie (*infml*), Scottish-terrier, Sealyham, setter, sheltie, shih tzu, springer spaniel, St Bernard, terrier, West Highland terrier, Westie (*infml*), whippet, wolfhound, Yorkshire terrier.

▶ *verb*
pursue, follow, trail, track, tail, hound, shadow, plague, harry, haunt, trouble, worry.

dogged *adjective*
determined, resolute, persistent, persevering, intent, tenacious, firm, steadfast, staunch, single-minded, indefatigable, steady, unshakable, stubborn, obstinate, relentless, unyielding.
🔁 irresolute, apathetic.

dogma *noun*
doctrine, creed, belief, precept (*fml*), principle, article (of faith), credo, tenet, conviction, teaching, opinion.

dogmatic *adjective*
opinionated, assertive, authoritative, positive, doctrinaire, dictatorial, doctrinal, categorical, emphatic, overbearing, arbitrary.

dole out *verb*
distribute, allocate, hand out, dish out, apportion, allot, mete out, share, divide, deal, issue, ration, dispense, administer, assign.

domain *noun*
1 the king's domain: dominion, kingdom, realm, territory, region, empire, lands, province.
2 his particular domain: field, area, speciality, concern, department, sphere, discipline, jurisdiction.

domestic *adjective*
1 domestic chores/animals: home, family, household, home-loving, stay-at-home, homely, house-trained, tame, pet, private.
2 domestic affairs: internal, indigenous, native.

domesticate *verb*
tame, house-train, break, train, accustom, familiarize.

dominant *adjective*
1 a dominant leader: authoritative, controlling, governing, ruling, powerful, assertive, influential.
2 the dominant species: principal, main, outstanding, chief, important, predominant, primary, prominent, leading, pre-eminent, prevailing, prevalent, commanding.
🔁 1 submissive. 2 subordinate.

dominate *verb*
1 the team dominates the Premiership: control, domineer, govern, rule, direct, monopolize, master, lead, overrule, prevail, overbear, tyrannize.
2 dominating the landscape: overshadow, eclipse, dwarf.

domineering *adjective*
overbearing, authoritarian, imperious, autocratic, bossy (*infml*), dictatorial, despotic, masterful, high-handed, oppressive, tyrannical, arrogant.
🔁 meek, servile.

dominion *noun*
1 had dominion over half of Europe: power, authority, domination, command, control, rule, sway, jurisdiction, government, lordship, mastery, supremacy, sovereignty.
2 man's dominion: domain, country, territory, province, colony, realm, kingdom, empire.

donate *verb*
give, contribute, present, bequeath, bestow, confer, subscribe.
🔁 receive.

donation noun
gift, present, offering, grant, gratuity, largess(e), contribution, presentation, subscription, alms, benefaction (fml), bequest.

done adjective
1 the job's done: finished, over, accomplished, completed, ended, concluded, settled, realized, executed.
2 not the done thing: conventional, acceptable, proper.
3 the meat's done: cooked, ready.

donor noun
giver, donator, benefactor, contributor, philanthropist, provider, fairy godmother (infml).
Ｅ beneficiary.

doom noun
fate, fortune, destiny, portion, lot, destruction, catastrophe, downfall, ruin, death, death-knell.

doomed adjective
condemned, damned, fated, ill-fated, ill-omened, cursed, destined, hopeless, luckless, ill-starred.

door noun
opening, entrance, entry, exit, doorway, portal, hatch.

dormant adjective
1 a dormant volcano: inactive, asleep, sleeping, inert, resting, slumbering, sluggish, torpid, hibernating, fallow, comatose.
2 a dormant bud: latent, unrealized, potential, undeveloped, undisclosed.
Ｅ 1 active, awake. 2 realized, developed.

dose noun
measure, dosage, amount, portion, quantity, draught, potion, prescription, shot (infml).

dot noun
point, spot, speck, mark, fleck, circle, pin-point, atom, decimal point, full stop, iota, jot.

double adjective
dual, twofold, twice, duplicate, twin, paired, doubled, coupled.
Ｅ single, half.
▶ verb
duplicate, enlarge, increase, repeat, multiply, fold, magnify.
▶ noun
twin, duplicate, copy, clone, replica, doppelgänger, lookalike, spitting image (infml), ringer (infml), image, counterpart, impersonator.

doubt verb
1 doubt his motives: distrust, mistrust, query, question, suspect, fear.
2 I don't doubt his ability: be uncertain, be dubious, hesitate, vacillate, waver.
Ｅ 1 believe, trust.
▶ noun
1 I have doubts about him: distrust, suspicion, mistrust, scepticism, reservation, misgiving, incredulity, apprehension, hesitation.
2 no doubt about the accuracy of his statement: uncertainty, difficulty, confusion, ambiguity, problem, indecision, perplexity, dilemma, quandary.
Ｅ 1 trust, faith. 2 certainty, belief.

doubtful adjective
1 doubtful about his future: uncertain, unsure, undecided, suspicious, irresolute, wavering, hesitant, vacillating, tentative, sceptical.
2 writing of doubtful origin: dubious, questionable, unclear, ambiguous, vague, obscure, debatable.
Ｅ 1 certain, decided. 2 definite, settled.

downfall noun
fall, ruin, failure, collapse, destruction, disgrace, debacle, undoing, overthrow.

downright adjective, adverb
absolute(ly), outright, plain(ly), utter(ly), clear(ly), complete(ly), out-and-out, frank(ly), explicit(ly).

downward adjective
descending, declining, downhill, sliding, slipping.
Ｅ upward.

doze verb
sleep, nod off, drop off, snooze (infml), kip (infml).

drab adjective
dull, dingy, dreary, dismal, gloomy, flat, grey, lacklustre, cheerless, sombre, shabby.
Ｅ bright, cheerful.

draft *verb*
draw (up), outline, sketch, plan, design, formulate, compose.
▶ *noun*
outline, sketch, plan, delineation, abstract, rough, blueprint.

drag *verb*
1 drag the box to the other room: draw, pull, haul, lug, tug, trail, tow.
2 time dragging by: go slowly, creep, crawl, lag.

drain *noun*
1 digging up the drains: channel, conduit, culvert, duct, outlet, trench, ditch, pipe, sewer.
2 a drain on their savings: depletion, exhaustion, sap, strain.
▶ *verb*
1 drained the tank: empty, remove, evacuate, draw off, strain, dry, milk, bleed.
2 draining into the sea: discharge, trickle, flow out, leak, ooze.
3 draining his energy: exhaust, consume, sap, use up, deplete, drink up, swallow.
F3 1 fill.

drama *noun*
1 study drama: play, acting, theatre, show, spectacle, stage-craft, scene, melodrama.
2 what's all the drama about?: excitement, crisis, turmoil.

dramatic *adjective*
1 a dramatic landscape: exciting, striking, stirring, thrilling, marked, significant, expressive, impressive.
2 don't be so dramatic!: histrionic, exaggerated, melodramatic, flamboyant.

drape *verb*
cover, wrap, hang, fold, drop, suspend.

drastic *adjective*
extreme, radical, strong, forceful, severe, harsh, far-reaching, desperate, dire.
F3 moderate, cautious.

draught *noun*
1 a draught from the window: puff, current, influx, flow.
2 take a long draught of ale: drink, potion, quantity.

draw *verb*
1 draw a crowd: attract, allure, entice, bring in, influence, persuade, elicit.
2 a caravan drawn by two horses: pull, drag, haul, tow, tug.
3 draw a diagram: delineate, map out, sketch, portray, trace, pencil, depict, design, outline.
4 the teams drew: tie, be equal, be even.
F3 1 repel. 2 push.
▶ *noun*
1 he's a big draw at the box-office: attraction, enticement, lure, appeal, bait, interest.
2 a 0-0 draw: tie, stalemate, dead-heat.
◆ **draw out** protract, extend, prolong, drag out, spin out, elongate, stretch, lengthen, string out.
F3 shorten.
◆ **draw up 1** draw up a plan: draft, compose, formulate, prepare, frame, write out.
2 a car drew up outside: pull up, stop, halt.

drawback *noun*
disadvantage, snag, hitch, obstacle, impediment, hindrance, difficulty, flaw, fault, fly in the ointment (*infml*), catch, stumbling block, nuisance, trouble, defect, handicap, deficiency, imperfection.
F3 advantage, benefit.

drawing *noun*
sketch, picture, outline, representation, delineation, portrayal, illustration, cartoon, graphic, portrait.

dread *verb*
fear, shrink from, quail, cringe at, flinch, shy, shudder, tremble.
▶ *noun*
fear, apprehension, misgiving, trepidation, dismay, alarm, horror, terror, fright, disquiet, worry, qualm.
F3 confidence, security.

dreadful *adjective*
awful, terrible, frightful, horrible, appalling, dire, shocking, ghastly, horrendous, tragic, grievous, hideous, tremendous.
F3 wonderful, comforting.

dream *noun*
1 have a bad dream/see them in his dreams: vision, illusion, reverie, trance, fantasy, daydream, nightmare, hallucination, delusion, imagination.
2 achieve his dream: aspiration, wish, hope, ambition, desire, pipe-dream, ideal, goal, design, speculation.
▶ *verb*
imagine, envisage, fancy, fantasize, daydream, hallucinate, conceive, visualize, conjure up, muse.
◆ **dream up** invent, devise, conceive, think up, imagine, concoct, hatch, create, spin, contrive.

dreary *adjective*
1 a dreary job: boring, tedious, uneventful, dull, humdrum, routine, monotonous, wearisome, commonplace, colourless, lifeless.
2 a dreary prospect: gloomy, depressing, drab, dismal, bleak, sombre, sad, mournful.
E3 1 interesting. 2 cheerful.

dregs *noun*
1 wash the dregs from the teacups: sediment, deposit, residue, lees, grounds, scum, dross, trash, waste.
2 the dregs of society: outcasts, rabble, riff-raff, scum, down-and-outs.

drench *verb*
soak, saturate, steep, wet, douse, souse, immerse, inundate, duck, flood, imbue, drown.

dress *verb*
1 dress for dinner: clothe, put on, garb, rig, robe, wear, don, decorate, deck, garnish, trim, adorn, fit, drape.
2 dressing the turkey/the shop window: arrange, adjust, dispose, prepare, groom, straighten.
3 dressing his wounds: bandage, tend, treat.
E3 1 strip, undress.
◆ **dress up** beautify, adorn, embellish, improve, deck, doll up, gild, disguise.

dribble *verb*
1 water dribbling down the walls: trickle, drip, leak, run, seep, drop, ooze.
2 dribbling saliva: drool, slaver, slobber, drivel.

drift *noun*
1 snow forming drifts: accumulation, mound, pile, bank, mass, heap.
2 the drift of history: trend, tendency, course, direction, flow, movement, current, rush, sweep.
3 get someone's drift: meaning, intention, implication, gist, tenor, thrust, significance, aim, design, scope.
▶ *verb*
1 drift past: wander, waft, stray, float, freewheel, coast.
2 snow drifting: gather, accumulate, pile up, drive.

drill *verb*
1 drilling the new recruits: teach, train, instruct, coach, practise, school, rehearse, exercise, discipline.
2 drill teeth/a hole: bore, pierce, penetrate, puncture, perforate.

drink *noun*
1 a cool drink: beverage, liquid, refreshment, draught, sip, swallow, swig (*infml*), gulp.
2 serve drinks/the demon drink: alcohol, spirits, booze (*infml*), liquor, tipple (*infml*), tot, the bottle (*infml*).
▶ *verb*
1 drinks only water: imbibe, swallow, sip, drain, down, gulp, swig (*infml*), knock back (*infml*), sup, quaff, absorb, swill.
2 he drinks: get drunk, booze (*infml*), tipple (*infml*), indulge, carouse, revel.

drip *noun*
drop, trickle, dribble, leak, bead, tear.
▶ *verb*
drop, dribble, trickle, plop, percolate, drizzle, splash, sprinkle, weep.

drive *verb*
1 driven by steam/greed: direct, control, manage, operate, run, handle, motivate.
2 he drove me to do it: force, compel, impel, coerce, constrain, press, push, urge, dragoon, goad, guide, oblige.
3 drive a tractor/driving home: steer, motor, propel, ride, travel.
▶ *noun*
1 need plenty of drive and enthusiasm: energy, enterprise, ambition, initiative,

get-up-and-go (*infml*), vigour, motivation, determination.

2 a drive to improve standards: campaign, crusade, appeal, effort, action.

3 a long drive: excursion, outing, journey, ride, spin, trip, jaunt.

4 the drive to succeed: urge, instinct, impulse, need, desire.

◆ **drive at** imply, allude to, intimate, mean, suggest, hint, get at, intend, refer to, signify, insinuate, indicate.

drop *noun*

1 a drop of water: droplet, bead, tear, drip, bubble, globule, trickle.

2 a few drops of vanilla essence: dash, pinch, spot, sip, trace, dab.

3 a drop in exports: fall, decline, falling-off, lowering, downturn, decrease, reduction, slump, plunge, deterioration.

4 a steep drop to the sea: descent, precipice, slope, chasm, abyss.

▶ *verb*

1 dropped to the ground/prices dropping: fall, sink, decline, plunge, plummet, tumble, dive, descend, lower, droop, depress, diminish.

2 drop the subject: abandon, forsake, desert, give up, relinquish, reject, leave, renounce, throw over, repudiate, cease, discontinue, quit.

₣₃ 1 rise.

◆ **drop off 1** grandad's dropped off again: nod off, doze, snooze (*infml*), have forty winks (*infml*).

2 orders have dropped off recently: decline, fall off, decrease, dwindle, lessen, diminish, slacken.

3 drop the parcel off: deliver, set down, leave.

₣₃ 1 wake up. **2** increase. **3** pick up.

◆ **drop out** back out, abandon, cry off, withdraw, forsake, leave, quit.

drown *verb*

1 nearly drowned while swimming/heavy rain drowning the garden: submerge, immerse, inundate, go under, flood, sink, deluge, engulf, drench.

2 loud music drowning their voices: overwhelm, overpower, overcome, swamp, wipe out, extinguish.

drowsy *adjective*

sleepy, tired, lethargic, nodding, dreamy, dozy, somnolent (*fml*).

₣₃ alert, awake.

drudgery *noun*

labour, donkey-work (*infml*), hack-work, slog (*infml*), grind (*infml*), slavery, sweat, sweated labour, toil, skivvying, chore.

drug *noun*

medication, medicine, remedy, potion.

▶ *verb*

medicate, sedate, tranquillize, dope (*infml*), anaesthetize, dose, knock out (*infml*), stupefy, deaden, numb.

drum *verb*

beat, pulsate, tap, throb, thrum, tattoo, reverberate, rap.

◆ **drum up** obtain, round up, collect, gather, solicit, canvass, petition, attract.

dry *adjective*

1 a dry throat/too dry to grow crops: arid, parched, thirsty, dehydrated, desiccated, barren.

2 the book was as dry as dust: boring, dull, dreary, tedious, monotonous.

3 dry humour: ironic, cynical, droll, deadpan, sarcastic, cutting.

₣₃ 1 wet. **2** interesting.

▶ *verb*

dehydrate, parch, desiccate, drain, shrivel, wither.

₣₃ soak.

dual *adjective*

double, twofold, duplicate, duplex, binary, combined, paired, twin, matched.

dubious *adjective*

1 was a bit dubious about it: doubtful, uncertain, undecided, unsure, wavering, unsettled, suspicious, sceptical, hesitant.

2 a dubious character: questionable, debatable, unreliable, ambiguous, suspect, obscure, fishy (*infml*), shady (*infml*).

₣₃ 1 certain. **2** trustworthy.

duck *verb*

1 duck down behind the wall: crouch, stoop, bob, bend.

2 duck one's responsibilities: avoid, dodge, evade, shirk, sidestep.

due *adjective*
1 the payment is due: owed, owing, payable, unpaid, outstanding, in arrears.
2 praise where praise is due: rightful, fitting, appropriate, proper, merited, deserved, justified, suitable.
3 give the due amount of attention to: adequate, enough, sufficient, ample, plenty of.
4 another train is due: expected, scheduled.
E3 1 paid. **3** inadequate.
▸ *adverb*
exactly, direct(ly), precisely, straight, dead (*infml*).

dull *adjective*
1 found it very dull: boring, uninteresting, unexciting, flat, dreary, monotonous, tedious, uneventful, humdrum, unimaginative, dismal, lifeless, plain, insipid, heavy.
2 a dull corner/dull weather: dark, gloomy, drab, murky, indistinct, grey, cloudy, lacklustre, opaque, dim, overcast.
3 a dull scholar: unintelligent, dense, dim, dimwitted (*infml*), thick (*infml*), stupid, slow.
E3 1 interesting, exciting. **2** bright. **3** intelligent, clever.

dumb *adjective*
silent, mute, soundless, speechless, tongue-tied, inarticulate, mum (*infml*).

dumbfounded *adjective*
astonished, amazed, astounded, overwhelmed, speechless, taken aback, thrown (*infml*), startled, overcome, confounded, flabbergasted (*infml*), staggered, confused, bowled over, dumb, floored (*infml*), paralysed.

dummy *adjective*
1 a dummy drawer: artificial, fake, imitation, false, bogus, mock, sham, phoney.
2 a dummy run: simulated, practice, trial.

dump *verb*
1 dumped it on the floor: deposit, drop, offload, throw down, let fall,
unload, empty out, discharge, park.
2 dump it overboard: get rid of, scrap, throw away, dispose of, ditch, tip, jettison.
▸ *noun*
1 throw it on the dump: rubbish-tip, junk-yard, rubbish-heap, tip.
2 (*infml*) live in a dump: hovel, slum, shack, shanty, hole (*infml*), joint (*infml*), pigsty, mess.

duplicate *adjective*
identical, matching, twin, twofold, corresponding, matched.
▸ *noun*
copy, replica, reproduction, photocopy, carbon (copy), match, facsimile.
▸ *verb*
copy, reproduce, repeat, photocopy, double, clone, echo.

durable *adjective*
lasting, enduring, long-lasting, abiding, hard-wearing, strong, sturdy, tough, unfading, substantial, sound, reliable, dependable, stable, resistant, persistent, constant, permanent, firm, fixed, fast.
E3 perishable, weak, fragile.

dusk *noun*
twilight, sunset, nightfall, evening, sundown, gloaming, darkness, dark, gloom, shadows, shade.
E3 dawn, brightness.

dutiful *adjective*
obedient, respectful, conscientious, devoted, filial, reverential, submissive.

duty *noun*
1 have a duty to perform/do one's duty: obligation, responsibility, assignment, calling, charge, role, task, job, business, function, work, office, service.
2 his duty to his king: obedience, respect, loyalty.
3 pay duty on imports: tax, toll, tariff, levy, customs, excise.
◆ **on duty** at work, engaged, busy.

dwell *verb*
live, inhabit, reside, stay, settle, populate, people, lodge, rest, abide (*fml*).

dwindle *verb*
diminish, decrease, decline, lessen, subside, ebb, fade, weaken, taper off, tail off, shrink, peter out, fall, wane, waste away, die out, wither, shrivel, disappear.
◨increase, grow.

dye *noun*
colour, colouring, stain, pigment, tint, tinge.

dying *adjective*
moribund, passing, final, going, mortal, not long for this world, perishing, failing, fading, vanishing.
◨reviving.

dynamic *adjective*
forceful, powerful, energetic, vigorous, go-ahead, high-powered, driving, self-starting, spirited, vital, lively, active.
◨inactive, apathetic.

Ee

eager *adjective*
1 eager to begin: keen, enthusiastic, fervent, intent, earnest, zealous.
2 eager for news: longing, yearning.
F3 1 unenthusiastic, indifferent.

ear *noun*
1 an ear for language: perception, sensitivity, discrimination, appreciation, hearing, skill, ability.
2 have the ear of the president: attention, heed, notice, regard.

early *adjective*
1 early symptoms: forward, advanced, premature, untimely, undeveloped.
2 early theatre: primitive, ancient, primeval.
▸ *adverb*
ahead of time, in good time, beforehand, in advance, prematurely.
F3 late.

earn *verb*
1 earn a good salary: receive, obtain, make, get, draw, bring in (*infml*), gain, realize, gross, reap.
2 have earned one's reputation: deserve, merit, warrant, win, rate.
F3 1 spend, lose.

earnest *adjective*
1 an earnest attempt/promise: resolute, firm, serious, sincere, solemn, grave, heartfelt.
2 an earnest pupil: devoted, ardent, conscientious, keen, fervent, eager, enthusiastic, steady.
F3 1 frivolous, flippant. **2** apathetic.

earth *noun*
1 all over the Earth: world, planet, globe, sphere.
2 planted in the earth: land, ground, soil, clay, loam, sod, humus.

ease *noun*
1 ease of doing: facility, effortlessness, skilfulness, deftness, dexterity, naturalness, cleverness.
2 living in ease: comfort, contentment, peace, affluence, repose, leisure, relaxation, rest, quiet, happiness.
F3 1 difficulty. **2** discomfort.
▸ *verb*
1 ease the pain: alleviate, moderate, lessen, lighten, relieve, mitigate, abate, relent, allay, assuage (*fml*), relax, comfort, calm, soothe, facilitate, smooth.
2 ease it into position: inch, steer, slide, slip.
F3 1 aggravate, intensify, worsen.

easily *adverb*
1 fits easily into the space: effortlessly, comfortably, readily, simply.
2 easily the best: by far, undoubtedly, indisputably, definitely, certainly, doubtless(ly), clearly, far and away, undeniably, simply, surely, probably, well.
F3 1 laboriously.

easy *adjective*
1 an easy task: effortless, simple, uncomplicated, undemanding, straightforward, manageable, cushy (*infml*).
2 an easy pace: relaxed, carefree, easy-going, comfortable, informal, calm, natural, leisurely.
F3 1 difficult, demanding, exacting. **2** tense, uneasy.
⇨ *See also* **Word Study** *panel.*

easy-going *adjective*
relaxed, tolerant, laid-back (*infml*), amenable, happy-go-lucky (*infml*),

WORD*study*   easy

There are many phrases used as alternative ways of expressing the idea of something being **easy**, or doing something with ease. Look at the panel on **difficulty** to check other phrases with the opposite meaning.

something that is easy to do

a breeze
a cinch
easy-peasy
a piece of cake

a cakewalk (*US*)
a walkover
duck soup (*US*)
a pushover

an easy situation

be as easy as pie
be plain sailing
be as easy as ABC
be no hassle
be child's play
a soft option

be as easy as falling off a log
there's nothing to it
be downhill all the way
be crystal clear
open-and-shut
second nature

to do something with ease

breeze through
sail through
at your leisure

waltz through
walk away with

be at your ease

be on easy street
have the life of Riley

be at home with something
be in clover

---

carefree, calm, even-tempered, serene.
F3 strict, intolerant, critical.

eat *verb*
1 eat breakfast/eat at 8 o'clock: consume, feed, swallow, devour, chew, scoff (*infml*), munch, dine, trough (*slang*), ingest (*fml*).
2 rust eating away the metal: corrode, erode, wear away, decay, rot, crumble, dissolve.
⇨ *See also* **Word Workshop** *panel.*

eccentric *adjective*
odd, peculiar, abnormal, unconventional, strange, quirky, weird,

way-out (*infml*), queer, outlandish, idiosyncratic, bizarre, freakish, erratic, singular, dotty (*infml*).
F3 conventional, orthodox, normal.

echo *verb*
1 voices echoing in the empty room: reverberate, resound, repeat, ring.
2 echoing what he had said: imitate, copy, reproduce, mirror, resemble, reflect, reiterate, mimic.

eclipse *noun*
1 an eclipse of the sun: obscuration, overshadowing, darkening, shading, dimming.
2 the eclipse of Britain as a great

WORD *workshop*   eat

There are many different words for **eat**. Aim to make your writing more colourful by using some of the synonyms used below.

eat eagerly

binge	gobble	scoff *(infml)*
bolt down *(infml)*	gulp down	tuck into *(infml)*
chomp	munch	wolf down *(infml)*
devour	pig out *(infml)*	
feast	polish off *(infml)*	

eat a little

chew	peck	snack
nibble	pick at	

eat meals

breakfast	have supper/tea
dine	lunch

animals

gnaw	graze

eat away at something

corrode	decay	rot
crumble	erode	rust

power: decline, failure, fall, loss.
▶ *verb*
1 the sun eclipsed by the moon: blot out, obscure, cloud, veil, darken, dim.
2 eclipsing his older brother's

achievements: outdo, overshadow, outshine, surpass, transcend.
economic *adjective*
1 economic growth: commercial, business, industrial.
2 an economic review: financial,

eat

WORD *workshop*

The following passage uses some alternative ways for expressing **eat**, **ate** and **eaten**.

> Maria and Rose went to the zoo. They brought bread for the
> ducks who ~~ate it~~ *gulped it down* very quickly. Then they watched the
> monkeys ~~eat~~ *tuck into* bananas and the sea lions perform tricks for fish,
> which they ~~ate~~ *devoured*. It was hot so the girls bought ice lollies to ~~eat~~ *chomp*
>
> and sat in the shade. The bars of the cage next to them had been
> ~~eaten~~ *corroded* by rust and an elephant was able to get his trunk through
> the bars and steal Maria's ice lolly. He had ~~eaten~~ *gobbled it up* it before she
>
> was able to stop him! When the girls got home they were so
> hungry they ~~ate~~ *wolfed down* a very big meal.

budgetary, fiscal, monetary.
3 an economic proposition: profitable, profit-making, money-making, productive, cost-effective, viable.

economical *adjective*
1 a very economical housekeeper: thrifty, careful, prudent, saving, sparing, frugal.
2 a more economical model of car: cheap, inexpensive, low-priced, reasonable, cost-effective,

modest, efficient.
⊨ 1 wasteful. **2** expensive, uneconomical.

economize *verb*
save, cut back, tighten one's belt (*infml*), cut costs.
⊨ waste, squander.

ecstasy *noun*
delight, rapture, bliss, elation, joy, euphoria, frenzy, exaltation, fervour.
⊨ misery, torment.

edge *noun*
1 the edge of the table/sea/sink:
border, rim, boundary, limit, brim,
threshold, brink, fringe, margin,
outline, side, verge, line, perimeter,
periphery, lip.
2 the local athlete had the edge over
the other competitors: advantage,
superiority, force.
▶ *verb*
creep, inch, ease, sidle.

edgy *adjective*
on edge, nervous, tense, anxious, ill at
ease, keyed-up, touchy, irritable.
Ⅎ calm.

edible *adjective*
eatable, palatable, digestible,
wholesome, good, harmless.
Ⅎ inedible.

edit *verb*
correct, emend, revise, rewrite,
reorder, rearrange, adapt, check,
compile, rephrase, select, polish,
annotate, censor.

educate *verb*
teach, train, instruct, tutor, coach,
school, inform, cultivate, edify, drill,
improve, discipline, develop.

educated *adjective*
learned, taught, schooled, trained,
knowledgeable, informed, instructed,
lettered, cultured, civilized, tutored,
refined, well-bred.
Ⅎ uneducated, uncultured.

education *noun*
teaching, training, schooling, tuition,
tutoring, coaching, guidance,
instruction, cultivation, culture,
scholarship, improvement,
enlightenment, knowledge, nurture,
development.

*Educational establishments
include:*

kindergarten, nursery school, infant
school; primary school, middle
school, combined school, community
school, foundation school, secondary
school, secondary modern, upper
school, high school, grammar school,
grant-maintained school, preparatory
school, public school, private school;
sixth-form college, college, city
technical college, CTC, technical
college, university; academy, adult-
education centre, boarding-school,
business school, convent school,
finishing school, secretarial college,
seminary, summer school, Sunday
school.

eerie *adjective*
weird, strange, uncanny, spooky
(*infml*), creepy, frightening, scary,
spine-chilling.

effect *noun*
1 the effects of the changes: outcome,
result, conclusion, consequence,
upshot, aftermath, issue.
2 have greater effect: power, force,
impact, efficacy, impression, strength.
3 words to that effect: meaning,
significance, import.
▶ *verb*
cause, execute, create, achieve,
accomplish, perform, produce, make,
initiate, fulfil, complete.
◆ **in effect** in fact, actually, really, in
reality, to all intents and purposes, for
all practical purposes, essentially,
effectively, virtually.
◆ **take effect** be effective, become
operative, come into force, come into
operation, be implemented, begin,
work.

effective *adjective*
1 an effective remedy: efficient,
efficacious, productive, adequate,
capable, useful.
2 when the measures become
effective: operative, in force,
functioning, current, active.
3 an effective argument: striking,
impressive, forceful, cogent, powerful,
persuasive, convincing, telling.
Ⅎ 1 ineffective, powerless.

effects *noun*
belongings, possessions, property,
goods, gear (*infml*), movables, chattels
(*fml*), things, trappings.

efficient *adjective*
effective, competent, proficient, skilful,
capable, able, productive, adept, well-

organized, businesslike, powerful,
well-conducted.
F3 inefficient, incompetent.

effort noun
1 too much effort involved: exertion,
strain, application, struggle, trouble,
energy, toil, striving, pains, travail
(*fml*).
2 make a good effort: attempt, try, go
(*infml*), endeavour, shot (*infml*), stab.
3 the result of their efforts: work,
achievement, accomplishment, feat,
exploit, production, creation, deed,
product.
⇨ *See also* **Word Study** *panel.*

effortless adjective
easy, simple, undemanding, facile,
painless, smooth.
F3 difficult.

egotistic adjective
egoistic, egocentric, self-centred, self-
important, conceited, vain, swollen-
headed (*infml*), bigheaded (*infml*),
boasting, bragging.
F3 humble.

eject verb
oust, evict, throw out, drive out, turn
out, expel, remove, banish, deport,
dismiss, exile, kick out (*infml*), fire
(*infml*), sack (*infml*).

elaborate adjective /i-**lab**-o-rat/
1 elaborate plans: detailed, careful,
thorough, exact, extensive,
painstaking, precise, perfected,
minute, laboured, studied.
2 elaborate design: intricate, complex,
complicated, involved, ornamental,
ornate, fancy, decorated, ostentatious,
showy, fussy.
F3 2 simple, plain.
▶ *verb* /i-**lab**-o-reit/
amplify, develop, enlarge, expand, flesh
out, polish, improve, refine, devise,
explain.
F3 précis, simplify.

elapse verb
pass, lapse, go by, slip away.

elastic adjective
1 an elastic band: pliable, flexible,
stretchable, supple, resilient, yielding,
springy, rubbery, pliant, plastic,
bouncy, buoyant.

2 the timetable is fairly elastic:
adaptable, accommodating, flexible,
tolerant, adjustable.
F3 1 rigid. **2** inflexible.

elated adjective
exhilarated, excited, euphoric, ecstatic,
exultant, jubilant, overjoyed, joyful.
F3 despondent, downcast.

elbow verb
jostle, nudge, push, shove, bump,
crowd, knock, shoulder.

elder adjective
older, senior, first-born, ancient.
F3 younger.

elderly adjective
aging, aged, old, hoary, senile.
F3 young, youthful.

elect verb
choose, pick, opt for, select, vote for,
prefer, adopt, designate, appoint,
determine.
▶ *adjective*
choice, elite, chosen, designated,
designate, picked, prospective,
selected, to be, preferred, hand-picked.

electric adjective
electrifying, exciting, stimulating,
thrilling, charged, dynamic, stirring,
tense, rousing.
F3 unexciting, flat.

electrify verb
thrill, excite, shock, invigorate,
animate, stimulate, stir, rouse, fire, jolt,
galvanize, amaze, astonish, astound,
stagger.
F3 bore.

elegant adjective
stylish, chic, fashionable, modish,
smart, refined, polished, genteel,
smooth, tasteful, fine, exquisite,
beautiful, graceful, handsome,
delicate, neat, artistic.
F3 inelegant, unrefined,
unfashionable.

element noun
factor, component, constituent,
ingredient, member, part, piece,
fragment, feature, trace.
F3 whole.

elementary adjective
1 an elementary mistake: simple,

WORD *study* effort

Here are some phrases that you might use to talk or write about the amount of **effort** involved in doing or achieving something. You could also take a look at the panels on **determination** and **work** for related phrases.

to put in a lot of effort

go all-out/flat-out
beaver away
sweat blood
bust a gut (*slang*)
go to great lengths
put your shoulder to the wheel
fight tooth and nail
go to a lot of trouble
do your utmost
pull your weight
break your back

do your bit
stay the course
huff and puff
be at pains
pull out all the stops
go to town on something
take the trouble to *or* go to the trouble of
go out of your way
put your back into

rudimentary, clear, easy, straightforward, uncomplicated.
2 his elementary education: basic, fundamental, primary, introductory.
Fa**2** advanced.

elevated *adjective*
raised, lofty, exalted, high, grand, noble, dignified, sublime.
Fa base.

eligible *adjective*
qualified, fit, appropriate, suitable, acceptable, worthy, proper, desirable.
Fa ineligible.

eliminate *verb*
remove, get rid of, cut out, take out, exclude, delete, dispense with, rub out, omit, reject, disregard, dispose of, drop, do away with, eradicate, expel, extinguish, stamp out, exterminate, knock out, kill, murder.
Fa include, accept.

elite *noun*
best, elect, aristocracy, upper classes, nobility, gentry, crème de la crème, establishment, high society.

▶ *adjective*
choice, best, exclusive, selected, first-class, aristocratic, noble, upper-class.

elongated *adjective*
lengthened, extended, prolonged, protracted, stretched, long.

eloquent *adjective*
articulate, fluent, well-expressed, glib, expressive, vocal, voluble, persuasive, moving, forceful, graceful, plausible, stirring, vivid.
Fa inarticulate, tongue-tied.

elusive *adjective*
1 an elusive quality: indefinable, intangible, unanalysable, subtle, puzzling, baffling, transient, transitory.
2 an elusive criminal: evasive, shifty, slippery, tricky.

emanate *verb*
1 emanating from the prime minister's office: originate, proceed, arise, derive, issue, spring, stem, flow, come, emerge.
2 smoke emanating from the chimney: discharge, send out, emit, give out, give off, radiate.

emancipate *verb*
free, liberate, release, set free, enfranchise, deliver, discharge, loose, unchain, unshackle, unfetter.
F3 enslave.

embargo *noun*
restriction, ban, prohibition, restraint, proscription, bar, barrier, interdiction (*fml*), impediment, check, hindrance, blockage, stoppage, seizure.

embark *verb*
board (ship), go aboard, take ship.
F3 disembark.
◆ **embark on** begin, start, commence, set about, launch, undertake, enter, initiate, engage.
F3 complete, finish.

embarrass *verb*
disconcert, mortify, show up, fluster, humiliate, shame, distress.

embarrassment *noun*
1 suffer from acute embarrassment: discomposure, self-consciousness, chagrin, mortification, humiliation, shame, awkwardness, confusion, bashfulness.
2 financial embarrassment: difficulty, constraint, predicament, distress, discomfort.
⇨ *See also* **Word Study** *panel.*

embellish *verb*
adorn, ornament, decorate, deck, dress up, beautify, gild, garnish, festoon, elaborate, embroider, enrich, exaggerate, enhance, varnish, grace.
F3 simplify, denude.

emblem *noun*
symbol, sign, token, representation, logo, insignia, device, crest, mark, badge, figure.

embodiment *noun*
incarnation, personification, exemplification, expression, epitome, example, incorporation, realization, representation, manifestation, concentration.

embrace *verb*
1 embrace each other: hug, clasp, cuddle, hold, grasp, squeeze.
2 embracing several topics: include, encompass, incorporate, contain, comprise, cover, involve.

3 embracing the new faith: accept, take up, welcome.

embryo *noun*
nucleus, germ, beginning, root.

embryonic *adjective*
undeveloped, rudimentary, immature, early, germinal, primary.
F3 developed.

emerge *verb*
1 see what will emerge at the next meeting: arise, rise, surface, appear, develop, crop up (*infml*), transpire, turn up, materialize.
2 emerging from the entrance: emanate, issue, proceed.

emergency *noun*
crisis, danger, difficulty, exigency (*fml*), predicament, plight, pinch, strait, quandary.

emigrate *verb*
migrate, relocate, move, depart.

eminent *adjective*
distinguished, famous, prominent, illustrious, outstanding, notable, pre-eminent, prestigious, celebrated, renowned, noteworthy, conspicuous, esteemed, important, well-known, elevated, respected, great, high-ranking, grand, superior.
F3 unknown, obscure, unimportant.

emit *verb*
discharge, issue, eject, emanate, exude, give out, give off, diffuse, radiate, release, shed, vent.
F3 absorb.

emotion *noun*
feeling, passion, sensation, sentiment, ardour, fervour, warmth, reaction, vehemence, excitement.

emotional *adjective*
1 she gets too emotional: feeling, passionate, sensitive, responsive, ardent, tender, warm, roused, demonstrative, excitable, enthusiastic, fervent, impassioned, moved, sentimental, zealous, hot-blooded, heated, tempestuous, overcharged, temperamental, fiery.
2 an emotional welcome: emotive, moving, poignant, thrilling, touching,

WORD study — embarrassment

There are many phrases used to express **embarrassment**, and you might want to try some of these out to add life to your written work.

do something embarrassing

drop a brick
drop a clanger
commit a faux pas
put a foot in your mouth

look a Charley
make an exhibition of yourself
make a fool of yourself
make a spectacle of yourself

feel/look embarrassed

want to curl up and die
go beetroot

want the ground to swallow you up

stirring, heart-warming, exciting, pathetic.
E3 1 unemotional, cold, detached, calm.

emphasis *noun*
stress, weight, significance, importance, priority, underscoring, accent, force, power, prominence, pre-eminence, attention, intensity, strength, urgency, positiveness, insistence, mark, moment.

emphasize *verb*
stress, accentuate, underline, highlight, accent, feature, dwell on, weight, point up, spotlight, play up, insist on, press home, intensify, strengthen, punctuate.
E3 play down, understate.

emphatic *adjective*
forceful, positive, insistent, certain, definite, decided, unequivocal, absolute, categorical, earnest, marked, pronounced, significant, strong, striking, vigorous, distinct, energetic, forcible, important, impressive, momentous, powerful, punctuated, telling, vivid, graphic, direct.
E3 tentative, hesitant, understated.

employ *verb*
1 employing school-leavers: engage, hire, take on, enlist, commission, recruit.
2 employing new techniques: use, utilize, make use of, apply, bring to bear, ply, exercise.

employment *noun*
1 have some form of employment: job, work, occupation, situation, business, calling, profession, line (*infml*), vocation, trade, pursuit, craft.
2 the employment of school-leavers: enlistment, employ, engagement, hire.
E3 1 unemployment.

empower *verb*
authorize, warrant, enable, license, sanction, permit, entitle, commission, delegate, qualify.

empty *adjective*
1 an empty space/house/landscape: vacant, void, unoccupied, uninhabited, unfilled, deserted, bare, hollow, desolate, blank, clear.
2 an empty gesture: futile, aimless, meaningless, senseless, trivial, vain, worthless, useless, insubstantial, ineffective, insincere.
3 an empty expression: vacuous, inane, expressionless, blank, vacant.

F3 1 full. 2 meaningful.
▶ *verb*
drain, exhaust, discharge, clear,
evacuate, vacate, pour out, unload,
void, gut.
F3 fill.

emulate *verb*
match, copy, mimic, follow, imitate,
echo, compete with, contend with,
rival, vie with.

enable *verb*
equip, qualify, empower, authorize,
sanction, warrant, allow, permit,
prepare, fit, facilitate, license,
commission, endue (*fml*).
F3 prevent, inhibit, forbid.

enact *verb*
1 enact a law : decree, ordain, order,
authorize, command, legislate,
sanction, ratify, pass, establish.
2 enact a play : act (out), perform, play,
portray, represent, depict.
F3 1 repeal, rescind.

enchanting *adjective*
captivating, charming, fascinating,
attractive, alluring, appealing,
delightful, enthralling, bewitching,
spellbinding, hypnotic.
F3 repellent.

enclose *verb*
encircle, encompass, surround, fence,
hedge, hem in, bound, encase,
embrace, envelop, confine, hold, shut
in, wrap, pen, cover, circumscribe,
incorporate, include, insert, contain,
comprehend.

encompass *verb*
1 encompassing her waist : encircle,
circle, ring, surround, gird, envelop,
circumscribe, hem in, enclose, hold.
2 encompassing the whole of
mankind : include, cover, embrace,
contain, comprise, admit, incorporate,
involve, embody, comprehend.

encounter *verb*
meet, come across, run into (*infml*),
happen on, chance upon, run across,
confront, face, experience.
▶ *noun*
1 an encounter with death : meeting,
brush, confrontation, rendezvous.
2 a titanic encounter between two

champions : clash, fight, combat,
conflict, contest, battle, set-to (*infml*),
dispute, engagement, action, skirmish,
run-in, collision.

encourage *verb*
1 encouraged them to continue :
hearten, exhort, stimulate, spur,
reassure, rally, inspire, incite, egg on
(*infml*), buoy up, cheer, urge, rouse,
comfort, console.
2 a scheme to encourage tourism in
the area : promote, advance, aid, boost,
forward, further, foster, support, help,
strengthen.
F3 1 discourage, depress. 2 discourage.

encouraging *adjective*
heartening, promising, hopeful,
reassuring, stimulating, uplifting,
auspicious, cheering, comforting,
bright, rosy, cheerful, satisfactory.
F3 discouraging.

encroach *verb*
intrude, invade, impinge, trespass,
infringe, usurp, overstep, make
inroads, muscle in (*infml*).

end *noun*
1 the end of the war : finish,
conclusion, termination, close,
completion, cessation, culmination,
dénouement.
2 the ends of the earth : extremity,
boundary, edge, limit, tip.
3 a cigarette end : remainder, tip, butt,
left-over, remnant, stub, scrap,
fragment.
4 with only one end in mind : aim,
object, objective, purpose, intention,
goal, point, reason, design.
5 to that end : result, outcome,
consequence, upshot.
6 the end was swift : death, demise,
destruction, extermination, downfall,
doom, ruin, dissolution.
F3 1 beginning, start. 6 birth.
▶ *verb*
1 ending the speech with a joke : finish,
close, cease, conclude, stop, terminate,
complete, culminate, wind up.
2 ending their lives : destroy,
annihilate, exterminate, extinguish,
ruin, abolish, dissolve.
F3 1 begin, start.

endanger *verb*
imperil, hazard, jeopardize, risk, expose, threaten, compromise.
F3 protect.

endearing *adjective*
lovable, charming, appealing, attractive, winsome, delightful, enchanting.

endeavour *verb*
attempt, try, strive, aim, aspire, undertake, venture, struggle, labour, take pains.
▸ *noun*
attempt, effort, go (*infml*), try, shot (*infml*), stab (*infml*), undertaking, enterprise, aim, venture.

ending *noun*
end, close, finish, completion, termination, conclusion, culmination, climax, resolution, consummation, dénouement, finale, epilogue.
F3 beginning, start.

endless *adjective*
1 the endless universe: infinite, boundless, unlimited, measureless.
2 endless love: everlasting, ceaseless, perpetual, constant, continual, continuous, undying, eternal, interminable, monotonous.
F3 1 finite, limited. 2 temporary.

endorse *verb*
1 endorse a candidate: approve, sanction, authorize, support, back, affirm, ratify, confirm, vouch for, advocate, warrant, recommend, subscribe to, sustain, adopt.
2 endorse a cheque: sign, countersign.

endow *verb*
bestow, bequeath, leave, will, give, donate, endue (*fml*), confer, grant, present, award, finance, fund, support, make over, furnish, provide, supply.

endurance *noun*
fortitude, patience, staying power, stamina, resignation, stoicism, tenacity, perseverance, resolution, stability, persistence, strength, toleration.

endure *verb*
1 endure hardship: bear, stand, put up with, tolerate, weather, brave, cope with, face, go through, experience, submit to, suffer, sustain, swallow, undergo, withstand, stick, stomach, allow, permit, support.
2 a love that will endure for ever: last, abide (*fml*), remain, live, survive, stay, persist, hold, prevail.

enemy *noun*
adversary, opponent, foe (*fml*), rival, antagonist, the opposition, competitor, opposer, other side.
F3 friend, ally.

energetic *adjective*
lively, vigorous, active, animated, dynamic, spirited, tireless, zestful, brisk, strong, forceful, potent, powerful, strenuous, high-powered.
F3 lethargic, sluggish, inactive, idle.

energy *noun*
liveliness, vigour, activity, animation, drive, dynamism, get-up-and-go (*infml*), life, spirit, verve, vivacity, vitality, zest, zeal, ardour, fire, efficiency, force, forcefulness, zip (*infml*), strength, power, intensity, exertion, stamina.
F3 lethargy, inertia, weakness.

enforce *verb*
impose, administer, implement, apply, execute, discharge, insist on, compel, oblige, urge, carry out, constrain, require, coerce, prosecute, reinforce.

engage *verb*
1 engaging in debate: participate, take part, embark on, take up, practise, involve.
2 engaged by her beauty: attract, allure, draw, captivate, charm, catch.
3 engaging their attention: occupy, engross, absorb, busy, tie up, grip.
4 engage a new cook: employ, hire, appoint, take on, enlist, enrol, commission, recruit, contract.
5 engage first gear: interlock, mesh, interconnect, join, interact, attach.
6 engage the enemy: fight, battle with, attack, take on, encounter, assail, combat.
F3 2 repel. 4 dismiss, discharge. 5 disengage.

engaged *adjective*
1 he's engaged until 5 o'clock: occupied, busy, engrossed, immersed,

absorbed, preoccupied, involved, employed.
2 the engaged couple: promised, betrothed (*fml*), pledged, spoken for, committed.
3 an engaged tone: busy, tied up, unavailable.

engagement *noun*
1 have several pressing engagements: appointment, meeting, date, arrangement, assignation, fixture, rendezvous.
2 announce their engagement: promise, pledge, betrothal (*fml*), commitment, obligation, assurance, vow, troth (*fml*).
3 the first engagement of the war: fight, battle, combat, conflict, action, encounter, confrontation, contest.

engaging *adjective*
charming, attractive, appealing, captivating, pleasing, delightful, winsome, lovable, likable, pleasant, fetching, fascinating, agreeable.
F3 repulsive, repellent.

engine *noun*
motor, machine, mechanism, appliance, contraption, apparatus, device, instrument, tool, locomotive, dynamo.

engineer *verb*
plan, contrive, devise, manoeuvre, cause, manipulate, control, bring about, mastermind, originate, orchestrate, effect, plot, scheme, manage, create, rig.

engrave *verb*
1 engrave a printing plate: inscribe, cut, carve, chisel, etch, chase.
2 engraved on her mind: imprint, impress, fix, stamp, lodge, ingrain.

engraving *noun*
print, impression, inscription, carving, etching, woodcut, plate, block, cutting, chiselling, mark.

engross *verb*
absorb, occupy, engage, grip, hold, preoccupy, rivet, fascinate, captivate, enthral, arrest, involve, intrigue.
F3 bore.

enhance *verb*
heighten, intensify, increase, improve,

elevate, magnify, swell, exalt, raise, lift, boost, strengthen, reinforce, embellish.
F3 reduce, minimize.

enigmatic *adjective*
mysterious, puzzling, cryptic, obscure, strange, perplexing.
F3 simple, straightforward.

enjoy *verb*
1 enjoy dancing: take pleasure in, delight in, appreciate, like, relish, revel in, rejoice in, savour.
2 enjoy a benefit: have, possess, be endowed with.
F3 1 dislike, hate. **2** lack.
◆ **enjoy oneself** have a good time, have fun, make merry.

enjoyable *adjective*
pleasant, agreeable, delightful, pleasing, gratifying, entertaining, amusing, fun, delicious, good, satisfying.
F3 disagreeable.

enjoyment *noun*
1 travelling for enjoyment: pleasure, delight, amusement, gratification, entertainment, relish, joy, fun, happiness, diversion, indulgence, recreation, zest, satisfaction.
2 (*fml*) **rights to the enjoyment of property**: possession, use, advantage, benefit.
F3 1 displeasure.

enlarge *verb*
increase, expand, augment, add to, grow, extend, magnify, inflate, swell, wax, stretch, multiply, develop, amplify, blow up, widen, broaden, lengthen, heighten, elaborate.
F3 diminish, shrink.

enlighten *verb*
instruct, edify, educate, inform, illuminate, teach, counsel, apprise, advise.
F3 confuse.

enlightened *adjective*
informed, aware, knowledgeable, educated, civilized, cultivated, refined, sophisticated, conversant (*fml*), wise, reasonable, liberal, open-minded, literate.
F3 ignorant, confused.

enlist *verb*
engage, enrol, register, sign up, recruit, conscript, employ, volunteer, join (up), gather, muster, secure, obtain, procure, enter.

enormous *adjective*
huge, immense, vast, gigantic, massive, colossal, gross, gargantuan, monstrous, mammoth, jumbo (*infml*), tremendous, prodigious.
F3 small, tiny.

enough *adjective*
sufficient, adequate, ample, plenty, abundant.
▶ *noun*
sufficiency, adequacy, plenty, abundance.
F3 insufficiency.
▶ *adverb*
sufficiently, adequately, reasonably, tolerably, passably, moderately, fairly, satisfactorily, amply.

enquire ⇨ *see* **inquire**.

enquiry ⇨ *see* **inquiry**.

enrage *verb*
incense, infuriate, anger, madden, provoke, incite, inflame, exasperate, irritate, rile.
F3 calm, placate.

enrol *verb*
register, enlist, sign on, sign up, join up, recruit, engage, admit.

ensemble *noun*
1 a wedding ensemble: outfit, costume, get-up (*infml*), rig-out (*infml*).
2 an ensemble of singers and musicians: group, band, company, troupe, chorus.

enslave *verb*
subjugate, subject, dominate, bind, enchain, yoke.
F3 free, emancipate.

ensue *verb*
follow, issue, proceed, succeed, result, arise, happen, turn out, befall, flow, derive, stem.
F3 precede.

ensure *verb*
certify, guarantee, warrant, protect, guard, safeguard, secure.

entail *verb*
involve, necessitate, occasion, require, demand, cause, give rise to, lead to, result in.

entangle *verb*
enmesh, ensnare, embroil, involve, implicate, snare, tangle, entrap, trap, catch, mix up, knot, ravel, muddle.
F3 disentangle.

enter *verb*
1 enter the room: come in, go in, arrive, insert, introduce, board, penetrate.
2 enter their names: record, log, note, register, take down, inscribe.
3 before entering university: join, embark upon, enrol, enlist, set about, sign up, participate, commence, start, begin.
F3 **1** depart. **2** delete.

enterprise *noun*
1 disapprove of the entire enterprise: undertaking, venture, project, plan, effort, operation, programme, endeavour.
2 show a lot of enterprise: initiative, resourcefulness, drive, boldness, adventurousness, get-up-and-go (*infml*), push, energy, enthusiasm, spirit.
3 start a new enterprise: business, company, firm, establishment, concern.
F3 **2** apathy.

enterprising *adjective*
venturesome, adventurous, bold, daring, go-ahead, imaginative, resourceful, self-reliant, enthusiastic, energetic, keen, ambitious, aspiring, spirited, active.
F3 unenterprising, lethargic.

entertain *verb*
1 entertaining them with magic tricks: amuse, divert, please, delight, cheer.
2 entertaining visitors: receive, have guests, accommodate, put up, treat.
3 entertain hopes of promotion: harbour, countenance, contemplate, consider, imagine, conceive.
F3 **1** bore. **3** reject.

entertaining *adjective*
amusing, diverting, fun, delightful,

interesting, pleasant, pleasing, humorous, witty.
Fa boring.

entertainment *noun*
1 get their entertainment at the cinema: amusement, diversion, recreation, enjoyment, play, pastime, fun, sport, distraction, pleasure.
2 plan a lavish entertainment: show, spectacle, performance, extravaganza.

Forms of entertainment include:

cartoon show, CD, cinema, DVD, radio, record, television, video; cabaret, casino, concert, dance, disco, discothèque, karaoke, musical, music hall, night-club, opera, pantomime, recital, revue, theatre, variety show; barbecue, carnival, circus, festival, fête, firework party, gymkhana. laser-light show, magic-show, pageant, Punch-and-Judy show, puppet show, rodeo, waxworks, zoo.

---

enthral *verb*
captivate, entrance, enchant, fascinate, charm, beguile, thrill, intrigue, hypnotize, mesmerize, engross.
Fa bore.

enthusiast *noun*
devotee, zealot, admirer, fan (*infml*), supporter, follower, buff (*infml*), freak (*infml*), fanatic, fiend (*infml*), lover.

enthusiastic *adjective*
keen, ardent, eager, fervent, vehement, passionate, warm, whole-hearted, zealous, vigorous, spirited, earnest, devoted, avid, excited, exuberant.
Fa unenthusiastic, apathetic.

entice *verb*
tempt, lure, attract, seduce, lead on, draw, coax, persuade, induce, sweet-talk (*infml*).

entire *adjective*
complete, whole, total, full, intact, perfect.
Fa incomplete, partial.

entirely *adverb*
completely, wholly, totally, fully, utterly, unreservedly, absolutely, in toto, thoroughly, altogether, perfectly, solely,

exclusively, every inch.
Fa partially.

entitle *verb*
1 entitling her to certain privileges: authorize, qualify, empower, enable, allow, permit, license, warrant.
2 the novel entitled 'Bleak House': name, call, term, title, style, christen, dub, label. designate.

entity *noun*
being, existence, thing, body, creature, individual, organism, substance.

entrance[1] *noun* /**en**-trans/
1 gain entrance to the castle: access, admission, admittance, entry, entrée.
2 the entrance of the United States into the war: arrival, appearance, debut, initiation, introduction, start.
3 the front/rear entrance: opening, way in, door, doorway, gate.
Fa 2 departure. 3 exit.

entrance[2] *verb* /in-**trahns**/
entrancing the audience: charm, enchant, enrapture, captivate, bewitch, spellbind, fascinate, delight, ravish, transport, hypnotize, mesmerize.
Fa repel.

entrant *noun*
1 entrants for the race/exam: competitor, candidate, contestant, contender, entry, participant, player.
2 a new entrant into the convent: novice, beginner, newcomer, initiate, convert, probationer.

entreat *verb*
beg, implore, plead with, beseech, crave, supplicate, pray, invoke, ask, petition, request, appeal to.

entry *noun*
1 made a dramatic entry: entrance, appearance, admittance, admission, access, entrée, introduction.
2 at the entry to the building: opening, entrance, door, doorway, access, threshold, way in, passage, gate.
3 an entry in his diary: record, item, minute, note, memorandum, statement, account.
4 a late entry into the race: entrant, competitor, contestant, candidate, participant, player.
Fa 2 exit.

envelop *verb* /in-**vel**-*o*p/
wrap, enfold, enwrap, encase, cover,
swathe, shroud, engulf, enclose,
encircle, encompass, surround, cloak,
veil, blanket, conceal, obscure, hide.

envelope *noun*
wrapper, wrapping, cover, case, casing,
sheath, covering, shell, skin, jacket,
coating.

enviable *adjective*
desirable, privileged, favoured,
blessed, fortunate, lucky,
advantageous, sought-after, excellent,
fine.
E₃ unenviable.

envious *adjective*
covetous, jealous, resentful, green (with
envy), dissatisfied, grudging,
jaundiced, green-eyed (*infml*).

environment *noun*
surroundings, conditions,
circumstances, milieu, atmosphere,
habitat, situation, element, medium,
background, ambience, setting,
context, territory, domain.

envoy *noun*
agent, representative, ambassador,
diplomat, messenger, legate, emissary,
minister, delegate, deputy, courier,
intermediary.

envy *noun*
covetousness, jealousy, resentfulness,
resentment, dissatisfaction, grudge, ill-
will, malice, spite.
▶ *verb*
covet, resent, begrudge, grudge, crave.

epidemic *noun*
plague, outbreak, spread, rash,
upsurge, wave.
▶ *adjective*
widespread, prevalent, rife, rampant,
pandemic, sweeping, wide-ranging,
prevailing.

episode *noun*
1 an unfortunate episode in her life :
incident, event, occurrence,
happening, occasion, circumstance,
experience, adventure, matter,
business.
2 the next episode of the soap opera :
instalment, part, chapter, passage,
section, scene.

epitome *noun*
personification, embodiment,
representation, model, archetype, type,
essence.

equal *adjective*
1 of equal strength : identical, the
same, alike, like, equivalent,
corresponding, commensurate,
comparable.
2 all things being equal : even,
uniform, regular, unvarying, balanced,
matched.
3 equal to the task : competent, able,
adequate, fit, capable, suitable.
E₃ 1 different. **2** unequal. **3** unsuitable.
▶ *noun*
peer, counterpart, equivalent, coequal,
match, parallel, twin, fellow.
▶ *verb*
match, parallel, correspond to,
balance, square with, tally with,
equalize, equate, rival, level, even.

equality *noun*
1 demonstrating equality between the
two systems : uniformity, evenness,
equivalence, correspondence, balance,
parity, par, symmetry, proportion,
identity, sameness, likeness.
2 equality of treatment : impartiality,
fairness, justice, egalitarianism.
E₃ 2 inequality.

equalize *verb*
level, even up, match, equal, equate,
draw level, balance, square,
standardize, compensate, smooth.

equate *verb*
compare, liken, match, pair,
correspond to, correspond with,
balance, parallel, equalize, offset,
square, agree, tally, juxtapose.

equilibrium *noun*
1 be in a state of equilibrium : balance,
poise, symmetry, evenness, stability.
2 maintaining her equilibrium
throughout : equanimity, self-
possession, composure, calmness,
coolness, serenity.
E₃ 1 imbalance.

equip *verb*
provide, fit out, supply, furnish,
prepare, arm, fit up, kit out, stock,
endow, rig, dress, array, deck out.

equipment noun
apparatus, gear (infml), supplies, tackle, rig-out (infml), tools, material, furnishings, baggage, outfit, paraphernalia, stuff (infml), things, accessories, furniture.

equivalent adjective
equal, same, similar, substitutable, corresponding, alike, comparable, interchangeable, even, tantamount, twin.
ⱻ unlike, different.

equivocal adjective
ambiguous, uncertain, obscure, vague, evasive, oblique, misleading, dubious, confusing, indefinite.
ⱻ unequivocal, clear.

era noun
age, epoch, period, date, day, days, time, aeon, stage, century.

eradicate verb
eliminate, annihilate, get rid of, remove, root out, suppress, destroy, exterminate, extinguish, weed out, stamp out, abolish, erase, obliterate.

erase verb
obliterate, rub out, expunge (fml), delete, blot out, cancel, efface (fml), get rid of, remove, eradicate.

erect adjective
upright, straight, vertical, upstanding, standing.
▶ verb
build, construct, put up, establish, set up, elevate, assemble, found, form, institute, initiate, raise, rear, lift, mount, pitch, create.

erode verb
wear away, eat away, wear down, corrode, abrade, consume, grind down, disintegrate, deteriorate, spoil.

erosion noun
wear, corrosion, abrasion, attrition, denudation, disintegration, deterioration, destruction, undermining.

errand noun
commission, charge, mission, assignment, message, task, job, duty.

erratic adjective
changeable, variable, fitful, fluctuating, inconsistent, irregular, unstable, shifting, inconstant, unpredictable, unreliable, aberrant (fml), abnormal, eccentric, desultory, meandering.
ⱻ steady, consistent, stable.

erroneous adjective
incorrect, wrong, mistaken, false, untrue, inaccurate, inexact, invalid, illogical, unfounded, faulty, flawed.
ⱻ correct, right.

error noun
mistake, inaccuracy, slip, slip-up (infml), blunder, howler (infml), gaffe, faux pas, solecism (fml), lapse, miscalculation, misunderstanding, misconception, misapprehension, misprint, oversight, omission, fallacy, flaw, fault, wrong.

erudite adjective
learned, scholarly, well-educated, knowledgeable, lettered, educated, well-read, literate, academic, cultured, wise, highbrow, profound.
ⱻ illiterate, ignorant.

erupt verb
break out, explode, belch, discharge, burst, gush, spout, eject, expel, emit, flare up.

eruption noun
1 volcanic eruptions/a sudden eruption of violence: outburst, discharge, ejection, emission, explosion, flare-up.
2 a skin eruption: rash, outbreak, inflammation.

escalate verb
increase, intensify, grow, accelerate, rise, step up, heighten, raise, spiral, magnify, enlarge, expand, extend, mount, ascend, climb, amplify.
ⱻ decrease, diminish.

escapade noun
adventure, exploit, fling, prank, caper, romp, spree, lark (infml), antic, stunt, trick.

escape verb
1 escape from prison: get away, break free, run away, bolt, abscond, flee, fly, decamp, break loose, break out, do a bunk (infml), flit, slip away, shake off, slip.
2 escape serious injury: avoid, evade,

elude, dodge, skip, shun.
3 gas escaping into the atmosphere:
leak, seep, flow, drain, gush, issue,
discharge, ooze, trickle, pour forth,
pass.

escort *noun*
1 her escort for the evening:
companion, chaperon(e), partner,
attendant, aide, squire, guide,
bodyguard, protector.
2 the king's official escort: entourage,
company, retinue, suite, train, guard,
convoy, cortège.
▶ *verb*
accompany, partner, chaperon(e),
guide, lead, usher, conduct, guard,
protect.

esoteric *adjective*
obscure, cryptic, inscrutable,
mysterious, mystic, mystical, occult,
hidden, secret, confidential, private,
inside.
Ⓔ well-known, familiar.

especially *adverb*
1 especially in the nineteenth century:
chiefly, mainly, principally, primarily,
pre-eminently, above all.
2 especially clever: particularly,
specially, markedly, notably,
exceptionally, outstandingly, expressly,
supremely, uniquely, unusually,
strikingly, very.

essay *noun*
composition, dissertation, paper,
article, assignment, thesis, piece,
commentary, critique, discourse,
treatise, review, leader, tract.

essence *noun*
1 what is the essence of his style?:
nature, being, quintessence, substance,
soul, spirit, core, centre, heart,
meaning, quality, significance, life,
entity, crux, kernel, marrow, pith,
character, characteristics, attributes,
principle.
2 almond essence: concentrate,
extract, distillation, spirits.

essential *adjective*
1 the essential message of his poem:
fundamental, basic, intrinsic, inherent,
principal, main, key, characteristic,
definitive, typical, constituent.

2 an essential job: crucial,
indispensable, necessary, vital,
requisite, required, needed,
important.
Ⓔ 1 incidental. **2** dispensable,
inessential.
▶ *noun*
necessity, prerequisite, must, requisite,
sine qua non (*fml*), requirement, basic,
fundamental, necessary, principle.
Ⓔ inessential.

establish *verb*
1 establish a colony: set up, found,
start, form, institute, create, organize,
inaugurate, introduce, install, plant,
settle, secure, lodge, base.
2 establish the truth: prove,
substantiate, demonstrate,
authenticate, ratify, verify, validate,
certify, confirm, affirm.
Ⓔ 1 uproot. **2** refute.

establishment *noun*
1 the establishment of rail links:
formation, setting up, founding,
creation, foundation, installation,
institution, inauguration.
2 an eating establishment: business,
company, firm, institute, organization,
concern, institution, enterprise.
3 part of the British establishment:
ruling class, the system, the authorities,
the powers that be.

estate *noun*
1 left his entire estate to his younger
son: possessions, effects, assets,
belongings, holdings, property, goods,
lands.
2 a country estate/housing estate:
area, development, land, manor.
3 (*fml*) men of low estate: status,
standing, situation, position, class,
place, condition, state, rank.

estimate *verb*
assess, reckon, evaluate, calculate,
gauge, guess, value, conjecture,
consider, judge, think, number, count,
compute, believe.
▶ *noun*
reckoning, valuation, judgement,
guess, approximation, assessment,
estimation, evaluation, computation,
opinion.

estimation *noun*
1 a rough estimation of the costs involved : judgement, opinion, belief, consideration, estimate, view, evaluation, assessment, reckoning, conception, calculation, computation.
2 he rose in our estimation : respect, regard, appreciation, esteem, credit.

estuary *noun*
inlet, mouth, firth, fjord, creek, arm, sea loch.

eternal *adjective*
1 eternal bliss : unending, endless, ceaseless, everlasting, never-ending, infinite, limitless, immortal, undying, imperishable.
2 eternal truths : unchanging, timeless, enduring, lasting, perennial, abiding.
3 (*infml*) eternal quarrelling : constant, continuous, perpetual, incessant, interminable.
E3 **1** ephemeral, temporary. **2** changeable.

eternity *noun*
1 the eternity of God : everlastingness, endlessness, everlasting, infinity, timelessness, perpetuity, imperishability, immutability.
2 last for an eternity : ages, age, aeon.

ethical *adjective*
moral, principled, just, right, proper, virtuous, honourable, fair, upright, righteous, seemly, honest, good, correct, commendable, fitting, noble.
E3 unethical.

ethics *noun*
moral values, morality, principles, standards, code, moral philosophy, rules, beliefs, propriety, conscience, equity.

ethnic *adjective*
racial, native, indigenous, traditional, tribal, folk, cultural, national, aboriginal.

ethos *noun*
attitude, beliefs, standards, manners, ethics, morality, code, principles, spirit, tenor, rationale, character, disposition.

etiquette *noun*
code, formalities, standards, correctness, conventions, customs, protocol, rules, manners, politeness, courtesy, civility, decorum, ceremony, decency.

euphemism *noun*
evasion, polite term, substitution, genteelism, politeness, understatement.

euphoria *noun*
elation, ecstasy, bliss, rapture, high spirits, well-being, high (*infml*), exhilaration, exultation, joy, intoxication, jubilation, transport, glee, exaltation, enthusiasm, cheerfulness.
E3 depression, despondency.

evacuate *verb*
leave, depart, withdraw, quit, remove, retire from, clear (out) (*infml*), abandon, desert, forsake, vacate, decamp, relinquish.

evade *verb*
1 evade one's responsibilities : elude, avoid, escape, dodge, shirk, steer clear of, shun, sidestep, duck (*infml*), balk, skive (*infml*), fend off, chicken out (*infml*), cop out (*infml*).
2 evade a question : equivocate, fence, prevaricate, fudge, parry, quibble, hedge.
E3 **1** confront, face.

evaluate *verb*
value, assess, appraise, estimate, reckon, calculate, gauge, judge, rate, size up, weigh, compute, rank.

evaporate *verb*
vaporize, disappear, dematerialize, vanish, melt (away), dissolve, disperse, dispel, dissipate, fade.

evasion *noun*
avoidance, escape, dodge, equivocation, excuse, prevarication, put-off, trickery, subterfuge, shirking.
E3 frankness, directness.

evasive *adjective*
equivocating, indirect, prevaricating, devious, shifty (*infml*), unforthcoming, slippery (*infml*), misleading, deceitful, deceptive, cagey (*infml*), oblique, secretive, tricky, cunning.
E3 direct, frank.

eve _noun_
day before, verge, brink, edge, threshold.

even _adjective_
1 an even surface: level, flat, smooth, horizontal, flush, parallel, plane.
2 an even pace: steady, unvarying, constant, regular, uniform.
3 scores are even: equal, balanced, matching, same, similar, like, symmetrical, fifty-fifty, level, side by side, neck and neck (_infml_).
F₃ 1 uneven. 3 unequal.
▸ _verb_
smooth, flatten, level, match, regularize, balance, equalize, align, square, stabilize, steady, straighten.

evening _noun_
nightfall, dusk, eve, eventide, twilight, sunset, sundown.

event _noun_
1 events in history: happening, occurrence, incident, occasion, affair, circumstance, episode, eventuality, experience, matter, case, adventure, business, fact, possibility, milestone.
2 stage an event: game, match, competition, contest, tournament, engagement.

eventful _adjective_
busy, exciting, lively, active, full, interesting, remarkable, significant, memorable, momentous, historic, crucial, critical, notable, noteworthy, unforgettable.
F₃ dull, ordinary.

eventual _adjective_
final, ultimate, resulting, concluding, ensuing, future, later, subsequent, prospective, projected, planned, impending.

eventually _adverb_
finally, ultimately, at last, in the end, at length, subsequently, after all, sooner or later.

ever _adverb_
1 yours ever: always, evermore, for ever, perpetually, constantly, at all times, continually, endlessly.
2 don't ever do that again: at any time, in any case, in any circumstances, at all, on any account.
F₃ 1 never.

everlasting _adjective_
eternal, undying, never-ending, endless, immortal, infinite, imperishable, constant, permanent, perpetual, indestructible, timeless.
F₃ temporary, transient.

everyday _adjective_
ordinary, common, commonplace, day-to-day, familiar, run-of-the-mill, regular, plain, routine, usual, workaday, common-or-garden (_infml_), normal, customary, stock, accustomed, conventional, daily, habitual, monotonous, frequent, simple, informal.
F₃ unusual, exceptional, special.

everyone _noun_
everybody, one and all, each one, all and sundry, the whole world.

everywhere _adverb_
all around, all over, throughout, far and near, far and wide, high and low, left, right and centre (_infml_).

evidence _noun_
1 the evidence of his own eyes/ written evidence: proof, verification, confirmation, affirmation, grounds, substantiation, documentation, data.
2 give evidence in court: testimony, declaration.
3 evidence of water on Mars: indication, manifestation, suggestion, sign, mark, hint, demonstration, token.

evident _adjective_
clear, obvious, manifest, apparent, plain, patent, visible, conspicuous, noticeable, clear-cut, unmistakable, perceptible, distinct, discernible, tangible, incontestable, indisputable, incontrovertible.

evidently _adverb_
clearly, apparently, plainly, patently, manifestly, obviously, seemingly, undoubtedly, doubtless(ly), indisputably.

evil _adjective_
1 an evil dictator: wicked, wrong, sinful, bad, immoral, vicious, vile, malevolent, iniquitous, cruel, base, corrupt, heinous (_fml_), malicious, malignant, devilish, depraved, mischievous, satanic.

2 an evil influence: harmful, pernicious, destructive, deadly, detrimental, hurtful, poisonous.
3 come the evil day: disastrous, ruinous, calamitous, catastrophic, adverse, dire, inauspicious.
4 an evil smell: offensive, noxious, foul.
▶ *noun*
1 do evil: wickedness, wrongdoing, wrong, immorality, badness, sin, sinfulness, vice, viciousness, iniquity (*fml*), depravity, baseness, corruption, malignity, mischief, heinousness.
2 deliver us from evil: adversity, affliction, calamity, disaster, misfortune, suffering, sorrow, ruin, catastrophe, blow, curse, distress, hurt, harm, ill, injury, misery, woe.

evolve *verb*
develop, grow, increase, mature, progress, unravel, expand, enlarge, emerge, descend, derive, result, elaborate.

exact *adjective*
1 an exact amount/account: precise, accurate, correct, faithful, literal, flawless, faultless, right, true, veracious (*fml*), definite, explicit, detailed, specific, strict, unerring, close, factual, identical, express, word-perfect, blow-by-blow (*infml*).
2 she's very exact: careful, scrupulous, particular, rigorous, methodical, meticulous, orderly, painstaking.
E3 1 inexact, imprecise.
▶ *verb*
extort, extract, claim, insist on, wrest (*fml*), wring, compel, demand, command, force, impose, require, squeeze, milk (*infml*).

exacting *adjective*
demanding, difficult, hard, laborious, arduous, rigorous, taxing, tough, harsh, painstaking, severe, strict, unsparing.
E3 easy.

exactly *adverb*
1 at two o'clock exactly/copy it exactly: precisely, accurately, literally, faithfully, correctly, specifically, rigorously, scrupulously, veraciously, verbatim, carefully, faultlessly, unerringly,

strictly, to the letter, particularly, methodically, explicitly, expressly, dead (*infml*).
2 exactly so: absolutely, definitely, precisely, indeed, certainly, truly, quite, just, unequivocally.
E3 1 inaccurately, roughly.

exaggerate *verb*
overstate, overdo, magnify, overemphasize, emphasize, embellish, embroider, enlarge, amplify, oversell, pile it on (*infml*).
E3 understate.

examination *noun*
1 examination of the evidence: inspection, enquiry, scrutiny, study, survey, search, analysis, exploration, investigation, probe, appraisal, observation, research, review, scan, once-over (*infml*), perusal, check, check-up, audit, critique.
2 a French examination: test, exam, quiz, questioning, cross-examination, cross-questioning, trial, inquisition, interrogation, viva.

examine *verb*
1 examine the body: inspect, investigate, scrutinize, study, survey, analyse, explore, enquire, consider, probe, review, scan, check (out), ponder, pore over, sift, vet, weigh up, appraise, assay, audit, peruse, case (*slang*).
2 examining them on their knowledge of anatomy: test, quiz, question, cross-examine, cross-question, interrogate, grill (*infml*), catechize (*fml*).

example *noun*
instance, case, case in point, illustration, exemplification, sample, specimen, model, pattern, ideal, archetype, prototype, standard, type, lesson, citation.

exasperate *verb*
infuriate, annoy, anger, incense, irritate, madden, provoke, get on someone's nerves, enrage, irk, rile, rankle, rouse, get to (*infml*), goad, vex.
E3 appease, pacify.

exceed *verb*
surpass, outdo, outstrip, beat, better, pass, overtake, top, outshine, eclipse,

outreach, outrun, transcend, cap, overdo, overstep.

excel *verb*
1 **excelling all previous records**: surpass, outdo, beat, outclass, outperform, outrank, eclipse, better.
2 **excel at sports**: be excellent, succeed, shine, stand out, predominate.

excellence *noun*
superiority, pre-eminence, distinction, merit, supremacy, quality, worth, fineness, eminence, goodness, greatness, virtue, perfection, purity.

excellent *adjective*
superior, first-class, first-rate, prime, superlative, unequalled, outstanding, surpassing, remarkable, distinguished, great, good, exemplary, select, superb, admirable, commendable, top-notch (*infml*), splendid, noteworthy, notable, fine, wonderful, worthy.
Ⓔ inferior, second-rate.

except *preposition*
excepting, but, apart from, other than, save, omitting, not counting, leaving out, excluding, except for, besides, bar, minus, less.
▸ *verb*
leave out, omit, bar, exclude, reject, rule out.

exception *noun*
oddity, anomaly, deviation, rarity, abnormality, irregularity, peculiarity, inconsistency, special case, quirk.

exceptional *adjective*
1 **this case is exceptional**: abnormal, unusual, anomalous, strange, odd, irregular, extraordinary, peculiar, special, rare, uncommon.
2 **an exceptional violinist**: outstanding, remarkable, phenomenal, prodigious, notable, noteworthy, superior, unequalled, marvellous.
Ⓔ 1 normal. 2 mediocre.

excerpt *noun*
extract, passage, portion, section, selection, quote, quotation, part, citation, scrap, fragment.

excess *noun*
1 **an excess of energy**: surfeit, overabundance, glut, plethora, superfluity, superabundance, surplus,

overflow, overkill, remainder, left-over.
2 **the excesses of the imperial court**: overindulgence, dissipation (*fml*), immoderateness, intemperance, extravagance, unrestraint, debauchery.
Ⓔ 1 deficiency. 2 restraint.
▸ *adjective*
extra, surplus, spare, redundant, remaining, residual, left-over, additional, superfluous, supernumerary.
Ⓔ inadequate.

excessive *adjective*
immoderate, inordinate, extreme, undue, uncalled-for, disproportionate, unnecessary, unneeded, superfluous, unreasonable, exorbitant, extravagant, steep (*infml*).
Ⓔ insufficient.

exchange *verb*
barter, change, trade, swap, switch, replace, interchange, convert, commute, substitute, reciprocate, bargain, bandy.
▸ *noun*
1 **an exchange between the two prime ministers**: conversation, discussion, chat.
2 **currency exchange**: trade, commerce, dealing, market, traffic, barter, bargain.
3 **the exchange of vows**: switch, interchange, swap, replacement, substitution, reciprocity.

excitable *adjective*
temperamental, volatile, passionate, emotional, highly-strung, fiery, hot-headed, hasty, nervous, hot-tempered, irascible, quick-tempered, sensitive, susceptible.
Ⓔ calm, stable.

excite *verb*
1 **excites the emotions**: move, agitate, disturb, upset, touch, stir up, thrill, elate, turn on (*infml*), impress.
2 **exciting a response**: arouse, rouse, animate, awaken, fire, inflame, kindle, motivate, stimulate, engender, inspire, instigate, incite, induce, ignite, galvanize, generate, provoke, sway, quicken (*fml*), evoke.
Ⓔ 1 calm.

excited *adjective*
aroused, roused, stimulated, stirred,
thrilled, elated, enthusiastic, eager,
moved, high (*infml*), worked up,
wrought-up, overwrought, restless,
frantic, frenzied, wild.
F3 calm, apathetic.

exciting *adjective*
stimulating, stirring, intoxicating,
exhilarating, thrilling, rousing,
moving, enthralling, electrifying, nail-
biting (*infml*), cliff-hanging (*infml*),
striking, sensational, provocative,
inspiring, interesting.
F3 dull, unexciting.

exclaim *verb*
cry (out), declare, blurt (out), call, yell,
shout, proclaim, utter.

exclude *verb*
1 **excluding VAT**: omit, leave out,
disallow, refuse, reject, ignore, rule out,
eliminate.
2 **excluding them from school**: expel,
eject, evict, excommunicate, ban, bar,
keep out, shut out, prohibit, veto,
proscribe, forbid, blacklist, ostracize.
F3 1 include. 2 admit.

exclusive *adjective*
1 **the exclusive right**: sole, single,
unique, only, undivided, unshared,
whole, total, peculiar.
2 **an exclusive restaurant**: restricted,
limited, closed, private, narrow,
restrictive, choice, select, cliquey,
discriminative, chic, classy (*infml*),
elegant, fashionable, posh (*infml*),
snobbish.

excruciating *adjective*
agonizing, painful, severe, tormenting,
unbearable, insufferable, acute,
intolerable, intense, sharp, piercing,
extreme, atrocious, racking,
harrowing, savage, burning, bitter.

excuse *verb* /eks-**kyooz**/
1 **can't excuse such behaviour**: forgive,
pardon, overlook, absolve, acquit,
exonerate, tolerate, ignore,
indulge.
2 **excusing him from games**: release,
free, discharge, liberate, let off, relieve,
spare, exempt.
F3 1 criticize. 2 punish.

▶ *noun* /eks-**kyoos**/
justification, explanation, grounds,
defence, plea, alibi, reason, apology,
pretext, pretence, exoneration, evasion,
cop-out (*infml*).

execute *verb*
1 **executed the murderer**: put to death,
kill, liquidate, hang, electrocute, shoot,
guillotine, decapitate, behead.
2 **execute a command**: carry out, do,
perform, accomplish, achieve, fulfil,
complete, discharge, effect, sign, enact,
deliver, enforce, finish, render, serve,
implement, administer, consummate,
realize, dispatch, expedite, validate.

executive *noun*
1 **a decision by the executive**:
administration, management,
government, leadership, hierarchy.
2 **the chief executive**: administrator,
manager, organizer, leader, controller,
director, governor, official.
▶ *adjective*
administrative, managerial,
controlling, supervisory, regulating,
decision-making, governing,
organizing, directing, directorial,
organizational, leading, guiding.

exemplary *adjective*
1 **exemplary behaviour**: model, ideal,
perfect, admirable, excellent, faultless,
flawless, correct, good, commendable,
praiseworthy, worthy, laudable,
estimable, honourable.
2 **an exemplary tale**: cautionary,
warning.
F3 1 imperfect, unworthy.

exemplify *verb*
illustrate, demonstrate, show, instance,
represent, typify, manifest, embody,
epitomize, exhibit, depict, display.

exempt *verb*
excuse, release, relieve, let off, free,
absolve, discharge, dismiss, liberate,
spare.
▶ *adjective*
excused, not liable, immune, released,
spared, absolved, discharged,
excluded, free, liberated, clear.
F3 liable.

exercise *verb*
1 **exercise a bit of self-control**: use,

utilize, employ, apply, exert, practise, wield, try, discharge.

2 must exercise regularly: train, drill, work out (*infml*), keep fit.

3 exercised by many difficult problems: worry, disturb, trouble, upset, burden, distress, vex, annoy, agitate, afflict.

▶ *noun*

1 a military exercise/violin exercises: training, drill, practice, task, lesson, work, discipline.

2 take regular exercise/do one's exercises: activity, physical jerks (*infml*), work-out (*infml*), aerobics, labour.

3 the exercise of power: use, utilization, employment, application, implementation, practice, operation, discharge, assignment, fulfilment, accomplishment.

exert *verb*

use, utilize, employ, apply, exercise, bring to bear, wield, expend.

◆ **exert oneself** strive, struggle, strain, make every effort, take pains, toil, labour, work, sweat (*infml*), endeavour, apply oneself.

exertion *noun*

effort, industry, labour, toil, work, struggle, diligence, assiduousness (*fml*), perseverance, pains, endeavour, attempt, strain, travail (*fml*), trial.

Fa idleness, rest.

exhaust *verb*

1 exhaust the supply of oxygen: consume, empty, deplete, drain, sap, spend, waste, squander, dissipate, impoverish, use up, finish, dry, bankrupt.

2 exhausting himself: tire (out), weary, fatigue, tax, strain, weaken, overwork, wear out.

Fa 1 renew. **2** refresh.

▶ *noun*

emission, exhalation, discharge, fumes.

exhausted *adjective*

1 exhausted by the climb: tired (out), dead tired, dead-beat (*infml*), all in (*infml*), done (in) (*infml*), fatigued, weak, washed-out, whacked (*infml*).

2 the mine/supply is exhausted:

empty, finished, depleted, spent, used up, drained, dry, worn out, void.

Fa 1 fresh. **2** vigorous.

exhausting *adjective*

tiring, strenuous, taxing, gruelling, arduous, hard, laborious, backbreaking, draining, severe, testing, punishing, formidable, debilitating.

Fa refreshing.

exhaustion *noun*

fatigue, tiredness, weariness, debility, feebleness, jet-lag.

Fa freshness, liveliness.

exhaustive *adjective*

comprehensive, all-embracing, all-inclusive, far-reaching, complete, extensive, encyclopedic, full-scale, thorough, full, in-depth, intensive, detailed, definitive, all-out, sweeping.

Fa incomplete, restricted.

exhibit *verb*

display, show, present, demonstrate, manifest, expose, parade, reveal, express, disclose, indicate, air, flaunt, offer.

Fa conceal.

▶ *noun*

display, exhibition, show, illustration, model.

exhibition *noun*

display, show, demonstration, exhibit, presentation, manifestation, spectacle, exposition, expo (*infml*), showing, fair, performance, airing, representation, showcase.

exhilarate *verb*

thrill, excite, elate, animate, enliven, invigorate, vitalize, stimulate.

Fa bore.

exile *noun*

1 in exile/the exile of Napoleon to Elba: banishment, deportation, expatriation, expulsion, ostracism, transportation.

2 an exile from his homeland: expatriate, refugee, émigré, deportee, outcast.

▶ *verb*

banish, expel, deport, expatriate, drive out, ostracize, oust.

exist *verb*

1 existing on the surface of the planet

be, live, abide (*fml*), continue, endure, have one's being, breathe, prevail.
2 exist on a diet of rice: subsist, survive.
3 existing in the bread and wine: be present, occur, happen, be available, remain.

existence *noun*
1 man's existence: being, life, reality, actuality, continuance, continuation, endurance, survival, breath, subsistence.
2 throughout existence: creation, the world.
F3 1 death, non-existence.

exit *noun*
1 make a rapid exit: departure, going, retreat, withdrawal, leave-taking, retirement, farewell, exodus.
2 leave by a side exit: door, way out, doorway, gate, vent.
F3 1 entrance, arrival. **2** entrance.
▸ *verb*
depart, leave, go, retire, withdraw, take one's leave, retreat, issue.
F3 arrive, enter.

exonerate *verb*
absolve, acquit, clear, vindicate, exculpate (*fml*), justify, pardon, discharge.
F3 incriminate.

exotic *adjective*
1 an exotic holiday/exotic fruits: foreign, alien, imported, introduced.
2 an exotic mixture: unusual, striking, different, unfamiliar, extraordinary, bizarre, curious, strange, fascinating, colourful, peculiar, outlandish.
F3 1 native. **2** ordinary.

expand *verb*
1 expand the boundaries of knowledge: stretch, swell, widen, lengthen, thicken, magnify, multiply, inflate, broaden, blow up, open out, fill out, fatten.
2 the universe is expanding/expanding the company: increase, grow, extend, enlarge, develop, amplify, spread, branch out, diversify, elaborate.
F3 1 contract.

expanse *noun*
extent, space, area, breadth, range, stretch, sweep, field, plain, tract.

expect *verb*
1 expect the money soon: anticipate, await, look forward to, hope for, look for, bank on, bargain for, envisage, predict, forecast, contemplate, project, foresee.
2 expect you to comply: require, want, wish, insist on, demand, rely on, count on.
3 expect you're right: suppose, surmise, assume, believe, think, presume, imagine, reckon, guess (*infml*), trust.

expectant *adjective*
1 an expectant silence: awaiting, anticipating, hopeful, in suspense, ready, apprehensive, anxious, watchful, eager, curious.
2 an expectant mother: pregnant, expecting (*infml*), with child (*fml*).

expedition *noun*
journey, excursion, trip, voyage, tour, exploration, trek, safari, hike, sail, ramble, raid, quest, pilgrimage, mission, crusade.

expel *verb*
1 expelling the invaders/expel them from school: drive out, eject, evict, banish, throw out, ban, bar, oust, exile, expatriate.
2 expelling waste into the sea: discharge, evacuate, void, cast out.

expend *verb*
1 expending precious energy: consume, use (up), dissipate, exhaust, employ.
2 expending many thousands of dollars: spend, pay, disburse (*fml*), fork out (*infml*).
F3 1 conserve. **2** save.

expenditure *noun*
spending, expense, outlay, outgoings, disbursement (*fml*), payment, output.
F3 income.

expense *noun*
spending, expenditure, disbursement (*fml*), outlay, payment, loss, cost, charge.

expensive *adjective*
dear, high-priced, costly, exorbitant, extortionate, steep (*infml*), extravagant, lavish.
F3 cheap, inexpensive.

experience *noun*
1 have some experience of children: knowledge, familiarity, know-how, involvement, participation, practice, understanding.
2 an interesting experience: incident, event, episode, happening, encounter, occurrence, adventure.
F3 1 inexperience.
▶ *verb*
undergo, go through, live through, suffer, feel, endure, encounter, face, meet, know, try, perceive, sustain.

experienced *adjective*
1 an experienced teacher: practised, knowledgeable, familiar, capable, competent, well-versed, expert, accomplished, qualified, skilled, tried, trained, professional.
2 an experienced soldier: seasoned, wise, veteran.
F3 1 inexperienced, unskilled.

experiment *noun*
trial, test, investigation, experimentation, research, examination, trial run, venture, trial and error, attempt, procedure, proof.
▶ *verb*
try, test, investigate, examine, research, sample, verify.

experimental *adjective*
trial, test, exploratory, empirical, tentative, provisional, speculative, pilot, preliminary, trial-and-error.

expert *noun*
specialist, connoisseur, authority, professional, pro (*infml*), dab hand (*infml*), maestro, virtuoso.
▶ *adjective*
proficient, adept, skilled, skilful, knowledgeable, experienced, able, practised, professional, masterly, specialist, qualified, virtuoso.
F3 amateurish, novice.

expertise *noun*
expertness, proficiency, skill, skilfulness, know-how, knack (*infml*), knowledge, mastery, dexterity, virtuosity.
F3 inexperience.

expire *verb*
end, cease, finish, stop, terminate, close, conclude, discontinue, run out, lapse, die, depart, decease, perish.
F3 begin.

explain *verb*
1 explaining his theory: interpret, clarify, describe, define, make clear, elucidate, simplify, resolve, solve, spell out, translate, unfold, unravel, untangle, illustrate, demonstrate, disclose, expound, teach.
2 explain yourself: justify, excuse, account for, rationalize.
F3 1 obscure, confound.

explanatory *adjective*
descriptive, interpretive, explicative, demonstrative, expository (*fml*), justifying.

explicit *adjective*
1 give explicit instructions: clear, distinct, exact, categorical, absolute, certain, positive, precise, specific, unambiguous, express, definite, declared, detailed, stated.
2 an explicit portrayal: open, direct, frank, outspoken, straightforward, unreserved, plain.
F3 1 implicit, unspoken, vague.

explode *verb*
1 exploding a bomb: blow up, burst, go off, set off, detonate, discharge, blast, erupt.
2 explode the myth: discredit, disprove, give the lie to, debunk, invalidate, refute, rebut, repudiate.
F3 2 prove, confirm.

exploit *noun*
deed, feat, adventure, achievement, accomplishment, attainment, stunt.
▶ *verb*
1 exploit an opportunity: use, utilize, capitalize on, profit by, turn to account, take advantage of, cash in on, make capital out of.
2 exploiting children: misuse, abuse, oppress, ill-treat, impose on, manipulate, rip off (*infml*), fleece (*infml*).

explore *verb*
1 explore the possibilities: investigate, examine, inspect, research, scrutinize, probe, analyse.
2 exploring the island: travel, tour,

search, reconnoitre, prospect, scout, survey.

explosion *noun*
detonation, blast, burst, outburst, discharge, eruption, bang, outbreak, clap, crack, fit, report.

explosive *adjective*
unstable, volatile, sensitive, tense, fraught, charged, touchy, overwrought, dangerous, hazardous, perilous, stormy.
F3 stable, calm.

expose *verb*
1 **expose the fraud**: reveal, show, exhibit, display, disclose, uncover, bring to light, present, manifest, detect, divulge, unveil, unmask, denounce.
2 **exposing his queen and losing the game**: endanger, jeopardize, imperil, risk, hazard.
F3 1 conceal.

exposed *adjective*
bare, open, revealed, laid bare, unprotected, vulnerable, exhibited, on display, on show, on view, shown, susceptible.
F3 covered, sheltered.

express *verb*
1 **expressing himself clearly**: articulate, verbalize, utter, voice, say, speak, state, communicate, pronounce, tell, assert, declare, put across, formulate, intimate, testify, convey.
2 **expressing disapproval**: show, manifest, exhibit, disclose, divulge, reveal, indicate, denote, depict, embody.
3 **expressing the horrors of war**: symbolize, stand for, represent, signify, designate.
▸ *adjective*
1 **against his express wishes**: specific, explicit, exact, definite, clear, categorical, precise, distinct, clear-cut, certain, plain, manifest, particular, stated, unambiguous.
2 **an express train**: fast, speedy, rapid, quick, high-speed, non-stop.
F3 1 vague.

expression *noun*
1 **a puzzled expression**: look, air, aspect, countenance, appearance, mien (*fml*).

2 **the artist's expression of emotion**: representation, manifestation, demonstration, indication, exhibition, embodiment, show, sign, symbol, style.
3 **a clear expression of his wishes**: utterance, verbalization, communication, articulation, statement, assertion, announcement, declaration, pronouncement, speech.
4 **put some expression into your voice**: tone, intonation, delivery, diction, enunciation, modulation.
5 **a Scottish expression**: phrase, term, turn of phrase, saying, set phrase, idiom.

expressionless *adjective*
dull, blank, dead-pan, impassive, straight-faced, poker-faced (*infml*), inscrutable, empty, vacuous, glassy.
F3 expressive.

expressive *adjective*
eloquent, meaningful, forceful, telling, revealing, informative, indicative, communicative, demonstrative, emphatic, moving, poignant, lively, striking, suggestive, significant, thoughtful, vivid, sympathetic.

expulsion *noun*
ejection, eviction, exile, banishment, removal, discharge, exclusion, dismissal.

exquisite *adjective*
1 **an exquisite collection of jade ornaments**: beautiful, attractive, dainty, delicate, charming, elegant, delightful, lovely, pleasing.
2 **an exquisite emerald**: perfect, flawless, fine, excellent, choice, precious, rare, outstanding.
3 **exquisite taste**: refined, discriminating, meticulous, sensitive, impeccable.
4 **the pain was exquisite**: intense, keen, sharp, poignant.
F3 1 ugly. 2 flawed. 3 unrefined.

extend *verb*
1 **extending to fifty acres**: spread, stretch, reach, continue.
2 **extending his power**: enlarge, increase, expand, develop, amplify, lengthen, widen, elongate, draw out, protract, prolong, spin out, unwind.

3 must extend our thanks to our hosts:
offer, give, grant, hold out, impart,
present, bestow, confer.
F3 2 contract, shorten. **3** withhold.

extension *noun*
1 extension of the empire:
enlargement, increase, stretching,
broadening, widening, lengthening,
expansion, elongation, development,
enhancement, protraction,
continuation.
2 an extension to the house: addition,
supplement, appendix, annexe,
addendum (*fml*).
3 ask for an extension: delay,
postponement.

extensive *adjective*
1 an extensive review: broad,
comprehensive, far-reaching, large-
scale, thorough, widespread, universal,
extended, all-inclusive, general,
pervasive, prevalent.
2 an extensive building: large, huge,
roomy, spacious, vast.
F3 1 restricted, narrow. **2** small.

extent *noun*
1 the extent of the universe:
dimension(s), amount, magnitude,
expanse, size, area, bulk, degree,
breadth, quantity, spread, stretch,
volume, width, measure, duration,
term, time.
2 the extent of his knowledge: limit,
bounds, lengths, range, reach, scope,
compass, sphere, play, sweep.

exterior *noun*
outside, surface, covering, coating,
face, façade, shell, skin, finish,
externals, appearance.
F3 inside, interior.
▶ *adjective*
outer, outside, outermost, surface,
external, superficial, surrounding,
outward, peripheral, extrinsic.
F3 inside, interior.

exterminate *verb*
annihilate, eradicate, destroy,
eliminate, massacre, abolish, wipe out.

external *adjective*
outer, surface, outside, exterior,
superficial, outward, outermost,
apparent, visible, extraneous, extrinsic,

extramural, independent.
F3 internal.

extinct *adjective*
1 dinosaurs became extinct: defunct,
dead, gone, obsolete, ended,
exterminated, terminated, vanished,
lost, abolished.
2 extinct volcano: extinguished,
quenched, inactive, out.
F3 1 living.

extinguish *verb*
1 extinguished the flames: put out,
blow out, snuff out, stifle, smother,
douse, quench.
2 extinguishing all life: annihilate,
exterminate, eliminate, destroy, kill,
eradicate, erase, expunge (*fml*),
abolish, remove, end, suppress.

extortionate *adjective*
exorbitant, excessive, grasping,
exacting, immoderate, rapacious,
unreasonable, oppressive, blood-
sucking (*infml*), rigorous, severe, hard,
harsh, inordinate.

extra *adjective*
1 an extra room: additional, added,
auxiliary, supplementary, new, more,
further, ancillary, fresh, other.
2 have no extra time to spare: excess,
spare, superfluous, supernumerary,
surplus, unused, unneeded, leftover,
reserve, redundant.
F3 1 integral. **2** essential.
▶ *noun*
addition, supplement, extension,
accessory, appendage, bonus,
complement, adjunct, addendum
(*fml*), attachment.
▶ *adverb*
especially, exceptionally, remarkably,
extraordinarily, particularly, unusually,
extremely.

extract *verb* /eks-trakt/
1 extract a tooth: remove, take out,
draw out, exact, uproot, withdraw.
2 extract some benefit: derive, draw,
distil, obtain, get, gather, glean, wrest
(*fml*), wring, elicit.
F3 1 insert.
▶ *noun* /**eks**-trakt/
1 lime extract: distillation, essence,
juice.

2 an extract from the play: excerpt, passage, selection, clip, cutting, quotation, abstract, citation.

extraordinary *adjective*
remarkable, unusual, exceptional, notable, noteworthy, outstanding, unique, special, strange, peculiar, rare, surprising, amazing, wonderful, unprecedented, marvellous, fantastic, significant, particular.
F3 commonplace, ordinary.

extravagant *adjective*
1 extravagant lifestyle: profligate, prodigal, spendthrift, thriftless, wasteful, reckless.
2 extravagant behaviour: immoderate, flamboyant, preposterous, outrageous, ostentatious, pretentious, lavish, ornate, flashy (*infml*), fanciful, fantastic, wild.
3 charge extravagant prices: exorbitant, expensive, excessive, costly.
F3 1 thrifty. **2** moderate. **3** reasonable.

extreme *adjective*
1 extreme cold: intense, great, immoderate, inordinate, utmost, utter, out-and-out, maximum, acute, downright, extraordinary, exceptional, greatest, highest, unreasonable, remarkable.
2 the extreme corners of the universe: farthest, far-off, faraway, distant, endmost, outermost, remotest, uttermost, final, last, terminal, ultimate.
3 extreme views: radical, zealous, extremist, fanatical.
4 extreme punishment: drastic, dire, uncompromising, stern, strict, rigid, severe, harsh.
F3 1 mild. **3** moderate.

▶ *noun*
extremity, limit, maximum, ultimate, utmost, excess, top, pinnacle, peak, height, end, climax, depth, edge, termination.

extremity *noun*
1 at the extremities: extreme, limit, boundary, brink, verge, bound, border, apex, height, tip, top, edge, excess, end, acme, termination, peak, pinnacle, margin, terminal, terminus, ultimate, pole, maximum, minimum, frontier, depth.
2 in extremity: crisis, danger, emergency, plight, hardship.

extrovert *adjective*
outgoing, friendly, sociable, amicable, amiable, exuberant.
F3 introvert.

exuberant *adjective*
lively, vivacious, spirited, zestful, high-spirited, effervescent, ebullient, enthusiastic, sparkling, excited, exhilarated, effusive, cheerful, fulsome.
F3 apathetic.

exult *verb*
rejoice, revel, delight, glory, celebrate, relish, crow, gloat, triumph.

eye *noun*
1 an eye for a bargain: appreciation, discrimination, discernment, perception, recognition.
2 it looks odd to my eye: viewpoint, opinion, judgement, mind.
3 keep an eye out for: watch, observation, lookout.
▶ *verb*
look at, watch, regard, observe, stare at, gaze at, glance at, view, scrutinize, scan, examine, peruse, study, survey, inspect, contemplate.

Ff

fable *noun*
allegory, parable, story, tale, yarn, myth, legend, fiction, fabrication, invention, lie, untruth, falsehood, tall story, old wives' tale.

fabric *noun*
1 a cotton fabric: cloth, material, textile, stuff, web, texture.
2 the fabric of society: structure, framework, construction, make-up, constitution, organization, infrastructure, foundations.

fabulous *adjective*
1 a fabulous holiday: wonderful, marvellous, fantastic (*infml*), superb, breathtaking, spectacular, phenomenal, amazing, astounding, unbelievable, incredible, inconceivable, terrific (*infml*), cool (*infml*).
2 a fabulous beast: mythical, legendary, fabled, fantastic, fictitious, invented, imaginary.
F 2 real.

face *noun*
1 a pretty face: features, countenance, visage, physiognomy.
2 modern farming has changed the face of the countryside: look, appearance, expression, air.
3 pull a face: grimace, frown, scowl, pout.
4 a building with a face of white marble: exterior, outside, surface, cover, front. façade, aspect, side.
▶ *verb*
1 facing south/the river: be opposite, give on to, front, overlook.
2 face danger: confront, face up to, deal with, cope with, tackle, brave, defy,

oppose, encounter, meet, experience.
3 faced with marble: cover, coat, dress, clad, overlay, veneer.
◆ **face to face** opposite, eye to eye, eyeball to eyeball, in confrontation.
◆ **face up to** accept, come to terms with, acknowledge, recognize, cope with, deal with, confront, meet head-on, stand up to.

facet *noun*
surface, plane, side, face, aspect, angle, point, feature, characteristic.

facetious *adjective*
flippant, frivolous, playful, jocular, jesting, tongue-in-cheek, funny, amusing, humorous, comical, witty.
F serious.

facilitate *verb*
ease, help, assist, further, promote, forward, expedite, speed up.

facilities *noun*
amenities, services, conveniences, resources, prerequisites, equipment, mod cons (*infml*), means, opportunities.

fact *noun*
1 facts and figures: information, datum, detail, particular, specific, point, item, circumstance, event, incident, occurrence, happening, act, deed, fait accompli.
2 the fact of the matter: reality, actuality, truth.
F 2 fiction.
◆ **in fact** actually, in actual fact, in point of fact, as a matter of fact, in reality, really, indeed.

factor *noun*
cause, influence, circumstance, contingency, consideration, element,

ingredient, component, part, point, aspect, fact, item, detail.

factual *adjective*
true, historical, actual, real, genuine, authentic, correct, accurate, precise, exact, literal, faithful, close, detailed, unbiased, objective.
E∃ false, fictitious, imaginary, fictional.

faculty *noun*
ability, capability, capacity, power, facility, knack, gift, talent, skill, aptitude, bent.

fad *noun*
craze, rage (*infml*), mania, fashion, mode, vogue, trend, whim, fancy, affectation.

fade *verb*
1 fade in the strong sunlight: discolour, bleach, blanch, blench, pale, whiten, dim, dull.
2 fade into obscurity: decline, fall, diminish, dwindle, ebb, wane, disappear, vanish, flag, weaken, droop, wilt, wither, shrivel, perish, die.

fail *verb*
1 the plot failed/fail an exam/his business failed: go wrong, miscarry, misfire, flop, miss, flunk (*infml*), fall through, come to grief, collapse, fold (*infml*), go bankrupt, go bust (*infml*), go under, founder, sink, decline, fall, weaken, dwindle, fade, wane, peter out, cease, die.
2 fail to pay the bill: omit, neglect, forget.
3 failed her parents: let down, disappoint, leave, desert, abandon, forsake.
E∃ 1 succeed, prosper.

failing *noun*
weakness, foible, fault, defect, imperfection, flaw, blemish, drawback, deficiency, shortcoming, failure, lapse, error.
E∃ strength, advantage.

failure *noun*
1 the play was a failure: flop, wash-out (*infml*), fiasco, disappointment.
2 the failure of his business: loss, defeat, downfall, decline, decay, deterioration, ruin, bankruptcy, crash, collapse, breakdown, stoppage.

3 a failure of the system: failing, shortcoming, deficiency.
E∃ 1 success. **2** prosperity.
⇨ *See also* **Word Study** *panel.*

faint *adjective*
1 a faint line/sound/light: slight, weak, feeble, soft, low, hushed, muffled, subdued, faded, bleached, light, pale, dull, dim, hazy, indistinct, vague.
2 feel faint: dizzy, giddy, woozy (*infml*), light-headed, weak, feeble, exhausted.
E∃ 1 strong, clear.
▶ *verb*
black out, pass out, swoon, collapse, flake out (*infml*), keel over (*infml*), drop.
▶ *noun*
blackout, swoon, collapse, unconsciousness.

fair¹ *adjective*
1 a fair contest/assessment/man: just, equitable, square, even-handed, dispassionate, impartial, objective, disinterested, unbiased, unprejudiced, right, proper, lawful, legitimate, honest, trustworthy, upright, honourable.
2 he's not dark, he's fair: fair-haired, fair-headed, blond(e), light.
3 fair weather: fine, dry, sunny, bright, clear, cloudless, unclouded.
4 not good, but fair: average, moderate, middling, not bad, all right, OK (*infml*), satisfactory, adequate, acceptable, tolerable, reasonable, passable, mediocre, so-so (*infml*).
E∃ 1 unfair. **2** dark. **3** inclement, cloudy. **4** excellent, poor.

fair² *noun*
a trade/country fair: show, exhibition, exposition, expo (*infml*), market, bazaar, fête, festival, carnival, gala.

faith *noun*
1 faith in himself: belief, credit, trust, reliance, dependence, conviction, confidence, assurance.
2 people of many faiths: religion, denomination, persuasion, church, creed, dogma.
3 in good faith: faithfulness, fidelity, loyalty, allegiance, honour, sincerity, honesty, truthfulness.
E∃ 1 mistrust. **3** unfaithfulness, treachery.

WORD *study*   failure

Here are some common fixed phrases that express **failure** of one sort or another. As with many other unpleasant subjects, people often prefer not to refer to failure directly. Note that these expressions also make it possible to emphasize the seriousness of the failure, or to make light of it. Check out the panel on **success** to find phrases with the opposite meaning.

to fail

go down like a lead balloon
have had your chips
bite the dust
come to grief
go up in smoke
go to the wall
go down the drain

draw a blank
come a cropper
fall flat
miss the mark
fall between two stools
come unstuck

to cause your own failure

blow it (*slang*)
blow your chance
fluff it
make a muck of something
miss the boat

burn your boats
sign your own death warrant
dig your own grave
make a pig's ear of something
score an own goal

to be doomed to failure

not have a hope in hell
not have a cat in hell's chance
be a dead duck
not have a ghost of a chance

be fighting a losing battle
not have a snowball's chance in hell
be a non-starter

faithful *adjective*
1 a faithful companion : loyal, devoted, staunch, strict, close, true, trusty, reliable, dependable, true.
2 a faithful copy : accurate, precise, exact, strict, close, true, truthful.
E3 1 disloyal, treacherous. **2** inaccurate, vague.

fake *noun*
forgery, copy, reproduction, replica, imitation, simulation, sham, hoax,

fraud, phoney (*infml*), impostor, charlatan.
▶ *adjective*
forged, counterfeit, false, spurious, phoney (*infml*), pseudo, bogus, assumed, affected, sham, artificial, simulated, mock, imitation, reproduction.
E3 genuine.
▶ *verb*
forge, fabricate, counterfeit, copy,

imitate, simulate, feign, sham, pretend, put on, affect, assume.

fall *verb*

1 fell to earth/fell from a great height: descend, go down, drop, slope, incline, slide, sink, dive, plunge, plummet, nose-dive.

2 she fell and broke her wrist: tumble, stumble, trip, topple, keel over, collapse, slump, crash.

3 crime rate is falling: decrease, lessen, decline, diminish, dwindle, fall off, subside.

Fa 2 rise. 3 increase.

▶ *noun*

1 have a fall/a fall in prices: tumble, descent, slope, incline, dive, plunge, decrease, reduction, lessening, drop, decline, dwindling, slump, crash.

2 the fall of Rome: defeat, conquest, overthrow, downfall, collapse, surrender, capitulation.

◆ **fall apart** break, go to pieces, shatter, disintegrate, crumble, decompose, decay, rot.

◆ **fall asleep** drop off, doze off, nod off (*infml*).

◆ **fall back on** resort to, have recourse to, use, turn to, look to.

◆ **fall behind** lag, trail, drop back.

◆ **fall in** cave in, come down, collapse, give way, subside, sink.

◆ **fall in with** agree with, assent to, go along with, accept, comply with, co-operate with.

◆ **fall off** decrease, lessen, drop, slump, decline, deteriorate, worsen, slow, slacken.

◆ **fall out** quarrel, argue, squabble, bicker, fight, clash, disagree, differ.

Fa agree.

◆ **fall through** come to nothing, fail, miscarry, founder, collapse.

Fa come off, succeed.

fallacy *noun*

misconception, delusion, mistake, error, flaw, inconsistency, falsehood.

Fa truth.

false *adjective*

1 a false assumption: wrong, incorrect, mistaken, erroneous, inaccurate, invalid, inexact, misleading, faulty, fallacious.

2 false eyelashes/a false name: unreal, artificial, synthetic, imitation, simulated, mock, fake, counterfeit, forged, feigned, pretended, sham, bogus, assumed, fictitious.

3 be false to one's principles: disloyal, unfaithful, faithless, lying, deceitful, insincere, hypocritical, two-faced, double-dealing, treacherous, unreliable.

Fa 1 true, right. 2 real, genuine. 3 faithful, reliable.

falsify *verb*

alter, cook (*infml*), tamper with, doctor, distort, pervert, misrepresent, misstate, forge, counterfeit, fake.

falter *verb*

totter, stumble, stammer, stutter, hesitate, waver, vacillate, flinch, quail, shake, tremble, flag, fail.

fame *noun*

renown, celebrity, stardom, prominence, eminence, illustriousness, glory, honour, esteem, reputation, name.

Fa infamy.

familiar *adjective*

1 a familiar sight: everyday, routine, household, common, ordinary, well-known, recognizable.

2 don't like to get too familiar with clients: intimate, close, confidential, friendly, informal, free, free-and-easy, relaxed.

3 familiar with the procedure: aware, acquainted, abreast, knowledgeable, versed, conversant (*fml*).

Fa 1 unfamiliar, strange. 2 formal, reserved. 3 unfamiliar, ignorant.

familiarity *noun*

1 a relaxed familiarity among friends: intimacy, liberty, closeness, friendliness, sociability, openness, naturalness, informality.

2 familiarity with the procedures: awareness, acquaintance, experience, knowledge, understanding, grasp.

familiarize *verb*

accustom, acclimatize, school, train, coach, instruct, prime, brief.

family *noun*

1 her close family: relatives, relations,

kin, kindred, kinsmen, people, folk (*infml*), ancestors, forebears, children, offspring, issue, progeny (*fml*), descendants.

Members of a family include:

ancestor, forebear, forefather, descendant, offspring, heir; husband, wife, spouse, parent, father, dad (*infml*), daddy (*infml*), old man (*infml*), mother, mum (*infml*), mummy (*infml*), mom (*US informal*), grandparent, grandfather, grandmother, granny (*infml*), nanny (*infml*), grandchild, son, daughter, brother, half-brother, sister, half-sister, sibling, uncle, aunt, nephew, niece, cousin, godfather, godmother, godchild, stepfather, stepmother, foster-parent, foster-child.

---

2 a family of aristocrats: clan, tribe, race, dynasty, house, pedigree, ancestry, parentage, descent, line, lineage, extraction, blood, stock, birth.
3 zoological/botanical family: class, group, classification.

famine *noun*
starvation, hunger, destitution, want, scarcity, death.
E∃ plenty.

famous *adjective*
well-known, famed, renowned, celebrated, noted, great, distinguished, illustrious, eminent, honoured, acclaimed, glorious, legendary, remarkable, notable, prominent, signal.
E∃ unheard-of, unknown, obscure.

fan[1] *noun*
used a fan on hot summer days: extractor fan, ventilator, air-conditioner, blower, propeller, vane.
▶ *verb*
1 fan oneself: cool, ventilate, air, air-condition, air-cool, blow, refresh.
2 fan the flames: increase, provoke, stimulate, rouse, arouse, excite, agitate, stir up, work up, whip up.

fan[2] *noun*
a football fan/she's a fan of his: enthusiast, admirer, supporter, follower, adherent, devotee, lover, buff (*infml*), fiend (*infml*), freak (*infml*).

fanatic *noun*
zealot, devotee, enthusiast, addict, fiend, freak, maniac, visionary, bigot, extremist, militant, activist.

fanatical *adjective*
overenthusiastic, extreme, passionate, zealous, fervent, burning, mad, wild, frenzied, rabid, obsessive, single-minded, bigoted, visionary.
E∃ moderate, unenthusiastic.

fanciful *adjective*
imaginary, mythical, fabulous, fantastic, visionary, romantic, fairy-tale, airy-fairy, vaporous, whimsical, wild, extravagant, curious.
E∃ real, ordinary.

fancy *verb*
1 fancy a nice piece of cheese: like, be attracted to, take a liking to, take to, go for, prefer, favour, desire, wish for, long for, yearn for.
2 he fancied himself as a bit of an actor: think, conceive, imagine, dream of, picture, conjecture, believe, suppose, reckon, guess.
E∃ **1** dislike.
▶ *adjective*
elaborate, ornate, decorated, ornamented, rococo, baroque, elegant, extravagant, fantastic, fanciful, far-fetched.
E∃ plain.
▶ *noun*
idea, notion, whim.

fantastic *adjective*
1 a fantastic sight: wonderful, marvellous, sensational, superb, excellent, first-rate, tremendous, terrific, great, incredible, unbelievable, overwhelming, enormous, extreme, cool (*infml*).
2 fantastic creatures: strange, weird, odd, exotic, outlandish, fanciful, fabulous, imaginative, visionary.
E∃ **1** ordinary. **2** real.

fantasy *noun*
dream, daydream, reverie, pipe-dream, nightmare, vision, hallucination, illusion, mirage, apparition, invention, fancy, flight of fancy, delusion,

misconception, imagination, unreality.
₣∃ reality.

far *adverb*
a long way, a good way, miles (*infml*),
much, greatly, considerably, extremely,
decidedly, incomparably.
₣∃ near, close.
▶ *adjective*
distant, far-off, faraway, far-flung,
outlying, remote, out-of-the-way, god-
forsaken, removed, far-removed,
further, opposite, other.
₣∃ nearby, close.

farce *noun*
1 tragedy and farce: comedy, slapstick,
buffoonery, satire, burlesque.
2 the whole thing was a farce: travesty,
sham, parody, joke, mockery,
ridiculousness, absurdity, nonsense.

fare *noun*
charge, cost, price, fee, passage.

far-fetched *adjective*
implausible, improbable, unlikely,
dubious, incredible, unbelievable,
fantastic, preposterous, crazy,
unrealistic.
₣∃ plausible.

farm *noun*
ranch, farmstead, grange, homestead,
station, land, holding, acreage, acres.
▶ *verb*
cultivate, till, work the land, plant,
operate.

fascinate *verb*
absorb, engross, intrigue, delight,
charm, captivate, spellbind, enthral,
rivet, transfix, hypnotize, mesmerize.
₣∃ bore, repel.

fascination *noun*
interest, attraction, lure, magnetism,
pull, charm, enchantment, spell,
sorcery, magic.
₣∃ boredom, repulsion.

fashion *noun*
1 the latest fashion(s): vogue, trend,
mode, style, fad, craze, rage (*infml*),
latest (*infml*), custom, convention.
2 in the same fashion: manner, way,
method, mode, style, shape, form,
pattern, line, cut, look, appearance,
type, sort, kind.
▶ *verb*

create, form, shape, mould, model,
design, fit, tailor, alter, adjust, adapt,
suit.

fashionable *adjective*
chic, smart, elegant, stylish, modish, à
la mode, in vogue, trendy (*infml*), in, all
the rage (*infml*), popular, prevailing,
current, latest, up-to-the-minute,
contemporary, modern, up-to-date.
₣∃ unfashionable.

fast[1] *adjective*
a fast car/pace: quick, swift, rapid,
brisk, accelerated, speedy, nippy
(*infml*), hasty, hurried, flying.
₣∃ slow, unhurried.
▶ *adverb*
run fast: quickly, swiftly, rapidly,
speedily, like a flash, like a shot, hastily,
hurriedly, apace, presto.
₣∃ slowly, gradually.
⇨ *See also* **Word Study** *panel.*

fast[2] *verb*
fast for a week: go hungry, diet, starve,
abstain.

fasten *verb*
fix, affix, attach, clamp, grip, anchor,
rivet, nail, pin, clip, tack, seal, close,
shut, lock, bolt, secure, tie, bind, chain,
link, interlock, connect, join, unite, do
up, button, lace, buckle.
₣∃ unfasten, untie.

fat *adjective*
plump, obese, tubby, stout, corpulent,
portly, round, rotund, paunchy, pot-
bellied, overweight, heavy, beefy, solid,
chubby, podgy, fleshy, flabby, gross.
₣∃ thin, slim, poor.

fatal *adjective*
deadly, lethal, mortal, killing,
incurable, malignant, terminal, final,
destructive, calamitous, catastrophic,
disastrous.
₣∃ harmless.

fate *noun*
destiny, providence, chance, future,
fortune, horoscope, stars, lot, doom,
end, outcome, ruin, destruction, death.

fateful *adjective*
crucial, critical, decisive, important,
momentous, significant, fatal, lethal,
disastrous.
₣∃ unimportant.

WORD study

fast

There are many colourful and informal phrases used to express how **fast** something happens or is done. Try out some of those listed below.

do something at a fast pace

as fast as your legs can carry you
at full pelt
fast and furious
like blazes
like crazy
like a shot

at breakneck speed
at full tilt
like a bat out of hell
like a bomb
like greased lightning

do something in very little time

in the blink/wink of an eye
in two shakes
just like that

quick as a flash
in no time at all
in the twinkling of an eye

father *noun*
1 this is my father : parent, begetter (*fml*), procreator (*fml*), progenitor (*fml*), sire (*fml*), papa, dad (*infml*), daddy (*infml*), old man (*infml*), patriarch, elder, forefather, ancestor, forebear, predecessor.
2 the father of steam : founder, creator, originator, inventor, maker, architect, author, patron, leader, prime mover.
3 the holy father : priest, padre.

fathom *verb*
understand, comprehend, grasp, see, work out, get to the bottom of, interpret.

fatigue *noun*
tiredness, weariness, exhaustion, lethargy, listlessness, lassitude, weakness, debility.
F∃ energy.
▶ *verb*
tire, wear out, weary, exhaust, drain, weaken, debilitate.

fault *noun*
1 we like her despite her faults : defect,

flaw, blemish, imperfection, deficiency, shortcoming, weakness, failing, foible, negligence, omission, oversight.
2 a fault in the manuscript : error, mistake, blunder, slip-up (*infml*), slip, lapse, misdeed, offence, wrong, sin.
3 it's your fault : responsibility, accountability, liability, culpability.
▶ *verb*
find fault with, pick holes in, criticize, knock (*infml*), impugn (*fml*), censure, blame, call to account.
F∃ praise.
◆ **at fault** (in the) wrong, blameworthy, to blame, responsible, guilty, culpable.

faultless *adjective*
perfect, flawless, unblemished, spotless, immaculate, unsullied, pure, blameless, exemplary, model, correct, accurate.
F∃ faulty, imperfect, flawed.

faulty *adjective*
imperfect, defective, flawed,

blemished, damaged, impaired, out of order, broken, wrong.
F3 faultless.

favour *noun*
1 find favour with some powerful people: approval, esteem, support, backing, sympathy, goodwill, patronage, favouritism, preference, partiality.
2 he did me a favour: kindness, service, good turn, courtesy.
F3 1 disapproval.
▸ *verb*
1 favoured the Labour candidate: prefer, choose, opt for, like, approve, support, back, advocate, champion.
2 favouring poorer workers: help, assist, aid, benefit, promote, encourage.
F3 1 dislike. **2** mistreat.
◆ **in favour of** for, supporting, on the side of.
F3 against.

favourable *adjective*
beneficial, advantageous, helpful, fit, suitable, convenient, timely, opportune, good, fair, promising, auspicious, hopeful, positive, encouraging, complimentary, enthusiastic, friendly, amicable, well-disposed, kind, sympathetic, understanding, reassuring.
F3 unfavourable, unhelpful, negative.

favourite *adjective*
preferred, favoured, pet, best-loved, dearest, beloved, esteemed, chosen.
F3 hated.
▸ *noun*
preference, choice, pick, pet, blue-eyed boy, teacher's pet, the apple of one's eye, darling, idol.
F3 bête noire, pet hate.

favouritism *noun*
nepotism, preferential treatment, preference, partiality, one-sidedness, partisanship, bias, injustice.
F3 impartiality.

fear *noun*
alarm, fright, terror, horror, panic, agitation, worry, anxiety, consternation, concern, dismay,

distress, uneasiness, qualms, misgivings, apprehension, trepidation, dread, foreboding, awe, phobia, nightmare.
F3 courage, bravery, confidence.
▸ *verb*
take fright, shrink from, dread, shudder at, tremble, worry, suspect, anticipate, expect, foresee, respect, venerate.
⇨ *See also* **Word Study** *panel.*

fearful *adjective*
1 fearful of the outcome: frightened, afraid, scared, alarmed, nervous, anxious, tense, uneasy, apprehensive, hesitant, nervy, panicky.
2 a fearful storm: terrible, fearsome, dreadful, awful, frightful, atrocious, shocking, appalling, monstrous, gruesome, hideous, ghastly, horrible.
F3 1 brave, courageous, fearless. **2** wonderful, delightful.

feasible *adjective*
practicable, practical, workable, achievable, attainable, realizable, viable, reasonable, possible, likely.
F3 impossible.

feat *noun*
exploit, deed, act, accomplishment, achievement, attainment, performance.

feature *noun*
1 one of its most appealing features: aspect, facet, point, factor, attribute, quality, property, trait, lineament, characteristic, peculiarity, mark, hallmark, speciality, highlight.
2 a magazine feature: column, article, report, story, piece, item, comment.
▸ *verb*
1 featuring the best of British craftsmanship: show, present, promote, emphasize, highlight, spotlight, play up.
2 featured in several of his films: appear, figure, participate, act, perform, star.

fee *noun*
charge, terms, bill, account, pay, remuneration, payment, retainer, subscription, reward, recompense, hire, toll.

WORD study

fear

Fixed phrases, or idioms are used a lot to express strong feelings and emotions, such as **fear**. Try using some of those listed below to add interest or emphasis to your speech or writing.

frightening someone

give someone the shivers
make someone's blood run cold
make someone jump out of their skin
scare the living daylights out of someone

give someone the willies (*slang*)
make someone's hair stand on end
put the fear of God into someone

being frightened

be a bundle of nerves
be rooted to the spot
be shaking in your shoes
have a chill running down your spine
have the heebie-jeebies (*slang*)
shake like a leaf

be in fear of your life
be scared out of your wits
have butterflies
have your heart in your mouth
shake like jelly
turn to jelly

giving in to fear

bottle out (*slang*)
lose your nerve
wimp out (*US*)

get cold feet
take fright

coping with fear

brave it out

pluck up the courage

feeble *adjective*
1 a feeble voice: weak, faint, exhausted, frail, delicate, puny, sickly, infirm, powerless, helpless.
2 a feeble excuse/attempt: inadequate, lame, poor, thin, flimsy, ineffective, incompetent, indecisive.
F3 1 strong, powerful.

feed *verb*
1 enough to feed everyone: nourish, cater for, provide for, supply, sustain, suckle, nurture, foster, strengthen, fuel.
2 cattle feeding contentedly: graze, pasture, eat, dine.
▸ *noun*
food, fodder, forage, pasture, silage.

◆ **feed on** eat, consume, devour, live on, exist on.

feel *verb*
1 feel pain: experience, go through, undergo, suffer, endure.
2 felt the texture: touch, finger, handle, manipulate, hold.
3 feel soft: seem, appear.
4 feel it is too soon: think, believe, consider, reckon, judge.
5 felt a presence: sense, perceive, notice, observe, know.
▸ *noun*
1 the feel of silk: texture, surface, finish, touch.
2 has a feel of home: sense,

impression, feeling, quality.
◆ **feel like** fancy, want, desire.

feeling *noun*
1 a feeling of freedom/have a feeling
about someone : sensation,
perception, sense, instinct, hunch,
suspicion, inkling, impression, idea,
notion, opinion, view, point of view.
2 show their feelings : emotion,
passion, intensity, warmth,
compassion, sympathy,
understanding, pity, concern,
affection, fondness, sentiment,
sentimentality, susceptibility,
sensibility, sensitivity, appreciation.
3 a feeling of space and light : air, aura,
atmosphere, mood, quality.

fell *verb*
cut down, hew, knock down, strike
down, floor, level, flatten, raze,
demolish.

fellow *noun*
person, man, boy, chap (*infml*), bloke
(*infml*), guy (*infml*), individual,
character.
▸ *adjective*
co-, associate, associated, related, like,
similar.

female *adjective*
feminine, she-, girlish, womanly.
F3 male.

feminine *adjective*
female, womanly, ladylike, graceful,
gentle, tender.
F3 masculine.

fence *noun*
barrier, railing, paling, wall, hedge,
windbreak, guard, defence, barricade,
stockade, rampart.
▸ *verb*
surround, encircle, bound, hedge, wall,
enclose, pen, coop, confine, restrict,
separate, protect, guard, defend,
fortify.

fend for *verb*
look after, take care of, shift for,
support, maintain, sustain, provide
for.

fend off *verb*
ward off, beat off, parry, deflect, avert,
resist, repel, repulse, hold at bay, keep
off, shut out.

ferocious *adjective*
vicious, savage, fierce, wild, barbarous,
barbaric, brutal, inhuman, cruel,
sadistic, murderous, bloodthirsty,
violent, merciless, pitiless, ruthless.
F3 gentle, mild, tame.

ferry *verb*
transport, ship, convey, carry, take,
shuttle, taxi, drive, run, move, shift.

fertile *adjective*
fruitful, productive, generative,
yielding, prolific, teeming, abundant,
plentiful, rich, lush, luxuriant, fat.
F3 infertile, barren, sterile,
unproductive.

fertilize *verb*
1 fertilizing the eggs : inseminate,
pollinate.
2 fertilize land : enrich, feed, dress,
compost, manure, dung.

fervent *adjective*
ardent, earnest, eager, enthusiastic,
whole-hearted, excited, energetic,
vigorous, fiery, spirited, intense,
vehement, passionate, full-blooded,
zealous, devout, heartfelt,
impassioned, emotional, warm.
F3 cool, indifferent, apathetic.

festival *noun*
celebration, commemoration,
anniversary, jubilee, holiday, feast,
gala, fête, carnival, fiesta, party,
merrymaking, entertainment,
festivities.

festive *adjective*
celebratory, festal, holiday, gala,
carnival, happy, joyful, merry, hearty,
cheery, jolly, jovial, cordial, convivial.
F3 gloomy, sombre, sober.

festivity *noun*
celebration, jubilation, feasting,
banqueting, fun, enjoyment, pleasure,
entertainment, sport, amusement,
merriment, merrymaking, revelry,
jollity, joviality, conviviality.

fetch *verb*
1 fetch a bucket/fetch the doctor : get,
collect, bring, carry, transport, deliver,
escort.
2 fetched nearly £100 : sell for, go for,
bring in, yield, realize, make, earn.

fetching *adjective*
attractive, pretty, sweet, cute, charming, enchanting, fascinating, captivating.

fever *noun*
1 the fever subsided : feverishness, (high) temperature, delirium.
2 a fever of excitement : agitation, turmoil, unrest, restlessness, heat, passion, ecstasy.

feverish *adjective*
1 feeling feverish : delirious, hot, burning, flushed.
2 feverish activity : excited, impatient, agitated, restless, nervous, frenzied, frantic, overwrought, hectic, hasty, hurried.
E∃ 1 cool. 2 calm.

few *adjective*
scarce, rare, uncommon, sporadic, infrequent, sparse, thin, scant, scanty, meagre, inconsiderable, inadequate, insufficient, in short supply.
E∃ many.
▶ *pronoun*
not many, hardly any, one or two, a couple, scattering, sprinkling, handful, some.
E∃ many.

fibre *noun*
1 cotton fibres/muscle fibres : filament, strand, thread, nerve, sinew, pile.
2 moral fibre : character, calibre, backbone, strength, stamina, toughness, courage, resolution, determination.

fickle *adjective*
inconstant, disloyal, unfaithful, faithless, treacherous, unreliable, unpredictable, changeable, capricious, mercurial, irresolute, vacillating.
E∃ constant, steady, stable.

fictional *adjective*
literary, invented, made-up, imaginary, make-believe, legendary, mythical, mythological, fabulous, non-existent, unreal.
E∃ factual, real.

fictitious *adjective*
false, untrue, invented, made-up, fabricated, apocryphal, imaginary, non-existent, bogus, counterfeit,

spurious, assumed, supposed.
E∃ true, genuine.

fiddle *verb*
1 fiddling with her necklace : play, tinker, toy, trifle, tamper, mess around, meddle, interfere, fidget.
2 fiddling the books : cheat, swindle, diddle, cook the books (*infml*), juggle, manoeuvre, racketeer, graft.

fidget *verb*
squirm, wriggle, shuffle, twitch, jerk, jump, fret, fuss, bustle, fiddle, mess about, play around.

field *noun*
1 a field of corn/a football field : grassland, meadow, pasture, paddock, playing-field, ground, pitch, green.
2 in one's field of vision : range, scope, bounds, limits, confines.
3 not my field/an expert in the field : territory, area, province, domain, sphere, environment, department, discipline, speciality, line, forte.
3 trailing the rest of the field : participants, entrants, contestants, competitors, contenders, runners, candidates, applicants, opponents, opposition, competition.

fiend *noun*
1 you little fiend! : evil spirit, demon, devil, monster.
2 (*infml*) a health fiend : enthusiast, fanatic, addict, devotee, freak (*infml*), nut (*infml*).

fiendish *adjective*
devilish, diabolical, infernal, wicked, malevolent, cunning, cruel, inhuman, savage, monstrous, unspeakable.

fierce *adjective*
1 a fierce fighter : ferocious, vicious, savage, cruel, brutal, merciless, aggressive, dangerous, murderous, frightening, menacing, threatening, stern, grim, relentless.
2 fierce criticism : intense, passionate, raging, wild, strong, powerful, relentless.
E∃ gentle, kind, calm.

fiery *adjective*
1 a fiery sun : burning, afire, flaming, aflame, blazing, ablaze, red-hot, glowing, aglow, flushed, hot, torrid, sultry.

2 a fiery temperament: passionate, inflamed, ardent, fervent, impatient, excitable, impetuous, impulsive, hot-headed, fierce, violent, heated.
F₃ 1 cold. **2** impassive.

fight *noun*
1 a hard fight/a street fight: bout, contest, duel, combat, action, battle, war, hostilities, brawl, scrap, scuffle, tussle, struggle, skirmish, set-to, clash, engagement, brush, encounter, conflict, fray, free-for-all, fracas, riot, fisticuffs.
2 have a fight with the boss: quarrel, row, argument, dispute.
3 the fight for freedom: campaign, battle, struggle, crusade, drive.
▸ *verb*
1 fight a battle/an opponent: wrestle, box, fence, joust, brawl, scrap, scuffle, tussle, skirmish, combat, battle, do battle, war, wage war, clash, cross swords, engage, grapple, struggle, strive, contend.
2 the brothers seem to fight continuously: quarrel, argue, dispute, squabble, bicker, wrangle.
3 fight the proposals: oppose, contest, campaign against, resist, withstand, defy, stand up to.
◆ **fight back 1 fighting back might discourage the bullies**: retaliate, defend oneself, resist, put up a fight, retort, reply.
2 fight back tears: hold back, restrain, curb, control, repress, bottle up, contain, suppress.
◆ **fight off** hold off, keep at bay, ward off, stave off, resist, repel, rebuff, beat off, rout, put to flight.

fighter *noun*
combatant, contestant, contender, disputant, boxer, wrestler, pugilist, prizefighter, soldier, trouper, mercenary, warrior, man-at-arms, swordsman, gladiator.

figurative *adjective*
metaphorical, symbolic, emblematic, representative, allegorical, parabolic, descriptive, pictorial.
F₃ literal.

figure *noun*
1 write the amount in figures: number, numeral, digit, integer, sum, amount.
2 a figure in the distance/have the figure of a supermodel: shape, form, outline, silhouette, body, frame, build, physique.
3 public figure: dignitary, celebrity, personality, character, person.
4 see figure 5 below: diagram, illustration, picture, drawing, sketch, image, representation, symbol.
▸ *verb*
1 he figured it was nearly lunchtime: reckon, guess, estimate, judge, think, believe.
2 his character figured in several stories: feature, appear, crop up.
◆ **figure out** work out, calculate, compute, reckon, puzzle out, resolve, fathom, understand, see, make out, decipher.

file¹ *verb*
file a rough surface: rub (down), sand, abrade, scour, scrape, grate, rasp, hone, whet, shave, plane, smooth, polish.

file² *verb*
file a complaint: record, register, note, enter, process, store, classify, categorize, pigeonhole, catalogue.
▸ *noun*
keep a file of possible improvements: folder, dossier, portfolio, binder, case, record, documents, data, information.

file³ *verb*
file past: march, troop, parade, stream, trail.
▸ *noun*
a file of armoured vehicles: line, queue, column, row, procession, cortège, train, string, stream, trail.

fill *verb*
1 fill the trolley with groceries/crowds of people filling the narrow streets: stock, supply, furnish, satisfy, pack, crowd, cram, stuff, load, congest, block, clog, plug, bung, cork, stop, close, seal.
2 happy children's voices filled the air: pervade, imbue, permeate, soak, impregnate.
3 fill a post: take up, hold, occupy, discharge, fulfil.
F₃ 1 empty, drain.

◆ **fill in 1** fill in a form : complete, fill out, answer.

2 (*infml*) fill in for someone : stand in, deputize, understudy, substitute, replace, represent, act for.

3 (*infml*) filled them in on what was happening : brief, inform, advise, acquaint, update, bring up to date.

film *noun*
1 a black-and-white film : motion picture, picture, movie (*infml*), video, DVD, feature film, blockbuster (*infml*), short, documentary.
2 a thin film of dust/grease : layer, covering, dusting, coat, coating, glaze, skin, membrane, tissue, sheet, veil, screen, cloud, mist, haze.
▸ *verb*
photograph, shoot, video, videotape.

filter *verb*
strain, sieve, sift, screen, refine, purify, clarify, percolate, ooze, seep, leak, trickle, dribble.

filth *noun*
dirt, grime, muck, dung, excrement, faeces, sewage, refuse, rubbish, garbage, trash, slime, sludge, effluent, pollution, contamination, corruption, impurity, uncleanness, foulness, sordidness, squalor.
E3 cleanness, cleanliness, purity.

filthy *adjective*
dirty, soiled, unwashed, grimy, grubby, mucky, muddy, slimy, sooty, unclean, impure, foul, gross, sordid, squalid, vile, low, mean, base, contemptible, despicable.
E3 clean, pure.

final *adjective*
last, latest, closing, concluding, finishing, end, ultimate, terminal, dying, last-minute, eventual, conclusive, definitive, decisive, definite, incontrovertible, irreversible.
E3 first, initial.

finale *noun*
end, conclusion, close, curtain, epilogue, climax, dénouement, culmination, crowning glory.

finalize *verb*
conclude, finish, complete, round off, resolve, settle, agree, decide,

close, clinch, sew up (*infml*), wrap up (*infml*).

finally *adverb*
lastly, in conclusion, ultimately, eventually, at last, at length, in the end, conclusively, once and for all, for ever, irreversibly, irrevocably, definitely.

finance *noun*
economics, money management, accounting, banking, investment, stock market, business, commerce, trade, money, funding, sponsorship, subsidy.
▸ *verb*
pay for, fund, sponsor, back, support, underwrite, guarantee, subsidize, capitalize, float, set up.

finances *noun*
accounts, affairs, budget, bank account, income, revenue, liquidity, resources, assets, capital, wealth, money, cash, funds, wherewithal.

financial *adjective*
monetary, money, pecuniary, economic, fiscal, budgetary, commercial.

find *verb*
1 find the source of the Nile/find the answer : discover, locate, track down, trace, retrieve, recover, unearth, uncover, expose, reveal, come across, chance on, stumble on, meet, encounter, detect, recognize, notice, observe, perceive, realize, learn.
2 find peace : attain, achieve, win, reach, gain, obtain, get.
3 find it difficult : consider, think, judge, declare.
◆ **find out 1** find out his name : learn, ascertain, discover, detect, note, observe, perceive, realize.
2 find someone out : unmask, expose, show up, uncover, reveal, disclose, catch, suss out (*infml*), rumble (*infml*), tumble to (*infml*).

finding *noun*
1 explain their findings : find, discovery, breakthrough.
2 the findings of the court : decision, conclusion, judgement, verdict, pronouncement, decree, recommendation, award.

fine¹ *adjective*
1 a fine young man : excellent, outstanding, exceptional, superior, exquisite, splendid, magnificent, brilliant, beautiful, handsome, attractive, elegant, lovely, nice, good.
2 fine thread/stitching : thin, slender, sheer, gauzy, powdery, flimsy, fragile, delicate, dainty.
3 it all seems fine : satisfactory, acceptable, all right, OK (*infml*).
4 fine weather : bright, sunny, clear, cloudless, dry, fair.
E3 2 thick, coarse.

fine² *noun*
a parking fine : penalty, punishment, forfeit, forfeiture, damages.

finish *verb*
1 finishing the job : end, terminate, stop, cease, complete, accomplish, achieve, fulfil, discharge, deal with, do, conclude, close, wind up, settle, round off, top off, culminate, perfect.
2 finished the milk : use (up), consume, devour, eat, drink, exhaust, drain, empty.
E3 1 begin, start.
▸ *noun*
1 in at the finish : end, termination, completion, conclusion, close, ending, finale, culmination.
2 gives the wood a good finish : surface, appearance, texture, grain, polish, shine, gloss, lustre, smoothness.
E3 1 beginning, start, commencement.

finite *adjective*
limited, restricted, bounded, demarcated, terminable, definable, fixed, measurable, calculable, countable, numbered.
E3 infinite.

fire *noun*
1 a blazing fire : flames, blaze, bonfire, conflagration, inferno, burning, combustion.
2 lit a fire in his heart : passion, feeling, excitement, enthusiasm, spirit, intensity, heat, radiance, sparkle.
▸ *verb*
1 fired the boiler : ignite, light, kindle, set fire to, set on fire, set alight.
2 fire a missile : shoot, launch, set off,

let off, detonate, explode, discharge.
3 (*infml*) fired his press officer : dismiss, discharge, sack (*infml*), eject.
4 firing them with enthusiasm : excite, whet, enliven, galvanize, electrify, stir, arouse, rouse, stimulate, inspire, incite, spark off, trigger off.
◆ **on fire** burning, alight, ignited, flaming, in flames, aflame, blazing, ablaze, fiery.

firm¹ *adjective*
1 a firm mattress : dense, compressed, compact, concentrated, set, solid, hard, unyielding, stiff, rigid, inflexible.
2 a firm foundation : fixed, embedded, fast, tight, secure, fastened, anchored, immovable, motionless, stationary, steady, stable, sturdy, strong.
3 firm control : adamant, unshakable, resolute, determined, dogged, unwavering, strict, constant, steadfast, staunch, dependable, true, sure, convinced, definite, settled, committed.
E3 1 soft, flabby. **2** unsteady. **3** hesitant.

firm² *noun*
a family firm : company, corporation, business, enterprise, concern, house, establishment, institution, organization, association, partnership, syndicate, conglomerate.

first *adjective*
1 the first day at school/not know the first thing about it : initial, opening, introductory, preliminary, elementary, primary, basic, fundamental.
2 the first humans : original, earliest, earlier, prior, primitive, primeval, oldest, eldest, senior.
3 Scotland's first minister : chief, main, key, cardinal, principal, head, leading, ruling, sovereign, highest, uppermost, paramount, prime, predominant, pre-eminent.
E3 1 last, final.
▸ *adverb*
initially, to begin with, to start with, at the outset, beforehand, originally, in preference, rather, sooner.

first name *noun*
forename, Christian name, baptismal name, given name.

fish

Types of fish, shellfish and crustaceans include:

bloater, brisling, cod, coley, Dover sole, haddock, hake, halibut, herring, kipper, mackerel, pilchard, plaice, rainbow trout, ray, salmon, sardine, sole, sprat, trout, tuna, turbot, whitebait; bass, Bombay duck, bream, brill, carp, catfish, chub, conger eel, cuttlefish, dab, dace, dogfish, dory, eel, goldfish, guppy, marlin, minnow, monkfish, mullet, octopus, perch, pike, piranha, roach, shark, skate, snapper, squid, stickleback, stingray, sturgeon, swordfish, tench, whiting; clam, cockle, crab, crayfish, crawfish (*US*), king prawn, lobster, mussel, oyster, prawn, scallop, shrimp, whelk.

► *verb*

angle, trawl, delve, hunt, seek, invite, solicit.

◆ **fish out** produce, take out, extract, find, come up with, dredge up, haul up.

fit¹ *adjective*

1 *fit for use*: suitable, appropriate, apt, fitting, correct, right, proper, ready, prepared, able, capable, competent, qualified, eligible, worthy.
2 *fit and well*: healthy, well, able-bodied, in good form, in good shape, sound, sturdy, strong, robust, hale and hearty.
E3 1 unsuitable, unworthy. 2 unfit.

► *verb*

1 *the key fits the lock/fits the description*: match, correspond, conform, follow, agree, concur, tally, suit, harmonize, go, belong, dovetail, interlock, join, meet, arrange, place, position, accommodate.
2 *fit the job to the person, not the person to the job*: alter, modify, change, adjust, adapt, tailor, shape, fashion.

fit² *noun*

have a fit: seizure, convulsion, spasm, paroxysm, attack, outbreak, bout, spell, burst, surge, outburst, eruption, explosion.

fitful *adjective*

sporadic, intermittent, occasional, spasmodic, erratic, irregular, uneven, broken, disturbed.
E3 steady, regular.

fitting *adjective*

apt, appropriate, suitable, fit, correct, right, proper, seemly, meet (*fml*), desirable, deserved.
E3 unsuitable, improper.

fix *verb*

1 *fixing it to the wall*: fasten, secure, tie, bind, attach, join, connect, link, couple, anchor, pin, nail, rivet, stick, glue, cement, set, harden, solidify, stiffen, stabilize, plant, root, implant, embed, establish, install, place, locate, position.
2 *fix a date*: arrange, set, specify, define, agree on, decide, determine, settle, resolve, finalize.
3 *fix the broken chair*: mend, repair, correct, rectify, adjust, restore.
E3 1 move, shift. 3 damage.

► *noun (infml)*

dilemma, quandary, plight, predicament, difficulty, hole (*infml*), corner, spot (*infml*), mess, muddle.

◆ **fix up** arrange, organize, plan, lay on, provide, supply, furnish, equip, settle, sort out, produce, bring about.

fixation *noun*

preoccupation, obsession, mania, fetish, thing (*infml*), infatuation, compulsion, hang-up (*infml*), complex.

fixed *adjective*

decided, settled, established, definite, arranged, planned, set, firm, rigid, inflexible, steady, secure, fast, rooted, permanent.
E3 variable.

fizzy *adjective*

effervescent, sparkling, aerated, carbonated, gassy, bubbly, bubbling, frothy, foaming.

flabby *adjective*

fleshy, soft, yielding, flaccid, limp, floppy, drooping, hanging, sagging, slack, loose, lax, weak, feeble.
E3 firm, strong.

flag *verb*

lessen, diminish, decline, fall (off),

abate, subside, sink, slump, dwindle, peter out, fade, fail, weaken, slow, falter, tire, weary, wilt, droop, sag, flop, faint, die.
F3 revive.

flair *noun*
skill, ability, aptitude, faculty, gift, talent, facility, knack, mastery, genius, feel, taste, discernment, acumen, style, elegance, stylishness, panache.
F3 inability, ineptitude.

flake *noun*
scale, peeling, paring, shaving, sliver, wafer, chip, splinter.

flamboyant *adjective*
showy, ostentatious, flashy, gaudy, colourful, brilliant, dazzling, striking, extravagant, rich, elaborate, ornate, florid.
F3 modest, restrained.

flame *noun*
1 held his frozen hands out to the flames: fire, blaze, light, brightness, heat, warmth.
2 the flame of nationalism: passion, ardour, fervour, enthusiasm, zeal, intensity, radiance.

flaming *adjective*
1 a flaming torch: burning, alight, aflame, blazing, fiery, brilliant, scintillating, red-hot, glowing, smouldering.
2 have a flaming row/flaming red hair: intense, vivid, aroused, impassioned, hot, raging, frenzied.

flammable *adjective*
inflammable, ignitable, combustible.
F3 non-flammable, incombustible, flameproof, fire-resistant.

flap *verb*
flutter, vibrate, wave, agitate, shake, wag, swing, swish, thrash, beat.
▸ *noun*
1 a flap of skin: fold, fly, lapel, tab, lug, tag, tail, skirt, aileron.
2 (*infml*) in a flap: panic, state (*infml*), fuss, commotion, fluster, agitation, flutter, dither, tizzy (*infml*).

flare *verb*
1 fire flared from the burning wells: flame, burn, blaze, glare, flash, flicker, burst, explode, erupt.

2 nostrils flaring: broaden, widen, flare out, spread out, splay.
◆ **flare up** erupt, break out, explode, blow up.

flash *noun*
beam, ray, shaft, spark, blaze, flare, burst, streak, gleam, glint, flicker, twinkle, sparkle, shimmer.
▸ *verb*
1 lightning flashed: beam, shine, light up, flare, blaze, glare, gleam, glint, flicker, twinkle, sparkle, glitter, shimmer.
2 the train flashed past: streak, fly, dart, race, dash.

flat[1] *adjective*
1 a flat plain/roof/colour: level, plane, even, smooth, uniform, unbroken, horizontal, low.
2 in a flat tone: dull, boring, monotonous, tedious, uninteresting, unexciting, stale, lifeless, dead, spiritless, lacklustre.
3 a flat refusal: absolute, utter, total, unequivocal, categorical, positive, unconditional, unqualified, point-blank, direct, straight, explicit, plain, final.
4 a flat tyre: punctured, burst, deflated, collapsed.
F3 1 bumpy, vertical. 3 equivocal.
◆ **flat out** at top speed, at full speed, all out, for all one is worth.

flat[2] *noun*
rent a flat: apartment, penthouse, maisonnette, tenement, flatlet, rooms, suite, bed-sit(ter).

flatten *verb*
1 flatten the ground with a roller: smooth, iron, press, roll, crush, squash, compress, level, even out.
2 flattened him with one punch: knock down, prostrate, floor, fell, demolish, raze, overwhelm, subdue.

flatter *verb*
praise, compliment, sweet-talk (*infml*), adulate, fawn, butter up (*infml*), wheedle, humour, play up to, court, curry favour with, soft-soap.
F3 criticize.

flavour *noun*
1 a sweet/fruity flavour: taste, tang,

smack, savour, relish, zest, zing (*infml*), aroma, odour.

2 has something of the flavour of an old cowboy movie: quality, property, character, style, aspect, feeling, feel, atmosphere.

3 the remark had a definite flavour of jealousy: hint, suggestion, touch, tinge, tone.

▶ *verb*

season, spice, ginger up, infuse, imbue.

flaw *noun*
defect, imperfection, fault, blemish, spot, mark, speck, crack, crevice, fissure, cleft, split, rift, break, fracture, weakness, shortcoming, failing, fallacy, lapse, slip, error, mistake.

flawed *adjective*
imperfect, defective, faulty, blemished, marked, damaged, spoilt, marred, cracked, chipped, broken, unsound, fallacious, erroneous.
F3 flawless, perfect.

flawless *adjective*
perfect, faultless, unblemished, spotless, immaculate, stainless, sound, intact, whole, unbroken, undamaged.
F3 flawed, imperfect.

fleck *noun, verb*
dot, spot, mark, speck, speckle, streak.

flee *verb*
run away, bolt, fly, take flight, take off, make off, cut and run, escape, get away, decamp, abscond, leave, depart, withdraw, retreat, vanish, disappear.
F3 stay.

fleeting *adjective*
short, brief, flying, short-lived, momentary, ephemeral, transient, transitory, passing, temporary.
F3 lasting, permanent.

flesh *noun*
body, tissue, fat, muscle, brawn, skin, meat, pulp, substance, matter, physicality.

flex *verb*
bend, bow, curve, angle, ply, double up, tighten, contract.
F3 straighten, extend.
▶ *noun*
cable, wire, lead, cord.

flexible *adjective*
1 flexible rod/limbs: bendable, bendy (*infml*), pliable, pliant, plastic, malleable, mouldable, elastic, stretchy, springy, yielding, supple, lithe, limber, double-jointed, mobile.
2 adopt a flexible approach: adaptable, adjustable, amenable, accommodating, variable, open, manageable, agreeable.
F3 1 inflexible, rigid. 2 inflexible.

flick *verb*
hit, strike, rap, tap, touch, dab, flip, jerk, whip, lash.
◆ **flick through** flip through, thumb through, leaf through, glance at, skim, scan.

flicker *verb*
flash, blink, wink, twinkle, sparkle, glimmer, shimmer, gutter, flutter, vibrate, quiver, waver.
▶ *noun*
flash, gleam, glint, twinkle, glimmer, spark, trace, drop, iota, atom, indication.

flight^1 *noun*
1 powered flight: flying, aviation, aeronautics, air transport, air travel.
2 a transatlantic flight: journey, trip, voyage.

flight^2 *noun*
the flight into Israel: fleeing, escape, getaway, breakaway, exit, departure, exodus, retreat.

flimsy *adjective*
thin, fine, light, slight, insubstantial, ethereal, fragile, delicate, shaky, rickety, makeshift, weak, feeble, meagre, inadequate, shallow, superficial, trivial, poor, unconvincing, implausible.
F3 sturdy.

flinch *verb*
wince, start, cringe, cower, quail, tremble, shake, quake, shudder, shiver, shrink, recoil, draw back, shy away, duck, shirk, withdraw, retreat, flee.

fling *verb*
throw, hurl, pitch, lob, toss, chuck (*infml*), cast, sling, catapult, launch, propel, send, let fly, heave, jerk.

flip *noun, verb*
flick, spin, twirl, twist, turn, toss, jerk,
flap.

flippant *adjective*
facetious, light-hearted, frivolous,
superficial, offhand, flip, glib, pert,
saucy (*infml*), cheeky (*infml*),
impudent, impertinent, rude,
disrespectful, irreverent.
F∃ serious, respectful.

flirt *verb*
chat up, make up to, lead on, philander,
dally.
◆ **flirt with** consider, entertain, toy
with, play with, trifle with, dabble in,
try.

flit *verb*
dart, speed, flash, fly, wing, flutter,
whisk, skim, slip, pass, bob, dance.

float *verb*
1 float in the air: glide, sail, swim, bob,
drift, waft, hover, hang.
2 float a company on the stock
exchange: launch, initiate, set up,
promote.
F∃ 1 sink.

flock *verb*
herd, swarm, troop, converge, mass,
bunch, cluster, huddle, crowd, throng,
group, gather, collect, congregate.
▶ *noun*
herd, pack, crowd, throng, multitude,
mass, bunch, cluster, group, gathering,
assembly, congregation.

flood *verb*
1 the river burst its banks, flooding the
surrounding farmland: deluge,
inundate, soak, drench, saturate, fill,
overflow, immerse, submerge, engulf,
swamp, overwhelm, drown.
2 water flooding into the lock: flow,
pour, stream, rush, surge, gush.
▶ *noun*
deluge, inundation, downpour, torrent,
flow, tide, stream, rush, spate,
outpouring, overflow, glut, excess,
abundance, profusion.
F∃ drought, trickle, dearth.

floor *noun*
1 a wooden floor: flooring, ground,
base, basis.
2 on the third floor: storey, level, stage,
landing, deck, tier.
▶ *verb* (*infml*)
defeat, overwhelm, beat, stump (*infml*),
frustrate, confound, perplex, baffle,
puzzle, bewilder, disconcert, throw.

flop *noun*
failure, non-starter, fiasco, debacle,
wash-out (*infml*), disaster.
▶ *verb*
1 the play flopped: fail, misfire, fall
flat, founder, fold.
2 hair flopping over her eyes/flop
down on the floor: droop, hang,
dangle, sag, drop, fall, topple, tumble,
slump, collapse.

flounder *verb*
wallow, struggle, grope, fumble,
blunder, stagger, stumble, falter.

flourish *verb*
1 the business flourished: thrive, grow,
wax, increase, flower, blossom, bloom,
develop, progress, get on, do well,
prosper, succeed, boom.
2 flourishing a big stick: brandish,
wave, shake, twirl, swing, display,
wield, flaunt, parade, vaunt.
F∃ 1 decline, languish, fail.
▶ *noun*
display, parade, show, gesture, wave,
sweep, fanfare, ornament, decoration,
panache, pizzazz (*infml*).

flout *verb*
defy, disobey, violate, break, disregard,
spurn, reject, scorn, jeer at, scoff at,
mock, ridicule.
F∃ obey, respect, regard.

flow *verb*
1 a river flowing to the sea/words
flowing from his pen: circulate, ooze,
trickle, ripple, bubble, well, spurt,
squirt, gush, spill, run, pour, cascade,
rush, stream, teem, flood, overflow,
surge, sweep, move, drift, slip, slide,
glide, roll, swirl.
2 flowing from our original discussion:
originate, derive, arise, spring, emerge,
issue, result, proceed, emanate.
▶ *noun*
course, flux, tide, current, drift,
outpouring, stream, deluge, cascade,
spurt, gush, flood, spate, abundance,
plenty.

flower noun

1 wild flowers: bloom, blossom, bud, floret.

Flowers include:

African violet, alyssum, anemone, aster, aubrietia, azalea, begonia, bluebell, busy lizzie, calendula, candytuft, carnation, chrysanthemum, cornflower, cowslip, crocus, cyclamen, daffodil, dahlia, daisy, delphinium, forget-me-not, foxglove, freesia, fuchsia, gardenia, geranium, gladioli, hollyhock, hyacinth, iris, lily, lily-of-the-valley, lobelia, lupin, marigold, narcissus, nasturtium, nemesia, nicotiana, night-scented stock, orchid, pansy, petunia, pink, phlox, poinsettia, polyanthus, poppy, primrose, primula, rose, salvia, snapdragon, snowdrop, stock, sunflower, sweet pea, sweet william, tulip, verbena, viola, violet, wallflower, zinnia. ⇨See also **plant**.

2 the flower of Britain's youth: best, cream, pick, choice, élite.

▶ verb

bud, burgeon, bloom, blossom, open, come out.

flowery adjective

florid, ornate, elaborate, fancy, baroque, rhetorical.
F3 plain, simple.

fluctuate verb

vary, change, alter, shift, rise and fall, seesaw, ebb and flow, alternate, swing, sway, oscillate, vacillate, waver.

fluent adjective

flowing, smooth, easy, effortless, articulate, eloquent, voluble, glib, ready.
F3 broken, inarticulate, tongue-tied.

fluffy adjective

furry, fuzzy, downy, feathery, fleecy, woolly, hairy, shaggy, velvety, silky, soft.

fluid noun

liquid, solution, liquor, juice, gas, vapour.

▶ adjective

1 fluid lava: liquid, liquefied, aqueous, watery, running, runny, melted, molten.
2 a fluid situation: variable, changeable, unstable, inconstant, shifting, mobile, adjustable, adaptable, flexible, open.
3 fluid movements: flowing, smooth, graceful.
F3 **1** solid. **2** stable.

flurry noun

1 a sudden flurry of snow: burst, outbreak, spell, spurt, gust, blast, squall.
2 a flurry of activity: bustle, hurry, fluster, fuss, to-do, commotion, tumult, whirl, disturbance, stir, flap (infml).

flush verb

1 flushing with embarrassment: blush, go red, redden, crimson, colour, burn, glow, suffuse.
2 flush the impurities out: cleanse, wash, rinse, hose, swab, clear, empty, evacuate.

▶ adjective

1 (infml) feeling flush: rich, wealthy, moneyed, prosperous, well-off, well-heeled, well-to-do, abundant, lavish, generous, full, overflowing.
2 the door isn't flush: level, even, smooth, flat, plane, square, true.

fluster verb

bother, upset, embarrass, disturb, perturb, agitate, ruffle, discompose, confuse, confound, unnerve, put off, disconcert, rattle (infml), distract.
F3 calm.

flutter verb

flap, wave, beat, bat, flicker, vibrate, palpitate, agitate, shake, tremble, quiver, shiver, ruffle, ripple, twitch, toss, waver, fluctuate.

flux noun

fluctuation, instability, change, alteration, modification, fluidity, flow, movement, motion, transition, development.
F3 stability, rest.

fly verb

1 fly from tree to tree: take off, rise,

foam *noun*

ascend, mount, soar, glide, float, hover, flit, wing.

2 flew down the road : race, sprint, dash, tear, rush, hurry, speed, zoom, shoot, dart, career.

◆ **fly at** attack, go for, fall upon.

foam *noun*

froth, lather, suds, head, bubbles, effervescence.

▶ *verb*

froth, lather, bubble, effervesce, fizz, boil, seethe.

fob off *verb*

foist, pass off, palm off (*infml*), get rid of, dump, unload, inflict, impose, deceive, put off.

focus *noun*

focal point, target, centre, heart, core, nucleus, kernel, crux, hub, axis, linchpin, pivot, hinge.

▶ *verb*

converge, meet, join, centre, concentrate, aim, direct, fix, spotlight, home in, zoom in, zero in (*infml*).

foggy *adjective*

misty, hazy, smoggy, cloudy, murky, dark, shadowy, dim, indistinct, obscure.

E3 clear.

foil[1] *verb*

foil a plot : defeat, outwit, frustrate, thwart, baffle, counter, nullify, stop, check, obstruct, block, circumvent, elude.

E3 abet.

foil[2] *noun*

an excellent foil for the bright red flowers : setting, background, relief, contrast, complement, balance.

fold *verb*

1 fold the paper in half : bend, ply, double, overlap, tuck, pleat, crease, crumple, crimp, crinkle.

2 (*infml*) **the business folded** : fail, go bust, shut down, collapse, crash.

3 folding her in his arms : enfold, embrace, hug, clasp, envelop, wrap (up), enclose, entwine, intertwine.

▶ *noun*

bend, turn, layer, ply, overlap, tuck, pleat, crease, knife-edge, line, wrinkle, furrow, corrugation.

folk *adjective*

ethnic, national, traditional, native, indigenous, tribal, ancestral.

follow *verb*

1 night follows day : come after, succeed, come next, replace, supersede, supplant.

2 following the scent : chase, pursue, go after, hunt, track, trail, shadow, tail, hound, catch.

3 Mary's lamb follows her everywhere : accompany, go (along) with, escort, attend, tag along with.

4 doesn't necessarily follow : result, ensue, develop, emanate, arise.

5 follow the rules : obey, comply with, adhere to, heed, mind, observe, conform to, carry out, practise.

6 can't follow these instructions : grasp, understand, comprehend, fathom.

E3 1 precede. **3** abandon, desert. **5** disobey.

◆ **follow through** continue, pursue, see through, finish, complete, conclude, fulfil, implement.

◆ **follow up** investigate, check out, continue, pursue, reinforce, consolidate.

follower *noun*

attendant, retainer, helper, companion, sidekick (*infml*), apostle, disciple, pupil, imitator, emulator, adherent, hanger-on (*infml*), believer, convert, backer, supporter, admirer, fan, devotee, freak (*infml*), buff (*infml*).

E3 leader, opponent.

following *adjective*

subsequent, next, succeeding, successive, resulting, ensuing, consequent, later.

E3 previous.

▶ *noun*

followers, suite, retinue, entourage, circle, fans, supporters, support, backing, patronage, clientele, audience, public.

folly *noun*

foolishness, stupidity, senselessness, rashness, recklessness, irresponsibility, indiscretion, craziness, madness, lunacy, insanity, idiocy, imbecility,

silliness, absurdity, nonsense.
Eɜ wisdom, prudence, sanity.

fond of *verb*
partial to, attached to, enamoured of,
keen on, addicted to, hooked on.

food *noun*
foodstuffs, comestibles (*fml*), eatables
(*infml*), provisions, stores, rations, eats
(*infml*), grub (*infml*), nosh (*infml*),
refreshment, sustenance, nourishment,
nutrition, nutriment, subsistence, feed,
fodder, diet, fare, cooking, cuisine,
menu, board, table, larder.

fool *noun*
blockhead, fat-head, nincompoop
(*infml*), ass (*infml*), chump (*infml*),
ninny (*infml*), clot (*infml*), dope (*infml*),
twit (*infml*), nitwit (*infml*), nit (*infml*),
dunce, dimwit, simpleton, halfwit,
idiot, imbecile, moron, dupe, sucker
(*infml*), mug (*infml*), stooge, clown,
buffoon, jester.
▶ *verb*
deceive, take in, delude, mislead, dupe,
gull, hoodwink, put one over on
(*infml*), trick, hoax, con (*infml*), cheat,
swindle, diddle (*infml*), string along
(*infml*), have on (*infml*), kid (*infml*),
tease, joke.
◆ **fool about** play about, mess about
(*infml*), mess around (*infml*), horse
around (*infml*), lark about.

foolhardy *adjective*
rash, reckless, imprudent, ill-advised,
irresponsible.
Eɜ cautious, prudent.

foolish *adjective*
stupid, senseless, unwise, ill-advised,
ill-considered, short-sighted, half-
baked, daft (*infml*), crazy, mad, insane,
idiotic, moronic, hare-brained, half-
witted, simple-minded, simple,
unintelligent, inept, inane, silly,
absurd, ridiculous, ludicrous,
nonsensical.
Eɜ wise, prudent.

foolproof *adjective*
idiot-proof, infallible, fail-safe, sure,
certain, sure-fire (*infml*), guaranteed.
Eɜ unreliable.

foot *noun*
1 an animal's foot: paw, hoof, pad,
trotter, leg, toe, sole, heel.
2 the foot of the hill: bottom, far end,
limit, foundation, base.
Eɜ 2 head, top, summit.

footing *noun*
base, foundation, basis, ground,
relations, relationship, terms,
conditions, state, standing, status,
grade, rank, position, balance,
foothold, purchase.

forbid *verb*
prohibit, disallow, ban, proscribe,
interdict (*fml*), veto, refuse, deny,
outlaw, debar, exclude, rule out,
preclude, prevent, block, hinder,
inhibit.
Eɜ allow, permit, approve.

forbidden *adjective*
prohibited, banned, proscribed, taboo,
vetoed, outlawed, out of bounds.

forbidding *adjective*
stern, formidable, awesome, daunting,
off-putting, uninviting, menacing,
threatening, ominous, sinister,
frightening.
Eɜ approachable, congenial.

force *verb*
1 forced to leave: compel, make,
oblige, necessitate, urge, coerce,
constrain, press, pressurize, lean on
(*infml*), press-gang, bulldoze, drive,
propel, push, thrust.
2 forced a confession from him: prise,
wrench, wrest (*fml*), extort, exact,
wring.
▶ *noun*
1 using force to get what they want:
compulsion, impulse, influence,
coercion, constraint, pressure, duress,
violence, aggression.
2 the force of his will: power, might,
strength, intensity, effort, energy,
vigour, drive, dynamism, stress,
emphasis.
3 a large force of infantry: army, troop,
body, corps, regiment, squadron,
battalion, division, unit, detachment,
patrol.
Eɜ 2 weakness.

forced *adjective*
unnatural, stiff, wooden, stilted,
laboured, strained, false, artificial,

contrived, feigned, affected, insincere.
ᴇᴬ spontaneous, sincere.

forceful *adjective*
strong, mighty, powerful, potent,
effective, compelling, convincing,
persuasive, cogent, telling, weighty,
urgent, emphatic, vehement, forcible,
dynamic, energetic, vigorous.
ᴇᴬ weak, feeble.

foreboding *noun*
misgiving, anxiety, worry, dread,
apprehension, fear, omen, sign, token,
premonition, warning, prediction,
prognostication, intuition, feeling.

forecast *verb*
predict, prophesy, foretell, foresee,
anticipate, expect, estimate, calculate.
▸ *noun*
prediction, prophecy, expectation,
prognosis, outlook, projection, guess,
guesstimate (*infml*).

forefront *noun*
front, front line, firing line, van,
vanguard, lead, fore, avant-garde,
cutting edge.
ᴇᴬ rear.

foreign *adjective*
alien, immigrant, imported,
international, external, outside,
overseas, exotic, faraway, distant,
remote, strange, unfamiliar, unknown,
uncharacteristic, incongruous,
extraneous, borrowed.
ᴇᴬ native, indigenous.

foremost *adjective*
first, leading, front, chief, main,
principal, primary, cardinal,
paramount, central, highest,
uppermost, supreme, prime, pre-
eminent.

foresee *verb*
envisage, anticipate, expect, forecast,
predict, prophesy, prognosticate,
foretell, forebode, divine.

foresight *noun*
anticipation, planning, forethought,
far-sightedness, vision, caution,
prudence, circumspection, care,
readiness, preparedness, provision,
precaution.
ᴇᴬ improvidence.

forever *adverb*
continually, constantly, persistently,
incessantly, perpetually, endlessly,
eternally, always, evermore, for all
time, permanently.

forfeit *verb*
lose, give up, surrender, relinquish,
sacrifice, forgo, renounce,
abandon.
▸ *noun*
loss, surrender, confiscation, fine,
sequestration, penalty, damages.

forge *verb*
1 forge an agreement: make, mould,
cast, shape, form, fashion, beat out,
hammer out, work, create, invent.
2 forge a document: fake, counterfeit,
falsify, copy, imitate, simulate, feign.

forgery *noun*
fake, counterfeit, copy, replica,
reproduction, imitation, dud (*infml*),
phoney (*infml*), sham, fraud.
ᴇᴬ original.

forget *verb*
omit, fail, neglect, let slip, overlook,
disregard, ignore, lose sight of, dismiss,
think no more of, unlearn.
ᴇᴬ remember, recall, recollect.

forgetful *adjective*
absent-minded, dreamy, inattentive,
oblivious, negligent, lax, heedless.
ᴇᴬ attentive, heedful.

forgive *verb*
pardon, absolve, excuse, exonerate,
exculpate (*fml*), acquit, remit, let off,
overlook, condone.
ᴇᴬ punish, censure.

forgiving *adjective*
merciful, clement, lenient, tolerant,
forbearing, indulgent, kind, humane,
compassionate, soft-hearted, mild.
ᴇᴬ merciless, censorious, harsh.

forgo *verb*
give up, yield, surrender, relinquish,
sacrifice, forfeit, waive, renounce,
abandon, resign, pass up, do without,
abstain from, refrain from.
ᴇᴬ claim, indulge in.

fork *verb*
split, divide, part, separate, diverge,
branch (off).

forlorn *adjective*
deserted, abandoned, forsaken, forgotten, bereft, friendless, lonely, lost, homeless, destitute, desolate, hopeless, unhappy, miserable, wretched, helpless, pathetic, pitiable.
Ea cheerful.

form *verb*
1 form circles/letters: shape, mould, model, fashion, make, manufacture, produce, create, found, establish, build, construct, assemble, put together, arrange, organize.
2 a nest formed from twigs and moss: comprise, constitute, make up, compose.
3 scum forming on the surface of the water: appear, take shape, materialize, crystallize, grow, develop.
▶ *noun*
1 in the form of a dove: appearance, shape, mould, cast, cut, outline, silhouette, figure, build, frame, structure, format, model, pattern, design, arrangement, organization, system.
2 a form of punishment: type, kind, sort, order, species, variety, genre, style, manner, nature, character, description.
3 the sixth form: class, year, grade, stream.
4 on top form: health, fitness, fettle, condition, spirits.
5 know the form: etiquette, protocol, custom, convention, ritual, behaviour, manners.
6 fill in a form: questionnaire, document, paper, sheet.

formal *adjective*
1 formal clothes/a formal occasion: official, ceremonial, stately, solemn, conventional, orthodox, correct, fixed, set, regular.
2 rather formal in his manner: prim, starchy, stiff, strict, rigid, precise, exact, punctilious, ceremonious, stilted, reserved.
Ea 2 informal, casual.

formality *noun*
custom, convention, ceremony, ritual, procedure, matter of form, bureaucracy, red tape, protocol, etiquette, form, correctness,
propriety, decorum, politeness.
Ea informality.

formation *noun*
1 rock formations: structure, construction, composition, constitution, configuration, format, organization, arrangement, grouping, pattern, design, figure.
2 formation of a new political alliance: creation, generation, production, manufacture, appearance, development, establishment.

former *adjective*
past, ex-, one-time, sometime, late, departed, old, old-time, ancient, bygone, earlier, prior, previous, preceding, antecedent, foregoing, above.
Ea current, present, future, following.

formerly *adverb*
once, previously, earlier, before, at one time, lately.
Ea currently, now, later.

formidable *adjective*
daunting, challenging, intimidating, threatening, frightening, terrifying, terrific, frightful, fearful, great, huge, tremendous, prodigious, impressive, awesome, overwhelming, staggering.

formula *noun*
recipe, prescription, proposal, blueprint, code, wording, rubric, rule, principle, form, procedure, technique, method, way.

formulate *verb*
create, invent, originate, found, form, devise, work out, plan, design, draw up, frame, define, express, state, specify, detail, develop, evolve.

forsake *verb*
desert, abandon, jilt, throw over, discard, jettison, reject, disown, leave, quit, give up, surrender, relinquish, renounce, forgo.

forthcoming *adjective*
1 their forthcoming wedding: impending, imminent, approaching, coming, future, prospective, projected, expected.
2 she wasn't very forthcoming: communicative, talkative, chatty, conversational, sociable, informative,

forthright *adjective*
direct, straightforward, blunt, frank, candid, plain, open, bold, outspoken.
F3 devious, secretive.

fortify *verb*
1 fortify the castle: strengthen, reinforce, brace, shore up, buttress, garrison, defend, protect, secure.
2 fortified by the news: invigorate, sustain, support, boost, encourage, hearten, cheer, reassure.
F3 1 weaken.

fortitude *noun*
courage, bravery, valour, grit, pluck, resolution, determination, perseverance, firmness, strength of mind, willpower, hardihood, endurance, stoicism.
F3 cowardice, fear.

fortuitous *adjective* (*fml*)
accidental, chance, random, arbitrary, casual, incidental, unforeseen, lucky, fortunate, providential.
F3 intentional, planned.

fortunate *adjective*
lucky, providential, happy, felicitous (*fml*), prosperous, successful, well-off, timely, well-timed, opportune, convenient, propitious, advantageous, favourable, auspicious.
F3 unlucky, unfortunate, unhappy.

fortune *noun*
1 make his/a fortune: wealth, riches, treasure, mint (*infml*), pile (*infml*), income, means, assets, estate, property, possessions, affluence, prosperity, success.
2 fortune did not favour them: luck, chance, accident, providence, fate, destiny, doom, lot, portion, life, history, future.

forward *adjective*
1 the forward edge/movement: first, head, front, fore, foremost, leading, onward, progressive, go-ahead, forward-looking, enterprising.
2 that child is becoming too forward: confident, assertive, pushy (*infml*), bold, audacious, brazen, brash, barefaced, cheeky (*infml*), impudent,

impertinent, fresh (*infml*), familiar, presumptuous.
3 the crops are well forward for the time of year: early, advance, precocious, premature, advanced, well-advanced, well-developed.
F3 1 backward, retrograde. 2 shy, modest. 3 late, retarded.
▸ *adverb*
forwards, ahead, on, onward, out, into view.
▸ *verb*
1 forward his career: advance, promote, further, foster, encourage, support, back, favour, help, assist, aid, facilitate, accelerate, speed, hurry, hasten, expedite.
2 forward mail to her new address: dispatch, send (on), post, transport, ship.
F3 1 impede, obstruct, hinder, slow.

foster *verb*
raise, rear, bring up, nurse, care for, take care of, nourish, feed, sustain, support, promote, advance, encourage, stimulate, cultivate, nurture, cherish, entertain, harbour.
F3 neglect, discourage.

foul *adjective*
1 a foul smell: dirty, filthy, unclean, tainted, polluted, contaminated, rank, fetid, stinking, smelly, putrid, rotten, nauseating, offensive, repulsive, revolting, disgusting, squalid.
2 foul language: obscene, lewd, smutty, indecent, coarse, vulgar, gross, blasphemous, abusive.
3 a foul thing to have done: nasty, disagreeable, wicked, vicious, vile, base, abhorrent (*fml*), disgraceful, shameful.
4 foul weather: bad, unpleasant, rainy, wet, stormy, rough.
F3 1 clean. 4 fine.
▸ *verb*
1 foul the pavements: dirty, soil, stain, sully (*fml*), defile (*fml*), taint, pollute, contaminate.
2 drains fouled by leaves and litter: block, obstruct, clog, choke, foul up.
3 fouling his line on a sunken boat: entangle, catch, snarl, twist, ensnare.
F3 1 clean. 2 clear. 3 disentangle.

found verb
1 found a children's charity: start, originate, create, initiate, institute, inaugurate, set up, establish, endow, organize.
2 founded on careful research: base, ground, bottom, rest, settle, fix, plant, raise, build, erect, construct.

foundation noun
1 the statement has no foundation in truth: base, foot, bottom, ground, bedrock, substance, basis, footing.
2 the foundation of a new college: setting up, establishment, institution, inauguration, endowment, organization, groundwork.

founder[1] noun
the founder of the college: originator, initiator, father, mother, benefactor, creator, author, architect, designer, inventor, maker, builder, constructor, organizer.

founder[2] verb
ships foundering on the rocks/the business foundered: sink, go down, submerge, subside, collapse, break down, fall, come to grief, fail, misfire, miscarry, fall through, come to nothing.

fountain noun
1 a fountain of water: spray, jet, spout, spring, well, wellspring, reservoir, waterworks.
2 the fountain of all knowledge: source, origin, fount, font, fountain-head, wellhead.

fracture noun
break, crack, fissure, cleft, rupture, split, rift, rent, schism, breach, gap, opening.
▶ verb
break, crack, rupture, split, splinter, chip.
E∃ join.

fragile adjective
brittle, breakable, frail, delicate, flimsy, dainty, fine, slight, insubstantial, weak, feeble, infirm.
E∃ robust, tough, durable.

fragment noun /**frag**-ment/
piece, bit, part, portion, fraction, particle, crumb, morsel, scrap,

remnant, shred, chip, splinter, shiver, sliver, shard.
▶ verb /frag-**ment**/
break, shatter, splinter, shiver, crumble, disintegrate, come to pieces, come apart, break up, divide, split (up), disunite.
E∃ hold together, join.

fragrance noun
perfume, scent, smell, odour, aroma, bouquet.

fragrant adjective
perfumed, scented, sweet-smelling, sweet, balmy, aromatic, odorous.

frail adjective
delicate, brittle, breakable, fragile, flimsy, insubstantial, slight, puny, weak, feeble, infirm, vulnerable.
E∃ robust, tough, strong.

frailty noun
weakness, foible, failing, deficiency, shortcoming, fault, defect, flaw, blemish, imperfection, fallibility, susceptibility.
E∃ strength, robustness, toughness.

frame verb
1 framing an idea: compose, formulate, conceive, devise, contrive, concoct, cook up, plan, map out, sketch, draw up, draft, shape, form, model, fashion, mould, forge, assemble, put together, build, construct, fabricate, make.
2 her face was framed by golden curls: surround, enclose, box in, case, mount.
3 I've been framed: set up, fit up (infml), trap.
▶ noun
1 built on a steel frame: structure, fabric, framework, skeleton, carcase, shell, casing, chassis, construction, bodywork, body, build, form.
2 a picture frame: mount, mounting, setting, surround, border, edge.
◆ frame of mind state of mind, mood, humour, temper, disposition, spirit, outlook, attitude.

framework noun
structure, fabric, bare bones, skeleton, shell, frame, outline, plan, foundation, groundwork.

frank adjective
honest, truthful, sincere, candid, blunt,

open, free, plain, direct, forthright, straight, straightforward, downright, outspoken.
F3 insincere, evasive.

frankly *adverb*
to be frank, to be honest, in truth, honestly, candidly, bluntly, openly, freely, plainly, directly, straight.
F3 insincerely, evasively.

frantic *adjective*
agitated, overwrought, fraught, desperate, beside oneself, furious, raging, mad, wild, raving, frenzied, berserk, hectic.
F3 calm, composed.

fraud *noun*
1 charged with fraud: deceit, deception, guile, cheating, swindling, double-dealing, sharp practice, fake, counterfeit, forgery, sham, hoax, trick.
2 (*infml*) the healer turned out to be a fraud: charlatan, impostor, pretender, phoney (*infml*), bluffer, hoaxer, cheat, swindler, double-dealer, con man (*infml*).

fraudulent *adjective*
dishonest, crooked (*infml*), criminal, deceitful, deceptive, false, bogus, phoney (*infml*), sham, counterfeit, swindling, double-dealing.
F3 honest, genuine.

fray *noun*
brawl, scuffle, dust-up (*infml*), free-for-all, set-to, clash, conflict, fight, combat, battle, quarrel, row, rumpus, disturbance, riot.

frayed *adjective*
ragged, tattered, worn, threadbare, unravelled.

freak *noun*
1 a freak of nature: monster, mutant, monstrosity, malformation, deformity, irregularity, anomaly, abnormality, aberration, oddity, curiosity, quirk, caprice, vagary, twist, turn.
2 (*infml*) a cricket freak: enthusiast, fanatic, addict, devotee, fan, buff (*infml*), fiend (*infml*), nut (*infml*).
▶ *adjective*
abnormal, atypical, unusual, exceptional, odd, queer, bizarre, aberrant (*fml*), capricious, erratic,

unpredictable, unexpected, surprise, chance, fortuitous (*fml*), flukey (*infml*).
F3 normal, common.

free *adjective*
1 the free peoples of the world/she was free at last: at liberty, at large, loose, unattached, unrestrained, liberated, emancipated, independent, democratic, self-governing.
2 free time/is this seat free?: spare, available, idle, unemployed, vacant, unoccupied, empty.
3 free tickets: gratis, without charge, free of charge, complimentary, on the house.
4 a free run to the coast: clear, unobstructed, unimpeded, open.
5 free with money: generous, liberal, open-handed, lavish, charitable, hospitable.
F3 1 imprisoned, confined, restricted. 2 busy, occupied.
▶ *verb*
release, let go, loose, turn loose, set free, untie, unbind, unchain, unleash, liberate, emancipate, rescue, deliver, save, ransom, disentangle, disengage, extricate, clear, rid, relieve, unburden, exempt, absolve, acquit.
F3 imprison, confine.
◆ **free of** lacking, devoid of, without, unaffected by, immune to, exempt from, safe from.

freedom *noun*
1 freedom from oppression: liberty, emancipation, deliverance, release, exemption, immunity, impunity.
2 win their freedom: independence, autonomy, self-government, home rule.
3 allow them a certain amount of freedom: range, scope, play, leeway, latitude, licence, privilege, power, free rein, free hand, opportunity, informality.
F3 1 captivity, confinement. 3 restriction.

freely *adverb*
1 come freely: readily, willingly, voluntarily, spontaneously, easily.
2 give freely: generously, liberally, lavishly, extravagantly, amply, abundantly.

3 speak freely: frankly, candidly, unreservedly, openly, plainly.
F∃ 2 grudgingly. **3** evasively, cautiously.

freeze *verb*
1 the sea froze: ice over, ice up, glaciate, congeal, solidify, harden, stiffen.
2 freeze the meat: deep-freeze, ice, refrigerate, chill, cool.
3 freeze wages: stop, suspend, fix, immobilize, hold.
▶ *noun*
1 a sudden freeze: frost, freeze-up.
2 a freeze on production: stoppage, halt, standstill, shutdown, suspension, interruption, postponement, stay, embargo, moratorium.

freezing *adjective*
icy, frosty, glacial, arctic, polar, Siberian, wintry, raw, bitter, biting, cutting, penetrating, numbing, cold, chilly.
F∃ hot, warm.

freight *noun*
cargo, load, lading, pay-load, contents, goods, merchandise, consignment, shipment, transportation, conveyance, carriage, haulage.

frenzied *adjective*
frantic, frenetic, hectic, feverish, desperate, furious, wild, uncontrolled, mad, demented, hysterical.
F∃ calm, composed.

frenzy *noun*
1 drive him into a frenzy: turmoil, agitation, distraction, derangement, madness, lunacy, mania, hysteria, delirium, fever.
2 in a frenzy of activity: burst, fit, spasm, paroxysm, convulsion, seizure, outburst, transport, passion, rage, fury.
F∃ 1 calm, composure.

frequent *adjective*
1 frequent storms: numerous, countless, incessant, constant, continual, persistent, repeated, recurring, regular.
2 a frequent visitor: common, commonplace, everyday, familiar, usual, customary.
F∃ 1 infrequent.

▶ *verb*
visit, patronize, attend, haunt, hang out at (*infml*), associate with, hang about with (*infml*), hang out with (*infml*).

fresh *adjective*
1 fresh supplies: additional, other, supplementary, extra, more, further.
2 a fresh approach: new, novel, innovative, original, different, unconventional, modern, up-to-date, recent, latest.
3 a fresh breeze: refreshing, bracing, invigorating, brisk, crisp, keen, cool, fair, bright, clear, pure.
4 fresh fruit: raw, natural, unprocessed.
5 feeling fresh and clean: refreshed, revived, restored, renewed, rested, invigorated, energetic, vigorous, lively, alert.
6 don't be so fresh!: pert, saucy (*infml*), cheeky (*infml*), disrespectful, impudent, insolent, bold, brazen, forward, familiar, presumptuous.
F∃ 2 old, hackneyed. **4** dried, processed. **5** tired, stale.

freshen *verb*
1 a cool breeze freshening the humid air: air, ventilate, purify.
2 change the water to freshen the flowers: refresh, restore, revitalize, reinvigorate, liven, enliven, spruce up.
F∃ 2 tire.

fret *verb*
worry, agonize, brood, pine.

friction *noun*
1 some friction between workers and management: disagreement, dissension, dispute, disharmony, conflict, antagonism, hostility, opposition, rivalry, animosity, ill feeling, bad blood, resentment.
2 damage caused by friction: rubbing, chafing, irritation, abrasion, scraping, grating, rasping, erosion, wearing away, resistance.

friend *noun*
mate (*infml*), pal (*infml*), chum (*infml*), buddy (*infml*), crony (*infml*), intimate, confidant(e), bosom friend, soul mate, comrade, ally, partner, sidekick (*infml*) associate, companion, playmate, pen-

friend, acquaintance, well-wisher, supporter.
E3 enemy, opponent.

friendly *adjective*
1 friendly neighbours: amiable, affable, genial, kind, kindly, neighbourly, helpful, sympathetic, fond, affectionate, familiar, intimate, close, matey (*infml*), pally (*infml*), chummy (*infml*), companionable, sociable, outgoing, approachable, receptive, amicable, peaceable, well-disposed, favourable.
2 a friendly atmosphere: convivial, congenial, cordial, welcoming, warm.
E3 1 hostile, unsociable. **2** cold.

friendship *noun*
closeness, intimacy, familiarity, affinity, rapport, attachment, affection, fondness, love, harmony, concord, goodwill, friendliness, alliance, fellowship, cameraderie, comradeship.
E3 enmity, animosity.

fright *noun*
shock, scare, alarm, consternation, dismay, dread, apprehension, trepidation, fear, terror, horror, panic.

frighten *verb*
alarm, daunt, unnerve, dismay, intimidate, terrorize, scare, startle, scare stiff, terrify, petrify, horrify, appal, shock.
E3 reassure, calm.

frightening *adjective*
alarming, daunting, formidable, fearsome, scary, terrifying, hair-raising, bloodcurdling, spine-chilling, petrifying, traumatic.

frightful *adjective*
unpleasant, disagreeable, awful, dreadful, fearful, terrible, appalling, shocking, harrowing, unspeakable, dire, grim, ghastly, hideous, horrible, horrid, grisly, macabre, gruesome.
E3 pleasant, agreeable.

frilly *adjective*
ruffled, crimped, gathered, frilled, trimmed, lacy, fancy, ornate.
E3 plain.

fringe *noun*
1 on the fringes of society/the town: margin, periphery, outskirts, edge,

perimeter, limits, borderline.
2 a fringe of lace: border, edging, trimming, tassel, frill, valance.
▶ *adjective*
unconventional, unorthodox, unofficial, alternative, avant-garde.
E3 conventional, mainstream.

frisky *adjective*
lively, spirited, high-spirited, frolicsome, playful, romping, rollicking, bouncy.
E3 quiet.

fritter *verb*
waste, squander, dissipate, idle, misspend, blow (*infml*).

frivolity *noun*
fun, gaiety, flippancy, facetiousness, jest, light-heartedness, levity, triviality, superficiality, silliness, folly, nonsense.
E3 seriousness.

frivolous *adjective*
trifling, trivial, unimportant, shallow, superficial, light, flippant, jocular, light-hearted, juvenile, puerile (*fml*), foolish, silly, idle, vain, pointless.
E3 serious, sensible.

frolic *verb*
gambol, caper, romp, play, lark around, rollick, make merry, frisk, prance, cavort, dance.

front *noun*
1 the front of the building: face, aspect, frontage, façade, outside, exterior, facing, cover, obverse, top, head, lead, vanguard, forefront, front line, foreground, forepart, bow.
2 put on a front: pretence, show, air, appearance, look, expression, manner, façade, cover, mask, disguise, pretext, cover-up.
E3 1 back, rear.
▶ *adjective*
fore, leading, foremost, head, first.
E3 back, rear, last.
◆ **in front** ahead, leading, first, in advance, before, preceding.
E3 behind.

frontier *noun*
border, boundary, borderline, limit, edge, perimeter, confines, marches, bounds, verge.

frosty *adjective*
1 a frosty morning: icy, frozen, freezing, frigid, wintry, cold, chilly.
2 a frosty reception: unfriendly, unwelcoming, cool, aloof, standoffish, stiff, discouraging.
E3 warm.

froth *noun*
bubbles, effervescence, foam, lather, suds, head, scum.

frown *noun*
scowl, glower, dirty look (*infml*), glare, grimace.
▶ *verb*
scowl, glower, lour, glare, grimace.
◆ **frown on** disapprove of, object to, dislike, discourage.
E3 approve of.

frozen *adjective*
iced, chilled, icy, icebound, ice-covered, arctic, ice-cold, frigid, freezing, numb, solidified, stiff, rigid, fixed.
E3 warm.

frugal *adjective*
thrifty, penny-wise, parsimonious, careful, provident, saving, economical, sparing, meagre.
E3 wasteful, generous.

fruit

Varieties of fruit include:

apple, Bramley, Cox's Orange Pippin, crab apple, Golden Delicious, Granny Smith; pear, Conference, William; orange, Jaffa, clementine, mandarin, minneola, satsuma, Seville, tangerine; apricot, avocado, cherry, damson, grape, gooseberry, goosegog (*infml*), greengage, nectarine, peach, plum, rhubarb, sloe, tomato; banana, date, fig, grapefruit, guava, lemon, lime, kiwi fruit, kumquat, lychee, mango, olive, papaya, pawpaw, pineapple, pomegranate, star fruit, Ugli® fruit; melon, cantaloupe, Galia, honeydew, watermelon; bilberry, blackberry, blueberry, boysenberry, cranberry, elderberry, loganberry, raspberry, strawberry; blackcurrant, redcurrant.

fruitful *adjective*
1 a lush and fruitful land: fertile, rich, teeming, plentiful, abundant, prolific, productive.
2 a fruitful meeting: rewarding, profitable, advantageous, beneficial, worthwhile, well-spent, useful, successful.
E3 1 barren. 2 fruitless.

fruitless *adjective*
unsuccessful, abortive, useless, futile, pointless, vain, idle, hopeless, barren, sterile.
E3 fruitful, successful, profitable.

frustrate *verb*
1 frustrating their hopes for promotion: thwart, foil, baffle, block, check, spike, defeat, circumvent, forestall, counter, nullify, neutralize, inhibit.
2 frustrated by his failure: disappoint, discourage, dishearten, depress.
E3 1 further, promote. 2 encourage.

fuel *noun*
combustible, propellant, motive power.
▶ *verb*
incite, inflame, fire, encourage, fan, feed, nourish, sustain, stoke up.
E3 discourage, damp down.

fugitive *noun*
escapee, runaway, deserter, refugee.

fulfil *verb*
complete, finish, conclude, consummate, perfect, realize, achieve, accomplish, perform, execute, discharge, implement, carry out, comply with, observe, keep, obey, conform to, satisfy, fill, answer.
E3 fail, break.

fulfilment *noun*
completion, perfection, consummation, realization, achievement, accomplishment, success, performance, execution, discharge, implementation, observance, satisfaction.
E3 failure.

full *adjective*
1 full of water/people: filled, loaded, packed, crowded, crammed, stuffed, jammed.
2 the full range of colours: entire,

whole, intact, total, complete, unabridged, unexpurgated.

3 a full report/list: thorough, comprehensive, exhaustive, all-inclusive, broad, vast, extensive, ample, generous, abundant, plentiful, copious, profuse.

4 a full sound: rich, resonant, loud, deep, clear, distinct.

5 at full speed: maximum, top, highest, greatest, utmost.

E3 1 empty. 2 partial, incomplete. 3 selective. 4 thin, reedy.

full-grown *adjective*
adult, grown-up, of age, mature, ripe, developed, full-blown, full-scale.

E3 young, undeveloped, immature.

fully *adverb*
completely, totally, utterly, wholly, entirely, thoroughly, altogether, quite, positively, without reserve, perfectly.

E3 partly.

fumble *verb*
grope, feel, bungle, botch, mishandle, mismanage.

fume *verb*
1 the volcano fumed: smoke, smoulder, boil, steam.

2 fume with indignation: rage, storm, rant, rave, seethe.

fumes *noun*
exhaust, smoke, gas, vapour, haze, fog, smog, pollution.

fun *noun*
enjoyment, pleasure, amusement, entertainment, diversion, distraction, recreation, play, sport, game, foolery, tomfoolery, horseplay, skylarking, romp, merrymaking, mirth, jollity, jocularity, joking, jesting.

◆ make fun of rag, jeer at, ridicule, laugh at, mock, taunt, tease, rib (*infml*).

function *noun*
1 what's his function?: role, part, office, duty, charge, responsibility, concern, job, task, occupation, business, activity, purpose, use.

2 a formal function: reception, party, gathering, affair, do (*infml*), dinner, luncheon.

▶ *verb*
work, operate, run, go, serve, act, perform, behave.

functional *adjective*
working, operational, practical, useful, utilitarian, utility, plain, hard-wearing.

E3 useless, decorative.

fund *noun*
pool, kitty, treasury, repository, storehouse, store, reserve, stock, hoard, cache, stack, mine, well, source, supply.

▶ *verb*
finance, capitalize, endow, subsidize, underwrite, sponsor, back, support, promote, float.

fundamental *adjective*
basic, primary, first, rudimentary, elementary, underlying, integral, central, principal, cardinal, prime, main, key, essential, indispensable, vital, necessary, crucial, important.

funds *noun*
money, finance, backing, capital, resources, savings, wealth, cash.

funeral *noun*
burial, interment, entombment, cremation, obsequies, wake.

funnel *verb*
channel, direct, convey, move, transfer, pass, pour, siphon, filter.

funny *adjective*
1 a funny story: humorous, amusing, entertaining, comic, comical, silly, hilarious, witty, facetious, droll, farcical, laughable, ridiculous, absurd.

2 funny behaviour: odd, strange, peculiar, curious, queer, weird, unusual, remarkable, puzzling, perplexing, mysterious, suspicious, dubious.

E3 1 serious, solemn, sad. 2 normal, ordinary, usual.

furious *adjective*
1 he was furious with us: angry, mad (*infml*), up in arms (*infml*), livid, enraged, infuriated, incensed, raging, fuming, boiling.

2 a furious wind: violent, wild, fierce, intense, vigorous, frantic, boisterous, stormy, tempestuous.

E3 1 calm, pleased.

furnish *verb*
equip, fit out, decorate, rig, stock, provide, supply, afford, grant, give, offer, present.
F3 divest.

furniture *noun*
equipment, appliances, furnishings, fittings, fitments, household goods, movables, possessions, effects, things.

furrow *noun*
groove, channel, trench, hollow, rut, track, line, crease, wrinkle.
▶ *verb*
seam, flute, corrugate, groove, crease, wrinkle, draw together, knit.

further *adjective*
more, additional, supplementary, extra, fresh, new, other.
▶ *verb*
advance, forward, promote, champion, push, encourage, foster, help, aid, assist, ease, facilitate, speed, hasten, accelerate, expedite.
F3 stop, frustrate.

furthermore *adverb*
moreover, what's more, in addition, further, besides, also, too, as well, additionally.

furthest *adjective*
farthest, furthermost, remotest, outermost, outmost, extreme, ultimate, utmost, uttermost.
F3 nearest.

furtive *adjective*
surreptitious, sly, stealthy, secretive, underhand, hidden, covert, secret.
F3 open.

fury *noun*
anger, rage, wrath, frenzy, madness, passion, vehemence, fierceness, ferocity, violence, wildness, turbulence, power.
F3 calm, peacefulness.

fusion *noun*
melting, smelting, welding, union, synthesis, blending, coalescence, amalgamation, integration, merger, federation.

fuss *noun*
bother, trouble, hassle (*infml*), palaver, to-do (*infml*), hoo-ha (*infml*), furore, squabble, row, commotion, stir, fluster, confusion, upset, worry, agitation, flap (*infml*), excitement, bustle, flurry, hurry.
F3 calm.
▶ *verb*
complain, grumble, fret, worry, flap (*infml*), take pains, bother, bustle, fidget.

fussy *adjective*
1 fussy about what she eats: particular, fastidious, scrupulous, finicky, pernickety, difficult, hard to please, choosy (*infml*), discriminating.
2 a fussy pattern: fancy, elaborate, ornate, cluttered.
F3 **1** casual, uncritical. **2** plain.

futile *adjective*
pointless, useless, worthless, vain, idle, wasted, fruitless, profitless, unavailing, unsuccessful, abortive, unprofitable, unproductive, barren, empty, hollow, forlorn.
F3 fruitful, profitable.

future *noun*
hereafter, tomorrow, outlook, prospects, expectations.
F3 past.
▶ *adjective*
prospective, designate, to be, fated, destined, to come, forthcoming, in the offing, impending, coming, approaching, expected, planned, unborn, later, subsequent, eventual.
F3 past.

fuzzy *adjective*
1 fuzzy hair: frizzy, fluffy, furry, woolly, fleecy, downy, velvety, napped.
2 a fuzzy outline: blurred, unfocused, ill-defined, unclear, vague, faint, hazy, shadowy, woolly, muffled, distorted.
F3 **2** clear, distinct.

G

gadget *noun*

tool, appliance, device, contrivance, contraption, thing, thingumajig (*infml*), invention, novelty, gimmick.

gag *noun* (*infml*)

joke, jest, quip, crack, wisecrack, one-liner, pun, witticism, funny (*infml*).

gaiety *noun*

1 the gaiety of the occasion: happiness, glee, cheerfulness, joie de vivre, jollity, merriment, mirth, hilarity, fun, merrymaking, revelry, festivity, celebration, joviality, high spirits, light-heartedness, liveliness.
2 the gaiety of their costumes: brightness, brilliance, sparkle, colour, colourfulness, show, showiness.
E꿈 sadness, drabness.

gaily *adverb*

1 whistling gaily as he worked: happily, joyfully, merrily, blithely.
2 gaily coloured costumes: brightly, brilliantly, colourfully, flamboyantly.
E꿈 1 sadly. 2 dully.

gain *verb*

1 gain a place at university: secure, net, obtain, acquire, procure, reap, harvest, win, capture.
2 shares gained 20%: earn, make, produce, gross, net, clear, profit, yield, bring in.
3 gain one's objective: reach, arrive at, come to, get to, attain, achieve, realize.
4 gain speed: increase, pick up, gather, collect, advance, progress, improve.
E꿈 1 lose. 2 lose. 4 reduce.

◆ **gain on** close with, narrow the gap, approach, catch up, level with, overtake, outdistance, leave behind.

gale *noun*

1 gales and heavy rain forecast: wind, squall, storm, hurricane, tornado, typhoon, cyclone.
2 gales of laughter: burst, outburst, outbreak, fit, eruption, explosion, blast.

gallant *adjective*

chivalrous, gentlemanly, courteous, polite, gracious, courtly, noble, dashing, heroic, valiant, brave, courageous, fearless, dauntless, bold, daring.
E꿈 ungentlemanly, cowardly.

gallop *verb*

bolt, run, sprint, race, career, fly, dash, tear, speed, zoom, shoot, dart, rush, hurry, hasten.
E꿈 amble.

gamble *verb*

bet, wager, have a flutter (*infml*), try one's luck, punt, play, game, stake, chance, take a chance, risk, hazard, venture, speculate, back.

game¹ *noun*

1 enjoy sports and games: recreation, play, sport, pastime, diversion, distraction, entertainment, amusement, fun, frolic, romp, joke, jest.
2 the Olympic Games: competition, contest, match, round, tournament, event, meeting.
3 shoot wild game: game birds, animals, meat, flesh, prey, quarry, bag, spoils.

game² *adjective* (*infml*)

1 game for anything: willing, inclined, ready, prepared, eager.
2 a game attempt: bold, daring,

intrepid, brave, courageous, fearless, resolute, spirited.
F∃ 1 unwilling. **2** cowardly.

gang *noun*
group, band, ring, pack, herd, mob, crowd, circle, clique, coterie, set, lot, posse, team, crew, squad, shift, party.

gaol ⇨ *see* **jail**.

gap *noun*
1 gap in the clouds: space, blank, void, hole, opening, crack, chink, crevice, cleft, breach, rift, divide, divergence, difference.
2 gap in the conversation: break, interruption, recess, pause, lull, interlude, intermission, interval.

gape *verb*
1 gaping at the TV: stare, gaze, gawp (*infml*), goggle, gawk (*infml*).
2 beaks gaping: open, yawn, part, split, crack.

garbled *adjective*
confused, muddled, jumbled, scrambled, mixed up.

garish *adjective*
gaudy, lurid, loud, glaring, flashy, showy, tawdry, tacky, vulgar, tasteless.
F∃ quiet, tasteful.

gash *verb*
cut, wound, slash, slit, incise, lacerate, tear, rend, split, score, gouge.
▶ *noun*
cut, wound, slash, slit, incision, laceration, tear, rent, split, score, gouge.

gasp *verb*
pant, puff, blow, breathe, wheeze, choke, gulp.
▶ *noun*
pant, puff, blow, breath, gulp, exclamation.

gate *noun*
barrier, door, doorway, gateway, opening, entrance, exit, access, passage.

gather *verb*
1 gathering at the concert venue: congregate, convene, muster, rally, round up, assemble, collect, group, amass, accumulate, hoard, stockpile, heap, pile up, build.

2 I gather he's leaving: infer, deduce, conclude, surmise, assume, understand, learn, hear.
3 gathering the fabric at the waist: fold, pleat, tuck, pucker.
4 gather flowers/information: pick, pluck, cull, select, reap, harvest, glean.
F∃ 1 scatter, dissipate.

gathering *noun*
assembly, convocation (*fml*), convention, meeting, round-up, rally, get-together, jamboree, party, group, company, congregation, mass, crowd, throng, turnout.

gaudy *adjective*
bright, brilliant, glaring, garish, loud, flashy, showy, ostentatious, tinselly, glitzy (*infml*), tawdry, vulgar, tasteless.
F∃ drab, plain.

gauge *verb*
estimate, guess, judge, assess, evaluate, value, rate, reckon, figure, calculate, compute, count, measure, weigh, determine, ascertain.
▶ *noun*
1 the gauge of excellence: standard, norm, criterion, benchmark, yardstick, rule, guideline, indicator, measure, meter, test, sample, example, model, pattern.
2 a wider gauge of barrel: size, magnitude, measure, capacity, bore, calibre, thickness, width, span, extent, scope, height, depth, degree.

gaunt *adjective*
haggard, hollow-eyed, angular, bony, thin, lean, lank, skinny, scraggy, scrawny, skeletal, emaciated, wasted.
F∃ plump.

gawky *adjective*
awkward, clumsy, maladroit, gauche, inept, ungainly, gangling, unco-ordinated, graceless.
F∃ graceful.

gaze *verb*
stare, contemplate, regard, watch, view, look, gape, wonder.
▶ *noun*
stare, look.

gear *noun*
1 lifting gear: equipment, kit, outfit,

tackle, apparatus, tools, instruments, accessories.

2 engage first gear: gearwheel, cogwheel, cog, gearing, mechanism, machinery, works.

3 (*infml*) **pack their gear**: belongings, possessions, things, stuff (*infml*), baggage, luggage, paraphernalia.

4 (*infml*) **trendy gear**: clothes, clothing, garments, attire, dress, garb (*infml*), togs (*infml*), get-up (*infml*).

gel, jell *verb*
set, congeal, coagulate, crystallize, harden, thicken, solidify, materialize, come together, finalize, form, take shape.

gem *noun*
gemstone, precious stone, stone, jewel, treasure, prize, masterpiece, pièce de résistance.

general *adjective*
1 a general statement: broad, blanket, sweeping, all-inclusive, comprehensive, universal, global, total, across-the-board, widespread, prevalent, extensive, overall, panoramic.
2 a general feeling of ill-ease: vague, ill-defined, indefinite, imprecise, inexact, approximate, loose, unspecific.
3 the general opinion: usual, regular, normal, typical, ordinary, everyday, customary, conventional, common, public.
E₃ 1 particular, limited. 2 specific. 3 rare.

generally *adverb*
usually, normally, as a rule, by and large, on the whole, mostly, mainly, chiefly, broadly, commonly, universally.

generate *verb*
produce, engender, whip up, arouse, cause, bring about, give rise to, create, originate, initiate, make, form, breed, propagate.
E₃ prevent.

generation *noun*
1 the younger/older generation: age group, age, era, epoch, period, time.
2 generation of profits: production, creation, origination, formation,

genesis, procreation, reproduction, propagation, breeding.

generosity *noun*
liberality, munificence, open-handedness, bounty, charity, magnanimity, philanthropy, kindness, big-heartedness, benevolence, goodness.
E₃ meanness, selfishness.

generous *adjective*
1 a generous gesture: liberal, free, bountiful, open-handed, unstinting, unsparing, lavish.
2 a generous person: magnanimous, charitable, philanthropic, public-spirited, unselfish, kind, big-hearted, benevolent, good, high-minded, noble.
3 a generous allowance: ample, full, plentiful, abundant, overflowing, copious.
E₃ 1 mean, miserly. 2 selfish. 3 meagre.

genial *adjective*
affable, amiable, friendly, convivial, cordial, kindly, kind, warm-hearted, warm, hearty, jovial, jolly, cheerful, happy, good-natured, easy-going (*infml*), agreeable, pleasant.
E₃ cold.

genius *noun*
1 she's a mathematical genius: virtuoso, maestro, master, past master, expert, adept, egghead (*infml*), intellectual, mastermind, brain, intellect.
2 Einstein's genius: intelligence, brightness, brilliance, ability, aptitude, gift, talent, flair, knack, bent, inclination, propensity, capacity, faculty.

gentle *adjective*
1 a gentle person: kind, kindly, amiable, tender, soft-hearted, compassionate, sympathetic, merciful, mild, placid, calm, tranquil.
2 a gentle slope: gradual, slow, easy, smooth, moderate, slight, light, imperceptible.
3 a gentle breeze: soothing, peaceful, serene, quiet, soft, balmy.
E₃ 1 unkind, rough. 3 harsh, wild.

genuine *adjective*
real, actual, natural, pure, original,

authentic, veritable (*fml*), true, bona
fide, legitimate, honest, sincere, frank,
candid, earnest.
F3 artificial, false, insincere.

geography

*Terms used in geography
include:*

archipelago, base level, bergschrund,
chorography, cirque, col, continental
drift, deforestation, denudation,
ecosystem, effluent, equator, erosion,
estuary, fjord, floodplain, glacial,
glaciate, glaciation, hanging valley,
headwaters, ice cap, inlet, line of
latitude, line of longitude, Mercator's
projection, meridian, moraine, oxbow
lake, peneplain, permafrost, plateau,
plate tectonics, prime meridian,
prograde, ria, roche moutonée, shield
volcano, shott, stratum, taiga,
tributary, tundra, water cycle,
weathering, zenithal projection.

germ *noun*
1 catch germs: micro-organism,
microbe, bacterium, bacillus, virus,
bug (*infml*).
2 the germ of an idea: beginning, start,
origin, source, cause, spark, rudiment,
nucleus, root, seed, embryo, bud,
sprout.

germinate *verb*
bud, sprout, shoot, develop, grow,
swell.

gesticulate *verb*
wave, signal, gesture, indicate, sign.

gesture *noun*
act, action, movement, motion,
indication, sign, signal, wave,
gesticulation.
▶ *verb*
indicate, sign, motion, beckon, point,
signal, wave, gesticulate.

get *verb*
1 get a job/rise/letter: obtain, acquire,
procure, come by, receive, earn, gain,
win, secure, achieve, realize.
2 it's getting dark: become, turn, go,
grow.
3 get him to help: persuade, coax,

induce, urge, influence, sway.
4 getting home: move, go, come, reach,
arrive.
5 get the newspaper/get a bite to eat:
fetch, collect, pick up, take, catch,
capture, seize, grab.
6 get mumps: contract, catch, pick up,
develop, come down with.
F3 1 lose. **4** leave.
⇨ *See also* **Word Workshop** *panel.*

◆ **get across** communicate, transmit,
convey, impart, put across, bring home
to.
◆ **get ahead** advance, progress, get on,
go places (*infml*), thrive, flourish,
prosper, succeed, make good, make it,
get there (*infml*).
F3 fall behind, fail.
◆ **get along 1 how is he getting
along?**: cope, manage, get by, survive,
fare, progress, develop.
2 they don't get along well: agree,
harmonize, get on, hit it off.
◆ **get at 1 get at the truth**: reach,
attain, find, discover.
2 (*infml*) **get at the judge**: bribe,
suborn, corrupt, influence.
3 (*infml*) **what was he getting at?**:
mean, intend, imply, insinuate, hint,
suggest.
4 (*infml*) **getting at me all the time**:
criticize, find fault with, pick on,
attack, make fun of.
◆ **get away** escape, get out, break out,
break away, run away, flee, depart, leave.
◆ **get back** recover, regain, recoup,
repossess, retrieve.
◆ **get down** depress, sadden,
dishearten, dispirit.
F3 encourage.
◆ **get in** enter, penetrate, infiltrate,
arrive, come, land, embark.
◆ **get off 1 get off a train**: alight,
disembark, dismount, descend, get
down.
2 get those wet boots off: remove,
detach, separate, shed.
F3 1 get on. **2** put on.
◆ **get on 1 get on the bus**: board,
embark, mount, ascend.
2 how is she getting on at school?:
cope, manage, fare, get along, make
out, prosper, succeed.

3 must get on or I'll be late: continue, proceed, press on, advance, progress.
F3 1 get off.

◆ **get out 1 get out of prison**: escape, flee, break out, extricate oneself, free oneself, leave, quit, vacate, evacuate, clear out, clear off (*infml*).
2 she got out a pen: take out, produce.
◆ **get over 1 just got over measles**: recover from, shake off, survive.
2 get over these problems: surmount, overcome, defeat, deal with.
3 get her message over: communicate, get across, convey, put over, impart, explain.
◆ **get round 1 try to get round the problem**: circumvent, bypass, evade, avoid.
2 get round him easily: persuade, win over, talk round, coax, prevail upon.
◆ **get together** assemble, collect, gather, congregate, rally, meet, join, unite, collaborate.
◆ **get up** stand (up), arise, rise, ascend, climb, mount, scale.

ghastly *adjective*
awful, dreadful, frightful, terrible, grim, gruesome, hideous, horrible, horrid, loathsome, repellent, shocking, appalling.
F3 delightful, attractive.

ghost *noun*
spectre, phantom, spook (*infml*), apparition, visitant, spirit, wraith, soul, shade, shadow.

ghostly *adjective*
eerie, spooky (*infml*), creepy, supernatural, unearthly, ghostlike, spectral, wraith-like, phantom, illusory.

giant *noun*
monster, titan, colossus, ogre, Goliath, Hercules.
▶ *adjective*
gigantic, colossal, titanic, mammoth, jumbo (*infml*), humungous (*infml*), king-size, huge, enormous, immense, vast, large.

gibe, jibe *noun*
jeer, sneer, mockery, ridicule, taunt, derision, scoff, dig (*infml*), crack (*infml*), poke, quip.

giddy *adjective*
1 feel giddy: dizzy, faint, light-headed, unsteady, reeling, vertiginous (*fml*).
2 he can be a bit giddy: silly, flighty, wild.

gift *noun*
1 birthday gifts: present, offering, donation, contribution, bounty, largess, gratuity, tip, bonus, freebie (*infml*), legacy, bequest, endowment.
2 have a real gift: talent, genius, flair, aptitude, bent, knack, power, faculty, attribute, ability, capability, capacity.

gifted *adjective*
talented, adept, skilful, expert, masterly, skilled, accomplished, able, capable, clever, intelligent, bright, brilliant.

gigantic *adjective*
huge, enormous, immense, vast, giant, colossal, titanic, mammoth, gargantuan, humungous (*infml*), Brobdingnagian.
F3 tiny, Lilliputian.

giggle *verb, noun*
titter, snigger, chuckle, chortle, laugh.

gimmick *noun*
attraction, ploy, stratagem, ruse, scheme, trick, stunt, dodge, device, contrivance, gadget.

gingerly *adverb*
tentatively, hesitantly, warily, cautiously, carefully, delicately.
F3 boldly, carelessly.

girl *noun*
lass, young woman, girlfriend, sweetheart, daughter.

girth *noun*
1 a gradually expanding girth: circumference, perimeter, measure, size, bulk.
2 tighten the girth: strap, band.

gist *noun*
pith, essence, marrow, substance, matter, meaning, significance, import, sense, idea, drift, direction, point, nub, core, quintessence.

give *verb*
1 giving the prizes: present, award, confer, offer, lend, donate, contribute, provide, supply, furnish, grant, bestow,

The verb **get** is often overused. Try to avoid repeating it too often by consulting the list of synonyms below.

get something, eg money

acquire	obtain
earn	receive

get something, eg a prize

achieve	gain	win

get someone to do something

coax	influence	urge
convince	persuade	
induce	sway	

get someone or something from somewhere

acquire	fetch	seize
catch	procure	
collect	secure	

get to a destination

arrive	reach

come to be (rich, etc)

become	grow

get to do something

arrange	organize
manage	succeed

understand something

comprehend   realize

get a disease

catch   contract   pick up
come down with   develop

In the following passage, there are some suggestions for how synonyms from the list might be used to avoid repeating **get** (and its forms **getting** and **got**).

From:	Emma
To:	Pete
Cc:	
Subject:	Paul's visit

I just ~~got~~ [received] an e-mail from Paul. He said he might be able to ~~get~~ [persuade] his parents to let him visit for my birthday. I hope he can ~~get~~ [manage] to do it. I've asked him to ~~get~~ [buy] the latest CD by that new French band. I'm not sure if he ~~got~~ [understood] what I was asking for, because my French isn't that good. He's supposed to ~~get~~ [arrive] here on the 28 June.

I must go, my mother has ~~got~~ [come down with] the flu and I have to ~~get~~ [fetch] my brother from football practice.

Talk soon

Emma

endow, gift, make over, hand over, deliver, entrust, commit, devote.
2 give news: communicate, transmit, impart, utter, announce, declare, pronounce, publish, set forth.
3 must give you that: concede, allow, admit, yield, give way, surrender.
4 give trouble: cause, occasion, make, produce, do, perform.
5 give under their weight: sink, yield, bend, give way, break, collapse, fall.
F3 1 take, withhold. **5** withstand.
◆ **give away** betray, inform on, expose, uncover, divulge, let slip, disclose, reveal, leak, let out.
◆ **give in** surrender, capitulate, submit, yield, give way, concede, give up, quit.
F3 hold out.
◆ **give off** emit, discharge, release, give out, send out, throw out, pour out, exhale, exude, produce.
◆ **give out 1 give out leaflets**: distribute, hand out, dole out, deal.
2 it has been given out that: announce, declare, broadcast, publish, disseminate, communicate, impart, notify, advertise.
◆ **give up 1 give up chocolate/trying**: stop, cease, quit, resign, abandon, renounce, relinquish, waive.
2 give up their arms: surrender, capitulate, give in.
F3 1 start. **2** hold out.

given *adjective*
1 a given number: specified, particular, definite.
2 given to sudden rages: inclined, disposed, likely, liable, prone.

glad *adjective*
1 glad to hear you are better: pleased, delighted, gratified, contented, happy, joyful, merry, cheerful, cheery, bright.
2 glad to help: willing, eager, keen, ready, inclined, disposed.
F3 1 sad, unhappy. **2** unwilling, reluctant.

glamorous *adjective*
smart, elegant, attractive, beautiful, gorgeous, enchanting, captivating, alluring, appealing, fascinating, exciting, dazzling, glossy, colourful.
F3 plain, drab, boring.

glamour *noun*
attraction, allure, appeal, fascination, charm, magic, beauty, elegance, glitter, prestige.

glance *verb*
peep, peek, glimpse, view, look, scan, skim, leaf, flip, thumb, dip, browse.
▸ *noun*
peep, peek, glimpse, look.

glare *verb*
1 she was glaring at us: glower, look daggers, frown, scowl, stare.
2 blinded by the sunlight glaring off the water: dazzle, blaze, flame, flare, shine, reflect.

glaring *adjective*
blatant, flagrant, open, conspicuous, manifest, patent, obvious, outrageous, gross.
F3 hidden, concealed, minor.

glaze *verb*
coat, enamel, gloss, varnish, lacquer, polish, burnish.
▸ *noun*
coat, coating, finish, enamel, varnish, lacquer, polish, shine, lustre, gloss.

gleam *noun, verb*
glint, flash, beam, ray, flicker, glimmer, shimmer, sparkle, glitter, gloss, glow.

glib *adjective*
fluent, easy, facile, quick, ready, talkative, plausible, insincere, smooth, slick, suave, smooth-tongued.
F3 tongue-tied, implausible.

glide *verb*
slide, slip, skate, skim, fly, float, drift, sail, coast, roll, run, flow.

glimmer *verb*
glow, shimmer, glisten, glitter, sparkle, twinkle, wink, blink, flicker, gleam, shine.
▸ *noun*
1 the faint glimmer of moonlight: glow, shimmer, sparkle, twinkle, flicker, glint, gleam.
2 not a glimmer of hope: trace, hint, suggestion, grain.

glimpse *noun*
peep, peek, squint, glance, look, sight, sighting, view.

▶ *verb*

spy, espy, spot, catch sight of, sight, view.

glint *verb*

flash, gleam, shine, reflect, glitter, sparkle, twinkle, glimmer.

▶ *noun*

flash, gleam, shine, reflection, glitter, sparkle, twinkle, glimmer.

glisten *verb*

shine, gleam, glint, glitter, sparkle, twinkle, glimmer, shimmer.

glitter *verb*

sparkle, spangle, scintillate, twinkle, shimmer, glimmer, glisten, glint, gleam, flash, shine.

▶ *noun*

sparkle, coruscation, scintillation, twinkle, shimmer, glimmer, glint, gleam, flash, shine, lustre, sheen, brightness, radiance, brilliance, splendour, showiness, glamour.

gloat *verb*

triumph, glory, exult, rejoice, revel in, relish, crow, boast, vaunt, rub it in (*infml*).

global *adjective*

universal, worldwide, international, general, all-encompassing, total, thorough, exhaustive, comprehensive, all-inclusive, encyclopedic, wide-ranging.

🖼 parochial, limited.

globe *noun*

world, earth, planet, sphere, ball, orb, round.

gloom *noun*

1 gloom descended on the company : depression, low spirits, despondency, dejection, sadness, unhappiness, glumness, melancholy, misery, desolation, despair.
2 see nothing through the gloom : dark, darkness, shade, shadow, dusk, twilight, dimness, obscurity, cloud, cloudiness, dullness.

🖼 1 cheerfulness, happiness. 2 brightness.

gloomy *adjective*

1 feel gloomy about the results : depressed, down, low, despondent, dejected, downcast, dispirited, down-hearted, sad, miserable, glum, morose, pessimistic, cheerless, dismal, depressing.
2 a gloomy corner : dark, sombre, shadowy, dim, obscure, overcast, dull, dreary.

🖼 1 cheerful. 2 bright.

glorious *adjective*

1 a glorious victory : illustrious, eminent, distinguished, famous, renowned, noted, great, noble, splendid, magnificent, grand, majestic, triumphant.
2 a glorious summer day : fine, bright, radiant, shining, brilliant, dazzling, beautiful, gorgeous, superb, excellent, wonderful, marvellous, delightful, heavenly.

🖼 1 unknown.

gloss *noun*

polish, varnish, lustre, sheen, shine, brightness, brilliance, show, appearance, semblance, surface, front, façade, veneer, window-dressing.

◆ **gloss over** conceal, hide, veil, mask, disguise, camouflage, cover up, whitewash, explain away.

glossy *adjective*

shiny, sheeny, lustrous, sleek, silky, smooth, glassy, polished, burnished, glazed, enamelled, bright, shining, brilliant.

🖼 matt.

glow *noun*

1 the glow from the lamp : light, gleam, glimmer, radiance, luminosity, brightness, vividness, brilliance, splendour.
2 romantic glow : ardour, fervour, intensity, warmth, passion, enthusiasm, excitement.
3 give a healthy glow to their skin : flush, blush, rosiness, redness, burning.

▶ *verb*

1 lamp glowing in the window : shine, radiate, gleam, glimmer, burn, smoulder.
2 their faces glowed : flush, blush, colour, redden.

glowing *adjective*

1 glowing embers : bright, luminous,

vivid, vibrant, rich, warm, flushed, red, flaming.

2 a glowing review: complimentary, enthusiastic, ecstatic, rhapsodic, rave (*infml*).

E3 1 dull, colourless. **2** restrained.

glue *noun*
adhesive, gum, paste, size, cement.
▸ *verb*
stick, affix, gum, paste, seal, bond, cement, fix.

glut *noun*
surplus, excess, superfluity, surfeit, overabundance, superabundance, saturation, overflow.

E3 scarcity, lack.

glutton *noun*
gourmand, gourmandizer (*fml*), guzzler, gorger, gobbler, pig.

E3 ascetic.

gnarled *adjective*
gnarly, knotted, knotty, twisted, contorted, distorted, rough, rugged, weather-beaten.

gnaw *verb*
1 mice gnawed a hole in the bag: bite, nibble, munch, chew, eat, devour, consume, erode, wear.

2 thought gnawing away at the back of his mind: worry, niggle, fret, trouble, plague, nag, prey, haunt.

go *verb*
1 go to school/go immediately: move, pass, advance, progress, proceed, make for, travel, journey, start, begin, depart, leave, take one's leave, retreat, withdraw, disappear, vanish.

2 the engine was still going: operate, function, work, run, act, perform.

3 going from left to right: extend, spread, stretch, reach, span, continue, unfold.

4 time goes quickly: pass, elapse, lapse, roll on.

E3 2 break down, fail.

⇨ *See also* **Word Workshop** *panel.*

▸ *noun* (*infml*)
1 have a go: attempt, try, shot (*infml*), bash (*infml*), stab (*infml*), turn.

2 full of go: energy, get-up-and-go (*infml*), vitality, life, spirit, dynamism, effort.

◆ **go about** approach, begin, set about, address, tackle, attend to, undertake, engage in, perform.

◆ **go ahead** begin, proceed, carry on, continue, advance, progress, move.

◆ **go away** depart, leave, clear off (*infml*), withdraw, retreat, disappear, vanish.

◆ **go back** return, revert, backslide, retreat.

◆ **go by 1 time went by**: pass, elapse, flow.

2 go by the rules: observe, follow, comply with, heed.

◆ **go down** descend, sink, set, fall, drop, decrease, decline, deteriorate, degenerate, fail, founder, go under, collapse, fold (*infml*).

◆ **go for 1** (*infml*) **go for the least expensive option**: choose, prefer, favour, like, admire, enjoy.

2 went for him with a knife: attack, assail, set about, lunge at.

◆ **go in for** enter, take part in, participate in, engage in, take up, embrace, adopt, undertake, practise, pursue, follow.

◆ **go into** discuss, consider, review, examine, study, scrutinize, investigate, inquire into, check out, probe, delve into, analyse, dissect.

◆ **go off 1 went off somewhere**: depart, leave, quit, abscond, vanish, disappear.

2 the bomb went off: explode, blow up, detonate.

3 the milk has gone off: deteriorate, turn, sour, go bad, rot.

◆ **go on 1 kept on working**: continue, carry on, proceed, persist, stay, endure, last.

2 going on and on: chatter, rabbit (*infml*), witter (*infml*), ramble on.

3 what's going on?: happen, occur, take place.

◆ **go out** exit, depart, leave.

◆ **go over** examine, peruse, study, revise, scan, read, inspect, check, review, repeat, rehearse, list.

◆ **go through 1 have to go through surgery**: suffer, undergo, experience, bear, tolerate, endure, withstand.

2 go through his papers: investigate, check, examine, look, search, hunt, explore.
3 go through money like water: use, consume, exhaust, spend, squander.
◆ **go together** match, harmonize, accord, fit.
◆ **go with 1 shoes to go with the outfit**: match, harmonize, co-ordinate, blend, complement, suit, fit, correspond.
2 go with her to the station: accompany, escort, take, usher.
E3 1 clash.
◆ **go without** abstain, forgo, do without, manage without, lack, want.

goad *verb*
prod, prick, spur, impel, push, drive, provoke, incite, instigate, arouse, stimulate, prompt, urge, nag, hound, harass, annoy, irritate, vex.

go-ahead *noun*
permission, authorization, clearance, green light (*infml*), sanction, assent, consent, OK (*infml*), agreement.
E3 ban, veto, embargo.
▶ *adjective*
enterprising, pioneering, progressive, ambitious, up-and-coming, dynamic, energetic.
E3 unenterprising, sluggish.

goal *noun*
target, mark, objective, aim, intention, object, purpose, end, ambition, aspiration.

gobble *verb*
bolt, guzzle, gorge, cram, stuff (*infml*), devour, consume, put away (*infml*), swallow, gulp.

godsend *noun*
blessing, boon, stroke of luck, windfall, miracle.
E3 blow, setback.

golden *adjective*
1 golden hair: gold, gilded, gilt, yellow, blond(e), fair, bright, shining, lustrous.
2 their golden years: prosperous, successful, glorious, excellent, happy, joyful, favourable, auspicious, promising, rosy.

good *adjective*
1 a good service/worker/degree: acceptable, satisfactory, pleasant, agreeable, nice, enjoyable, pleasing, commendable, excellent, great (*infml*), super (*infml*), first-class, first-rate, superior, advantageous, beneficial, favourable, auspicious, helpful, useful, worthwhile, profitable, appropriate, suitable, fitting.
2 good at her job: competent, proficient, skilled, expert, accomplished, professional, skilful, clever, talented, gifted, fit, able, capable, dependable, reliable.
3 good of you: kind, considerate, gracious, benevolent, charitable, philanthropic.
4 a good man: virtuous, exemplary, moral, upright, honest, trustworthy, worthy, righteous.
5 you've been a good boy today: well-behaved, obedient, well-mannered.
6 have a good look: thorough, complete, whole, substantial, considerable.
E3 1 bad, poor. **2** incompetent. **3** unkind, inconsiderate. **4** wicked, immoral. **5** naughty, disobedient.
⇨ *See also* **Word Workshop** *panel.*
▶ *noun*
1 the good and the bad in everyone: virtue, morality, goodness, righteousness, right.
2 it's no good: use, purpose, avail, advantage, profit, gain, worth, merit, usefulness, service.
3 for your own good: welfare, well-being, interest, sake, behalf, benefit, convenience.

good-bye *noun*
farewell, adieu, au revoir, valediction, leave-taking, parting.

good-natured *adjective*
kind, kindly, kind-hearted, sympathetic, benevolent, helpful, neighbourly, gentle, good-tempered, approachable, friendly, tolerant, patient.
E3 ill-natured.

goodness *noun*
virtue, uprightness, rectitude, honesty, probity (*fml*), kindness, compassion, graciousness, goodwill, benevolence,

Try not to repeat the verb **go** (or its forms **going**, **gone** and **went**) too often. Aim to make your speech or writing more interesting by using some of the alternatives listed here.

to move

advance	pass	travel
journey	proceed	
make for	progress	

to leave

depart	retreat	withdraw
leave	take one's leave	

go from one point to another

continue	span	unfold
extend	spread	
reach	stretch	

to become

change into	grow
get	turn

to work

act	operate	run
function	perform	

to take or use up

disappear	vanish

to proceed

| develop | manage | progress |
| end up | occur | result |

to be given to

| award | grant |
| distribute | present |

talking about time

| elapse | lapse | pass |

Instead of repeating **go** in the following passage, you might use some of the synonyms discussed opposite.

> The day had *passed* ~~gone~~ very quickly. Diane had been visiting her elderly grandmother as usual and was just about to *leave* ~~go~~ when she heard on the radio that all London-bound trains had been cancelled. She had to get home by six o'clock, but when she checked the time on her watch she noticed that it wasn't *working* ~~going~~. Daylight was *disappearing* ~~going~~ fast, the sky was *growing* ~~going~~ dark and she decided not to *travel* ~~go~~ to London until the next day.

WORD *workshop* good

The adjective **good** is often overused, but there are many synonyms that can be used instead to add variety to your writing. Try out some of those in the lists below.

a person's ability

accomplished	expert	skilled
clever	gifted	talented
competent	proficient	

a person's character

capable	moral	virtuous
dependable	reliable	worthy
exemplary	trustworthy	
honest	upright	

a person's personality

considerate	gracious	sympathetic
friendly	kind	

something that has a positive effect

advantageous	profitable	valuable
beneficial	rewarding	worthwhile

good behaviour

obedient	respectful	well-mannered
polite	well-behaved	

unselfishness, generosity, friendliness, helpfulness.
E∃ badness, wickedness.

goods *noun*
1 all their worldly goods: property,

chattels (*fml*), effects, possessions, belongings, paraphernalia, stuff (*infml*), things, gear (*infml*).
2 sell their goods at the market:

good WORD *workshop*

an event, eg a holiday

agreeable	first-class	superb
enjoyable	pleasant	wonderful
excellent	pleasing	
fine	pleasurable	

something large

considerable	sizeable	substantial

The following postcard shows ways in which some of the synonyms opposite can be used instead of repeating **good**.

Dear Hazel

We're having a really ~~good~~ ^{wonderful} time on
holidays. The weather is ~~good~~ ^{lovely} and the
hotel is ~~good.~~ ^{superb} Julie has been learning to
swim but she's not very ~~good~~ ^{proficient} yet. The
twins are not being too ~~good~~ ^{well-behaved} but the
staff are very ~~good.~~ ^{friendly} On the whole the
holiday has been very ~~good~~ ^{worthwhile} for us.
Hope you are feeling ~~good.~~ ^{fine} See you next
week,

Kate

Hazel Black
3 Sunnymeadows
Hopeville
HV3 6ZY

merchandise, wares, commodities, stock, freight.

goodwill *noun*
benevolence, kindness, generosity, favour, friendliness, friendship, zeal.

Ea ill-will.

gorge *noun*
canyon, ravine, gully, defile (*fml*), chasm, abyss, cleft, fissure, gap, pass.

▶ *verb*
feed, guzzle, gobble, devour, bolt, wolf, gulp, swallow, cram, stuff (*infml*), fill, sate, surfeit, glut, overeat.
🗲 fast.

gorgeous *adjective*
magnificent, splendid, grand, glorious, superb, fine, rich, sumptuous, luxurious, brilliant, dazzling, showy, glamorous, attractive, beautiful, handsome, good-looking, delightful, pleasing, lovely, enjoyable, good.
🗲 dull, plain.

gory *adjective*
bloody, sanguinary, bloodstained, blood-soaked, grisly, brutal, savage, murderous.

gossip *noun*
1 don't listen to gossip: idle talk, prattle, chitchat, tittle-tattle, rumour, hearsay, report, scandal.
2 the local gossip: gossip-monger, scandalmonger, whisperer, prattler, babbler, chatterbox, nosey parker (*infml*), busybody, talebearer, tell-tale, tattler.
▶ *verb*
talk, chat, natter, chatter, gabble, tell tales, prattle, tattle, whisper, rumour.

gouge *verb*
chisel, cut, hack, incise, score, groove, scratch, claw, gash, slash, dig, scoop, hollow, extract.

gourmet *noun*
gastronome, epicure, epicurean, connoisseur, bon vivant.

govern *verb*
1 governing most of Europe: rule, reign, direct, manage, superintend, supervise, oversee, preside, lead, head, command, influence, guide, conduct, steer, pilot.
2 govern one's temper: dominate, master, control, regulate, curb, check, restrain, contain, quell, subdue, tame, discipline.

government *noun*
1 blame the government: administration, executive, ministry, Establishment, authorities, powers that be, state, régime.
2 government by the people: rule, sovereignty, sway, direction, management, superintendence, supervision, surveillance, command, charge, authority, guidance, conduct, domination, dominion, control, regulation, restraint.

governor *noun*
ruler, commissioner, administrator, executive, director, manager, leader, head, chief, commander, superintendent, supervisor, overseer, controller, boss.

gown *noun*
robe, dress, frock, dressing-gown, habit, costume.

grab *verb*
seize, snatch, take, nab (*infml*), pluck, snap up, catch hold of, grasp, clutch, grip, catch, bag (*infml*), capture, collar (*infml*), commandeer, appropriate, usurp, annex.

grace *noun*
1 move with grace: gracefulness, poise, beauty, attractiveness, loveliness, shapeliness, elegance, tastefulness, refinement, polish, breeding, manners, etiquette, decorum, decency, courtesy, charm.
2 the grace of God: kindness, kindliness, compassion, consideration, goodness, virtue, generosity, charity, benevolence, goodwill, favour, forgiveness, indulgence, mercy, leniency, pardon, reprieve.
3 say grace: blessing, benediction, thanksgiving, prayer.
🗲 **2** cruelty, harshness.
▶ *verb*
favour, honour, dignify, distinguish, embellish, enhance, set off, trim, garnish, decorate, ornament, adorn.
🗲 spoil, detract from.

graceful *adjective*
easy, flowing, smooth, supple, agile, deft, natural, slender, fine, tasteful, elegant, beautiful, charming, suave.
🗲 graceless, awkward, clumsy, ungainly.

gracious *adjective*
elegant, refined, polite, courteous, well-mannered, considerate, sweet,

obliging, accommodating, kind,
compassionate, kindly, benevolent,
generous, magnanimous, charitable,
hospitable, forgiving, indulgent,
lenient, mild, clement, merciful.
F3 ungracious.

grade noun
rank, status, standing, station, place,
position, level, stage, degree, step,
rung, notch, mark, brand, quality,
standard, condition, size, order, group,
class, category.
► verb
sort, arrange, categorize, order, group,
class, rate, size, rank, range, classify,
evaluate, assess, value, mark, brand,
label, pigeonhole, type.

gradient noun
slope, incline, hill, bank, rise, declivity
(fml).

gradual adjective
slow, leisurely, unhurried, easy, gentle,
moderate, regular, even, measured,
steady, continuous, progressive, step-
by-step.
F3 sudden, precipitate (fml).

gradually adverb
little by little, bit by bit, imperceptibly,
inch by inch, step by step, progressively,
by degrees, piecemeal, slowly, gently,
cautiously, gingerly, moderately, evenly,
steadily.

graduate verb
pass, qualify.

graft noun
implant, implantation, transplant,
splice, bud, sprout, shoot, scion.
► verb
engraft, implant, insert, transplant,
join, splice.

grain noun
1 a grain of sand: bit, piece, fragment,
scrap, morsel, crumb, granule, particle,
molecule, atom, jot, iota, mite, speck,
modicum, trace.
2 making flour from the grain: seed,
kernel, corn, cereals.
3 the grain of the wood: texture, fibre,
weave, pattern, marking, surface.

grand adjective
1 a grand house/in the grand manner:
majestic, regal, stately, splendid,

magnificent, glorious, superb, sublime,
fine, excellent, outstanding, first-rate,
impressive, imposing, striking,
monumental, large, noble, lordly, lofty,
pompous, pretentious, grandiose,
ambitious.
2 a chess grand master: supreme, pre-
eminent, leading, head, chief, arch,
highest, senior, great, illustrious.
F3 1 humble, common, poor.

grandeur noun
majesty, stateliness, pomp, state,
dignity, splendour, magnificence,
nobility, greatness, illustriousness,
importance.
F3 humbleness, lowliness, simplicity.

grandiose adjective
pompous, pretentious, high-flown,
lofty, ambitious, extravagant,
ostentatious, showy, flamboyant,
grand, majestic, stately, magnificent,
impressive, imposing, monumental.
F3 unpretentious.

grant verb
1 grant them leave to appeal: give,
donate, present, award, confer, bestow,
impart, transmit, dispense, apportion,
assign, allot, allocate, provide,
supply.
2 grant that it is likely: admit,
acknowledge, concede, allow, permit,
consent to, agree to, accede to.
F3 1 withhold. 2 deny.
► noun
allowance, subsidy, concession, award,
bursary, scholarship, gift, donation,
endowment, bequest, annuity, pension,
honorarium.

granular adjective
grainy, granulated, gritty, sandy, lumpy,
rough, crumbly, friable.

graph noun
diagram, chart, table, grid.

graphic adjective
vivid, descriptive, expressive, striking,
telling, lively, realistic, explicit, clear,
lucid, specific, detailed, blow-by-blow,
visual, pictorial, diagrammatic,
illustrative.
F3 vague, impressionistic.

grapple verb
seize, grasp, snatch, grab, grip, clutch,

clasp, hold, wrestle, tussle, struggle, contend, fight, combat, clash, engage, encounter, face, confront, tackle, deal with, cope with.
F3 release, avoid, evade.

grasp *verb*
1 grasping the rope in both hands: hold, clasp, clutch, grip, grapple, seize, snatch, grab, catch.
2 grasp a concept: understand, comprehend, get (*infml*), follow, see, realize.
▸ *noun*
1 a firm grasp: grip, clasp, hold, embrace, clutches, possession, control, power.
2 a good grasp of grammar: understanding, comprehension, apprehension, mastery, familiarity, knowledge.

grasping *adjective*
avaricious, greedy, rapacious, acquisitive, mercenary, mean, selfish, miserly, close-fisted, tight-fisted, parsimonious.
F3 generous.

grass *noun*
turf, lawn, green, grassland, field, meadow, pasture, prairie, pampas, savanna, steppe.

grate *verb*
1 grate the cheese: grind, shred, mince, pulverize, rub, rasp, scrape.
2 grate on one's nerves: jar, set one's teeth on edge, annoy, irritate, aggravate (*infml*), get on one's nerves, vex, irk, exasperate.

grateful *adjective*
thankful, appreciative, indebted, obliged, obligated, beholden.
F3 ungrateful.

gratify *verb*
satisfy, fulfil, indulge, pander to, humour, favour, please, gladden, delight, thrill.
F3 frustrate, thwart.

grating[1] *adjective*
a grating noise: harsh, rasping, scraping, squeaky, strident, discordant, jarring, annoying, irritating, unpleasant, disagreeable.
F3 harmonious, pleasing.

grating[2] *noun*
fit a grating over the drain: grate, grill, grid, lattice, trellis.

gratitude *noun*
gratefulness, thankfulness, thanks, appreciation, acknowledgement, recognition, indebtedness, obligation.
F3 ingratitude, ungratefulness.

gratuitous *adjective*
wanton, unnecessary, needless, superfluous, unwarranted, unjustified, groundless, undeserved, unprovoked, uncalled-for, unasked-for, unsolicited, voluntary, free, gratis, complimentary.
F3 justified, provoked.

grave[1] *noun*
mark the graves with crosses: burial-place, tomb, vault, crypt, sepulchre, mausoleum, pit, barrow, tumulus, cairn.

grave[2] *adjective*
1 a grave mistake: important, significant, weighty, momentous, serious, critical, vital, crucial, urgent, acute, severe, dangerous, hazardous.
2 look grave: solemn, dignified, sober, sedate, serious, thoughtful, pensive, grim, long-faced, quiet, reserved, subdued, restrained.
F3 1 trivial, light, slight. **2** cheerful.

gravity *noun*
1 realize the gravity of their predicament: importance, significance, seriousness, urgency, acuteness, severity, danger.
2 the gravity of his expression: solemnity, dignity, sobriety, seriousness, thoughtfulness, sombreness, reserve, restraint.
3 force of gravity: gravitation, attraction, pull, weight, heaviness.
F3 1 triviality. **2** levity.

graze *verb*
scratch, scrape, skin, abrade, rub, chafe, shave, brush, skim, touch.
▸ *noun*
scratch, scrape, abrasion.

grease *noun*
oil, lubrication, fat, lard, dripping, tallow.

greasy *adjective*
oily, fatty, lardy, buttery, smeary, slimy, slippery, smooth, waxy.

great *adjective*
1 a great house/the Great Plains: large, big, huge, enormous, massive, colossal, gigantic, mammoth, immense, vast, impressive.
2 with great care: considerable, pronounced, extreme, excessive, inordinate.
3 a great actor: famous, renowned, celebrated, illustrious, eminent, distinguished, prominent, noteworthy, notable, remarkable, outstanding, grand, glorious, fine.
4 a great discovery: important, significant, serious, major, principal, primary, main, chief, leading.
5 (*infml*) that's great!: excellent, first-rate, superb, wonderful, marvellous, tremendous, terrific, fantastic (*infml*), (*infml*), cool (*infml*), wicked (*infml*).
F3 **1** small. **2** slight. **3** unknown. **4** unimportant, insignificant.
⇨ *See also* **Word Workshop** *panel.*

greedy *adjective*
1 a greedy boy: hungry, starving, ravenous, gluttonous, gourmandizing (*fml*), voracious, insatiable.
2 greedy for money and power: acquisitive, covetous, desirous, craving, eager, impatient, avaricious, grasping, selfish.
F3 **1** abstemious.

green *adjective*
1 a green field: grassy, leafy, verdant, unripe, unseasoned, tender, fresh, budding, blooming, flourishing.
2 green with envy: envious, covetous, jealous, resentful.
3 too green to know better: immature, naïve, unsophisticated, ignorant, inexperienced, untrained, raw, new, recent, young.
4 green issues: ecological, environmental, eco-friendly, environmentally aware.
▶ *noun*
common, lawn, grass, turf.

greenhouse *noun*
glasshouse, hothouse, conservatory, pavilion, vinery, orangery.

greet *verb*
hail, salute, acknowledge, address, accost, meet, receive, welcome.
F3 ignore.

greeting *noun*
salutation, acknowledgement, wave, hallo, the time of day, address, reception, welcome.

greetings *noun*
regards, respects, compliments, salutations, best wishes, good wishes, love.

gregarious *adjective*
sociable, outgoing, extrovert, friendly, affable, social, convivial, cordial, warm.
F3 unsociable.

grey *adjective*
1 a grey colour/day: neutral, colourless, pale, ashen, leaden, dull, cloudy, overcast, dim, dark, murky.
2 a grey industrial landscape: gloomy, dismal, cheerless, depressing, dreary, bleak.

grief *noun*
sorrow, sadness, unhappiness, depression, dejection, desolation, distress, misery, woe, heartbreak, mourning, bereavement, heartache, anguish, agony, pain, suffering, affliction, trouble, regret, remorse.
F3 happiness, delight.

grievance *noun*
complaint, moan (*infml*), grumble (*infml*), resentment, objection, protest, charge, wrong, injustice, injury, damage, trouble, affliction, hardship, trial, tribulation.

grieve *verb*
1 grieving for his dead wife: sorrow, mope, lament, mourn, wail, cry, weep.
2 grieves me that he didn't take my advice: sadden, upset, dismay, distress, afflict, pain, hurt, wound.
F3 **1** rejoice. **2** please, gladden.

grim *adjective*
1 a grim sight: unpleasant, horrible, horrid, ghastly, gruesome, grisly, sinister, frightening, fearsome, terrible, shocking.
2 a grim expression: stern, severe, harsh, dour, forbidding, surly, sullen, morose, gloomy, depressing, unattractive.
F3 **1** pleasant. **2** attractive.

Beware of using **great** too often in your writing. Try out some of the following instead.

large in size

big	huge	mammoth
colossal	immense	massive
enormous	impressive	vast
gigantic	large	

important or well-known in a particular field

celebrated	fine	prominent
distinguished	glorious	remarkable
eminent	noteworthy	renowned
famous	outstanding	

good at something

able	practised	skilled
experienced	professional	talented
expert	skilful	

important

chief	major	serious
leading	primary	significant
main	principal	

very good

excellent	first-rate *(infml)*	tremendous
fabulous *(infml)*	marvellous	terrific *(infml)*
fantastic	superb	wonderful

great   WORD *workshop*

doing something with, eg great care

considerable   extreme
excessive   pronounced

Instead of using **great** in the following passage, you might use some of the synonyms discussed.

huge
The Museum of Film shows classic films on a ~~great~~
expert
screen. The ~~great~~ staff make sure that everything runs smoothly.
significant
In the exhibitions, all the ~~great~~ actors in film history are
celebrated
represented, right up to the ~~great~~ stars of the present day.
considerable
The museum has taken ~~great~~ care to make sure that there is
marvellous
something of interest for everyone and it is a ~~great~~ place to visit

for the day.

grimace *noun*
frown, scowl, pout, smirk, sneer, face.
▶ *verb*
make a face, pull a face, frown, scowl, pout, smirk, sneer.

grimy *adjective*
dirty, mucky, grubby, soiled, filthy, sooty, smutty, dusty, smudgy.
₣ clean.

grind *verb*
crush, pound, pulverize, powder, mill, grate, scrape, gnash, rut, abrade, sand, file, smooth, polish, sharpen, whet.

grip *noun*
hold, grasp, clasp, embrace, clutches, control, power.
▶ *verb*
1 grip the rock: hold, grasp, clasp, clutch, seize, grab, catch.
2 gripped by the film: fascinate, thrill, enthral, spellbind, mesmerize, hypnotize, rivet, engross, absorb, involve, engage, compel.

grisly *adjective*
gruesome, gory, grim, macabre, horrid, horrible, ghastly, awful, frightful, terrible, dreadful,

abominable, appalling, shocking.
F3 delightful.

grit *noun*
gravel, pebbles, shingle, sand, dust.
▸ *verb*
clench, gnash, grate, grind.

groan *noun*
moan, sigh, cry, whine, wail, lament,
complaint, objection, grumble,
protest, outcry.
F3 cheer.
▸ *verb*
moan, sigh, cry, whine, wail, lament,
complain, object, protest, grumble.
F3 cheer.

groom *verb*
1 grooming the horses: smarten,
neaten, tidy, spruce up, clean, brush,
curry, preen, dress.
2 groomed for her new post: prepare,
train, school, educate, drill.

groove *noun*
furrow, rut, track, slot, channel, gutter,
trench, hollow, indentation, score.
F3 ridge.

grope *verb*
feel, fumble, scrabble, flounder, cast
about, fish, search, probe.

gross *adjective*
1 gross misconduct: serious, grievous,
blatant, flagrant, glaring, obvious,
plain, sheer, utter, outright, shameful,
shocking.
2 don't be so gross!: obscene, lewd,
improper, indecent, offensive, rude,
coarse, crude, vulgar, tasteless.
3 a gross body: fat, obese, overweight,
big, large, huge, colossal, hulking,
bulky, heavy.
4 gross earnings: inclusive, all-
inclusive, total, aggregate, entire,
complete, whole.
F3 3 slight. 4 net.

grotesque *adjective*
bizarre, odd, weird, unnatural,
freakish, monstrous, hideous, ugly,
unsightly, misshapen, deformed,
distorted, twisted, fantastic, fanciful,
extravagant, absurd, surreal, macabre.
F3 normal, graceful.

ground *noun*
1 feet on the ground: bottom,

foundation, surface, land, terrain, dry
land, terra firma, earth, soil, clay,
loam, dirt, dust.
2 football ground: field, pitch,
stadium, arena, park.

groundless *adjective*
baseless, unfounded, unsubstantiated,
unsupported, empty, imaginary, false,
unjustified, unwarranted, unprovoked,
uncalled-for.
F3 well-founded, reasonable, justified.

grounds[1] *noun*
the castle grounds: land, terrain,
holding, estate, property, territory,
domain, gardens, park, campus,
surroundings, fields, acres.

grounds[2] *noun*
have grounds for complaint: base,
foundation, justification, excuse,
vindication, reason, motive,
inducement, cause, occasion, call,
score, account, argument, principle,
basis.

group *noun*
band, gang, pack, team, crew, troop,
squad, detachment, party, faction, set,
circle, clique, club, society, association,
organization, company, gathering,
congregation, crowd, collection,
bunch, clump, cluster,
conglomeration, constellation, batch,
lot, combination, formation, grouping,
class, classification, category, genus,
species.
▸ *verb*
1 grouped around their parents:
gather, collect, assemble, congregate,
mass, cluster, clump, bunch.
2 group them according to size: sort,
range, arrange, marshal, organize,
order, class, classify, categorize, band,
link, associate.

grovel *verb*
crawl, creep, ingratiate oneself, toady,
suck up (*infml*), flatter, fawn, cringe,
cower, kowtow, defer, demean oneself.

grow *verb*
1 grow in size: increase, rise, expand,
enlarge, swell, spread, extend, stretch,
develop, proliferate, mushroom.
2 grow from seed: originate, arise,
issue, spring, germinate, shoot, sprout

bud, flower, mature, develop, progress, thrive, flourish, prosper.
3 grow crops: cultivate, farm, produce, propagate, breed, raise.
4 grow cold: become, get, go, turn.
F3 1 decrease, shrink.

growl *verb*
snarl, snap, yap, rumble, roar.

grown-up *adjective*
adult, mature, of age, full-grown, fully-fledged.
F3 young, immature.
▶ *noun*
adult, man, woman.
F3 child.

growth *noun*
1 the growth in prosperity: increase, rise, extension, enlargement, expansion, spread, proliferation, development, evolution, progress, advance, improvement, success, prosperity.
2 a malignant growth: tumour, lump, swelling, protuberance (*fml*), outgrowth.
F3 1 decrease, decline, failure.

grub *noun*
maggot, worm, larva, pupa, caterpillar, chrysalis.

grubby *adjective*
dirty, soiled, unwashed, mucky, grimy, filthy, squalid, seedy, scruffy.
F3 clean.

grudge *noun*
resentment, bitterness, envy, jealousy, spite, malice, enmity, antagonism, hate, dislike, animosity, ill-will, hard feelings, grievance.
F3 favour.
▶ *verb*
begrudge, resent, envy, covet, dislike, take exception to, object to, mind.

grudging *adjective*
reluctant, unwilling, hesitant, half-hearted, unenthusiastic, resentful, envious, jealous.

gruelling *adjective*
hard, difficult, taxing, demanding, tiring, exhausting, laborious, arduous, strenuous, backbreaking, harsh, severe, tough, punishing.
F3 easy.

gruesome *adjective*
horrible, disgusting, repellent, repugnant, repulsive, hideous, grisly, macabre, grim, ghastly, awful, terrible, horrific, shocking, monstrous, abominable.
F3 pleasant.

gruff *adjective*
1 a gruff manner: curt, brusque, abrupt, blunt, rude, surly, sullen, grumpy, bad-tempered.
2 a gruff voice: rough, harsh, rasping, guttural, throaty, husky, hoarse.
F3 1 friendly, courteous.

grumble *verb*
complain, moan, whine, bleat, grouch, gripe, mutter, murmur, carp, find fault.

grumpy *adjective*
bad-tempered, ill-tempered, crotchety, crabbed, cantankerous, cross, irritable, surly, sullen, sulky, grouchy, discontented.
F3 contented.

guarantee *noun*
warranty, insurance, assurance, promise, word of honour, pledge, oath, bond, security, collateral, surety, endorsement, testimonial.
▶ *verb*
assure, promise, pledge, swear, vouch for, answer for, warrant, certify, underwrite, endorse, secure, protect, insure, ensure, make sure, make certain.

guard *verb*
protect, safeguard, save, preserve, shield, screen, shelter, cover, defend, patrol, police, escort, supervise, oversee, watch, look out, mind, beware.
▶ *noun*
1 an armed guard: protector, defender, custodian, warder, escort, bodyguard, minder (*infml*), watchman, lookout, sentry, picket, patrol, security.
2 a guard against infection: protection, safeguard, defence, wall, barrier, screen, shield, bumper, buffer, pad.

guarded *adjective*
cautious, wary, careful, watchful, discreet, non-committal, reticent, reserved, secretive, cagey (*infml*).
F3 communicative, frank.

guardian *noun*
trustee, curator, custodian, keeper, warden, protector, preserver, defender, champion, guard, warder, escort, attendant.

guess *verb*
speculate, conjecture, predict, estimate, judge, reckon, work out, suppose, assume, surmise, think, believe, imagine, fancy, feel, suspect.
▶ *noun*
prediction, estimate, speculation, conjecture, supposition, assumption, belief, fancy, idea, notion, theory, hypothesis, opinion, feeling, suspicion, intuition.

guesswork *noun*
speculation, conjecture, estimation, reckoning, supposition, assumption, surmise, intuition.

guest *noun*
visitor, caller, boarder, lodger, resident, patron, regular.

guidance *noun*
leadership, direction, management, control, teaching, instruction, advice, counsel, counselling, help, instructions, directions, guidelines, indications, pointers, recommendations.

guide *verb*
lead, conduct, direct, navigate, point, steer, pilot, manoeuvre, usher, escort, accompany, attend, control, govern, manage, oversee, supervise, superintend, advise, counsel, influence, educate, teach, instruct, train.
▶ *noun*
1 a tour guide: leader, courier, navigator, pilot, helmsman, steersman, usher, escort, chaperon(e), attendant, companion, adviser, counsellor, mentor, guru, teacher, instructor.
2 a guide to the Lake District: manual, handbook, guidebook, catalogue, directory.
3 the lighthouse serves as a guide to ships: indication, pointer, signpost, sign, marker.
4 serve as a guide to others: guideline, example, model, standard, criterion.

guilt *noun*
1 he confessed his guilt: culpability, responsibility, blame, disgrace, dishonour.
2 a feeling of guilt: guilty conscience, conscience, shame, self-condemnation, self-reproach, regret, remorse, contrition.
F3 1 innocence, righteousness. 2 shamelessness.

guilty *adjective*
1 the guilty party: culpable, responsible, blamable, blameworthy, offending, wrong, sinful, wicked, criminal, convicted.
2 feel guilty: conscience-stricken, ashamed, shamefaced, sheepish, sorry, regretful, remorseful, contrite, penitent, repentant.
F3 1 innocent, guiltless, blameless. 2 shameless.

gulf *noun*
bay, bight, basin, gap, opening, separation, rift, split, breach, cleft, chasm, gorge, abyss, void.

gullible *adjective*
credulous, suggestible, impressionable, trusting, unsuspecting, foolish, naïve, green, unsophisticated, innocent.
F3 astute.

gully *noun*
channel, watercourse, gutter, ditch, ravine.

gulp *verb*
swallow, swig, swill, knock back (*infml*), bolt, wolf (*infml*), gobble, guzzle, devour, stuff (*infml*).
F3 sip, nibble.
▶ *noun*
swallow, swig, draught, mouthful.

gum *noun*
adhesive, glue, paste, cement.
▶ *verb*
stick, glue, paste, fix, cement, seal, clog.

gun *noun*
firearm, handgun, pistol, revolver, shooter (*infml*), rifle, shotgun, bazooka, howitzer, cannon.

gurgle *verb*
bubble, babble, burble, murmur, ripple, lap, splash, crow.

▸ *noun*
babble, murmur, ripple.

gush *verb*
1 oil gushing from the bore hole: flow, run, pour, stream, cascade, flood, rush, burst, spurt, spout, jet, well.
2 'how splendid you look!' she gushed: enthuse, chatter, babble, jabber, go on (*infml*).
▸ *noun*
flow, outflow, stream, torrent, cascade, flood, tide, rush, burst, outburst, spurt, spout, jet.

gust *noun*
blast, burst, rush, flurry, blow, puff, breeze, wind, gale, squall.

gusto *noun*
zest, relish, appreciation, enjoyment, pleasure, delight, enthusiasm, exuberance, élan, verve, zeal.

Fꝫ distaste, apathy.

gut *verb*
1 gut fish: disembowel, draw, clean (out).
2 (*infml*) gut the house: strip, clear, empty, rifle, ransack, plunder, loot, sack, ravage.

guts *noun*
1 remove the guts from the game: intestines, bowels, viscera, entrails, insides, innards (*infml*), belly, stomach.
2 (*infml*) have a lot of guts: courage, bravery, pluck, grit, nerve, mettle.

gutter *noun*
drain, sluice, ditch, trench, trough, channel, duct, conduit, passage, pipe, tube.

gyrate *verb*
turn, revolve, rotate, twirl, pirouette, spin, whirl, wheel, circle, spiral.

H

habit *noun*
custom, usage, practice, routine, rule, second nature, way, manner, mode, wont, inclination, tendency, bent, mannerism, quirk, addiction, dependence, fixation, obsession, weakness.

habitat *noun*
home, abode (*fml*), domain, element, environment, surroundings, locality, territory, terrain.

habitual *adjective*
1 his habitual route: customary, traditional, wonted, routine, usual, ordinary, common, natural, normal, standard, regular, recurrent, fixed, established, familiar.
2 habitual smoker: confirmed, inveterate, hardened, addicted, dependent, persistent.
F3 1 occasional, infrequent.

hack *verb*
cut, chop, hew, notch, gash, slash, lacerate, mutilate, mangle.

hackneyed *adjective*
stale, overworked, tired, worn-out, time-worn, threadbare, unoriginal, corny (*infml*), clichéd, stereotyped, stock, banal, trite, commonplace, common, pedestrian, uninspired.
F3 original, new, fresh.

haggard *adjective*
drawn, gaunt, careworn, thin, wasted, shrunken, pinched, pale, wan, ghastly.
F3 hale.

haggle *verb*
bargain, negotiate, barter, wrangle, squabble, bicker, quarrel, dispute.

hail¹ *noun*
a hail of bullets: barrage, bombardment, volley, torrent, shower, rain, storm.
▸ *verb*
pelt, bombard, shower, rain, batter, attack, assail.

hail² *verb*
hailed a taxi: greet, address, acknowledge, salute, wave, signal to, flag down, shout, call, acclaim, cheer, applaud, honour, welcome.

hair-raising *adjective*
frightening, scary, terrifying, horrifying, shocking, bloodcurdling, spine-chilling, eerie, alarming, startling, thrilling.

hairstyle *noun*
style, coiffure, hairdo (*infml*), cut, haircut, set, perm (*infml*), barnet (*infml*).

hairy *adjective*
hirsute, bearded, shaggy, bushy, fuzzy, furry, woolly.
F3 bald, clean-shaven.

half *noun*
fifty per cent, bisection, hemisphere, semicircle, section, segment, portion, share, fraction.
▸ *adjective*
semi-, halved, divided, fractional, part, partial, incomplete, moderate, limited.
F3 whole.
▸ *adverb*
partly, partially, incompletely, moderately, slightly.
F3 completely.

half-hearted *adjective*
lukewarm, cool, weak, feeble, passive, apathetic, uninterested, indifferent, neutral.
F3 whole-hearted, enthusiastic.

hall *noun*
hallway, corridor, passage, passageway, entrance-hall, foyer, vestibule, lobby, concert-hall, auditorium, chamber, assembly room.

hallmark *noun*
stamp, mark, trademark, brand-name, sign, indication, symbol, emblem, device, badge.

hallucination *noun*
illusion, mirage, vision, apparition, dream, daydream, fantasy, figment, delusion.

halt *verb*
stop, draw up, pull up, pause, wait, rest, break off, discontinue, cease, desist, quit, end, terminate, check, stem, curb, obstruct, impede.
F₃ start, continue.
▶ *noun*
stop, stoppage, arrest, interruption, break, pause, rest, standstill, end, close, termination.
F₃ start, continuation.

halting *adjective*
hesitant, stuttering, stammering, faltering, stumbling, broken, imperfect, laboured, awkward.
F₃ fluent.

halve *verb*
bisect, cut in half, split in two, divide, split, share, cut down, reduce, lessen.

hammer *verb*
hit, strike, beat, drum, bang, bash, pound, batter, knock, drive, shape, form, make.
▶ *noun*
mallet, gavel.
◆ **hammer out** settle, sort out, negotiate, thrash out, produce, bring about, accomplish, complete, finish.

hamper *verb*
hinder, impede, obstruct, slow down, hold up, frustrate, thwart, prevent, handicap, hamstring, shackle, cramp, restrict, curb, restrain.
F₃ aid, facilitate.

hand *noun*
1 holding it in his hand: fist, palm, paw (*infml*), mitt (*infml*).
2 give me a hand: help, aid, assistance, support, participation, part, influence.

3 a farm hand: worker, employee, operative, workman, labourer, farm-hand, hireling.
▶ *verb*
give, pass, offer, submit, present, yield, deliver, transmit, conduct, convey.
◆ **at hand** near, close, to hand, handy, accessible, available, ready, imminent.
◆ **hand down** bequeath, will, pass on, transfer, give, grant.
◆ **hand out** distribute, deal out, give out, share out, dish out (*infml*), mete out, dispense.
◆ **hand over** yield, relinquish, surrender, turn over, deliver, release, give, donate, present.
F₃ keep, retain.

handbook *noun*
manual, instruction book, guide, guidebook, companion.

handful *noun*
few, sprinkling, scattering, smattering.
F₃ a lot, many.

handicap *noun*
obstacle, block, barrier, impediment, stumbling block, hindrance, drawback, disadvantage, restriction, limitation, penalty, disability, impairment, defect, shortcoming.
F₃ assistance, advantage.
▶ *verb*
impede, hinder, disadvantage, hold back, retard, hamper, burden, encumber, restrict, limit, disable.
F₃ help, assist.

handiwork *noun*
work, doing, responsibility, achievement, product, result, design, invention, creation, production, skill, workmanship, craftsmanship, artisanship.

handle *noun*
grip, handgrip, knob, stock, shaft, hilt.
▶ *verb*
1 don't handle the fruit: touch, finger, feel, fondle, pick up, hold, grasp.
2 handle a situation: tackle, treat, deal with, manage, cope with, control, supervise.

handout *noun*
1 live on handouts: charity, alms, dole,

largess(e), share, issue, free sample,
freebie (*infml*).
2 a press handout: leaflet, circular,
bulletin, statement, press release,
literature.

handsome *adjective*
1 a handsome youth: good-looking,
attractive, fair, personable, elegant.
2 a handsome amount: generous,
liberal, large, considerable, ample.
E3 1 ugly, unattractive. **2** mean.

handwriting *noun*
writing, script, hand, fist (*infml*),
penmanship, scrawl, calligraphy.

handy *adjective*
1 keep it handy/a handy guide:
available, to hand, ready, at hand, near,
accessible, convenient, practical,
useful, helpful.
2 he's quite handy about the house:
skilful, proficient, expert, skilled,
clever, practical.
E3 1 inconvenient. **2** clumsy.

hang *verb*
1 hang from a branch/long hair
hanging down over his eyes: suspend,
dangle, swing, drape, drop, flop, droop,
sag, trail.
2 hang a picture: fasten, attach, fix,
stick.
3 hang in the air: float, drift, hover,
linger, remain, cling.
◆ **hang about** hang around, linger,
loiter, dawdle, waste time, associate
with, frequent, haunt.
◆ **hang back** hold back, demur,
hesitate, shy away, recoil.
◆ **hang on 1** hang on till the bus
arrives: wait, hold on, remain, hold
out, endure, continue, carry on,
persevere, persist.
2 hang on with both hands: grip,
grasp, hold fast.
3 Labour victory hangs on gaining this
seat: depend on, hinge on, turn on.
E3 1 give up.

hang-up *noun*
inhibition, difficulty, problem,
obsession, preoccupation, thing
(*infml*), block, mental block.

hanker *verb*
crave, hunger for, thirst for, wish for,

desire, yearn for, pine for, long for,
want, need.

haphazard *adjective*
random, chance, casual, arbitrary, hit-
or-miss, unsystematic, disorganized,
disorderly, careless, slapdash, slipshod.
E3 methodical, orderly.

happen *verb*
occur, take place, arise, crop up,
develop, materialize (*infml*), come
about, result, ensue, follow, turn out,
transpire.

happening *noun*
occurrence, phenomenon, event,
incident, episode, occasion, adventure,
experience, accident, chance,
circumstance, case, affair.

happiness *noun*
joy, joyfulness, gladness, cheerfulness,
contentment, pleasure, delight, glee,
elation, bliss, ecstasy, euphoria.
E3 unhappiness, sadness.
⇨ See also **Word Study** panel.

happy *adjective*
1 very happy to see her: joyful, jolly,
merry, cheerful, glad, pleased,
delighted, thrilled, elated, satisfied,
content, contented.
2 a happy coincidence: lucky,
fortunate, felicitous (*fml*), favourable,
apt, appropriate, fitting.
E3 1 unhappy, sad, discontented. **2**
unfortunate, inappropriate.
⇨ See also **Word Workshop** panel.

harass *verb*
pester, badger, harry, plague, torment,
persecute, exasperate, vex, annoy,
irritate, bother, disturb, nag, hassle
(*infml*), trouble, worry, stress, tire, wear
out, exhaust, fatigue.

harbour *noun*
port, dock, quay, wharf, marina,
mooring, anchorage, haven, shelter.
▶ *verb*
1 harbour a criminal: hide, conceal,
protect, shelter.
2 harbour a feeling: hold, retain, cling
to, entertain, foster, nurse, nurture,
cherish, believe, imagine.

hard *adjective*
1 a hard surface: solid, firm,
unyielding, tough, strong, dense,

WORD *study* happiness

There are many ways of expressing **happiness**. You might try using some of those listed below to add variety to your writing. Check out the panel at **sadness** for ideas on how to express the opposite emotion.

being happy

be walking on air
be on cloud nine
be as happy as a sandboy
be as happy as the day is long
be in seventh heaven
be as pleased as Punch
be on top of the world

be thrilled to bits
be as happy as a pig in muck
be as happy as Larry
be full of the joys of spring
be over the moon
be in high spirits
be tickled pink

making someone happy

do someone's heart good
make someone's day

warm the cockles of someone's
heart

impenetrable, stiff, rigid, inflexible.
2 found the exam quite hard: difficult,
arduous, strenuous, laborious, tiring,
exhausting, backbreaking, complex,
complicated, involved, knotty, baffling,
puzzling, perplexing.
3 a hard taskmaster: harsh, severe,
strict, callous, unfeeling,
unsympathetic, cruel, pitiless,
merciless, ruthless, unrelenting,
distressing, painful, unpleasant,
heartless.
E3 1 soft, yielding. **2** easy, simple. **3**
kind, pleasant.
▶ *adverb*
industriously, diligently, assiduously
(*fml*), doggedly, steadily, laboriously,
strenuously, earnestly, keenly, intently,
strongly, violently, intensely,
energetically, vigorously.
◆ **hard up** poor, broke (*infml*),
penniless, impoverished, in the red,
bankrupt, bust, short, lacking.
E3 rich.

harden *verb*
solidify, set, freeze, bake, stiffen,

strengthen, reinforce, fortify, buttress,
brace, steel, nerve, toughen, season,
accustom, train.
E3 soften, weaken.

hard-headed *adjective*
shrewd, astute, businesslike, level-
headed, clear-thinking, sensible,
realistic, pragmatic, practical, hard-
boiled, tough, unsentimental.
E3 unrealistic.

hard-hearted *adjective*
callous, unfeeling, cold, hard, stony,
heartless, unsympathetic, cruel,
inhuman, pitiless, merciless.
E3 soft-hearted, kind, merciful.

hard-hitting *adjective*
condemnatory, critical, unsparing, no
holds barred, vigorous, forceful, tough.
E3 mild.

hardly *adverb*
barely, scarcely, just, only just, not
quite, not at all, by no means.

hardship *noun*
misfortune, adversity, trouble,
difficulty, affliction, distress, suffering,

WORD workshop

happy

There are many words that you can use to avoid repeating **happy** too often in your writing. The lists below show some synonyms that you might choose to use instead to add more variety to your speech or writing.

joyful

cheerful	glad	pleased
delighted	gleeful	rapturous
ecstatic	jolly	thrilled
elated	merry	
euphoric	overjoyed	

contented

carefree	light-hearted	untroubled
comfortable	relaxed	unworried
content	satisfied	
in a good mood	unconcerned	

lucky

advantageous	favourable	fortunate
convenient	felicitous	opportune

---

trial, tribulation, want, need, privation (*fml*), austerity, poverty, destitution, misery.
F3 ease, comfort, prosperity.

hard-wearing *adjective*
durable, lasting, strong, tough, sturdy, stout, rugged, resilient.
F3 delicate.

hardworking *adjective*
industrious, diligent, assiduous (*fml*), conscientious, zealous, busy, energetic.
F3 idle, lazy.

hardy *adjective*
strong, tough, sturdy, robust, vigorous, fit, sound, healthy.
F3 weak, unhealthy.

harm *noun*
damage, loss, injury, hurt, detriment, ill, misfortune, wrong, abuse.
F3 benefit.
► *verb*
damage, impair, blemish, spoil, mar, ruin, hurt, injure, wound, ill-treat, maltreat, abuse, misuse.
F3 benefit, improve.

happy

WORD *workshop*

Instead of repeating **happy** in the following passage, you might use some of the synonyms discussed opposite.

Ultrazap®

satisfied
Are you ~~happy~~ with your microwave? Does it heat your food the way it should?

pleased
At Ultrazap® we are ~~happy~~ to announce that over 90% of our
delighted
customers have said that they are ~~happy~~ with our new deluxe model. New technology means that it heats your food even
content
faster. You can relax, ~~happy~~ in the knowledge that your food will be piping hot within minutes.

fortunate
By a ~~happy~~ coincidence, this month is our anniversary. To celebrate, the price of the deluxe model will be cut by 25%. All new customers will be entered for a draw – some lucky
thrilled
person will be ~~happy~~ to win a holiday in the sun.

harmful *adjective*
damaging, detrimental, pernicious, noxious, unhealthy, unwholesome, injurious, dangerous, hazardous, poisonous, toxic, destructive.
Fऄ harmless, safe.

harmless *adjective*
safe, innocuous, non-toxic, inoffensive, gentle, innocent.
Fऄ harmful, dangerous, destructive.

harmonious *adjective*
1 harmonious sounds: melodious,
tuneful, musical, sweet-sounding.
2 harmonious colours/relationship: matching, co-ordinated, balanced, compatible, like-minded, agreeable, cordial, amicable, peaceable, friendly, sympathetic.
Fऄ 1 discordant. **2** inharmonious.

harmonize *verb*
match, co-ordinate, balance, fit in, suit, tone, blend (in), correspond, agree, reconcile, accommodate, adapt, arrange, compose.
Fऄ clash.

harmony *noun*
1 the harmony of his playing: tunefulness, tune, melody, euphony.
2 live in harmony: agreement, unanimity, accord, concord, unity, compatibility, like-mindedness, peace, goodwill, rapport, sympathy, understanding, amicability, friendliness, co-operation, co-ordination, balance, symmetry, correspondence, conformity.
F3 1 discord. **2** conflict.

harness *noun*
tackle, gear, equipment, reins, straps, tack.
▶ *verb*
control, channel, use, utilize, exploit, make use of, employ, mobilize, apply.

harrowing *adjective*
distressing, upsetting, heart-rending, disturbing, alarming, frightening, terrifying, nerve-racking, traumatic, agonizing, excruciating.

harry *verb*
badger, pester, nag, chivvy, harass, plague, torment, persecute, annoy, vex, worry, trouble, bother, hassle (*infml*), disturb, molest.

harsh *adjective*
1 a harsh punishment: severe, strict, Draconian, unfeeling, cruel, hard, pitiless, austere, Spartan, bleak, grim, comfortless.
2 a harsh sound: rough, coarse, rasping, croaking, guttural, grating, jarring, discordant, strident, raucous, sharp, shrill, unpleasant.
3 harsh colour: bright, dazzling, glaring, gaudy, lurid.
F3 1 lenient. **2** soft. **3** subdued.

harvest *noun*
1 an early harvest: harvest-time, ingathering, reaping, collection.
2 a good harvest of grapes: crop, yield, return, produce, fruits, result, consequence.
▶ *verb*
reap, mow, pick, gather, collect, accumulate, amass.

haste *noun*
hurry, rush, hustle, bustle, speed, velocity, rapidity, swiftness, quickness, briskness, urgency, rashness, recklessness, impetuosity.
F3 slowness.

hasten *verb*
hurry, rush, make haste, run, sprint, dash, tear, race, fly, bolt, accelerate, speed (up), quicken, expedite, dispatch, precipitate (*fml*), urge, press, advance, step up.
F3 dawdle, delay.

hasty *adjective*
hurried, rushed, impatient, headlong, rash, reckless, heedless, thoughtless, impetuous, impulsive, hot-headed, fast, quick, rapid, swift, speedy, brisk, prompt, short, brief, cursory.
F3 slow, careful, deliberate.

hatch *verb*
1 hatching her eggs: incubate, brood, breed.
2 hatch a plot: concoct, formulate, originate, think up, dream up, conceive, devise, contrive, plot, scheme, design, plan, project.

hate *verb*
dislike, despise, detest, loathe, abhor, abominate, execrate (*fml*).
F3 like, love.
▶ *noun*
hatred, aversion, dislike, loathing, abhorrence (*fml*), abomination.
F3 liking, love.

hatred *noun*
hate, aversion, dislike, detestation, loathing, repugnance, revulsion, abhorrence (*fml*), abomination, execration (*fml*), animosity, ill-will, antagonism, hostility, enmity, antipathy.
F3 liking, love.

haughty *adjective*
lofty, imperious, high and mighty, supercilious, cavalier, snooty (*infml*), contemptuous, disdainful, scornful, superior, snobbish, arrogant, proud, stuck-up (*infml*), conceited.
F3 humble, modest.

haul *verb*
pull, heave, tug, draw, tow, drag, trail, move, transport, convey, carry, cart, lug, hump (*infml*).
F3 push.

▶ *noun*
loot, booty, plunder, swag (*slang*), spoils, takings, gain, yield, find.

haunt *verb*
1 haunting the art galleries: frequent, patronize, visit.
2 memories haunted her: plague, torment, trouble, disturb, recur, prey on, beset, obsess, possess.

▶ *noun*
resort, hangout (*infml*), stamping-ground, den, meeting-place, rendezvous.

haunting *adjective*
memorable, unforgettable, persistent, recurrent, evocative, nostalgic, poignant.

have *verb*
1 have a job: own, possess, get, obtain, gain, acquire, procure, secure, receive, accept, keep, hold.
2 have a good time/a heart attack: feel, experience, enjoy, suffer, undergo, endure, put up with.
3 have two bedrooms: contain, include, comprise, incorporate, consist of.
4 have a baby: give birth to, bear.
F3 1 lack.

◆ **have to** must, be forced, be compelled, be obliged, be required, ought, should.

haven *noun*
harbour, port, anchorage, shelter, refuge, sanctuary, asylum, retreat.

havoc *noun*
chaos, confusion, disorder, disruption, damage, destruction, ruin, wreck, rack and ruin, devastation, waste, desolation.

haywire *adjective* (*infml*)
wrong, tangled, out of control, crazy, mad, wild, chaotic, confused, disordered, disorganized, topsy-turvy.

hazard *noun*
risk, danger, peril, jeopardy, threat, death-trap, accident, chance.
F3 safety.

hazardous *adjective*
risky, dangerous, unsafe, perilous, precarious, insecure, chancy, difficult, tricky.
F3 safe, secure.

hazy *adjective*
misty, foggy, smoky, clouded, cloudy, milky, fuzzy, blurred, ill-defined, veiled, obscure, dim, faint, unclear, indistinct, vague, indefinite, uncertain.
F3 clear, bright, definite.

head *noun*
1 bump his head/all in his head/have a good head on her shoulders: skull, cranium, brain, mind, mentality, brains (*infml*), intellect, intelligence, understanding, thought.
2 the head of the queue: top, peak, summit, crown, tip, apex, height, climax, front, fore, lead.
3 the head of the school: leader, chief, captain, commander, boss, director, manager, superintendent, principal, head teacher, ruler.
F3 2 base, foot, end. **3** subordinate.

▶ *adjective*
leading, front, foremost, first, chief, main, prime, principal, top, highest, supreme, premier, dominant, pre-eminent.

▶ *verb*
lead, rule, govern, command, direct, manage, run, superintend, oversee, supervise, control, guide, steer.

◆ **head for** make for, go towards, direct towards, aim for, point to, turn for, steer for.

◆ **head off** forestall, intercept, intervene, interpose, deflect, divert, fend off, ward off, avert, prevent, stop.

heading *noun*
title, name, headline, rubric, caption, section, division, category, class.

headland *noun*
promontory, cape, head, point, foreland.

headlong *adjective*
hasty, precipitate (*fml*), impetuous, impulsive, rash, reckless, dangerous, breakneck, head-first.

▶ *adverb*
head first, hurriedly, hastily, precipitately, rashly, recklessly, heedlessly, thoughtlessly, wildly.

headquarters *noun*
HQ, base (camp), head office, nerve centre.

headstrong *adjective*
stubborn, obstinate, intractable, pigheaded, wilful, self-willed, perverse, contrary.
E3 tractable, docile.

headway *noun*
advance, progress, way, improvement.

heady *adjective*
intoxicating, strong, stimulating, exhilarating, thrilling, exciting.

heal *verb*
cure, remedy, mend, restore, treat, soothe, salve, settle, reconcile, patch up.

health *noun*
fitness, constitution, form, shape, trim, fettle, condition, tone, state, healthiness, good condition, well-being, welfare, soundness, robustness, strength, vigour.
E3 illness, infirmity.
⇨ *See also* **Word Study** *panel.*

healthy *adjective*
1 a healthy child/stay healthy: well, fit, good, fine, in condition, in good shape, in fine fettle, sound, sturdy, robust, strong, vigorous, hale and hearty, blooming, flourishing, thriving.
2 healthy food: wholesome, nutritious, nourishing, bracing, invigorating, healthful.
E3 1 ill, sick, infirm.

heap *noun*
pile, stack, mound, mountain, lot, mass, accumulation, collection, hoard, stockpile, store.
▶ *verb*
pile, stack, mound, bank, build, amass, accumulate, collect, gather, hoard, stockpile, store, load, burden, shower, lavish.

hear *verb*
1 hear him calling: listen, catch, pick up, overhear, eavesdrop, heed, pay attention.
2 I heard she's going to Australia: learn, find out, discover, ascertain, understand, gather.
3 hear the case: judge, try, examine, investigate.

hearing *noun*
1 said in his hearing: earshot, sound, range, reach, ear, perception.
2 a preliminary hearing: trial, inquiry, investigation, inquest, audition, interview, audience.

hearsay *noun*
rumour, word of mouth, talk, gossip, tittle-tattle, report, buzz (*infml*).

heart *noun*
1 have no heart: soul, mind, character, disposition, nature, temperament, feeling, emotion, sentiment, love, tenderness, compassion, sympathy, pity.
2 lose heart: courage, bravery, boldness, spirit, resolution, determination.
3 the heart of the countryside/the matter: centre, middle, core, kernel, nucleus, nub, crux, essence.
E3 2 cowardice. 3 periphery.
◆ **by heart** by rote, parrot-fashion, pat, off pat, word for word, verbatim.

heartbreaking *adjective*
distressing, sad, tragic, harrowing, heart-rending, pitiful, agonizing, grievous, bitter, disappointing.
E3 heartwarming, heartening.

heartbroken *adjective*
broken-hearted, desolate, sad, miserable, dejected, despondent, downcast, crestfallen, disappointed, dispirited, grieved, crushed.
E3 delighted, elated.

hearten *verb*
comfort, console, reassure, cheer (up), buck up (*infml*), encourage, boost, inspire, stimulate, rouse, pep up (*infml*).
E3 dishearten, depress, dismay.

heartfelt *adjective*
deep, profound, sincere, honest, genuine, earnest, ardent, fervent, whole-hearted, warm.
E3 insincere, false.

heartless *adjective*
unfeeling, uncaring, cold, hard, hard-hearted, callous, unkind, cruel, inhuman, brutal, pitiless, merciless.
E3 kind, considerate, sympathetic, merciful.

heart-rending *adjective*
harrowing, heartbreaking, agonizing,

WORD *study*   health

When talking or writing about your own or someone else's **health**, you might choose to use one of the phrases from the lists below.

feeling ill or unhealthy

be at a low ebb
be/feel off-colour
be/feel out of sorts
be in a bad way
be out of shape
be a nervous wreck
look like death warmed up
not look yourself

be/feel below par
be out of condition
be/feel under the weather
be out of joint
be pale/green around the gills
feel like nothing on earth
not feel yourself
overdo it

recovering from illness

be on the mend

be up and about

strong and healthy

alive and kicking
have the constitution of an ox
in shape
right as rain

fit as a fiddle
hale and hearty
on top form

---

pitiful, piteous, pathetic, tragic, sad, distressing, moving, affecting, poignant.

heartwarming *adjective*
pleasing, gratifying, satisfying, cheering, heartening, encouraging, touching, moving, affecting.
E3 heartbreaking.

hearty *adjective*
1 a hearty welcome/laugh: enthusiastic, whole-hearted, unreserved, heartfelt, sincere, genuine, warm, friendly, cordial, jovial, cheerful, ebullient, exuberant, boisterous, energetic, vigorous.
2 a hearty breakfast: large, sizable, substantial, filling, ample, generous.
E3 1 half-hearted, cool, cold.

heat *noun*
1 the heat of the day: hotness, warmth,

sultriness, closeness, high temperature.
2 in the heat of the moment: ardour, fervour, fieriness, passion, intensity, vehemence, fury, excitement, impetuosity, earnestness, zeal.
E3 1 cold(ness). **2** coolness.
▶ *verb*
warm, boil, toast, cook, bake, roast, reheat, warm up, inflame, excite, animate, rouse, stimulate, flush, glow.
E3 cool, chill.

heated *adjective*
angry, furious, raging, passionate, fiery, stormy, tempestuous, bitter, fierce, intense, vehement, violent, frenzied.
E3 calm.

heave *verb*
1 heave the piano up a flight of stairs: pull, haul, drag, tug, raise, lift, hitch, hoist, lever, rise, surge.

2 heave a brick through the window: throw, fling, hurl, cast, toss, chuck, let fly.

heavy *adjective*
1 a heavy load/a heavy chocolate pudding: weighty, hefty, ponderous, burdensome, massive, large, bulky, solid, dense, stodgy.
2 heavy work: hard, difficult, tough, arduous, laborious, strenuous, demanding, taxing, harsh, severe.
3 a heavy atmosphere: oppressive, intense, serious, dull, tedious.
Fa 1 light. **2** easy.

hectic *adjective*
busy, frantic, frenetic, chaotic, fast, feverish, excited, heated, furious, wild.
Fa leisurely.

hedge *noun*
hedgerow, screen, windbreak, barrier, fence, dike, boundary.
▶ *verb*
1 hedged in by problems: surround, enclose, hem in, confine, restrict, fortify, guard, shield, protect, safeguard, cover.
2 he always hedges when asked a direct question: stall, temporize, equivocate, dodge, sidestep, evade, duck.

heed *verb*
listen, pay attention, mind, note, regard, observe, follow, obey.
Fa ignore, disregard.

heedless *adjective*
oblivious, unthinking, careless, negligent, rash, reckless, inattentive, unobservant, thoughtless, unconcerned.
Fa mindful, attentive.

hefty *adjective*
heavy, weighty, big, large, burly, hulking, beefy, brawny, strong, powerful, vigorous, robust, strapping, solid, substantial, massive, colossal, bulky, unwieldy.
Fa slight, small.

height *noun*
1 the height of Everest: highness, altitude, elevation, tallness, loftiness, stature.
2 when the sun is at its height: top, summit, peak, pinnacle, apex, crest, crown, zenith, apogee, culmination, climax, extremity, maximum, limit, ceiling.
Fa 1 depth.

heighten *verb*
raise, elevate, increase, add to, magnify, intensify, strengthen, sharpen, improve, enhance.
Fa lower, decrease, diminish.

helm *noun*
tiller, wheel, driving seat, reins, saddle, command, control, leadership, direction.

help *verb*
1 can you help me, please: aid, assist, lend a hand, serve, be of use, collaborate, co-operate, back, stand by, support.
2 shouting won't help the situation: improve, ameliorate (*fml*), relieve, alleviate, mitigate, ease, facilitate.
Fa 1 hinder. **2** worsen.
noun
aid, assistance, collaboration, co-operation, support, advice, guidance, service, use, utility, avail, benefit.
Fa hindrance.
⇨ *See also* **Word Study** *panel.*

helper *noun*
assistant, deputy, auxiliary, subsidiary, attendant, right-hand man, PA, mate, partner, associate, colleague, collaborator, accomplice, aide, ally, supporter, second.

helpful *adjective*
1 made some helpful comments: useful, practical, constructive, worthwhile, valuable, beneficial, advantageous.
2 a helpful person: co-operative, obliging, neighbourly, friendly, caring, considerate, kind, sympathetic, supportive.
Fa 1 useless, futile.

helping *noun*
serving, portion, share, ration, amount, plateful, piece, dollop (*infml*).

helpless *adjective*
weak, feeble, powerless, dependent, vulnerable, exposed, unprotected, defenceless, abandoned, friendless,

WORD *study*

help

Try out some of these phrases when you are talking or writing about **help** given or received, or when you are describing someone as **helpful**.

helping someone

aid and abet
come to the aid of someone *or* come to someone's aid
do someone a good turn
give someone a leg up

be of service to someone
come through for someone
give/lend a hand
lighten someone's load

doing all you can to help

lean/bend over backwards

take great pains

someone who is helpful

a life-saver
an angel of mercy

a tower of strength
worth their weight in gold

destitute, forlorn, incapable, incompetent, infirm, disabled, paralysed.
F∃ strong, independent, competent.

hem *noun*
edge, border, margin, fringe, trimming.
◆ **hem in** surround, enclose, box in, confine, restrict.

herald *noun*
messenger, courier, harbinger, forerunner, precursor, omen, token, signal, sign, indication.
▶ *verb*
announce, proclaim, broadcast, advertise, publicize, trumpet, pave the way, precede, usher in, show, indicate, promise.

herd *noun*
flock, swarm, pack, press, crush, mass, horde, throng, multitude, crowd, mob, the masses, rabble.

hereditary *adjective*
inherited, bequeathed, handed down,

family, ancestral, inborn, inbred, innate, natural, congenital, genetic.

heritage *noun*
history, past, tradition, culture.

hero *noun*
protagonist, lead, celebrity, star, superstar, idol, paragon, goody (*infml*), champion, conqueror.

heroic *adjective*
brave, courageous, fearless, dauntless, undaunted, lion-hearted, stout-hearted, valiant, bold, daring, intrepid, adventurous, gallant, chivalrous, noble, selfless.
F∃ cowardly, timid.

heroism *noun*
bravery, courage, valour, boldness, daring, intrepidity, gallantry, prowess, selflessness.
F∃ cowardice, timidity.

hesitant *adjective*
hesitating, reluctant, half-hearted, uncertain, unsure, indecisive, irresolute, vacillating, wavering,

tentative, wary, shy, timid, halting, stammering, stuttering.
E3 decisive, resolute, confident, fluent.

hesitate *verb*
pause, delay, wait, be reluctant, be unwilling, think twice, hold back, shrink from, scruple, boggle, demur, vacillate, waver, be uncertain, dither, shilly-shally, falter, stumble, halt, stammer, stutter.
E3 decide.

hesitation *noun*
pause, delay, reluctance, unwillingness, hesitance, scruple(s), qualm(s), misgivings, doubt, second thoughts, vacillation, uncertainty, indecision, irresolution, faltering, stumbling, stammering, stuttering.
E3 eagerness, assurance.

heyday *noun*
peak, prime, flush, bloom, flowering, golden age, boom time.

hidden *adjective*
1 a hidden door : concealed, covered, shrouded, veiled, disguised, camouflaged, unseen, secret.
2 hidden meaning : obscure, dark, occult, secret, covert, close, cryptic, mysterious, abstruse (*fml*), mystical, latent, ulterior.
E3 1 showing, apparent. 2 obvious.

hide[1] *verb*
1 hiding the key/truth : conceal, cover, cloak, shroud, veil, screen, mask, disguise, camouflage, obscure, shadow, eclipse, bury, stash (*infml*), secrete (*fml*), withhold, keep dark, suppress.
2 hid behind some rocks : take cover, shelter, lie low, go to ground, hole up (*infml*).
E3 1 reveal, show, display.

hide[2] *noun*
cow hide : skin, pelt, fell, fur, leather.

hideous *adjective*
ugly, repulsive, grotesque, monstrous, horrid, ghastly, awful, dreadful, frightful, terrible, grim, gruesome, macabre, terrifying, shocking, appalling, disgusting, revolting, horrible.
E3 beautiful, attractive.

hiding[1] *noun*
given a good hiding : beating, flogging, whipping, caning, spanking, thrashing, walloping (*infml*).

hiding[2] *noun*
remain in hiding : concealment, cover, veiling, screening, disguise, camouflage.

hiding-place *noun*
hide-away, hideout, lair, den, hole, hide, cover, refuge, haven, sanctuary, retreat.

hierarchy *noun*
pecking order, ranking, grading, scale, series, ladder, echelons, strata.

high *adjective*
1 a high cliff : tall, lofty, elevated, soaring, towering.
2 a high wind : great, strong, intense, extreme.
3 a high official : important, influential, powerful, eminent, distinguished, prominent, chief, leading, senior.
4 a high voice : high-pitched, soprano, treble, sharp, shrill, piercing.
5 a high price : expensive, dear, costly, exorbitant, excessive.
E3 1 low, short. 2 light, gentle. 3 lowly. 4 deep. 5 cheap.

highbrow *noun*
intellectual, egghead (*infml*), scholar, academic.
▶ *adjective*
intellectual, sophisticated, cultured, cultivated, academic, bookish, brainy (*infml*), deep, serious, classical.
E3 lowbrow.

high-class *adjective*
upper-class, posh (*infml*), classy (*infml*), top-class, top-flight, high-quality, quality, de luxe, superior, excellent, first-rate, choice, select, exclusive.
E3 ordinary, mediocre.

high-handed *adjective*
overbearing, domineering, bossy (*infml*), imperious, dictatorial, autocratic, despotic, tyrannical, oppressive, arbitrary.

highlight *noun*
high point, high spot, peak, climax, best, cream.

▶ *verb*
underline, emphasize, stress, accentuate, play up, point up, spotlight, illuminate, show up, set off, focus on, feature.

highly *adverb*
very, greatly, considerably, decidedly, extremely, immensely, tremendously, exceptionally, extraordinarily, enthusiastically, warmly, well.

highly-strung *adjective*
sensitive, neurotic, nervy, jumpy, edgy, temperamental, excitable, restless, nervous, tense.
F3 calm.

high-powered *adjective*
powerful, forceful, driving, aggressive, dynamic, go-ahead, enterprising, energetic, vigorous.

high-spirited *adjective*
boisterous, bouncy, exuberant, bold, effervescent, frolicsome, ebullient, sparkling, vibrant, vivacious, lively, energetic, spirited, dashing, daring.
F3 quiet, sedate.

hijack *verb*
commandeer, expropriate (*fml*), skyjack, seize, take over.

hike *verb*
ramble, walk, trek, tramp, trudge, plod.
▶ *noun*
ramble, walk, trek, tramp, march.

hilarious *adjective*
funny, amusing, comical, side-splitting, hysterical (*infml*), uproarious, noisy, rollicking, merry, jolly, jovial.
F3 serious, grave.

hill *noun*
1 *rolling hills*: hillock, knoll, mound, prominence, eminence, elevation, foothill, down, fell, mountain, height.
2 *a steep hill*: slope, incline, gradient, ramp, rise, ascent, acclivity (*fml*), drop, descent, declivity (*fml*).

hinder *verb*
hamper, obstruct, impede, encumber, handicap, hamstring, hold up, delay, retard, slow down, hold back, check, curb, stop, prevent, frustrate, thwart, oppose.
F3 help, aid, assist.

hindrance *noun*
obstruction, impediment, handicap, encumbrance, obstacle, stumbling block, barrier, bar, check, restraint, restriction, limitation, difficulty, drag, snag, hitch, drawback, disadvantage, inconvenience, deterrent.
F3 help, aid, assistance.

hinge *verb*
centre, turn, revolve, pivot, hang, depend, rest.

hint *noun*
1 *give them a hint*: tip, advice, suggestion, help, clue, inkling, suspicion, tip-off, reminder, indication, sign, pointer, mention, allusion, intimation, insinuation, implication, innuendo.
2 *a hint of garlic*: touch, trace, tinge, taste, dash, soupçon, speck.
▶ *verb*
suggest, prompt, tip off, indicate, imply, insinuate, intimate, allude, mention.

hire *verb*
rent, let, lease, charter, commission, book, reserve, employ, take on, sign up, engage, appoint, retain.
F3 dismiss, fire (*infml*).
▶ *noun*
rent, rental, fee, charge, cost, price.

historic *adjective*
momentous, consequential, important, significant, epoch-making, notable, remarkable, outstanding, extraordinary, celebrated, renowned, famed, famous.
F3 unimportant, insignificant, unknown.

historical *adjective*
real, actual, authentic, factual, documented, recorded, attested, verifiable.
F3 legendary, fictional.

history *noun*
1 *characters from history*: past, olden days, days of old, antiquity.
2 *a history of the twentieth century*: chronicle, record, annals, archives, chronology, account, narrative, story, tale, saga, biography, life, autobiography, memoirs.

hit verb
1 hit the ball: strike, knock, tap, smack, slap, thrash, whack (*infml*), bash, thump, clout, punch, belt (*infml*), wallop (*infml*), beat, batter.
2 hit his head: bump, collide with, bang, crash, smash, damage, harm.
▶ *noun*
1 several good hits to make 20 more runs: stroke, shot, blow, knock, tap, slap, smack, bash, bump, collision, impact, crash, smash.
2 be a great hit: success, triumph, winner (*infml*).
F∃ 2 failure.
◆ **hit back** retaliate, reciprocate, counter-attack, strike back.
◆ **hit on** chance on, stumble on, light on, discover, invent, realize, arrive at, guess.
◆ **hit out** lash out, assail, attack, rail, denounce, condemn, criticize.

hitch noun
delay, hold-up, trouble, problem, difficulty, mishap, setback, hiccup, drawback, snag, catch, impediment, hindrance.
▶ *verb*
1 hitch the horse to the wagon: fasten, attach, tie, harness, yoke, couple, connect, join, unite.
2 hitching up her dress: pull, heave, yank (*infml*), tug, jerk, hoist, hike (up) (*infml*).
F∃ 1 unhitch, unfasten.

hoard noun
collection, accumulation, mass, heap, pile, fund, reservoir, supply, reserve, store, stockpile, cache, treasure-trove.
▶ *verb*
collect, gather, amass, accumulate, save, put by, lay up, store, stash away (*infml*), stockpile, keep, treasure.
F∃ use, spend, squander.

hoarse adjective
husky, croaky, throaty, guttural, gravelly, gruff, growling, rough, harsh, rasping, grating, raucous, discordant.
F∃ clear, smooth.

hoax noun
trick, prank, practical joke, put-on (*infml*), joke, leg-pull (*infml*), spoof,
fake, fraud, deception, bluff, humbug, cheat, swindle, con (*infml*).

hobble verb
limp, stumble, falter, stagger, totter, dodder, shuffle.

hobby noun
pastime, diversion, recreation, relaxation, pursuit, sideline.

hoist verb
lift, elevate, raise, erect, jack up, winch up, heave, rear, uplift.

hold verb
1 hold her hand: grip, grasp, clutch, clasp, embrace, have, own, possess, keep, retain.
2 hold a meeting: conduct, carry on, continue, call, summon, convene, assemble.
3 (*fml*) he holds that it just wasn't possible: consider, deem, judge, reckon, think, believe, maintain.
4 hold fifty passengers: bear, support, sustain, carry, comprise, contain, accommodate.
5 holding him for questioning: imprison, detain, stop, arrest, check, curb, restrain.
6 fetch me a nail - these screws aren't holding: cling, stick, adhere, stay.
F∃ 1 drop. **5** release, free, liberate.
▶ *noun*
1 keep a tight hold: grip, grasp, clasp, embrace.
2 have a hold over him: influence, power, sway, mastery, dominance, authority, control, leverage.
◆ **hold back 1** hold back her tears: control, curb, check, restrain, suppress, stifle, retain, withhold, repress, inhibit.
2 don't hold back if you have something to say: hesitate, delay, desist, refrain, shrink, refuse.
F∃ 1 release.
◆ **hold forth** speak, talk, lecture, discourse, orate, preach, declaim.
◆ **hold off 1** hold off the attack: fend off, ward off, stave off, keep off, repel, rebuff.
2 hold off until September: put off, postpone, defer, delay, wait.
◆ **hold out 1** he held out his hand to me: give, present, extend.

2 they held out until help arrived: last, continue, persist, endure, persevere, stand fast, hang on.
F∃ 2 give in, yield.

◆ **hold up 1 holding up the roof**: support, sustain, brace, shore up, lift, raise.

2 holding up the traffic: delay, detain, retard, slow, hinder, impede.

◆ **hold with** agree with, go along with, approve of, countenance, support, subscribe to, accept.

hole *noun*

1 a hole in the pipe: aperture, opening, orifice, pore, puncture, perforation, eyelet, tear, split, vent, outlet, shaft, slot, gap, breach, break, crack, fissure, fault, defect, flaw.

2 a hole in the ground: dent, dimple, depression, hollow, cavity, crater, pit, excavation, cavern, cave, chamber, pocket, niche, recess, burrow, nest, lair, retreat.

holiday *noun*

vacation, recess, leave, time off, day off, break, rest, half-term, bank-holiday, feast-day, festival, celebration, anniversary.

hollow *adjective*

1 a hollow tube: empty, vacant, unfilled, concave, indented, depressed, sunken, deep, cavernous.

2 a hollow victory: false, artificial, deceptive, insincere, meaningless, empty, vain, futile, fruitless, worthless.
F∃ 1 solid. **2** real.

▶ *noun*

hole, pit, well, cavity, crater, excavation, cavern, cave, depression, concavity, basin, bowl, cup, dimple, dent, indentation, groove, channel, trough, valley.

holy *adjective*

1 holy ground: sacred, hallowed, consecrated, sanctified, dedicated, blessed, venerated, revered, spiritual, divine, evangelical.

2 a holy man: pious, religious, devout, godly, God-fearing, saintly, virtuous, good, righteous, faithful, pure, perfect.
F∃ 1 unsanctified. **2** impious, irreligious.

home *noun*

residence, domicile, dwelling-place, abode (*fml*), base, house, pied-à-terre, hearth, fireside, birthplace, home town, home ground, territory, habitat, element.

▶ *adjective*

domestic, household, family, internal, local, national, inland.
F∃ foreign, international.

◆ **at home 1 feel at home here**: comfortable, relaxed, at ease.

2 at home with all these technical terms: familiar, knowledgeable, experienced, skilled.

homeless *adjective*

itinerant, travelling, nomadic, wandering, vagrant, rootless, unsettled, displaced, dispossessed, evicted, exiled, outcast, abandoned, forsaken, destitute, down-and-out.

▶ *noun*

travellers, vagabonds, vagrants, tramps, down-and-outs, dossers (*infml*), squatters.

homely *adjective*

homelike, homey, comfortable, cosy, snug, relaxed, informal, friendly, intimate, familiar, everyday, ordinary, domestic, natural, plain, simple, modest, unassuming, unpretentious, unsophisticated, folksy, homespun.
F∃ grand, formal.

hone *verb*

sharpen, whet, point, edge, grind, file, polish.

honest *adjective*

1 an honest answer: truthful, sincere, frank, candid, blunt, outspoken, direct, straight, outright, forthright, straightforward, plain, simple, open, above-board, legitimate, legal, lawful, on the level (*infml*), fair, just, impartial, objective.

2 an honest citizen: law-abiding, virtuous, upright, ethical, moral, high-minded, scrupulous, honourable, reputable, respectable, reliable, trustworthy, true, genuine, real.
F∃ 1 dishonest. **2** dishonourable.

honorary *adjective*
unpaid, unofficial, titular, nominal, in name only, honorific, formal.
E3 paid.

honour *noun*
1 the honour of his family : reputation, good name, repute, renown, distinction, esteem, regard, respect, credit, dignity, self-respect, pride, integrity, morality, decency, rectitude, probity (*fml*).
2 military honours : award, accolade, commendation, acknowledgement, recognition, tribute, privilege.
3 in her honour : praise, acclaim, homage, admiration, reverence, worship, adoration.
E3 **1** dishonour, disgrace.
▸ *verb*
1 honouring the saint : praise, acclaim, exalt, glorify, pay homage to, decorate, crown, celebrate, commemorate, remember, admire, esteem, respect, revere, worship, prize, value.
2 honour a promise : keep, observe, respect, fulfil, carry out, discharge, execute, perform.
E3 **1** dishonour, disgrace.

honourable *adjective*
great, eminent, distinguished, renowned, respected, worthy, prestigious, trusty, reputable, respectable, virtuous, upright, upstanding, straight, honest, trustworthy, true, sincere, noble, principled, moral, ethical, fair, just, right, proper, decent.
E3 dishonourable, unworthy, dishonest.

hop *verb*
jump, leap, spring, bound, vault, skip, dance, prance, frisk.

hope *noun*
hopefulness, optimism, ambition, aspiration, wish, desire, longing, dream, expectation, anticipation, prospect, promise, belief, confidence, assurance, conviction, faith.
E3 pessimism, despair.
▸ *verb*
aspire, wish, desire, long, expect, await, look forward, anticipate, contemplate,

foresee, believe, trust, rely, reckon on, assume.
E3 despair.

hopeful *adjective*
1 hopeful that it will turn out well : optimistic, bullish (*infml*), confident, assured, expectant, sanguine, cheerful, buoyant.
2 a hopeful sign : encouraging, heartening, reassuring, favourable, auspicious, promising, rosy, bright.
E3 **1** pessimistic, despairing. **2** discouraging.

hopeless *adjective*
1 felt hopeless about the future : pessimistic, defeatist, negative, despairing, demoralized, downhearted, dejected, despondent, forlorn, wretched.
2 a hopeless dream : unattainable, unachievable, impracticable, impossible, vain, foolish, futile, useless, pointless.
3 a hopeless failure/case : worthless, poor, helpless, lost, irremediable, irreparable, incurable.
E3 **1** hopeful, optimistic. **2** possible. **3** curable.

horde *noun*
band, gang, pack, herd, drove, flock, swarm, crowd, mob, throng, multitude, host.

horizon *noun*
skyline, vista, prospect, compass, range, scope, perspective.

horrible *adjective*
unpleasant, disagreeable, nasty, unkind, horrid, disgusting, revolting, offensive, repulsive, hideous, grim, ghastly, awful, dreadful, frightful, fearful, terrible, abominable, shocking, appalling, horrific.
E3 pleasant, agreeable, lovely, attractive.

horrific *adjective*
horrifying, shocking, appalling, awful, dreadful, ghastly, gruesome, terrifying, frightening, scary, harrowing, bloodcurdling.

horrify *verb*
shock, outrage, scandalize, appal,

disgust, sicken, dismay, alarm, startle, scare, frighten, terrify.
E3 please, delight.

horror *noun*
1 recoil in horror: shock, outrage, disgust, revulsion, repugnance, abhorrence (*fml*), loathing, dismay, consternation, alarm, fright, fear, terror, panic, dread, apprehension.
2 the horrors of war: ghastliness, awfulness, frightfulness, hideousness.
E3 1 approval, delight.

hospitable *adjective*
friendly, sociable, welcoming, receptive, cordial, amicable, congenial, convivial, genial, kind, gracious, generous, liberal.
E3 inhospitable, unfriendly, hostile.

hostile *adjective*
belligerent, warlike, ill-disposed, unsympathetic, unfriendly, inhospitable, inimical, antagonistic, opposed, adverse, unfavourable, contrary, opposite.
E3 friendly, welcoming, favourable.

hot *adjective*
1 a hot climate/hot soup: warm, heated, fiery, burning, scalding, blistering, scorching, roasting, baking, boiling, steaming, sizzling, sweltering, sultry, torrid, tropical.
2 a hot curry: spicy, peppery, piquant, sharp, pungent, strong.
E3 1 cold, cool. 2 mild.

hotel *noun*
boarding-house, guest-house, pension, motel, inn, public house, pub (*infml*), hostel.

hotheaded *adjective*
headstrong, impetuous, impulsive, hasty, rash, reckless, fiery, volatile, hot-tempered, quick-tempered.
E3 cool, calm.

hound *verb*
chase, pursue, hunt (down), drive, goad, prod, chivvy, nag, pester, badger, harry, harass, persecute.

house *noun*
1 rows of neat little houses: building, dwelling, residence, home.

> *Types of house include:*
>
> bungalow, cottage, council house, detached, pied-à-terre, prefab (*infml*), semi-detached, semi (*infml*), terraced, thatched cottage, town house; apartment, bedsit, condominium (*US*), duplex (*US*), flat, granny flat, maisonette, penthouse, studio; chalet, croft, farmhouse, grange, hacienda, hall, homestead, lodge, manor, manse, mansion, parsonage, ranch house, rectory, shack, shanty, treehouse, vicarage, villa; hut, igloo, log cabin, tepee, wigwam, yurt. ⇨ *See also* **accommodation**; **building**.

2 the house of Stuart: dynasty, family, clan, tribe.
▶ *verb*
1 soldiers housed with local families: lodge, quarter, billet, board, accommodate, put up, take in, shelter, harbour.
2 housing the crown jewels: hold, contain, protect, cover, sheathe, place, keep, store.

household *noun*
family, family circle, house, home, ménage, establishment, set-up.
▶ *adjective*
domestic, home, family, ordinary, plain, everyday, common, familiar, well-known, established.

hover *verb*
1 a hawk hovering above: hang, poise, float, drift, fly, flutter, flap.
2 he hovered by the door: pause, linger, hang about, hesitate, waver, fluctuate, seesaw.

however *conjunction*
nevertheless, nonetheless, still, yet, even so, notwithstanding, though, anyhow.

howl *noun, verb*
wail, cry, shriek, scream, shout, yell, roar, bellow, bay, yelp, hoot, moan, groan.

hub *noun*
centre, middle, focus, focal point, axis, pivot, linchpin, nerve centre, core, heart.

hubbub *noun*
noise, racket, din, clamour, commotion, disturbance, riot, uproar, hullabaloo, rumpus, confusion, disorder, tumult, hurly-burly, chaos, pandemonium.
≠ peace, quiet.

huddle *noun*
1 sheep stood in a huddle by the gate: cluster, clump, knot, mass, crowd, muddle, jumble.
2 go into a huddle: conclave, conference, meeting.
▶ *verb*
cluster, gravitate, converge, meet, gather, congregate, crowd, flock, throng, press, cuddle, snuggle, nestle, curl up, crouch, hunch.
≠ disperse.

hue *noun*
colour, shade, tint, dye, tinge, nuance, tone, complexion, aspect, light.

huff *noun*
pique, sulks, mood, bad mood, anger, rage, passion.

hug *verb*
embrace, cuddle, squeeze, enfold, hold, clasp, clutch, grip, cling to, enclose.
▶ *noun*
embrace, cuddle, squeeze, clasp, hold, clinch.

huge *adjective*
immense, vast, enormous, massive, colossal, titanic, giant, gigantic, mammoth, monumental, tremendous, great, big, large, bulky, unwieldy.
≠ tiny, minute.

hulking *adjective*
massive, heavy, unwieldy, bulky, awkward, ungainly.
≠ small, delicate.

hum *verb*
buzz, whirr, purr, drone, thrum, croon, sing, murmur, mumble, throb, pulse, vibrate.

human *adjective*
1 he's only human: mortal, fallible, susceptible, reasonable, rational.
2 he's quite human once you get to know him: kind, considerate, understanding, humane, compassionate.

≠ **2** inhuman.
▶ *noun*
human being, mortal, homo sapiens, man, woman, child, person, individual, body, soul.

humane *adjective*
kind, compassionate, sympathetic, understanding, kind-hearted, good-natured, gentle, tender, loving, mild, lenient, merciful, forgiving, forbearing, kindly, benevolent, charitable, humanitarian, good.
≠ inhumane, cruel.

humanitarian *adjective*
benevolent, charitable, philanthropic, public-spirited, compassionate, humane, altruistic, unselfish.
≠ selfish, self-seeking.

humanity *noun*
1 affecting the whole of humanity: human race, humankind, mankind, womankind, mortality, people.
2 the humanity of their actions: humaneness, kindness, compassion, fellow-feeling, understanding, tenderness, benevolence, generosity, goodwill.
≠ **2** inhumanity, cruelty.

humble *adjective*
1 try to be humble: meek, submissive, unassertive, self-effacing, polite, respectful, deferential, servile, subservient, sycophantic, obsequious.
2 their humble home: lowly, low, mean, insignificant, unimportant, common, commonplace, ordinary, plain, simple, modest, unassuming, unpretentious, unostentatious.
≠ **1** proud, assertive. **2** important, pretentious.
▶ *verb*
bring down, lower, bring low, abase, demean, sink, discredit, disgrace, shame, humiliate, mortify, chasten, crush, deflate, subdue, belittle.
≠ exalt.

humdrum *adjective*
boring, tedious, monotonous, routine, dull, dreary, uninteresting, uneventful, ordinary, mundane, everyday, commonplace.
≠ lively, unusual, exceptional.

humid *adjective*
damp, moist, dank, clammy, sticky, muggy, sultry, steamy.
≠dry.

humiliate *verb*
mortify, embarrass, confound, crush, break, deflate, chasten, shame, disgrace, discredit, degrade, demean, humble, bring low.
≠dignify, exalt.

humility *noun*
meekness, submissiveness, deference, self-abasement (*fml*), servility, humbleness, lowliness, modesty, unpretentiousness.
≠pride, arrogance, assertiveness.

humorous *adjective*
funny, amusing, comic, entertaining, witty, satirical, jocular, facetious, playful, waggish, droll, whimsical, comical, farcical, zany (*infml*), ludicrous, absurd, hilarious, side-splitting.
≠serious, humourless.

humour *noun*
1 enjoy his kind of humour: wit, drollery, jokes, jesting, badinage, repartee, facetiousness, satire, comedy, farce, fun, amusement.
2 in a bad humour: mood, temper, frame of mind, spirits, disposition, temperament.
▶ *verb*
go along with, comply with, accommodate, gratify, indulge, pamper, spoil, favour, please, mollify, flatter.

humourless *adjective*
boring, tedious, dull, dry, solemn, serious, glum, morose.
≠humorous, witty.

hunch *noun*
premonition, presentiment, intuition, suspicion, feeling, impression, idea, guess.
▶ *verb*
hump, bend, curve, arch, stoop, crouch, squat, huddle, draw in, curl up.

hunger *noun*
1 die from hunger: hungriness, emptiness, starvation, malnutrition, famine, appetite, ravenousness.

2 hunger for power: desire, craving, longing, yearning, itch, thirst.

hungry *adjective*
1 I feel hungry: starving, peckish (*infml*), empty, hollow, famished, ravenous.
2 hungry for knowledge: desirous, craving, longing, aching, thirsty, eager, avid.
≠1 satisfied, full.

hunk *noun*
chunk, lump, piece, block, slab, wedge, mass, clod.

hunt *verb*
1 police hunting the killer: chase, pursue, hound, dog, stalk, track, trail.
2 hunt for her umbrella: seek, look for, search, scour, rummage, forage, investigate.
▶ *noun*
chase, pursuit, search, quest, investigation.

hurdle *noun*
jump, fence, wall, hedge, barrier, barricade, obstacle, obstruction, stumbling block, hindrance, impediment, handicap, problem, snag, difficulty, complication.

hurl *verb*
throw, toss, fling, sling, catapult, project, propel, fire, launch, send.

hurried *adjective*
rushed, hectic, hasty, precipitate (*fml*), speedy, quick, swift, rapid, passing, brief, short, cursory, superficial, shallow, careless, slapdash.
≠leisurely.

hurry *verb*
rush, dash, fly, get a move on (*infml*), hasten, quicken, speed up, hustle, push.
≠slow down, delay.
▶ *noun*
rush, haste, quickness, speed, urgency, hustle, bustle, flurry, commotion.
≠leisureliness, calm.
⇨ *See also* **Word Study** *panel.*

hurt *verb*
1 my leg hurts: ache, pain, throb, sting, smart.
2 hurt her head: injure, wound, maltreat, ill-treat, bruise, cut, burn, torture, maim, disable.

WORD *study*

There are many rather informal phrases for describing being in a **hurry**, and many ways of telling someone to **hurry up**. Try some of these in your speech or writing.

go in a hurry

beat a retreat   hightail it
press on

tell someone to hurry up

chop-chop!   get a move on!
get cracking!   get your skates on!
jump to it!   look alive/lively!
look sharp!   look smart!
make it snappy!   put your foot down!
shake a leg!   show your heels!
step on it!

be in a hurry

be pressed for time   be pushed for time
be rushed off your feet

do or make something in a hurry

bang something out   dash something off
throw something together

3 hurt his chances: damage, impair, harm, mar, spoil.
4 hurts me when he behaves like that: upset, sadden, grieve, distress, afflict, offend, wound, annoy.
▶ *noun*
pain, soreness, discomfort, suffering, injury, wound, damage, harm, distress, sorrow.
▶ *adjective*
1 how many people were hurt?: injured, wounded, bruised, grazed, cut, scarred, maimed.
2 hurt feelings: upset, sad, saddened, distressed, aggrieved, annoyed, offended, affronted, wounded.

hurtful *adjective*
upsetting, wounding, vicious, cruel, mean, unkind, nasty, malicious, spiteful, catty, derogatory, scathing, cutting.
F3 kind.

hurtle *verb*
dash, tear, race, fly, shoot, speed, rush, charge, plunge, dive, crash, rattle.

hush *verb*
quieten, silence, still, settle, compose, calm, soothe, subdue.
F3 disturb, rouse.
▶ *noun*
quietness, silence, peace, stillness, repose, calm, calmness, tranquillity, serenity.
F3 noise, clamour.
▶ *interjection*
quiet, hold your tongue, shut up (*infml*) not another word.

◆ **hush up** keep dark, suppress, conceal, cover up, stifle, gag.
🔁 publicize.

husk *noun*
covering, case, shell, pod, hull, rind, bran, chaff.

husky *adjective*
hoarse, croaky, croaking, low, throaty, guttural, gruff, rasping, rough, harsh.

hustle *verb*
hasten, rush, hurry, bustle, force, push, shove, thrust, bundle, elbow, jostle.

hut *noun*
cabin, shack, shanty, booth, shed, lean-to, shelter, den.

hybrid *adjective*
crossbred, mongrel, composite, combined, mixed, heterogeneous (*fml*), compound.
🔁 pure-bred.

hygiene *noun*
sanitariness, sanitation, sterility, disinfection, cleanliness, purity, wholesomeness.
🔁 insanitariness.

hygienic *adjective*
sanitary, sterile, aseptic, germ-free, disinfected, clean, pure, salubrious (*fml*), healthy, wholesome.
🔁 unhygienic, insanitary.

hyperbole *noun*
overstatement, exaggeration, magnification, extravagance.
🔁 understatement.

hypnotic *adjective*
mesmerizing, soporific (*fml*), sleep-inducing, spellbinding, fascinating, compelling, irresistible, magnetic.

hypnotize *verb*
mesmerize, spellbind, bewitch, enchant, entrance, fascinate, captivate, magnetize.

hypocritical *adjective*
insincere, two-faced, self-righteous, double-dealing, false, hollow, deceptive, spurious, deceitful, dissembling (*fml*), pharisaic(al) (*fml*).
🔁 sincere, genuine.

hypothetical *adjective*
theoretical, imaginary, supposed, assumed, proposed, conjectural, speculative.
🔁 real, actual.

hysterical *adjective*
1 become hysterical : frantic, frenzied, berserk, uncontrollable, mad, raving, crazed, demented, overwrought, neurotic.
2 (*infml*) hysterical laughter/the show's hysterical : hilarious, uproarious, side-splitting, priceless (*infml*), rich (*infml*).
🔁 1 calm, composed, self-possessed.

I i

ice *noun*
frost, rime, icicle, glacier, iciness, frostiness, coldness, chill.

icon *noun*
image, representation, symbol, idol, portrait.

icy *adjective*
1 *icy wind:* ice-cold, arctic, polar, glacial, freezing, frozen, raw, bitter, biting, cold, chill, chilly.
2 *icy roads:* frosty, slippery, glassy, frozen, icebound, frostbound.
3 *an icy silence:* hostile, cold, stony, cool, indifferent, aloof, distant, formal.
⬛ 1 hot. **3** friendly, warm.

idea *noun*
1 *have an idea:* thought, concept, notion, theory, hypothesis, guess, conjecture, belief, opinion, view, viewpoint, judgement, conception, vision, image, impression, perception, interpretation, understanding, inkling, suspicion, clue.
2 *a good idea:* brainwave, suggestion, proposal, proposition, plan, scheme, recommendation, design.
3 *that was the general idea:* aim, intention, purpose, reason, point, object.

ideal *noun*
perfection, epitome, acme, paragon, exemplar, example, model, pattern, archetype, prototype, type, image, criterion, standard, principle.
▶ *adjective*
perfect, dream, utopian, best, optimum, optimal, supreme, highest, model, archetypal.

idealistic *adjective*
perfectionist, utopian, visionary, romantic, quixotic, starry-eyed, optimistic, unrealistic, impractical, impracticable.
⬛ realistic, pragmatic.

identical *adjective*
same, self-same, indistinguishable, interchangeable, twin, duplicate, like, alike, corresponding, matching, equal, equivalent.
⬛ different.

identify *verb*
recognize, know, pick out, single out, distinguish, perceive, make out, discern, notice, detect, diagnose, name, label, tag, specify, pinpoint, place, catalogue, classify.
◆ **identify with** empathize with, relate to, associate with, respond to, sympathize with, feel for.

identity *noun*
individuality, particularity, singularity, uniqueness, self, personality, character, existence.

ideology *noun*
philosophy, world-view, ideas, principles, tenets, doctrine(s), convictions, belief(s), faith, creed, dogma.

idiom *noun*
phrase, expression, colloquialism, language, turn of phrase, phraseology, style, usage, jargon, vernacular.

idiosyncrasy *noun*
characteristic, peculiarity, singularity, oddity, eccentricity, freak, quirk, habit, mannerism, trait, feature.

idiotic *adjective*
foolish, stupid, silly, absurd, senseless, daft (*infml*), lunatic, insane, foolhardy, harebrained, halfwitted, moronic,

cretinous, crazy.
F≣ sensible, sane.

idle *adjective*
1 machines lying idle/he's been idle for three months: inactive, inoperative, unused, unoccupied, unemployed, jobless, redundant.
2 an idle layabout: lazy, work-shy, indolent.
3 idle talk: empty, trivial, casual, futile, vain, pointless, unproductive.
F≣ **1** active. **2** busy.

idol *noun*
icon, effigy, image, graven image, god, deity, fetish, favourite, darling, hero, heroine, pin-up, superstar, heart-throb (*infml*).

idolize *verb*
hero-worship, lionize, exalt, glorify, worship, venerate, revere, admire, adore, love, dote on.
F≣ despise.

idyllic *adjective*
perfect, idealized, heavenly, delightful, charming, picturesque, pastoral, rustic, unspoiled, peaceful, happy.
F≣ unpleasant.

ignite *verb*
set fire to, set alight, catch fire, flare up, burn, conflagrate, fire, kindle, touch off, spark off.
F≣ quench.

ignominious *adjective*
humiliating, mortifying, degrading, undignified, shameful, dishonourable, disreputable, disgraceful, despicable, scandalous.
F≣ triumphant, honourable.

ignorance *noun*
unintelligence, illiteracy, unawareness, unconsciousness, oblivion, innocence, unfamiliarity, inexperience, naïvety.
F≣ knowledge, wisdom.

ignorant *adjective*
uneducated, illiterate, unread, untaught, untrained, inexperienced, stupid, clueless (*infml*), uninitiated, unenlightened, uninformed, ill-informed, unwitting, unaware, unconscious, oblivious.
F≣ educated, knowledgeable, clever, wise.

ignore *verb*
disregard, take no notice of, shut one's eyes to, overlook, pass over, neglect, omit, reject, snub, cold-shoulder.
F≣ notice, observe.

ill *adjective*
1 feel/look ill: sick, poorly, unwell, indisposed, laid up, ailing, off-colour, out of sorts (*infml*), under the weather (*infml*), seedy, queasy, diseased, unhealthy, infirm, frail.
2 an ill omen: bad, evil, damaging, harmful, injurious, detrimental, adverse, unfavourable, inauspicious, unpromising, sinister, ominous, threatening, unlucky, unfortunate, difficult, harsh, severe, unkind, unfriendly, antagonistic.
F≣ **1** well. **2** good, favourable, fortunate.

illegal *adjective*
unlawful, illicit, criminal, wrong, forbidden, prohibited, banned, outlawed, unauthorized, under-the-counter, black-market, unconstitutional, wrongful.
F≣ legal, lawful.

illegible *adjective*
unreadable, indecipherable, scrawled, obscure, faint, indistinct.
F≣ legible.

ill-fated *adjective*
doomed, ill-starred, ill-omened, unfortunate, unlucky, luckless, unhappy.
F≣ lucky.

illicit *adjective*
illegal, unlawful, criminal, wrong, illegitimate, improper, forbidden, prohibited, unauthorized, unlicensed, black-market, contraband, ill-gotten, under-the-counter, furtive, clandestine.
F≣ legal, permissible.

illness *noun*
disease, disorder, complaint, ailment, sickness, ill health, ill-being, indisposition, infirmity, disability, affliction.

ill-treat *verb*
maltreat, abuse, injure, harm, damage, neglect, mistreat, mishandle, misuse, wrong, oppress.

illusion *noun*
apparition, mirage, hallucination, figment, fantasy, fancy, delusion, misapprehension, misconception, error, fallacy.
F3 reality, truth.

illusory *adjective*
illusive, deceptive, misleading, apparent, seeming, deluding, delusive, unreal, unsubstantial, sham, false, fallacious, untrue, mistaken.
F3 real.

illustrate *verb*
draw, sketch, depict, picture, show, exhibit, demonstrate, exemplify, explain, interpret, clarify, elucidate, illuminate, decorate, ornament, adorn.

illustration *noun*
1 book with full-colour illustrations: picture, plate, half-tone, photograph, drawing, sketch, figure, representation, decoration.
2 an illustration of what I mean: example, specimen, instance, case, analogy, demonstration, explanation, interpretation.

illustrious *adjective*
great, noble, eminent, distinguished, celebrated, famous, famed, renowned, noted, prominent, outstanding, remarkable, notable, brilliant, excellent, splendid, magnificent, glorious, exalted.
F3 ignoble, inglorious.

image *noun*
1 an image in his mind: idea, notion, concept, impression, perception.
2 images of the saints: representation, likeness, picture, portrait, icon, effigy, figure, statue, idol, replica, reflection.

imaginary *adjective*
imagined, fanciful, illusory, hallucinatory, visionary, pretend, make-believe, unreal, non-existent, fictional, fabulous, legendary, mythological, made-up, invented, fictitious, assumed, supposed, hypothetical.
F3 real.

imagination *noun*
imaginativeness, creativity, inventiveness, originality, inspiration,

insight, ingenuity, resourcefulness, enterprise, wit, vision, mind's eye, fancy, illusion.
F3 unimaginativeness, reality.

imaginative *adjective*
creative, inventive, innovative, original, inspired, visionary, ingenious, clever, resourceful, enterprising, fanciful, fantastic, vivid.
F3 unimaginative.

imagine *verb*
1 imagining what it would be like: picture, visualize, envisage, conceive, fancy, fantasize, pretend, make believe, conjure up, dream up, think up, invent, devise, create, plan, project.
2 I imagine so: think, believe, judge, suppose, guess, conjecture, assume, take it, gather.

imitate *verb*
copy, emulate, follow, ape, mimic, impersonate, take off, caricature, parody, send up, spoof, mock, parrot, repeat, echo, mirror, duplicate, reproduce, simulate, counterfeit, forge.

imitation *noun*
1 do an imitation of the prime minister: mimicry, impersonation, impression, take-off, caricature, parody, send-up, spoof, mockery, travesty.
2 cheap imitations of designer clothing: copy, duplicate, reproduction, replica, simulation, counterfeit, fake, forgery, sham, likeness, resemblance, reflection, dummy.
▸ *adjective*
artificial, synthetic, man-made, ersatz, fake, phoney (*infml*), mock, pseudo, reproduction, simulated, sham, dummy.
F3 genuine.

immaculate *adjective*
perfect, unblemished, flawless, faultless, impeccable, spotless, clean, spick and span, pure, unsullied, undefiled, untainted, stainless, blameless, innocent.
F3 blemished, stained, contaminated.

immaterial *adjective*
irrelevant, insignificant, unimportant,

minor, trivial, trifling, inconsequential.
 ≠ relevant, important.

immature *adjective*
young, under-age, adolescent, juvenile, childish, puerile (*fml*), infantile, babyish, raw, crude, callow, inexperienced, green, unripe, undeveloped.
 ≠ mature.

immediate *adjective*
1 an immediate response: instant, instantaneous, direct, prompt, swift, current, present, existing, urgent, pressing.
2 our immediate neighbours: nearest, next, adjacent, near, close, recent.
 ≠ 1 delayed. 2 distant.

immediately *adverb*
now, straight away, right away, at once, instantly, directly, forthwith, without delay, promptly, unhesitatingly.
 ≠ eventually, never.

immense *adjective*
vast, great, huge, enormous, massive, giant, gigantic, tremendous, monumental.
 ≠ tiny, minute.

immerse *verb*
plunge, submerge, submerse, sink, duck, dip, douse, bathe.

immigrant *noun*
incomer, settler, newcomer, alien.
 ≠ emigrant.

imminent *adjective*
impending, forthcoming, in the offing, approaching, coming, near, close, looming, menacing, threatening, brewing, in the air.
 ≠ remote, far-off.

immobilize *verb*
stop, halt, fix, freeze, transfix, paralyse, cripple, disable.
 ≠ mobilize.

immoral *adjective*
unethical, wrong, bad, sinful, evil, wicked, unscrupulous, unprincipled, dishonest, corrupt, depraved, degenerate, dissolute, lewd, indecent, pornographic, obscene, impure.
 ≠ moral, right, good.

immortal *adjective*
undying, imperishable, eternal, everlasting, perpetual, endless, ceaseless, lasting, enduring, abiding, timeless, ageless.
 ≠ mortal.

immune *adjective*
invulnerable, unsusceptible, resistant, proof, protected, safe, exempt, free, clear.
 ≠ susceptible.

immunize *verb*
vaccinate, inoculate, inject, protect, safeguard.

impact *noun*
1 the impact of the reforms: effect, consequences, repercussions, impression, power, influence, significance, meaning.
2 flung forward by the impact: collision, crash, smash, bang, bump, blow, knock, contact, jolt, shock, brunt.

impair *verb*
damage, harm, injure, hinder, mar, spoil, worsen, undermine, weaken, reduce, lessen, diminish, blunt.
 ≠ improve, enhance.

impartial *adjective*
objective, dispassionate, detached, disinterested, neutral, non-partisan, unbiased, unprejudiced, open-minded, fair, fair-minded, just, equitable, even-handed, equal.
 ≠ biased, prejudiced.

impassive *adjective*
expressionless, calm, composed, unruffled, unconcerned, cool, unfeeling, unemotional, unmoved, imperturbable, unexcitable, stoical, indifferent, dispassionate.
 ≠ responsive, moved.

impatient *adjective*
eager, keen, restless, fidgety, fretful, edgy, irritable, snappy, hot-tempered, quick-tempered, intolerant, brusque, abrupt, impetuous, hasty, precipitate (*fml*), headlong.
 ≠ patient.

impeccable *adjective*
perfect, faultless, precise, exact, flawless, unblemished, stainless,

immaculate, pure, irreproachable,
blameless, innocent.
F3 faulty, flawed, corrupt.

impede *verb*
hinder, hamper, obstruct, block, clog,
slow, retard, hold up, delay, check, curb,
restrain, thwart, disrupt, stop, bar.
F3 aid, promote, further.

impediment *noun*
hindrance, obstacle, obstruction,
barrier, bar, block, stumbling block,
snag, difficulty, handicap, check, curb,
restraint, restriction.
F3 aid.

impel *verb*
urge, force, oblige, compel, constrain,
drive, propel, push, spur, goad,
prompt, stimulate, excite, instigate,
motivate, inspire, move.
F3 deter, dissuade.

impending *adjective*
imminent, forthcoming, approaching,
coming, close, near, looming,
menacing, threatening.
F3 remote.

impenetrable *adjective*
1 **impenetrable jungle**: solid, thick,
dense, impassable.
2 **impenetrable logic**: unintelligible,
incomprehensible, unfathomable,
baffling, mysterious, cryptic,
enigmatic, obscure, dark, inscrutable.
F3 1 accessible. 2 understandable.

imperative *adjective*
compulsory, obligatory, essential, vital,
crucial, pressing, urgent.
F3 optional, unimportant.

imperceptible *adjective*
inappreciable, indiscernible, inaudible,
faint, slight, negligible, infinitesimal,
microscopic, minute, tiny, small, fine,
subtle, gradual.
F3 perceptible, obvious.

imperfect *adjective*
faulty, flawed, defective, damaged,
broken, chipped, deficient, incomplete.
F3 perfect.

impersonal *adjective*
formal, official, businesslike,
bureaucratic, faceless, aloof, remote,
distant, detached, neutral, objective,

dispassionate, cold, frosty, glassy.
F3 informal, friendly.

impersonate *verb*
imitate, mimic, take off, parody, ape,
caricature, mock, masquerade as, pose
as, act, portray.

impertinent *adjective*
rude, impolite, ill-mannered,
discourteous, disrespectful, insolent,
impudent, cheeky (*infml*), pert, bold,
brazen, forward, presumptuous, fresh.
F3 polite, respectful.

impervious *adjective*
1 **impervious to water**: impermeable,
waterproof, damp-proof, watertight,
hermetic, closed, sealed, impenetrable.
2 **impervious to criticism** immune,
invulnerable, untouched, unaffected,
unmoved, resistant.
F3 1 porous, pervious. 2 responsive,
vulnerable.

impetuous *adjective*
impulsive, spontaneous, unplanned,
unpremeditated, hasty, precipitate
(*fml*), rash, reckless, thoughtless,
unthinking.
F3 cautious, wary, circumspect (*fml*).

impetus *noun*
impulse, momentum, force, energy,
power, drive, boost, push, spur,
stimulus, incentive, motivation.

impinge *verb*
hit, touch (on), affect, influence,
encroach, infringe, intrude, trespass,
invade.

implement *noun*
tool, instrument, utensil, gadget,
device, apparatus, appliance.
▶ *verb*
enforce, effect, bring about, carry out,
execute, discharge, perform, do, fulfil,
complete, accomplish, realize.

implicate *verb*
involve, embroil, entangle, incriminate,
compromise, include, concern,
connect, associate.
F3 exonerate.

implication *noun*
1 **the implication is that we are
incompetent**: inference, insinuation,
suggestion, meaning, significance,

ramification, repercussion.
2 implication in the crimes:
involvement, entanglement,
incrimination, connection,
association.

implicit *adjective*
1 an implicit suggestion: implied,
inferred, insinuated, indirect, unsaid,
unspoken, tacit, understood.
2 implicit belief: unquestioning, utter,
total, full, complete, absolute,
unqualified, unreserved,
wholehearted.
F3 1 explicit. **2** half-hearted.

imply *verb*
suggest, insinuate, hint, intimate,
mean, signify, point to, indicate,
involve, require.
F3 state.

importance *noun*
momentousness, significance,
consequence, substance, matter,
concern, interest, usefulness, value,
worth, weight, influence, mark,
prominence, eminence, distinction,
esteem, prestige, status, standing.
F3 unimportance.

important *adjective*
1 an important point/discovery/exam:
momentous, noteworthy, significant,
meaningful, relevant, material, salient,
urgent, vital, essential, key, primary,
major, substantial, valuable, seminal,
weighty, serious, grave, far-reaching.
2 an important person: leading,
foremost, high-level, high-ranking,
influential, powerful, pre-eminent,
prominent, outstanding, eminent,
noted.
F3 1 unimportant, insignificant, trivial.

impose *verb*
1 imposing taxes: introduce, institute,
enforce, promulgate, exact, levy, set,
fix, put, place, lay, inflict, burden,
encumber, saddle.
2 impose on their hospitality: intrude,
butt in, encroach, trespass, obtrude,
force oneself, presume, take liberties.

imposing *adjective*
impressive, striking, grand, stately,
majestic, dignified.
F3 unimposing, modest.

impossible *adjective*
hopeless, impracticable, unworkable,
unattainable, unachievable,
unobtainable, insoluble, unreasonable,
unacceptable, inconceivable,
unthinkable, preposterous, absurd,
ludicrous, ridiculous.
F3 possible.

impostor *noun*
fraud, fake, phoney (*infml*), quack,
charlatan, impersonator, pretender,
con man (*infml*), swindler, cheat,
rogue.

impress *verb*
1 tried to impress me: strike, move,
touch, affect, influence, stir, inspire,
excite, grab (*infml*).
**2 must impress on them the
importance of this**: stamp, imprint,
mark, indent, instil, inculcate.

impression *noun*
**1 get the impression he doesn't want
to come**: feeling, awareness,
consciousness, sense, illusion, idea,
notion, opinion, belief, conviction,
suspicion, hunch, memory,
recollection.
2 do an impression of someone:
impersonation, imitation, take-off,
parody, send-up.
3 make a good impression: effect,
impact, influence.

impressionable *adjective*
naïve, gullible, susceptible, vulnerable,
sensitive, responsive, open, receptive.

impressive *adjective*
striking, imposing, grand, powerful,
effective, stirring, exciting, moving,
touching.
F3 unimpressive, uninspiring.

imprison *verb*
jail, incarcerate, intern, detain, send
down (*infml*), put away (*infml*), lock up,
cage, confine, shut in.
F3 release, free.

impromptu *adjective*
improvised, extempore (*fml*), ad-lib,
off the cuff, unscripted, unrehearsed,
unprepared, spontaneous.
F3 rehearsed.
▸ *adverb*
extempore (*fml*), ad lib, off the cuff, off

the top of one's head, spontaneously, on the spur of the moment.

improper *adjective*
wrong, incorrect, irregular, unsuitable, inappropriate, inopportune, incongruous, out of place, indecent, rude, vulgar, unseemly, unbecoming, shocking.
F∃ proper, appropriate, decent.

improve *verb*
better, ameliorate (*fml*), enhance, polish, touch up, mend, rectify, correct, amend, reform, upgrade, increase, rise, pick up, develop, look up, advance, progress, get better, recover, recuperate, rally, perk up, mend one's ways, turn over a new leaf.
F∃ worsen, deteriorate, decline.

improvement *noun*
betterment, amelioration (*fml*), enhancement, rectification, correction, amendment, reformation, increase, rise, upswing, gain, development, advance, progress, furtherance, recovery, rally.
F∃ deterioration, decline.

improvise *verb*
1 improvised a stage using a curtain: contrive, devise, concoct, invent, throw together, make do.
2 an actor who improvises a lot: extemporize (*fml*), ad-lib, play by ear, vamp.

impudent *adjective*
impertinent, cheeky (*infml*), saucy (*infml*), bold, forward, shameless, cocky, insolent, rude, presumptuous, fresh.
F∃ polite.

impulse *noun*
1 resisting an impulse to slap him: urge, wish, desire, inclination, whim, notion, instinct, feeling, passion.
2 the impulse behind the movement of peoples: impetus, momentum, force, pressure, drive, thrust, push, incitement, stimulus, motive.

impulsive *adjective*
impetuous, rash, reckless, hasty, quick, spontaneous, automatic, instinctive, intuitive.
F∃ cautious, premeditated.

impurity *noun*
adulteration, contamination, pollution, infection, corruption, dirtiness, contaminant, dirt, filth, foreign body, mark, spot.
F∃ purity.

inability *noun*
incapability, incapacity, powerlessness, impotence, inadequacy, weakness, handicap, disability.
F∃ ability.

inaccessible *adjective*
isolated, remote, unfrequented, unapproachable, unget-at-able (*infml*), unreachable, unattainable.
F∃ accessible.

inaccurate *adjective*
incorrect, wrong, erroneous, mistaken, faulty, flawed, defective, imprecise, inexact, loose, unreliable, unfaithful, untrue.
F∃ accurate, correct.

inadequate *adjective*
1 an inadequate supply of food: insufficient, short, wanting, deficient, scanty, sparse, meagre, niggardly.
2 feel inadequate/an inadequate attempt: incompetent, incapable, unequal, unqualified, ineffective, faulty, defective, imperfect, unsatisfactory.
F∃ 1 adequate. 2 satisfactory.

inadvertently *adverb*
accidentally, by chance, unintentionally, carelessly.
F∃ deliberately, consciously, carefully.

inane *adjective*
senseless, foolish, stupid, unintelligent, silly, idiotic, fatuous, frivolous, trifling, puerile (*fml*), mindless, vapid, empty, vacuous, vain, worthless, futile.
F∃ sensible.

inappropriate *adjective*
unsuitable, inapt, ill-suited, ill-fitted, irrelevant, incongruous, out of place, untimely, ill-timed, tactless, improper, unseemly, unbecoming, unfitting.
F∃ appropriate, suitable.

inaudible *adjective*
silent, noiseless, imperceptible, faint, indistinct, muffled, muted, low, mumbled.
F∃ audible, loud.

incapable *adjective*
unable, powerless, impotent, helpless, weak, feeble, unfit, unsuited, unqualified, incompetent, inept, inadequate, ineffective.
F3 capable.

incapacitated *adjective*
disabled, crippled, paralysed, immobilized, out of action.

incarnation *noun*
personification, embodiment, manifestation, impersonation.

incentive *noun*
bait, lure, enticement, carrot (*infml*), sweetener (*infml*), reward, encouragement, inducement, reason, motive, impetus, spur, stimulus, motivation.
F3 disincentive, discouragement, deterrent.

incessant *adjective*
ceaseless, unceasing, endless, never-ending, interminable, continual, persistent, constant, perpetual, eternal, everlasting, continuous, unbroken, unremitting, non-stop.
F3 intermittent, sporadic, periodic, temporary.

incidence *noun*
frequency, commonness, prevalence, extent, range, amount, degree, rate, occurrence.

incident *noun*
1 in a separate incident, two people were killed: occurrence, happening, event, episode, adventure, affair, occasion, instance.
2 a nasty incident involving a knife: disturbance, scene, upset, mishap, confrontation, clash, fight, skirmish, commotion.

incidental *adjective*
accidental, chance, random, minor, non-essential, secondary, subordinate, subsidiary, ancillary, supplementary, accompanying, attendant, related, contributory.
F3 important, essential.

incisive *adjective*
cutting, keen, sharp, acute, trenchant (*fml*), piercing, penetrating,

biting, caustic, acid, astute, perceptive.
F3 vague.

incite *verb*
prompt, instigate, rouse, foment, stir up, whip up, work up, excite, animate, provoke, stimulate, spur, goad, impel, drive, urge, encourage, egg on (*infml*).
F3 restrain.

inclement *adjective*
intemperate, harsh, severe, stormy, tempestuous, rough.
F3 fine.

incline *verb*
dispose, influence, persuade, affect, bias, prejudice.
▶ *noun*
slope, gradient, ramp, hill, rise, ascent, acclivity (*fml*), dip, descent, declivity (*fml*).

inclined *adjective*
liable, likely, given, apt, disposed, of a mind, willing.

include *verb*
comprise, incorporate, embody, comprehend, contain, enclose, embrace, encompass, cover, subsume, take in, add, allow for, take into account, involve, rope in.
F3 exclude, omit, eliminate.

inclusive *adjective*
comprehensive, full, all-in, all-inclusive, all-embracing, blanket, across-the-board, general, catch-all, overall, sweeping.
F3 exclusive, narrow.

incognito *adjective*
in disguise, disguised, masked, veiled, unmarked, unidentified, unrecognizable, unknown.
F3 undisguised.

income *noun*
revenue, returns, proceeds, gains, profits, interest, takings, receipts, earnings, pay, salary, wages, means.
F3 expenditure, expenses.

incoming *adjective*
arriving, entering, approaching, coming, homeward, returning, ensuing, succeeding, next, new.
F3 outgoing.

incompatible *adjective*
irreconcilable, contradictory, conflicting, at variance, inconsistent, clashing, mismatched, unsuited.
E∃ compatible.

incompetent *adjective*
incapable, unable, unfit, inefficient, inexpert, unskilful, bungling, stupid, useless, ineffective.
E∃ competent, able.

incomplete *adjective*
deficient, lacking, short, unfinished, abridged, partial, part, fragmentary, broken, imperfect, defective.
E∃ complete, exhaustive.

inconceivable *adjective*
unthinkable, unimaginable, mind-boggling (*infml*), staggering, unheard-of, unbelievable, incredible, implausible.
E∃ conceivable.

inconclusive *adjective*
unsettled, undecided, open, uncertain, indecisive, ambiguous, vague, unconvincing, unsatisfying.
E∃ conclusive.

incongruous *adjective*
inappropriate, unsuitable, out of place, out of keeping, inconsistent, conflicting, incompatible, irreconcilable, contradictory, contrary.
E∃ consistent, compatible.

inconsiderate *adjective*
unkind, uncaring, unconcerned, selfish, self-centred, intolerant, insensitive, tactless, rude, thoughtless, unthinking, careless, heedless.
E∃ considerate.

inconsistent *adjective*
1 a fact that is inconsistent with their theory: conflicting, at variance, at odds, incompatible, contradictory, contrary, incongruous, discordant.
2 he can be very inconsistent: changeable, variable, irregular, unpredictable, varying, unstable, unsteady, inconstant, fickle.
E∃ 2 constant.

inconspicuous *adjective*
hidden, concealed, camouflaged, plain, ordinary, unobtrusive, discreet, low-key, modest, unassuming, quiet, retiring, insignificant.
E∃ conspicuous, noticeable, obtrusive.

inconvenience *noun*
awkwardness, difficulty, annoyance, nuisance, hindrance, drawback, bother, trouble, fuss, upset, disturbance, disruption.
E∃ convenience.

inconvenient *adjective*
awkward, ill-timed, untimely, inopportune, unsuitable, difficult, embarrassing, annoying, troublesome, unwieldy, unmanageable.
E∃ convenient.

incorporate *verb*
include, embody, contain, subsume, take in, absorb, assimilate, integrate, combine, unite, merge, blend, mix, fuse, coalesce, consolidate.
E∃ separate.

increase *verb*
raise, boost, add to, improve, enhance, advance, step up, intensify, strengthen, heighten, grow, develop, build up, wax, enlarge, extend, prolong, expand, spread, swell, magnify, multiply, proliferate, rise, mount, soar, escalate.
E∃ decrease, reduce, decline.
▶ *noun*
rise, surge, upsurge, upturn, gain, boost, addition, increment, advance, step-up, intensification, growth, development, enlargement, extension, expansion, spread, proliferation, escalation.
E∃ decrease, reduction, decline.

incredible *adjective*
unbelievable, improbable, implausible, far-fetched, preposterous, absurd, impossible, inconceivable, unthinkable, unimaginable, extraordinary, amazing, astonishing, astounding.
E∃ credible, believable.

incredulous *adjective*
unbelieving, disbelieving, unconvinced, sceptical, doubting, distrustful, suspicious, dubious, doubtful, uncertain.
E∃ credulous.

incriminate *verb*
inculpate, implicate, involve, accuse,

charge, impeach, indict, point the
finger at, blame.
F∃ exonerate.

incur *verb*
suffer, sustain, provoke, arouse, bring
upon oneself, expose oneself to, meet
with, run up, gain, earn.

incurable *adjective*
1 an incurable disease: terminal, fatal,
untreatable, inoperable, hopeless.
2 an incurable romantic: incorrigible,
inveterate, hardened, dyed-in-the-wool.
F∃ 1 curable.

indebted *adjective*
obliged, grateful, thankful.

indecent *adjective*
improper, immodest, impure,
indelicate, offensive, obscene,
pornographic, lewd, licentious, vulgar,
coarse, crude, dirty, filthy, foul, gross,
outrageous, shocking.
F∃ decent, modest.

indecisive *adjective*
undecided, irresolute, undetermined,
vacillating, wavering, in two minds,
hesitating, faltering, tentative,
uncertain, unsure, doubtful,
inconclusive, indefinite, indeterminate,
unclear.
F∃ decisive.

indeed *adverb*
really, actually, in fact, certainly,
positively, truly, undeniably,
undoubtedly, to be sure.

indefinite *adjective*
unknown, uncertain, unsettled,
unresolved, undecided, undetermined,
undefined, unspecified, unlimited, ill-
defined, vague, indistinct, unclear,
obscure, ambiguous, imprecise,
inexact, loose, general.
F∃ definite, limited, clear.

indefinitely *adverb*
for ever, eternally, endlessly,
continually, ad infinitum.

independence *noun*
autonomy, self-government, self-
determination, self-rule, home rule,
sovereignty, freedom, liberty,
individualism, separation.
F∃ dependence.

independent *adjective*
1 an independent nation: autonomous,
self-governing, self-determining,
sovereign, absolute, non-aligned,
neutral, impartial, unbiased.
2 a very independent person: free,
liberated, unconstrained,
individualistic, unconventional, self-
sufficient, self-supporting, self-reliant,
unaided.
3 independent evidence: individual,
self-contained, separate, unconnected,
unrelated.
F∃ 1 dependent.

indescribable *adjective*
indefinable, inexpressible, unutterable,
unspeakable.
F∃ describable.

indestructible *adjective*
unbreakable, durable, tough, strong,
lasting, enduring, abiding, permanent,
eternal, everlasting, immortal,
imperishable.
F∃ breakable, mortal.

indicate *verb*
register, record, show, reveal, display,
manifest, point to, designate, specify,
point out, mark, signify, mean, denote,
express, suggest, imply.

indication *noun*
mark, sign, manifestation, evidence,
symptom, signal, warning, omen,
intimation, suggestion, hint, clue, note,
explanation.

indict *verb*
charge, accuse, arraign, impeach,
summon, summons, prosecute,
incriminate.
F∃ exonerate.

indifferent *adjective*
1 indifferent to their distress:
uninterested, unenthusiastic,
unexcited, apathetic, unconcerned,
unmoved, uncaring, unsympathetic,
cold, cool, distant, aloof, detached,
uninvolved, neutral, disinterested.
2 an indifferent meal: mediocre,
average, middling, passable, moderate,
fair, ordinary.
F∃ 1 interested, caring. 2 excellent.

indigenous *adjective*
native, aboriginal, original,

local, home-grown.
F₃ foreign.

indignant *adjective*
annoyed, angry, irate, heated, fuming,
livid, furious, incensed, infuriated,
exasperated, outraged.
F₃ pleased, delighted.

indignation *noun*
annoyance, anger, ire, wrath, rage, fury,
exasperation, outrage, scorn,
contempt.
F₃ pleasure, delight.

indirect *adjective*
1 an indirect route: roundabout,
circuitous, wandering, rambling,
winding, meandering, zigzag,
tortuous.
2 an indirect effect: secondary,
incidental, unintended, subsidiary,
ancillary.
F₃ 1 direct. 2 primary.

indiscreet *adjective*
tactless, undiplomatic, impolitic,
injudicious, imprudent, unwise,
foolish, rash, reckless, hasty, careless,
heedless, unthinking.
F₃ discreet, cautious.

indiscriminate *adjective*
general, sweeping, wholesale, random,
haphazard, hit or miss, aimless,
unsystematic, unmethodical, mixed,
motley, miscellaneous.
F₃ selective, specific, precise.

indispensable *adjective*
vital, essential, basic, key, crucial,
imperative, required, requisite, needed,
necessary.
F₃ dispensable, unnecessary.

indistinct *adjective*
unclear, ill-defined, blurred, fuzzy,
misty, hazy, shadowy, obscure, dim,
faint, muffled, confused, unintelligible,
vague, woolly, ambiguous, indefinite.
F₃ distinct, clear.

individual *noun*
person, being, creature, party, body,
soul, character, fellow.
▶ *adjective*
distinctive, characteristic,
idiosyncratic, peculiar, singular,
unique, exclusive, special, personal,
own, proper, respective, several,

separate, distinct, specific,
personalized, particular, single.
F₃ collective, shared, general.

individuality *noun*
character, personality, distinctiveness,
peculiarity, singularity, uniqueness,
separateness, distinction.
F₃ sameness.

indoctrinate *verb*
brainwash, teach, instruct, school,
ground, train, drill.

induce *verb*
1 inducing a violent response: cause,
effect, bring about, occasion, give rise
to, lead to, incite, instigate, prompt,
provoke, produce, generate.
2 induce him to stay: coax, prevail
upon, encourage, press, persuade, talk
into, move, influence, draw, tempt.
F₃ 2 discourage, deter.

indulge *verb*
gratify, satisfy, humour, pander to, go
along with, give in to, yield to, favour,
pet, cosset, mollycoddle, pamper,
spoil, treat, regale.

indulgence *noun*
extravagance, luxury, excess,
immoderation, intemperance, favour,
tolerance.

indulgent *adjective*
tolerant, easy-going (*infml*), lenient,
permissive, generous, liberal, kind,
fond, tender, understanding,
patient.
F₃ strict, harsh.

industrious *adjective*
busy, productive, hardworking,
diligent, assiduous (*fml*),
conscientious, zealous, active,
energetic, tireless, persistent,
persevering.
F₃ lazy, idle.

industry *noun*
1 the steel industry: business, trade,
commerce, manufacturing,
production.
2 the industry of the worker ants:
industriousness, diligence,
application, effort, labour, toil,
persistence, perseverance,
determination.

inedible *adjective*
uneatable, unpalatable, indigestible,
harmful, noxious, poisonous, deadly.
F3 edible.

ineffective *adjective*
useless, worthless, vain, idle, futile,
unavailing, fruitless, unproductive,
unsuccessful, powerless, impotent,
ineffectual, inadequate, weak, feeble,
inept, incompetent.
F3 effective, effectual.

inefficient *adjective*
uneconomic, wasteful, money-wasting,
time-wasting, incompetent, inexpert,
unworkmanlike, slipshod, sloppy,
careless, negligent.
F3 efficient.

inept *adjective*
awkward, clumsy, bungling,
incompetent. unskilful, inexpert,
foolish, stupid.
F3 competent, skilful.

inequality *noun*
unequalness, difference, diversity,
dissimilarity, disparity, unevenness,
disproportion, bias, prejudice.
F3 equality.

inert *adjective*
immobile, motionless, unmoving, still,
inactive, inanimate, lifeless, dead,
passive, unresponsive, apathetic,
dormant, idle, lazy, lethargic, sluggish,
torpid, sleepy.
F3 lively, animated.

inertia *noun*
immobility, stillness, inactivity,
passivity, unresponsiveness, apathy,
idleness, laziness, lethargy, torpor,
listlessness.
F3 activity, liveliness.

inevitable *adjective*
unavoidable, inescapable, necessary,
definite, certain, sure, decreed,
ordained, destined, fated, automatic,
assured, fixed, unalterable,
irrevocable, inexorable.
F3 avoidable, uncertain, alterable.

inexhaustible *adjective*
unlimited, limitless, boundless,
unbounded, infinite, endless, never-
ending, abundant.
F3 limited.

inexpensive *adjective*
cheap, low-priced, reasonable,
modest, bargain, budget, low-cost,
economical.
F3 expensive, dear.

inexperienced *adjective*
inexpert, untrained, unskilled,
amateur, probationary, apprentice,
unfamiliar, unacquainted,
unaccustomed, new, fresh, raw, callow,
young, immature, naïve,
unsophisticated, innocent.
F3 experienced, mature.

inexplicable *adjective*
unexplainable, unaccountable, strange,
mystifying, puzzling, baffling,
mysterious, enigmatic, unfathomable,
incomprehensible, incredible,
unbelievable, miraculous.
F3 explicable.

infallible *adjective*
accurate, unerring, unfailing,
foolproof, fail-safe, sure-fire (*infml*),
certain, sure, reliable, dependable,
trustworthy, sound, perfect, faultless,
impeccable.
F3 fallible.

infamous *adjective*
notorious, ill-famed, disreputable,
disgraceful, shameful, shocking,
outrageous, scandalous, wicked,
iniquitous.
F3 illustrious, glorious.

infancy *noun*
1 died in infancy: babyhood,
childhood, youth.
2 when computers were in their
infancy: beginning, start,
commencement, inception, outset,
birth, dawn, genesis, emergence,
origins, early stages.
F3 1 adulthood.

infant *noun*
baby, toddler, tot (*infml*), child, babe
(*fml*), babe in arms (*fml*).
F3 adult.
▶ *adjective*
newborn, baby, young, youthful,
juvenile, immature, growing,
developing, rudimentary, early, initial,
new.
F3 adult, mature.

infantile *adjective*
babyish, childish, puerile (*fml*),
juvenile, young, youthful, adolescent,
immature.
🔁 adult, mature.

infatuated *adjective*
besotted, obsessed, enamoured,
smitten (*infml*), crazy (*infml*),
spellbound, mesmerized, captivated,
fascinated, enraptured, ravished.
🔁 indifferent, disenchanted.

infect *verb*
contaminate, pollute, defile (*fml*),
taint, blight, poison, corrupt, pervert,
influence, affect, touch, inspire.

infectious *adjective*
contagious, communicable,
transmissible, infective, catching,
spreading, epidemic, virulent, deadly,
contaminating, polluting, defiling,
corrupting.

infer *verb*
derive, extrapolate, deduce, conclude,
assume, presume, surmise, gather,
understand.

inferior *adjective*
1 an inferior position: lower, lesser,
minor, secondary, junior, subordinate,
subsidiary, second-class, low, humble,
menial.
2 an inferior product: substandard,
second-rate, mediocre, bad, poor,
unsatisfactory, slipshod, shoddy.
🔁 **1** superior. **2** excellent.
▶ *noun*
subordinate, junior, underling (*infml*),
minion, vassal, menial.
🔁 superior.

infest *verb*
swarm, teem, throng, flood, overrun,
invade, infiltrate, penetrate, permeate,
pervade, ravage.

infinite *adjective*
limitless, unlimited, boundless,
unbounded, endless, never-ending,
inexhaustible, bottomless, innumerable,
numberless, uncountable, countless,
untold, incalculable, inestimable,
immeasurable, unfathomable, vast,
immense, enormous, huge, absolute,
total.
🔁 finite, limited.

infinitesimal *adjective*
tiny, minute, microscopic, minuscule,
inconsiderable, insignificant,
negligible, inappreciable,
imperceptible. .
🔁 great, large, significant.

infinity *noun*
eternity, perpetuity, limitlessness,
boundlessness, endlessness,
inexhaustibility, countlessness,
immeasurableness, vastness,
immensity.
🔁 finiteness, limitation.

infirm *adjective*
weak, feeble, frail, ill, unwell, poorly,
sickly, failing, faltering, unsteady,
shaky, wobbly, doddery, lame.
🔁 healthy, strong.

inflame *verb*
anger, enrage, infuriate, incense,
exasperate, madden, provoke,
stimulate, excite, rouse, arouse, agitate,
foment, kindle, ignite, fire, heat, fan,
fuel, increase, intensify, worsen,
aggravate.
🔁 cool, quench.

inflammable *adjective*
flammable, combustible, burnable.
🔁 non-flammable, incombustible,
flameproof.

inflammation *noun*
soreness, painfulness, tenderness,
swelling, abscess, infection, redness,
heat, rash, sore, irritation.

inflate *verb*
blow up, pump up, blow out, puff out,
swell, distend, bloat, expand, enlarge,
increase, boost, exaggerate.
🔁 deflate.

inflation *noun*
expansion, increase, rise, escalation,
hyperinflation.
🔁 deflation.

inflict *verb*
impose, enforce, perpetrate, wreak,
administer, apply, deliver, deal, mete
out, lay, burden, exact, levy.

influence *noun*
power, sway, rule, authority,
domination, mastery, hold, control,
direction, guidance, bias, prejudice,

pull, pressure, effect, impact, weight, importance, prestige, standing.

▶ *verb*

dominate, control, manipulate, direct, guide, manoeuvre, change, alter, modify, affect, impress, move, stir, arouse, rouse, sway, persuade, induce, incite, instigate, prompt, motivate, dispose, incline, bias, prejudice, predispose.

influential *adjective*

dominant, controlling, leading, authoritative, charismatic, persuasive, convincing, compelling, inspiring, moving, powerful, potent, effective, telling, strong, weighty, momentous, important, significant, instrumental, guiding.

F3 ineffective, unimportant.

influx *noun*

inflow, inrush, invasion, arrival, stream, flow, rush, flood, inundation.

inform *verb*

tell, advise, notify, communicate, impart, leak, tip off, acquaint, fill in (*infml*), brief, instruct, enlighten, illuminate.

◆ **inform on** betray, incriminate, shop (*slang*), tell on (*infml*), squeal (*infml*), blab (*infml*), grass (*slang*), denounce.

informal *adjective*

unofficial, unceremonious, casual, relaxed, easy, free, natural, simple, unpretentious, familiar, colloquial.

F3 formal, solemn.

information *noun*

facts, data, input, gen (*infml*), bumf (*infml*), intelligence, news, report, bulletin, communiqué, message, word, advice, notice, briefing, instruction, knowledge, dossier, database, databank, clues, evidence.

informative *adjective*

educational, instructive, edifying, enlightening, illuminating, revealing, forthcoming, communicative, chatty, gossipy, newsy, helpful, useful, constructive.

F3 uninformative.

informed *adjective*

1 we'll keep you informed: familiar, conversant (*fml*), acquainted,

enlightened, briefed, primed, posted, up to date, abreast, au fait, in the know (*infml*).

2 an informed opinion: well-informed, authoritative, expert, versed, well-read, erudite, learned, knowledgeable, well-researched.

F3 1 ignorant, unaware.

infringe *verb*

1 infringing the rules: break, violate, contravene, transgress, overstep, disobey, defy, flout, ignore.

2 infringing on their territory: intrude, encroach, trespass, invade.

infuriate *verb*

anger, vex, enrage, incense, exasperate, madden, provoke, rouse, annoy, irritate, rile, antagonize.

F3 calm, pacify.

ingenious *adjective*

clever, shrewd, cunning, crafty, skilful, masterly, imaginative, creative, inventive, resourceful, original, innovative.

F3 unimaginative.

ingrained *adjective*

fixed, rooted, deep-rooted, deep-seated, entrenched, immovable, ineradicable, permanent, inbuilt, inborn, inbred.

ingratiate *verb*

curry favour, flatter, creep, crawl, grovel, fawn, get in with.

ingratitude *noun*

ungratefulness, thanklessness, unappreciativeness, ungraciousness.

F3 gratitude, thankfulness.

ingredient *noun*

constituent, element, factor, component, part.

inhabit *verb*

live, dwell, reside, occupy, possess, colonize, settle, people, populate, stay.

inhabitant *noun*

resident, dweller, citizen, native, occupier, occupant, inmate, tenant, lodger.

inherent *adjective*

inborn, inbred, innate, inherited, hereditary, native, natural, inbuilt,

built-in, intrinsic, ingrained, essential,
fundamental, basic.

inherit verb
succeed to, accede to, assume, come
into, be left, receive.

inheritance noun
legacy, bequest, heritage, birthright,
heredity, descent, succession.

inhibit verb
discourage, repress, hold back,
suppress, curb, check, restrain, hinder,
impede, obstruct, interfere with,
frustrate, thwart, prevent, stop, stanch,
stem.
Ⓕ encourage, assist.

inhibited adjective
repressed, self-conscious, shy, reticent,
withdrawn, reserved, guarded,
subdued.
Ⓕ uninhibited, open, relaxed.

inhibition noun
repression, hang-up (infml), self-
consciousness, shyness, reticence,
reserve, restraint, curb, check,
hindrance, impediment, obstruction,
bar.
Ⓕ freedom.

inhuman adjective
barbaric, barbarous, animal, bestial,
vicious, savage, sadistic, cold-blooded,
brutal, cruel, inhumane.
Ⓕ human.

inhumane adjective
unkind, insensitive, callous, unfeeling,
heartless, cold-hearted, hard-hearted,
pitiless, ruthless, cruel, brutal,
inhuman.
Ⓕ humane, kind, compassionate.

initial adjective
first, beginning, opening, introductory,
inaugural, original, primary, early,
formative.
Ⓕ final, last.

initially adverb
at first, at the beginning, to begin with,
to start with, originally, first, firstly,
first of all.
Ⓕ finally, in the end.

initiate verb
begin, start, commence, originate,
pioneer, institute, set up, introduce,

launch, open, inaugurate, instigate,
activate, trigger, prompt, stimulate,
cause.

initiative noun
1 show some initiative: energy, drive,
dynamism, get-up-and-go (infml),
ambition, enterprise, resourcefulness,
inventiveness, originality,
innovativeness.
2 a government initiative: suggestion,
recommendation, action, lead, first
move, first step.

inject verb
1 injected into the vein: inoculate,
vaccinate.
2 inject a little humour into the
discussion: introduce, insert, add,
bring, infuse, instil.

injure verb
hurt, harm, damage, impair, spoil,
mar, ruin, disfigure, deface, mutilate,
wound, cut, break, fracture, maim,
disable, cripple, lame, ill-treat,
maltreat, abuse, offend, wrong, upset,
put out.

injury noun
wound, cut, lesion, fracture, trauma,
hurt, mischief, ill, harm, damage,
impairment, ruin, disfigurement,
mutilation, ill-treatment, abuse, insult,
offence, wrong, injustice.

injustice noun
unfairness, inequality, disparity,
discrimination, oppression, bias,
prejudice, one-sidedness,
partisanship, partiality, favouritism,
wrong, iniquity (fml).
Ⓕ justice, fairness.

inkling noun
suspicion, idea, notion, faintest (infml),
glimmering, clue, hint, intimation,
suggestion, allusion, indication, sign,
pointer.

inlet noun
bay, cove, creek, fjord, opening,
entrance, passage.

inn noun
public house, pub (infml), local (infml),
tavern, hostelry, hotel.

innate adjective
inborn, inbred, inherent, intrinsic,

native, natural, instinctive, intuitive.
F3 acquired, learnt.

inner *adjective*
internal, interior, inside, inward,
innermost, central, middle, concealed,
hidden, secret, private, personal,
intimate, mental, psychological,
spiritual, emotional.
F3 outer, outward.

innocent *adjective*
1 innocent of the crime: guiltless,
blameless, irreproachable,
unimpeachable, honest, upright,
virtuous, righteous, faultless,
impeccable, stainless, spotless,
immaculate, unsullied, untainted,
uncontaminated, pure, chaste,
virginal, inoffensive, harmless,
innocuous.
2 too innocent to understand: artless,
guileless, ingenuous, naïve, green,
inexperienced, fresh, natural, simple,
unsophisticated, unworldly, childlike,
credulous, gullible, trusting.
F3 1 guilty. **2** experienced.

innocuous *adjective*
harmless, safe, inoffensive,
unobjectionable, innocent.
F3 harmful.

innovative *adjective*
new, fresh, original, creative,
imaginative, inventive, resourceful,
enterprising, go-ahead, progressive,
reforming, groundbreaking, bold,
daring, adventurous.
F3 conservative, unimaginative.

innuendo *noun*
insinuation, aspersion (*fml*), slur,
whisper, hint, intimation, suggestion,
implication.

inoculation *noun*
vaccination, immunization,
protection, injection, shot (*infml*), jab
(*infml*).

inoffensive *adjective*
harmless, innocuous, innocent,
peaceable, mild, unobtrusive,
unassertive, quiet, retiring.
F3 offensive, harmful, provocative.

inordinate *adjective*
excessive, immoderate, unwarranted,
undue, unreasonable,

disproportionate, great.
F3 moderate, reasonable.

inquire, enquire *verb*
ask, question, quiz, query, investigate,
look into, probe, examine, inspect,
scrutinize, search, explore.

inquiry, enquiry *noun*
question, query, investigation, inquest,
hearing, inquisition, examination,
inspection, scrutiny, study, survey, poll,
search, probe, exploration.

inquisitive *adjective*
curious, questioning, probing,
searching, prying, peeping, snooping,
nosey, interfering, meddlesome,
intrusive.

insane *adjective*
1 go insane: mad, crazy, mentally ill,
lunatic, mental (*slang*), demented,
deranged, unhinged, disturbed.
2 an insane thing to do: foolish, stupid,
senseless, impractical.
F3 1 sane. **2** sensible.

insanity *noun*
madness, craziness, lunacy, mental
illness, neurosis, psychosis, mania,
dementia, derangement, folly,
stupidity, senselessness,
irresponsibility.
F3 sanity.

insatiable *adjective*
unquenchable, unsatisfiable, ravenous,
voracious, immoderate, inordinate.

inscription *noun*
engraving, epitaph, caption, legend,
lettering, words, writing, signature,
autograph, dedication.

inscrutable *adjective*
incomprehensible, unfathomable,
impenetrable, deep, inexplicable,
unexplainable, baffling, mysterious,
enigmatic, cryptic, hidden.
F3 comprehensible, expressive.

insect

Insects include:

cranefly, daddy longlegs (*infml*),
dragonfly, fly, gnat, horsefly, locust,
mayfly, midge, mosquito, tsetse-fly;
butterfly, red admiral, cabbage-white,
moth, tiger moth; bee, bumblebee,

hornet, wasp; aphid, blackfly, greenfly, froghopper, lacewing, ladybird, lady bug (*US*), water boatman, whitefly; beetle, cockroach, roach (*US*), earwig, grasshopper, cricket, cicada, flea, glow-worm, leatherjacket, louse, nit, stick insect, termite, woodworm, weevil, woodlouse.

Arachnids include:

spider, black widow, redback, tarantula; mite, scorpion, tick.

insecure *adjective*
1 feeling insecure: anxious, worried, nervous, uncertain, unsure, afraid.
2 an insecure position: unsafe, dangerous, hazardous, perilous, precarious, unsteady, shaky, loose, unprotected, defenceless, exposed, vulnerable.
Ea 1 confident, self-assured. **2** secure, safe.

insensitive *adjective*
hardened, tough, resistant, impenetrable, impervious, immune, unsusceptible, thick-skinned, unfeeling, impassive, indifferent, unaffected, unmoved, untouched, uncaring, unconcerned, callous, thoughtless, tactless, crass.
Ea sensitive.

inseparable *adjective*
indivisible, indissoluble, inextricable, close, intimate, bosom, devoted.
Ea separable.

insert *verb*
put, place, put in, stick in, push in, introduce, implant, embed, engraft, set, inset, let in, interleave, intercalate, interpolate, interpose.
▶ *noun*
insertion, enclosure, inset, notice, advertisement, supplement, addition.

inside *noun*
interior, content, contents, middle, centre, heart, core.
Ea outside.

▶ *adverb*
within, indoors, internally, inwardly, secretly, privately.
Ea outside.
▶ *adjective*
interior, internal, inner, innermost, inward, secret, classified, confidential, private.

insides *noun*
entrails, guts, intestines, bowels, innards (*infml*), organs, viscera, belly, stomach.

insidious *adjective*
subtle, sly, crafty, cunning, wily, deceptive, devious, stealthy, surreptitious, furtive, sneaking, treacherous.
Ea direct, straightforward.

insight *noun*
awareness, knowledge, comprehension, understanding, grasp, apprehension, perception, intuition, sensitivity, discernment, judgement, acumen, penetration, observation, vision, wisdom, intelligence.

insignificant *adjective*
unimportant, irrelevant, meaningless, inconsequential, minor, trivial, trifling, petty, paltry, small, tiny, insubstantial, inconsiderable, negligible, non-essential.
Ea significant, important.

insincere *adjective*
hypocritical, two-faced, double-dealing, lying, untruthful, dishonest, deceitful, devious, unfaithful, faithless, untrue, false, feigned, pretended, phoney (*infml*), hollow.
Ea sincere.

insinuate *verb*
imply, suggest, allude, hint, intimate, get at (*infml*), indicate.

insipid *adjective*
tasteless, flavourless, unsavoury, dry, unappetizing, watery, weak, bland, wishy-washy (*infml*), colourless, drab, dull, monotonous, boring, lifeless, uninteresting, tame, flat, spiritless, characterless, trite, unimaginative.
Ea tasty, spicy, piquant, appetizing.

insist *verb*
demand, require, urge, stress,

emphasize, repeat, reiterate, dwell on, harp on, assert, maintain, claim, contend, hold (*fml*), vow, swear, persist, stand firm.

insistent *adjective*
demanding, importunate (*fml*), emphatic, forceful, pressing, urgent, dogged, tenacious, persistent, persevering, relentless, unrelenting, unremitting, incessant.

insolent *adjective*
rude, abusive, insulting, disrespectful, cheeky (*infml*), impertinent, impudent, saucy (*infml*), bold, forward, fresh, presumptuous, arrogant, defiant, insubordinate.
F∃ polite, respectful.

insoluble *adjective*
unsolvable, unexplainable, inexplicable, incomprehensible, unfathomable, impenetrable, obscure, mystifying, puzzling, perplexing, baffling.
F∃ explicable.

inspect *verb*
check, vet, look over, examine, search, investigate, scrutinize, study, scan, survey, superintend, supervise, oversee, visit.

inspection *noun*
check, check-up, examination, scrutiny, scan, study, survey, review, search, investigation, supervision, visit.

inspiration *noun*
1 lacking inspiration: creativity, imagination, genius, muse, influence, encouragement, stimulation, motivation, spur, stimulus.
2 a flash of inspiration: idea, brainwave, insight, illumination, revelation, awakening.

inspire *verb*
encourage, hearten, influence, impress, animate, enliven, quicken (*fml*), galvanize, fire, kindle, stir, arouse, trigger, spark off, prompt, spur, motivate, provoke, stimulate, excite, exhilarate, thrill, enthral, enthuse, imbue, infuse.

inspiring *adjective*
encouraging, heartening, uplifting,

invigorating, stirring, rousing, stimulating, exciting, exhilarating, thrilling, enthralling, moving, affecting, memorable, impressive.
F∃ uninspiring, dull.

instability *noun*
unsteadiness, shakiness, vacillation, wavering, irresolution, uncertainty, unpredictability, changeableness, variability, fluctuation, volatility, capriciousness, fickleness, inconstancy, unreliability, insecurity, unsafeness, unsoundness.
F∃ stability.

install *verb*
fix, fit, lay, put, place, position, locate, site, situate, station, plant, settle, establish, set up, introduce, institute, inaugurate, invest, induct, ordain.

instalment *noun*
1 pay in instalments: payment, repayment, portion.
2 find out in the next instalment: episode, chapter, part, section, division.

instant *noun*
flash, twinkling, trice, moment, tick (*infml*), split second, second, minute, time, occasion.
▶ *adjective*
instantaneous, immediate, on-the-spot, direct, prompt, urgent, unhesitating, quick, fast, rapid, swift.
F∃ slow.

instead *adverb*
alternatively, preferably, rather.
◆ **instead of** in place of, in lieu of, on behalf of, in preference to, rather than.

instigate *verb*
initiate, set on, start, begin, cause, generate, inspire, move, influence, encourage, urge, spur, prompt, provoke, stimulate, incite, stir up, whip up, foment, rouse, excite.

instil *verb*
infuse, imbue, insinuate, introduce, inject, implant, inculcate, impress, din into (*infml*).

instinct *noun*
intuition, sixth sense, gut reaction (*infml*), impulse, urge, feeling, hunch, flair, knack, gift, talent, feel, faculty,

ability, aptitude, predisposition, tendency.

instinctive *adjective*
natural, native, inborn, innate, inherent, intuitive, impulsive, involuntary, automatic, mechanical, reflex, spontaneous, immediate, unthinking, unpremeditated, gut (*infml*), visceral.
E3 conscious, voluntary, deliberate.

institute *verb*
originate, initiate, introduce, enact, begin, start, commence, create, establish, set up, organize, found, inaugurate, open, launch, appoint, install, invest, induct, ordain.
E3 cancel, discontinue, abolish.
▶ *noun*
school, college, academy, conservatory, foundation, institution.

instruct *verb*
1 instructing them in safety procedures: teach, educate, tutor, coach, train, drill, ground, school, discipline.
2 instructed him to remain where he was: order, command, direct, mandate, tell, inform, notify, advise, counsel, guide.

instruction *noun*
1 follow the instructions: direction, recommendation, advice, guidance, information, order, command, injunction, mandate, directive, ruling.
2 computer instruction: education, schooling, lesson(s), tuition, teaching, training, coaching, drilling, grounding, preparation.

instructive *adjective*
informative, educational, edifying, enlightening, illuminating, helpful, useful.
E3 unenlightening.

instrument *noun*
tool, implement, utensil, appliance, gadget, contraption, device, contrivance, apparatus, mechanism.

instrumental *adjective*
active, involved, contributory, conducive, influential, useful, helpful, auxiliary, subsidiary.
E3 obstructive, unhelpful.

insufferable *adjective*
intolerable, unbearable, detestable, loathsome, dreadful, impossible.
E3 pleasant, tolerable.

insufficient *adjective*
inadequate, short, deficient, lacking, sparse, scanty, scarce.
E3 sufficient, excessive.

insular *adjective*
parochial, provincial, cut off, detached, isolated, remote, withdrawn, inward-looking, blinkered, closed, narrow-minded, narrow, limited, petty.
E3 cosmopolitan.

insulate *verb*
cushion, pad, lag, cocoon, protect, shield, shelter, isolate, separate, cut off.

insult *verb*
abuse, call names, disparage (*fml*), revile, libel, slander, slight, snub, injure, affront, offend, outrage.
E3 compliment, praise.
▶ *noun*
abuse, rudeness, insolence, defamation (*fml*), libel, slander, slight, snub, affront, indignity, offence, outrage.
E3 compliment, praise.

insurance *noun*
cover, protection, safeguard, security, provision, assurance, indemnity, guarantee, warranty, policy, premium.

intact *adjective*
unbroken, all in one piece, whole, complete, integral, entire, perfect, sound, undamaged, unhurt, uninjured.
E3 broken, incomplete, damaged.

intangible *adjective*
insubstantial, imponderable, elusive, fleeting, airy, shadowy, vague, indefinite, abstract, unreal, invisible.
E3 tangible, real.

integral *adjective*
intrinsic, constituent, elemental, basic, fundamental, necessary, essential, indispensable.
E3 extra, additional, unnecessary.

integrate *verb*
assimilate, merge, join, unite, combine, amalgamate, incorporate, coalesce, fuse, knit, mesh, mix,

blend, harmonize.
Ⓔ divide, separate.

integrity *noun*
1 I doubt his integrity: honesty,
uprightness, probity (*fml*),
incorruptibility, purity, morality,
principle, honour, virtue, goodness,
righteousness.
2 the integrity of the system:
completeness, wholeness, unity,
coherence, cohesion.
Ⓔ 1 dishonesty. 2 incompleteness.

intellect *noun*
mind, brain(s), brainpower,
intelligence, genius, reason,
understanding, sense, wisdom,
judgement.
Ⓔ stupidity.

intellectual *adjective*
academic, scholarly, intelligent,
studious, thoughtful, cerebral, mental,
highbrow, cultural.
Ⓔ lowbrow.
▶ *noun*
thinker, academic, highbrow, egghead,
mastermind, genius.
Ⓔ lowbrow.

intelligence *noun*
1 high/low intelligence: intellect,
reason, wit(s), brain(s) (*infml*),
brainpower, cleverness, brightness,
aptitude, quickness, alertness,
discernment, perception,
understanding, comprehension.
2 military intelligence: information,
facts, data, lowdown (*infml*),
knowledge, findings, news, report,
warning, tip-off.
Ⓔ 1 stupidity, foolishness.

intelligent *adjective*
clever, bright, smart, brainy (*infml*),
quick, alert, quick-witted, sharp, acute,
knowing, knowledgeable, well-
informed, thinking, rational, sensible.
Ⓔ unintelligent, stupid, foolish.

intend *verb*
aim, have a mind, contemplate, mean,
propose, plan, project, scheme, plot,
design, purpose, resolve, determine,
destine, mark out, earmark, set apart.

intense *adjective*
great, deep, profound, strong,

powerful, forceful, fierce, harsh, severe,
acute, sharp, keen, eager, earnest,
ardent, fervent, fervid, passionate,
vehement, energetic, violent, intensive,
concentrated, heightened.
Ⓔ moderate, mild, weak.

intensify *verb*
increase, step up, escalate, heighten,
hot up (*infml*), fire, boost, fuel,
aggravate, add to, strengthen,
reinforce, sharpen, whet, quicken
(*fml*), deepen, concentrate, emphasize,
enhance.
Ⓔ reduce, weaken.

intensive *adjective*
concentrated, thorough, exhaustive,
comprehensive, detailed, in-depth,
thoroughgoing, all-out, intense.
Ⓔ superficial.

intent *adjective*
determined, resolved, resolute, set,
bent, concentrated, eager, earnest,
committed, steadfast, fixed, alert,
attentive, concentrating, preoccupied,
engrossed, wrapped up, absorbed,
occupied.
Ⓔ absent-minded, distracted.

intention *noun*
aim, purpose, object, end, point,
target, goal, objective, idea, plan,
design, view, intent, meaning.

intentional *adjective*
designed, wilful, conscious, planned,
deliberate, prearranged, premeditated,
calculated, studied, intended, meant.
Ⓔ unintentional, accidental.

intercede *verb*
mediate, arbitrate, intervene, plead,
entreat, beseech, speak.

intercept *verb*
head off, ambush, interrupt, cut off,
stop, arrest, catch, take, seize, check,
block, obstruct, delay, frustrate,
thwart.

interchangeable *adjective*
reciprocal, equivalent, similar,
identical, the same, synonymous,
standard.
Ⓔ different.

interest *noun*
1 of great/little interest: importance,

significance, note, concern.
2 show some interest: attention, notice, curiosity, involvement, participation, care, concern.
3 leisure interests: activity, pursuit, pastime, hobby, diversion, amusement.
▶ *verb*
concern, involve, touch, move, attract, appeal to, divert, amuse, occupy, engage, absorb, engross, fascinate, intrigue.
Ea bore.

interested *adjective*
1 keep the audience interested: attentive, curious, absorbed, engrossed, fascinated, enthusiastic, keen, attracted.
2 an interested party: concerned, involved, affected.
Ea 1 uninterested, indifferent, apathetic. **2** disinterested, unaffected.

interesting *adjective*
attractive, appealing, entertaining, engaging, absorbing, engrossing, fascinating, intriguing, compelling, gripping, stimulating, thought-provoking, curious, unusual.
Ea uninteresting, boring, monotonous, tedious.

interfere *verb*
1 don't interfere: intrude, poke one's nose in (*infml*), pry, butt in, interrupt, intervene, meddle, tamper.
2 interfere with the proceedings: hinder, hamper, obstruct, block, impede, handicap, cramp, inhibit, conflict, clash.
Ea 2 assist.

interim *adjective*
temporary, provisional, stopgap, makeshift, improvised, stand-in, acting, caretaker.
▶ *noun*
meantime, meanwhile, interval.

interior *adjective*
1 interior view/life: internal, inside, inner, central, inward, mental, spiritual, private, secret, hidden.
2 interior design: home, domestic.
Ea 1 exterior, external.

▶ *noun*
inside, centre, middle, core, heart, depths.
Ea exterior, outside.

interjection *noun*
exclamation, ejaculation, cry, shout, call, interpolation.

intermediary *noun*
mediator, go-between, middleman, broker, agent.

intermediate *adjective*
midway, halfway, in-between, mean, middle, mid, median, intermediary, intervening, transitional.
Ea extreme.

interminable *adjective*
endless, never-ending, ceaseless, perpetual, limitless, unlimited, long, long-winded, long-drawn-out, dragging, wearisome.
Ea limited, brief.

intermission *noun*
interval, entr'acte, interlude, break, recess, rest, respite, breather (*infml*), breathing-space, pause, lull, let-up (*infml*), remission, suspension, interruption, halt, stop, stoppage, cessation.

intermittent *adjective*
occasional, periodic, sporadic, spasmodic, fitful, erratic, irregular, broken.
Ea continuous, constant.

internal *adjective*
inside, inner, interior, inward, intimate, private, personal, domestic, in-house.
Ea external.

international *adjective*
global, worldwide, intercontinental, cosmopolitan, universal, general.
Ea national, local, parochial.

interplay *noun*
exchange, interchange, interaction, reciprocation, give-and-take.

interpret *verb*
explain, expound, elucidate, clarify, throw light on, define, paraphrase, translate, render, decode, decipher, solve, make sense of, understand, construe, read, take.

interpretation *noun*
explanation, clarification, analysis, translation, rendering, version, performance, reading, understanding, sense, meaning.

interrogate *verb*
question, quiz, examine, cross-examine, grill, give the third degree, pump, debrief.

interrupt *verb*
intrude, barge in (*infml*), butt in, interject, break in, heckle, disturb, disrupt, interfere, obstruct, check, hinder, hold up, stop, halt, suspend, discontinue, cut off, disconnect, punctuate, separate, divide, cut, break.

interruption *noun*
intrusion, interjection, disturbance, disruption, obstruction, impediment, obstacle, hitch, pause, break, halt, stop, stoppage, suspension, discontinuance, disconnection, separation, division.

intersect *verb*
cross, criss-cross, cut across, bisect, divide, meet, converge.

intersection *noun*
junction, interchange, crossroads, crossing.

interval *noun*
interlude, intermission, break, rest, pause, delay, wait, interim, meantime, meanwhile, gap, opening, space, distance, period, spell, time, season.

intervene *verb*
step in, mediate, arbitrate, interfere, interrupt, intrude.

intervention *noun*
involvement, interference, intrusion, mediation, agency, intercession.

interview *noun*
audience, consultation, talk, dialogue, meeting, conference, press conference, oral examination.
▶ *verb*
question, interrogate, examine, vet.

intestines *noun*
bowels, guts, entrails, insides, innards (*infml*), offal, viscera, vitals.

intimacy *noun*
friendship, closeness, familiarity, confidence, confidentiality, privacy.
€∃ distance.

intimate[1] *verb* / **in**-tim-eit/
intimating that he may call an election: hint, insinuate, imply, suggest, indicate, communicate, impart, tell, state, declare, announce.

intimate[2] *adjective* / **in**-tim-*a*t/
an intimate dinner for two: friendly, informal, familiar, cosy, warm, affectionate, dear, bosom, close, near, confidential, secret, private, personal, internal, innermost, deep, penetrating, detailed, exhaustive.
€∃ unfriendly, cold, distant.

intimidate *verb*
daunt, cow, overawe, appal, dismay, alarm, scare, frighten, terrify, threaten, menace, terrorize, bully, browbeat, bulldoze, coerce, pressure, pressurize, lean on (*infml*).

intolerable *adjective*
unbearable, unendurable, insupportable, unacceptable, insufferable, impossible.
€∃ tolerable.

intolerant *adjective*
impatient, prejudiced, bigoted, narrow-minded, small-minded, opinionated, dogmatic, illiberal, uncharitable.
€∃ tolerant.

intonation *noun*
modulation, tone, accentuation, inflection.

intoxicating *adjective*
1 intoxicating liquor: alcoholic, strong.
2 an intoxicating atmosphere: exciting, stimulating, heady, exhilarating, thrilling.
€∃ **2** sobering.

intrepid *adjective*
bold, daring, brave, courageous, plucky, valiant, lion-hearted, fearless, dauntless, undaunted, stout-hearted, stalwart, gallant, heroic.
€∃ cowardly, timid.

intricate *adjective*
elaborate, fancy, ornate, rococo, complicated, complex, sophisticated, involved, convoluted, tortuous, tangled, entangled, knotty, perplexing, difficult.
€∃ simple, plain, straightforward.

intriguing *adjective*
fascinating, puzzling, tantalizing, attractive, charming, captivating.

introduce *verb*
1 *introduce a new product*: institute, begin, start, commence, establish, found, inaugurate, launch, open, bring in.
2 *introduce the next act*: present, announce.
3 *introduce him to classical music*: acquaint, familiarize, initiate.
4 *introduce legislation*: put forward, advance, submit, offer, propose, suggest.
F∃ 1 end, conclude. 4 remove, take away.

introduction *noun*
1 *introduction of new taxes*: institution, beginning, start, commencement, establishment, inauguration, launch, presentation, debut, initiation.
2 *the introduction to the book*: foreword, preface, preamble, prologue, preliminaries, overture, prelude, lead-in, opening.
F∃ 1 removal, withdrawal. 2 appendix, conclusion.

introductory *adjective*
preliminary, preparatory, opening, inaugural, first, initial, early, elementary, basic.

introspective *adjective*
inward-looking, contemplative, meditative, pensive, thoughtful, brooding, introverted, self-centred, reserved, withdrawn.
F∃ outward-looking.

introverted *adjective*
introspective, inward-looking, self-centred, withdrawn, shy, reserved, quiet.
F∃ extroverted.

intrude *verb*
interrupt, butt in, meddle, interfere, violate, infringe, encroach, trespass.
F∃ withdraw, stand back.

intruder *noun*
trespasser, prowler, burglar, raider, invader, infiltrator, interloper, gatecrasher.

intuition *noun*
instinct, sixth sense, perception, discernment, insight, hunch, feeling, gut feeling (*infml*).
F∃ reasoning.

intuitive *adjective*
instinctive, spontaneous, involuntary, innate, untaught.
F∃ reasoned.

inundate *verb*
flood, deluge, swamp, engulf, submerge, immerse, drown, bury, overwhelm, overrun.

invade *verb*
enter, penetrate, infiltrate, burst in, descend on, attack, raid, seize, occupy, overrun, swarm over, infest, pervade, encroach, infringe, violate.
F∃ withdraw, evacuate.

invalid[1] *noun* /**in**-val-id/
how's the invalid today?: patient, convalescent.
▸ *adjective*
looking after his invalid wife: sick, ill, poorly, ailing, sickly, weak, feeble, frail, infirm, disabled, bedridden.
F∃ healthy.

invalid[2] *adjective* /in-**val**-id/
1 *an invalid argument*: false, fallacious, unsound, ill-founded, unfounded, baseless, illogical, irrational, unscientific, wrong, incorrect.
2 *declare the result invalid*: illegal, null, void, worthless.
F∃ 1 valid. 2 legal.

invaluable *adjective*
priceless, inestimable, incalculable, precious, valuable, useful.
F∃ worthless, cheap.

invariably *adverb*
always, without exception, without fail, unfailingly, consistently, regularly, habitually.
F∃ never.

invasion *noun*
attack, offensive, onslaught, raid, incursion, foray, breach, penetration, infiltration, intrusion, encroachment, infringement, violation.
F∃ withdrawal, evacuation.

invent *verb*
conceive, think up, design, discover, create, originate, formulate, frame,

devise, contrive, improvise, fabricate, make up, concoct, cook up, trump up, imagine, dream up.

invention noun
1 her latest invention: design, creation, brainchild, discovery, development, device, gadget.
2 a mere invention: lie, falsehood, deceit, fabrication, fiction, tall story, fantasy, figment.
F3 2 truth.

inventive adjective
imaginative, creative, innovative, original, ingenious, resourceful, fertile, inspired, gifted, clever.

inventor noun
designer, discoverer, creator, originator, author, architect, maker, scientist, engineer.

invert verb
upturn, turn upside down, overturn, capsize, upset, transpose, reverse.
F3 right.

invertebrate

Invertebrates include:

sponges: calcareous, glass, horny; jellyfish, corals and sea anemones: box jellyfish, dead-men's fingers, Portuguese man-of-war, sea pansy, sea gooseberry, sea wasp, Venus's girdle; echinoderms: brittle star, crown-of-thorns, feather star, sand dollar, sea cucumber, sea lily, sea urchin, starfish; worms: annelid worm, arrow worm, blood fluke, bristle worm, earthworm, eelworm, flatworm, fluke, hookworm, leech, liver fluke, lugworm, peanut worm, pinworm, ragworm, ribbonworm, roundworm, sea mouse, tapeworm, threadworm; crustaceans: acorn barnacle, barnacle, brine shrimp, crayfish, daphnia, fairy shrimp, fiddler crab, fish louse, goose barnacle, hermit crab, krill, lobster, mantis shrimp, mussel shrimp, pill bug, prawn, sand hopper, seed shrimp, spider crab, spiny lobster, tadpole shrimp, water flea, whale louse, woodlouse; centipede, millipede, velvet worm. ⇨ See also **insect; mollusc.**

invest verb
1 invest in property: spend, lay out, put in, sink.
2 investing them with powers: provide, supply, endow, vest, empower, authorize, sanction.

investigate verb
inquire into, look into, consider, examine, study, inspect, scrutinize, analyse, go into, probe, explore, search, sift.

investigation noun
inquiry, inquest, hearing, examination, study, research, survey, review, inspection, scrutiny, analysis, probe, exploration, search.

investment noun
asset, speculation, venture, stake, contribution, outlay, expenditure, transaction.

invigorate verb
vitalize, energize, animate, enliven, liven up, quicken (fml), strengthen, fortify, brace, stimulate, inspire, exhilarate, perk up, refresh, freshen, revitalize, rejuvenate.
F3 tire, weary, dishearten.

invincible adjective
unbeatable, unconquerable, insuperable, unsurmountable, indomitable, unassailable, impregnable, impenetrable, invulnerable, indestructible.
F3 beatable.

invisible adjective
unseen, out of sight, hidden, concealed, disguised, inconspicuous, indiscernible, imperceptible, infinitesimal, microscopic, imaginary, non-existent.
F3 visible.

invitation noun
request, solicitation, call, summons, temptation, enticement, allurement, encouragement, inducement, provocation, incitement, challenge.

invite verb
ask, call, summon, welcome, encourage, lead, draw, attract, tempt, entice, allure, bring on, provoke, ask for, request, solicit, seek.

inviting *adjective*
welcoming, appealing, attractive, tempting, seductive, enticing, alluring, pleasing, delightful, captivating, fascinating, intriguing, tantalizing.
E3 uninviting, unappealing.

involuntary *adjective*
spontaneous, unconscious, automatic, mechanical, reflex, instinctive, conditioned, impulsive, unthinking, blind, uncontrolled, unintentional.
E3 deliberate, intentional.

involve *verb*
1 involve some careful thought: require, necessitate, mean, imply, entail.
2 involve the family: include, incorporate, embrace, cover, take in, affect, concern.
3 involving others in the fraud: implicate, incriminate, inculpate, draw in, mix up, embroil, associate.
4 involving the audience: engage, occupy, absorb, engross, preoccupy, hold, grip, rivet.
E3 2 exclude.

involved *adjective*
1 the people involved: concerned, implicated, mixed up, caught up in (*infml*), participating.
2 the explanation was too involved to be easily understood: complicated, complex, intricate, elaborate, tangled, knotty, tortuous, confusing.
E3 1 uninvolved. **2** simple.

involvement *noun*
concern, interest, responsibility, association, connection, participation, implication, entanglement.

inward *adjective*
incoming, entering, inside, interior, internal, inner, innermost, inmost, personal, private, secret, confidential.
E3 outward, external.

iota *noun*
scrap, bit, mite, jot, speck, trace, hint, grain, particle, atom.

irate *adjective*
annoyed, irritated, indignant, up in arms, angry, enraged, mad (*infml*), furious, infuriated, incensed, worked up, fuming, livid, exasperated.
E3 calm, composed.

iron *adjective*
rigid, inflexible, adamant, determined, hard, steely, tough, strong.
E3 pliable, weak.
▶ *verb*
press, smooth, flatten.
◆ **iron out** resolve, settle, sort out, straighten out, clear up, put right, reconcile, deal with, get rid of, eradicate, eliminate.

ironic *adjective*
ironical, sarcastic, sardonic, scornful, contemptuous, derisive, sneering, scoffing, mocking, satirical, wry, paradoxical.

irony *noun*
sarcasm, mockery, satire, paradox, contrariness, incongruity.

irrational *adjective*
unreasonable, unsound, illogical, absurd, crazy, wild, foolish, silly, senseless, unwise.
E3 rational.

irrefutable *adjective*
undeniable, incontrovertible, indisputable, incontestable, unquestionable, unanswerable, certain, sure.

irregular *adjective*
1 an irregular surface: rough, bumpy, uneven, crooked.
2 at irregular intervals: variable, fluctuating, wavering, erratic, fitful, intermittent, sporadic, spasmodic, occasional, random, haphazard, disorderly, unsystematic.
3 this is quite irregular: abnormal, unconventional, unorthodox, improper, unusual, exceptional, anomalous.
E3 1 smooth, level. **2** regular. **3** conventional.

irrelevant *adjective*
immaterial, beside the point, inapplicable, inappropriate, unrelated, unconnected, inconsequent, peripheral, tangential.
E3 relevant.

irreplaceable *adjective*
indispensable, essential, vital, unique, priceless, peerless, matchless, unmatched.
E3 replaceable.

irresistible *adjective*
overwhelming, overpowering,
unavoidable, inevitable, inescapable,
uncontrollable, potent, compelling,
imperative, pressing, urgent, tempting,
seductive, ravishing, enchanting,
charming, fascinating.
F3 resistible, avoidable.

irresponsible *adjective*
unreliable, untrustworthy, careless,
negligent, thoughtless, heedless,
ill-considered, rash, reckless,
wild, carefree, light-hearted,
immature.
F3 responsible, cautious.

irreverent *adjective*
1 an irreverent act: impious, godless,
irreligious, profane, sacrilegious,
blasphemous.
2 an irreverent impersonation:
disrespectful, discourteous, rude,
impudent, impertinent, mocking,
flippant.
F3 1 reverent. **2** respectful.

irritable *adjective*
cross, bad-tempered, ill-tempered,
crotchety, crusty, cantankerous, crabby,
testy, short-tempered, snappish,
snappy, short, impatient, touchy, edgy,
prickly, peevish, fretful, fractious,
tetchy.
F3 good-tempered, cheerful.

irritate *verb*
1 try not to irritate her: annoy, get on
one's nerves, aggravate (*infml*), bother,
harass, rouse, provoke, rile, anger, vex,
enrage, infuriate, incense, exasperate,
peeve, put out.
2 irritating the skin: inflame, chafe,
rub, tickle, itch.
F3 1 please, gratify.

irritation *noun*
displeasure, dissatisfaction,
annoyance, aggravation, provocation,
anger, vexation, indignation, fury,
exasperation, irritability,
crossness, testiness, snappiness,
impatience.
F3 pleasure, satisfaction, delight.

isolate *verb*
set apart, sequester, seclude, keep
apart, segregate, quarantine, insulate,

cut off, detach, remove, disconnect,
separate, divorce, alienate, shut
out, ostracize, exclude.
F3 assimilate, incorporate.

isolated *adjective*
1 an isolated community: remote, out-
of-the-way, outlying, god-forsaken,
deserted, unfrequented, secluded,
detached, cut off, lonely, solitary,
single.
2 an isolated occurrence: unique,
special, exceptional, atypical, unusual,
freak, abnormal, anomalous.
F3 1 populous. **2** typical.

issue *noun*
1 a political issue: matter, affair,
concern, problem, point, subject,
topic, question, debate, argument,
dispute, controversy.
2 a special issue of stamps:
publication, release, distribution,
supply, delivery, circulation,
promulgation, broadcast,
announcement.
3 last week's issue: copy, number,
instalment, edition, impression,
printing.
▶ *verb*
1 issue a statement/summons:
publish, release, distribute, supply,
deliver, give out, deal out, circulate,
promulgate, broadcast, announce, put
out, emit, produce.
2 issuing from a mountain lake:
originate, stem, spring, rise, emerge,
burst forth, gush, flow, proceed,
emanate, arise.

itch *verb*
tickle, irritate, tingle, prickle, crawl.
▶ *noun*
1 scratch an itch: itchiness, tickle,
irritation, prickling.
2 an itch to travel: eagerness, keenness,
desire, longing, yearning, hankering,
craving.

item *noun*
1 an item of jewellery/go on to the
next item: object, article, thing, piece,
component, ingredient, element,
factor, point, detail, particular,
aspect, feature, consideration,
matter.

2 an item in the local paper: article, piece, report, account, notice, entry, paragraph.

itinerant *adjective*
travelling, peripatetic, roving, roaming, wandering, rambling, nomadic, migratory, rootless, unsettled.

▣ stationary, settled.

itinerary *noun*
route, course, journey, tour, circuit, plan, programme, schedule.

Jj

jab *verb*
poke, prod, dig, nudge, stab, push, elbow, lunge, punch, tap, thrust.

jaded *adjective*
fatigued, exhausted, dulled, played-out, tired, tired out, weary, spent, bored, fagged (*infml*).
🖃 fresh, refreshed.

jagged *adjective*
uneven, irregular, notched, indented, rough, serrated, saw-edged, toothed, ragged, pointed, ridged, craggy, barbed, broken.
🖃 even, smooth.

jail, gaol *noun*
prison, jailhouse, custody, lock-up, penitentiary, guardhouse, inside (*infml*), nick (*infml*), clink (*slang*).
▶ *verb*
imprison, incarcerate, lock up, put away, send down, confine, detain, intern, impound, immure.

jam¹ *verb*
1 jamming them into a tiny space: cram, pack, wedge, squash, squeeze, press, crush, crowd, congest, ram, stuff, confine, force.
2 jamming the road/the door jammed: block, clog, obstruct, stall, stick.
▶ *noun*
1 trying to clear the jam: crush, crowd, press, congestion, pack, mob, throng, bottle-neck, traffic jam, obstruction, gridlock.
2 in a bit of a jam: predicament, trouble, quandary, plight, fix (*infml*).

jam² *noun*
strawberry jam: conserve, preserve, jelly, spread, marmalade.

jangle *verb*
clank, clash, jar, clatter, jingle, chime, rattle, vibrate.

jar¹ *noun*
an earthenware jar: pot, container, vessel, receptacle, crock, pitcher, urn, vase, flagon, jug, mug.

jar² *verb*
1 jarred her spine: jolt, agitate, rattle, shake, vibrate, jangle, rock, disturb, discompose.
2 a harsh voice jarring on the ears of the listeners: annoy, irritate, grate, nettle (*infml*), offend, upset, irk.

jargon *noun*
1 legal jargon: parlance, cant, argot, vernacular, idiom.
2 full of meaningless jargon: nonsense, gobbledegook (*infml*), mumbo-jumbo (*infml*), gibberish.

jaunty *adjective*
sprightly, lively, perky, breezy, buoyant, high-spirited, self-confident, carefree, airy, cheeky, debonair, dapper, smart, showy, spruce.
🖃 depressed, dowdy.

jealous *adjective*
1 jealous of her sister: envious, green (*infml*), green-eyed (*infml*), covetous, grudging, resentful.
2 a jealous husband/wife: suspicious, wary, distrustful, anxious, possessive, protective.
🖃 **1** contented, satisfied.

jeer *verb*
mock, scoff, taunt, jibe, ridicule, sneer, deride, make fun of, chaff, barrack, twit, knock (*infml*), heckle, banter, boo.
▶ *noun*
mockery, derision, ridicule, taunt, jibe,

sneer, scoff, abuse, catcall, dig (*infml*), hiss, hoot.

jell ⇨ *see* **gel**.

jeopardize *verb*
endanger, imperil, risk, hazard, venture, gamble, chance, threaten, menace, expose, stake.
F∃ protect, safeguard.

jerk *noun, verb*
jolt, tug, twitch, jar, jog, yank, wrench, pull, pluck, lurch, throw, thrust, shrug.

jerky *adjective*
fitful, twitchy, spasmodic, jumpy, jolting, convulsive, disconnected, bumpy, bouncy, shaky, rough, unco-ordinated, uncontrolled, incoherent.
F∃ smooth.

jet¹ *noun*
a jet of water: gush, spurt, spout, spray, spring, sprinkler, sprayer, fountain, flow, stream, squirt.

jet² *adjective*
jet-black: black, pitch-black, ebony, sable, sooty.

jetty *noun*
breakwater, pier, dock, groyne, quay, wharf.

jewel *noun*
1 precious jewels: gem, precious stone, gemstone, ornament, rock (*infml*).
2 the jewel of the east: treasure, find, prize, rarity, paragon, pearl.

jibe ⇨ *see* **gibe**.

jilt *verb*
abandon, reject, desert, discard, brush off, ditch (*infml*), drop, spurn, betray.

jingle *verb*
clink, tinkle, ring, chime, chink, jangle, clatter, rattle.
▸ *noun*
1 the jingle of bells: clink, tinkle, ringing, clang, rattle, clangour.
2 a catchy jingle: rhyme, verse, song, tune, ditty, doggerel, melody, poem, chant, chorus.

jinx *noun* (*infml*)
spell, curse, evil eye, hex, voodoo, hoodoo, black magic, gremlin (*infml*), charm, plague.

job *noun*
1 she has a good job: work,

employment, occupation, position, post, situation, profession, career, calling, vocation, trade, métier, capacity, business, livelihood.
2 it's a difficult job: task, chore, duty, responsibility, charge, commission, mission, activity, affair, concern, proceeding, project, enterprise, office, pursuit, role, undertaking, venture, province, part, place, share, errand, function, contribution, stint, assignment, consignment.

jobless *adjective*
unemployed, out of work, laid off, on the dole (*infml*), inactive, redundant.
F∃ employed.

jog *verb*
1 jogged his arm: jolt, jar, bump, jostle, jerk, joggle, nudge, poke, shake, prod, bounce, push, rock.
2 jogged her memory: prompt, remind, stir, arouse, activate, stimulate.
3 jogs to work every morning: run, trot.
▸ *noun*
1 gave her arm a jog: jolt, bump, jerk, nudge, shove, push, poke, prod, shake.
2 go for a jog: run, trot.

join *verb*
1 join the two pieces together: unite, connect, combine, conjoin, attach, link, amalgamate, fasten, merge, marry, couple, yoke, tie, splice, knit, cement, add, adhere, annex.
2 where it joins the neighbouring estate: abut, adjoin, border (on), verge on, touch, meet, coincide, march with.
3 join a club: associate, affiliate, accompany, ally, enlist, enrol, enter, sign up, team.
F∃ 1 divide, separate. 3 leave.

joint *noun*
junction, connection, union, juncture, intersection, hinge, knot, articulation, seam.
▸ *adjective*
combined, common, communal, joined, shared, united, collective, amalgamated, mutual, co-operative, co-ordinated, consolidated, concerted.

oke noun
1 crack a few jokes: jest, quip, crack (infml), gag (infml), witticism, wisecrack (infml), one-liner (infml), pun, hoot, whimsy, yarn.
2 play a joke on him: trick, jape, lark, prank, spoof, fun.
▸ verb
jest, quip, clown, fool, pun, wisecrack (infml), kid (infml), tease, banter, mock, laugh, frolic, gambol.

oker noun
comedian, comic, wit, humorist, jester, trickster, wag, clown, buffoon, kidder (infml), droll, card (infml), character, sport.

olly adjective
jovial, merry, cheerful, playful, hearty, happy, exuberant.
F∃ sad.

olt verb
1 jolting his arm: jar, jerk, jog, bump, jostle, knock, bounce, shake, push.
2 jolted by the news: upset, startle, shock, surprise, stun, discompose, disconcert, disturb.
▸ noun
1 a sudden jolt: jar, jerk, jog, bump, blow, impact, lurch, shake.
2 gave her a bit of a jolt: shock, surprise, reversal, setback, start.

ostle verb
push, shove, jog, bump, elbow, hustle, jolt, crowd, shoulder, joggle, shake, squeeze, throng.

ot down verb
write down, take down, note, list, record, scribble, register, enter.

ournal noun
newspaper, periodical, magazine, paper, publication, review, weekly, monthly, register, chronicle, diary, gazette, daybook, log, record.

ournalist noun
reporter, news-writer, hack, correspondent, editor, columnist, feature-writer, commentator, broadcaster, contributor.

ourney noun
voyage, trip, travel, expedition, passage, trek, tour, ramble, outing, wanderings, safari, progress.

jovial adjective
jolly, cheery, merry, affable, cordial, genial.
F∃ gloomy.

joy noun
happiness, gladness, delight, pleasure, bliss, ecstasy, elation, joyfulness, exultation, gratification, rapture.
F∃ despair, grief.

joyful adjective
happy, pleased, delighted, glad, elated, ecstatic, triumphant.
F∃ sorrowful.

jubilant adjective
joyful, rejoicing, overjoyed, delighted, elated, triumphant, exuberant, excited, euphoric, thrilled.

judge noun
1 a High Court judge: justice, Law Lord, magistrate, arbiter, adjudicator, arbitrator, mediator, moderator, referee, umpire, beak (infml).
2 a good judge of wine: connoisseur, authority, expert, evaluator, assessor, critic.
▸ verb
1 judging the case: adjudicate, arbitrate, try, referee, umpire, decree, mediate, examine, sentence, review, rule, find.
2 judge if it is safe: ascertain, determine, decide, assess, appraise, evaluate, estimate, value, distinguish, discern, reckon, believe, think, consider, conclude, rate.
3 shouldn't judge him: condemn, criticize, doom.

judgement noun
1 deliver his judgement: verdict, sentence, ruling, decree, conclusion, decision, arbitration, finding, result, mediation, order.
2 good judgement: discernment, discrimination, understanding, wisdom, prudence, common sense, sense, intelligence, taste, shrewdness, penetration, enlightenment.
3 judgement of the risks and benefits: assessment, evaluation, appraisal, estimate, opinion, view, belief, diagnosis.
4 a harsh judgement: conviction,

damnation, punishment, retribution, doom, fate, misfortune.

judicial *adjective*
legal, judiciary, magistral, forensic, official, discriminating, critical, impartial.

juggle *verb*
alter, change, manipulate, falsify, rearrange, rig, doctor (*infml*), cook (*infml*), disguise.

juice *noun*
liquid, fluid, extract, essence, sap, secretion, nectar, liquor.

juicy *adjective*
1 a juicy orange : succulent, moist, lush, watery.
2 (*infml*) some juicy gossip : interesting, colourful, sensational, racy, risqué, suggestive, lurid.
F∃ 1 dry.

jumble *verb*
disarrange, confuse, disorganize, mix (up), muddle, shuffle, tangle.
F∃ order.
▶ *noun*
disorder, disarray, confusion, mess, chaos, mix-up, muddle, clutter, mixture, hotch-potch, mishmash (*infml*), medley.

jump *verb*
1 jumping the gate : leap, spring, bound, vault, clear, bounce, skip, hop, prance, frolic, gambol.
2 nearly jumped out of his skin : start, flinch, jerk, recoil, jump out of one's skin (*infml*), wince, quail.
3 jumped a few verses : omit, leave out, miss, skip, pass over, bypass, disregard, ignore, avoid, digress.
4 jump in price : rise, increase, gain, appreciate, ascend, escalate, mount, advance, surge, spiral.

jumpy *adjective*
nervous, anxious, agitated, apprehensive, jittery, tense, edgy, fidgety, shaky.
F∃ calm, composed.

junction *noun*
joint, join, joining, connection, juncture, union, intersection, linking, coupling, meeting-point, confluence.

junior *adjective*
younger, minor, lesser, lower, subordinate, secondary, subsidiary, inferior.
F∃ senior.

junk *noun*
rubbish, refuse, trash, debris, garbage, waste, scrap, litter, clutter, oddments, rummage, dregs, wreckage.

jurisdiction *noun*
power, authority, control, influence, dominion, province, sovereignty, command, domination, rule, prerogative, sway, orbit, bounds, area, field, scope, range, reach, sphere, zone.

just *adjective*
1 a just ruler : fair, equitable, impartial, unbiased, unprejudiced, fair-minded, even-handed, objective, righteous, upright, virtuous, honourable, good, honest, irreproachable.
2 a just punishment : deserved, merited, fitting, well-deserved, appropriate, suitable, due, proper, reasonable, rightful, lawful, legitimate
F∃ 1 unjust. **2** undeserved.

justice *noun*
1 can see the justice in that : fairness, equity, impartiality, objectivity, equitableness, justness, legitimacy, honesty, right, justifiableness, reasonableness, rectitude.
2 trying to get justice/flee justice : legality, law, penalty, recompense, reparation, satisfaction.
3 come before the justices : judge, Justice of the Peace, JP, magistrate.
F∃ 1 injustice, unfairness.

justifiable *adjective*
defensible, excusable, warranted, reasonable, justified, lawful, legitimate acceptable, explainable, forgivable, pardonable, understandable, valid, well-founded, right, proper, explicable fit, tenable.

justify *verb*
vindicate, exonerate, warrant, substantiate, defend, acquit, absolve, excuse, forgive, explain, pardon, validate, uphold, sustain, support, maintain, establish.

jut (out) *verb*
project, protrude, stick out, overhang,
extend.
F₃recede.

juvenile *noun*
child, youth, minor, young person,
youngster, adolescent, teenager, boy,
girl, kid (*infml*), infant.

▸ *adjective*
young, youthful, immature, childish,
puerile (*fml*), infantile, adolescent,
babyish, unsophisticated.
F₃mature.

juxtaposition *noun*
contiguity, proximity, nearness,
closeness, contact, vicinity, immediacy.

K k

keen *adjective*
1 a keen gardener: eager, avid, fervent, enthusiastic, earnest, devoted, diligent, industrious.
2 a keen mind: astute, shrewd, clever, perceptive, wise, discerning, quick, deep, sensitive.
3 keen eyesight/understanding: sharp, piercing, penetrating, incisive, acute, pointed.
⊟ 1 apathetic. **2** superficial. **3** dull.

keep *verb*
1 keep the receipt: retain, hold, preserve, hold on to, hang on to, store, stock, possess, amass, accumulate, collect, stack, conserve, deposit, heap, pile, place, maintain, furnish.
2 keep walking/in step: carry on, keep on, continue, persist, remain.
3 keep pigs and chickens/keep two houses: look after, tend, care for, have charge of, have custody of, maintain, provide for, subsidize, support, sustain, be responsible for, foster, mind, protect, shelter, guard, defend, watch (over), shield, safeguard, feed, nurture, manage.
4 keep us waiting: detain, delay, retard, check, hinder, hold (up), impede, obstruct, prevent, block, curb, interfere with, restrain, limit, inhibit, deter, hamper, keep back, control, constrain, arrest, withhold.
5 keep to the rules/keep faith with: observe, comply with, respect, obey, fulfil, adhere to, recognize, keep up, keep faith with, commemorate, celebrate, hold, maintain, perform, perpetuate, mark, honour.
▶ *noun*
1 earn one's keep: subsistence, board,

livelihood, living, maintenance, support, upkeep, means, food, nourishment, nurture.
2 the ruined keep: fort, fortress, tower, castle, citadel, stronghold, dungeon.
◆ keep back 1 keeping us back: restrain, check, constrain, curb, impede, limit, prohibit, retard, stop, control, delay.
2 kept things back from us: hold back, restrict, suppress, withhold, conceal, censor, hide, hush up, stifle, reserve, retain.
◆ keep in 1 keeping in her rage: repress, keep back, inhibit, bottle up, conceal, stifle, suppress, hide, control, restrain, stay, stop up.
2 kept in after school: confine, detain, shut in, coop up.
⊟ 1 declare. **2** release.
◆ keep on continue, carry on, endure, persevere, persist, keep at it, last, remain, stay, stay the course, soldier on (*infml*), hold on, retain, maintain.
◆ keep up keep pace, equal, contend, compete, vie, rival, match, emulate, continue, maintain, persevere, support, sustain, preserve.

keepsake *noun*
memento, souvenir, remembrance, relic, reminder, token, pledge, emblem.

key *noun*
1 the key to the mystery: clue, cue, indicator, pointer, explanation, sign, answer, solution, interpretation, means, secret.
2 a key to the symbols: guide, glossary, translation, legend, code, table, index.
▶ *adjective*
important, essential, vital, crucial,

necessary, principal, decisive, central, chief, main, major, leading, basic, fundamental.

kick *verb*

1 kick a ball: boot, hit, strike, jolt.
2 (*infml*) kicking the habit: give up, quit, stop, leave off, abandon, desist from, break.

▸ *noun*

1 the first kick of the engine: blow, recoil, jolt, striking.
2 (*infml*) get a kick out of it: stimulation, thrill, excitement.

◆ **kick off** (*infml*) begin, commence, start, open, get under way, open the proceedings, set the ball rolling, introduce, inaugurate, initiate.

◆ **kick out** (*infml*) eject, evict, expel, oust, remove, chuck out (*infml*), discharge, dismiss, get rid of, sack (*infml*), throw out, reject.

kid[1] *noun* (*infml*)

a group of kids: child, youngster, youth, juvenile, infant, girl, boy, teenager, lad, nipper (*infml*), tot (*infml*).

kid[2] *verb* (*infml*)

just kidding: tease, joke, have on (*infml*), hoax, fool, pull someone's leg (*infml*), pretend, trick, delude, dupe, con (*infml*), jest, hoodwink, humbug, bamboozle.

kidnap *verb*

abduct, capture, seize, hold to ransom, snatch, hijack, steal.

kill *verb*

1 killing thousands of people: slaughter, murder, slay (*fml*), put to death, exterminate, assassinate, do to death, do in (*infml*), bump off (*infml*), finish off, massacre, execute, eliminate, destroy, dispatch, do away with (*infml*), butcher, annihilate, liquidate (*infml*).
2 killing the engine: stifle, deaden, smother, quash, quell, suppress.

kind *noun*

sort, type, class, category, set, variety, character, genus, genre, style, brand, family, breed, race, nature, persuasion, description, species, stamp, temperament, manner.

▸ *adjective*

benevolent, kind-hearted, kindly,

good-hearted, good-natured, helpful, obliging, humane, generous, compassionate, charitable, amiable, friendly, congenial, soft-hearted, thoughtful, warm, warm-hearted, considerate, courteous, sympathetic, tender-hearted, understanding, lenient, mild, hospitable, gentle, indulgent, neighbourly, tactful, giving, good, loving, gracious.
🖃 cruel, inconsiderate, unhelpful.

kindly *adjective*

benevolent, kind, compassionate, charitable, good-natured, helpful, warm, generous, cordial, favourable, giving, indulgent, pleasant, sympathetic, tender, gentle, mild, patient, polite.
🖃 cruel, uncharitable.

kindness *noun*

1 thank them for their kindness: benevolence, kindliness, charity, magnanimity, compassion, generosity, hospitality, humanity, loving-kindness (*fml*), courtesy, friendliness, good will, goodness, grace, indulgence, tolerance, understanding, gentleness.
2 did me a kindness: favour, good turn, assistance, help, service.
🖃 **1** cruelty, inhumanity. **2** disservice.

king *noun*

monarch, ruler, sovereign, majesty, emperor, chief, chieftain, prince, supremo (*infml*), leading light (*infml*).

kingdom *noun*

monarchy, sovereignty, reign, realm, empire, dominion, commonwealth, nation, principality, state, country, domain, dynasty, province, sphere, territory, land, division.

kiosk *noun*

booth, stall, stand, news-stand, bookstall, cabin, box, counter.

kiss *verb*

1 kiss and cuddle: caress, peck (*infml*), smooch (*infml*), neck (*infml*), snog (*slang*).
2 the cue ball kissed the pink: touch, graze, glance, brush, lick, scrape, fan.

▸ *noun*

peck (*infml*), smack (*infml*), smacker (*infml*).

kit *noun*
equipment, gear, strip, apparatus, supplies, tackle, provisions, outfit, implements, set, tools, trappings, rig, instruments, paraphernalia, utensils, effects, luggage, baggage.

◆ **kit out** equip, fit out, outfit, supply, fix up, furnish, prepare, arm, deck out, dress.

knack *noun*
flair, faculty, facility, hang (*infml*), bent, skill, talent, genius, gift, trick, propensity, ability, expertise, skilfulness, forte, capacity, handiness, dexterity, quickness, turn.

knead *verb*
manipulate, press, massage, work, ply, squeeze, shape, rub, form, mould, knuckle.

knife *noun*
blade, cutter, carver, dagger, penknife, pocket-knife, switchblade, jack-knife, flick-knife, machete.

▶ *verb*
cut, rip, slash, stab, pierce, wound.

knit *verb*
1 *the bones are knitting well*: join, unite, secure, connect, tie, fasten, link, mend, interlace, intertwine.
2 *knit a cardigan*: knot, loop, crotchet, weave.
3 *knitting his brows*: wrinkle, furrow.

knock *verb*
hit, strike, rap, thump, pound, slap, smack.

▶ *noun*
blow, box, rap, thump, cuff, clip, pounding, hammering, slap, smack.

◆ **knock about 1** *knock about all over Europe*: wander, travel, roam, rove, saunter, traipse, ramble, range.
2 *knocking about with two other boys*: associate, go around.
3 *they knocked him about*: beat up, batter, abuse, mistreat, hurt, hit, bash, damage, maltreat, manhandle, bruise, buffet.

◆ **knock down** demolish, destroy, fell, floor, level, wreck, raze, pound, batter, clout, smash.

◆ **knock off 1** (*infml*) *knock off work*: finish, cease, stop, pack (it) in, clock off, clock out, terminate.
2 *knock £20 off the price*: deduct, take away.

knot *verb*
tie, secure, bind, entangle, tangle, knit, entwine, ravel, weave.

▶ *noun*
1 *a reef knot*: tie, bond, joint, fastening, loop, splice, hitch.
2 *a knot of people*: bunch, cluster, clump, group.

know *verb*
1 *know French*: understand, comprehend, apprehend, perceive, notice, be aware, fathom, experience, realize, see, undergo.
2 *I know George*: be acquainted with, be familiar with, recognize, identify.
3 *know a good wine*: distinguish, discriminate, discern, differentiate, make out, tell.

knowledge *noun*
1 *I have the knowledge but not the experience*: learning, scholarship, erudition, education, schooling, instruction, tuition, information, enlightenment, know-how.
2 *a good knowledge of wine*: acquaintance, familiarity, awareness, cognizance, intimacy, consciousness.
3 *test your knowledge*: understanding, comprehension, cognition, apprehension, recognition, judgement, discernment, ability, grasp, wisdom, intelligence.

E31, 3 ignorance.

knowledgeable *adjective*
educated, scholarly, learned, well-informed, lettered, intelligent, well-read.

E3ignorant.

known *adjective*
acknowledged, recognized, well-known, noted, obvious, patent, plain, admitted, familiar, avowed, commonplace, published, confessed, celebrated, famous.

L

label *noun*
1 the maker's label: tag, ticket, docket, mark, marker, sticker, trademark.
2 give him the label 'delinquent': description, categorization, identification, characterization, classification, badge, brand.
► *verb*
1 labelling their goods: tag, mark, stamp.
2 labelled him a liar: define, describe, classify, categorize, characterize, identify, class, designate, brand, call, dub, name.

laborious *adjective*
hard, arduous, difficult, strenuous, tough, backbreaking, wearisome, tiresome, uphill, onerous, heavy, toilsome (*fml*).
F∃easy, effortless.

labour *noun*
1 hard labour: work, task, job, chore, toil, effort, exertion, drudgery, grind (*infml*), slog (*infml*), sweat (*infml*).
2 hire new labour: workers, employees, workforce, labourers.
3 in labour: childbirth, birth, delivery, labour pains, contractions.
F∃1 ease, leisure. **2** management.
► *verb*
1 laboured for six days: work, toil, drudge, slave, strive, endeavour, struggle, grind (*infml*), sweat (*infml*), plod, travail (*fml*).
2 labour the point: overdo, overemphasize, dwell on, elaborate, overstress, strain.
F∃1 laze, idle, lounge.

lack *noun*
need, want, scarcity, shortage, insufficiency, dearth, deficiency, absence, scantiness, vacancy, void, privation (*fml*), deprivation, destitution, emptiness.
F∃abundance, profusion.
► *verb*
need, want, require, miss.

lag *verb*
dawdle, loiter, hang back, linger, straggle, trail, saunter, delay, shuffle, tarry, idle, dally.
F∃hurry, lead.

lake *noun*
lagoon, reservoir, loch, mere, tarn, lough.

lame *adjective*
1 become/go lame: crippled, limping, hobbling.
2 a lame excuse: weak, feeble, flimsy, inadequate, unsatisfactory, poor.
F∃2 convincing, pathetic (*infml*).

lament *noun*
lamentation, dirge, elegy, requiem, threnody (*fml*), complaint, moan, wail.
► *verb*
mourn, bewail, bemoan, grieve, sorrow, weep, wail, complain, deplore, regret.
F∃rejoice, celebrate.

land *noun*
1 reach land: earth, (solid) ground, terra firma.
2 till the land: dirt, earth, soil.
3 buy land: property, grounds, estate, real estate (*US*), country, countryside, farmland, tract.
4 a foreign land: country, nation, region, territory, province.
► *verb*
1 land on the runway: alight,

disembark, dock, berth, touch down,
come to rest, arrive, deposit, wind up,
end up, drop, settle, turn up.
2 land a big contract: obtain, secure,
gain, get, acquire, net, capture, achieve,
win.

landscape *noun*
scene, scenery, view, panorama,
outlook, vista, prospect, countryside,
aspect.

language *noun*
1 learn languages: speech, tongue,
dialect, lingo (*infml*).
2 medical language: vocabulary,
terminology, parlance, jargon.
3 the language of love: talk,
conversation, discourse.
4 use complicated language: wording,
style, phraseology, phrasing,
expression, utterance, diction.

*Terms used when talking about
language include:*

applied linguistics, argot, brogue,
buzz word, cant, colloquialism,
creole, dialect, dialectology,
doublespeak, etymology, idiom,
jargon, journalese, legalese,
lexicography, lingua franca,
linguistics, localism, orthography,
phonetics, patois, pidgin,
regionalism, semantics, slang,
sociolingustics, syntax, vernacular.

languish *verb*
wilt, droop, fade, fail, flag, wither,
waste away, weaken, sink, faint,
decline, mope, waste, grieve, sorrow,
sigh, sicken.

lap[1] *verb*
lapping the milk: drink, sip, sup, lick.

lap[2] *noun*
do four laps of the track: circuit,
round, orbit, tour, loop, course, circle,
distance.

lapse *noun*
1 an unfortunate lapse on his part:
error, slip, mistake, negligence,
omission, oversight, fault, failing,
indiscretion, aberration, backsliding,
relapse.

2 a lapse in demand: fall, descent,
decline, drop, deterioration.
3 a lapse of a few weeks: break, gap,
interval, lull, interruption,
intermission, pause.
▸ *verb*
1 lapsed into a coma: decline, fall, sink,
drop, deteriorate, slide, slip, fail,
worsen, degenerate, backslide.
2 policy lapsed: expire, run out, end,
stop, terminate.

large *adjective*
1 a large nose/country/amount: big,
huge, immense, massive, vast, sizable,
great, giant, gigantic, bulky, enormous,
king-sized, broad, considerable,
monumental, substantial, whopping
(*infml*), mega (*infml*).
2 large house/grounds: extensive,
generous, liberal, roomy, plentiful,
spacious, capacious, grand, sweeping,
grandiose.
E3 1 small, tiny. **2** modest.
◆ **at large** free, at liberty, on the loose,
on the run, independent.

largely *adverb*
mainly, principally, chiefly, generally,
primarily, predominantly, mostly,
considerably, by and large, widely,
extensively, greatly.

lash[1] *verb*
1 lashing the horses: whip, flog, beat,
hit, thrash, strike, scourge.
2 lash out at someone: attack, criticize,
lay into, scold.

lash[2] *verb*
**lash the boxes down to stop them
moving about**: tie, bind, fasten, secure,
make fast, join, affix, rope, tether, strap.

last[1] *adjective*
the last day of term: final, ultimate,
closing, latest, rearmost, terminal,
furthest, concluding, remotest, utmost,
extreme, conclusive, definitive.
E3 first, initial.
▸ *adverb*
finally, ultimately, behind, after.
E3 first, firstly.
◆ **at last** eventually, finally, in the end,
in due course, at length.

last[2] *verb*
last for centuries: continue, endure,

remain, persist, keep (on), survive, hold out, carry on, wear, stay, hold on, stand up, abide (*fml*).
F3 cease, stop, fade.

lasting *adjective*
enduring, unchanging, unceasing, unending, continuing, permanent, perpetual, lifelong, long-standing, long-term.
F3 brief, fleeting, short-lived.

late *adjective*
1 late for work: overdue, behind, behind-hand, slow, unpunctual, delayed, last-minute.
2 his late wife: former, previous, departed, dead, deceased, past, preceding, old.
F3 1 early, punctual.

lately *adverb*
recently, of late, latterly.

latent *adjective*
potential, dormant, undeveloped, unrealized, lurking, unexpressed, unseen, secret, concealed, hidden, invisible, underlying, veiled.
F3 active, conspicuous.

later *adverb*
next, afterwards, subsequently, after, successively.
F3 earlier.

lateral *adjective*
sideways, side, oblique, sideward, edgeways, marginal, flanking.

lather *noun*
1 makes a good lather: foam, suds, soap-suds, froth, bubbles, soap, shampoo.
2 (*infml*) **getting herself into a lather**: agitation, fluster, fuss, dither, state (*infml*), flutter, flap (*infml*), fever.
▶ *verb*
foam, froth, soap, shampoo, whip up.

latter *adjective*
last-mentioned, last, later, closing, concluding, ensuing, succeeding, successive, second.
F3 former.

laugh *verb*
chuckle, giggle, guffaw, snigger, titter, chortle, split one's sides, fall about (*infml*), crease up (*infml*).

▶ *noun*
giggle, chuckle, snigger, titter, guffaw, chortle, lark, scream (*infml*), hoot (*infml*), joke.
◆ **laugh at** mock, ridicule, deride, jeer, make fun of, scoff at, scorn, taunt.

laughable *adjective*
ridiculous, absurd, ludicrous, preposterous, nonsensical, derisory, derisive.
F3 serious.

laughter *noun*
laughing, giggling, chuckling, chortling, guffawing, tittering, hilarity, amusement, merriment, mirth, glee, convulsions.

launch *verb*
1 launch a rocket: propel, dispatch, discharge, send off, project, float, set in motion, throw, fire.
2 launch a campaign: begin, commence, start, embark on, establish, found, open, initiate, inaugurate, introduce, instigate.

lavatory *noun*
toilet, loo (*infml*), WC, bathroom, cloakroom, washroom, water-closet (*old*), public convenience, ladies (*infml*), gents (*infml*), urinal, powder-room.

lavish *adjective*
1 give it lavish praise: abundant, plentiful, profuse, unlimited, prolific.
2 lavish in her gifts to charity: generous, liberal, open-handed, extravagant, thriftless, prodigal, immoderate, intemperate, unstinting.
F3 1 scant. 2 frugal, thrifty.

law *noun*
1 a law against trespass/the law of the land: rule, act, decree, edict, order, statute, regulation, command, ordinance, charter, constitution, enactment.
2 a law of physics: principle, axiom, criterion, standard, precept (*fml*), formula, code, canon.
3 work at the law/go to law: jurisprudence, legislation, litigation.

law-abiding *adjective*
obedient, upright, orderly, lawful, honest, honourable, decent, good.
F3 lawless.

lawful *adjective*
legal, legitimate, permissible, legalized, authorized, allowable, warranted, valid, proper, rightful.
Fa illegal, unlawful, illicit.

lawless *adjective*
disorderly, rebellious, anarchic(al), unruly, riotous, mutinous, unrestrained, chaotic, wild, reckless.
Fa law-abiding.

lawsuit *noun*
litigation, suit, action, proceedings, case, prosecution, dispute, process, trial, argument, contest, cause.

lawyer *noun*
solicitor, barrister, advocate, attorney, counsel, QC, brief (*infml*).

lax *adjective*
casual, careless, easy-going, slack, lenient, negligent, remiss.
Fa strict.

lay¹ *verb*
1 lay the book down: put, place, deposit, set down, settle, lodge, plant, set, leave.
2 lay the table for dinner: arrange, position, set out, locate, devise, prepare, present.
3 lay the blame firmly on them: attribute, ascribe, assign, charge.
◆ **lay in** store (up), stock up, amass, accumulate, hoard, stockpile, gather, collect, build up, glean.
◆ **lay off 1** laid twenty men off: dismiss, discharge, make redundant, sack (*infml*), pay off, let go.
2 (*infml*) lay off the sweets: give up, drop, stop, quit, cease, desist, leave off, leave alone, let up.
◆ **lay on** provide, supply, cater, furnish, give, set up.
◆ **lay out 1** laid out the plan/garden: display, set out, spread out, exhibit, arrange, plan, design.
2 (*infml*) laid him out: knock out, fell, flatten, demolish.
3 (*infml*) laid out a lot of money: spend, pay, shell out (*infml*), fork out (*infml*), give, invest.

lay² *adjective*
a lay preacher: laic, secular.
Fa clergy.

layer *noun*
1 a thin layer of snow: cover, coating, coat, covering, film, blanket, mantle, sheet, lamina.
2 a layer of peat: stratum, seam, thickness, tier, bed, plate.

layout *noun*
arrangement, design, outline, plan, sketch, draft, map.

laze *verb*
idle, loaf (*infml*), lounge, sit around, lie around, loll, relax, veg (*infml*).

lazy *adjective*
idle, slothful, slack, work-shy, inactive, lethargic.
Fa industrious.

lead *verb*
1 lead him by the hand: guide, conduct, escort, steer, pilot, usher.
2 lead the country: rule, govern, head, preside over, direct, supervise.
3 leads me to believe: influence, persuade, incline.
4 leading by three lengths: come/be/ go first, surpass, outdo, excel, outstrip, transcend.
5 lead a quiet life: pass, spend, live, undergo.
Fa 1 follow.
▶ *noun*
1 I have a five-point lead: advantage, edge, priority, precedence, first place, start, van, vanguard.
2 follow the lead of the United States: guidance, direction, leadership, example, model.
3 give the police a lead: clue, hint, indication, guide, tip, suggestion.
4 the lead in the movie: title role, starring part, principal.
◆ **lead off** begin, commence, open, get going, start (off), inaugurate, initiate, kick off (*infml*), start the ball rolling.
◆ **lead on** entice, lure, seduce, tempt, draw on, beguile, persuade, string along, deceive, trick.
◆ **lead to** cause, result in, produce, bring about, bring on, contribute to, tend towards.
◆ **lead up to** prepare (the way) for, approach, introduce, make overtures, pave the way.

leader *noun*
head, chief, director, ruler, principal, commander, captain, boss (*infml*), superior, chieftain, ringleader, guide, conductor.
F∃ follower.

leadership *noun*
direction, control, command, management, authority, guidance, domination, pre-eminence, premiership, administration, sway, directorship.

leading *adjective*
main, principal, chief, primary, first, supreme, outstanding, foremost, dominant, ruling, superior, greatest, highest, governing, pre-eminent, number one.
F∃ subordinate.

league *noun*
1 the football league: association, confederation, alliance, union, federation, confederacy, coalition, combination, band, syndicate, guild, consortium, cartel, combine, partnership, fellowship, compact.
2 not in the same league: category, class, level, group.

leak *verb*
1 water leaking out of the tank: seep, drip, ooze, escape, spill, trickle, percolate, exude, discharge.
2 leak the information to the press: divulge, disclose, reveal, let slip, make known, make public, tell, give away, pass on.
▸ *noun*
1 a leak in the gutter: crack, hole, opening, puncture, crevice, chink.
2 leaks of harmful gases: leakage, leaking, seepage, drip, oozing, percolation.
3 a government leak: disclosure, divulgence.

lean¹ *verb*
1 leaning to the left: slant, slope, bend, tilt, list, tend.
2 leaning against the wall: recline, prop, rest.
3 lean towards the opposite view: incline, favour, prefer.

lean² *adjective*
1 a lean athlete: thin, skinny, bony, gaunt, lank, angular, slim, scraggy, scrawny, emaciated.
2 lean times: scanty, inadequate, bare, barren.
F∃ 1 fat. 2 plentiful.

leap *verb*
1 leaping the wall: jump (over), bound, spring, vault, clear, skip, hop, bounce, caper, gambol.
2 prices leaping upwards: soar, surge, increase, rocket, escalate, rise.
F∃ 2 drop, fall.
▸ *noun*
1 in one leap: jump, bound, spring, vault, hop, skip, caper.
2 a leap in the price of oil: increase, upsurge, upswing, surge, rise, escalation.

learn *verb*
1 learns quickly: grasp, comprehend, understand, master, acquire, pick up, gather, assimilate, discern.
2 learn a poem: memorize, learn by heart.
3 learn about his misfortune: discover, find out, ascertain, hear, detect, determine.

learner *noun*
novice, beginner, student, trainee, pupil, scholar, apprentice.

learning *noun*
scholarship, erudition, education, schooling, knowledge, information, letters, study, wisdom, tuition, culture, edification, research.

lease *verb*
let, loan, rent, hire, sublet, charter.

least *adjective*
smallest, lowest, minimum, fewest, slightest, poorest.
F∃ most.

leave¹ *verb*
1 he left around midnight: depart, go, go away, set out, take off, decamp, exit, move, quit, retire, withdraw, disappear, do a bunk (*infml*), clear off (*infml*).
2 leave school: abandon, desert, forsake, give up, drop, relinquish, renounce, pull out, surrender, desist, cease.

3 leave him money in her will: assign, commit, entrust, consign, bequeath, will, hand down, leave behind, give over, transmit.

⊟ 1 arrive. **3** receive.

◆ **leave off** stop, cease, discontinue, desist, abstain, refrain, lay off (*infml*), quit, terminate, break off, end, halt, give over.

◆ **leave out** omit, exclude, overlook, ignore, except, disregard, pass over, count out, cut (out), eliminate, neglect, reject, cast aside, bar.

leave² *noun*
1 get leave to go: permission, authorization, consent, allowance, sanction, concession, dispensation, indulgence, liberty, freedom.
2 take a few days' leave: holiday, time off, vacation, sabbatical, furlough.
⊟ 1 refusal, rejection.

lecture *noun*
1 gives lectures on anatomy: discourse, address, lesson, speech, talk, instruction.
2 gave him a lecture: reprimand, rebuke, reproof, scolding, harangue, censure, chiding, telling-off (*infml*), talking-to (*infml*), dressing-down (*infml*).
▸ *verb*
1 policeman lectured us all on road safety: talk, teach, hold forth, speak, expound, address.
2 she's always lecturing me about being late: reprimand, reprove, scold, admonish, harangue, chide, censure, tell off (*infml*).

left *adjective*
1 on the left side: left-hand, port, sinistral.
2 he was more left than centrist: left-wing, socialist, radical, progressive, revolutionary, liberal, communist, red (*infml*).
⊟ 1 right. **2** right-wing.

leg *noun*
1 broke her leg: limb, member, shank, pin (*infml*), stump (*infml*).
2 a leg at each corner: support, prop, upright, brace.
3 the last leg of the journey: stage,

part, section, portion, stretch, segment, lap.

legacy *noun*
bequest, endowment, gift, heritage, heritance, inheritance, birthright, estate, heirloom.

legal *adjective*
1 is it legal?: lawful, legitimate, permissible, sanctioned, allowed, authorized, allowable, legalized, constitutional, valid, warranted, above board, proper, rightful.
2 a legal inquiry: judicial, judiciary, forensic.
⊟ 1 illegal.

legalize *verb*
legitimize, license, permit, sanction, allow, authorize, warrant, validate, approve.

legend *noun*
1 the legend of St George: myth, story, tale, folk-tale, fable, fiction, narrative.
2 displaying the legend 'Buy British': inscription, caption, key, motto.

legendary *adjective*
1 legendary monsters: mythical, fabulous, story-book, fictitious, traditional.
2 a legendary win: famous, celebrated, renowned, well-known, illustrious.

legible *adjective*
readable, intelligible, decipherable, clear, distinct, neat.
⊟ illegible.

legislate *verb*
enact, ordain, authorize, codify, constitutionalize, prescribe, establish.

legislation *noun*
law, statute, regulation, bill, act, charter, authorization, ruling, measure.

legislative *adjective*
law-making, law-giving, judicial, parliamentary, congressional, senatorial.

legislature *noun*
assembly, chamber, house, parliament, congress, senate.

legitimate *adjective*
1 a legitimate claim: legal, lawful, authorized, statutory, rightful,

proper, correct, real, acknowledged.
2 have a legitimate reason to call:
reasonable, sensible, admissible,
acceptable, justifiable, warranted,
well-founded, valid, true.
F3 1 illegal, illegitimate. **2** invalid.

leisure *noun*
relaxation, rest, spare time, time off,
ease, freedom, liberty, recreation,
retirement, holiday, vacation.
F3 work.

leisurely *adjective*
unhurried, slow, relaxed, comfortable,
easy, unhasty, tranquil, restful, gentle,
carefree, laid-back (*infml*), lazy, loose.
F3 rushed, hectic.

lend *verb*
1 lend him the money: loan, advance.
2 lends truth to his statement: give,
grant, bestow, provide, furnish, confer,
supply, impart, contribute.
F3 1 borrow.

length *noun*
1 the length of a piece of string: extent,
distance, measure, reach, piece,
portion, section, segment.
2 a short length of time: duration,
period, term, stretch, space, span.

lengthen *verb*
stretch, extend, elongate, draw out,
prolong, protract, spin out, eke (out),
pad out, increase, expand, continue.
F3 reduce, shorten.

lengthy *adjective*
long, prolonged, protracted, extended,
lengthened, overlong, long-drawn-out,
long-winded, rambling, diffuse,
verbose, drawn-out, interminable.
F3 brief, concise.

lenient *adjective*
tolerant, forbearing, sparing, indulgent,
merciful, forgiving, soft-hearted, kind,
mild, gentle, compassionate.
F3 strict, severe.

lessen *verb*
decrease, reduce, diminish, lower, ease,
abate, contract, die down, dwindle,
lighten, slow down, weaken, shrink,
abridge, de-escalate, erode, minimize,
narrow, moderate, slack, flag, fail,
deaden, impair.
F3 grow, increase.

lesser *adjective*
lower, secondary, inferior, smaller,
subordinate, slighter, minor.
F3 greater.

lesson *noun*
1 a piano lesson: class, period,
instruction, lecture, tutorial, teaching,
coaching.
2 finish your lessons before watching
TV: assignment, exercise, homework,
practice, task, drill.
3 a lesson to us all: example, model,
warning, deterrent.

let *verb*
1 let him go: permit, allow, give leave,
give permission, authorize, consent to,
agree to, sanction, grant, OK, enable,
tolerate.
2 let the flat: lease, hire, rent.
F3 1 prohibit, forbid.
◆ **let in** admit, accept, receive, take in,
include, incorporate, welcome.
F3 prohibit, bar, forbid.
◆ **let off 1** let him off with a warning:
excuse, absolve, pardon, exempt,
forgive, acquit, exonerate, spare,
ignore, liberate, release.
2 letting off fireworks: discharge,
detonate, fire, explode, emit.
F3 1 punish.
◆ **let out 1** letting the hens out/let out
a scream: free, release, let go,
discharge.
2 let out that they were leaving:
reveal, disclose, make known, utter,
betray, let slip, leak (*infml*).
F3 1 keep in.
◆ **let up** abate, subside, ease (up),
moderate, slacken, diminish, decrease,
stop, end, cease, halt.
F3 continue.

lethal *adjective*
fatal, deadly, deathly, mortal,
dangerous, poisonous, noxious,
destructive, devastating.
F3 harmless, safe.

lethargy *noun*
lassitude, listlessness, sluggishness,
torpor, dullness, inertia, slowness,
apathy, inaction, indifference,
sleepiness, drowsiness, stupor.
F3 liveliness.

letter *noun*
1 send him a letter: note, message, line, missive (*fml*), epistle (*fml*), dispatch, communication, acknowledgement, chit.
2 a capital letter: character, symbol, sign, grapheme.

level *adjective*
1 make sure it's level: flat, smooth, even, flush, horizontal, aligned, plane.
2 the teams were level at half-time: equal, balanced, even, on a par, neck and neck, matching, uniform.
E3 1 uneven. **2** unequal.
▶ *verb*
1 levelling the buildings: demolish, destroy, devastate, flatten, knock down, raze, pull down, bulldoze, tear down, lay low.
2 level the ground/score: even out, flush, plane, smooth, equalize.
3 level criticism/a gun at: direct, point.
▶ *noun*
1 at the same level: height, elevation, altitude.
2 the next level up: position, rank, status, class, degree, grade, standard, standing, plane, echelon, layer, stratum, storey, stage, zone.

lever *verb*
force, prise, pry, raise, dislodge, jemmy, shift, move, heave.
▶ *noun*
bar, crowbar, jemmy, joy-stick, handle.

liability *noun*
1 the insurers accepted liability: accountability, duty, obligation, responsibility, onus.
2 assets and liabilities: debt, arrears, indebtedness.
3 a bit of a liability: drawback, disadvantage, hindrance, impediment, drag (*infml*).

liable *adjective*
1 liable to lose his temper: inclined, likely, apt, disposed, prone, tending, susceptible.
2 liable for any damage: responsible, answerable, accountable, amenable.

liar *noun*
falsifier, perjurer, deceiver, fibber (*infml*).

libel *noun*
defamation (*fml*), slur, smear, slander, vilification (*fml*), aspersion (*fml*), calumny (*fml*).
▶ *verb*
defame (*fml*), slur, smear, slander, vilify (*fml*), malign.

liberal *adjective*
1 a liberal attitude: broad-minded, open-minded, tolerant, lenient.
2 liberal politicians: progressive, reformist, moderate.
3 a liberal amount: generous, ample, bountiful, lavish, plentiful, handsome.
E3 1 narrow-minded. **2** conservative. **3** mean, miserly.

liberate *verb*
free, emancipate, release, let loose, let go, let out, set free, deliver, unchain, discharge, rescue, ransom.
E3 imprison, enslave.

liberty *noun*
1 give them their liberty: freedom, emancipation, release, independence, autonomy.
2 liberty to roam: licence, permission, sanction, right, authorization, dispensation, franchise.
3 take liberties: familiarity, disrespect, overfamiliarity, presumption, impertinence, impudence.
E3 1 imprisonment. **3** respect.
◆ **at liberty** free, unconstrained, unrestricted, not confined.

licence *noun*
1 a driving licence: permission, permit, leave, warrant, authorization, authority, certificate, charter.
2 licence to roam: right, entitlement, privilege, dispensation, carte blanche, freedom, liberty, exemption, independence.
E3 1 prohibition. **2** restriction.

license *verb*
permit, allow, authorize, certify, warrant, entitle, empower, sanction, commission, accredit (*fml*).
E3 ban, prohibit.

lick *verb*
tongue, touch, wash, lap, taste, dart, flick, flicker, play over, smear, brush.

lie¹ verb
lie under oath: perjure, misrepresent, fabricate, falsify, fib (*infml*), invent, equivocate, prevaricate, forswear oneself (*fml*).

▶ *noun*

tell a lie: falsehood, untruth, falsification, fabrication, invention, fiction, deceit, fib (*infml*), falsity, white lie, prevarication, whopper (*infml*), porky (*infml*).

F⋥ truth.

lie² verb
lies west of here: be, exist, dwell, belong, extend, remain.

◆ **lie down** repose, rest, recline, stretch out, lounge, couch, laze.

life noun
1 a long and happy life: being, existence, animation, breath, viability, entity, soul.

2 the life of the parliament: duration, course, span, career.

3 full of life: liveliness, vigour, vitality, vivacity, verve, zest, energy, élan, spirit, sparkle, activity.

lifeless adjective
1 her lifeless body: dead, deceased, defunct, cold, unconscious, inanimate, insensible, stiff.

2 feel lifeless: lethargic, listless, sluggish, dull, apathetic, passive, insipid, colourless, slow.

3 a lifeless desert: barren, bare, empty, desolate, arid.

F⋥ 1 alive. **2** lively. **3** fertile.

lifelike adjective
realistic, true-to-life, real, true, vivid, natural, authentic, faithful, exact, graphic.

F⋥ unrealistic, unnatural.

lifelong adjective
lifetime, long-lasting, long-standing, persistent, lasting, enduring, abiding, permanent, constant.

F⋥ impermanent, temporary.

lift verb
1 she lifted the chair: raise, elevate, hoist, upraise.

2 it lifted their spirits: uplift, exalt, buoy up, boost.

3 the ban was lifted: revoke, cancel, relax.

F⋥ 1 drop. **2** lower.

light¹ noun
1 full of light: illumination, brightness, brilliance, luminescence, radiance, glow, ray, shine, glare, gleam, glint, lustre, flash, blaze.

2 bring a light: lamp, lantern, lighter, match, torch, candle, bulb, beacon.

3 at first light: day, daybreak, daylight, daytime, dawn, sunrise.

4 see the light: enlightenment, explanation, elucidation, understanding.

F⋥ 1 darkness. **3** night.

▶ *verb*

1 light the fire: ignite, fire, set alight, set fire to, kindle.

2 lighting up the sky: illuminate, light up, lighten, brighten, animate, cheer, switch on, turn on, put on.

F⋥ 1 extinguish. **2** darken.

▶ *adjective*

1 a light corner: illuminated, bright, brilliant, luminous, glowing, shining, well-lit, sunny.

2 light skin/hair: pale, pastel, fair, blond, blonde, bleached, faded, faint.

F⋥ 1 dark. **2** dark, colourful.

light² adjective
1 light as a feather: weightless, insubstantial, delicate, airy, buoyant, flimsy, feathery, slight.

2 light punishment: trivial, inconsiderable, trifling, inconsequential, worthless.

3 a light mood: cheerful, cheery, carefree, lively, merry, blithe.

4 light entertainment: amusing, funny, humorous, frivolous, witty, pleasing.

F⋥ 1 heavy, weighty. **2** important, serious. **3** solemn. **4** serious.

lighten¹ verb
lightening the sky: illuminate, illumine, brighten, light up, shine.

F⋥ darken.

lighten² verb
1 lightening his burden: ease, lessen, unload, lift, relieve, reduce, mitigate, alleviate.

2 lightening their hearts: brighten,

cheer, encourage, hearten, inspirit, uplift, gladden, revive, elate, buoy up, inspire.
F3 1 burden. 2 depress.

light-hearted *adjective*
cheerful, joyful, jolly, happy-go-lucky, bright, carefree, untroubled, merry, sunny, glad, elated, jovial, playful.
F3 sad, unhappy, serious.

likable *adjective*
pleasing, appealing, agreeable, charming, engaging, winsome, pleasant, amiable, congenial, attractive, sympathetic.
F3 unpleasant, disagreeable.

like[1] *adjective*
she's like her mother: similar, resembling, alike, same, identical, equivalent, akin, corresponding, related, relating, parallel, allied, analogous, approximating.
F3 unlike, dissimilar.

like[2] *verb*
1 like a good film/like her immensely: enjoy, delight in, care for, admire, appreciate, hold dear, love, esteem, cherish, prize, relish, revel in, approve, take (kindly) to.
2 would you like coffee or tea?: prefer, choose, select, feel inclined, go for (*infml*), desire, want, wish.
F3 1 dislike. 2 reject.
⇒ *See also* **Word Study** *panel.*

likelihood *noun*
likeliness, probability, possibility, chance, prospect, liability.
F3 improbability, unlikeliness.

likely *adjective*
1 it is likely to rain: probable, possible, anticipated, expected, liable, prone, tending, predictable, odds-on (*infml*), inclined, foreseeable.
2 a likely explanation: credible, believable, plausible, feasible, reasonable.
3 a likely candidate: promising, hopeful, pleasing, appropriate, proper, suitable.
F3 1, 2 unlikely. 3 unsuitable.
▸ *adverb*
probably, presumably, like as not, in all probability, no doubt, doubtlessly.

liken *verb*
compare, equate, match, parallel, relate, juxtapose, associate, set beside.

likeness *noun*
1 bears a remarkable likeness to the one I lost: similarity, resemblance, affinity, correspondence.
2 a likeness of the king: image, representation, copy, reproduction, replica, facsimile, effigy, picture, portrait, photograph, counterpart.
F3 1 dissimilarity, unlikeness.

likewise *adverb*
similarly, also, moreover, furthermore, in addition, further, besides, by the same token, too.

liking *noun*
fondness, affection, preference, partiality, affinity, predilection, penchant, taste, attraction, love, appreciation, proneness, propensity, inclination, tendency, bias, desire, weakness, fancy, soft spot (*infml*).
F3 dislike, aversion, hatred.

limb *noun*
arm, leg, member, appendage, branch, projection, offshoot, wing, fork, extension, part, spur, extremity, bough.

limelight *noun*
fame, celebrity, spotlight, stardom, recognition, renown, attention, prominence, publicity, public eye.

limit *noun*
1 the outer limits of the solar system: boundary, bound, border, frontier, confines, edge, brink, threshold, verge, brim, end, perimeter, rim, compass, termination, ultimate, utmost, terminus, extent.
2 a limit on spending/a time limit: check, curb, restraint, restriction, limitation, ceiling, maximum, cut-off point, saturation point, deadline.
▸ *verb*
check, curb, restrict, restrain, constrain, confine, demarcate, delimit, bound, hem in, ration, specify, hinder.

limitation *noun*
1 a limitation on imports: check, restriction, curb, control, constraint, restraint, delimitation, demarcation, block.

WORD *study* like

Here some common phrases used to express one's **like** of someone or something are grouped together under their broad meanings.

liking someone or something a great deal
be bowled over by
take a shine to something

have a weakness for
take someone's breath away

liking someone or something a little
have a thing about/for

have a soft spot for

being suitable to one's tastes
someone's cup of tea
to someone's liking

suit someone down to the ground
up someone's street

2 has its limitations: inadequacy, shortcoming, disadvantage, drawback, condition, qualification, reservation.
F3 1 extension.

limited *adjective*
restricted, circumscribed, constrained, controlled, confined, checked, defined, finite, fixed, minimal, narrow, inadequate, insufficient.
F3 limitless.

limitless *adjective*
unlimited, unbounded, boundless, illimited, undefined, immeasurable, incalculable, infinite, countless, endless, never-ending, unending, inexhaustible, untold, vast.
F3 limited.

limp¹ *verb*
limping badly: hobble, falter, stumble, hop, shuffle, shamble.

limp² *adjective*
1 a limp handshake: flabby, drooping, flaccid, floppy, loose, slack, relaxed, lax, soft, flexible, pliable, limber.
2 feel weak and limp: tired, weary, exhausted, spent, weak, worn out, lethargic, debilitated, enervated.
F3 1 stiff. **2** vigorous.

line¹ *noun*
1 draw a line: stroke, band, bar, stripe, mark, strip, rule, dash, strand, streak, underline, score, scratch.
2 a line of people/cars: row, rank, queue, file, column, sequence, series, procession, chain, trail.
3 the front line: limit, boundary, border, borderline, edge, frontier, demarcation.
4 plastic line: string, rope, cord, cable, thread, filament, wire.
5 the line of her chin: profile, contour, outline, silhouette, figure, formation, configuration.
6 lines on his face: crease, wrinkle, furrow, groove, corrugation.
7 his line of sight: course, path, direction, track, route, axis.
8 take a different line: approach, avenue, course (of action), belief, ideology, policy, system, position, practice, procedure, method, scheme.
9 in a different line (of work): occupation, business, trade, profession, vocation, job, activity, interest, employment, department, calling, field, province, forte, area, pursuit, specialization, specialty, specialism, speciality.
10 the female line: ancestry, family,

descent, extraction, lineage, pedigree, stock, race, breed.

◆ **line up 1** lined them up in rows on the shelves: align, range, straighten, marshal, order, regiment, queue up, form ranks, fall in, array, assemble. **2** have lined up a lift to the match: organize, lay on, arrange, prepare, produce, procure, secure, obtain.

line² *verb*
lined it with silk: fill, pad, stuff, reinforce.

linger *verb*
loiter, delay, dally, tarry, wait, remain, stay, hang on, lag, procrastinate, dawdle, dilly-dally (*infml*), idle, stop, endure, hold out, last, persist, survive.
F∃leave, rush.

lining *noun*
inlay, interfacing, padding, backing, stiffening.

link *noun*
1 I could find no link to the other crimes: connection, bond, tie, association, joint, relationship, tie-up, union, knot, liaison, attachment, communication.
2 a link in the chain: part, piece, element, member, constituent, component, division.
▶ *verb*
connect, join, couple, tie, fasten, unite, bind, amalgamate, merge, associate, ally, bracket, identify, relate, yoke, attach, hook up, join forces, team up.
F∃separate, unfasten.

lip *noun*
edge, brim, border, brink, rim, margin, verge.

liquid *noun*
liquor, fluid, juice, drink, sap, solution, lotion.
▶ *adjective*
fluid, flowing, liquefied, watery, wet, runny, melted, molten, thawed, clear, smooth.
F∃solid.

list¹ *noun*
a list of names: catalogue, roll, inventory, register, enumeration, schedule, index, listing, record, file, directory, table, tabulation, tally, series, syllabus, invoice.

▶ *verb*
listing items for sale: enumerate, register, itemize, catalogue, index, tabulate, record, file, enrol, enter, note, bill, book, set down, write down.

list² *verb*
ship was listing heavily: lean, incline, tilt, slope, heel (over), tip.

listen *verb*
hark, attend, pay attention, hear, heed, hearken, hang on (someone's) words, prick up one's ears, take notice, lend an ear, eavesdrop, overhear, give ear.

listless *adjective*
sluggish, lethargic, languid, torpid, enervated, spiritless, limp, lifeless, inert, inactive, impassive, indifferent, uninterested, vacant, apathetic, indolent, depressed, bored, heavy.
F∃energetic, enthusiastic.

literal *adjective*
1 a literal translation: verbatim, word-for-word, strict, close, actual, precise, faithful, exact, accurate, factual, true, genuine, unexaggerated.
2 a literal interpretation: prosaic, unimaginative, uninspired, matter-of-fact, down-to-earth, humdrum.
F∃1 imprecise, loose. **2** imaginative.

literary *adjective*
bookish, cultured, cultivated, refined, formal.

literate *adjective*
educated, well-read, learned, erudite, scholarly, lettered.
F∃ illiterate.

literature *noun*
1 English literature: writings, letters, paper(s).

Types of literature include:

allegory, anti-novel, autobiography, belles-lettres (*fml*), biography, classic novel, criticism, drama, epic, epistle, essay, fiction, Gothic novel, lampoon, libretto, magnum opus, non-fiction, novel, novella, parody, pastiche, penny dreadful, picaresque novel, poetry, polemic, prose, roman, saga, satire, thesis, tragedy, treatise, triad, trilogy, verse. ⇨ *See also* **poem**; **story**.

Terms used in literature include:

act, alliteration, anthology, assonance, bathos, blank verse, bucolic, characterization, cliché, comedy, couplet, critic, eclogue, epigram, epilogue, epode, epopee, essay, female or feminine rhyme, fiction, free verse, genre, georgic, imagery, internal rhyme, irony, lampoon, lay, libretto, lipogram, male or masculine rhyme, metaphor, metre, monody, monologue, motif, onomatopoeia, oxymoron, narrator, palinode, paradox, parody, pastiche, pathetic fallacy, plot, postil, prologue, protagonist, rhyme, rhythm, rondeau, scene, simile, stanza, style, sub-plot.

2 get all the available literature: information, leaflet(s), pamphlet(s), circular(s), brochure(s), handout(s), bumf (*infml*).

litigation *noun*
lawsuit, action, suit, case, prosecution, process, contention.

litter *noun*
1 clear up other people's litter: rubbish, debris, refuse, waste, mess, disorder, clutter, confusion, disarray, untidiness, junk (*infml*), muck, jumble, fragments, shreds.
2 a litter of pups: offspring, young, progeny (*fml*), brood, family.
▶ *verb*
strew, scatter, mess up, disorder, clutter.
E3 tidy.

little *adjective*
1 a little man/car/creature: small, short, tiny, wee (*infml*), minute, teeny (*infml*), diminutive, miniature, infinitesimal, mini, microscopic, petite, pint-size(d) (*infml*), slender.
2 a little pause: short-lived, brief, fleeting, passing, transient.
3 had little water/money: insufficient, sparse, scant, meagre, paltry, skimpy.
4 a little detail: insignificant, inconsiderable, negligible, trivial, petty, trifling, unimportant.

E3 1 big. 2 lengthy. 3 ample.
4 considerable.
▶ *adverb*
barely, hardly, scarcely, rarely, seldom, infrequently, not much.
E3 frequently.
▶ *noun*
bit, dash, pinch, spot, trace, drop, dab, speck, touch, taste, particle, hint, fragment, modicum, trifle.
E3 lot.

live¹ *verb* /liv/
1 live for seventy years: be, exist, breathe, draw breath.
2 his achievements will live on after his death: last, endure, continue, remain, persist, survive.
3 live in a tent: dwell, inhabit, reside, lodge, abide (*fml*).
4 live a quiet life: pass, spend, lead.
E3 1 die. 2 cease, disappear.

live² *adjective* /laiv/
1 live births: alive, living, existent.
2 he's a live wire: lively, vital, active, energetic, dynamic, alert, vigorous.
3 live electric cable: burning, glowing, blazing, ignited.
4 live issue: relevant, current, topical, pertinent, controversial, pressing.
E3 1 dead. 2 apathetic.

livelihood *noun*
occupation, employment, job, living, means, income, maintenance, work, support, subsistence, sustenance.

lively *adjective*
1 lively discussion: animated, alert, active, energetic, spirited, vivacious, vigorous, sprightly, spry, agile, nimble, quick, keen.
2 she's very lively for her age: cheerful, blithe, merry, frisky, perky, breezy, chirpy (*infml*), frolicsome.
3 a lively market: busy, bustling, brisk, crowded, eventful, exciting, buzzing.
4 a lively scene: vivid, bright, colourful, stimulating, stirring, invigorating, racy, refreshing, sparkling.
E3 1 moribund, apathetic. 2 lethargic. 3 inactive. 4 dull.

liven (up) *verb*
enliven, vitalize, put life into, rouse,

invigorate, animate, energize, brighten, stir (up), buck up (*infml*), pep up (*infml*), perk up (*infml*), hot up (*infml*).
F3 dishearten.

livid *adjective*
1 (*infml*) was absolutely livid: angry, furious, infuriated, irate, outraged, enraged, raging, fuming, indignant, incensed, exasperated, mad (*infml*).
2 a livid purple: leaden, black-and-blue, bruised, discoloured, greyish, pale, ashen, purple.
F3 1 calm.

living *adjective*
alive, breathing, existing, live, current, extant, operative, strong, vigorous, active, lively, vital, animated.
F3 dead, sluggish.
▸ *noun*
livelihood, maintenance, support, income, subsistence, sustenance, work, job, occupation, profession, benefice, way of life.

load *noun*
1 carry heavy loads: burden, onus, encumbrance, weight, pressure, oppression, millstone.
2 spilling its load: cargo, consignment, shipment, goods, lading, freight.
▸ *verb*
1 she arrived loaded with packages: burden, weigh down, encumber, overburden, oppress, trouble, weight, saddle with.
2 load the crates into the van: pack, pile, heap, freight, fill, stack.

loan *noun*
advance, credit, mortgage, allowance.
▸ *verb*
lend, advance, credit, allow.

loathe *verb*
hate, detest, abominate, abhor, despise, dislike.
F3 adore, love.

loathing *noun*
hatred, detestation, abhorrence (*fml*), abomination, repugnance, revulsion, repulsion, dislike, disgust, aversion, horror.
F3 affection, love.

lobby *verb*
campaign for, press for, demand,

persuade, call for, urge, push for, influence, solicit, pressure, promote.
▸ *noun*
1 the hotel lobby: vestibule, foyer, porch, anteroom, hall, hallway, waiting room, entrance hall, corridor, passage.
2 the tobacco lobby: pressure group, campaign, ginger group.

local *adjective*
regional, provincial, community, district, neighbourhood, parochial, vernacular, small-town, limited, narrow, restricted, parish(-pump).
F3 national.
▸ *noun*
1 one of the locals: inhabitant, citizen, resident, native.
2 (*infml*) go down the local: pub.

locality *noun*
neighbourhood, vicinity, district, area, locale, region, position, place, site, spot, scene, setting.

locate *verb*
1 can't locate the file: find, discover, unearth, run to earth (*infml*), track down, detect, lay one's hands on (*infml*), pinpoint, identify.
2 located near the station: situate, settle, fix, establish, place, put, set, seat.

location *noun*
position, situation, place, locus, whereabouts, venue, site, locale, bearings, spot, point.

lock *noun*
fastening, bolt, clasp, padlock.
▸ *verb*
1 lock the gates: fasten, secure, bolt, latch, seal, shut.
2 locking the two pieces together: join, unite, engage, link, mesh, entangle, entwine, clench.
3 locking arms: clasp, hug, embrace, grasp, encircle, enclose, clutch, grapple.
F3 unlock.
◆ **lock out** shut out, refuse admittance to, keep out, exclude, bar, debar.
◆ **lock up** imprison, jail, confine, shut in, shut up, incarcerate, secure, cage, pen, detain, close up.
F3 free.

lodge *noun*
hut, cabin, cottage, chalet, shelter,
retreat, den, gatehouse, house,
hunting-lodge, meeting-place, club,
haunt.
▶ *verb*
1 lodging with an elderly couple: live,
stay, reside.
**2 house that lodged two whole
families**: accommodate, put up (*infml*),
quarter, board, billet, shelter.
3 lodged between the boards: fix,
imbed, implant, get stuck.
**4 lodge funds in the account/lodge a
complaint**: deposit, place, put, submit,
register.

log *noun*
1 put some logs on the fire: timber,
trunk, block, chunk.
2 the captain's log: record, diary,
journal, logbook, daybook, account,
tally.
▶ *verb*
record, register, write up, note, book,
chart, tally.

logic *noun*
reasoning, reason, sense, deduction,
rationale, argumentation.

logical *adjective*
reasonable, rational, reasoned,
coherent, consistent, valid, sound,
well-founded, clear, sensible,
deducible, methodical, well-
organized.
E3 illogical, irrational.

loiter *verb*
dawdle, hang about, idle, linger, dally,
dilly-dally (*infml*), delay, mooch, lag,
saunter.

lone *adjective*
single, sole, one, only, isolated, solitary,
separate, separated, unattached,
unaccompanied, unattended.
E3 accompanied.

lonely *adjective*
1 a lonely old woman: alone,
friendless, lonesome, solitary,
abandoned, forsaken, companionless,
unaccompanied, destitute.
2 a lonely farmhouse: isolated,
uninhabited, remote, out-of-the-
way, unfrequented, secluded,

abandoned, deserted, forsaken,
desolate.
E3 1 popular. 2 accessible.

long *adjective*
lengthy, extensive, extended, expanded,
prolonged, protracted, stretched,
spread out, sustained, expansive, far-
reaching, long-drawn-out,
interminable, slow.
E3 brief, short, fleeting, abbreviated.
◆ **long for** yearn for, crave, want, wish,
desire, dream of, hanker for, pine,
thirst for, lust after, covet, itch for, yen
for (*infml*).

longing *noun*
craving, desire, yearning, hungering,
hankering, yen, thirst, wish, urge,
coveting, aspiration, ambition.

long-suffering *adjective*
uncomplaining, forbearing, forgiving,
tolerant, easy-going, patient, stoical.

long-winded *adjective*
lengthy, overlong, prolonged, diffuse,
verbose, wordy, voluble, long-drawn-
out, discursive, repetitious, rambling,
tedious.
E3 brief, terse.

look *verb*
1 looking through the window: watch,
see, observe, view, survey, regard, gaze,
study, stare, examine, inspect,
scrutinize, glance, contemplate, scan,
peep, gawp (*infml*).
2 looking very smart: seem, appear,
show, exhibit, display.
▶ *noun*
1 take a good look: view, survey,
inspection, examination, observation,
sight, review, once-over (*infml*), glance,
glimpse, gaze, peek.
2 has a frightening look: appearance,
aspect, manner, semblance, mien
(*fml*), expression, bearing, face,
complexion.
◆ **look after** take care of, mind, care
for, attend to, take charge of, tend, keep
an eye on, watch over, protect,
supervise, guard.
E3 neglect.
◆ **look down on** despise, scorn,
sneer at, hold in contempt, disdain,
look down one's nose at (*infml*), turn

one's nose up at (*infml*).
F3 esteem, approve.

◆ **look forward to** anticipate, await, expect, hope for, long for, envisage, envision, count on, wait for, look for.

◆ **look into** investigate, probe, research, study, go into, examine, enquire about, explore, check out, inspect, scrutinize, look over, plumb, fathom.

◆ **look out** pay attention, watch out, beware, be careful, keep an eye out.

◆ **look up 1** look up a word in the dictionary: search for, research, hunt for, find, track down.
2 look us up next time you come: visit, call on, drop in on, look in on, pay a visit to, stop by, drop by.
3 things are looking up: improve, get better, pick up, progress, come on.

◆ **look up to** admire, esteem, respect, revere, honour, have a high opinion of.

look-alike *noun*
double, replica, twin, spitting image (*infml*), living image, clone, spit (*infml*), dead ringer (*infml*), doppelgänger.

loom *verb*
appear, emerge, take shape, menace, threaten, impend, hang over, dominate, tower, overhang, rise, soar, overshadow, overtop.

loop *noun*
hoop, ring, circle, noose, coil, eyelet, loophole, spiral, curve, curl, kink, twist, whorl, twirl, turn, bend.
▸ *verb*
coil, encircle, roll, bend, circle, curve round, turn, twist, spiral, connect, join, knot, fold, braid.

loophole *noun*
let-out, escape, evasion, excuse, pretext, plea, pretence.

loose *adjective*
1 a loose tooth: free, unfastened, untied, movable, unattached, insecure, wobbly.
2 loose clothing: slack, lax, baggy, hanging.
3 a loose description: imprecise, vague, inexact, ill-defined, indefinite, inaccurate, indistinct.
F3 **1** firm, secure. **2** tight. **3** precise.

loosen *verb*
1 loosen his collar: ease, relax, loose, slacken, undo, unbind, untie, unfasten.
2 loosening his tongue: free, set free, release, let go, let out, deliver.
F3 **1** tighten.

loot *verb*
plunder, pillage, rob, sack, rifle, raid, maraud, ransack, ravage.
▸ *noun*
spoils, booty, plunder, haul, swag (*infml*), prize.

lop-sided *adjective*
asymmetrical, unbalanced, askew, off balance, uneven.
F3 balanced, symmetrical.

lord *noun*
1 my noble lords: peer, noble, earl, duke, count, baron.
2 the lord of all he surveys: master, ruler, superior, overlord, leader, commander, governor, king.

lore *noun*
knowledge, wisdom, learning, erudition, scholarship, traditions, teaching, beliefs, sayings.

lose *verb*
1 lose his pen: mislay, misplace, forget, miss, forfeit.
2 lose money: waste, squander, dissipate, use up, exhaust, expend, drain.
3 lose the race: fail, fall short, suffer defeat.
F3 **1** find. **2** make, gain. **3** win.
⇨ *See also* **Word Study** *panel.*

loss *noun*
1 loss of liberty: deprivation, disadvantage, defeat, failure, losing, bereavement, damage, destruction, ruin, hurt.
2 have large losses: waste, depletion, disappearance, deficiency, deficit.
F3 gain.

lost *adjective*
1 lost property: mislaid, missing, vanished, disappeared, misplaced, astray.
2 look lost: confused, disoriented, bewildered, puzzled, baffled, perplexed, preoccupied.

WORD*study* losing

There are many expressions that describe how a person or team can **lose** or be defeated. Try out some of those listed below, but remember that many phrases are only appropriate for informal contexts.

lose

come off worst
slip up

go down

be close to defeat

be on your last legs
be on your knees

be on the ropes

lose decisively

take a hammering/thrashing

meet your Waterloo

a heavy loss

a drubbing
a whitewash

a pasting

admit defeat or retire

bottle out (*slang*)
lose your nerve
throw in the towel

lick your wounds
throw in your hand
throw up the cards

3 lost time: wasted, squandered, ruined, destroyed.
F3 1 found.

lot *noun*
1 lots of food/a lot of people: large amount, great number, many, a quantity, a good/great deal, shedload (*infml*).
2 an interesting lot: collection, batch, assortment, quantity, group, set, crowd.
3 accept our lot: share, portion, allowance, ration, quota, part, piece, parcel.
⇨ *See also* **Word Workshop** *panel*.

lotion *noun*
ointment, balm, cream, salve.

loud *adjective*
1 a loud voice: noisy, deafening,

booming, resounding, ear-piercing, ear-splitting, piercing, thundering, blaring, clamorous, vociferous.
2 a loud tie: garish, gaudy, glaring, flashy, brash, showy, ostentatious, tasteless.
F3 1 quiet. **2** subdued.

lounge *verb*
relax, loll, idle, laze, waste time, kill time, lie about, take it easy, sprawl, recline, lie back, slump.
▶ *noun*
sitting room, living room, drawing room, day room, parlour.

lovable *adjective*
adorable, endearing, winsome, captivating, charming, engaging,

WORD *work shop*   lot

Beware of using **a lot** or **lots** too often in your writing as your readers may find it boring. Try out some of the following synonyms instead:

a lot

abundance	great number	wealth
glut	large amount	
good deal	profusion	

lots

countless	numerous	several
many	plenty	

you can use these synonyms when you speak, but not when you write!

dozens	masses	stacks
heaps	millions	thousands
hundreds	oodles	tons
loads	piles	

attractive, fetching, sweet, lovely, pleasing, delightful.
≠ detestable, hateful.

love *verb*
1 he loves his children: adore, cherish, dote on, treasure, hold dear, idolize, worship.
2 I love dancing: like, take pleasure in, enjoy, delight in, appreciate, desire, fancy.
≠ detest, hate.
▶ *noun*
adoration, affection, fondness, attachment, regard, liking, amorousness, ardour, devotion,

adulation, passion, rapture, tenderness, warmth, inclination, infatuation, delight, enjoyment, soft spot (*infml*), weakness, taste, friendship.
≠ detestation, hate, loathing.

love affair *noun*
affair, romance, liaison, relationship, love, passion, fling (*infml*).

lovely *adjective*
beautiful, charming, delightful, attractive, enchanting, pleasing, pleasant, pretty, adorable, agreeable, enjoyable, sweet, winning, exquisite.
≠ ugly, hideous.

lot   WORD *workshop*

Instead of repeating **a lot** or **lots** in the following passage, you might use some of the synonyms suggested opposite.

> *large number*
> "A ~~lot~~ of people will be attending the school open day," announced the headteacher, "and ~~lots~~ *many* of those people will be important, so I want everyone to help make the school look its best."
>
> *good deal*
> "That will take a ~~lot~~ of work," thought the caretaker, "and we will need ~~lots~~ *plenty* of time too."
>
> *great deal*
> "So let's get busy," exclaimed the head, "there's a ~~lot~~ to be done!"

loving *adjective*
amorous, affectionate, devoted, doting, fond, ardent, passionate, warm, warm-hearted, tender.

low *adjective*
1 a low wall: short, small, squat, stunted, little, shallow, deep, depressed, sunken.
2 supplies are low: inadequate, deficient, poor, sparse, meagre, paltry, scant, insignificant.
3 feeling a bit low: unhappy, depressed, downcast, gloomy.
4 a low trick: base, coarse, vulgar, mean, contemptible.

5 low prices: cheap, inexpensive, reasonable.
6 low lighting: subdued, muted, soft.
Ea 1 high. **2** plentiful. **3** cheerful.
4 honourable. **5** exorbitant, high. **6** harsh.

lower *adjective*
inferior, lesser, subordinate, secondary, minor, second-class, low-level, lowly, junior.
Ea higher.
▶ *verb*
1 lower the flag: drop, depress, sink, descend, let down.
2 lowering interest rates: reduce,

decrease, cut, lessen, diminish.
F3 1 raise. **2** increase, raise.

lowly *adjective*
humble, low-born, obscure, poor,
plebeian, plain, simple, modest,
ordinary, inferior, meek, mild, mean,
submissive, subordinate.
F3 lofty, noble.

loyal *adjective*
true, faithful, steadfast, staunch,
devoted, trustworthy, sincere,
patriotic.
F3 disloyal, treacherous.

loyalty *noun*
allegiance, faithfulness, fidelity,
devotion, steadfastness, constancy,
trustworthiness, reliability, patriotism.
F3 disloyalty, treachery.

luck *noun*
1 *trust to luck:* chance, fortune,
accident, fate, fortuity (*fml*), fluke
(*infml*), destiny.
2 *have the luck to be in the right place
at the right time:* good fortune,
success, break (*infml*), godsend.
F3 1 design. **2** misfortune.

lucky *adjective*
fortunate, favoured, auspicious,
successful, prosperous, timely, jammy
(*infml*).
F3 unlucky.

lucrative *adjective*
profitable, well-paid, remunerative,
advantageous.
F3 unprofitable.

ludicrous *adjective*
absurd, ridiculous, preposterous,
nonsensical, laughable, farcical, silly,
comical, funny, outlandish, crazy
(*infml*).
F3 serious.

lukewarm *adjective*
cool, half-hearted, apathetic, tepid,
indifferent, unenthusiastic,
uninterested, unresponsive,
unconcerned.

lull *verb*
soothe, subdue, calm, hush, pacify,
quieten down, quiet, quell,
compose.
F3 agitate.

▸ *noun*
calm, peace, quiet, tranquillity,
stillness, let-up, pause, hush,
silence.
F3 agitation.

lumber *verb*
clump, shamble, plod, shuffle, stump,
trundle.

luminous *adjective*
glowing, illuminated, lit, lighted,
radiant, shining, fluorescent, brilliant,
lustrous, bright.

lump *noun*
1 *a lump of sugar/rock:* mass, cluster,
clump, clod, ball, bunch, piece, chunk,
cake, hunk, nugget, wedge.
2 *a lump on his head:* swelling, growth,
bulge, bump, protuberance (*fml*),
protrusion, tumour, nodule.
▸ *verb*
collect, mass, gather, cluster, combine,
coalesce, group, consolidate, unite.

lunacy *noun*
madness, insanity, aberration,
derangement, mania, craziness (*infml*),
idiocy, imbecility, folly, absurdity,
stupidity.
F3 sanity.

lunge *verb*
thrust, jab, stab, pounce, plunge, pitch
into, charge, dart, dash, dive, poke,
strike (at), fall upon, grab (at), hit (at),
leap.

lurch *verb*
roll, rock, pitch, sway, stagger, reel,
list.

lure *verb*
tempt, entice, draw, attract, allure,
seduce, ensnare, lead on.
▸ *noun*
temptation, enticement, attraction,
bait, inducement.

lurid *adjective*
1 *lurid headlines:* sensational,
shocking, startling, graphic,
exaggerated.
2 *lurid details:* macabre, gruesome,
gory, ghastly, grisly.
3 *a lurid shade of pink:* brightly
coloured, garish, glaring, loud,
vivid.

lurk *verb*
skulk, prowl, lie in wait, crouch, lie low, hide, snoop.

luxurious *adjective*
sumptuous, opulent, lavish, de luxe, plush, magnificent, splendid, expensive, costly, self-indulgent, pampered.

⊞ austere, spartan.

luxury *noun*
sumptuousness, opulence, hedonism, splendour, affluence, richness, magnificence, pleasure, indulgence, gratification, comfort, extravagance, satisfaction.

⊞ austerity.

Mm

macabre *adjective*
gruesome, grisly, grim, horrible, frightful, dreadful, ghostly, eerie.

machine *noun*
1 a flying machine/washing machine/photocopying machine: instrument, device, contrivance, tool, mechanism, engine, apparatus, appliance.
2 the government's publicity machine: agency, organization, structure, system.

machinery *noun*
1 farm machinery: instruments, mechanism, tools, apparatus, equipment, tackle, gear.
2 the machinery of government: organization, channels, structure, system, procedure.

mad *adjective*
1 went mad with grief: insane, lunatic, unbalanced, psychotic, deranged, demented, out of one's mind, crazy (*infml*), nuts (*infml*), barmy (*infml*), bonkers (*infml*).
2 (*infml*) she got really mad: angry, furious, enraged, infuriated, incensed.
3 a mad idea: irrational, illogical, unreasonable, absurd, preposterous, foolish, crazy (*infml*).
4 mad about cars/football: fanatical, enthusiastic, infatuated, ardent.
E∃ 1 sane. 2 calm. 3 sensible.
4 apathetic.

madden *verb*
anger, enrage, infuriate, incense, exasperate, provoke, annoy, irritate.
E∃ calm, pacify.

madly *adverb*
1 rolling his eyes madly: insanely, dementedly, hysterically, wildly.

2 waving her arms about madly: excitedly, frantically, furiously, recklessly, violently, energetically, rapidly, hastily, hurriedly.
3 madly in love: intensely, extremely, exceedingly, fervently, devotedly.

magazine *noun*
1 a fashion magazine: journal, periodical, paper, weekly, monthly, quarterly.
2 a magazine of bullets: arsenal, storehouse, ammunition dump, depot, ordnance.

magic *noun*
1 black/white magic: sorcery, enchantment, occultism, black art, witchcraft, wizardry, spell, necromancy.
2 perform magic: conjuring, illusion, sleight of hand, legerdemain, trickery.
3 islands have a certain indefinable magic: charm, fascination, glamour, allure.
▶ *adjective*
charming, enchanting, bewitching, fascinating, spellbinding.

magician *noun*
sorcerer, miracle-worker, conjuror, enchanter, enchantress, wizard, witch, warlock, spellbinder, wonder-worker.

magnetic *adjective*
attractive, alluring, fascinating, charming, mesmerizing, seductive, irresistible, entrancing, captivating, gripping, absorbing, charismatic.
E∃ repellent, repulsive.

magnificent *adjective*
splendid, grand, imposing, impressive, glorious, gorgeous, brilliant, excellent, majestic, superb, sumptuous, noble,

elegant, fine, rich.
F3 modest, humble, poor.

magnify *verb*
enlarge, amplify, increase, expand,
intensify, boost, enhance, greaten,
heighten, deepen, build up, exaggerate,
dramatize, overemphasize, overplay,
overstate, overdo, blow up (*infml*).
F3 belittle, play down.

magnitude *noun*
1 the magnitude of a star: size, extent,
measure, amount, expanse,
dimensions, mass, proportions,
quantity, volume, bulk, largeness,
space, strength, amplitude.
2 a decision of great magnitude:
importance, consequence,
significance, weight, greatness,
moment, intensity.

mail *noun*
post, letters, correspondence,
packages, parcels, delivery.
▶ *verb*
post, send, dispatch, forward.

maim *verb*
mutilate, wound, incapacitate, injure,
disable, hurt, impair, cripple, lame.

main *adjective*
principal, chief, leading, first,
foremost, predominant, pre-eminent,
primary, prime, supreme, paramount,
central, cardinal, outstanding,
essential, critical, crucial, necessary,
vital.
F3 minor, unimportant, insignificant.
▶ *noun*
pipe, duct, conduit, channel, cable,
line.

mainly *adverb*
primarily, principally, chiefly, in the
main, mostly, on the whole, for the
most part, generally, in general,
especially, as a rule, above all, largely,
overall.

maintain *verb*
**1 maintain the same rate of
production**: carry on, continue, keep
(up), sustain, retain.
2 work to maintain one's family: care
for, conserve, look after, take care of,
preserve, support, finance, supply.
3 maintains that he never received the

letter: assert, affirm, claim, contend,
declare, hold (*fml*), state, insist, believe,
fight for.
F3 2 neglect. **3** deny.

maintenance *noun*
**1 long-term maintenance of low
inflation**: continuation, continuance,
perpetuation.
**2 house required constant
maintenance**: care, conservation,
preservation, support, repairs,
protection, upkeep, running.
3 paying child maintenance: keep,
subsistence, living, livelihood,
allowance, alimony.
F3 2 neglect.

majestic *adjective*
magnificent, grand, dignified, noble,
royal, stately, splendid, imperial,
impressive, exalted, imposing, regal,
sublime, superb, lofty, monumental,
pompous.
F3 lowly, unimpressive, unimposing.

major *adjective*
greater, chief, main, larger, bigger,
higher, leading, outstanding, notable,
supreme, uppermost, significant,
crucial, important, key, keynote, great,
senior, older, superior, pre-eminent,
vital, weighty.
F3 minor, unimportant, trivial.

majority *noun*
1 the majority of households: bulk,
mass, preponderance, most, greater
part.
2 reach his/her majority: adulthood,
maturity, manhood, womanhood,
years of discretion.
F3 1 minority.

make *verb*
1 make cars/cakes/music: create,
manufacture, fabricate, construct,
build, produce, put together, originate,
compose, form, shape.
2 made trouble/a scene/a mistake:
cause, bring about, effect, accomplish,
occasion, give rise to, generate, render,
perform.
3 they made him do it: coerce, force,
oblige, constrain, compel, prevail
upon, pressurize, press, require.
4 made her a partner in the firm:

appoint, elect, designate, nominate, ordain, install.
5 make money/a profit: earn, gain, net, obtain, acquire.
6 two and two makes four: compose, constitute, comprise, add up to, amount to.
▶ *noun*
brand, sort, type, style, variety, manufacture, model, mark, kind, form, structure.

◆ **make off** run off, run away, depart, bolt, leave, fly, cut and run (*infml*), beat a hasty retreat (*infml*), clear off (*infml*).

◆ **make out 1 couldn't quite make it/ him out:** discern, perceive, decipher, distinguish, recognize, see, detect, discover, understand, work out, grasp, follow, fathom.
2 make out a cheque: draw up, complete, fill in, write out.
3 they tried to make out that I was at fault: maintain, imply, claim, assert, describe, demonstrate, prove.
4 how is he making out at college?: manage, get on, progress, succeed, fare.

◆ **make up 1 make up a story/excuse:** create, invent, devise, fabricate, construct, originate, formulate, dream up, compose.
2 make up the difference: complete, fill, supply, meet, supplement.
3 made up of three distinct elements: comprise, constitute, compose, form.
4 kiss and make up: be reconciled, make peace, settle differences, bury the hatchet (*infml*), forgive and forget, call it quits (*infml*).

◆ **make up for** compensate for, make good, make amends for, redress, recompense, redeem, atone for.

make-believe *noun*
pretence, imagination, fantasy, unreality, play-acting, role-play, dream, charade.
F3 reality.

makeshift *adjective*
temporary, improvised, rough and ready, provisional, substitute, stop-gap, expedient, make-do.
F3 permanent.

make-up *noun*
1 wearing a lot of make-up: cosmetics, paint, powder, maquillage, war paint (*infml*).
2 the political make-up of the committee: constitution, nature, composition, character, construction, form, format, formation, arrangement, organization, style, structure, assembly.

male *adjective*
masculine, manly, virile, boyish, he-.
F3 female.

malice *noun*
malevolence, enmity, animosity, ill-will, hatred, hate, spite, vindictiveness, bitterness.
F3 love.

malicious *adjective*
malevolent, ill-natured, malign, spiteful, venomous, vicious, vengeful, evil-minded, bitter, resentful.
F3 kind, friendly.

malign *adjective*
malignant, malevolent, bad, evil, harmful, hurtful, injurious, destructive, hostile.
F3 benign.
▶ *verb*
defame (*fml*), slander, libel, disparage (*fml*), abuse, run down (*infml*), harm, injure.
F3 praise.

malignant *adjective*
1 a malignant tumour: fatal, deadly, incurable, dangerous, cancerous, uncontrollable, virulent.
2 a malignant person: malevolent, malicious, spiteful, evil, hostile, vicious, venomous, destructive, harmful, hurtful, pernicious.
F3 1 benign. 2 kind.

mammal

Mammals include:

aardvark, African black rhinoceros, African elephant, anteater, antelope, armadillo, baboon, Bactrian camel, badger, bat, bear, beaver, bushbaby, cat, chimpanzee, chipmunk, cow, deer, dog, dolphin, duck-billed platypus, dugong, echidna, flying lemur, fox, gerbil, gibbon, giraffe, goat, gorilla, guinea pig, hamster, hare, hedgehog, hippopotamus, horse, human being, hyena, Indian elephant, kangaroo, koala, lemming, leopard, lion, manatee, marmoset, marmot, marsupial mouse, mole, mouse, opossum, orang-utan, otter, pig, porcupine, porpoise, rabbit, raccoon, rat, sea cow, seal, sea lion, sheep, shrew, sloth, squirrel, tamarin, tapir, tiger, vole, wallaby, walrus, weasel, whale, wolf, zebra. ⇨ *See also* **animal**; **cat**; **dog**; **marsupial**; **rodent**.

man *noun*
1 *don't know that man*: male, gentleman, fellow, bloke (*infml*), chap (*infml*), guy (*infml*).
2 *all men are created equal*: human being, person, individual, adult, human.
3 *the evolution of man*: humanity, humankind, mankind, human race, people, Homo sapiens, mortals.
▶ *verb*
staff, crew, take charge of, operate, occupy.

manage *verb*
1 *managed the task quite easily*: accomplish, succeed, bring about, bring off, effect.
2 *managing a small workforce*: administer, direct, run, command, govern, preside over, rule, superintend, supervise, oversee, conduct.
3 *manage money*: control, influence, deal with, handle, operate, manipulate, guide.
4 *can't manage on less than £200 per week*: cope, fare, survive, get by, get along, get on, make do.
E3 1 fail. **2** mismanage.

management *noun*
1 *the overall management of the project*: administration, direction, control, government, command, running, superintendence, supervision, charge, care, handling.
2 *management versus unions*: managers, directors, directorate, executive, executives, governors, board, bosses (*infml*), supervisors.
E3 1 mismanagement. **2** workers.

manager *noun*
director, executive, administrator, controller, superintendent, supervisor, overseer, governor, organizer, head, boss (*infml*).

mangle *verb*
mutilate, disfigure, mar, maim, spoil, butcher, destroy, deform, wreck, twist, maul, distort, crush, cut, hack, tear, rend.

mania *noun*
1 *suffer from persecution mania*: madness, insanity, lunacy, psychosis, derangement, disorder, aberration, craziness (*infml*), frenzy.
2 *have a mania for collecting Chinese porcelain*: passion, craze, rage, obsession, compulsion, enthusiasm, fad (*infml*), infatuation, fixation, craving.

Manias (by name of disorder) include:

dipsomania (*alcohol*), bibliomania (*books*), ailuromania (*cats*), demomania (*crowds*), necromania (*dead bodies*), thanatomania (*death*), cynomania (*dogs*), narcomania (*drugs*), pyromania (*fire-raising*), anthomania (*flowers*), hippomania (*horses*), mythomania (*lying and exaggerating*), egomania (*oneself*), ablutomania (*personal cleanliness*), hedonomania (*pleasure*), megalomania (*power*), theomania (*religion*), monomania (*single idea or thing*), kleptomania (*stealing*), tomomania (*surgery*), logomania (*talking*), ergomania (*work*). ⇨ *See also* **phobia.**

maniac *noun*
1 *attacked by a maniac*: lunatic, madman, madwoman, psychotic, psychopath, loony (*infml*), nutter (*infml*).
2 *a bit of a football maniac*: enthusiast, fan (*infml*), fanatic, fiend (*infml*), freak (*infml*).

manifestation *noun*
display, exhibition, demonstration, show, revelation, exposure, disclosure, appearance, expression, sign, indication.

manipulate *verb*
1 manipulating the clay/an audience:
handle, control, wield, operate, use,
manoeuvre, influence, engineer, guide,
direct, steer, negotiate, work.
2 manipulate the figures: falsify, rig,
juggle with, doctor (*infml*), cook
(*infml*), fiddle (*infml*).

manner *noun*
1 address him in the correct manner:
way, method, means, fashion, style,
procedure, process, form.
2 her manner is a little offhand:
behaviour, conduct, bearing,
demeanour, air, appearance, look,
character.

mannerism *noun*
idiosyncrasy, peculiarity,
characteristic, quirk, trait, feature,
foible, habit.

manners *noun*
behaviour, conduct, demeanour,
etiquette, politeness, bearing, courtesy,
formalities, social graces, p's and q's.

manoeuvre *noun*
**1 reversing round a corner can be a
tricky manoeuvre**: move, movement,
operation.
2 a political manoeuvre: action,
exercise, plan, ploy, plot, ruse,
stratagem, machination, gambit,
tactic, trick, scheme, dodge (*infml*).
▶ *verb*
move, manipulate, handle, guide, pilot,
steer, navigate, jockey, direct, drive.

manual *noun*
handbook, guide, guidebook,
instructions, Bible, vade mecum,
directions.
▶ *adjective*
hand-operated, by hand, physical,
human.
E∃ automatic.

manufacture *verb*
1 manufacturing steel/cars: make,
produce, construct, build, fabricate,
create, assemble, mass-produce, turn
out, process, forge, form.
2 manufacture an excuse: invent, make
up, concoct, fabricate, think up.
▶ *noun*
production, making, construction,

fabrication, mass-production,
assembly, creation, formation.

many *adjective*
numerous, countless, lots of (*infml*),
manifold (*fml*), various, varied,
sundry, diverse, umpteen (*infml*).
E∃ few.

mar *verb*
spoil, impair, harm, hurt, damage,
deface, disfigure, mutilate, injure,
maim, scar, detract from, mangle, ruin,
wreck, tarnish.
E∃ enhance.

march *verb*
walk, stride, parade, pace, file, tread,
stalk.
▶ *noun*
1 advance at a slow march: step, pace,
stride.
2 the long march home: walk, trek,
hike, footslog (*infml*).
3 a peace march: procession, parade,
demonstration, demo (*infml*).
4 the march of time: advance,
development, progress, evolution,
passage.

margin *noun*
1 the margin of the lake: border, edge,
boundary, bound, periphery,
perimeter, rim, brink, limit, confine,
verge, side, skirt.
2 win by a narrow margin: allowance,
play, leeway, latitude, scope, room,
space, surplus, extra.

marginal *adjective*
borderline, peripheral, negligible,
minimal, insignificant, minor, slight,
doubtful, low, small.
E∃ central, core.

marital *adjective*
conjugal, matrimonial, married,
wedded, nuptial (*fml*), connubial (*fml*).

maritime *adjective*
marine, nautical, naval, seafaring, sea,
seaside, oceanic, coastal.

mark *noun*
**1 leave marks on the table/skin/
paintwork**: spot, stain, blemish, blot,
blotch, smudge, dent, impression, scar,
scratch, bruise, line.
2 a mark of good quality: symbol, sign,
indication, emblem, brand, stamp,

token, characteristic, feature, proof, evidence, badge.
3 hit the mark: target, goal, aim, objective, purpose.
▶ *verb*
1 marked the paintwork: stain, blemish, blot, smudge, dent, scar, scratch, bruise.
2 marked with a kite symbol: brand, label, stamp, characterize, identify, distinguish.
3 marking the exam papers: evaluate, assess, correct, grade.

marked *adjective*
1 a marked difference: noticeable, obvious, conspicuous, evident, pronounced, distinct, decided, emphatic, considerable, remarkable, apparent, glaring.
2 a marked man: suspected, watched, doomed.
E∃ 1 unnoticeable, slight.

marriage *noun*
1 joined in marriage/his first marriage: matrimony, wedlock, wedding, nuptials (*fml*).
2 a marriage of styles: union, alliance, merger, coupling, amalgamation, link, association, confederation.
E∃ 1 divorce. **2** separation.

marry *verb*
1 marry young: wed, join in matrimony, tie the knot (*infml*), get hitched (*infml*), get spliced (*infml*).
2 successfully marry the two styles: unite, ally, join, merge, match, link, knit.
E∃ 1 divorce. **2** separate.

marsh *noun*
marshland, bog, swamp, fen, morass, quagmire, slough.

marsupial

Marsupials include:

bandicoot, cuscus, kangaroo, rat kangaroo, tree kangaroo, wallaroo, koala, marsupial anteater, marsupial mouse, marsupial mole, marsupial rat, opossum, pademelon, phalanger, Tasmanian Devil, Tasmanian wolf, wallaby, rock wallaby, wombat.

marvel *noun*
wonder, miracle, phenomenon, prodigy, spectacle, sensation, genius.
▶ *verb*
wonder, gape, gaze, be amazed at.

marvellous *adjective*
1 had a marvellous holiday: wonderful, excellent, splendid, superb, magnificent, terrific (*infml*), super, fantastic (*infml*).
2 a marvellous sight: extraordinary, amazing, astonishing, astounding, miraculous, remarkable, surprising, unbelievable, incredible, glorious.
E∃ 1 terrible, awful. **2** ordinary, run-of-the-mill.

masculine *adjective*
male, manlike, manly, mannish, virile, macho, strong, muscular, powerful, vigorous.
E∃ feminine, girly (*infml*).

mash *verb*
crush, pulp, beat, pound, pulverize, pummel, grind, smash.

mask *noun*
disguise, camouflage, façade, front, concealment, cover-up, cover, guise, pretence, semblance, cloak, veil, blind, show, veneer, visor.

mass *noun*
1 a mass of rubbish/masses of clothes: heap, pile, load, accumulation, aggregate, collection, conglomeration, combination, entirety, whole, totality, sum, lot, group, batch, bunch.
2 moved forward in a mass: multitude, throng, troop, crowd, band, horde, mob.
3 the greater mass of the population: majority, body, bulk.
4 measure its mass: size, dimension, magnitude, immensity.
5 forming a solid mass: lump, piece, chunk, block, hunk.
▶ *adjective*
widespread, large-scale, extensive, comprehensive, general, indiscriminate, popular, across-the-board, sweeping, wholesale, blanket.
E∃ limited, small-scale.
▶ *verb*
collect, gather, assemble, congregate,

crowd, rally, cluster, muster, swarm, throng.
F3 separate.

massacre *noun*
slaughter, murder, extermination, carnage, butchery, holocaust, bloodbath, annihilation, killing.
▶ *verb*
slaughter, butcher, murder, mow down, wipe out, exterminate, annihilate, kill, decimate.

massive *adjective*
huge, immense, enormous, vast, colossal, gigantic, big, bulky, monumental, solid, substantial, heavy, large-scale, extensive, whopping (*infml*).
F3 tiny, small.

master *noun*
1 obey one's master: ruler, chief, governor, head, lord, captain, boss (*infml*), employer, commander, controller, director, manager, superintendent, overseer, principal, overlord, owner.
2 a chess master: expert, genius, virtuoso, past master, maestro, dab hand (*infml*), ace (*infml*), pro (*infml*).
3 the science master: teacher, tutor, instructor, schoolmaster, guide, guru, preceptor (*fml*).
F3 1 servant, underling. 2 amateur. 3 learner, pupil.
▶ *adjective*
1 master key: chief, principal, main, leading, foremost, prime, predominant, controlling, great, grand.
2 master builder/craftsman: expert, masterly, skilled, skilful, proficient.
F3 1 subordinate. 2 inept.
▶ *verb*
1 master one's fear: conquer, defeat, subdue, subjugate, vanquish (*fml*), triumph over, overcome, quell, rule, control.
2 master the basics: learn, grasp, acquire, get the hang of (*infml*), manage.

masterful *adjective*
arrogant, authoritative, domineering, overbearing, high-handed, despotic, dictatorial, autocratic, bossy (*infml*), tyrannical, powerful.
F3 humble, servile.

masterly *adjective*
expert, skilled, skilful, dexterous, adept, adroit, first-rate, ace (*infml*), excellent, superb, superior, supreme.
F3 inept, clumsy.

masterpiece *noun*
masterwork, magnum opus, pièce de résistance, jewel.

match *noun*
1 a football/hockey match: contest, competition, bout, game, test, trial.
2 meet one's match: equal, equivalent, peer, counterpart, fellow, mate, rival, copy, double, replica, look-alike, twin, duplicate.
3 wanted her daughter to make a good match: marriage, alliance, union, partnership, affiliation.
▶ *verb*
1 match its speed: equal, compare, measure up to, rival, compete, oppose, contend, vie, pit against.
2 colour matches your eyes: fit, go with, accord, agree, suit, correspond, harmonize, tally, co-ordinate, blend, adapt, go together, relate, tone with, accompany.
3 matching the girls up with suitable partners: join, marry, unite, mate, link, couple, combine, ally, pair, yoke, team.
F3 2 clash. 3 separate.

matching *adjective*
corresponding, comparable, equivalent, like, identical, co-ordinating, similar, duplicate, same, twin.
F3 clashing.

mate *noun*
1 my best mate: friend, companion, comrade, pal (*infml*), colleague, partner, fellow-worker, co-worker, associate, buddy (*infml*), chum (*infml*).
2 find a mate for life: spouse, partner, husband, wife.
3 a carpenter and his mate: assistant, helper, subordinate.

material *noun*
1 material from the comet's tail: stuff, substance, body, matter.

2 a material similar to velvet: fabric, textile, cloth.
3 it would make good material for a novel: information, facts, data, evidence, constituents, work, notes.

▶ *adjective*

1 a material being: physical, concrete, tangible, substantial.
2 the material facts: relevant, significant, important, meaningful, pertinent, essential, vital, indispensable, serious.

F₃ 1 abstract. **2** immaterial, irrelevant.

mathematics

Terms used in mathematics include:

acute angle, addition, algebra, algorithm, analysis, angle, apex, approximate, arc, area, arithmetic, arithmetic progression, asymmetrical, average, axis, axis of symmetry, bar chart, bar graph, base, bearing, binary, binomial, breadth, calculus, cardinal number, Carroll diagram, Cartesian co-ordinates, circumference, coefficient, combination, complement, complementary angle, complex number, concave, concentric circles, congruent, conjugate angles, constant, converse, convex, co-ordinate, correlation, cosine, cross-section, cube, cube root, cuboid, curve, decimal, degree, denominator, determinant, diagonal, diameter, differentiation, distribution, dividend, division, equation, equidistant, even number, exponent, exponential, factor, factorial, Fibonacci sequence, formula, fraction, function, geometric progression, geometry, gradient, graph, helix, histogram, horizontal, hyperbola, hypotenuse, imperial unit, infinity, integer, integration, intersecting, irrational number, line graph, locus, logarithm, longitude, magic square, matrix, maximum, mean, measure, median, metric unit, Möbius strip, mode, modulus, multiple, natural logarithm, natural number, negative number, numerator, oblique, obtuse angle, ordinal number, origin, parabola, parallel lines, parallel planes, parameter, percentage, percentile, perimeter, permutation, perpendicular, pi, pie chart, plane figure, positive number, prime number, prism, probability, product, proportion, protractor, Pythagoras' theorem, quadrant, quadratic equation, quadrilateral, quartile, quotient, radian, radius, ratio, rational number, real numbers, reciprocal, recurring decimal, reflex angle, remainder, right-angle, right-angled triangle, root, rotation, rotational symmetry, scalar segment, sector, set, simultaneous equation, sine, square, square root, statistics, subset, subtractor, supplementary angles, symmetry, tangent, tangram, three-dimensional, triangulation, trigonometry, unit, universal set, variable, variance, vector, velocity, volume, whole number. ⇨ *See also* **shape**.

matrimonial *adjective*
marital, nuptial (*fml*), marriage, wedding, married, wedded, conjugal.

matter *noun*
1 a very serious matter: subject, issue, topic, question, affair, business, concern, event, episode, incident.
2 it's of no matter: importance, significance, consequence, note.
3 what's the matter?: trouble, problem, difficulty, worry.
4 organic matter: substance, stuff, material, body, content.

▶ *verb*

count, be important, make a difference, mean something.

matter-of-fact *adjective*
unemotional, prosaic, emotionless, straightforward, sober, unimaginative, flat, deadpan (*infml*).

F₃ emotional.

mature *adjective*
1 a mature young man/attitude: adult, grown-up, grown, full-grown, fully

fledged, complete, perfect, perfected, well-thought-out.
2 mature wood: ripe, ripened, seasoned, mellow, ready.
F⁊ 1 childish. **2** immature.
▸ *verb*
grow up, come of age, develop, mellow, ripen, perfect, age, bloom, fall due.

maximum *adjective*
greatest, highest, largest, biggest, most, utmost, supreme.
F⁊ minimum.
▸ *noun*
most, top (point), utmost, upper limit, peak, pinnacle, summit, height, ceiling, extremity, zenith.
F⁊ minimum.

maybe *adverb*
perhaps, possibly, perchance (*fml*).
F⁊ definitely.

meagre *adjective*
1 a meagre allowance: scanty, sparse, inadequate, deficient, skimpy, paltry, negligible, poor.
2 their meagre little faces: thin, puny, insubstantial, bony, emaciated, scrawny, slight.
F⁊ 1 ample. **2** fat.

meal

Meals include:

afternoon tea, banquet, barbecue, barbie (*infml*), blow-out (*slang*), breakfast, brunch, buffet, cream tea, dinner, elevenses (*infml*), evening meal, feast, fork supper, harvest supper, high tea, lunch, luncheon, picnic, snack, spread, supper, take-away, tea, tea break, tea party, tiffin, TV dinner, wedding breakfast.

mean¹ *adjective*
1 too mean to spend the money: miserly, niggardly, parsimonious, selfish, tight (*infml*), tight-fisted, stingy (*infml*), penny-pinching (*infml*).
2 a mean thing to say: unkind, unpleasant, nasty, bad-tempered, cruel.
3 they lived in a mean little cottage: lowly, base, poor, humble, wretched.
F⁊ 1 generous. **2** kind. **3** splendid.

mean² *verb*
1 what does this word mean?: signify, represent, denote, stand for, symbolize, suggest, indicate, imply.
2 what do you mean to do?: intend, aim, propose, design.
3 it will mean severe cutbacks: cause, give rise to, involve, entail.

mean³ *adjective*
the mean point on the scale: average, intermediate, middle, halfway, median, normal.
F⁊ extreme.
▸ *noun*
average, middle, mid-point, norm, median, compromise, middle course, middle way, happy medium, golden mean.
F⁊ extreme.

meaning *noun*
1 the meaning of the phrase: significance, sense, import, implication, gist, trend, explanation, interpretation.
2 what's the meaning of this behaviour?: aim, intention, purpose, object, idea.
3 gives her life some meaning: value, worth, point.

meaningful *adjective*
1 a meaningful look: expressive, significant, suggestive, warning, pointed.
2 meaningful employment: important, relevant, valid, useful, worthwhile, material, purposeful, serious.
F⁊ 2 unimportant, worthless.

meaningless *adjective*
1 a meaningless statement: senseless, pointless, purposeless, useless, insignificant, aimless, futile, insubstantial, trifling, trivial.
2 a meaningless existence: empty, hollow, vacuous, vain, worthless, nonsensical, absurd.
F⁊ 1 important, meaningful. **2** worthwhile.

means *noun*
1 the means of production/a means of travel: method, mode, way, medium, course, agency, process, instrument, channel, vehicle.

2 a man of means/have the means to buy a house: resources, funds, money, income, wealth, riches, substance, wherewithal, fortune, affluence.

measure   *noun*
1 short measure: size, quantity, magnitude, amount, degree, extent, range, scope.
2 a tape measure/a measure of efficiency: rule, gauge, scale, standard, criterion, norm, touchstone, yardstick, test, meter.
3 introduce new measures to control imports: step, course, action, deed, procedure, method, act, bill, statute.
4 has had his fair measure of bad luck: portion, ration, share, allocation, quota, proportion.
▶ *verb*
quantify, evaluate, assess, weigh, value, gauge, judge, sound, fathom, determine, calculate, estimate, plumb, survey, compute, measure out, measure off.

measurement   *noun*
1 take the measurements of the hall: dimension, size, extent, amount, magnitude, area, capacity, height, depth, length, width, weight, volume.
2 a good measurement of the scheme's success: assessment, evaluation, estimation, computation, calculation, calibration, gauging, judgement, appraisal, appreciation, survey.

mechanical   *adjective*
automatic, involuntary, instinctive, routine, habitual, impersonal, emotionless, cold, matter-of-fact, unfeeling, lifeless, dead, dull.
E∃ conscious.

mechanism   *noun*
1 the clock's mechanism: machine, machinery, engine, appliance, instrument, tool, motor, works, workings, gadget, device, apparatus, contrivance, gears, components.
2 find some mechanism for making quick payments: means, method, agency, process, procedure, system, technique, medium, structure, operation, functioning, performance.

meddle   *verb*
interfere, intervene, pry, snoop (*infml*), intrude, butt in, tamper.

medicinal   *adjective*
therapeutic, healing, remedial, curative, restorative, medical.

medicine   *noun*
medication, drug, cure, remedy, medicament, prescription, pharmaceutical, panacea.

mediocre   *adjective*
ordinary, average, middling, medium, indifferent, unexceptional, undistinguished, so-so (*infml*), run-of-the-mill, commonplace, insignificant, second-rate, inferior, uninspired.
E∃ exceptional, extraordinary, distinctive.

medium[1]   *adjective*
of medium height: average, middle, median, mean, medial, intermediate, middling, midway, standard, fair.

medium[2]   *noun*
1 a medium for informing local people: means, agency, channel, vehicle, instrument, way, mode, form, avenue, organ (*fml*).
2 a spiritual medium: psychic, spiritualist, spiritist, clairvoyant.

meek   *adjective*
modest, long-suffering, forbearing, humble, docile, patient, unassuming, unpretentious, resigned, gentle, peaceful, tame, timid, submissive, spiritless.
E∃ arrogant, assertive, rebellious.

meet   *verb*
1 met him in the street: encounter, come across, run across, run into, chance on, bump into (*infml*).
2 met with an accident: experience, encounter, face, go through, undergo, endure.
3 meet at the station: gather, collect, assemble, congregate, convene.
4 meet the target: fulfil, satisfy, match, answer, measure up to, equal, discharge, perform.
5 meet in the middle: join, converge, come together, connect, cross, intersect, touch, abut, unite.
E∃ 3 scatter. **5** diverge.

meeting *noun*
1 their first meeting: encounter, confrontation, rendezvous, engagement, assignation, introduction, tryst (*fml*).
2 call a meeting of the council: assembly, gathering, congregation, conference, convention, rally, get-together, forum, conclave, session.
3 a meeting of minds: convergence, confluence, junction, intersection, union.

melancholy *adjective*
depressed, dejected, downcast, down, down-hearted, gloomy, low, low-spirited, heavy-hearted, sad, unhappy, despondent, dispirited, miserable, mournful, dismal, sorrowful, moody.
E⊰ cheerful, elated, joyful.
▸ *noun*
depression, dejection, gloom, despondency, low spirits, blues (*infml*), sadness, unhappiness, sorrow.
E⊰ elation, joy.

mellow *adjective*
1 tastes warm and mellow: mature, smooth, ripe, juicy, full-flavoured, sweet, tender, mild.
2 became more mellow as he got older: genial, cordial, affable, pleasant, relaxed, easy-going, placid, serene, tranquil, cheerful, happy, jolly.
3 a mellow sound: melodious, rich, rounded, soft.
E⊰ **1** unripe. **2** cold. **3** harsh.
▸ *verb*
mature, ripen, improve, sweeten, soften, temper, season, perfect.

melodramatic *adjective*
histrionic, theatrical, overdramatic, exaggerated, overemotional, sensational, hammy (*infml*).

melt *verb*
liquefy, dissolve, thaw, fuse, deliquesce (*fml*).
E⊰ freeze, solidify.
◆ **melt away** disappear, vanish, fade, evaporate, dissolve, disperse.

member *noun*
adherent, associate, subscriber, representative, comrade, fellow.

memento *noun*
souvenir, keepsake, remembrance, reminder, token, memorial, record, relic.

memoirs *noun*
reminiscences, recollections, autobiography, life story, diary, chronicles, annals, journals, records, confessions, experiences.

memorable *adjective*
unforgettable, remarkable, significant, impressive, notable, noteworthy, extraordinary, important, outstanding, momentous.
E⊰ forgettable, trivial, unimportant.

memorial *noun*
remembrance, monument, souvenir, memento, record, stone, plaque, mausoleum.
▸ *adjective*
commemorative, celebratory.

memorize *verb*
learn, learn by heart, commit to memory, remember.
E⊰ forget.

memory *noun*
recall, retention, recollection, remembrance, reminiscence, commemoration.
E⊰ forgetfulness.

menace *noun*
1 voice full of menace: intimidation, threat, terrorism, warning.
2 combat the menace of drinking and driving: danger, peril, hazard, jeopardy, risk.
3 cats are becoming a menace: nuisance, annoyance, pest.

mend *verb*
1 mend a road/tear/shoes: repair, renovate, restore, refit, fix, patch, cobble, darn, heal.
2 he's mending slowly: recover, get better, improve.
3 mend the mistakes of the past: remedy, correct, rectify, reform, revise.
E⊰ **1** break. **2** deteriorate. **3** destroy.

mental *adjective*
1 mental exercises/processes: intellectual, abstract, conceptual, cognitive, cerebral, theoretical, rational.

2 (*infml*) go mental: mad, insane, lunatic, crazy, unbalanced, deranged, psychotic, disturbed, loony (*infml*).
F3 **1** physical. **2** sane.

mentality *noun*
frame of mind, attitude, character, disposition, personality, psychology, outlook.

mention *verb*
refer to, speak of, allude to, touch on, name, cite, acknowledge, bring up, report, make known, impart, declare, communicate, broach, divulge, disclose, intimate, point out, reveal, state, hint at, quote.
▸ *noun*
reference, allusion, citation, observation, recognition, remark, acknowledgement, announcement, notification, tribute, indication.

merchant *noun*
trader, dealer, broker, trafficker, wholesaler, retailer, seller, shopkeeper, vendor.

merciful *adjective*
compassionate, forgiving, forbearing, humane, lenient, sparing, tender-hearted, pitying, gracious, humanitarian, kind, liberal, sympathetic, generous, mild.
F3 hard-hearted, merciless.

merciless *adjective*
pitiless, relentless, unmerciful, ruthless, hard-hearted, hard, heartless, implacable, inhumane, unforgiving, remorseless, unpitying, unsparing, severe, cruel, callous, inhuman.
F3 compassionate, merciful.

mercy *noun*
1 show mercy to the prisoner: compassion, clemency, forgiveness, forbearance, leniency, pity, humanitarianism, kindness, grace.
2 was a mercy he wasn't hurt: blessing, godsend, good luck, relief.
F3 **1** cruelty, harshness.

mere *adjective*
sheer, plain, simple, bare, utter, pure, absolute, complete, stark, unadulterated, common, paltry, petty.

merge *verb*
join, unite, combine, converge, amalgamate, blend, coalesce, mix, intermix, mingle, melt into, fuse, meet, meld, incorporate, consolidate.

merit *noun*
worth, excellence, value, quality, good, goodness, virtue, asset, credit, advantage, strong point, talent, justification, due, claim.
F3 fault.
▸ *verb*
deserve, be worthy of, earn, justify, warrant.

merry *adjective*
jolly, light-hearted, mirthful, joyful, happy, convivial, festive, cheerful, glad.
F3 gloomy, melancholy, sober.

mesh *noun*
net, network, netting, lattice, web, tangle, entanglement, snare, trap.
▸ *verb*
engage, interlock, dovetail, fit, connect, harmonize, co-ordinate, combine, come together.

mess *noun*
1 clearing up the mess after the party: chaos, untidiness, disorder, disarray, confusion, muddle, jumble, clutter, disorganization, mix-up, shambles (*infml*).
2 got himself into a mess financially: difficulty, trouble, predicament, fix (*infml*), jam (*infml*), pickle (*infml*).
F3 **1** order, tidiness.
◆ **mess about** mess around, fool around, play, play around, play about, muck about (*infml*), interfere, tamper, trifle.
◆ **mess up 1** messing up her hair: disarrange, jumble, muddle, tangle, dishevel, disrupt.
2 I'm afraid I've messed it up: botch, bungle, spoil, muck up (*infml*).

message *noun*
1 got an urgent message: communication, bulletin, dispatch, communiqué, report, missive (*fml*), errand, letter, memorandum, note, notice, cable, fax, e-mail, text.
2 the message in the song: meaning, idea, point, theme, moral.

messenger *noun*
courier, emissary, envoy, go-between,

herald, runner, carrier, bearer, harbinger, agent, ambassador.

messy *adjective*
untidy, unkempt, dishevelled, disorganized, chaotic, sloppy, slovenly, confused, dirty, grubby, muddled, cluttered.
F∃ neat, ordered, tidy.

metamorphosis *noun*
change, alteration, transformation, rebirth, regeneration, transfiguration, conversion, modification, change-over.

metaphor *noun*
figure of speech, allegory, analogy, symbol, picture, image.

meteoric *adjective*
rapid, speedy, swift, sudden, overnight, instantaneous, momentary, brief, spectacular, brilliant, dazzling.

method *noun*
1 teaching methods: way, approach, means, course, manner, mode, fashion, process, procedure, route, technique, style, plan, scheme, programme.
2 need to apply some method to your work: organization, order, structure, system, pattern, form, planning, regularity, routine.

methodical *adjective*
systematic, structured, organized, ordered, orderly, tidy, regular, planned, efficient, disciplined, businesslike, deliberate, neat, scrupulous, precise, meticulous, painstaking.
F∃ chaotic, irregular, confused.

meticulous *adjective*
precise, scrupulous, exact, punctilious, fussy, detailed, accurate, thorough, fastidious, painstaking, strict.
F∃ careless, slapdash.

microscopic *adjective*
minute, tiny, minuscule, infinitesimal, indiscernible, imperceptible, negligible.
F∃ huge, enormous.

middle *adjective*
central, halfway, mean, median, inner, intermediate, inside, intervening.
▶ *noun*
centre, halfway point, mid-point, mean,

heart, core, midst, inside, bull's eye.
F∃ extreme, end, edge, beginning, border.

middling *adjective*
mediocre, medium, ordinary, moderate, average, unexceptional, unremarkable, run-of-the-mill, indifferent, modest, passable, tolerable, so-so (*infml*), OK (*infml*).

midget *noun*
person of restricted growth, pygmy, dwarf, Tom Thumb.
F∃ giant.
▶ *adjective*
tiny, small, miniature, little, pocket, pocket-size(d).
F∃ giant.

midst *noun*
middle, centre, mid-point, heart, hub, interior.

migrate *verb*
move, resettle, relocate, wander, roam, rove, journey, emigrate, travel, voyage, trek, drift.

mild *adjective*
1 mild manners: gentle, calm, peaceable, placid, tender, soft, good-natured, kind, amiable, lenient, compassionate.
2 mild weather: calm, temperate, warm, balmy, clement, fair, pleasant.
3 mild curry: bland, mellow, smooth, subtle, soothing.
F∃ 1 harsh, fierce. 2 stormy. 3 strong.

militant *adjective*
aggressive, belligerent, vigorous, fighting, warring.
F∃ pacifist, peaceful.
▶ *noun*
activist, combatant, fighter, struggler, warrior, aggressor, belligerent.

military *adjective*
martial, armed, soldierly, warlike, service.
▶ *noun*
army, armed forces, soldiers, forces, services.

militate against *verb*
oppose, counter, counteract, count against, tell against, weigh against, contend, resist.

milk *verb*
drain, bleed, tap, extract, draw off, exploit, use, express, press, pump, siphon, squeeze, wring.

milky *adjective*
white, milk-white, chalky, opaque, clouded, cloudy.

mill *noun*
1 woollen mill/steel mill: factory, plant, works, workshop, foundry.
2 pepper mill: grinder, crusher, quern, roller.
▶ *verb*
grind, pulverize, powder, pound, crush, roll, press, grate.

mimic *verb*
imitate, parody, caricature, take off (*infml*), ape, parrot, impersonate, echo, mirror, simulate, look like.

mind *noun*
1 using your mind: intelligence, intellect, brains, reason, sense, understanding, wits, mentality, thinking, thoughts, grey matter (*infml*), head, genius, concentration, attention, spirit, psyche.
2 come to mind: memory, remembrance, recollection.
3 we're of the same mind: opinion, view, point of view, belief, attitude, judgement, feeling, sentiment.
4 have a good mind to object: inclination, disposition, tendency, will, wish, intention, desire.
▶ *verb*
1 didn't mind the noise: care, object, take offence, resent, disapprove, dislike.
2 mind the step: regard, heed, pay attention, pay heed to, note, obey, listen to, comply with, follow, observe, be careful, watch.
3 minding the shop: look after, take care of, watch over, guard, have charge of, keep an eye on (*infml*).
◆ **bear in mind** consider, remember, note.
◆ **make up one's mind** decide, choose, determine, settle, resolve.

mindless *adjective*
1 mindless violence: thoughtless, senseless, illogical, irrational, stupid, foolish, gratuitous, negligent.
2 a mindless task: mechanical, automatic, tedious.
Fa 1 thoughtful, intelligent.

mine *noun*
1 a coal/gold/diamond mine: pit, colliery, coalfield, excavation, vein, seam, shaft, trench, deposit.
2 a mine of information: supply, source, stock, store, reserve, fund, hoard, treasury, wealth.
▶ *verb*
excavate, dig for, dig up, delve, quarry, extract, unearth, tunnel, remove, undermine.

mingle *verb*
1 joy mingled with a touch of regret: mix, intermingle, intermix, combine, blend, merge, unite, alloy, coalesce, join, compound.
2 mingling with the crowd: associate, socialize, circulate, hobnob (*infml*), rub shoulders (*infml*).

miniature *adjective*
tiny, small, scaled-down, minute, diminutive, baby, pocket-size(d), pint-size(d) (*infml*), little, mini (*infml*).
Fa giant.

minimal *adjective*
least, smallest, minimum, slightest, littlest, negligible, minute, token.

minimize *verb*
1 minimize the risk of failure: reduce, decrease, diminish.
2 minimized his achievements: belittle, make light of, make little of, disparage (*fml*), deprecate (*fml*), discount, play down, underestimate, underrate.
Fa 1 maximize.

minimum *noun*
least, lowest point, slightest, bottom.
Fa maximum.
▶ *adjective*
minimal, least, lowest, slightest, smallest, littlest, tiniest.
Fa maximum.

minister *noun*
1 a government minister: official, office-holder, politician, dignitary, diplomat, ambassador, delegate, envoy, consul, cabinet minister, agent, aide, administrator, executive.

2 a local minister conducted the service: clergyman, clergywoman, churchman, churchwoman, cleric, parson, priest, pastor, vicar, preacher, ecclesiastic (*fml*), divine.

minor *adjective*
lesser, secondary, smaller, inferior, subordinate, subsidiary, junior, younger, insignificant, inconsiderable, negligible, petty, trivial, trifling, second-class, unclassified, slight, light.
☞ major, significant, important.

mint *adjective*
perfect, brand-new, fresh, immaculate, unblemished, excellent, first-class.

minute[1] *noun* /**min**-it/
wait a minute: moment, second, instant, flash, jiffy (*infml*), tick (*infml*).

minute[2] *adjective* /mai-**nyoot**/
1 minute particles of dust: tiny, infinitesimal, minuscule, microscopic, miniature, inconsiderable, negligible, small.
2 a minute examination: detailed, precise, meticulous, painstaking, close, critical, exhaustive.
☞ **1** gigantic, huge. **2** cursory, superficial.

miraculous *adjective*
wonderful, marvellous, phenomenal, extraordinary, amazing, astounding, astonishing, unbelievable, supernatural, incredible, inexplicable, unaccountable, superhuman.
☞ natural, normal.

mirror *noun*
1 checked her make-up in the mirror: glass, looking-glass, reflector.
2 the eyes are said to be the mirror of the soul: reflection, likeness, image, double, copy.
▶ *verb*
reflect, echo, imitate, copy, represent, show, depict, mimic.

misbehave *verb*
offend, transgress, trespass (*fml*), get up to mischief, mess about (*infml*), muck about (*infml*), play up (*infml*), act up (*infml*).

miscalculate *verb*
misjudge, get wrong, slip up, blunder,

boob (*infml*), miscount, overestimate, underestimate.

miscellaneous *adjective*
mixed, varied, various, assorted, diverse, diversified, sundry, motley, jumbled, indiscriminate.

mischievous *adjective*
1 a mischievous child: naughty, impish, rascally, roguish, playful, teasing.
2 a mischievous lie: malicious, evil, spiteful, vicious, wicked, pernicious, destructive, injurious.
☞ **1** well-behaved, good. **2** kind.

miserable *adjective*
1 the news made him miserable: unhappy, sad, dejected, despondent, downcast, heartbroken, wretched, distressed, crushed.
2 a miserable wet day: cheerless, depressing, dreary, impoverished, shabby, gloomy, dismal, forlorn, joyless.
3 a miserable state of affairs: contemptible, despicable, ignominious, detestable, disgraceful, deplorable, shameful.
4 a miserable offer: meagre, paltry, niggardly, worthless, pathetic, pitiful.
☞ **1** cheerful, happy. **2** pleasant. **4** generous.

miserly *adjective*
mean, niggardly, tight, stingy (*infml*), sparing, parsimonious, cheese-paring, beggarly, penny-pinching (*infml*), mingy (*infml*).
☞ generous, spendthrift.

misery *noun*
1 her expression was one of complete misery: unhappiness, sadness, suffering, distress, depression, despair, gloom, grief, wretchedness, affliction.
2 lived a life of misery in terrible conditions: privation (*fml*), hardship, deprivation, poverty, want, oppression, destitution.
3 (*infml*) don't be such an old misery!: spoilsport, pessimist, killjoy, wet blanket (*infml*).
☞ **1** contentment. **2** comfort.

misfortune *noun*
bad luck, mischance, mishap, ill-luck, setback, reverse, calamity, catastrophe,

disaster, blow, accident, tragedy, trouble, hardship, trial, tribulation.
F3 luck, success.

misguided *adjective*
misled, misconceived, ill-considered, ill-advised, ill-judged, imprudent, rash, misplaced, deluded, foolish, erroneous.
F3 sensible, wise.

misinterpret *verb*
misconstrue, misread, misunderstand, mistake, distort, garble.

misjudge *verb*
miscalculate, mistake, misinterpret, misconstrue, misunderstand, overestimate, underestimate.

mislay *verb*
lose, misplace, miss, lose sight of.

mislead *verb*
misinform, misdirect, deceive, delude, lead astray, fool.

misleading *adjective*
deceptive, confusing, unreliable, ambiguous, biased, loaded, evasive, tricky (*infml*).
F3 unequivocal, authoritative, informative.

miss *verb*
1 missed his chance/missed the point: fail, miscarry, lose, let slip, let go, omit, overlook, pass over, slip, leave out, mistake, trip, misunderstand, err.
2 just missed a pedestrian/missed a couple of pages: avoid, escape, evade, dodge, forego, skip, bypass, circumvent.
3 missing his family: pine for, long for, yearn for, regret, grieve for, mourn, sorrow for, want, wish, need, lament.
▸ *noun*
failure, error, blunder, mistake, omission, oversight, fault, flop (*infml*), fiasco.

missile *noun*
projectile, shot, guided missile, arrow, shaft, dart, rocket, bomb, shell, flying bomb, grenade, torpedo, weapon.

missing *adjective*
absent, lost, lacking, gone, mislaid, unaccounted-for, wanting,

disappeared, astray, strayed, misplaced.
F3 found, present.

mission *noun*
1 a peace mission: task, undertaking, assignment, operation, campaign, crusade, business, errand.
2 his mission in life: calling, duty, purpose, vocation, raison d'être, aim, goal, quest, pursuit, charge, office, job, work.

mist *noun*
haze, fog, vapour, smog, cloud, condensation, film, spray, drizzle, dew, steam, veil, dimness.
◆ **mist over** cloud over, fog, dim, blur, steam up, obscure, veil.
F3 clear.

mistake *noun*
error, inaccuracy, slip, slip-up (*infml*), oversight, lapse, blunder, clanger (*infml*), boob (*infml*), gaffe, fault, faux pas, solecism (*fml*), indiscretion, misjudgement, miscalculation, misunderstanding, misprint, misspelling, misreading, mispronunciation, howler (*infml*).
▸ *verb*
misunderstand, misapprehend, misconstrue, misjudge, misread, miscalculate, confound, confuse, slip up, blunder, err.

mistaken *adjective*
wrong, incorrect, erroneous, inaccurate, inexact, untrue, inappropriate, ill-judged, inauthentic, false, deceived, deluded, misinformed, misled, faulty.
F3 correct, right.

mistreat *verb*
abuse, ill-treat, ill-use, maltreat, harm, hurt, batter, injure, knock about, molest.

misty *adjective*
hazy, foggy, cloudy, blurred, fuzzy, murky, smoky, unclear, dim, indistinct, obscure, opaque, vague, veiled.
F3 clear.

misunderstanding *noun*
1 a misunderstanding of the instructions: mistake, error, misapprehension, misconception,

misjudgement, misinterpretation, misreading, mix-up.

2 they've had a slight misunderstanding: disagreement, argument, dispute, conflict, clash, difference, breach, quarrel, discord, rift.

🖃 **1** understanding. **2** agreement.

misuse *noun*
mistreatment, maltreatment, abuse, harm, ill-treatment, misapplication, misappropriation, waste, perversion, corruption, exploitation.
▶ *verb*
abuse, misapply, misemploy, ill-use, ill-treat, harm, mistreat, wrong, distort, injure, corrupt, pervert, waste, squander, misappropriate, exploit, dissipate.

mix *verb*
1 mix the ingredients in a bowl: combine, blend, mingle, intermingle, intermix, amalgamate, compound, homogenize, synthesize, merge, join, unite, coalesce, fuse, incorporate, fold in.
2 doesn't mix with the locals much: associate, consort, fraternize, socialize, mingle, join, hobnob (*infml*).
🖃 **1** divide, separate.
◆ **mix up 1 mix up all the letters and then pick seven**: mix, jumble.
2 try not to mix the two things up: confuse, muddle, garble, jumble.
3 she mixes me up when she keeps changing the subject: confuse, bewilder, muddle, perplex, confound.
4 mixed up in the affair: involve, implicate.

mixed *adjective*
1 of mixed race: combined, hybrid, mingled, crossbred, mongrel, blended, composite, compound, incorporated, united, alloyed, amalgamated, fused.
2 mixed biscuits: assorted, varied, miscellaneous, diverse, diversified, motley.
3 have mixed feelings: ambivalent, equivocal, conflicting, contradicting, uncertain.

mixture *noun*
mix, blend, combination,

amalgamation, amalgam, compound, conglomeration, composite, coalescence, alloy, brew, synthesis, union, fusion, concoction, cross, hybrid, assortment, variety, miscellany, medley, mélange, mixed bag, pot-pourri, jumble, hotchpotch.

moan *verb*
1 women crying and moaning: lament, wail, sob, weep, howl, groan, whimper, mourn, grieve.
2 (*infml*) **always moaning about something**: complain, grumble, whine, whinge (*infml*), gripe (*infml*), carp.
🖃 **1** rejoice.

mob *noun*
crowd, mass, throng, multitude, horde, host, swarm, gathering, group, collection, flock, herd, pack, set, tribe, troop, company, crew, gang.
▶ *verb*
crowd, crowd round, surround, swarm round, jostle, overrun, set upon, besiege, descend on, throng, pack, pester, charge.

mobile *adjective*
1 a mobile home: moving, movable, portable, peripatetic, travelling, roaming, roving, itinerant, wandering, migrant.
2 exercises to keep the joints mobile: flexible, agile, active, energetic, nimble.
3 the mime artist's mobile features: changing, changeable, ever-changing, expressive, lively.
🖃 **1** immobile, static.

mock *verb*
1 mocked by the other children: ridicule, jeer, make fun of, laugh at, disparage (*fml*), deride, scoff, sneer, taunt, scorn, tease.
2 cleverly mocking the prime minister's characteristic gestures: imitate, simulate, mimic, ape, caricature, satirize.
▶ *adjective*
imitation, counterfeit, artificial, sham, simulated, synthetic, false, fake, forged, fraudulent, bogus, phoney (*infml*), pseudo, spurious, feigned, faked, pretended, dummy, faux.

mocking *adjective*
scornful, derisive, contemptuous, sarcastic, satirical, taunting, scoffing, sardonic, snide (*infml*), insulting, irreverent, impudent, disrespectful, disdainful, cynical.

model *noun*
1 a cardboard model of the ship: copy, replica, representation, facsimile, imitation, mock-up.
2 a model of what a soldier ought to be: example, exemplar, pattern, standard, ideal, mould, prototype, template.
3 buy the latest model: design, style, type, version, mark.
4 a fashion model/an artist's model: mannequin, supermodel, dummy, sitter, subject, poser.
► *adjective*
exemplary, perfect, typical, ideal.
► *verb*
1 modelling it from clay: make, form, fashion, mould, sculpt, carve, cast, shape, work, create, design, plan.
2 modelling the designer's latest collection: display, wear, show off.

moderate *adjective*
1 the accommodation was good but the weather was only moderate: medium, ordinary, fair, indifferent, average, middle-of-the-road, middling.
2 take a more moderate view: reasonable, restrained, sensible, calm, controlled, cool, mild, well-regulated.
F₃ 1 exceptional. 2 immoderate.

moderately *adverb*
somewhat, quite, rather, fairly, slightly, reasonably, passably, to some extent.
F₃ extremely.

modern *adjective*
current, contemporary, up-to-date, new, fresh, latest, late, novel, present, present-day, recent, up-to-the-minute, newfangled (*infml*), advanced, avant-garde, progressive, modernistic, innovative, inventive, state-of-the-art, go-ahead, fashionable, stylish, in vogue, in style, modish, trendy (*infml*), hip (*infml*).
F₃ old-fashioned, old, out-of-date, antiquated.

modernize *verb*
renovate, refurbish, rejuvenate, regenerate, streamline, revamp, renew, update, improve, do up, redesign, reform, remake, remodel, refresh, transform, modify, progress.
F₃ regress.

modest *adjective*
1 a modest man: unassuming, humble, self-effacing, quiet, reserved, retiring, unpretentious, discreet, bashful, shy.
2 makes a modest living: moderate, ordinary, unexceptional, fair, reasonable, limited, small.
F₃ 1 immodest, conceited. 2 exceptional, excessive.

modify *verb*
1 modified their plans: change, alter, redesign, revise, vary, adapt, adjust, tweak (*infml*), transform, reform, convert, improve, reorganize.
2 modify the aggressive tone of the letter: moderate, reduce, temper, tone down, limit, soften, qualify.

moist *adjective*
damp, clammy, humid, wet, dewy, rainy, muggy, marshy, drizzly, watery, soggy.
F₃ dry, arid.

moisten *verb*
moisturize, dampen, damp, wet, water, lick, irrigate.
F₃ dry.

moisture *noun*
water, liquid, wetness, wateriness, damp, dampness, dankness, humidity, vapour, dew, mugginess, condensation, steam, spray.
F₃ dryness.

mollusc

Molluscs include:

abalone, conch, cowrie, cuttlefish, clam, cockle, limpet, mussel, nautilus, nudibranch, octopus, oyster, periwinkle, scallop, sea slug, slug, freshwater snail, land snail, marine snail, squid, tusk shell, whelk. ⇨ *See also* **invertebrate**.

moment *noun*
second, instant, minute, split second, trice, jiffy (*infml*), tick (*infml*).

momentary *adjective*
brief, short, short-lived, temporary,
transient, transitory, fleeting,
ephemeral, hasty, quick, passing.
F3 lasting, permanent.

momentum *noun*
impetus, force, energy, impulse, drive,
power, thrust, speed, velocity, impact,
incentive, stimulus, urge, strength,
push.

money *noun*
currency, cash, legal tender,
banknotes, coin, funds, capital, dough
(*infml*), dosh (*infml*), riches, wealth.
⇨ *See also* **Word Study** *panel.*

mongrel *noun*
cross, crossbreed, hybrid, half-breed.
▶ *adjective*
crossbred, hybrid, half-breed, bastard,
mixed, ill-defined.
F3 pure-bred, pedigree.

monitor *noun*
1 a computer monitor: screen, display,
VDU, recorder, scanner.
2 a class monitor: supervisor,
watchdog, overseer, invigilator,
adviser, prefect.
▶ *verb*
check, watch, keep track of, keep under
surveillance, keep an eye on, follow,
track, supervise, observe, note, survey,
trace, scan, record, plot, detect.

monopolize *verb*
dominate, take over, appropriate,
corner, control, hog (*infml*), engross,
occupy, preoccupy, take up, tie up.
F3 share.

monotonous *adjective*
boring, dull, tedious, uninteresting,
tiresome, wearisome, unchanging,
uneventful, unvaried, uniform,
toneless, flat, colourless, repetitive,
routine, plodding, humdrum, soul-
destroying.
F3 lively, varied, colourful.

monster *noun*
beast, fiend, brute, barbarian, savage,
villain, giant, ogre, ogress, troll,
mammoth, freak, monstrosity, mutant.
▶ *adjective*
huge, gigantic, giant, colossal,
enormous, immense, massive,

monstrous, jumbo, mammoth, vast,
tremendous.
F3 tiny, minute.

monstrous *adjective*
1 that was a monstrous thing to do:
wicked, evil, vicious, cruel, criminal,
heinous (*fml*), outrageous, scandalous,
disgraceful, atrocious, abhorrent (*fml*),
dreadful, frightful, horrible,
horrifying, terrible.
2 a monstrous appearance: unnatural,
inhuman, freakish, grotesque, hideous,
deformed, malformed, misshapen.
3 monstrous trees: huge, enormous,
colossal, gigantic, vast, immense,
massive, mammoth.

monument *noun*
memorial, cenotaph, headstone,
gravestone, tombstone, shrine,
mausoleum, cairn, barrow, cross,
marker, obelisk, pillar, statue, relic,
remembrance, commemoration,
testament, reminder, record, memento,
evidence, token.

monumental *adjective*
1 a monumental decision: impressive,
imposing, awe-inspiring, awesome,
overwhelming, significant, important,
epoch-making, historic, magnificent,
majestic, memorable, notable,
outstanding, abiding, immortal,
lasting, classic.
2 a monumental mistake: huge,
immense, enormous, colossal, vast,
tremendous, massive, great.
3 monumental statues:
commemorative, memorial.
F3 1 insignificant, unimportant.

mood *noun*
1 gauge the mood of the nation:
disposition, frame of mind, state of
mind, temper, humour, spirit, tenor,
whim.
2 in one of his moods: bad temper,
sulk, the sulks, pique, melancholy,
depression, blues (*infml*), doldrums,
dumps (*infml*).

moody *adjective*
changeable, temperamental,
unpredictable, capricious, irritable,
short-tempered, crabby (*infml*),
crotchety, crusty (*infml*), testy, touchy,

The important subjects of **money**, what something costs, and making a living, can be referred to, especially informally, using some of the phrases shown here.

expensive

beyond your means
cost a bomb
cost a packet

cost an arm and a leg
cost the earth
daylight robbery

not expensive

cheap as chips
for peanuts
not cost a penny

dirt cheap
(going) for a song
a steal

making money

bring home the bacon
make a bundle
make a good living

hit the jackpot
make a fortune

having money

be rolling in it
be in the black
be well off

have money to burn
be in the money

not having money

feel the pinch
not have two pennies to rub together
be skint
be strapped (for cash)

be in the red
be on your uppers
be stony-broke

spending money

go Dutch
pay through the nose for something
put your hand in your pocket
spend money like it was going out of
    fashion

go halves
pay over the odds for something
spend money like water
throw money around

being mean

be a cheapskate
be tight-fisted

be a skinflint
be penny-pinching

morose, angry, broody, mopey, sulky, sullen, gloomy, melancholy, miserable, downcast, doleful, glum, impulsive, fickle, flighty.
Fa equable, cheerful.

moor¹ *verb*
mooring the yacht: fasten, secure, tie up, drop anchor, anchor, berth, dock, make fast, fix, hitch, bind.
Fa loose.

moor² *noun*
heather-covered moors: moorland, heath, fell, upland.

mop *verb*
swab, sponge, wipe, clean, wash, absorb, soak.

mope *verb*
brood, fret, sulk, pine, languish, droop, despair, grieve, idle.

moral *adjective*
ethical, virtuous, good, right, principled, honourable, decent, upright, upstanding, straight, righteous, high-minded, honest, incorruptible, proper, blameless, chaste, clean-living, pure, just, noble.
Fa immoral.
▶ *noun*
lesson, message, teaching, dictum, meaning, maxim, adage, precept (*fml*), saying, proverb, aphorism, epigram.

morale *noun*
confidence, spirits, esprit de corps, self-esteem, state of mind, heart, mood.

morality *noun*
ethics, morals, ideals, principles, standards, virtue, rectitude, righteousness, decency, goodness, honesty, integrity, justice, uprightness, propriety, conduct, manners.
Fa immorality.

morals *noun*
morality, ethics, principles, standards, ideals, integrity, scruples, behaviour, conduct, habits, manners.

morbid *adjective*
1 a morbid story of death and destruction: ghoulish, ghastly, gruesome, macabre, hideous, horrid, grim.

2 a morbid view of life: gloomy, pessimistic, melancholy, sombre.
3 a morbid obsession: sick, unhealthy, unwholesome, insalubrious (*fml*).

more *adjective*
further, extra, additional, added, new, fresh, increased, other, supplementary, repeated, alternative, spare.
Fa less.
▶ *adverb*
further, longer, again, besides, moreover, better.
Fa less.

moreover *adverb*
furthermore, further, besides, in addition, as well, also, additionally, what is more.

morsel *noun*
bit, scrap, piece, fragment, crumb, bite, mouthful, nibble, taste, soupçon, titbit, slice, fraction, modicum, grain, atom, part.

mortal *adjective*
1 his mortal remains: worldly, earthly, bodily, human, perishable, temporal.
2 a mortal wound: fatal, lethal, deadly.
3 in mortal terror: extreme, great, severe, intense, grave, awful.
Fa **1** immortal.
▶ *noun*
human being, human, individual, person, being, body, creature.
Fa immortal, god.

mortality *noun*
1 aware of one's own mortality: humanity, death, impermanence, perishability.
2 high/low mortality: fatality, death rate.
Fa **1** immortality.

mostly *adverb*
mainly, on the whole, principally, chiefly, generally, usually, largely, for the most part, as a rule.

mother *noun*
parent, procreator (*fml*), progenitress (*fml*), dam, mamma (*infml*), mum (*infml*), mummy (*infml*), ma (*infml*), matriarch, ancestor, matron, old woman (*infml*).

▶ *verb*
pamper, spoil, baby, indulge,
overprotect, fuss over.

motherly *adjective*
maternal, caring, comforting,
affectionate, kind, loving, protective,
warm, tender, gentle, fond.
Ⅎ neglectful, uncaring.

motif *noun*
theme, idea, topic, concept, pattern,
design, figure, form, logo, shape,
device, ornament, decoration.

motion *noun*
1 in constant motion: movement,
action, mobility, moving, activity,
locomotion, travel, progress, change,
flow.
2 put forward a motion: proposal,
suggestion, recommendation,
proposition.
▶ *verb*
signal, gesture, gesticulate, sign, wave,
nod, beckon, direct, usher.

motionless *adjective*
unmoving, still, stationary, static,
immobile, at a standstill, fixed, halted,
at rest, resting, standing, paralysed,
inanimate, lifeless, frozen, rigid,
stagnant.
Ⅎ active, moving.

motivate *verb*
prompt, incite, impel, spur, provoke,
stimulate, drive, lead, stir, urge, push,
propel, persuade, move, inspire,
encourage, cause, trigger, induce,
kindle, draw, arouse, bring.
Ⅎ deter, discourage.

motive *noun*
ground(s), cause, reason, purpose,
motivation, object, intention, urge,
influence, rationale, thinking,
incentive, impulse, stimulus, desire,
inspiration, incitement, design,
encouragement, consideration.
Ⅎ deterrent, disincentive.

motto *noun*
saying, slogan, maxim, watchword,
catchword, byword, precept (*fml*),
proverb, adage, formula, rule, golden
rule, dictum.

mould *noun*
1 pouring the metal into a mould: cast,

form, die, template, pattern, matrix.
2 a government of a different mould:
shape, form, format, pattern, structure,
style, type, build, construction, cut,
design, kind, model, sort, stamp,
arrangement, brand, frame, character,
nature, quality, line, make.
▶ *verb*
1 moulding the clay: forge, cast, shape,
stamp, make, form, create, design,
construct, sculpt, model, work.
2 moulding young minds: influence,
direct, control.

mouldy *adjective*
mildewed, blighted, musty, decaying,
corrupt, rotten, fusty, putrid, bad,
spoiled, stale, off.
Ⅎ fresh, wholesome.

mound *noun*
heap, pile, bank, stack.

mount *verb*
1 mount a campaign: produce, put on,
set up, prepare, stage, exhibit, display,
launch.
2 tension was mounting: increase,
grow, accumulate, multiply, rise,
intensify, soar, swell.
3 mounting the stairs/his horse:
climb, ascend, get up, go up, get on,
clamber up, scale, get astride.
Ⅎ 2 decrease, descend. **3** descend,
dismount, go down.

mountain *noun*
1 snow-capped mountains: height,
elevation, mount, peak, mound, alp,
tor, massif.
2 a mountain of paperwork: heap, pile,
stack, mass, abundance, backlog.

mourn *verb*
grieve, lament, sorrow, bemoan, miss,
regret, deplore, weep, wail.
Ⅎ rejoice.

mournful *adjective*
sorrowful, sad, unhappy, desolate,
grief-stricken, heavy-hearted,
heartbroken, broken-hearted, cast-
down, downcast, miserable, tragic,
woeful, melancholy, sombre,
depressed, dejected, gloomy, dismal.
Ⅎ joyful.

mouth *noun*
1 open one's mouth to speak: lips,

jaws, trap (*infml*), gob (*slang*).
2 the mouth of the cave: opening, aperture, orifice, cavity, entrance, gateway.
3 the mouth of the river: inlet, estuary.
▶ *verb*
enunciate, articulate, utter, pronounce, whisper, form.

movable *adjective*
mobile, portable, transportable, changeable, alterable, adjustable, flexible, transferable.
E3 fixed, immovable.

move *verb*
1 move suddenly/move forward: stir, go, advance, budge, change, proceed, progress, make strides.
2 moving goods: transport, carry, transfer.
3 they're moving to London: depart, go away, leave, decamp, migrate, remove, move house, relocate.
4 was moved to object: prompt, stimulate, urge, impel, drive, propel, motivate, incite, persuade, induce, inspire.
5 moved her to tears: affect, touch, agitate, stir, impress, excite.
▶ *noun*
1 work out what the next move should be: movement, motion, step, manoeuvre, action, device, stratagem.
2 a move to the city: removal, relocation, migration, transfer.

movement *noun*
1 movement of traffic: repositioning, move, moving, relocation, activity, act, action, agitation, stirring, transfer, passage.
2 movement towards a settlement: change, development, advance, evolution, current, drift, flow, shift, progress, progression, trend, tendency.
3 the Green movement: campaign, crusade, drive, group, organization, party, faction.

moving *adjective*
1 moving traffic: mobile, active, in motion.
2 a moving story: touching, affecting, poignant, impressive, emotive,

arousing, stirring, inspiring, inspirational, exciting, thrilling, persuasive, stimulating.
E3 1 immobile. **2** unemotional.

much *adverb*
greatly, considerably, a lot, frequently, often.
▶ *adjective*
copious, plentiful, ample, considerable, a lot, abundant, great, substantial.

muck *noun*
dirt, grime, dung, manure, mire, filth, mud, sewage, slime, gunge (*infml*), ordure, scum, sludge.

muddle *verb*
1 muddled clean and dirty clothes: disorganize, disorder, mix up, mess up, jumble, scramble, tangle.
2 you're deliberately trying to muddle me: confuse, bewilder, bemuse, perplex.
▶ *noun*
chaos, confusion, disorder, mess, mix-up, jumble, clutter, tangle.

muddy *adjective*
1 muddy boots/field: dirty, foul, miry, mucky, marshy, boggy, swampy, quaggy, grimy.
2 a muddy colour: cloudy, indistinct, obscure, opaque, murky, hazy, blurred, fuzzy, dull.
E3 1 clean. **2** clear.

muffle *verb*
1 muffled in long scarves and woolly hats: wrap, envelop, cloak, swathe, cover.
2 their voices were muffled: deaden, dull, quieten, silence, stifle, dampen, muzzle, suppress.
E3 2 amplify.

mug *verb*
set upon, attack, assault, waylay, steal from, rob, beat up, jump (on).

muggy *adjective*
humid, sticky, stuffy, sultry, close, clammy, oppressive, sweltering, moist, damp.
E3 dry.

multiple *adjective*
many, numerous, manifold (*fml*), various, several, sundry, collective.

multiply *verb*
increase, proliferate, expand, spread, reproduce, propagate, breed, accumulate, intensify, extend, build up, augment, boost.
F3 decrease, lessen.

multitude *noun*
crowd, throng, horde, swarm, mob, mass, herd, congregation, host, lot, lots, legion, public, people, populace.
F3 few, scattering.

munch *verb*
eat, chew, crunch, masticate (*fml*).

mundane *adjective*
banal, ordinary, everyday, commonplace, prosaic, humdrum, workaday, routine.
F3 extraordinary.

murder *noun*
homicide, killing, manslaughter, slaying, assassination, massacre, bloodshed.
▶ *verb*
kill, slaughter, slay (*fml*), assassinate, butcher, massacre.

murderous *adjective*
1 murderous pirates: homicidal, brutal, barbarous, bloodthirsty, bloody, cut-throat, killing, lethal, cruel, savage, ferocious, deadly.
2 (*infml*) the heat/climb was murderous: difficult, exhausting, strenuous, arduous, punishing, unpleasant, dangerous.

murky *adjective*
dark, dingy, dismal, gloomy, dreary, cheerless, dull, overcast, misty, foggy, dim, cloudy, obscure, veiled, grey.
F3 bright, clear.

murmur *noun*
mumble, muttering, whisper, undertone, undercurrent, humming, rumble, drone, buzz, hum, grumble, susurration (*fml*).
▶ *verb*
mutter, mumble, whisper, buzz, hum, rumble, purr, burble.

muscular *adjective*
brawny, beefy (*infml*), sinewy, athletic, powerfully built, strapping, hefty, powerful, hunky (*infml*), robust, stalwart, vigorous, strong.
F3 puny, flabby, weak.

music

Types of music include:

acid house, ambient, ballet, ballroom, bebop, bhangra, Big Beat, bluegrass, blues, boogie-woogie, chamber, choral, classical, country-and-western, dance, disco, Dixieland, doo-wop, electronic, folk, folk rock, funk, garage, gospel, grunge, hard rock, heavy metal, hip-hop, honky-tonk, house, incidental, indie, instrumental, jazz, jazz-funk, jazz-pop, jazz-rock, jive, karaoke, lounge music, muzak, nu-metal, operatic, orchestral, pop, punk rock, ragtime, rap, reggae, rhythm and blues (R & B), rock and roll, rock, sacred, salsa, ska, skiffle, soft rock, soul, swing, techno, thrash metal, trance, trip-hop, world music.

Terms used in music include:

accelerando, acciaccatura, accidental, acoustic, adagio, ad lib, a due, affettuoso, agitato, al fine, al segno, alla breve, alla cappella, allargando, allegretto, allegro, alto, alto clef, amoroso, andante, animato, appoggiatura, arco, arpeggio, arrangement, a tempo, attacca, bar, bar line, baritone, bass clef, beat, bis, breve, buffo, cadence, cantabile, cantilena, chord, chromatic, clef, coda, col canto, compound time, con brio, con fuoco, con moto, consonance, contralto, counterpoint, crescendo, cross-fingering, crotchet, cue, da capo, decrescendo, demisemiquaver, descant, diatonic, diminuendo, dissonance, dolce, doloroso, dotted note, dotted rest, double bar line, double flat, double sharp, double trill, downbeat, drone, duet, duo, duplet, encore, ensemble, finale, fine, fingerboard, flat, forte, fortissimo, four-four time, fret, glissando, grave, harmonics, harmony, hemidemisemiquaver, improvisation, interval, intonation, key, key signature, langsam, larghetto, largo, leading note, ledger line, legato, lento, lyric, maestoso, maestro, major, marcato, mediant, metre, mezza voce, mezzo forte, microtone, middle C, minim, minor, mode, moderato, modulation, molto, mordent, motif, movement, non troppo, nonet, obbligato, octave, ostinato, pentatonic, percussion, perdendo, phrase, pianissimo, piano, pitch, pizzicato, presto, prima donna, quarter tone, quartet, quaver, quintet, quintuplet, rallentando, reed, rhythm, rinforzando, ritenuto, root, scale, score, semibreve, semiquaver, semitone, semplice, sempre, senza, sequence, sextet, sextuplet, sharp, simple time, six-eight time, smorzando, solo, soprano, sostenuto, sotto voce, spiritoso, staccato, staff, stave, string, subdominant, subito, submediant, sul ponticello, supertonic, syncopation, tablature, tacet, tanto, tempo, tenor clef, tenuto, theme, three-four time, tie, timbre, time signature, tonic sol-fa, transposition, treble clef, tremolo, triad, trill, trio, triplet, tutti, two-two time, unison, upbeat, vibrato, vigoroso, virtuoso, vivace.

musical *adjective*
tuneful, melodious, melodic, harmonious, dulcet, sweet-sounding, lyrical.
E3 discordant, unmusical.

musical instruments

Musical instruments include:

balalaika, banjo, cello, clarsach, double bass, guitar, harp, hurdy-gurdy, lute, lyre, mandolin, sitar, spinet, ukulele, viola, violin, fiddle (*infml*), zither; accordion, concertina, squeeze-box (*infml*), clavichord, harmonium, harpsichord, keyboard, melodeon, organ, Wurlitzer®, piano, grand piano, Pianola®, player-piano, synthesizer, virginals; bagpipes,

bassoon, bugle, clarinet, cor anglais, cornet, didgeridoo, euphonium, fife, flugelhorn, flute, French horn, harmonica, horn, kazoo, mouth-organ, oboe, Pan-pipes, piccolo, recorder, saxophone, sousaphone, trombone, trumpet, tuba, uillean pipes; castanets, cymbal, glockenspiel, maracas, marimba, tambourine, triangle, tubular bells, xylophone; bass drum, bodhran, bongo, kettledrum, snare-drum, tenor-drum, timpani, tom-tom.

muster *verb*
assemble, convene, gather, call together, mobilize, round up, marshal, come together, congregate, collect, group, meet, rally, mass, throng, call up, summon, enrol.

musty *adjective*
mouldy, mildewy, stale, stuffy, fusty, dank, airless, decayed, smelly.

mutation *noun*
change, alteration, variation, modification, transformation, deviation, anomaly, evolution.

mute *adjective*
silent, dumb, voiceless, wordless, speechless, mum (*infml*), unspoken, noiseless, unexpressed, unpronounced.
E3 vocal, talkative.

mutilate *verb*
maim, injure, dismember, disable, disfigure, lame, mangle, cut to pieces, cut up, butcher.

mutiny *noun*
rebellion, insurrection, revolt, revolution, rising, uprising, insubordination, disobedience, defiance, resistance, riot, strike.
▶ *verb*
rebel, revolt, rise up, resist, protest, disobey, strike.

mutter *verb*
mumble, murmur, rumble.

mutual *adjective*
reciprocal, shared, common, joint, interchangeable, interchanged, exchanged, complementary.

mysterious *adjective*
enigmatic, cryptic, mystifying,
inexplicable, incomprehensible,
puzzling, perplexing, obscure, strange,
unfathomable, unsearchable, mystical,
baffling, curious, hidden, insoluble,
secret, weird, secretive, veiled, dark,
furtive.
Fa straightforward, comprehensible.

mystery *noun*
1 solve a mystery: enigma, puzzle,
secret, riddle, conundrum, question.
2 cloaked in mystery: obscurity,
secrecy, ambiguity.

mystical *adjective*
occult, arcane, mystic, esoteric,
supernatural, paranormal,
transcendental, metaphysical, hidden,
mysterious.

mystify *verb*
puzzle, bewilder, baffle, perplex,
confound, confuse.

myth *noun*
legend, fable, fairy tale, allegory,
parable, saga, story, fiction, tradition,
fancy, fantasy, superstition.

mythical *adjective*
1 mythical beasts: mythological,
legendary, fabled, fairy-tale.
2 his wealth turned out to be entirely
mythical: fictitious, imaginary, made-
up, invented, make-believe, non-
existent, unreal, pretended, fanciful.
Fa **1** historical. **2** actual, real.

mythology *noun*
legend, myths, lore, tradition(s),
folklore, folk tales, tales.

nag *verb*
scold, berate, irritate, annoy, pester, badger, plague, torment, harass, henpeck (*infml*), harry, vex, upbraid (*fml*), goad.

nail *noun*
1 hammer in the nail: fastener, pin, tack, spike, skewer.
2 long painted nails: talon, claw.
▸ *verb*
fasten, attach, secure, pin, tack, fix, join.

naïve *adjective*
unsophisticated, ingenuous, innocent, unaffected, artless, guileless, simple, natural, childlike, open, trusting, unsuspecting, gullible, credulous, wide-eyed.
🔁 experienced, sophisticated.

naked *adjective*
1 a naked body: nude, bare, undressed, unclothed, uncovered, stripped, stark naked, disrobed, denuded, in the altogether (*infml*).
2 naked aggression: open, unadorned, undisguised, unqualified, plain, stark, overt, blatant, exposed.
🔁 **1** clothed, covered. **2** hidden.

name *noun*
1 what's your name?: title, appellation (*fml*), designation, label, term, epithet, handle (*infml*).
2 have a name for efficient service: reputation, character, repute, renown, esteem, eminence, fame, honour, distinction, note.
▸ *verb*
1 name the baby: call, christen, baptize, term, title, entitle, dub, label, style.

2 name your price: designate, nominate, cite, choose, select, specify, classify, commission, appoint.

namely *adverb*
that is, ie, specifically, viz, that is to say.

nap *noun*
rest, sleep, siesta, snooze (*infml*), catnap, forty winks (*infml*), kip (*infml*).
▸ *verb*
doze, sleep, snooze (*infml*), nod (off), drop off, rest, kip (*infml*).

narrate *verb*
tell, relate, report, recount, describe, unfold, recite, state, detail.

narrative *noun*
story, tale, chronicle, account, history, report, detail, statement.

narrow *adjective*
1 a narrow passage/bridge/waist/ margin: tight, confined, constricted, cramped, slim, slender, thin, fine, tapering, close.
2 a narrow brief: limited, restricted, circumscribed.
3 a narrow outlook: narrow-minded, biased, bigoted, exclusive, dogmatic.
🔁 **1** wide. **2** broad. **3** broad-minded, tolerant.
▸ *verb*
constrict, limit, tighten, reduce, diminish, simplify.
🔁 broaden, widen, increase.

narrow-minded *adjective*
illiberal, biased, bigoted, prejudiced, reactionary, small-minded, conservative, intolerant, insular, petty.
🔁 broad-minded.

nasty *adjective*
1 a nasty smell: unpleasant, repellent, repugnant, repulsive, objectionable,

offensive, disgusting, sickening, horrible, filthy, foul, polluted, obscene.
2 a nasty remark: malicious, mean, spiteful, vicious, malevolent.
E3 1 agreeable, pleasant, decent.
2 benevolent, kind.

nation *noun*
country, people, race, state, realm, population, community, society.

national *adjective*
countrywide, civil, domestic, nationwide, state, internal, general, governmental, public, widespread, social.
▸ *noun*
citizen, native, subject, inhabitant, resident.

nationalism *noun*
patriotism, allegiance, loyalty, chauvinism, xenophobia, jingoism.

nationality *noun*
race, nation, ethnic group, birth, tribe, clan.

native *adjective*
1 native species/land/customs: local, indigenous, domestic, vernacular, home, aboriginal, mother, original.
2 native cunning: inborn, inherent, innate, inbred, hereditary, inherited, congenital, instinctive, natural, intrinsic, natal.
▸ *noun*
inhabitant, resident, national, citizen, dweller, aborigine.
E3 foreigner, outsider, stranger.

natural *adjective*
1 in his natural voice: ordinary, normal, common, regular, standard, usual, typical.
2 a natural ability: innate, inborn, instinctive, intuitive, inherent, congenital, native, indigenous.
3 natural materials/in its natural state: genuine, pure, authentic, unrefined, unprocessed, unmixed, real.
4 she's always so natural: sincere, unaffected, genuine, artless, ingenuous, guileless, simple, unsophisticated, open, candid, spontaneous.
E3 1 unnatural. **2** acquired. **3** artificial, synthetic. **4** affected, disingenuous.

naturalistic *adjective*
natural, realistic, true-to-life, representational, lifelike, graphic, real-life, photographic.

naturally *adverb*
1 naturally, he was shocked at their behaviour: of course, as a matter of course, simply, obviously, logically, typically, certainly, absolutely.
2 speaking quite naturally: normally, genuinely, instinctively, spontaneously.

nature *noun*
1 a pleasant nature: essence, quality, character, features, disposition, attributes, personality, make-up, constitution, temperament, mood, outlook, temper.
2 of a different nature: kind, sort, type, description, category, variety, style, species.
3 not found anywhere in nature: universe, world, creation, earth, environment.
4 study nature: natural history.

naughty *adjective*
1 a naughty child: bad, badly behaved, mischievous, disobedient, wayward, exasperating, playful, roguish.
2 a naughty word: indecent, obscene, bawdy, risqué, smutty.
E3 1 good, well-behaved. **2** decent.

nauseate *verb*
sicken, disgust, revolt, repel, offend, turn one's stomach (*infml*).

nautical *adjective*
naval, marine, maritime, sea-going, seafaring, sailing, oceanic, boating.

navigate *verb*
steer, drive, direct, pilot, guide, handle, manoeuvre, cruise, sail, skipper, voyage, journey, cross, helm, plot, plan.

near *adjective*
1 near neighbours: nearby, close, bordering, adjacent, adjoining, alongside, neighbouring.
2 the exams are near: imminent, impending, forthcoming, coming, approaching.
3 a near relation: dear, familiar, close, related, intimate, akin.
E3 1 far. **2** distant. **3** remote.

nearby *adjective*
near, neighbouring, adjoining, adjacent, accessible, convenient, handy.
🗲 faraway.
▶ *adverb*
near, within reach, at close quarters, close at hand, not far away.

nearly *adverb*
almost, practically, virtually, closely, approximately, more or less, as good as, just about, roughly, well-nigh.
🗲 completely, totally.

neat *adjective*
1 a neat appearance: tidy, orderly, smart, spruce, trim, clean, spick-and-span (*infml*), shipshape.
2 a neat trick: deft, clever, adroit, skilful, expert.
🗲 1 untidy. 2 clumsy.

necessary *adjective*
needed, required, essential, compulsory, indispensable, vital, imperative, mandatory, obligatory, needful, unavoidable, inevitable, inescapable, inexorable, certain.
🗲 unnecessary, inessential, unimportant.

necessitate *verb*
require, involve, entail, call for, demand, oblige, force, constrain, compel.

necessity *noun*
requirement, obligation, prerequisite, essential, fundamental, need, want, compulsion, demand.

need *verb*
miss, lack, want, require, demand, call for, necessitate, have need of, have to, crave.
▶ *noun*
1 a need for caution: call, demand, obligation, requirement.
2 the family's needs: essential, necessity, requisite, prerequisite.
3 a need for equipment: want, lack, insufficiency, inadequacy, neediness, shortage.

needless *adjective*
unnecessary, gratuitous, uncalled-for, unwanted, redundant, superfluous, useless, pointless, purposeless.
🗲 necessary, essential.

needy *adjective*
poor, destitute, impoverished, penniless, disadvantaged, deprived, poverty-stricken, underprivileged.
🗲 affluent, wealthy, well-off.

negate *verb*
1 negate any gains made: nullify, annul, cancel, invalidate, undo, countermand, abrogate (*fml*), neutralize, quash, retract, reverse, revoke, rescind, wipe out, void, repeal.
2 negating his argument: deny, contradict, oppose, disprove, refute, repudiate.
🗲 2 affirm.

negative *adjective*
1 a negative answer: contradictory, contrary, denying, opposing, invalidating, neutralizing, nullifying, annulling.
2 a negative attitude: unco-operative, cynical, pessimistic, unenthusiastic, uninterested, unwilling.
🗲 1 affirmative, positive.
2 constructive, positive.
▶ *noun*
contradiction, denial, opposite, refusal.

neglect *verb*
1 neglect one's family: disregard, ignore, leave alone, abandon, pass by, rebuff, scorn, disdain, slight, spurn.
2 neglect one's duty: forget, fail (in), omit, overlook, let slide, shirk, skimp.
🗲 1 cherish, appreciate. 2 remember.
▶ *noun*
negligence, disregard, carelessness, failure, inattention, indifference, slackness, dereliction of duty, forgetfulness, heedlessness, oversight, slight, disrespect.
🗲 care, attention, concern.

negligent *adjective*
neglectful, inattentive, remiss, thoughtless, casual, lax, careless, indifferent, offhand, nonchalant, slack, uncaring, forgetful.
🗲 attentive, careful, scrupulous.

negligible *adjective*
unimportant, insignificant, small, imperceptible, trifling, trivial, minor, minute.
🗲 significant.

negotiate *verb*
1 negotiate with the union: confer, deal, mediate, arbitrate, bargain, arrange, transact, work out, manage, settle, consult, contract.
2 negotiate the bend: get round, cross, surmount, traverse, pass.

neighbouring *adjective*
adjacent, bordering, near, nearby, adjoining, connecting, next, surrounding.
Fd distant, remote.

neighbourly *adjective*
sociable, friendly, amiable, kind, helpful, genial, hospitable, obliging, considerate, companionable.

nerve *noun*
1 lose one's nerve: courage, bravery, mettle, pluck, guts (*infml*), spunk (*infml*), spirit, vigour, intrepidity, daring, fearlessness, firmness, resolution, fortitude, steadfastness, will, determination, endurance, force.
2 (*infml*) **what a nerve he's got!:** audacity, impudence, cheek (*infml*), effrontery, brazenness, boldness, chutzpah (*infml*), impertinence, insolence.
Fd 1 weakness. **2** timidity.

nerve-racking *adjective*
harrowing, distressing, trying, stressful, tense, maddening, worrying, difficult, frightening.

nerves *noun*
nervousness, tension, stress, anxiety, worry, strain, fretfulness.

nervous *adjective*
highly-strung, excitable, anxious, agitated, nervy (*infml*), on edge, edgy, jumpy (*infml*), jittery (*infml*), tense, fidgety, apprehensive, neurotic, shaky, uneasy, worried, flustered, fearful.
Fd calm, relaxed.

nest *noun*
1 an eagle's nest: breeding-ground, den, roost, eyrie, lair.
2 a cosy nest: retreat, refuge, haunt, hideaway.

nestle *verb*
snuggle, huddle, cuddle, curl up.

net[1] *noun*
mesh, web, network, netting, open-work, lattice, lace.
▶ *verb*
catch, trap, capture, bag, ensnare, entangle, nab (*infml*).

net[2] *adjective*
nett, clear, after tax, final, lowest.
▶ *verb*
bring in, clear, earn, make, realize, receive, gain, obtain, accumulate.

network *noun*
system, organization, arrangement, structure, interconnections, complex, grid, net, maze, mesh, labyrinth, channels, circuitry, convolution, grill, tracks.

neutral *adjective*
1 a neutral country: impartial, uncommitted, unbiased, non-aligned, disinterested, unprejudiced, undecided, non-partisan, non-committal, objective, indifferent, dispassionate, even-handed.
2 a neutral colour: dull, nondescript, colourless, drab, expressionless, indistinct.
Fd 1 biased, partisan. **2** colourful.

neutralize *verb*
counteract, counterbalance, offset, negate, cancel, nullify, invalidate, undo, frustrate.

nevertheless *adverb*
nonetheless, notwithstanding, still, anyway, even so, yet, however, anyhow, but, regardless.

new *adjective*
1 a new approach/car/day/lamb: novel, original, fresh, different, unfamiliar, unusual, brand-new, mint, unknown, unused, newborn.
2 new technology: modern, contemporary, current, latest, recent, up-to-date, up-to-the-minute, topical, trendy (*infml*), ultra-modern, advanced, newfangled (*infml*).
3 the new face of politics: changed, altered, modernized, improved, renewed, restored, redesigned.
4 new vigour: added, additional, extra, more, supplementary.

1 usual. **2** outdated, out-of-date.
3 old.

news *noun*

report, account, information,
intelligence, dispatch, communiqué,
bulletin, gossip, hearsay, rumour,
statement, story, word, tidings, latest,
release, scandal, revelation, lowdown
(*infml*), exposé, disclosure, gen (*infml*),
advice.

next *adjective*

1 the next street: adjacent, adjoining,
neighbouring, nearest, closest.
2 the next day: following, subsequent,
succeeding, ensuing, later.
2 previous, preceding.

▶ *adverb*

afterwards, subsequently, later, then.

nice *adjective*

1 a nice person: pleasant, agreeable,
delightful, charming, likable,
attractive, good, kind, friendly, well-
mannered, polite, respectable.
2 (*fml*) **a nice distinction**: subtle,
delicate, fine, fastidious,
discriminating, scrupulous, precise,
exact, accurate, careful, strict.
1 nasty, disagreeable, unpleasant.
2 careless.

⇨ *See also* **Word Workshop** *panel*.

niche *noun*

1 a niche in the wall: recess, alcove,
hollow, nook, cubby-hole, corner,
opening.
2 find one's niche in life: position,
place, vocation, calling, métier, slot.

nick *noun*

notch, indentation, chip, cut, groove,
dent, scar, scratch, mark.

▶ *verb*

notch, cut, dent, indent, chip, score,
scratch, scar, mark, damage, snick.

nickname *noun*

pet name, sobriquet (*fml*), epithet,
diminutive.

night *noun*

night-time, darkness, dark, dead of
night.
day, daytime.

nightfall *noun*

sunset, dusk, twilight, evening, gloaming.
dawn, sunrise.

nightmare *noun*

1 in his worst nightmare: bad dream,
hallucination.
2 the journey was a nightmare: ordeal,
horror, torment, trial.

nil *noun*

nothing, zero, none, nought, naught,
love, duck, zilch (*infml*).

nimble *adjective*

agile, active, lively, sprightly, spry,
smart, quick, brisk, nippy (*infml*), deft,
alert, light-footed, prompt, ready,
swift, quick-witted.
clumsy, slow.

nip *verb*

bite, pinch, squeeze, snip, clip, tweak,
catch, grip, nibble.

nobility *noun*

1 the nobility of his actions: nobleness,
dignity, grandeur, illustriousness,
stateliness, majesty, magnificence,
eminence, excellence, superiority,
uprightness, honour, virtue,
worthiness.
2 belong to the nobility: aristocracy,
peerage, nobles, gentry, élite, lords,
high society.
1 baseness. **2** proletariat.

noble *adjective*

1 a noble family: aristocratic, highborn, titled, high-ranking, patrician,
blue-blooded (*infml*).
2 a noble brow: magnificent,
magnanimous, splendid, stately,
generous, dignified, distinguished,
eminent, grand, great, honoured,
honourable, imposing, impressive,
majestic, virtuous, worthy, excellent,
elevated, fine, gentle.
1 low-born. **2** ignoble, base,
contemptible.

nod *verb*

1 nodding and waving: gesture,
indicate, sign, signal, salute,
acknowledge.
2 he nodded but said nothing: agree,
assent.
3 nodding off: sleep, doze, drowse,
nap.

▶ *noun*

gesture, indication, sign, signal, salute,
greeting, beck, acknowledgement.

nominal *adjective*
1 the nominal head: titular, supposed, purported, professed, ostensible, so-called, theoretical, self-styled, puppet, symbolic.
2 a nominal amount: token, minimal, trifling, trivial, insignificant, small.
F₃ **1** actual, genuine, real.

noise *noun*
sound, din, racket, row, clamour, clash, clatter, commotion, outcry, hubbub, uproar, cry, blare, talk, pandemonium, tumult, babble.
F₃ quiet, silence.
▶ *verb*
report, rumour, publicize, announce, circulate.

noisy *adjective*
loud, deafening, ear-splitting, clamorous, piercing, vocal, vociferous, tumultuous, boisterous, obstreperous.
F₃ quiet, silent, peaceful.

nominate *verb*
propose, choose, select, name, designate, submit, suggest, recommend, put up, present, elect, appoint, assign, commission, elevate, term.

nonchalant *adjective*
unconcerned, detached, dispassionate, offhand, blasé, indifferent, casual, cool, collected, apathetic, careless, insouciant.
F₃ concerned, careful.

none *pronoun*
no-one, not any, not one, nobody, nil, zero.

nonsense *noun*
rubbish, trash, drivel, balderdash, gibberish, gobbledygook, senselessness, stupidity, silliness, foolishness, folly, rot (*infml*), blather, twaddle (*infml*), ridiculousness, claptrap (*infml*), cobblers (*slang*).
F₃ sense, wisdom.

nonsensical *adjective*
ridiculous, meaningless, senseless, foolish, inane, irrational, silly, incomprehensible, ludicrous, absurd, fatuous, crazy (*infml*).
F₃ reasonable, sensible, logical.

non-stop *adjective*
never-ending, uninterrupted,

continuous, incessant, constant, endless, interminable, unending, unbroken, round-the-clock, ongoing.
F₃ intermittent, occasional.

nook *noun*
recess, alcove, corner, cranny, niche, cubby-hole, hideout, retreat, shelter, cavity.

norm *noun*
average, mean, standard, rule, pattern, criterion, model, yardstick, benchmark, measure, reference.

normal *adjective*
usual, standard, general, common, ordinary, conventional, average, regular, routine, typical, mainstream, natural, accustomed, well-adjusted, straight, rational, reasonable.
F₃ abnormal, irregular, peculiar.

normality *noun*
usualness, commonness, ordinariness, regularity, routine, conventionality, balance, adjustment, typicality, naturalness, reason, rationality.
F₃ abnormality, irregularity, peculiarity.

normally *adverb*
ordinarily, usually, as a rule, typically, commonly, characteristically.
F₃ abnormally, exceptionally.

nosey *adjective* (*infml*)
inquisitive, meddlesome, prying, interfering, snooping, curious, eavesdropping.

nostalgic *adjective*
yearning, longing, wistful, emotional, regretful, sentimental, homesick.

notable *adjective*
noteworthy, remarkable, noticeable, striking, extraordinary, impressive, outstanding, marked, unusual, celebrated, distinguished, famous, eminent, well-known, notorious, renowned, rare.
F₃ ordinary, commonplace, usual.
▶ *noun*
celebrity, notability, VIP, personage, somebody, dignitary, luminary, worthy.
F₃ nobody, nonentity.

Nice is a rather uninteresting adjective, especially if it is used too often. When you are thinking of using **nice** to describe something, consider other words that you might use instead. Some alternative words are listed here:

a person's appearance

attractive	good-looking	pretty
cute	handsome	

a person's personality

agreeable	good	polite
amiable	good-natured	sweet
charming	helpful	thoughtful
considerate	kind	warm
friendly	likeable	wonderful
generous	pleasant	

for an object, eg a painting, or a place

beautiful	charming	lovely

for a piece of clothing, eg a dress

elegant	glamorous	stylish
fashionable	smart	

for a room, house, etc

comfortable	homely
cosy	snug

for a meal

delicious	scrumptious	yummy
mouth-watering	tasty	

for the weather

fine	pleasant	warm
mild	sunny	

for an event or occasion, eg a holiday

delightful	glorious	wonderful
enjoyable	lovely	

Instead of repeating **nice** in the following passage, you might use some of the synonyms discussed opposite.

Dear Sheena

     kind
It was really ~~nice~~ of you to invite me to your birthday party
        wonderful   *pretty*
yesterday. I had a really ~~nice~~ time. You looked ~~nice~~ in your
      delicious
new dress. The food was ~~nice~~, especially your birthday
          sunny
cake. We were also lucky that the weather was ~~nice~~ and we
   beautiful
could play in your ~~nice~~ garden.
                  generous
I would also like to thank your parents for being so ~~nice~~ to
        lovely
all of us. I hope you enjoyed all the ~~nice~~ presents you
received.

Thank you again,

Mary

Write a thank-you card to someone thanking them for a present which they have given you or a party or event to which they invited you. Try to think of as many substitutes as you can for the word **nice**.

notably *adverb*
markedly, noticeably, particularly, remarkably, strikingly, conspicuously, distinctly, especially, impressively, outstandingly, eminently.

notch *noun*
1 cut a notch in a piece of wood: cut, nick, indentation, incision, score, groove, cleft, mark, snip.
2 tension between the two countries moved up another notch: degree, grade, step.

note *noun*
1 a note of absence: communication, letter, message, memorandum, reminder, memo (*infml*), line, jotting, record.
2 a note in the margin: annotation, comment, gloss, remark.
3 a note of distinction: indication, signal, token, mark, symbol.
4 of considerable note: eminence, distinction, consequence, fame, renown, reputation.
5 take note: heed, attention, regard, notice, observation.
▶ *verb*
1 noted his absence: notice, observe, perceive, heed, detect, mark, remark, mention, see, witness.
2 noted down the details: record, register, write down, enter.

noted *adjective*
famous, well-known, renowned, notable, celebrated, eminent, prominent, great, acclaimed, illustrious, distinguished, respected, recognized.
E3 obscure, unknown.

noteworthy *adjective*
remarkable, significant, important, notable, memorable, exceptional, extraordinary, unusual, outstanding.
E3 commonplace, unexceptional, ordinary.

nothing *noun*
nought, zero, nothingness, zilch (*infml*), nullity, non-existence, emptiness, void, nobody, nonentity.
E3 something.

notice *verb*
note, remark, perceive, observe, mind,

see, discern, distinguish, mark, detect heed, spot.
E3 ignore, overlook.
▶ *noun*
1 notice to quit: notification, announcement, information, declaration, communication, intelligence, news, warning, instruction.
2 a notice in the paper: advertisement poster, sign, bill.
3 reading the notices for the play: review, comment, criticism.
4 take some notice: attention, observation, awareness, note, regard, consideration, heed.

noticeable *adjective*
perceptible, observable, appreciable, unmistakable, conspicuous, evident, manifest, clear, distinct, significant, striking, plain, obvious, measurable.
E3 inconspicuous, unnoticeable.

notification *noun*
announcement, information, notice, declaration, advice, warning, intelligence, message, publication, statement, communication.

notify *verb*
inform, tell, advise, announce, declare warn, acquaint, alert, publish, disclose reveal.

notion *noun*
1 a strange notion: idea, thought, concept, conception, belief, impression, view, opinion, understanding, apprehension.
2 have a notion for some ice-cream: inclination, wish, whim, fancy, caprice.

notorious *adjective*
infamous, disreputable, scandalous, dishonourable, disgraceful, ignominious, flagrant, well-known.

nought *noun*
zero, nil, zilch (*infml*), naught, nothing nothingness.

nourish *verb*
1 nourishing the parched land: nurture, feed, foster, care for, provide for, sustain, support, tend, nurse, maintain, cherish.
2 nourishing a general sense of

injustice: strengthen, encourage, promote, cultivate, stimulate.

nourishment *noun*
nutrition, food, sustenance, diet.

novel *adjective*
new, original, fresh, innovative, unfamiliar, unusual, uncommon, different, imaginative, unconventional, strange.
🔁 hackneyed, familiar, ordinary.
▶ *noun*
fiction, story, tale, narrative, romance.

novelty *noun*
1 the novelty of the situation: newness, originality, freshness, innovation, unfamiliarity, uniqueness, difference, strangeness.
2 selling toys and novelties: gimmick, gadget, trifle, memento, knick-knack, curiosity, souvenir, trinket, bauble, gimcrack.

novice *noun*
beginner, tiro, learner, pupil, trainee, probationer, apprentice, neophyte (*fml*), amateur, newcomer, rookie (*US infml*).
🔁 expert.

now *adverb*
1 do it now: immediately, at once, directly, instantly, straight away, promptly, next.
2 here and now: at present, nowadays, these days.

nuance *noun*
subtlety, suggestion, shade, hint, suspicion, gradation, distinction, overtone, refinement, touch, trace, tinge, degree, nicety.

nucleus *noun*
centre, heart, nub, core, focus, kernel, pivot, basis, crux.

nude *adjective*
naked, bare, undressed, unclothed, stripped, stark-naked, uncovered, starkers (*infml*), in one's birthday suit (*infml*).
🔁 clothed, dressed.

nudge *verb, noun*
poke, prod, shove, dig, jog, prompt, push, elbow, bump.

nuisance *noun*
annoyance, inconvenience, bother, irritation, pest, pain (*infml*), drag (*infml*), bore, problem, trial, trouble, drawback.

numb *adjective*
benumbed, insensible, unfeeling, deadened, insensitive, frozen, immobilized.
🔁 sensitive.
▶ *verb*
deaden, anaesthetize, freeze, immobilize, paralyse, dull, stun.
🔁 sensitize.

number *noun*
1 a list of numbers: figure, numeral, digit, integer, unit.
2 a large number: total, sum, aggregate, collection, amount, quantity, several, many, company, crowd, multitude, throng, horde.
3 the latest number of the magazine: copy, issue, edition, impression, volume, printing.
▶ *verb*
count, calculate, enumerate, reckon, total, add, compute, include.

numerous *adjective*
many, abundant, several, plentiful, copious, profuse, sundry.
🔁 few.

nurse *verb*
1 nurse the sick: tend, care for, look after, treat.
2 mother nursing her baby: breast-feed, feed, suckle, nurture, nourish.
3 have to nurse it along: preserve, sustain, support, cherish, encourage, keep, foster, promote.
▶ *noun*
sister, matron, nursemaid, nanny.

nurture *noun*
rearing, upbringing, training, care, cultivation, development, education, discipline.
▶ *verb*
1 nurture the plants: feed, nourish, nurse, tend, care for, foster, support, sustain.
2 nurturing the next generation: bring up, rear, cultivate, develop, educate, instruct, train, school, discipline.

nutrition *noun*
food, nourishment, sustenance.

nutritious *adjective*
nourishing, nutritive, wholesome, healthful, health-giving, good, beneficial, strengthening, substantial, invigorating.
🔁 bad, unwholesome.

oasis *noun*
1 an oasis in the desert: spring, watering-hole.
2 an oasis of peace: refuge, haven, island, sanctuary, retreat.

oath *noun*
1 an oath of loyalty: vow, pledge, promise, word, affirmation, assurance, word of honour.
2 shouting oaths: curse, imprecation, swear-word, profanity, expletive, blasphemy.

obedient *adjective*
compliant, docile, acquiescent, submissive, tractable, yielding, dutiful, law-abiding, deferential, respectful, subservient, observant.
F3 disobedient, rebellious, wilful.

obese *adjective*
fat, overweight, corpulent, stout, gross, plump, portly, bulky.
F3 thin, slender, skinny.

obey *verb*
1 obey the rules: comply, submit, surrender, yield, be ruled by, bow to, take orders from, defer (to), give way, follow, observe, abide by, adhere to, conform, heed, keep, mind, respond.
2 obey a command: carry out, discharge, execute, act upon, fulfil, perform.
F3 **1** disobey.

object¹ *noun* /ob-jekt/
1 a valuable object: thing, entity, article, body.
2 the object of the exercise: aim, objective, purpose, goal, target, intention, motive, end, reason, point, design.

3 an object of fun: target, recipient, butt, victim.

object² *verb* /ob-jekt/
object to that remark: protest, oppose, demur, take exception, disapprove, refuse, complain, rebut, repudiate.
F3 agree, acquiesce.

objection *noun*
protest, dissent, disapproval, opposition, demur, complaint, challenge, scruple.
F3 agreement, assent.

objectionable *adjective*
unacceptable, unpleasant, offensive, obnoxious, repugnant, disagreeable, abhorrent (*fml*), detestable, deplorable, despicable.
F3 acceptable.

objective *adjective*
impartial, unbiased, detached, unprejudiced, open-minded, equitable, dispassionate, even-handed, neutral, disinterested, just, fair.
F3 subjective.
▶ *noun*
object, aim, goal, end, purpose, ambition, mark, target, intention, design.

obligation *noun*
duty, responsibility, onus, charge, commitment, liability, requirement, bond, contract, debt, burden, trust.

obligatory *adjective*
compulsory, mandatory, statutory, re-quired, binding, essential, necessary, enforced.
F3 optional.

oblige *verb*
1 was obliged to go: compel,

obliging *adjective*

constrain, coerce, require, make,
necessitate, force, bind.
2 happy to oblige: help, assist,
accommodate, do a favour, serve,
gratify, please.

obliging *adjective*
accommodating, co-operative, helpful,
considerate, agreeable, friendly, kind,
civil.
F3 unhelpful.

oblivious *adjective*
unaware, unconscious, inattentive,
careless, heedless, blind, insensible,
negligent.
F3 aware.

obnoxious *adjective*
unpleasant, disagreeable, disgusting,
loathsome, nasty, horrid, odious,
repulsive, revolting, repugnant,
sickening, nauseating.
F3 pleasant.

obscene *adjective*
indecent, improper, immoral, impure,
filthy, dirty, bawdy, lewd, licentious,
pornographic, scurrilous, suggestive,
disgusting, foul, shocking, shameless,
offensive.
F3 decent, wholesome.

obscure *adjective*
1 an obscure poet: unknown,
unimportant, little-known, unheard-
of, undistinguished, nameless,
inconspicuous, humble, minor.
2 an obscure remark: cryptic,
incomprehensible, enigmatic,
recondite (*fml*), arcane, esoteric,
mysterious, deep, abstruse (*fml*),
confusing.
**3 shape was too obscure to make out
what it was**: indistinct, unclear,
indefinite, shadowy, blurred, cloudy,
faint, hazy, dim, misty, shady, vague,
murky, gloomy, dusky.
F3 1 famous, renowned. **2** intelligible,
straightforward. **3** clear, definite.
▶ *verb*
conceal, cloud, obfuscate (*fml*), hide,
cover, blur, disguise, mask,
overshadow, shadow, shade, cloak, veil,
shroud, darken, dim, eclipse, screen,
block out.
F3 clarify, illuminate.

observant *adjective*
attentive, alert, vigilant, watchful,
perceptive, eagle-eyed, wide-awake,
heedful.
F3 unobservant.

observation *noun*
1 learn by observation: attention,
notice, examination, inspection,
scrutiny, monitoring, study, watching,
consideration, discernment.
**2 he made an interesting observation
about the situation**: remark,
comment, utterance, thought,
statement, pronouncement, reflection,
opinion, finding, note.

observe *verb*
1 observing wildlife: watch, see, study,
notice, contemplate, keep an eye on,
perceive.
2 'that's odd,' she observed: remark,
comment, say, mention.
3 observe the rules: abide by, comply
with, honour, keep, fulfil, celebrate,
perform.
F3 1 miss. **3** break, violate.

obsession *noun*
preoccupation, fixation, idée fixe,
ruling passion, compulsion, fetish,
hang-up (*infml*), infatuation, mania,
enthusiasm.

obsessive *adjective*
consuming, compulsive, gripping,
fixed, haunting, tormenting,
maddening.

obsolete *adjective*
outmoded, disused, out of date, old-
fashioned, passé, dated, outworn, old,
antiquated, antique, dead, extinct.
F3 modern, current, up-to-date.

obstacle *noun*
barrier, bar, obstruction, impediment,
hurdle, hindrance, check, snag,
stumbling block, drawback, difficulty,
hitch, catch, stop, interference,
interruption.
F3 advantage, help.

obstinate *adjective*
stubborn, inflexible, immovable,
intractable, pig-headed (*infml*),
unyielding, intransigent, persistent,
dogged, headstrong, bloody-minded,
strong-minded, self-willed, steadfast,

firm, determined, wilful.
F3 flexible, tractable.

obstruct *verb*
block, impede, hinder, prevent, check,
frustrate, hamper, clog, choke, bar,
barricade, stop, stall, retard, restrict,
thwart, inhibit, hold up, curb, arrest,
slow down, interrupt, interfere with,
shut off, cut off, obscure.
F3 assist, further.

obstruction *noun*
barrier, blockage, bar, barricade,
hindrance, impediment, check, stop,
stoppage, difficulty.
F3 help.

obtain *verb*
1 obtain a passport: acquire, get, gain,
come by, attain, procure, secure, earn,
achieve.
2 (*fml*) situation that obtained at that
time: prevail, exist, hold, be in force, be
the case, stand, reign, rule, be
prevalent.

obvious *adjective*
evident, self-evident, manifest, patent,
clear, plain, distinct, transparent,
undeniable, unmistakable,
conspicuous, glaring, apparent, open,
unconcealed, visible, noticeable,
perceptible, pronounced,
recognizable, self-explanatory,
straightforward, prominent.
F3 unclear, indistinct, obscure.

occasion *noun*
1 on the occasion of their marriage/on
each occasion: event, occurrence,
incident, time, instance, chance, case,
opportunity.
2 gave him occasion to pause: reason,
cause, excuse, justification, ground(s).
3 it was quite an occasion: celebration,
function, affair, party.

occasional *adjective*
periodic, intermittent, irregular,
sporadic, infrequent, uncommon,
incidental, odd, rare, casual.
F3 frequent, regular, constant.

occasionally *adverb*
sometimes, on occasion, from time to
time, at times, at intervals, now and
then, now and again, irregularly,
periodically, every so often, once in a

while, off and on, infrequently.
F3 frequently, often, always.

occupant *noun*
occupier, holder, inhabitant, resident,
householder, tenant, user, lessee,
squatter, inmate.

occupation *noun*
1 what's his occupation?: job,
profession, work, vocation,
employment, trade, post, calling,
business, line, pursuit, craft, walk of
life, activity.
2 occupation of the country by the
enemy: invasion, seizure, conquest,
control, takeover.
3 owner occupation: occupancy,
possession, holding, tenancy, tenure,
residence, habitation, use.

occupy *verb*
1 occupying the house next door:
inhabit, live in, possess, reside in, stay
in, take possession of, own.
2 occupied by the task: absorb, take
up, engross, engage, hold, involve,
preoccupy, amuse, busy, interest.
3 occupying the country: invade, seize,
capture, overrun, take over.
4 occupy one's time: fill, take up, use.

occur *verb*
happen, come about, take place,
transpire, turn out, chance, come to
pass, materialize, befall, develop, crop
up, arise, appear, turn up, obtain (*fml*),
result, exist, be present, be found.

odd *adjective*
1 odd smell/behaviour: unusual,
strange, uncommon, peculiar,
abnormal, exceptional, curious,
atypical, different, queer, bizarre,
eccentric, remarkable,
unconventional, weird, irregular,
extraordinary, outlandish, rare.
2 have the odd drink: occasional,
incidental, irregular, random, casual.
3 odd socks: unmatched, unpaired,
single, spare, surplus, left-over,
remaining, sundry, various,
miscellaneous.
F3 1 normal, usual. **2** regular.

oddity *noun*
1 the oddity of his appearance:
abnormality, peculiarity, rarity,

eccentricity, idiosyncrasy, phenomenon, quirk.
2 a bit of an oddity: curiosity, character, freak, misfit.

odds noun
1 what are the odds of rain?: likelihood, probability, chances.
2 against the odds: advantage, edge, lead, superiority.

odour noun
smell, scent, fragrance, aroma, perfume, redolence, stench, stink (infml), pong (infml).

off adjective
1 this milk is off: rotten, bad, sour, turned, rancid, mouldy, decomposed.
2 the match is off: cancelled, postponed.
3 he's off somewhere: away, absent, gone.
4 have an off day: substandard, below par, disappointing, unsatisfactory.
▶ adverb
away, elsewhere, out, at a distance, apart, aside.

offence noun
1 a criminal offence: misdemeanour, transgression, violation, wrong, wrongdoing, infringement, crime, misdeed, sin, trespass (fml).
2 an offence to decency: affront, insult, injury.
3 take offence: resentment, indignation, pique, umbrage, outrage, hurt, hard feelings.

offend verb
1 offended him by laughing: hurt, insult, injure, affront, wrong, wound, displease, snub, upset, annoy, outrage.
2 offending the senses: disgust, repel, sicken.
3 offended repeatedly: transgress, sin, violate, err.
F3 1 please.

offender noun
transgressor, wrongdoer, culprit, criminal, miscreant (fml), guilty party, law-breaker, delinquent.

offensive adjective
1 an offensive remark: disagreeable, unpleasant, objectionable, displeasing,

disgusting, odious, obnoxious, repellent, repugnant, revolting, loathsome, vile, nauseating, nasty, detestable, abominable.
2 don't be offensive: insolent, abusive, rude, insulting, impertinent.
F3 1 pleasant. **2** polite.
▶ noun
attack, assault, onslaught, invasion, raid, sortie.

offer verb
1 offered him a drink: present, make available, advance, extend, put forward, submit, suggest, hold out, provide, sell.
2 offered his hand in marriage: proffer, propose, bid, tender.
3 offered their services: volunteer, come forward, show willing (infml).
▶ noun
proposal, bid, submission, tender, suggestion, proposition, overture, approach, attempt, presentation.

offering noun
present, gift, donation, contribution.

offhand adjective
casual, unconcerned, uninterested, take-it-or-leave-it (infml), brusque, abrupt, perfunctory (fml), informal, cavalier, careless.
▶ adverb
impromptu, off the cuff, extempore (fml), off the top of one's head, immediately.
F3 calculated, planned.

office noun
1 high office: responsibility, duty, obligation, charge, commission, occupation, situation, post, employment, function, appointment, business, role, service.
2 go into the office: workplace, workroom, bureau.

officer noun
official, office-holder, public servant, functionary, dignitary, bureaucrat, administrator, representative, executive, agent, appointee.

official adjective
authorized, authoritative, legitimate, formal, licensed, accredited, certified, approved, authenticated, authentic,

bona fide, proper.

F3 unofficial.

▸ *noun*

office-bearer, officer, functionary, bureaucrat, executive, representative, agent.

offload *verb*

unburden, unload, jettison, dump, drop, deposit, get rid of, discharge.

often *adverb*

frequently, repeatedly, regularly, generally, again and again, time after time, time and again, much.

F3 rarely, seldom, never.

oil *verb*

grease, lubricate, anoint.

oily *adjective*

1 oily food : greasy, fatty.

2 an oily manner : unctuous (*fml*), smooth, obsequious, ingratiating, smarmy (*infml*), glib, flattering.

OK *adjective* (*infml*)

acceptable, all right, fine, permitted, in order, fair, satisfactory, reasonable, tolerable, passable, not bad, good, adequate, convenient, correct, accurate.

▸ *noun* (*infml*)

authorization, approval, endorsement, go-ahead, permission, green light, consent, agreement.

▸ *verb* (*infml*)

approve, authorize, pass, give the go-ahead to, give the green light to (*infml*), rubber-stamp, agree to.

▸ *interj* (*infml*)

all right, fine, very well, agreed, right, yes.

old *adjective*

1 an old person : aged, elderly, advanced in years, grey, senile.

2 an old manuscript : ancient, original, primitive, antiquated, mature.

3 an old friend : long-standing, long-established, time-honoured, traditional.

4 an old model : obsolete, old-fashioned, out of date, worn-out, decayed, decrepit.

5 an old girlfriend : former, previous, earlier, one-time, ex-.

F3 1 young. 2 new. 4 modern. 5 current.

old-fashioned *adjective*

outmoded, out of date, outdated, dated, unfashionable, obsolete, behind the times, antiquated, archaic, passé, obsolescent, retro (*infml*).

F3 modern, up-to-date.

omen *noun*

portent, sign, warning, premonition, foreboding, augury, indication.

ominous *adjective*

portentous, inauspicious, foreboding, menacing, sinister, fateful, unpromising, threatening.

F3 auspicious, favourable.

omission *noun*

exclusion, gap, oversight, failure, lack, neglect, default, avoidance.

omit *verb*

leave out, exclude, miss out, pass over, overlook, drop, skip, eliminate, forget, neglect, leave undone, fail, disregard, edit out.

F3 include.

once *adverb*

formerly, previously, in the past, at one time, long ago, in times past, once upon a time, in the old days.

◆ **at once** **1** do it at once : immediately, instantly, directly, right away, straightaway, without delay, now, promptly, forthwith.

2 all arrived at once : simultaneously, together, at the same time.

one *adjective*

1 the one person who knows : single, solitary, lone, individual, only.

2 of one mind : united, harmonious, like-minded, whole, entire, complete, equal, identical, alike.

one-sided *adjective*

1 a one-sided grin : unbalanced, unequal, lopsided.

2 a one-sided argument : unfair, unjust, prejudiced, biased, partial, partisan.

3 a one-sided decision : unilateral, independent.

F3 1 balanced. 2 impartial. 3 bilateral, multilateral.

only *adverb*

just, at most, merely, simply, purely, barely, exclusively, solely.

▶ *adjective*

sole, single, solitary, lone, unique, exclusive, individual.

onset *noun*

beginning, start, commencement, inception, outset, outbreak.
E3 end, finish.

onus *noun*

burden, responsibility, load, obligation, duty, liability, task.

onward(s) *adverb*

forward, on, ahead, in front, beyond, forth.
E3 backward(s).

ooze *verb*

seep, exude, leak, escape, dribble, drip, drop, discharge, bleed, secrete, emit, overflow with, filter, drain.

opaque *adjective*

1 opaque glass: cloudy, clouded, murky, dull, dim, hazy, muddied, muddy, turbid.
2 a less opaque definition: obscure, unclear, impenetrable, incomprehensible, unintelligible, enigmatic, difficult.
E3 1 transparent. **2** clear, obvious, transparent.

open *adjective*

1 an open door: unclosed, ajar, gaping, uncovered, unfastened, unlocked, unsealed, yawning, lidless.
2 an open meeting/outlook: unrestricted, free, unobstructed, clear, accessible, exposed, unprotected, unsheltered, vacant, wide, available.
3 open opposition: overt, obvious, plain, evident, manifest, noticeable, flagrant, conspicuous.
4 an open question: undecided, unresolved, unsettled, debatable, problematic, moot.
5 an open manner: frank, candid, honest, guileless, natural, ingenuous, unreserved.
E3 1 shut. **2** restricted. **3** hidden. **4** decided. **5** reserved.
▶ *verb*

1 open the window/road: unfasten, undo, unlock, uncover, unseal, unblock, uncork, clear, expose.
2 opening her heart: explain,

divulge, disclose, lay bare.
3 flower opening: extend, spread (out), unfold, separate, split.
4 open the campaign: begin, start, commence, inaugurate, initiate, set in motion, launch.
E3 1 close, shut. **2** hide. **4** end, finish.

opening *noun*

1 an opening in the hedge: aperture, breach, gap, orifice, break, chink, crack, fissure, cleft, chasm, hole, split, vent, rupture.
2 the opening of discussions: start, onset, beginning, inauguration, inception, birth, dawn, launch.
3 looking for an opening in advertising: opportunity, chance, occasion, break (*infml*), place, vacancy.
E3 2 close, end.
▶ *adjective*

beginning, commencing, starting, first, inaugural, introductory, initial, early, primary.
E3 closing.

openly *adverb*

overtly, frankly, candidly, blatantly, flagrantly, plainly, unashamedly, unreservedly, glaringly, in public, in full view, shamelessly.
E3 secretly, slyly.

operate *verb*

1 torch operates on batteries: function, act, perform, run, work, go.
2 people who operate heavy machinery: control, handle, manage, use, utilize, manoeuvre.

operation *noun*

1 the operation of government/the machine: functioning, action, running, motion, movement, performance, working.
2 operation of the controls: influence, manipulation, handling, management, use, utilization.
3 runs an international mining operation: undertaking, enterprise, affair, procedure, proceeding, process, business, deal, transaction, effort.
4 a military operation: campaign, action, task, manoeuvre, exercise.

opinion *noun*

belief, judgement, view, point of view,

idea, perception, stance, theory, impression, feeling, sentiment, estimation, assessment, conception, mind, notion, way of thinking, persuasion, attitude.

opponent *noun*
adversary, enemy, antagonist, foe (*fml*), competitor, contestant, challenger, opposer, opposition, rival, objector, dissident.
F3 ally.

opportunity *noun*
chance, opening, break (*infml*), occasion, possibility, hour, moment.

oppose *verb*
1 opposing the plan: resist, withstand, counter, attack, combat, contest, stand up to, take a stand against, take issue with, confront, defy, face, fight, fly in the face of, hinder, obstruct, bar, check, prevent, thwart.
2 oppose one thing with the other: compare, contrast, match, offset, counterbalance, play off.
F3 1 defend, support.

opposed *adjective*
in opposition, against, hostile, conflicting, opposing, opposite, antagonistic, clashing, contrary, incompatible, anti.
F3 in favour.

opposite *adjective*
1 on the opposite bank: facing, fronting, corresponding.
2 opposite views: opposed, antagonistic, conflicting, contrary, hostile, adverse, contradictory, antithetical, irreconcilable, unlike, reverse, inconsistent, different, contrasted, differing.
F3 2 same.
▶ *noun*
reverse, converse, contrary, antithesis, contradiction, inverse.
F3 same.

opposition *noun*
1 met with a great deal of opposition: antagonism, hostility, resistance, obstructiveness, unfriendliness, disapproval.
2 beat the opposition: opponent, antagonist, rival, foe (*fml*), other side.

F3 1 co-operation, support. **2** ally, supporter.

oppression *noun*
tyranny, subjugation, subjection, repression, despotism, suppression, injustice, cruelty, brutality, abuse, persecution, maltreatment, harshness, hardship.

oppressive *adjective*
1 an oppressive atmosphere: airless, stuffy, close, stifling, suffocating, sultry, muggy, heavy.
2 an oppressive regime: tyrannical, despotic, overbearing, overwhelming, repressive, harsh, unjust, inhuman, cruel, brutal, burdensome, onerous, intolerable.
F3 1 airy. **2** just, gentle.

optimistic *adjective*
confident, assured, sanguine, hopeful, positive, cheerful, buoyant, bright, idealistic, expectant, upbeat (*infml*).
F3 pessimistic.

option *noun*
choice, alternative, preference, possibility, selection.

optional *adjective*
voluntary, discretionary, elective, free, unforced.
F3 compulsory.

orbit *noun*
1 circuit, cycle, circle, course, path, trajectory, track, revolution, rotation.
2 range, scope, domain, influence, sphere of influence, compass.
▶ *verb*
revolve, circle, encircle, circumnavigate.

ordeal *noun*
trial, test, tribulation(s), affliction, trouble(s), suffering, anguish, agony, pain, persecution, torture, nightmare.

order *noun*
1 an order of the court: command, directive, decree, injunction, instruction, direction, edict, ordinance, mandate, regulation, rule, precept (*fml*), law.
2 deal with your order immediately: requisition, request, booking, commission, reservation, application, demand.

3 change the order: arrangement, organization, grouping, disposition, sequence, categorization, classification, method, pattern, plan, system, array, layout, line-up, structure.
4 restore order: peace, quiet, calm, tranquillity, harmony, law and order, discipline.
5 a religious order: association, society, community, fraternity, brotherhood, sisterhood, lodge, guild, company, organization, denomination, sect, union.
6 an order of the animal kingdom: class, kind, sort, type, rank, species, hierarchy, family.
F3 3 confusion, disorder. **4** anarchy.
▶ *verb*
1 ordered them to go: command, instruct, direct, bid, decree, require, authorize.
2 ordered a taxi: request, reserve, book, apply for, requisition.
3 ordering the books according to author: arrange, organize, dispose, classify, group, marshal, sort out, lay out, manage, control, catalogue.
◆ **out of order 1 phone is out of order**: broken, broken down, not working, inoperative.
2 files are out of order: disordered, disorganized, out of sequence.

orderly *adjective*
1 an orderly system: ordered, systematic, neat, tidy, regular, methodical, in order, well-organized, well-regulated.
2 orderly conduct: well-behaved, controlled, disciplined, law-abiding.
F3 1 chaotic. **2** disorderly.

ordinary *adjective*
common, commonplace, regular, routine, standard, average, everyday, run-of-the-mill, usual, unexceptional, unremarkable, typical, normal, customary, common-or-garden, plain, familiar, habitual, simple, conventional, modest, mediocre, indifferent, pedestrian, prosaic, undistinguished.
F3 extraordinary, unusual.

organ *noun*
1 internal organs: device, instrument,

implement, tool, element, process, structure, unit, member.
2 (*fml*) **an organ of the state**: medium, agency, forum, vehicle, voice, mouthpiece, publication, newspaper, periodical, journal.

organization *noun*
1 a religious organization: association, institution, society, company, firm, corporation, federation, group, league, club, confederation, consortium.
2 efficient organization/the organization of society: arrangement, system, classification, methodology, order, formation, grouping, method, plan, structure, pattern, composition, configuration, design.

organize *verb*
1 organize the library: structure, co-ordinate, arrange, order, group, marshal, classify, systematize, tabulate, catalogue.
2 organize a strike: establish, found, set up, develop, form, frame, construct, shape, run.
F3 1 disorganize.

origin *noun*
1 the origin of the story: source, spring, fount, foundation, base, cause, derivation, provenance, roots, well-spring.
2 the origins of man: beginning, commencement, start, inauguration, launch, dawning, creation, emergence.
3 of Welsh origin: ancestry, descent, extraction, heritage, family, lineage, parentage, pedigree, birth, paternity, stock.
F3 2 end, termination.

original *adjective*
1 the original version: first, early, earliest, initial, primary, archetypal, rudimentary, embryonic, starting, opening, commencing, first-hand.
2 a very original piece of work: novel, innovative, new, creative, fresh, imaginative, inventive, unconventional, unusual, unique.
F3 1 latest. **2** hackneyed, unoriginal.
▶ *noun*
prototype, master, paradigm, model, pattern, archetype, standard, type.

originate *verb*
1 where does it originate from?: rise, arise, spring, stem, issue, flow, proceed, derive, come, evolve, emerge, be born.
2 the person who originated the idea: create, invent, inaugurate, introduce, give birth to, develop, discover, establish, begin, commence, start, set up, launch, pioneer, conceive, form, produce, generate.
F3 1 end, terminate.

ornament *noun*
decoration, adornment, embellishment, garnish, trimming, accessory, frill, trinket, bauble, jewel.
– *verb*
decorate, adorn, embellish, garnish, trim, beautify, brighten, dress up, deck, gild.

ornamental *adjective*
decorative, embellishing, adorning, attractive, showy.

ornate *adjective*
elaborate, ornamented, fancy, decorated, baroque, rococo, florid, flowery, fussy, busy, sumptuous.
F3 plain.

orthodox *adjective*
conformist, conventional, accepted, official, traditional, usual, well-established, established, received, customary, conservative, recognized, authoritative.
F3 nonconformist, unorthodox.

ostentatious *adjective*
showy, flashy, pretentious, vulgar, loud, garish, gaudy, flamboyant, conspicuous, extravagant.
F3 restrained.

ostracize *verb*
exclude, banish, exile, expel, excommunicate, reject, segregate, send to Coventry, shun, snub, boycott, avoid, cold-shoulder (*infml*), cut.
F3 accept, welcome.

other *adjective*
1 prefer some other method: different, dissimilar, unlike, separate, distinct, contrasting.
2 is there any other business?: more, further, extra, additional, supplementary, spare, alternative.

oust *verb*
expel, eject, depose, displace, turn out, throw out, overthrow, evict, drive out, unseat, dispossess, disinherit, replace, topple.
F3 install, settle.

out *adjective*
1 he's out at the moment: away, absent, elsewhere, not at home, gone, outside, abroad.
2 it will all be out in the open: revealed, exposed, disclosed, public, evident, manifest.
3 that's definitely out: forbidden, unacceptable, impossible, disallowed, excluded.
4 high heels are out now: out-of-date, unfashionable, old-fashioned, dated, passé, antiquated.
5 the fire is out: extinguished, finished, expired, dead, used up.
F3 1 in. **2** concealed. **3** allowed. **4** up-to-date, fashionable.

outbreak *noun*
eruption, outburst, explosion, flare-up, upsurge, flash, rash, burst, epidemic.

outburst *noun*
outbreak, eruption, explosion, flare-up, outpouring, burst, fit, gush, surge, storm, spasm, seizure, gale, attack, fit of temper.

outcast *noun*
castaway, exile, pariah, outsider, untouchable, refugee, reject, persona non grata.

outcome *noun*
result, consequence, upshot, conclusion, effect, end result.

outcry *noun*
protest, complaint, protestation, objection, dissent, indignation, uproar, cry, exclamation, clamour, row, commotion, noise, hue and cry, hullabaloo (*infml*), outburst.

outdated *adjective*
out-of-date, old-fashioned, dated, unfashionable, outmoded, behind the times, obsolete, obsolescent, antiquated, archaic.
F3 fashionable, modern.

outdo *verb*
surpass, exceed, beat, excel, outstrip,

outshine, get the better of, overcome, outclass, outdistance.

outer *adjective*
1 the outer wall: external, exterior, outside, outward, surface, peripheral.
2 the outer regions: outlying, distant, remote, further.
F3 1 internal. 2 inner.

outfit *noun*
1 a wedding outfit: clothes, costume, ensemble, get-up (*infml*), togs (*infml*), garb.
2 a picnic outfit: equipment, gear (*infml*), kit, rig, trappings, paraphernalia.
3 (*infml*) runs an outfit offering cheap travel: organization, firm, business, corporation, company, group, team, unit, set, set-up, crew, gang, squad.

outgoing *adjective*
1 an outgoing personality: sociable, friendly, unreserved, amiable, warm, approachable, expansive, open, extrovert, cordial, easy-going, communicative, demonstrative, sympathetic.
2 the outgoing chairman: departing, retiring, former, last, past, ex-.
F3 1 reserved. 2 incoming.

outlaw *noun*
bandit, brigand, robber, desperado, highwayman, criminal, marauder, pirate, fugitive.
▸ *verb*
ban, disallow, forbid, prohibit, exclude, embargo, bar, debar, banish, condemn.
F3 allow, legalize.

outlet *noun*
1 the outlet from the boiler: exit, way out, vent, egress, escape, opening, release, safety valve, channel.
2 open several outlets nationwide: retailer, shop, store, market.
F3 1 entry, inlet.

outline *noun*
1 an outline of the story: summary, synopsis, précis, bare facts, sketch, thumbnail sketch, abstract.
2 the outline of the hills: profile, form, contour, silhouette, shape.

▸ *verb*
sketch, summarize, draft, trace, rough out.

outlook *noun*
1 have a different outlook on life: view, viewpoint, point of view, attitude, perspective, frame of mind, angle, slant, standpoint, opinion.
2 the outlook is good: expectations, future, forecast, prospect, prognosis.

out-of-date *adjective*
old-fashioned, unfashionable, outdated, obsolete, dated, outmoded, antiquated, passé.
F3 fashionable, modern.

output *noun*
production, productivity, product, yield, manufacture, achievement.

outrage *noun*
1 wrote letters expressing their outrage: anger, fury, rage, indignation, shock, affront, horror.
2 their prices are an outrage: atrocity, offence, injury, enormity, barbarism, crime, violation, evil, scandal.
▸ *verb*
anger, infuriate, affront, incense, enrage, madden, disgust, injure, offend, shock, scandalize.

outrageous *adjective*
1 outrageous behaviour: atrocious, abominable, shocking, scandalous, offensive, disgraceful, monstrous, heinous (*fml*), unspeakable, horrible.
2 outrageous prices: excessive, exorbitant, immoderate, unreasonable, extortionate, inordinate, preposterous.
F3 2 acceptable, reasonable.

outright *adjective*
total, utter, absolute, complete, pure, downright, out-and-out, unqualified, unconditional, perfect, thorough, direct, definite, categorical, straightforward.
F3 ambiguous, indefinite.
▸ *adverb*
1 win outright: totally, absolutely, completely, utterly, thoroughly, openly, without restraint, straightforwardly, positively, directly, explicitly.
2 killed outright: instantaneously, at once, there and then, instantly, immediately.

outset *noun*
start, beginning, opening, inception, commencement, inauguration, kick-off (*infml*).
F∃ end, conclusion.

outside *adjective*
1 the outside world: external, exterior, outer, surface, superficial, outward, extraneous, outdoor, outermost, extreme.
2 an outside chance: remote, marginal, distant, faint, slight, slim, negligible.
F∃ 1 inside.
▶ *noun*
exterior, façade, front, surface, face, appearance, cover.
F∃ inside.

outsider *noun*
stranger, intruder, alien, non-member, non-resident, foreigner, newcomer, visitor, interloper, misfit, odd man out.

outskirts *noun*
suburbs, vicinity, periphery, fringes, borders, boundary, edge, margin.
F∃ centre.

outspoken *adjective*
candid, frank, forthright, blunt, unreserved, plain-spoken, direct, explicit.
F∃ diplomatic, reserved.

outstanding *adjective*
1 an outstanding success/ performance: excellent, distinguished, eminent, pre-eminent, celebrated, exceptional, superior, remarkable, prominent, superb, great, notable, impressive, striking, superlative, important, noteworthy, memorable, special, extraordinary.
2 the amount outstanding: owing, unpaid, due, unsettled, unresolved, uncollected, pending, payable, remaining, ongoing, leftover.
F∃ 1 ordinary, unexceptional. 2 paid, settled.

outstrip *verb*
surpass, exceed, better, outdo, beat, top, transcend, outshine, pass, gain on, leave behind, leave standing, outrun, outdistance, overtake, eclipse.

outward *adjective*
external, exterior, outer, outside, surface, superficial, visible, apparent, observable, evident, supposed, professed, public, obvious, ostensible.
F∃ inner, private.

outwit *verb*
outsmart, outthink, get the better of, trick, better, beat, dupe, cheat, deceive, defraud, swindle.

oval *adjective*
egg-shaped, elliptical, ovoid, ovate.

over *adjective*
finished, ended, done with, concluded, past, gone, completed, closed, in the past, settled, up, forgotten, accomplished.
▶ *adverb*
1 it sailed over our heads: above, beyond, overhead, on high.
2 there were six left over: extra, remaining, surplus, superfluous, left, unclaimed, unused, unwanted, in excess, in addition.
▶ *preposition*
1 the roof over our heads: higher than, above.
2 the person over me: above, in charge of, in command of.
3 over the odds: exceeding, more than, in excess of.

overall *adjective*
total, all-inclusive, all-embracing, comprehensive, inclusive, general, universal, global, broad, blanket, complete, all-over.
F∃ narrow, specific.
▶ *adverb*
in general, on the whole, by and large, broadly, generally speaking.

overcast *adjective*
cloudy, grey, dull, dark, sombre, sunless, hazy, lowering.
F∃ bright, clear.

overcharge *verb*
surcharge, short-change, cheat, extort, rip off (*infml*), sting (*infml*), do (*infml*), diddle (*infml*).
F∃ undercharge.

overcome *verb*
conquer, defeat, beat, surmount, triumph over, vanquish (*fml*), rise above, master, overpower, overwhelm, overthrow, subdue.

overcrowded *adjective*
congested, packed (out), jam-packed, crammed full, chock-full, overpopulated, overloaded, swarming.
₣₃ deserted, empty.

overdo *verb*
exaggerate, go too far, carry to excess, go overboard (*infml*), lay it on thick (*infml*), overindulge, overstate, overact, overplay, overwork.

overdue *adjective*
late, behindhand, behind schedule, delayed, owing, unpunctual, slow.
₣₃ early.

overflow *verb*
spill, overrun, run over, pour over, well over, brim over, bubble over, surge, flood, inundate, deluge, shower, submerge, soak, swamp, teem.
▶ *noun*
overspill, spill, inundation, flood, overabundance, surplus.

overhang *verb*
jut, project, bulge, protrude, stick out, extend.

overhaul *verb*
1 overhaul the engine: renovate, repair, service, recondition, mend, examine, inspect, check, survey, re-examine, fix.
2 was overhauled by a more powerful car: overtake, pull ahead of, outpace, outstrip, gain on, pass.
▶ *noun*
reconditioning, repair, renovation, check, service, examination, inspection, going-over (*infml*).

overhead *adverb*
above, up above, on high, upward.
₣₃ below, underfoot.
▶ *adjective*
elevated, aerial, overhanging, raised.

overload *verb*
burden, oppress, strain, tax, weigh down, overcharge, encumber.

overlook *verb*
1 overlooking the sea: front on to, face, look on to, look over, command a view of.
2 overlooked several spelling mistakes: miss, disregard, ignore, omit, neglect, pass over, let pass, let ride.
3 overlook your lateness this once:

excuse, forgive, pardon, condone, wink at, turn a blind eye to.
₣₃ **2** notice. **3** penalize.

overpowering *adjective*
overwhelming, powerful, strong, forceful, irresistible, uncontrollable, compelling, extreme, oppressive, suffocating, unbearable, nauseating, sickening.

overrule *verb*
overturn, override, countermand, revoke, reject, rescind, reverse, invalidate, cancel, vote down.

overrun *verb*
1 country was overrun by the enemy troops: invade, occupy, infest, overwhelm, inundate, run riot, spread over, swamp, swarm over, surge over, ravage, overgrow.
2 overrun the time allowed: exceed, overshoot, overstep, overreach.

overshadow *verb*
1 overshadowing her face: obscure, cloud, darken, dim, spoil, veil.
2 overshadowed by his more talented brother: outshine, eclipse, excel, surpass, dominate, dwarf, put in the shade, rise above, tower above.

oversight *noun*
1 an oversight on his part: lapse, omission, fault, error, slip-up (*infml*), mistake, blunder, carelessness, neglect.
2 left to the oversight of the committee: supervision, responsibility, care, charge, control, custody, keeping, administration, management, direction.

overt *adjective*
open, manifest, plain, evident, observable, obvious, apparent, public, professed, unconcealed.
₣₃ covert, secret.

overtake *verb*
1 overtake a lorry: pass, catch up with, outdistance, outstrip, draw level with, pull ahead of, overhaul.
2 overtaken by events: come upon, befall, happen, strike, engulf.

overthrow *verb*
depose, oust, bring down, topple, unseat, displace, dethrone, conquer,

vanquish (*fml*), beat, defeat, crush, overcome, overpower, overturn, overwhelm, subdue, master, abolish, upset.

E install, protect, reinstate, restore.

▶ *noun*

ousting, unseating, defeat, deposition, dethronement, fall, rout, undoing, suppression, downfall, end, humiliation, destruction, ruin.

overtone *noun*

suggestion, intimation, nuance, hint, undercurrent, insinuation, connotation, association, feeling, implication, sense, flavour.

overturn *verb*

1 car overturned : capsize, upset, upturn, tip over, topple, overbalance, keel over, knock over, spill.

2 overturned the decision : overthrow, repeal, rescind, reverse, annul, abolish, destroy, quash, set aside.

overwhelm *verb*

1 problems threatened to overwhelm them : overcome, overpower, destroy, defeat, crush, rout, devastate.

2 their troops were overwhelmed by a stronger force : overrun, inundate, snow under, submerge, swamp, engulf.

3 your generosity overwhelms me : confuse, bowl over, stagger, floor.

overwork *verb*

overstrain, overload, exploit, exhaust, overuse, overtax, strain, wear out, oppress, burden, weary.

owing *adjective*

unpaid, due, owed, in arrears, outstanding, payable, unsettled, overdue.

◆ **owing to** because of, as a result of, on account of, thanks to.

own *adjective*

personal, individual, private, particular, idiosyncratic.

▶ *verb*

possess, have, hold, retain, keep, enjoy.

◆ **own up** admit, confess, come clean (*infml*), tell the truth, acknowledge.

owner *noun*

possessor, holder, landlord, landlady, proprietor, proprietress, master, mistress, freeholder.

P p

pace *noun*
step, stride, walk, gait, tread, movement, motion, progress, rate, speed, velocity, celerity, quickness, rapidity, tempo, measure.
▶ *verb*
step, stride, walk, march, tramp, pound, patrol, mark out, measure.

pacify *verb*
appease, conciliate, placate, mollify, calm, compose, soothe, assuage (*fml*), allay, moderate, soften, lull, still, quiet, silence, quell, crush, put down, tame, subdue.
🖃 anger.

pack *noun*
1 **a pack of cigarettes:** packet, box, carton, parcel, package, bundle, burden, load, backpack, rucksack, haversack, knapsack, kitbag.
2 **a pack of wolves:** group, company, troop, herd, flock, band, crowd, gang, mob.
▶ *verb*
1 **pack books into boxes:** wrap, parcel, package, bundle, stow, store.
2 **packed them into the theatre:** cram, stuff, crowd, throng, press, ram, wedge, compact, compress, fill, load, charge.

package *noun*
parcel, pack, packet, box, carton, bale, consignment.

packed *adjective*
filled, full, jam-packed, chock-a-block, crammed, crowded, congested.
🖃 empty, deserted.

packet *noun*
pack, carton, box, bag, package, parcel, case, container, wrapper, wrapping, packing.

pact *noun*
treaty, convention, covenant, bond, alliance, cartel, contract, deal, bargain, compact, agreement, arrangement, understanding.
🖃 disagreement, quarrel.

pad *verb*
fill, stuff, wad, pack, wrap, line, cushion, protect.
◆ **pad out** expand, inflate, fill out, augment, amplify, elaborate, flesh out, lengthen, stretch, protract, spin out.

paddle[1] *verb*
paddle a canoe: row, oar, scull, propel, steer.
▶ *noun*
oar, scull.

paddle[2] *verb*
paddle in the sea: wade, splash, slop, dabble.

pagan *noun*
heathen, atheist, unbeliever, infidel, idolater.
🖃 believer.
▶ *adjective*
heathen, irreligious, atheistic, godless, infidel, idolatrous.

page *noun*
leaf, sheet, folio, side.

pageantry *noun*
pomp, ceremony, grandeur, magnificence, splendour, glamour, glitter, spectacle, parade, display, show, extravagance, theatricality, drama, melodrama.

pain *noun*
1 **a pain in his stomach/feel pain:** hurt, ache, throb, cramp, spasm, twinge, pang, stab, sting, smart, soreness, tenderness, discomfort, distress,

suffering, affliction, trouble, anguish, agony, torment, torture.
2 (*infml*) it's a pain: nuisance, bother, bore (*infml*), annoyance, vexation, burden, headache (*infml*).
► *verb*
hurt, afflict, torment, torture, agonize, distress, upset, sadden, grieve.
🖃 please, delight, gratify.

painful *adjective*
1 a painful wound: sore, tender, aching, throbbing, smarting, stabbing, agonizing, excruciating.
2 a painful experience: unpleasant, disagreeable, distressing, upsetting, saddening, harrowing, traumatic.
🖃 **1** painless, soothing. **2** pleasant, agreeable.

painkiller *noun*
analgesic, anodyne, anaesthetic, palliative (*fml*), sedative, drug, remedy.

painless *adjective*
pain-free, trouble-free, effortless, easy, simple, undemanding.
🖃 painful, difficult.

pains *noun*
trouble, bother, effort, labour, care, diligence.

painstaking *adjective*
careful, meticulous, scrupulous, thorough, conscientious, diligent, assiduous (*fml*), industrious, hardworking, dedicated, devoted, persevering.
🖃 careless, negligent.

paint *noun*
colour, colouring, pigment, dye, tint, stain.
► *verb*
1 paint the ceiling: colour, dye, tint, stain, lacquer, varnish, glaze, apply, daub, coat, cover, decorate.
2 paint a portrait: portray, depict, describe, recount, picture, represent.

Terms used in painting include:

abstract, acrylics, alla prima, aquarelle, aquatint, canvas, canvas board, capriccio, chiaroscuro, collage, composition, craquelure, diptych, drawing, easel, encaustic, facture, figurative, filbert brush, flat brush,

foreground, foreshortening, fresco, frieze, frottage, genre painting, gesso, gouache, grisaille, grotesque, icon, impasto, landscape, mahlstick, miniature, monochrome, montage, mural, oil painting, palette, palette knife, pastels, pastoral, paysage, pentimento, perspective, pieta, pigment, pochade box, pointillism, portrait, primer, round brush, sable brush, scumble, seascape, secco, sfumato, sgraffito, silhouette, sketch, skyscape, still life, stipple, tempera, tint, tondo, tone, triptych, trompe l'œil, turpentine, underpainting, vanishing point, vignette, wash, watercolour.

pair *noun*
couple, brace, twosome, duo, twins, two of a kind.
► *verb*
match (up), twin, team, mate, marry, wed, splice, join, couple, link, bracket, put together.
🖃 separate, part.

palatable *adjective*
tasty, appetizing, eatable, edible, acceptable, satisfactory, pleasant, agreeable, enjoyable, attractive.
🖃 unpalatable, unacceptable, unpleasant, disagreeable.

pale *adjective*
1 I went/look pale: pallid, livid, ashen, ashy, white, chalky, pasty, pasty-faced, waxen, waxy, wan, sallow, anaemic.
2 pale blue: light, pastel, faded, washed-out, bleached, colourless, insipid, vapid, weak, feeble, faint, dim.
🖃 **1** ruddy. **2** dark.
► *verb*
whiten, blanch, bleach, fade, dim.
🖃 colour, blush.

pall[1] *noun*
a pall of dust: shroud, veil, mantle, cloak, cloud, shadow, gloom, damper.

pall[2] *verb*
quite exciting at first, but soon palled: tire, weary, jade, sate, satiate, cloy, sicken.

palpable *adjective*
solid, substantial, material, real,

paltry *adjective*
meagre, derisory, contemptible, mean, low, miserable, wretched, poor, sorry, small, slight, trifling, inconsiderable, negligible, trivial, minor, petty, unimportant, insignificant, worthless.
F3 substantial, significant, valuable.

pamper *verb*
cosset, coddle, mollycoddle, humour, gratify, indulge, overindulge, spoil, pet, fondle.
F3 neglect, ill-treat.

pamphlet *noun*
leaflet, brochure, booklet, folder, circular, handout, notice.

panache *noun*
flourish, flamboyance, ostentation, style, flair, élan, dash, spirit, enthusiasm, zest, energy, vigour, verve.

pandemonium *noun*
chaos, disorder, confusion, rumpus, commotion, turmoil, turbulence, tumult, uproar, din, bedlam, hubbub, hullabaloo, hue and cry, to-do (*infml*).
F3 order, calm, peace.

pander to *verb*
humour, indulge, pamper, please, gratify, satisfy, fulfil, provide, cater to.

panel *noun*
board, committee, jury, team.

pang *noun*
pain, ache, twinge, stab, sting, prick, stitch, gripe, spasm, throe, agony, anguish, discomfort, distress.

panic *noun*
agitation, flap (*infml*), alarm, dismay, consternation, fright, fear, horror, terror, frenzy, hysteria.
F3 calmness, confidence.
▸ *verb*
lose one's nerve, lose one's head, go to pieces, flap (*infml*), overreact.
F3 relax.

panic-stricken *adjective*
alarmed, frightened, horrified, terrified, petrified, scared stiff, in a cold sweat, panicky, frantic, frenzied, hysterical.
F3 relaxed, confident.

panoramic *adjective*
scenic, wide, sweeping, extensive, far-reaching, widespread, overall, general, universal.
F3 narrow, restricted, limited.

pant *verb*
puff, blow, gasp, wheeze, breathe, sigh, heave, throb, palpitate.

pants *noun*
1 **wearing a vest and pants**: underpants, drawers, panties, briefs, knickers (*infml*), thong, Y-fronts, boxer shorts, trunks, shorts.
2 (*US*) **he put his wallet in the back pocket of his pants**: trousers, slacks, jeans.

paper *noun*
1 **a daily paper/the Sunday papers**: newspaper, daily, broadsheet, tabloid, rag (*infml*), journal, organ (*fml*).
2 **personal/travel/legal papers**: document, credential, authorization, identification, certificate, deed.
3 **a paper on alternative medicine**: essay, composition, dissertation, thesis, treatise, article, report.

parade *noun*
procession, cavalcade, motorcade, march, column, file, train, review, ceremony, spectacle, pageant, show, display, exhibition.
▸ *verb*
1 **parade down the high street**: march, process, file past.
2 **parading his recently-acquired wealth**: show, display, exhibit, show off, vaunt, flaunt, brandish.

paradise *noun*
heaven, utopia, Shangri-La, Elysium, Eden, bliss, nirvana, delight.
F3 hell, Hades.

parallel *adjective*
equidistant, aligned, coextensive, alongside, analogous, equivalent, corresponding, matching, like, similar, resembling.
F3 divergent, different.
▸ *noun*
1 **have no parallel**: match, equal, twin,

duplicate, analogue, equivalent, counterpart.
2 draw a parallel: similarity, resemblance, likeness, correspondence, correlation, equivalence, analogy, comparison.
▶ *verb*
match, echo, conform, agree, correspond, correlate, compare, liken.
F∃ diverge, differ.

paralyse *verb*
cripple, lame, disable, incapacitate, immobilize, anaesthetize, numb, deaden, freeze, transfix, halt, stop.

paralysed *adjective*
paralytic, paraplegic, quadriplegic, crippled, lame, disabled, incapacitated, immobilized, numb.
F∃ able-bodied.

paralysis *noun*
1 paralysis in the legs: paraplegia, quadriplegia, palsy, numbness, deadness, immobility.
2 paralysis of the transport system: halt, standstill, stoppage, shutdown.

paraphernalia *noun*
equipment, gear (*infml*), tackle, apparatus, accessories, trappings, bits and pieces, odds and ends, belongings, effects, stuff (*infml*), things, baggage.

paraphrase *noun*
rewording, rephrasing, restatement, version, interpretation, rendering, translation.
▶ *verb*
reword, rephrase, restate, interpret, render, translate.

parcel *noun*
package, packet, pack, box, carton, bundle.

parch *verb*
dry (up), desiccate, dehydrate, bake, burn, scorch, sear, blister, wither, shrivel.

parched *adjective*
1 a parched landscape: arid, waterless, dry, dried up, dehydrated, scorched, withered, shrivelled.
2 (*infml*) **I'm absolutely parched**: thirsty, gasping (*infml*).

pardon *verb*
forgive, condone, overlook, excuse, vindicate, acquit, absolve, remit, let off, reprieve, free, liberate, release.
F∃ punish, discipline.
▶ *noun*
forgiveness, mercy, clemency, indulgence, amnesty, excuse, acquittal, absolution, reprieve, release, discharge.
F∃ punishment, condemnation.

pare *verb*
peel, skin, shear, clip, trim, crop, cut, dock, lop, prune, cut back, reduce, decrease.

parent *noun*
father, mother, dam, sire (*fml*), progenitor (*fml*), begetter (*fml*), procreator (*fml*), guardian.

park *noun*
grounds, estate, parkland, gardens, woodland, reserve, pleasure-ground.
▶ *verb*
put, position, deposit, leave.

parliament *noun*
legislature, senate, congress, house, assembly, convocation (*fml*), council, diet.

parody *noun*
caricature, lampoon, burlesque, satire, send-up, spoof, skit, mimicry, imitation, take-off, travesty, distortion.

part *noun*
1 have some parts missing: component, constituent, element, factor, piece, bit, particle, fragment, scrap, segment, fraction, portion, share.
2 a different part of the organization/ country: section, division, department, branch, sector, district, region, territory.
3 get a part in a film: role, character.
4 did his part to make it a success: duty, task, responsibility, office, function, capacity.
F∃ 1 whole, totality.
▶ *verb*
1 part on the best of terms: separate, part company, split up, break up, disband, leave, depart, withdraw, go away.
2 part the curtains: separate, divide,

detach, disconnect, sever, split, tear, break, take apart, dismantle, come apart, disunite.
◆ **part with** relinquish, let go of, give up, yield, surrender, renounce, forgo, abandon, discard, jettison.

partial *adjective*
1 a partial victory: incomplete, limited, restricted, imperfect, fragmentary, unfinished.
2 someone less partial should judge: biased, prejudiced, partisan, one-sided, discriminatory, unfair, unjust, predisposed, coloured, affected.
F∃ 1 complete, total. 2 impartial, disinterested, unbiased, fair.
◆ **partial to** fond of, keen on, crazy about (*infml*), mad about (*infml*).

participate *verb*
take part, join in, contribute, engage, be involved, enter, share, partake, co-operate, help, assist.

particle *noun*
bit, piece, fragment, scrap, shred, sliver, speck, morsel, crumb, iota, whit, jot, tittle, atom, grain, drop.

particular *adjective*
1 on that particular day: specific, precise, exact, distinct, special, peculiar.
2 made a particular effort to be polite: exceptional, remarkable, notable, marked, thorough, unusual, uncommon.
3 not very particular about hygiene: fussy, discriminating, choosy (*infml*), finicky, fastidious.
F∃ 1 general.
▶ *noun*
detail, specific, point, feature, item, fact, circumstance.

particularly *adverb*
especially, exceptionally, remarkably, notably, extraordinarily, unusually, uncommonly, surprisingly, in particular, specifically, explicitly, distinctly.

parting *noun*
1 an emotional parting: departure, going, leave-taking, farewell, goodbye, adieu.

2 a parting of the ways: divergence, separation, division, partition, rift, split, rupture, breaking.
F∃ 1 meeting. 2 convergence.
▶ *adjective*
departing, farewell, last, dying, final, closing, concluding.
F∃ first.

partition *noun*
1 build a partition in one corner: divider, barrier, wall, panel, screen, room-divider.
2 the partition of the country: division, break-up, splitting, separation, parting, severance.
▶ *verb*
separate, divide, subdivide, wall off, fence off, screen.

partly *adverb*
somewhat, to some extent, to a certain extent, up to a point, slightly, fractionally, moderately, relatively, in part, partially, incompletely.
F∃ completely, totally.

partner *noun*
1 partner in crime: associate, ally, confederate, colleague, team-mate, collaborator, accomplice, helper, mate, sidekick (*infml*), companion, comrade.
2 my life partner: spouse, husband, wife, consort, boyfriend, girlfriend, other half (*infml*), significant other.

partnership *noun*
1 go into partnership: alliance, confederation, affiliation, combination, union, syndicate, co-operative, association, society, corporation, company, firm, fellowship, fraternity, brotherhood, sisterhood.
2 partnership in government: collaboration, co-operation, participation, sharing.

party *noun*
1 a birthday party: celebration, festivity, social, do (*infml*), knees-up (*infml*), rave-up (*infml*), bash (*infml*), get-together, gathering, reunion, function, reception, at-home, housewarming.

Kinds of party include:

acid-house party, barbecue, bash (*infml*), beanfeast (*infml*), beano (*infml*), birthday party, bunfight (*infml*), ceilidh, cocktail party, dinner party, disco, discotheque, do (*infml*), flatwarming, garden party, gathering of the clan (*infml*), Hallowe'en party, hen party, hooley (*infml*), hootenanny (*US infml*), housewarming, knees-up (*infml*), picnic, pyjama party, rave, rave-up (*infml*), shindig (*infml*), shivoo (*infml*), shower (*US infml*), sleepover, slumber party (*US*), social, soirée, stag night, stag party, supper party, tea party, thrash (*infml*), welcoming party. ⇨*See also* **celebration**.

2 a search party: team, squad, crew, gang, band, group, company, detachment.

3 a political party: faction, side, league, cabal, alliance, association, grouping, combination.

4 the other party: person, individual, litigant, plaintiff, defendant.

pass[1] *verb*
1 passed the other runners and went on to win: surpass, exceed, go beyond, outdo, outstrip, overtake, leave behind.
2 passing the time: spend, while away, fill, occupy.
3 time passing slowly: go past, go by, elapse, lapse, proceed, roll, flow, run, move, go, disappear, vanish.
4 passed him the butter/passed secrets to the enemy: give, hand, transfer, transmit.
5 legislation passed by parliament: enact, ratify, validate, adopt, authorize, sanction, approve.
6 pass an exam: succeed, get through, qualify, graduate.
▶ *noun*
1 a good pass to the midfielder: throw, kick, move, lunge, swing.
2 a 24-hour pass: permit, passport, identification, ticket, licence, authorization, warrant, permission.
◆ **pass away** die, pass on, expire, decease, give up the ghost.
◆ **pass out 1** he passed out when he

saw the blood: faint, lose consciousness, black out, collapse, flake out, keel over (*infml*), drop.
2 passed out the exam papers: give out, hand out, dole out, distribute, deal out, share out.
◆ **pass over** disregard, ignore, overlook, miss, omit, leave, neglect.

pass[2] *noun*
a mountain pass: col, defile (*fml*), gorge, ravine, canyon, gap, passage.

passable *adjective*
1 gave a passable performance: satisfactory, acceptable, allowable, tolerable, average, ordinary, unexceptional, moderate, fair, adequate, all right, OK (*infml*), mediocre.
2 the road is now passable: clear, unobstructed, unblocked, open, navigable.
F3 1 unacceptable, excellent. **2** obstructed, blocked, impassable.

passage *noun*
1 a long unlit passage: passageway, aisle, corridor, hall, hallway.
2 read a short passage from the Bible: extract, excerpt, quotation, text, paragraph, section, piece, clause, verse.
3 book a passage to Australia: journey, voyage, trip, crossing.

passing *adjective*
ephemeral, transient, short-lived, temporary, momentary, fleeting, brief, short, cursory, hasty, quick, slight, superficial, shallow, casual, incidental.
F3 lasting, permanent.

passion *noun*
feeling, emotion, love, adoration, infatuation, fondness, affection, lust, itch, desire, craving, fancy, mania, obsession, craze, eagerness, keenness, avidity, zest, enthusiasm, fanaticism, zeal, ardour, fervour, warmth, heat, fire, spirit, intensity, vehemence, anger, indignation, fury, rage, outburst.
F3 coolness, indifference, self-possession.

passionate *adjective*
1 feel passionate about the subject: ardent, fervent, eager, keen, avid,

enthusiastic, fanatical, zealous, warm, hot, fiery, inflamed, aroused, excited, impassioned, intense, strong, fierce, vehement, violent, stormy, tempestuous, wild, frenzied.
2 a passionate nature : emotional, excitable, hot-headed, impetuous, impulsive, quick-tempered, irritable.
Eᴈ 1 phlegmatic, laid-back (*infml*).

passive *adjective*
receptive, unassertive, submissive, docile, unresisting, non-violent, patient, resigned, long-suffering, indifferent, apathetic, lifeless, inert, inactive, non-participating.
Eᴈ active, lively, responsive, involved.

past *adjective*
1 the time is past : over, ended, finished, completed, done, over and done with.
2 past experiences : former, previous, preceding, foregoing, late, recent.
3 past times : ancient, bygone, olden, early, gone, no more, extinct, defunct, forgotten.
Eᴈ 2 future.
▶ *noun*
1 in the past : history, former times, olden days, antiquity.
2 know nothing about her past : life, background, history, experience, track record.
Eᴈ 1 future.

paste *noun*
adhesive, glue, gum, mastic, putty, cement.
▶ *verb*
stick, glue, gum, cement, fix.

pastime *noun*
hobby, activity, game, sport, recreation, play, fun, amusement, entertainment, diversion, distraction, relaxation.
Eᴈ work, employment.

pastoral *adjective*
1 a pastoral landscape : rural, country, rustic, bucolic (*fml*), agricultural, agrarian, idyllic.
2 pastoral duties/a pastoral visit : ecclesiastical, clerical, priestly, ministerial.
Eᴈ 1 urban.

pasture *noun*
grass, grassland, meadow, field, paddock, pasturage, grazing.

pasty *adjective*
pale, pallid, wan, anaemic, pasty-faced, sickly, unhealthy.
Eᴈ ruddy, healthy.

pat *verb*
tap, dab, slap, touch, stroke, caress, fondle, pet.
▶ *noun*
tap, dab, slap, touch, stroke, caress.
▶ *adverb*
precisely, exactly, perfectly, flawlessly, faultlessly, fluently.
Eᴈ imprecisely, inaccurately, wrongly.
▶ *adjective*
glib, fluent, smooth, slick, ready, easy, facile, simplistic.

patch *noun*
piece, bit, scrap, spot, area, stretch, tract, plot, lot, parcel.
▶ *verb*
mend, repair, fix, cover, reinforce.

patchy *adjective*
uneven, irregular, inconsistent, variable, random, fitful, erratic, sketchy, bitty, spotty, blotchy.
Eᴈ even, uniform, regular, consistent.

path *noun*
route, course, direction, way, passage, road, avenue, lane, footpath, bridleway, trail, track, walk.

pathetic *adjective*
1 a pathetic sight : pitiable, poor, sorry, lamentable, miserable, sad, distressing, moving, touching, poignant, plaintive, heart-rending, heartbreaking.
2 (*infml*) **a pathetic attempt at humour** : contemptible, derisory, deplorable, useless, worthless, inadequate, meagre, feeble.
Eᴈ 1 cheerful. **2** admirable, excellent, valuable.

patience *noun*
calmness, composure, self-control, restraint, tolerance, forbearance, endurance, fortitude, long-suffering, submission, resignation, stoicism, persistence, perseverance, diligence.
Eᴈ impatience, intolerance, exasperation.

patient *adjective*
calm, composed, self-possessed, self-controlled, restrained, even-tempered, mild, lenient, indulgent, understanding, forgiving, tolerant, accommodating, forbearing, long-suffering, uncomplaining, submissive, resigned, philosophical, stoical, persistent, persevering.
F3 impatient, restless, intolerant, exasperated.
▸ *noun*
invalid, sufferer, case, client.

patriotic *adjective*
nationalistic, chauvinistic, jingoistic, loyal, flag-waving.

patrol *verb*
police, guard, protect, defend, go the rounds, tour, inspect.

patron *noun*
1 a patron of the arts: benefactor, philanthropist, sponsor, backer, supporter, sympathizer, advocate, champion, defender, protector, guardian, helper.
2 the shop's regular patrons: customer, client, frequenter, regular, shopper, buyer, purchaser, subscriber.

patronize *verb*
1 patronize the arts: sponsor, fund, back, support, maintain, help, assist, promote, foster, encourage.
2 doesn't patronize the local shops: frequent, shop at, buy from, deal with.

patronizing *adjective*
condescending, stooping, overbearing, high-handed, haughty, superior, snobbish, supercilious, disdainful.
F3 humble, lowly.

patter *noun*
1 the patter of tiny feet: pattering, tapping, pitter-patter, beating.
2 a salesman's patter: chatter, gabble, jabber, line, pitch, spiel (*infml*), jargon, lingo (*infml*).

pattern *noun*
1 a pattern of behaviour: system, method, order, plan.
2 a striped pattern: decoration, ornamentation, ornament, figure, motif, design, style.
3 was the pattern for many other

schemes: model, template, stencil, guide, original, prototype, standard, norm.

pause *verb*
halt, stop, cease, discontinue, break off, interrupt, take a break, rest, wait, delay, hesitate.
▸ *noun*
halt, stoppage, interruption, break, rest, breather (*infml*), lull, let-up (*infml*), respite, gap, interval, interlude, intermission, wait, delay, hesitation.

pay *verb*
1 pay £30/the bill: remit, settle, discharge, reward, remunerate, recompense, reimburse, repay, refund, spend, pay out.
2 the business didn't pay: benefit, profit, pay off, bring in, yield, return.
3 pay for one's mistakes: atone, make amends, compensate, answer, suffer.
▸ *noun*
remuneration, wages, salary, earnings, income, fee, stipend, honorarium, emoluments, payment, reward, recompense, compensation, reimbursement.
◆ **pay back 1 pay back a loan**: repay, refund, reimburse, recompense, settle, square.
2 I'll pay him back for that: retaliate, get one's own back, take revenge, get even with, reciprocate, counter-attack.
◆ **pay off 1 pay off a debt**: discharge, settle, square, clear.
2 had to pay off half the workforce: dismiss, fire (*infml*), sack (*infml*), lay off.
3 the preparations paid off: succeed, work.

payment *noun*
remittance, settlement, discharge, premium, outlay, advance, deposit, instalment, contribution, donation, allowance, reward, remuneration, pay, fee, hire, fare, toll.

peace *noun*
1 peace, perfect peace: silence, quiet, hush, stillness, rest, relaxation, tranquillity, calm, calmness, composure, contentment.
2 negotiate a lasting peace: armistice, truce, ceasefire, conciliation, concord,

harmony, agreement, treaty.
F3 1 noise, disturbance. **2** war, disagreement.

peaceable *adjective*
pacific, peace-loving, unwarlike, non-violent, conciliatory, friendly, amicable, inoffensive, gentle, placid, easy-going (*infml*), mild.
F3 belligerent, aggressive.

peaceful *adjective*
quiet, still, restful, relaxing, tranquil, serene, calm, placid, unruffled, undisturbed, untroubled, friendly, amicable, peaceable, pacific, gentle.
F3 noisy, disturbed, troubled, violent.

peak *noun*
top, summit, pinnacle, crest, crown, zenith, height, maximum, climax, culmination, apex, tip, point.
F3 nadir, trough.
▶ *verb*
climax, culminate, come to a head.

peal *noun*
chime, carillon, toll, knell, ring, clang, ringing, crash, reverberation, rumble, roar, clap.
▶ *verb*
chime, toll, ring, clang, resonate, crash, reverberate, resound, rumble, roll, roar.

peculiar *adjective*
1 *a peculiar person*: strange, odd, curious, funny, weird, bizarre, extraordinary, unusual, abnormal, exceptional, unconventional, offbeat, eccentric, way-out (*infml*), outlandish, exotic.
2 *a peculiar way of pronouncing certain words*: characteristic, distinctive, specific, particular, special, individual, personal, idiosyncratic, unique, singular.
F3 1 ordinary, normal. **2** general, normal.

pedestrian *noun*
walker, foot-traveller.
▶ *adjective*
dull, boring, flat, uninspired, banal, mundane, run-of-the-mill, commonplace, ordinary, mediocre, indifferent, prosaic, stodgy, plodding.
F3 exciting, imaginative.

pedigree *noun*
genealogy, family tree, lineage, ancestry, descent, line, family, parentage, derivation, extraction, race, breed, stock, blood.

peel *verb*
pare, skin, strip, scale, flake (off).
▶ *noun*
skin, rind, zest, peeling.

peep *verb*
look, peek, glimpse, spy, squint, peer, emerge, issue, appear.
▶ *noun*
look, peek, glimpse, glance, squint.

peer[1] *verb*
peering through the dirty window: look, gaze, scan, scrutinize, examine, inspect, spy, snoop, peep, squint.

peer[2] *noun*
1 *a peer of the realm*: aristocrat, noble, nobleman, lord, lady, duke, duchess, marquess, marquis, earl, count, viscount, baron.
2 *amongst one's peers*: equal, counterpart, equivalent, match, fellow.

peevish *adjective*
petulant, querulous (*fml*), fractious, fretful, touchy, complaining, irritable, cross, grumpy, ratty (*infml*), crotchety, ill-tempered, crabbed, cantankerous, crusty, snappy, short-tempered, surly, sullen, sulky.
F3 good-tempered.

peg *verb*
1 *I pegged the washing to the line*: fasten, secure, fix, attach, join.
2 *peg prices*: control, stabilize, limit, freeze, fix, set.
▶ *noun*
pin, dowel, hook, knob, marker, post, stake.

pelt *verb*
1 *pelted them with rotten fruit*: throw, hurl, bombard, shower, assail, batter, beat, hit, strike.
2 *it's pelting outside*: pour, teem, rain cats and dogs (*infml*).
3 *came pelting down the street*: rush, hurry, charge, belt (*infml*), tear, dash, speed, career.

penalize *verb*
punish, discipline, correct, fine, handicap.
F3 reward.

penalty *noun*
punishment, retribution, fine, forfeit, handicap, disadvantage.
F3 reward.

penance *noun*
atonement, reparation, punishment, penalty, mortification.

pending *adjective*
impending, in the offing, forthcoming, imminent, undecided, in the balance.
F3 finished, settled.

penetrate *verb*
pierce, stab, prick, puncture, probe, sink, bore, enter, infiltrate, permeate, seep, pervade, suffuse.

penetrating *adjective*
1 *a penetrating wind*: piercing, stinging, biting, sharp, keen.
2 *a penetrating remark*: acute, incisive, shrewd, discerning, perceptive, observant, profound, deep, searching, probing.
F3 blunt.

penitent *adjective*
repentant, contrite, sorry, apologetic, remorseful, regretful, conscience-stricken, shamefaced, humble.
F3 unrepentant, hard-hearted, callous.

penniless *adjective*
poor, poverty-stricken, impoverished, destitute, bankrupt, ruined, bust, broke (*infml*), stony-broke (*infml*), skint (*infml*).
F3 rich, wealthy, affluent.

pension *noun*
annuity, superannuation, allowance, benefit.

pensive *adjective*
thoughtful, reflective, contemplative, meditative, ruminative, absorbed, preoccupied, absent-minded, wistful, solemn, serious, sober.
F3 carefree.

pent-up *adjective*
repressed, inhibited, restrained, bottled-up, suppressed, stifled.

people *noun*
persons, individuals, humans, human beings, mankind, humanity, folk, public, general public, populace, rank and file, population, inhabitants, citizens, community, society, race, nation.
▶ *verb*
populate, inhabit, occupy, settle, colonize.

pep up *verb* (*infml*)
invigorate, vitalize, liven up, quicken (*fml*), stimulate, excite, exhilarate, inspire.
F3 tone down.

perceive *verb*
1 *I could just perceive faint marks on the surface*: see, discern, make out, detect, discover, spot, catch sight of, notice, observe, view, remark, note, distinguish, recognize.
2 *perceiving that she was upset*: sense, feel, apprehend, learn, realize, appreciate, be aware of, know, grasp, understand, gather, deduce, conclude.

perceptible *adjective*
perceivable, discernible, detectable, appreciable, distinguishable, observable, noticeable, obvious, evident, conspicuous, clear, plain, apparent, visible.
F3 imperceptible, inconspicuous.

perception *noun*
sense, feeling, impression, idea, conception, apprehension, awareness, consciousness, observation, recognition, grasp, understanding, insight, discernment, taste.

perceptive *adjective*
discerning, observant, sensitive, responsive, aware, alert, quick, sharp, astute, shrewd.
F3 unobservant.

perennial *adjective*
lasting, enduring, everlasting, eternal, immortal, undying, imperishable, unceasing, incessant, never-ending, constant, continual, uninterrupted, perpetual, persistent, unfailing.

perfect *adjective*
1 *a perfect performance/trying to be perfect*: faultless, impeccable, flawless, immaculate, spotless, blameless, pure,

superb, excellent, matchless, incomparable.
2 a perfect circle : exact, precise, accurate, right, correct, true.
3 he would make a perfect partner for her : ideal, model, exemplary, ultimate, consummate, expert, accomplished, experienced, skilful.
4 felt a perfect fool : utter, absolute, sheer, complete, entire, total.
F3 1 imperfect, flawed, blemished. 2 inaccurate, wrong. 3 inexperienced, unskilled.

▶ *verb*
fulfil, consummate, complete, finish, polish, refine, elaborate.
F3 spoil, mar.

perfection *noun*
faultlessness, flawlessness, excellence, superiority, ideal, model, paragon, crown, pinnacle, acme, consummation, completion.
F3 imperfection, flaw.

perform *verb*
1 perform a task/one's duty : do, carry out, execute, discharge, fulfil, satisfy, complete, achieve, accomplish, bring off, pull off, effect, bring about.
2 performing a play/Hamlet : stage, put on, present, enact, represent, act, play, appear as.
3 car performs well in wet conditions : function, work, operate, behave, produce.

performance *noun*
1 a performance of Macbeth : show, act, play, appearance, presentation, production, interpretation, rendition, representation, portrayal, acting.
2 in the performance of his duty : action, deed, doing, carrying out, execution, implementation, discharge, fulfilment, completion, achievement, accomplishment.
3 the engine's performance : functioning, operation, behaviour, conduct.

performer *noun*
actor, actress, player, artiste, entertainer.

perfume *noun*
scent, fragrance, smell, odour, aroma, bouquet, sweetness, balm, essence, cologne, toilet water, incense.

perhaps *adverb*
maybe, possibly, conceivably, feasibly.

perimeter *noun*
circumference, edge, border, boundary, frontier, limit, bounds, confines, fringe, margin, periphery.
F3 middle, centre, heart.

period *noun*
era, epoch, age, generation, date, years, time, term, season, stage, phase, stretch, turn, session, interval, space, span, spell, cycle.

peripheral *adjective*
1 of peripheral importance : minor, secondary, incidental, unimportant, irrelevant, unnecessary, marginal, borderline, surface, superficial.
2 affecting the entire city and peripheral area : outlying, outer, outermost.
F3 1 major, crucial. 2 central.

perish *verb*
rot, decay, decompose, disintegrate, crumble, collapse, fall, die, expire, pass away.

perishable *adjective*
destructible, biodegradable, decomposable, short-lived.
F3 imperishable, durable.

perk *noun* (*infml*)
perquisite (*fml*), fringe benefit, benefit, bonus, dividend, gratuity, tip, extra, plus (*infml*).

perk up *verb* (*infml*)
brighten, cheer up, buck up (*infml*), revive, liven up, pep up (*infml*), rally, recover, improve, look up.

permanent *adjective*
fixed, stable, unchanging, imperishable, indestructible, unfading, eternal, everlasting, lifelong, perpetual, constant, steadfast, perennial, long-lasting, lasting, enduring, durable.
F3 temporary, ephemeral, fleeting.

permeable *adjective*
porous, absorbent, absorptive, penetrable.
F3 impermeable, watertight.

permeate *verb*
pass through, soak through, filter through, seep through, penetrate, infiltrate, pervade, imbue, saturate, impregnate, fill.

permissible *adjective*
permitted, allowable, allowed, admissible, all right, acceptable, proper, authorized, sanctioned, lawful, legal, legitimate.
F∃ prohibited, banned, forbidden.

permission *noun*
consent, assent, agreement, approval, go-ahead, green light (*infml*), authorization, sanction, leave, warrant, permit, licence, dispensation, freedom, liberty.
F∃ prohibition.

permit *verb* /per-mit/
allow, let, consent, agree, admit, grant, authorize, sanction, warrant, license.
F∃ prohibit, forbid.
▶ *noun* /per-mit/
pass, passport, visa, licence, warrant, authorization, sanction, permission.
F∃ prohibition.

perpendicular *adjective*
vertical, upright, erect, straight, sheer, plumb.
F∃ horizontal.

perpetrate *verb*
commit, carry out, execute, do, perform, inflict, wreak.

perpetual *adjective*
eternal, everlasting, infinite, endless, unending, never-ending, interminable, ceaseless, unceasing, incessant, continuous, uninterrupted, constant, persistent, continual, repeated, recurrent, perennial, permanent, lasting, enduring, abiding, unchanging.
F∃ intermittent, temporary, ephemeral, transient.

perpetuate *verb*
continue, keep up, maintain, preserve, keep alive, immortalize, commemorate.

perplex *verb*
puzzle, baffle, mystify, stump (*infml*), confuse, muddle, confound, bewilder, dumbfound.

persecute *verb*
hound, pursue, hunt, bother, worry, annoy, pester, harass, molest, abuse, ill-treat, maltreat, oppress, tyrannize, victimize, martyr, distress, afflict, torment, torture, crucify.
F∃ pamper, spoil.

persevere *verb*
continue, carry on, stick at it (*infml*), keep going, soldier on, persist, plug away (*infml*), remain, stand firm, stand fast, hold on, hang on.
F∃ give up, stop, discontinue.

persist *verb*
remain, linger, last, endure, abide (*fml*), continue, carry on, keep at it, persevere, insist.
F∃ desist, stop.

persistent *adjective*
1 a persistent knocking sound: incessant, endless, never-ending, interminable, continuous, unrelenting, relentless, unremitting, constant, steady, continual, repeated, perpetual, lasting, enduring.
2 persistent effort: persevering, determined, resolute, dogged, tenacious, stubborn, obstinate, steadfast, zealous, tireless, unflagging, indefatigable.

person *noun*
individual, being, human being, human, man, woman, body, soul, character, type.

personal *adjective*
own, private, confidential, intimate, special, particular, individual, exclusive, idiosyncratic, distinctive.
F∃ public, general, universal.

personality *noun*
1 an attractive personality: character, nature, disposition, temperament, individuality, psyche, traits, make-up, charm, charisma, magnetism.
2 a TV personality: celebrity, notable, personage, public figure, VIP (*infml*), star.

personify *verb*
embody, epitomize, typify, exemplify, symbolize, represent, mirror.

personnel *noun*
staff, workforce, workers, employees,

crew, human resources, manpower, people, members.

perspective *noun*
aspect, angle, slant, attitude, standpoint, viewpoint, point of view, view, vista, scene, prospect, outlook, proportion, relation.

perspire *verb*
sweat, exude, secrete, swelter, drip.

persuade *verb*
coax, prevail upon, lean on, cajole, wheedle, inveigle (*fml*), talk into, induce, bring round, win over, convince, convert, sway, influence, lead on, incite, prompt, urge.
F∃ dissuade, deter, discourage.

persuasion *noun*
1 used persuasion to get what she wants: coaxing, cajolery, wheedling, inducement, enticement, pull, power, influence, conviction, conversion.
2 of a different religious persuasion: opinion, school (of thought), party, faction, side, conviction, faith, belief, denomination, sect.

persuasive *adjective*
convincing, plausible, cogent, sound, valid, influential, forceful, weighty, effective, telling, potent, compelling, moving, touching.
F∃ unconvincing.

pertinent *adjective*
appropriate, suitable, fitting, apt, apposite, relevant, to the point, material, applicable.
F∃ inappropriate, unsuitable, irrelevant.

perturb *verb*
disturb, bother, trouble, upset, worry, alarm, disconcert, unsettle, discompose, ruffle, fluster, agitate, vex.
F∃ reassure, compose.

pervasive *adjective*
prevalent, common, extensive, widespread, general, universal, inescapable, omnipresent, ubiquitous.

perverse *adjective*
contrary, wayward, wrong-headed, wilful, headstrong, stubborn, obstinate, unyielding, intransigent, disobedient, rebellious, troublesome,

unmanageable, ill-tempered, cantankerous, unreasonable, incorrect, improper.
F∃ obliging, co-operative, reasonable.

pessimistic *adjective*
negative, cynical, fatalistic, defeatist, resigned, hopeless, despairing, despondent, dejected, downhearted, glum, morose, melancholy, depressed, dismal, gloomy, bleak.
F∃ optimistic.

pest *noun*
nuisance, bother, annoyance, irritation, vexation, trial, curse, scourge, bane, blight, bug.

pester *verb*
nag, badger, hound, hassle (*infml*), harass, plague, torment, provoke, worry, bother, disturb, annoy, irritate, pick on, get at (*infml*).

pet *adjective*
favourite, favoured, preferred, dearest, cherished, special, particular, personal.
▶ *verb*
stroke, caress, fondle, cuddle, kiss, neck (*infml*), snog (*slang*).

peter out *verb*
dwindle, taper off, fade, wane, ebb, fail, cease, stop.

petition *noun*
appeal, round robin, application, request, solicitation, plea, entreaty, prayer, supplication, invocation.
▶ *verb*
appeal, call upon, ask, crave, solicit, bid, urge, press, implore, beg, plead, entreat, beseech, supplicate, pray.

petrified *adjective*
terrified, horrified, appalled, paralysed, numb.

petty *adjective*
1 a petty offence: minor, unimportant, insignificant, trivial, secondary, lesser, small, little, slight, trifling, paltry, inconsiderable, negligible.
2 don't be so petty!: small-minded, mean, ungenerous, grudging, spiteful.
F∃1 important, significant. **2** generous.

petulant *adjective*
fretful, peevish, cross, irritable,

snappish, bad-tempered, ill-humoured, moody, sullen, sulky, sour, ungracious.

phantom *noun*
ghost, spectre, spirit, apparition, vision, hallucination, illusion, figment.

phase *noun*
stage, step, time, period, spell, season, chapter, position, point, aspect, state, condition.
◆ **phase out** wind down, run down, ease off, taper off, eliminate, dispose of, get rid of, remove, withdraw, close, terminate.

phenomenal *adjective*
marvellous, sensational, stupendous, amazing, remarkable, extraordinary, exceptional, unusual, unbelievable, incredible.

phenomenon *noun*
1 a natural phenomenon: occurrence, happening, event, incident, episode, fact, appearance, sight.
2 an infant phenomenon: wonder, marvel, miracle, prodigy, rarity, curiosity, spectacle, sensation.

philanthropy *noun*
humanitarianism, public-spiritedness, altruism, unselfishness, benevolence, kind-heartedness, charity, alms-giving, patronage, generosity, liberality, open-handedness.
Ｅ misanthropy.

philosophical *adjective*
1 a philosophical discussion: metaphysical, abstract, theoretical, analytical, rational, logical, erudite, learned, wise, thoughtful.
2 was philosophical about his failure: resigned, patient, stoical, unruffled, calm, composed.

philosophy *noun*
metaphysics, rationalism, reason, logic, thought, thinking, wisdom, knowledge, ideology, world-view, doctrine, beliefs, convictions, values, principles, attitude, viewpoint.

phobia *noun*
fear, terror, dread, anxiety, neurosis, obsession, hang-up (*infml*), thing (*infml*), aversion, dislike, hatred, horror, loathing, revulsion, repulsion.
Ｅ love, liking.

Phobias (by name of fear) include:

zoophobia (*animals*), apiphobia (*bees*), haemophobia (*blood*), ailurophobia (*cats*), necrophobia (*corpses*), demophobia/ochlophobia (*crowds*), scotophobia (*darkness*), thanatophobia (*death*), cynophobia (*dogs*), claustrophobia (*enclosed places*), panphobia (*everything*), pyrophobia (*fire*), xenophobia (*foreigners*), bacteriophobia/spermophobia (*germs*), phasmophobia (*ghosts*), acrophobia (*high places*), hippophobia (*horses*), entomophobia (*insects*), astraphobia (*lightning*), autophobia (*loneliness*), agoraphobia (*open spaces*), toxiphobia (*poison*), herpetophobia (*reptiles*), ophiophobia (*snakes*), tachophobia (*speed*), arachnophobia (*spiders*), triskaidekaphobia (*thirteen*), brontophobia (*thunder*), hodophobia (*travel*), hydrophobia (*water*). ⇨*See also* **mania**.

phone *verb*
telephone, ring (up), call (up), dial, contact, get in touch, give a buzz (*infml*), give a tinkle (*infml*).

phoney *adjective* (*infml*)
fake, counterfeit, forged, bogus, trick, false, spurious, assumed, affected, put-on, sham, pseudo, imitation.
Ｅ real, genuine.

photograph *noun*
photo, snap, snapshot, print, shot, slide, transparency, picture, image, likeness.
▶ *verb*
snap, take, film, shoot, video, record.

phrase *noun*
construction, clause, idiom, expression, saying, utterance, remark.
▶ *verb*
word, formulate, frame, couch, present, put, express, say, utter, pronounce.

physical *adjective*
1 physical pain: bodily, corporeal, fleshy, incarnate, mortal, earthly.
2 the physical world: material, concrete, solid, substantial,

tangible, visible, real, actual.
F3 mental, spiritual.

physics

Terms used in physics include:

absolute zero, acceleration, acoustics, alpha particles, Archimedes principle, atom, beta particles, Big Bang theory, capillary action, centrifugal force, circuit, circuit-breaker, critical mass, cryogenics, density, diffraction, elasticity, electric current, electric discharge, electricity, electrodynamics, electromagnetic spectrum, electromagnetic waves, electron, energy, entropy, evaporation, force, formula, freezing point, frequency, friction, gamma ray, gravity, half-life, heavy water, hydraulics, hydrodynamics, hydrostatics, incandescence, inertia, infrared, ion, Kelvin effect, kinetic energy, kinetic theory, laser (light amplification by stimulated emission of radiation), latent heat, lens, light emission, light intensity, longitudinal wave, luminescence, Mach number, magnetic field, magnetism, mass, mechanics, microwaves, Mohs scale, molecule, neutron, nuclear, nuclear fission, nuclear fusion, nuclear physics, nucleus, optical centre, optics, oscillation, parallel motion, particle, periodic law, perpetual motion, phonon, photon, photosensitivity, polarity, potential energy, proton, quantum chromodynamics (QCD), quantum electrodynamics (QED), quantum mechanics, quantum theory, quark, radiation, radioactive element, radioactivity, radioisotope, reflection, refraction, relativity, resistance, resonance, semiconductor, sensitivity, separation, SI unit, specific gravity, specific heat capacity, spectroscopy, spectrum, statics, surface tension, theory of relativity, thermodynamics, Thomson effect, transverse wave, ultrasound, ultraviolet, velocity, viscosity, visible spectrum, volume, wave, white heat, X-ray.

physique *noun*
body, figure, shape, form, build, frame, structure, constitution, make-up.

pick *verb*
1 pick a number : select, choose, opt for, decide on, settle on, single out.
2 pick strawberries : gather, collect, pluck, harvest.
▶ *noun*
1 take your pick : choice, selection, option, decision, preference.
2 the pick of the crop : best, cream, flower, élite, elect.
◆ **pick on** bully, torment, persecute, nag, get at (*infml*), needle (*infml*), bait.
◆ **pick out** spot, notice, perceive, recognize, distinguish, tell apart, separate, single out, hand-pick, choose, select.
◆ **pick up** 1 picking the box up : lift, raise, hoist.
2 I'll pick you up at eight : call for, fetch, collect.
3 picked up a little French : learn, master, grasp, gather.
4 business is now picking up : improve, rally, recover, perk up (*infml*).
5 pick up a bargain : buy, purchase.
6 pick up information : obtain, acquire, gain.
7 pick up an infection : catch, contract, get.

picket *verb*
protest, demonstrate, boycott, blockade, enclose, surround.

pickle *verb*
preserve, conserve, souse, marinade, steep, cure, salt.

pictorial *adjective*
graphic, diagrammatic, schematic, representational, vivid, expressive, illustrated, picturesque, scenic.

picture *noun*
1 hang pictures on the wall : painting, portrait, landscape, drawing, sketch, illustration, engraving, photograph, print, representation, likeness, image, effigy.
2 gives a good picture of the overall situation : depiction, portrayal, description, account, report, impression.

3 the picture of health: embodiment, personification, epitome, archetype, essence.
4 a cowboy picture: film, movie (*infml*), motion picture.
▶ *verb*
1 picture the scene: imagine, envisage, envision, conceive, visualize, see.
2 was pictured sitting on a wall: depict, describe, represent, show, portray, draw, sketch, paint, photograph, illustrate.

picturesque *adjective*
1 a picturesque view: attractive, beautiful, pretty, charming, quaint, idyllic, scenic.
2 his account was picturesque: descriptive, graphic, vivid, colourful, striking.
⊟ 1 unattractive. **2** dull.

piece *noun*
1 a piece of orange/fabric/the jigsaw: fragment, bit, scrap, morsel, mouthful, bite, lump, chunk, slice, sliver, snippet, shred, offcut, sample, component, constituent, element, part, segment, section, division, fraction, share, portion, quantity.
2 a piece in the paper: article, item, report, study, work, composition, creation, specimen, example.

pierce *verb*
penetrate, enter, stick into, puncture, drill, bore, probe, perforate, punch, prick, stab, lance, bayonet, run through, spear, skewer, spike, impale, transfix.

piercing *adjective*
1 a piercing cry: shrill, high-pitched, loud, ear-splitting, sharp.
2 piercing eyes: penetrating, probing, searching.
3 a piercing wind: cold, bitter, raw, biting, keen, fierce, severe, wintry, frosty, freezing.
4 a piercing pain: agonizing, excruciating, stabbing, lacerating.

pig *noun*
1 pigs in the farmyard: swine, hog, sow, boar.
2 a pig of a man: animal, beast, brute.
3 made a pig of herself: glutton, gourmand.

pigeonhole *noun*
compartment, niche, slot, cubby-hole, cubicle, locker, box, place, section, class, category, classification.
▶ *verb*
compartmentalize, label, classify, sort, file, catalogue, alphabetize, shelve, defer.

pigment *noun*
colour, hue, tint, dye, stain, paint, colouring, tincture.

pile *noun*
stack, heap, mound, mountain, mass, accumulation, collection, assortment, hoard, stockpile.
▶ *verb*
stack, heap, mass, amass, accumulate, build up, gather, assemble, collect, hoard, stockpile, store, load, pack, jam, crush, crowd, flock, flood, stream, rush, charge.

pilfer *verb*
steal, pinch (*infml*), nick (*infml*), knock off (*infml*), filch, lift, shoplift, rob, thieve.

pilgrimage *noun*
crusade, mission, expedition, journey, trip, tour.

pillar *noun*
column, shaft, post, mast, pier, upright, pile, support, prop, mainstay, bastion, tower of strength.

pilot *noun*
1 a fighter pilot: flyer, aviator, airman.
2 a ship's pilot: navigator, steersman, helmsman, coxswain, captain, leader, director, guide.
▶ *verb*
fly, drive, steer, direct, control, handle, manage, operate, run, conduct, lead, guide, navigate.
▶ *adjective*
experimental, trial, test, model.

pin *verb*
tack, nail, fix, affix, attach, join, staple, clip, fasten, secure, hold down, restrain, immobilize.
▶ *noun*
tack, nail, screw, spike, rivet, bolt, peg, fastener, clip, staple, brooch.
◆ **pin down 1 pin down the source of the leak**: pinpoint, identify, determine, specify.

2 pin him down to a specific time:
force, make, press, pressurize.

pinch *verb*
1 pinched her cheek: squeeze,
compress, crush, press, tweak, nip,
hurt, grip, grasp.
2 (*infml*) **his bike was pinched:** steal,
nick (*infml*), pilfer, filch, snatch.
► *noun*
1 gave him a pinch: squeeze, tweak,
nip.
2 a pinch of salt: dash, soupçon, taste,
bit, speck, jot, mite.
3 in a pinch: emergency, crisis,
predicament, difficulty, hardship,
pressure, stress.

pine *verb*
long, yearn, ache, sigh, grieve, mourn,
wish, desire, crave, hanker, hunger,
thirst.

pinnacle *noun*
1 a rocky pinnacle: peak, summit, top,
cap, crown, crest, apex, vertex, acme,
zenith, height, eminence.
2 the pinnacle of the roof: spire,
steeple, turret, pyramid, cone, obelisk,
needle.

pinpoint *verb*
identify, spot, distinguish, locate, place,
home in on, zero in on (*infml*), pin
down, determine, specify, define.

pioneer *noun*
colonist, settler, frontiersman,
frontierswoman, explorer, developer,
pathfinder, trail-blazer, leader,
innovator, inventor, discoverer,
founder.

pious *adjective*
1 a good and pious man: devout, godly,
saintly, holy, spiritual, religious,
reverent, virtuous, righteous, moral.
2 a pious attitude: sanctimonious,
holier-than-thou (*infml*), self-righteous,
goody-goody (*infml*), hypocritical.
E3 1 impious, irreligious, irreverent.

pipe *noun*
tube, hose, piping, tubing, pipeline,
line, main, flue, duct, conduit, channel,
passage, conveyor.

pit *noun*
mine, coalmine, excavation, trench,
ditch, hollow, depression, indentation,

dent, hole, cavity, crater, pothole, gulf,
chasm, abyss.

pitch *verb*
1 pitching the ball: throw, fling, toss,
chuck (*infml*), lob, bowl, hurl, heave,
sling, fire, launch, aim, direct.
2 ship pitched and rolled: plunge, dive,
plummet, drop, fall headlong, tumble,
lurch, roll, wallow.
3 pitch camp: erect, put up, set up,
place, station, settle, plant, fix.
► *noun*
1 cricket pitch: ground, field, playing-
field, arena, stadium.
2 played at the correct pitch: sound,
tone, timbre, modulation, frequency,
level.
3 pitch of the roof: gradient, incline,
slope, tilt, angle, degree, steepness.

pitfall *noun*
danger, peril, hazard, trap, snare,
stumbling block, catch, snag,
drawback, difficulty.

pitiful *adjective*
1 a pitiful example: contemptible,
despicable, low, mean, vile, shabby,
deplorable, lamentable, woeful,
inadequate, hopeless, pathetic (*infml*),
insignificant, paltry, worthless.
2 a pitiful wail: piteous, doleful,
mournful, distressing, heart-rending,
pathetic, pitiable, sad, miserable,
wretched, poor, sorry.

pity *noun*
1 feel pity for them: sympathy,
commiseration, regret, understanding,
fellow-feeling, compassion, kindness,
tenderness, mercy, forbearance.
2 what a pity!: shame, misfortune, bad
luck.
E3 1 cruelty, anger, scorn.
► *verb*
feel sorry for, feel for, sympathize with,
commiserate with, grieve for, weep for.

pivot *noun*
axis, hinge, fulcrum, axle, spindle,
kingpin, linchpin, swivel, hub, focal
point, centre, heart.
► *verb*
1 windows that pivot inwards: swivel,
turn, spin, revolve, rotate, swing.
2 success or failure pivots on his

performance today: depend, rely, hinge, hang, lie.

place *noun*
1 broken in several places: site, locale, venue, location, situation, spot, point, position.
2 a place at table/take your place: seat, space, room.
3 a place on the map: city, town, village, locality, neighbourhood, district, area, region.
4 a big place in town: building, property, dwelling, residence, house, flat, apartment, home.
▸ *verb*
put, set, plant, fix, position, locate, situate, rest, settle, lay, stand, deposit, leave.
◆ **out of place** inappropriate, unsuitable, unfitting, unbecoming, unseemly.
◆ **take place** happen, occur, come about.

placid *adjective*
calm, composed, unruffled, laid-back (*infml*), untroubled, cool, self-possessed, level-headed, imperturbable, phlegmatic, mild, gentle, equable, even-tempered, serene, tranquil, still, quiet, peaceful, restful. ⫽excitable, agitated, disturbed.

plagiarize *verb*
crib, copy, reproduce, imitate, counterfeit, pirate, infringe copyright, poach, steal, lift, appropriate, borrow.

plague *noun*
1 thousands died from plague: pestilence, epidemic, disease, infection, contagion.
2 a plague of biting flies: nuisance, annoyance, infestation, invasion, scourge, torment.
▸ *verb*
annoy, vex, bother, disturb, trouble, distress, upset, pester, harass, hound, haunt, bedevil, afflict, torment, torture, persecute.

plain *adjective*
1 good plain cooking: ordinary, basic, simple, unpretentious, modest, unadorned, unelaborate, restrained.
2 it was plain to see: obvious, evident,

patent, clear, understandable, apparent, visible, unmistakable.
3 plain speaking: frank, candid, blunt, outspoken, direct, forthright, straightforward, unambiguous, plain-spoken, open, honest, truthful.
4 a plain face: unattractive, ugly, unprepossessing, unlovely.
5 plain fabric: unpatterned, unvariegated, uncoloured, self-coloured.
⫽**1** fancy, elaborate. **2** unclear, obscure. **3** devious, deceitful. **4** attractive, good-looking. **5** patterned.
▸ *noun*
grassland, prairie, steppe, lowland, flat, plateau, tableland.

plan *noun*
1 the plans for the extension: blueprint, layout, diagram, chart, map, drawing, sketch, representation, design.
2 have a cunning plan: idea, suggestion, proposal, proposition, project, scheme, plot, system, method, procedure, strategy, programme, schedule, scenario.
▸ *verb*
1 planning the attack: plot, scheme, design, invent, devise, contrive, formulate, frame, draft, outline, prepare, organize, arrange.
2 plan to be a lawyer: aim, intend, propose, contemplate, envisage, foresee.

plant *noun*
1 garden plants: flower, shrub, herb, bush, greenery.

Plants include:
annual, biennial, perennial; cultivar, evergreen, herbaceous plant, house plant, hybrid, pot plant, succulent; air-plant, algae, bush, cactus, cereal, grass, fern, flower, fungus herb, lichen, moss, shrub, tree, vegetable, vine, water-plant, weed, wild flower; bulb, bush, climber, corm, sapling, seedling. ⇨*See also* **flower**.

2 he worked in the industrial plant: factory, works, foundry, mill, shop, yard, workshop, machinery, apparatus, equipment, gear.

▶ *verb*

1 plant seeds: sow, seed, bury, transplant.

2 plant an idea in his head: insert, put, place, set, fix, lodge, root, settle, found, establish.

plaster *verb*
daub, smear, coat, cover, spread.

plastic *adjective*
soft, pliable, flexible, supple, malleable, mouldable, ductile, receptive, impressionable, manageable.

E∃ rigid, inflexible.

plate *noun*

1 a plate of mince: dish, platter, salver, helping, serving, portion.

2 a colour plate: illustration, picture, print, lithograph.

▶ *verb*

coat, cover, overlay, veneer, laminate, electroplate, anodize, galvanize, platinize, gild, silver, tin.

platform *noun*

1 take the platform: stage, podium, dais, rostrum, stand.

2 the party's platform: policy, party line, principles, tenets, manifesto, programme, objectives.

plausible *adjective*
credible, believable, reasonable, logical, likely, possible, probable, convincing, persuasive, smooth-talking, glib.

E∃ implausible, unlikely, improbable.

play *verb*

1 play games: amuse oneself, have fun, enjoy oneself, revel, sport, romp, frolic, caper.

2 play a part: participate, take part, join in, compete.

3 France played Italy: oppose, vie with, challenge, take on.

4 played Hamlet: act, perform, portray, represent, impersonate.

E∃ 1 work.

▶ *noun*

1 all work and no play: fun, amusement, entertainment, diversion, recreation, sport, game, hobby, pastime.

2 a part in a play: drama, tragedy, comedy, farce, show, performance.

3 too much play in the steering: movement, action, flexibility, give, leeway, latitude, margin, scope, range, room, space.

E∃ 1 work.

◆ **play down** minimize, make light of, gloss over, underplay, understate, undervalue, underestimate.

E∃ exaggerate.

◆ **play on** exploit, take advantage of, turn to account, profit by, trade on, capitalize on.

player *noun*

1 a football player: contestant, competitor, participant, sportsman, sportswoman.

2 the players took a bow: performer, entertainer, artiste, actor, actress, musician, instrumentalist.

playful *adjective*
sportive, frolicsome, lively, spirited, mischievous, roguish, impish, puckish, kittenish, good-natured, jesting, teasing, humorous, tongue-in-cheek.

E∃ serious.

plea *noun*

1 a plea for mercy: appeal, petition, request, entreaty, supplication, prayer, invocation.

2 a plea of temporary insanity: defence, justification, excuse, explanation, claim.

plead *verb*

1 pleading with him to let them go: beg, implore, beseech, entreat, appeal, petition, ask, request.

2 plead ignorance: assert, maintain, claim, allege.

pleasant *adjective*
agreeable, nice, fine, lovely, delightful, charming, likable, amiable, friendly, affable, good-humoured, cheerful, congenial, enjoyable, amusing, pleasing, gratifying, satisfying, acceptable, welcome, refreshing.

E∃ unpleasant, nasty, unfriendly.

please *verb*

1 it pleases me to see them so happy: delight, charm, captivate, entertain, amuse, cheer, gladden, humour, indulge, gratify, satisfy, content, suit.

2 if you please: want, will, wish, desire, like, prefer, choose, think fit.

F3 1 displease, annoy, anger, sadden.

pleased *adjective*
contented, satisfied, gratified, glad, happy, delighted, thrilled, euphoric.
F3 displeased, annoyed.

pleasing *adjective*
gratifying, satisfying, acceptable, good, pleasant, agreeable, nice, delightful, charming, attractive, engaging, winning.
F3 unpleasant, disagreeable.

pleasure *noun*
amusement, entertainment, recreation, fun, enjoyment, gratification, satisfaction, contentment, happiness, joy, delight, comfort, solace.
F3 sorrow, pain, trouble, displeasure.

pleat *noun, verb*
tuck, fold, crease, flute, crimp, gather, pucker.

pledge *noun*
1 make a pledge of loyalty: promise, vow, word of honour, oath, bond, covenant, guarantee, warrant, assurance, undertaking.
2 a pledge of £1000: deposit, security, surety, bail.
▶ *verb*
promise, vow, swear, contract, engage, undertake, vouch, guarantee, secure.

plentiful *adjective*
ample, abundant, profuse, copious, overflowing, lavish, generous, liberal, bountiful, fruitful, productive.
F3 scarce, scanty, rare.

plenty *noun*
abundance, profusion, plethora, lots (*infml*), loads (*infml*), masses (*infml*), heaps (*infml*), piles (*infml*), stacks (*infml*), enough, sufficiency, quantity, mass, volume, fund, mine, store.
F3 scarcity, lack, want, need.

pliable *adjective*
pliant, flexible, bendable, bendy (*infml*), supple, lithe, malleable, plastic, yielding, adaptable, accommodating,

manageable, tractable, docile, compliant, biddable, persuadable, responsive, receptive, impressionable, susceptible.
F3 rigid, inflexible, headstrong.

plight *noun*
predicament, quandary, dilemma, extremity, trouble, difficulty, straits, state, condition, situation, circumstances, case.

plod *verb*
1 plod through the mud: trudge, tramp, stump, lumber, plough through.
2 keep plodding on regardless: drudge, labour, toil, grind, slog, persevere, soldier on.

plot *noun*
1 the Gunpowder Plot: conspiracy, intrigue, machination, scheme, plan, stratagem.
2 couldn't follow the plot: story, narrative, subject, theme, storyline, thread, outline, scenario.
3 plot of land: patch, tract, area, allotment, lot, parcel.
▶ *verb*
1 plotting against him: conspire, intrigue, machinate, scheme, hatch, lay, cook up, devise, contrive, plan, project, design, draft.
2 plotting their route: chart, map, mark, locate, draw, calculate.

ploy *noun*
manoeuvre, stratagem, tactic, move, device, contrivance, scheme, game, trick, artifice, dodge, wile, ruse, subterfuge.

pluck *verb*
1 plucking the feathers from the bird: pull, draw, tug, snatch, pull off, remove, pick, collect, gather, harvest.
2 pluck a guitar: pick, twang, strum.

plucky *adjective*
brave, courageous, bold, daring, intrepid, heroic, valiant, spirited, feisty (*infml*).
F3 cowardly, weak, feeble.

plug *noun*
1 a bath plug: stopper, bung, cork, spigot.
2 (*infml*) **giving his new book a plug**:

advertisement, publicity, mention,
puff.
▶ *verb*
1 plug the hole: stop (up), bung, cork,
block, choke, close, seal, fill, pack,
stuff.
2 (*infml*) **plugging their new album**:
advertise, publicize, promote, push,
mention.

plummet *verb*
plunge, dive, nosedive, descend, drop,
fall, tumble.
F3 soar.

plump *adjective*
fat, dumpy, tubby, stout, round, rotund,
portly, chubby, podgy, fleshy, full,
ample, buxom.
F3 thin, skinny.

plump for *verb*
opt for, choose, select, favour, back,
support.

plunder *verb*
loot, pillage, ravage, devastate, sack,
raid, ransack, rifle, steal, rob,
strip.
▶ *noun*
loot, pillage, booty, swag (*slang*),
spoils, pickings, ill-gotten gains, prize.

plunge *verb*
1 plunged to earth: dive, jump,
nosedive, swoop, dive-bomb, plummet,
descend, go down, sink, drop, fall,
pitch, tumble, hurtle, career, charge,
dash, rush, tear.
2 plunge your hand into cold water:
immerse, submerge, dip.
▶ *noun*
dive, jump, swoop, descent, drop, fall,
tumble, immersion, submersion.

poach *verb*
steal, pilfer, appropriate, trespass,
encroach, infringe.

pocket *noun*
pouch, bag, envelope, receptacle,
compartment, hollow, cavity.
▶ *adjective*
small, little, mini (*infml*), concise,
compact, portable, miniature.
▶ *verb*
take, appropriate, help oneself to, lift,
pilfer, filch, steal, nick (*infml*), pinch
(*infml*).

poem

Types of poem include:

ballad, clerihew, elegy, epic, haiku,
idyll, lay, limerick, lyric, madrigal,
nursery-rhyme, ode, pastoral,
roundelay, saga, sonnet, tanka, triolet,
verselet, versicle. ⇒*See also* **literature**;
song.

poet *noun*
versifier, rhymer, rhymester, lyricist,
bard, minstrel.

poetic *adjective*
poetical, lyrical, moving, artistic,
graceful, flowing, metrical,
rhythmical, rhyming.
F3 prosaic.

poignant *adjective*
moving, touching, affecting, tender,
distressing, upsetting, heartbreaking,
heart-rending, piteous, pathetic, sad,
painful, agonizing.

point *noun*
1 has several good points: feature,
attribute, aspect, facet, detail,
particular, item, subject, topic.
2 what's the point?: use, purpose,
motive, reason, object, intention, aim,
end, goal, objective.
3 the point of the story: essence, crux,
core, pith, gist, thrust, meaning, drift,
burden.
4 a point on the route: place, position,
situation, location, site, spot.
5 at this point in time: moment,
instant, juncture, stage, time, period.
6 a point of light: dot, spot, mark,
speck, full stop.
▶ *verb*
1 point a gun: aim, direct, train,
level.
2 point to the culprit: indicate, signal,
show, signify, denote, designate.
◆ **point out** show, indicate, draw
attention to, point to, reveal, identify,
specify, mention, bring up, allude to,
remind.

point-blank *adjective*
direct, forthright, straightforward,
plain, explicit, open, unreserved,
blunt, frank, candid.

▶ *adverb*

directly, forthrightly, straightforwardly, plainly, explicitly, openly, bluntly, frankly, candidly.

pointed *adjective*

sharp, keen, edged, barbed, cutting, incisive, trenchant (*fml*), biting, penetrating, telling.

pointless *adjective*

useless, futile, vain, fruitless, aimless, unproductive, unprofitable, worthless, senseless, absurd, meaningless.
🔁 useful, profitable, meaningful.

point of view *noun*

opinion, view, belief, judgement, attitude, position, standpoint, viewpoint, outlook, perspective, approach, angle, slant.

poised *adjective*

1 a poised performance: dignified, graceful, calm, composed, unruffled, collected, self-possessed, cool, self-confident, assured.
2 poised for action: prepared, ready, set, waiting, expectant.

poison *noun*

toxin, venom, bane, blight, cancer, malignancy, contagion, contamination, corruption.
▶ *verb*

infect, contaminate, pollute, taint, adulterate, corrupt, deprave, pervert, warp.

poisonous *adjective*

toxic, venomous, lethal, deadly, fatal, mortal, noxious, pernicious, malicious.

poke *verb*

prod, stab, jab, stick, thrust, push, shove, nudge, elbow, dig, butt, hit, punch.
▶ *noun*

prod, jab, thrust, shove, nudge, dig, butt, punch.

police *noun*

police force, constabulary, the law (*infml*), the cops (*infml*).
▶ *verb*

check, control, regulate, monitor, watch, observe, supervise, oversee, patrol, guard, protect, defend, keep the peace.

policy *noun*

1 not our policy: code of practice, rules, guidelines, procedure, method, practice, custom, protocol.
2 government policy: course of action, line, course, plan, programme, scheme, stance, position.

polish *verb*

1 polish your shoes: shine, brighten, smooth, rub, buff, burnish, clean, wax.
2 polishing their act: improve, enhance, brush up, touch up, finish, perfect, refine, cultivate.
🔁 1 tarnish, dull.
▶ *noun*

1 a tin of polish: wax, varnish.
2 a high polish: shine, gloss, sheen, lustre, brightness, brilliance, sparkle, smoothness, finish, glaze, veneer.
3 performance showed polish and insight: refinement, cultivation, class, breeding, sophistication, finesse, style, elegance, grace, poise.
🔁 2 dullness.

polished *adjective*

1 a polished surface: shining, shiny, glossy, lustrous, gleaming, burnished, smooth, glassy, slippery.
2 a polished performance: faultless, flawless, impeccable, perfect, outstanding, superlative, masterly, expert, professional, skilful, accomplished, perfected.
3 polished manners: refined, cultivated, genteel, well-bred, polite, sophisticated, urbane, suave, elegant, graceful.
🔁 1 tarnished. 2 inexpert. 3 gauche.

polite *adjective*

courteous, well-mannered, respectful, civil, well-bred, refined, cultured, gentlemanly, ladylike, gracious, obliging, thoughtful, considerate, tactful, diplomatic.
🔁 impolite, discourteous, rude.

politics *noun*

public affairs, civics, affairs of state, statecraft, government, diplomacy, statesmanship, political science.

Terms used in politics include:

alliance, apartheid, assembly, ballot, bill, blockade, cabinet, campaign, civil service, coalition, constitution, council, coup d'état, détente, devolution, election, electoral register, ethnic cleansing, first minister, general election, go to the country, government, green paper, Hansard, judiciary, left wing, lobby, local government, majority, mandate, manifesto, nationalization, parliament, party, party line, prime minister's question time, privatization, propaganda, proportional representation, rainbow coalition, referendum, right wing, sanction, shadow cabinet, sovereignty, state, summit, summit conference, term of office, trade union, veto, vote, welfare state, whip, three-line whip, white paper.

poll *noun*
ballot, vote, voting, plebiscite, referendum, straw-poll, sampling, canvass, opinion poll, survey, census, count, tally.

pollution *noun*
impurity, contamination, infection, taint, adulteration, corruption, dirtiness, foulness, defilement.
E3 purification, purity, cleanness.

pomp *noun*
ceremony, ceremonial, ritual, solemnity, formality, ceremoniousness, state, grandeur, splendour, magnificence, pageantry, show, display, parade, ostentation, flourish.
E3 austerity, simplicity.

pompous *adjective*
self-important, arrogant, grandiose, supercilious, overbearing, imperious, magisterial, bombastic, high-flown, overblown, windy, affected, pretentious, ostentatious, stuffy.
E3 unassuming, modest, simple, unaffected.

pool[1] *noun*
a deep pool: puddle, pond, lake, mere, tarn, watering-hole, paddling-pool, swimming-pool.

pool[2] *noun*
put money into the pool: fund, reserve, accumulation, bank, kitty, purse, pot, jackpot.
▶ *verb*
contribute, chip in (*infml*), combine, amalgamate, merge, share, muck in (*infml*).

poor *adjective*
1 a poor country: impoverished, poverty-stricken, badly off, hard-up, broke (*infml*), stony-broke (*infml*), skint (*infml*), bankrupt, penniless, destitute, miserable, wretched, distressed, straitened, needy, lacking, deficient, insufficient, scanty, skimpy, meagre, sparse, depleted, exhausted.
2 a poor mark: bad, substandard, unsatisfactory, inferior, mediocre, below par, low-grade, second-rate, third-rate, shoddy, imperfect, faulty, weak, feeble, pathetic (*infml*), sorry, worthless, fruitless.
3 the poor souls: unfortunate, unlucky, luckless, ill-fated, unhappy, miserable, pathetic, pitiable, pitiful.
E3 1 rich, wealthy, affluent. **2** superior, impressive. **3** fortunate, lucky.

poorly *adjective*
ill, sick, unwell, indisposed, ailing, sickly, off colour, below par, out of sorts (*infml*), under the weather (*infml*), seedy, groggy, rotten (*infml*).
E3 well, healthy.

pop *verb*
burst, explode, go off, bang, crack, snap.
▶ *noun*
bang, crack, snap, burst, explosion.

popular *adjective*
well-liked, favourite, liked, favoured, approved, in demand, sought-after, fashionable, modish, trendy (*infml*), prevailing, current, accepted, conventional, standard, stock, common, prevalent, widespread, universal, general, household, famous, well-known, celebrated, idolized.
E3 unpopular.

popularize *verb*
spread, propagate, universalize, democratize, simplify.

populate *verb*
people, occupy, settle, colonize, inhabit, live in, overrun.

population *noun*
inhabitants, natives, residents, citizens, occupants, community, society, people, folk.

porous *adjective*
permeable, pervious, penetrable, absorbent, spongy, honeycombed, pitted.
E3 impermeable, impervious.

portable *adjective*
movable, transportable, compact, lightweight, manageable, handy, convenient.
E3 fixed, immovable.

porter[1] *noun*
a station porter: bearer, carrier, baggage-attendant, baggage-handler.

porter[2] *noun*
the porter let us in: doorman, door-keeper, commissionaire, gatekeeper, janitor, caretaker, concierge.

portion *noun*
share, allocation, allotment, parcel, allowance, ration, quota, measure, part, section, division, fraction, percentage, bit, fragment, morsel, piece, segment, slice, serving, helping.

portrait *noun*
picture, painting, drawing, sketch, caricature, miniature, icon, photograph, likeness, image, representation, vignette, profile, characterization, description, depiction, portrayal.

portray *verb*
draw, sketch, paint, illustrate, picture, represent, depict, describe, evoke, play, impersonate, characterize, personify.

pose *verb*
1 posing for the camera: model, sit, position.
2 posing as a salesman: pretend, feign, affect, put on an act, masquerade, pass oneself off, impersonate.
3 pose a question: set, put forward, submit, present.
▶ *noun*
1 adopt a relaxed pose: position,

stance, air, bearing, posture, attitude.
2 just a pose: pretence, sham, affectation, façade, front, masquerade, role, act.

poser[1] *noun* (*infml*)
that's a bit of a poser: puzzle, riddle, conundrum, brain-teaser, mystery, enigma, problem, vexed question.

poser[2] *noun*
he's a real poser: poseur, poseuse, posturer, attitudinizer, exhibitionist, show-off, pseud (*infml*), phoney (*infml*).

posh *adjective* (*infml*)
smart, stylish, fashionable, high-class, upper-class, la-di-da (*infml*), grand, luxurious, lavish, swanky (*infml*), luxury, deluxe, up-market, exclusive, select, classy (*infml*), swish (*infml*).
E3 inferior, cheap.

position *noun*
1 what's the ship's position?: place, situation, location, site, spot, point.
2 sitting in an awkward position: posture, stance, pose, arrangement, disposition.
3 was offered the position of nanny: job, post, occupation, employment, office, duty, function, role.
4 a high position in government: rank, grade, level, status, standing.
5 take a position on the issue: opinion, point of view, belief, view, outlook, viewpoint, standpoint, stand.
▶ *verb*
put, place, set, fix, stand, arrange, dispose, lay out, deploy, station, locate, situate, site.

positive *adjective*
1 positive I saw him: sure, certain, convinced, confident, assured.
2 positive criticism: helpful, constructive, practical, useful, optimistic, hopeful, promising.
3 a positive answer: definite, decisive, conclusive, clear, unmistakable, explicit, unequivocal, express, firm, emphatic, categorical, undeniable, irrefutable, indisputable, incontrovertible.
4 it's a positive scandal!: absolute, utter, sheer, complete, perfect.

1 uncertain. **2** negative. **3** indefinite, vague.

possess *verb*
1 I don't possess an umbrella: own, have, hold, enjoy, be endowed with.
2 possessed by demons: seize, take, obtain, acquire, take over, occupy, control, dominate, bewitch, haunt.

possessions *noun*
belongings, property, things, paraphernalia, effects, goods, chattels (*fml*), movables, assets, estate, wealth, riches.

possessive *adjective*
selfish, clinging, overprotective, domineering, dominating, jealous, covetous, acquisitive, grasping.
unselfish, sharing.

possibility *noun*
likelihood, probability, odds, chance, risk, danger, hope, prospect, potentiality, conceivability, practicability, feasibility.
impossibility, impracticability.

possible *adjective*
potential, promising, likely, probable, imaginable, conceivable, practicable, feasible, viable, tenable, workable, achievable, attainable, accomplishable, realizable.
impossible, unthinkable, impracticable, unattainable.

possibly *adverb*
perhaps, maybe, hopefully (*infml*), by any means, at all, by any chance.

post¹ *noun*
a wooden post: pole, stake, picket, pale, pillar, column, shaft, support, baluster, upright, stanchion, strut, leg.
▶ *verb*
post a notice: display, stick up, pin up, advertise, publicize, announce, make known, report, publish.

post² *noun*
1 apply for the post of production controller: office, job, employment, position, situation, place, vacancy, appointment.
2 took up his usual post at the window: station, location, position.
▶ *verb*
was posted abroad: station, locate,

situate, position, place, put, appoint, assign, second, transfer, move, send.

post³ *noun*
arrived by the first post: mail, letters, dispatch, collection, delivery.
▶ *verb*
post a parcel: mail, send, dispatch, transmit.

poster *noun*
notice, bill, sign, placard, sticker, advertisement, announcement.

postpone *verb*
put off, defer, put back, hold over, delay, adjourn, suspend, shelve, pigeonhole, freeze, put on ice.
advance, forward.

postscript *noun*
PS (*infml*), addition, supplement, afterthought, addendum, codicil, appendix, afterword, epilogue.
introduction, prologue.

posture *noun*
position, stance, pose, attitude, disposition, bearing, carriage, deportment.

potent *adjective*
powerful, mighty, strong, intoxicating, pungent, effective, impressive, cogent, convincing, persuasive, compelling, forceful, dynamic, vigorous, authoritative, commanding, dominant, influential, overpowering.
impotent, weak.

potential *adjective*
possible, likely, probable, prospective, future, aspiring, would-be, promising, budding, embryonic, undeveloped, dormant, latent, hidden, concealed, unrealized.
▶ *noun*
possibility, ability, capability, capacity, aptitude, talent, powers, resources.

potion *noun*
mixture, concoction, brew, beverage, drink, draught, dose, medicine, tonic, elixir.

potter *verb*
tinker, fiddle, mess about (*infml*), dabble, loiter, fritter.

pounce *verb*
fall on, dive on, swoop, drop, attack,

strike, ambush, spring, jump, leap, snatch, grab.

pound *verb*
1 *pounding at the door*: strike, thump, beat, drum, pelt, hammer, batter, bang, bash, smash.
2 *pounding the rock into dust*: pulverize, powder, grind, mash, crush.
3 *his heart was pounding*: throb, pulsate, palpitate, thump, thud.

pour *verb*
1 *pour a drink*: serve, decant, tip.
2 *pouring into the football ground*: spill, issue, discharge, flow, stream, run, rush, spout, spew, gush, cascade, crowd, throng, swarm.

pout *verb*
scowl, glower, grimace, pull a face, sulk, mope.
🔁 grin, smile.

poverty *noun*
poorness, impoverishment, insolvency, bankruptcy, pennilessness, penury (*fml*), destitution, distress, hardship, privation (*fml*), need, necessity, want, lack, deficiency, shortage, inadequacy, insufficiency, depletion, scarcity, meagreness, paucity (*fml*), dearth.
🔁 wealth, richness, affluence, plenty.

powdery *adjective*
dusty, sandy, grainy, granular, powdered, pulverized, ground, fine, loose, dry, crumbly, friable, chalky.

power *noun*
1 *political power*: command, authority, sovereignty, rule, dominion, control, influence.
2 *powers of arrest*: right, privilege, prerogative, authorization, warrant.
3 *engine is losing power*: potency, strength, intensity, force, vigour, energy.
4 *the power of speech*: ability, capability, capacity, potential, faculty, competence.
🔁 1 subjection. 3 weakness. 4 inability.

powerful *adjective*
dominant, prevailing, leading, influential, high-powered, authoritative, commanding, potent, effective, strong, mighty, robust, muscular, energetic, forceful, telling, impressive, convincing, persuasive, compelling, winning, overwhelming.
🔁 impotent, ineffective, weak.

powerless *adjective*
impotent, incapable, ineffective, weak, feeble, frail, infirm, incapacitated, disabled, paralysed, helpless, vulnerable, defenceless, unarmed.
🔁 powerful, potent, able.

practicable *adjective*
possible, feasible, performable, achievable, attainable, viable, workable, practical, realistic.
🔁 impracticable.

practical *adjective*
1 *a practical idea/person*: realistic, sensible, commonsense, practicable, workable, feasible, down-to-earth, matter-of-fact, pragmatic, hardnosed (*infml*), hard-headed, businesslike, experienced, trained, qualified, skilled, accomplished, proficient, hands-on, applied.
2 *designed to be practical rather than beautiful*: useful, handy, serviceable, utilitarian, functional, working, everyday, ordinary.
🔁 1 impractical, unskilled, theoretical.

practically *adverb*
1 *practically grown up*: almost, nearly, well-nigh, virtually, pretty well, all but, just about, in principle, in effect, essentially, fundamentally, to all intents and purposes.
2 *not practically possible*: realistically, sensibly, reasonably, rationally, pragmatically.

practice *noun*
1 *our normal practice*: custom, tradition, convention, usage, habit, routine, way, method, system, procedure, policy.
2 *need practice*: rehearsal, run-through, dry run, dummy run, try-out, training, drill, exercise, work-out, study, experience.
3 *in practice*: effect, reality, actuality, action, operation, performance, use, application.
🔁 3 theory, principle.

practise *verb*
1 *practising medicine/law*: do,

perform, execute, implement, carry out, apply, put into practice, follow, pursue, engage in, undertake.
2 practising the violin : rehearse, run through, repeat, drill, exercise, train, study, perfect.

practised *adjective*
experienced, seasoned, veteran, trained, qualified, accomplished, skilled, versed, knowledgeable, able, proficient, expert, masterly, consummate, finished.
E3 unpractised, inexperienced, inexpert.

praise *noun*
approval, admiration, commendation, congratulation, compliment, flattery, adulation, eulogy, applause, ovation, cheering, acclaim, recognition, testimonial, tribute, accolade, homage, honour, glory, worship, adoration, devotion, thanksgiving.
E3 criticism, revilement.
▶ *verb*
commend, congratulate, admire, compliment, flatter, eulogize (*fml*), wax lyrical, rave over (*infml*), extol (*fml*), promote, applaud, cheer, acclaim, hail, recognize, acknowledge, pay tribute to, honour, laud (*fml*), glorify, magnify, exalt, worship, adore, bless.
E3 criticize, revile.

pray *verb*
invoke, call on, supplicate, entreat, implore, plead, beg, beseech, petition, ask, request, crave, solicit.

prayer *noun*
collect, litany, devotion, communion, invocation, supplication, entreaty, plea, appeal, petition, request.

preach *verb*
address, lecture, harangue, pontificate, sermonize, evangelize, moralize, exhort, urge, advocate.

precarious *adjective*
unsafe, dangerous, treacherous, risky, hazardous, chancy, uncertain, unsure, dubious, doubtful, unpredictable, unreliable, unsteady, unstable, shaky, wobbly, insecure, vulnerable.
E3 safe, certain, stable, secure.

precaution *noun*
safeguard, security, protection, insurance, providence, forethought, caution, prudence, foresight, anticipation, preparation, provision.

precede *verb*
come before, lead, come first, go before, take precedence, introduce, herald, usher in.
E3 follow, succeed.

precedent *noun*
example, instance, pattern, model, standard, criterion.

precious *adjective*
1 very precious to her : valued, treasured, prized, cherished, beloved, dearest, darling, favourite, loved, adored, idolized.
2 a precious stone : valuable, expensive, costly, dear, priceless, inestimable, rare, choice, fine.

precipitate *verb* (*fml*)
hasten, hurry, speed, accelerate, quicken, expedite, advance, further, bring on, induce, trigger, cause, occasion.
▶ *adjective* (*fml*)
sudden, unexpected, abrupt, quick, swift, rapid, brief, hasty, hurried, headlong, breakneck, frantic, violent, impatient, hot-headed, impetuous, impulsive, rash, reckless, heedless, indiscreet.
E3 cautious, careful.

precipitous *adjective*
steep, sheer, perpendicular, vertical, high.
E3 gradual.

precise *adjective*
exact, accurate, right, punctilious, correct, factual, faithful, authentic, literal, word-for-word, express, definite, explicit, unequivocal, unambiguous, clear-cut, distinct, detailed, blow-by-blow, minute, nice (*fml*), particular, specific, fixed, rigid, strict, careful, meticulous, scrupulous, fastidious.
E3 imprecise, inexact, ambiguous, careless.

precisely *adverb*
exactly, absolutely, just so, accurately,

correctly, literally, verbatim, word for word, strictly, minutely, clearly, distinctly.

precocious *adjective*
forward, ahead, advanced, early, premature, mature, developed, gifted, clever, bright, smart, quick, fast.
F3 backward.

preconception *noun*
presupposition, presumption, assumption, conjecture, anticipation, expectation, prejudgement, bias, prejudice.

predecessor *noun*
ancestor, forefather, forebear, antecedent, forerunner, precursor.
F3 successor, descendant.

predetermined *adjective*
1 believe everything is predetermined :
predestined, destined, fated, doomed, ordained, foreordained.
2 a predetermined time : prearranged, arranged, agreed, fixed, set.

predicament *noun*
situation, plight, trouble, mess, fix, spot (*infml*), quandary, dilemma, impasse, crisis, emergency.

predict *verb*
foretell, prophesy, foresee, forecast, prognosticate, project.

predictable *adjective*
foreseeable, expected, anticipated, likely, probable, imaginable, foreseen, foregone, certain, sure, reliable, dependable.
F3 unpredictable, uncertain.

pre-empt *verb*
anticipate, obviate, forestall.

preface *noun*
foreword, introduction, preamble, prologue, prelude, preliminaries.
F3 epilogue, postscript.
▸ *verb*
precede, prefix, lead up to, introduce, launch, open, begin, start.
F3 end, finish, complete.

prefer *verb*
favour, like better, would rather, would sooner, want, wish, desire, choose, select, pick, opt for, go for, plump for, single out, advocate, recommend,

back, support, fancy, elect, adopt.
F3 reject.

preferable *adjective*
better, superior, nicer, preferred, favoured, chosen, desirable, advantageous, advisable, recommended.
F3 inferior, undesirable.

preference *noun*
1 this would be my preference :
favourite, first choice, choice, pick, selection, option, wish, desire.
2 have a preference for : liking, fancy, inclination, predilection, partiality, favouritism, preferential treatment.

preferential *adjective*
better, superior, favoured, privileged, special, favourable, advantageous.
F3 equal.

pregnant *adjective*
1 a pregnant woman : expectant, expecting, with child (*fml*).
2 a pregnant pause : meaningful, significant, eloquent, expressive, suggestive, charged, loaded, full.

prejudice *noun*
1 racial/religious prejudice : bias, partiality, partisanship, discrimination, unfairness, injustice, intolerance, narrow-mindedness, bigotry, chauvinism, racism, sexism.
2 without prejudice to any subsequent discussion : harm, damage, impairment, hurt, injury, detriment, disadvantage, loss, ruin.
F3 1 fairness, tolerance. 2 benefit, advantage.
▸ *verb*
1 prejudicing the jury against the witness : bias, predispose, incline, sway, influence, condition, colour, slant, distort, load, weight.
2 prejudice his chances of getting a job : harm, damage, impair, hinder, undermine, hurt, injure, mar, spoil, ruin, wreck.
F3 2 benefit, help, advance.

prejudiced *adjective*
biased, partial, predisposed, subjective, partisan, one-sided, discriminatory, unfair, unjust, loaded, weighted, intolerant, narrow-minded,

bigoted, chauvinist, racist, sexist, jaundiced, distorted, warped, influenced, conditioned.
F3 impartial, fair, tolerant.

preliminary *adjective*
preparatory, prior, advance, exploratory, experimental, trial, test, pilot, early, earliest, first, initial, primary, qualifying, inaugural, introductory, opening.
F3 final, closing.

prelude *noun*
overture, introduction, preface, foreword, preamble, prologue, opening, opener, preliminary, preparation, beginning, start, commencement, precursor, curtain-raiser.
F3 finale, epilogue.

premature *adjective*
early, immature, green, unripe, embryonic, half-formed, incomplete, undeveloped, abortive, hasty, ill-considered, rash, untimely, inopportune, ill-timed.
F3 late, tardy.

premeditated *adjective*
planned, intended, intentional, deliberate, wilful, conscious, cold-blooded, calculated, considered, contrived, preplanned, prearranged, predetermined.
F3 unpremeditated, spontaneous.

premise *noun*
proposition, statement, assertion, postulate, thesis, argument, basis, supposition, hypothesis, presupposition, assumption.

premises *noun*
building, property, establishment, office, grounds, estate, site, place.

premonition *noun*
presentiment, feeling, intuition, hunch, idea, suspicion, foreboding, misgiving, fear, apprehension, anxiety, worry, warning, omen, sign.

preoccupied *adjective*
1 preoccupied with work: obsessed, intent, immersed, engrossed, engaged, taken up, wrapped up, involved.
2 a preoccupied look: distracted, abstracted, absent-minded,

daydreaming, absorbed, faraway, heedless, oblivious, pensive.

preparation *noun*
1 do the preparation/in preparation for: readiness, provision, precaution, safeguard, foundation, groundwork, spadework, basics, rudiments, preliminaries, plans, arrangements.
2 a medical preparation: mixture, compound, concoction, potion, medicine, lotion, application.

preparatory *adjective*
preliminary, introductory, opening, initial, primary, basic, fundamental, rudimentary, elementary.

prepare *verb*
1 preparing them for the match: get ready, warm up, train, coach, study, make ready, adapt, adjust, plan, organize, arrange, pave the way.
2 prepare a meal: make, produce, construct, assemble, concoct, contrive, devise, draft, draw up, compose.
3 to prepare a room for visitors: provide, supply, equip, fit out, rig out.

prepared *adjective*
ready, waiting, set, fit, inclined, disposed, willing, planned, organized, arranged.
F3 unprepared, unready.

prescribe *verb*
ordain, decree, dictate, rule, command, order, require, direct, assign, specify, stipulate, lay down, set, appoint, impose, fix, define, limit.

prescription *noun*
medicine, drug, preparation, mixture, remedy, treatment.

presence *noun*
1 the presence of oxygen in the atmosphere/in the judge's presence: attendance, company, occupancy, residence, existence.
2 have a certain presence: aura, air, demeanour, bearing, carriage, appearance, poise, self-assurance, personality, charisma.
3 could feel her presence: nearness, closeness, proximity, vicinity.
F3 1 absence. **3** remoteness.

present[1] *adjective* /**prez**-ent/
1 present at the meeting: attending,

here, there, near, at hand, to hand,
available, ready.
2 at the present time: current,
contemporary, present-day,
immediate, instant, existent, existing.
F3 1 absent. **2** past, out-of-date.

present² *verb* /pri-zent/
1 present a play: show, display, exhibit,
demonstrate, mount, stage, put on,
introduce, announce.
2 present him with the award: award,
confer, bestow, grant, give, donate,
hand over, entrust, extend, hold out,
offer, tender, submit.

present³ *noun* /prez-ent/
a birthday present: gift, prezzie
(*infml*), offering, donation, grant,
endowment, benefaction (*fml*), bounty,
largess, gratuity, tip, favour.

presentable *adjective*
neat, tidy, clean, respectable, decent,
proper, suitable, acceptable,
satisfactory, tolerable.
F3 unpresentable, untidy, shabby.

presentation *noun*
1 presentation is important: show,
performance, production, staging,
representation, display, exhibition,
demonstration, talk, delivery,
appearance, arrangement.
2 made a presentation to the queen:
award, conferral, bestowal, investiture.

presently *adverb*
1 be there presently: soon, shortly, in a
minute, before long, by and by.
2 not working presently: currently, at
present, now.

preserve *verb*
1 preserve our customs: protect,
safeguard, guard, defend, shield,
shelter, care for, maintain, uphold,
sustain, continue, perpetuate, keep,
retain, conserve, save, store.
2 preserve food: bottle, tin, can,
pickle, salt, cure, dry, smoke, treat.
F3 1 destroy, ruin.
▶ *noun*
1 home-made preserves: conserve,
jam, marmalade, jelly, pickle.
2 not his preserve: domain, realm,
sphere, area, field, speciality.
3 a preserve for endangered species:
reservation, sanctuary, game reserve,
safari park.

preside *verb*
chair, officiate, conduct, direct,
manage, administer, control, run,
head, lead, govern, rule.

press *verb*
1 press flowers: crush, squash,
squeeze, compress, stuff, cram, crowd,
push, depress.
2 press clothes: iron, smooth, flatten.
3 pressed her in his arms: hug,
embrace, clasp, squeeze.
4 pressed him for an answer: urge,
plead, petition, campaign, demand,
insist on, compel, constrain, force,
pressure, pressurize, harass.
▶ *noun*
1 a press of people: crowd, throng,
multitude, mob, horde, swarm, pack,
crush, push.
2 a member of the press: journalists,
reporters, correspondents, the media,
newspapers, papers, Fleet Street,
fourth estate.

pressing *adjective*
urgent, high-priority, burning, crucial,
vital, essential, imperative, serious,
important.
F3 unimportant, trivial.

pressure *noun*
1 under pressure: force, power, load,
burden, weight, heaviness,
compression, squeezing, stress, strain.
2 the pressures of modern living:
difficulty, problem, demand,
constraint, stress, obligation, urgency.

pressurize *verb*
force, compel, constrain, oblige, drive,
bulldoze, coerce, press, pressure, lean
on (*infml*), browbeat, bully.

prestige *noun*
status, reputation, standing, stature,
eminence, distinction, esteem, regard,
importance, authority, influence, fame,
renown, kudos, credit, honour.
F3 humbleness, unimportance.

prestigious *adjective*
esteemed, respected, reputable,
important, influential, great, eminent,
prominent, illustrious, renowned,
celebrated, exalted, imposing,

impressive, up-market.
E3 humble, modest.

presume *verb*
1 presume this is correct: assume, take
it, think, believe, suppose, surmise,
infer, presuppose, take for granted,
count on, rely on, depend on, bank on,
trust.
2 presume to criticize: dare, make so
bold, go so far, venture, undertake.

presumptuous *adjective*
bold, audacious, impertinent,
impudent, insolent, over-familiar,
forward, pushy (*infml*), arrogant, over-
confident, conceited.
E3 humble, modest.

pretence *noun*
show, display, appearance, cover, front,
façade, veneer, cloak, veil, mask, guise,
sham, feigning, faking, simulation,
deception, trickery, wile, ruse, excuse,
pretext, bluff, falsehood, deceit,
fabrication, invention, make-believe,
charade, acting, play-acting,
posturing, posing, affectation,
pretension, pretentiousness.
E3 honesty, openness.

pretend *verb*
1 pretend to be pleased: affect, put on,
assume, feign, sham, counterfeit, fake,
simulate, bluff, impersonate, pass
oneself off, act, play-act, mime, go
through the motions.
2 pretending to the throne: claim,
allege, profess, purport.
3 pretend this is a castle: imagine,
make believe, suppose.

pretentious *adjective*
pompous, self-important, conceited,
immodest, snobbish, affected,
mannered, showy, ostentatious,
extravagant, over-the-top, exaggerated,
magniloquent, high-sounding, inflated,
grandiose, ambitious, overambitious.
E3 modest, humble, simple,
straightforward.

pretext *noun*
excuse, ploy, ruse, cover, cloak, mask,
guise, semblance, appearance,
pretence, show.

pretty *adjective*
attractive, good-looking, beautiful,

fair, lovely, bonny, cute, winsome,
appealing, charming, dainty, graceful,
elegant, fine, delicate, nice.
E3 plain, unattractive, ugly.
▸ *adverb*
fairly, somewhat, rather, quite,
reasonably, moderately, tolerably.

prevail *verb*
1 the opinion that prevails:
predominate, preponderate, abound.
2 our soldiers will prevail: win,
triumph, succeed, overcome, overrule,
reign, rule.
E3 2 lose.
◆ **prevail upon** persuade, talk into,
prompt, induce, incline, sway,
influence, convince, win over.

prevailing *adjective*
predominant, preponderant, main,
principal, dominant, controlling,
powerful, compelling, influential,
reigning, ruling, current, fashionable,
popular, mainstream, accepted,
established, set, usual, customary,
common, prevalent, widespread.
E3 minor, subordinate.

prevalent *adjective*
widespread, extensive, rampant, rife,
frequent, general, customary, usual,
universal, ubiquitous, common,
everyday, popular, current, prevailing.
E3 uncommon, rare.

prevent *verb*
stop, avert, avoid, head off, ward off,
stave off, intercept, forestall,
anticipate, frustrate, thwart, check,
restrain, inhibit, hinder, hamper,
impede, obstruct, block, bar.
E3 cause, help, foster, encourage,
allow.

prevention *noun*
avoidance, frustration, check,
hindrance, impediment, obstruction,
obstacle, bar, elimination, precaution,
safeguard, deterrence.
E3 cause, help.

preventive *adjective*
preventative, anticipatory, pre-
emptive, inhibitory, obstructive,
precautionary, protective,
counteractive, deterrent.
E3 causative.

previous *adjective*
preceding, foregoing, earlier, prior, past, former, ex-, one-time, sometime, erstwhile.
F≡ following, subsequent, later.

previously *adverb*
formerly, once, earlier, before, beforehand.
F≡ later.

prey *noun*
quarry, victim, game, kill.
◆ **prey on 1** preying on small animals : hunt, kill, devour, feed on, live off, exploit.
2 prey on one's mind : haunt, trouble, distress, worry, burden, weigh down, oppress.

price *noun*
value, worth, cost, expense, outlay, expenditure, fee, charge, levy, toll, rate, bill, assessment, valuation, estimate, quotation, figure, amount, sum, payment, reward, penalty, forfeit, sacrifice, consequences.
▸ *verb*
value, rate, cost, evaluate, assess, estimate.

priceless *adjective*
1 a priceless manuscript : invaluable, inestimable, incalculable, expensive, costly, dear, precious, valuable, prized, treasured, irreplaceable.
2 (*infml*) joke was priceless : funny, amusing, comic, hilarious, riotous, side-splitting, killing (*infml*), rich (*infml*).
F≡ **1** cheap, run-of-the-mill.

prick *verb*
pierce, puncture, perforate, punch, jab, stab, sting, bite, prickle, itch, tingle.
▸ *noun*
puncture, perforation, pinhole, stab, pang, twinge, sting, bite.

prickly *adjective*
1 a prickly bush : thorny, brambly, spiny, barbed, spiky, bristly, rough, scratchy.
2 he can be a bit prickly : irritable, edgy, touchy, grumpy, short-tempered.
F≡ **1** smooth. **2** relaxed, easy-going (*infml*).

pride *noun*
1 pride goes before a fall : conceit,
vanity, egotism, bigheadedness, boastfulness, smugness, arrogance, self-importance, presumption, haughtiness, superciliousness, snobbery, pretentiousness.
2 for her pride's sake : dignity, self-respect, self-esteem, honour.
3 take pride in something : satisfaction, gratification, pleasure, delight.
F≡ **1** humility, modesty. **2** shame.

priest *noun*
minister, vicar, padre, father, man of God, man of the cloth, clergyman, clergywoman, churchman, churchwoman.

prim *adjective*
prudish, strait-laced, formal, demure, proper, priggish, prissy, fussy, particular, precise, fastidious.
F≡ informed, relaxed, easy-going (*infml*).

primarily *adverb*
chiefly, principally, mainly, mostly, basically, fundamentally, especially, particularly, essentially.

primary *adjective*
1 primary school : first, earliest, original, initial, introductory, beginning, basic, fundamental, essential, radical, rudimentary, elementary, simple.
2 primary reason : chief, principal, main, dominant, leading, foremost, supreme, cardinal, capital, paramount, greatest, highest, ultimate.
F≡ **2** secondary, subsidiary, minor.

prime *adjective*
best, choice, select, quality, first-class, first-rate, excellent, top, supreme, pre-eminent, superior, senior, leading, ruling, chief, principal, main, predominant, primary.
F≡ second-rate, secondary.
▸ *noun*
height, peak, zenith, heyday, flower, bloom, maturity, perfection.

primeval *adjective*
earliest, first, original, primordial, early, old, ancient, prehistoric, primitive, instinctive.
F≡ modern.

primitive *adjective*
1 primitive paintings: crude, rough, unsophisticated, uncivilized, barbarian, savage.
2 primitive man: early, elementary, rudimentary, primary, first, original, earliest.
F3 1 advanced, sophisticated, civilized.

principal *adjective*
main, chief, key, essential, cardinal, primary, first, foremost, leading, dominant, prime, paramount, pre-eminent, supreme, highest.
F3 minor, subsidiary, lesser, least.
▶ *noun*
head, head teacher, headmaster, headmistress, chief, leader, boss, director, manager, superintendent.

principally *adverb*
mainly, mostly, chiefly, primarily, predominantly, above all, particularly, especially.

principle *noun*
1 go against all principles of morality and decency: rule, formula, law, canon, axiom, dictum, precept (*fml*), maxim, truth, tenet, doctrine, creed, dogma, code, standard, criterion, proposition, fundamental, essential.
2 a man of principle: honour, integrity, rectitude, uprightness, virtue, decency, morality, morals, ethics, standards, scruples, conscience.

print *verb*
mark, stamp, imprint, impress, engrave, copy, reproduce, run off, publish, issue.
▶ *noun*
1 appear in print: letters, characters, lettering, type, typescript, typeface, fount.
2 find the lion's prints: mark, impression, fingerprint, footprint.
3 make a series of prints of the painting: copy, reproduction, picture, engraving, lithograph, photograph, photo.

prior *adjective*
earlier, preceding, foregoing, previous, former.
F3 later.

◆ **prior to** before, preceding, earlier than.
F3 after, following.

priority *noun*
right of way, precedence, seniority, rank, superiority, pre-eminence, supremacy, the lead, first place, urgency.
F3 inferiority.

prison *noun*
jail, nick (*infml*), clink (*slang*), cooler (*slang*), penitentiary, cell, lock-up, cage, dungeon, imprisonment, confinement, detention, custody.

prisoner *noun*
captive, hostage, convict, jail-bird (*infml*), inmate, internee, detainee.

privacy *noun*
secrecy, confidentiality, independence, solitude, isolation, seclusion, concealment, retirement, retreat.

private *adjective*
1 private discussion: secret, classified, hush-hush (*infml*), off the record, unofficial, confidential.
2 private life: intimate, personal, individual, own, secret, independent, solitary, reserved, withdrawn.
3 private place: isolated, secluded, hidden, concealed, exclusive, particular, special, separate, remote.
F3 1 public, open.
◆ **in private** privately, in confidence, secretly, in secret, behind closed doors, in camera.
F3 publicly, openly.

privilege *noun*
advantage, benefit, concession, birthright, title, due, right, prerogative, entitlement, freedom, liberty, franchise, licence, sanction, authority, immunity, exemption.
F3 disadvantage.

privileged *adjective*
advantaged, favoured, special, sanctioned, authorized, immune, exempt, élite, honoured, ruling, powerful.
F3 disadvantaged, underprivileged.

prize *noun*
reward, trophy, medal, award, winnings, jackpot, purse, premium,

stake(s), honour, accolade.
▶ *adjective*
best, top, first-rate, excellent,
outstanding, champion, winning,
prize-winning, award-winning, plum,
top-notch (*infml*).
F3 second-rate.
▶ *verb*
treasure, value, appreciate, esteem,
revere, cherish, hold dear.
F3 despise.

probability *noun*
likelihood, odds, chances, expectation,
prospect, chance, possibility.
F3 improbability.

probable *adjective*
likely, odds-on, expected, credible,
believable, plausible, feasible, possible,
apparent, seeming.
F3 improbable, unlikely.

probation *noun*
apprenticeship, trial period, trial,
test.

probe *verb*
prod, poke, pierce, penetrate, sound,
plumb, explore, examine, scrutinize,
investigate, go into, look into, search,
sift, test.

problem *noun*
1 what's the problem here?: trouble,
worry, predicament, quandary,
dilemma, difficulty, complication,
snag.
2 a mathematical problem: question,
poser (*infml*), puzzle, brain-teaser,
conundrum, riddle, enigma.
▶ *adjective*
difficult, unmanageable,
uncontrollable, unruly, delinquent.
F3 well-behaved, manageable.

procedure *noun*
routine, process, method, system,
technique, custom, practice, policy,
formula, course, scheme, strategy, plan
of action, move, step, action, conduct,
operation, performance.

proceed *verb*
1 permission to proceed: advance, go
ahead, move on, progress, continue,
carry on, press on.
2 proceeding from our discussions:
originate, derive, flow, start, stem,

spring, arise, issue, result, ensue,
follow, come.
F3 **1** stop, retreat.

proceedings *noun*
1 court proceedings: matters, affairs,
business, dealings, transactions,
report, account, minutes, records,
archives, annals.
2 watch the proceedings with interest:
events, happenings, deeds, doings,
moves, steps, measures, action, course
of action.

proceeds *noun*
revenue, income, returns, receipts,
takings, earnings, gain, profit, yield,
produce.
F3 expenditure, outlay.

process *noun*
1 the smelting process: procedure,
operation, practice, method, system,
technique, means, manner, mode, way,
stage, step.
2 in the process of developing: course,
progression, advance, progress,
development, evolution, formation,
growth, movement, action,
proceeding.
▶ *verb*
deal with, handle, treat, prepare, refine,
transform, convert, change, alter.

procession *noun*
march, parade, cavalcade, motorcade,
cortège, file, column, train, succession,
series, sequence, course, run.

proclaim *verb*
announce, declare, pronounce, affirm,
give out, publish, advertise, make
known, profess, testify, show, indicate.

procure *verb*
acquire, buy, purchase, get, obtain,
find, come by, pick up, lay hands on,
earn, gain, win, secure, appropriate,
requisition.
F3 lose.

prod *verb*
poke, jab, dig, elbow, nudge, push,
shove, goad, spur, urge, egg on (*infml*),
prompt, stimulate, motivate.
▶ *noun*
poke, jab, dig, elbow, nudge, push,
shove, prompt, reminder, stimulus,
motivation.

prodigy *noun*
genius, virtuoso, wonder, marvel, miracle, phenomenon, sensation, freak, curiosity, rarity, child genius, wonder child, whizz kid (*infml*).

produce *verb*
1 **produce gases/milk**: cause, occasion, give rise to, provoke, bring about, result in, effect, create, originate, invent, make, manufacture, fabricate, construct, compose, generate, yield, bear, deliver.
2 **produced a letter from his pocket**: advance, put forward, present, offer, give, supply, provide, furnish, bring out, bring forth, show, exhibit, demonstrate.
3 **produce a play**: direct, stage, mount, put on.
▶ *noun*
crop, harvest, yield, output, product.

product *noun*
1 **dairy/manufactured products**: commodity, merchandise, goods, end-product, artefact, work, creation, invention, production, output, yield, produce, fruit, return.
2 **the accident was a product of carelessness**: result, consequence, outcome, issue, upshot, offshoot, spin-off, by-product, legacy.
⊟ 2 cause.

production *noun*
1 **the production of oil and gas**: making, manufacture, fabrication, construction, assembly, creation, origination, preparation, formation.
2 **an amateur production**: staging, presentation, direction, management.
⊟ 1 consumption.

productive *adjective*
fruitful, profitable, rewarding, valuable, worthwhile, useful, constructive, creative, inventive, fertile, rich, teeming, busy, energetic, vigorous, efficient, effective.
⊟ unproductive, fruitless, useless.

productivity *noun*
productiveness, yield, output, work rate, efficiency.

profession *noun*
1 **one of the caring professions**: career, job, occupation, employment, business, line (of work), trade, vocation, calling, métier, craft, office, position.
2 **a profession of guilt**: admission, confession, acknowledgement, declaration, announcement, statement, testimony, assertion, affirmation, claim.

professional *adjective*
qualified, licensed, trained, experienced, practised, skilled, expert, masterly, proficient, competent, businesslike, efficient.
⊟ amateur, unprofessional.
▶ *noun*
expert, authority, specialist, pro (*infml*), master, virtuoso, dab hand (*infml*).
⊟ amateur.

proficient *adjective*
able, capable, skilled, qualified, trained, experienced, accomplished, expert, masterly, gifted, talented, clever, skilful, competent, efficient.
⊟ unskilled, incompetent.

profile *noun*
1 **viewed in profile**: side view, outline, contour, silhouette, shape, form, figure, sketch, drawing, diagram, chart, graph.
2 **a profile of the candidate**: biography, curriculum vitae, thumbnail sketch, vignette, portrait, study, analysis, examination, survey, review.

profit *noun*
gain, surplus, excess, bottom line, revenue, return, yield, proceeds, receipts, takings, earnings, winnings, interest, advantage, benefit, use, avail, value, worth.
⊟ loss.
▶ *verb*
gain, make money, pay, serve, avail, benefit.
⊟ lose.

profitable *adjective*
cost-effective, economic, commercial, money-making, lucrative, remunerative, paying, rewarding, successful, fruitful, productive, advantageous, beneficial, useful,

valuable, worthwhile.
E3 unprofitable, loss-making, non-profit-making.

profound *adjective*
1 profound sadness : deep, great, intense, extreme, heartfelt, marked, far-reaching, extensive, exhaustive.
2 a profound remark : serious, weighty, penetrating, thoughtful, philosophical, wise, learned, erudite, abstruse (*fml*).
E3 1 shallow, slight, mild.

profusion *noun*
abundance, plenty, wealth, multitude, plethora, glut, excess, surplus, superfluity, extravagance.
E3 inadequacy, scarcity.

programme *noun*
1 a teaching/study programme : schedule, timetable, agenda, calendar, order of events, listing, line-up, plan, scheme, project, syllabus, curriculum.
2 radio programme : broadcast, transmission, show, performance, production, presentation.

progress *noun*
movement, progression, passage, journey, way, advance, headway, step forward, breakthrough, development, evolution, growth, increase, improvement, betterment, promotion.
E3 recession, deterioration, decline.
▸ *verb*
proceed, advance, go forward, forge ahead, make progress, make headway, come on, develop, grow, mature, blossom, improve, better, prosper, increase.
E3 deteriorate, decline.

progression *noun*
cycle, chain, string, succession, series, sequence, order, course, advance, headway, progress, development.

progressive *adjective*
1 a progressive school : modern, avant-garde, advanced, forward-looking, enlightened, liberal, radical, revolutionary, reformist, dynamic, enterprising, go-ahead, up-and-coming.
2 progressive disease : advancing, continuing, developing, growing, increasing, intensifying.
E3 1 regressive.

prohibit *verb*
forbid, ban, bar, veto, proscribe, outlaw, rule out, preclude, prevent, stop, hinder, hamper, impede, obstruct, restrict.
E3 permit, allow, authorize.

project *noun* /proj-ekt/
assignment, contract, task, job, work, occupation, activity, enterprise, undertaking, venture, plan, scheme, programme, design, proposal, idea, conception.
▸ *verb* /pro-**jekt**/
1 project into the future : predict, forecast, extrapolate, estimate, reckon, calculate.
2 missiles projected at the cities : throw, fling, hurl, launch, propel.
3 projecting from the surface : protrude, stick out, bulge, jut out, overhang.

projection *noun*
1 a projection from the wall : protuberance (*fml*), bulge, overhang, ledge, sill, shelf, ridge.
2 a budget projection : prediction, forecast, extrapolation, estimate, reckoning, calculation, computation.

prolific *adjective*
productive, fruitful, fertile, profuse, copious, abundant.
E3 unproductive.

prolong *verb*
lengthen, extend, stretch, protract, draw out, spin out, drag out, delay, continue, perpetuate.
E3 shorten.

prominent *adjective*
1 put it in a prominent position : noticeable, conspicuous, obvious, unmistakable, striking, eye-catching.
2 prominent eyes : bulging, protuberant, projecting, jutting, protruding, obtrusive.
3 a prominent writer : famous, well-known, celebrated, renowned, noted, eminent, distinguished, respected, leading, foremost, chief, main, important, popular, outstanding.
E3 1 inconspicuous. **3** unknown, unimportant, insignificant.

promise *verb*
1 promise to pay: vow, pledge, swear, take an oath, contract, undertake, give one's word, vouch, warrant, guarantee, assure.
2 dark clouds promising rain: augur, presage, indicate, suggest, hint at.
▶ *noun*
1 make a promise: vow, pledge, oath, word of honour, bond, compact, covenant, guarantee, assurance, undertaking, engagement, commitment.
2 show promise: potential, ability, capability, aptitude, talent.

promising *adjective*
auspicious, propitious, favourable, rosy, bright, encouraging, hopeful, talented, gifted, budding, up-and-coming.
E3 unpromising, inauspicious, discouraging.

promote *verb*
1 promote their products/promote a healthy lifestyle: advertise, plug (*infml*), publicize, hype (*infml*), popularize, market, sell, push, recommend, advocate, champion, endorse, sponsor, support, back, help, aid, assist, foster, nurture, further, forward, encourage, boost, stimulate, urge.
2 promoted to head teacher: upgrade, advance, move up, raise, elevate, exalt, honour.
E3 1 disparage (*fml*), hinder. **2** demote.

promotion *noun*
1 ask for/get promotion: advancement, upgrading, rise, preferment, elevation, exaltation.
2 an advertising promotion: advertising, plugging (*infml*), publicity, hype (*infml*), campaign, propaganda, marketing, pushing, support, backing, furtherance, development, encouragement, boosting.
E3 1 demotion. **2** disparagement (*fml*), obstruction.

prompt[1] *adjective*
a prompt payer: punctual, on time, immediate, instantaneous, instant, direct, quick, swift, rapid, speedy, unhesitating, willing, ready, alert, responsive, timely, early.
E3 slow, hesitant, late.
▶ *adverb*
promptly, punctually, exactly, on the dot, to the minute, sharp.

prompt[2] *verb*
prompting him to reply: cause, give rise to, result in, occasion, produce, instigate, call forth, elicit, provoke, incite, urge, encourage, inspire, move, stimulate, motivate, spur, prod, remind.
E3 deter, dissuade.
▶ *noun*
reminder, cue, hint, help, jolt, prod, spur, stimulus.

prone *adjective*
1 prone to jealousy: likely, given, inclined, disposed, predisposed, bent, apt, liable, subject, susceptible, vulnerable.
2 she lay prone: face down, prostrate, flat, horizontal, full-length, stretched, recumbent.
E3 1 unlikely, immune. **2** upright, supine.

pronounce *verb*
1 pronounce words correctly: say, utter, speak, express, voice, vocalize, sound, enunciate, articulate, stress.
2 pronounced herself satisfied: declare, announce, proclaim, decree, judge, affirm, assert.

pronounced *adjective*
clear, distinct, definite, positive, decided, marked, noticeable, conspicuous, evident, obvious, striking, unmistakable, strong, broad.
E3 faint, vague.

pronunciation *noun*
speech, diction, elocution, enunciation, articulation, delivery, accent, stress, inflection, intonation, modulation.

proof *noun*
evidence, documentation, demonstration, verification, confirmation, corroboration, substantiation.

prop *verb*
1 propping up the wall: support,

sustain, uphold, maintain, shore, stay, buttress, bolster, underpin, set.
2 propped against the wall: lean, rest, stand.
▶ *noun*
support, stay, mainstay, strut, buttress, brace, truss.

propaganda *noun*
advertising, publicity, hype (*infml*), indoctrination, brainwashing, disinformation.

propagate *verb*
1 propagating rumours: spread, transmit, broadcast, diffuse, disseminate, circulate, publish, promulgate, publicize, promote.
2 propagating plants: increase, multiply, proliferate, generate, produce, breed, beget (*fml*), spawn, procreate, reproduce.

propel *verb*
move, drive, impel, force, thrust, push, shove, launch, shoot, send.
F∃ stop.

proper *adjective*
1 the proper way to do it: right, correct, accurate, exact, precise, true, genuine, real, actual.
2 proper behaviour: accepted, correct, suitable, appropriate, fitting, decent, respectable, polite, formal.
F∃ 1 wrong. **2** improper, indecent.

property *noun*
1 own property: estate, land, real estate (*US*), acres, premises, buildings, house(s), wealth, riches, resources, means, capital, assets, holding(s), belongings, possessions, effects, goods, chattels (*fml*).
2 a property of the chemical: feature, trait, quality, attribute, characteristic, idiosyncrasy, peculiarity, mark.

prophecy *noun* / **prof**-*es*-i/
prediction, augury, forecast, prognosis.

prophesy *verb* / **prof**-*es*-ai/
predict, foresee, augur, foretell, forewarn, forecast.

prophet *noun*
seer, soothsayer, foreteller, forecaster, oracle, clairvoyant, fortune-teller.

proportion *noun*
1 a large proportion: percentage, fraction, part, division, share, quota, amount.
2 in proportion: ratio, relationship, correspondence, symmetry, balance, distribution.
F∃ 2 disproportion, imbalance.

proportional *adjective*
proportionate, relative, commensurate, consistent, corresponding, analogous, comparable, equitable, even.
F∃ disproportionate.

proportions *noun*
dimensions, measurements, size, magnitude, volume, capacity.

proposal *noun*
proposition, suggestion, motion, recommendation, plan, scheme, project, design, programme, manifesto, presentation, bid, offer, tender, terms.

propose *verb*
1 propose a motion: suggest, recommend, move, advance, put forward, introduce, bring up, table, submit, present, offer, tender.
2 when do you propose to leave?: intend, mean, aim, purpose, plan, design.
3 propose him for chairman: nominate, put up.
4 propose marriage: ask to marry, ask for someone's hand (in marriage), pop the question (*infml*), go down on bended knee (*infml*).
F∃ 1 withdraw.

proprietor *noun*
landlord, landlady, title-holder, freeholder, leaseholder, landowner, owner, possessor.

prosecute *verb*
accuse, indict, sue, prefer charges, take to court, litigate, summon, put on trial, try.
F∃ defend.

prospect *noun*
chance, odds, probability, likelihood, possibility, hope, expectation, anticipation, outlook, future.
F∃ unlikelihood.

prospective *adjective*
future, -to-be, intended, designate,

destined, forthcoming, approaching, coming, imminent, awaited, expected, anticipated, likely, possible, probable, potential, aspiring, would-be.
E3 current.

prosper *verb*
boom, thrive, flourish, flower, bloom, succeed, get on, advance, progress, grow rich.
E3 fail.

prosperity *noun*
boom, plenty, affluence, wealth, riches, fortune, well-being, luxury, the good life, success, good fortune.
E3 adversity, poverty.

prosperous *adjective*
booming, thriving, flourishing, blooming, successful, fortunate, lucky, rich, wealthy, affluent, well-off, well-to-do.
E3 unfortunate, poor.

prostrate *adjective* /praw-streit/
flat, horizontal, prone, fallen, overcome, overwhelmed, crushed, paralysed, powerless, helpless, defenceless.
E3 triumphant.
▶ *verb* /praw-**streit**/
lay low, overcome, overwhelm, crush, overthrow, tire, wear out, fatigue, exhaust, drain, ruin.
E3 strengthen.

protagonist *noun*
hero, heroine, lead, principal, leader, prime mover, champion, advocate, supporter, proponent, exponent.

protect *verb*
safeguard, defend, guard, escort, cover, screen, shield, secure, watch over, look after, care for, support, shelter, harbour, keep, conserve, preserve, save.
E3 attack, neglect.

protection *noun*
1 protection of the environment : care, custody, charge, guardianship, safekeeping, conservation, preservation, safety, safeguard.
2 flood protection : barrier, buffer, bulwark, defence, guard, shield, armour, screen, cover, shelter,

refuge, security, insurance.
E3 1 neglect, attack.

protective *adjective*
1 protective parents : possessive, defensive, motherly, maternal, fatherly, paternal, watchful, vigilant, careful.
2 protective clothing : waterproof, fireproof, insulating, weatherproof.
E3 1 aggressive, threatening.

protest *noun* /**proh**-test/
objection, disapproval, opposition, dissent, complaint, protestation, outcry, appeal, demonstration.
E3 acceptance.
▶ *verb* /pro-**test**/
1 protest against the new road : object, take exception, complain, appeal, demonstrate, oppose, disapprove, disagree, argue.
2 protest one's innocence : assert, maintain, contend, insist, profess.
E3 1 accept.

protracted *adjective*
long, lengthy, prolonged, extended, drawn-out, long-drawn-out, overlong, interminable.
E3 brief, shortened.

protrude *verb*
stick out, poke out, come through, bulge, jut out, project, extend, stand out, obtrude.

proud *adjective*
1 a proud man : conceited, vain, egotistical, bigheaded, boastful, smug, complacent, arrogant, self-important, cocky, presumptuous, haughty, high and mighty, overbearing, supercilious, snooty (*infml*), snobbish, toffee-nosed (*infml*), stuck-up (*infml*).
2 proud of his achievements : satisfied, contented, gratified, pleased, delighted, honoured.
3 a proud tradition : dignified, noble, honourable, worthy, self-respecting.
E3 1 humble, modest, unassuming.
2 ashamed. **3** deferential, ignoble.

prove *verb*
show, demonstrate, attest (*fml*), verify, confirm, corroborate, substantiate, bear out, document, certify, authenticate, validate, justify, establish, determine, ascertain, try,

test, check, examine, analyse.
F3 disprove, discredit, falsify.

proverb *noun*
saying, adage, aphorism, maxim,
byword, dictum, precept (*fml*).

proverbial *adjective*
axiomatic, accepted, conventional,
traditional, customary, time-
honoured, famous, well-known,
legendary, notorious, typical,
archetypal.

provide *verb*
1 provide her with a place to stay:
supply, furnish, stock, equip, outfit,
prepare for, cater, serve, present, give,
contribute, yield, lend, add, bring.
2 provide for the future: plan for,
allow, make provision, accommodate,
arrange for, take precautions.
3 provided by law: state, specify,
stipulate, lay down, require.
F3 1 take, remove.

providential *adjective*
timely, opportune, convenient,
fortunate, lucky, happy, welcome,
heaven-sent.
F3 untimely.

providing *conjunction*
provided, with the proviso, given, as
long as, on condition, on the
understanding.

province *noun*
1 a province of France: region, area,
district, zone, county, shire,
department, territory, colony,
dependency.
2 not his province: responsibility,
concern, duty, office, role, function,
field, sphere, domain, department,
line.

provincial *adjective*
1 a provincial theatre: regional, local,
rural, rustic, country.
2 provincial attitudes: parochial,
home-grown, small-town, parish-
pump, insular, inward-looking,
limited, narrow, narrow-minded,
small-minded.
F3 national, cosmopolitan, urban,
sophisticated.

provision *noun*
1 make provision for old age: plan,

arrangement, preparation, measure,
precaution.
2 a provision of the contract:
stipulation, specification, proviso,
condition, term, requirement.

provisional *adjective*
temporary, interim, transitional,
stopgap, makeshift, conditional,
tentative.
F3 permanent, fixed, definite.

provisions *noun*
food, foodstuff, groceries, eatables
(*infml*), sustenance, rations, supplies,
stocks, stores.

proviso *noun*
condition, term, requirement,
stipulation, qualification, reservation,
restriction, limitation, provision,
clause, rider.

provocative *adjective*
annoying, aggravating (*infml*), galling,
outrageous, offensive, insulting,
abusive.
F3 conciliatory.

provoke *verb*
1 don't provoke him: annoy, irritate,
rile, aggravate (*infml*), offend, insult,
anger, enrage, infuriate, incense,
madden, exasperate, tease, taunt.
2 provoke debate: cause, occasion,
give rise to, produce, generate, induce,
elicit, evoke, excite, inspire, move, stir,
prompt, stimulate, motivate, incite,
instigate.
F3 1 please, pacify.

prowess *noun*
accomplishment, attainment, ability,
aptitude, skill, expertise, mastery,
command, talent, genius.

proximity *noun*
closeness, nearness, vicinity,
neighbourhood, adjacency,
juxtaposition.
F3 remoteness.

prudent *adjective*
wise, sensible, politic, judicious,
shrewd, discerning, careful, cautious,
wary, vigilant, circumspect, discreet,
provident, far-sighted, thrifty.
F3 imprudent, unwise, careless,
rash.

pry *verb*
meddle, interfere, poke one's nose in,
intrude, peep, peer, snoop, nose, ferret,
dig, delve.
F3 mind one's own business.

pseudonym *noun*
false name, assumed name, alias,
incognito, pen name, nom de plume,
stage name.

psychic *adjective*
spiritual, supernatural, occult,
mystic(al), clairvoyant, extra-sensory,
telepathic, mental, psychological,
intellectual, cognitive.

psychological *adjective*
mental, cerebral, intellectual,
cognitive, emotional, subjective,
subconscious, unconscious,
psychosomatic, irrational, unreal.
F3 physical, real.

puberty *noun*
pubescence, adolescence, teens, youth,
growing up, maturity.

public *adjective*
1 public buildings: state, national, civil,
community, social, collective,
communal, common, general,
universal, open, unrestricted.
2 public figure/knowledge: known,
well-known, recognized,
acknowledged, overt, open, exposed,
published.
F3 **1** private, personal. **2** secret.
▶ *noun*
people, nation, country, population,
populace, masses, citizens, society,
community, voters, electorate,
followers, supporters, fans, audience,
patrons, clientele, customers, buyers,
consumers.

publication *noun*
1 a new publication: book, newspaper,
magazine, periodical, booklet, leaflet,
pamphlet, handbill.
2 publication of the figures:
announcement, declaration,
notification, disclosure, release, issue,
printing, publishing.

publicity *noun*
advertising, plug (*infml*), hype (*infml*),
promotion, build-up, boost, attention,
limelight, splash.

publicize *verb*
advertise, plug (*infml*), hype (*infml*),
promote, push, spotlight, broadcast,
make known, blaze.

publish *verb*
1 publish a book: produce, print, issue,
bring out, distribute, circulate, spread,
diffuse.
2 publish the banns: announce,
declare, communicate, make known,
divulge, disclose, reveal, release,
publicize, advertise.

pucker *verb*
gather, ruffle, wrinkle, shrivel, crinkle,
crumple, crease, furrow, purse, screw
up, contract, compress.

puff *noun*
1 not a puff of wind: breath, waft,
whiff, draught, flurry, gust, blast.
2 a few puffs on his pipe: pull, drag.
▶ *verb*
1 puff and blow: breathe, pant, gasp,
gulp, wheeze, blow, waft, inflate,
expand, swell.
2 puff a cigarette: smoke, pull, drag,
draw, suck.

puffy *adjective*
puffed up, inflated, swollen, bloated,
distended, enlarged.

pull *verb*
1 pull a caravan: tow, drag, haul, draw,
tug, jerk, yank (*infml*).
2 pull a tooth: remove, take out,
extract, pull out, pluck, uproot, pull up,
rip, tear.
3 pull the crowds: attract, draw, lure,
allure, entice, tempt, magnetize.
4 pull a muscle: dislocate, sprain,
wrench, strain.
F3 **1** push, press. **3** repel, deter,
discourage.
▶ *noun*
1 give it a pull: tow, drag, tug, jerk,
yank (*infml*).
2 the pull of London: attraction, lure,
allurement, drawing power,
magnetism, influence, weight.
◆ **pull apart** separate, part,
dismember, dismantle, take to pieces.
F3 join.
◆ **pull down** destroy, demolish, knock
down, bulldoze.

build, erect, put up.
◆ **pull off 1** pull off a marketing coup:
accomplish, achieve, bring off,
succeed, manage, carry out.
2 pull the petals off: detach, remove.
1 fail. **2** attach.
◆ **pull out** retreat, withdraw, leave,
depart, quit, move out, evacuate,
desert, abandon.
join, arrive.
◆ **pull through** recover, rally,
recuperate, survive, weather.
◆ **pull together** co-operate, work
together, collaborate, team up.
fight.
◆ **pull up 1** pull up by the side of the
road: stop, halt, park, draw up, pull in,
pull over, brake.
2 (*infml*) ref pulled him up for tackling
too hard: reprimand, tell off (*infml*),
tick off (*infml*), take to task, rebuke,
criticize.

pulp *noun*
flesh, marrow, paste, purée, mash,
mush, pap.
▸ *verb*
crush, squash, pulverize, mash, purée,
liquidize.

pulsate *verb*
pulse, beat, throb, pound, hammer,
drum, thud, thump, vibrate, oscillate,
quiver.

pulse *noun*
beat, stroke, rhythm, throb, pulsation,
beating, pounding, drumming,
vibration, oscillation.

pulverize *verb*
1 pulverize the dried spices: crush,
pound, grind, mill, powder.
2 pulverizing the opposition: defeat,
destroy, demolish, annihilate.

pump *verb*
push, drive, force, inject, siphon, draw,
drain.
◆ **pump up** blow up, inflate, puff up,
fill.

pun *noun*
play on words, double entendre,
witticism, quip.

punch[1] *verb*
punched him in the face: hit, strike,
pummel, jab, bash, clout, cuff, box,

thump, sock (*infml*), wallop (*infml*).
▸ *noun*
1 a punch in the face: blow, jab, bash,
clout, thump, wallop (*infml*).
2 has plenty of punch: force, impact,
effectiveness, drive, vigour, verve,
panache.

punch[2] *verb*
punched her ticket: perforate, pierce,
puncture, prick, bore, drill, stamp, cut.

punctilious *adjective*
scrupulous, conscientious, meticulous,
careful, exact, precise, strict, formal,
proper, particular, finicky, fussy.
lax, informal.

punctual *adjective*
prompt, on time, on the dot, exact,
precise, early, in good time.
unpunctual, late.

punctuation

Punctuation marks include:
apostrophe, asterisk, backslash,
brace, brackets, colon, comma,
daggerdash, ellipsis, exclamation
mark, forward slash, full stop, hyphen,
inverted commas, oblique stroke,
parentheses, period, question mark,
quotation marks, quotes (*infml*),
semicolon, speech marks, square
brackets, star, stop, solidus.

puncture *noun*
1 car had a puncture: flat tyre, flat
(*infml*), blow-out.
2 a small puncture in the skin: leak,
hole, perforation, cut, nick.
▸ *verb*
prick, pierce, penetrate, perforate,
hole, cut, nick, burst, rupture, flatten,
deflate.

pungent *adjective*
1 a pungent cheese: strong, hot,
peppery, spicy, aromatic, tangy,
piquant, sharp, sour, bitter, acrid,
stinging.
2 a pungent remark: biting, caustic,
cutting, keen, acute, incisive, pointed,
piercing, penetrating, sarcastic,
scathing.
1 mild, bland, tasteless.

punish *verb*
penalize, discipline, correct, chastise, castigate (*fml*), scold, beat, flog, lash, cane, spank, fine, imprison.
F⊒ reward.

punishment *noun*
discipline, correction, chastisement, beating, flogging, penalty, fine, imprisonment, sentence, deserts, retribution, revenge.
F⊒ reward.

puny *adjective*
weak, feeble, frail, sickly, undeveloped, underdeveloped, stunted, undersized, diminutive, little, tiny, insignificant.
F⊒ strong, sturdy, large, important.

pupil *noun*
student, scholar, schoolboy, schoolgirl, learner, apprentice, beginner, novice, disciple, protégé(e).
F⊒ teacher.

purchase *verb*
buy, pay for, invest in (*infml*), procure, acquire, obtain, get, secure, gain, earn, win.
F⊒ sell.
▸ *noun*
acquisition, buy (*infml*), investment, asset, possession, property.
F⊒ sale.

pure *adjective*
1 pure gold : unadulterated, unalloyed, unmixed, undiluted, neat, solid, simple, natural, real, authentic, genuine, true.
2 pure water : sterile, uncontaminated, unpolluted, germ-free, aseptic, antiseptic, disinfected, sterilized, hygienic, sanitary, clean, immaculate, spotless, clear.
3 pure nonsense : sheer, utter, complete, total, thorough, absolute, perfect, unqualified.
4 young and pure : chaste, virginal, undefiled, unsullied, moral, upright, virtuous, blameless, innocent.
5 pure mathematics : theoretical, abstract, conjectural, speculative, academic.
F⊒ 1 impure, adulterated.
2 contaminated, polluted, impure.
4 immoral, impure. **5** applied.

purely *adverb*
1 not purely accurate : utterly, completely, totally, entirely, wholly, thoroughly, absolutely.
2 purely out of interest : only, simply, merely, just, solely, exclusively.

purge *verb*
1 purged of sin : purify, cleanse, clean out, scour, clear, absolve.
2 purging those who didn't agree : oust, remove, get rid of, eject, expel, root out, eradicate, exterminate, wipe out, kill.
▸ *noun*
removal, ejection, expulsion, witch hunt, eradication, extermination.

purify *verb*
refine, filter, clarify, clean, cleanse, decontaminate, sanitize, disinfect, sterilize, fumigate, deodorize.
F⊒ contaminate, pollute, defile (*fml*).

purist *noun*
pedant, literalist, formalist, stickler, quibbler, nit-picker.

puritanical *adjective*
puritan, moralistic, disciplinarian, ascetic, abstemious, austere, severe, stern, strict, strait-laced, prim, proper, prudish, disapproving, stuffy, stiff, rigid, narrow-minded, bigoted, fanatical, zealous.
F⊒ hedonistic, liberal, indulgent, broad-minded.

purity *noun*
1 purity of the water : clearness, clarity, cleanness, cleanliness, untaintedness, wholesomeness.
2 purity of line : simplicity, authenticity, genuineness, truth.
3 purity of spirit : chastity, decency, morality, integrity, rectitude, uprightness, virtue, innocence, blamelessness.
F⊒ 1 impurity. **3** immorality.

purpose *noun*
1 have a purpose in life : intention, aim, objective, end, goal, target, plan, design, vision, idea, point, object, reason, motive, rationale, principle, result, outcome.
2 full of purpose : determination, resolve, resolution, drive, single-

mindedness, dedication, devotion, constancy, steadfastness, persistence, tenacity, zeal.

3 what purpose will it serve?: use, function, application, good, advantage, benefit, value.

◆ **on purpose** purposely, deliberately, intentionally, consciously, knowingly, wittingly, wilfully.

F∃ accidentally, impulsively, spontaneously.

purposeful *adjective*
determined, decided, resolved, resolute, single-minded, constant, steadfast, persistent, persevering, tenacious, strong-willed, positive, firm, deliberate.

F∃ purposeless, aimless.

purse *noun*
1 lost her purse: money-bag, wallet, pouch.
2 the public purse: money, means, resources, finances, funds, coffers, treasury, exchequer.
3 a purse of a million dollars: reward, award, prize.

▶ *verb*
pucker, wrinkle, draw together, close, tighten, contract, compress.

pursue *verb*
1 pursue an activity: perform, engage in, practise, conduct, carry on, continue, keep on, keep up, maintain, persevere in, persist in, hold to, aspire to, aim for, strive for, try for.
2 pursued by the press: chase, go after, follow, track, trail, shadow, tail, dog, harass, harry, hound, hunt, seek, search for, investigate, inquire into.

pursuit *noun*
1 join the pursuit: chase, hue and cry, tracking, stalking, trail, hunt, quest, search, investigation.
2 interesting pursuits: activity, interest, hobby, pastime, occupation, trade, craft, line, speciality, vocation.

push *verb*
1 pushed along by the wind/push the button: propel, thrust, ram, shove, jostle, elbow, prod, poke, press, depress, squeeze, squash, drive, force, constrain.

2 pushing his products: promote, advertise, publicize, boost, encourage, urge, egg on (*infml*), incite, spur, influence, persuade, pressurize, bully.
F∃ 1 pull. 2 discourage, dissuade.

▶ *noun*
1 gave him a push: knock, shove, nudge, jolt, prod, poke, thrust.
2 doesn't have much push: energy, vigour, vitality, go (*infml*), drive, effort, dynamism, enterprise, initiative, ambition, determination.

pushy *adjective* (*infml*)
assertive, self-assertive, ambitious, forceful, aggressive, over-confident, forward, bold, brash, arrogant, presumptuous, assuming, bossy (*infml*), in-your-face (*infml*).
F∃ unassertive, unassuming.

put *verb*
1 put it over there: place, lay, deposit, plonk (*infml*), set, fix, settle, establish, stand, position, dispose, situate, station, post.
2 put all the blame on me: apply, impose, inflict, levy, assign, subject.
3 put it another way: word, phrase, formulate, frame, couch, express, voice, utter, state.
4 put a suggestion: submit, present, offer, suggest, propose.

◆ **put across** put over, communicate, convey, express, explain, spell out, bring home to, get through to.

◆ **put aside** put by, set aside, keep, retain, save, reserve, store, stow, stockpile, stash (*infml*), hoard, salt away.

◆ **put back 1 put the meeting back for a week**: delay, defer, postpone, reschedule.
2 put the money back: replace, return.
F∃ 1 bring forward.

◆ **put down 1 put down on paper**: write down, transcribe, enter, log, register, record, note.
2 put down a rebellion: crush, quash, suppress, defeat, quell, silence, squash.
3 they put him down for being unfashionable: deflate, humble, take down a peg, shame, humiliate, mortify, snub, slight.

4 put the old dog down: kill, put to sleep.

5 put it down to nerves: ascribe, attribute, blame, charge.

◆ **put forward** advance, suggest, recommend, nominate, propose, move, table, introduce, present, submit, offer, tender.

◆ **put in** insert, enter, input, submit, install, fit.

◆ **put off 1 put it off for a fortnight**: delay, defer, postpone, reschedule.

2 wasn't put off in the least: deter, dissuade, discourage, dishearten, demoralize, daunt, dismay, intimidate, disconcert, confuse, distract.
E3 2 encourage.

◆ **put on 1 put on the badge**: attach, affix, apply, place, add.

2 put on an act: pretend, feign, sham, fake, simulate, affect, assume.

3 put on a play: stage, mount, produce, present, do, perform.

◆ **put out 1 put out leaflets**: publish, announce, broadcast, circulate.

2 put the fire/lights out: extinguish, quench, douse, smother, switch off, turn off.

3 don't want to put you out: inconvenience, impose on, bother, disturb, trouble, upset, hurt, offend, annoy, irritate, irk, anger, exasperate.
E3 2 light.

◆ **put up 1 put up a tent**: erect, build, construct, assemble.

2 can put you up for a couple of nights: accomodate, house, lodge, shelter.

3 put up prices: raise, increase.

4 put up the bulk of the money: pay, invest, give, advance, float, provide, supply, pledge, offer.

◆ **put up to** prompt, incite, encourage, egg on (*infml*), urge, goad.
E3 discourage, dissuade.

◆ **put up with** stand, bear, abide, stomach, endure, suffer, tolerate, allow, accept, stand for, take, take lying down.
E3 object to, reject.

putrid *adjective*
rotten, decayed, decomposed, mouldy, off, bad, rancid, addled, corrupt, contaminated, tainted, polluted, foul, rank, fetid, stinking.
E3 fresh, wholesome.

puzzle *verb*
1 their behaviour always puzzled him: baffle, mystify, perplex, confound, stump (*infml*), floor (*infml*), confuse, bewilder, flummox (*infml*).

2 puzzling over the problem: think, ponder, meditate, consider, mull over, deliberate, figure, rack one's brains.
▶ *noun*
question, poser (*infml*), brain-teaser, mind-bender, crossword, rebus, anagram, riddle, conundrum, mystery, enigma, paradox.

puzzled *adjective*
baffled, mystified, perplexed, confounded, at a loss, beaten, stumped (*infml*), confused, bewildered, nonplussed, lost, at sea, flummoxed (*infml*).
E3 clear.

quagmire *noun*
bog, marsh, fen, swamp, morass, quicksand.

quail *verb*
recoil, back away, shy away, shrink, flinch, cringe, cower, tremble, quake, shudder, falter.

quaint *adjective*
picturesque, charming, twee (*infml*), old-fashioned, antiquated, old-world, olde-worlde (*infml*), unusual, strange, odd, curious, bizarre, fanciful, whimsical.
Fa modern.

quake *verb*
shake, tremble, shudder, quiver, shiver, quail, vibrate, wobble, rock, sway, move, convulse, heave.

qualification *noun*
1 good qualifications: certificate, diploma, training, skill, competence, ability, capability, capacity, aptitude, suitability, fitness, eligibility.
2 without qualification: restriction, limitation, reservation, exception, exemption, condition, caveat, provision, proviso, stipulation, modification.

qualified *adjective*
1 a qualified doctor: certified, chartered, licensed, professional, trained, experienced, practised, skilled, accomplished, expert, knowledgeable, skilful, talented, proficient, competent, efficient, able, capable, fit, eligible.
2 qualified praise: reserved, guarded, cautious, restricted, limited, bounded, contingent (*fml*), conditional, provisional, equivocal.

Fa 1 unqualified. **2** unconditional, whole-hearted.

qualify *verb*
1 qualify as a doctor: train, prepare, equip, fit, pass, graduate, certify, empower, entitle, authorize, sanction, permit.
2 qualify the last statement: moderate, reduce, lessen, diminish, temper, soften, weaken, mitigate, ease, adjust, modify, restrain, restrict, limit, delimit, define, classify.
Fa 1 disqualify.

quality *noun*
1 has many good qualities: property, characteristic, peculiarity, attribute, aspect, feature, trait, mark.
2 of poor quality: standard, grade, class, kind, sort, nature, character, calibre, status, rank, value, worth, merit, condition.
3 shows real quality: excellence, superiority, pre-eminence, distinction, refinement.

qualm *noun*
misgiving, apprehension, fear, anxiety, worry, disquiet, uneasiness, scruple, hesitation, reluctance, uncertainty, doubt.

quandary *noun*
dilemma, predicament, impasse, perplexity, bewilderment, confusion, mess, fix, hole (*infml*), problem, difficulty.

quantity *noun*
amount, number, sum, total, aggregate, mass, lot, share, portion, quota, allotment, measure, dose, proportion, part, content, capacity, volume, weight, bulk, size,

magnitude, expanse, extent, length, breadth.

quarrel noun
row, argument, slanging match (*infml*), wrangle, squabble, tiff, misunderstanding, disagreement, dispute, dissension, controversy, difference, conflict, clash, contention, strife, fight, scrap, brawl, feud, vendetta, schism.
🖅 agreement, harmony.
▶ verb
row, argue, bicker, squabble, wrangle, be at loggerheads, fall out, disagree, dispute, dissent, differ, be at variance, clash, contend, fight, scrap, feud.
🖅 agree.

quarrelsome adjective
argumentative, disputatious, contentious, belligerent, ill-tempered, irritable.
🖅 peaceable, placid.

quarter noun
district, sector, zone, neighbourhood, locality, vicinity, area, region, province, territory, division, section, part, place, spot, point, direction, side.
▶ verb
station, post, billet, accommodate, put up, lodge, board, house, shelter.

quarters noun
accommodation, lodgings, billet, digs (*infml*), residence, dwelling, habitation, domicile, rooms, barracks, station, post.

quash verb
annul, revoke, rescind, overrule, cancel, nullify, void, invalidate, reverse, set aside, squash, crush, quell, suppress, subdue, defeat, overthrow.
🖅 confirm, vindicate, reinstate.

quaver verb
shake, tremble, quake, shudder, quiver, vibrate, pulsate, oscillate, flutter, flicker, trill, warble.

queasy adjective
sick, ill, unwell, queer, groggy, green, nauseated, sickened, bilious, squeamish, faint, dizzy, giddy.

queen noun
1 monarch, sovereign, ruler, majesty, princess, empress, consort.
2 beauty, belle.

queer adjective
odd, mysterious, strange, unusual, uncommon, weird, unnatural, bizarre, eccentric, peculiar, funny, puzzling, curious, remarkable.
🖅 ordinary, usual, common.

quell verb
subdue, quash, crush, squash, suppress, put down, overcome, conquer, defeat, overpower, moderate, mitigate, allay, alleviate, soothe, calm, pacify, hush, quiet, silence, stifle, extinguish.

quench verb
1 quench one's thirst : slake, satisfy, sate, cool.
2 quenching the flames : extinguish, douse, put out, snuff out.

query verb
ask, inquire, question, challenge, dispute, quarrel with, doubt, suspect, distrust, mistrust, disbelieve.
🖅 accept.
▶ noun
question, inquiry, problem, uncertainty, doubt, suspicion, scepticism, reservation, hesitation.

quest noun
search, hunt, pursuit, investigation, inquiry, mission, crusade, enterprise, undertaking, venture, journey, voyage, expedition, exploration, adventure.

question verb
interrogate, quiz, grill, pump, interview, examine, cross-examine, debrief, ask, inquire, investigate, probe, query, challenge, dispute, doubt, disbelieve.
▶ noun
1 have a couple of questions : query, inquiry, poser (*infml*), problem, difficulty.
2 that's not the question we're dealing with at the moment : issue, matter, subject, topic, point, proposal, proposition, motion, debate, dispute, controversy.

questionable adjective
debatable, disputable, unsettled, undetermined, unproven, uncertain, arguable, controversial, vexed, dodgy (*infml*), doubtful, dubious, suspicious,

suspect, shady (*infml*), fishy (*infml*), iffy (*infml*).

F3 unquestionable, indisputable, certain.

questionnaire *noun*
quiz, test, survey, opinion poll.

queue *noun*
line, tailback, file, crocodile, procession, train, string, succession, series, sequence, order.

quibble *verb*
carp, cavil, split hairs, nit-pick, equivocate, prevaricate.
▸ *noun*
complaint, objection, criticism, query.

quick *adjective*
1 a quick look / phone call : fast, swift, rapid, speedy, express, hurried, hasty, cursory, fleeting, brief, prompt, ready, immediate, instant, instantaneous, sudden, brisk, nimble, sprightly, agile.
2 she's very quick at picking things up : clever, intelligent, quick-witted, smart, sharp, keen, shrewd, astute, discerning, perceptive, responsive, receptive.
F3 1 slow, sluggish, lethargic. **2** unintelligent, dull.

quicken *verb*
1 pace quickened : accelerate, speed, hurry, hasten, precipitate (*fml*), expedite, dispatch, advance.
2 (*fml*) **flame quickened into life** : animate, enliven, invigorate, energize, galvanize, activate, rouse, arouse, stimulate, excite, inspire, revive, refresh, reinvigorate, reactivate.
F3 1 slow, retard. **2** dull.

quiet *adjective*
1 quiet as a mouse / in a quiet voice : silent, noiseless, inaudible, hushed, soft, low.
2 quiet surroundings : peaceful, still, tranquil, serene, calm, composed, undisturbed, untroubled, placid.
3 a quiet person : shy, reserved, reticent, uncommunicative, taciturn, unforthcoming, retiring, withdrawn, thoughtful, subdued, meek.
4 a quiet spot : isolated, unfrequented, lonely, secluded, private.

F3 1 noisy, loud. **2** excitable. **3** extrovert.
▸ *noun*
quietness, silence, hush, peace, lull, stillness, tranquillity, serenity, calm, rest, repose.
F3 noise, loudness, disturbance, bustle.

quieten *verb*
1 quieten the children : silence, hush, mute, soften, lower, diminish, reduce, stifle, muffle, deaden, dull.
2 he's quietened down a lot : subdue, pacify, quell, quiet, still, smooth, calm, soothe, compose, sober.
F3 2 disturb, agitate.

quirk *noun*
freak, eccentricity, curiosity, oddity, peculiarity, idiosyncrasy, mannerism, habit, trait, foible, whim, caprice, turn, twist.

quit *verb*
1 quit his job : leave, depart, go, exit, decamp, desert, forsake, abandon, renounce, relinquish, surrender, give up, resign, retire, withdraw.
2 quit smoking : stop, cease, end, discontinue, desist, drop, give up, pack in (*infml*).

quite *adverb*
1 quite good : moderately, rather, somewhat, fairly, relatively, comparatively.
2 quite awful : utterly, absolutely, totally, completely, entirely, wholly, fully, perfectly, exactly, precisely.

quiver *verb*
shake, tremble, shudder, shiver, quake, quaver, vibrate, palpitate, flutter, flicker, oscillate, wobble.

quiz *noun*
questionnaire, test, examination, competition.
▸ *verb*
question, interrogate, grill, pump, examine, cross-examine.

quizzical *adjective*
questioning, inquiring, curious, amused, humorous, teasing, mocking, satirical, sardonic, sceptical.

quota *noun*
ration, allowance, allocation, assignment, share, portion, part, slice, cut (*infml*), percentage, proportion.

quotation *noun*
1 a quotation from Shakespeare: citation, quote (*infml*), extract, excerpt, passage, piece, cutting, reference.
2 a quotation from a builder: estimate, quote (*infml*), tender, figure, price, cost, charge, rate.

quote *verb*
cite, refer to, mention, name, reproduce, echo, repeat, recite, recall, recollect.

rabble *noun*
crowd, throng, horde, herd, mob, masses, populace, riff-raff.

race¹ *noun*
a race against time: sprint, steeplechase, marathon, scramble, regatta, competition, contest, contention, rivalry, chase, pursuit, quest.
▶ *verb*
run, sprint, dash, tear, fly, gallop, speed, career, dart, zoom, rush, hurry, hasten.

race² *noun*
people of all races: nation, people, tribe, clan, house, dynasty, family, kindred, ancestry, line, blood, stock, genus, species, breed.

racial *adjective*
national, tribal, ethnic, folk, genealogical, ancestral, inherited, genetic.

racism *noun*
racialism, xenophobia, chauvinism, jingoism, discrimination, prejudice, bias.

racket *noun*
1 stop that terrible racket!: noise, din, uproar, row, fuss, outcry, clamour, commotion, disturbance, pandemonium, hurly-burly, hubbub.
2 running a racket: swindle, con (*infml*), fraud, fiddle, deception, trick, dodge, scheme, business, game.

radiant *adjective*
1 radiant as if lit with a thousand candles: bright, luminous, shining, gleaming, glowing, beaming, glittering, sparkling, brilliant, resplendent, splendid, glorious.

2 a radiant smile: happy, joyful, delighted, ecstatic.
F3 1 dull. **2** miserable.

radiate *verb*
1 heat radiating from the sun: shine, gleam, glow, beam, shed, pour, give off, emit, emanate, diffuse, issue, disseminate, scatter, spread (out).
2 lines radiating from a central point: diverge, branch.

radical *adjective*
1 radical change/investigation: drastic, comprehensive, thorough, sweeping, far-reaching, fundamental, thoroughgoing, complete, total, entire.
2 radical views: fanatical, militant, extreme, extremist, revolutionary.
F3 1 superficial. **2** moderate.
▶ *noun*
fanatic, militant, extremist, revolutionary, reformer, reformist, fundamentalist.

rage *noun*
1 in a rage/white with rage: anger, wrath, fury, frenzy, tantrum, temper.
2 (*infml*) **all the rage**: craze, fad, thing (*infml*), fashion, vogue, style, passion, enthusiasm, obsession.
▶ *verb*
fume, seethe, rant, rave, storm, thunder, explode, rampage.

ragged *adjective*
1 ragged clothes: frayed, torn, ripped, tattered, worn-out, threadbare, tatty, shabby, scruffy, unkempt, down-at-heel.
2 a ragged edge: jagged, serrated, indented, notched, rough, uneven, irregular.
3 a ragged group of protestors: fragmented, erratic, disorganized.

raid *noun*
attack, onset, onslaught, invasion, inroad, incursion, foray, sortie, strike, blitz, swoop, bust (*infml*), robbery, break-in, hold-up.
▶ *verb*
loot, pillage, plunder, ransack, rifle, maraud, attack, descend on, invade, storm.

rain *noun*
rainfall, precipitation, raindrops, drizzle, shower, cloudburst, downpour, deluge, torrent, storm, thunderstorm, squall.
▶ *verb*
spit, drizzle, shower, pour, teem, pelt, bucket (*infml*), deluge.

raise *verb*
1 raising defensive walls: lift, elevate, hoist, jack up, erect, build, construct.
2 raise prices: increase, augment, escalate, magnify, heighten, strengthen, intensify, amplify, boost, enhance.
3 raise funds: get, obtain, collect, gather, assemble, rally, muster, recruit.
4 raise a family: bring up, rear, breed, propagate, grow, cultivate, develop.
5 raise a subject: bring up, broach, introduce, present, put forward, moot, suggest.
E3 **1** lower. **2** decrease, reduce.
5 suppress.

rake *verb*
1 rake the dug earth: hoe, scratch, scrape, graze, comb, level.
2 raking through their belongings: search, scour, hunt, ransack.
3 raking money in: gather, collect, amass, accumulate.

rally *verb*
1 rallied an army/rallied to the cause: gather, collect, assemble, congregate, convene, muster, summon, round up, unite, marshal, organize, mobilize, reassemble, regroup, reorganize.
2 rallied for a short time before relapsing: recover, recuperate, revive, improve, pick up.
▶ *noun*
gathering, assembly, convention, convocation (*fml*), conference,

meeting, jamboree, reunion, march, demonstration.

ram *verb*
1 ramming the car in front: hit, strike, butt, hammer, pound, drum, crash, smash, slam.
2 rammed his hands into his pockets: force, drive, thrust, cram, stuff, pack, crowd, jam, wedge.

ramble *verb*
1 rambling along the road: walk, hike, trek, tramp, traipse, stroll, amble, saunter, straggle, wander, roam, rove, meander, wind, zigzag.
2 he rambles on for hours: chatter, babble, rabbit (on) (*infml*), witter (on) (*infml*), expatiate, digress, drift.
▶ *noun*
walk, hike, trek, tramp, stroll, saunter, tour, trip, excursion.

rambling *adjective*
1 a rambling rose: spreading, sprawling, straggling, trailing.
2 a rambling explanation: circuitous, roundabout, digressive, wordy, long-winded, long-drawn-out, disconnected, incoherent.
E3 **2** direct.

rampage *verb*
run wild, run amok, run riot, rush, tear, storm, rage, rant, rave.
▶ *noun*
rage, fury, frenzy, storm, uproar, violence, destruction.

rampant *adjective*
unrestrained, uncontrolled, unbridled, unchecked, wanton, excessive, fierce, violent, raging, wild, riotous, rank, profuse, rife, widespread, prevalent.

ramshackle *adjective*
dilapidated, tumbledown, broken-down, crumbling, ruined, derelict, jerry-built, unsafe, rickety, shaky, unsteady, tottering, decrepit.
E3 solid, stable.

rancid *adjective*
sour, off, bad, musty, stale, rank, foul, fetid, putrid, rotten.
E3 sweet.

random *adjective*
arbitrary, chance, fortuitous (*fml*), casual, incidental, haphazard,

irregular, unsystematic, unplanned, accidental, aimless, purposeless, indiscriminate, stray.
F3 systematic, deliberate.

range noun
1 across the entire range: scope, compass, scale, gamut, spectrum, sweep, spread, extent, distance, reach, span, limits, bounds, parameters, area, field, domain, province, sphere, orbit.
2 a range of colours: variety, diversity, assortment, selection, sort, kind, class, order, series, string, chain.
▶ verb
1 ranges from dark to light: extend, stretch, reach, spread, vary, fluctuate.
2 ranging the books along the shelf: align, arrange, order, rank, classify, catalogue.

rank[1] noun
1 high rank/an army rank: grade, degree, class, caste, status, standing, position, station, condition, estate (fml), echelon, level, stratum, tier, classification, sort, type, group, division.
2 ranks of shelves: row, line, range, column, file, series, order, formation.
▶ verb
grade, class, rate, place, position, range, sort, classify, categorize, order, arrange, organize, marshal.

rank[2] adjective
1 a rank smell: foul, repulsive, disgusting, revolting, stinking, putrid, rancid, stale.
2 rank nonsense: utter, total, complete, absolute, unmitigated, thorough, sheer, downright, out-and-out, arrant, gross, flagrant, glaring, outrageous.

ransack verb
search, scour, comb, rummage, rifle, raid, sack, strip, despoil, ravage, loot, plunder, pillage.

ransom noun
price, money, payment, pay-off, redemption, deliverance, rescue, liberation, release.
▶ verb
buy off, redeem, deliver, rescue, liberate, free, release.

rap verb
1 rap on the window: knock, hit, strike, tap, thump.
2 (infml) rap over the knuckles: reprove, reprimand, criticize, censure.
▶ noun
1 a rap on the door: knock, blow, tap, thump.
2 (infml) take the rap: rebuke, reprimand, censure, blame, punishment.

rapid adjective
swift, speedy, quick, fast, express, lightning, prompt, brisk, hurried, hasty, precipitate (fml), headlong.
F3 slow, leisurely, sluggish.

rapport noun
bond, link, affinity, relationship, empathy, sympathy, understanding, harmony.

rapture noun
delight, happiness, joy, bliss, ecstasy, euphoria, exaltation.

rare adjective
1 a rare animal/pleasure: uncommon, unusual, scarce, sparse, sporadic, infrequent.
2 a rare example: exquisite, superb, excellent, superlative, incomparable, exceptional, remarkable, precious.
F3 1 common, abundant, frequent.

rarely adverb
seldom, hardly ever, infrequently, little.
F3 often, frequently.

raring adjective
eager, keen, enthusiastic, ready, willing, impatient, longing, itching, desperate.

rarity noun
1 something of a rarity: curiosity, curio, gem, pearl, treasure, find.
2 sought after for its rarity: uncommonness, unusualness, strangeness, scarcity, shortage, sparseness, infrequency.
F3 2 commonness, frequency.

rash adjective
reckless, ill-considered, foolhardy, ill-advised, madcap, hare-brained, hot-headed, headstrong, impulsive, impetuous, hasty, headlong, unguarded, unwary, indiscreet,

imprudent, careless, heedless,
unthinking.
E3 cautious, wary, careful.

rate *noun*
1 rate of change: speed, velocity,
tempo, time, ratio, proportion,
relation, degree, grade, rank, rating,
standard, basis, measure, scale.
2 rate of pay/interest: charge, fee, hire,
toll, tariff, price, cost, value, worth,
tax, duty, amount, figure, percentage.
▶ *verb*
1 rated B+/'parental guidance': judge,
regard, consider, deem, count, reckon,
figure, estimate, evaluate, assess,
weigh, measure, grade, rank, class,
classify.
2 don't rate it at all: admire, respect,
esteem, value, prize.
3 rate a second look: deserve, merit.

rather *adverb*
1 rather funny: moderately, relatively,
slightly, a bit, somewhat, fairly, quite,
pretty, noticeably, significantly, very.
2 rather you than me: preferably,
sooner, instead.

rating *noun*
class, rank, degree, status, standing,
position, placing, order, grade, mark,
evaluation, assessment, classification,
category.

ratio *noun*
percentage, fraction, proportion,
relation, relationship, correspondence,
correlation.

ration *noun*
quota, allowance, allocation,
allotment, share, portion, helping,
part, measure, amount.
▶ *verb*
apportion, allot, allocate, share, deal
out, distribute, dole out, dispense,
supply, issue, control, restrict, limit,
conserve, save.

rational *adjective*
logical, reasonable, sound, well-
founded, realistic, sensible, clear-
headed, judicious (*fml*), wise, sane,
normal, balanced, lucid, reasoning,
thinking, intelligent, enlightened.
E3 irrational, illogical, insane,
crazy.

rationale *noun*
logic, reasoning, philosophy, principle,
basis, grounds, explanation, reason,
motive, motivation, theory.

rattle *verb*
clatter, jingle, jangle, clank, shake,
vibrate, jolt, jar, bounce, bump.
◆ **rattle off** reel off, list, run through,
recite, repeat.

raucous *adjective*
harsh, rough, hoarse, husky, rasping,
grating, jarring, strident, noisy,
loud.

ravage *verb*
destroy, devastate, lay waste, demolish,
raze, wreck, ruin, spoil, damage, loot,
pillage, plunder, sack, despoil.

rave *verb*
rage, storm, thunder, roar, rant,
ramble, babble, splutter.
▶ *adjective* (*infml*)
enthusiastic, rapturous, favourable,
excellent, wonderful.

ravenous *adjective*
hungry, starving, starved, famished,
greedy, voracious, insatiable.

raving *adjective*
mad, insane, crazy, hysterical,
delirious, wild, frenzied, furious,
berserk.

ravishing *adjective*
delightful, enchanting, charming,
lovely, beautiful, gorgeous, stunning
(*infml*), radiant, dazzling, alluring,
seductive.

raw *adjective*
1 raw vegetables: uncooked, fresh.
2 raw cotton: unprocessed, unrefined,
untreated, crude, natural.
3 the raw truth: plain, bare, naked,
basic, harsh, brutal, realistic.
4 raw skin: scratched, grazed, scraped,
open, bloody, sore, tender, sensitive.
5 it's raw outside: cold, chilly, bitter,
biting, piercing, freezing, bleak.
6 a raw recruit: new, green, immature,
callow, inexperienced, untrained,
unskilled.
E3 1 cooked, done. 2 processed,
refined. 5 warm. 6 experienced,
skilled.

ray *noun*
beam, shaft, flash, gleam, flicker, glimmer, glint, spark, trace, hint, indication.

re *preposition*
about, concerning, regarding, with regard to, with reference to.

reach *verb*
arrive at, get to, attain, achieve, make, amount to, hit, strike, touch, contact, stretch, extend, grasp.
▶ *noun*
range, scope, compass, distance, spread, extent, stretch, grasp, jurisdiction, command, power, influence.

react *verb*
respond, retaliate, reciprocate, reply, answer, acknowledge, act, behave.

reaction *noun*
response, effect, reply, answer, acknowledgement, feedback, counteraction, reflex, recoil, reciprocation, retaliation.

reactionary *adjective*
conservative, right-wing, rightist, diehard, counter-revolutionary.
F3 progressive, revolutionary.
▶ *noun*
conservative, right-winger, rightist, diehard, counter-revolutionary.
F3 progressive, revolutionary.

read *verb*
1 read a book/read French: study, peruse, pore over, scan, skim, decipher, decode, interpret, construe, understand, comprehend.
2 read us a story: recite, declaim, deliver, speak, utter.
3 the gauge read zero: indicate, show, display, register, record.

readable *adjective*
1 machine-readable language: legible, decipherable, intelligible, clear, understandable, comprehensible.
2 his style is very readable: interesting, enjoyable, entertaining, gripping, unputdownable (*infml*).
F3 1 illegible. 2 unreadable.

readily *adverb*
willingly, unhesitatingly, gladly, eagerly, promptly, quickly, freely,

smoothly, easily, effortlessly.
F3 unwillingly, reluctantly.

ready *adjective*
1 ready to go: prepared, waiting, set, fit, arranged, organized, completed, finished.
2 ready and able: willing, inclined, disposed, happy, game (*infml*), eager, keen.
3 ready cash/in ready amounts: available, to hand, present, near, accessible, convenient, handy.
4 a ready response: prompt, immediate, quick, sharp, astute, perceptive, alert.
F3 1 unprepared. 2 unwilling, reluctant, disinclined. 3 unavailable, inaccessible. 4 slow.

real *adjective*
actual, existing, physical, material, substantial, tangible, genuine, authentic, bona fide, official, rightful, legitimate, valid, true, factual, certain, sure, positive, veritable (*fml*), honest, sincere, heartfelt, unfeigned, unaffected.
F3 unreal, imaginary, false.

realistic *adjective*
1 not a realistic proposal: practical, down-to-earth, commonsense, sensible, level-headed, clear-sighted, businesslike, hard-headed, pragmatic, matter-of-fact, rational, logical, objective, detached, unsentimental, unromantic.
2 a realistic portrayal: lifelike, faithful, truthful, true, genuine, authentic, natural, real, real-life, graphic, representational.
F3 1 unrealistic, impractical, irrational, idealistic.

reality *noun*
truth, fact, certainty, realism, actuality, existence, materiality, tangibility, genuineness, authenticity, validity.

realize *verb*
1 realize what he meant: understand, comprehend, grasp, catch on, cotton on (*infml*), recognize, accept, appreciate.
2 realize her dreams: achieve, accomplish, fulfil, complete,

implement, perform.
3 realize the highest prices: sell for, fetch, make, earn, produce, net, clear.

really *adverb*
actually, truly, honestly, sincerely, genuinely, positively, certainly, absolutely, categorically, very, indeed.
⇨ *See also* **Word Workshop** *panel.*

realm *noun*
kingdom, monarchy, principality, empire, country, state, land, territory, area, region, province, domain, sphere, orbit, field, department.

rear *noun*
back, stern, end, tail, rump, buttocks, posterior, behind, bottom, backside (*infml*).
F∃ front.
▶ *adjective*
back, hind, hindmost, rearmost, last.
F∃ front.
▶ *verb*
1 rear a child: bring up, raise, breed, grow, cultivate, foster, nurse, nurture, train, educate.
2 rearing up out of the mist: rise, tower, soar, raise, lift.

reason *noun*
1 the reason for his silence/their reason for leaving: cause, motive, incentive, rationale, explanation, excuse, justification, defence, warrant, ground, basis, case, argument, aim, intention, purpose, object, end, goal.
2 using reason: sense, logic, reasoning, rationality, sanity, mind, wit, brain, intellect, understanding, wisdom, judgement, common sense, gumption.
▶ *verb*
work out, solve, resolve, conclude, deduce, infer, think.
◆ **reason with** urge, persuade, move, remonstrate with, argue with, debate with, discuss with.

reasonable *adjective*
1 a reasonable suggestion: sensible, wise, well-advised, sane, intelligent, rational, logical, practical, sound, reasoned, well-thought-out, plausible, credible, possible, viable.
2 a reasonable price: acceptable, satisfactory, tolerable, moderate,

average, fair, just, modest, inexpensive.
F∃ **1** irrational, unreasonable.
2 exorbitant.

reassure *verb*
comfort, cheer, encourage, hearten, inspirit, brace, bolster.
F∃ alarm.

rebate *noun*
refund, repayment, reduction, discount, deduction, allowance.

rebel *verb* /ri-bel/
revolt, mutiny, rise up, run riot, dissent, disobey, defy, resist, recoil, shrink.
F∃ conform.
▶ *noun* / **reb**-el/
revolutionary, insurrectionary, mutineer, dissenter, nonconformist, schismatic, heretic.

rebellion *noun*
revolt, revolution, coup (d'état), rising, uprising, insurrection, insurgence, mutiny, resistance, opposition, defiance, disobedience, insubordination, dissent, heresy.

rebound *verb*
recoil, backfire, return, bounce, ricochet, boomerang.

rebuke *verb*
reprove, castigate (*fml*), chide, scold, tell off (*infml*), admonish, tick off (*infml*), reprimand, upbraid (*fml*), berate, censure, blame, reproach.
F∃ praise, compliment.
▶ *noun*
reproach, reproof, reprimand, lecture, dressing-down (*infml*), telling-off (*infml*), ticking-off (*infml*), admonition, censure, blame.
F∃ praise, commendation.

recall *verb*
remember, recollect, cast one's mind back, evoke, bring back.

recede *verb*
go back, return, retire, withdraw, retreat, ebb, wane, sink, decline, diminish, dwindle, decrease, lessen, shrink, slacken, subside, abate.
F∃ advance.

receipt *noun*
1 issue a receipt: voucher, ticket, slip, counterfoil, stub, acknowledgement.

2 on receipt of your letter: receiving, reception, acceptance, delivery.

receive *verb*
1 receiving a salary: take, accept, get, obtain, derive, acquire, pick up, collect, inherit.
2 receive guests: admit, let in, greet, welcome, entertain, accommodate.
3 receive a blow to the head: experience, undergo, suffer, sustain, meet with, encounter.
4 wasn't received favourably: react to, respond to, hear, perceive, apprehend.
F3 1 give, donate.

recent *adjective*
late, latest, current, present-day, contemporary, modern, up-to-date, new, novel, fresh, young.
F3 old, out-of-date.

recently *adverb*
lately, newly, freshly.

reception *noun*
1 got a great reception: welcome, treatment, acceptance, admission, greeting, recognition, response, reaction, acknowledgement, receipt.
2 attend the reception: party, function, do (*infml*), entertainment.

receptive *adjective*
open-minded, amenable, accommodating, suggestible, susceptible, sensitive, responsive, open, accessible, approachable, friendly, hospitable, welcoming, sympathetic, favourable, interested.
F3 narrow-minded, resistant, unresponsive.

recess *noun*
1 during recess: break, interval, intermission, rest, respite, holiday, vacation.
2 a recess in the wall: alcove, niche, nook, corner, bay, cavity, hollow, depression, indentation.

recession *noun*
slump, depression, downturn, decline.
F3 boom, upturn.

recipe *noun*
formula, prescription, ingredients, instructions, directions, method, system, procedure, technique.

reciprocate *verb*
respond, reply, requite, return, exchange, swap, trade, match, equal, correspond, interchange, alternate.

recite *verb*
repeat, tell, narrate, relate, recount, speak, deliver, articulate, declaim, perform, reel off, itemize, enumerate.

reckless *adjective*
heedless, thoughtless, mindless, careless, negligent, irresponsible, imprudent, ill-advised, indiscreet, rash, hasty, foolhardy, daredevil, wild.
F3 cautious, wary, careful, prudent.

reckon *verb*
1 reckoning the cost: calculate, compute, figure out, work out, add up, total, tally, count, number, enumerate.
2 reckoned to be quite good: deem, regard, consider, esteem, value, rate, judge, evaluate, assess, estimate, gauge.
3 I reckon that will be OK: think, believe, imagine, fancy, suppose, surmise, assume, guess, conjecture.

reckoning *noun*
1 by my reckoning: calculation, computation, estimate.
2 bill, account, charge, due, score, settlement.
3 the day of reckoning: judgement, retribution, doom.

reclaim *verb*
recover, regain, recapture, retrieve, salvage, rescue, redeem, restore, reinstate, regenerate.

recognition *noun*
1 damaged beyond all recognition: identification, detection, discovery, recollection, recall, remembrance, awareness, perception, realization, understanding.
2 recognition of his failings/nod in recognition: confession, admission, acceptance, acknowledgement, gratitude, appreciation, honour, respect, greeting, salute.

recognize *verb*
1 recognized him immediately: identify, know, remember, recollect, recall, place, see, notice, spot, perceive.
2 recognize I may have been wrong: confess, own, acknowledge, accept,

WORD *workshop* really/very

Try to avoid using **really** and **very** too often in your writing. Here are some words that you could use instead to give emphasis.

absolutely	extremely	remarkably
acutely	greatly	severely
deeply	highly	truly
exceptionally	incredibly	unbelievably
exceedingly	noticeably	uncommonly
excessively	particularly	unusually

admit, grant, concede, allow, appreciate, understand, realize.

recollect *verb*
recall, remember, cast one's mind back, reminisce.

recollection *noun*
recall, remembrance, memory, souvenir, reminiscence, impression.

recommend *verb*
advocate, urge, exhort, advise, counsel, suggest, propose, put forward, advance, praise, commend, plug (*infml*), endorse, approve, vouch for.
E3 disapprove.

recommendation *noun*
advice, counsel, suggestion, proposal, advocacy, endorsement, approval, sanction, blessing, praise, commendation, plug (*infml*), reference, testimonial.
E3 disapproval.

recompense *noun*
compensation, indemnification, damages, reparation, restitution, amends, requital, repayment, reward, payment, remuneration, pay, wages.

reconcile *verb*
reunite, conciliate, pacify, appease, placate, propitiate, accord, harmonize, accommodate, adjust, resolve, settle, square.
E3 estrange, alienate.

record *noun* / **rek-awd**/
1 a record of events: register, log, report, account, minutes, memorandum, note, entry, document, file, dossier, diary, journal, memoir, history, annals, archives, documentation, evidence, testimony, trace.
2 make a pop record: recording, disc, single, CD, compact disc, album, release, LP.
3 break the record: fastest time, best performance, personal best, world record.
4 has a good record in the industry: background, track record, curriculum vitae, career.
▶ *verb* /ri-**kawd**/
1 recording dates and times: note, enter, inscribe, write down, transcribe, register, log, put down, enrol, report,

The passage that follows has some suggestions for synonyms you might choose to avoid using **really** and **very** too often.

"

Due to ~~very~~ *exceptionally* heavy freezing rain and fog, driving conditions are ~~very~~ *highly* dangerous, especially on ~~very~~ *particularly* isolated or high roads. Police are asking motorists to be ~~really~~ *exceedingly* careful because visibility is ~~very~~ *severely* limited. They also advise avoiding travelling unless journeys are ~~really~~ *absolutely* necessary.

There is no end in sight to the ~~very~~ *unusually* bad weather so travelling conditions will remain ~~very~~ *extremely* hazardous for the new few days.

"

---

minute, chronicle, document, keep, preserve.
2 recording their performance: tape-record, tape, videotape, video, cut.

recording *noun*
release, performance, record, disc, CD, cassette, tape, video, DVD, MP3, Mini Disc®.

recoup *verb*
recover, retrieve, regain, get back, make good, repay, refund, reimburse, compensate.

recover *verb*
1 recover from illness: get better, improve, pick up, rally, mend, heal, pull through, get over, recuperate, revive, convalesce, come round.

2 recover stolen goods: regain, get back, recoup, retrieve, retake, recapture, repossess, reclaim, restore.
🔁 **1** worsen. **2** lose, forfeit.

recovery *noun*
1 make a rapid recovery: recuperation, convalescence, rehabilitation, mending, healing, improvement, upturn, rally, revival, restoration.
2 recovery of the wreckage: retrieval, salvage, reclamation, repossession, recapture.
🔁 **1** worsening. **2** loss, forfeit.

recreation *noun*
fun, enjoyment, pleasure, amusement, diversion, distraction, entertainment, hobby, pastime, game, sport, play, leisure, relaxation, refreshment.

recruit *verb*
enlist, draft, conscript, enrol, sign up, engage, take on, mobilize, raise, gather, obtain, procure.
▶ *noun*
beginner, novice, initiate, learner, trainee, apprentice, conscript, convert.

rectify *verb*
correct, put right, right, remedy, cure, repair, fix, mend, improve, amend, adjust, reform.

recuperate *verb*
recover, get better, improve, pick up, rally, revive, mend, convalesce.
E⅃ worsen.

recur *verb*
repeat, persist, return, reappear.

recurrent *adjective*
recurring, chronic, persistent, repeated, repetitive, regular, periodic, frequent, intermittent.

recycle *verb*
reuse, reprocess, reclaim, recover, salvage, save.

red *adjective*
1 red as blood: scarlet, vermilion, cherry, ruby, crimson, maroon, pink, reddish, bloodshot, inflamed.
2 a red face: ruddy, florid, glowing, rosy, flushed, blushing, embarrassed, shamefaced.
3 red hair: ginger, carroty, auburn, chestnut, Titian.

redden *verb*
blush, flush, colour, go red, crimson.

redeem *verb*
1 redeem a pledge: buy back, repurchase, cash (in), exchange, change, trade, ransom, reclaim, regain, repossess, recoup, recover, recuperate, retrieve, salvage.
2 did nothing to redeem himself: compensate for, make up for, offset, outweigh, atone for, expiate, absolve, acquit, discharge, release, liberate, emancipate, free, deliver, rescue, save.

reduce *verb*
1 reduce the power: lessen, decrease, contract, shrink, slim, shorten, curtail, trim, cut, slash, discount, rebate, lower, moderate, weaken, diminish, impair.

2 reduce her to tears/reduced to begging: drive, force, degrade, downgrade, demote, humble, humiliate, impoverish, subdue, overpower, master, vanquish (*fml*).
E⅃ 1 increase, raise, boost.

reduction *noun*
decrease, drop, fall, decline, lessening, moderation, weakening, diminution, contraction, compression, shrinkage, narrowing, shortening, curtailment, restriction, limitation, cutback, cut, discount, rebate, devaluation, depreciation, deduction, subtraction, loss.
E⅃ increase, rise, enlargement.

redundant *adjective*
1 was made redundant: unemployed, out of work, laid off, dismissed.
2 a redundant factory: superfluous, surplus, excess, extra, supernumerary, unneeded, unnecessary, unwanted.
3 a redundant phrase: wordy, verbose, repetitious, tautological.
E⅃ 2 necessary, essential. 3 concise.

reel *verb*
stagger, totter, wobble, rock, sway, waver, falter, stumble, lurch, pitch, roll, revolve, gyrate, spin, wheel, twirl, whirl, swirl.

refer *verb*
1 refer it to the committee: send, direct, point, guide, pass on, transfer, commit, deliver.
2 refer to a catalogue: consult, look up, turn to, resort to.
3 refer to him by name: allude, mention, touch on, speak of, bring up, recommend, cite, quote.
4 what does this refer to?: apply, concern, relate, belong, pertain.

referee *noun*
umpire, judge, adjudicator, arbitrator, mediator, ref (*infml*).

reference *noun*
1 several references to his family: allusion, remark, mention, citation, quotation, illustration, instance, note.
2 need at least three references: testimonial, recommendation, endorsement, character.
3 in reference to your letter: relation, regard, respect, connection, bearing.

refine *verb*
process, treat, purify, clarify, filter, distil, polish, hone, improve, perfect, elevate, exalt.

refined *adjective*
civilized, cultured, cultivated, polished, sophisticated, urbane, genteel, gentlemanly, ladylike, well-bred, well-mannered, polite, civil, elegant, fine, delicate, subtle, precise, exact, sensitive, discriminating.
E∃ coarse, vulgar, rude.

reflect *verb*
1 image reflected in the water: mirror, echo, imitate, reproduce, portray, depict, show, reveal, display, exhibit, manifest, demonstrate, indicate, express, communicate.
2 reflect on what she had done: think, ponder, consider, mull (over), deliberate, contemplate, meditate, muse.

reflection *noun*
1 a reflection of their views: image, likeness, echo, impression, indication, manifestation, observation, view, opinion.
2 on reflection: thinking, thought, study, consideration, deliberation, contemplation, meditation, musing.

reform *verb*
change, amend, improve, ameliorate (*fml*), better, rectify, correct, mend, repair, rehabilitate, rebuild, reconstruct, remodel, revamp, renovate, restore, regenerate, reconstitute, reorganize, shake up (*infml*), revolutionize, purge.
▶ *noun*
change, amendment, improvement, rectification, correction, rehabilitation, renovation, reorganization, shake-up (*infml*), purge.

refresh *verb*
1 refreshed by the breeze: cool, freshen, enliven, invigorate, fortify, revive, restore, renew, rejuvenate, revitalize, reinvigorate.
2 refresh one's memory: jog, stimulate, prompt, prod.
E∃ 1 tire, exhaust.

refreshing *adjective*
1 a refreshing drink/shower: cool,

thirst-quenching, bracing, invigorating, energizing, reviving, stimulating.
2 a refreshing change from routine: fresh, new, novel, different.

refreshment *noun*
sustenance, food, drink, snack, revival, restoration, renewal, reanimation, reinvigoration, revitalization.

refuge *noun*
sanctuary, asylum, shelter, protection, security, retreat, hideout, hide-away, resort, harbour, haven.

refugee *noun*
exile, émigré, displaced person, fugitive, runaway, escapee.

refund *verb*
repay, reimburse, rebate, return, restore.
▶ *noun*
repayment, reimbursement, rebate, return.

refusal *noun*
rejection, no, rebuff, repudiation, denial, negation.
E∃ acceptance.

refuse[1] *verb* /ri-**fyooz**/
refuse to go/tell: reject, turn down, decline, spurn, repudiate, rebuff, repel, deny, withhold.
E∃ accept, allow, permit.

refuse[2] *noun* /**ref**-yoos/
dispose of our refuse: rubbish, waste, trash, garbage, junk, litter.

refute *verb*
disprove, rebut, confute, give the lie to, discredit, counter, negate.

regain *verb*
recover, get back, recoup, reclaim, repossess, retake, recapture, retrieve, return to.

regal *adjective*
majestic, kingly, queenly, princely, imperial, royal, sovereign, stately, magnificent, noble, lordly.

regard *verb*
consider, deem, judge, rate, value, think, believe, suppose, imagine, look upon, view, observe, watch.
▶ *noun*
care, concern, consideration, attention, notice, heed, respect, deference, honour, esteem, admiration,

affection, love, sympathy.
F3 disregard, contempt.

regarding *preposition*
with regard to, as regards, concerning,
with reference to, re, about, as to.

regardless *adjective*
disregarding, heedless, unmindful,
neglectful, inattentive, unconcerned,
indifferent.
F3 heedful, mindful, attentive.
▸ *adverb*
anyway, nevertheless, nonetheless,
despite everything, come what may.

regime *noun*
government, rule, administration,
management, leadership, command,
control, establishment, system.

region *noun*
land, terrain, territory, country,
province, area, district, zone, sector,
neighbourhood, range, scope, expanse,
domain, realm, sphere, field, division,
section, part, place.

*Types of geographical region
include:*

Antarctic, Arctic, basin, belt, coast,
colony, continent, country,
countryside, desert, forest, grassland,
green belt, heartland, heath,
hemisphere, interior, jungle,
lowlands, marshland, outback,
pampas, plain, prairie, region,
reservation, riviera, savannah,
scrubland, seaside, settlement, steppe,
subcontinent, territory, time zone,
tract, tropics, tundra, veld, wasteland,
wilderness, woodland, zone.

Administrative regions include:

bailiwick, banana republic, borough,
burgh, capital city, county, county
town, diocese, district, dominion,
duchy, emirate, empire, free state,
kingdom, municipality, nation,
parish, postal district, principality,
protectorate, province, realm,
republic, riding, shire, state, town,
township, urban district.

register *noun*
roll, roster, list, index, catalogue,
directory, log, record, chronicle,
annals, archives, file, ledger, schedule,
diary, almanac.
▸ *verb*
1 register for the vote : record, note,
log, enter, inscribe, mark, list,
catalogue, chronicle, enrol, enlist, sign
on, check in.
2 registering ten degrees : show, reveal,
betray, display, exhibit, manifest,
express, say, read, indicate.

regret *verb*
rue, repent, lament, mourn, grieve,
deplore.
▸ *noun*
remorse, contrition, compunction,
self-reproach, shame, sorrow, grief,
disappointment, bitterness.

regretful *adjective*
remorseful, rueful, repentant, contrite,
penitent, conscience-stricken,
ashamed, sorry, apologetic, sad,
sorrowful, disappointed.
F3 impenitent, unashamed.

regrettable *adjective*
unfortunate, unlucky, unhappy, sad,
disappointing, upsetting, distressing,
lamentable, deplorable, shameful,
wrong, ill-advised.
F3 fortunate, happy.

regular *adjective*
1 a regular event/not the regular
thing : routine, habitual, typical, usual,
customary, time-honoured,
conventional, orthodox, correct,
official, standard, normal, ordinary,
common, commonplace, everyday.
2 a regular pulse : periodic, rhythmic,
steady, constant, fixed, set, unvarying,
uniform, even, level, smooth,
balanced, symmetrical, orderly,
systematic, methodical.
F3 **1** unusual, unconventional.
2 irregular.

regulate *verb*
control, direct, guide, govern, rule,
administer, manage, handle, conduct,
run, organize, order, arrange, settle,
square, monitor, set, adjust, tune,
moderate, balance.

regulation *noun*
rule, statute, law, ordinance, edict, decree, order, commandment, precept (*fml*), dictate, requirement, procedure.
▶ *adjective*
standard, official, statutory, prescribed, required, orthodox, accepted, customary, usual, normal.

rehearsal *noun*
practice, drill, exercise, dry run, run-through, preparation, reading, recital, narration, account, enumeration, list.

rehearse *verb*
practise, drill, train, go over, prepare, try out, repeat, recite, recount, relate.

reign *noun*
rule, sway, monarchy, empire, sovereignty, supremacy, power, command, dominion, control, influence.
▶ *verb*
rule, govern, command, prevail, predominate, influence.

reinforce *verb*
strengthen, fortify, toughen, harden, stiffen, steel, brace, support, buttress, shore, prop, stay, supplement, augment, increase, emphasize, stress, underline.
E3 weaken, undermine.

reinstate *verb*
restore, return, replace, recall, reappoint, reinstall, re-establish.

reject *verb* /ri-jekt/
refuse, deny, decline, turn down, veto, disallow, condemn, despise, spurn, rebuff, jilt, exclude, repudiate, repel, renounce, eliminate, scrap, discard, jettison, cast off.
E3 accept, choose, select.
▶ *noun* /**ree**-jekt/
failure, second, discard, cast-off.

rejoice *verb*
celebrate, revel, delight, glory, exult, triumph.

relapse *verb*
worsen, deteriorate, degenerate, weaken, sink, fail, lapse, revert, regress, backslide.
▶ *noun*
worsening, deterioration, setback,

recurrence, weakening, lapse, reversion, regression, backsliding.

relate *verb*
1 related to each other: link, connect, join, couple, ally, associate, correlate.
2 related to your last statement: refer, apply, concern, pertain, appertain.
3 a book relating their adventures: tell, recount, narrate, report, describe, recite.
4 can relate to his experiences: identify, sympathize, empathize, understand, feel for.

related *adjective*
kindred, akin, affiliated, allied, associated, connected, linked, interrelated, interconnected, accompanying, concomitant, joint, mutual.
E3 unrelated, unconnected.

relation *noun*
1 a close relation: relative, family, kin, kindred.
2 has no relation to the events of yesterday: link, connection, bond, relationship, correlation, comparison, similarity, affiliation, interrelation, interconnection, interdependence, regard, reference.

relations *noun*
1 all our friends and relations: relatives, family, kin, kindred.
2 establish friendly relations with other countries: relationship, terms, rapport, liaison, intercourse, affairs, dealings, interaction, communications, contact, associations, connections.

relationship *noun*
bond, link, connection, association, liaison, rapport, affinity, closeness, similarity, parallel, correlation, ratio, proportion.

relative *adjective*
comparative, proportional, proportionate, commensurate, corresponding, respective, appropriate, relevant, applicable, related, connected, interrelated, reciprocal, dependent.
▶ *noun*
relation, family, kin.

relax *verb*
slacken, loosen, lessen, reduce, diminish, weaken, lower, soften, moderate, abate, remit, relieve, ease, rest, unwind, calm, tranquillize, sedate.
F3 tighten, intensify.

relaxed *adjective*
informal, casual, laid-back (*infml*), easy-going (*infml*), carefree, happy-go-lucky, cool, calm, composed, collected, unhurried, leisurely.
F3 tense, nervous, formal.

relay *verb*
broadcast, transmit, communicate, send, spread, carry, supply.

release *verb*
loose, unloose, unleash, unfasten, extricate, free, liberate, deliver, emancipate, acquit, absolve, exonerate, excuse, exempt, discharge, issue, publish, circulate, distribute, present, launch, unveil.
F3 imprison, detain, check.
▶ *noun*
freedom, liberty, liberation, deliverance, emancipation, acquittal, absolution, exoneration, exemption, discharge, issue, publication, announcement, proclamation.
F3 imprisonment, detention.

relent *verb*
give in, give way, yield, capitulate, unbend, relax, slacken, soften, weaken.

relentless *adjective*
unrelenting, unremitting, incessant, persistent, unflagging, ruthless, remorseless, implacable, merciless, pitiless, unforgiving, cruel, harsh, fierce, grim, hard, punishing, uncompromising, inflexible, unyielding, inexorable.
F3 merciful, yielding.

relevant *adjective*
pertinent, material, significant, germane, related, applicable, apposite, apt, appropriate, suitable, fitting, proper, admissible.
F3 irrelevant, inapplicable, inappropriate, unsuitable.

reliable *adjective*
unfailing, certain, sure, dependable,

responsible, trusty, trustworthy, honest, true, faithful, constant, staunch, solid, safe, sound, stable, predictable, regular.
F3 unreliable, doubtful, untrustworthy.

relic *noun*
memento, souvenir, keepsake, token, survival, remains, remnant, scrap, fragment, vestige, trace.

relief *noun*
1 relief from pain: alleviation, cure, remedy.
2 smile with relief: reassurance, consolation, comfort, ease, release.
3 famine relief: deliverance, help, aid, assistance, support, sustenance, refreshment.
4 relief from the merciless sun: diversion, relaxation, rest, respite, break, breather (*infml*), remission, let-up (*infml*), abatement.

relieve *verb*
1 relieve suffering: alleviate, mitigate, cure, soothe, calm, reassure, console, comfort, ease.
2 relieve the poor: help, aid, assist, support, sustain.
3 relieve overcrowding: release, deliver, free, unburden, lighten, soften, slacken, relax.
F3 aggravate, intensify.

religion

Religions include:

Amish, Anglicanism, Baptists, Calvinism, Catholicism, Christianity, Church of England, Church of Scotland, Congregationalism, evangelicalism, Free Church, Jehovah's Witnesses, Methodism, Mormonism, Presbyterianism, Protestantism, Quakerism; Baha'ism, Buddhism, Confucianism, Hinduism, Islam, Jainism, Judaism, Sikhism, Taoism, Shintoism, Zen, Zoroastrianism; druidism, New Age, paganism, Scientology, voodoo.

religious *adjective*
1 religious texts: sacred, holy, divine, spiritual, devotional, scriptural, theological, doctrinal.

2 a religious person: devout, godly, pious, God-fearing, church-going, reverent, righteous.
F3 1 secular. 2 irreligious, ungodly.

relinquish *noun*
let go, release, hand over, surrender, yield, cede, give up, resign, renounce, repudiate, waive, forgo, abandon, desert, forsake, drop, discard.
F3 keep, retain.

relish *verb*
like, enjoy, savour, appreciate, revel in.
▸ *noun*
1 hamburger with relish: seasoning, condiment, sauce, pickle, spice, piquancy, tang.
2 did it with a great deal of relish: enjoyment, pleasure, delight, gusto, zest.

reluctant *adjective*
unwilling, disinclined, indisposed, hesitant, slow, backward, loth, averse, unenthusiastic, grudging.
F3 willing, ready, eager.

rely *verb*
depend, lean, count, bank, reckon, trust, swear by.

remain *verb*
stay, rest, stand, dwell, abide (*fml*), last, endure, survive, prevail, persist, continue, linger, wait.
F3 go, leave, depart.

remainder *noun*
rest, balance, surplus, excess, remnant, remains.

remaining *adjective*
left, unused, unspent, unfinished, residual, outstanding, surviving, persisting, lingering, lasting, abiding.

remains *noun*
1 she cleared the remains of the breakfast: rest, remainder, residue, debris, dregs, leavings, leftovers, scraps, crumbs, fragments, remnants, oddments, traces, vestiges.
2 remains of the dead: body, corpse, relics, carcass, ashes.

remark *noun*
comment, observation, opinion, reflection, mention, utterance, statement, assertion, declaration.
▸ *verb*
comment, observe, note, mention, say, state, declare.

remarkable *adjective*
striking, impressive, noteworthy, surprising, amazing, strange, odd, unusual, uncommon, extraordinary, phenomenal, exceptional, outstanding, notable, conspicuous, prominent, distinguished.
F3 average, ordinary, commonplace, usual.

remedy *noun*
cure, antidote, countermeasure, corrective, restorative, medicine, treatment, therapy, relief, solution, answer, panacea.
▸ *verb*
correct, rectify, put right, redress, counteract, cure, heal, restore, treat, help, relieve, soothe, ease, mitigate, mend, repair, fix, solve.

remember *verb*
1 remember his name: recall, recollect, summon up, think back, reminisce, recognize, place.
2 remembering her lines: memorize, learn, retain.
F3 1 forget.

remind *verb*
prompt, nudge, hint, jog one's memory, refresh one's memory, bring to mind, call to mind, call up.

reminder *noun*
prompt, nudge, hint, suggestion, memorandum, memo, souvenir, memento, keepsake.

reminiscence *noun*
memory, remembrance, memoir, anecdote, recollection, recall, retrospection, review, reflection.

reminiscent *adjective*
suggestive, evocative, nostalgic.

remnant *noun*
scrap, piece, bit, fragment, end, offcut, leftover, remainder, balance, residue, shred, trace, vestige.

remorse *noun*
regret, compunction, ruefulness, repentance, penitence, contrition, self-

reproach, shame, guilt, bad
conscience, sorrow, grief.

remote *adjective*
1 a remote island : distant, far, faraway,
far-off, outlying, out-of-the-way,
inaccessible, god-forsaken, isolated,
secluded, lonely.
2 she's a little remote sometimes :
detached, aloof, standoffish,
uninvolved, reserved, withdrawn.
3 a remote possibility : slight, small,
slim, slender, faint, negligible, unlikely,
improbable.
E3 1 close, nearby, accessible. **2** friendly.

remove *verb*
1 remove a tooth/one's hat : detach,
pull off, amputate, cut off, extract, pull
out, withdraw, take away, take off, strip,
shed, doff.
2 remove all trace of it : expunge (*fml*),
efface (*fml*), erase, delete, strike out, get
rid of, abolish, purge, eliminate.
3 remove the dictator : dismiss,
discharge, eject, throw out, oust,
depose.
4 removed to a quieter place where I
could paint in peace : displace,
dislodge, shift, move, transport,
transfer, relocate.

render *verb*
1 rendered it harmless : make, cause to
be, leave.
2 tree rendering its sap : give, provide,
supply, tender, present, submit, hand
over, deliver.
3 render it into plain English : translate,
transcribe, interpret, explain, clarify,
represent.

renew *verb*
1 renew the spring in the watch :
renovate, modernize, refurbish, refit,
recondition, mend, repair, overhaul,
remodel, reform, transform, recreate,
reconstitute, re-establish, regenerate,
revive, resuscitate, refresh, rejuvenate,
reinvigorate, revitalize, restore, replace,
replenish, restock.
2 renewing calls for his resignation :
repeat, restate, reaffirm, extend, prolong,
continue, recommence, restart, resume.

renounce *verb*
abandon, forsake, give up, resign,

relinquish, surrender, discard, reject,
spurn, disown, repudiate, disclaim,
deny, recant, abjure.

renovate *verb*
restore, renew, recondition, repair,
overhaul, modernize, refurbish, refit,
redecorate, do up, remodel, reform,
revamp, improve.

renown *noun*
fame, celebrity, stardom, acclaim,
glory, eminence, illustriousness,
distinction, note, mark, esteem,
reputation, honour.
E3 obscurity, anonymity.

renowned *adjective*
famous, well-known, celebrated,
acclaimed, famed, noted, eminent,
distinguished, illustrious, notable.
E3 unknown, obscure.

rent *noun*
rental, lease, hire, payment, fee.
▶ *verb*
let, sublet, lease, hire, charter.

repair *verb*
mend, fix, patch up, overhaul, service,
rectify, redress, restore, renovate, renew.
▶ *noun*
mend, patch, darn, overhaul, service,
maintenance, restoration, adjustment,
improvement.

repay *verb*
refund, reimburse, compensate,
recompense, reward, remunerate, pay,
settle, square, get even with, retaliate,
reciprocate, revenge, avenge.

repeal *verb*
revoke, rescind, abrogate (*fml*), quash,
annul, nullify, void, invalidate, cancel,
countermand, reverse, abolish.
E3 enact.

repeat *verb*
restate, reiterate, recapitulate, echo,
quote, recite, relate, retell, reproduce,
duplicate, renew, rebroadcast, reshow,
replay, rerun, redo.
▶ *noun*
repetition, echo, reproduction,
duplicate, rebroadcast, reshowing,
replay, rerun.

repeatedly *adverb*
time after time, time and (time) again,

again and again, over and over,
frequently, often.

repel *verb*
1 repelled their attackers: drive back,
repulse, check, hold off, ward off, parry,
resist, oppose, fight, refuse, decline,
reject, rebuff.
2 he repels me: disgust, revolt,
nauseate, sicken, offend.
E∃ 1 attract. **2** delight.

repent *noun*
regret, rue, sorrow, lament, deplore,
atone.

repentant *adjective*
penitent, contrite, sorry, apologetic,
remorseful, regretful, rueful,
chastened, ashamed.
E∃ unrepentant.

repercussion *noun*
result, consequence, backlash,
reverberation, echo, rebound,
recoil.

repetition *noun*
restatement, reiteration,
recapitulation, echo, return,
reappearance, recurrence, duplication,
tautology.

repetitive *adjective*
recurrent, monotonous, tedious,
boring, dull, mechanical, unchanging,
unvaried.

replace *verb*
1 replace the lid: put back, return,
restore, make good, reinstate, re-
establish.
2 replacing the outgoing chairman:
supersede, succeed, follow, supplant,
oust, deputize, substitute.

replacement *noun*
substitute, stand-in, understudy,
fill-in, supply, proxy, surrogate,
successor.

replenish *verb*
refill, restock, reload, recharge,
replace, restore, renew, supply, provide,
furnish, stock, fill, top up.

replica *noun*
model, imitation, reproduction,
facsimile, copy, duplicate, clone.

reply *verb*
answer, respond, retort, rejoin, react,

acknowledge, return, echo,
reciprocate, counter, retaliate.
▶ *noun*
answer, response, retort, rejoinder,
riposte, repartee, reaction, comeback,
acknowledgement, return, echo,
retaliation.

report *noun*
article, piece, write-up, record,
account, relation, narrative,
description, story, tale, gossip, hearsay,
rumour, talk, statement, communiqué,
declaration, announcement,
communication, information, news,
word, message, note.
▶ *verb*
state, announce, declare, proclaim, air,
broadcast, relay, publish, circulate,
communicate, notify, tell, recount,
relate, narrate, describe, detail, cover,
document, record, note.

reporter *noun*
journalist, correspondent, columnist,
newspaperman, newspaperwoman,
hack, newscaster, commentator,
announcer.

represent *verb*
stand for, symbolize, designate, denote,
mean, express, evoke, depict, portray,
describe, picture, draw, sketch,
illustrate, exemplify, typify, epitomize,
embody, personify, appear as, act as,
enact, perform, show, exhibit, be,
amount to, constitute.

representation *noun*
likeness, image, icon, picture, portrait,
illustration, sketch, model, statue,
bust, depiction, portrayal, description,
account, explanation.

representative *noun*
delegate, deputy, proxy, stand-in,
spokesperson, spokesman,
spokeswoman, ambassador,
commissioner, agent, salesman,
saleswoman, rep (*infml*), traveller.
▶ *adjective*
typical, illustrative, exemplary,
archetypal, characteristic, usual,
normal, symbolic.
E∃ unrepresentative, atypical.

repress *verb*
inhibit, check, control, curb,

restrain, suppress, bottle up, hold back, stifle, smother, muffle, silence, quell, crush, quash, subdue, overpower, overcome, master, subjugate, oppress.

repressive *adjective*
oppressive, authoritarian, despotic, tyrannical, dictatorial, autocratic, totalitarian, absolute, harsh, severe, tough, coercive.

reprieve *verb*
pardon, let off, spare, rescue, redeem, relieve, respite.
▶ *noun*
pardon, amnesty, suspension, abeyance, postponement, deferment, remission, respite, relief, let-up (*infml*), abatement.

reprimand *noun*
rebuke, reproof, reproach, admonition, telling-off (*infml*), ticking-off (*infml*), lecture, talking-to (*infml*), dressing-down (*infml*), censure, blame.

reprisal *noun*
retaliation, counter-attack, retribution, requital, revenge, vengeance.

reproach *verb*
rebuke, reprove, reprimand, upbraid (*fml*), scold, chide, reprehend (*fml*), blame, censure, condemn, criticize, disparage (*fml*), defame (*fml*).

reproduce *verb*
1 *reproducing his achievements*: copy, transcribe, print, duplicate, clone, mirror, echo, repeat, imitate, emulate, match, simulate, recreate, reconstruct.
2 *animals reproduce*: breed, spawn, procreate, generate, propagate, multiply.

reproduction *noun*
1 *a reproduction of the painting*: copy, print, picture, duplicate, facsimile, replica, clone, imitation.
2 *sexual reproduction*: breeding, procreation, generation, propagation, multiplication.
E3 1 original.

reproductive *adjective*
procreative, generative, sexual, sex, genital.

reptile

Reptiles include:

adder, puff adder, grass snake, tree snake, asp, viper, rattlesnake, sidewinder, anaconda, boa constrictor, cobra, king cobra, mamba, python; lizard, chameleon, frilled lizard, gecko, iguana, monitor lizard, skink, slow-worm, worm lizard; turtle, green turtle, hawksbill turtle, snapping turtle, terrapin, tortoise, giant tortoise; alligator, crocodile. ⇨ *See also* **amphibian**.

repulsive *adjective*
repellent, repugnant, revolting, disgusting, nauseating, sickening, offensive, distasteful, objectionable, obnoxious, foul, vile, loathsome, abominable, abhorrent (*fml*), hateful, horrid, unpleasant, disagreeable, ugly, hideous, forbidding.
E3 attractive, pleasant, delightful.

reputable *adjective*
respectable, reliable, dependable, trustworthy, upright, honourable, creditable, worthy, good, excellent, irreproachable.
E3 disreputable, infamous.

reputation *noun*
honour, character, standing, stature, esteem, opinion, credit, repute, fame, renown, celebrity, distinction, name, good name, bad name, infamy, notoriety.

reputed *adjective*
alleged, supposed, said, rumoured, believed, thought, considered, regarded, estimated, reckoned, held, seeming, apparent, ostensible.
E3 actual, true.

request *verb*
ask for, solicit, demand, require, seek, desire, beg, entreat, supplicate, petition, appeal.
▶ *noun*
appeal, call, demand, requisition, desire, application, solicitation, suit, petition, entreaty, supplication, prayer.

require *verb*
1 *is there anything you require?*: need,

want, wish, desire, lack, miss.
2 you are required to attend: oblige, force, compel, constrain, make, ask, request, instruct, direct, order, demand, necessitate, take, involve.

requirement *noun*
need, necessity, essential, must, requisite, prerequisite, demand, stipulation, condition, term, specification, proviso, qualification, provision.

requisite *adjective*
required, needed, necessary, essential, obligatory, compulsory, set, prescribed.

requisition *verb*
request, put in for, demand, commandeer, appropriate, take, confiscate, seize, occupy.

rescue *verb*
save, recover, salvage, deliver, free, liberate, release, redeem, ransom.
F≡ capture, imprison.
▶ *noun*
saving, recovery, salvage, deliverance, liberation, release, redemption, salvation.
F≡ capture.

research *noun*
investigation, inquiry, fact-finding, groundwork, examination, analysis, scrutiny, study, search, probe, exploration, experimentation.
▶ *verb*
investigate, examine, analyse, scrutinize, study, search, probe, explore, experiment.

resemblance *noun*
likeness, similarity, sameness, parity, conformity, closeness, affinity, parallel, comparison, analogy, correspondence, image, facsimile.
F≡ dissimilarity.

resemble *verb*
be like, look like, take after, favour, mirror, echo, duplicate, parallel.
F≡ differ from.

resent *verb*
grudge, begrudge, envy, take offence at, take umbrage at, take amiss, object to, grumble at, take exception to, dislike.
F≡ accept, like.

resentful *adjective*
grudging, envious, jealous, bitter, embittered, hurt, wounded, offended, aggrieved, put out, miffed (*infml*), peeved (*infml*), indignant, angry, vindictive.
F≡ satisfied, contented.

resentment *noun*
grudge, envy, jealousy, bitterness, spite, malice, ill-will, ill-feeling, animosity, hurt, umbrage, pique, displeasure, irritation, indignation, vexation, anger, vindictiveness.
F≡ contentment, happiness.

reservation *noun*
1 have some reservations about the scheme: doubt, scepticism, misgiving, qualm, scruple, hesitation, second thought.
2 agree without reservation: proviso, stipulation, qualification.
3 live on the reservation: reserve, preserve, park, sanctuary, homeland, enclave.
4 make a reservation: booking, engagement, appointment.

reserve *verb*
1 reserved for VIPs: set apart, earmark, keep, retain, hold back, save, store, stockpile.
2 reserve a seat: book, engage, order, secure.
F≡ **1** use up.
▶ *noun*
1 a reserve of money: store, stock, supply, fund, stockpile, cache, hoard, savings.
2 her reserve made her difficult to talk to: shyness, reticence, secretiveness, coolness, aloofness, modesty, restraint.
3 a game reserve: reservation, preserve, park, sanctuary.
4 he's the second reserve: replacement, substitute, stand-in.
F≡ **2** friendliness, openness.

reserved *adjective*
1 a reserved table: booked, engaged, taken, spoken for, set aside, earmarked, meant, intended, designated, destined, saved, held, kept, retained.

2 he's very reserved: shy, retiring, reticent, unforthcoming, uncommunicative, secretive, silent, taciturn, unsociable, cool, aloof, standoffish, unapproachable, modest, restrained, cautious.
F3 1 unreserved, free, available. 2 friendly, open.

residence *noun*
dwelling, habitation, domicile, abode (*fml*), seat, place, home, house, lodgings, quarters, hall, manor, mansion, palace, villa, country house, country seat.

resident *noun*
inhabitant, citizen, local, householder, occupier, tenant, lodger, guest.
F3 non-resident.

residual *adjective*
remaining, leftover, unused, unconsumed, net.

resign *verb*
stand down, leave, quit, abdicate, vacate, renounce, relinquish, forgo, waive, surrender, yield, abandon, forsake.
F3 join.
◆ **resign oneself** reconcile oneself, accept, bow, submit, yield, comply, acquiesce.
F3 resist.

resignation *noun*
1 offered his resignation: standing-down, abdication, retirement, departure, notice, renunciation, relinquishment.
2 resignation to their fate: acceptance, acquiescence, surrender, submission, non-resistance, passivity, patience, stoicism, defeatism.
F3 2 resistance.

resigned *adjective*
reconciled, philosophical, stoical, patient, unprotesting, unresisting, submissive, defeatist.
F3 resistant.

resilient *adjective*
1 resilient material: flexible, pliable, supple, plastic, elastic, springy, bouncy.
2 a resilient person: strong, tough, hardy, adaptable, buoyant.
F3 1 rigid, brittle.

resist *verb*
oppose, defy, confront, fight, combat, weather, withstand, repel, counteract, check, avoid, refuse.
F3 submit, accept.

resistant *adjective*
1 resistant to change: opposed, antagonistic, defiant, unyielding, intransigent, unwilling.
2 water-resistant: proof, impervious, immune, invulnerable, tough, strong.
F3 1 compliant, yielding.

resolute *adjective*
determined, resolved, set, fixed, unwavering, staunch, firm, steadfast, relentless, single-minded, persevering, dogged, tenacious, stubborn, obstinate, strong-willed, undaunted, unflinching, bold.
F3 irresolute, weak-willed, half-hearted.

resolution *noun*
1 his resolution never wavered: determination, resolve, willpower, commitment, dedication, devotion, firmness, steadfastness, persistence, perseverance, doggedness, tenacity, zeal, courage, boldness.
2 vote on the resolution: decision, judgement, finding, declaration, proposition, motion.
F3 1 half-heartedness, uncertainty, indecision.

resolve *verb*
decide, make up one's mind, determine, fix, settle, conclude, sort out, work out, solve.

resort *verb*
go, visit, frequent, patronize, haunt.
▶ *noun*
recourse, refuge, course (of action), alternative, option, chance, possibility.
◆ **resort to** turn to, use, utilize, employ, exercise.

resounding *adjective*
1 a resounding bang: resonant, reverberating, echoing, ringing, sonorous, booming, thunderous, full, rich, vibrant.
2 a resounding victory: decisive, conclusive, crushing, thorough.
F3 1 faint.

resource *noun*
1 natural resources: supply, reserve, stockpile, source, expedient, contrivance, device.
2 shows great resource: resourcefulness, initiative, ingenuity, inventiveness, talent, ability, capability.

resourceful *adjective*
ingenious, imaginative, creative, inventive, innovative, original, clever, bright, sharp, quick-witted, able, capable, talented.

resources *noun*
materials, supplies, reserves, holdings, funds, money, wealth, riches, capital, assets, property, means.

respect *noun*
1 respect for their elders: admiration, esteem, appreciation, recognition, honour, deference, reverence, veneration, politeness, courtesy.
2 in every respect: point, aspect, facet, feature, characteristic, particular, detail, sense, way, regard, reference, relation, connection.
F3 1 disrespect.
▶ *verb*
1 respect his judgement: admire, esteem, regard, appreciate, value.
2 respect the law: obey, observe, heed, follow, honour, fulfil.
F3 1 despise, scorn. 2 ignore, disobey.

respectable *adjective*
1 a respectable family: honourable, worthy, respected, dignified, upright, honest, decent, clean-living.
2 make a respectable living: acceptable, tolerable, passable, adequate, fair, reasonable, appreciable, considerable.
F3 1 dishonourable, disreputable. 2 inadequate, paltry.

respectful *adjective*
deferential, reverential, humble, polite, well-mannered, courteous, civil.
F3 disrespectful.

respective *adjective*
corresponding, relevant, various, several, separate, individual, personal, own, particular, special.

respond *verb*
answer, reply, retort, acknowledge, react, return, reciprocate.

response *noun*
answer, reply, retort, comeback, acknowledgement, reaction, feedback.
F3 query.

responsibility *noun*
fault, blame, guilt, culpability, answerability, accountability, duty, obligation, burden, onus, charge, care, trust, authority, power.

responsible *adjective*
1 are you responsible for this mess?: guilty, culpable, at fault, to blame, liable, answerable, accountable.
2 a responsible adult: dependable, reliable, conscientious, trustworthy, honest, sound, steady, sober, mature, sensible, rational.
3 the body responsible for this: authoritative, executive, decision-making.
F3 2 irresponsible, unreliable, untrustworthy.

rest[1] *noun*
1 get some rest: leisure, relaxation, repose, lie-down, sleep, snooze, nap, siesta, idleness, inactivity, motionlessness, standstill, stillness, tranquillity, calm.
2 need a rest: break, pause, breathing-space, breather (*infml*), intermission, interlude, interval, recess, holiday, vacation, halt, cessation, lull, respite.
3 an arm rest: support, prop, stand, base.
F3 1 action, activity. 2 work.
▶ *verb*
1 rest for a moment: pause, halt, stop, cease.
2 rest in bed: relax, repose, sit, recline, lounge, laze, lie down, sleep, snooze, doze.
3 rests on his decision: depend, rely, hinge, hang, lie.
4 rested his hand on her shoulder: lean, prop, support, stand.
F3 1 continue. 2 work.

rest[2] *noun*
the rest of the day: remainder, others, balance, surplus, excess, residue, remains, leftovers, remnants.

restaurant *noun*
eating-house, bistro, steakhouse, grill room, dining room, snack bar, buffet, cafeteria, café.

restful *adjective*
relaxing, soothing, calm, tranquil, serene, peaceful, quiet, undisturbed, relaxed, comfortable, leisurely, unhurried.
E3 tiring, restless.

restless *adjective*
fidgety, unsettled, disturbed, troubled, agitated, nervous, anxious, worried, uneasy, fretful, edgy, jumpy, restive, unruly, turbulent, sleepless.
E3 calm, relaxed, comfortable.

restore *verb*
1 *restoring law and order*: return, reinstate, rehabilitate, re-establish, reintroduce, re-enforce.
2 *restore a building*: renovate, renew, rebuild, reconstruct, refurbish, retouch, recondition, repair, mend, fix.
3 *restoring his strength*: revive, refresh, rejuvenate, revitalize, strengthen.
E3 1 remove. 2 damage. 3 weaken.

restrain *verb*
hold back, keep back, suppress, subdue, repress, inhibit, check, curb, bridle, stop, arrest, prevent, bind, tie, chain, fetter, manacle, imprison, jail, confine, restrict, regulate, control, govern.
E3 encourage, liberate.

restrained *adjective*
moderate, temperate, mild, subdued, muted, quiet, soft, low-key, unobtrusive, discreet, tasteful, calm, controlled, steady, self-controlled.
E3 unrestrained.

restraint *noun*
moderation, inhibition, self-control, self-discipline, hold, grip, check, curb, rein, bridle, suppression, bondage, captivity, confinement, imprisonment, bonds, chains, fetters, straitjacket, restriction, control, constraint, limitation, tie, hindrance, prevention.
E3 liberty.

restrict *verb*
limit, bound, demarcate, control,

regulate, confine, contain, cramp, constrain, impede, hinder, hamper, handicap, tie, restrain, curtail.
E3 broaden, free.

restriction *noun*
limit, bound, confine, limitation, constraint, handicap, check, curb, restraint, ban, embargo, control, regulation, rule, stipulation, condition, proviso.
E3 freedom.

result *noun*
effect, consequence, sequel, repercussion, reaction, outcome, upshot, issue, end-product, fruit, score, answer, verdict, judgement, decision, conclusion.
E3 cause.
▸ *verb*
follow, ensue, happen, occur, issue, emerge, arise, spring, derive, stem, flow, proceed, develop, end, finish, terminate, culminate.
E3 cause.

resume *verb*
restart, recommence, reopen, reconvene, continue, carry on, go on, proceed.
E3 cease.

resurrection *noun*
restoration, revival, resuscitation, renaissance, rebirth, renewal, resurgence, reappearance, return, comeback.

retain *verb*
1 *retain a copy for your files*: keep, hold, reserve, hold back, save, preserve.
2 *retain information*: remember, memorize, recall.
3 *retaining his services*: employ, engage, hire, commission.
E3 1 release. 2 forget. 3 dismiss.

retaliate *verb*
reciprocate, counter-attack, hit back, strike back, fight back, get one's own back, get even with, take revenge.

reticent *adjective*
reserved, shy, uncommunicative, unforthcoming, tight-lipped, secretive, taciturn, silent, quiet.
E3 communicative, forward, frank.

retire *verb*
leave, depart, withdraw, retreat, recede.
F∃ join, enter, advance.

retirement *noun*
withdrawal, retreat, solitude, loneliness, seclusion, privacy, obscurity.

retiring *adjective*
shy, bashful, timid, shrinking, quiet, reticent, reserved, self-effacing, unassertive, diffident, modest, unassuming, humble.
F∃ bold, forward, assertive.

retort *verb*
answer, reply, respond, rejoin, return, counter, retaliate.
▶ *noun*
answer, reply, response, rejoinder, riposte, repartee, quip.

retract *verb*
take back, withdraw, recant, reverse, revoke, rescind, cancel, repeal, repudiate, disown, disclaim, deny.
F∃ assert, maintain.

retreat *verb*
draw back, recoil, shrink, turn tail (*infml*), withdraw, retire, leave, depart, quit.
F∃ advance.
▶ *noun*
1 *army is in retreat*: withdrawal, departure, evacuation, flight.
2 *provide a retreat from the world*: seclusion, privacy, hideaway, den, refuge, asylum, sanctuary, shelter, haven.
F∃ 1 advance, charge.

retrieve *verb*
fetch, bring back, regain, get back, recapture, repossess, recoup, recover, salvage, save, rescue, redeem, restore, return.
F∃ lose.

retrograde *adjective*
retrogressive, backward, reverse, negative, downward, declining, deteriorating.
F∃ progressive.

retrospect *noun*
hindsight, afterthought, re-examination, review, recollection, remembrance.
F∃ prospect.

return *verb*
1 *return home*: come back, reappear, recur, go back, backtrack, regress, revert.
2 *return his letters*: give back, hand back, send back, deliver, put back, replace, restore.
3 *return a favour*: reciprocate, requite, repay, refund, reimburse, recompense.
F∃ 1 leave, depart. 2 take.
▶ *noun*
1 *on his return*: reappearance, recurrence, comeback, home-coming.
2 *the return of a favour*: repayment, recompense, replacement, restoration, reinstatement, reciprocation.
3 *make a good return on their investment*: revenue, income, proceeds, takings, yield, gain, profit, reward, advantage, benefit.
F∃ 1 departure, disappearance.
2 removal. 3 payment, expense, loss.

reveal *verb*
expose, uncover, unveil, unmask, show, display, exhibit, manifest, disclose, divulge, betray, leak, tell, impart, communicate, broadcast, publish, announce, proclaim.
F∃ hide, conceal, mask.

revel in *verb*
enjoy, relish, savour, delight in, thrive on, bask in, glory in, lap up, indulge in, wallow in, luxuriate in.

revelation *noun*
uncovering, unveiling, exposure, unmasking, show, display, exhibition, manifestation, disclosure, confession, admission, betrayal, giveaway, leak, news, information, communication, broadcasting, publication, announcement, proclamation.

revenge *noun*
vengeance, satisfaction, reprisal, retaliation, requital, retribution.
▶ *verb*
avenge, repay, retaliate, get one's own back.

revenue *noun*
income, return, yield, interest, profit, gain, proceeds, receipts, takings.
F∃ expenditure.

reverberate *verb*
echo, re-echo, resound, resonate, ring, boom, vibrate.

revere *verb*
respect, esteem, honour, pay homage to, venerate, worship, adore, exalt.
F3 despise, scorn.

reverence *noun*
respect, deference, honour, homage, admiration, awe, veneration, worship, adoration, devotion.
F3 contempt, scorn.

reverent *adjective*
reverential, respectful, deferential, humble, dutiful, awed, solemn, pious, devout, adoring, loving.
F3 irreverent, disrespectful.

reversal *noun*
negation, cancellation, annulment, nullification, countermanding, revocation, rescinding, repeal, reverse, turnabout, turnaround, U-turn, volte-face, upset.
F3 advancement, progress.

reverse *verb*
1 reverse into the garage/reverse an order: back, retreat, backtrack, undo, negate, cancel, annul, invalidate, countermand, overrule, revoke, rescind, repeal, retract, quash, overthrow.
2 mirror reverses the image:
transpose, turn round, invert, up-end, overturn, upset, change, alter.
F3 1 advance, enforce.
▶ *noun*
1 the reverse of the coin: underside, back, rear, inverse, converse, contrary, opposite, antithesis.
2 suffer a major reverse of fortunes: misfortune, mishap, misadventure, adversity, affliction, hardship, trial, blow, disappointment, setback, check, delay, problem, difficulty, failure, defeat.
▶ *adjective*
opposite, contrary, converse, inverse, inverted, backward, back, rear.

revert *verb*
return, go back, resume, lapse, relapse, regress.

review *verb*
1 review the play: criticize, assess,

evaluate, judge, weigh, discuss, examine, inspect, scrutinize, study, survey, recapitulate.
2 review the situation: reassess, re-evaluate, re-examine, reconsider, rethink, revise.
▶ *noun*
criticism, critique, assessment, evaluation, judgement, report, commentary, examination, scrutiny, analysis, study, survey, recapitulation, reassessment, re-evaluation, re-examination, revision.

revise *verb*
1 revise one's opinion: change, alter, modify, amend, correct, update, adjust, edit, rewrite, reword, recast, revamp, reconsider, re-examine, review.
2 revising for the exams: study, learn, swot up (*infml*), cram (*infml*).

revival *noun*
resuscitation, revitalization, restoration, renewal, renaissance, rebirth, reawakening, resurgence, upsurge.

revive *verb*
resuscitate, reanimate, revitalize, restore, renew, refresh, animate, invigorate, quicken (*fml*), rouse, awaken, recover, rally, reawaken, rekindle, reactivate.
F3 weary.

revoke *verb*
repeal, rescind, quash, abrogate (*fml*), annul, nullify, invalidate, negate, cancel, countermand, reverse, retract, withdraw.
F3 enforce.

revolt *noun*
revolution, rebellion, mutiny, rising, uprising, insurrection, putsch, coup (d'état), secession, defection.
▶ *verb*
1 revolt against authority: rebel, mutiny, rise, riot, resist, dissent, defect.
2 it revolted him: disgust, sicken, nauseate, repel, offend, shock, outrage, scandalize.
F3 1 submit. **2** please, delight.

revolting *adjective*
disgusting, sickening, nauseating, repulsive, repellent, obnoxious, nasty, horrible, foul, loathsome, abhorrent

fml), distasteful, offensive, shocking,
appalling.
≠ pleasant, delightful, attractive,
palatable.

revolution *noun*
1 the French Revolution : revolt,
rebellion, mutiny, rising, uprising,
insurrection, putsch, coup (d'état),
reformation, change, transformation,
innovation, upheaval, cataclysm.
2 allow the engine to go through
several revolutions : rotation, turn,
spin, cycle, circuit, round, circle, orbit,
gyration.

revolutionary *noun*
rebel, mutineer, insurgent, anarchist,
revolutionist.
▸ *adjective*
1 a revolutionary leader : rebel,
rebellious, mutinous, insurgent,
subversive, seditious, anarchistic.
2 revolutionary ideas : new, innovative,
avant-garde, different, drastic, radical,
thoroughgoing.
≠ 1 conservative.

revolve *verb*
rotate, turn, pivot, swivel, spin, wheel,
whirl, gyrate, circle, orbit.

revulsion *noun*
repugnance, disgust, distaste, dislike,
aversion, hatred, loathing, abhorrence
(*fml*), abomination.
≠ delight, pleasure, approval.

reward *noun*
prize, honour, medal, decoration,
bounty, pay-off, bonus, premium,
payment, remuneration, recompense,
repayment, requital, compensation,
gain, profit, return, benefit, merit,
desert, retribution.
≠ punishment.
▸ *verb*
pay, remunerate, recompense, repay,
requite, compensate, honour, decorate.
≠ punish.

rewarding *adjective*
profitable, remunerative, lucrative,
productive, fruitful, worthwhile,
valuable, advantageous, beneficial,
satisfying, gratifying, pleasing,
fulfilling, enriching.
≠ unrewarding.

rhetoric *noun*
eloquence, oratory, grandiloquence,
magniloquence, bombast, pomposity,
hyperbole, verbosity, wordiness.

rhetorical *adjective*
oratorical, grandiloquent,
magniloquent, bombastic,
declamatory, pompous, high-
sounding, grand, high-flown, flowery,
florid, flamboyant, showy, pretentious,
artificial, insincere.
≠ simple.

rhyme *noun*
poetry, verse, poem, ode, limerick,
jingle, song, ditty.

rhythm *noun*
beat, pulse, time, tempo, metre,
measure, movement, flow, lilt, swing,
accent, cadence, pattern.

rhythmic *adjective*
rhythmical, metric, metrical,
pulsating, throbbing, flowing, lilting,
periodic, regular, steady.

rich *adjective*
1 a rich family : wealthy, affluent,
moneyed, prosperous, well-to-do, well-
off, loaded (*infml*).
2 a rich crop : plentiful, abundant,
copious, profuse, prolific, ample, full.
3 rich soil : fertile, fruitful, productive,
lush.
4 rich food : creamy, fatty, full-bodied,
heavy, full-flavoured, strong, spicy,
savoury, tasty, delicious, luscious, juicy,
sweet.
5 rich colours : deep, intense, vivid,
bright, vibrant, warm.
6 rich fabrics : expensive, precious,
valuable, lavish, sumptuous, opulent,
luxurious, splendid, gorgeous, fine,
elaborate, ornate.
≠ 1 poor, impoverished. 3 barren.
4 plain, bland. 5 dull, soft. 6 plain.

riches *noun*
wealth, affluence, money, gold,
treasure, fortune, assets, property,
substance, resources, means.
≠ poverty.

rickety *adjective*
unsteady, wobbly, shaky, unstable,
insecure, flimsy, jerry-built, decrepit,
ramshackle, broken-down,

dilapidated, derelict.
F₃ stable, strong.

rid *verb*
clear, purge, free, deliver, relieve,
unburden.

riddle¹ *noun*
solve the riddle: enigma, mystery,
conundrum, brain-teaser, puzzle,
poser (*infml*), problem.

riddle² *verb*
1 riddled with bullet holes: perforate,
pierce, puncture, pepper, fill,
permeate, pervade, infest.
2 riddle the soil to remove small
stones: sift, sieve, strain, filter, winnow.

ride *verb*
sit, move, progress, travel, journey,
gallop, trot, pedal, drive, steer, control,
handle, manage.
▶ *noun*
journey, trip, outing, jaunt, spin, drive,
lift.

ridicule *noun*
satire, irony, sarcasm, mockery,
jeering, scorn, derision, taunting,
teasing, chaff, banter, badinage,
laughter.
F₃ praise.
▶ *verb*
satirize, send up, caricature, lampoon,
burlesque, parody, mock, make fun of,
jeer, scoff, deride, sneer, tease, rib
(*infml*), humiliate, taunt.
F₃ praise.

ridiculous *adjective*
ludicrous, absurd, nonsensical, silly,
foolish, stupid, contemptible, derisory,
laughable, farcical, comical, funny,
hilarious, outrageous, preposterous,
incredible, unbelievable.
F₃ sensible.

rife *adjective*
abundant, rampant, teeming, raging,
epidemic, prevalent, widespread,
general, common, frequent.
F₃ scarce.

rift *noun*
1 a rift in the rock: split, breach, break,
fracture, crack, fault, chink, cleft,
cranny, crevice, gap, space, opening.
2 cause a rift between them:
disagreement, difference, separation,

division, schism, alienation.
F₃ 2 unity.

right *adjective*
1 the right answer: correct, accurate,
exact, precise, true, factual, actual,
real.
2 the right thing to do: proper, fitting
seemly, becoming, appropriate,
suitable, fit, admissible, satisfactory,
reasonable, desirable, favourable,
advantageous.
3 a right decision: fair, just, equitable,
lawful, honest, upright, good, virtuous
righteous, moral, ethical, honourable.
4 right-wing: conservative, Tory.
F₃ 1 wrong, incorrect. 2 improper,
unsuitable. 3 unfair, wrong. 4 left-wing
▶ *adverb*
1 do it right: correctly, accurately,
exactly, precisely, factually, properly,
satisfactorily, well, fairly.
2 right to the bottom: straight,
directly, completely, utterly.
F₃ 1 wrongly, incorrectly, unfairly.
▶ *noun*
1 human rights: privilege, prerogative,
due, claim, business, authority, power.
2 legal/moral rights: justice, legality,
good, virtue, righteousness, morality,
honour, integrity, uprightness.
F₃ 2 wrong.
▶ *verb*
rectify, correct, put right, fix, repair,
redress, vindicate, avenge, settle,
straighten, stand up.
◆ **right away** straight away,
immediately, at once, now, instantly,
directly, forthwith, without delay,
promptly.
F₃ later, eventually.

rightful *adjective*
legitimate, lawful, legal, just, bona fide
true, real, genuine, valid, authorized,
correct, proper, suitable, due.
F₃ wrongful, unlawful.

rigid *adjective*
stiff, inflexible, unbending, cast-iron,
hard, firm, set, fixed, unalterable,
invariable, austere, harsh, severe,
unrelenting, strict, rigorous, stringent
stern, uncompromising, unyielding.
F₃ flexible, elastic.

rigorous *adjective*
strict, stringent, rigid, firm, exact, precise, accurate, meticulous, painstaking, scrupulous, conscientious, thorough.
F3 lax, superficial.

rile *verb*
annoy, irritate, nettle, pique, peeve (*infml*), put out, upset, irk, vex, anger, exasperate.
F3 calm, soothe.

rim *noun*
lip, edge, brim, brink, verge, margin, border, circumference.
F3 centre, middle.

ring[1] *noun*
1 a ring of gold: circle, round, loop, hoop, halo, band, girdle, collar, circuit, arena, enclosure.
2 a drug ring: group, cartel, syndicate, association, organization, gang, crew, mob, band, cell, clique, coterie.
► *verb*
surround, encircle, gird, circumscribe, encompass, enclose.

ring[2] *verb*
1 front doorbell bell rang: chime, peal, toll, tinkle, clink, jingle, clang, sound, resound, resonate, reverberate, buzz.
2 ring him: telephone, phone, call, ring up.
► *noun*
1 gave two short rings: chime, peal, toll, tinkle, clink, jingle, clang.
2 give me a ring: phone call, call, buzz (*infml*), tinkle (*infml*).

rinse *verb*
swill, bathe, wash, clean, cleanse, flush, wet, dip.

riot *noun*
insurrection, rising, uprising, revolt, rebellion, anarchy, lawlessness, affray, disturbance, turbulence, disorder, confusion, commotion, tumult, turmoil, uproar, row, quarrel, strife.
F3 order, calm.
► *verb*
revolt, rebel, rise up, run riot, run wild, rampage.

rip *verb*
tear, rend, split, separate, rupture, burst, cut, slit, slash, gash, lacerate, hack.

► *noun*
tear, rent, split, cleavage, rupture, cut, slit, slash, gash, hole.
◆ **rip off** (*infml*) overcharge, swindle, defraud, cheat, diddle, do (*infml*), fleece, sting (*infml*), con (*infml*), trick, dupe, exploit.

ripe *adjective*
1 ripe fruit: ripened, mature, mellow, seasoned, grown, developed, complete, finished, perfect.
2 ripe for change: ready, suitable, right, favourable, auspicious, propitious, timely, opportune.
F3 2 untimely, inopportune.

ripen *verb*
develop, mature, mellow, season, age.

rise *verb*
1 rising above the horizon: go up, ascend, climb, mount, slope (up), soar, tower, grow, increase, escalate, intensify.
2 all rise: stand up, get up, arise, jump up, spring up.
3 living standards are rising: advance, progress, improve, prosper.
4 stream rising in the mountains: originate, spring, flow, issue, emerge, appear.
F3 1 fall, descend. **2** sit down.
► *noun*
1 over the next rise: ascent, climb, slope, incline, hill, elevation.
2 a rise in prices: increase, increment, upsurge, upturn, advance, progress, improvement, advancement, promotion.
F3 1 descent, valley. **2** fall.

risk *noun*
danger, peril, jeopardy, hazard, chance, possibility, uncertainty, gamble, speculation, venture, adventure.
F3 safety, certainty.
► *verb*
endanger, imperil, jeopardize, hazard, chance, gamble, venture, dare.

risky *adjective*
dangerous, unsafe, perilous, hazardous, chancy, uncertain, touch-and-go, dicey (*infml*), tricky, precarious.
F3 safe.

ritual noun
custom, tradition, convention, usage, practice, habit, wont, routine, procedure, ordinance, prescription, form, formality, ceremony, ceremonial, solemnity, rite, sacrament, service, liturgy, observance, act.
▶ adjective
customary, traditional, conventional, habitual, routine, procedural, prescribed, set, formal, ceremonial.
E3 informal.

rival noun
competitor, contestant, contender, challenger, opponent, adversary, antagonist, match, equal, peer.
E3 colleague, associate.
▶ adjective
competitive, competing, opposed, opposing, conflicting.
E3 associate.
▶ verb
compete with, contend with, vie with, oppose, emulate, match, equal.
E3 co-operate.

rivalry noun
competitiveness, competition, contest, contention, conflict, struggle, strife, opposition, antagonism.
E3 co-operation.

river noun
waterway, watercourse, tributary, stream, brook, beck, creek, estuary.

road noun
roadway, motorway, bypass, highway, thoroughfare, street, avenue, boulevard, crescent, drive, lane, track, route, course, way, direction.

roam verb
wander, rove, range, travel, walk, ramble, stroll, amble, prowl, drift, stray.
E3 stay.

roar verb, noun
bellow, yell, shout, cry, bawl, howl, hoot, guffaw, thunder, crash, blare, rumble.
E3 whisper.

rob verb
steal from, hold up, raid, burgle, loot, pillage, plunder, sack, rifle, ransack, swindle, rip off (infml), do (infml), cheat, defraud, deprive.

robbery noun
theft, stealing, larceny, hold-up, stick-up (infml), heist (infml), raid, burglary, pillage, plunder, fraud, embezzlement, swindle, rip-off (infml).

robust adjective
strong, sturdy, tough, hardy, vigorous, powerful, muscular, athletic, fit, healthy, well.
E3 weak, feeble, unhealthy.

rock[1] noun
made of rock : boulder, stone, pebble, crag, outcrop.

rock[2] verb
1 rocked from side to side : sway, swing, tilt, tip, shake, wobble, roll, pitch, toss, lurch, reel, stagger, totter.
2 news that rocked the nation : shock, stun, daze, dumbfound, astound, astonish, surprise, startle.

rocky[1] adjective
a rocky slope : stony, pebbly, craggy, rugged, rough, hard, flinty.
E3 smooth, soft.

rocky[2] adjective
the chair/business is rocky : unsteady, shaky, wobbly, staggering, tottering, unstable, unreliable, uncertain, weak.
E3 steady, stable, dependable, strong.

rod noun
bar, shaft, strut, pole, stick, baton, wand, cane, switch, staff, mace, sceptre.

rodent

Kinds of rodent include:

agouti, bandicoot, beaver, black rat, brown rat, cane rat, capybara, cavy, chinchilla, chipmunk, cony, coypu, dormouse, ferret, fieldmouse, gerbil, gopher, grey squirrel, groundhog, guinea pig, hamster, hare, harvest mouse, hedgehog, jerboa, kangaroo rat, lemming, marmot, meerkat, mouse, muskrat, musquash, pika, porcupine, prairie dog, rabbit, rat, red squirrel, squirrel, vole, water rat, water vole, woodchuck.

rogue noun
scoundrel, rascal, scamp, villain, miscreant (fml), crook (infml),

swindler, fraud, cheat, con man (*infml*), reprobate, wastrel, ne'er-do-well.

role *noun*
part, character, representation, portrayal, impersonation, function, capacity, task, duty, job, post, position.

roll *verb*
1 rolling a hoop: rotate, revolve, turn, spin, wheel, twirl, whirl, gyrate, move, run, pass.
2 rolled up into a ball: wind, coil, furl, twist, curl, wrap, envelop, enfold, bind.
3 the ship rolled: rock, sway, swing, pitch, toss, lurch, reel, wallow, undulate.
4 rolling the lawn: press, flatten, smooth, level.
5 thunder rolled: rumble, roar, thunder, boom, resound, reverberate.
▶ *noun*
1 a roll of paper: roller, cylinder, drum, reel, spool, bobbin, scroll.
2 the electoral roll: register, roster, census, list, inventory, index, catalogue, directory, schedule, record, chronicle, annals.
3 roll of the dice: rotation, revolution, cycle, turn, spin, wheel, twirl, whirl, gyration, undulation.
4 the roll of thunder: rumble, roar, thunder, boom, resonance, reverberation.
◆ **roll up** (*infml*) arrive, assemble, gather, congregate, convene.
🔁 leave.

romance *noun*
1 her latest romance: love affair, affair, relationship, liaison, intrigue, passion.
2 write romances: love story, novel, story, tale, fairy tale, legend, idyll, fiction, fantasy.
3 the romance of living on a tropical island: adventure, excitement, melodrama, mystery, charm, fascination, glamour, sentiment.

romantic *adjective*
1 a romantic figure/notion: imaginary, fictitious, fanciful, fantastic, legendary, fairy tale, idyllic, utopian, idealistic, quixotic, visionary, starry-eyed, dreamy, unrealistic, impractical, improbable, wild, extravagant,

exciting, fascinating.
2 wrote romantic letters: sentimental, loving, amorous, passionate, tender, fond, lovey-dovey (*infml*), soppy, mushy, sloppy.
🔁 1 real, practical. 2 unromantic, unsentimental.
▶ *noun*
sentimentalist, dreamer, visionary, idealist, utopian.
🔁 realist.

room *noun*
space, volume, capacity, headroom, legroom, elbow-room, scope, range, extent, leeway, latitude, margin, allowance, chance, opportunity.

Types of room include:

attic, basement, bathroom, bedroom, boudoir, boxroom, breakfast room, cellar, chamber, cloakroom, conservatory, den (*infml*), dining room, drawing room, dressing-room, en suite bathroom, family room, front room, guest room, hall, kitchen, kitchen-diner, kitchenette, landing, larder, laundry, lavatory, library, living room, loft, loo (*infml*), lounge, lounge-diner, lumber room, morning room, nursery, pantry, parlour, playroom, porch, reception room, rest room (*US*), rumpus room (*US*), salon, scullery, sitting room, spare room, study, sun lounge, toilet, utility room, WC; anteroom, assembly room, boardroom, buttery, cabin, cell, chambers, classroom, common room, consulting room, control room, courtroom, cubicle, darkroom, day room, dormitory, engine-room, fitting-room, foyer, games room, greenroom, guardroom, laboratory, lobby, locker room, mezzanine, music-room, office, reading-room, recreation room, saddleroom, sickroom, smoking room, staffroom, stateroom, stockroom, storeroom, strongroom, studio, tack room, waiting room, washroom, workroom, workshop.

roomy *adjective*
spacious, capacious, large, sizable,

broad, wide, extensive, ample, generous.
 F3 cramped, small, tiny.

root¹ *noun*
1 edible roots: tuber, rhizome, stem.
2 get to the root of the problem: origin, source, derivation, cause, starting point, fount, fountainhead, seed, germ, nucleus, heart, core, nub, essence, seat, base, bottom, basis, foundation.
 ▶ *verb*
anchor, moor, fasten, fix, set, stick, implant, embed, entrench, establish, ground, base.

root² *verb*
enjoys rooting around in antique shops: dig, delve, burrow, forage, hunt, rummage, ferret, poke, pry, nose.
 ◆ **root out** unearth, dig out, uncover, discover, uproot, eradicate, extirpate, eliminate, exterminate, destroy, abolish, clear away, remove.

roots *noun*
beginning(s), origins, family, heritage, background, birthplace, home.

rope *noun*
line, cable, cord, string, strand.
 ▶ *verb*
tie, bind, lash, fasten, hitch, moor, tether.
 ◆ **rope in** enlist, engage, involve, persuade, inveigle (*fml*).

rot *verb*
decay, decompose, putrefy, fester, perish, corrode, spoil, go bad, go off, degenerate, deteriorate, crumble, disintegrate, taint, corrupt.
 ▶ *noun*
1 find rot in the timbers: decay, decomposition, putrefaction, corrosion, rust, mould.
2 (*infml*) talking rot: nonsense, rubbish, poppycock (*infml*), drivel, claptrap.

rotate *verb*
revolve, turn, spin, gyrate, pivot, swivel, roll.

rotten *adjective*
1 rotten wood/fruit: decayed, decomposed, putrid, addled, bad, off, mouldy, fetid, stinking, rank, foul,

rotting, decaying, disintegrating.
2 a rotten job: inferior, bad, poor, inadequate, low-grade, lousy, crummy (*infml*), ropy (*infml*), mean, nasty, beastly, dirty, despicable, contemptible dishonourable, wicked.
 F3 1 fresh. 2 good.

rough *adjective*
1 a rough surface: uneven, bumpy, lumpy, rugged, craggy, jagged, irregular, coarse, bristly, scratchy.
2 rough treatment: harsh, severe, tough, hard, cruel, brutal, drastic, extreme, brusque, curt, sharp.
3 a rough guess: approximate, estimated, imprecise, inexact, vague, general, cursory, hasty, incomplete, unfinished, crude, rudimentary.
4 rough sea: choppy, agitated, turbulent, stormy, tempestuous, violent, wild.
 F3 1 smooth. 2 mild. 3 accurate. 4 calm

round *adjective*
1 a round coin: spherical, globular, ball-shaped, circular, ring-shaped, disc-shaped, cylindrical, rounded, curved.
2 she's rather small and round: rotund, plump, stout, portly.
 ▶ *noun*
1 a round of golf: cycle, series, sequence, succession, period, bout, session.
2 security guard doing his rounds: beat, circuit, lap, course, routine.
 ▶ *verb*
circle, skirt, flank, bypass.
 ◆ **round off** finish (off), complete, end close, conclude, cap, crown.
 F3 begin.
 ◆ **round on** turn on, attack, lay into, abuse.
 ◆ **round up** herd, marshal, assemble, gather, rally, collect, group.
 F3 disperse, scatter.

roundabout *adjective*
circuitous, tortuous, twisting, winding, indirect, oblique, devious, evasive.
 F3 straight, direct.

rouse *verb*
wake (up), awaken, arouse, call, stir, move, start, disturb, agitate, anger,

rout noun
defeat, conquest, overthrow, beating, thrashing, flight, stampede.
F₃ win.

route noun
course, run, path, road, avenue, way, direction, itinerary, journey, passage, circuit, round, beat.

routine noun
1 part of their daily routine: procedure, way, method, system, order, pattern, formula, practice, usage, custom, habit.
2 a comedy routine: act, piece, programme, performance.
▸ adjective
customary, habitual, usual, typical, ordinary, run-of-the-mill, normal, standard, conventional, unoriginal, predictable, familiar, everyday, banal, humdrum, dull, boring, monotonous, tedious.
F₃ unusual, different, exciting.

row¹ noun /roh/
rows of seats: line, tier, bank, rank, range, column, file, queue, string, series, sequence.

row² noun /row/
1 have a row with someone: argument, quarrel, dispute, disagreement, controversy, squabble, tiff, slanging match (infml), fight, brawl.
2 stop that row immediately!: noise, racket, din, uproar, commotion, disturbance, rumpus, fracas.
F₃ 2 calm.
▸ verb
argue, quarrel, wrangle, bicker, squabble, fight, scrap.

rowdy adjective
noisy, loud, rough, boisterous, disorderly, unruly, riotous, wild.
F₃ quiet, peaceful.

royal adjective
regal, majestic, kingly, queenly, princely, imperial, monarchical, sovereign, august, grand, stately, magnificent, splendid, superb.

rub verb
apply, spread, smear, stroke, caress, massage, knead, chafe, grate, scrape, abrade, scour, scrub, clean, wipe, smooth, polish, buff, shine.
◆ **rub out** erase, efface (fml), obliterate, delete, cancel.

rubbish noun
1 rubbish scattered on the beach: refuse, garbage, trash, junk, litter, waste, dross, debris, flotsam and jetsam.
2 talking rubbish: nonsense, drivel, claptrap, twaddle, gibberish, gobbledegook (infml), balderdash, poppycock (infml), rot (infml).
F₃ 2 sense.

rude adjective
1 was rude to the teacher: impolite, discourteous, disrespectful, impertinent, impudent, cheeky (infml), insolent, offensive, insulting, abusive, ill-mannered, uncivil, curt, brusque, abrupt, sharp, short, ill-bred, uncouth, uncivilized.
2 made a rude noise: obscene, vulgar, coarse, dirty, naughty, gross.
F₃ 1 polite, courteous, civil.

rudimentary adjective
primary, initial, introductory, elementary, basic, fundamental, primitive, undeveloped, embryonic.
F₃ advanced, developed.

rudiments noun
basics, fundamentals, essentials, principles, elements, ABC, beginnings, foundations.

ruin noun
1 the ruin of all their hopes: destruction, devastation, wreckage, havoc, damage, disrepair, decay, disintegration, breakdown, collapse, fall, downfall, failure, defeat, overthrow, ruination, undoing.
2 financial ruin: insolvency, bankruptcy, crash.
F₃ 1 development, reconstruction.
▸ verb
spoil, mar, botch, mess up (infml), damage, break, smash, shatter, wreck, destroy, demolish, raze, devastate, overwhelm, overthrow, defeat, crush,

impoverish, bankrupt.
E₃ develop, restore.

rule *noun*
1 that's against the rules: regulation, law, statute, ordinance, decree, order, direction, guide, precept (*fml*), tenet, canon, maxim, axiom, principle, formula, guideline, standard, criterion.
2 the rule of law: reign, sovereignty, supremacy, dominion, mastery, power, authority, command, control, influence, regime, government, leadership.
▸ *verb*
1 rule a country: reign, govern, command, lead, administer, manage, direct, guide, control, regulate, prevail, dominate.
2 court ruled in our favour: judge, adjudicate, decide, find, determine, resolve, establish, decree, pronounce.
◆ **as a rule** usually, normally, ordinarily, generally.
◆ **rule out** exclude, eliminate, reject, dismiss, preclude, prevent, ban, prohibit, forbid, disallow.

ruling *noun*
judgement, adjudication, verdict, decision, finding, resolution, decree, pronouncement.
▸ *adjective*
reigning, sovereign, supreme, governing, commanding, leading, main, chief, principal, dominant, predominant, controlling.

rumour *noun*
hearsay, gossip, talk, whisper, word, news, report, story, grapevine, bush telegraph.

run *verb*
1 run for the bus: sprint, jog, race, career, tear, dash, hurry, rush, speed, bolt, dart, scoot, scuttle.
2 route runs through the village: go, pass, move, proceed, issue.
3 leave the engine running: function, work, operate, perform.
4 run a company: head, lead, administer, direct, manage, superintend, supervise, oversee, control, regulate.

5 run for president: compete, contend, stand, challenge.
6 the series ran for ten years: last, continue, extend, reach, stretch, spread, range.
7 can hear water running: flow, stream, pour, gush.
▸ *noun*
1 go for a run every morning: jog, gallop, race, sprint, spurt, dash, rush.
2 take the family for a run in the car: drive, ride, spin, jaunt, excursion, outing, trip, journey.
3 a run of bad luck: sequence, series, string, chain, course.
◆ **run away** escape, flee, abscond, bolt, scarper (*infml*), beat it (*infml*), run off, make off, clear off (*infml*).
E₃ stay.
◆ **run down 1** running down the government: criticize, belittle, disparage (*fml*), denigrate, defame (*fml*).
2 child was run down by a motorcyclist: run over, knock over, hit, strike.
3 run down by work and worry: tire, weary, exhaust, weaken.
4 run down production: reduce, decrease, drop, cut, trim, curtail.
E₃ 1 praise. **3** pep up. **4** increase, expand.
◆ **run out** expire, terminate, end, cease, close, finish, dry up, fail.

runner *noun*
jogger, sprinter, athlete, competitor, participant, courier, messenger.

running *adjective*
successive, consecutive, unbroken, uninterrupted, continuous, constant, perpetual, incessant, unceasing, moving, flowing.
E₃ broken, occasional.

runny *adjective*
flowing, fluid, liquid, liquefied, melted, molten, watery, diluted.
E₃ solid.

run-of-the-mill *adjective*
ordinary, common, everyday, average, unexceptional, unremarkable, undistinguished, unimpressive, mediocre.
E₃ exceptional.

rupture *noun*
split, tear, burst, puncture, break, breach, fracture, crack, separation, division, estrangement, schism, rift, disagreement, quarrel, falling-out, bust-up (*infml*).
verb
split, tear, burst, puncture, break, fracture, crack, sever, separate, divide.

rural *adjective*
country, rustic, pastoral, agricultural, agrarian.
🗗 urban.

rush *verb*
hurry, hasten, quicken, accelerate, speed (up), press, push, dispatch, bolt, dart, shoot, fly, tear, career, dash, race, run, sprint, scramble, stampede, charge.
noun
hurry, haste, urgency, speed, swiftness, dash, race, scramble, stampede, charge, flow, surge.

rustic *adjective*
a charming rustic scene: pastoral,
sylvan (*fml*), bucolic (*fml*), countrified, country, rural.
2 rustic furniture: plain, simple, rough, crude, coarse, rude, clumsy, awkward, artless, unsophisticated, unrefined, uncultured, provincial, uncouth, boorish, oafish.
🗗 1 urban. 2 urbane, sophisticated, cultivated, polished.

rusty *adjective*
1 a rusty old car: corroded, rusted, rust-covered, oxidized, tarnished, discoloured, dull.
2 my German is a bit rusty: unpractised, weak, poor, deficient, dated, old-fashioned, outmoded, antiquated, stale, stiff, creaking.

ruthless *adjective*
merciless, pitiless, hard-hearted, hard, heartless, unfeeling, callous, cruel, inhuman, brutal, savage, cut-throat, fierce, ferocious, relentless, unrelenting, inexorable, implacable, harsh, severe.
🗗 merciful, compassionate.

sabotage *verb*

damage, spoil, mar, disrupt, vandalize, wreck, destroy, thwart, scupper, cripple, incapacitate, disable, undermine, weaken.

▶ *noun*

vandalism, wilful damage, impairment, disruption, wrecking, destruction.

sack *verb* (*infml*)

dismiss, fire (*infml*), discharge, axe (*infml*), lay off, make redundant.

▶ *noun* (*infml*)

dismissal, discharge, one's cards, notice, the boot (*infml*), the push (*infml*), the elbow (*infml*), the axe (*infml*), the chop (*infml*).

sacred *adjective*

holy, divine, heavenly, blessed, hallowed, sanctified, consecrated, dedicated, religious, devotional, ecclesiastical, priestly, saintly, godly, venerable, revered, sacrosanct, inviolable.

E3 temporal, profane.

sacrifice *verb*

1 sacrificed his precious time: surrender, forfeit, relinquish, let go, abandon, renounce, give up, forgo.
2 sacrificed a goat to appease the gods: offer, kill, slaughter.

sad *adjective*

1 don't look so sad: unhappy, sorrowful, tearful, grief-stricken, heavy-hearted, upset, distressed, miserable, low-spirited, downcast, doleful, glum, long-faced, crestfallen, dejected, down-hearted, down (*infml*), despondent, melancholy, depressed, low, gloomy, dismal, blue (*infml*), woebegone.

2 sad news/a sad state of affairs: upsetting, distressing, painful, depressing, touching, poignant, heart rending, tragic, grievous, lamentable, regrettable, sorry, unfortunate, seriou[s] grave, disastrous.

E3 1 happy, cheerful. **2** fortunate, lucky.

⤷ *See also* **Word Study** *panel.*

safe *adjective*

1 is the water safe to drink?: harmles[s] innocuous, non-toxic, non-poisonous uncontaminated.
2 make your property safe from burglars: secure, protected, guarded, impregnable, invulnerable, immune.
3 they were found safe and well: unharmed, undamaged, unscathed, uninjured, unhurt, intact.
4 take the safe course of action/a saf[e] pair of hands: unadventurous, cautious, prudent, conservative, sure, proven, tried, tested, sound, dependable, reliable, trustworthy.

E3 1 dangerous, harmful, unsafe.
2 vulnerable, exposed. **4** risky.

safeguard *verb*

protect, preserve, defend, guard, shield, screen, shelter, secure.
E3 endanger, jeopardize.

safe-keeping *noun*

protection, care, custody, keeping, charge, trust, guardianship, surveillance, supervision.

safety *noun*

protection, refuge, sanctuary, shelter, cover, security, safeguard, immunity, impregnability, safeness, harmlessnes[s] reliability, dependability.

E3 danger, jeopardy, risk.

WORD *study* sad

There are many ways of describing how **sad** someone is. You might consider using some of those listed below to add variety to your speech or writing.

feeling sad

be cut up
be down in the dumps
be in low spirits
have a heavy heart
hit rock bottom

be in the doldrums
be down in the mouth
(have) got the blues
have your heart in your boots

being upset

be in a state
cry or sob your heart out

cry your eyes out
weep buckets

sag *verb*
bend, give, bag, droop, hang, fall, drop, sink, dip, decline, slump, flop, fail, flag, weaken, wilt.
Fâ bulge, rise.

sail *verb*
1 sail for France: embark, set sail, weigh anchor, put to sea, cruise, voyage.
2 sailed the yacht around the world: captain, skipper, pilot, navigate, steer.
3 it sailed over our heads: glide, plane, sweep, float, skim, scud, fly.

sailor *noun*
seafarer, mariner, seaman, marine, rating, yachtsman, yachtswoman.

saintly *adjective*
godly, pious, devout, God-fearing, holy, religious, blessed, angelic, pure, spotless, innocent, blameless, sinless, virtuous, upright, worthy, righteous.
Fâ godless, unholy, wicked.

sake *noun*
benefit, advantage, good, welfare, well-being, gain, profit, behalf, interest, account.

salary *noun*
pay, payment, remuneration, emolument (*fml*), stipend, wages, earnings, income.

sale *noun*
selling, marketing, vending, disposal, trade, traffic, transaction, deal, auction.

salient *adjective*
important, significant, chief, main, principal, striking, conspicuous, noticeable, obvious, prominent, outstanding, remarkable.

sallow *adjective*
yellowish, pale, pallid, wan, pasty, sickly, unhealthy, anaemic, colourless.
Fâ rosy, healthy.

salty *adjective*
salt, salted, saline, briny, brackish, savoury, spicy, piquant, tangy.
Fâ fresh, sweet.

salutary *adjective*
good, beneficial, advantageous, profitable, valuable, helpful, useful, practical, timely.

salute *verb*
greet, acknowledge, recognize, wave, hail, address, nod, bow, honour.
▶ *noun*
greeting, acknowledgement, recognition, wave, gesture, hail, address, handshake, nod, bow, tribute.

salvage *verb*
save, preserve, conserve, rescue, recover, retrieve, reclaim, redeem, repair, restore.
Fa waste, abandon.

salvation *noun*
deliverance, liberation, rescue, saving, preservation, redemption, reclamation.
Fa loss, damnation.

same *adjective*
1 gave the same excuse yesterday: identical, twin, duplicate, indistinguishable, selfsame.
2 these words have much the same meaning: alike, like, similar, comparable, equivalent, matching, corresponding, mutual, reciprocal, interchangeable, substitutable, synonymous.
3 stuck to the same theme throughout: consistent, uniform, unvarying, changeless, unchanged.
Fa 1 different. **2** different, opposite.
3 inconsistent, variable, changeable.

sample *noun*
specimen, example, cross-section, model, pattern, swatch, piece, demonstration, illustration, instance, sign, indication, foretaste.
▶ *verb*
try, test, taste, sip, inspect, experience.

sanctions *noun*
restrictions, boycott, embargo, ban, prohibition, penalty.

sanctity *noun*
holiness, sacredness, inviolability, piety, godliness, religiousness, devotion, grace, spirituality, purity, goodness, righteousness.
Fa unholiness, secularity, worldliness, godlessness.

sane *adjective*
normal, rational, right-minded, all there (*infml*), balanced, stable, sound, sober, level-headed, sensible, judicious (*fml*), reasonable, moderate.
Fa insane, mad, crazy, foolish.

sanitary *adjective*
clean, pure, uncontaminated, unpolluted, aseptic, germ-free, disinfected, hygienic, salubrious

(*fml*), healthy, wholesome.
Fa insanitary, unwholesome.

sanity *noun*
normality, rationality, reason, sense, common sense, balance of mind, stability, soundness, level-headedness, judiciousness.
Fa insanity, madness.

sap *verb*
bleed, drain, exhaust, weaken, undermine, deplete, reduce, diminish, impair.
Fa strengthen, build up, increase.

sarcastic *adjective*
ironical, satirical, mocking, taunting, sneering, derisive, scathing, disparaging, cynical, incisive, cutting, biting, caustic.

sardonic *adjective*
mocking, jeering, sneering, derisive, scornful, sarcastic, biting, cruel, heartless, malicious, cynical, bitter.

satanic *adjective*
satanical, diabolical, devilish, demonic, fiendish, hellish, infernal, inhuman, malevolent, wicked, evil.
Fa holy, divine, godly, saintly, benevolent.

satire *noun*
ridicule, irony, sarcasm, wit, burlesque, skit, send-up, spoof, take-off, parody, caricature, travesty.

satirical *adjective*
ironical, sarcastic, mocking, irreverent, taunting, derisive, sardonic, incisive, cutting, biting, caustic, cynical, bitter.

satirize *verb*
ridicule, mock, make fun of, burlesque, lampoon, send up, take off, parody, caricature, criticize, deride.
Fa acclaim, honour.

satisfaction *noun*
1 felt some satisfaction at her achievements: gratification, contentment, happiness, pleasure, enjoyment, comfort, ease, well-being, fulfilment, self-satisfaction, pride.
2 demand satisfaction from the company: settlement, compensation, reimbursement, indemnification,

damages, reparation, amends, redress, recompense, requital, vindication.
F3 1 dissatisfaction, displeasure.

satisfactory *adjective*
acceptable, passable, up to the mark, all right, OK (*infml*), fair, average, competent, adequate, sufficient, suitable, proper.
F3 unsatisfactory, unacceptable, inadequate.

satisfy *verb*
1 nothing seems to satisfy him/satisfy their hunger : gratify, indulge, content, please, delight, quench, slake, sate, satiate, surfeit.
2 satisfy requirements : meet, fulfil, discharge, settle, answer, fill, suffice, serve, qualify.
3 satisfy herself that it was true : assure, convince, persuade.
F3 1 dissatisfy. **2** fail.

saturate *verb*
soak, steep, souse, drench, waterlog, impregnate, permeate, imbue, suffuse, fill.

saunter *verb*
stroll, amble, mosey (*infml*), mooch (*infml*), wander, ramble, meander.
► *noun*
stroll, walk, constitutional, ramble.

savage *adjective*
wild, untamed, undomesticated, uncivilized, primitive, barbaric, barbarous, fierce, ferocious, vicious, beastly, cruel, inhuman, brutal, sadistic, bloodthirsty, bloody, murderous, pitiless, merciless, ruthless, harsh.
F3 tame, civilized, humane, mild.

save *verb*
1 save money/time : economize, cut back, conserve, preserve, keep, retain, hold, reserve, store, lay up, set aside, put by, hoard, stash (*infml*), collect, gather.
2 saving them from a watery grave : rescue, deliver, liberate, free, salvage, recover, reclaim.
3 build a wall to save the village from the floods : protect, guard, screen, shield, safeguard, spare, prevent, hinder.
F3 1 spend, squander, waste, discard.

► *noun*
economy, thrift, discount, reduction, bargain, cut, conservation, preservation.
F3 expense, waste, loss.

savings *noun*
capital, investments, nest egg, fund, store, reserves, resources.

saviour *noun*
rescuer, deliverer, redeemer, liberator, emancipator, guardian, protector, defender, champion.
F3 destroyer.

savour *verb*
relish, enjoy, delight in, revel in, like, appreciate.
F3 shrink from.

savoury *adjective*
1 makes a very savoury soup : tasty, appetizing, delicious, mouthwatering, luscious, palatable.
2 sweet or savoury pancakes : salty, spicy, aromatic, piquant, tangy.
F3 1 unappetizing, tasteless, insipid. **2** sweet.

say *verb*
1 say the words aloud/said his name : express, phrase, put, render, utter, voice, articulate, enunciate, pronounce, mention, deliver, speak, orate, recite, repeat, read.
2 she said, 'Hi, I haven't seen you for ages!' : exclaim, comment, remark, observe.
3 what would you say to a weekend in Paris?/I'd say 'yes, please!' : answer, reply, respond, rejoin, retort.
4 what does it say in the papers/the instruction manual? : tell, instruct, order, communicate, convey, intimate, report, announce, declare, state.
5 it's said they are very rich : assert, affirm, maintain, claim, allege, rumour.
6 what do these figures say to you? : suggest, imply, signify, reveal, disclose, divulge.
7 I'd say it was about two o'clock/can't say yet how much it will be : guess, estimate, reckon, judge, imagine, suppose, assume, presume, surmise.
⇨ *See also* **Word Workshop** *panel*.

When you are writing down what people have said it can become boring if you repeat the words **say** and **said**. Try out some of the following instead to indicate more about the way in which people speak.

to express something in words

phrase	put into words
put	render

to guess

estimate	judge	reckon
imagine	presume	suppose

to report

affirm	convey	relate
announce	declare	state
assert	inform	tell
communicate		

to ask

demand	interrogate	question
inquire	query	

to reply

answer	respond
counter	return

to speak unclearly

babble	mutter	whisper
mumble	stutter	

to speak angrily

nag	snap	yell
shout	snarl	

to speak happily		
chuckle	joke	
giggle	laugh	

to complain or speak sadly		
cry	grumble	whine
groan	protest	sob

Instead of repeating **say/said** in the following passage, you might use some of the synonyms discussed opposite.

"

"Where have you been?" ~~said~~ *demanded* Peter.

"It's none of your business!" ~~said~~ *snapped* Chloe.

"We're in trouble now," ~~said~~ *murmured* Sheila.

"You've been gone for hours, I've been worried!" ~~said~~ *cried* Peter.

"You worry too much," Chloe ~~said~~ *grumbled*.

"Of course I do, it's late and I didn't know where you were," ~~said~~ *replied* Peter.

"Stop panicking. You can always reach us on our mobiles!" ~~said~~ *laughed* Sheila.

"I tried them but they were switched off," Peter ~~said~~ *protested*.

"That's because we were in the cinema," ~~said~~ *responded* Chloe.

"Well, let me know the next time if you are going to be late," Peter ~~said~~ *insisted*.

"

saying *noun*
adage, proverb, dictum, precept (*fml*), axiom, aphorism, maxim, motto, slogan, phrase, expression, quotation, statement, remark.

scale[1] *noun*
on a scale of one to ten : ratio, proportion, measure, degree, extent, spread, reach, range, scope, compass, spectrum, gamut, sequence, series, progression, order, hierarchy, ranking, ladder, steps, gradation, graduation, calibration, register.

scale[2] *verb*
scaling the mountain : climb, ascend, mount, clamber, scramble, shin up, conquer, surmount.

scamper *verb*
scuttle, scurry, scoot, dart, dash, run, sprint, rush, hurry, hasten, fly, romp, frolic, gambol.

scan *verb*
1 scan the horizon : examine, scrutinize, study, search, survey, sweep, investigate, check.
2 scanning the pages of the book : skim, glance at, flick through, thumb through.

scandal *noun*
outrage, offence, outcry, uproar, furore, gossip, stir, rumours, smear, dirt, discredit, dishonour, disgrace, shame, embarrassment, ignominy.

scandalize *verb*
shock, horrify, appal, dismay, disgust, repel, revolt, offend, affront, outrage.

scandalous *adjective*
shocking, appalling, atrocious, abominable, monstrous, unspeakable, outrageous, disgraceful, shameful, disreputable, infamous, improper, unseemly, defamatory, scurrilous, slanderous, libellous, untrue.

scanty *adjective*
deficient, short, inadequate, insufficient, scant, little, limited, restricted, narrow, poor, meagre, insubstantial, thin, skimpy, sparse, bare.
E3 adequate, sufficient, ample, plentiful, substantial.

scar *noun*
mark, lesion, wound, injury, blemish, stigma.
▶ *verb*
mark, disfigure, spoil, damage, brand, stigmatize.

scarce *adjective*
few, rare, infrequent, uncommon, unusual, sparse, scanty, insufficient, deficient, lacking.
E3 plentiful, common.

scarcely *adverb*
hardly, barely, only just.

scarcity *noun*
lack, shortage, dearth, deficiency, insufficiency, paucity (*fml*), rareness, rarity, infrequency, uncommonness, sparseness, scantiness.
E3 glut, plenty, abundance, sufficiency, enough.

scare *verb*
frighten, startle, alarm, dismay, daunt, intimidate, unnerve, threaten, menace, terrorize, shock, appal, panic, terrify.
E3 reassure, calm.
▶ *noun*
fright, start, shock, alarm, panic, hysteria, terror.
E3 reassurance, comfort.

scared *adjective*
frightened, fearful, nervous, anxious, worried, startled, shaken, panic-stricken, terrified.
E3 confident, reassured.

scary *adjective*
frightening, alarming, daunting, intimidating, disturbing, shocking, horrifying, terrifying, hair-raising, bloodcurdling, spine-chilling, chilling, creepy, eerie, spooky (*infml*).

scathing *adjective*
sarcastic, scornful, critical, trenchant (*fml*), cutting, biting, caustic, acid, vitriolic, bitter, harsh, brutal, savage, unsparing.
E3 complimentary.

scatter *verb*
disperse, dispel, dissipate, disband, disunite, separate, divide, break up, disintegrate, diffuse, broadcast, disseminate, spread, sprinkle,

sow, strew, fling, shower.
☒ gather, collect.

scatterbrained *adjective*
forgetful, absent-minded, empty-
headed, feather-brained, scatty (*infml*),
careless, inattentive, thoughtless,
unreliable, irresponsible, frivolous.
☒ sensible, sober, efficient, careful.

scattering *noun*
sprinkling, few, handful, smattering.
☒ mass, abundance.

scavenge *verb*
forage, rummage, rake, search, scrounge.

scenario *noun*
outline, synopsis, summary, résumé,
storyline, plot, scheme, plan,
programme, projection, sequence,
situation, scene.

scene *noun*
1 the scene of the crime : place, area,
spot, locale, site, situation, position,
whereabouts, location, locality,
environment, milieu, setting, contact,
background, backdrop, set, stage.
2 rural scene/a battle scene :
landscape, panorama, view, vista,
prospect, sight, spectacle, picture,
tableau, pageant.
3 a scene from the film : episode,
incident, part, division, act, clip.
4 don't make a scene : fuss, commotion,
to-do (*infml*), performance, drama,
exhibition, display, show.

scenery *noun*
landscape, terrain, panorama, view,
vista, outlook, scene, background,
setting, surroundings, backdrop, set.

scenic *adjective*
panoramic, picturesque, attractive,
pretty, beautiful, grand, striking,
impressive, spectacular, breathtaking,
awe-inspiring.
☒ dull, dreary.

scent *noun*
1 the scent of roses : perfume,
fragrance, aroma, bouquet, smell,
odour.
2 follow the scent : track, trail.
☒ **1** stink.
▸ *verb*
smell, sniff (out), nose (out), sense,
perceive, detect, discern, recognize.

scented *adjective*
perfumed, fragrant, sweet-smelling,
aromatic.
☒ malodorous, stinking.

sceptic *noun*
doubter, unbeliever, disbeliever,
agnostic, atheist, rationalist,
questioner, scoffer, cynic.
☒ believer.

sceptical *adjective*
doubting, doubtful, unconvinced,
unbelieving, disbelieving, questioning,
distrustful, mistrustful, hesitating,
dubious, suspicious, scoffing, cynical,
pessimistic.
☒ convinced, confident, trusting.

schedule *noun*
timetable, programme, agenda, diary,
calendar, itinerary, plan, scheme, list,
inventory, catalogue, table, form.
▸ *verb*
timetable, time, table, programme, plan,
organize, arrange, appoint,
assign, book, list.

scheme *noun*
1 draw up a traffic-calming scheme :
programme, schedule, plan, project,
idea, proposal, proposition,
suggestion, draft, outline, blueprint,
schema, diagram, chart, layout,
pattern, design, shape, configuration,
arrangement.
2 hatch a scheme for defrauding the
company : intrigue, plot, conspiracy,
device, stratagem, ruse, ploy, shift,
manoeuvre, tactic(s), strategy,
procedure, system, method.
▸ *verb*
plot, conspire, connive, collude,
intrigue, machinate, manoeuvre,
manipulate, pull strings, mastermind,
plan, project, contrive, devise, frame,
work out.

schism *noun*
division, split, rift, rupture, break,
breach, disunion, separation,
severance, estrangement, discord.

scholar *noun*
pupil, student, academic, intellectual,
egghead (*infml*), authority, expert.

scholarly *adjective*
learned, erudite, lettered, academic,

scholastic, school, intellectual, highbrow, bookish, studious, knowledgeable, well-read, analytical, scientific.

F3 uneducated, illiterate.

scholarship *noun*

1 his scholarship impressed us: erudition, learnedness, learning, knowledge, wisdom, education, schooling.

2 a scholarship to a public school: grant, award, bursary, endowment, fellowship, exhibition.

school *noun*

college, academy, institute, institution, seminary, faculty, department, discipline, class, group, pupils, students.

▶ *verb*

educate, teach, instruct, tutor, coach, train, discipline, drill, verse, prime, prepare, indoctrinate.

schooling *noun*

education, book-learning, teaching, instruction, tuition, coaching, training, drill, preparation, grounding, guidance, indoctrination.

science

Sciences include:

acoustics, aerodynamics, aeronautics, agricultural science, anatomy, anthropology, archaeology, astronomy, astrophysics, behavioural science, biochemistry, biology, biophysics, botany, chemistry, chemurgy, climatology, computer science, cybernetics, diagnostics, dietetics, domestic science, dynamics, earth science, ecology, economics, electrodynamics, electronics, engineering, entomology, environmental science, food science, genetics, geochemistry, geographical science, geology, geophysics, graphology, hydraulics, information technology, inorganic chemistry, life science, linguistics, macrobiotics, materials science, mathematics, mechanical engineering, mechanics, medical science, metallurgy,

meteorology, microbiology, mineralogy, morphology, natural science, nuclear physics, organic chemistry, ornithology, pathology, pharmacology, physics, physiology, political science, psychology, radiochemistry, robotics, sociology, space technology, telecommunications, thermodynamics, toxicology, ultrasonics, veterinary science, zoology.

scientific *adjective*

methodical, systematic, controlled, regulated, analytical, mathematical, exact, precise, accurate, scholarly, thorough.

scoff[1] *verb*

scoffed at their efforts: mock, ridicule, poke fun, taunt, tease, rib (*infml*), jeer, sneer, pooh-pooh, scorn, despise, revile, deride, belittle, disparage (*fml*), knock (*infml*).

F3 praise, compliment, flatter.

scoff[2] *verb* (*infml*)

scoffed all the chocolates: eat, consume, devour, put away (*infml*), gobble, guzzle, wolf (*infml*), bolt, gulp.

F3 fast, abstain.

scold *verb*

chide, tell off (*infml*), tick off (*infml*), reprimand, reprove, rebuke, take to task, admonish, upbraid (*fml*), reproach, blame, censure, lecture, nag.

F3 praise, commend.

scoop *verb*

gouge, scrape, hollow, empty, excavate, dig, shovel, ladle, spoon, dip, bail.

▶ *noun*

1 a large metal scoop: ladle, spoon, dipper, bailer, bucket, shovel.

2 (*infml*) get a scoop for his newspaper: exclusive, coup, inside story, revelation, exposé, sensation.

scope *noun*

1 the scope of the enquiry: range, compass, field, area, sphere, ambit, terms of reference, confines, reach, extent, span, breadth, coverage.

2 scope for improvement: room, space,

capacity, elbow-room, latitude, leeway,
freedom, liberty, opportunity.

scorch *verb*
burn, singe, char, blacken, scald, roast,
sear, parch, shrivel, wither.

scorching *adjective*
burning, boiling, baking, roasting,
sizzling, blistering, sweltering, torrid,
tropical, searing, red-hot.

score *noun*
1 *what's the latest score?*: result, total,
sum, tally, points, marks.
2 *making deep scores in the rock*:
scratch, line, groove, mark, nick, notch.
▶ *verb*
1 *score a goal/point*: record, register,
chalk up, notch up, count, total, make,
earn, gain, achieve, attain, win, have
the advantage, have the edge, be one up.
2 *blade scored the table top*: scratch,
scrape, graze, mark, groove, gouge, cut,
incise, engrave, indent, nick, slash.

scorn *noun*
contempt, scornfulness, disdain,
sneering, derision, mockery, ridicule,
sarcasm, disparagement (*fml*), disgust.
Ea admiration, respect. *verb*
mock, disdain, deride, laugh at, hold in
contempt, scoff at, slight, sneer at,
dismiss.
Ea admire, respect.

scornful *adjective*
contemptuous, disdainful,
supercilious, haughty, arrogant,
sneering, scoffing, derisive, mocking,
jeering, sarcastic, scathing,
disparaging, insulting, slighting,
dismissive.
Ea admiring, respectful.

scour[1] *verb*
scoured the pots and pans: scrape,
abrade, rub, polish, burnish, scrub,
clean, wash.

scour[2] *verb*
*scouring the countryside looking for
the missing boy*: search, hunt, comb,
drag, ransack, rummage, forage.

scourge *noun*
affliction, misfortune, torment, terror,
bane, evil, curse, plague, penalty,
punishment.
Ea blessing, godsend, boon.

scout *verb*
spy out, reconnoitre, explore,
investigate, check out, survey, case
(*slang*), spy, snoop, search, seek, hunt,
probe, look, watch, observe.

scowl *verb, noun*
frown, glower, glare, grimace, pout.
Ea smile, grin, beam.

scramble *verb*
1 *scrambling up the rocks*: climb, scale,
clamber, crawl, shuffle, scrabble,
grope.
2 *scrambling to get on the bus*: rush,
hurry, hasten, run, push, jostle,
struggle, strive, vie, contend.
▶ *noun*
rush, hurry, race, dash, hustle, bustle,
commotion, confusion, muddle,
struggle, free-for-all, mêlée.

scrap[1] *noun*
1 *scraps of paper/material/food*: bit,
piece, fragment, part, fraction, crumb,
morsel, bite, mouthful, sliver, shred,
snippet.
2 *not a single scrap remained*: atom,
iota, grain, particle, mite, trace,
vestige, remnant, morsel.
3 *a heap of scrap/sell the old car for
scrap*: waste, junk, rubbish, refuse.
▶ *verb*
discard, throw away, jettison, shed,
abandon, drop, dump, ditch (*infml*),
cancel, axe, demolish, break up, write
off.
Ea recover, restore.

scrap[2] *noun*
had a bit of a scrap in the playground:
fight, scuffle, brawl, dust-up (*infml*),
quarrel, row, argument, squabble,
wrangle, dispute, disagreement.
Ea peace, agreement.

scrape *verb*
grate, grind, rasp, file, abrade, scour,
rub, clean, remove, erase, scrabble,
claw, scratch, graze, skin, bark, scuff.

scrappy *adjective*
bitty, disjointed, piecemeal,
fragmentary, incomplete, sketchy,
superficial, slapdash, slipshod.
Ea complete, finished.

scratch *verb*
claw, gouge, score, mark, cut, incise,

etch, engrave, scrape, rub, scuff, graze, gash, lacerate.

▶ *noun*

mark, line, scrape, scuff, abrasion, graze, gash, laceration.

scream *verb, noun*
shriek, screech, cry, shout, yell, bawl, roar, howl, wail, squeal, yelp.

screen *verb*
1 screening a film: show, present, broadcast.
2 hedge screening the garden: shield, protect, safeguard, defend, guard, cover, mask, veil, cloak, shroud, hide, conceal, shelter, shade.
3 screen the candidates: vet, evaluate, sort, grade, sift, sieve, filter, process, gauge, examine, scan.
F∃ 2 uncover, expose.

▶ *noun*

partition, divider, shield, guard, cover, mask, veil, cloak, shroud, concealment, shelter, shade, awning, canopy, net, mesh.

screw *verb*
fasten, adjust, tighten, contract, compress, squeeze, extract, extort, force, constrain, pressurize, turn, wind, twist, wring, distort, wrinkle.

scribble *verb*
write, pen, jot, dash off, scrawl, doodle.

script *noun*
1 a film script: text, lines, words, dialogue, screenplay, libretto, book.
2 old-fashioned copperplate script: writing, handwriting, hand, longhand, calligraphy, letters, manuscript, copy.

scrub *verb*
1 scrub the floor: rub, brush, clean, wash, cleanse, scour.
2 (*infml*) scrub all the arrangements: abolish, cancel, delete, abandon, give up, drop, discontinue.

scruffy *adjective*
untidy, messy, unkempt, dishevelled, bedraggled, run-down, tattered, shabby, disreputable, worn-out, ragged, seedy, squalid, slovenly.
F∃ tidy, well-dressed.

scruples *noun*
standards, principles, morals, ethics.

scrupulous *adjective*
1 a scrupulous examination: painstaking, meticulous, conscientious, careful, rigorous, strict, exact, precise, minute, nice (*fml*).
2 he wasn't very scrupulous about his associates: principled, moral, ethical, honourable, upright.
F∃ 1 superficial, careless, reckless.
2 unscrupulous, unprincipled.

scrutinize *verb*
examine, inspect, study, scan, analyse, sift, investigate, probe, search, explore.

scuff *verb*
scrape, scratch, graze, abrade, rub, brush, drag.

scuffle *noun*
fight, scrap, tussle, brawl, fray, set-to, rumpus, commotion, disturbance, affray.

sculpt *verb*
sculpture, carve, chisel, hew, cut, model, mould, cast, form, shape, fashion.

scum *noun*
1 scum rising to the surface of the water: froth, foam, film, impurities.
2 he described them as the scum of the earth: dross, dregs, rubbish, trash.

scurrilous *adjective*
rude, vulgar, coarse, foul, obscene, indecent, salacious, offensive, abusive, insulting, disparaging, defamatory, slanderous, libellous, scandalous.
F∃ polite, courteous, complimentary.

scurry *verb*
dash, rush, hurry, hasten, bustle, scramble, scuttle, scamper, scoot, dart, run, sprint, trot, race, fly, skim, scud.

sea *noun*
1 go to sea/sail the seven seas: ocean, main, deep, briny (*infml*).
2 a sea of faces: multitude, abundance, profusion, mass.

▶ *adjective*

marine, maritime, ocean, oceanic, salt, saltwater, aquatic, seafaring.
F∃ land, air.

◆ **at sea** adrift, lost, confused, bewildered, baffled, puzzled, perplexed, mystified.

seal *verb*
1 seal a jar : close, shut, stop, plug, cork, stopper, waterproof, fasten, secure.
2 seal the bargain : settle, conclude, finalize, stamp.
F3 1 unseal.
▶ *noun*
stamp, signet, insignia, imprimatur, authentication, assurance, attestation, confirmation, ratification.
◆ **seal off** block up, close off, shut off, fence off, cut off, segregate, isolate, quarantine.
F3 open up.

seam *noun*
1 burst along the back seam : join, joint, weld, closure, line.
2 coal seam : layer, stratum, vein, lode.

sear *verb*
burn, scorch, brown, fry, sizzle, seal, cauterize, brand, parch, shrivel, wither.

search *verb*
seek, look, hunt, rummage, rifle, ransack, scour, comb, sift, probe, explore, frisk (*infml*), examine, scrutinize, inspect, check, investigate, inquire, pry.
▶ *noun*
hunt, quest, pursuit, rummage, probe, exploration, examination, scrutiny, inspection, investigation, inquiry, research, survey.

searching *adjective*
penetrating, piercing, keen, sharp, close, intent, probing, thorough, minute.
F3 vague, superficial.

season *noun*
period, spell, phase, term, time, span, interval.
▶ *verb*
1 season food : flavour, spice, salt.
2 seasoning the wood : age, mature, ripen, harden, toughen, train, prepare, condition, treat, temper.

seasoned *adjective*
mature, experienced, practised, well-versed, veteran, old, hardened, toughened, conditioned, acclimatized, weathered.
F3 inexperienced, novice.

seasoning *noun*
flavouring, spice, condiment, salt, pepper, relish, sauce, dressing.

seat *noun*
1 a garden seat : chair, bench, pew, stool, throne.
2 their country seat : residence, abode (*fml*), house, mansion.
3 the seat of government : place, site, situation, location, headquarters, centre, heart, hub, axis, source, cause, bottom, base, foundation, footing, ground.

seating *noun*
seats, chairs, places, room, accommodation.

secluded *adjective*
private, cloistered, sequestered, shut away, cut off, isolated, lonely, solitary, remote, out-of-the-way, sheltered, hidden, concealed.
F3 public, accessible.

second[1] *adjective*
1 a second helping/a second chance : duplicate, twin, double, repeated, additional, further, extra, supplementary, alternative, other, alternate, next, following, subsequent, succeeding.
2 the first and second places : secondary, subordinate, lower, inferior, lesser, supporting.
▶ *noun*
helper, assistant, backer, supporter.
▶ *verb*
approve, agree with, endorse, back, support, help, assist, aid, further, advance, forward, promote, encourage.

second[2] *noun*
will only take a second : moment, minute, tick (*infml*), instant, flash, jiffy (*infml*).

secondary *adjective*
subsidiary, subordinate, lower, inferior, lesser, minor, unimportant, ancillary, auxiliary, supporting, relief, back-up, reserve, spare, extra, second, alternative, indirect, derived, resulting.
F3 primary, main, major.

second-rate *adjective*
inferior, substandard, second-class, second-best, poor, low-grade, shoddy,

cheap, tawdry, mediocre,
undistinguished, uninspired,
uninspiring.
F∃ first-rate.

secret *adjective*
1 kept it secret/secret activities:
private, discreet, covert, hidden,
concealed, unseen, shrouded, covered,
disguised, camouflaged, undercover,
furtive, surreptitious, stealthy, sly,
underhand, under-the-counter, hole-
and-corner, cloak-and-dagger,
clandestine, underground.
2 a secret mission/file marked 'secret':
classified, restricted, confidential,
hush-hush (*infml*), unpublished,
undisclosed, unrevealed, unknown.
3 secret code: cryptic, mysterious,
occult, arcane, recondite (*fml*), deep.
4 a secret place in his heart: secretive,
close, retired, secluded, out-of-the-
way.
F∃ 1 public, open. 2 well-known.
▶ *noun*
confidence, mystery, enigma, code,
key, formula, recipe.

secretary *noun*
personal assistant, PA, typist,
stenographer, clerk.

secrete[1] *verb*
secreting a sticky substance: exude,
discharge, release, give off, emit,
emanate, produce.

secrete[2] (*fml*) *verb*
secreted the letters in a hidden
drawer: hide, conceal, stash away
(*infml*), bury, cover, screen, shroud,
veil, disguise, take, appropriate.
F∃ uncover, reveal, disclose.

secretive *adjective*
tight-lipped, close, cagey (*infml*),
uncommunicative, unforthcoming,
reticent, reserved, withdrawn, quiet,
deep, cryptic, enigmatic.
F∃ open, communicative, forthcoming.

sectarian *adjective*
factional, partisan, cliquish, exclusive,
narrow, limited, parochial, insular,
narrow-minded, bigoted, fanatical,
doctrinaire, dogmatic, rigid.
F∃ non-sectarian, cosmopolitan,
broad-minded.

section *noun*
division, subdivision, chapter,
paragraph, passage, instalment, part,
component, fraction, fragment, bit,
piece, slice, portion, segment, sector,
zone, district, area, region,
department, branch, wing.
F∃ whole.

sector *noun*
zone, district, quarter, area, region,
section, division, subdivision, part.
F∃ whole.

secular *adjective*
lay, temporal, worldly, earthly, civil,
state, non-religious, profane.
F∃ religious.

secure *adjective*
1 keep valuables in a secure place: safe,
protected, sheltered, shielded,
immune, impregnable, fortified, fast,
tight, fastened, locked, fixed,
immovable.
2 secure foundations/a secure income:
stable, steady, solid, firm, well-
founded, reliable, dependable,
steadfast.
3 secure in the knowledge: certain,
sure, confident, assured, reassured.
F∃ 1 insecure, vulnerable. 2 unstable,
unreliable. 3 uneasy, ill at ease.
▶ *verb*
1 secure their agreement: obtain,
acquire, gain, get.
2 secure the lid/rope/gates: fasten,
attach, fix, make fast, tie, moor, lash,
chain, lock (up), padlock, bolt, batten
down, nail, rivet.
F∃ 1 lose. 2 unfasten.

sedate *adjective*
staid, dignified, solemn, grave, serious,
sober, decorous, proper, seemly,
demure, composed, unruffled, serene,
tranquil, calm, quiet, cool, collected,
imperturbable, unflappable (*infml*),
deliberate, slow-moving.
F∃ undignified, lively, agitated.

sedentary *adjective*
sitting, seated, desk-bound, inactive,
still, stationary, immobile, unmoving.
F∃ active.

sediment *noun*
deposit, residue, grounds, lees, dregs.

see *verb*
1 see it in the distance: perceive, glimpse, discern, spot, make out, distinguish, identify, sight, notice, observe, watch, view, look at, mark, note.
2 could see it in her mind's eye/could see it coming: imagine, picture, visualize, envisage, foresee, anticipate.
3 I see your point: understand, comprehend, grasp, fathom, follow, realize, recognize, appreciate, regard, consider, deem.
4 just couldn't see the answer: discover, find out, learn, ascertain, determine, decide.
5 see them into the study: lead, usher, accompany, escort.
6 seeing another woman: court, go out with, date.
7 going to see his family: visit, meet, spend time with.
8 see her about it: interview, consult.
◆ **see to** attend to, deal with, take care of, look after, arrange, organize, manage, do, fix, repair, sort out.

seed *noun*
pip, stone, kernel, nucleus, grain, germ, sperm, ovum, egg, ovule, spawn, embryo, source, start, beginning.

seedy *adjective*
1 a seedy little café: shabby, scruffy, tatty, mangy, sleazy, squalid, grotty (*infml*), crummy (*infml*), run-down, dilapidated, decaying.
2 feel extremely seedy: unwell, ill, sick, poorly, ailing, off-colour.
F3 **2** well.

seek *verb*
look for, search for, hunt, pursue, follow, inquire, ask, invite, request, solicit, petition, entreat, want, desire, aim, aspire, try, attempt, endeavour, strive.

seem *verb*
appear, look, feel, sound, pretend to be.

seeming *adjective*
apparent, ostensible, outward, superficial, surface, quasi-, pseudo, specious.
F3 real.

seep *verb*
ooze, leak, exude, well, trickle, dribble, percolate, permeate, soak.

seethe *verb*
1 ocean seething beneath the tiny yacht/street seething with people: boil, simmer, bubble, effervesce, fizz, foam, froth, ferment, rise, swell, surge, teem, swarm.
2 mind seething with powerful emotions: rage, fume, smoulder, storm.

segment *noun*
section, division, compartment, part, bit, piece, slice, portion, wedge.
F3 whole.

segregate *verb*
separate, keep apart, cut off, isolate, quarantine, set apart, exclude.
F3 unite, join.

seize *verb*
grab, snatch, grasp, clutch, grip, hold, take, confiscate, impound, appropriate, commandeer, hijack, annex, abduct, catch, capture, arrest, apprehend, nab (*infml*), collar (*infml*).
F3 let go, release, hand back.

seizure *noun*
fit, attack, convulsion, paroxysm, spasm.

seldom *adverb*
rarely, infrequently, occasionally, hardly ever.
F3 often, usually.

select *verb*
choose, pick, single out, decide on, appoint, elect, prefer, opt for.
▶ *adjective*
selected, choice, top, prime, first-class, first-rate, hand-picked, élite, exclusive, limited, privileged, special, excellent, superior, posh (*infml*).
F3 second-rate, ordinary, general.

selective *adjective*
particular, choosy (*infml*), careful, discerning, discriminating.
F3 indiscriminate.

self *noun*
ego, personality, identity, person.

self-conscious *adjective*
uncomfortable, ill at ease, awkward, embarrassed, shamefaced, sheepish,

shy, bashful, coy, retiring, shrinking, self-effacing, nervous, insecure.
F3 natural, unaffected, confident.

self-control noun
calmness, composure, cool (infml), patience, self-restraint, restraint, self-denial, temperance, self-discipline, self-mastery, will-power.

self-indulgent adjective
hedonistic, dissolute, dissipated, profligate, extravagant, intemperate, immoderate.
F3 abstemious.

selfish adjective
self-interested, self-seeking, self-serving, mean, miserly, mercenary, greedy, covetous, self-centred, egocentric, egotistic(al).
F3 unselfish, selfless, generous, considerate.

selfless adjective
unselfish, altruistic, self-denying, self-sacrificing, generous, philanthropic.
F3 selfish, self-centred.

self-respect noun
pride, dignity, self-esteem, self-assurance, self-confidence.

sell verb
barter, exchange, trade, auction, vend, retail, stock, handle, deal in, trade in, traffic in, merchandise, hawk, peddle, push, advertise, promote, market.
F3 buy.

seller noun
vendor, merchant, trader, dealer, supplier, stockist, retailer, shopkeeper, salesman, saleswoman, agent, representative, rep (infml), traveller.
F3 buyer, purchaser.

send verb
1 send a letter/payment : post, mail, dispatch, consign, remit, forward, convey, deliver.
2 message was sent out by radio : transmit, broadcast, communicate.
3 sending them flying/sending out smoke and flames : propel, drive, move, throw, fling, hurl, launch, fire, shoot, discharge, emit, direct.
◆ **send for** summon, call for, request, order, command.
F3 dismiss.

◆ **send up** satirize, mock, ridicule, parody, take off, mimic, imitate.

senile adjective
old, aged, doddering, decrepit, failing, confused.

senior adjective
older, elder, higher, superior, high-ranking, major, chief.
F3 junior.

seniority noun
priority, precedence, rank, standing, status, age, superiority, importance.

sensation noun
1 a sensation of falling/no sensation in his limbs : feeling, sense, impression, perception, awareness, consciousness.
2 the report caused a sensation : commotion, stir, agitation, excitement, thrill, furore, outrage, scandal.

sensational adjective
1 a sensational success : exciting, thrilling, electrifying, breathtaking, startling, amazing, astounding, staggering, dramatic, spectacular, impressive, exceptional, excellent, wonderful, marvellous, smashing (infml).
2 sensational headlines : scandalous, shocking, horrifying, revealing, melodramatic, lurid.
F3 1 ordinary, run-of-the-mill.

sense noun
1 the five senses/a sense of longing : feeling, sensation, impression, perception, awareness, consciousness, appreciation, faculty.
2 had the sense to realize what was happening : reason, logic, mind, brain(s), wit(s), wisdom, intelligence, cleverness, understanding, discernment, judgement, intuition.
3 get the sense of what he was saying/in another sense : meaning, significance, definition, interpretation, implication, point, purpose, substance.
F3 2 foolishness.
▶ verb
feel, suspect, intuit, perceive, detect, notice, observe, realize, appreciate, understand, comprehend, grasp.

senseless adjective
1 a senseless thing to do : foolish,

stupid, unwise, silly, idiotic, mad, crazy, daft (*infml*), ridiculous, ludicrous, absurd, meaningless, nonsensical, fatuous, irrational, illogical, unreasonable, pointless, purposeless, futile.
2 knocked senseless: unconscious, out, stunned, anaesthetized, deadened, numb, unfeeling.
F3 1 sensible, meaningful. 2 conscious.

sensible *adjective*
wise, prudent, judicious (*fml*), well-advised, shrewd, far-sighted, intelligent, level-headed, down-to-earth, commonsense, sober, sane, rational, logical, reasonable, realistic, practical, functional, sound.
F3 senseless, foolish, unwise.

sensitive *adjective*
1 sensitive to heat/sensitive about one's appearance: susceptible, vulnerable, impressionable, tender, emotional, thin-skinned, temperamental, touchy, irritable, sensitized, responsive, aware, perceptive, discerning, appreciative.
2 sensitive instruments: delicate, fine, exact, precise.
F3 1 insensitive, thick-skinned. 2 imprecise, approximate.

sensual *adjective*
self-indulgent, voluptuous, worldly, physical, animal, carnal, fleshly, bodily, sexual, erotic.
F3 ascetic.

sensuous *adjective*
pleasurable, gratifying, voluptuous, rich, lush, luxurious, sumptuous.
F3 ascetic, plain, simple.

sentence *noun*
judgement, decision, verdict, condemnation, pronouncement, ruling, decree, order.
▶ *verb*
judge, pass judgement on, condemn, doom, punish, penalize.

sentiment *noun*
1 I agree with that sentiment: thought, idea, feeling, opinion, view, judgement, belief, persuasion, attitude.
2 full of flowery sentiment: emotion, sensibility, tenderness, soft-heartedness, romanticism, sentimentality, mawkishness.

sentimental *adjective*
tender, soft-hearted, emotional, gushing, touching, pathetic, tear-jerking, weepy (*infml*), maudlin, mawkish, nostalgic, romantic, lovey-dovey (*infml*), slushy, mushy, sloppy, schmaltzy, soppy, corny (*infml*).
F3 unsentimental, realistic, cynical.

separate *verb*
divide, sever, part, split (up), divorce, part company, diverge, disconnect, uncouple, disunite, disaffiliate, disentangle, segregate, isolate, cut off, abstract, remove, detach, withdraw, secede.
F3 join, unite, combine.
▶ *adjective*
single, individual, particular, independent, alone, solitary, segregated, isolated, apart, divorced, divided, disunited, disconnected, disjointed, detached, unattached, unconnected, unrelated, different, disparate, distinct, discrete, several, sundry.
F3 together, attached.

septic *adjective*
infected, poisoned, festering, putrefying, putrid.

sequel *noun*
follow-up, continuation, development, result, consequence, outcome, issue, upshot, pay-off, end, conclusion.

sequence *noun*
succession, series, run, progression, chain, string, train, line, procession, order, arrangement, course, track, cycle, set.

serene *adjective*
calm, tranquil, cool, composed, placid, untroubled, undisturbed, still, quiet, peaceful.
F3 troubled, disturbed.

series *noun*
set, cycle, succession, sequence, run, progression, chain, string, line, train, order, arrangement, course.

serious *adjective*
1 a serious error: important, significant, weighty, momentous, crucial.

2 a serious accident/illness: grave, severe, dangerous, acute.
3 had a serious effect: severe, critical, deep, far-reaching.
4 she wore a serious expression/was not a serious attempt: unsmiling, long-faced, humourless, grim, solemn, sober, stern, thoughtful, pensive, earnest, sincere.
1 trivial, slight. **2** minor, slight, trivial. **3** minor, marginal. **4** smiling, facetious, frivolous.

servant *noun*
domestic, maid, valet, steward, attendant, retainer, hireling, lackey, menial, skivvy (*infml*), slave, help, helper, assistant, ancillary.
master, mistress.

serve *verb*
1 serve two masters/serving their own ends: wait on, attend, minister to, work for, help, aid, assist, benefit, further.
2 serve a purpose: fulfil, complete, answer, satisfy, discharge, perform, act, function.
3 serve the lunch: distribute, dole out, present, deliver, provide, supply.

service *noun*
1 in the service of the king/do a service for someone: employment, work, labour, business, duty, function.
2 be of service to them: use, usefulness, utility, advantage, benefit, help, assistance.
3 car needs a service: servicing, maintenance, overhaul, check.
4 church service: worship, observance, ceremony, rite.
▶ *verb*
maintain, overhaul, check, repair, recondition, tune.

serviceable *adjective*
usable, useful, helpful, profitable, advantageous, beneficial, utilitarian, simple, plain, unadorned, strong, tough, durable, hard-wearing, dependable, efficient, functional, practical, convenient.
unserviceable, unusable.

servile *adjective*
obsequious, sycophantic, toadying, cringing, fawning, grovelling,

bootlicking, slavish, subservient, subject, submissive, humble, abject, low, mean, base, menial.
assertive, aggressive.

session *noun*
sitting, hearing, meeting, assembly, conference, discussion, period, time, term, semester, year.

set *verb*
1 set it down on the floor: put, place, locate, situate, position, arrange, prepare, lodge, fix, stick, park, deposit.
2 set a time/limit: schedule, appoint, designate, specify, name, prescribe, ordain, assign, allocate, impose, fix, establish, determine, decide, conclude, settle, resolve.
3 set the clocks: adjust, regulate, synchronize, co-ordinate.
4 the sun sets: go down, sink, dip, subside, disappear, vanish.
5 when the jam has set: congeal, thicken, gel, stiffen, solidify, harden, crystallize.
4 rise.
▶ *noun*
batch, series, sequence, kit, outfit, compendium, assortment, collection, class, category, group, band, gang, crowd, circle, clique, faction.
▶ *adjective*
scheduled, appointed, arranged, prepared, prearranged, fixed, established, definite, decided, agreed, settled, firm, strict, rigid, inflexible, prescribed, formal, conventional, traditional, customary, usual, routine, regular, standard, stock, stereotyped, hackneyed.
movable, free, spontaneous, undecided.
◆ **set about** begin, start, embark on, undertake, tackle, attack.
◆ **set back** delay, hold up, slow, retard, hinder, impede.
◆ **set off 1** set off down the street: leave, depart, set out, start (out), begin. **2** set off a firework: detonate, light, ignite, touch off, trigger off, explode. **3** hat sets off the outfit perfectly: display, show off, enhance, contrast.
◆ **set out 1** set out on their journey: leave, depart, set off, start (out), begin.

2 set out the rules: lay out, arrange, display, exhibit, present, describe, explain.

◆ **set up**
raise, elevate, erect, build, construct, assemble, compose, form, create, establish, institute, found, inaugurate, initiate, begin, start, introduce, organize, arrange, prepare.

setback *noun*
delay, hold-up, problem, snag, hitch, hiccup, reverse, misfortune, upset, disappointment, defeat.
Ⅎ boost, advance, help, advantage.

setting *noun*
mounting, frame, surroundings, milieu, environment, background, context, perspective, period, position, location, locale, site, scene, scenery.

settle *verb*
1 settled the dispute: arrange, order, adjust, reconcile, resolve, complete, conclude.
2 settled on a branch/the bottom of the tank: sink, subside, drop, fall, descend, land, alight.
3 I settled for the blue one: choose, appoint, fix, establish, determine, decide, agree, confirm.
4 settled in the States: colonize, occupy, populate, people, inhabit, live, reside.
5 settle a bill: pay, clear, discharge.

set-up *noun*
system, structure, organization, arrangement, business, conditions, circumstances.

sever *verb*
cut, cleave, split, rend, part, separate, divide, cut off, amputate, detach, disconnect, disjoin, disunite, dissociate, estrange, alienate, break off, dissolve, end, terminate.
Ⅎ join, unite, combine, attach.

several *adjective*
some, many, various, assorted, sundry, diverse, different, distinct, separate, particular, individual.

severe *adjective*
1 severe discipline/a severe expression: stern, disapproving, sober, strait-laced, strict, rigid, unbending, harsh, tough, hard, difficult, demanding, arduous, punishing, rigorous, grim, forbidding, cruel, biting, cutting, scathing, pitiless, merciless, oppressive, relentless, inexorable, acute, bitter, intense, extreme, fierce, violent, distressing, serious, grave, critical, dangerous.
2 a severe black dress: plain, simple, unadorned, unembellished, functional, restrained, austere, ascetic.
Ⅎ 1 kind, compassionate, sympathetic, lenient, mild. **2** decorated, ornate.

sew *verb*
stitch, tack, baste, hem, darn, embroider.

shabby *adjective*
1 shabby clothes: ragged, tattered, frayed, worn, worn-out, mangy, moth-eaten, scruffy, tatty, disreputable, dilapidated, run-down, seedy, dirty, dingy, poky.
2 a shabby trick: contemptible, despicable, rotten, mean, low, cheap, shoddy, shameful, dishonourable.
Ⅎ 1 smart. **2** honourable, fair.

shade *noun*
1 sit in the shade: shadiness, shadow, darkness, obscurity, semi-darkness, dimness, gloom, gloominess, twilight, dusk, gloaming.
2 a shade for his eyes: awning, canopy, cover, shelter, screen, blind, curtain, shield, visor, umbrella, parasol.
3 a bright shade of pink: colour, hue, tint, tone, tinge.
4 had a shade of jealousy in her voice: trace, dash, hint, suggestion, suspicion, nuance, gradation, degree, amount, variety.
5 the shades of the dead: ghost, spectre, phantom, spirit, apparition, semblance.
▶ *verb*
shield, screen, protect, cover, shroud, veil, hide, conceal, obscure, cloud, dim, darken, shadow, overshadow.

shadow *noun*
1 room was in shadow: shade, darkness, obscurity, semi-darkness, dimness, gloom, twilight, dusk, gloaming, cloud, cover, protection.

2 see his shadow through the mist: silhouette, shape, image, representation.

3 not a shadow of doubt: trace, hint, suggestion, suspicion, vestige, remnant.

▸ *verb*

1 shadowing the garden: overshadow, overhang, shade, shield, screen, obscure, darken.

2 shadowing the man through the town: follow, tail, dog, stalk, trail, watch.

shady *adjective*

1 a shady nook: shaded, shadowy, dim, dark, cool, leafy.

2 (*infml*) a shady character: dubious, questionable, suspect, suspicious, fishy (*infml*), dishonest, crooked, unreliable, untrustworthy, disreputable, unscrupulous, unethical, underhand.

⊟ 1 sunny, sunlit, bright. **2** honest, trustworthy, honourable.

shaft *noun*

handle, shank, stem, upright, pillar, pole, rod, bar, stick, arrow, dart, beam, ray, duct, passage.

shake *verb*

1 shaking his fist/wind shaking the branches/the earth shook under them: wave, flourish, brandish, wag, waggle, agitate, rattle, joggle, jolt, jerk, twitch, convulse, heave, throb, vibrate, oscillate, fluctuate, waver, wobble, totter, sway, rock, tremble, quiver, quake, shiver, shudder.

2 the news shook her: upset, distress, shock, frighten, unnerve, intimidate, disturb, discompose, unsettle, agitate, stir, rouse.

◆ shake off get rid of, dislodge, lose, elude, give the slip, leave behind, outdistance, outstrip.

shaky *adjective*

1 a shaky hand/start: trembling, quivering, faltering, tentative, uncertain.

2 a shaky bridge: unstable, unsteady, insecure, precarious, wobbly, rocky, tottery, rickety, weak.

3 company looks rather shaky: dubious, questionable, suspect,

unreliable, unsound, unsupported.

⊟ 1 steady. **2** firm, strong. **3** sound.

shallow *adjective*

superficial, surface, skin-deep, one-dimensional, slight, flimsy, trivial, frivolous, foolish, idle, empty, meaningless, unscholarly, ignorant, simple.

⊟ deep, profound.

sham *noun*

pretence, fraud, counterfeit, forgery, fake, imitation, simulation, hoax, humbug.

shame *noun*

disgrace, dishonour, discredit, stain, stigma, disrepute, infamy, scandal, ignominy, humiliation, degradation, shamefacedness, remorse, guilt, embarrassment, mortification.

⊟ honour, credit, distinction, pride.

▸ *verb*

embarrass, mortify, abash, confound, humiliate, ridicule, humble, put to shame, show up, disgrace, dishonour, discredit, debase, degrade, sully (*fml*), taint, stain.

shameful *adjective*

1 a shameful waste of money: disgraceful, outrageous, scandalous, indecent, abominable, atrocious, wicked, mean, low, vile, reprehensible, contemptible, unworthy, ignoble.

2 was shameful for the whole family: embarrassing, mortifying, humiliating, ignominious.

⊟ 1 honourable, creditable, worthy.

shameless *adjective*

unashamed, unabashed, unrepentant, impenitent, barefaced, flagrant, blatant, brazen, brash, audacious, insolent, defiant, hardened, incorrigible.

⊟ ashamed, shamefaced, contrite.

shape *noun*

1 a square shape/could see the shape of a ship through the fog: form, outline, silhouette, profile, model, mould, pattern, cut, lines, contours, figure, physique, build, frame, format, configuration.

Geometrical shapes include:

circle, crescent, ellipse, oval, quadrant, semicircle; triangle, equilateral triangle, isosceles triangle, scalene triangle; oblong, quadrilateral, rectangle, square; decagon, diamond, hexagon, heptagon, kite, nonagon, octagon, parallelogram, pentagon, polygon, rhombus, trapezium; cone, cube, cuboid, cylinder, hemisphere, octahedron, pentahedron, polyhedron, prism, pyramid, sphere, tetrahedron.

2 adopted the shape of a swan: appearance, guise, likeness, semblance. **3** in good shape: condition, state, form, health, trim, fettle.

verb
form, fashion, model, mould, cast, forge, sculpt, carve, whittle, make, produce, construct, create, devise, frame, plan, prepare, adapt, adjust, regulate, accommodate, modify, remodel.

shapeless *adjective*
formless, amorphous, unformed, nebulous, unstructured, irregular, misshapen, deformed, dumpy.

share *verb*
divide, split, go halves, partake, participate, share out, distribute, dole out, give out, deal out, apportion, allot, allocate, assign.
▶ *noun*
portion, ration, quota, allowance, allocation, allotment, lot, part, division, proportion, percentage, cut (*infml*), dividend, due, contribution, whack (*infml*).

sharp *adjective*
1 a sharp needle: pointed, keen, edged, knife-edged, razor-sharp, cutting, serrated, jagged, barbed, spiky. **2** a sharp outline: clear, clear-cut, well-defined, distinct, marked, crisp. **3** a sharp operator: quick-witted, alert, shrewd, astute, perceptive, observant, discerning, penetrating, clever, crafty, cunning, artful, sly.

4 sharp pain: sudden, abrupt, violent, fierce, intense, extreme, severe, acute, piercing, stabbing. **5** sharp-tasting: pungent, piquant, sour, tart, vinegary, bitter, acerbic, acid. **6** sharp wit: trenchant (*fml*), incisive, cutting, biting, caustic, sarcastic, sardonic, scathing, vitriolic, acrimonious.
E3 1 blunt. **2** blurred. **3** slow, stupid. **4** gentle. **5** bland. **6** mild.
▶ *adverb*
punctually, promptly, on the dot, exactly, precisely, abruptly, suddenly, unexpectedly.
E3 approximately, roughly.

sharpen *verb*
edge, whet, hone, grind, file.
E3 blunt.

shatter *verb*
break, smash, splinter, shiver, crack, split, burst, explode, blast, crush, demolish, destroy, devastate, wreck, ruin, overturn, upset.

shed¹ *verb*
1 snake shed its skin: cast (off), moult, slough, discard. **2** lorry shed its load: drop, spill, pour, shower, scatter. **3** shedding a pale light: diffuse, emit, radiate, shine, throw.

shed² *noun*
a garden shed: outhouse, lean-to, hut, shack.

sheen *noun*
lustre, gloss, shine, shimmer, brightness, brilliance, shininess, polish, burnish.
E3 dullness, tarnish.

sheer *adjective*
1 sheer nonsense: utter, complete, total, absolute, thorough, mere, pure, unadulterated, downright, out-and-out, rank, thoroughgoing, unqualified, unmitigated. **2** a sheer drop: vertical, perpendicular, precipitous, abrupt, steep. **3** sheer fabric: thin, fine, flimsy, gauzy, gossamer, translucent, transparent, see-through.
E3 2 gentle, gradual. **3** thick, heavy.

sheet *noun*
cover, blanket, covering, coating, coat, film, layer, stratum, skin, membrane, lamina, veneer, overlay, plate, leaf, page, folio, piece, panel, slab, pane, expanse, surface.

shelf *noun*
ledge, mantelpiece, sill, step, bench, counter, bar, bank, sandbank, reef, terrace.

shell *noun*
covering, hull, husk, pod, rind, crust, case, casing, body, chassis, frame, framework, structure, skeleton.
▶ *verb*
1 shell nuts: hull, husk, pod.
2 shelling the city: bomb, bombard, barrage, blitz, attack.

shelter *verb*
cover, shroud, screen, shade, shadow, protect, safeguard, defend, guard, shield, harbour, hide, accommodate, put up.
E∃ expose.
▶ *noun*
cover, roof, shade, shadow, protection, defence, guard, security, safety, sanctuary, asylum, haven, refuge, retreat, accommodation, lodging.
E∃ exposure.

sheltered *adjective*
covered, shaded, shielded, protected, cosy, snug, warm, quiet, secluded, isolated, retired, withdrawn, reclusive, cloistered, unworldly.
E∃ exposed.

shield *verb*
defend, guard, protect, safeguard, screen, shade, shadow, cover, shelter.
E∃ expose.

shift *verb*
change, vary, fluctuate, alter, adjust, move, budge, remove, dislodge, displace, relocate, reposition, rearrange, transpose, transfer, switch, swerve, veer.

shifty *adjective*
untrustworthy, dishonest, deceitful, scheming, contriving, tricky, wily, crafty, cunning, devious, evasive, slippery, furtive, underhand, dubious, shady (*infml*).
E∃ dependable, honest, open.

shimmer *verb*
glisten, gleam, glimmer, glitter, scintillate, twinkle.

shine *verb*
1 sun shining on the sea: beam, radiate, glow, flash, glare, gleam, glint, glitter, sparkle, twinkle, shimmer, glisten, glimmer.
2 shining their shoes: polish, burnish, buff, brush, rub.
3 shine at athletics: excel, stand out.

shining *adjective*
1 shining armour: bright, radiant, glowing, beaming, flashing, gleaming, glittering, glistening, shimmering, twinkling, sparkling, brilliant, resplendent, splendid, glorious.
2 a shining example: conspicuous, outstanding, leading, eminent, celebrated, distinguished, illustrious.
E∃ 1 dark.

shiny *adjective*
polished, burnished, sheeny, lustrous, glossy, sleek, bright, gleaming, glistening.
E∃ dull, matt.

ship *noun*
vessel, craft, liner, steamer, tanker, ferry.

shirk *verb*
dodge, evade, avoid, duck (*infml*), shun, slack, skive (*infml*).

shiver *verb*
shudder, tremble, quiver, quake, shake, vibrate, palpitate, flutter.
▶ *noun*
shudder, quiver, shake, tremor, twitch, start, vibration, flutter.

shock *verb*
disgust, revolt, sicken, offend, appal, outrage, scandalize, horrify, astound, stagger, stun, stupefy, numb, paralyse, traumatize, jolt, jar, shake, agitate, unsettle, disquiet, unnerve, confound, dismay.
E∃ delight, please, gratify, reassure.
▶ *noun*
fright, start, jolt, impact, collision, surprise, bombshell, thunderbolt, blow, trauma, upset, distress, dismay, consternation, disgust, outrage.
E∃ delight, pleasure, reassurance.

shocking *adjective*
appalling, outrageous, scandalous, horrifying, disgraceful, deplorable, intolerable, unbearable, atrocious, abominable, monstrous, unspeakable, detestable, abhorrent (*fml*), dreadful, awful, terrible, frightful, ghastly, hideous, horrible, disgusting, revolting, repulsive, sickening, nauseating, offensive, distressing.
F϶ acceptable, satisfactory, pleasant, delightful.

shoddy *adjective*
inferior, second-rate, cheap, tawdry, tatty, trashy, rubbishy, poor, careless, slipshod, slapdash.
F϶ superior, well-made.

shoot *verb*
1 shooting arrows/a gun: fire, discharge, launch, propel, hurl, fling, project.
2 shoot forwards: dart, bolt, dash, tear, rush, race, sprint, speed, charge, hurtle.
3 shoot rabbits/shot him in the back: hit, kill, blast, bombard, gun down, snipe at, pick off.
▶ *noun*
sprout, bud, offshoot, branch, twig, sprig, slip, scion.

shop

Types of shop include:
bazaar, cash-and-carry, corner shop, department store, e-shop, hypermarket, indoor market, market, mini-market, shopping mall, supermarket, superstore; baker, butcher, candy store (*US*), confectioner, dairy, delicatessen, farm shop, fish and chip shop, fishmonger, greengrocer, grocer, health-food shop, off-licence, sweet shop, take-away, tobacconist, tuck shop; bookshop, boutique, charity shop, chemist, draper, dress shop, drugstore (*US*), florist, haberdasher, hardware shop, ironmonger, jeweller, milliner, newsagent, outfitter, pharmacy, radio and TV shop, saddler, shoe shop, stationer, tailor, toy shop, video shop; barber, betting shop, bookmaker, bookie (*infml*), hairdresser, launderette, pawnbroker, post office.

shore¹ *noun*
a sandy shore/on the shores of the lake: seashore, beach, sand(s), shingle, strand, waterfront, front, promenade, coast, seaboard, lakeside, bank.

shore² *verb*
shore (up) crumbling walls/a failing business: support, hold, prop, stay, underpin, buttress, brace, strengthen, reinforce.

short *adjective*
1 a short stay/story: brief, cursory, fleeting, momentary, transitory, ephemeral, concise, succinct, terse, pithy, compact, compressed, shortened, curtailed, abbreviated, abridged, summarized.
2 was rather short with me: brusque, curt, gruff, snappy, sharp, abrupt, blunt, direct, rude, impolite, discourteous, uncivil.
3 a short person: small, little, low, petite, diminutive, squat, dumpy.
4 short supply/rations: inadequate, insufficient, deficient, lacking, wanting, low, poor, meagre, scant, sparse.
F϶ 1 long, lasting. 2 polite. 3 tall. 4 adequate, ample.

shortage *noun*
inadequacy, insufficiency, deficiency, shortfall, deficit, lack, want, need, scarcity, paucity (*fml*), poverty, dearth, absence.
F϶ sufficiency, abundance, surplus.

shortcoming *noun*
defect, imperfection, fault, flaw, drawback, failing, weakness, foible.

shorten *verb*
cut, trim, prune, crop, dock, curtail, truncate, abbreviate, abridge, reduce, lessen, decrease, diminish, take up.
F϶ lengthen, enlarge, amplify.

shortly *adverb*
soon, before long, presently, by and by.

short-sighted *adjective*
1 becoming more short-sighted as she gets older: myopic, near-sighted.
2 a short-sighted view/attitude: improvident (*fml*), imprudent, injudicious, unwise, impolitic, ill-

advised, careless, hasty, ill-considered.
E₃ 1 long-sighted, far-sighted.

shot *noun*
1 a shot from a gun : bullet, missile,
projectile, ball, pellet, slug (*infml*),
discharge, blast.
2 (*infml*) have a shot on his bike/at the
answer : attempt, try, effort, endeavour,
go (*infml*), bash (*infml*), crack (*infml*),
stab (*infml*), guess, turn.

shoulder *verb*
1 shouldered his way through the
crowd : push, shove, jostle, thrust,
press.
2 shouldered the responsibility :
accept, assume, take on, bear, carry,
sustain.

shout *noun, verb*
call, cry, scream, shriek, yell, roar,
bellow, bawl, howl, bay, cheer.

shove *verb*
push, thrust, drive, propel, force, barge,
jostle, elbow, shoulder, press, crowd.

show *noun*
1 all show/did it for show : ostentation,
parade, display, flamboyance, panache,
pizzazz (*infml*), showiness,
exhibitionism, affectation, pose,
pretence, illusion, semblance, façade,
impression, appearance, air.
2 a show of strength/a West End
show : demonstration, presentation,
exhibition, exposition, fair, display,
parade, pageant, extravaganza,
spectacle, entertainment,
performance, production, staging,
showing, representation.
▶ *verb*
1 show how it is done/show good
judgement : reveal, expose, uncover,
disclose, divulge, present, offer,
exhibit, manifest, display, indicate,
register, demonstrate, prove, illustrate,
exemplify, explain, instruct, teach,
clarify, elucidate.
2 show him out : lead, guide, conduct,
usher, escort, accompany, attend.
E₃ 1 hide, cover.
◆ **show off** parade, strut, swagger,
brag, boast, swank (*infml*), flaunt,
brandish, display, exhibit, demonstrate,
advertise, set off, enhance.

◆ **show up 1** (*infml*) band didn't show
up : arrive, come, turn up, appear,
materialize (*infml*).
2 don't show me up in front of the
others! : humiliate, embarrass, mortify,
shame, disgrace, let down.
3 show up its faults : reveal, show,
expose, unmask, lay bare, highlight,
pinpoint.

shower *noun*
rain, stream, torrent, deluge, hail,
volley, barrage.
▶ *verb*
spray, sprinkle, rain, pour, deluge,
inundate, overwhelm, load, heap,
lavish.

showy *adjective*
flashy, flamboyant, ostentatious, gaudy,
garish, loud, tawdry, fancy, ornate,
pretentious, pompous, swanky (*infml*),
flash (*infml*).
E₃ quiet, restrained.

shred *noun*
ribbon, tatter, rag, scrap, snippet,
sliver, bit, piece, fragment, jot, iota,
atom, grain, mite, whit, trace.

shrewd *adjective*
astute, judicious (*fml*), well-advised,
calculated, far-sighted, smart, clever,
intelligent, sharp, keen, acute, alert,
perceptive, observant, discerning,
discriminating, knowing, calculating,
cunning, crafty, artful, sly.
E₃ unwise, obtuse, naïve,
unsophisticated.

shriek *verb, noun*
scream, screech, squawk, squeal, cry,
shout, yell, wail, howl.

shrill *adjective*
high, high-pitched, treble, sharp, acute,
piercing, penetrating, screaming,
screeching, strident, ear-splitting.
E₃ deep, low, soft, gentle.

shrink *verb*
1 shrink in size : contract, shorten,
narrow, decrease, lessen, diminish,
dwindle, shrivel, wrinkle, wither.
2 shrink from the blows/direct
confrontation : recoil, back away, shy
away, withdraw, retire, balk, quail,
cower, cringe, wince, flinch, shun.
E₃ 1 expand, stretch. **2** accept, embrace.

shrivel *verb*
wrinkle, pucker, wither, wilt, shrink, dwindle, parch, dehydrate, desiccate, scorch, sear, burn, frizzle.

shudder *verb*
shiver, shake, tremble, quiver, quake, heave, convulse.
▶ *noun*
shiver, quiver, tremor, spasm, convulsion.

shuffle *verb*
1 shuffle the playing cards: mix (up), intermix, jumble, confuse, disorder, rearrange, reorganize, shift around, switch.
2 shuffle across the room: shamble, scuffle, scrape, drag, limp, hobble.

shun *verb*
avoid, evade, elude, steer clear of, shy away from, spurn, ignore, cold-shoulder, ostracize.
F3 accept, embrace.

shut *verb*
close, slam, seal, fasten, secure, lock, latch, bolt, bar.
F3 open.
◆ **shut down** close, stop, cease, terminate, halt, discontinue, suspend, switch off, deactivate.
◆ **shut off** seclude, isolate, cut off, separate, segregate.
◆ **shut out 1** shut him out of their discussions: exclude, bar, debar, lock out, ostracize, banish.
2 shutting out their cries of pain: hide, conceal, cover, mask, screen, veil.
◆ **shut up 1** (*infml*) do shut up!: silence, gag, quiet, hush up, pipe down (*infml*), hold one's tongue, clam up (*infml*).
2 shut up in prison: confine, coop up, imprison, incarcerate, jail, intern.

shy *adjective*
timid, bashful, reticent, reserved, retiring, diffident, coy, self-conscious, inhibited, modest, self-effacing, shrinking, hesitant, cautious, chary, suspicious, nervous.
F3 bold, assertive, confident.

sick *adjective*
1 a sick child: ill, unwell, indisposed, laid up, poorly, ailing, sickly, under

the weather, weak, feeble.
2 I feel sick: vomiting, queasy, nauseous, bilious, seasick, airsick.
3 sick of waiting: bored, fed up (*infml*), tired, weary, disgusted, nauseated.
F3 1 well, healthy.

sickening *adjective*
nauseating, revolting, disgusting, offensive, distasteful, foul, vile, loathsome, repulsive.
F3 delightful, pleasing, attractive.

sickly *adjective*
1 a sickly child: unhealthy, infirm, delicate, weak, feeble, frail, wan, pallid, ailing, indisposed, sick, faint, languid.
2 a sickly green/taste: nauseating, revolting, sweet, syrupy, cloying, mawkish.
F3 1 healthy, robust, sturdy, strong.

sickness *noun*
1 recovering from a long sickness: illness, disease, malady, ailment, complaint, affliction, ill-health, indisposition, infirmity.
2 symptoms are sickness and dizziness: vomiting, nausea, queasiness, biliousness.
F3 1 health.

side *noun*
1 the side of the lake/shape has four sides: edge, margin, fringe, periphery, border, boundary, limit, verge, brink, bank, shore, quarter, region, flank, hand, face, facet, surface.
2 standpoint, viewpoint, view, aspect, angle, slant.
3 team, party, faction, camp, cause, interest.
▶ *adjective*
lateral, flanking, marginal, secondary, subsidiary, subordinate, lesser, minor, incidental, indirect, oblique.
◆ **side with** agree with, team up with, support, vote for, favour, prefer.

sidetrack *verb*
deflect, head off, divert, distract.

sideways *adverb*
sidewards, edgeways, laterally, obliquely.
▶ *adjective*
sideward, side, lateral, slanted, oblique, indirect, sidelong.

sidle *verb*
slink, edge, inch, creep, sneak.

sift *verb*
1 sift the flour and sugar: sieve, strain, filter, riddle, screen, winnow, separate, sort.
2 sifting through a pile of papers: examine, scrutinize, investigate, analyse, probe, review.

sigh *verb*
breathe, exhale, moan, complain, lament, grieve.

sight *noun*
1 lose his sight: vision, eyesight, seeing, observation, perception.
2 out of sight: view, look, glance, glimpse, range, field of vision, visibility.
3 what a sight!: appearance, spectacle, show, display, exhibition, scene, eyesore, monstrosity, fright (*infml*).
▶ *verb*
see, observe, spot, glimpse, perceive, discern, distinguish, make out.

sign *noun*
1 a sign of peace: symbol, token, character, figure, representation, emblem, badge, insignia, logo.
2 no sign of her anywhere: indication, mark, signal, gesture, evidence, manifestation, clue, pointer, hint, suggestion, trace.
3 the sign said 'Keep off the grass': notice, poster, board, placard.
4 a sign of things to come: portent, omen, forewarning, foreboding, harbinger (*fml*).
▶ *verb*
autograph, initial, endorse, write.
◆ **sign up** enlist, enrol, join (up), volunteer, register, sign on, recruit, take on, hire, engage, employ.

signal *noun*
sign, indication, mark, gesture, cue, go-ahead, password, light, indicator, beacon, flare, rocket, alarm, alert, warning, tip-off.
▶ *verb*
wave, gesticulate, gesture, beckon, motion, nod, sign, indicate, communicate.

signature *noun*
autograph, initials, mark, endorsement, inscription.

significant *adjective*
1 significant improvement: important, relevant, consequential, momentous, weighty, serious, noteworthy, critical, vital, marked, considerable, appreciable.
2 significant gesture: meaningful, symbolic, expressive, suggestive, indicative, symptomatic.
₣₃ 1 insignificant, unimportant, trivial.
2 meaningless.

signify *verb*
1 the colour red signifies danger: mean, denote, symbolize, represent, stand for, indicate, show, express, convey, transmit, communicate, intimate, imply, suggest.
2 that doesn't signify: matter, count.

silence *noun*
quiet, quietness, hush, peace, stillness, calm, lull, noiselessness, soundlessness, muteness, dumbness, speechlessness, taciturnity, reticence, reserve.
₣₃ noise, sound, din, uproar.
▶ *verb*
quiet, quieten, hush, mute, deaden, muffle, stifle, gag, muzzle, suppress, subdue, quell, still, dumbfound.

silent *adjective*
inaudible, noiseless, soundless, quiet, peaceful, still, hushed, muted, mute, dumb, speechless, tongue-tied, taciturn, mum, reticent, reserved, tacit, unspoken, unexpressed, understood, voiceless, wordless.
₣₃ noisy, loud, talkative.

silhouette *noun*
outline, contour, delineation, shape, form, configuration, profile, shadow.

silky *adjective*
silken, fine, sleek, lustrous, glossy, satiny, smooth, soft, velvety.

silly *adjective*
foolish, stupid, imprudent, senseless, pointless, idiotic, daft (*infml*), ridiculous, ludicrous, preposterous, absurd, meaningless, irrational, illogical, childish, puerile (*fml*),

immature, irresponsible, scatterbrained.
F∃ wise, sensible, sane, mature, clever, intelligent.

silt *noun*
sediment, deposit, alluvium, sludge, mud, ooze.

similar *adjective*
like, alike, close, related, akin, corresponding, equivalent, analogous, comparable, uniform, homogeneous.
F∃ dissimilar, different.

similarity *noun*
likeness, resemblance, similitude, closeness, relation, correspondence, congruence, equivalence, analogy, comparability, compatibility, agreement, affinity, homogeneity, uniformity.
F∃ dissimilarity, difference.

simmer *verb*
boil, bubble, seethe, stew, burn, smoulder, fume, rage.
◆ **simmer down** calm down, cool down, control oneself, collect oneself, chill (out) (*infml*).

simple *adjective*
1 a simple question: easy, elementary, straightforward, uncomplicated, uninvolved, clear, lucid, plain, understandable, comprehensible.
2 a simple peasant: unsophisticated, natural, innocent, artless, guileless, ingenuous, naïve, green.
3 he's a bit simple: foolish, stupid, silly, idiotic, half-witted, simple-minded, feeble-minded, backward.
F∃ 1 difficult, hard, complicated, intricate. **2** sophisticated, worldly.

simplicity *noun*
simpleness, ease, straightforwardness, clarity, purity, plainness, restraint, naturalness, innocence, artlessness, candour, openness, sincerity, directness.
F∃ difficulty, complexity, intricacy, sophistication.

simplify *verb*
disentangle, untangle, decipher, clarify, paraphrase, abridge, reduce, streamline.
F∃ complicate, elaborate.

simplistic *adjective*
oversimplified, superficial, shallow, sweeping, facile, simple, naïve.
F∃ analytical, detailed.

simply *adverb*
1 he was simply asking: merely, just, only, solely, purely.
2 that's simply ridiculous: utterly, completely, totally, wholly, absolutely, quite, really, undeniably, unquestionably, clearly, plainly, obviously.
3 simply made/put: easily, straightforwardly, directly, intelligibly.

simultaneous *adjective*
synchronous, synchronic, concurrent, contemporaneous, coinciding, parallel.
F∃ asynchronous.

sin *noun*
wrong, offence, transgression, trespass (*fml*), misdeed, lapse, fault, error, crime, wrongdoing, sinfulness, wickedness, iniquity (*fml*), evil, impiety, ungodliness, unrighteousness, guilt.
▶ *verb*
offend, transgress, trespass (*fml*), lapse, err, misbehave, stray, go astray, fall, fall from grace.

sincere *adjective*
honest, truthful, candid, frank, open, direct, straightforward, plain-spoken, serious, earnest, heartfelt, wholehearted, real, true, genuine, pure, unadulterated, unmixed, natural, unaffected, artless, guileless, simple.
F∃ insincere, hypocritical, affected.

sing *verb*
chant, intone, vocalize, croon, serenade, yodel, trill, warble, chirp, pipe, whistle, hum.

singe *verb*
scorch, char, blacken, burn, sear.

single *adjective*
one, unique, singular, individual, particular, exclusive, sole, only, lone, solitary, separate, distinct, free, unattached, unmarried, celibate, unshared, undivided, unbroken, simple, one-to-one, man-to-man.
F∃ multiple.

◆ single out
choose, select, pick, hand-pick, distinguish, identify, separate, set apart, isolate, highlight, pinpoint.

single-handed *adjective, adverb*
solo, alone, unaccompanied, unaided, unassisted, independent(ly).

single-minded *adjective*
determined, resolute, dogged, persevering, tireless, unwavering, fixed, unswerving, undeviating, steadfast, dedicated, devoted.

sinister *adjective*
ominous, menacing, threatening, disturbing, disquieting, unlucky, inauspicious, malevolent, evil.
E3 auspicious, harmless, innocent.

sink *verb*
1 sinking to her knees/sinking below the waves: descend, slip, fall, drop, slump, lower, stoop, succumb, lapse, droop, sag, dip, set, disappear, vanish.
2 hope is sinking fast: decrease, lessen, subside, abate, dwindle, diminish, ebb, fade, flag, weaken, fail, decline, worsen, degenerate, degrade, decay, collapse.
3 sink like a stone/sinking it in concrete: dive, plunge, plummet, submerge, immerse, engulf, drown.
4 sink a well: bore, drill, penetrate, dig, excavate, lay, conceal.
E3 1 rise. 2 increase. 3 float.

sinuous *adjective*
lithe, slinky, curved, wavy, undulating, tortuous, twisting, winding, meandering, serpentine, coiling.
E3 straight.

sip *verb*
taste, sample, drink, sup.
▶ *noun*
taste, drop, spoonful, mouthful.

sit *verb*
1 sit on a branch: settle, rest, perch, roost.
2 table sits twelve: seat, accommodate, hold, contain.
3 when the parliament sits: meet, assemble, gather, convene, deliberate.

site *noun*
location, place, spot, position, situation, station, setting, scene, plot, lot, ground, area.
▶ *verb*
locate, place, position, situate, station, set, install.

sitting *noun*
session, period, spell, meeting, assembly, hearing, consultation.

situation *noun*
1 an attractive situation: site, location, position, place, spot, seat, locality, locale, setting, scenario.
2 what's the latest situation?: state of affairs, case, circumstances, predicament, state, condition, status.

sizable *adjective*
large, substantial, considerable, respectable, goodly, largish, biggish, decent, generous.
E3 small, tiny.

size *noun*
magnitude, measurement(s), dimensions, proportions, volume, bulk, mass, height, length, extent, range, scale, amount, greatness, largeness, bigness, vastness, immensity.
◆ size up gauge, assess, evaluate, weigh up, measure.

skeleton *noun*
bones, frame, structure, framework, bare bones, outline, draft, sketch.

sketch *verb*
draw, depict, portray, represent, pencil, paint, outline, delineate, draft, rough out, block out.
▶ *noun*
drawing, vignette, design, plan, diagram, outline, delineation, skeleton, draft.

sketchy *adjective*
rough, vague, incomplete, unfinished, scrappy, bitty, imperfect, inadequate, insufficient, slight, superficial, cursory, hasty.
E3 full, complete.

skilful *adjective*
able, capable, adept, competent, proficient, deft, adroit, handy, expert, masterly, accomplished, skilled, practised, experienced, professional, clever, tactical, cunning.
E3 inept, clumsy, awkward.

skill *noun*
skilfulness, ability, aptitude, facility, handiness, talent, knack, art, technique, training, experience, expertise, expertness, mastery, proficiency, competence, accomplishment, cleverness, intelligence.

skilled *adjective*
trained, schooled, qualified, professional, experienced, practised, accomplished, expert, masterly, proficient, able, skilful.
Ǝ unskilled, inexperienced.

skim *verb*
1 skimming the surface of the water: brush, touch, skate, plane, float, sail, glide, fly.
2 skim through the documents: scan, look through, skip.
3 skim milk: cream, separate.

skimp *verb*
economize, scrimp, pinch, cut corners, stint, withhold.
Ǝ squander, waste.

skin *noun*
hide, pelt, membrane, film, coating, surface, outside, peel, rind, husk, casing, crust.
► *verb*
flay, fleece, strip, peel, scrape, graze.

skinny *adjective*
thin, lean, scrawny, scraggy, skeletal, skin-and-bone, emaciated, underfed, undernourished.
Ǝ fat, plump.

skip *verb*
1 skipped down the street: hop, jump, leap, dance, gambol, frisk, caper, prance.
2 skip a page: miss, omit, leave out, cut.

skirmish *noun*
fight, combat, battle, engagement, encounter, conflict, clash, brush, scrap, tussle, set-to, dust-up (*infml*).

skirt *verb*
circle, circumnavigate, border, edge, flank, bypass, avoid, evade, circumvent.

skulk *verb*
lurk, hide, prowl, sneak, creep, slink.

sky *noun*
space, atmosphere, air, heavens, the blue.

slab *noun*
piece, block, lump, chunk, hunk, wodge (*infml*), wedge, slice, portion.

slack *adjective*
1 trousers are too slack: loose, limp, sagging, baggy.
2 a slack period: quiet, idle, inactive, sluggish, slow.
3 a slack attitude to his studies: neglectful, negligent, careless, inattentive, remiss, permissive, lax, relaxed, easy-going (*infml*).
Ǝ **1** tight, taut, stiff, rigid. **2** busy. **3** diligent.
► *noun*
looseness, give, play, room, leeway, excess.
► *verb*
idle, shirk, skive (*infml*), neglect.

slacken off *verb*
loosen, release, relax, ease, moderate, reduce, lessen, decrease, diminish, abate, slow (down).
Ǝ tighten, increase, intensify, quicken.

slam *verb*
1 slamming the door: bang, crash, dash, smash, throw, hurl, fling.
2 (*infml*) slammed their political opponents: criticize, slate (*infml*), pan (*infml*).

slander *noun*
defamation (*fml*), calumny (*fml*), misrepresentation, libel, scandal, smear, slur, aspersion (*fml*), backbiting.
► *verb*
defame (*fml*), vilify (*fml*), malign, denigrate, disparage (*fml*), libel, smear, slur, backbite.
Ǝ praise, compliment.

slanderous *adjective*
defamatory, false, untrue, libellous, damaging, malicious, abusive, insulting.

slant *verb*
tilt, slope, incline, lean, list, skew, angle.
► *noun*
1 a downwards slant: slope, incline,

gradient, ramp, camber, pitch, tilt, angle, diagonal.

2 give the story a different slant: bias, emphasis, attitude, viewpoint.

slanting *adjective*
sloping, tilted, oblique, diagonal.

slap *noun*
smack, spank, cuff, blow, bang, clap.
▶ *verb*
1 slap someone's face: smack, spank, hit, strike, cuff, clout, bang, clap.
2 slap on paint: daub, plaster, spread, apply.

slash *verb*
cut, slit, gash, lacerate, rip, tear, rend.
▶ *noun*
cut, incision, slit, gash, laceration, rip, tear, rent.

slaughter *noun*
killing, murder, massacre, extermination, butchery, carnage, blood-bath, bloodshed.
▶ *verb*
kill, slay (*fml*), murder, massacre, exterminate, liquidate, butcher.

slave *noun*
servant, drudge, vassal, serf, villein, captive.
▶ *verb*
toil, labour, drudge, sweat, grind, slog.

slavery *noun*
servitude, bondage, captivity, enslavement, serfdom, thraldom, subjugation.
E3 freedom, liberty.

slavish *adjective*
1 a slavish copy: unoriginal, imitative, unimaginative, uninspired, literal, strict.
2 was too slavish in his attitude: servile, abject, submissive, sycophantic, grovelling, cringing, fawning, menial, low, mean.
E3 1 original, imaginative.
2 independent, assertive.

sleek *adjective*
shiny, glossy, lustrous, smooth, silky, well-groomed.
E3 rough, unkempt.

sleep *verb*
doze, snooze, slumber, kip (*infml*), doss

(down) (*infml*), hibernate, drop off, nod off, rest, repose.
▶ *noun*
doze, snooze, nap, forty winks, shut-eye (*infml*), kip (*infml*), slumber, hibernation, rest, repose, siesta.

sleepless *adjective*
unsleeping, awake, wide-awake, alert, vigilant, watchful, wakeful, restless, disturbed, insomniac.

sleepy *adjective*
drowsy, somnolent (*fml*), tired, weary, heavy, slow, sluggish, torpid, lethargic, inactive, quiet, dull, soporific (*fml*), hypnotic.
E3 awake, alert, wakeful, restless.

slender *adjective*
1 tall and slender: slim, thin, lean, slight, svelte, graceful.
2 a slender chance: faint, remote, slight, inconsiderable, tenuous, flimsy, feeble, inadequate, insufficient, meagre, scanty.
E3 1 fat. **2** appreciable, considerable, ample.

slice *noun*
piece, sliver, wafer, rasher, tranche, slab, wedge, segment, section, share, portion, helping, cut (*infml*), whack (*infml*).
▶ *verb*
carve, cut, chop, divide, segment.

slick *adjective*
1 a slick operator: glib, plausible, deft, adroit, dexterous, skilful, professional.
2 slick hair: smooth, sleek, glossy, shiny, polished.

slide *verb*
slip, slither, skid, skate, ski, toboggan, glide, plane, coast, skim.

slight *adjective*
1 a slight mistake/bump: minor, unimportant, insignificant, negligible, trivial, paltry, modest, small, little, inconsiderable, insubstantial.
2 a slight figure: slender, slim, diminutive, petite, delicate.
E3 1 major, significant, noticeable, considerable. **2** large, muscular.
▶ *noun*
insult, affront, slur, snub, rebuff, rudeness, discourtesy, disrespect,

contempt, disdain, indifference, disregard, neglect.
F3 respect, praise, compliment, flattery.

slim *adjective*
1 a slim waist: slender, thin, lean, svelte, trim.
2 a slim chance of success: slight, remote, faint, poor.
F3 **1** fat, chubby. **2** strong, considerable.
▸ *verb*
lose weight, diet, reduce.

slimy *adjective*
1 slimy mud: mucous, viscous, oily, greasy, slippery.
2 I hate the slimy way he talks to the boss: servile, obsequious, sycophantic, toadying, smarmy, oily, unctuous (*fml*).

sling *verb*
1 slinging it away: throw, hurl, fling, catapult, heave, pitch, lob, toss, chuck (*infml*).
2 slinging his bow over his shoulder: hang, suspend, dangle, swing.

slink *verb*
sneak, steal, creep, sidle, slip, prowl, skulk.

slip[1] *verb*
1 slipped on the ice: slide, glide, skate, skid, stumble, trip, fall, slither.
2 slipped into the room unseen: slink, sneak, steal, creep.
▸ *noun*
mistake, error, slip-up (*infml*), bloomer (*infml*), blunder, fault, indiscretion, omission, oversight, failure.

slip[2] *noun*
a slip of paper: piece, strip, voucher, chit, coupon, certificate.

slippery *adjective*
1 a slippery surface: slippy, icy, greasy, glassy, smooth, dangerous, treacherous, perilous.
2 a slippery character: dishonest, untrustworthy, false, duplicitous, two-faced, crafty, cunning, devious, evasive, smooth, smarmy.
F3 **1** rough. **2** trustworthy, reliable.

slipshod *adjective*
careless, slapdash, sloppy, slovenly, untidy, negligent, lax, casual.
F3 careful, fastidious, neat, tidy.

slit *verb*
cut, gash, slash, slice, split, rip, tear.
▸ *noun*
opening, aperture, vent, cut, incision, gash, slash, split, tear, rent.

slither *verb*
slide, slip, glide, slink, creep, snake, worm.

sliver *noun*
flake, shaving, paring, slice, wafer, shred, fragment, chip, splinter, shiver, shard.

slogan *noun*
jingle, motto, catch-phrase, catchword, watchword, battle-cry, war cry.

slop *verb*
spill, overflow, slosh, splash, splatter, spatter.

slope *verb*
slant, lean, tilt, tip, pitch, incline, rise, fall.
▸ *noun*
incline, gradient, ramp, hill, ascent, descent, slant, tilt, pitch, inclination.

sloppy *adjective*
1 a sloppy mixture: watery, wet, liquid, runny, mushy, slushy.
2 sloppy work: careless, hit-or-miss, slapdash, slipshod, slovenly, untidy, messy, clumsy, amateurish.
3 sloppy song: soppy, sentimental, schmaltzy, slushy, mushy.
F3 **1** solid. **2** careful, exact, precise.

slot *noun*
hole, opening, aperture, slit, vent, groove, channel, gap, space, time, vacancy, place, spot, position, niche.
▸ *verb*
insert, fit, place, position, assign, pigeonhole.

slouch *verb*
stoop, hunch, droop, slump, lounge, loll, shuffle, shamble.

slovenly *adjective*
sloppy, careless, slipshod, untidy, messy, disorganized, scruffy, slatternly, sluttish.
F3 neat, smart.

slow *adjective*
1 a slow pace: leisurely, unhurried, lingering, loitering, dawdling, lazy,

WORD study

slowly

There are many colourful phrases used to express how **slowly** something happens or is done. Try out some of those listed below to add variety to your speech or writing.

---

slowly

at a crawl
at a snail's pace

at crawling pace
be a slowcoach

slow down

put the brakes on
wind down

throttle back

telling someone to slow down

hold your horses!
take it easy!

not so fast!

---

sluggish, slow-moving, creeping, gradual, deliberate, measured, plodding.
2 too slow to understand what you meant: stupid, slow-witted, dim, thick (*infml*).
3 a slow journey: prolonged, protracted, long-drawn-out, tedious, boring, dull, uninteresting, uneventful.
F3 1 quick, fast, swift, rapid, speedy. **2** clever, intelligent. **3** brisk, lively, exciting.
▶ *verb*
brake, decelerate, delay, hold up, retard, handicap, check, curb, restrict.
F3 speed, accelerate.

slowly *adverb*
leisurely, gradually, lazily, sluggishly, unhurriedly.
⇨ *See also* **Word Study** *panel.*

sluggish *adjective*
lethargic, listless, torpid, heavy, dull, slow, slow-moving, slothful, lazy, idle, inactive, lifeless, unresponsive.
F3 brisk, vigorous, lively, dynamic.

slump *verb*
1 trade slumped: collapse, fall, drop, plunge, plummet, sink, decline, deteriorate, worsen, crash, fail.
2 he slumped against the wall: droop, sag, bend, stoop, slouch, loll, lounge, flop.
▶ *noun*
recession, depression, stagnation, downturn, low, trough, decline, deterioration, worsening, fall, drop, collapse, crash, failure.
F3 boom.

sly *adjective*
wily, foxy, crafty, cunning, artful, guileful, clever, canny, shrewd, astute, knowing, subtle, devious, shifty, tricky, furtive, stealthy, surreptitious, underhand, covert, secretive, scheming, conniving, mischievous, roguish.
F3 honest, frank, candid, open.

smack *verb*
hit, strike, slap, spank, whack (*infml*), thwack (*infml*), clap, box, cuff, pat, tap.
▶ *noun*
blow, slap, spank, whack (*infml*),

thwack (*infml*), box, cuff, pat, tap.
▶ *adverb*
bang, slap-bang, right, plumb, straight,
directly, exactly, precisely.

small *adjective*
1 a small man/dog/house/child : little,
tiny, minute, minuscule, short, slight,
puny, petite, diminutive, pint-size(d)
(*infml*), miniature, mini, pocket,
pocket-sized, young.
2 a small fee/amount : petty, trifling,
trivial, unimportant, insignificant,
minor, inconsiderable, negligible.
3 a person of small means : inadequate,
insufficient, scanty, meagre, paltry,
mean, limited.
F⊒ 1 large, big, huge. **2** great,
considerable. **3** ample.
⇨ *See also* **Word Workshop** *panel.*

small-minded *adjective*
petty, mean, ungenerous, illiberal,
intolerant, bigoted, narrow-minded,
parochial, insular, rigid, hidebound.
F⊒ liberal, tolerant, broad-minded.

smarmy *adjective*
smooth, oily, unctuous (*fml*), servile,
obsequious, sycophantic, toadying,
ingratiating, crawling, fawning.

smart *adjective*
1 smart clothes/appearance : elegant,
stylish, chic, fashionable, modish, neat,
tidy, spruce, trim, well-groomed.
2 a smart fellow/move : clever,
intelligent, bright, sharp, acute,
shrewd, astute.
F⊒ 1 dowdy, unfashionable, untidy,
scruffy. **2** stupid, slow.
▶ *verb*
sting, hurt, prick, burn, tingle, twinge,
throb.

smash *verb*
1 smash a window : break, shatter,
shiver, ruin, wreck, demolish, destroy,
defeat, crush.
2 smashed his fist down on the table :
crash, collide, strike, bang, bash,
thump.

smattering *noun*
bit, modicum, dash, sprinkling, basics,
rudiments, elements.

smear *verb*
1 smeared their faces with mud : daub,

plaster, spread, cover, coat, rub,
smudge, streak.
2 smearing him in the press : defame
(*fml*), malign, vilify (*fml*), blacken,
sully (*fml*), stain, tarnish.

smell *noun*
odour, whiff, scent, perfume,
fragrance, bouquet, aroma, stench,
stink, pong (*infml*).

---

*Words used for types of smell
include:*

pleasant: aroma, bouquet, fragrance,
incense, nose, odour, pot pourri,
perfume, redolence, scent; *unpleasant*:
b.o. (body odour), fetor, funk (*US*),
hum, malodour, mephitis, miasma,
niff (*infml*), pong (*infml*), pungency,
reek, sniff, stench, stink, whiff.

▶ *verb*
sniff, nose, scent, stink, reek, pong
(*infml*).

smelly *adjective*
malodorous, pongy (*infml*), stinking,
reeking, foul, bad, off, fetid, putrid,
high, strong.

smile *noun, verb*
grin, beam, simper, smirk, leer,
laugh.

smoke *noun*
fumes, exhaust, gas, vapour, mist, fog,
smog.

smooth *adjective*
1 a nice smooth surface : level, plane,
even, flat, horizontal, flush.
2 a smooth ride/landing : steady,
unbroken, flowing, regular, uniform,
rhythmic, easy, effortless.
3 smooth water : shiny, polished,
glossy, silky, glassy, calm, undisturbed,
serene, tranquil, peaceful.
4 a smooth operator : suave, agreeable,
smooth-talking, glib, plausible,
persuasive, slick, smarmy, unctuous
(*fml*), ingratiating.
F⊒ 1 rough, lumpy. **2** bumpy,
irregular, erratic, unsteady. **3** rough,
choppy.
▶ *verb*
1 smooth out any wrinkles/bumps :

WORD workshop

small

The adjective **small** tends to be overused. Try out some of the synonyms listed below to add variety to your writing.

a person's age

infant	junior	young

a person's size

petite	short	slim
puny	slight	

small in size

diminutive	miniscule	pocket-sized
little	miniature	tiny
mini	minute	

small amount

inadequate	meagre	scanty
limited	paltry	

of little importance

insignificant	petty	trivial
minor	slight	unimportant
negligible	trifling	

feeling small

ashamed	humiliated	unimportant
embarrassed	stupid	

iron, press, roll, flatten, level, plane, file, sand, polish.
2 smooth their feelings: ease, alleviate, assuage (*fml*), allay, mitigate, calm, mollify.
F₃ 1 roughen, wrinkle, crease.

small

WORD workshop

Instead of repeating **small** in the following passage, you might use some of the synonyms discussed opposite

"

"Oh look, it's horrible!" screamed Michelle.

"It's only a ~~small~~ *little* spider," said Clare, "it won't hurt you!"

"I've been scared of spiders since I was ~~small~~ *young*," explained Michelle. "I've never liked them, even the really ~~small~~ *tiny* ones frighten me."

"You shouldn't still be scared of them at your age," scoffed Clare. "It really is quite silly."

"It may be a ~~small~~ *trivial* matter to you," replied Michelle, "but to me it's very serious!"

"I don't mean to make you feel ~~small~~ *embarrassed*," Clare assured her, "but only a ~~small~~ *paltry* number of spiders are dangerous. This one is more scared of you than you are of him!"

"

smother *verb*
suffocate, asphyxiate, strangle, throttle, choke, stifle, extinguish, snuff, muffle, suppress, repress, hide, conceal, cover, shroud, envelop, wrap.

smoulder *verb*
burn, smoke, fume, rage, seethe, simmer.

smudge *verb*
blur, smear, daub, mark, spot, stain, dirty, soil.
▶ *noun*
blot, stain, spot, blemish, blur, smear, streak.

smug *adjective*
complacent, self-satisfied, superior, holier-than-thou, self-righteous,

priggish, conceited.
F3 humble, modest.

snack *noun*
refreshment(s), bite, nibble, titbit, elevenses (*infml*).

snag *noun*
disadvantage, inconvenience, drawback, catch, problem, difficulty, complication, setback, hitch, obstacle, stumbling block.
▶ *verb*
catch, rip, tear, hole, ladder.

snap *verb*
1 the twig snapped : break, crack, split, separate.
2 dog snapped at him : bite, nip, bark, growl, snarl.
3 snapped it up : snatch, seize, catch, grasp, grip.
▶ *noun*
break, crack, bite, nip, flick, fillip, crackle, pop.
▶ *adjective*
immediate, instant, on-the-spot, abrupt, sudden.

snappy *adjective*
1 a snappy dresser : smart, stylish, chic, fashionable, modish, trendy (*infml*).
2 make it snappy! : quick, hasty, brisk, lively, energetic.
3 a snappy comment : cross, irritable, edgy, touchy, brusque, quick-tempered, ill-natured, crabbed, testy.
F3 1 dowdy. 2 slow.

snare *verb*
trap, ensnare, entrap, catch, net.
▶ *noun*
trap, wire, net, noose, catch, pitfall.

snarl[1] *verb*
he snarled back at me : growl, grumble, complain.

snarl[2] *verb*
line snarled on a tree : tangle, knot, ravel, entangle, enmesh, embroil, confuse, muddle, complicate.

snatch *verb*
grab, seize, kidnap, take, nab (*infml*), pluck, pull, wrench, wrest (*fml*), gain, win, clutch, grasp, grip.

sneak *verb*
1 sneaked away under cover of darkness : creep, steal, slip, slink, sidle, skulk, lurk, prowl, smuggle, spirit.
2 sneaked to his parents : tell tales, split (*infml*), inform on, grass on (*slang*).
▶ *noun*
tell-tale, informer, grass (*slang*).

sneaking *adjective*
private, secret, furtive, surreptitious, hidden, lurking, suppressed, grudging, nagging, niggling, persistent, worrying, uncomfortable, intuitive.

sneer *verb*
scorn, disdain, look down on, deride, scoff, jeer, mock, ridicule, gibe, laugh, snigger.

snide *adjective*
derogatory, disparaging, sarcastic, cynical, scornful, sneering, hurtful, unkind, nasty, mean, spiteful, malicious, ill-natured.
F3 complimentary.

sniff *verb*
breathe, inhale, snuff, snuffle, smell, nose, scent.

snigger *verb, noun*
laugh, giggle, titter, chuckle, sneer.

snippet *noun*
piece, scrap, cutting, clipping, fragment, particle, shred, snatch, part, portion, segment, section.

snobbish *adjective*
supercilious, disdainful, snooty (*infml*), stuck-up (*infml*), toffee-nosed (*infml*), superior, lofty, high and mighty, arrogant, pretentious, affected, condescending, patronizing.

snoop *verb*
spy, sneak, pry, nose, interfere, meddle.

snooze *verb*
nap, doze, sleep, kip (*infml*).
▶ *noun*
nap, catnap, forty winks, doze, siesta, sleep, kip (*infml*).

snub *verb*
rebuff, brush off, cut, cold-shoulder, slight, rebuke, put down, squash, humble, shame, humiliate, mortify.

snug *adjective*
cosy, warm, comfortable, homely, friendly, intimate, sheltered, secure, tight, close-fitting.

soak *verb*
wet, drench, saturate, penetrate, permeate, infuse, bathe, marinate, souse, steep, submerge, immerse.

soaking *adjective*
soaked, drenched, sodden, waterlogged, saturated, sopping, wringing, dripping, streaming.
F3 dry.

soar *verb*
fly, wing, glide, plane, tower, rise, ascend, climb, mount, escalate, spiral, rocket.
F3 fall, plummet.

sob *verb*
cry, weep, bawl, howl, blubber, snivel.

sober *adjective*
1 stay sober: teetotal, temperate, moderate, abstinent, abstemious.
2 a sober attitude/group of gentlemen: solemn, dignified, serious, staid, steady, sedate, quiet, serene, calm, composed, unruffled, unexcited, cool, dispassionate, level-headed, practical, realistic, reasonable, rational, clear-headed.
3 sober dark suit: sombre, drab, dull, plain, subdued, restrained.
F3 **1** drunk, intemperate. **2** frivolous, excited, unrealistic, irrational. **3** flashy, garish.

so-called *adjective*
alleged, supposed, purported, ostensible, nominal, self-styled, professed, would-be, pretended.

sociable *adjective*
outgoing, gregarious, friendly, affable, companionable, genial, convivial, cordial, warm, hospitable, neighbourly, approachable, accessible, familiar.
F3 unsociable, withdrawn, unfriendly, hostile.

social *adjective*
communal, public, community, common, general, collective, group, organized.

socialize *verb*
mix, mingle, fraternize, get together, go out, entertain.

society *noun*
1 study society: community, population, culture, civilization, nation, people, mankind, humanity.
2 the Royal Society/form a society: club, circle, group, association, organization, company, corporation, league, union, guild, fellowship, fraternity, brotherhood, sisterhood, sorority.
3 the society of his peers: friendship, companionship, camaraderie, fellowship, company.
4 high society: upper classes, aristocracy, gentry, nobility, élite.

soft *adjective*
1 a soft bed: yielding, pliable, flexible, elastic, plastic, malleable, spongy, squashy, pulpy.
2 soft colours: pale, light, pastel, delicate, subdued, muted, quiet, low, dim, faint, diffuse, mild, bland, gentle, soothing, sweet, mellow, melodious, dulcet, pleasant.
3 soft fur/skin: furry, downy, velvety, silky, smooth.
4 you're too soft with that boy: lenient, lax, permissive, indulgent, tolerant, easy-going (*infml*), kind, generous, gentle, merciful, soft-hearted, tender.
5 don't go soft on us now!: sensitive, weak, spineless.
F3 **1** hard. **2** harsh. **3** rough. **4** strict, severe. **5** tough.

soften *verb*
1 soften the blow: moderate, temper, mitigate, lessen, diminish, abate, alleviate, ease, soothe, palliate (*fml*), quell, assuage (*fml*), subdue, mollify, appease, calm, still, relax.
2 soften the butter in a pan: melt, liquefy, dissolve, reduce.

soft-hearted *adjective*
sympathetic, compassionate, kind, benevolent, charitable, generous, warm-hearted, tender, sentimental.
F3 hard-hearted, callous.

soggy *adjective*
wet, damp, moist, soaked, drenched, sodden, waterlogged, saturated, sopping, dripping, heavy, boggy, spongy, pulpy.

soil[1] *noun*
dig in the soil: earth, clay, loam,

humus, dirt, dust, ground, land,
region, country.

soil² *verb*
soil one's clothes: dirty, stain, spot,
smudge, smear, foul, muddy, pollute,
defile (*fml*), besmirch (*fml*), sully (*fml*),
tarnish.

sole *adjective*
only, unique, exclusive, individual,
single, singular, one, lone, solitary,
alone.
🖃 shared, multiple.

solemn *adjective*
1 a solemn expression/vow: serious,
grave, sober, sedate, sombre, glum,
thoughtful, earnest, awed, reverential.
2 a solemn occasion: grand, stately,
majestic, ceremonial, ritual, formal,
ceremonious, pompous, dignified,
august, venerable, awe-inspiring,
impressive, imposing, momentous.
🖃 **1** light-hearted. **2** frivolous.

solicit *verb*
ask (for), request, seek, crave, beg,
beseech, entreat, implore, plead, pray,
apply (for), supplicate, sue, petition,
canvass, importune.

solid *adjective*
1 solid rock/foundation: hard, firm,
dense, compact, strong, sturdy,
substantial, sound, unshakable.
2 a solid wall of people/a solid white
line: unbroken, continuous,
uninterrupted.
3 a solid person: reliable, dependable,
trusty, worthy, decent, upright, sensible,
level-headed, stable, serious, sober.
4 even solid flesh must decay: real,
genuine, pure, concrete, tangible.
🖃 **1** liquid, gaseous, hollow. **2** broken,
dotted. **3** unreliable, unstable. **4** unreal.

solidarity *noun*
unity, agreement, accord, unanimity,
consensus, harmony, concord,
cohesion, like-mindedness,
camaraderie, team spirit, soundness,
stability.
🖃 discord, division, schism.

solidify *verb*
harden, set, jell, congeal, coagulate,
clot, cake, crystallize.
🖃 soften, liquefy, dissolve.

solitary *adjective*
sole, single, lone, alone, lonely,
lonesome, friendless, unsociable,
reclusive, withdrawn, retired,
sequestered, cloistered, secluded,
separate, isolated, remote, out-of-the-
way, inaccessible, unfrequented,
unvisited, untrodden.
🖃 accompanied, gregarious, busy.

solitude *noun*
aloneness, loneliness, reclusiveness,
retirement, privacy, seclusion,
isolation, remoteness.
🖃 companionship.

solution *noun*
1 answer, result, explanation,
resolution, key, remedy.
2 mixture, blend, compound,
suspension, emulsion, liquid.

solve *verb*
work out, figure out, puzzle out,
decipher, crack, disentangle, unravel,
answer, resolve, settle, clear up, clarify,
explain, interpret.

sombre *adjective*
dark, funereal, drab, dull, dim,
obscure, shady, shadowy, gloomy,
dismal, melancholy, mournful, sad,
joyless, sober, serious, grave.
🖃 bright, cheerful, happy.

someday *adverb*
sometime, one day, eventually.
🖃 never.

sometimes *adverb*
occasionally, now and again, now and
then, once in a while, from time to time.
🖃 always, never.

song *noun*
ballad, madrigal, lullaby, shanty,
anthem, hymn, carol, chant, chorus,
air, tune, melody, lyric, number,
ditty.

Types of song include:
air, anthem, aria, ballad, barcarole,
bird call, bird song, blues, calypso,
cantata, canticle, cantilena, canzone,
canzonet, carol, chanson,
chansonette, chant, chorus, descant,
dirge, dithyramb, ditty, elegy,
epinikion, epithalamium, folk-song,

gospel song, hymn, jingle, lay, love-song, lied, lilt, lullaby, lyric(s), madrigal, melody, number, nursery rhyme, ode, plainchant, plainsong, pop song, psalm, rap, recitative, refrain, requiem, rock and roll, roundelay, serenade, shanty, spiritual, threnody, tune, war song, wassail, yodel. ⇨*See also* **poem.**

soon *adverb*
shortly, presently, in a minute, before long, in the near future.

soothe *verb*
alleviate, relieve, ease, salve, comfort, allay, calm, compose, tranquillize, settle, still, quiet, hush, lull, pacify, appease, mollify, assuage (*fml*), mitigate, soften.
F3 aggravate, irritate, annoy, vex.

sophisticated *adjective*
1 *a sophisticated lifestyle/appearance:* urbane, cosmopolitan, worldly, worldly-wise, cultured, cultivated, refined, polished.
2 *sophisticated technology:* advanced, highly-developed, complicated, complex, intricate, elaborate, delicate, subtle.
F3 1 unsophisticated, naïve.
2 primitive, simple.

soppy *adjective*
sentimental, lovey-dovey (*infml*), weepy (*infml*), sloppy, slushy, mushy, corny (*infml*), mawkish, cloying, soft (*infml*), silly, daft (*infml*).

sordid *adjective*
dirty, filthy, unclean, foul, vile, squalid, sleazy, seamy, seedy, disreputable, shabby, tawdry, corrupt, degraded, degenerate, debauched, low, base, despicable, shameful, wretched, mean, miserly, niggardly, grasping, mercenary, selfish, self-seeking.
F3 pure, honourable, upright.

sore *adjective*
1 *a sore head:* painful, hurting, aching, smarting, stinging, tender, sensitive, inflamed, red, raw.
2 *sore about his insulting comments:* annoyed, irritated, vexed, angry, upset, hurt, wounded, afflicted, aggrieved, resentful.

F3 2 pleased, happy.
▶ *noun*
wound, lesion, swelling, inflammation, boil, abscess, ulcer.

sorrow *noun*
sadness, unhappiness, grief, mourning, misery, woe, distress, affliction, anguish, heartache, heartbreak, misfortune, hardship, trouble, worry, trial, tribulation, regret, remorse.
F3 happiness, joy.

sorry *adjective*
1 *said he was sorry for what he'd done:* apologetic, regretful, remorseful, contrite, penitent, repentant, conscience-stricken, guilt-ridden, shamefaced.
2 *in a sorry state:* pathetic, pitiful, poor, wretched, miserable, sad, unhappy, dismal.
3 *sorry to hear the sad news:* sympathetic, compassionate, understanding, pitying, concerned, moved.
F3 1 impenitent, unashamed. **2** happy, cheerful. **3** uncaring.

sort *noun*
kind, type, genre, ilk, family, race, breed, species, genus, variety, order, class, category, group, denomination (*fml*), style, make, brand, stamp, quality, nature, character, description.
▶ *verb*
class, group, categorize, distribute, divide, separate, segregate, sift, screen, grade, rank, order, classify, catalogue, arrange, organize, systematize.
◆ **sort out** resolve, clear up, clarify, tidy up, neaten, choose, select.

soul *noun*
1 *touched his soul:* spirit, psyche, mind, reason, intellect, character, inner being, essence, life, vital force.
2 *ship carrying two hundred souls:* individual, person, man, creature.

sound¹ *noun*
1 *the sound of hammering:* noise, din, report, resonance, reverberation, tone, timbre.
2 *by the sound of it, he isn't very optimistic:* tenor, description.

▶ *verb*

1 sound the alarm: ring, toll, chime, peal, resound, resonate, reverberate, echo.

2 don't sound the 'b' in 'dumb': articulate, enunciate, pronounce, voice, express, utter.

sound² *adjective*

1 sound in wind and limb: fit, well, healthy, vigorous, robust, sturdy, firm, solid, whole, complete, intact, perfect, unbroken, undamaged, unimpaired, unhurt, uninjured.

2 a sound argument: valid, well-founded, reasonable, rational, logical, orthodox, right, true, proven, reliable, trustworthy, secure, substantial, thorough, good.

E3 1 unfit, ill, shaky. **2** unsound, unreliable, poor.

sour *adjective*

1 sour lemon/sour milk: tart, sharp, acid, pungent, vinegary, bitter, rancid.

2 a sour expression: embittered, acrimonious, ill-tempered, peevish, crabbed, crusty, disagreeable.

E3 1 sweet, sugary. **2** good-natured, generous.

source *noun*

origin, derivation, beginning, start, commencement, cause, root, rise, spring, fountainhead, wellhead, supply, mine, originator, authority, informant.

souvenir *noun*

memento, reminder, remembrance, keepsake, relic, token.

sovereign *noun*

ruler, monarch, king, queen, emperor, empress, potentate, chief.

▶ *adjective*

ruling, royal, imperial, absolute, unlimited, supreme, paramount, predominant, principal, chief, dominant, independent, autonomous.

sow *verb*

plant, seed, scatter, strew, spread, disseminate, lodge, implant.

space *noun*

1 space to grow/move: room, place, seat, accommodation, capacity, volume, extent, expansion, scope,

range, play, elbow-room, leeway, margin.

2 an empty space: blank, omission, gap, opening, lacuna, interval, intermission, chasm.

spacious *adjective*

roomy, capacious, ample, big, large, sizable, broad, wide, huge, vast, extensive, open, uncrowded.

E3 small, narrow, cramped, confined.

span *noun*

spread, stretch, reach, range, scope, compass, extent, length, distance, duration, term, period, spell.

▶ *verb*

arch, vault, bridge, link, cross, traverse, extend, cover.

spare *adjective*

reserve, emergency, extra, additional, leftover, remaining, unused, over, surplus, superfluous, supernumerary, unwanted, free, unoccupied.

E3 necessary, vital, used.

▶ *verb*

1 no one was spared in the attack: pardon, let off, reprieve, release, free.

2 can spare £5: grant, allow, afford, part with.

sparing *adjective*

economical, thrifty, careful, prudent, frugal, meagre, miserly.

E3 unsparing, liberal, lavish.

spark *noun*

flash, flare, gleam, glint, flicker, hint, trace, vestige, scrap, atom, jot.

▶ *verb*

kindle, set off, trigger, start, cause, occasion, prompt, provoke, stimulate, stir, excite, inspire.

sparkle *verb*

1 diamonds sparkled: twinkle, glitter, scintillate, flash, gleam, glint, glisten, shimmer, coruscate, shine, beam.

2 champagne sparkles: effervesce, fizz, bubble.

▶ *noun*

twinkle, glitter, flash, gleam, glint, flicker, spark, radiance, brilliance, dazzle, spirit, vitality, life, animation.

sparse *adjective*

scarce, scanty, meagre, scattered,

infrequent, sporadic.
E3 plentiful, thick, dense.

spasm *noun*
burst, eruption, outburst, frenzy, fit,
convulsion, seizure, attack,
contraction, jerk, twitch, tic.

spasmodic *adjective*
sporadic, occasional, intermittent,
erratic, irregular, fitful, jerky.
E3 continuous, uninterrupted.

spate *noun*
flood, deluge, torrent, rush,
outpouring, flow.

speak *verb*
talk, converse, say, state, declare,
express, utter, voice, articulate,
enunciate, pronounce, tell,
communicate, address, lecture,
harangue, hold forth, declaim, argue,
discuss.

speaker *noun*
lecturer, orator, spokesperson,
spokesman, spokeswoman.

special *adjective*
1 a special occasion: important,
significant, momentous, major,
noteworthy, distinguished, memorable,
remarkable, extraordinary,
exceptional.
2 her own special way of doing things:
different, distinctive, characteristic,
peculiar, singular, individual, unique,
exclusive, select, choice, particular,
specific, unusual, precise, detailed.
E3 1 normal, ordinary, usual. 2 general,
common.

speciality *noun*
forte, talent, strength, field, specialty,
pièce de résistance.

specific *adjective*
precise, exact, fixed, limited,
particular, special, definite,
unequivocal, clear-cut, explicit,
express, unambiguous.
E3 vague, approximate.

specification *noun*
requirement, condition, qualification,
description, listing, item, particular,
detail.

specify *verb*
stipulate, spell out, define,

particularize, detail, itemize,
enumerate, list, mention, cite, name,
designate, indicate, describe, delineate.

specimen *noun*
sample, example, instance, illustration,
model, pattern, paradigm, exemplar,
representative, copy, exhibit.

spectacle *noun*
show, performance, display, exhibition,
parade, pageant, extravaganza, scene,
sight, curiosity, wonder, marvel,
phenomenon.

spectacular *adjective*
grand, splendid, magnificent,
sensational, impressive, striking,
stunning, staggering, amazing,
remarkable, dramatic, daring,
breathtaking, dazzling, eye-catching,
colourful.
E3 unimpressive, ordinary.

spectator *noun*
watcher, viewer, onlooker, looker-on,
bystander, passer-by, witness, eye-
witness, observer.
E3 player, participant.

speculate *verb*
wonder, contemplate, meditate,
muse, reflect, consider, deliberate,
theorize, suppose, guess, conjecture,
surmise, gamble, risk, hazard,
venture.

speech *noun*
1 slurred speech/typical speech of a
countryman: diction, articulation,
enunciation, elocution, delivery,
utterance, voice, language, tongue,
parlance, dialect, jargon.
2 make a speech: oration (*fml*),
address, discourse, talk, lecture,
harangue, spiel (*infml*), conversation,
dialogue, monologue, soliloquy.

speechless *adjective*
dumbfounded, thunderstruck,
amazed, aghast, tongue-tied,
inarticulate, mute, dumb, silent,
mum.
E3 talkative.

speed *noun*
velocity, rate, pace, tempo, quickness,
swiftness, rapidity, celerity, alacrity,
haste, hurry, dispatch, rush,
acceleration.

◨slowness, delay.

verb

race, tear, belt (*infml*), zoom, career, bowl along, sprint, gallop, hurry, rush, hasten, accelerate, quicken, put one's foot down (*infml*), step on it (*infml*).

◨slow, delay.

spell[1] *noun*

a spell in the army: period, time, bout, session, term, season, interval, stretch, patch, turn, stint.

spell[2] *noun*

cast a spell on them: charm, incantation, magic, sorcery, witchery, bewitchment, enchantment, fascination, glamour.

spellbound *adjective*

transfixed, hypnotized, mesmerized, fascinated, enthralled, gripped, entranced, captivated, bewitched, enchanted, charmed.

spend *verb*

1 spend money: disburse (*fml*), pay out, fork out (*infml*), shell out (*infml*), invest, lay out, splash out (*infml*), waste, squander, fritter, expend, consume, use up, exhaust.

2 spend time/the day: pass, fill, occupy, use, employ, apply, devote.

◨1 save, hoard.

spendthrift *adjective*

extravagant, improvident (*fml*), prodigal, wasteful.

sphere *noun*

1 a golden sphere: ball, globe, orb.

2 not within its sphere of influence: domain, realm, province, department, territory, field, range, scope, compass, rank, function, capacity.

spherical *adjective*

round, rotund, ball-shaped, globe-shaped.

spicy *adjective*

piquant, hot, pungent, tangy, seasoned, aromatic, fragrant.

◨bland, insipid.

spike *noun*

point, prong, tine, spine, barb, nail, stake.

spill *verb*

overturn, upset, slop, overflow, disgorge, pour, tip, discharge, shed, scatter.

spin *verb*

turn, revolve, rotate, twist, gyrate, twirl, pirouette, wheel, whirl, swirl, reel.

◆**spin out** prolong, protract, extend, lengthen, amplify, pad out.

▶ *noun*

1 a spin of the wheel: turn, revolution, twist, gyration, twirl, pirouette, whirl, swirl.

2 get in a spin: commotion, agitation, panic, flap (*infml*), state (*infml*), tizzy (*infml*).

3 go for a spin: drive, ride, run.

spine *noun*

1 curvature of the spine: backbone, spinal column, vertebral column, vertebrae.

2 a porcupine's spines: horn, barb, prickle, bristle, quill.

spineless *adjective*

weak, feeble, irresolute, ineffective, cowardly, faint-hearted, lily-livered, yellow (*infml*), soft (*infml*), wet, submissive, weak-kneed.

◨strong, brave.

spiral *adjective*

winding, coiled, corkscrew, helical, whorled, scrolled, circular.

▶ *noun*

coil, helix, corkscrew, screw, whorl, convolution.

spirit *noun*

1 balm for the spirit: soul, psyche, mind, breath, life.

2 haunted by spirits: ghost, spectre, phantom, apparition, angel, demon, fairy, sprite.

3 have a lot of spirit: liveliness, vivacity, animation, sparkle, vigour, energy, zest, fire, ardour, motivation, enthusiasm, zeal, enterprise, resolution, willpower, courage, backbone, mettle.

4 the spirit of the law: meaning, sense, substance, essence, gist, tenor, character, quality.

5 in good spirits: mood, humour, temper, disposition, temperament, feeling, morale, attitude, outlook.

spirited *adjective*
lively, vivacious, animated, sparkling, high-spirited, vigorous, energetic, active, ardent, zealous, bold, courageous, mettlesome, plucky, feisty (*infml*).
F∃spiritless, lethargic, cowardly.

spiritual *adjective*
unworldly, incorporeal (*fml*), immaterial, otherworldly, heavenly, divine, holy, sacred, religious, ecclesiastical.
F∃physical, material.

spit *verb*
expectorate, eject, discharge, splutter, hiss.

spite *noun*
spitefulness, malice, venom, gall, bitterness, rancour, animosity, ill feeling, grudge, malevolence, malignity, ill nature, hate, hatred.
F∃goodwill, compassion, affection.

spiteful *adjective*
malicious, venomous, catty, snide, barbed, cruel, vindictive, vengeful, malevolent, malignant, ill-natured, ill-disposed, nasty.
F∃charitable, affectionate.

splash *verb*
1 *splashing in the water/splashed over the edge of the bucket*: bathe, wallow, paddle, wade, dabble, plunge, wet, wash, shower, spray, squirt, sprinkle, spatter, splatter, splodge (*infml*), spread, daub, plaster, slop, slosh, plop, surge, break, dash, strike, buffet.
2 *splashed the story all over the front page*: publicize, flaunt, blazon, trumpet.
▸ *noun*
1 *a splash of colour*: spot, patch, splatter, splodge, burst, touch, dash.
2 *make a splash in the tabloid press*: publicity, display, ostentation, effect, impact, stir, excitement, sensation.

splendid *adjective*
brilliant, dazzling, glittering, lustrous, bright, radiant, glowing, glorious, magnificent, gorgeous, resplendent, sumptuous, luxurious, lavish, rich, fine, grand, stately, imposing, impressive, great, outstanding, remarkable, exceptional, sublime, supreme, superb, excellent, first-class, wonderful, marvellous, admirable.
F∃drab, ordinary, run-of-the-mill.

splendour *noun*
brightness, radiance, brilliance, dazzle, lustre, glory, resplendence, magnificence, richness, grandeur, majesty, solemnity, pomp, ceremony, display, show, spectacle.
F∃drabness, squalor.

splinter *noun*
sliver, shiver, chip, shard, fragment, flake, shaving, paring.
▸ *verb*
split, fracture, smash, shatter, shiver, fragment, disintegrate.

split *noun*
1 *a split in the rock*: division, separation, partition, break, breach, gap, cleft, crevice, crack, fissure, rupture, tear, rent, rip, rift, slit, slash.
2 *a split in the party/church*: schism, disunion, dissension, discord, difference, divergence, break-up.
▸ *adjective*
divided, cleft, cloven, bisected, dual, twofold, broken, fractured, cracked, ruptured.
▸ *verb*
divide, separate, partition, part, disunite, disband, open, gape, fork, diverge, break, splinter, shiver, snap, crack, burst, rupture, tear, rend, rip, slit, slash, cleave, halve, slice up, share, distribute, parcel out.
◆**split up** part, part company, disband, break up, separate, divorce.

spoil *verb*
1 *spoiled his good looks*: mar, upset, wreck, ruin, destroy, damage, impair, harm, hurt, injure, deface, disfigure, blemish.
2 *spoil the child*: indulge, pamper, cosset, coddle, mollycoddle, baby, spoon-feed.
3 *food will spoil in this heat*: deteriorate, go bad, go off, sour, turn, curdle, decay, decompose.

spongy *adjective*
soft, cushioned, yielding, elastic, springy, porous, absorbent, light.

sponsor *noun*
patron, backer, angel (*infml*), promoter, underwriter, guarantor, surety.
▶ *verb*
finance, fund, bankroll, subsidize, patronize, back, promote, underwrite, guarantee.

spontaneous *adjective*
natural, unforced, untaught, instinctive, impulsive, unpremeditated, free, willing, unhesitating, voluntary, unprompted, impromptu, extempore.
🖃 forced, studied, planned, deliberate.

sport *noun*
1 the sport of kings/enjoy several sports: exercise, activity, pastime, amusement, entertainment, diversion, recreation, play.

Sports include:

badminton, fives, lacrosse, ping-pong (*infml*), squash, table-tennis, tennis; American football, Australian rules football, baseball, basketball, billiards, boules, bowls, cricket, croquet, football, Gaelic football, golf, handball, hockey, hurling, netball, pétanque, pitch and putt, polo, pool, putting, rounders, Rugby, shinty, snooker, soccer, tenpin bowling, volleyball; athletics, cross-country, decathlon, discus, high-jump, hurdling, javelin, long-jump, marathon, pentathlon, pole vault, running, shot put, triple-jump; angling, canoeing, diving, fishing, rowing, sailing, skin-diving, surfing, swimming, synchronized swimming, water polo, water-skiing, windsurfing, yachting; bobsleigh, curling, ice-hockey, ice-skating, skiing, snowboarding, speed skating, tobogganing (luging); aerobics, aqua aerobics, fencing, gymnastics, jogging, keep-fit, roller-skating, trampolining; archery, darts, quoits; boxing, judo, jujitsu, karate, tae kwon do, weightlifting, wrestling; climbing, mountaineering, orienteering, pot-holing, rock-climbing, walking; cycle racing, drag-racing, go-karting, greyhound racing, motor racing, speedway racing, stock-car racing; clay-pigeon shooting, shooting; horse-racing, hunting, show-jumping; gliding, paragliding, sky-diving.

sporting *adjective*
sportsmanlike, gentlemanly, decent, considerate, fair.
🖃 unsporting, ungentlemanly, unfair.

sporty *adjective*
1 she's very sporty/a sporty type: athletic, fit, energetic, outdoor.
2 a sporty little car/a sporty jacket: stylish, trendy (*infml*), jaunty, natty (*infml*), snazzy (*infml*), showy, loud, flashy, casual, informal.

2 (*fml*) made sport of him: fun, mirth, humour, joking, jesting, banter, teasing, mockery, ridicule.

sporting *adjective*
sportsmanlike, gentlemanly, decent, considerate, fair.
🖃 unsporting, ungentlemanly, unfair.

sporty *adjective*
1 she's very sporty/a sporty type: athletic, fit, energetic, outdoor.
2 a sporty little car/a sporty jacket: stylish, trendy (*infml*), jaunty, natty (*infml*), snazzy (*infml*), showy, loud, flashy, casual, informal.

spot *noun*
1 spots of blood/colour: dot, speckle, fleck, mark, speck, blotch, blot, smudge, daub, splash, stain, discoloration.
2 a spot on her chin: pimple, blemish, flaw, zit (*slang*).
3 find a secluded spot: place, point, position, situation, location, site, scene, locality.
4 (*infml*) in a tight spot: plight, predicament, quandary, difficulty, trouble, mess.
▶ *verb*
see, notice, observe, detect, discern, identify, recognize.

spotless *adjective*
immaculate, clean, gleaming, spick and span, unmarked, unstained, unblemished, unsullied, pure, chaste,

virgin, untouched, innocent,
blameless, faultless, irreproachable.
F3 dirty, impure.

spotted *adjective*
dotted, speckled, flecked, mottled,
dappled, pied.

spotty *adjective*
pimply, pimpled, blotchy, spotted.

spout *verb*
jet, spurt, squirt, spray, shoot, gush,
stream, surge, erupt, emit, discharge.

sprawl *verb*
spread, straggle, trail, ramble, flop,
slump, slouch, loll, lounge, recline,
repose.

spray[1] *verb*
spraying water everywhere: shower,
spatter, sprinkle, scatter, diffuse, wet,
drench.
▶ *noun*
1 *a fine salt spray*: moisture, drizzle,
mist, foam, froth.
2 *paint sold in sprays*: aerosol,
atomizer, sprinkler.

spray[2] *noun*
a spray of apple blossom: sprig,
branch, corsage, posy, bouquet,
garland, wreath.

spread *verb*
1 *spreading outwards*: stretch, extend,
sprawl, broaden, widen, dilate, expand,
swell, mushroom, proliferate, escalate.
2 *spreading its wings/sails*: open,
unroll, unfurl, unfold, fan out, cover,
lay out, arrange.
3 *spreading panic/disease/gossip*:
scatter, strew, diffuse, radiate,
disseminate, broadcast, transmit,
communicate, promulgate, propagate,
publicize, advertise, publish, circulate,
distribute.
F3 **1** contract. **2** fold, furl. **3** suppress.
▶ *noun*
1 *the spread of its wings*: stretch,
reach, span, extent, expanse, sweep,
compass.
2 *the spread of disease*: advance,
development, expansion, increase,
proliferation, escalation, diffusion,
dissemination, dispersion.

sprightly *adjective*
agile, nimble, spry, active, energetic,

lively, spirited, vivacious, hearty, brisk,
jaunty, cheerful, blithe, airy.
F3 doddering, inactive, lifeless.

spring[1] *verb*
1 *spring back/spring to his feet*: jump,
leap, vault, bound, hop, bounce,
rebound, recoil.
2 *springing from the earth*: originate,
derive, come, stem, arise, start,
proceed, issue, emerge, emanate,
appear, sprout, grow, develop.
▶ *noun*
1 *sudden spring into the air*: jump,
leap, vault, bound.
2 *need a bed with a more spring in it/
had a spring in his step*: springiness,
resilience, give, flexibility, elasticity,
bounce, buoyancy.

spring[2] *noun*
hot springs: source, origin, beginning,
cause, root, fountainhead, wellhead,
wellspring, well, geyser, spa.

springy *adjective*
bouncy, resilient, flexible, elastic,
stretchy, rubbery, spongy, buoyant.
F3 hard, stiff.

sprinkle *verb*
shower, spray, spatter, scatter, strew,
dot, pepper, dust, powder.

sprint *verb*
run, race, dash, tear, belt (*infml*), dart,
shoot.

sprout *verb*
shoot, bud, germinate, grow, develop,
come up, spring up.

spruce *adjective*
smart, elegant, neat, trim, dapper,
well-dressed, well-turned-out, well-
groomed, sleek.
F3 scruffy, untidy.
◆ **spruce up** neaten, tidy, smarten up,
groom.

spur *verb*
goad, prod, poke, prick, stimulate,
prompt, incite, drive, propel, impel,
urge, encourage, motivate.
F3 curb, discourage.
▶ *noun*
incentive, encouragement,
inducement, motive, stimulus,
incitement, impetus, fillip.
F3 curb, disincentive.

spurious *adjective*
false, fake, counterfeit, forged, bogus, phoney (*infml*), mock, sham, feigned, pretended, simulated, imitation, artificial.
F3 genuine, authentic, real.

spurt *verb*
gush, squirt, jet, shoot, burst, erupt, surge.

spy *noun*
secret agent, undercover agent, double agent, mole (*infml*), fifth columnist, scout, snooper.
► *verb*
spot, glimpse, notice, observe, discover.

squabble *verb*
bicker, wrangle, quarrel, row, argue, dispute, clash, brawl, scrap, fight.

squalid *adjective*
dirty, filthy, unclean, foul, disgusting, repulsive, sordid, seedy, dingy, untidy, slovenly, unkempt, broken-down, run-down, neglected, uncared-for, low, mean, nasty.
F3 clean, pleasant, attractive.

squander *verb*
waste, misspend, misuse, lavish, blow (*infml*), fritter away, throw away, dissipate, scatter, spend, expend, consume.

square *verb*
settle, reconcile, tally, agree, accord, harmonize, correspond, match, balance, straighten, level, align, adjust, regulate, adapt, tailor, fit, suit.
► *adjective*
1 **a square edge**: quadrilateral, rectangular, right-angled, perpendicular, straight, true, even, level.
2 **a square deal**: fair, equitable, just, ethical, honourable, honest, genuine, above board, on the level (*infml*).

squash *verb*
1 **squashed the tomatoes**: crush, flatten, press, squeeze, compress, crowd, trample, stamp, pound, pulp, smash, distort.
2 **squashing any protest/his ego**: suppress, silence, quell, quash, annihilate, put down, snub, humiliate.
F3 1 stretch, expand.

squat *verb*
crouch, stoop, bend, sit.
► *adjective*
short, stocky, thickset, dumpy, chunky, stubby.
F3 slim, lanky.

squeak *verb, noun*
squeal, whine, creak, peep, cheep.

squeal *verb, noun*
cry, shout, yell, yelp, wail, scream, screech, shriek, squawk.

squeamish *adjective*
queasy, nauseated, sick, delicate, fastidious, particular, prudish.

squeeze *verb*
1 **squeeze a lemon/squeezing her tight**: press, squash, crush, pinch, nip, compress, grip, clasp, clutch, hug, embrace, enfold, cuddle.
2 **squeeze into a corner**: cram, stuff, pack, crowd, wedge, jam, force, ram, push, thrust, shove, jostle.
3 **squeeze information/money out of**: wring, wrest (*fml*), extort, milk, bleed, force, lean on (*infml*).
► *noun*
press, squash, crush, crowd, congestion, jam.

squirt *verb*
spray, spurt, jet, shoot, spout, gush, discharge, emit, eject, expel.

stab *verb*
pierce, puncture, cut, wound, injure, gore, knife, spear, stick, jab, thrust.
► *noun*
1 **felt a stab of pain**: ache, pang, twinge, prick, puncture, cut, incision, gash, wound, jab.
2 (*infml*) **have a stab at it**: try, attempt, endeavour, bash (*infml*).

stable *adjective*
steady, firm, secure, fast, sound, sure, constant, steadfast, reliable, established, well-founded, deep-rooted, strong, sturdy, durable, lasting, enduring, abiding, permanent, unchangeable, unalterable, invariable, immutable, fixed, static, balanced.
F3 unstable, wobbly, shaky, weak.

stack *noun*
heap, pile, mound, mass, load,

accumulation, hoard, stockpile.
▸ *verb*
heap, pile, load, amass, accumulate, assemble, gather, save, hoard, stockpile.

staff *noun*
personnel, workforce, employees, workers, crew, team, teachers, officers.

stage *noun*
point, juncture, step, phase, period, division, lap, leg, length, level, floor.
▸ *verb*
mount, put on, present, produce, give, do, perform, arrange, organize, stage-manage, orchestrate, engineer.

stagger *verb*
1 staggering to its feet: lurch, totter, teeter, wobble, sway, rock, reel, falter, hesitate, waver.
2 the price staggered me: surprise, amaze, astound, astonish, stun, stupefy, dumbfound, flabbergast (*infml*), shake, shock, confound, overwhelm.

stagnant *adjective*
still, motionless, standing, brackish, stale, sluggish, torpid, lethargic.
F∃ fresh, moving.

stagnate *verb*
vegetate, idle, languish, decline, deteriorate, degenerate, decay, rot, rust.

staid *adjective*
sedate, calm, composed, sober, demure, solemn, serious, grave, quiet, steady.
F∃ jaunty, debonair, frivolous, adventurous.

stain *verb*
1 stained the tablecloth/his reputation: mark, spot, blemish, blot, smudge, discolour, dirty, soil, taint, contaminate, sully (*fml*), tarnish, blacken, disgrace.
2 stained her hair/lips/fingernails red: dye, tint, tinge, colour, paint, varnish.
▸ *noun*
mark, spot, blemish, blot, smudge, discoloration, smear, slur, disgrace, shame, dishonour.

stake *noun*
1 a major stake in the football club:

bet, wager, pledge, interest, concern, involvement, share, investment, claim.
2 a stake supporting a sapling: cane, post, pole.
▸ *verb*
gamble, bet, wager, pledge, risk, chance, hazard, venture.

stale *adjective*
1 stale bread: dry, hard, old, musty, fusty, flat, insipid, tasteless.
2 stale phrases: overused, hackneyed, clichéd, stereotyped, jaded, worn-out, unoriginal, trite, banal, commonplace.
F∃ 1 crisp. 2 new.

stalemate *noun*
draw, tie, deadlock, impasse, standstill, halt.
F∃ progress.

stalk[1] *verb*
stalking its prey: track, trail, hunt, follow, pursue, shadow, tail, haunt.

stalk[2] *noun*
stalks of corn: stem, twig, branch, trunk.

stall *verb*
play for time, delay, hedge, equivocate, obstruct, stonewall, temporize.

stalwart *adjective*
strong, sturdy, robust, rugged, stout, strapping, muscular, athletic, vigorous, valiant, daring, intrepid, indomitable, determined, resolute, staunch, steadfast, reliable, dependable.
F∃ weak, feeble, timid.

stamina *noun*
energy, vigour, strength, power, force, grit, resilience, resistance, endurance, indefatigability, staying power.
F∃ weakness.

stammer *verb*
stutter, stumble, falter, hesitate, splutter.

stamp *verb*
1 horse stamped on my foot: trample, crush, beat, pound.
2 stamping his passport: imprint, impress, print, inscribe, engrave, emboss, mark.
3 stamping them as terrorists: brand, label, categorize, identify, characterize.

▶ *noun*

print, imprint, impression, seal, signature, authorization, mark, hallmark, attestation, brand, cast, mould, cut, form, fashion, sort, kind, type, breed, character, description.

stampede *noun*

charge, rush, dash, sprint, flight, rout.
▶ *verb*

charge, rush, dash, tear, run, sprint, gallop, shoot, fly, flee, scatter.

stance *noun*

posture, deportment, carriage, bearing, position, standpoint, angle, viewpoint, point of view, attitude.

stand *verb*

1 *stand it in the corner*: put, place, set, erect, up-end, position, station.
2 *I can't stand it*: bear, tolerate, abide, endure, suffer, experience, undergo, withstand, weather.
3 *stand for the national anthem*: rise, get up, stand up.
▶ *noun*

base, pedestal, support, frame, rack, table, stage, platform, place, stall, booth.
◆ **stand by** support, back, champion, defend, stick up for, uphold, adhere to, hold to, stick by.
🖅 let down.
◆ **stand down** step down, resign, abdicate, quit, give up, retire, withdraw.
🖅 join.
◆ **stand for** represent, symbolize, mean, signify, denote, indicate.
◆ **stand in for** deputize for, cover for, understudy, replace, substitute for.
◆ **stand out** show, catch the eye, stick out, jut out, project.
◆ **stand up for** defend, stick up for, side with, fight for, support, protect, champion, uphold.
🖅 attack.
◆ **stand up to** defy, oppose, resist, withstand, endure, face, confront, brave.
🖅 give in to.

standard *noun*

1 *not up to their usual standard*: norm, average, type, model, pattern, example, sample, guideline, benchmark, touchstone, yardstick, rule, measure, gauge, level, criterion, requirement, specification, grade, quality.
2 *the royal standard*: flag, ensign, pennant, pennon, colours, banner.
▶ *adjective*

normal, average, typical, stock, classic, basic, staple, usual, customary, popular, prevailing, regular, approved, accepted, recognized, official, orthodox, set, established, definitive.
🖅 abnormal, unusual, irregular.

standardize *verb*

normalize, equalize, homogenize, stereotype, mass-produce.
🖅 differentiate.

standards *noun*

principles, ideals, morals, ethics.

standpoint *noun*

position, station, vantage point, stance, viewpoint, angle, point of view.

standstill *noun*

stop, halt, pause, lull, rest, stoppage, jam, log-jam, hold-up, impasse, deadlock, stalemate.
🖅 advance, progress.

staple *adjective*

basic, fundamental, primary, key, main, chief, major, principal, essential, necessary, standard.
🖅 minor.

star *noun*

celebrity, personage, luminary, idol, lead, leading man, leading lady, superstar.

stare *verb*

gaze, look, watch, gape, gawp, gawk, goggle, glare.

stark *adjective*

1 *a stark landscape/the stark truth*: bare, barren, bleak, bald, plain, simple, austere, harsh, severe, grim, dreary, gloomy, depressing.
2 *stark nonsense*: utter, unmitigated, total, consummate, absolute, sheer, downright, out-and-out, flagrant, arrant.

start *verb*

1 *start a business/walking/the singing*: begin, commence, originate, initiate, introduce, pioneer, create,

found, establish, set up, institute,
inaugurate, launch, open, kick off
(*infml*), instigate, activate, trigger, set off,
set out, leave, depart, appear, arise, issue.
2 started at the sudden noise: jump,
jerk, twitch, flinch, recoil.
F3 1 stop, finish, end.
▶ *noun*
1 the start of business: beginning,
commencement, outset, inception,
dawn, birth, break, outburst, onset,
origin, initiation, introduction,
foundation, inauguration, launch,
opening, kick-off (*infml*).
2 gave a start: jump, jerk, twitch,
spasm, convulsion.
F3 1 stop, finish, end.

startle *verb*
surprise, amaze, astonish, astound,
shock, scare, frighten, alarm, agitate,
upset, disturb.
F3 calm.

starving *adjective*
hungry, underfed, undernourished,
ravenous, famished.

state *verb*
say, declare, announce, report,
communicate, assert, aver, affirm,
specify, present, express, put,
formulate, articulate, voice.
▶ *noun*
1 his state of health: condition, shape,
situation, position, circumstances,
case.
2 co-operation between states:
nation, country, land, territory,
kingdom, republic, government.
3 (*infml*) **got into a state**: panic, flap
(*infml*), tizzy (*infml*), bother, plight,
predicament.
4 lie in state: pomp, ceremony, dignity,
majesty, grandeur, glory, splendour.
▶ *adjective*
national, governmental, public, official,
formal, ceremonial, pompous, stately.

stately *adjective*
grand, imposing, impressive, elegant,
majestic, regal, royal, imperial, noble,
august, lofty, pompous, dignified,
measured, deliberate, solemn,
ceremonious.
F3 informal, unimpressive.

statement *noun*
account, report, bulletin,
communiqué, announcement,
declaration, proclamation,
communication, utterance, testimony.

static *adjective*
stationary, motionless, immobile,
unmoving, still, inert, resting, fixed,
constant, changeless, unvarying,
stable.
F3 dynamic, mobile, varying.

station *noun*
place, location, position, post,
headquarters, base, depot.
▶ *verb*
locate, set, establish, install, garrison,
post, send, appoint, assign.

stationary *adjective*
motionless, immobile, unmoving, still,
static, inert, standing, resting, parked,
moored, fixed.
F3 mobile, moving, active.

statue *noun*
figure, head, bust, effigy, idol, statuette,
carving, bronze.

status *noun*
rank, grade, degree, level, class,
station, standing, position, state,
condition, prestige, eminence,
distinction, importance, consequence,
weight.
F3 unimportance, insignificance.

staunch *adjective*
loyal, faithful, hearty, strong, stout,
firm, sound, sure, true, trusty, reliable,
dependable, steadfast.
F3 unfaithful, weak, unreliable.

stay *verb*
1 staying the same: continue, endure,
abide (*fml*), remain, linger, persist.
2 stay in London: reside, dwell, live,
settle, sojourn (*fml*).
F3 1 go, leave.
▶ *noun*
visit, holiday, stopover, sojourn (*fml*).

steady *adjective*
stable, balanced, poised, fixed,
immovable, firm, settled, still, calm,
imperturbable, equable, even, uniform,
consistent, unvarying, unchanging,
constant, persistent, unremitting,
incessant, uninterrupted, unbroken,

regular, rhythmic, steadfast, unwavering.
E3 unsteady, unstable, variable, wavering.
▸ *verb*
balance, stabilize, fix, secure, brace, support.

steal *verb*
1 *steal a car/his ideas*: thieve, pilfer, filch, pinch (*infml*), nick (*infml*), take, appropriate, snatch, swipe, shoplift, poach, embezzle, lift, plagiarize.
2 *steal out of the room*: creep, tiptoe, slip, slink, sneak.
E3 1 return, give back.

stealthy *adjective*
surreptitious, clandestine, covert, secret, unobtrusive, secretive, quiet, furtive, sly, cunning, sneaky, underhand.
E3 open.

steam *noun*
vapour, mist, haze, condensation, moisture, dampness.

steep *adjective*
1 *a steep slope*: sheer, precipitous, headlong, abrupt, sudden, sharp.
2 (*infml*) *prices are a little too steep for me*: excessive, extreme, stiff, unreasonable, high, exorbitant, extortionate, overpriced.
E3 1 gentle, gradual. 2 moderate, low.

steer *verb*
pilot, guide, direct, control, govern, conduct.

stem[1] *noun*
the main stem of the shrub: stalk, shoot, stock, branch, trunk.

stem[2] *verb*
stem the flow of refugees: stop, halt, arrest, stanch, staunch, block, dam, check, curb, restrain, contain, resist, oppose.

step *noun*
1 *take a step back/heard his step on the stairs*: pace, stride, footstep, tread, footprint, print, trace, track.
2 *what's the next step?*: move, act, action, deed, measure, procedure, process, proceeding, progression, movement, stage, phase, degree.
3 *the next step up*: rung, stair, level, rank, point.

▸ *verb*
pace, stride, tread, stamp, walk, move.
◆ **step down** stand down, resign, abdicate, quit, leave, retire, withdraw.
E3 join.
◆ **step up** increase, raise, augment, boost, build up, intensify, escalate, accelerate, speed up.
E3 decrease.

stereotype *verb*
categorize, pigeonhole, typecast, standardize, formalize, conventionalize, mass-produce.
E3 differentiate.

sterile *adjective*
1 *operate in sterile conditions*: germ-free, aseptic, sterilized, disinfected, antiseptic, uncontaminated.
2 *a sterile plant/a sterile argument*: infertile, barren, arid, bare, unproductive, fruitless, pointless, useless, abortive.
E3 1 septic, contaminated. 2 fertile, fruitful.

sterilize *verb*
disinfect, fumigate, purify, clean, cleanse.
E3 contaminate, infect.

stern *adjective*
strict, severe, authoritarian, rigid, inflexible, unyielding, hard, tough, rigorous, stringent, harsh, cruel, unsparing, relentless, unrelenting, grim, forbidding, stark, austere.
E3 kind, gentle, mild, lenient.

stew *verb*
boil, simmer, braise, casserole.

stick[1] *verb*
1 *sticking his head through the window*: thrust, poke, stab, jab, pierce, penetrate, puncture, spear, transfix.
2 *sticking the two edges together*: glue, gum, paste, cement, bond, fuse, weld, solder, adhere, cling, hold.
3 *mud sticking to his clothes*: attach, affix, fasten, secure, fix, pin, join, bind.
4 *stick it down over there*: put, place, position, set, install, deposit, drop.
◆ **stick at** persevere, plug away (*infml*), persist, continue.
E3 give up.

◆**stick out** protrude, jut out, project, extend.

◆**stick up for** stand up for, speak up for, defend, champion, support, uphold.

F3attack.

stick² *noun*
gather sticks for a fire: branch, twig, wand, baton, staff, sceptre, cane, birch, rod, pole, stake.

sticky *adjective*
1 a sticky substance: adhesive, gummed, tacky, gluey, gummy, viscous, glutinous, gooey (*infml*).
2 (*infml*) a sticky situation: difficult, tricky, thorny, unpleasant, awkward, embarrassing, delicate.
3 weather was hot and sticky: humid, clammy, muggy, close, oppressive, sultry.

F3 1 dry. 2 easy. 3 fresh, cool.

stiff *adjective*
1 stiff joints: rigid, inflexible, unbending, unyielding, hard, solid, hardened, solidified, firm, tight, taut, tense.
2 his manner was very stiff: formal, ceremonious, pompous, stand-offish, cold, prim, priggish, austere, strict, severe, harsh.
3 a stiff test: difficult, hard, tough, arduous, laborious, awkward, exacting, rigorous.

F3 1 flexible. 2 informal. 3 easy.

stiffen *verb*
harden, solidify, tighten, tense, brace, reinforce, starch, thicken, congeal, coagulate, jell, set.

stifle *verb*
smother, suffocate, asphyxiate, strangle, choke, extinguish, muffle, dampen, deaden, silence, hush, suppress, quell, check, curb, restrain, repress.

F3encourage.

stigma *noun*
brand, mark, stain, blot, spot, blemish, disgrace, shame, dishonour.

F3credit, honour.

still *adjective*
stationary, motionless, lifeless, stagnant, smooth, undisturbed,
unruffled, calm, tranquil, serene, restful, peaceful, hushed, quiet, silent, noiseless.

F3active, disturbed, agitated, noisy.
▶ *verb*
calm, soothe, allay, tranquillize, subdue, restrain, hush, quieten, silence, pacify, settle, smooth.

F3agitate, stir up.
▶ *adverb*
yet, even so, nevertheless, nonetheless, notwithstanding, however.

stilted *adjective*
artificial, unnatural, stiff, wooden, forced, constrained.

F3fluent, flowing.

stimulate *verb*
rouse, arouse, animate, quicken (*fml*), fire, inflame, inspire, motivate, encourage, induce, urge, impel, spur, prompt, goad, provoke, incite, instigate, trigger off.

F3discourage, hinder, prevent.

stimulus *noun*
incentive, encouragement, inducement, spur, goad, provocation, incitement.

F3discouragement.

sting *verb*
1 bee stung him on the nose: bite, prick, hurt, injure, wound.
2 eyes were stinging with the smoke: smart, tingle, burn, pain.
▶ *noun*
bite, nip, prick, smart, tingle.

stingy *adjective*
mean, miserly, niggardly, tight-fisted (*infml*), parsimonious, penny-pinching.

F3generous, liberal.

stink *verb*
smell, reek, pong (*infml*), hum (*infml*).
▶ *noun*
smell, odour, stench, pong (*infml*), niff (*infml*).

stint *noun*
spell, stretch, period, time, shift, turn, bit, share, quota.

stir *verb*
1 breeze stirring the leaves: move, budge, touch, affect, inspire, excite, thrill, disturb, agitate, shake, tremble,

quiver, flutter, rustle.
2 stir the cake mixture: mix, blend, beat.

◆ **stir up** rouse, arouse, awaken, animate, quicken (*fml*), kindle, fire, inflame, stimulate, spur, prompt, provoke, incite, instigate, agitate.
F3 calm, discourage.

stock *noun*
1 put new stock on the shelves/a good stock of tinned food: goods, merchandise, wares, commodities, capital, assets, inventory, repertoire, range, variety, assortment, source, supply, fund, reservoir, store, reserve, stockpile, hoard.
2 of Welsh and Irish stock: parentage, ancestry, descent, extraction, family, line, lineage, pedigree, race, breed, species, blood.
3 the farmer's stock: livestock, animals, cattle, horses, sheep, herds, flocks.
▶ *adjective*
standard, basic, regular, routine, ordinary, run-of-the-mill, usual, customary, traditional, conventional, set, stereotyped, hackneyed, overused, banal, trite.
F3 original, unusual.
▶ *verb*
keep, carry, sell, trade in, deal in, handle, supply, provide.

◆ **stock up** gather, accumulate, amass, lay in, provision, fill, replenish, store (up), save, hoard, pile up.

stocky *adjective*
sturdy, solid, thickset, chunky, short, squat, dumpy, stubby.
F3 tall, skinny.

stoical *adjective*
patient, long-suffering, uncomplaining, resigned, philosophical, indifferent, impassive, unemotional, phlegmatic, dispassionate, cool, calm, imperturbable.
F3 excitable, anxious.

stomach *noun*
tummy (*infml*), gut, inside(s), belly, abdomen, paunch, pot.

▶ *verb*
tolerate, bear, stand, abide, endure, suffer, submit to, take.

stony *adjective*
1 a stony expression/silence: blank, expressionless, hard, cold, frigid, icy, indifferent, unfeeling, heartless, callous, merciless, pitiless, inexorable, hostile.
2 stony beach: pebbly, shingly, rocky.
F3 1 warm, soft-hearted, friendly.

stoop *verb*
1 he stooped to get under the low fence: hunch, bow, bend, incline, lean, duck, squat, crouch.
2 even stooped to blackmail: descend, sink, lower oneself, resort, go so far as, condescend, deign.

stop *verb*
1 stop shouting/stop the train: halt, cease, end, finish, conclude, terminate, discontinue, suspend, interrupt, quit, pause, refrain, desist, pack in (*infml*).
2 stop him entering: prevent, bar, frustrate, thwart, intercept, hinder, impede, check, restrain.
3 stop up the hole in the pipe/stop the bleeding: seal, close, plug, block, obstruct, arrest, stem, stanch.
F3 1 start, continue.
▶ *noun*
1 get off at the next stop: station, terminus, destination.
2 a short stop: rest, break, pause, stage.
3 come to a stop: halt, standstill, stoppage, cessation, end, finish, conclusion, termination, discontinuation.
F3 3 start, beginning, continuation.

stoppage *noun*
stop, halt, standstill, arrest, blockage, obstruction, check, hindrance, interruption, shutdown, closure, strike, walk-out, sit-in.
F3 start, continuation.

stopper *noun*
cork, bung, plug.

store *verb*
save, keep, put aside, lay by, reserve, stock, lay in, deposit, lay down, lay up, accumulate, hoard, salt away,

stockpile, stash (*infml*).

F3 use.

▶ *noun*

1 a good store of food for the winter:
stock, supply, provision, fund, reserve,
mine, reservoir, hoard, cache,
stockpile, accumulation, quantity,
abundance, plenty, lot.

2 keep all the old files in the store:
storeroom, storehouse, warehouse,
repository, depository.

F3 1 scarcity.

storey *noun*
floor, level, stage, tier, flight, deck.

storm *noun*

1 winter storms: tempest,
thunderstorm, squall, blizzard, gale,
hurricane, whirlwind, tornado,
cyclone.

Kinds of storm include:

blizzard, buran, cloudburst, cyclone,
downpour, dust devil, dust storm,
electrical storm, gale, haboob,
hailstorm, hurricane, ice storm,
monsoon, rainstorm, sand storm,
snow storm, squall, tempest,
thunderstorm, tornado, typhoon,
whirlwind.

2 a storm of protest: outburst, uproar,
furore, outcry, row, rumpus,
commotion, tumult, disturbance,
turmoil, stir, agitation, rage, outbreak,
attack, assault.

F3 2 calm.

verb
charge, rush, attack, assault, assail,
roar, thunder, rage, rant, rave, fume.

stormy *adjective*
tempestuous, squally, rough, choppy,
turbulent, wild, raging, windy, gusty,
blustery, foul.

F3 calm.

story *noun*

1 tell us a story/write a story: tale,
fairy tale, fable, myth, legend, novel,
romance, fiction, yarn, anecdote,
episode, plot, narrative, history,
chronicle, record, account, relation,
recital, report, article, feature.

Types of story include:

adventure story, anecdote, bedtime
story, blockbuster (*infml*), children's
story, comedy, black comedy, crime
story, detective story, fable, fairy story,
fairy tale, fantasy, folk tale, ghost
story, historical novel, horror story,
interactive story, legend, love story,
Mills & Boon®, mystery, myth, novel,
novella, parable, romance, saga,
science fiction, sci-fi (*infml*), short
story, spiel, spine-chiller, spy story,
supernatural tale, tall story, thriller,
western, whodunnit (*infml*), yarn
(*infml*). ⇨ *See also* **literature**.

2 she tells stories: lie, falsehood,
untruth, fib.

stout *adjective*

1 getting rather stout/stout arms: fat,
plump, fleshy, portly, corpulent,
overweight, heavy, bulky, big, brawny,
beefy, hulking, burly, muscular,
athletic.

2 stout packaging: strong, tough,
durable, thick, sturdy, robust, hardy,
vigorous.

3 a stout defence: brave, courageous,
valiant, plucky, fearless, bold, intrepid,
dauntless, resolute, stalwart.

F3 1 thin, lean, slim. **2** weak.
3 cowardly, timid.

stow *verb*
put away, store, load, pack, cram, stuff,
stash (*infml*).

F3 unload.

straight *adjective*

1 a straight line: level, even, flat,
horizontal, upright, vertical, aligned,
direct, undeviating, unswerving, true,
right.

2 keep things straight: tidy, neat,
orderly, shipshape, organized.

3 he's absolutely straight: honourable,
honest, law-abiding, respectable,
upright, trustworthy, reliable,
straightforward, fair, just.

4 a straight answer: frank, candid,
blunt, forthright, direct.

5 straight whisky: undiluted, neat,
unadulterated, unmixed.

E∃1 bent, crooked. **2** untidy. **3** bent (*infml*), dishonest. **4** evasive. **5** diluted.
▶ *adverb*

directly, point-blank, honestly, frankly, candidly.

◆**straight away** at once, immediately, instantly, right away, directly, now, there and then.
E∃later, eventually.

straighten   *verb*
unbend, align, tidy, neaten, order, arrange.
E∃bend, twist.

◆**straighten out** clear up, sort out, settle, resolve, correct, rectify, disentangle, regularize.
E∃confuse, muddle.

straightforward   *adjective*
1 first part of the exam was quite straightforward: easy, simple, uncomplicated, clear, elementary.
2 a very straightforward person: honest, truthful, sincere, genuine, open, frank, candid, direct, forthright.
E∃1 complicated. **2** evasive, devious.

strain¹   *verb*
1 strain a muscle: pull, wrench, twist, sprain, tear, stretch, extend, tighten, tauten.
2 strain the gravy: sieve, sift, screen, separate, filter, purify, drain, wring, squeeze, compress, express.
3 don't strain yourself: weaken, tire, tax, overtax, overwork, labour, try, endeavour, struggle, strive, exert, force, drive.
▶ *noun*

stress, anxiety, burden, pressure, tension, tautness, pull, sprain, wrench, injury, exertion, effort, struggle, force.
E∃relaxation.

strain²   *noun*
1 a different strain of the virus: stock, ancestry, descent, extraction, family, lineage, pedigree, blood, variety, type.
2 has a strain of black humour: trait, streak, vein, tendency, trace, suggestion, suspicion.

strained   *adjective*
forced, constrained, laboured, false, artificial, unnatural, stiff, tense, unrelaxed, uneasy, uncomfortable,

awkward, embarrassed, self-conscious.
E∃natural, relaxed.

strand   *noun*
fibre, filament, wire, thread, string, piece, length.

stranded   *adjective*
marooned, high and dry, abandoned, forsaken, in the lurch, helpless, aground, grounded, beached, shipwrecked, wrecked.

strange   *adjective*
1 strange feeling/behaviour: odd, peculiar, funny (*infml*), curious, queer, weird, bizarre, eccentric, abnormal, irregular, uncommon, unusual, exceptional, remarkable, extraordinary, mystifying, perplexing, unexplained.
2 visit strange places: new, novel, untried, unknown, unheard-of, unfamiliar, unacquainted, foreign, alien, exotic.
E∃1 ordinary, common. **2** well-known, familiar.

stranger   *noun*
newcomer, visitor, guest, non-member, outsider, foreigner, alien.
E∃local, native.

strangle   *noun*
throttle, choke, asphyxiate, suffocate, stifle, smother, suppress, gag, repress, inhibit.

strap   *noun*
thong, tie, band, belt, leash.

stratagem   *noun*
plan, scheme, plot, intrigue, ruse, ploy, trick, dodge, manoeuvre, device, artifice, wile, subterfuge.

strategic   *adjective*
important, key, critical, decisive, crucial, vital, tactical, planned, calculated, deliberate, politic, diplomatic.
E∃unimportant.

strategy   *noun*
tactics, planning, policy, approach, procedure, plan, programme, design, scheme.

stray   *verb*
wander (off), get lost, err, ramble, roam, rove, range, meander,

straggle, drift, diverge, deviate, digress.
▶ *adjective*
1 stray cats and dogs: lost, abandoned, homeless, wandering, roaming.
2 hit by a stray bullet: random, chance, accidental, freak, odd, erratic.

streak *noun*
line, stroke, smear, band, stripe, strip, layer, vein, trace, dash, touch, element, strain.
▶ *verb*
1 streaks of red and white: band, stripe, fleck, striate, smear, daub.
2 streaked past us: speed, tear, hurtle, sprint, gallop, fly, dart, flash, whistle, zoom, whizz, sweep.

stream *noun*
1 fishing in the stream: river, creek, brook, beck, burn, rivulet, tributary.
2 the Gulf Stream: current, drift.
3 a steady stream of letters: flow, run, gush, flood, deluge, cascade, torrent.
▶ *verb*
issue, well, surge, run, flow, course, pour, spout, gush, flood, cascade.

streamlined *adjective*
aerodynamic, smooth, sleek, graceful, efficient, well-run, smooth-running, rationalized, time-saving, organized, slick.
E3clumsy, inefficient.

strength *noun*
toughness, robustness, sturdiness, lustiness, brawn, muscle, sinew, power, might, force, vigour, energy, stamina, health, fitness, courage, fortitude, spirit, resolution, firmness, effectiveness, potency, concentration, intensity, vehemence.
E3weakness, feebleness, impotence.

strengthen *verb*
reinforce, brace, steel, fortify, buttress, bolster, support, toughen, harden, stiffen, consolidate, substantiate, corroborate, confirm, encourage, hearten, refresh, restore, invigorate, nourish, increase, heighten, intensify.
E3weaken, undermine.

strenuous *adjective*
1 strenuous work: hard, tough, demanding, gruelling, taxing,

laborious, uphill, arduous, tiring, exhausting.
2 made a strenuous effort: active, energetic, vigorous, eager, earnest, determined, resolute, spirited, tireless, indefatigable.
E3 1 easy, effortless.

stress *noun*
1 suffer from stress: pressure, strain, tension, worry, anxiety, weight, burden, trauma, hassle (*infml*).
2 putting the stress on the second syllable: emphasis, accent, accentuation, beat, force, weight, importance, significance.
E3 1 relaxation.
▶ *verb*
emphasize, accentuate, highlight, underline, underscore, repeat.
E3understate, downplay.

stretch *verb*
pull, tighten, tauten, strain, tax, extend, lengthen, elongate, expand, spread, unfold, unroll, inflate, swell, reach.
E3compress.
▶ *noun*
1 a stretch of water: expanse, spread, sweep, reach, extent, distance, space, area, tract.
2 a short stretch in prison: period, time, term, spell, stint, run.
◆ **stretch out** extend, relax, hold out, put out, lie down, reach.
E3draw back

strict *adjective*
1 a strict disciplinarian: stern, authoritarian, no-nonsense, firm, rigid, inflexible, stringent, rigorous, harsh, severe, austere.
2 strict examination of their methods: exact, precise, accurate, literal, faithful, true, absolute, utter, total, complete, thoroughgoing, meticulous, scrupulous, particular, religious.
E3 1 easy-going (*infml*), flexible. **2** loose.

strident *adjective*
loud, clamorous, vociferous, harsh, raucous, grating, rasping, shrill, screeching, unmusical, discordant, clashing, jarring, jangling.
E3quiet, soft.

strife noun
conflict, discord, dissension,
controversy, animosity, friction, rivalry,
contention, quarrel, row, wrangling,
struggle, fighting, combat, battle,
warfare.
E3 peace.

strike noun
1 go on strike: industrial action, work-
to-rule, go-slow, stoppage, sit-in, walk-
out, mutiny, revolt.
2 strikes against enemy targets: hit,
blow, stroke, raid, attack.
▶ verb
1 strike in protest: stop work, down
tools, work to rule, walk out, protest,
mutiny, revolt.
2 striking the gong: hit, knock, collide
with, slap, smack, cuff, clout, thump,
wallop (infml), beat, pound, hammer
(infml), buffet.
3 striking at the enemy: raid, attack,
afflict.
3 struck me as odd: impress, affect,
touch, register.
4 strike gold/oil: find, discover,
unearth, uncover, encounter, reach.
◆ **strike out** cross out, delete, strike
through, cancel, strike off, remove.
E3 add.

striking adjective
noticeable, conspicuous, salient,
outstanding, remarkable,
extraordinary, memorable, impressive,
dazzling, arresting, astonishing,
stunning (infml).
E3 unimpressive.

string noun
1 a piece of string: twine, cord, rope,
cable, line, strand, fibre.
2 a string of disasters: series,
succession, sequence, chain, line, row,
file, queue, procession, train.
▶ verb
thread, link, connect, tie up, hang,
suspend, festoon, loop.

stringent adjective
binding, strict, severe, rigorous, tough,
rigid, inflexible, tight.
E3 lax, flexible.

strip[1] verb
strip naked/strip the bark off the tree:

peel, skin, flay, denude, divest, deprive,
undress, disrobe, unclothe, uncover,
expose, lay bare, bare, empty, clear, gut,
ransack, pillage, plunder, loot.
E3 dress, clothe, cover.

strip[2] noun
a strip of leather: ribbon, thong, strap,
belt, sash, band, stripe, lath, slat, piece,
bit, slip, shred.

stripe noun
band, line, bar, chevron, flash, streak,
fleck, strip, belt.

strive verb
try, attempt, endeavour, struggle,
strain, work, toil, labour, fight,
contend, compete.

stroke verb
caress, fondle, pet, touch, pat, rub,
massage.
▶ noun
1 give the cat a stroke: caress, pat, rub.
2 a single stroke of the axe: blow, hit,
knock, swipe.
3 removed with a stroke of the pen:
sweep, flourish, movement, action,
move, line.

stroll verb
saunter, amble, dawdle, ramble,
wander.
▶ noun
saunter, amble, walk, constitutional,
turn, ramble.

strong adjective
1 strong shoes/arms: tough, resilient,
durable, hard-wearing, heavy-duty,
robust, sturdy, firm, sound, lusty,
strapping, stout, burly, well-built,
beefy, brawny, muscular, sinewy,
athletic, fit, healthy, hardy, powerful,
mighty, potent.
2 strong feelings/colours/support:
intense, deep, vivid, fierce, violent,
vehement, keen, eager, zealous,
fervent, ardent, dedicated, staunch,
stalwart, determined, resolute,
tenacious, strong-minded, strong-
willed, self-assertive.
3 strong taste/drink: highly-flavoured,
piquant, hot, spicy, highly-seasoned,
sharp, pungent, undiluted,
concentrated.
4 strong argument: convincing,

persuasive, cogent, effective, telling, forceful, weighty, compelling, urgent.
F3 1 weak, feeble. **2** indecisive. **3** mild, bland. **4** unconvincing.

stronghold *noun*
citadel, bastion, fort, fortress, castle, keep, refuge.

structure *noun*
construction, erection, building, edifice, fabric, framework, form, shape, design, configuration, conformation, make-up, formation, arrangement, organization, set-up.

struggle *verb*
strive, work, toil, labour, strain, agonize, fight, battle, wrestle, grapple, contend, compete, vie.
F3 yield, give in.
▶ *noun*
difficulty, problem, effort, exertion, pains, agony, work, labour, toil, clash, conflict, strife, fight, battle, skirmish, encounter, combat, hostilities, contest.
F3 ease, submission, co-operation.

stub *noun*
end, stump, remnant, counterfoil.

stubborn *adjective*
obstinate, stiff-necked, mulish, pig-headed, obdurate, intransigent, rigid, inflexible, unbending, unyielding, dogged, persistent, tenacious, headstrong, self-willed, wilful, refractory, difficult, unmanageable.
F3 compliant, flexible, yielding.

stuck *adjective*
1 door is stuck: fast, jammed, firm, fixed, fastened, joined, glued, cemented.
2 stuck for an answer: beaten, stumped (*infml*), baffled.
F3 1 loose.

stuck-up *adjective* (*infml*)
snobbish, toffee-nosed (*infml*), supercilious, snooty (*infml*), haughty, high and mighty, condescending, proud, arrogant, conceited, bigheaded (*infml*).
F3 humble, modest.

student *noun*
undergraduate, postgraduate, scholar, schoolboy, schoolgirl, pupil, disciple, learner, trainee, apprentice.

studious *adjective*
scholarly, academic, intellectual, bookish, serious, thoughtful, reflective, diligent, hardworking, industrious, assiduous (*fml*), careful, attentive, earnest, eager.
F3 lazy, idle, negligent.

study *verb*
read, learn, revise, cram, swot (*infml*), mug up (*infml*), read up, research, investigate, analyse, survey, scan, examine, scrutinize, peruse, pore over, contemplate, meditate, ponder, consider, deliberate.
▶ *noun*
1 needs further study: reading, homework, preparation, learning, revision, cramming, swotting (*infml*), research, investigation, inquiry, analysis, examination, scrutiny, inspection, contemplation, consideration, attention.

Subjects of study include:
accountancy, agriculture, anatomy, anthropology, archaeology, architecture, art, astrology, astronomy, biology, botany, building studies, business studies, calligraphy, chemistry, citizenship, civil engineering, the Classics, commerce, computer studies, cosmology, craft, creative writing, dance, design, design and technology (D & T), drama, dressmaking, driving, ecology, economics, education, electronics, engineering, environmental studies, ethnology, eugenics, fashion, fitness, food technology, forensics, gender studies, genetics, geography, geology, heraldry, history, home economics, horticulture, information and communication technology (ICT), information technology (IT), journalism, languages, law, leisure studies, lexicography, librarianship, linguistics, literature, logistics, management studies, marine studies, marketing, mathematics, mechanics, media studies, medicine, metallurgy, metaphysics, meteorology, music,

mythology, natural history, oceanography, ornithology, pathology, penology, personal and social education (PSE), personal, health and social education (PHSE), pharmacology, philosophy, photography, physics, physiology, politics, pottery, psychology, religious studies, science, shorthand, social sciences, sociology, sport, statistics, surveying, technology, theology, tourism & hospitality, typewriting, visual arts, web design, word processing, zoology.

2 a study of the causes of crime: report, essay, thesis, paper, monograph, survey, review, critique.

3 my father's study: office, den (*infml*).

stuff *verb*

1 stuff some clothes into a bag: pack, stow, load, fill, cram, crowd, force, push, shove, ram, wedge, jam, squeeze, compress.

2 (*infml*) stuff themselves with sweets: gorge, gourmandize (*fml*), overindulge, guzzle, gobble, sate, satiate.

F3**1** unload, empty. **2** nibble.

▸ *noun*

1 what's this stuff for?: material, fabric, matter, substance.

2 (*infml*) don't touch my stuff: belongings, possessions, things, objects, articles, goods, luggage, paraphernalia, gear (*infml*), clobber (*infml*), kit, tackle, equipment, materials.

stuffy *adjective*

1 a stuffy room: musty, stale, airless, unventilated, suffocating, stifling, oppressive, heavy, close, muggy, sultry.

2 had to visit our stuffy old relatives: staid, strait-laced, prim, conventional, old-fashioned, pompous, dull, dreary, uninteresting, stodgy.

F3**1** airy, well-ventilated. **2** informal, modern, lively.

stumble *verb*

1 stumble on the uneven ground: trip, slip, fall, lurch, reel, stagger, flounder, blunder.

2 stumbled at the difficult words: stammer, stutter, hesitate, falter.

◆**stumble on** come across, chance upon, happen upon, find, discover, encounter.

stump *noun*

end, remnant, trunk, stub.

▸ *verb* (*infml*)

defeat, outwit, confound, perplex, puzzle, baffle, mystify, confuse, bewilder, flummox (*infml*), bamboozle (*infml*), dumbfound.

F3assist.

◆**stump up** (*infml*) pay, hand over, fork out (*infml*), shell out (*infml*), donate, contribute, cough up (*infml*).

F3receive.

stun *verb*

amaze, astonish, astound, stagger, shock, daze, stupefy, dumbfound, flabbergast (*infml*), overcome, confound, confuse, bewilder.

stunning *adjective* (*infml*)

beautiful, lovely, gorgeous, ravishing, dazzling, brilliant, striking, impressive, spectacular, remarkable, wonderful, marvellous, great, sensational.

F3ugly, awful.

stunt[1] *noun*

a dangerous stunt: feat, exploit, act, deed, enterprise, trick, turn, performance.

stunt[2] *verb*

stunting its growth: stop, arrest, check, restrict, slow, retard, hinder, impede, dwarf.

F3promote, encourage.

stupid *adjective*

1 too stupid to know any better/that was a really stupid thing to do/say: silly, foolish, irresponsible, ill-advised, indiscreet, foolhardy, rash, senseless, mad, lunatic, brainless, half-witted, idiotic, imbecilic, moronic, feeble-minded, simple-minded, slow, dim, dull, dense, thick, dumb, dopey, crass, inane, puerile (*fml*), mindless, futile, pointless, meaningless, nonsensical, absurd, ludicrous, ridiculous, laughable.

2 stupid with exhaustion: dazed,

groggy, stupefied, stunned, sluggish, semiconscious.
F3 1 sensible, wise, clever, intelligent. 2 alert.

sturdy *adjective*
strong, robust, durable, well-made, stout, substantial, solid, well-built, powerful, muscular, athletic, hardy, vigorous, flourishing, hearty, staunch, stalwart steadfast, firm, resolute, determined.
F3 weak, flimsy, puny.

stutter *verb*
stammer, hesitate, falter, stumble, mumble.

style *noun*
1 a style of jacket/architecture/painting: appearance, cut, design, pattern, shape, form, sort, type, kind, genre, variety, category.
2 have style: elegance, smartness, chic, flair, panache, stylishness, taste, polish, refinement, sophistication, urbanity, fashion, vogue, trend, mode, dressiness, flamboyance, affluence, luxury, grandeur.
3 a different style of management: technique, approach, method, manner, mode, fashion, way, custom.
F3 2 inelegance, tastelessness.
▶ *verb*
1 styled her hair: design, cut, tailor, fashion, shape, adapt.
2 styles himself Lord Greenmarch: designate, term, name, call, address, title, dub, label.

stylish *adjective*
chic, fashionable, à la mode, modish, in vogue, voguish, trendy (*infml*), snappy, natty (*infml*), snazzy (*infml*), dressy, smart, elegant, classy (*infml*), polished, refined, sophisticated, urbane.
F3 old-fashioned, shabby.

suave *adjective*
polite, courteous, charming, agreeable, affable, soft-spoken, smooth, unctuous (*fml*), sophisticated, urbane, worldly.
F3 rude, unsophisticated.

subconscious *adjective*
subliminal, unconscious, intuitive, inner, innermost, hidden, latent, repressed, suppressed.
F3 conscious.

subdue *verb*
overcome, quell, suppress, repress, overpower, crush, defeat, conquer, vanquish (*fml*), overrun, subject, subjugate, humble, break, tame, master, discipline, control, check, moderate, reduce, soften, quieten, damp, mellow.
F3 arouse, awaken.

subdued *adjective*
1 looking rather subdued: sad, downcast, dejected, crestfallen, quiet, serious, grave, solemn.
2 a subdued murmur: quiet, muted, hushed, soft, dim, shaded, sombre, sober, restrained, unobtrusive, low-key, subtle.
F3 1 lively, excited. 2 striking, obtrusive.

subject *noun* /**sub**-jekt/
topic, theme, matter, issue, question, point, case, affair, business, discipline, field.
▶ *adjective*
1 subject to change: liable, disposed, prone, susceptible, vulnerable, open, exposed.
2 a subject nation: subjugated, captive, bound, obedient, answerable, subordinate, inferior, subservient, submissive.
3 subject to the weather: dependent, contingent on (*fml*), conditional.
F3 1 vulnerable. 2 free, superior.
3 unconditional.
▶ *verb* /sub-**jekt**/
expose, lay open, submit, subjugate, subdue.

subjective *adjective*
biased, prejudiced, personal, individual, idiosyncratic, emotional, intuitive, instinctive.
F3 objective, unbiased, impartial.

sublime *adjective*
exalted, elevated, high, lofty, noble, majestic, great, grand, imposing, magnificent, glorious, transcendent, spiritual.
F3 lowly, base.

submerge *verb*
submerse, immerse, plunge, duck, dip, sink, drown, engulf, overwhelm, swamp, flood, inundate, deluge.
F3 surface.

submissive *adjective*
yielding, unresisting, resigned, patient,
uncomplaining, accommodating,
biddable, obedient, deferential,
ingratiating, subservient, humble,
meek, docile, subdued, passive.
Ｆ∃ intransigent, intractable.

submit *verb*
1 **submit to pressure/the enemy**: yield,
give in, surrender, capitulate, knuckle
under, bow, bend, stoop, succumb,
agree, comply.
2 **submit an application**: present,
tender, offer, put forward, suggest,
propose, table, state, claim, argue.
Ｆ∃ 1 resist. 2 withdraw.

subordinate *adjective*
secondary, auxiliary, ancillary,
subsidiary, dependent, inferior, lower,
junior, minor, lesser.
Ｆ∃ superior, senior.
▶ *noun*
inferior, junior, assistant, attendant,
second, aide, dependant, underling
(*infml*).
Ｆ∃ superior, boss.

subscribe *verb*
1 **subscribe to a theory**: support,
endorse, back, advocate, approve,
agree.
2 **subscribe to several charities**: give,
donate, contribute.

subscription *noun*
membership fee, dues, payment,
donation, contribution, offering, gift.

subsequent *adjective*
following, later, future, next,
succeeding, consequent, resulting,
ensuing.
Ｆ∃ previous, earlier.

subside *verb*
sink, collapse, settle, descend, fall,
drop, lower, decrease, lessen, diminish,
dwindle, decline, wane, ebb, recede,
moderate, abate, die down, quieten,
slacken, ease.
Ｆ∃ rise, increase.

subsidiary *adjective*
auxiliary, supplementary, additional,
ancillary, assistant, supporting,
contributory, secondary, subordinate,
lesser, minor.

Ｆ∃ primary, chief, major.
▶ *noun*
branch, offshoot, division, section,
part.

subsidize *verb*
support, back, underwrite, sponsor,
finance, fund, aid, promote.

subsidy *noun*
grant, allowance, assistance, help, aid,
contribution, sponsorship, finance,
support, backing.

subsistence *noun*
living, survival, existence, livelihood,
maintenance, support, keep,
sustenance, nourishment, food,
provisions, rations.

substance *noun*
1 **a slimy substance**: matter, material,
stuff, fabric.
2 **a being with no substance**: essence,
pith, entity, body, solidity, concreteness,
reality, actuality, ground, foundation.
3 **the sum and substance of his
argument**: subject, subject-matter,
theme, gist, meaning, significance,
force.

substantial *adjective*
large, big, sizable, ample, generous,
great, considerable, significant,
important, worthwhile, massive, bulky,
hefty, well-built, stout, sturdy, strong,
sound, durable.
Ｆ∃ small, insignificant, weak.

substitute *verb*
1 **substitute one thing for another**:
change, exchange, swap, switch,
interchange, replace.
2 **substituting for the manager**: stand
in, fill in (*infml*), cover, deputize,
understudy, relieve.
▶ *noun*
reserve, stand-by, temp (*infml*), supply,
locum, understudy, stand-in,
replacement, relief, surrogate, proxy,
agent, deputy, makeshift, stopgap.
▶ *adjective*
reserve, temporary, acting, surrogate,
proxy, replacement, alternative.

subtle *adjective*
1 **subtle colours/taste/humour**:
delicate, understated, implied,
indirect, slight, tenuous, faint, mild,

fine, nice (*fml*), refined, sophisticated, deep, profound.
2 subtle argument: artful, cunning, crafty, sly, devious, shrewd, astute.
E3 1 blatant, obvious. 2 artless, open.

subtract *verb*
deduct, take away, remove, withdraw, debit, detract, diminish.
E3 add.

subversive *adjective*
seditious, treasonous, treacherous, traitorous, inflammatory, incendiary, disruptive, riotous, weakening, undermining, destructive.
E3 loyal.

succeed *verb*
1 succeed in life/the attempt: triumph, make it, get on, thrive, flourish, prosper, make good.
2 winter succeeds autumn: follow, replace.
E3 1 fail. 2 precede.

succeeding *adjective*
following, next, subsequent, ensuing, coming, to come, later, successive.
E3 previous, earlier.

success *noun*
1 owed her success to hard work: triumph, victory, luck, fortune, prosperity, fame, eminence.
2 he/she/it was a success: celebrity, star, somebody, winner, bestseller, hit, sensation.
E3 1 failure, disaster.
⇨ *See also* **Word Study** *panel*.

successful *adjective*
1 successful candidate/team/ business/businessman: victorious, winning, lucky, fortunate, prosperous, wealthy, thriving, flourishing, booming, moneymaking, lucrative, profitable, rewarding, satisfying, fruitful, productive.
2 a successful writer: famous, well-known, popular, leading, bestselling, top, unbeaten.
E3 1 unsuccessful, unprofitable, fruitless. 2 unknown.

succession *noun*
sequence, series, order, progression, run, chain, string, cycle, continuation, flow, course, line, train, procession.

successive *adjective*
consecutive, sequential, following, succeeding.

succinct *adjective*
short, brief, terse, pithy, concise, compact, condensed, summary.
E3 long, lengthy, wordy, verbose.

succulent *adjective*
fleshy, juicy, moist, luscious, mouthwatering, lush, rich, mellow.
E3 dry.

succumb *verb*
give way, yield, give in, submit, knuckle under, surrender, capitulate, collapse, fall.
E3 overcome, master.

suck *verb*
draw in, absorb, soak up, extract, drain.

sudden *adjective*
unexpected, unforeseen, surprising, startling, abrupt, sharp, quick, swift, rapid, prompt, hurried, hasty, rash, impetuous, impulsive, snap (*infml*).
E3 expected, predictable, gradual, slow.

sue *verb*
prosecute, charge, indict, summon, solicit, appeal.

suffer *verb*
1 suffer in silence: hurt, ache, agonize, grieve, sorrow.
2 suffer humiliation: bear, support, tolerate, endure, sustain, experience, undergo, go through, feel.

suffering *noun*
pain, discomfort, agony, anguish, affliction, distress, misery, hardship, ordeal, torment, torture.
E3 ease, comfort.

sufficient *adjective*
enough, adequate, satisfactory, effective.
E3 insufficient, inadequate.

suffocate *verb*
asphyxiate, smother, stifle, choke, strangle, throttle.

suggest *verb*
1 suggest a solution: propose, put forward, advocate, recommend, advise, counsel.
2 what are you suggesting?: imply,

WORD study

success

Success is something that makes most people feel good. The phrases that are used to talk and write about it often contain positive images that reflect the degree of pleasure or satisfaction they feel.

being successful

carry the day
come into your own
go the distance
go up in the world
have the world at your feet
make it
make your mark
strike gold

carry it off
fall on your feet
go from strength to strength
hit the mark
make it big
make your name *or* make a name for yourself
pass with flying colours

having a chance of success

have a fighting/sporting chance
be looking good

be in with a chance

insinuate, hint, intimate, evoke, indicate.

suggestion *noun*
1 make a good suggestion: proposal, proposition, motion, recommendation, idea, plan.
2 the suggestion was that she was incompetent: implication, insinuation, innuendo, hint, intimation, suspicion, trace, indication.

suit *verb*
1 suit their needs: satisfy, gratify, please, answer, match, tally, agree, correspond, harmonize.
2 suiting the word to the deed: fit, befit, become, tailor, adapt, adjust, accommodate, modify.
E31 displease, clash.
▶ *noun*
outfit, costume, dress, clothing.

suitable *adjective*
appropriate, fitting, convenient, opportune, suited, due, apt, apposite, relevant, applicable, fit, adequate, satisfactory, acceptable, befitting,

becoming, seemly, proper, right.
E3unsuitable, inappropriate.

sulk *verb*
mope, brood, pout.

sulky *adjective*
brooding, moody, morose, resentful, grudging, disgruntled, put out, cross, bad-tempered, sullen, aloof, unsociable.
E3cheerful, good-tempered, sociable.

sullen *adjective*
1 a sullen expression: sulky, moody, morose, glum, gloomy, silent, surly, sour, perverse, obstinate, stubborn.
2 a sullen sky: dark, gloomy, sombre, dismal, cheerless, dull, leaden, heavy.
E31 cheerful, happy. **2** fine, clear.

sultry *adjective*
hot, sweltering, stifling, stuffy, oppressive, close, humid, muggy, sticky.
E3cool, cold.

sum *noun*
total, sum total, aggregate, whole, entirety, number, quantity, amount,

tally, reckoning, score, result.
◆**sum up** summarize, review, recapitulate, conclude, close.

summarize *verb*
outline, précis, condense, abridge, abbreviate, shorten, sum up, encapsulate, review.
F∃expand (on).

summary *noun*
synopsis, résumé, outline, abstract, précis, condensation, digest, compendium, abridgement, summing-up, review, recapitulation.
▸ *adjective*
short, succinct, brief, cursory, hasty, prompt, direct, unceremonious, arbitrary.
F∃lengthy, careful.

summit *noun*
top, peak, pinnacle, apex, point, crown, head, zenith, acme, culmination, height.
F∃bottom, foot, nadir.

summon *verb*
call, send for, invite, bid, beckon, gather, assemble, convene, rally, muster, mobilize, rouse, arouse.
F∃dismiss.

sundry *adjective*
various, diverse, miscellaneous, assorted, varied, different, several, some, a few.

sunken *adjective*
submerged, buried, recessed, lower, depressed, concave, hollow, haggard, drawn.

sunny *adjective*
1 a sunny day: fine, cloudless, clear, summery, sunshiny, sunlit, bright, brilliant.
2 a sunny disposition: cheerful, happy, joyful, smiling, beaming, radiant, light-hearted, buoyant, optimistic, pleasant.
F∃1 sunless, dull. **2** gloomy.

sunrise *noun*
dawn, crack of dawn, daybreak, daylight.

sunset *noun*
sundown, dusk, twilight, gloaming, evening, nightfall.

superb *adjective*
excellent, first-rate, first-class, superior, choice, fine, exquisite, gorgeous, magnificent, splendid, grand, wonderful, marvellous, admirable, impressive, breathtaking.
F∃bad, poor, inferior.

superficial *adjective*
surface, external, exterior, outward, apparent, seeming, cosmetic, skin-deep, shallow, slight, trivial, lightweight, frivolous, casual, cursory, sketchy, hasty, hurried, passing, one-dimensional.
F∃internal, deep, thorough.

superfluous *adjective*
extra, spare, excess, surplus, remaining, redundant, supernumerary, unnecessary, needless, unwanted, uncalled-for, excessive.
F∃necessary, needed, wanted.

superior *adjective*
1 superior accommodation: excellent, first-class, first-rate, top-notch (*infml*), top-flight (*infml*), high-class, exclusive, choice, select, fine, de luxe, admirable, distinguished, exceptional, unrivalled, par excellence.
2 superior to mine: better, preferred, greater, higher, senior.
3 a superior air: haughty, lordly, pretentious, snobbish, snooty (*infml*), supercilious, disdainful, condescending, patronizing.
F∃1 inferior, average. **2** worse, lower. **3** humble.
▸ *noun*
senior, elder, better, boss, chief, principal, director, manager, foreman, supervisor.
F∃inferior, junior, assistant.

superiority *noun*
advantage, lead, edge, supremacy, ascendancy, pre-eminence, predominance.
F∃inferiority.

superlative *adjective*
best, greatest, highest, supreme, transcendent, unbeatable, unrivalled, unparalleled, matchless, peerless, unsurpassed, unbeaten, consummate, excellent, outstanding.
F∃poor, average.

supernatural *adjective*
paranormal, unnatural, abnormal, metaphysical, spiritual, psychic, mystic, occult, hidden, mysterious, miraculous, magical, phantom, ghostly.
F3 natural, normal.

supersede *verb*
succeed, replace, supplant, usurp, oust, displace, remove.

superstition *noun*
myth, old wives' tale, fallacy, delusion, illusion.

superstitious *adjective*
mythical, false, fallacious, irrational, groundless, delusive, illusory.
F3 rational, logical.

supervise *verb*
oversee, watch over, look after, superintend, run, manage, administer, direct, conduct, preside over, control, handle.

supervision *noun*
surveillance, care, charge, superintendence, oversight, running, management, administration, direction, control, guidance, instruction.

supervisor *noun*
overseer, inspector, superintendent, boss, chief, director, administrator, manager, foreman, forewoman.

supple *adjective*
flexible, bending, pliant, pliable, plastic, lithe, graceful, loose-limbed, double-jointed, elastic.
F3 stiff, rigid, inflexible.

supplement *noun*
addition, extra, insert, pull-out, addendum, appendix, codicil, postscript, sequel.
▶ *verb*
add to, augment, boost, reinforce, fill up, top up, complement, extend, eke out.
F3 deplete, use up.

supplementary *adjective*
additional, extra, auxiliary, secondary, complementary, accompanying.

supplies *noun*
stores, provisions, food, equipment, materials, necessities.

supply *verb*
provide, furnish, equip, outfit, stock, fill, replenish, give, donate, grant, endow, contribute, yield, produce, sell.
F3 take, receive.
▶ *noun*
source, amount, quantity, stock, fund, reservoir, store, reserve, stockpile, hoard, cache.
F3 lack.

support *verb*
1 support one's team/local charities: back, second, defend, champion, advocate, promote, foster, help, aid, assist, rally round, finance, fund, subsidize, underwrite.
2 supporting the roof: hold up, bear, carry, sustain, brace, reinforce, strengthen, prop, buttress, bolster.
3 support his family: maintain, keep, provide for, feed, nourish.
4 evidence supporting his statement: endorse, confirm, verify, authenticate, corroborate, substantiate.
F3 1 oppose. **3** live off. **4** contradict.
▶ *noun*
1 have the support of the majority: backing, allegiance, loyalty, defence, protection, patronage, sponsorship, approval, encouragement, comfort, relief, help, aid, assistance.
2 a roof support: prop, stay, post, pillar, brace, crutch, foundation, underpinning.
F3 1 opposition, hostility.

supporter *noun*
fan, follower, adherent, advocate, champion, defender, seconder, patron, sponsor, helper, ally, friend.
F3 opponent.

supportive *adjective*
helpful, caring, attentive, sympathetic, understanding, comforting, reassuring, encouraging.
F3 discouraging.

suppose *verb*
assume, presume, expect, infer, conclude, guess, conjecture, surmise, believe, think, consider, judge, imagine, conceive, fancy, pretend, postulate, hypothesize.
F3 know.

supposed *adjective*
alleged, reported, rumoured,
assumed, presumed, reputed, putative
(*fml*), imagined, hypothetical.
E3 known, certain.
◆ **supposed to** meant to, intended to,
expected to, required to, obliged to.

supposition *noun*
assumption, presumption, guess,
conjecture, speculation, theory,
hypothesis, idea, notion.
E3 knowledge.

suppress *verb*
crush, stamp out, quash, quell, subdue,
stop, silence, censor, stifle, smother,
strangle, conceal, withhold, hold back,
contain, restrain, check, repress,
inhibit.
E3 encourage, incite.

supreme *adjective*
best, greatest, highest, top, crowning,
culminating, first, leading, foremost,
chief, principal, head, sovereign, pre-
eminent, predominant, prevailing,
world-beating, unsurpassed, second-
to-none, incomparable, matchless,
consummate, transcendent,
superlative, prime, ultimate, extreme,
final.
E3 lowly, poor.

sure *adjective*
1 a sure sign/sure to know: certain,
convinced, assured, confident,
decided, positive, definite,
unmistakable, clear, accurate, precise,
unquestionable, indisputable,
undoubted, undeniable, irrevocable,
inevitable, bound.
2 guided by his sure hand: safe, secure,
fast, solid, firm, steady, stable,
guaranteed, reliable, dependable,
trustworthy, steadfast, unwavering,
unerring, unfailing, infallible,
effective.
E3 1 unsure, uncertain, doubtful.
2 unsafe, insecure.

surface *noun*
outside, exterior, façade, veneer,
covering, skin, top, side, face, plane.
E3 inside, interior.
▶ *verb*
rise, arise, come up, emerge,

appear, materialize, come to light.
E3 sink, disappear, vanish.

surly *adjective*
gruff, brusque, churlish, ungracious,
bad-tempered, cross, crabbed,
grouchy, crusty, sullen, sulky, morose.
E3 friendly, polite.

surpass *verb*
beat, outdo, exceed, outstrip, better,
excel, transcend, outshine, eclipse.

surplus *noun*
excess, residue, remainder, balance,
superfluity, glut, surfeit.
E3 lack, shortage.
▶ *adjective*
excess, superfluous, redundant, extra,
spare, remaining, unused.

surprise *verb*
startle, amaze, astonish, astound,
stagger, flabbergast (*infml*), bewilder,
confuse, nonplus, disconcert, dismay.
▶ *noun*
amazement, astonishment, incredulity,
wonder, bewilderment, dismay, shock,
start, bombshell, revelation.
E3 composure.
⇨ *See also* **Word Study** panel.

surprised *adjective*
startled, amazed, astonished,
astounded, staggered, flabbergasted
(*infml*), thunderstruck, dumbfounded,
speechless, shocked, nonplussed.
E3 unsurprised, composed.

surprising *adjective*
amazing, astonishing, astounding,
staggering, stunning, incredible,
extraordinary, remarkable, startling,
unexpected, unforeseen.
E3 unsurprising, expected.

surrender *verb*
capitulate, submit, resign, concede,
yield, give in, cede, give up, quit,
relinquish, abandon, renounce, forgo,
waive.

surreptitious *adjective*
furtive, stealthy, sly, covert, veiled,
hidden, secret, clandestine,
underhand, unauthorized.
E3 open, obvious.

surround *verb*
encircle, ring, girdle, encompass,

WORD study

surprise

When you are **surprised** by something or it was unexpected, you can express your feelings using the phrases listed below.

things people say when they are surprised

I don't believe it!
fancy that!
I'll be blowed!
I can't get over ...
it's beyond belief
that's a new one on me
what is the world coming to?
who does so-and-so think they're kidding?
words fail me
you won't believe your ears
you don't say!
you're kidding!

bless my soul!
funnily enough
in all my born days
in heaven's name!
fancy meeting you here!
that's news to me
to think
well I never!
wonders will never cease
would you believe
you won't believe your eyes
you're joking!

be surprising

come as a surprise
come out of the blue

be a bombshell

---

envelop, encase, enclose, hem in, besiege.

surrounding *adjective*
encircling, bordering, adjacent, adjoining, neighbouring, nearby.

surroundings *noun*
neighbourhood, vicinity, locality, setting, environment, background, milieu, ambience.

survey *verb*
view, contemplate, observe, supervise, scan, scrutinize, examine, inspect, study, research, review, consider, estimate, evaluate, assess, measure, plot, plan, map, chart, reconnoitre.
▶ *noun*
review, overview, scrutiny, examination, inspection, study, appraisal, assessment, measurement.

survive *verb*
outlive, outlast, endure, last, stay, remain, live, exist, withstand, weather.
F∃ succumb, die.

susceptible *adjective*
liable, prone, inclined, disposed, given, subject, receptive, responsive, impressionable, suggestible, weak, vulnerable, open, sensitive, tender.
F∃ resistant, immune.

suspect *verb*
1 *no cause to suspect the truth of what he says*: doubt, distrust, mistrust, call into question.
2 *I suspect he's not happy*: believe, fancy, feel, guess, conjecture, speculate, surmise, suppose, consider, conclude, infer.
▶ *adjective*
suspicious, doubtful, dubious, questionable, debatable, unreliable, iffy (*infml*), dodgy (*infml*), fishy (*infml*).
F∃ acceptable, reliable.

suspend *verb*
1 suspended from the ceiling: hang, dangle, swing.
2 suspend the hearing: adjourn, interrupt, discontinue, cease, delay, defer, postpone, put off, shelve.
3 suspend them from school: expel, dismiss, exclude, debar.
F2 continue. **3** restore, reinstate.

suspense *noun*
uncertainty, insecurity, anxiety, tension, apprehension, anticipation, expectation, expectancy, excitement.
F2 certainty, knowledge.

suspicion *noun*
1 filled with suspicion: doubt, scepticism, distrust, mistrust, wariness, caution, misgiving, apprehension.
2 just a suspicion of garlic: trace, hint, suggestion, soupçon, touch, tinge, shade, glimmer, shadow.
3 had a suspicion something was wrong: idea, notion, hunch.
F2 trust.

suspicious *adjective*
1 a suspicious look: doubtful, sceptical, unbelieving, suspecting, distrustful, mistrustful, wary, chary, apprehensive, uneasy.
2 a suspicious character: dubious, questionable, suspect, irregular, shifty, shady (*infml*), dodgy (*infml*), fishy (*infml*).
F2 trustful, confident. **2** trustworthy, innocent.

sustain *verb*
1 sustaining them through the winter: nourish, provide for, nurture, foster, help, aid, assist, comfort, relieve, support, uphold, endorse, bear, carry.
2 can't sustain that pace: maintain, keep going, keep up, continue, prolong, hold.

sustained *adjective*
prolonged, protracted, long-drawn-out, steady, continuous, constant, perpetual, unremitting.
F2 broken, interrupted, intermittent, spasmodic.

swagger *verb*
bluster, boast, crow, brag, swank

(*infml*), parade, strut.
▸ *noun*
bluster, show, ostentation, arrogance.

swallow *verb*
1 swallow the medicine: consume, devour, eat, gobble up, guzzle, drink, quaff, knock back (*infml*), gulp, down (*infml*).
2 swallowed in the fog: engulf, enfold, envelop, swallow up, absorb, assimilate.
3 didn't swallow that story, did you?: accept, believe.

swamp *noun*
bog, marsh, fen, slough, quagmire, quicksand, mire, mud.
▸ *verb*
flood, inundate, deluge, engulf, submerge, sink, drench, saturate, waterlog, overload, overwhelm, besiege, beset.

swap, swop *verb*
exchange, transpose, switch, interchange, barter, trade, traffic.

swarm *noun*
crowd, throng, mob, mass, multitude, myriad, host, army, horde, herd, flock, drove, shoal.
▸ *verb*
1 swarmed into the stadium: flock, flood, stream, mass, congregate, crowd, throng.
2 swarming with tourists: teem, crawl, bristle, abound.

sway *verb*
1 sway from side to side: rock, roll, lurch, swing, wave, oscillate, fluctuate, bend, incline, lean, divert, veer, swerve.
2 swaying public opinion: influence, affect, persuade, induce, convince, convert, overrule, dominate, govern.

swear *verb*
1 swearing revenge: vow, promise, pledge, avow, attest (*fml*), asseverate (*fml*), testify, affirm, assert, declare, insist.
2 swearing at the top of his voice: curse, blaspheme.

swear word *noun*
expletive, four-letter word, curse, oath, imprecation, obscenity, profanity, blasphemy, swearing, bad language.

sweat *noun*
1 soaking with sweat: perspiration, moisture, stickiness.
2 get into a sweat about it: anxiety, worry, agitation, panic.
3 takes a lot of sweat to achieve: toil, labour, drudgery, chore.
▶ *verb*
perspire, swelter, exude.

sweep *verb*
1 sweep the floor: brush, dust, clean, clear, remove.
2 swept through the room: pass, sail, fly, glide, scud, skim, glance, whisk, tear, hurtle.
▶ *noun*
arc, curve, bend, swing, stroke, movement, gesture, compass, scope, range, extent, span, stretch, expanse, vista.

sweeping *adjective*
general, global, all-inclusive, all-embracing, blanket, across-the-board, broad, wide-ranging, extensive, far-reaching, comprehensive, thoroughgoing, radical, wholesale, indiscriminate, oversimplified, simplistic.
E₃ specific, narrow.

sweet *adjective*
1 a sweet taste: sugary, syrupy, sweetened, honeyed, saccharine, luscious, delicious.
2 a sweet nature: pleasant, delightful, lovely, attractive, beautiful, pretty, winsome, cute, appealing, lovable, charming, agreeable, amiable, affectionate, tender, kind, treasured, precious, dear, darling.
3 sweet-smelling: fresh, clean, wholesome, pure, clear, perfumed, fragrant, aromatic, balmy.
4 sweet music: melodious, tuneful, harmonious, euphonious, musical, dulcet, soft, mellow.
E₃ 1 savoury, salty, sour, bitter.
2 unpleasant, nasty, ugly. **3** foul.
4 discordant.
▶ *noun*
dessert, pudding, afters (*infml*).

sweeten *verb*
sugar, honey, mellow, soften, soothe, appease, temper, cushion.
E₃ sour, embitter.

swell *verb*
expand, dilate, inflate, blow up, puff up, bloat, distend, fatten, bulge, balloon, billow, surge, rise, mount, increase, enlarge, extend, grow, augment, heighten, intensify.
E₃ shrink, contract, decrease, dwindle.
▶ *noun*
billow, wave, undulation, surge, rise, increase, enlargement.

swelling *noun*
lump, tumour, bump, bruise, blister, boil, inflammation, bulge, protuberance (*fml*), puffiness, distension (*fml*), enlargement.

sweltering *adjective*
hot, tropical, baking, scorching, stifling, suffocating, airless, oppressive, sultry, steamy, sticky, humid.
E₃ cold, cool, fresh, breezy, airy.

swerve *verb*
turn, bend, incline, veer, swing, shift, deviate, stray, wander, diverge, deflect, sheer.

swift *adjective*
fast, quick, rapid, speedy, express, flying, hurried, hasty, short, brief, sudden, prompt, ready, agile, nimble, nippy (*infml*).
E₃ slow, sluggish, unhurried.

swindle *verb*
cheat, defraud, diddle, do (*infml*), overcharge, fleece, rip off (*infml*), trick, deceive, dupe, con (*infml*), bamboozle (*infml*).
▶ *noun*
fraud, fiddle, racket, sharp practice, double-dealing, trickery, deception, con (*infml*), rip-off (*infml*).

swing *verb*
hang, suspend, dangle, wave, brandish, sway, rock, oscillate, vibrate, fluctuate, vary, veer, swerve, turn, whirl, twirl, spin, rotate.
▶ *noun*
sway, rock, oscillation, vibration, fluctuation, variation, change, shift, movement, motion, rhythm.

swingeing *adjective*
harsh, severe, stringent, drastic,

punishing, devastating, excessive, extortionate, oppressive, heavy.
E3 mild.

swipe *verb*
1 *swiped at the ball*: hit, strike, lunge, lash out, slap, whack (*infml*), wallop (*infml*), sock (*infml*).
2 (*infml*) *who's swiped my trainers?*: steal, pilfer, lift, pinch (*infml*).
▶ *noun*
stroke, blow, slap, smack, clout, whack (*infml*), wallop (*infml*).

swirl *verb*
churn, agitate, spin, twirl, whirl, wheel, eddy, twist, curl.

switch *verb*
change, exchange, swap, trade, interchange, transpose, substitute, replace, shift, rearrange, turn, veer, deviate, divert, deflect.
▶ *noun*
change, alteration, shift, exchange, swap, interchange, substitution, replacement.

swivel *verb*
pivot, spin, rotate, revolve, turn, twirl, pirouette, gyrate, wheel.

swollen *adjective*
bloated, distended, inflated, tumid, puffed up, puffy, inflamed, enlarged, bulbous, bulging.
E3 shrunken, shrivelled.

swoop *verb*
dive, plunge, drop, fall, descend, stoop, pounce, lunge, rush.

swop ⇨ *see* **swap**.

sword *noun*
blade, foil, rapier, sabre, scimitar.

swot *verb* (*infml*)
study, work, learn, memorize, revise, cram, mug up (*infml*), bone up (*infml*).

syllabus *noun*
curriculum, course, programme, schedule, plan.

symbol *noun*
sign, token, representation, mark, emblem, badge, logo, character, ideograph, figure, image.

symbolic *adjective*
symbolical, representative, emblematic, token, figurative,

metaphorical, allegorical, meaningful, significant.

symbolize *verb*
represent, stand for, denote, mean, signify, typify, exemplify, epitomize, personify.

symmetry *noun*
balance, evenness, regularity, parallelism, correspondence, proportion, harmony, agreement.
E3 asymmetry, irregularity.

sympathetic *adjective*
understanding, appreciative, supportive, comforting, consoling, commiserating, pitying, interested, concerned, solicitous, caring, compassionate, tender, kind, warm-hearted, well-disposed, affectionate, agreeable, friendly, congenial, like-minded, compatible.
E3 unsympathetic, indifferent, callous, antipathetic.

sympathize *verb*
understand, comfort, commiserate, pity, feel for, empathize, identify with, respond to.
E3 ignore, disregard.

sympathy *noun*
1 *feel sympathy for them*:
understanding, comfort, consolation, condolences, commiseration, pity, compassion, tenderness, kindness, warmth, thoughtfulness, empathy, fellow-feeling, affinity, rapport.
2 *was in sympathy with their aims*:
agreement, accord, correspondence, harmony.
E3 1 indifference, insensitivity, callousness. **2** disagreement.

symptom *noun*
sign, indication, evidence, manifestation, expression, feature, characteristic, mark, token, warning.

synonymous *adjective*
interchangeable, substitutable, the same, identical, similar, comparable, tantamount, equivalent, corresponding.
E3 antonymous, opposite.

synopsis *noun*
outline, abstract, summary, résumé, précis, condensation, digest, abridgement, review, recapitulation.

synthesize *verb*
unite, combine, amalgamate, integrate, merge, blend, compound, alloy, fuse, weld, coalesce, unify.
Fₐseparate, analyse, resolve.

synthetic *adjective*
manufactured, man-made, simulated, artificial, ersatz, imitation, fake, bogus, mock, sham, pseudo.
Fₐgenuine, real, natural.

system *noun*
1 a good system of government: method, mode, technique, procedure, process, routine, practice, usage, rule.
2 have to have some sort of system: organization, structure, set-up, systematization, co-ordination, orderliness, methodology, logic, classification, arrangement, order.

systematic *adjective*
methodical, logical, ordered, well-ordered, planned, well-planned, organized, well-organized, structured, systematized, standardized, orderly, businesslike, efficient.
Fₐunsystematic, arbitrary, disorderly, inefficient.

T t

table *noun*
1 a work table: board, slab, counter, worktop, desk, bench, stand.
2 a table of contents: diagram, chart, graph, timetable, schedule, programme, list, inventory, catalogue, index, register, record.
► *verb*
propose, suggest, submit, put forward.

taboo *adjective*
forbidden, prohibited, banned, proscribed, unacceptable, unmentionable, unthinkable.
E3 permitted, acceptable.
► *noun*
ban, interdiction (*fml*), prohibition, restriction, anathema, curse.

tack *noun*
1 carpet tacks: nail, pin, drawing pin, staple.
2 go off on a different tack: course, path, bearing, heading, direction, line, approach, method, way, technique, procedure, plan, tactic, attack.
► *verb*
add, append, attach, affix, fasten, fix, nail, pin, staple, stitch, baste.

tackle *noun*
1 a rugby tackle: attack, challenge, interception, intervention, block.
2 all their climbing/fishing tackle: equipment, tools, implements, apparatus, rig, outfit, gear (*infml*), trappings, paraphernalia.
► *verb*
1 tackle the problem immediately: begin, embark on, set about, try, attempt, undertake, take on, challenge, confront, encounter, face up to, grapple

with, deal with, attend to, handle, grab, seize, grasp.
2 tackling one of the forwards: intercept, block, halt, stop.
E3 1 avoid, sidestep.

tactful *adjective*
diplomatic, discreet, politic, judicious (*fml*), prudent, careful, delicate, subtle, sensitive, perceptive, discerning, understanding, thoughtful, considerate, polite, skilful, adroit.
E3 tactless, indiscreet, thoughtless, rude.

tactic *noun*
approach, course, way, means, method, procedure, plan, stratagem, scheme, ruse, ploy, subterfuge, trick, device, shift, move, manoeuvre.

tactical *adjective*
strategic, planned, calculated, artful, cunning, shrewd, skilful, clever, smart, prudent, politic, judicious (*fml*).

tactics *noun*
strategy, campaign, plan, policy, approach, line of attack, moves, manoeuvres.

tactless *adjective*
undiplomatic, indiscreet, indelicate, inappropriate, impolitic, imprudent, careless, clumsy, blundering, insensitive, unfeeling, hurtful, unkind, thoughtless, inconsiderate, rude, impolite, discourteous.
E3 tactful, diplomatic, discreet.

tag *noun*
label, sticker, tab, ticket, mark, identification, note, slip, docket.
► *verb*
1 tag all the boxes to be moved: label, mark, identify, designate.

2 was tagged 'Little Mo' by the press: call, name, christen, nickname, style, dub.

3 tagged on at the end: add, append, annex, adjoin, affix, fasten.

◆ **tag along** follow, shadow, tail, trail, accompany.

tail *noun*
end, extremity, rear, rear end, rump, behind (*infml*), posterior (*infml*), appendage.
▶ *verb*
follow, pursue, shadow, dog, stalk, track, trail.

◆ **tail off** decrease, decline, drop, fall away, fade, wane, dwindle, taper off, peter out, die (out).
Eಃ increase, grow.

tailor *verb*
fit, suit, cut, trim, style, fashion, shape, mould, alter, modify, adapt, adjust, accommodate.

tailor-made *adjective*
made-to-measure, custom-built, ideal, perfect, right, suited, fitted.
Eಃ unsuitable.

taint *verb*
contaminate, infect, pollute, adulterate, corrupt, deprave, stain, blemish, blot, smear, tarnish, blacken, dirty, soil, muddy, defile (*fml*), sully (*fml*), harm, damage, blight, spoil, ruin, shame, disgrace, dishonour.

take *verb*
1 took his hand/a seat/the next three games/his mother's name: seize, grab, snatch, grasp, hold, catch, capture, get, obtain, acquire, secure, gain, win, derive, adopt, assume, pick, choose, select, accept, receive.
2 take five from ten: remove, eliminate, take away, subtract, deduct.
3 taking anything that wasn't nailed down: steal, filch, purloin (*fml*), nick (*infml*), pinch (*infml*), appropriate, abduct, carry off.
4 takes courage: need, necessitate, require, demand, call for.
5 take me home: convey, carry, bring, transport, ferry, accompany, escort, lead, guide, conduct, usher.
6 can't take pain: bear, tolerate, stand, stomach, abide, endure, suffer, undergo, withstand.
Eಃ 1 leave, refuse. **2** add, put back.

◆ **take aback** surprise, astonish, astound, stagger, stun, startle, disconcert, bewilder, dismay, upset.

◆ **take apart** take to pieces, dismantle, disassemble, analyse.

◆ **take back** reclaim, repossess, withdraw, retract, recant, repudiate, deny, eat one's words.

◆ **take down 1 take down the scaffolding:** dismantle, disassemble, demolish, raze, level, lower.
2 taking down the details: note, record, write down, put down, set down, transcribe.

◆ **take in 1 take in carbon dioxide:** absorb, assimilate.
2 didn't take it in at first/couldn't take it all in: digest, realize, appreciate, understand, comprehend, grasp.
3 offered to take the children in: admit, receive, shelter, accommodate.
4 takes in all of London: contain, include, comprise, incorporate, embrace, encompass, cover.
5 was completely taken in by his charm: deceive, fool, dupe, con (*infml*), mislead, trick, hoodwink, bamboozle (*infml*), cheat, swindle.

◆ **take off 1 took off his hat:** remove, doff, divest, shed, discard, drop.
2 took off as soon as the police arrived: leave, depart, go, decamp, disappear.
3 taking off the prime minister: imitate, mimic, parody, caricature, satirize, mock, send up.

◆ **take on 1 take on the job:** accept, assume, acquire, undertake, tackle, face, contend with, fight, oppose.
2 take on staff: employ, hire, enlist, recruit, engage, retain.

◆ **take up 1 take up all their time:** occupy, fill, engage, engross, absorb, monopolize, use up.
2 take up a hobby: start, begin, embark on, pursue, carry on, continue.
3 take up an offer: accept, adopt, assume.

takeover *noun*
merger, amalgamation, combination, incorporation, coup.

takings *noun*
receipts, gate, proceeds, profits, gain, returns, revenue, yield, income, earnings, pickings.

tale *noun*
story, yarn, anecdote, spiel (*infml*), narrative, account, report, rumour, tall story, old wives' tale, superstition, fable, myth, legend, saga, lie, fib, falsehood, untruth, fabrication.

talent *noun*
gift, endowment, genius, flair, feel, knack, bent, aptitude, faculty, skill, ability, capacity, power, strength, forte.
F3 inability, weakness.

talented *adjective*
gifted, brilliant, well-endowed, versatile, accomplished, able, capable, proficient, adept, adroit, deft, clever, skilful.
F3 inept.

talk *verb*
speak, utter, articulate, say, communicate, converse, chat, gossip, natter (*infml*), chatter, discuss, confer, negotiate.
▶ *noun*
1 a lot of talk about nothing/have a long talk: conversation, dialogue, discussion, conference, meeting, consultation, negotiation, chat, chatter, natter (*infml*), gossip, hearsay, rumour, tittle-tattle.
2 give a talk: lecture, seminar, symposium, speech, address, discourse, sermon, spiel (*infml*).
3 baby talk: language, dialect, slang, jargon, speech, utterance, words.
◆ **talk into** encourage, coax, sway, persuade, convince, bring round, win over.
F3 dissuade.
◆ **talk out of** discourage, deter, put off, dissuade.
F3 persuade, convince.

talkative *adjective*
garrulous, voluble, vocal, communicative, forthcoming, unreserved, expansive, chatty, gossipy, verbose, wordy.
F3 taciturn, quiet, reserved.

tall *adjective*
high, lofty, elevated, soaring, towering, big, great, giant, gigantic.
F3 short, low, small.

tally *verb*
1 two versions don't tally: agree, concur, tie in, square, accord, harmonize, coincide, correspond, match, conform, suit, fit.
2 tally the figures: add (up), total, count, reckon, figure.
F3 1 disagree, differ.
▶ *noun*
record, count, total, score, reckoning, account.

tame *adjective*
1 a tame owl: domesticated, broken in, trained, disciplined, manageable, tractable, amenable, gentle, docile, meek, submissive, unresisting, obedient, biddable.
2 party was pretty tame: dull, boring, tedious, uninteresting, humdrum, flat, bland, insipid, weak, feeble, uninspired, unadventurous, unenterprising, lifeless, spiritless.
F3 1 wild, unmanageable, rebellious.
2 exciting.
▶ *verb*
domesticate, house-train, break in, train, discipline, master, subjugate, conquer, bridle, curb, repress, suppress, quell, subdue, temper, soften, mellow, calm, pacify, humble.

tamper *verb*
interfere, meddle, mess (*infml*), tinker, fiddle, fix, rig, manipulate, juggle, alter, damage.

tang *noun*
sharpness, bite, piquancy, pungency, taste, flavour, savour, smack, smell, aroma, scent, whiff, tinge, touch, trace, hint, suggestion, overtone.

tangible *adjective*
touchable, tactile, palpable, solid, concrete, material, substantial, physical, real, actual, perceptible, discernible, evident, manifest, definite, positive.
F3 intangible, abstract, unreal.

tangle *noun*
knot, snarl-up, twist, coil, convolution,

mesh, web, maze, labyrinth, mess, muddle, jumble, mix-up, confusion, entanglement, embroilment, complication.
▸ *verb*
entangle, knot, snarl, ravel, twist, coil, interweave, interlace, intertwine, catch, ensnare, entrap, enmesh, embroil, implicate, involve, muddle, confuse.
Fᴇ disentangle.

tantalize *verb*
tease, taunt, torment, torture, provoke, lead on, titillate, tempt, entice, bait, balk, frustrate, thwart.
Fᴇ gratify, satisfy, fulfil.

tantamount *adjective*
as good as, equivalent, commensurate, equal, synonymous, the same as.

tantrum *noun*
temper, rage, fury, storm, outburst, fit, scene.

tap¹ *verb*
tapping on the door: hit, strike, knock, rap, beat, drum, pat, touch.
▸ *noun*
knock, rap, beat, pat, touch.

tap² *noun*
turn on the tap: stopcock, valve, faucet, spigot, spout.
▸ *verb*
use, utilize, exploit, mine, quarry, siphon, bleed, milk, drain.

tape *noun*
band, strip, binding, ribbon, video, cassette.
▸ *verb*
record, video, bind, secure, stick, seal.

taper *verb*
narrow, attenuate (*fml*), thin, slim, decrease, reduce, lessen, dwindle, fade, wane, peter out, tail off, die away.
Fᴇ widen, flare, swell, increase.
▸ *noun*
spill, candle, wick.

target *noun*
aim, object, end, purpose, intention, ambition, goal, destination, objective, butt, mark, victim, prey, quarry.

tariff *noun*
price list, schedule, charges, rate, toll, tax, levy, customs, excise, duty.

tarnish *verb*
discolour, corrode, rust, dull, dim, darken, blacken, sully (*fml*), taint, stain, blemish, spot, blot, mar, spoil.
Fᴇ polish, brighten.

tart¹ *noun*
an apple tart: pie, flan, pastry, tartlet, patty.

tart² *adjective*
1 if it's too tart, add some sugar: sharp, acid, sour, bitter, vinegary, tangy, piquant, pungent.
2 got a tart response to my question: biting, cutting, trenchant (*fml*), incisive, caustic, astringent, acerbic, scathing, sardonic.
Fᴇ bland, sweet.

task *noun*
job, chore, duty, charge, imposition, assignment, exercise, mission, errand, undertaking, enterprise, business, occupation, activity, employment, work, labour, toil, burden.

taste *noun*
1 a taste of garlic: flavour, savour, relish, smack, tang.

> *Ways of describing taste include:*
>
> acid, acrid, appetizing, bitter, bittersweet, citrus, creamy, delicious, flavoursome, fruity, hot, meaty, moreish, mouthwatering (*infml*), peppery, piquant, pungent, salty, sapid, savoury, scrumptious (*infml*), sharp, sour, spicy, sugary, sweet, tangy, tart, tasty, vinegary, yummy (*infml*).

2 a taste of things to come: sample, bit, piece, morsel, titbit, bite, nibble, mouthful, sip, drop, dash, soupçon.
3 a taste for adventure: liking, fondness, partiality, preference, inclination, leaning, desire, appetite.
4 have good taste/shows taste: discrimination, discernment, judgement, perception, appreciation, sensitivity, refinement, polish, culture, cultivation, breeding, decorum, finesse, style, elegance, tastefulness.
Fᴇ **1** blandness. **3** distaste.
4 tastelessness.

▶ *verb*

savour, relish, sample, nibble, sip, try, test, differentiate, distinguish, discern, perceive, experience, undergo, feel, know.

tasteful *adjective*

refined, polished, cultured, cultivated, elegant, smart, stylish, aesthetic, artistic, harmonious, beautiful, exquisite, delicate, graceful, restrained, well-judged, judicious (*fml*), correct, fastidious, discriminating.
E3 tasteless, garish, tawdry.

tasteless *adjective*

1 **soup is tasteless:** flavourless, insipid, bland, mild, weak, watery, flat, stale, dull, boring, uninteresting, vapid.
2 **tasteless comment/decoration:** inelegant, graceless, unseemly, improper, indiscreet, crass, rude, crude, vulgar, kitsch, tacky (*infml*), naff (*slang*), cheap, tawdry, flashy, gaudy, garish, loud.
E3 1 tasty. 2 tasteful, elegant.

tasty *adjective*

luscious, palatable, appetizing, mouthwatering, delicious, flavoursome, succulent, scrumptious (*infml*), yummy (*infml*), tangy, piquant, savoury, sweet.
E3 tasteless, insipid.

tattered *adjective*

ragged, frayed, threadbare, ripped, torn, tatty, shabby, scruffy.
E3 smart, neat.

taunt *verb*

tease, torment, provoke, bait, goad, jeer, mock, ridicule, gibe, rib (*infml*), deride, sneer, insult, revile, reproach.
▶ *noun*

jeer, catcall, gibe, dig, sneer, insult, reproach, taunting, teasing, provocation, ridicule, sarcasm, derision, censure.

taut *adjective*

tight, stretched, contracted, strained, tense, unrelaxed, stiff, rigid.
E3 slack, loose, relaxed.

tax *noun*

levy, charge, rate, tariff, customs, contribution, imposition, burden, load.

▶ *verb*

levy, charge, demand, exact, assess, impose, burden, load, strain, stretch, try, tire, weary, exhaust, drain, sap, weaken.

teach *verb*

instruct, train, coach, tutor, lecture, drill, ground, verse, discipline, school, educate, enlighten, edify, inform, impart, inculcate, advise, counsel, guide, direct, show, demonstrate.
E3 learn.

teacher *noun*

schoolteacher, schoolmaster, master, schoolmistress, mistress, educator, pedagogue, tutor, lecturer, professor, don, instructor, trainer, coach, adviser, counsellor, mentor, guide, guru.
E3 pupil.

teaching *noun*

1 **the teaching of English/teaching as a profession:** instruction, tuition, training, grounding, schooling, education, pedagogy.
2 **the church's teachings:** dogma, doctrine, tenet, precept (*fml*), principle.

team *noun*

side, line-up, squad, shift, crew, gang, band, group, company, stable.
◆ **team up** join, unite, couple, combine, band together, co-operate, collaborate, work together.

tear *verb*

1 **tearing his sleeve on the wire/tore it into shreds:** rip, rend, divide, rupture, sever, shred, scratch, claw, gash, lacerate, mutilate, mangle.
2 **tore the book out of his hand:** pull, snatch, grab, seize, wrest (*fml*).
3 **tear down the street:** dash, rush, hurry, speed, race, run, sprint, fly, shoot, dart, bolt, belt (*infml*), career, charge.
▶ *noun*

rip, rent, slit, hole, split, rupture, scratch, gash, laceration.

tearful *adjective*

crying, weeping, sobbing, whimpering, blubbering, sad, sorrowful, upset, distressed, emotional, weepy (*infml*).
E3 happy, smiling, laughing.

tease *verb*
taunt, provoke, bait, annoy, irritate, aggravate (*infml*), needle (*infml*), badger, worry, pester, plague, torment, tantalize, mock, ridicule, gibe, banter, rag (*infml*), rib (*infml*).

technical *adjective*
mechanical, technological, scientific, electronic, computerized, specialized, expert, professional.

technique *noun*
method, system, procedure, manner, fashion, style, mode, way, means, approach, course, performance, execution, delivery, artistry, craftsmanship, skill, facility, proficiency, expertise, know-how (*infml*), art, craft, knack, touch.

tedious *adjective*
boring, monotonous, uninteresting, unexciting, dull, dreary, drab, banal, humdrum, tiresome, wearisome, tiring, laborious, long-winded, long-drawn-out.
E3 lively, interesting, exciting.

teenage *adjective*
teenaged, adolescent, young, youthful, juvenile, immature.

telepathy *noun*
mind-reading, thought transference, sixth sense, ESP, clairvoyance.

telephone *verb*
phone, ring (up), call (up), dial, buzz (*infml*), contact, get in touch.

tell *verb*
1 tell him the news: inform, notify, let know, acquaint, impart, communicate, speak, utter, say, state, confess, divulge, disclose, reveal.
2 tell a story: narrate, recount, relate, report, announce, describe, portray, mention.
3 told them to wait: order, command, direct, instruct, authorize.
4 tell them apart/tell which is which: differentiate, distinguish, discriminate, discern, recognize, identify, discover, see, understand, comprehend.
◆ **tell off** (*infml*) scold, chide, tick off (*infml*), upbraid (*fml*), reprimand, rebuke, reprove, lecture, berate, dress down (*infml*), reproach, censure.

temper *noun*
1 the temper of the meeting: mood, humour, nature, temperament, character, disposition.
2 in a temper: anger, rage, fury, passion, tantrum, paddy (*infml*), annoyance, irritability, ill-humour.
3 lose one's temper: calm, composure, self-control, cool (*infml*).
E3 2 calmness, self-control. **3** anger, rage.
▶ *verb*
1 tempering his threats with some encouraging words: moderate, lessen, reduce, calm, soothe, allay, assuage (*fml*), palliate (*fml*), mitigate, modify, soften.
2 tempering the steel: harden, toughen, strengthen.

temperament *noun*
nature, character, personality, disposition, tendency, bent, constitution, make-up, soul, spirit, mood, humour, temper, state of mind, attitude, outlook.

temperamental *adjective*
moody, emotional, neurotic, highly-strung, sensitive, touchy, irritable, impatient, passionate, fiery, excitable, explosive, volatile, mercurial, capricious, unpredictable, unreliable.
E3 calm, level-headed, steady.

temperate *adjective*
mild, clement, balmy, fair, equable, balanced, stable, gentle, pleasant, agreeable.

tempestuous *adjective*
stormy, windy, gusty, blustery, squally, turbulent, tumultuous, rough, wild, violent, furious, raging, heated, passionate, intense.
E3 calm.

temple *noun*
shrine, sanctuary, church, tabernacle, mosque, pagoda, synagogue, chapel.

tempo *noun*
time, rhythm, metre, beat, pulse, speed, velocity, rate, pace.

temporary *adjective*
impermanent, provisional, interim, makeshift, stopgap, temporal, transient, transitory, passing,

ephemeral, evanescent, fleeting, brief, short-lived, momentary.
F3 permanent, everlasting.

tempt *verb*
entice, coax, persuade, woo, bait, lure, allure, attract, draw, seduce, invite, tantalize, provoke, incite.
F3 discourage, dissuade, repel.

temptation *noun*
enticement, inducement, coaxing, persuasion, bait, lure, allure, appeal, attraction, draw, pull, seduction, invitation.

tenant *noun*
renter, lessee, leaseholder, occupier, occupant, resident, inhabitant.

tend¹ *verb*
tends towards the left of the party/ tends to be lazy: incline, lean, bend, bear, head, aim, lead, go, move, gravitate.

tend² *verb*
tending the sick: look after, care for, cultivate, keep, maintain, manage, handle, guard, protect, watch, mind, nurture, nurse, minister to, serve, attend.
F3 neglect, ignore.

tendency *noun*
trend, drift, movement, course, direction, bearing, heading, bias, partiality, predisposition, propensity, readiness, liability, susceptibility, proneness, inclination, leaning, bent, disposition.

tender¹ *adjective*
1 a tender caress: kind, gentle, caring, humane, considerate, compassionate, sympathetic, warm, fond, affectionate, loving, amorous, romantic, sentimental, emotional, sensitive, tender-hearted, soft-hearted.
2 of tender years: youthful, immature, green, raw, new, inexperienced, impressionable, vulnerable.
3 tender meat: soft, succulent, fleshy, dainty, delicate.
4 skin is still a bit tender: sore, painful, aching, smarting, bruised, inflamed, raw.
F3 **1** hard-hearted, callous. **2** mature. **3** tough, hard.

tender² *verb*
tender one's resignation: offer, proffer, extend, give, present, submit, propose, suggest, advance, volunteer.
▸ *noun*
1 legal tender: currency, money.
2 submit a tender for the contract: offer, bid, estimate, quotation, proposal, proposition, suggestion, submission.

tense *adjective*
1 muscles were tense: tight, taut, stretched, strained, stiff, rigid.
2 feel tense: nervous, anxious, worried, jittery, uneasy, apprehensive, edgy, fidgety, restless, jumpy, overwrought, keyed up.
3 a tense moment: stressful, exciting, worrying, fraught.
F3 **1** loose, slack. **2** calm, relaxed.
▸ *verb*
tighten, contract, brace, stretch, strain.
F3 loosen, relax.

tension *noun*
1 increase the tension on the rope: tightness, tautness, stiffness, strain, stress, pressure.
2 suffering from nervous tension: nervousness, anxiety, worry, uneasiness, apprehension, edginess, restlessness, suspense.
F3 **1** looseness. **2** calm(ness), relaxation.

tentative *adjective*
experimental, exploratory, speculative, hesitant, faltering, cautious, unsure, uncertain, doubtful, undecided, provisional, indefinite, unconfirmed.
F3 definite, decisive, conclusive, final.

tenuous *adjective*
thin, slim, slender, fine, slight, insubstantial, flimsy, fragile, delicate, weak, shaky, doubtful, dubious, questionable.
F3 strong, substantial.

tepid *adjective*
lukewarm, cool, half-hearted, unenthusiastic, apathetic.
F3 cold, hot, passionate.

term *noun*
1 a Scottish term: word, name, designation, appellation (*fml*), title,

epithet, phrase, expression.
2 in his second term at university: time, period, course, duration, spell, span, stretch, interval, space, semester, session, season.
▶ *verb*
call, name, dub, style, designate, label, tag, title, entitle.

terminal *adjective*
1 the terminal event: last, final, concluding, ultimate, extreme, utmost.
2 terminal illness: fatal, deadly, lethal, mortal, incurable.
E₃1 initial.

terminology *noun*
language, jargon, phraseology, vocabulary, words, terms, nomenclature.

terms *noun*
1 on good terms: relations, relationship, footing, standing, position.
2 the terms of the agreement: conditions, specifications, stipulations, provisos, provisions, qualifications, particulars.
3 our terms are very reasonable: rates, charges, fees, prices, tariff.

terrain *noun*
land, ground, territory, country, countryside, landscape, topography.

terrestrial *adjective*
earthly, worldly, global, mundane.
E₃ extraterrestrial, cosmic, heavenly.

terrible *adjective*
bad, awful, frightful, dreadful, shocking, appalling, outrageous, disgusting, revolting, repulsive, offensive, abhorrent (*fml*), hateful, horrid, horrible, unpleasant, obnoxious, foul, vile, hideous, gruesome, horrific, harrowing, distressing, grave, serious, severe, extreme, desperate.
E₃ excellent, wonderful, superb.

terrific *adjective* (*infml*)
1 a terrific show: excellent, wonderful, marvellous, super, smashing (*infml*), outstanding, brilliant, magnificent, superb, fabulous (*infml*), fantastic (*infml*), cool (*infml*), sensational, amazing, stupendous, breathtaking.

2 a terrific monster/price: huge, enormous, gigantic, tremendous, great, intense, extreme, excessive.
E₃1 awful, terrible, appalling.

terrify *verb*
petrify, horrify, appal, shock, terrorize, intimidate, frighten, scare, alarm, dismay.

territory *noun*
country, land, state, dependency, province, domain, preserve, jurisdiction, sector, region, area, district, zone, tract, terrain.

terror *noun*
fear, panic, dread, trepidation, horror, shock, fright, alarm, dismay, consternation, terrorism, intimidation.

terrorize *verb*
threaten, menace, intimidate, oppress, coerce, bully, browbeat, frighten, scare, alarm, terrify, petrify, horrify, shock.

terse *adjective*
short, brief, succinct, concise, compact, condensed, epigrammatic, pithy, incisive, snappy, curt, brusque, abrupt, laconic.
E₃ long-winded, verbose.

test *verb*
try, experiment, examine, assess, evaluate, check, investigate, analyse, screen, prove, verify.
▶ *noun*
trial, try-out, experiment, examination, assessment, evaluation, check, investigation, analysis, proof, probation, ordeal.

testify *verb*
give evidence, depose, state, declare, assert, swear, avow, attest (*fml*), vouch, certify, corroborate, affirm, show, bear witness.

testimony *noun*
evidence, statement, affidavit, submission, deposition, declaration, profession, attestation, affirmation, support, proof, verification, confirmation, witness, demonstration, manifestation, indication.

text *noun*
words, wording, content, matter, body,

subject, topic, theme, reading, passage, paragraph, sentence, book, textbook, source.

texture *noun*
consistency, feel, surface, grain, weave, tissue, fabric, structure, composition, constitution, character, quality.

thank *verb*
say thank you, be grateful, appreciate, acknowledge, recognize, credit.

thankful *adjective*
grateful, appreciative, obliged, indebted, pleased, contented, relieved.
Ⅎungrateful, unappreciative.

thankless *adjective*
unrecognized, unappreciated, unrequited, unrewarding, unprofitable, fruitless.
Ⅎrewarding, worthwhile.

thanks *noun*
gratitude, gratefulness, appreciation, acknowledgement, recognition, credit, thanksgiving, thank-offering.
◆ **thanks to** because of, owing to, due to, on account of, as a result of, through.

thaw *verb*
melt, defrost, de-ice, soften, liquefy, dissolve, warm, heat up.
Ⅎfreeze.

theatrical *adjective*
1 theatrical props: dramatic, thespian.

Theatrical forms include:

ballet, burlesque, cabaret, circus, comedy, black comedy, comedy of humours, comedy of manners, comedy of menace, commedia dell'arte, duologue, farce, fringe theatre, Grand Guignol, kabuki, kitchen-sink, legitimate drama, masque, melodrama, mime, miracle play, monologue, morality play, mummery, music hall, musical, musical comedy, mystery play, Noh, opera, operetta, pageant, pantomime, play, Punch and Judy, puppet theatre, revue, street theatre, tableau, theatre-in-the-round, Theatre of the Absurd, Theatre of Cruelty, tragedy.

2 theatrical behaviour: melodramatic,

histrionic, mannered, affected, artificial, pompous, ostentatious, showy, extravagant, exaggerated, overdone.

theft *noun*
robbery, thieving, stealing, pilfering, larceny, shoplifting, kleptomania, fraud, embezzlement.

theme *noun*
subject, topic, thread, motif, keynote, idea, gist, essence, burden, argument, thesis, dissertation, composition, essay, text, matter.

theorem *noun*
formula, principle, rule, statement, deduction, proposition, hypothesis.

theoretical *adjective*
hypothetical, conjectural, speculative, abstract, academic, pure, ideal.
Ⅎpractical, applied, concrete.

theory *noun*
hypothesis, supposition, assumption, presumption, surmise, guess, conjecture, speculation, idea, notion, abstraction, philosophy, thesis, plan, proposal, scheme, system.
Ⅎcertainty, practice.

therapeutic *adjective*
remedial, curative, healing, restorative, tonic, medicinal, corrective, good, beneficial.
Ⅎharmful, detrimental.

therapy *noun*
treatment, remedy, cure, healing, tonic.

therefore *adverb*
so, then, consequently, as a result, thus (*fml*).

thick *adjective*
1 thick waist/sweater/forest: wide, broad, fat, heavy, solid, dense, impenetrable, close, compact.
2 thick cream/soup: concentrated, condensed, viscous, coagulated, clotted.
3 thick with shoppers: full, packed, crowded, chock-a-block, swarming, teeming, bristling, brimming, bursting, numerous, abundant.
4 (*infml*) can be a bit thick sometimes: stupid, foolish, slow, dull, dim-witted, brainless, simple.

E3 1 thin, slim, slender, slight. **3** sparse. **4** clever, brainy (*infml*).

thicken *verb*
condense, stiffen, congeal, coagulate, clot, cake, gel, jell, set.
E3 thin.

thicket *noun*
wood, copse, coppice, grove, spinney.

thickness *noun*
1 wood/paint of the right thickness: width, breadth, diameter, density, viscosity, bulk, body.
2 several thicknesses of material: layer, stratum, ply, sheet, coat.
E3 1 thinness.

thief *noun*
robber, bandit, mugger, pickpocket, shoplifter, burglar, house-breaker, plunderer, poacher, stealer, pilferer, filcher, kleptomaniac, swindler, embezzler.

thin *adjective*
1 thin arms/a few thin sheep: lean, slim, slender, narrow, attenuated (*fml*), slight, skinny, bony, skeletal, scraggy, scrawny, lanky, gaunt, spare, underweight, undernourished, emaciated.
2 thin fabric: fine, delicate, light, flimsy, filmy, gossamer, sheer, see-through, transparent, translucent.
3 thin pickings: sparse, scarce, scattered, scant, meagre, poor, inadequate, deficient, scanty, skimpy.
4 thin soup: weak, feeble, runny, watery, diluted.
E3 1 fat, broad. **2** thick, dense, solid. **3** plentiful, abundant. **4** strong.
▸ *verb*
1 thinning out towards the end/thin out the plants: narrow, attenuate (*fml*), diminish, reduce, trim, weed out.
2 thin the paint: weaken, dilute, water down.

thing *noun*
1 make things out of wood article, object, entity, creature, body, substance.
2 one of the things we need to discuss: item, detail, particular, feature, factor, element, point, fact, concept, thought.
3 the thing that turns the wheels: device, contrivance, gadget, tool, implement, instrument, apparatus, machine, mechanism.
4 have things to do act, deed, feat, action, task.
5 a strange thing happened: circumstance, eventuality, happening, occurrence, event, incident, phenomenon, affair, proceeding.
6 (*infml*) cars are his thing/have a thing about spiders: obsession, preoccupation, fixation, fetish, phobia, hang-up (*infml*).
⇨ *See also* **Word Workshop** *panel.*

things *noun*
belongings, possessions, effects, paraphernalia, stuff (*infml*), goods, luggage, baggage, equipment, gear (*infml*), clobber (*infml*), odds and ends, bits and pieces.

think *verb*
1 think it was true: believe, hold (*fml*), consider, regard, esteem, deem, judge, estimate, reckon, calculate, determine, conclude, reason.
2 think of the consequences: conceive, imagine, suppose, presume, surmise, expect, foresee, envisage, anticipate.
3 think it over: ponder, mull over, chew over, ruminate, meditate, contemplate, muse, cogitate, reflect, deliberate, weigh up, recall, recollect, remember.
◆ **think up** devise, contrive, dream up, imagine, foresee, visualize, invent, design, create, concoct.

thinking *noun*
reasoning, philosophy, thoughts, conclusions, theory, idea, opinion, view, outlook, position, judgement, assessment.
▸ *adjective*
reasoning, rational, intellectual, intelligent, cultured, sophisticated, philosophical, analytical, reflective, contemplative, thoughtful.

thirst *noun*
1 dying of thirst: thirstiness, dryness, drought.
2 a thirst for knowledge: desire, longing, yearning, hankering, craving, hunger, appetite, lust, passion, eagerness, keenness.

thirsty *adjective*
1 hungry and thirsty: dry, parched
(*infml*), gasping (*infml*), dehydrated,
arid.
2 thirsty for knowledge: desirous,
longing, yearning, hankering, craving,
hungry, burning, itching, dying, eager,
avid, greedy.

thorn *noun*
spike, point, barb, prickle, spine,
bristle, needle.

thorough *adjective*
full, complete, total, entire, utter,
absolute, perfect, pure, sheer,
unqualified, unmitigated, out-and-
out, downright, sweeping, all-
embracing, comprehensive, all-
inclusive, exhaustive, thoroughgoing,
intensive, in-depth, conscientious,
efficient, painstaking, scrupulous,
meticulous, careful.
E3 partial, superficial, careless.

though *conjunction*
although, even if, notwithstanding,
while, allowing, granted.
▶ *adverb*
however, nevertheless, nonetheless,
yet, still, even so, all the same, for all
that.

thought *noun*
1 give it some thought: thinking,
attention, heed, regard, consideration,
study, scrutiny, introspection,
meditation, contemplation, cogitation,
reflection, deliberation.
**2 had thoughts of being a lawyer/
what are your thoughts on this?**: idea,
notion, concept, conception, belief,
conviction, opinion, view, judgement,
assessment, conclusion, plan, design,
intention, purpose, aim, hope, dream,
expectation, anticipation.
3 have some thought for others:
thoughtfulness, consideration,
kindness, care, concern, compassion,
sympathy, gesture, touch.

thoughtful *adjective*
1 in thoughtful silence: pensive,
wistful, dreamy, abstracted, reflective,
contemplative, introspective, thinking,
absorbed, studious, serious, solemn.
2 a thoughtful act: considerate, kind,

unselfish, helpful, caring, attentive,
heedful, mindful, careful, prudent,
cautious, wary.
E3 2 thoughtless, insensitive, selfish.

thoughtless *adjective*
1 a thoughtless thing to say:
inconsiderate, callous, unthinking,
insensitive, unfeeling, tactless,
undiplomatic, unkind, selfish,
uncaring.
2 in a thoughtless moment: absent-
minded, inattentive, heedless,
mindless, foolish, stupid, silly, rash,
reckless, ill-considered, imprudent,
careless, negligent, remiss.
E3 1 thoughtful, considerate. **2** careful.

thrash *verb*
1 was thrashed severely: punish, beat,
whip, lash, flog, scourge, cane, belt,
spank, clobber, wallop (*infml*), lay into.
2 thrashed the opposition: defeat,
beat, trounce, hammer (*infml*),
slaughter (*infml*), crush, overwhelm,
rout.
3 thrashing about in the water: thresh,
flail, toss, jerk.
◆ **thrash out** discuss, debate, negotiate,
settle, resolve.

thread *noun*
1 sewing thread: cotton, yarn, strand,
fibre, filament, string, line.
2 lose the thread of the argument:
course, direction, drift, tenor, theme,
motif, plot, storyline.

threadbare *adjective*
1 threadbare clothes: worn, frayed,
ragged, moth-eaten, scruffy, shabby.
2 a threadbare excuse: hackneyed,
overused, old, stale, tired, trite, stock.
E3 1 new. **2** fresh.

threat *noun*
menace, warning, omen, portent,
presage, foreboding, danger, risk,
hazard, peril.

threaten *verb*
menace, intimidate, browbeat,
pressurize, bully, terrorize, warn,
portend, presage, forebode,
foreshadow, endanger, jeopardize,
imperil.

threatening *adjective*
menacing, warning, cautionary,

The words **thing** or **things** are rather vague and uninteresting.
Try to use more specific words instead, especially in your
writing. Some suggestions for alternatives are listed below.

device

apparatus	implement	mechanism
contrivance	instrument	tool
gadget	machine	

an act or duty

action	feat	responsibility
deed	problem	task

a situation or something that happens

affair	eventuality	phenomenon
circumstance	incident	proceeding
event	occurrence	

a specific thing

article	entity	object
body	item	substance
creature		

a detail or part of something

aspect	factor	particular
characteristic	feature	point

idea

concept	fact	thought

gear

baggage	clothes	possessions
belongings	odds and ends	stuff
bits and pieces		

The following passage shows how some of the synonyms
listed opposite might be used instead of repeating **thing**.

"

"On our first night camping, I heard this ~~thing~~ *creature*
breathing," said Peter. "I was petrified. Des decided that
the only sensible ~~thing~~ *approach* was to look outside the tent to
see what it was. When he told me it was only a cow I
couldn't believe it!"

"Still, we had a good holiday, and the new cooking
~~things~~ *apparatus* worked well. The best ~~thing~~ *aspect* was the peace and
quiet in the countryside. And after the ~~thing~~ *incident* with the cow,
the only other exciting ~~thing~~ *event* was the flood on the last
night. The biggest ~~thing~~ *problem* we discovered was that the tent
wasn't waterproof, and all our ~~things~~ *belongings* got soaked!"

ominous, inauspicious, sinister, grim, looming, impending.

threshold *noun*
doorstep, sill, doorway, door, entrance, brink, verge, starting-point, dawn, beginning, start, outset, opening.

thrifty *adjective*
economical, saving, frugal, sparing, prudent, careful.
🖃 extravagant, profligate, prodigal, wasteful.

thrill *noun*
excitement, adventure, pleasure, stimulation, charge, kick (*infml*), buzz (*infml*), sensation, glow, tingle, throb, shudder, quiver, tremor.
▶ *verb*
excite, electrify, galvanize, exhilarate, rouse, arouse, move, stir, stimulate, flush, glow, tingle, throb, shudder, tremble, quiver, shake.
🖃 bore.

thrive *verb*
flourish, prosper, boom, grow, increase, advance, develop, bloom, blossom, gain, profit, succeed.
🖃 languish, stagnate, fail, die.

throb *verb*
pulse, pulsate, beat, palpitate, vibrate, pound, thump.
▶ *noun*
pulse, pulsation, beat, palpitation, vibration, pounding, thumping.

throttle *verb*
strangle, choke, asphyxiate, suffocate, smother, stifle, gag, silence, suppress, inhibit.

through *preposition*
1 through the streets: between, by, via, by way of, by means of, using.
2 all through the night: throughout, during, in.
3 through his efforts: because of, as a result of, thanks to.
▶ *adjective*
1 (*infml*) are you through yet?: finished, ended, completed, done.
2 through train: direct, express, non-stop.

throw *verb*
1 throw a stone: hurl, heave, lob, pitch, chuck (*infml*), sling, cast, fling,

toss, launch, propel, send.
2 throw light on something: shed, cast, project, direct.
3 was thrown to the ground: bring down, floor, upset, overturn, dislodge, unseat, unsaddle, unhorse.
4 (*infml*) threw him for a moment: perplex, baffle, confound, confuse, disconcert, astonish, dumbfound.
▶ *noun*
heave, lob, pitch, sling, fling, toss, cast.
◆ **throw away 1** throw away old letters: discard, jettison, dump, ditch (*infml*), scrap, dispose of, throw out.
2 throw money away: waste, squander, fritter away, blow (*infml*).
🖃 1 keep, preserve, salvage, rescue.
◆ **throw out 1** threw them out of their house: evict, turn out, expel, turf out (*infml*), eject, emit, radiate, give off.
2 throwing out all the old magazines: reject, discard, dismiss, turn down, jettison, dump, ditch (*infml*), throw away, scrap.
◆ **throw up 1** (*infml*) feel as if I'm going to throw up: vomit, regurgitate, disgorge, retch, heave.
2 threw up his job: give up, abandon, renounce, relinquish, resign, quit, leave.

thrust *verb*
push, shove, butt, ram, jam, wedge, stick, poke, prod, jab, lunge, pierce, stab, plunge, press, force, impel, drive, propel.
▶ *noun*
push, shove, poke, prod, lunge, stab, drive, impetus, momentum.

thud *noun, verb*
thump, clump, knock, clunk, smack, wallop (*infml*), crash, bang, thunder.

thump *noun*
knock, blow, punch, clout, box, cuff, smack, whack (*infml*), wallop (*infml*), crash, bang, thud, beat, throb.
▶ *verb*
hit, strike, knock, punch, clout, box, cuff, smack, thrash, whack (*infml*), wallop (*infml*), crash, bang, thud, batter, pound, hammer, beat, throb.

thunder *noun*
boom, reverberation, crash, bang,

crack, clap, peal, rumble, roll, roar, blast, explosion.

▶ *verb*

boom, resound, reverberate, crash, bang, crack, clap, peal, rumble, roll, roar, blast.

thus *adverb*

so, hence, therefore, consequently, then, accordingly, like this, in this way, as follows.

thwart *verb*

frustrate, foil, stymie, defeat, hinder, impede, obstruct, block, check, baffle, stop, prevent, oppose.

₣ help, assist, aid.

tick *noun*

1 the tick of the clock: click, tap, stroke, tick-tock.

2 (*infml*) **wait a tick**: moment, instant, flash, jiffy (*infml*), second, minute.

▶ *verb*

1 tick the box: mark, indicate, choose, select.

2 clock ticking: click, tap, beat.

◆ **tick off** (*infml*) scold, chide, reprimand, rebuke, reproach, reprove, upbraid (*fml*), tell off (*infml*).

₣ praise, compliment.

ticket *noun*

pass, card, certificate, token, voucher, coupon, docket, slip, label, tag, sticker.

tickle *verb*

excite, thrill, delight, please, gratify, amuse, entertain, divert.

tide *noun*

current, ebb, flow, stream, flux, movement, course, direction, drift, trend, tendency.

tidy *adjective*

1 a tidy cupboard/appearance: neat, orderly, methodical, systematic, organized, clean, spick-and-span, shipshape, smart, spruce, trim, well-kept, ordered, uncluttered.

2 (*infml*) **a tidy sum**: large, substantial, sizable, considerable, good, generous, ample.

₣ **1** untidy, messy, disorganized. **2** small, insignificant.

▶ *verb*

neaten, straighten, order, arrange, clean, smarten, spruce up, groom.

tie *verb*

knot, fasten, secure, moor, tether, attach, join, connect, link, unite, rope, lash, strap, bind, restrain, restrict, confine, limit, hamper, hinder.

▶ *noun*

1 breaking all his family ties: connection, link, liaison, relationship, bond, affiliation, obligation, commitment, duty, restraint, restriction, limitation, hindrance.

2 a tie between the two teams: draw, dead heat, stalemate, deadlock.

◆ **tie up 1 tie up at the jetty**: moor, tether, attach, secure, rope, lash, bind, truss, wrap up, restrain.

2 tie up all the loose ends: conclude, terminate, wind up, settle.

3 tied up all this week: occupy, engage, engross.

tier *noun*

floor, storey, level, stage, stratum, layer, belt, zone, band, echelon, rank, row, line.

tight *adjective*

1 keep the line tight/tight clothes/a tight space: taut, stretched, tense, rigid, stiff, firm, fixed, fast, secure, close, cramped, constricted, compact, snug, close-fitting.

2 a tight seal: hermetic, -proof, impervious, airtight, watertight.

3 (*infml*) **tight with money**: mean, stingy, miserly, niggardly, parsimonious, tight-fisted (*infml*).

4 tight security: strict, severe, stringent, rigorous.

₣ **1** loose, slack. **2** open. **3** generous. **4** lax.

tilt *verb*

slope, incline, slant, pitch, list, tip, lean.

▶ *noun*

slope, incline, angle, inclination, slant, pitch, list.

timber *noun*

wood, trees, forest, beam, lath, plank, board, log.

time *noun*

1 stay for a short/long time: spell, stretch, period, term, season, session, span, duration, interval, space, while.

2 in time with the music: tempo, beat, rhythm, metre, measure.
3 at that time in his life: moment, point, juncture, stage, instance, occasion, date, day, hour.
4 in Roman times/in the time of Napoleon: age, era, epoch, life, lifetime, generation, heyday, peak.

Periods of time include:

eternity, era, eon, age, generation, period, epoch, millennium, chiliad, century, lifetime, quinquennium, year, light-year, yesteryear, quarter, month, fortnight, week, midweek, weekend, long weekend, day, today, tonight, yesterday, tomorrow, morrow, weekday, hour, minute, second, moment, instant, millisecond, microsecond, nanosecond; dawn, sunrise, sun-up, the early hours, wee small hours (*infml*), morning, morn, a.m., daytime, midday, noon, high noon, p.m., afternoon, teatime, evening, twilight, dusk, sunset, nightfall, bedtime, night, night-time; season, spring, summer, midsummer, autumn, fall (*US*), winter.

verb
clock, measure, meter, regulate, control, set, schedule, timetable.

timeless *adjective*
ageless, immortal, everlasting, eternal, endless, permanent, lasting, enduring, changeless, unchanging, unending, abiding (*fml*).

timely *adjective*
well-timed, seasonable, suitable, appropriate, convenient, opportune, propitious, prompt, punctual.
F∃ ill-timed, unsuitable, inappropriate.

timetable *noun*
schedule, programme, agenda, calendar, diary, rota, roster, list, listing, curriculum.

timid *adjective*
shy, bashful, modest, shrinking, retiring, nervous, apprehensive, afraid, timorous, fearful, cowardly, faint-hearted, spineless, irresolute.
F∃ brave, bold, audacious.

tinge *noun*
tint, dye, colour, shade, touch, trace, suggestion, hint, smack, flavour, pinch, drop, dash, bit, sprinkling, smattering.
▸ *verb*
tint, dye, stain, colour, shade, suffuse, imbue.

tingle *verb*
sting, prickle, tickle, itch, thrill, throb, quiver, vibrate.

tinker *verb*
fiddle, play, toy, trifle, potter, dabble, meddle, tamper.

tint *noun*
dye, stain, rinse, wash, colour, hue, shade, tincture, tinge, tone, cast, streak, trace, touch.

tiny *adjective*
minute, microscopic, infinitesimal, teeny (*infml*), small, little, slight, negligible, insignificant, diminutive, petite, dwarfish, pint-sized (*infml*), pocket, miniature, mini (*infml*).
F∃ huge, enormous, immense.

tip[1] *noun*
the tip of her finger: end, extremity, point, nib, apex, peak, pinnacle, summit, acme, top, cap, crown, head.
▸ *verb*
cap, crown, top, surmount.

tip[2] *verb*
tipping it up on end: lean, incline, slant, list, tilt, topple over, capsize, upset, overturn, spill, pour out, empty, unload, dump.

tip[3] *noun*
1 gave us a few useful tips: clue, pointer, hint, suggestion, advice, warning, tip-off, information, inside information, forecast.
2 gave the waiter a tip: gratuity, gift, perquisite (*fml*).
▸ *verb*
1 tipped us off: advise, suggest, warn, caution, forewarn, tip off, inform, tell.
2 tip the driver: reward, remunerate.

tire *verb*
weary, fatigue, wear out, exhaust, drain, enervate.
F∃ enliven, invigorate, refresh.

tired *adjective*
1 felt very tired: weary, drowsy, sleepy, flagging, fatigued, worn out, exhausted, dog-tired, drained, jaded, bushed (*infml*), whacked (*infml*), shattered (*infml*), beat (*infml*), deadbeat (*infml*), all in (*infml*), knackered (*infml*).
2 tired of waiting: fed up, bored, sick.
F3 1 lively, energetic, rested, refreshed.

tireless *adjective*
untiring, unwearied, unflagging, indefatigable, energetic, vigorous, diligent, industrious, resolute, determined.
F3 tired, lazy.

tiresome *adjective*
troublesome, trying, annoying, irritating, exasperating, wearisome, dull, boring, tedious, monotonous, uninteresting, tiring, fatiguing, laborious.
F3 interesting, stimulating, easy.

tiring *adjective*
wearying, fatiguing, exhausting, draining, demanding, exacting, taxing, arduous, strenuous, laborious.

title *noun*
1 what's her (job) title?: name, appellation (*fml*), denomination (*fml*), term, designation, label, epithet, nickname, pseudonym, rank, status, office, position.
2 the title of the play: heading, headline, caption, legend, inscription.
3 title to the land: right, prerogative, privilege, claim, entitlement, ownership, deeds.
▶ *verb*
entitle, name, call, dub, style, term, designate, label.

toast *verb*
grill, brown, roast, heat, warm.
▶ *noun*
drink, pledge, tribute, salute, compliment, health.

together *adverb*
jointly, in concert, side by side, shoulder to shoulder, in unison, as one, simultaneously, at the same time, all at once, collectively, en masse, closely, continuously, consecutively,

successively, in succession, in a row, hand in hand.
F3 separately, individually, alone.

toil *noun*
labour, hard work, donkey-work, drudgery, sweat, graft (*infml*), industry, application, effort, exertion, elbow grease.
▶ *verb*
labour, work, slave, drudge, sweat, grind, slog, graft (*infml*), plug away (*infml*), persevere, strive, struggle.

token *noun*
1 a love token: symbol, emblem, representation, mark, sign, indication, manifestation, demonstration, expression, evidence, proof, clue, warning, reminder, memorial, memento, souvenir, keepsake.
2 gift token: voucher, coupon, counter, disc.
▶ *adjective*
symbolic, emblematic, nominal, minimal, perfunctory (*fml*), superficial, cosmetic, hollow, insincere.

tolerable *adjective*
bearable, endurable, sufferable, acceptable, passable, adequate, reasonable, fair, average, all right, OK (*infml*), not bad, mediocre, indifferent, so-so (*infml*), unexceptional, ordinary, run-of-the-mill.
F3 intolerable, unbearable, insufferable.

tolerant *adjective*
patient, forbearing, long-suffering, open-minded, fair, unprejudiced, broad-minded, liberal, charitable, kind-hearted, sympathetic, understanding, forgiving, lenient, indulgent, easy-going (*infml*), permissive, lax, soft.
F3 intolerant, biased, prejudiced, bigoted, unsympathetic.

tolerate *verb*
endure, suffer, put up with, bear, stand, abide, stomach, swallow, take, receive, accept, admit, allow, permit, condone, countenance, indulge.

toll[1] *verb*
bell tolled: ring, peal, chime, knell, sound, strike, announce, call.

toll² *noun*

pay a toll on the motorway: charge, fee, payment, levy, tax, duty, tariff, rate, cost, penalty, demand.

tomb *noun*

grave, burial-place, vault, crypt, sepulchre, catacomb, mausoleum, cenotaph.

tone *noun*

1 tone of voice: note, timbre, pitch, volume, intonation, modulation, inflection, accent, stress, emphasis, force, strength.

2 brown tones: tint, tinge, colour, hue, shade, cast, tonality.

3 gauge the tone of the meeting: air, manner, attitude, mood, spirit, humour, temper, character, quality, feel, style, effect, vein, tenor, drift.

▸ *verb*

match, co-ordinate, blend, harmonize.

◆ **tone down** moderate, temper, subdue, restrain, soften, dim, dampen, play down, reduce, alleviate, assuage (*fml*), mitigate.

tongue *noun*

language, speech, discourse, talk, utterance, articulation, parlance, vernacular, idiom, dialect, patois.

tonic *noun*

cordial, pick-me-up, restorative, refresher, bracer, stimulant, shot in the arm (*infml*), boost, fillip.

too *adverb*

1 like him too: also, as well, in addition, besides, moreover, likewise.

2 too expensive: excessively, inordinately, unduly, over, overly, unreasonably, ridiculously, extremely, very.

tool *noun*

1 gardening tools: implement, instrument, utensil, gadget, device, contrivance, contraption, apparatus, appliance.

2 he was the tool of corrupt politicians: puppet, pawn, dupe, stooge, minion, hireling.

top *noun*

1 top of the class/hill: head, tip, vertex, apex, crest, crown, peak, pinnacle, summit, acme, zenith, culmination, height.

2 put the top back on the toothpaste: lid, cap, cover, cork, stopper.

F3 1 bottom, base, nadir.

▸ *adjective*

highest, topmost, upmost, uppermost, upper, superior, head, chief, leading, first, foremost, principal, sovereign, ruling, pre-eminent, dominant, prime, paramount, greatest, maximum, best, finest, supreme, crowning, culminating.

F3 bottom, lowest, inferior.

▸ *verb*

1 ice cream topped with raspberry sauce: tip, cap, crown, cover, finish (off), decorate, garnish.

2 that tops everything: beat, exceed, outstrip, better, excel, best, surpass, eclipse, outshine, outdo, surmount, transcend.

topic *noun*

subject, theme, issue, question, matter, point, thesis, text.

topical *adjective*

current, contemporary, up-to-date, up-to-the-minute, recent, newsworthy, relevant, popular, familiar.

topple *verb*

totter, overbalance, tumble, fall, collapse, upset, overturn, capsize, overthrow, oust.

torment *verb*

tease, provoke, annoy, vex, trouble, worry, harass, hound, pester, bother, bedevil, plague, afflict, distress, harrow, pain, torture, persecute.

torrent *noun*

stream, volley, outburst, gush, rush, flood, spate, deluge, cascade, downpour.

F3 trickle.

torture *verb*

pain, agonize, excruciate, crucify, rack, martyr, persecute, torment, afflict, distress.

▸ *noun*

pain, agony, suffering, affliction, distress, misery, anguish, torment, martyrdom, persecution.

toss *verb*

1 toss a coin/toss it away: flip, cast,

fling, throw, chuck (*infml*), sling, hurl, lob.
2 tossed from side to side: roll, heave, pitch, lurch, jolt, shake, agitate, rock, thrash, squirm, wriggle.
▶ *noun*
flip, cast, fling, throw, pitch.

total *noun*
sum, whole, entirety, totality, all, lot, mass, aggregate, amount.
▶ *adjective*
full, complete, entire, whole, integral, all-out, utter, absolute, unconditional, unqualified, outright, undisputed, perfect, consummate, thoroughgoing, sheer, downright, thorough.
F3 partial, limited, restricted.
▶ *verb*
add (up), sum (up), tot (up), count (up), reckon, amount to, come to, reach.

touch *noun*
1 the touch of her hand: feel, texture, brush, stroke, caress, pat, tap, contact.
2 a touch of garlic: trace, spot, dash, pinch, soupçon, suspicion, hint, suggestion, speck, jot, tinge, smack.
3 has the right touch: skill, art, knack, flair, style, method, manner, technique, approach.
▶ *verb*
1 touched his face: feel, handle, finger, brush, graze, stroke, caress, fondle, pat, tap, hit, strike.
2 touching on either side: contact, meet, abut, adjoin, border.
3 touched her heart: move, stir, upset, disturb, impress, inspire, influence, affect.
4 her letters touched on the subject more than once: mention, concern, regard.
5 couldn't touch him for sheer skill: reach, attain, equal, match, rival, better.
◆ **touch on** mention, broach, speak of, remark on, refer to, allude to, cover, deal with.

touchy *adjective*
irritable, irascible, quick-tempered, bad-tempered, grumpy, grouchy, crabbed, cross, peevish, captious, edgy, over-sensitive.
F3 calm, imperturbable.

tough *adjective*
1 a tough material: strong, durable, resilient, resistant, hardy, sturdy, solid, rigid, stiff, inflexible, hard, leathery.
2 tough character: rough, violent, vicious, callous, hardened, obstinate.
3 a tough regime: harsh, severe, strict, stern.
4 had to be pretty tough to survive: firm, resolute, determined, tenacious.
5 a tough job/problem: arduous, laborious, exacting, hard, difficult, puzzling, perplexing, baffling, knotty, thorny, troublesome.
F3 1 fragile, delicate, weak, tender. 2 gentle, soft. 3 gentle. 5 easy, simple.
▶ *noun*
brute, thug, bully, ruffian, hooligan, lout, yob (*slang*).

tour *noun*
circuit, round, visit, expedition, journey, trip, outing, excursion, drive, ride, course.
▶ *verb*
visit, go round, sightsee, explore, travel, journey, drive, ride.

tourist *noun*
holidaymaker, visitor, sightseer, tripper, excursionist, traveller, voyager, globetrotter.

tournament *noun*
championship, series, competition, contest, match, event, meeting.

tow *verb*
pull, tug, draw, trail, drag, lug, haul, transport.

towards *preposition*
1 towards the end: to, approaching, nearing, close to, nearly, almost.
2 his feelings towards her: regarding, with regard to, with respect to, concerning, about, for.

tower *noun*
steeple, spire, belfry, turret, fortification, bastion, citadel, fort, fortress, castle, keep.

towering *adjective*
soaring, tall, high, lofty, elevated, monumental, colossal, gigantic, great, magnificent, imposing, impressive, sublime, supreme, surpassing,

overpowering, extreme, inordinate.
F∃small, tiny, minor, trivial.

toxic *adjective*
poisonous, harmful, noxious,
unhealthy, dangerous, deadly, lethal.
F∃harmless, safe.

toy *noun*
plaything, game, doll, knick-knack.
▶ *verb*
play, tinker, fiddle, sport, trifle, dally.

trace *noun*
trail, track, spoor, footprint, footmark,
mark, token, sign, indication,
evidence, record, relic, remains,
remnant, vestige, shadow, hint,
suggestion, suspicion, soupçon, dash,
drop, spot, bit, jot, touch, tinge,
smack.
▶ *verb*
1 trace the picture/trace the outline
with his finger: copy, draw, sketch,
outline, delineate, depict, mark,
record, map, chart.
2 trace his missing family: find,
discover, detect, unearth, track (down),
trail, stalk, hunt, seek, follow, pursue,
shadow.

track *noun*
footstep, footprint, footmark, scent,
spoor, trail, wake, mark, trace, slot,
groove, rail, path, way, route, orbit,
line, course, drift, sequence.
▶ *verb*
stalk, trail, hunt, trace, follow, pursue,
chase, dog, tail, shadow.
◆ **track down** find, discover, trace,
hunt down, run to earth, sniff out,
ferret out, dig up, unearth, expose,
catch, capture.

trade *noun*
1 the trade in manufactured goods/
trade is brisk: commerce, traffic,
business, dealing, buying, selling,
shopkeeping, barter, exchange,
transactions, custom.
2 learning his trade: occupation, job,
business, profession, calling, craft,
skill.
▶ *verb*
traffic, peddle, do business, deal,
transact, buy, sell, barter, exchange,
swap, switch, bargain.

trademark *noun*
brand, label, name, sign, symbol, logo,
insignia, crest, emblem, badge,
hallmark.

trader *noun*
merchant, tradesman, broker, dealer,
buyer, seller, vendor, supplier,
wholesaler, retailer, shopkeeper,
trafficker, peddler.

traditional *adjective*
conventional, customary, habitual,
usual, accustomed, established, fixed,
long-established, time-honoured, old,
historic, folk, oral, unwritten.
F∃unconventional, innovative, new,
modern, contemporary.

traffic *noun*
1 road/air traffic: vehicles, shipping,
transport, transportation, freight.
2 the traffic in endangered species:
trade, commerce, business, dealing,
trafficking, barter, exchange.
3 traffic between nations:
communication, dealings, relations.
▶ *verb*
peddle, buy, sell, trade, do business,
deal, bargain, barter, exchange.

tragedy *noun*
adversity, misfortune, unhappiness,
affliction, blow, calamity, disaster,
catastrophe.

tragic *adjective*
sad, sorrowful, miserable, unhappy,
unfortunate, unlucky, ill-fated, pitiable,
pathetic, heartbreaking, shocking,
appalling, dreadful, awful, dire,
calamitous, disastrous, catastrophic,
deadly, fatal.
F∃happy, comic, successful.

trail *verb*
1 trailing along behind: drag, pull, tow,
droop, dangle, extend, stream, straggle,
dawdle, lag, loiter, linger.
2 trailing the thieves to their hideout:
track, stalk, hunt, follow, pursue,
chase, shadow, tail.
▶ *noun*
track, footprints, footmarks, scent,
trace, path, footpath, road, route, way.

train *verb*
1 training the new recruits/training
her voice: teach, instruct, coach, tutor,

educate, improve, school, discipline, prepare, drill, exercise, work out, practise, rehearse.
2 all eyes were trained on the horizon: point, direct, aim, level.
▶ *noun*
1 train of events: sequence, succession, series, progression, order, string, chain, line, file, procession, convoy, cortège, caravan.
2 the queen and her train of courtiers: retinue, entourage, attendants, court, household, staff, followers, following.

training *noun*
teaching, instruction, coaching, tuition, education, schooling, discipline, preparation, grounding, drill, exercise, working-out, practice, learning, apprenticeship.

trait *noun*
feature, attribute, quality, characteristic, idiosyncrasy, peculiarity, quirk.

traitor *noun*
betrayer, informer, deceiver, double-crosser, turncoat, renegade, deserter, defector, quisling, collaborator.
☒loyalist, supporter, defender.

tramp *verb*
walk, march, tread, stamp, stomp, stump, plod, trudge, traipse, trail, trek, hike, ramble, roam, rove.
▶ *noun*
vagrant, vagabond, hobo, down-and-out, dosser (*infml*).

trample *verb*
tread, stamp, crush, squash, flatten.

trance *noun*
dream, reverie, daze, stupor, unconsciousness, spell, ecstasy, rapture.

tranquil *adjective*
calm, composed, cool, imperturbable, unexcited, placid, sedate, relaxed, laid-back (*infml*), serene, peaceful, restful, still, undisturbed, untroubled, quiet, hushed, silent.
☒agitated, disturbed, troubled, noisy.

transaction *noun*
deal, bargain, agreement, arrangement, negotiation, business, affair, matter, proceeding, enterprise,

undertaking, deed, action, execution, discharge.

transfer *verb*
change, transpose, move, shift, remove, relocate, transplant, transport, carry, convey, transmit, consign, grant, hand over.
▶ *noun*
change, changeover, transposition, move, shift, removal, relocation, displacement, transmission, handover, transference.

transfix *verb*
fascinate, spellbind, mesmerize, hypnotize, paralyse.

transform *verb*
change, alter, adapt, convert, remodel, reconstruct, transfigure, revolutionize.
☒preserve, maintain.

transit *noun*
passage, journey, travel, movement, transfer, transportation, conveyance, carriage, haulage, shipment.

transition *noun*
passage, passing, progress, progression, development, evolution, flux, change, alteration, conversion, transformation, shift.

transitional *adjective*
provisional, temporary, passing, intermediate, developmental, changing, fluid, unsettled.
☒initial, final.

translate *verb*
interpret, render, paraphrase, simplify, decode, decipher, transliterate, transcribe, change, alter, convert, transform, improve.

translation *noun*
rendering, version, interpretation, gloss, crib, rewording, rephrasing, paraphrase, simplification, transliteration, transcription, change, alteration, conversion, transformation.

transmission *noun*
1 transmission of diseases: broadcasting, diffusion, spread, communication, conveyance, carriage, transport, shipment, sending, dispatch, relaying, transfer.
2 a live transmission: broadcast,

programme, show, signal.
E₃ 1 reception.

transmit *verb*
communicate, impart, convey, carry,
bear, transport, send, dispatch,
forward, relay, transfer, broadcast,
radio, disseminate, network, diffuse,
spread.
E₃ receive.

transparent *adjective*
1 transparent plastic: clear, see-
through, translucent, sheer.
2 meaning was transparent: plain,
distinct, clear, lucid, explicit,
unambiguous, unequivocal, apparent,
visible, obvious, evident, manifest,
patent, undisguised, open, candid,
straightforward.
E₃ 1 opaque. 2 unclear, ambiguous.

transplant *verb*
move, shift, displace, remove, uproot,
transfer, relocate, resettle, repot.
E₃ leave.

transport *verb*
convey, carry, bear, take, fetch, bring,
move, shift, transfer, ship, haul,
remove, deport.
▶ *noun*
conveyance, carriage, transfer,
transportation, shipment, shipping,
haulage, removal.

transverse *adjective*
cross, crosswise, transversal, diagonal,
oblique.

trap *noun*
snare, net, noose, springe, gin, booby-
trap, pitfall, danger, hazard, ambush,
trick, wile, ruse, stratagem, device,
trickery, artifice, deception.
▶ *verb*
snare, net, entrap, ensnare, enmesh,
catch, take, ambush, corner, trick,
deceive, dupe.

trash *noun*
rubbish, garbage, refuse, junk, waste,
litter, sweepings, scum, dregs.

trauma *noun*
injury, wound, hurt, damage, pain,
suffering, anguish, agony, torture,
ordeal, shock, jolt, upset, disturbance,
upheaval, strain, stress.
E₃ healing.

traumatic *adjective*
painful, hurtful, injurious, shocking,
upsetting, distressing, disturbing,
unpleasant, frightening, stressful.
E₃ healing, relaxing.

travel *verb*
journey, voyage, go, wend, move,
proceed, progress, wander, ramble,
roam, rove, tour, cross, traverse.
E₃ stay, remain.

Methods of travel include:
aviate, bike (*infml*), bus, commute,
cruise, cycle, drive, fly, freewheel, hike,
hitch-hike, march, motor, orienteer,
paddle, pilot, punt, ramble, ride, row,
sail, shuttle, skate, ski, steam, swim,
trek, walk.

noun
travelling, touring, tourism,
globetrotting.

Forms of travel include:
circumnavigation, cruise, drive,
excursion, expedition, exploration,
flight, hike, holiday, jaunt, journey,
march, migration, mission, outing,
pilgrimage, ramble, ride, safari, sail,
tour, trek, trip, visit, voyage, walk.

traveller *noun*
1 a seasoned traveller: tourist,
explorer, voyager, globetrotter,
holidaymaker, tripper (*infml*),
excursionist, passenger, commuter,
wanderer, rambler, hiker, wayfarer,
migrant, nomad.
2 a commercial traveller: salesman,
saleswoman, representative, rep
(*infml*), agent.

travelling *adjective*
touring, wandering, roaming, roving,
wayfaring, migrating, migrant,
migratory, nomadic, itinerant,
peripatetic, mobile, moving, vagrant,
homeless, unsettled.
E₃ fixed.

treacherous *adjective*
1 a treacherous plot: traitorous,
disloyal, unfaithful, faithless,
unreliable, untrustworthy, false,

untrue, deceitful, double-crossing.
2 treacherous roads: dangerous, hazardous, risky, perilous, precarious, icy, slippery.
F3 1 loyal, faithful, dependable. 2 safe, stable.

tread *verb*
walk, step, pace, stride, march, tramp, trudge, plod, stamp, trample, walk on, press, crush, squash.
▶ *noun*
walk, footfall, footstep, step, pace, stride.

treason *noun*
treachery, perfidy, disloyalty, duplicity, subversion, sedition, mutiny, rebellion.
F3 loyalty.

treasure *noun*
fortune, wealth, riches, money, cash, gold, jewels, hoard, cache.
▶ *verb*
prize, value, esteem, revere, worship, love, adore, idolize, cherish, preserve, guard.
F3 disparage, belittle.

treat *noun*
indulgence, gratification, pleasure, delight, enjoyment, fun, entertainment, excursion, outing, party, celebration, feast, banquet, gift, surprise, thrill.
▶ *verb*
1 how will you treat this question?: deal with, manage, handle, use, regard, consider, discuss, cover.
2 treat the patient: tend, nurse, minister to, attend to, care for, heal, cure.
3 treat you to lunch: pay for, buy, stand, give, provide, entertain, regale, feast.

treatment *noun*
1 treatment of disease: healing, cure, remedy, medication, therapy, surgery, care, nursing.
2 the treatment of waste/the paper's treatment of the story: management, handling, use, usage, conduct, discussion, coverage.

treaty *noun*
pact, convention, agreement,

covenant, compact, negotiation, contract, bond, alliance.

tree *noun*
bush, shrub, evergreen, conifer.

Trees include:

acacia, acer, alder, almond, apple, ash, aspen, balsa, bay, beech, birch, blackthorn, blue gum, box, cedar, cherry, chestnut, coconut palm, cottonwood, cypress, date palm, dogwood, Dutch elm, ebony, elder, elm, eucalyptus, fig, fir, gum, hawthorn, hazel, hickory, hornbeam, horse chestnut, Japanese maple, larch, laurel, lime, linden, mahogany, maple, monkey puzzle, mountain ash, oak, palm, pear, pine, plane, plum, poplar, prunus, pussy willow, redwood, rowan, rubber tree, sandalwood, sapele, sequoia, silver birch, silver maple, spruce, sycamore, teak, walnut, weeping willow, whitebeam, willow, witch hazel, yew, yucca; bonsai, conifer, deciduous, evergreen, fruit, hardwood, ornamental, palm, softwood. ⇨*See also* **wood**.

trek *noun*
hike, walk, march, tramp, journey, expedition, safari.
▶ *verb*
hike, walk, march, tramp, trudge, plod, journey, rove, roam.

tremble *verb*
shake, vibrate, quake, shiver, shudder, quiver, wobble, rock.

tremendous *adjective*
wonderful, marvellous, stupendous, sensational, spectacular, extraordinary, amazing, incredible, terrific, impressive, huge, immense, vast, colossal, gigantic, towering, formidable.
F3 ordinary, unimpressive.

tremor *noun*
shake, quiver, tremble, shiver, quake, quaver, wobble, vibration, agitation, thrill, shock, earthquake.
F3 steadiness.

trend *noun*
course, flow, drift, tendency,

inclination, leaning, craze, rage (*infml*), fashion, vogue, mode, style, look.

trespass *verb*
invade, intrude, encroach, poach, infringe, violate, offend, wrong.
E3 obey, keep to.

trial *noun*
1 on trial/go to trial: litigation, lawsuit, hearing, inquiry, tribunal.
2 medical trials: experiment, test, examination, check, dry run, dummy run, practice, rehearsal, audition, contest.
3 the trials of life: affliction, suffering, grief, misery, distress, adversity, hardship, ordeal, trouble, nuisance, vexation, tribulation.
E3 relief, happiness.
▸ *adjective*
experimental, test, pilot, exploratory, provisional, probationary.

tribe *noun*
race, nation, people, clan, family, house, dynasty, blood, stock, group, caste, class, division, branch.

tribute *noun*
praise, commendation, compliment, accolade, homage, respect, honour, credit, acknowledgement, recognition, gratitude.

trick *noun*
fraud, swindle, deception, deceit, artifice, illusion, hoax, practical joke, joke, leg-pull (*infml*), prank, antic, caper, frolic, feat, stunt, ruse, wile, dodge, subterfuge, trap, device, knack, technique, secret.
▸ *verb*
deceive, delude, dupe, fool, hoodwink, beguile, mislead, bluff, hoax, pull someone's leg (*infml*), cheat, swindle, diddle, defraud, con (*infml*), trap, outwit.

trickery *noun*
deception, illusion, sleight-of-hand, pretence, artifice, guile, deceit, dishonesty, cheating, swindling, fraud, imposture, double-dealing, monkey business, funny business (*infml*), chicanery, skulduggery, hocus-pocus.
E3 straightforwardness, honesty.

trickle *verb*
dribble, run, leak, seep, ooze, exude, drip, drop, filter, percolate.
E3 stream, gush.
▸ *noun*
dribble, drip, drop, leak, seepage.
E3 stream, gush.

tricky *adjective*
1 a tricky problem: difficult, awkward, problematic, complicated, knotty, thorny, delicate, ticklish.
2 a tricky fraud: crafty, artful, cunning, sly, wily, foxy, subtle, devious, slippery, scheming, deceitful.
E3 1 easy, simple. **2** honest.

trifle *noun*
1 turn the sound up a trifle: little, bit, spot, drop, dash, touch, trace.
2 bought you a little trifle for your jewellery box: toy, plaything, trinket, bauble, knick-knack, triviality, nothing.
▸ *verb*
toy, play, sport, flirt, dally, dabble, fiddle, meddle, fool.

trigger *verb*
cause, start, initiate, activate, set off, spark off, provoke, prompt, elicit, generate, produce.
▸ *noun*
lever, catch, switch, spur, stimulus.

trim *adjective*
1 a trim little craft/a trim appearance: neat, tidy, orderly, shipshape, spick-and-span, spruce, smart, dapper.
2 a trim waist: slim, slender, streamlined, compact.
E3 1 untidy, scruffy.
▸ *verb*
1 trim his hair/beard/the hedge: cut, clip, crop, dock, prune, pare, shave, neaten, tidy.
2 trim the dress with lace: decorate, ornament, embellish, garnish, dress.
▸ *noun*
condition, state, order, form, shape, fitness, health.

trimmings *noun*
1 roast beef with all the trimmings: garnish, decorations, ornaments, frills, extras, accessories.
2 fabric trimmings: cuttings, clippings, parings, ends.

trio *noun*
threesome, triad, triumvirate, trinity, triplet, trilogy.

trip *noun*
outing, excursion, tour, jaunt, ride, drive, spin, journey, voyage, expedition, foray.
▸ *verb*
stumble, slip, fall, tumble, stagger, totter, blunder.

triple *adjective*
treble, triplicate, threefold, three-ply, three-way.
▸ *verb*
treble, triplicate.

trite *adjective*
banal, commonplace, ordinary, run-of-the-mill, stale, tired, worn, threadbare, unoriginal, hackneyed, overused, stock, stereotyped, clichéd, corny (*infml*).
F⁊ original, new, fresh.

triumph *noun*
1 fresh from his triumph in the Olympics: win, victory, conquest, walk-over, success, achievement, accomplishment, feat, coup, masterstroke, hit, sensation.
2 couldn't disguise the triumph in her voice: exultation, jubilation, rejoicing, celebration, elation, joy, happiness.
F⁊ 1 failure.
▸ *verb*
win, succeed, prosper, conquer, vanquish (*fml*), overcome, overwhelm, prevail, dominate, celebrate, rejoice, glory, gloat.
F⁊ lose, fail.

triumphant *adjective*
winning, victorious, conquering, successful, exultant, jubilant, rejoicing, celebratory, glorious, elated, joyful, proud, boastful, gloating, swaggering.
F⁊ defeated, humble.

trivial *adjective*
unimportant, insignificant, inconsequential, incidental, minor, petty, paltry, trifling, small, little, inconsiderable, negligible, worthless, meaningless, frivolous, banal, trite, commonplace, everyday.
F⁊ important, significant, profound.

troop *noun*
contingent, squadron, unit, division, company, squad, team, crew, gang, band, bunch, group, body, pack, herd, flock, horde, crowd, throng, multitude.
▸ *verb*
go, march, parade, stream, flock, swarm, throng.

troops *noun*
army, military, soldiers, servicemen, servicewomen.

trophy *noun*
cup, prize, award, souvenir, memento.

tropical *adjective*
hot, torrid, sultry, sweltering, stifling, steamy, humid.
F⁊ arctic, cold, cool, temperate.

trot *verb*
jog, run, scamper, scuttle, scurry.

trouble *noun*
1 have a lot of trouble/tell her his troubles: problem, difficulty, struggle, annoyance, irritation, bother, nuisance, inconvenience, misfortune, adversity, trial, tribulation, pain, suffering, affliction, distress, grief, woe, heartache, concern, uneasiness, worry, anxiety, agitation.
2 trouble in the streets: unrest, strife, tumult, commotion, disturbance, disorder, upheaval.
3 back trouble: disorder, complaint, ailment, illness, disease, disability, defect.
4 too much trouble to do it: effort, exertion, pains, care, attention, thought.
F⁊ 1 relief, calm. 2 order. 3 health.
▸ *verb*
annoy, vex, harass, torment, bother, inconvenience, disturb, upset, distress, sadden, pain, afflict, burden, worry, agitate, disconcert, perplex.
F⁊ reassure, help.

troublemaker *noun*
agitator, rabble-rouser, instigator, ringleader, stirrer, mischief-maker.
F⁊ peacemaker.

troublesome *adjective*
1 a troublesome problem: annoying, irritating, vexatious, irksome, bothersome, inconvenient, difficult,

hard, tricky, thorny, taxing, demanding, laborious, tiresome, wearisome.

2 class was being especially troublesome that day: unruly, rowdy, turbulent, trying, unco-operative, insubordinate, rebellious.

F3 1 easy, simple. **2** helpful.

trough *noun*
gutter, conduit, trench, ditch, gully, channel, groove, furrow, hollow, depression.

truant *noun*
absentee, deserter, runaway, idler, shirker, skiver (*infml*), dodger.

▸ *adjective*
absent, missing, runaway.

truce *noun*
ceasefire, peace, armistice, cessation, moratorium, suspension, stay, respite, let-up (*infml*), lull, rest, break, interval, intermission.

F3 war, hostilities.

truck *noun*
lorry, van, wagon, juggernaut, float.

trudge *verb*
tramp, plod, clump, stump, lumber, traipse, slog, labour, trek, hike, walk, march.

true *adjective*
1 the true facts: real, genuine, authentic, actual, veritable (*fml*), exact, precise, accurate, correct, right, factual, truthful, veracious (*fml*), sincere, honest, legitimate, valid, rightful, proper.

2 a true friend: faithful, loyal, constant, steadfast, staunch, firm, trustworthy, trusty, honourable, dedicated, devoted.

F3 1 false, wrong, incorrect, inaccurate. **2** unfaithful, faithless.

truly *adverb*
very, greatly, extremely, really, genuinely, sincerely, honestly, truthfully, undeniably, indubitably, indeed, in fact, in reality, exactly, precisely, correctly, rightly, properly.

F3 slightly, falsely, incorrectly.

trumpet *noun*
bugle, horn, clarion, blare, blast, roar, bellow, cry, call.

▸ *verb*
blare, blast, roar, bellow, shout, proclaim, announce, broadcast, advertise.

trunk *noun*
1 pack a large trunk: case, suitcase, chest, coffer, box, crate.

2 trunk of a tree: shaft, stock, stem, stalk.

3 spots appear mainly round the waist and on the trunk: torso, body.

truss *verb*
tie, strap, bind, pinion, fasten, secure, bundle, pack.

F3 untie, loosen.

▸ *noun*
binding, bandage, support, brace, prop, stay, shore, strut, joist.

trust *noun*
1 have trust in God/betray someone's trust: faith, belief, credence, credit, hope, expectation, reliance, confidence, assurance, conviction, certainty.

2 hold the money in trust: care, charge, custody, safekeeping, guardianship, protection, responsibility, duty.

F3 1 distrust, mistrust, scepticism, doubt.

▸ *verb*
1 trust in providence: believe, imagine, assume, presume, suppose, surmise, hope, expect, rely on, depend on, count on, bank on, swear by.

2 trusted him with a large sum of money: entrust, commit, consign, confide, give, assign, delegate.

F3 1 distrust, mistrust, doubt, disbelieve.

trusting *adjective*
trustful, credulous, gullible, naïve, innocent, unquestioning, unsuspecting, unguarded, unwary.

F3 distrustful, suspicious, cautious.

trustworthy *adjective*
honest, upright, honourable, principled, dependable, reliable, steadfast, true, responsible, sensible.

F3 untrustworthy, dishonest, unreliable, irresponsible.

truth *noun*
1 spoke with truth and reason: truthfulness, veracity, candour,

frankness, honesty, sincerity, genuineness, authenticity, realism, exactness, precision, accuracy, validity, legitimacy, honour, integrity, uprightness, faithfulness, fidelity.
2 the truth of the matter/discover the truth: facts, reality, actuality, fact, axiom, maxim, principle, truism.
F3 1 deceit, dishonesty, falseness. 2 lie, falsehood.

truthful *adjective*
veracious (*fml*), frank, candid, straight, honest, sincere, true, veritable (*fml*), exact, precise, accurate, correct, realistic, faithful, trustworthy, reliable.
F3 untruthful, deceitful, false, untrue.

try *verb*
1 try to escape: attempt, endeavour, venture, undertake, seek, strive.
2 try the case: hear, judge.
3 trying it out: test, sample, taste, inspect, examine, investigate, evaluate, appraise.
▶ *noun*
1 have another try: attempt, endeavour, effort, go (*infml*), bash (*infml*), crack (*infml*), shot (*infml*), stab (*infml*).
2 give it a try: test, trial, sample, taste.

trying *adjective*
annoying, irritating, aggravating (*infml*), vexatious, exasperating, troublesome, tiresome, wearisome, difficult, hard, tough, arduous, taxing, demanding, testing.
F3 easy.

tub *noun*
bath, basin, vat, tun, butt, cask, barrel, keg.

tube *noun*
hose, pipe, cylinder, duct, conduit, spout, channel.

tuck *verb*
1 tucked it into her pocket: insert, push, thrust, stuff, cram.
2 tucked around the waist fold, pleat, gather, crease.

tuft *noun*
crest, beard, tassel, knot, clump, cluster, bunch.

tug *verb*
pull, draw, tow, haul, drag, lug, heave, wrench, jerk, pluck.

tuition *noun*
teaching, instruction, coaching, training, lessons, schooling, education.

tumble *verb*
fall, stumble, trip, topple, overthrow, drop, flop, collapse, plummet, pitch, roll, toss.

tumultuous *adjective*
turbulent, stormy, raging, fierce, violent, wild, hectic, boisterous, rowdy, noisy, disorderly, unruly, riotous, restless, agitated, troubled, disturbed, excited.
F3 calm, peaceful, quiet.

tune *noun*
melody, theme, motif, song, air, strain.
▶ *verb*
pitch, harmonize, set, regulate, adjust, adapt, temper, attune, synchronize.

tuneful *adjective*
melodious, melodic, catchy, musical, euphonious, harmonious, pleasant, mellow, sonorous.
F3 tuneless, discordant.

tunnel *noun*
passage, passageway, gallery, subway, underpass, burrow, hole, mine, shaft, chimney.

turbulent *adjective*
rough, choppy, stormy, blustery, tempestuous, raging, furious, violent, wild, tumultuous, unbridled, boisterous, rowdy, disorderly, unruly, undisciplined, obstreperous, rebellious, mutinous, riotous, agitated, unsettled, unstable, confused, disordered.
F3 calm, composed.

turmoil *noun*
confusion, disorder, tumult, commotion, disturbance, trouble, disquiet, agitation, turbulence, stir, ferment, flurry, bustle, chaos, pandemonium, bedlam, noise, din, hubbub, row, uproar.
F3 calm, peace, quiet.

turn *verb*
1 turn round and round/turn left: revolve, circle, spin, twirl, whirl, twist, gyrate, pivot, hinge, swivel, rotate, roll, move, shift, invert, reverse, bend, veer, swerve, divert.

2 turned into a butterfly: make, transform, change, alter, modify, convert, adapt, adjust, fit, mould, shape, form, fashion, remodel.

3 turn cold: go, become, grow.

4 turn to them in a crisis: resort, have recourse, apply, appeal.

5 milk has turned: sour, curdle, spoil, go off, go bad.

▸ *noun*

1 give it a couple of turns/a turn in the road: revolution, cycle, round, circle, rotation, spin, twirl, twist, gyration, bend, curve, loop, reversal.

2 a turn for the worse: change, alteration, shift, deviation.

3 it's your turn: go, chance, opportunity, occasion, stint, period, spell.

4 comedy turn: act, performance, performer.

◆ **turn away** reject, avert, deflect, deviate, depart.

F3 accept, receive.

◆ **turn down 1** turn down an offer: reject, decline, refuse, spurn, rebuff, repudiate.

2 turn down the heat/volume: lower, lessen, quieten, soften, mute, muffle.

F3 1 accept. **2** turn up.

◆ **turn in 1** said he was going to turn in: go to bed, retire.

2 turn in their weapons to the police: hand over, give up, surrender, deliver, hand in, tender, submit, return, give back.

F3 1 get up. **2** keep.

◆ **turn off 1** turn off to the right: branch off, leave, quit, depart from, deviate, divert.

2 turn off the lights: switch off, turn out, stop, shut down, unplug, disconnect.

3 (*infml*) that sort of behaviour really turns me off: repel, sicken, nauseate, disgust, offend, displease, disenchant, alienate, bore, discourage, put off.

F3 1 join.

◆ **turn on 1** turn on the heater: switch on, start (up), activate, connect.

2 it all turns on the grades I get: hinge on, depend on, rest on.

3 dog turned on me: attack, round on, fall on.

F3 1 turn off.

◆ **turn out 1** turned out well: happen, come about, transpire, ensue, result, end up, become, develop, emerge.

2 turn out the lights: switch off, turn off, unplug, disconnect.

3 turn out in full dress uniform: appear, present, dress, clothe.

4 turning out millions of cheap toys: produce, make, manufacture, fabricate, assemble.

5 turned out into the street: evict, throw out, expel, deport, banish, dismiss, discharge, drum out, kick out (*infml*), sack (*infml*).

6 turn out the attic: empty, clear, clean out.

F3 2 turn on. **5** admit. **6** fill.

◆ **turn up 1** turn up at the party: attend, come, arrive, appear, show up (*infml*).

2 turn up the volume: amplify, intensify, raise, increase.

3 turned up some interesting fossils: discover, find, unearth, dig up, expose, disclose, reveal, show.

F3 1 stay away. **2** turn down.

turning *noun*

turn-off, junction, crossroads, fork, bend, curve, turn.

turnout *noun*

attendance, audience, gate, crowd, gathering, assembly, congregation, number.

tutor *noun*

teacher, instructor, coach, educator, lecturer, supervisor, guide, mentor, guru, guardian.

▸ *verb*

teach, instruct, train, drill, coach, educate, school, lecture, supervise, direct, guide.

tweak *verb, noun*

twist, pinch, squeeze, nip, pull, tug, jerk, twitch.

twilight *noun*

dusk, half-light, gloaming, gloom, dimness, sunset, evening.

twin *noun*

double, look-alike, likeness, duplicate, clone, match, counterpart,

corollary, fellow, mate.
▶ *adjective*
identical, matching, corresponding,
symmetrical, parallel, matched,
paired, double, dual, duplicate,
twofold.

twine *noun*
string, cord, thread, yarn.
▶ *verb*
wind, coil, spiral, loop, curl, bend,
twist, wreathe, wrap, surround,
encircle, entwine, plait, braid, knit,
weave.

twinge *noun*
pain, pang, throb, spasm, throe, stab,
stitch, pinch, prick.

twinkle *verb*
sparkle, glitter, shimmer, glisten,
glimmer, flicker, wink, flash, glint,
gleam, shine.
▶ *noun*
sparkle, scintillation, glitter, shimmer,
glisten, glimmer, flicker, wink, flash,
glint, gleam, light.

twirl *verb*
spin, whirl, pirouette, wheel, rotate,
revolve, swivel, pivot, turn, twist,
gyrate, wind, coil.

twist *verb*
1 twisting from left to right: turn,
screw, wring, spin, swivel, wind,
zigzag, bend, coil, spiral, curl, wreathe,
twine, entwine, intertwine, weave,
entangle, wriggle, squirm, writhe.
2 twisted his ankle: wrench, rick,
sprain, strain.
3 twisting my words: change, alter,
garble, misquote, misrepresent, distort,
contort, warp, pervert.
▶ *noun*
1 twists in the road: turn, screw, spin,
roll, bend, curve, arc, curl, loop,
zigzag, coil, spiral, convolution,
squiggle, tangle.
2 a twist of fate: change, variation.
3 gave the story a fascinating twist:
surprise, quirk, oddity, peculiarity.

twitch *verb*
jerk, jump, start, blink, tremble, shake,
pull, tug, tweak, snatch, pluck.

▶ *noun*
spasm, convulsion, tic, tremor, jerk,
jump, start.

twitter *verb*
chirp, chirrup, tweet, cheep, sing,
warble, whistle, chatter.

two-faced *adjective*
hypocritical, insincere, false, lying,
deceitful, treacherous, double-dealing,
devious, untrustworthy.
Fɜhonest, candid, frank.

tycoon *noun*
industrialist, entrepreneur, captain of
industry, magnate, mogul, baron,
supremo, capitalist, financier.

type *noun*
1 types of people/animals/plants: sort,
kind, form, genre, variety, strain,
species, breed, group, class, category,
subdivision, classification,
description, designation, stamp, mark,
order, standard.
2 conform to type: archetype,
embodiment, prototype, original,
model, pattern, specimen, example.
3 set in type: print, printing,
characters, letters, lettering, face,
fount, font.

typical *adjective*
standard, normal, usual, average,
conventional, orthodox, stock, model,
representative, illustrative, indicative,
characteristic, distinctive.
Fɜatypical, unusual.

typify *verb*
embody, epitomize, encapsulate,
personify, characterize, exemplify,
symbolize, represent, illustrate.

tyrannical *adjective*
dictatorial, despotic, autocratic,
absolute, arbitrary, authoritarian,
domineering, overbearing, high-
handed, imperious, magisterial,
ruthless, harsh, severe, oppressive,
overpowering, unjust, unreasonable.
Fɜliberal, tolerant.

tyrant *noun*
dictator, despot, autocrat, absolutist,
authoritarian, bully, oppressor, slave-
driver, taskmaster.

U

ugly adjective
1 an ugly face: unattractive, unsightly, plain, unprepossessing, ill-favoured, hideous, monstrous, deformed.
2 an ugly scene: unpleasant, disagreeable, nasty, horrid, objectionable, offensive, disgusting, revolting, repulsive, vile, frightful, terrible.
F3 1 attractive, beautiful, handsome, pretty. 2 pleasant.

ulterior adjective
secondary, hidden, concealed, undisclosed, unexpressed, covert, secret, private, personal, selfish.
F3 overt.

ultimate adjective
1 the ultimate round in the competition: final, last, closing, concluding, eventual, terminal, furthest, remotest, extreme.
2 the ultimate adventure: utmost, greatest, highest, supreme, superlative, perfect.
3 the ultimate priority: radical, fundamental, primary.

ultimately adverb
finally, eventually, at last, in the end, after all.

umpire noun
referee, linesman, judge, adjudicator, arbiter, arbitrator, mediator, moderator.

umpteen adjective (infml)
a good many, numerous, plenty, millions, countless, innumerable.
F3 few.

unable adjective
incapable, powerless, impotent, unequipped, unqualified, unfit,
incompetent, inadequate.
F3 able, capable.

unacceptable adjective
intolerable, inadmissible, unsatisfactory, unsuitable, disappointing, undesirable, unwelcome, objectionable, offensive, unpleasant.
F3 acceptable, satisfactory.

unaccompanied adjective
alone, unescorted, unattended, lone, solo, single-handed.
F3 accompanied.

unanimous adjective
united, concerted, joint, common, as one, in agreement, in accord, harmonious.
F3 disunited, divided.

unapproachable adjective
inaccessible, remote, distant, aloof, standoffish, withdrawn, reserved, unsociable, unfriendly, forbidding.
F3 approachable, friendly.

unasked adjective
uninvited, unbidden, unrequested, unsought, unsolicited, unwanted, voluntary, spontaneous.
F3 invited, wanted.

unassuming adjective
unassertive, self-effacing, retiring, modest, humble, meek, unobtrusive, unpretentious, simple, restrained.
F3 presumptuous, assertive, pretentious.

unattached adjective
unmarried, single, free, available, footloose, fancy-free, independent, unaffiliated.
F3 engaged, committed.

unattended *adjective*
ignored, disregarded, unguarded, unwatched, unsupervised, unaccompanied, unescorted, alone.
⯲ attended, escorted.

unauthorized *adjective*
unofficial, unlawful, illegal, illicit, illegitimate, irregular, unsanctioned.
⯲ authorized, legal.

unavoidable *adjective*
inevitable, inescapable, inexorable, certain, sure, fated, destined, obligatory, compulsory, mandatory, necessary.
⯲ avoidable.

unaware *adjective*
oblivious, unconscious, ignorant, uninformed, unknowing, unsuspecting, unmindful, heedless, blind, deaf.
⯲ aware, conscious.

unbalanced *adjective*
1 *mind became unbalanced*: insane, mad, crazy, lunatic, deranged, disturbed, demented, irrational, unsound.
2 *an unbalanced report*: biased, prejudiced, one-sided, partisan, unfair, unjust, unequal, uneven, asymmetrical, lopsided, unsteady, unstable.
⯲ 1 sane. 2 unbiased.

unbeatable *adjective*
invincible, unconquerable, unstoppable, unsurpassable, matchless, supreme, excellent.

unbecoming *adjective*
unseemly, improper, unsuitable, inappropriate, unbefitting, ungentlemanly, unladylike, unattractive, unsightly.
⯲ suitable, attractive.

unbelievable *adjective*
incredible, inconceivable, unthinkable, unimaginable, astonishing, staggering, extraordinary, impossible, improbable, unlikely, implausible, unconvincing, far-fetched, preposterous.
⯲ believable, credible.

unborn *adjective*
embryonic, expected, awaited, coming, future.

unbreakable *adjective*
indestructible, shatterproof, toughened, resistant, proof, durable, strong, tough, rugged, solid.
⯲ breakable, fragile.

unbridled *adjective*
immoderate, excessive, uncontrolled, unrestrained, unchecked.

uncalled-for *adjective*
gratuitous, unprovoked, unjustified, unwarranted, undeserved, unnecessary, needless.
⯲ timely.

uncanny *adjective*
weird, strange, queer, bizarre, mysterious, unaccountable, incredible, remarkable, extraordinary, fantastic, unnatural, unearthly, supernatural, eerie, creepy, spooky (*infml*).

uncertain *adjective*
1 *uncertain what to do*: unsure, unconvinced, doubtful, dubious, undecided, ambivalent, hesitant, wavering, vacillating.
2 *weather is uncertain*: inconstant, changeable, variable, erratic.
3 *a few uncertain steps*: irregular, shaky, unsteady, unreliable.
4 *outcome is uncertain*: unpredictable, unforeseeable, undetermined, unsettled, unresolved, unconfirmed, indefinite, vague, insecure, risky, iffy (*infml*).
⯲ 1 certain, sure. 3 steady.
4 predictable.

uncharitable *adjective*
unkind, cruel, hard-hearted, callous, unfeeling, insensitive, unsympathetic, unfriendly, mean, ungenerous.
⯲ kind, sensitive, charitable, generous.

uncharted *adjective*
unexplored, undiscovered, unplumbed, foreign, alien, strange, unfamiliar, new, virgin.
⯲ familiar.

unclear *adjective*
indistinct, hazy, dim, obscure, vague, indefinite, ambiguous, equivocal, uncertain, unsure, doubtful, dubious.
⯲ clear, evident.

uncomfortable *adjective*
1 *uncomfortable conditions/bed/*

shoes: cramped, hard, cold, ill-fitting, irritating, painful, disagreeable.
2 an uncomfortable silence followed: awkward, embarrassed, self-conscious, uneasy, troubled, worried, disturbed, distressed, disquieted, conscience-stricken.
F∃1 comfortable. **2** relaxed.

unconcerned *adjective*
indifferent, apathetic, uninterested, nonchalant, carefree, relaxed, complacent, cool, composed, untroubled, unworried, unruffled, unmoved, uncaring, unsympathetic, callous, aloof, remote, distant, detached, dispassionate, uninvolved, oblivious.
F∃concerned, worried, interested.

unconditional *adjective*
unqualified, unreserved, unrestricted, unlimited, absolute, utter, full, total, complete, entire, whole-hearted, thoroughgoing, downright, outright, positive, categorical, unequivocal.
F∃conditional, qualified, limited.

unconscious *adjective*
1 was unconscious for several minutes: stunned, knocked out, out, out cold (*infml*), out for the count (*infml*), concussed, comatose, senseless, insensible.
2 unconscious of his surroundings: unaware, oblivious, blind, deaf, heedless, unmindful, ignorant.
3 an unconscious reaction: involuntary, automatic, reflex, instinctive, impulsive, innate, subconscious, subliminal, repressed, suppressed, latent, unwitting, inadvertent, accidental, unintentional.
F∃1 conscious. **2** aware. **3** intentional.

uncouth *adjective*
coarse, crude, vulgar, rude, ill-mannered, unseemly, improper, clumsy, awkward, gauche, graceless, unrefined, uncultivated, uncultured, uncivilized, rough.
F∃polite, refined, urbane.

uncover *verb*
unveil, unmask, unwrap, strip, bare, open, expose, reveal, show, disclose, divulge, leak, unearth,

exhume, discover, detect.
F∃cover, conceal, suppress.

undaunted *adjective*
undeterred, undiscouraged, undismayed, unbowed, resolute, steadfast, brave, courageous, fearless, bold, intrepid, dauntless, indomitable.
F∃discouraged, timorous.

undecided *adjective*
uncertain, unsure, in two minds, ambivalent, doubtful, hesitant, wavering, irresolute, uncommitted, indefinite, vague, dubious, debatable, moot, unsettled, open.
F∃decided, certain, definite.

undeniable *adjective*
irrefutable, unquestionable, incontrovertible, sure, certain, undoubted, proven, clear, obvious, patent, evident, manifest, unmistakable.
F∃questionable.

under *preposition*
below, underneath, beneath, lower than, less than, inferior to, subordinate to.
F∃over, above.
◆ **under way** moving, in motion, going, in operation, started, begun, in progress, afoot.

undercover *adjective*
secret, hush-hush (*infml*), private, confidential, spy, intelligence, underground, clandestine, surreptitious, furtive, covert, hidden, concealed.
F∃open, unconcealed.

underestimate *verb*
underrate, undervalue, misjudge, miscalculate, minimize, belittle, disparage (*fml*), dismiss.
F∃overestimate, exaggerate.

undergo *verb*
experience, suffer, sustain, submit to, bear, stand, endure, weather, withstand.

underground *adjective*
1 an underground passage: subterranean, buried, sunken, covered, hidden, concealed.
2 an underground movement: secret, covert, undercover, revolutionary,

undergrowth *noun*
brush, scrub, vegetation, ground cover, bracken, bushes, brambles, briars.

underhand *adjective*
unscrupulous, unethical, immoral, improper, sly, crafty, sneaky, stealthy, surreptitious, furtive, clandestine, devious, dishonest, deceitful, deceptive, fraudulent, crooked (*infml*), shady (*infml*).
F3 honest, open, above board.

underline *verb*
mark, underscore, stress, emphasize, accentuate, italicize, highlight, point up.
F3 play down, soft-pedal.

underlying *adjective*
basic, fundamental, essential, primary, elementary, root, intrinsic, latent, hidden, lurking, veiled.

undermine *verb*
mine, tunnel, excavate, erode, wear away, weaken, sap, sabotage, subvert, vitiate, mar, impair.
F3 strengthen, fortify.

underprivileged *adjective*
disadvantaged, deprived, poor, needy, impoverished, destitute, oppressed.
F3 privileged, fortunate, affluent.

underrate *verb*
underestimate, undervalue, belittle, disparage (*fml*), depreciate, dismiss.
F3 overrate, exaggerate.

understand *verb*
1 understand what you mean: grasp, comprehend, take in, follow, get (*infml*), cotton on (*infml*), fathom, penetrate, make out, discern, perceive, see, realize, recognize, appreciate, accept.
2 understand their distress: sympathize, empathize, commiserate.
3 I understood everyone was invited: believe, think, know, hear, learn, gather, assume, presume, suppose, conclude.
F3 1 misunderstand.

understanding *noun*
1 shows little understanding of the subject: grasp, comprehension, knowledge, wisdom, intelligence, intellect, sense, judgement, discernment, insight, appreciation, awareness, impression, perception, belief, idea, notion, opinion, interpretation.
2 come to an understanding: agreement, arrangement, pact, accord, harmony.
3 show patience and understanding: sympathy, empathy.
▶ *adjective*
sympathetic, compassionate, kind, considerate, sensitive, tender, loving, patient, tolerant, forbearing, forgiving.
F3 unsympathetic, insensitive, impatient, intolerant.

understood *adjective*
accepted, assumed, presumed, implied, implicit, inferred, tacit, unstated, unspoken, unwritten.

understudy *noun*
stand-in, double, substitute, replacement, reserve, deputy.

undertake *verb*
1 undertake to pay the loan: pledge, promise, guarantee, agree, contract, covenant.
2 undertaking a new venture: begin, commence, embark on, tackle, try, attempt, endeavour, take on, accept, assume.

undertaking *noun*
1 a whole new undertaking: enterprise, venture, business, affair, task, project, operation, attempt, endeavour, effort.
2 gave me an undertaking: pledge, commitment, promise, vow, word, assurance.

undertone *noun*
hint, suggestion, whisper, murmur, trace, tinge, touch, flavour, feeling, atmosphere, undercurrent.

underwater *adjective*
subaquatic, undersea, submarine, submerged, sunken.

underwrite *verb*
endorse, authorize, sanction, approve,

back, guarantee, insure, sponsor, fund, finance, subsidize, subscribe, sign, initial, countersign.

undisputed *adjective*
uncontested, unchallenged, unquestioned, undoubted, indisputable, incontrovertible, undeniable, irrefutable, accepted, acknowledged, recognized, sure, certain, conclusive.
▪ debatable, uncertain.

undivided *adjective*
solid, unbroken, intact, whole, entire, full, complete, combined, united, unanimous, concentrated, exclusive, whole-hearted.

undo *verb*
1 undo the fastenings: untie, unbuckle, unbutton, unzip, unlock, unwrap, unwind, open, loose, loosen, separate.
2 will undo all our hard work: annul, nullify, invalidate, cancel, offset, neutralize, reverse, overturn, upset, quash, defeat, undermine, subvert, mar, spoil, ruin, wreck, shatter, destroy.
▪ **1** fasten, do up.

undoing *noun*
downfall, ruin, ruination, collapse, destruction, defeat, overthrow, reversal, weakness, shame, disgrace.

undone *adjective*
1 leave tasks undone: unaccomplished, unfulfilled, unfinished, uncompleted, incomplete, outstanding, left, omitted, neglected, forgotten.
2 shirt/button is undone: unfastened, untied, unlaced, unbuttoned, unlocked, open, loose.
▪ **1** done, accomplished, complete.
2 fastened.

undress *verb*
strip, peel off (*infml*), disrobe, take off, divest, remove, shed.

undue *adjective*
unnecessary, needless, uncalled-for, unwarranted, undeserved, unreasonable, disproportionate, excessive, immoderate, inordinate, extreme, extravagant, improper.
▪ reasonable, moderate, proper.

unduly *adverb*
too, over, excessively, immoderately, inordinately, disproportionately, unreasonably, unjustifiably, unnecessarily.
▪ moderately, reasonably.

unearth *verb*
dig up, exhume, disinter, excavate, uncover, expose, reveal, find, discover, detect.
▪ bury.

unearthly *adjective*
1 an unearthly screech: supernatural, ghostly, eerie, uncanny, weird, strange, spine-chilling.
2 at an unearthly hour: unreasonable, outrageous, ungodly.
▪ **2** reasonable.

uneasy *adjective*
uncomfortable, anxious, worried, apprehensive, tense, strained, nervous, agitated, shaky, jittery, edgy, upset, troubled, disturbed, unsettled, restless, impatient, unsure, insecure.
▪ calm, composed.

unemployed *adjective*
jobless, out of work, laid off, redundant, unwaged, on the dole (*infml*), idle, unoccupied.
▪ employed, occupied.

unending *adjective*
endless, never-ending, unceasing, ceaseless, incessant, interminable, constant, continual, perpetual, everlasting, eternal, undying.
▪ transient, intermittent.

unequal *adjective*
different, varying, dissimilar, unlike, unmatched, uneven, unbalanced, disproportionate, asymmetrical, irregular, unfair, unjust, biased, discriminatory.
▪ equal.

unequivocal *adjective*
unambiguous, explicit, clear, plain, evident, distinct, unmistakable, express, direct, straight, definite, positive, categorical, incontrovertible, absolute, unqualified, unreserved.
▪ ambiguous, vague, qualified.

unethical *adjective*
unprofessional, immoral, improper,

wrong, unscrupulous, unprincipled, dishonourable, disreputable, illegal, illicit, dishonest, underhand, shady (*infml*).
F3 ethical.

uneven *adjective*
1 uneven ground: rough, bumpy.
2 uneven number/teeth: odd, unequal, inequitable, unfair, unbalanced, one-sided, asymmetrical, lopsided, crooked.
3 results were uneven: irregular, intermittent, spasmodic, fitful, jerky, unsteady, variable, changeable, fluctuating, erratic, inconsistent, patchy.
F3 1 flat, level. 2 even, equal. 3 regular.

uneventful *adjective*
uninteresting, unexciting, quiet, unvaried, boring, monotonous, tedious, dull, routine, humdrum, ordinary, commonplace, unremarkable, unexceptional, unmemorable.
F3 eventful, memorable.

unexpected *adjective*
unforeseen, unanticipated, unpredictable, chance, accidental, fortuitous (*fml*), sudden, abrupt, surprising, startling, amazing, astonishing, unusual.
F3 expected, predictable.

unfair *adjective*
unjust, inequitable, partial, biased, prejudiced, bigoted, discriminatory, unbalanced, one-sided, partisan, arbitrary, undeserved, unmerited, unwarranted, uncalled-for, unethical, unscrupulous, unprincipled, wrongful, dishonest.
F3 fair, just, unbiased, deserved.

unfaithful *adjective*
disloyal, treacherous, false, untrue, deceitful, dishonest, untrustworthy, unreliable, fickle, inconstant, adulterous, two-timing, duplicitous, double-dealing.
F3 faithful, loyal, reliable.

unfamiliar *adjective*
strange, unusual, uncommon, curious, alien, foreign, uncharted, unexplored, unknown, different, new, novel,

unaccustomed, unacquainted, inexperienced, unpractised, unskilled, unversed.
F3 familiar, customary, conversant (*fml*).

unfashionable *adjective*
outmoded, dated, out-of-date, out, passé, old-fashioned, antiquated, obsolete.
F3 fashionable.

unfasten *verb*
undo, untie, loosen, unlock, open, uncouple, disconnect, separate, detach.
F3 fasten.

unfavourable *adjective*
inauspicious, unpromising, ominous, threatening, discouraging, inopportune, untimely, unseasonable, ill-suited, unfortunate, unlucky, disadvantageous, bad, poor, adverse, contrary, negative, hostile, unfriendly, uncomplimentary.
F3 favourable, auspicious, promising.

unfinished *adjective*
incomplete, uncompleted, half-done, sketchy, rough, crude, imperfect, lacking, wanting, deficient, undone, unaccomplished, unfulfilled.
F3 finished, perfect.

unfit *adjective*
1 unfit for consumption/service: unsuitable, inappropriate, unsuited, ill-equipped, unqualified, ineligible, untrained, unprepared, unequal, incapable, incompetent, inadequate, ineffective, useless.
2 too unfit to run for a bus: unhealthy, out of condition, flabby, feeble, decrepit.
F3 1 fit, suitable, competent. 2 healthy.

unfold *verb*
1 history unfolding: develop, evolve.
2 as the plot unfolds: reveal, disclose, show, present, describe, explain, clarify, elaborate.
3 unfold a map: open, spread, flatten, straighten, stretch out, undo, unfurl, unroll, uncoil, unwrap, uncover.
F3 2 withhold, suppress. 3 fold, wrap.

unforeseen *adjective*
unpredicted, unexpected,

unanticipated, surprising, startling, sudden, unavoidable.
Ea expected, predictable.

unforgivable *adjective*
unpardonable, inexcusable, unjustifiable, indefensible, reprehensible, shameful, disgraceful, deplorable.
Ea forgivable, venial.

unfortunate *adjective*
1 the unfortunate family/an unfortunate mistake: unlucky, luckless, hapless, unsuccessful, poor, wretched, unhappy, doomed, ill-fated, hopeless, calamitous, disastrous, ruinous.
2 made an unfortunate remark: regrettable, lamentable, deplorable, adverse, unfavourable, unsuitable, inappropriate, inopportune, untimely, ill-timed.
Ea 1 fortunate, happy. 2 favourable, appropriate.

unfounded *adjective*
baseless, groundless, unsupported, unsubstantiated, unproven, unjustified, idle, false, spurious, trumped-up, fabricated.
Ea substantiated, justified.

unfriendly *adjective*
unsociable, standoffish, aloof, distant, unapproachable, inhospitable, uncongenial, unneighbourly, unwelcoming, cold, chilly, hostile, aggressive, quarrelsome, inimical, antagonistic, ill-disposed, disagreeable, surly, sour.
Ea friendly, amiable, agreeable.

ungainly *adjective*
clumsy, awkward, gauche, inelegant, gawky, unco-ordinated, lumbering, unwieldy.
Ea graceful, elegant.

ungrateful *adjective*
unthankful, unappreciative, ill-mannered, ungracious, selfish, heedless.
Ea grateful, thankful.

unguarded *adjective*
1 in an unguarded moment: unwary, careless, incautious, imprudent, impolitic, indiscreet, undiplomatic,

thoughtless, unthinking, heedless, foolish, foolhardy, rash, ill-considered.
2 an unguarded entrance: undefended, unprotected, exposed, vulnerable, defenceless.
Ea 1 guarded, cautious. 2 defended, protected.

unhappy *adjective*
1 could tell that she was unhappy: sad, sorrowful, miserable, melancholy, depressed, dispirited, despondent, dejected, downcast, crestfallen, long-faced, gloomy.
2 an unhappy combination of circumstances: unfortunate, unlucky, ill-fated, unsuitable, inappropriate, inapt, ill-chosen, tactless, awkward, clumsy.
Ea 1 happy. 2 fortunate, suitable.

unharmed *adjective*
undamaged, unhurt, uninjured, unscathed, whole, intact, safe, sound.
Ea harmed, damaged.

unhealthy *adjective*
1 most unhealthy nation in Europe: unwell, sick, ill, poorly, ailing, sickly, infirm, invalid, weak, feeble, frail, unsound.
2 an unhealthy climate: unwholesome, insanitary, unhygienic, harmful, detrimental, morbid, unnatural.
Ea 1 healthy, fit. 2 wholesome, hygienic, natural.

unheard-of *adjective*
1 unheard-of riches: unthinkable, inconceivable, unimaginable, undreamed-of, unprecedented, unacceptable, offensive, shocking, outrageous, preposterous.
2 unheard-of before now: unknown, unfamiliar, new, unusual, obscure.
Ea 1 normal, acceptable. 2 famous.

unidentified *adjective*
unknown, unrecognized, unmarked, unnamed, nameless, anonymous, incognito, unfamiliar, strange, mysterious.
Ea identified, known, named.

uniform *noun*
outfit, costume, livery, insignia, regalia, robes, dress, suit.

▸ *adjective*
same, identical, like, alike, similar, homogeneous, consistent, regular, equal, smooth, even, flat, monotonous, unvarying, unchanging, constant, unbroken.
⊟ different, varied, changing.

unify *verb*
unite, join, bind, combine, integrate, merge, amalgamate, consolidate, coalesce, fuse, weld.
⊟ separate, divide, split.

unimportant *adjective*
insignificant, inconsequential, irrelevant, immaterial, minor, trivial, trifling, petty, slight, negligible, worthless.
⊟ important, significant, relevant, vital.

uninhabited *adjective*
unoccupied, vacant, empty, deserted, abandoned, unpeopled, unpopulated.

uninhibited *adjective*
unconstrained, unreserved, unselfconscious, liberated, free, unrestricted, uncontrolled, unrestrained, abandoned, natural, spontaneous, irrepressible, frank, candid, open, relaxed, informal.
⊟ inhibited, repressed, constrained, restrained.

uninterested *adjective*
indifferent, unconcerned, uninvolved, bored, listless, apathetic, impassive, unenthusiastic, blasé, unresponsive.
⊟ interested, concerned, enthusiastic, responsive.

uninteresting *adjective*
boring, tedious, monotonous, humdrum, dull, drab, dreary, dry, flat, tame, uneventful, unexciting, uninspiring, unimpressive.
⊟ interesting, exciting.

uninterrupted *adjective*
unbroken, continuous, non-stop, unending, constant, continual, steady, sustained, undisturbed, peaceful.
⊟ broken, intermittent.

uninvited *adjective*
unasked, unsought, unsolicited, unwanted, unwelcome.
⊟ invited.

union *noun*
alliance, coalition, league, association, federation, confederation, confederacy, merger, combination, amalgamation, blend, mixture, synthesis, fusion, unification, unity.
⊟ separation, alienation, estrangement.

unique *adjective*
single, one-off, sole, only, lone, solitary, unmatched, matchless, peerless, unequalled, unparalleled, unrivalled, incomparable, inimitable.
⊟ common.

unit *noun*
item, part, element, constituent, piece, component, module, section, segment, portion, entity, whole, one, system, assembly.

unite *verb*
join, link, couple, marry, ally, co-operate, band, associate, federate, confederate, combine, pool, amalgamate, merge, blend, unify, consolidate, coalesce, fuse.
⊟ separate, sever.

united *adjective*
allied, affiliated, corporate, unified, combined, pooled, collective, concerted, one, unanimous, agreed, in agreement, in accord, like-minded.
⊟ disunited.

universal *adjective*
worldwide, global, all-embracing, all-inclusive, general, common, across-the-board, total, whole, entire, all-round, unlimited.

unjust *adjective*
unfair, inequitable, wrong, partial, biased, prejudiced, one-sided, partisan, unreasonable, unjustified, undeserved.
⊟ just, fair, reasonable.

unkempt *adjective*
dishevelled, tousled, rumpled, uncombed, ungroomed, untidy, messy, scruffy, shabby, slovenly.
⊟ well-groomed, tidy.

unkind *adjective*
cruel, inhuman, inhumane, callous, hard-hearted, unfeeling, insensitive,

thoughtless, inconsiderate, uncharitable, nasty, malicious, spiteful, mean, malevolent, unfriendly, uncaring, unsympathetic.
F3 kind, considerate.

unknown *adjective*
unfamiliar, unheard-of, strange, alien, foreign, mysterious, dark, obscure, hidden, concealed, undisclosed, secret, untold, new, uncharted, unexplored, undiscovered, unidentified, unnamed, nameless, anonymous, incognito.
F3 known, familiar.

unlawful *adjective*
illegal, criminal, illicit, illegitimate, unconstitutional, outlawed, banned, prohibited, forbidden, unauthorized.
F3 lawful, legal.

unlikely *adjective*
1 an unlikely story: improbable, implausible, far-fetched, unconvincing, unbelievable, incredible, unimaginable, unexpected, doubtful, dubious, questionable, suspect, suspicious.
2 an unlikely chance: slight, faint, remote, distant.
F3 1 likely, plausible.

unlimited *adjective*
limitless, unrestricted, unbounded, boundless, infinite, endless, countless, incalculable, immeasurable, vast, immense, extensive, great, indefinite, absolute, unconditional, unqualified, all-encompassing, total, complete, full, unconstrained, unhampered.
F3 limited.

unlucky *adjective*
unfortunate, luckless, unhappy, miserable, wretched, ill-fated, ill-starred, jinxed, doomed, cursed, unfavourable, inauspicious, ominous, unsuccessful, disastrous.
F3 lucky.

unmanageable *adjective*
1 large suitcase would be too unmanageable: unwieldy, bulky, cumbersome, awkward, inconvenient, unhandy.
2 an unmanageable child: uncontrollable, wild, unruly,

disorderly, difficult.
F3 1 manageable. 2 controllable.

unmistakable *adjective*
clear, plain, distinct, pronounced, obvious, evident, manifest, patent, glaring, explicit, unambiguous, unequivocal, positive, definite, sure, certain, unquestionable, indisputable, undeniable.
F3 unclear, ambiguous.

unmoved *adjective*
unaffected, untouched, unshaken, dry-eyed, unfeeling, cold, dispassionate, indifferent, impassive, unresponsive, unimpressed, firm, adamant, inflexible, unbending, undeviating, unwavering, steady, unchanged, resolute, resolved, determined.
F3 moved, affected, shaken.

unnatural *adjective*
1 unnatural behaviour: abnormal, anomalous, freakish, irregular, unusual, strange, odd, peculiar, queer, bizarre, extraordinary, uncanny, supernatural, inhuman, perverted.
2 an unnatural voice: affected, feigned, artificial, false, insincere, contrived, laboured, stilted, forced, strained, self-conscious, stiff.
F3 1 natural, normal. 2 sincere, fluent.

unnecessary *adjective*
unneeded, needless, uncalled-for, unwanted, non-essential, dispensable, expendable, superfluous, redundant, tautological.
F3 necessary, essential, indispensable.

unnoticed *adjective*
unobserved, unremarked, unseen, unrecognized, undiscovered, overlooked, ignored, disregarded, neglected, unheeded.
F3 noticed, noted.

unobtrusive *adjective*
inconspicuous, unnoticeable, unassertive, self-effacing, humble, modest, unostentatious, unpretentious, restrained, low-key, subdued, quiet, retiring.
F3 obtrusive, ostentatious.

unoccupied *adjective*
uninhabited, vacant, empty, free, idle,

inactive, workless, jobless, unemployed.
🔁 occupied, busy.

unofficial *adjective*
unauthorized, illegal, informal, off-the-record, personal, private, confidential, undeclared, unconfirmed.
🔁 official.

unorthodox *adjective*
unconventional, nonconformist, heterodox, alternative, fringe, irregular, abnormal, unusual.
🔁 orthodox, conventional.

unpaid *adjective*
1 unpaid bills: outstanding, overdue, unsettled, owing, due, payable.
2 unpaid work: voluntary, honorary, unsalaried, unwaged, unremunerative, free.
🔁 1 paid.

unpalatable *adjective*
1 mixed flour and water into an unpalatable goo: unappetizing, distasteful, insipid, bitter, uneatable, inedible.
2 found the truth pretty unpalatable: unpleasant, disagreeable, unattractive, offensive, repugnant.
🔁 1 palatable. 2 pleasant.

unparalleled *adjective*
unequalled, unmatched, matchless, peerless, incomparable, unrivalled, unsurpassed, supreme, superlative, rare, exceptional, unprecedented.

unpleasant *adjective*
disagreeable, ill-natured, nasty, objectionable, offensive, distasteful, unpalatable, unattractive, repulsive, bad, troublesome.
🔁 pleasant, agreeable, nice.

unpopular *adjective*
disliked, hated, detested, unloved, unsought-after, unfashionable, undesirable, unwelcome, unwanted, rejected, shunned, avoided, neglected.
🔁 popular, fashionable.

unprecedented *adjective*
new, original, revolutionary, unknown, unheard-of, exceptional, remarkable, extraordinary, abnormal, unusual, freakish, unparalleled, unrivalled.
🔁 usual.

unpredictable *adjective*
unforeseeable, unexpected, changeable, variable, inconstant, unreliable, fickle, unstable, erratic, random, chance.
🔁 predictable, foreseeable, constant.

unprepared *adjective*
unready, surprised, unsuspecting, ill-equipped, unfinished, incomplete, half-baked, unplanned, unrehearsed, spontaneous, improvised, ad-lib, off-the-cuff.
🔁 prepared, ready.

unprofessional *adjective*
amateurish, inexpert, unskilled, sloppy, incompetent, inefficient, casual, negligent, lax, unethical, unprincipled, improper, unseemly, unacceptable, inadmissible.
🔁 professional, skilful.

unprotected *adjective*
unguarded, unattended, undefended, unfortified, unarmed, unshielded, unsheltered, uncovered, exposed, open, naked, vulnerable, defenceless, helpless.
🔁 protected, safe, immune.

unqualified *adjective*
1 unqualified to comment: untrained, inexperienced, amateur, ineligible, unfit, incompetent, incapable, unprepared, ill-equipped.
2 an unqualified success: absolute, categorical, utter, total, complete, thorough, consummate, downright, unmitigated, unreserved, whole-hearted, outright, unconditional, unrestricted.
🔁 1 qualified, professional.
2 conditional, tentative.

unravel *verb*
unwind, undo, untangle, disentangle, free, extricate, separate, resolve, sort out, solve, work out, figure out, puzzle out, penetrate, interpret, explain.
🔁 tangle, complicate.

unreal *adjective*
false, artificial, synthetic, mock, fake, sham, imaginary, visionary, fanciful, make-believe, pretend (*infml*), fictitious, made-up, fairy-tale, legendary, mythical, fantastic, illusory,

immaterial, insubstantial, hypothetical.
F3 real, genuine.

unrealistic *adjective*
impractical, idealistic, romantic, quixotic, impracticable, unworkable, unreasonable, impossible.
F3 realistic, pragmatic.

unreasonable *adjective*
1 *an unreasonable punishment*: unfair, unjust, biased, unjustifiable, unjustified, unwarranted, undue, uncalled-for.
2 *unreasonable behaviour*: irrational, illogical, inconsistent, arbitrary, absurd, nonsensical, far-fetched, preposterous, mad, senseless, silly, foolish, stupid, headstrong, opinionated, perverse.
3 *unreasonable demands*: excessive, immoderate, extravagant, exorbitant, extortionate.
F3 1 reasonable, fair. 2 rational, sensible. 3 moderate.

unrecognizable *adjective*
unidentifiable, disguised, incognito, changed, altered.

unrefined *adjective*
raw, untreated, unprocessed, unfinished, unpolished, crude, coarse, vulgar, unsophisticated, uncultivated, uncultured.
F3 refined, finished.

unrelated *adjective*
unconnected, unassociated, irrelevant, extraneous, different, dissimilar, unlike, disparate, distinct, separate, independent.
F3 related, similar.

unrelenting *adjective*
relentless, unremitting, uncompromising, inexorable, incessant, unceasing, ceaseless, endless, unbroken, continuous, constant, continual, perpetual, steady, unabated, remorseless, unmerciful, merciless, pitiless, unsparing.
F3 spasmodic, intermittent.

unreliable *adjective*
unsound, fallible, deceptive, false, mistaken, erroneous, inaccurate, unconvincing, implausible, uncertain,

undependable, untrustworthy, unstable, fickle, irresponsible.
F3 reliable, dependable, trustworthy.

unrest *noun*
protest, rebellion, turmoil, agitation, restlessness, dissatisfaction, dissension, disaffection, worry.
F3 peace, calm.

unrivalled *adjective*
unequalled, unparalleled, unmatched, matchless, peerless, incomparable, inimitable, unsurpassed, supreme, superlative.

unruly *adjective*
uncontrollable, unmanageable, ungovernable, intractable, disorderly, wild, rowdy, riotous, rebellious, mutinous, lawless, insubordinate, disobedient, wayward, wilful, headstrong, obstreperous.
F3 manageable, orderly.

unsatisfactory *adjective*
unacceptable, imperfect, defective, faulty, inferior, poor, weak, inadequate, insufficient, deficient, unsuitable, displeasing, dissatisfying, unsatisfying, frustrating, disappointing.
F3 satisfactory, pleasing.

unscathed *adjective*
unhurt, uninjured, unharmed, undamaged, untouched, whole, intact, safe, sound.
F3 hurt, injured.

unscrupulous *adjective*
unprincipled, ruthless, shameless, dishonourable, dishonest, crooked (*infml*), corrupt, immoral, unethical, improper.
F3 scrupulous, ethical, proper.

unseemly *adjective*
improper, indelicate, indecorous, unbecoming, undignified, unrefined, disreputable, discreditable, undue, inappropriate, unsuitable.
F3 seemly, decorous.

unseen *adjective*
unnoticed, unobserved, undetected, invisible, hidden, concealed, veiled, obscure.
F3 visible.

unsettled *adjective*
1 was unsettled by the noise: disturbed, upset, troubled, agitated, anxious, uneasy, tense, edgy, flustered, shaken, unnerved, disoriented, confused.
2 an unsettled question: unresolved, undetermined, undecided, open, uncertain, doubtful.
3 unsettled weather: changeable, variable, unpredictable, inconstant, unstable, insecure, unsteady, shaky.
4 unsettled bills: unpaid, outstanding, owing, payable, overdue.
F3 1 composed. 2 certain. 3 settled. 4 paid.

unshakable *adjective*
firm, well-founded, fixed, stable, immovable, unassailable, unwavering, constant, steadfast, staunch, sure, resolute, determined.
F3 insecure.

unsightly *adjective*
ugly, unattractive, unprepossessing, hideous, repulsive, repugnant, off-putting, unpleasant, disagreeable.
F3 attractive.

unsociable *adjective*
unfriendly, aloof, distant, standoffish, withdrawn, introverted, reclusive, retiring, reserved, taciturn, unforthcoming, uncommunicative, cold, chilly, uncongenial, unneighbourly, inhospitable, hostile.
F3 sociable, friendly.

unsolicited *adjective*
unrequested, unsought, uninvited, unasked, unwanted, unwelcome, uncalled-for, voluntary, spontaneous.
F3 requested, invited.

unsound *adjective*
1 reasoning is unsound: faulty, flawed, defective, ill-founded, fallacious, false, erroneous, invalid, illogical.
2 of unsound mind: unhealthy, unwell, ill, diseased, weak, frail, unbalanced, deranged, unhinged.
F3 1 sound. 2 sound, well.

unspeakable *adjective*
unutterable, inexpressible, indescribable, awful, dreadful, frightful, terrible, horrible, shocking, appalling, monstrous, inconceivable, unbelievable.

unspoilt *adjective*
preserved, unchanged, untouched, natural, unaffected, unsophisticated, unharmed, undamaged, unimpaired, unblemished, perfect.
F3 spoilt, affected.

unspoken *adjective*
unstated, undeclared, unuttered, unexpressed, unsaid, voiceless, wordless, silent, tacit, implicit, implied, inferred, understood, assumed.
F3 stated, explicit.

unsung *adjective*
unhonoured, unpraised, unacknowledged, unrecognized, overlooked, disregarded, neglected, forgotten, unknown, anonymous, obscure.
F3 honoured, famous, renowned.

unsure *adjective*
uncertain, doubtful, dubious, suspicious, sceptical, unconvinced, unpersuaded, undecided, hesitant, tentative.
F3 sure, certain, confident.

unsurpassed *adjective*
surpassing, supreme, transcendent, unbeaten, unexcelled, unequalled, unparalleled, unrivalled, incomparable, matchless, superlative, exceptional.

unsuspecting *adjective*
unwary, unaware, unconscious, trusting, trustful, unsuspicious, credulous, gullible, ingenuous, naïve, innocent.
F3 suspicious, knowing.

unthinkable *adjective*
inconceivable, unimaginable, unheard-of, unbelievable, incredible, impossible, improbable, unlikely, implausible, unreasonable, illogical, absurd, preposterous, outrageous, shocking.

untimely *adjective*
early, premature, unseasonable, ill-timed, inopportune, inconvenient, awkward, unsuitable, inappropriate, unfortunate, inauspicious.
F3 timely, opportune.

untold *adjective*
uncounted, unnumbered, unreckoned, incalculable, innumerable, uncountable, countless, infinite, measureless, boundless, inexhaustible, undreamed-of, unimaginable.

untouched *adjective*
unharmed, undamaged, unimpaired, unhurt, uninjured, unscathed, safe, intact, unchanged, unaltered, unaffected.

unused *adjective*
leftover, remaining, surplus, extra, spare, available, new, fresh, blank, clean, untouched, unexploited, unemployed, idle.
F3 used.

unusual *adjective*
uncommon, rare, unfamiliar, strange, odd, curious, queer, bizarre, unconventional, irregular, abnormal, extraordinary, remarkable, exceptional, different, surprising, unexpected.
F3 usual, normal, ordinary.

unveil *verb*
uncover, expose, bare, reveal, disclose, divulge, discover.
F3 cover, hide.

unwanted *adjective*
undesired, unsolicited, uninvited, unwelcome, outcast, rejected, unrequired, unneeded, unnecessary, surplus, extra, superfluous, redundant.
F3 wanted, needed, necessary.

unwelcome *adjective*
1 unwelcome visitors: unwanted, undesirable, unpopular, uninvited, excluded, rejected.
2 unwelcome news: unpleasant, disagreeable, upsetting, worrying, distasteful, unpalatable, unacceptable.
F3 1 welcome, desirable. **2** pleasant.

unwieldy *adjective*
unmanageable, inconvenient, awkward, clumsy, ungainly, bulky, massive, hefty, weighty, ponderous, cumbersome.
F3 handy, dainty.

unwilling *adjective*
reluctant, disinclined, indisposed, resistant, opposed, averse, lo(a)th,

slow, unenthusiastic, grudging.
F3 willing, enthusiastic.

unwind *verb*
1 unwind the spool: unroll, unreel, unwrap, undo, uncoil, untwist, unravel, disentangle.
2 (*infml*) **unwind in front of the TV:** relax, wind down, calm down.
F3 1 wind, roll.

unwitting *adjective*
unaware, unknowing, unsuspecting, unthinking, unconscious, involuntary, accidental, chance, inadvertent, unintentional, unintended, unplanned.
F3 knowing, conscious, deliberate.

unwarranted *adjective*
unjustified, undeserved, unprovoked, uncalled-for, groundless, unreasonable, unjust, wrong.
F3 warranted, justifiable, deserved.

unwritten *adjective*
verbal, oral, word-of-mouth, unrecorded, tacit, implicit, understood, accepted, recognized, traditional, customary, conventional.
F3 written, recorded.

upbringing *noun*
bringing-up, raising, rearing, breeding, parenting, care, nurture, cultivation, education, training, instruction, teaching.

update *verb*
modernize, revise, amend, correct, renew, renovate, revamp.

upgrade *verb*
promote, advance, elevate, raise, improve, enhance.
F3 downgrade, demote.

upheaval *noun*
disruption, disturbance, upset, chaos, confusion, disorder, turmoil, shake-up (*infml*), revolution, overthrow.

uphill *adjective*
hard, difficult, arduous, tough, taxing, strenuous, laborious, tiring, wearisome, exhausting, gruelling, punishing.
F3 easy.

uphold *verb*
support, maintain, hold to, stand by,

defend, champion, advocate, promote, back, endorse, sustain, fortify, strengthen, justify, vindicate.
F∃ abandon, reject.

upkeep *noun*
maintenance, preservation, conservation, care, running, repair, support, sustenance, subsistence, keep.
F∃ neglect.

upper *adjective*
higher, loftier, superior, senior, top, topmost, uppermost, high, elevated, exalted, eminent, important.
F∃ lower, inferior, junior.

uppermost *adjective*
highest, loftiest, top, topmost, greatest, supreme, first, primary, foremost, leading, principal, main, chief, dominant, predominant, paramount, pre-eminent.
F∃ lowest.

upright *adjective*
1 an upright post: vertical, perpendicular, erect, straight.
2 upright citizens: righteous, good, virtuous, upstanding, noble, honourable, ethical, principled, incorruptible, honest, trustworthy.
F∃ 1 horizontal, flat. 2 dishonest.

uprising *noun*
rebellion, revolt, mutiny, rising, insurgence, insurrection, revolution.

uproar *noun*
noise, din, racket, hubbub, hullabaloo, pandemonium, tumult, turmoil, turbulence, commotion, confusion, disorder, clamour, outcry, furore, riot, rumpus.

uproot *verb*
pull up, rip up, root out, weed out, remove, displace, eradicate, destroy, wipe out.

upset *verb*
1 upsetting his parents: distress, grieve, dismay, trouble, worry, agitate, disturb, bother, fluster, ruffle, discompose, shake, unnerve, disconcert, confuse, disorganize.
2 upset the milk jug: tip, spill, overturn, capsize, topple, overthrow, destabilize, unsteady.
▸ *noun*

1 a bit of an upset in the government: trouble, worry, agitation, disturbance, bother, disruption, upheaval, shake-up (*infml*), reverse, surprise, shock.
2 stomach upset: disorder, complaint, bug (*infml*), illness, sickness.
▸ *adjective*
distressed, grieved, hurt, annoyed, dismayed, troubled, worried, agitated, disturbed, bothered, shaken, disconcerted, confused.

upshot *noun*
result, consequence, outcome, issue, end, conclusion, finish, culmination.

upside down *adjective, adverb*
inverted, upturned, wrong way up, upset, overturned, disordered, muddled, jumbled, confused, topsy-turvy, chaotic.

up-to-date *adjective*
current, contemporary, modern, fashionable, trendy (*infml*), latest, recent, new, state-of-the-art.
F∃ out-of-date, old-fashioned.

urban *adjective*
town, city, inner-city, metropolitan, municipal, civic, built-up.
F∃ country, rural.

urge *verb*
1 urged him to accept: advise, counsel, recommend, advocate, encourage, exhort.
2 'Please say yes,' she urged: implore, beg, beseech, entreat, plead.
3 urged them on: push, drive, goad, impel, spur, hasten, induce, incite, instigate, press, constrain, compel, force.
F∃ 1 discourage, dissuade. 3 deter, hinder.
▸ *noun*
desire, wish, inclination, fancy, longing, yearning, itch, impulse, compulsion, impetus, drive, eagerness.
F∃ disinclination.

urgent *adjective*
immediate, instant, top-priority, important, critical, crucial, imperative, exigent, pressing, compelling, persuasive, earnest, eager, insistent, persistent.
F∃ unimportant.

usage *noun*
1 usage of resources: treatment, handling, management, control, running, operation, employment, application, use.
2 normal usage: tradition, custom, practice, habit, convention, etiquette, rule, regulation, form, routine, procedure, method.

use *verb*
utilize, employ, exercise, practise, operate, work, apply, wield, handle, treat, manipulate, exploit, enjoy, consume, exhaust, expend, spend.
▸ *noun*
utility, usefulness, value, worth, profit, advantage, benefit, good, avail, help, service, point, object, end, purpose, reason, cause, occasion, need, necessity, usage, application, employment, operation, exercise.
◆ **use up** finish, exhaust, drain, sap, deplete, consume, devour, absorb, waste, squander, fritter.

used *adjective*
second-hand, cast-off, hand-me-down, nearly new, worn, dog-eared, soiled.
E∃ unused, new, fresh.

useful *adjective*
handy, convenient, all-purpose, practical, effective, productive, fruitful, profitable, valuable, worthwhile, advantageous, beneficial, helpful.
E∃ useless, ineffective, worthless.

useless *adjective*
futile, fruitless, unproductive, vain, idle, unavailing, hopeless, pointless, worthless, unusable, broken-down, clapped-out (*infml*), unworkable, impractical, ineffective, inefficient, incompetent, weak.
E∃ useful, helpful, effective.

usual *adjective*
normal, typical, stock, standard, regular, routine, habitual, customary, conventional, accepted, recognized, accustomed, familiar, common, everyday, general, ordinary, unexceptional, expected, predictable.
E∃ unusual, strange, rare.

usually *adverb*
normally, generally, as a rule, ordinarily, typically, traditionally, regularly, commonly, by and large, on the whole, mainly, chiefly, mostly.
E∃ exceptionally.

utensil *noun*
tool, implement, instrument, device, contrivance, gadget, apparatus, appliance.

utmost *adjective*
1 with the utmost care: extreme, maximum, greatest, highest, supreme, paramount.
2 the utmost limit: farthest, furthermost, remotest, outermost, ultimate, final, last.
▸ *noun*
best, hardest, most, maximum.

utter[1] *adjective*
felt an utter fool: absolute, complete, total, entire, thoroughgoing, out-and-out, downright, sheer, stark, arrant, unmitigated, unqualified, perfect, consummate.

utter[2] *verb*
didn't utter another word: speak, say, voice, vocalize, verbalize, express, articulate, enunciate, sound, pronounce, deliver, state, declare, announce, proclaim, tell, reveal, divulge.

utterly *adverb*
absolutely, completely, totally, fully, entirely, wholly, thoroughly, downright, perfectly.

U-turn *noun*
about-turn, volte-face, reversal, backtrack.

vacancy *noun*
opportunity, opening, position, post, job, place, room, situation.

vacant *adjective*
1 is this seat vacant?: empty, unoccupied, unfilled, free, available, void, not in use, unused, uninhabited.
2 a vacant stare: blank, expressionless, vacuous, inane, inattentive, absent, absent-minded, unthinking, dreamy.
F₃1 occupied, engaged.

vacuum *noun*
emptiness, void, nothingness, vacuity, space, chasm, gap.

vague *adjective*
1 a vague outline: ill-defined, blurred, indistinct, hazy, dim, shadowy, misty, fuzzy, nebulous, obscure.
2 a vague feeling of nausea: indefinite, imprecise, unclear, uncertain, undefined, undetermined, unspecific, generalized, inexact, ambiguous, evasive, loose, woolly.
F₃1 clear. **2** definite.

vain *adjective*
1 a vain attempt: useless, worthless, futile, abortive, fruitless, pointless, unproductive, unprofitable, unavailing, hollow, groundless, empty, trivial, unimportant.
2 a vain little man: conceited, proud, self-satisfied, arrogant, self-important, egotistical, bigheaded (*infml*), swollen-headed (*infml*), stuck-up (*infml*), affected, pretentious, ostentatious, swaggering.
F₃1 fruitful, successful. **2** modest, self-effacing.

valid *adjective*
1 a valid argument: logical, well-founded, well-grounded, sound, good, cogent, convincing, telling, conclusive, reliable, substantial, weighty, powerful, just.
2 a valid passport: official, legal, lawful, legitimate, authentic, bona fide, genuine, binding, proper.
F₃1 false, weak. **2** unofficial, invalid.

valley *noun*
dale, vale, dell, glen, hollow, cwm, depression, gulch.

valuable *adjective*
1 necklace is very valuable: precious, prized, valued, costly, expensive, dear, high-priced, treasured, cherished, estimable.
2 valuable advice: helpful, worthwhile, useful, beneficial, invaluable, constructive, fruitful, profitable, important, serviceable, worthy, handy.
F₃1 worthless. **2** useless.

value *noun*
1 what's the value of the painting?: cost, price, rate, worth.
2 of little value: worth, use, usefulness, utility, merit, importance, desirability, benefit, advantage, significance, good, profit.
▶ *verb*
1 value his opinion highly: prize, appreciate, treasure, esteem, hold dear, respect, cherish.
2 valuing the house: evaluate, assess, estimate, price, appraise, survey, rate.
F₃1 disregard, neglect.

vanish *verb*
disappear, fade, dissolve, evaporate, disperse, melt, die out, depart, exit, fizzle out, peter out.
F₃ appear, materialize.

vanity *noun*
conceit, conceitedness, pride, arrogance, self-conceit, self-love, self-satisfaction, narcissism, egotism, pretension, ostentation, affectation, airs, bigheadedness (*infml*), swollen-headedness (*infml*).
E₃ modesty.

vapour *noun*
steam, mist, fog, smoke, breath, fumes, haze, damp, dampness, exhalation.

variable *adjective*
changeable, inconstant, varying, shifting, mutable, unpredictable, fluctuating, fitful, unstable, unsteady, wavering, vacillating, temperamental, fickle, flexible.
E₃ fixed, invariable, stable.

variation *noun*
diversity, variety, deviation, discrepancy, diversification, alteration, change, difference, departure, modification, modulation, inflection, novelty, innovation.
E₃ monotony, uniformity.

varied *adjective*
assorted, diverse, miscellaneous, mixed, various, sundry, heterogeneous (*fml*), different, wide-ranging.
E₃ standardized, uniform.

variegated *adjective*
multi-coloured, many-coloured, parti-coloured, varicoloured, speckled, mottled, dappled, pied, streaked, motley.
E₃ monochrome, plain.

variety *noun*
1 sell a variety of cold meats: assortment, miscellany, mixture, collection, medley, pot-pourri, range.
2 nature displays endless variety: difference, diversity, dissimilarity, discrepancy, variation, multiplicity.
3 a new variety of rose: sort, kind, class, category, species, type, breed, brand, make, strain.
E₃ 2 uniformity, similitude (*fml*).

various *adjective*
different, differing, diverse, varied, varying, assorted, miscellaneous, heterogeneous (*fml*), distinct, diversified, mixed, many, several.

varnish *noun*
lacquer, glaze, resin, polish, gloss, coating.

vary *verb*
1 vary the order/his route: change, alter, modify, modulate, diversify, reorder, transform, alternate, permutate.
2 opinions vary: diverge, differ, disagree, depart, fluctuate.

vast *adjective*
huge, immense, massive, gigantic, enormous, great, colossal, extensive, tremendous, sweeping, unlimited, fathomless, immeasurable, never-ending, monumental, monstrous, far-flung.

vault¹ *verb*
vaulting the gate: leap, spring, bound, clear, jump, hurdle, leap-frog.

vault² *noun*
1 keep the gold in a sealed vault: cellar, crypt, strongroom, repository, cavern, depository, wine-cellar, tomb, mausoleum.
2 a barrel vault: arch, roof, span, concave.

veer *verb*
swerve, swing, change, shift, diverge, deviate, wheel, turn, sheer, tack.

vegetable

Vegetables include:

artichoke, asparagus, aubergine, baby corn, bean, bean sprout, beetroot, bok choy, broad bean, broccoli, Brussels sprout, butter bean, cabbage, calabrese, capsicum, carrot, cassava or manioc, cauliflower, celeriac, celery, chicory, courgette, cress, cucumber, eggplant (*US*), endive, fennel, French bean, garlic, Jerusalem artichoke, jicama, kale, kohlrabi, leek, lentil, lettuce, mangetout, marrow, mooli, mushroom, okra, onion, pak-choi, parsnip, pea, pepper, petit pois, potato, spud (*infml*), pumpkin, radish, runner bean, shallot, soya bean, spinach, spring onion, squash, swede, sweetcorn, sweet potato, turnip, water chestnut, watercress, yam, zucchini (*US*).

vegetate *verb*
stagnate, degenerate, deteriorate,

rusticate, go to seed, idle, rust, languish.

vehement *adjective*
impassioned, passionate, ardent, fervent, intense, forceful, emphatic, heated, strong, powerful, urgent, enthusiastic, animated, eager, earnest, forcible, fierce, violent, zealous.
E₃ apathetic, indifferent.

vehicle

Vehicles include:

barouche, bicycle, bike (*infml*), boat, bobsleigh, boneshaker (*infml*), brougham, bus, cab, camper, car, caravan, caravanette, charabanc, coach, cycle, dog-cart, double-decker, dray, fork-lift truck, four-in-hand, gig, hackney carriage, hansom, juggernaut, landau, litter, lorry, maglev, minibus, monorail, motorcycle, motorbike, omnibus, pantechnicon, penny-farthing, phaeton, plane, post-chaise, Pullman, rickshaw, scooter, sedan chair, ship, sled, sledge, sleeper, sleigh, stagecoach, steam-roller, sulky, surrey, tandem, tank, taxi, toboggan, tractor, trailer, train, tram, Transit®, trap, tricycle, troika, trolleybus, truck, tube, van, Vespa®, wagon, wagon-lit.

veil *verb*
screen, cloak, cover, mask, shadow, shield, obscure, conceal, hide, disguise, shade.
E₃ expose, uncover.
▶ *noun*
cover, cloak, curtain, mask, screen, disguise, film, blind, shade, shroud.

vein *noun*
mode, style, tendency, bent, strain, temper, tenor, tone, frame of mind.

vendetta *noun*
feud, blood-feud, enmity, rivalry, quarrel, bad blood, bitterness.

veneer *noun*
front, façade, appearance, coating, surface, show, mask, gloss, pretence, guise, finish.

vengeance *noun*
retribution, revenge, retaliation, reprisal, requital, tit for tat.
E₃ forgiveness.

venom *noun*
1 snake venom: poison, toxin.
2 a voice filled with venom: rancour, ill-will, malice, malevolence, spite, bitterness, acrimony, hate, virulence.

venomous *adjective*
1 venomous toad: poisonous, toxic, virulent, harmful, noxious.
2 venomous look: malicious, spiteful, vicious, vindictive, baleful, hostile, malignant, rancorous, baneful.
E₃ 1 harmless.

vent *noun*
opening, hole, aperture, outlet, passage, orifice, duct.
▶ *verb*
air, express, voice, utter, release, discharge, emit.

ventilate *verb*
air, aerate, freshen.

venture *verb*
1 venture to suggest: dare, advance, make bold, put forward, presume, suggest, volunteer.
2 venturing money on the race: risk, hazard, endanger, imperil, jeopardize, speculate, wager, stake.
▶ *noun*
risk, chance, hazard, speculation, gamble, undertaking, project, adventure, endeavour, enterprise, operation, fling.

verbal *adjective*
spoken, oral, verbatim, unwritten, word-of-mouth.

verbatim *adverb*
word for word, exactly, literally, to the letter, precisely.

verdict *noun*
decision, judgement, conclusion, finding, adjudication, assessment, opinion, sentence.

verge *noun*
border, edge, margin, limit, rim, brim, brink, boundary, threshold, extreme, edging.

◆ **verge on** approach, border on, come close to, near.

verify *verb*
confirm, corroborate, substantiate, authenticate, bear out, prove, support, validate, testify, attest (*fml*).
🔁 invalidate, discredit.

versatile *adjective*
adaptable, flexible, all-round, multipurpose, multifaceted, adjustable, many-sided, general-purpose, functional, resourceful, handy, variable.
🔁 inflexible.

verse *noun*
poetry, rhyme, stanza, metre, doggerel, jingle.

versed *adjective*
skilled, proficient, practised, experienced, familiar, acquainted, learned, knowledgeable, conversant (*fml*), seasoned, qualified, competent, accomplished.

version *noun*
1 a modern version of Hamlet: rendering, reading, interpretation, account, translation, paraphrase, adaptation, portrayal.
2 create an updated version: type, kind, variant, form, model, style, design.

vertical *adjective*
upright, perpendicular, upstanding, erect, on end.
🔁 horizontal.

very *adverb*
extremely, greatly, highly, deeply, truly, terribly (*infml*), remarkably, excessively, exceedingly, acutely, particularly, really, absolutely, noticeably, unusually.
🔁 slightly, scarcely.
⇒ *See also* **Word Workshop** *panel at* **really**.
▶ *adjective*
actual, real, same, selfsame, identical, true, genuine, simple, utter, sheer, pure, perfect, plain, mere, bare, exact, appropriate.

vet *verb*
investigate, examine, check, scrutinize, scan, inspect, survey, review, appraise, audit.

veteran *noun*
master, past master, old hand, old stager, old-timer, pro (*infml*), war-horse.
🔁 novice, recruit.
▶ *adjective*
experienced, practised, seasoned, long-serving, expert, adept, proficient, old.
🔁 inexperienced.

veto *verb*
reject, turn down, forbid, disallow, ban, prohibit, rule out, block.
🔁 approve, sanction.
▶ *noun*
rejection, ban, embargo, prohibition, thumbs-down (*infml*).
🔁 approval, assent.

vexed *adjective*
1 I'm vexed that you didn't call me: irritated, annoyed, provoked, upset, troubled, worried, nettled, put out, exasperated, bothered, confused, perplexed, aggravated (*infml*), harassed, hassled (*infml*), ruffled, riled, disturbed, distressed, displeased, agitated.
2 a vexed question: difficult, controversial, contested, disputed.

viable *adjective*
feasible, practicable, possible, workable, usable, operable, achievable, sustainable.
🔁 impossible, unworkable.

vibrant *adjective*
animated, vivacious, vivid, bright, brilliant, colourful, lively, responsive, sparkling, spirited, thrilling, dynamic, electrifying, electric.

vibrate *verb*
quiver, pulsate, shudder, shiver, resonate, reverberate, throb, oscillate, tremble, undulate, sway, swing, shake.

vice *noun*
1 stamp out vice: evil, evil-doing, depravity, immorality, wickedness, sin, corruption, iniquity (*fml*), profligacy (*fml*), degeneracy.
2 smoking is one of his vices: fault, failing, defect, shortcoming, weakness, imperfection, blemish, bad habit, besetting sin.
🔁 **1** virtue, morality.

vicinity *noun*
neighbourhood, area, locality, district, precincts, environs, proximity.

vicious *adjective*
1 a vicious crime: wicked, bad, wrong, immoral, depraved, unprincipled, diabolical, corrupt, debased, perverted, profligate (*fml*), vile, heinous (*fml*).
2 a vicious lie: malicious, spiteful, vindictive, virulent, cruel, mean, nasty, slanderous, venomous, defamatory.
3 a vicious dog: savage, wild, violent, barbarous, brutal, dangerous.
E3 1 virtuous. 2 kind.

victim *noun*
sufferer, casualty, prey, scapegoat, martyr, sacrifice, fatality.
E3 offender, attacker.

victimize *verb*
oppress, persecute, discriminate against, pick on, prey on, bully, exploit.

victorious *adjective*
conquering, champion, triumphant, winning, unbeaten, successful, prize-winning, top, first.
E3 defeated, unsuccessful.

victory *noun*
conquest, win, triumph, success, superiority, mastery, vanquishment (*fml*), subjugation, overcoming.
E3 defeat, loss.

vie *verb*
strive, compete, contend, struggle, contest, fight, rival.

view *noun*
1 hold the opposite view: opinion, attitude, belief, judgement, estimation, feeling, sentiment, impression, notion.
2 a view of the sea: sight, scene, vision, vista, outlook, prospect, perspective, panorama, landscape.
3 hold a private view: survey, inspection, examination, observation, scrutiny, scan.
▶ *verb*
1 viewed it in a different light: consider, regard, contemplate, judge, think about, speculate.
2 viewed the scene: observe, watch, see, examine, inspect, look at, scan, survey, witness, perceive.

viewer *noun*
spectator, watcher, observer, onlooker.

viewpoint *noun*
attitude, position, perspective, slant, standpoint, stance, opinion, angle, feeling.

vigilant *adjective*
watchful, alert, attentive, observant, on one's guard, on the lookout, cautious, wide-awake, sleepless, unsleeping.
E3 careless.

vigorous *adjective*
energetic, active, lively, healthy, strong, strenuous, robust, lusty, sound, vital, brisk, dynamic, forceful, forcible, powerful, stout, spirited, full-blooded, effective, efficient, enterprising, flourishing, intense.
E3 weak, feeble.

vigour *noun*
energy, vitality, liveliness, health, robustness, stamina, strength, resilience, soundness, spirit, verve, gusto, activity, animation, power, potency, force, forcefulness, might, dash, dynamism.
E3 weakness.

vile *adjective*
1 a vile sinner: base, contemptible, debased, depraved, degenerate, bad, wicked, wretched, worthless, sinful, miserable, mean, evil, impure, corrupt, despicable, disgraceful, degrading, vicious, appalling.
2 the coffee was vile: disgusting, foul, nauseating, sickening, repulsive, repugnant, revolting, noxious, offensive, nasty, loathsome, horrid.
E3 1 pure, worthy. 2 pleasant, lovely.

villain *noun*
evil-doer, miscreant (*fml*), scoundrel, rogue, malefactor (*fml*), criminal, reprobate, rascal.

villainous *adjective*
wicked, bad, criminal, evil, sinful, vicious, notorious, cruel, inhuman, vile, depraved, disgraceful, terrible.
E3 good.

vindicate *verb*
justify, uphold, support, maintain, defend, establish, advocate, assert, verify.

vindictive *adjective*
spiteful, unforgiving, implacable, vengeful, relentless, unrelenting, revengeful, resentful, punitive, venomous, malevolent, malicious.
F3 forgiving.

vintage *noun*
year, period, era, epoch, generation, origin, harvest, crop.
▶ *adjective*
choice, best, fine, prime, select, superior, rare, mature, old, ripe, classic, venerable, veteran.

violate *verb*
contravene, disobey, disregard, transgress, break, flout, infringe.
F3 observe.

violence *noun*
1 the violence of the attack was shocking: force, strength, power, vehemence, might, intensity, ferocity, fierceness, severity, tumult, turbulence, wildness.
2 prevent violence: brutality, destructiveness, cruelty, bloodshed, murderousness, savagery, passion, fighting, frenzy, fury, hostilities.

violent *adjective*
1 a violent storm: intense, strong, severe, sharp, acute, extreme, harmful, destructive, devastating, injurious, powerful, painful, agonizing, forceful, forcible, harsh, ruinous, rough, vehement, tumultuous, turbulent.
2 a violent attack: cruel, brutal, aggressive, bloodthirsty, impetuous, hot-headed, headstrong, murderous, savage, wild, vicious, unrestrained, uncontrollable, ungovernable, passionate, furious, intemperate, maddened, outrageous, riotous, fiery.
F3 1 calm, moderate. **2** peaceful, gentle.

virtual *adjective*
effective, essential, practical, implied, implicit, potential.

virtually *adverb*
practically, in effect, almost, nearly, as good as, in essence.

virtue *noun*
1 her goodness and virtue: morality, rectitude, uprightness, worthiness, righteousness, probity (*fml*), integrity,

honour, incorruptibility, justice, high-mindedness, excellence.
2 the plan has many virtues: quality, worth, merit, advantage, asset, credit, strength.
F3 1 vice.

virtuoso *noun*
expert, master, maestro, prodigy, genius.

virtuous *adjective*
good, moral, righteous, upright, worthy, honourable, irreproachable, incorruptible, exemplary, unimpeachable, high-principled, blameless, clean-living, excellent, innocent.
F3 immoral, vicious.

virulent *adjective*
1 a virulent poison: toxic, venomous, deadly, lethal, malignant, injurious, pernicious, intense.
2 virulent attack: hostile, resentful, spiteful, acrimonious, bitter, vicious, vindictive, malevolent, malicious.
F3 1 harmless.

visible *adjective*
perceptible, discernible, detectable, apparent, noticeable, observable, distinguishable, discoverable, evident, unconcealed, undisguised, unmistakable, conspicuous, clear, obvious, manifest, open, palpable, plain, patent.
F3 invisible, indiscernible, hidden.

vision *noun*
1 saw a vision: apparition, hallucination, illusion, delusion, mirage, phantom, ghost, chimera, spectre, wraith.
2 had a vision of his perfect house: idea, ideal, conception, insight, view, picture, image, fantasy, dream, daydream.
3 have excellent vision: sight, seeing, eyesight, perception, discernment, far-sightedness, foresight, penetration.

visionary *adjective*
idealistic, impractical, romantic, dreamy, unrealistic, utopian, unreal, fanciful, prophetic, speculative, unworkable, illusory, imaginary.

▶ *noun*
idealist, romantic, dreamer,
daydreamer, fantasist, prophet, mystic,
seer, utopian, rainbow-chaser,
theorist.
E3 pragmatist.

visit *verb*
call on, call in, stay with, stay at, drop
in on (*infml*), stop by (*infml*), look in,
look up, pop in (*infml*), see.
▶ *noun*
call, stay, stop, excursion, sojourn
(*fml*).

visitor *noun*
caller, guest, company, tourist,
holidaymaker.

visualize *verb*
picture, envisage, imagine, conceive.

vital *adjective*
1 *a vital factor*: critical, crucial,
important, imperative, key, significant,
basic, fundamental, essential,
necessary, requisite, indispensable,
urgent, life-or-death, decisive, forceful.
2 *strong and vital*: living, alive, lively,
life-giving, invigorating, spirited,
vivacious, vibrant, vigorous, dynamic,
animated, energetic, quickening
(*fml*).
E3 1 inessential, peripheral. 2 dead.

vitality *noun*
life, liveliness, animation, vigour,
energy, vivacity, spirit, sparkle, go
(*infml*), exuberance, strength, stamina.

vivacious *adjective*
lively, animated, spirited, high-
spirited, effervescent, ebullient,
cheerful, sparkling, bubbly, light-
hearted.

vivid *adjective*
1 *a vivid shade of orange*: bright,
colourful, intense, strong, rich, vibrant,
brilliant, glowing, dazzling, vigorous,
dramatic, flamboyant, animated, lively.
2 *have vivid memories*: memorable,
powerful, graphic, clear, distinct,
striking, sharp, realistic.
E3 1 colourless, dull. 2 vague.

vocabulary *noun*
language, words, glossary, lexicon,
dictionary, word-book, thesaurus.

vocal *adjective*
1 *vocal tradition*: spoken, said, oral,
uttered, voiced.
2 *a very vocal minority*: articulate,
eloquent, expressive, noisy, clamorous,
shrill, strident, outspoken, frank,
forthright, plain-spoken.
E3 1 unspoken. 2 inarticulate.

vocation *noun*
calling, pursuit, career, métier,
mission, profession, trade,
employment, work, role, post, job,
business, office.

vogue *noun*
fashion, mode, style, craze, popularity,
trend, prevalence, acceptance, custom,
fad (*infml*), the latest (*infml*), the rage
(*infml*), the thing (*infml*).

voice *noun*
1 *a deep voice/the voice of the people*:
speech, utterance, articulation,
language, words, sound, tone,
intonation, inflection, expression,
mouthpiece, medium, instrument,
organ (*fml*).
2 *have a voice*: say, vote, opinion, view,
decision, option, will.
▶ *verb*
express, say, utter, air, articulate, speak
of, verbalize, assert, convey, disclose,
divulge, declare, enunciate.

void *noun*
emptiness, vacuity, vacuum, chasm,
blank, blankness, space, lack, want,
cavity, gap, hollow, opening.
▶ *adjective*
annulled, inoperative, invalid,
cancelled, ineffective, futile, useless,
vain, worthless.
E3 valid.

volatile *adjective*
changeable, inconstant, unstable,
variable, erratic, temperamental,
unsteady, unsettled, fickle, mercurial,
unpredictable, capricious, restless,
giddy, flighty, up and down (*infml*),
lively.
E3 constant, steady.

voluble *adjective*
fluent, glib, articulate, loquacious
(*fml*), talkative, forthcoming,
garrulous.

volume *noun*
1 volume of the tank: bulk, size, capacity, dimensions, amount, mass, quantity, aggregate, amplitude, body.
2 in two volumes: book, tome, publication.

voluntary *adjective*
1 voluntary work: free, gratuitous, optional, spontaneous, unforced, willing, unpaid, honorary.
2 decision was voluntary: conscious, deliberate, purposeful, intended, intentional, wilful.
1 compulsory. **2** involuntary.

volunteer *verb*
offer, propose, put forward, present, suggest, step forward, advance.

vomit *verb*
be sick, bring up, heave, retch, puke (*infml*), throw up (*infml*).

vote *noun*
ballot, poll, election, franchise, referendum.
▸ *verb*
elect, ballot, choose, opt, plump for, declare, return.

vouch for *verb*
guarantee, support, back, endorse, confirm, certify, affirm, assert, attest to, speak for, swear to, uphold.

vow *verb*
promise, pledge, swear, dedicate, devote, profess, consecrate, affirm.
▸ *noun*
promise, oath, pledge.

voyage *noun*
journey, trip, passage, expedition, crossing.

vulgar *adjective*
1 decoration was vulgar: tasteless, flashy, gaudy, tawdry, cheap and nasty (*infml*).
2 vulgar manners: unrefined, uncouth, coarse, common, crude, ill-bred, impolite, indecorous.
3 a vulgar word: indecent, suggestive, risqué, rude, indelicate.
4 vulgar Latin: ordinary, general, popular, vernacular.
1 tasteful. **2** correct. **3** decent.

vulnerable *adjective*
unprotected, exposed, defenceless, susceptible, weak, sensitive, wide open.
protected, strong, invulnerable.

waddle *verb*
toddle, totter, wobble, sway, rock, shuffle.

waffle *verb*
jabber, prattle, blather, rabbit on (*infml*), witter on (*infml*).

▶ *noun*
blather, prattle, wordiness, padding, nonsense, gobbledegook (*infml*), hot air (*infml*).

waft *verb*
drift, float, blow, transport, transmit.

wag *verb*
shake, waggle, wave, sway, swing, bob, nod, wiggle, oscillate, flutter, vibrate, quiver, rock.

wage *noun*
pay, fee, earnings, salary, wage-packet, payment, stipend, remuneration, emolument (*fml*), allowance, reward, hire, compensation, recompense.

▶ *verb*
carry on, conduct, engage in, undertake, practise, pursue.

wail *verb*
moan, cry, howl, lament, weep, complain, yowl (*infml*).

wait *verb*
delay, linger, hold back, hesitate, pause, hang around, hang fire, remain, rest, stay.

F₃ proceed, go ahead.

▶ *noun*
hold-up, hesitation, delay, interval, pause, halt.

waive *verb*
renounce, relinquish, forgo, resign, surrender, yield.

wake¹ *verb*
1 wake from the anaesthetic: rise, get up, arise, rouse, come to, bring round.

2 woke forgotten feelings: stimulate, stir, activate, arouse, animate, excite, fire, galvanize.

F₃1 sleep.

▶ *noun*
funeral, death-watch, vigil, watch.

wake² *noun*
1 in the wake of the election: trail, track, path, aftermath.

2 the ship's wake: backwash, wash, rear, train, waves.

walk *verb*
step, stride, pace, proceed, advance, march, plod, tramp, traipse, trek, trudge, saunter, amble, stroll, tread, hike, promenade, move, hoof it (*infml*), accompany, escort.

⇨ *See also* **Word Workshop** *panel.*

▶ *noun*
1 a funny walk: carriage, gait, step, pace, stride.

2 go for a walk: stroll, amble, ramble, saunter, march, hike, tramp, trek, traipse, trudge, trail.

3 a tree-lined walk: footpath, path, walkway, avenue, pathway, promenade, alley, esplanade, lane, pavement, sidewalk.

◆ **walk of life** field, area, sphere, line, activity, arena, course, pursuit, calling, métier, career, vocation, profession, trade.

walk-out *noun*
strike, stoppage, industrial action, protest, rebellion, revolt.

walk-over *noun*
pushover (*infml*), doddle (*infml*), child's play, piece of cake (*infml*), cinch (*infml*).

WORD workshop

walk

There are many different ways of **walking**. We can tell a lot about a person or creature by the way they walk. Aim to make your writing more interesting by using some of the synonyms listed.

walk at your ease

amble	roam	stroll
ramble	saunter	wander

walk quickly

hike	pace	troop
march	stride	

walk quietly

creep	slink	tiptoe
prowl	sneak	

walk with difficulty

hobble	stagger	trek
limp	stumble	trudge
plod	tramp	

walk with pride

parade	strut
promenade	swagger

how creatures walk

pad	trot
scuttle	waddle

wall *noun*
1 cell wall/garden wall/walls of steel: partition, screen, panel, divider, fence, hedge, enclosure, membrane, bulkhead.

2 the castle walls: fortification, barricade, rampart, parapet, stockade, embankment, bulwark, palisade.

walk   WORD *workshop*

The following passage shows how some of the synonyms listed opposite can be used instead of repeating **walk**.

> As it was a warm evening, Sara decided to ~~walk~~ *stroll* home through the park. As she watched the ducks ~~walk~~ *waddle* along the edge of the pond, she caught sight of Donald ~~walking~~ *striding* in the direction of his house. "You're in a hurry," she remarked. "Yes," Donald replied, "I got home very late last night and my mother heard me ~~walking~~ *sneaking* upstairs. I was warned I would have to get home quickly tonight." As they were chatting, Trevor ~~walked~~ *paraded* past, showing off his new trainers. Just then, a big black dog, which Trevor didn't see, ~~walked~~ *trotted* across the footpath, knocking him over. Donald and Sara couldn't help laughing as Trevor picked himself up and ~~walked~~ *hobbled* away.

3 wall of people: obstacle, obstruction, barrier, block, impediment.

wallow *verb*
1 wallow in mud: loll, lie, roll, wade, welter, lurch, flounder, splash.
2 wallow in nostalgia: indulge, luxuriate, relish, revel, bask, enjoy, glory, delight.

wander *verb*
1 wander the countryside/wander home: roam, rove, ramble, meander, saunter, stroll, prowl, drift, range, stray, straggle.
2 wander from the point: digress, diverge, deviate, depart, go astray, swerve, veer, err.

3 wandering in his mind: ramble, rave, babble, gibber.
▶ *noun*
excursion, ramble, stroll, saunter, meander, prowl, cruise.

wanderer *noun*
itinerant, traveller, voyager, drifter, rover, rambler, stroller, stray, straggler, ranger, nomad, gypsy, vagrant, vagabond, rolling stone (*infml*).

wane *verb*
diminish, decrease, decline, weaken, subside, fade, dwindle, ebb, lessen, abate, sink, drop, taper off, dim, droop, contract, shrink, fail, wither.
E∃ increase, wax.

want *verb*
1 wants something to eat/wanted peace: desire, wish, crave, covet, fancy, long for, pine for, yearn for, hunger for, thirst for.
2 wants a lick of paint: need, require, demand, lack, miss, call for.
⇨ *See also* **Word Workshop** *panel.*
▶ *noun*
1 satisfy their wants: desire, demand, longing, requirement, wish, need, appetite.
2 a want of decent restaurants: lack, dearth, insufficiency, deficiency, shortage, inadequacy.
3 suffer want: poverty, privation (*fml*), destitution.

wanton *adjective*
malicious, immoral, shameless, arbitrary, unprovoked, unjustifiable, unrestrained, rash, reckless, wild.

war *noun*
warfare, hostilities, fighting, battle, combat, conflict, strife, struggle, bloodshed, contest, contention, enmity.
E∃ peace, ceasefire.
▶ *verb*
wage war, fight, take up arms, battle, clash, combat, strive, skirmish, struggle, contest, contend.

ward *noun*
1 a hospital ward: room, apartment, unit.
2 an electoral ward: division, area, district, quarter, precinct, zone.

3 a ward of court: charge, dependant, protégé(e), minor.
◆ **ward off** avert, fend off, deflect, parry, repel, stave off, thwart, beat off, forestall, evade, turn away, block, avoid.

wares *noun*
goods, merchandise, commodities, stock, products, produce, stuff.

warfare *noun*
war, fighting, hostilities, battle, arms, combat, strife, struggle, passage of arms, contest, conflict, contention, discord, blows.
E∃ peace.

warlike *adjective*
belligerent, aggressive, bellicose, pugnacious (*fml*), combative, bloodthirsty, war-mongering, militaristic, hostile, antagonistic, unfriendly.
E∃ friendly, peaceable.

warm *adjective*
1 warm water: heated, tepid, lukewarm.
2 warm support: ardent, passionate, fervent, vehement, earnest, zealous.
3 warm colours: rich, intense, mellow, cheerful.
4 a warm welcome: friendly, amiable, cordial, affable, kindly, genial, hearty, hospitable, sympathetic, affectionate, tender.
5 a warm climate: fine, sunny, balmy, temperate, close.
E∃1 cool. **2** indifferent. **3** cold.
4 unfriendly. **5** cool.
▶ *verb*
1 warm the milk: heat (up), reheat, melt, thaw.
2 warming her heart: animate, interest, please, delight, stimulate, stir, rouse, excite.
E∃1 cool.

warmth *noun*
1 the warmth of its body: warmness, heat.
2 the warmth of the people: friendliness, affection, cordiality, tenderness.
3 replied with some warmth: ardour, enthusiasm, passion, fervour, zeal, eagerness.

F≡ 1 coldness. **2** unfriendliness.
3 indifference.

warn *verb*
caution, alert, admonish, advise,
notify, counsel, put on one's guard,
inform, tip off (*infml*).

warning *noun*
1 give them some warning/sound a
warning: caution, alert, admonition,
advice, notification, notice, advance
notice, counsel, hint, lesson, alarm,
threat, tip-off (*infml*).
2 dark clouds were the first warning of
a storm brewing: omen, augury,
premonition, presage, sign, signal,
portent.

warp *verb*
twist, bend, contort, deform, distort,
kink, misshape, pervert, corrupt,
deviate.
F≡ straighten.

warrant *noun*
authorization, authority, sanction,
permit, permission, licence,
guarantee, warranty, security, pledge,
commission, voucher.

wary *adjective*
cautious, guarded, careful, chary, on
one's guard, on the lookout, prudent,
distrustful, suspicious, heedful,
attentive, alert, watchful, vigilant,
wide-awake.
F≡ unwary, careless, heedless.

wash *verb*
1 wash clothes/the floors: clean,
cleanse, launder, scrub, swab down,
rinse, swill.
2 wash before dinner: bathe, bath,
shower, douche, shampoo.

waste *verb*
1 don't waste your money: squander,
misspend, misuse, fritter away,
dissipate, lavish, spend, throw away,
blow (*infml*).
2 wasting energy: consume, erode,
exhaust, drain, destroy, spoil.
F≡ 1 economize. **2** preserve.
▸ *noun*
1 a waste of money: squandering,
dissipation (*fml*), prodigality (*fml*),
wastefulness, extravagance, loss.
2 a waste of his talent: misapplication,

misuse, abuse, neglect.
3 dispose of waste: rubbish, refuse,
trash, garbage, leftovers, debris, dregs,
effluent, litter, scrap, slops, dross.
▸ *adjective*
1 waste materials: useless, worthless,
unwanted, unused, left-over,
superfluous, supernumerary, extra.
2 waste land: barren, desolate, empty,
uninhabited, bare, devastated,
uncultivated, unprofitable, wild,
dismal, dreary.

wasted *adjective*
1 wasted effort: unnecessary,
needless, useless.
2 thin and wasted faces: emaciated,
withered, shrivelled, shrunken, gaunt,
washed-out, spent.

wasteful *adjective*
extravagant, spendthrift, prodigal,
profligate, uneconomical, thriftless,
unthrifty, ruinous, lavish, improvident
(*fml*).
F≡ economical, thrifty.

wasteland *noun*
wilderness, desert, barrenness, waste,
wild(s), void.

watch *verb*
1 watch him closely: observe, see, look
at, regard, note, notice, mark, stare at,
peer at, gaze at, view.
2 watch my bag: guard, look after,
keep an eye on, mind, protect,
superintend, take care of, keep.
3 watch for those holes in the road:
pay attention, be careful, take heed,
look out.
▸ *noun*
1 wearing a watch: timepiece,
wristwatch, clock, chronometer.
2 keep (a) watch: vigilance,
watchfulness, vigil, observation,
surveillance, notice, lookout, attention,
heed, alertness, inspection,
supervision.
◆ **watch out** notice, be vigilant, look
out, keep one's eyes open.
◆ **watch over** guard, protect, stand
guard over, keep an eye on, look after,
mind, shield, defend, shelter, preserve.

watchful *adjective*
vigilant, attentive, heedful, observant,

WORD *workshop*

If the word **want** is used too often in the same piece of writing, it can bore the reader. Try varying the verbs you use, choosing some of the synonyms listed below to help you.

wish for

covet	hanker for	thirst for
crave	hunger for	wish (for)
desire	long (for)	yearn (for)
fancy	pine for	

need

be without	call for	miss
be deficient in	demand	need
be in need of	lack	require

---

alert, guarded, on one's guard, wide awake, suspicious, wary, chary, cautious.
E3 unobservant, inattentive.

water *noun*
rain, sea, ocean, lake, river, stream.
▸ *verb*
wet, moisten, dampen, soak, spray, sprinkle, irrigate, drench, flood, hose.
E3 dry out, parch.
◆ **water down 1** water the beer down: dilute, thin, water, weaken, adulterate, mix.
2 water down his remarks somewhat: tone down, soften, qualify.

waterfall *noun*
fall, cascade, chute, cataract, torrent.

watertight *adjective*
1 hull is watertight: waterproof, sound, hermetic.
2 a watertight alibi: impregnable, unassailable, airtight, flawless,

foolproof, firm, incontrovertible.
E3 **1** leaky.

watery *adjective*
1 watery eyes/grave: liquid, fluid, moist, wet, damp.
2 a rather watery soup: weak, watered-down, diluted, insipid, tasteless, thin, runny, soggy, flavourless, washy, wishy-washy (*infml*).
E3 **1** dry.

wave *verb*
1 waved to his parents: beckon, gesture, gesticulate, indicate, sign, signal, direct.
2 waving a stick: brandish, flourish, flap, flutter, shake, sway, swing.
3 waving in the wind: waft, quiver, ripple.
▸ *noun*
1 waves crashing on the shore: breaker, roller, billow, ripple, tidal wave, wavelet, undulation, white horse (*infml*).

want

WORD *workshop*

Instead of repeating **want** in the following advert, you might use some of the synonyms discussed opposite.

Do you ~~want~~ *desire* the perfect holiday? Do you ~~want~~ *hanker after* long sandy beaches and palm trees? Do you ~~want~~ *long* to relax and enjoy the sound of the sea? Do you ~~want~~ *yearn* to escape from the hustle and bustle of everyday life and people constantly ~~wanting~~ *demanding* your attention?

At Palm Tree Holidays we have just what you ~~want~~ *wish for*. We offer luxury hotels in exotic locations where our staff can provide everything you ~~want~~ *require*. You are one phone call away from paradise!

2 a wave of relief/protest: surge, sweep, swell, upsurge, groundswell, current, drift, movement, rush, tendency, trend, stream, flood, outbreak, rash.

waver *verb*
1 wavering between one and the other: vacillate, falter, hesitate, dither, fluctuate, vary, seesaw.
2 wavering on the edge: oscillate, shake, sway, wobble, tremble, totter, rock.
F₃ 1 decide.

wavy *adjective*
undulating, rippled, curly, curvy, ridged, sinuous, winding, zigzag.

wax *verb*
grow, increase, rise, swell, develop, enlarge, expand, magnify, mount, fill out, become.
F₃ decrease, wane.

way *noun*
1 the usual way: method, approach, manner, technique, procedure, means, mode, system, fashion.
2 study their ways/it's just his way: custom, practice, habit, usage, characteristic, idiosyncrasy, trait, style, conduct, nature.
3 the way home: direction, course, route, path, road, channel, access, avenue, track, passage, highway,

street, thoroughfare, lane.
◆ **by the way** incidentally, in passing.

wayward *adjective*
wilful, capricious, perverse, contrary, changeable, fickle, unpredictable, stubborn, self-willed, unmanageable, headstrong, obstinate, disobedient, rebellious, insubordinate, intractable, unruly, incorrigible.
🗉 tractable, good-natured.

weak *adjective*
1 *a weak excuse/chest*: feeble, frail, infirm, unhealthy, sickly, delicate, debilitated, exhausted, fragile, flimsy.
2 *a weak spot*: vulnerable, unprotected, unguarded, defenceless, exposed.
3 *a weak government/argument*: powerless, impotent, spineless, cowardly, indecisive, ineffectual, irresolute, poor, lacking, lame, inadequate, defective, deficient, inconclusive, unconvincing, untenable.
4 *a weak signal*: faint, slight, low, soft, muffled, dull, imperceptible.
5 *weak tea*: insipid, tasteless, watery, thin, diluted, runny.
🗉 1 strong. 2 secure. 3 powerful.
4 strong. 5 strong.

weaken *verb*
1 *weaken their hold*: enfeeble, exhaust, debilitate, sap, undermine, dilute, diminish, lower, lessen, reduce, moderate, mitigate, temper, soften (up), thin, water down.
2 *storm weakened*: tire, flag, fail, give way, droop, fade, abate, ease up, dwindle.
🗉 1 strengthen.

weakness *noun*
1 *weakness of body*: feebleness, debility, infirmity, impotence, frailty, powerlessness, vulnerability.
2 *have many weaknesses*: fault, failing, flaw, shortcoming, blemish, defect, deficiency, foible.
3 *a weakness for chocolate*: liking, inclination, fondness, penchant, passion, soft spot (*infml*).
🗉 1 strength. 2 strength. 3 dislike.

wealth *noun*
1 *have considerable wealth*: money,

cash, riches, assets, affluence, prosperity, funds, mammon, fortune, capital, opulence, means, substance, resources, goods, possessions, property, estate.
2 *a wealth of reading material*: abundance, plenty, bounty, fullness, profusion, store.
🗉 1 poverty.

wealthy *adjective*
rich, prosperous, affluent, well-off, moneyed, opulent, comfortable, well-heeled, well-to-do, flush (*infml*), loaded (*infml*), rolling in it (*infml*).
🗉 poor, impoverished.

wear *verb*
1 *wearing green/a hat*: dress in, have on, put on, don, sport, carry, bear, display, show.
2 *wear away/down*: deteriorate, erode, corrode, consume, fray, rub, abrade, waste, grind.
▸ *noun*
1 *men's wear*: clothes, clothing, dress, garments, outfit, costume, attire.
2 *wear and tear*: deterioration, erosion, corrosion, wear and tear, friction, abrasion.
◆ **wear off** decrease, abate, dwindle, diminish, subside, wane, weaken, fade, lessen, ebb, peter out, disappear.
🗉 increase.
◆ **wear out 1** *journey wore him out*: exhaust, fatigue, tire (out), enervate, sap.
2 *wear out the carpet*: deteriorate, wear through, erode, impair, consume, fray.

wearing *adjective*
exhausting, fatiguing, tiresome, tiring, wearisome, trying, taxing, oppressive, irksome, exasperating.
🗉 refreshing.

weary *adjective*
tired, exhausted, fatigued, sleepy, worn out, drained, drowsy, jaded, all in (*infml*), done in (*infml*), dead beat (*infml*), dog-tired (*infml*), whacked (*infml*).
🗉 refreshed.

weather *noun*
climate, conditions, temperature.

Types of weather include:

black ice, breeze, chinook, cloud, cyclone, deluge, dew, downpour, drizzle, drought, fog, frost, gale, hail, haze, heatwave, hurricane, hoar frost, ice, lightning, mist, mistral, monsoon, rain, rainbow, shower, sleet, slush, smog, snow, snowstorm, squall, storm, sunshine, tempest, thaw, thunder, tornado, twister (*infml*), typhoon, whirlwind, wind.

verb

1 weather the storm: endure, survive, live through, come through, ride out, rise above, stick out, withstand, surmount, stand, brave, overcome, resist, pull through, suffer.
2 face weathered by sun, wind, and rain: expose, toughen, season, harden.
E3 1 succumb.

weave *verb*

1 weaving the strands together: interlace, lace, plait, braid, intertwine, spin, knit, entwine, intercross, fuse, merge, unite.
2 weaving a complicated story: create, compose, construct, contrive, put together, fabricate.
3 weaving from side to side: wind, twist, zigzag, criss-cross.

web *noun*

network, net, netting, lattice, mesh, webbing, interlacing, weft, snare, tangle, trap.

wedding *noun*

marriage, matrimony, nuptials (*fml*), wedlock, bridal.
E3 divorce.

wedge *noun*

lump, block, chunk, wodge, chock.
▸ *verb*
jam, cram, pack, ram, squeeze, stuff, push, lodge, block, thrust, crowd, force.

weep *verb*

cry, sob, moan, lament, wail, mourn, grieve, bawl, blubber, snivel, whimper, blub (*infml*).
E3 rejoice.

weigh *verb*

1 weighing heavily on them: bear down, oppress.
2 weigh the odds: consider, contemplate, evaluate, meditate on, mull over, ponder, think over, examine, reflect on, deliberate.
◆ **weigh down** oppress, overload, load, burden, bear down, weigh upon, press down, get down (*infml*), depress, afflict, trouble, worry.
E3 lighten, hearten.
◆ **weigh up** assess, examine, size up, balance, consider, contemplate, deliberate, mull over, ponder, think over, discuss, chew over (*infml*).

weight *noun*

1 the great weight made his legs buckle: heaviness, gravity, burden, load, pressure, mass, force, ballast, tonnage, poundage.
2 add weight to his statement: importance, significance, substance, consequence, impact, moment, influence, value, authority, clout (*infml*), power, preponderance, consideration.
E3 1 lightness.
▸ *verb*
bias, unbalance, slant, prejudice.

weighty *adjective*

1 several weighty volumes: heavy, burdensome, substantial, bulky.
2 a weighty decision: important, significant, consequential, crucial, critical, momentous, serious, grave, solemn.
3 a weighty problem: demanding, difficult, exacting, taxing.
E3 1 light. **2** unimportant.

weird *adjective*

strange, uncanny, bizarre, eerie, creepy, supernatural, unnatural, ghostly, freakish, mysterious, queer, grotesque, spooky (*infml*), far-out (*infml*), way-out (*infml*).
E3 normal, usual.

welcome *adjective*

acceptable, desirable, pleasing, pleasant, agreeable, gratifying, appreciated, delightful, refreshing.
E3 unwelcome.

▸ *noun*

reception, greeting, salutation (*infml*), acceptance, hospitality, red carpet (*infml*).

▸ *verb*

greet, hail, receive, salute, meet, accept, approve of, embrace.
F3 reject, snub.

weld *verb*

fuse, unite, bond, join, solder, bind, connect, seal, link, cement.
F3 separate.

welfare *noun*

wellbeing, health, prosperity, happiness, benefit, good, advantage, interest, profit, success.

well[1] *noun*

get water from the well: spring, well-spring, fountain, fount, source, reservoir, wellhead, waterhole.

▸ *verb*

flow, spring, surge, gush, stream, brim over, jet, spout, spurt, swell, pour, flood, ooze, run, trickle, rise, seep.

well[2] *adverb*

do something well/get on well: rightly, correctly, properly, skilfully, ably, expertly, successfully, adequately, sufficiently, suitably, easily, satisfactorily, thoroughly, greatly, fully, considerably, completely, agreeably, pleasantly, happily, kindly, favourably, splendidly, substantially, comfortably, readily, carefully, clearly, highly, deeply, justly.
F3 badly, inadequately, incompetently, wrongly.

▸ *adjective*

1 feel well: healthy, in good health, fit, able-bodied, sound, robust, strong, thriving, flourishing.
2 all is well: satisfactory, right, all right, good, pleasing, proper, agreeable, fine, lucky, fortunate.
F3 1 ill. 2 bad.

wellbeing *noun*

welfare, happiness, comfort, good.

wellbred *adjective*

well-mannered, polite, well-brought-up, mannerly, courteous, civil, refined, cultivated, cultured, genteel.
F3 ill-bred.

well-worn *adjective*

timeworn, stale, tired, trite, overused, unoriginal, hackneyed, commonplace, stereotyped, threadbare, corny (*infml*).
F3 original.

wet *adjective*

1 wet clothes/ground: damp, moist, soaked, soaking, sodden, saturated, soggy, sopping, watery, waterlogged, drenched, dripping, spongy, dank, clammy.
2 a wet day: raining, rainy, showery, teeming, pouring, drizzling, humid.
3 (*infml*) don't be so wet!: weak, feeble, weedy, wimpish (*infml*), spineless, soft, ineffectual, namby-pamby, irresolute, timorous.
F3 1 dry. 2 dry. 3 strong.

▸ *verb*

moisten, damp, dampen, soak, saturate, drench, steep, water, irrigate, spray, splash, sprinkle, imbue, dip.
F3 dry.

whack *verb*

hit, strike, smack, thrash, slap, beat, bash (*infml*), bang, cuff, thump, box, buffet, rap, wallop (*infml*), belt (*infml*), clobber (*infml*), clout (*infml*), sock (*infml*).

▸ *noun*

smack, slap, blow, hit, rap, stroke, thump, cuff, box, bang, clout (*infml*), bash (*infml*), wallop (*infml*).

wheedle *verb*

cajole, coax, persuade, inveigle (*fml*), charm, flatter, entice, court, draw.
F3 force.

wheel *noun*

turn, revolution, circle, rotation, gyration, pivot, roll, spin, twirl, whirl.

▸ *verb*

turn, rotate, circle, gyrate, orbit, spin, twirl, whirl, swing, roll, revolve, swivel.

wheeze *verb*

pant, gasp, cough, hiss, rasp, whistle.

whereabouts *noun*

location, position, place, situation, site, vicinity.

whet *verb*

1 whet the blade: sharpen, hone, file, grind.
2 whet their appetite: stimulate, stir,

rouse, arouse, provoke, kindle, quicken (*fml*), incite, awaken, increase.
E31 blunt. **2** dampen.

whiff *noun*
breath, puff, hint, trace, blast, draught, odour, smell, aroma, sniff, scent, reek, stink, stench.

whim *noun*
fancy, caprice, notion, quirk, freak, humour, conceit, fad, vagary, urge.

whimper *verb*
cry, sob, weep, snivel, whine, grizzle, mewl, moan, whinge (*infml*).
▶ *noun*
sob, snivel, whine, moan.

whimsical *adjective*
fanciful, capricious, playful, impulsive, eccentric, funny, droll, curious, queer, unusual, weird, odd, peculiar, quaint, dotty (*infml*).

whine *noun*
1 dog whining: cry, whimper, moan, wail.
2 whining about the cost: complaint, grumble, grouse, gripe (*infml*), grouch (*infml*).
▶ *verb*
1 dog gave a pathetic whine: cry, sob, whimper, grizzle, moan, wail.
2 always has some whine or other: complain, carp, grumble, whinge (*infml*), gripe (*infml*), grouch (*infml*).

whip *verb*
1 whipping the horses: beat, flog, lash, flagellate, scourge, birch, cane, strap, thrash, punish, chastise, discipline, castigate (*fml*).
2 whipped it away/whipped past: pull, jerk, snatch, whisk, dash, dart, rush, tear, flit, flash, fly.
3 whipping up trouble: goad, drive, spur, push, urge, stir, rouse, agitate, incite, provoke, instigate.
▶ *noun*
lash, scourge, switch, birch, cane, horsewhip, riding-crop, cat-o'-nine-tails.

whirl *verb*
swirl, spin, turn, twist, twirl, pivot, pirouette, swivel, wheel, rotate, revolve, reel, roll, gyrate, circle.

▶ *noun*
1 did a whirl: spin, twirl, twist, gyration, revolution, pirouette, swirl, turn, wheel, rotation, circle, reel, roll.
2 a whirl of excitement: confusion, daze, flurry, commotion, agitation, bustle, hubbub, hurly-burly, giddiness, tumult, uproar.

whisk *verb*
1 whisk the eggs: whip, beat.
2 whisked down to the shops: dart, dash, rush, hurry, speed, hasten, race.
3 whisking the flies away: brush, sweep, flick, wipe, twitch.

whisper *verb*
1 whispered his name/wind whispering: murmur, mutter, mumble, breathe, hiss, rustle, sigh.
2 people are already whispering that she'll have to resign: hint, intimate, insinuate, gossip, divulge.
E31 shout.
▶ *noun*
1 the whisper of the wind in the trees: murmur, undertone, sigh, hiss, rustle.
2 not a whisper: hint, suggestion, suspicion, breath, whiff, rumour, report, innuendo, insinuation, trace, tinge, soupçon, buzz.

whittle *verb*
1 whittling wood: carve, cut, scrape, shave, trim, pare, hew, shape.
2 whittling away at their lead: erode, eat away, wear away, diminish, consume, reduce, undermine.

whole *adjective*
1 the whole day/text: complete, entire, integral, full, total, unabridged, uncut, undivided, unedited.
2 a whole dinosaur skeleton: intact, unharmed, undamaged, unbroken, inviolate, perfect, in one piece, mint, unhurt.
3 felt whole again: well, healthy, fit, sound, strong.
E31 partial. **2** damaged. **3** ill.
▶ *noun*
total, aggregate, sum total, entirety, all, fullness, totality, ensemble, entity, unit, lot, piece, everything.
E3 part.
◆ **on the whole** generally, mostly, in

general, generally speaking, as a rule, for the most part, all in all, all things considered, by and large.

whole-hearted *adjective*
unreserved, unstinting, unqualified, passionate, enthusiastic, earnest, committed, dedicated, devoted, heartfelt, emphatic, warm, sincere, unfeigned, genuine, complete, true, real, zealous.
F3 half-hearted.

wholesale *adjective*
comprehensive, far-reaching, extensive, sweeping, wide-ranging, mass, broad, outright, total, massive, indiscriminate.
F3 partial.

wholesome *adjective*
1 wholesome food: healthy, hygienic, salubrious (*fml*), sanitary, nutritious, nourishing, beneficial, salutary, invigorating, bracing.
2 wholesome entertainment: moral, decent, clean, proper, improving, edifying, uplifting, pure, virtuous, righteous, honourable, respectable.
F3 1 unhealthy. **2** unwholesome.

wholly *adverb*
completely, entirely, fully, purely, absolutely, totally, utterly, comprehensively, altogether, perfectly, thoroughly, all, exclusively, only.
F3 partly.

wicked *adjective*
1 a wicked man/crime: evil, sinful, immoral, depraved, corrupt, vicious, unprincipled, iniquitous, heinous (*fml*), debased, abominable, ungodly, unrighteous, shameful.
2 a wicked smell: bad, unpleasant, harmful, offensive, vile, worthless, difficult, dreadful, distressing, awful, atrocious, severe, intense, nasty, foul, injurious, troublesome, terrible, fierce.
3 a wicked grin: naughty, mischievous, roguish.
F3 1 good, upright. **2** harmless.

wide *adjective*
1 a wide street: broad, roomy, spacious, vast, immense.
2 wide eyes: dilated, expanded, full.
3 wide influence: extensive, wide-

ranging, comprehensive, far-reaching, general.
4 wide trousers: loose, baggy.
5 a wide shot: off-target, distant, remote.
F3 1 narrow. **3** restricted. **5** near.
▶ *adverb*
1 shot went wide: astray, off course, off target, off the mark.
2 travel far and wide: fully, completely, all the way.
F3 1 on target.

widen *verb*
distend, dilate, expand, extend, spread, stretch, enlarge, broaden.
F3 narrow.

widespread *adjective*
extensive, prevalent, rife, general, sweeping, universal, wholesale, far-reaching, unlimited, broad, common, pervasive, far-flung.
F3 limited.

width *noun*
breadth, diameter, wideness, compass, thickness, span, scope, range, measure, girth, beam, amplitude, extent, reach.

wield *verb*
1 wield a weapon: brandish, flourish, swing, wave, handle, ply, manage, manipulate.
2 wield power: have, hold, possess, employ, exert, exercise, use, utilize, maintain, command.

wild *adjective*
1 a wild horse: untamed, undomesticated, feral, savage, barbarous, primitive, uncivilized, natural, ferocious, fierce.
2 wild country: uncultivated, desolate, waste, uninhabited.
3 wild behaviour: unrestrained, unruly, unmanageable, violent, turbulent, rowdy, lawless, disorderly, riotous, boisterous.
4 a wild night: stormy, tempestuous, rough, blustery, choppy.
5 wild hair: untidy, unkempt, messy, dishevelled, tousled.
6 a wild guess: reckless, rash, imprudent, foolish, foolhardy, impracticable, irrational, outrageous, preposterous, wayward, extravagant.

7 go wild: mad, crazy (*infml*), frenzied, distraught, demented.
F₃ 1 civilized, tame. **2** cultivated. **3** restrained. **4** calm. **5** tidy. **6** sensible. **7** sane.

wilderness *noun*
desert, wasteland, waste, wilds, jungle.

wiles *noun*
trick, stratagem, ruse, ploy, device, contrivance, guile, manoeuvre, subterfuge, cunning, dodge (*infml*), deceit, cheating, trickery, fraud, craftiness, chicanery.
F₃ guilelessness.

wilful *adjective*
1 wilful damage: deliberate, conscious, intentional, voluntary, premeditated.
2 a wilful child: self-willed, obstinate, stubborn, pig-headed, obdurate, intransigent, inflexible, perverse, wayward, contrary.
F₃ 1 unintentional. **2** good-natured.

will *noun*
1 of their own free will: volition, choice, option, preference, decision, discretion.
2 the will to live: wish, desire, inclination, feeling, fancy, disposition, mind.
3 have a strong will: purpose, resolve, resolution, determination, will-power, aim, intention, command.
▸ *verb*
1 willed that it was so: want, desire, choose, compel, command, decree, order, ordain.
2 willed his entire estate to his son: bequeath, leave, hand down, pass on, transfer, confer, dispose of.

willing *adjective*
disposed, inclined, agreeable, compliant, ready, prepared, consenting, content, amenable, biddable, pleased, well-disposed, favourable, happy, eager, enthusiastic.
F₃ unwilling, disinclined, reluctant.

wilt *verb*
droop, sag, wither, shrivel, flop, flag, dwindle, weaken, diminish, fail, fade, languish, ebb, sink, wane.
F₃ perk up.

wily *adjective*
shrewd, cunning, scheming, artful, crafty, foxy, intriguing, tricky, underhand, shifty, deceitful, deceptive, astute, sly, guileful, designing, crooked, fly (*infml*).
F₃ guileless.

win *verb*
1 win the race: be victorious, triumph, succeed, prevail, overcome, conquer, come first, carry off, finish first.
2 win a place at Cambridge: gain, acquire, achieve, attain, accomplish, receive, procure, secure, obtain, get, earn, catch, net.
F₃ 1 fail, lose.
⇨ *See also* **Word Study** *panel.*
▸ *noun*
victory, triumph, conquest, success, mastery.
F₃ defeat.
◆ **win over** persuade, prevail upon, convince, influence, convert, sway, talk round, charm, allure, attract.

wind¹ *noun* /wind/
a cold wind from the Arctic: air, breeze, draught, gust, puff, breath, air-current, blast, current, bluster, gale, hurricane, tornado, cyclone.

wind² *verb* /waind/
winding the wool round and round: coil, twist, turn, curl, curve, bend, loop, spiral, zigzag, twine, encircle, furl, deviate, meander, ramble, wreathe, roll, reel.
◆ **wind down 1 winding down the business**: slow (down), slacken off, lessen, reduce, subside, diminish, dwindle, decline.
2 wind down after a hard day's work: relax, unwind, quieten down, ease up, calm down.
F₃ 1 increase.
◆ **wind up 1 wind up the business**: close (down), end, conclude, terminate, finalize, finish, liquidate.
2 wind up in Orkney: end up, finish up, find oneself, settle.
3 (*infml*) **don't wind him up**: annoy, irritate, disconcert, fool, trick, kid (*infml*).
F₃ 1 begin.

WORD *study* win

There are many expressions that describe how someone **wins**. Try out some of those listed below, but remember that many phrases are only appropriate for informal contexts.

win

have beginner's luck
come up *or* turn up trumps

come on top

win easily

beat the socks off someone
beat someone hollow
give someone a drubbing/hammering
make a clean sweep
romp home
walk away with
win in a canter
wipe the floor with someone

beat someone hands down
get the better of someone
have the last laugh
make mincemeat of someone
sweep the board
whitewash someone
win hands down

win narrowly

edge someone out
pip someone at the post
win by a head

inch someone out
shade it

windfall *noun*
bonanza, godsend, jackpot, treasure-trove, stroke of luck, find.

window *noun*
pane, light, opening, skylight, rose-window, casement, oriel, dormer.

windy *adjective*
breezy, blowy, blustery, squally, windswept, stormy, tempestuous, gusty.
F∃ calm.

wing *noun*
branch, arm, section, faction, group, grouping, flank, circle, coterie, set, segment, side, annexe, adjunct, extension.

wink *verb*
blink, flutter, glimmer, glint, twinkle, gleam, sparkle, flicker, flash.

▶ *noun*
1 the first wink of sunshine: blink, flutter, sparkle, twinkle, glimmering, gleam, glint.
2 in the wink of an eye: instant, second, split second, flash.

winner *noun*
champion, victor, prizewinner, world-beater, medallist, title-holder, conqueror.
F∃ loser.

winning *adjective*
1 the winning team: conquering, triumphant, unbeaten, undefeated, victorious, successful.
2 winning ways: winsome, charming, attractive, captivating, engaging, fetching, enchanting, endearing, delightful, amiable, alluring, lovely, pleasing, sweet.
F∃ 1 losing. 2 unappealing.

wintry *adjective*
cold, chilly, bleak, cheerless, desolate,
dismal, harsh, snowy, frosty, freezing,
frozen, icy.

wipe *verb*
1 wiped his mouth/the table: rub,
clean, dry, dust, brush, mop, swab,
sponge, clear.
2 wiped the smile off her face: remove,
erase, take away, take off.
◆ **wipe out** eradicate, obliterate,
destroy, massacre, exterminate,
annihilate, erase, expunge (*fml*), raze,
abolish, blot out, efface (*fml*).

wiry *adjective*
muscular, sinewy, lean, tough, strong.
E3 puny.

wisdom *noun*
discernment, penetration, sagacity
(*fml*), reason, sense, astuteness,
comprehension, enlightenment,
judgement, judiciousness,
understanding, knowledge, learning,
intelligence, erudition, foresight,
prudence.
E3 folly, stupidity.

wise *adjective*
1 a wise old man: discerning,
sagacious (*fml*), perceptive, rational,
informed, well-informed,
understanding, erudite, enlightened,
knowing, intelligent, clever, aware,
experienced.
2 a wise decision: well-advised,
judicious (*fml*), prudent, reasonable,
sensible, sound, long-sighted, shrewd.
E3 1 foolish, stupid. 2 ill-advised.

wish *verb*
1 wishing for success/rain: desire,
want, yearn, long, hanker, covet, crave,
aspire, hope, hunger, thirst, prefer,
need.
2 do as she wishes: ask, bid, require,
order, instruct, direct, command.
▶ *noun*
1 I have a wish for a better life: desire,
want, hankering, aspiration,
inclination, hunger, thirst, liking,
preference, yearning, urge, whim,
hope.
2 carry out his wishes: request,
bidding, order, command, will.

wisp *noun*
shred, strand, thread, twist, piece,
lock.

wistful *adjective*
1 a wistful expression: thoughtful,
pensive, musing, reflective, wishful,
contemplative, dreamy, dreaming,
meditative.
2 a wistful sigh: melancholy, sad,
forlorn, disconsolate, longing, mournful.

wit *noun*
1 her writing is full of subtle wit:
humour, repartee, facetiousness,
drollery, banter, jocularity, levity.
2 have the wit to realize what was
happening: intelligence, cleverness,
brains, sense, reason, common sense,
wisdom, understanding, judgement,
insight, intellect.
3 he's a bit of a wit: humorist,
comedian, comic, satirist, joker, wag.
E3 1 seriousness. 2 stupidity.

witchcraft *noun*
sorcery, magic, wizardry, occultism,
the occult, the black art, black magic,
enchantment, necromancy, voodoo,
spell, incantation, divination,
conjuration.

withdraw *verb*
1 withdrew her hand quickly: recoil,
shrink back, draw back, pull back.
2 withdrew the accusation: recant,
disclaim, take back, revoke, rescind,
retract, cancel, abjure, recall, take
away.
3 withdrew from the world: depart, go
(away), absent oneself, retire, remove,
leave, back out, fall back, drop out,
retreat, secede.
4 withdrew the cork: draw out, extract,
pull out.

withdrawn *adjective*
reserved, unsociable, shy, introvert,
quiet, retiring, aloof, detached,
shrinking, uncommunicative,
unforthcoming, taciturn, silent.
E3 extrovert, outgoing.

wither *verb*
shrink, shrivel, dry, wilt, droop, decay,
disintegrate, wane, perish, fade,
languish, decline, waste.
E3 flourish, thrive.

withering *adjective*
scornful, contemptuous, scathing, snubbing, humiliating, mortifying, wounding.
₣₃ encouraging, supportive.

withhold *verb*
keep back, retain, hold back, suppress, restrain, repress, control, check, reserve, deduct, refuse, hide, conceal.
₣₃ give, accord.

withstand *verb*
resist, oppose, stand fast, stand one's ground, stand, stand up to, confront, brave, face, cope with, take on, thwart, defy, hold one's ground, hold out, last out, hold off, endure, bear, tolerate, put up with, survive, weather.
₣₃ give in, yield.

witness *noun*
1 call the next witness: testifier, attestant (*fml*), deponent (*fml*).
2 a witness to the accident: onlooker, eye-witness, looker-on, observer, spectator, viewer, watcher, bystander.
▸ *verb*
1 witness the accident: see, observe, notice, note, view, watch, look on, mark, perceive.
2 witness his signature: endorse, sign, countersign.

witty *adjective*
humorous, amusing, comic, sharp-witted, droll, whimsical, original, brilliant, clever, ingenious, lively, sparkling, funny, facetious, fanciful, jocular.
₣₃ dull, unamusing.

wizened *adjective*
shrivelled, shrunken, dried up, withered, wrinkled, gnarled, thin, worn, lined.

wobble *verb*
shake, oscillate, tremble, quake, sway, teeter, totter, rock, seesaw, vibrate, waver, dodder, fluctuate, hesitate, dither, vacillate, shilly-shally.

wobbly *adjective*
unstable, shaky, rickety, unsteady, wonky (*infml*), teetering, tottering, doddering, doddery, uneven, unbalanced, unsafe.
₣₃ stable, steady.

woman *noun*
female, lady, girl, matriarch, maiden, maid.

wonder *noun*
1 one of the wonders of the world: marvel, phenomenon, miracle, prodigy, sight, spectacle, rarity, curiosity.
2 watch it with wonder: awe, amazement, astonishment, admiration, wonderment, fascination, surprise, bewilderment.
▸ *verb*
1 wonder what he's doing: meditate, speculate, ponder, ask oneself, question, conjecture, puzzle, enquire, query, doubt, think.
2 wonder at its size: marvel, gape, be amazed, be surprised.

wonderful *adjective*
1 had a wonderful time: marvellous, magnificent, outstanding, excellent, superb, admirable, delightful, phenomenal, sensational, stupendous, tremendous, super (*infml*), terrific (*infml*), brilliant (*infml*), great (*infml*), fabulous (*infml*), fantastic (*infml*).
2 a wonderful sight: amazing, astonishing, astounding, startling, surprising, extraordinary, incredible, remarkable, staggering, strange.
₣₃ 1 appalling, dreadful. 2 ordinary.

wood *noun*
1 cut the wood: timber, lumber, planks.

Types of wood include:

bitterwood, brushwood, chipboard, cordwood, driftwood, firewood, fruitwood, green wood, hardboard, hardwood, heartwood, kindling, lumber (*US*), matchwood, nutwood, plywood, pulpwood, sapwood, seasoned wood, softwood, timber, whitewood, wood veneer; afrormosia, ash, balsa, beech, cedar, cherry, chestnut, cottonwood, deal, ebony, elm, fir, hazel, mahogany, African mahogany, maple, oak, pine, poplar, redwood, rosewood, sandalwood, sapele, satinwood, sycamore, teak, walnut, willow. ⇨*See also* **tree**.

2 an oak wood: forest, woods, woodland, trees, plantation, thicket, grove, coppice, copse, spinney.

wooded *adjective*
forested, timbered, woody, tree-covered, sylvan (*fml*).

wooden *adjective*
1 wooden planks: timber, woody.
2 a wooden expression: emotionless, expressionless, awkward, clumsy, stilted, lifeless, spiritless, unemotional, stiff, rigid, leaden, deadpan, blank, empty, slow.
E3 2 lively.

wool *noun*
fleece, down, yarn.

woolly *adjective*
1 a woolly coat: woollen, fleecy, woolly-haired, downy, shaggy, fuzzy, frizzy.
2 a bit woolly about yesterday's events: unclear, ill-defined, hazy, blurred, confused, muddled, vague, indefinite, nebulous.
E3 2 clear, distinct.
▸ *noun*
jumper, sweater, jersey, pullover, cardigan.

word *noun*
1 what does this word mean?: name, term, expression, designation, utterance, vocable (*fml*).
2 have a word with him later: conversation, chat, talk, discussion, consultation.
3 get word to his family: information, news, report, communication, notice, message, bulletin, communiqué, statement, dispatch, declaration, comment, assertion, account, remark, advice, warning.
4 give you my word: promise, pledge, oath, assurance, vow, guarantee.
5 just give the word: command, order, decree, commandment, go-ahead (*infml*), green light (*infml*).
▸ *verb*
phrase, express, couch, put, say, explain, write.

words *noun*
1 have words with someone: argument, dispute, quarrel,

disagreement, altercation (*fml*), bickering, row, squabble.
2 write the words of a song: lyrics, libretto, text, book.

wordy *adjective*
verbose, long-winded, loquacious (*fml*), garrulous, prolix, rambling, diffuse, discursive.
E3 concise.

work *noun*
1 what line of work are you in?: occupation, job, employment, profession, trade, business, career, calling, vocation, line, line of business, métier, livelihood, craft, skill.
2 doing important work for the government: task, assignment, undertaking, job, chore, responsibility, duty, commission.
3 takes a lot of hard work: toil, labour, drudgery, effort, exertion, industry, slog (*infml*), graft (*infml*), elbow grease (*infml*).
4 Beethoven's orchestral works: creation, production, achievement, composition, opus.
▸ *verb*
1 not working at the moment: be employed, have a job, earn one's living.
2 working hard: labour, toil, drudge, slave.
3 machine isn't working/working the controls: function, go, operate, perform, run, handle, manage, use, control.
4 work a minor miracle: bring about, accomplish, achieve, create, cause, pull off (*infml*).
5 work the land: cultivate, farm, dig, till.
6 working the clay in his hands: manipulate, knead, mould, shape, form, fashion, make, process.
E3 1 be unemployed. **2** play, rest. **3** fail.
⇨ *See also* **Word Study** *panel.*
◆ **work out 1 work the sum out in his head**: solve, resolve, calculate, figure out, puzzle out, sort out, understand, clear up.
2 working out well: develop, evolve, go well, succeed, prosper, turn out, pan out (*infml*).
3 work out what to do: plan, devise,

WORD study work

Like so many of the basic things in life, there are lots of expressions that refer to **work**. Try using some of those listed below, but remember that many would not be suitable in more formal contexts.

being busy

be up to your eyeballs
be up to your neck
have your hands full

be up to your eyes
busy as a bee
be rushed off your feet

working very hard

beaver away
burn the midnight oil
keep your nose to the grindstone
work like a dog

burn the candle at both ends
hard at it
pull your weight
work your fingers to the bone

get on with it

get down to business
knuckle down

get cracking
put your shoulder to the wheel

arrange, contrive, invent, construct, put together.
4 bill works out at £10 each: add up to, amount to, total, come out.
◆ **work up** incite, stir up, rouse, arouse, animate, excite, move, stimulate, inflame, spur, instigate, agitate, generate.

worker *noun*
employee, labourer, working man, working woman, artisan, craftsman, tradesman, hand, operative, wage-earner, breadwinner, proletarian.

workforce *noun*
workers, employees, personnel, labour force, staff, labour, work-people, shop-floor.

working *noun*
functioning, operation, running, routine, manner, method, action.
▶ *adjective*
1 working mines: functioning, operational, running, operative, going.

2 working man: employed, active.
E₃1 inoperative. **2** idle.

workmanship *noun*
skill, craft, craftsmanship, expertise, art, handicraft, handiwork, technique, execution, manufacture, work, finish.

works *noun*
1 a textile works: factory, plant, workshop, mill, foundry, shop.
2 the devil and all his works: actions, acts, doings.
3 the works of Shakespeare: productions, output, oeuvre, writings, books.
4 water got into the works: machinery, mechanism, workings, action, movement, parts, installations.

workshop *noun*
1 will find him in his workshop: works, workroom, atelier, studio, factory, plant, mill, shop.
2 organize a theatre workshop: study

group, seminar, symposium, discussion group, class.

world *noun*
1 all over the world: earth, globe, planet, star, universe, cosmos, creation, nature.
2 the world and his wife: everybody, everyone, people, human race, humankind, humanity.
3 in his own little world: sphere, realm, field, area, domain, division, system, society, province, kingdom.
4 the Roman world: times, epoch, era, period, age, days, life.

worldly *adjective*
1 worldly concerns: temporal, earthly, mundane, terrestrial, physical, secular, unspiritual, profane.
2 became more worldly when she moved to the city: worldly-wise, sophisticated, urbane, cosmopolitan, experienced, knowing, streetwise (*infml*).
3 too worldly for my taste: materialistic, selfish, ambitious, grasping, greedy, covetous, avaricious.
Ⓔ1 spiritual, eternal.
2 unsophisticated, unworldly.

worn *adjective*
1 worn carpet/cuffs: shabby, threadbare, worn-out, tatty, tattered, frayed, ragged.
2 a worn expression: exhausted, tired, weary, spent, fatigued, careworn, drawn, haggard, jaded.
Ⓔ1 new, unused. **2** fresh.
◆ worn out 1 worn out slippers: shabby, threadbare, useless, used, tatty, tattered, on its last legs, ragged, moth-eaten, frayed, decrepit.
2 was too worn out to object: tired out, exhausted, weary, done in (*infml*), all in (*infml*), dog-tired (*infml*).
Ⓔ1 new, unused. **2** fresh.

worried *adjective*
anxious, troubled, uneasy, ill at ease, apprehensive, concerned, bothered, upset, fearful, afraid, frightened, on edge, overwrought, tense, strained, nervous, disturbed, distraught, distracted, fretful, distressed, agonized.
Ⓔ calm, unworried, unconcerned.

worry *verb*
1 worry unnecessarily: be anxious, be troubled, be distressed, agonize, fret.
2 stop worrying your father!: irritate, plague, pester, torment, upset, unsettle, annoy, bother, disturb, vex, tease, nag, harass, harry, perturb, hassle (*infml*).
3 dog worrying sheep: attack, go for, savage.
Ⓔ1 be unconcerned. **2** comfort.
▶ *noun*
1 have a lot of worry/worries: problem, trouble, responsibility, burden, concern, care, trial, annoyance, irritation, vexation.
2 worry showed on her face: anxiety, apprehension, unease, misgiving, fear, disturbance, agitation, torment, misery, perplexity.
Ⓔ2 comfort, reassurance.
⇨ *See also* **Word Study** *panel.*

worsen *verb*
1 worsening the anger they felt: exacerbate, aggravate, intensify, heighten.
2 their condition worsened: get worse, weaken, deteriorate, degenerate, decline, sink, go downhill (*infml*).
Ⓔ improve.

worship *verb*
venerate, revere, reverence, adore, exalt, glorify, honour, praise, idolize, adulate, love, respect, pray to, deify.
Ⓔ despise, hate.
▶ *noun*
veneration, reverence, adoration, devotion(s), homage, honour, glory, glorification, exaltation, praise, prayer(s), respect, regard, love, adulation, deification, idolatry.

worth *noun*
worthiness, merit, value, benefit, advantage, importance, significance, use, usefulness, utility, quality, good, virtue, excellence, credit, desert(s), cost, rate, price, help, assistance, avail.
Ⓔ worthlessness.

worthless *adjective*
1 a worthless piece of junk: valueless, useless, pointless, meaningless, futile,

WORD *study*

worry

You might want to try some of these phrases when you are talking about feelings of **worry**.

being nervous

be a bundle of nerves
have butterflies in your stomach
be like a cat on hot bricks

be jittery
have kittens
be on edge

being worried

be at the end of your tether
be in a stew
be worried to death
go out of your mind
sweat it out
wait with bated breath

be beside yourself with something
be stressed out
be worried sick
have something on your mind
tear your hair out over something
be on tenterhooks

unavailing, unimportant, insignificant, trivial, unusable, cheap, poor, rubbishy, trashy, trifling, paltry.
2 *that worthless fellow*: contemptible, despicable, good-for-nothing, vile.
F3 1 valuable. **2** worthy.

worthwhile *adjective*
profitable, useful, valuable, worthy, good, helpful, beneficial, constructive, gainful, justifiable, productive.
F3 worthless.

worthy *adjective*
praiseworthy, laudable, creditable, commendable, valuable, worthwhile, admirable, fit, deserving, appropriate, respectable, reputable, good, honest, honourable, excellent, decent, upright, righteous.
F3 unworthy, disreputable.

wound *noun*
1 *a head wound*: injury, trauma, hurt, cut, gash, lesion, laceration, scar.
2 *a wound to the heart*: hurt, distress, trauma, torment, heartbreak, harm, damage, anguish, grief, shock.
▶ *verb*
1 *wounding the skin*: damage, harm,

hurt, injure, hit, cut, gash, lacerate, slash, pierce.
2 *remark wounded them deeply*: distress, offend, insult, pain, mortify, upset, slight, grieve.

wrangle *noun*
argument, quarrel, dispute, controversy, squabble, tiff, row (*infml*), bickering, disagreement, clash, altercation (*fml*), contest, slanging match (*infml*), set-to (*infml*).
F3 agreement.
▶ *verb*
argue, quarrel, disagree, dispute, bicker, altercate, contend, fall out (*infml*), row (*infml*), squabble, scrap, fight, spar.
F3 agree.

wrap *verb*
envelop, fold, enclose, cover, pack, shroud, wind, surround, package, muffle, cocoon, cloak, roll up, bind, bundle up, immerse.
F3 unwrap.
◆ **wrap up 1** *wrap up the presents*: wrap, pack up, package, parcel.
2 (*infml*) *that just about wraps it up*:

conclude, finish off, end, bring to a close, terminate, wind up, complete, round off.

wrapper noun
wrapping, packaging, envelope, cover, jacket, dust jacket, sheath, sleeve, paper.

wreak verb
inflict, exercise, create, cause, bring about, perpetrate, vent, unleash, express, execute, carry out, bestow.

wreath noun
garland, coronet, chaplet, festoon, crown, band, ring.

wreck verb
destroy, ruin, demolish, devastate, shatter, smash, break, spoil, play havoc with, ravage, write off.
E3 conserve, repair.
► noun
ruin, destruction, devastation, mess, demolition, ruination, write-off, disaster, loss, disruption.

wreckage noun
debris, remains, rubble, ruin(s), fragments, flotsam, pieces.

wrench verb
yank, wrest (fml), jerk, pull, tug, force, sprain, strain, rick, tear, twist, wring, rip, distort.
► verb
struggle, strive, fight, scuffle, grapple, tussle, combat, contend, contest, vie, battle.

wretch noun
scoundrel, rogue, villain, good-for-nothing, ruffian, rascal, vagabond, miscreant (fml), outcast.

wretched adjective
1 in a wretched state: atrocious, awful, deplorable, appalling.
2 she was wretched for a whole month: unhappy, sad, miserable, melancholy, depressed, dejected, disconsolate, downcast, forlorn, gloomy, doleful, distressed, broken-hearted, crestfallen.
3 a wretched attempt: pathetic, pitiable, pitiful, unfortunate, sorry, hopeless, poor.
4 where's that wretched dog?: contemptible, despicable, vile,

worthless, shameful, inferior, low, mean, paltry.
E3 1 excellent. 2 happy. 3 enviable. 4 worthy.

wriggle verb
squirm, writhe, wiggle, worm, twist, snake, slink, crawl, edge, sidle, manoeuvre, squiggle, dodge, extricate, zigzag, waggle, turn.

wring verb
1 wringing her hands: squeeze, twist, wrench, wrest (fml), extract, mangle, screw.
2 will get the answer if I have to wring it out of him: exact, extort, coerce, force.

wrinkle noun
furrow, crease, corrugation, line, fold, gather, pucker, crumple.
► verb
crease, corrugate, furrow, fold, crinkle, crumple, shrivel, gather, pucker.

write verb
pen, inscribe, record, jot down, set down, take down, transcribe, scribble, scrawl, correspond, communicate, draft, draw up, copy, compose, create.
◆ **write off 1** write off a debt: delete, cancel, cross out, disregard.
2 wrote off the car: wreck, destroy, crash, smash up.

writer noun
author, scribe, wordsmith, novelist, dramatist, essayist, playwright, columnist, diarist, hack, penpusher, scribbler, secretary, copyist, clerk.

Writers include:

annalist, author, autobiographer, bard, biographer, calligraphist, chronicler, clerk, columnist, composer, contributor, copyist, copywriter, correspondent, court reporter, diarist, dramatist, editor, essayist, fabler, fiction writer, ghost writer, hack, historian, journalist, leader-writer, lexicographer, librettist, lyricist, novelist, pen-friend, penman, pen-pal, penpusher (infml), penwoman, playwright, poet, poet laureate, reporter, rhymer, satirist, scribbler, scribe, scriptwriter, short-story writer, sonneteer, stenographer, storyteller, technical writer, web author.

writhe *verb*
squirm, wriggle, thresh, thrash, twist, wiggle, toss, coil, contort, struggle.

writing *noun*
1 can't read the writing: handwriting, calligraphy, script, penmanship, scrawl, scribble, hand, print.
2 one of his many writings on the subject: document, letter, book, composition, letters, literature, work, publication.

wrong *adjective*
1 the wrong date: inaccurate, incorrect, mistaken, erroneous, false, fallacious, in error, imprecise.
2 what you did was wrong: inappropriate, unsuitable, unseemly, improper, indecorous, unconventional, unfitting, incongruous, inapt.
3 a wrong act: unjust, unethical, unfair, unlawful, immoral, illegal, illicit, dishonest, criminal, crooked (*infml*), reprehensible, blameworthy, guilty, to blame, bad, wicked, sinful, iniquitous, evil.
4 something is wrong: defective, faulty, out of order, amiss, awry.
🗲1 correct, right. 2 suitable, right. 3 good, moral.
▸ *adverb*
amiss, astray, awry, inaccurately, incorrectly, wrongly, mistakenly,

faultily, badly, erroneously, improperly.
🗲 right.
▸ *noun*
sin, misdeed, offence, crime, immorality, sinfulness, transgression, wickedness, wrongdoing, trespass (*fml*), injury, grievance, abuse, injustice, iniquity (*fml*), inequity (*fml*), infringement, unfairness, error.
🗲 right.
▸ *verb*
abuse, ill-treat, mistreat, maltreat, injure, ill-use, hurt, harm, discredit, dishonour, misrepresent, malign, oppress, cheat.

wrongdoer *noun*
offender, law-breaker, transgressor, criminal, delinquent, felon, miscreant (*fml*), evil-doer, sinner, trespasser, culprit.

wrongful *adjective*
immoral, improper, unfair, unethical, unjust, unlawful, illegal, illegitimate, illicit, dishonest, criminal, blameworthy, dishonourable, wrong, reprehensible, wicked, evil.
🗲 rightful.

wry *adjective*
1 wry humour: ironic, sardonic, dry, sarcastic, mocking, droll.
2 a wry neck: twisted, distorted, deformed, contorted, warped, uneven, crooked.
🗲2 straight.

yank *verb, noun*
jerk, tug, pull, wrench, snatch, haul, heave.

yardstick *noun*
measure, gauge, criterion, standard, benchmark, touchstone, comparison.

yarn *noun*
1 cotton yarn: thread, fibre, strand.
2 tells some really good yarns: story, tale, anecdote, fable, fabrication, tall story, cock-and-bull story (*infml*).

yawning *adjective*
gaping, wide, wide-open, huge, vast, cavernous.

yearly *adjective*
annual, per year, per annum, perennial.
▶ *adverb*
annually, every year, once a year, perennially.

yearn for *verb*
long for, pine for, desire, want, wish for, crave, covet, hunger for, hanker for, ache for, languish for, itch for.

yell *verb*
shout, scream, bellow, roar, bawl, shriek, squeal, howl, holler (*infml*), screech, squall, yelp, yowl, whoop.
E3 whisper.
▶ *noun*
shout, scream, cry, roar, bellow, shriek, howl, screech, squall, whoop.
E3 whisper.

yelp *verb*
yap, bark, squeal, cry, yell, yowl, bay.
▶ *noun*
yap, bark, yip, squeal, cry, yell, yowl.

yield *verb*
1 yield to the enemy: surrender, renounce, abandon, abdicate, cede, part with, relinquish.
2 yield to temptation: give way, capitulate, concede, submit, succumb, give (in), admit defeat, bow, cave in, knuckle under, resign oneself, go along with, permit, allow, acquiesce, accede, agree, comply, consent.
3 yield fruit/an income: produce, bear, supply, provide, generate, bring in, bring forth, furnish, return, earn, pay.
E3 1 hold. **2** resist, withstand.
▶ *noun*
return, product, earnings, harvest, crop, produce, output, profit, revenue, takings, proceeds, income.

yoke *noun*
1 tied together with a wooden yoke: harness, bond, link.
2 cast off the yoke of slavery: burden, bondage, oppression, subjugation, servility.
▶ *verb*
couple, link, join, tie, harness, hitch, bracket, connect, unite.

young *adjective*
1 young lambs/people: youthful, juvenile, baby, infant, junior, adolescent.
2 young shoots: immature, early, new, recent, green, growing, fledgling, unfledged, inexperienced.
E3 1 adult, old. **2** mature, old.
▶ *noun*
offspring, babies, issue, litter, progeny (*fml*), brood, children, family.

youngster *noun*
child, boy, girl, toddler, youth,
teenager, kid (*infml*).

youth *noun*
1 arrested a youth: adolescent,
youngster, juvenile, teenager, kid
(*infml*), boy, young man.
2 the youth of today: young people,
the young, younger generation.

3 in her/his youth: adolescence,
childhood, immaturity, boyhood,
girlhood.
E3 3 adulthood.

youthful *adjective*
young, boyish, girlish, childish,
immature, juvenile, inexperienced,
fresh, active, lively, well-preserved.
E3 aged.

zany *adjective* (*infml*)
comical, funny, amusing, eccentric, droll, crazy (*infml*), clownish, loony (*infml*), wacky (*infml*).
≢ serious.

zeal *noun*
ardour, fervour, passion, warmth, fire, enthusiasm, devotion, spirit, keenness, zest, eagerness, earnestness, dedication, fanaticism, gusto, verve.
≢ apathy, indifference.

zealous *adjective*
ardent, fervent, impassioned, passionate, devoted, burning, enthusiastic, intense, fanatical, militant, keen, eager, earnest, spirited.
≢ apathetic, indifferent.

zenith *noun*
summit, peak, height, pinnacle, apex, high point, top, optimum, climax, culmination, acme, meridian, vertex.
≢ nadir.

zero *noun*
nothing, nought, nil, nadir, bottom, cipher, zilch (*infml*), duck, love.

zest *noun*
1 zest for life: gusto, appetite, enthusiasm, enjoyment, keenness, zeal, exuberance, interest.
2 lemon zest: flavour, taste, relish, savour, spice, tang, piquancy.
≢ 1 apathy.

zigzag *verb*
meander, snake, wind, twist, curve.
► *adjective*
meandering, crooked, serpentine, sinuous, twisting, winding.
≢ straight.

zodiac

> *The signs of the zodiac (with their symbols) are:*
>
> Aries (Ram), Taurus (Bull), Gemini (Twins), Cancer (Crab), Leo (Lion), Virgo (Virgin), Libra (Balance), Scorpio (Scorpion), Sagittarius (Archer), Capricorn (Goat), Aquarius (Water-bearer), Pisces (Fishes).

zone *noun*
region, area, district, territory, section, sector, belt, sphere, tract, stratum.

zoom *verb*
race, rush, tear, dash, speed, fly, hurtle, streak, flash, shoot, whirl, dive, buzz, zip.

SUPPLEMENTS

USING WORDS WELL

This supplement is aimed to help you get the most from *Chambers School Thesaurus*. It helps you to choose the right vocabulary for the context and express yourself creatively and accurately.

CHOOSING THE RIGHT WORD

Our choice of word can depend on:

- **where** we are, and in what kind of situation
- **who** we are communicating with, and their relationship to us
- **what** effect we wish to have on our audience, and the result we want to achieve

We have to think of all these things before we even open our mouths, or put pen to paper. When we use a thesaurus, we must take care in choosing the appropriate word. This is especially true if we are using words which are new to us.

Context

The most important factor to remember when choosing a word from the *School Thesaurus* is the situation in which you will use it. No matter how suitable a word may appear, if it is used out of context it will be inappropriate, and may even have the opposite effect to the one that you hoped for. Using a slang expression in an essay may lose marks, but using a very formal term amongst friends will make them laugh.

Examples of the right and wrong context are given throughout this section to help you choose the right word for the situation.

Audience

Your audience is the person or people who will be hearing or reading your words: a teacher, your classmates, or anyone else that you wish to communicate with. You might ask yourself:

- what does the audience already know or understand about the subject?
- will they understand and enjoy simple or more complicated vocabulary?
- what is their relationship to you – are they in authority, or your classmates?

Think about who your audience is, and then match your choice of words to them.

Aim

You might have different aims when you write or speak. You might want to express the right information so you get a good mark in an essay; you might want to make people laugh, or persuade them that your point of view is the right one. Think carefully about your aim when choosing words, so that you can achieve the result you want.

✗ 'I **deserve** a good mark for this essay because I **worked** hard on it.'

✓ 'I have **earned** a good mark for this essay because I **researched** it, **studied** the issues closely, and have **presented** them clearly.'

The first example says what you think. The second example has more chance of persuading someone, because the words emphasize *why* you think this – and so you have a better chance of achieving your aim.

Choosing the most suitable word

Considering the context, your audience and your aim will help you to choose the right word. But it is also important to check the meaning of any word that you are unsure about in a dictionary, such as *Chambers School Dictionary*, before using it. Not all synonyms listed are identical, and so not all can be used in the same situation.

Look at this sentence:

✓ She was **accustomed** to his whining by now, so ignored him as they drove along the rough track, the mud becoming **caked** on the **reinforced** tyres.

Although in their own way each of these words means *harden*, each only applies to certain forms of hardening, and if you use them inappropriately your sentence can become nonsense:

✗ She was **caked** to his whining by now, so ignored him as they drove along the rough track, the mud becoming **reinforced** on the **accustomed** tyres.

LOOKING AT THE LABELS

The italic labels used in the *School Thesaurus* indicate, for example, the register of a term, eg whether it is formal (*fml*) or informal (*infml*), or the place or country where it is most used, eg the United States (*US*). A word may have more than one element in its label, for example (*US slang*).

The labels are there as a *guide* to help you in your choice of words, and to help you choose the most appropriate word for any situation.

REGISTER

What is register?

Register is the style of language that is suitable for certain situations or subjects. People use different words in a formal situation, for example at an interview or in an exam, from those that they use when chatting with friends. Most of the time, people choose which words to use without thinking. When using a thesaurus to choose words that might be new or strange to you, you have to be careful. If a word is used in the wrong context, it may have the wrong effect – or even cause offence.

Register labels

Most of the words in the *School Thesaurus* are Standard English. However, some words are marked by register labels, which indicate the context in which word might be used.

- *fml* (formal) – words which would be used in a more formal context (eg in an essay, talking to people in authority etc)
- *infml* (informal) – words which would be suitable in an informal context (with your classmates and friends)
- *slang* – words which should only be used in a very informal context (with people you know well)

The synonyms given for a word in the *School Thesaurus* may include words from several different registers:

> **eat** *verb*
> **1 eat breakfast/eat at 8 o'clock:**
> consume, feed, swallow, devour, chew,
> scoff (*infml*), munch, dine, trough
> (*slang*), ingest (*fml*).

standard	'Try and *eat* something,' she said, offering me the sandwiches.
formal	'Fiddler crabs *ingest* particles of sand and mud, using their mouthparts to scrape food materials from the sediment,' explained the zoologist.
informal	'I *scoffed* too many sweets and feel a bit ill,' groaned John.
slang	'Rab, you greedy pig! Have you been *troughing* all the chocolates?' demanded Fiona.

These different registers are discussed in more detail below.

STANDARD ENGLISH

Standard English is the form of English generally used throughout the English-speaking world in education, business, newspapers and television, and in all other everyday speech and writing. It is understood by all speakers of English, and is much the same from one English-speaking country to another. Standard English terms are not labelled in the *School Thesaurus*.

FORMAL LANGUAGE

Formal language is often used in official or business situations, eg in the office, in courts, by politicians etc. Like Standard English, it is strictly correct with regard to grammar, style and choice of words. Standard English words can be used in a formal context, but informal or slang words are not suitable.

➤ Structure

The structure of formal language is more limited than language used in conversation. Abbreviations and short forms (words like *I'm*, *can't*) are seldom used. Both the words and sentences may be longer:

✗ We hope that he'll phone in, as we don't have much time to put this right.

✓ It is to be hoped that he will telephone the office, given the time constraints within which the situation must be rectified.

➤ Vocabulary

Formal words are not frequently used in everyday conversation. However, they may come in useful when addressing someone in authority, or for making an argument more serious:

✗ 'Your Honour, I solemnly swear that I did not *rip anyone off* and that the evidence against me is a *pile of rubbish*.'

✓ 'Your Honour, I solemnly swear that I did not *defraud anyone* and that the evidence against me is *fabricated*.'

➤ *Possible difficulties*

It is important not to overuse formal words, as there is a risk of sounding pompous or pretentious, or of being unclear:

✗ He had a *propensity* for *loquaciousness* in his *oration*, for which he was *denigrated*.

✓ He was *criticized* for being too *talkative* and *long-winded*.

➤ *Context*

The context of formal words is also very important. They are unlikely, for example, to be dropped casually into everyday conversation:

✗ 'My brother is a real *miscreant* and always getting into *altercations*!' laughed four-year-old Debbie.

✓ 'It was wrong of you *miscreants* to become involved in this *altercation*,' lectured the headmaster, as John and Jo stared out the window.

INFORMAL LANGUAGE

Informal language is sometimes called colloquial language. It is used when you know your audience quite well and are in a more relaxed or familiar situation. Informal language uses words and idioms of everyday language. It should not be used in a formal context.

> **leave**[1] *verb*
> **1** he left around midnight: depart, go, go away, set out, take off, decamp, exit, move, quit, retire, withdraw, disappear, do a bunk (*infml*), clear off (*infml*).

✗ 'Prince Charles Edward Stuart *did a bunk* to Skye,' said the eminent historian.

✓ The tea stain wouldn't come out of the carpet, so Kieran *did a bunk* before his mother came home.

Remember that not only should informal words only be used in an informal context, but that not all the words listed mean exactly the same thing:

✗ 'The train will *clear off* at 16.20 – so we'd better run!' he shouted.

✓ They grabbed the box of chocolates and *cleared off* as fast as their legs could carry them.

➤ Idioms

Informal language often contains idioms. An idiom is an expression with a meaning that cannot be understood from the usual meanings of the words which form it. Idioms can add colour to your speech and writing, making it more lively and interesting. However, as with all informal language, such idioms are often inappropriate in more formal situations. See the **Word Study panels** for more examples of idioms.

suddenly becoming angry

go up in the air	go mental (*slang*)	go spare (*slang*)
go ballistic (*slang*)	fly off the handle	blow your stack
raise Cain	lose your head	throw a tantrum
cut up rough	blow/flip your lid	lose your temper
go off the deep end	lose your rag	blow your top
fly into a rage	throw a wobbly (*slang*)	hit the roof
blow a fuse/gasket	see red	

✗ The Chief Executive shocked the Board of Directors when she *threw a wobbly* on seeing the sales figures.

✓ Caitlin *threw a wobbly* when Helen sneakily finished off the last of the chocolate fudge cake.

Be careful not to overuse idioms or the effectiveness will be lost and the meaning will be unclear.

SLANG

The most informal of all language is **slang**. Slang has been around for hundreds of years, but the words that are considered to be slang are constantly changing. Many terms that were once slang are now thought to be Standard English. *Donkey*, for example, was a slang term in the 1800s! As a general rule, slang should not be used in a formal context, and should always be used with caution. It can also be very specific to one region or group of people.

> **mouth** *noun*
> **1 open one's mouth to speak**: lips, jaws, trap (*infml*), gob (*slang*).

✗ 'Please open your *gob* so I can examine your teeth,' said the dentist.

✓ 'Shut your *gob* and don't make a sound,' growled the infamous gangster, 'Red' Rogers.

GEOGRAPHICAL LABELS

English is spoken by millions of people around the world, but varies slightly from country to country, as it is influenced by the other languages spoken there and the particular culture of each country. For example, there are differences between the English spoken in the United Kingdom and the English spoken in the United States of America. Terms that are used mainly in the United States are labelled (*US*) in the *School Thesaurus*.

There are many differences of meaning, pronunciation, spelling and sentence structure between British and US English. Some words may be difficult to understand for someone from the other country.

'The dish of the day is vegetable lasagne with *eggplant* and *zucchini*,' said the waitress in the New York diner.

'For the harvest supper, I'm going to make a casserole with *aubergine* and *courgette*,' announced Harriet.

USING WORDS CREATIVELY

USING LIVELY LANGUAGE

The more creative your choice of words, the more interesting your speech or writing will be, and the more influence it will have on your audience. Lively language gets a response from the audience: it arouses their emotions or changes their point of view. Choose the right word to add interest, impact and a deeper meaning to your speech or writing.

Colourful descriptions

Colourful descriptions can create a vivid mental image for the audience. It is tempting to rely on overused words because they can often be used in a variety of contexts – *big*, for example, can mean *sizable*, *elder*, *significant*, *famous* or *generous*. Use the **Word Workshop** panels in the *School Thesaurus* to exchange dull or common words for ones with impact and interest which will give your writing pep and zest. This is an extract from the **Word Workshop** panel **nice**:

---

a person's appearance

attractive	cute	good-looking	handsome
pretty			

a person's personality

agreeable	amiable	charming	considerate
friendly	generous	good	good-natured
helpful	kind	likeable	pleasant
polite	sweet	thoughtful	warm
wonderful			

✗ 'He's a *nice* guy,' said Claire.

✓ 'He's *attractive*, *polite*, *good-humoured*, *sympathetic*, *understanding* and *kind*,' said Claire.

You should also be careful not to pepper your work with words such as *really* or *very* because these will actually reduce the impact of what you want to say.

USING WORDS CREATIVELY

Substituting colourful words for dull ones is especially useful for descriptive writing but can be used (carefully) in most contexts to make your work more expressive.

✗ The *big*, *dry* desert was *hot* and the *lost* explorers were *very thirsty*.

✓ The *vast*, *arid* desert was *sweltering* and the *disorientated* explorers were *extremely dehydrated*.

Vigorous verbs

Many commonly overused verbs, such as *say*, *do* and *like*, are the simplest way of expressing an idea, but they are also rather bland. To add interest you can use an adverb to describe the tone or way in which the action is performed. However, this can still lack impact. Try using a more forceful verb in place of the overused word:

✗ 'You told her my secret!' he *said accusingly*.

✓ 'You told her my secret!' he *accused*.

The second example is more likely to grab the reader's attention. Throughout the *School Thesaurus* **Word Study** panels list these useful verbs. Use them to make your writing more lively. Take a look at this extract from the panel **walk**:

---

walk at your ease

amble	ramble	roam	saunter
stroll	wander		

walk quickly

hike	march	pace	stride
troop			

walk quietly

crawl	creep	prowl	slink
sneak	tiptoe		

walk with difficulty

hobble	limp	plod	stagger
stumble	trudge		

✗ Russell *walked* out of the house.

✓ Russell *sneaked* out of the house.

✓ Russell *marched* out of the house.

The first example lacks interest because it provides little information and does not arouse much interest. But the other sentences capture the reader's attention. He sneaks (why does he not want people to see him?) and he marches (has he just had an argument?). A careful word choice adds meaning to the sentence, and something about tone, atmosphere and character can all be conveyed in this way. The **Word Study** panel **talk** lists many alternative verbs:

to express something in words			
phrase	put	put into words	render
to guess			
estimate	imagine	judge	presume
reckon	suppose		
to report			
affirm	announce	assert	communicate
convey	declare	inform	relate
state	tell		
to ask			
demand	inquire	interrogate	query
question			
to reply			
answer	counter	respond	return
to speak unclearly			
babble	mumble	mutter	stutter
whisper			
to speak angrily			
nag	shout	snap	snarl
yell			

✗ 'I'm not afraid of you!' he *said*.

✓ 'I'm not afraid of you!' he *announced*.

✓ 'I'm not afraid of you!' he *mumbled*.

✓ 'I'm not afraid of you!' he *snarled*.

✓ 'I'm not afraid of you!' he *yelled*.

By varying the verb, the entire situation changes. Is the speaker brave or terrified? Making your audience think about your meaning rather than simply stating the information keeps their attention. Your words will have more power if you let them draw conclusions for themselves.

ASSOCIATIONS AND CONNOTATIONS

Just as some synonyms in a list can have a very specific meaning, some words can carry certain connotations or associations.

● A *connotation* is an idea or feeling suggested in addition to the literal meaning of a word.

● An *association* is a connection in the mind between a word and emotions, feelings or sensations.

The connotations or associations of a word often vary from person to person, and words which seem positive to one person can seem negative to another. This is because your own personal experiences provide different impressions. However, many words have widely recognized connotations shared by most people. This means that many words have both a literal meaning and other associations.

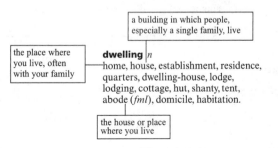

a building in which people, especially a single family, live

the place where you live, often with your family

dwelling *n*
home, house, establishment, residence, quarters, dwelling-house, lodge, lodging, cottage, hut, shanty, tent, abode (*fml*), domicile, habitation.

the house or place where you live

The definitions of these words are very similar. But the connotations vary. A *home* carries associations of security and happiness. A *house* on the other hand is associated more with the actual building than with the emotions. An *abode* is a formal term which does not have any emotional effect.

✓ Hannah bought candles, bright curtains, colourful rugs and comfy cushions to turn her drab new *house* into a *home*.

Use these connotations and associations to add extra meaning and depth to your words, or to help you create a certain effect.

PRESENTING FACTS AND OPINIONS

Many newspaper articles, television programmes, Internet sites and conversations between friends or colleagues are made up of a mixture of facts and opinions.

● A *fact* is a thing that is known to be true, exist, or have happened.

● An *opinion* is a belief or judgement which seems likely to be true, but which is not based on proof. It is what someone thinks about somebody or something.

Often a writer will mingle facts and opinions, and will use language skilfully to blur the distinctions between the two.

✓ The Hungry Moose Steakhouse on the High Street serves a varied and interesting menu at reasonable prices. The steak was deliciously tender, in a mouthwatering peppercorn sauce and accompanied by a mound of golden fries, whilst my companion's beefburger came loaded with crispy lettuce, smooth mayonnaise and dripping with melted cheese.

In this review, the restaurant critic has mixed facts (for example that the restaurant is on the High Street, that the steak was served with chips, and that his or her companion had a burger) and opinions (for example that the prices are reasonable, that the lettuce was crispy). Keep an eye out for words such as *varied*, *interesting* or *delicious* as these words are indicating personal opinion rather than stating a fact.

USING WORDS CREATIVELY

The restaurant critic did not point out which words were facts and which were opinions, but there are words you can use in your own writing to identify what is fact and what is your own opinion. This might be useful if writing an essay, as you must be careful not to state an idea as a fact just because *you* believe it to be right.

You can look under these key headwords in the *School Thesaurus* for:

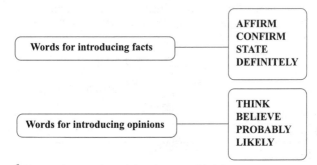

✓ The teacher *confirmed* that there would *definitely* be a question about Henry VIII in the test.

✓ Jia-Ling *believed* that there would *probably* be a question about Henry VIII in the test.

USING LANGUAGE FOR EMOTIONAL EFFECT

You may not be able to change the facts of a situation, but through a skilful use of words you can change the way in which your audience views them.

● *Objective language* presents facts without opinion. It does not encourage the audience to become emotionally involved.

● *Subjective language* is intended to arouse emotion to influence the audience.

You should be aware of how reports and articles are sometimes biased towards one side of a situation. (If necessary, you should then be able to use the same techniques to persuade and influence in your own work.)

Imagine that a construction company have applied for permission to build houses on a green field. The local newspaper could report this as:

against   A development scheme which *threatens* to *devastate* a wildlife reserve was revealed today.

for   A development scheme which *promises* to *create* homes and jobs was revealed today.

The focus of the article can change from the effect on the nature and wildlife to the effect on the people living there. By changing the highlighted text from words with *negative* associations to words with *positive* associations, the writer changes the tone of the piece.

Many entries in the *School Thesaurus* give antonyms, words which mean the opposite of the headword. Antonyms are useful if you want to change the bias of a report. For example:

against   The *selfish* schemes of *greedy* developers will mean destruction for the environment.

for   The *public-spirited* schemes of *generous* developers will provide jobs and homes.

Purpose

Objective or subjective language, mixing facts and opinions, using emotive words – these are all techniques used by the writer to achieve results. Look for characteristics which indicate the writer's aim.

PERSUADE/ARGUE

- using colourful language
- giving a mixture of opinions and facts, but not showing the difference between them
- using language which is emotional and biased
- using words which possibly have several meanings

EXPLAIN/DESCRIBE

- using language that is less emotional
- giving a balanced point of view
- using mainly facts
- presenting facts and opinions clearly so that the reader is able to tell the difference
- using straightforward and clear layout

MATCH THE SYNONYMS

Below you will find two lists of words. The words in List B are all
SYNONYMS of the words in List A – but they are jumbled up. Can you
find the correct pairs?

A	B
ill	sadness
legend	large
grief	irritate
run	conceal
scare	dwell
ready	meadow
big	myth
grab	difficult
confess	prepared
live	frighten
friend	sick
annoy	snatch
hard	sprint
hide	chum
field	admit

MATCH THE ANTONYMS

This time the words in List B are all ANTONYMS of the words in List A – but they are jumbled up. Can you find the correct pairs?

A	B
different	artificial
begin	fiction
smooth	punishment
obey	cease
scold	delight
increase	sturdy
genuine	rarely
afraid	rough
reward	thrifty
fact	defy
horrible	reduce
disgust	similar
flimsy	lovely
often	brave
extravagant	praise

WORD GAMES: CONFUSABLES

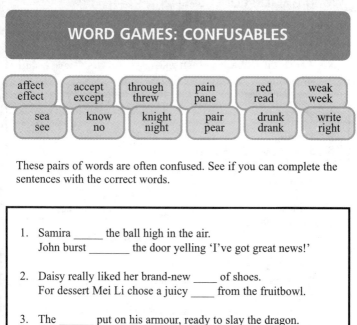

affect
effect

accept
except

through
threw

pain
pane

red
read

weak
week

sea
see

know
no

knight
night

pair
pear

drunk
drank

write
right

These pairs of words are often confused. See if you can complete the
sentences with the correct words.

1. Samira _____ the ball high in the air.
   John burst _____ the door yelling 'I've got great news!'

2. Daisy really liked her brand-new ____ of shoes.
   For dessert Mei Li chose a juicy ____ from the fruitbowl.

3. The _____ put on his armour, ready to slay the dragon.
   It was a frosty _____ and the stars were twinkling in the sky.

4. Thabo ____ the latest Harry Potter book in one day.
   ___ sky at night, shepherd's delight.

5. From the top of the hill, Murad could ___ for miles.
   He sat down on the beach and gazed at the calm ___.

6. 'Have you _____ all the milk?' Chloe demanded.
   'I _____ two glasses for breakfast,' Ewan replied.

7. The doctor treated him for the ____ in his stomach.
   With a loud crash, the football smashed through the ____ of
   glass.

8. After his illness Arif still felt quite ____ and wasn't able to do any sport.
   The family were really looking forward to spending a ____ in Spain.

9. The magic potion had no _____ on the little prince – to his horror he was still a frog.
   Scientists forecast that global warming could seriously _____ the climate.

10. For homework, Sara had to _____ an essay on Florence Nightingale.
    'You were _____,' he admitted, 'I should have taken the other route. Now we're lost.'

11. He was alone in a strange city and had __ idea how to get back to the hotel.
    She looked blankly at the test paper and realized that she did not ____ anything about Henry VIII.

12. 'I hope you have learned a lesson from this. I am happy to _____ your apology,' said the teacher.
    The museum is open daily at 9am, _____ on Sundays when it opens at 10.30am.

Everyone has played the game **Hangman** at some point. In this game, the solutions are all idioms from the **Word Study** panels. One person knows the answer and the other person must guess the correct letters to find out what the idiom is. We have started you off with some letters.

1. If you criticize someone severely you

   ____ ____ ____ ___ C____

2. A difficult situation is sometimes called

    V
_ _____ _____

3. Something which is doomed to failure is said to

           LL
___ ____ _ ____ __ __

4. Someone who is mad is sometimes described as

  TT   T
__ _ __ _ ____ ____

5. If someone works very hard, we say that they

        D   D
____ ___ ___ __ __ ____ __ D_

Now come up with your own idioms and clues!

WORD GAMES: RHYMING SYNONYMS

Find the rhyming synonyms from the following clues. For example a **famous dog** is a **renowned hound**. Some are tricky!

1. wealthy magician   _____
2. cheerful nest   _____
3. shy lad   _____
4. sad friend   _____
5. tired question   _____
6. uninterested crowd   _____
7. red lake   _____
8. conceited fool   _____
9. grisly tale   _____
10. dead animal   _____
11. prudent crook   _____
12. angry chief   _____
13. delirious visionary   _____
14. desolate mountain   _____
15. lazy journalist   _____

Can you come up with more?

WORD GAMES: STARTERS

Find synonyms for the clues. All the answers to the clues begin with the same three letters **RES**. Fill in the missing letters in the grid to reveal another jumbled word down the ladder. Rearrange the letters to find the word. (Hint: it also begins with the letters **RES**.)

R	E	S						
		R	E	S				
	R	E	S					
R	E	S						
		R	E	S				
R	E	S						
	R	E	S					
	R	E	S					
		R	E	S				
	R	E	S					
R	E	S						

1.   unsettled, agitated
2.   admiration, reverence
3.   defiant, unyielding
4.   set aside, retained
5.   quit, abdicate
6.   decide, determine
7.   study, examine
8.   look like, take after
9.   echo, reverberate
10. elastic, springy; tough, hardy
11. citizen, inhabitant

WORD GAMES: ANTONYM WORD LADDER

On each ladder, remove ONE letter from the first word and replace it with another letter to make the second word; then remove ONE letter from the second word and replace it with another letter to make the third word. Continue until you finally end up with an **antonym** for the first word.

The first one has been done for you.

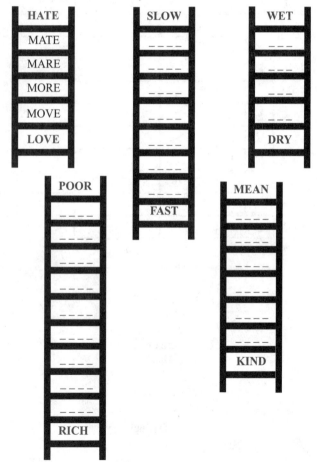

HATE	SLOW	WET
MATE	_ _ _ _	_ _ _
MARE	_ _ _ _	_ _ _
MORE	_ _ _ _	_ _ _
MOVE	_ _ _ _	_ _ _
LOVE	_ _ _ _	DRY
	_ _ _ _	
	FAST	

POOR	MEAN
_ _ _ _	_ _ _ _
_ _ _ _	_ _ _ _
_ _ _ _	_ _ _ _
_ _ _ _	_ _ _ _
_ _ _ _	_ _ _ _
_ _ _ _	_ _ _ _
_ _ _ _	KIND
_ _ _ _	
RICH	

634

WORD GAMES: WORD SEARCH

Can you find synonyms for walk in the following grid? The words are all written across, down, backwards and forwards. We've started you off with the first one – "plod".

C	A	M	B	L	E	C	A	R	R	Y	C	J
A	C	A	C	A	R	M	I	N	E	O	A	C
P	A	R	A	S	T	R	O	L	L	S	R	R
A	R	C	S	C	T	I	P	T	O	E	E	O
R	G	H	C	A	R	P	E	T	R	C	F	A
A	O	C	A	R	E	D	R	C	N	A	R	M
D	C	A	T	B	H	O	B	B	L	E	E	Y
E	A	R	T	O	O	L	A	R	T	A	E	S
A	H	I	J	N	C	P	R	P	I	V	Z	T
R	I	B	C	N	A	C	D	E	O	A	C	A
D	K	O	W	A	D	D	L	E	N	N	A	G
I	E	D	I	R	T	S	G	T	Q	X	R	G
N	E	F	V	R	O	A	A	E	Y	J	T	E
A	G	H	E	E	N	S	N	E	A	K	T	R
L	C	T	R	O	O	P	Y	C	A	R	O	L

Clues:

1. to walk slowly: PLOD

2. to walk without hurrying: A _ _ _ _

3. to walk with a limp: H _ _ _ _ _

4. how an army walks: M _ _ _ _

5. to wander: R _ _ _

6. how a duck walks: W _ _ _ _ _

7. to walk quietly: T _ _ _ _ _

8. to walk so that nobody sees you: S _ _ _ _ _

9. to walk through the countryside: H _ _ _

10. to walk in procession: P _ _ _ _ _ _

11. to walk with long steps: S _ _ _ _ _

12. to walk unsteadily: S _ _ _ _ _ _

13. to walk quickly in a group: T _ _ _ _

14. to walk in a leisurely way: S _ _ _ _ _

Match the Synonyms

ill - sick
legend - myth
grief - sadness
run - sprint
scare - frighten
ready - prepared
big - large
grab - snatch

confess - admit
live - dwell
friend - chum
annoy - irritate
hard - difficult
hide - conceal
field - meadow

Match the Antonyms

different - similar
begin - cease
smooth - rough
obey - defy
scold - praise
increase - reduce
genuine - artificial
afraid - brave

reward - punishment
fact - fiction
horrible - lovely
disgust - delight
flimsy - sturdy
often - rarely
extravagant - thrifty

Confusables

1. threw
   through
2. pair
   pear
3. knight
   night
4. read
   red
5. see
   sea
6. drunk
   drank

7. pain
   pane
8. weak
   week
9. effect
   affect
10. write
    right
11. no
    know
12. accept
    except

Idiom Hangman

1. Haul them over the coals
2. A vicious circle
3. Not have a hope in hell
4. Nutty as a fruitcake
5. Burn the candle at both ends

Rhyming Synonyms

1. rich witch
2. cheery eyrie
3. coy boy
4. glum chum
5. weary query
6. bored horde
7. maroon lagoon
8. smug mug
9. gory story
10. deceased beast
11. discreet cheat
12. cross boss
13. frantic romantic
14. bleak peak
15. slack hack

Starters

1	R	E	S	T	L	E	S	S		
2				R	E	S	P	E	C	T
3			R	E	S	I	S	T	A	N	T
4	R	E	S	E	R	V	E	D		
5				R	E	S	I	G	N	
6	R	E	S	O	L	V	E			
7		R	E	S	E	A	R	C	H	
8		R	E	S	E	M	B	L	E	
9				R	E	S	O	U	N	D	
10		R	E	S	I	L	I	E	N	T	
11	R	E	S	I	D	E	N	T		

The unjumbled word is: **RESPONSIBLE**

Antonym Word Ladder

1. **SLOW**	1. **WET**	1. **POOR**	1. **MEAN**
2. FLOW	2. PET	2. POUR	2. MEAT
3. FLAW	3. PAT	3. POUT	3. SEAT
4. FLAT	4. PAY	4. POST	4. SENT
5. FEAT	5. PRY	5. MOST	5. SEND
6. PEAT	6. **DRY**	6. MUST	6. MEND
7. PEST		7. RUST	7. MIND
8. PAST		8. RUSE	8. **KIND**
9. **FAST**		9. RISE	
		10. RICE	
		11. **RICH**	

Word Search

C	A	M	B	L	E	C	A	R	R	Y	C	J
A	C	A	C	A	R	M	I	N	E	O	A	C
P	A	R	A	S	T	R	O	L	L	S	R	R
A	R	C	S	C	T	I	P	T	O	E	E	O
R	G	H	C	A	R	P	E	T	R	C	F	A
A	O	C	A	R	E	D	R	C	N	A	R	M
D	C	A	T	B	H	O	B	B	L	E	E	Y
E	A	R	T	O	O	L	A	R	T	A	E	S
A	H	I	J	N	C	P	R	P	I	V	Z	T
R	I	B	C	N	A	C	D	E	O	A	C	A
D	K	O	W	A	D	D	L	E	N	N	A	G
I	E	D	I	R	T	S	G	T	Q	X	R	G
N	E	F	V	R	O	A	A	E	Y	J	T	E
A	G	H	E	E	N	S	N	E	A	K	T	R
L	C	T	R	O	O	P	Y	C	A	R	O	L